I give thanks to my God at every remembrance

of you, praying always with joy

in my every prayer for all of you.

Philippians 1, 3–4

Presented to

_____

By

_____

On

_____

PRAY IT!

This book can change your life.
The Bible's essential message is this: God
LOVES us and wants to be in a lifelong
friendship with us. The Bible tells the story
of God's love, revealed most perfectly in
Jesus' **life**, **death**, and **RESURRECTION**.
Through Christ, God offers us forgiveness,
freedom, companionship, and **new** life. It is a
wonderful gift, but we must choose to
ACCEPT it. How will you **respond** to that
invitation?

Lord God, here I am!

You created me and know me completely.

You know all about my life—my joys and my
sufferings, my questions and my dreams.

I know you love me, even when I feel my sins
and mistakes make me unlovable.

Help me to love you, God, with all my heart,
mind, and soul, and to love all people,
even as I love myself.

Jesus, thank you for showing me how to live.

I know you want only the best for my life,
and I believe following you is the way to a
full and abundant life.

Holy Spirit, give me the courage and wisdom
to be Jesus' follower, even when it isn't easy.

Fill me with the joy and peace that comes
from doing your will.

Amen.

THE Catholic Youth Bible

Article and introduction writers: Eduardo Arnouil; Lisa-Marie Calderone-Stewart; Carmen María Cervantes; Catherine Cory; Gary Dreier; Karen Emmerich; Carole Goodwin; Ron Kenney; Edward P. Kunzman; Judi Lanciotti; Joseph A. Morris, C.M.; Daniel Ponsetto; Rosa Sanchez; Larry Schatz, F.S.C.; Valerie Shields; Brian Singer-Towns; and Michael Theisen

The acknowledgments continue on page 1695.

Produced with the assistance of The Livingstone Corporation. Project staff include: Christopher D. Hudson, Ashley Taylor, Thomas Ristow, Troy Ristow, Kathleen Ristow, Rosalie Krusemark, and Katie Gieser.

Printed in the United States of America

Printing: 9 8 7 6 5 4 3 2

Year: 2010 09 08 07 06 05 04 03 02

ISBN 0-88489-744-3, paper
ISBN 0-88489-745-1, hardcover
ISBN 0-88489-746-X, bonded leather

Library of Congress Cataloging-in-Publication Data

Bible. English. New American. 2002.
    The Catholic Youth Bible: New American Bible including the revised Psalms and the revised New Testament translated from the original languages with critical use of all the ancient sources.
        p. cm.
        Includes index.
        ISBN 0-88489-745-1—ISBN 0-88489-744-3 (pbk.)—ISBN 0-88489-746-X (bonded leather)
        I. Title.

BS192.3.A1 2002 W56
220.5'2054—dc21

2002001981

THE
Catholic
Youth
Bible

New Amercian Bible
Including the Revised Psalms and the Revised New Testament
Translated from the Original Languages with Critical Use of
All the Ancient Sources

Saint Mary's Press
Christian Brothers Publications
Winona, Minnesota

Contents

The Old Testament

The New Testament

Welcome!

THIS UNIQUE BIBLE IS FOR YOU.

The Catholic Youth Bible (CYB) is filled with things that will make it easier for you to understand the Bible's message. The authors, editors, designers, and artists involved in creating its special features were focused on you—a young person seeking answers to life's important questions. The CYB can be a true companion, helping you find the answers you seek and perhaps raising new questions along the way. It will help you see yourself in God's image and likeness, *A VITAL PART OF GOD'S SAVING WORK IN THE WORLD.*

WHAT MAKES THIS YOUTH BIBLE *CATHOLIC*?
For starters, its introductions and articles reflect Catholic interpretation of the Bible and make connections to Catholic beliefs and traditions. In addition, this Bible contains all seventy-three books and letters that form a complete Catholic Bible, seven more than most other Bibles (see "The Case of the Missing Books," near Tb 1, 16). Does this mean that other Christians cannot use *The Catholic Youth Bible?* Not at all. When it comes to the Scriptures, Christians from all cultures and denominations have more in common than they have differences.

AS YOU USE THIS BIBLE, keep in mind two important points. The first is that the Bible is for everyone. Wherever you are in your relationship with God, *the Bible can speak to you.* The articles in the *CYB* invite you to consider what the church teaches about God's message in the Bible whether you are a committed Christian or a searcher with lots of questions.

The second point is that all the special features in *The Catholic Youth Bible* are designed to encourage you *to read the Bible itself.* It is the Bible's stories, poems, prophecies, and letters that carry this central message: *God desires a loving relationship with us.* The special features of this Bible can help you understand God's message. *BUT IT IS GOD'S WORD IN THE BIBLE THAT CAN CHANGE YOUR LIFE.*

Love one another

SPECIAL FEATURES

The Catholic Youth Bible is loaded with special features to help make it easier for you to read and understand the Bible. Here is a list of some of those features and where to find them.

HOW TO READ AND STUDY THE BIBLE

The chapter that follows this general introduction gives advice for interpreting the Bible and a process for studying the Bible alone or with a group.

How to **Read AND Study** THE BIBLE

SUGGESTED READING PLANS

This chapter offers some great reading plans to get you started in studying the Bible.

Suggested **Reading Plans**

SECTION INTRODUCTIONS

Each major section of the Bible (the Pentateuch, the historical books, the wisdom books, the prophetic books, the Gospels and the Acts of the Apostles, and the Letters and Revelation) begins with background on the books in that section.

Gospels
Gospels
Gospels
Gospels

BOOK INTRODUCTIONS

Introductions at the beginning of most books (sometimes two or three books share a single introduction) give insight into each book's central message and an overview of its contents. You can find more extensive book introductions in other editions of the New American Bible.

The Book of *Genesis*

LIVE IT!

The "Live It!" articles apply the Bible's messages to situations you may be facing now or will face in the future.

LIVE IT!

PRAY IT!

The "Pray It!" articles can help you use the Bible for personal prayer. They show the biblical basis for the prayer and sacramental life of the Catholic church.

PRAY IT!

DID YOU KNOW?

The "Did You Know?" articles provide background from biblical scholars to help you understand the culture and traditions of biblical times, or the church's interpretation of certain passages.

INTRODUCING . . .

The "Introducing . . ." articles give a quick introduction to the lives of important biblical people.

CATHOLIC CONNECTIONS

The "Catholic Connections" articles show the biblical basis for many Catholic Christian beliefs and practices.

WHERE DO I FIND IT?

Several indexes are located at the back of the Bible, before the maps. The first index contains several lists that can help you locate Bible passages on events, people, and teachings of Jesus. The second index helps you find Bible passages related to each sacrament. The third index helps you find Bible passages related to specific life and faith issues. The fourth index leads you to articles on specific topics throughout *The Catholic Youth Bible.* The first three indexes generally use Bible citations to guide you, and the fourth index uses page numbers.

STUDY AIDS

Color maps, a timeline, and pictures are found at the back of the Bible. The timeline and maps will help you locate where and when different biblical events occurred.

The Bible Is MULTICULTURAL

THE BIBLE developed in the midst of great cultural diversity. In fact, the Bible was originally written in at least two languages, Hebrew and Greek. The people of the Old Testament were influenced by Arabic, Egyptian, and other Middle Eastern cultures that surrounded them. Later, they and the early Christian church were influenced by the Greek and Roman cultures. In the Bible, God is revealed as the God of *all* nations and *all* cultures.

Christians believe that the Bible's core message of God's love for human beings speaks to people of any culture. That is one reason the Bible has been translated into more languages than any other book in the world. Christians also believe that God is at work in the lives of people of every culture, whether or not they have been formally introduced to the Christian message. Listening to other cultures' experience of God can deepen Christian people's appreciation of God's message present in the Bible.

We also live in a multicultural world. *The Catholic Youth Bible* responds to this reality in two main ways. First, all the articles attempt to speak in a way that people of all cultures can appreciate and understand. Second, some articles have been specially written to represent one of four distinct cultural perspectives: African American, Asian American, Hispanic and Latino, and Native American. These articles share cultural experiences and traditions, religious symbols, prayers, and poetry, and they connect all these elements to the Bible. The article subject index at the back of this book lists the location of the articles for each of these cultural perspectives.

The four major cultural perspectives represented in *The Catholic Youth Bible* are actually a small sampling of the many unique cultures in the world. Because of space restrictions, most of these cultures are not included. Despite these limitations, the multicultural articles can deepen your appreciation of the Bible's message and the rich ways different cultures live that message.

NAVIGATING *The Catholic Youth Bible*

THE CATHOLIC YOUTH BIBLE has several aids to help you locate references to Bible books and the Bible's special features. The contents on pages iv–v will be your main guide in locating the different books and features. However, the last page in the color section (facing the back cover) lists all the Bible books alphabetically and gives their abbreviations and beginning page numbers. You will find this a useful and easy-to-locate guide. Also, as mentioned previously, the section "Where Do I Find It?" offers several types of indexes to help you locate specific passages and articles.

Throughout *The Catholic Youth Bible,* there are many references to specific Bible passages. These references are given in shorthand form, such as Jn 3, 16–17. The initial letters are the abbreviation for (or, in a few cases, the full name of) the Bible book. The number before the comma stands for the chapter and the number(s) after the comma stands for the verse(s). So Jn 3, 16–17 refers to the Gospel According to John, chapter 3, verses 16 to 17.

NAME OF BOOK   VERSE(S)

Jn 3, 16–17

CHAPTER

Most of the articles end with a citation identifying the Bible passage the article is based on. It is important to read the passage before reading the article.

In addition to the Bible text, you will find footnotes and Scripture cross-references printed along the bottom of each page. Every time you see an obelisk (†) in the Bible text, you will find a corresponding footnote labeled with the same chapter and verse numbers at the bottom of the page. The footnotes provide you with added information about words and phrases mentioned in the Bible. Every time you see an asterisk (*) in the Bible text, you will find a corresponding cross-reference labeled with the same chapter and verse numbers at the bottom of the page. The cross-references direct you to similar Scripture passages.

QUESTIONS AND ANSWERS About the Bible

THE BIBLE—which is also called the sacred Scriptures—tells the story of the loving relationship between God and humankind. It brings people to a deeper relationship with God, teaches important truths about Christian faith, and challenges how we live our life and relate with other people. However, studying the Bible raises questions for many people. This section gives some answers to key questions from Catholic Christian teaching. Because these are brief answers to important questions, you may want to talk more about them with someone in your family, church, or school.

What does it mean to say that God inspired the Bible? Did God speak directly to the Bible's authors?

Christians make a fantastic claim about the Bible: God is the author of the sacred Scriptures. They believe the Bible is God's word, containing the truths that God wishes to reveal to humankind for our salvation. Through the Holy Spirit, God inspired the human authors of the Bible's books to reveal these truths in their writings. These two concepts—God's **inspiration** of the biblical authors and God's **revelation** in their writings of the truths about God and God's will for us—are two important Christian beliefs about the Bible.

To say that biblical authors were inspired by God does not mean that they took dictation directly from God. They were true authors using creative literary forms to communicate the people's experience of God. In fact, many of the books had more than one author. Some books went through several decades of development in which the stories were told and retold, written down, combined, and edited. The church believes the Holy Spirit was guiding the many people involved throughout this whole process.

How do I know that what is in the Bible is true? Aren't there mistakes in the Bible?

Christians believe that the Bible is true and without errors when it teaches the things God wishes to reveal for the sake of our salvation. This is called the **inerrancy** of the Bible.

Some Christians also believe that the Bible is without error in every respect, including all references to scientific and historical facts. But Catholic Christians, along with others, are cautious about making this claim. The Catholic church teaches that in order to interpret the Bible correctly, we must understand what the human authors intended to communicate at the time of their writing. To know what God wants to reveal through their words, we must take into account "the conditions of their time and culture, the literary genres in use at that time, and the modes of feeling, speaking, and narrating then current" (*Catechism of the Catholic Church*, no. 110).

In other words, from our modern viewpoint, some statements in the Bible may seem like mistakes. But these "mistakes" may be due to the difference between a biblical author's cultural perspective and our cultural perspective. Or they may be due to our misunderstanding of a biblical author's use of literary devices such as metaphors, fiction, and poetry. Or perhaps they are due to a biblical author's different understanding of science or history. In its introductions and articles, *The Catholic Youth Bible* will help you understand the biblical authors' intentions and the church's teaching about what God is revealing through them.

Why do Catholics believe that the Bible alone isn't enough to teach all the truths about the Christian faith?

All Christians believe that God's complete revelation—all that people need to know about God and about their relation to God—is expressed in Jesus Christ. They believe that Jesus is the living Word of God, "the image of the invisible God" (Col 1, 15). All Christians believe that the Bible is a primary way of communicating God's revelation, which has its ultimate source in Christ.

But Catholic Christians believe that God's revelation is also communicated through **sacred Tradition.** Sacred Tradition, which is sometimes simply called Tradition, is all that the first Apostles learned from Jesus and the Holy Spirit. Under the guidance of the Holy Spirit, it is preserved, taught, and reinterpreted for each new generation by the Apostles' successors—the pope and bishops. Scripture and Tradition are closely related and support each other, having their common source in Jesus Christ. Some of the articles in *The Catholic Youth Bible* expand on the Bible's message with teaching from sacred Tradition.

Why does the Bible have two testaments?

The Bible reveals God's plan for humanity. It is divided into two parts. The Old Testament records the relationship between God and the descendants of Abraham, particularly the descendants of Abraham's grandson Jacob. At different times in their history, these descendants are called the Hebrews, the Israelites, and the Jews. The Old Testament contains their religious history, laws, and sacred stories. Because the Old Testament contains the sacred Scriptures of the Jewish people, many Christians also call the Old Testament the Hebrew Scriptures.

The New Testament presents Jesus as the full revelation of God. Jesus was a Jew, and he affirmed the core beliefs of the Jewish faith. He knew and cherished the Hebrew Scriptures. But he also revealed new insights into God's desired relationship with human beings. After his Resurrection, as his followers lived out the implications of his teachings, they eventually formed a new religious faith that came to

be called Christianity. The books and letters in the New Testament record their central teachings and beliefs about Jesus.

The church teaches that there is a profound unity to the Old and New Testaments in relation to God's revelation. "The Old Testament prepares for the New and the New Testament fulfills the Old; the two shed light on each other; both are true Word of God" (*Catechism*, no. 140). This is why both the Old and New Testaments are used in Catholic liturgy and catechism.

The Bible was written a long time ago. What does it have to do with my life today?

Christians believe the Bible's core message of God's desire to be in a loving relationship with human beings is greater than the difficulties caused by the passing of time and by cultural differences between the biblical era and our time. They believe that the more people read, reflect on, and study the Bible, the more they can discover what God is saying to people today. The Bible's message does not wear out or become obsolete. However, the Bible was originally written by and for people who lived in different historical circumstances. In order to make the Bible relevant to our time, people need to interpret it in its proper context (see the next chapter, "How to Read and Study the Bible," for help with this). This process of making the Bible's message current for our time is called **actualization.**

Each person, community, and culture brings its life experiences to interact with God's revelation in the Bible. God's word sheds light on our hopes and struggles and in so doing becomes a source of new life for us. Knowing that God forgives our sins, liberates us from the things that oppress and enslave us, and rejoices in our successes gives us the inner peace we all seek. The Bible tells us that we are entrusted with Jesus' mission to share God's peace, justice, and love—a mission that gives true meaning to our life.

Of course, the best way to discover what the Bible has to do with your life is to read and study it yourself. The same Holy Spirit who inspired the original authors will also be your companion as you spend time with the Bible—comforting, exciting, challenging, and encouraging you along your way.

How to Read AND Study THE BIBLE

MAKING SENSE OF THE BIBLE

> "And the Word became flesh and made his dwelling among us" (Jn 1, 14).

God's Word came to earth as a person, Jesus Christ. Jesus was fully human so that people could experience God's love firsthand. He was also fully God so that through him death is overcome and new life is breathed into sinful humanity.

The Bible is called God's word because it is closely linked to Jesus. Like Jesus, it can be said to be both human and divine. It is divine because it reveals to us God and God's plan. But it is also the work of human authors and reflects their knowledge, culture, and biases. It is through their words that the Bible reveals God's nature, God's saving work in the world (often called salvation history), and God's purpose for humanity—including our lives. It follows that an important part of understanding the Bible is understanding the human authors' intentions.

However, understanding the authors' intentions isn't enough either. We must also look at the message of any individual book or passage within the bigger picture of the entire Bible's message and the church's interpretation of it. Here are some suggestions for considering these different contexts when you read the Bible.

Consider the Book's Central Themes

The Bible's authors usually had a central theme or themes in mind when writing their particular book or letter. So when you are confused about the meaning of a particular verse or passage, it often helps to go back and read the whole chapter or even check out the introduction to the book. For example, you may wonder what Jesus is trying to teach us in the story of the prodigal son, Lk 15, 11–32. You might try reading from the beginning of chapter 15. You'll find that Jesus told the story in response to people who criticized him for welcoming sinners. This helps us understand that the prodigal son story teaches that we are supposed to welcome sinners too.

Consider the Historical Situation and the Audience

Certain Bible passages do not make sense unless we understand the historical situation the author was trying to address. The introductions to each of the books in *The Catholic Youth Bible* help you with this. For example, in Am 5, 21.23 God tells the people: "I hate, I spurn your feasts, I take no pleasure in your solemnities; . . . / Away with your noisy songs!" Doesn't God like worship? In the introduction to Amos, we learn that God sent Amos to speak against the rich people who exploited the poor and then attended elaborate religious festivals to worship God. The hypocrisy was what God hated.

Consider the Teaching of the Whole Bible

An old saying calls us to "use the Bible to interpret the Bible." Some people focus on a single verse from the Bible and ignore other passages on the same subject. For example, some churches will not allow women in any position of leadership. They base this on 1 Cor 14, 34, which says, "women should keep silent in the churches." But in doing this, they disregard other passages, such as those in which Paul pays respect to women who were ministers and leaders in the church.

Consider the Church's Interpretation

Most Christian churches have traditions and teachings for interpreting the Bible and applying its message. For Roman Catholics, bishops ultimately have the responsibility for properly interpreting God's revelation in the Bible. Many other people (Scripture scholars, priests, parish ministers, and teachers, for example) help us understand the bishops' interpretation of Scripture and how to apply it to our lives. *The Catholic Youth Bible* points out the Catholic church's established teaching for important passages, especially in the "Catholic Connections" articles. When in doubt, ask a priest, minister, parish leader, teacher, or parent for help in looking for the correct interpretation of a confusing passage.

HEAD AND HEART

Sometimes when you pick up the Bible, you want to study and learn. Maybe you want to learn some Bible history or understand more about Baptism. Maybe you want to know why the Gospel of John is so different from the other Gospels. These are things of the head, the intellect.

Sometimes when you pick up the Bible, you are hungry to grow closer to God. You want to experience God's presence in your life or receive guidance about a problem. These are things of the heart, the soul.

Ask God to touch both your head and heart when you read the Bible. It's important to be open to both because we were created to be whole people. *The Catholic Youth Bible* can help. Some of the articles, particularly the introductions to the books, the "Did You Know?" articles, and the "Catholic Connections" articles, give background to help your understanding for head reading. The "Live It!" and "Pray It!" articles are more for your heart reading.

THE PRIMA PROCESS

Prima is the Latin word for "first." In the PRIMA process, each letter of the word stands for a step in reading and studying the Bible individually or with a group. Using the PRIMA process helps you remember to keep God first in your life!

Pray. Begin with a prayer that your time with the Bible will draw you closer to God.

Read attentively, trusting that God will give you what you need to learn or grow.

Imagine what was going on when the passage was first written. What is its cultural and historical context? Try to put yourself into the story. What was the author trying to get across?

Meditate on what you have read. How does this fit in the context of the rest of the Bible's teaching? with the church's teaching? What do you think God is teaching you?

Apply what you have read to your life. God may be calling you to address a particular issue or relationship. Or you may find words of comfort and support you need at this particular time. Carry God's word into the rest of your day, the rest of your life!

PERSONAL AND GROUP STUDY

Personal Reading and Study

Faith is personal. Reading the Bible by yourself can help you grow in both your head and heart relationships with God. Choose a time that fits for you and make a commitment to read *The Catholic Youth Bible* regularly, at least once a week if not every day. The PRIMA process and the Bible reading plans in the next chapter will give you a structure for your personal reading.

Group Reading and Study

Your faith is personal, but it is not private. The Bible itself teaches that God calls us to be part of a Christian community. Reading and studying the Bible with a group can feed you and teach you in an exciting way. Consider starting a group Bible study by inviting some friends or family members to meet with you. Or check at your parish to see what Bible studies might already be going on.

Again, the PRIMA process and the Bible reading plans in this book can provide a structure for reading the Bible with a group. Check with your parish or school for other resources you can use with a group.

MAKING A PLAN

Note: All the reading plans described in this section are found in the next chapter, "Suggested Reading Plans."

The Catholic church has an excellent plan for reading and studying the Bible, called the lectionary. The lectionary includes a cycle of Scripture passages read at Sunday Eucharist in the liturgy of the word. It is inspiring to know that other Catholics all over the world are hearing and reflecting on the same Scriptures at the same time. Studying the Sunday lectionary readings can make a big difference in your appreciation of the Eucharist. You can use reading plan 1, "Reading the Bible with the Church," to help you do this for part of the year. It lists the Sunday lectionary readings for the seasons of Advent, Christmas, Lent, and Easter.

Reading whole books of the Bible is important to fully understanding the Bible in context. But it rarely works to say, "I'm going to read the whole Bible cover to cover." Most people quit when they hit the detailed laws in the Book of Exodus. So as a start, you can use reading plan 2, "A Walk Through the Bible," which gives a four-week overview of the important events in the Bible. After that you might read one of the four Gospels—Mark is good because it is short and filled with action. Then try the Acts of the Apostles. Follow this by one of the letters from the New Testament—1 Corinthians is a good one to start with. Eventually, move on to Genesis and Exodus from the Old Testament to see how their themes are connected to the New Testament books you have read.

You could also make a plan to study themes in the Bible. To get started, pick from reading plans 3 to 8, which cover topics such as sin and salvation, suffering, God's call, and women in the Bible. Or use the article subject index in the back of *The Catholic Youth Bible* to create your own reading plan on a topic that interests you.

Suggested Reading Plans

READING PLAN 1: Reading the Bible with the Church

This reading plan lists the Sunday readings for the liturgical seasons of Advent, Christmas, Lent, and Easter.

ADVENT AND CHRISTMAS

Cycle A (2001, 2004, 2007)	Cycle B (2002, 2005, 2008)	Cycle C (2000, 2003, 2006)
The First Sunday of Advent		
Is 2, 1–5	Is 63, 16–17.19; 64, 2–7	Jer 33, 14–16
Rom 13, 11–14	1 Cor 1, 3–9	1 Thes 3, 12—4, 2
Mt 24, 37–44	Mk 13, 33–37	Lk 21, 25–28.34–36
The Second Sunday of Advent		
Is 11, 1–10	Is 40, 1–5.9–11	Bar 5, 1–9
Rom 15, 4–9	2 Pt 3, 8–14	Phil 1, 4–6.8–11
Mt 3, 1–12	Mk 1, 1–8	Lk 3, 1–6
The Third Sunday of Advent		
Is 35, 1–6.10	Is 61, 1–2.10–11	Zep 3, 14–18
Jas 5, 7–10	1 Thes 5, 16–24	Phil 4, 4–7
Mt 11, 2–11	Jn 1, 6–8.19–28	Lk 3, 10–18
The Fourth Sunday of Advent		
Is 7, 10–14	2 Sm 7, 1–5.8–11.16	Mi 5, 1–4
Rom 1, 1–7	Rom 16, 25–27	Heb 10, 5–10
Mt 1, 18–24	Lk 1, 26–38	Lk 1, 39–45
Midnight Mass *(25 December, every year, readings are the same for all cycles)*		
Is 9, 1–6	Is 9, 1–6	Is 9, 1–6
Ti 2, 11–14	Ti 2, 11–14	Ti 2, 11–14
Lk 2, 1–14	Lk 2, 1–14	Lk 2, 1–14
Feast of the Holy Family		
Sir 3, 2–6.12–14	Sir 3, 2–6.12–14	Sir 3, 2–6.12–14
Col 3, 12–21	Col 3, 12–21	Col 3, 12–21
Mt 2, 13–15.19–23	Lk 2, 22–40 or 2, 22.39–40	Lk 2, 41–52
Solemnity of Mary, Mother of God *(1 January, every year, readings are the same for all cycles)*		
Nm 6, 22–27	Nm 6, 22–27	Nm 6, 22–27
Gal 4, 4–7	Gal 4, 4–7	Gal 4, 4–7
Lk 2, 16–21	Lk 2, 16–21	Lk 2, 16–21
Epiphany *(readings are the same for all cycles)*		
Is 60, 1–6	Is 60, 1–6	Is 60, 1–6
Eph 3, 2–3.5–6	Eph 3, 2–3.5–6	Eph 3, 2–3.5–6
Mt 2, 1–12	Mt 2, 1–12	Mt 2, 1–12
Baptism of the Lord		
Is 42, 1–4.6–7	Is 42, 1–4.6–7	Is 42, 1–4.6–7
Acts 10, 34–38	Acts 10, 34–38	Acts 10, 34–38
Mt 3, 13–17	Mk 1, 7–11	Lk 3, 15–16.21–22

LENT AND EASTER

Cycle A (2002, 2005, 2008)	Cycle B (2000, 2003, 2006)	Cycle C (2001, 2004, 2007)
Ash Wednesday *(readings are the same for all cycles)*		
Jl 2, 12–18	Jl 2, 12–18	Jl 2, 12–18
2 Cor 5, 20—6, 2	2 Cor 5, 20—6, 2	2 Cor 5, 20—6, 2
Mt 6, 1–6.16–18	Mt 6, 1–6.16–18	Mt 6, 1–6.16–18
The First Sunday of Lent		
Gn 2, 7–9; 3, 1–7	Gn 9, 8–15	Dt 26, 4–10
Rom 5, 12–19	1 Pt 3, 18–22	Rom 10, 8–13
Mt 4, 1–11	Mk 1, 12–15	Lk 4, 1–13

Cycle A (2002, 2005, 2008)	Cycle B (2000, 2003, 2006)	Cycle C (2001, 2004, 2007)
The Second Sunday of Lent		
Gn. 12, 1–4	Gn 22, 1–2.9.10–13.15–18	Gn 15, 5–12.17–18
2 Tm 1, 8–10	Rom 8, 31–34	Phil 3, 17—4, 1
Mt 17, 1–9	Mk 9, 2–10	Lk 9, 28–36
The Third Sunday of Lent		
Ex 17, 3–7	Ex 20, 1–17	Ex 3, 1–8.13–15
Rom 5, 1–2.5–8	1 Cor 1, 22–25	1 Cor 10, 1–6.10–12
Jn 4, 5–42	Jn 2, 13–25	Lk 13, 1–9
The Fourth Sunday of Lent		
1 Sm 16, 1.6–7.10–13	2 Chr 36, 14–17.19–23	Jos 5, 9.10–12
Eph 5, 8–14	Eph 2, 4–10	2 Cor 5, 17–21
Jn 9, 1–41	Jn 3, 14–21	Lk 15, 1–3.11–32
The Fifth Sunday of Lent		
Ez 37, 12–14	Jer 31, 31–34	Is 43, 16–21
Rom 8, 8–11	Heb 5, 7–9	Phil 3, 8–14
Jn 11, 1–45	Jn 12, 20–33	Jn 8, 1–11
Passion Sunday (Palm Sunday)		
Is 50, 4–7	Is 50, 4–7	Is 50, 4–7
Phil 2, 6–11	Phil 2, 6–11	Phil 2, 6–11
Mt 26, 14—27, 66	Mk 14, 1—15, 47	Lk 22, 14—23, 56
Holy Thursday *(readings are the same for all cycles)*		
Ex 12, 1–8.11–14	Ex 12, 1–8.11–14	Ex 12, 1–8.11–14
1 Cor 11, 23–26	1 Cor 11, 23–26	1 Cor 11, 23–26
Jn 13, 1–15	Jn 13, 1–15	Jn 13, 1–15
Good Friday *(readings are the same for all cycles)*		
Is 52, 13—53, 12	Is 52, 13—53, 12	Is 52, 13—53, 12
Heb 4, 14–16; 5, 7–9	Heb 4, 14–16; 5, 7–9	Heb 4, 14–16; 5, 7–9
Jn 18, 1—19, 42	Jn 18, 1—19, 42	Jn 18, 1—19, 42
Easter Sunday *(readings are the same for all cycles)*		
Acts 10, 34.37–43	Acts 10, 34.37–43	Acts 10, 34.37–43
Col 3, 1–4 or 1 Cor 5, 6–8	Col 3, 1–4 or 1 Cor 5, 6–8	Col 3, 1–4 or 1 Cor 5, 6–8
Jn 20, 1–9	Jn 20, 1–9	Jn 20, 1–9
Second Sunday of Easter		
Acts 2, 42–47	Acts 4, 32–35	Acts 5, 12–16
1 Pt 1, 3–9	1 Jn 5, 1–6	Rv 1, 9–11.12–13.17–19
Jn 20, 19–31	Jn 20, 19–31	Jn 20, 19–31
Third Sunday of Easter		
Acts 2, 14.22–28	Acts 3, 13–15.17–19	Acts 5, 27–32.40–41
1 Pt 1, 17–21	1 Jn 2, 1–5	Rv 5, 11–14
Lk 24, 13–35	Lk 24, 35–48	Jn 21, 1–19 or 1–14
Fourth Sunday of Easter		
Acts 2, 14.36–41	Acts 4, 8–12	Acts 13, 14.43–52
1 Pt 2, 20–25	1 Jn 3, 1–2	Rv 7, 9.14–17
Jn 10, 1–10	Jn 10, 11–18	Jn 10, 27–30
Fifth Sunday of Easter		
Acts 6, 1–7	Acts 9, 26–31	Acts 14, 21–27
1 Pt 2, 4–9	1 Jn 3, 18–24	Rv 21, 1–5
Jn 14, 1–12	Jn 15, 1–8	Jn 13, 31–35
Sixth Sunday of Easter		
Acts 8, 5–8.14–17	Acts 10, 25–26.34–35.44–48	Acts 15, 1–2.22–29
1 Pt 3, 15–18	1 Jn 4, 7–10	Rv 21, 10–14.22–23
Jn 14, 15–21	Jn 15, 9–17	Jn 14, 23–29
Seventh Sunday of Easter		
Acts 1, 12–14	Acts 1, 15–17.20–26	Acts 7, 55–60
1 Pt 4, 13–16	1 Jn 4, 11–16	Rv 22, 12–14.16–17.20
Jn 17, 1–11	Jn 17, 11–19	Jn 17, 20–26
Pentecost Sunday *(readings are the same for all cycles)*		
Acts 2, 1–11	Acts 2, 1–11	Acts 2, 1–11
1 Cor 12, 3–7.12–13	1 Cor 12, 3–7.12–13	1 Cor 12, 3–7.12–13
Jn 20, 19–23	Jn 20, 19–23	Jn 20, 19–23

READING PLAN 2:
A Walk Through the Bible

In four weeks, you can visit some of the highlights of the Bible in chronological order.

Day	Bible Reading	Story
❏ 1	Gn, chs 1–2	Creation
❏ 2	Gn, ch 3	the first sin
❏ 3	Gn 6, 5—9, 17	the Flood
❏ 4	Gn 17, 1—18, 15	God's covenant with Abraham
❏ 5	Gn, chs 37. 42–45	Joseph and his brothers
❏ 6	Ex, chs 2–4	the birth and call of Moses
❏ 7	Ex, chs 12–14	God's victory over Pharaoh
❏ 8	Ex, chs 19–20	the Covenant at Sinai and the Ten Commandments
❏ 9	Jgs, chs 13–16	Sampson
❏ 10	1 Sm, ch 17	David and Goliath
❏ 11	2 Sm, chs 6–7	God's promise to David
❏ 12	2 Chr, chs 1–3	King Solomon
❏ 13	2 Chr, chs 34–36	from King Josiah to the fall of Jerusalem
❏ 14	Ps 51, 139	David's repentance and God's presence

Day	Bible Reading	Story
❏ 15	Wis, chs 7–9	God's wisdom
❏ 16	Mi, chs 1–3	the sins of Judah and Israel
❏ 17	Is, chs 11–12	promises of hope
❏ 18	Mal, ch 3	the day of the Lord
❏ 19	Lk, ch 2	the birth and childhood of Jesus
❏ 20	Mt, chs 5–7	Jesus' Sermon on the Mount
❏ 21	Lk, chs 15–16	Jesus' parables
❏ 22	Mk, ch 15	the death of Jesus
❏ 23	Jn, ch 20	the Resurrection of Jesus
❏ 24	Acts 9, 1–22	the conversion of Saul (Paul)
❏ 25	1 Cor, chs 12–14	Christian community
❏ 26	Gal, chs 1–3	faith and the Law
❏ 27	Jas	Christian living
❏ 28	Rv, chs 21.22. Epilogue	the new heaven and the new earth

READING PLAN 5:
The Justice of God

God, it seems, has a preference for the poor. Spend a week reading about God's justice in the Old Testament, and a week in the New Testament.

Day	Bible Reading	Theme
❏ 1	Gn 1, 1—2, 3	God's Creation is good.
❏ 2	Gn, ch 45	God sides with the youngest.
❏ 3	Ex 3, 7–10	God sides with the oppressed.
❏ 4	Lv, ch 25	the Jubilee year
❏ 5	Dt 24, 10–21	God is with the least.
❏ 6	Ps 82	justice to the needy
❏ 7	Am 5, 21–24; 8, 4–10	Let justice roll down.
❏ 8	Mt 5, 43–48	Love your enemies.
❏ 9	Mt 19, 13–15	Jesus welcomes little children.
❏ 10	Mt 25, 31–46	Jesus identifies with the least.
❏ 11	Lk 1, 46–55; 6, 20–26	God reverses the world's order.
❏ 12	Lk 16, 19–31	a rich man and poor Lazarus
❏ 13	Lk 22, 24–27	Who is the greatest?
❏ 14	Jas 2, 1–13	showing favorites?

READING PLAN 6:
Sin and Salvation

The truth is, none of us is perfect—we are all sinners. But God has a plan to save us. Take a two-week journey as you walk from sin to salvation.

Day	Bible Reading	Theme
❏ 1	Gn, ch 3	the first sin
❏ 2	Gn, ch 6	evil everywhere
❏ 3	Gn 12, 1–9	God starts a relationship.
❏ 4	Ex 6, 1–9	God rescues God's people.
❏ 5	Lv, ch 4	a sacrifice for sin
❏ 6	Jn 3, 1–21	for God so loved the world
❏ 7	Mk 8, 31–38	a new sacrifice
❏ 8	Rom 7, 13–25	the predicament
❏ 9	Rom 6, 1–8. 20–23	the promise
❏ 10	Gal 3, 23–29	children of God
❏ 11	Jl 2, 12–13; 1 Jn 1, 8—2, 2	return, repent, and confess
❏ 12	Ps 51	confession prayer
❏ 13	Heb 10, 8–15	the only sacrifice
❏ 14	Mt 26, 26–28	the Eucharist

READING PLAN 3:
Images of God

God has revealed the divine self to us in many wonderful ways. Enjoy two weeks of "seeing" the different pictures of our God.

Day	Bible Reading	Picture of God
☐ 1	Gn 1, 26—3, 24	Creator
☐ 2	Ex 3, 13–15; 6, 2–3	"I AM"
☐ 3	Lv 11, 44–45; Mt 25, 31–46	holy one and judge
☐ 4	Dt, ch 20	warrior and defender
☐ 5	Ps 12, 6	advocate of the poor
☐ 6	Ps 23	great shepherd
☐ 7	Jb 42, 1–6; Jer 18, 1–11	mysterious awesome one
☐ 8	Wis 6, 12–20	feminine, wise
☐ 9	Is 49, 14–15	faithful mother
☐ 10	Jon 1, 1–2; 3, 5–10	universal God of all
☐ 11	Lk 11, 1–4	father
☐ 12	Lk, ch 15	domestic God
☐ 13	Jn 1, 1–18; Col 1, 15–20	Jesus, the Word made flesh
☐ 14	1 Cor, ch 13; 1 Jn 4, 7–8	love

READING PLAN 4:
Called by God

Throughout the Bible, God calls people to serve. You too are called to be a disciple. Take two weeks and pray about your call.

Day	Bible Reading	The One Called
☐ 1	Gn 12, 1–9	Abram (Abraham)
☐ 2	Ex 3, 1—4, 17	Moses
☐ 3	Ru	Ruth
☐ 4	1 Sm, ch 3	Samuel
☐ 5	1 Sm, ch 16	David
☐ 6	Is 43, 1–7	Isiah
☐ 7	Jer 1, 4–10	Jeremiah
☐ 8	Mt 4, 18–22	the first disciples
☐ 9	Mk 8, 31–38	any disciple
☐ 10	Lk 9, 1–6	any disciple
☐ 11	Lk 18, 18–30	a rich ruler
☐ 12	Acts 9, 1–19	Saul (Paul)
☐ 13	Eph 5, 1–20	any disciple
☐ 14	1 Pt 2, 9–17	you!

READING PLAN 7:
Why Do We Suffer?

Why God allows suffering has been a question for many of the Bible's authors. During this two-week study, look for the growing awareness that God is with us in our suffering.

Day	Bible Reading	Theme or Article Title
☐ 1	introduction to Tb	God rescues the suffering?
☐ 2	Tb, ch 3	suffering and suicide
☐ 3	Jb 1, 13–21	suffering and faith
☐ 4	the article near Job 24, 1	"A Long Debate"
☐ 5	the article near Jb 38, 1—42, 6	"Why?"
☐ 6	Ps 6	praying for deliverance
☐ 7	the article near Lam 5, 22	"Growing Through Loss"
☐ 8	Is 52, 13—53, 12	the suffering servant
☐ 9	Jn 12, 24–26	the paschal mystery
☐ 10	the article near Mk 15, 16–20	"Facing the Hard Times"
☐ 11	the article near Mt 27, 27–44	"Suffering Prayer"
☐ 12	2 Cor 1, 3–11	God's presence
☐ 13	2 Cor 11, 16–29	Paul's suffering
☐ 14	1 Pt 3, 13—4, 19	suffering as a Christian

READING PLAN 8:
Women in the Bible

In the ancient world, many people considered women to be inferior to men. But throughout the Bible, God shows otherwise. Here is a two-week look at women who have served God and the church.

Day	Bible Reading	Woman or Women
☐ 1	Gn 2, 18—3, 20	Eve
☐ 2	Gn 17, 15–16; 21, 1–7	Sarai (Sarah)
☐ 3	Ex 15, 19–21	Miriam
☐ 4	Jgs, chs 4–5	Deborah
☐ 5	Ru	Ruth
☐ 6	1 Sm 1, 1—2, 10	Hannah
☐ 7	Est, ch 8	Esther
☐ 8	Lk 1, 5–25.57–66	Elizabeth
☐ 9	Lk 1, 26—2, 20	Mary, the mother of our Lord
☐ 10	Lk 2, 36–38	Anna
☐ 11	Jn 20, 1–18	Mary Magdalene
☐ 12	Jn 11, 1–44; 12, 1–8	Mary and Martha
☐ 13	Acts 16, 11–15; ch 18	Lydia and Priscilla
☐ 14	Rom 16, 1–7	Phoebe and Junia

Preface to the New American Bible:
The Old Testament

On September 30, 1943, His Holiness Pope Pius XII issued his now famous encyclical on scripture studies, *Divino afflante Spiritu*. He wrote: "We ought to explain the original text which was written by the inspired author himself and has more authority and greater weight than any, even the very best, translation whether ancient or modern. This can be done all the more easily and fruitfully if to the knowledge of languages be joined a real skill in literary criticism of the same text."

Early in 1944, in conformity with the spirit of the encyclical, and with the encouragement of Archbishop Cicognani, Apostolic Delegate to the United States, the Bishops' Committee of the Confraternity of Christian Doctrine requested members of The Catholic Biblical Association of America to translate the sacred scriptures from the original languages or from the oldest extant form of the text, and to present the sense of the biblical text in as correct a form as possible.

The first English Catholic version of the Bible, the Douay-Rheims (1582-1609/10), and its revision by Bishop Challoner (1750) were based on the Latin Vulgate. In view of the relative certainties more recently attained by textual and higher criticism, it has become increasingly desirable that contemporary translations of the sacred books into English be prepared in which due reverence for the text and strict observance of the rules of criticism would be combined.

The New American Bible has accomplished this in response to the need of the church in America today. It is the achievement of some fifty biblical scholars, the greater number of whom, though not all, are Catholics. In particular, the editors-in-chief have devoted twenty-five years to this work. The collaboration of scholars who are not Catholic fulfills the directive of the Second Vatican Council, not only that "correct translations be made into different languages especially from the original texts of the sacred books," but that, "with the approval of the church authority, these translations be produced in cooperation with separated brothers" so that "all Christians may be able to use them."

The text of the books contained in *The New American Bible* is a completely new translation throughout. From the original and the oldest available texts of the sacred books, it aims to convey as directly as possible the thought and individual style of the inspired writers. The better understanding of Hebrew and Greek, and the steady development of the science of textual criticism, the fruit of patient study since the time of St. Jerome, have allowed the translators and editors in their use of all available materials to approach more closely than ever before the sense of what the sacred authors actually wrote.

Where the translation supposes the received text—Hebrew, Aramaic, or Greek, as the case may be— ordinarily contained in the best-known editions, as the original or the oldest extant form, no additional remarks are necessary. But for those who are happily able to study the original text of the scriptures at first-hand, a supplementary series of textual notes pertaining to the Old Testament was added originally in an appendix to the typical edition. (It is now obtainable in a separate booklet from The Catholic Biblical Association of America, The Catholic University of America, Washington, DC 20064.) These notes furnish a guide in those cases in which the editorial board judges that the manuscripts in the original languages, or the evidence of the ancient versions, or some similar source, furnish the correct reading of a passage, or at least a reading more true to the original than that customarily printed in the available editions.

The Massoretic text of 1 and 2 Samuel has in numerous instances been corrected by the more ancient manuscripts Samuel a, b, and c from Cave 4 of Qumran, with the aid of important evidence from the Septuagint in both its oldest form and its Lucianic recension. Fragments of the lost Book of Tobit in Aramaic and in Hebrew, recovered from Cave 4 of Qumran, are in substantial agreement with the Sinaiticus Greek recension used for the translation of this book. The lost original Hebrew text of 1 Maccabees is replaced by its oldest extant form in Greek. Judith, 2 Maccabees, and parts of Esther are also translated from the Greek.

The basic text for the Psalms is not the Massoretic but one which the editors considered closer to the original inspired form, namely the Hebrew text underlying the new Latin Psalter of the Church, the *Liber Psalmorum* (1944[1], 1945[2]). Nevertheless they retained full liberty to establish the reading of the original text on sound critical principles.

The translation of Sirach, based on the original Hebrew as far as it is preserved and corrected from the ancient versions, is often interpreted in the light of the traditional Greek text. In the Book of Baruch the basic text is the Greek of the Septuagint, with some readings derived from an underlying Hebrew form no longer extant. In the deuterocanonical sections of Daniel (3, 24–91, chapter 13 and chapter 14 [these are Azariah, Susanna, and Bel and the Dragon respectively in WORDsearch]), the basic text is the Greek text of Theodotion, occasionally revised according to the Greek text of the Septuagint.

In some instances in the Book of Job, in Proverbs, Sirach, Isaiah, Jeremiah, Ezekiel, Hosea, Amos, Micah, Nahum, Habakkuk, and Zechariah there is good reason to believe that the original order of lines was accidentally disturbed in the transmission of the text. The verse numbers given in such cases are always those of the current Hebrew text, though the arrangement differs. In these instances the textual notes advise the reader of the difficulty. Cases of exceptional dislocation are called to the reader's attention by footnotes.

The Books of *Genesis* to *Ruth* were first published in 1952; the Wisdom Books, *Job* to *Sirach*, in 1955; the Prophetic Books, *Isaiah* to *Malachi*, in 1961; and the Historical Books, *Samuel* to *Maccabees*, in 1969. In the present edition of *Genesis* to *Ruth* there are certain new features: a general introduction to the Pentateuch, a retranslation of the text of Genesis with an introduction, cross-references, and revised textual notes, besides new and expanded exegetical notes which take into consideration the various sources or literary traditions.

The revision of *Job* to *Sirach* includes changes in strophe division in Job and Proverbs and in titles of principal parts and sections of Wisdom and Ecclesiastes. Corrections in the text of Sirach are made in Sir 39, 27—44, 17 on the basis of the Masada text, and in 51, 13–30 on the basis of the occurrence of this canticle in the Psalms scroll from Qumran Cave 11. In this typical edition, new corrections are reflected in the textual notes of Job, Proverbs, Wisdom, and Sirach. In the Psalms, the enumeration found in the Hebrew text is followed instead of the double enumeration, according to both the Hebrew and the Latin Vulgate texts, contained in the previous edition of this book.

In the Prophetic Books *Isaiah* to *Malachi*, only minor revisions have been made in the structure and wording of the texts, and in the textual notes.

The spelling of proper names in *The New American Bible* follows the customary forms found in most English Bibles since the Authorized Version.

The work of translating the Bible has been characterized as "the sacred and apostolic work of interpreting the word of God and of presenting it to the laity in translations as clear as the difficulty of the matter and the limitations of human knowledge permit" (A. G. Cicognani, Apostolic Delegate, in *The Catholic Biblical Quarterly*, 6, [1944], 389–90). In the appraisal of the present work, it is hoped that the words of the encyclical *Divino afflante Spiritu* will serve as a guide: "Let all the sons of the church bear in mind that the efforts of these resolute laborers in the vineyard of the Lord should be judged not only with equity and justice but also with the greatest charity; all moreover should abhor that intemperate zeal which imagines that whatever is new should for that very reason be opposed or suspected."

Conscious of their personal limitations for the task thus defined, those who have prepared this text cannot expect that it will be considered perfect; but they can hope that it may deepen in its readers "the right understanding of the divinely given Scriptures," and awaken in them "that piety by which it behooves us to be grateful to the God of all providence, who from the throne of his majesty has sent these books as so many personal letters to his own children" *(Divino afflante Spiritu).*

THE *Old Testament*

Introduction to the
Pentateuch

Did you ever get to a movie late? Did you end up bothering your friends who got there on time by asking: "What's happening? Why did he do that? What did she mean by that?" Like the first crucial minutes of a movie, the five books of the Pentateuch set the stage for much of what happens in the rest of the Bible. If you are not familiar with their wonderful stories, you might find yourself asking: "What's happening? Why is he doing that? Why did she say that?" when reading later books.

In-depth

THE NAME PENTATEUCH LITERALLY MEANS A "five-part writing." Thus, the Pentateuch is the first five books of the Old Testament: Genesis, Exodus, Leviticus, Numbers, and Deuteronomy. These books are special to Jewish and Christian believers because they tell of the origins of God's people and their unique relationship with God—sometimes called salvation history. They are the blueprint needed for properly understanding the rest of the Bible. The Pentateuch introduces the idea of a single God who is responsible for all creation. It also tells that this God is active in the world and in the lives of its people, and that the Israelites have been called into a special relationship with this God.

One of the central elements of the special relationship between God and the Israelites described in the Pentateuch is the Sinai Covenant. A covenant is a solemn promise between two parties, where both parties agree to fulfill certain obligations. The Sinai Covenant is the most famous one between God and Israel, with Moses as the mediator, which you will read about in Exodus. In Genesis, you will read about the covenants God makes with Noah, Abraham, and Jacob, which lead to the Sinai Covenant.

Reading the Pentateuch is like appreciating a fine tapestry. When you view a tapestry from the front, all the threads combine to make a beautiful, coherent image. In the same way, an overall look at the covenants, stories, and laws in the Pentateuch combine to form a picture of the love relationship between God and the people of Israel. A close look at the back of a tapestry shows a more chaotic mix of colors and yarn. So too a closer look at the writings in the Pentateuch reveals not one story but many.

Biblical scholars speak of four primary sources for the stories and traditions in the Pentateuch. The sources reflect four different schools of thought about Israel's relationship with God. For convenience, each source is referred to as an individual author.

- The Yahwist used Yahweh as God's name. This writer focused on the southern kingdom of Judah, used lots of stories, emphasized God's closeness to humanity, and portrayed God acting as a human person.
- The Elohist referred to God as Elohim or Lord. The Elohist wrote about the northern kingdom of Israel and was concerned about idolatry and morality. The writings of the Elohist present God speaking through symbols such as a burning bush.
- The Deuteronomist emphasized the Law as the foundation of the kingdom of Judah. The Deuteronomist emerged toward the end of the monarchy (the time of the Israelite kings), when the Covenant Law seemed to have been forgotten.
- Finally, the Priestly writer emphasized religious rituals and the role of the priesthood. This writer portrayed God as more distant and used a more formal style. This source was written after the Babylonian Exile.

Knowing that these four sources contributed to the final form of the Pentateuch can help us understand that the Pentateuch books are not simply records of events as they occurred, but rather faith accounts about the Israelites' growing relationship with God, inspired by God and told from different perspectives.

In the Pentateuch, God reveals how much God loves the human race collectively and how much God loves us personally. God wishes to be in a relationship with us today just as much as God did back then. The Pentateuch reminds us that we are all children of God.

Other Background

- Some of the most familiar stories and people of the Old Testament are found in Genesis and Exodus. Genesis includes the stories of Creation, Adam and Eve, Noah and the Flood, Abraham and Sarah, and Joseph and his brothers. Exodus contains the stories of Moses and the burning bush, Pharaoh and the ten plagues, the parting of the Red Sea, and the Ten Commandments.

- The Jews also refer to the five books of the Pentateuch as the Torah, meaning "teaching" or "instruction."

- An ancient tradition named Moses as the author of the Pentateuch. This was no doubt due to Moses' importance in the Pentateuch itself. But evidence suggests that most of the Pentateuch was written hundreds of years after Moses' death.

- The two types of writing in the Pentateuch are stories and laws. Genesis is all stories, Leviticus and Deuteronomy are mostly laws, and Exodus and Numbers are about half stories and half laws.

Displays of awesome cosmic power, tender love stories, tearful family reunions, and tales of deceit, rape, murder, and worldwide destruction. Does this sound like the script for next summer's blockbuster movie? No, it's the Book of Genesis! It is the story of how a world created for love and harmony goes astray because of human sin. Through it all, God is at work, forming a people to restore what was lost.

At a Glance

I. The Primeval History (1, 1—11, 26).

II. The Patriarch Abraham (11, 27—25, 18).

III. The Patriarchs Isaac and Jacob (25, 19—36, 43).

IV. Joseph and His Brothers (37, 1—50, 26).

In-depth

Genesis gathers together inspired stories and traditions that reveal God's nature and purpose, and the beginning of the Israelites' special relationship with God. Genesis has four main sections. The first section, (1, 1—11, 26) contains some of the Bible's most memorable stories about Creation and the effect of sin. Chapters 1–2 tell two stories of Creation that portray the beauty and wonder of the natural world and emphasize the goodness and harmony that God intended in Creation. Creation culminates in human beings, made in God's own image. Those first human beings, Adam and Eve, live in a wonderful garden in harmony with God, Creation, and each other. But in chapter 3, sin enters the world, and as a result, Adam and Eve will experience separation, suffering, and ultimately death.

And sin spreads, first to the family (Cain and Abel in chapter 4), then to all society (Noah and the Flood in chapters 6–9). Even after the Flood and God's covenant with Noah, the story of the tower of Babel demonstrates that sin pits nation against nation. As you read these chapters, remember that they were written not as historical accounts or scientific explanations but as symbolic stories that shared faith experiences and taught important religious truths.

Sections two through four of Genesis (11, 27—50, 26) tell the story of the origins of the Israelite people. The story begins with Abraham and Sarah (originally called Abram and Sarai) and continues with Ishmael and Isaac and with Isaac and Rebekah's children, Esau and Jacob. Genesis ends with Joseph, one of Jacob's twelve sons, cleverly saving Egypt and Israel from famine. These sections introduce the covenant God makes with Abraham and remind the reader that God's plans will overcome human sin and weakness.

Quick Facts

Period Covered

The stories in the first eleven chapters are primeval history. Genesis 11, 27—50, 26 covers the period of the ancestors, or patriarchs and matriarchs (from 2000 to 1500 B.C.).

Author

An unknown author gathered oral traditions and stories from tribal peoples sometime from 1225 to 1000 B.C. (see Introduction to the Pentateuch).

Themes

the goodness of Creation, human responsibility, the effects of sin, covenant, God's bringing good out of evil

Genesis

I: The Primeval History

First Story of Creation

1 1*† In the beginning, when God created the heavens and the earth, 2*† the earth was a formless wasteland, and darkness covered the abyss, while a mighty wind swept over the waters.

3* Then God said, "Let there be light," and there was light. 4 God saw how good the light was. God then separated the light from the darkness. 5† God called the light "day," and the darkness he called "night." Thus evening came, and morning followed—the first day.

6 Then God said, "Let there be a dome in the middle of the waters, to separate one body of water from the other." And so it happened: 7* God made the dome, and it separated the water above the dome from the water below it. 8 God called the dome "the sky." Evening came, and morning followed—the second day.

9* Then God said, "Let the water under the sky be gathered into a single basin, so that the dry land may appear." And so it happened: the water under the sky was gathered into its basin, and the dry land appeared. 10 God called the dry land "the earth," and the basin of the water he called "the sea." God saw how good it was. 11* Then God said, "Let the earth bring forth vegetation: every kind of plant that bears seed and every kind of fruit tree on earth that bears fruit with its seed in it." And so it happened: 12 the earth brought forth every kind of plant that bears seed and every kind of fruit tree on earth that bears fruit with its seed in it. God saw how good it was. 13 Evening came, and morning followed—the third day.

14* Then God said: "Let there be lights in the dome of the sky, to separate day from night. Let them mark the fixed times, the days and the years, 15 and serve as luminaries in the dome of the sky, to shed light upon the earth." And so it happened: 16* God made the two great lights, the greater one to govern the day, and the lesser one to govern the night; and he made the stars. 17 God set them in the dome of the sky, to shed light upon the earth, 18 to govern the day and the night, and to separate the light from the darkness. God saw how good it was.

---

† **1, 1—2, 4a:** This section introduces the whole Pentateuch. It shows how God brought an orderly universe out of primordial chaos.

1, 2: *The abyss:* the primordial ocean according to the ancient Semitic cosmogony. After God's creative activity, part of this vast body forms the salt-water seas (vv 9f); part of it is the fresh water under the earth (Ps 33, 7; Ez 31, 4), which wells forth on the earth as springs and fountains (Gn 7, 11; 8, 2; Prv 3, 20). Part of it, "the upper water" (Ps 148, 4; Dn 3, 60), is held up by the dome of the sky (Gn 1, 6f) from which rain descends on the earth (Gn 7, 11; 2 Kgs 7, 2.19; Ps 104, 13). *A mighty wind:* literally, "a wind of God," or "a spirit of God"; cf Gn 8, 1.

1, 5: In ancient Israel a day was considered to begin at sunset. Ac-

cording to the highly artificial literary structure of Gn 1, 1—2, 4a, God's creative activity is divided into six days to teach the sacredness of the sabbath rest on the seventh day in the Israelite religion (Gn 2, 2f).

1, 1: Gn 2, 1.4; Pss 8, 4; 38—39; 90, 2; Wis 11, 17; Sir 16, 24; Jer 10, 12; 2 Mc 7, 28; Acts 14, 15; Col 1, 16f; Heb 1, 2f; 3, 4; 11, 3; Rv 4, 11.
1, 2: Jer 4, 23.
1, 3: 2 Cor 4, 6.

1, 7: Prv 8, 27f; 2 Pt 3, 5.
1, 9: Jb 38, 8; Ps 33, 7; Jer 5, 22.
1, 11: Ps 104, 14.
1, 14: Jb 26, 10; Ps 19, 1f; Bar 3, 33.
1, 16: Dt 4, 19; Ps 136, 7ff; Wis 13, 2ff; Jer 31, 35.

19 Evening came, and morning followed—the fourth day.

20* Then God said, "Let the water teem with an abundance of living creatures, and on the earth let birds fly beneath the dome of the sky." And so it happened: 21 God created the great sea monsters and all kinds of swimming creatures with which the water teems, and all kinds of winged birds. God saw how good it was, 22* and God blessed them, saying, "Be fertile, multiply, and fill the water of the seas; and let the birds multiply on the earth." 23 Evening came, and morning followed—the fifth day.

?did you KNOW?

Literary Genres

Some Christians believe that God actually created the world in seven twenty-four-hour days. Such a belief comes from a literal reading of the first chapter of Genesis, as though it were a scientific textbook. However, Genesis was written not as a science article but as symbolic stories, sometimes called mythic stories, that convey great moral and spiritual truths. We should not try to come to any scientific conclusions about the creation of the world from reading these stories.

Mythic stories are one literary type, or genre. You just have to look in a newspaper to see examples of different literary genres: news stories, advice columns, editorials, and comics. Each genre has different rules for interpreting its meaning. The Bible also contains many types of literary genres, including hero stories, poetry, laws, legends, fictional satire, debates, and letters. To properly understand the Bible, pay attention to the literary genre—otherwise, you might believe the Bible is saying something God doesn't intend.

▸ Gn 1, 1—2, 4

IN THE BEGINNING

"In the beginning, when God created the heavens and the earth . . ." (Gn 1, 1). This simple verse is one of the foundational beliefs of Christianity. We are not a random collection of atoms. The world is not a lucky combination of cosmic circumstances. The universe did not just accidentally happen.

The beginning of wisdom is acknowledging that a higher power is at work in our life, that the universe has purpose, and that everything was created by God. The ancient writers and editors of Genesis expressed these ideas in the Creation stories. The church affirms these beliefs. They are expressed in a prayer called the Apostles' Creed, which begins, "I believe in God the father almighty, creator of heaven and earth."

Genesis expresses another foundational belief: God created everything good! Read the story in chapter 1 and see how this belief is constantly repeated: And humankind is "very good," created in God's own image. This is God's message to you in the first chapter of the Bible: You carry God's image within you. You are very good! Don't let anyone ever convince you otherwise.

▸ Gn 1, 1—2, 4

24* Then God said, "Let the earth bring forth all kinds of living creatures: cattle, creeping things, and wild animals of all kinds." And so it happened: 25 God made all kinds of wild animals, all kinds of cattle, and all kinds of creeping things of the earth. God saw how good it was. 26*† Then God said: "Let us make man in our image, after our likeness. Let them have dominion over the fish of the sea, the birds of the air, and the cattle, and over all the wild animals and all the creatures that crawl on the ground."

27   God created man in his image;
        in the divine image he created him;
        male and female he created them.

1, 26: Man is here presented as the climax of God's creative activity; he resembles God primarily because of the dominion God gives him over the rest of creation.

1, 20: Jb 12, 7–10.
1, 22: Gn 8, 17.
1, 24: Sir 16, 27f; Bar 3, 32.
1, 26f: Gn 5, 1.3; 9, 6; Ps 8, 5f;

Wis 2, 23; 10, 2; Sir 17, 1.3f; Jas 3, 7; 1 Cor 11, 7; Eph 4, 24; Col 3, 10; Mt 19, 4; Mk 10, 6.

In God's Image

God does not make mistakes; people do. Some people might be tempted to deny their racial heritage, to even change their physical appearance in order to fit into the latest fad or the dominant cultural image of beauty. We must remember that physical features are not accidents. God planned for them—we are all made in God's image.

If we are to authentically love ourselves, we must love our whole selves. This includes a love for dark skin or light skin; straight hair or tight curly hair; wide nose or pug nose; and all the variation in between. Whatever our appearance, we are all blessed of God.

Dear God, I praise you for who I am on the inside and on the outside. Amen.

▸ Gn 1, 26–27

28* God blessed them, saying to them: "Be fertile and multiply; fill the earth and subdue it. Have dominion over the fish of the sea, the birds of the air, and all the living things that move on the earth." 29* God also said: "See, I give you every seed-bearing plant all over the earth and every tree that has seed-bearing fruit on it to be your food; 30 and to all the animals of the land, all the birds of the air, and all the living creatures that crawl on the ground, I give all the green plants for food." And so it happened. 31* God looked at everything he had made, and he found it very good. Evening came, and morning followed—the sixth day.

2 1* Thus the heavens and the earth and all their array were completed. 2* Since on the seventh day God was finished with the work he had been doing, he rested on the seventh day from all the work he had undertaken. 3* So God blessed the seventh day and made it holy, because

on it he rested from all the work he had done in creation.

4 Such is the story of the heavens and the earth at their creation.

Second Story of Creation

† At the time when the LORD God made the earth and the heavens— 5 while as yet there was no field shrub on earth and no grass of the field had sprouted, for the LORD God had sent no rain upon the earth and there was no man to till the soil, 6 but a stream was welling up out of the earth and was

The Sabbath

Even God needed to take a rest. The writer of Genesis makes this point to remind readers to set aside a day for rest and prayer, which Jewish people call the Sabbath. Honoring the Sabbath is an act of trust in God. It means we believe that the world will not fall apart if we stop our activity. The world is in God's hands. We can hear this truth echoed in Jesus' words:

Notice how the flowers grow. They do not toil or spin. But I tell you, not even Solomon in all his splendor was dressed like one of them. If God so clothes the grass in the field that grows today and is thrown into the oven tomorrow, will he not much more provide for you, O you of little faith? (Lk 12, 27–28)

Traditionally, Christians rest and pray on Sunday because it is the day Jesus was resurrected. In our culture today, it seems that many people are losing this practice. What could we gain if we recommitted ourselves to a day of rest, celebration, and prayer? What can you do personally to more fully honor the concept of "Sabbath" rest?

▸ Gn 2, 1–3

2, 4b–25: This section is chiefly concerned with the creation of man. It is much older than the narrative of Gn 1, 1—2, 4a. Here God is depicted as creating man before the rest of his creatures, which are made for man's sake.

1, 28: Gn 8, 17; 9, 1; Pss 8, 6–9; 115, 16; Wis 9, 2.
1, 29f: Gn 9, 3; Ps 104, 14f.
1, 31: 1 Tm 4, 4.
2, 1: Is 45, 12; Jn 1, 3.

2, 2: Ex 20, 9ff; 31, 17; Heb 4, 4.10.
2, 3: Ex 20, 11; Dt 5, 14; Neh 9, 14.

GN

¡Dios es nuestro Creador!

HISPANIC

GOD IS OUR CREATOR!

According to Genesis, chapters 1–2, God created the universe and is the source of order in all creation. Creation is good, and its goodness is reflected in the harmony, peace, and love between the Creator and his creatures, and among the creatures themselves. In Hispanic theological traditions, this ideal relationship—symbolized by the way God and Adam and Eve relate in the Garden of Eden—is considered the foundation in which salvation history is rooted.

- How are your relationships with God, your friends, your family, and nature characterized by harmony, peace, and love?
- Reflect on how you can improve some of your strained relationships, and ask God's help to do it.

Human beings are created in God's image and likeness and share God's attributes: freedom, love, knowledge, and the ability to create. With these gifts comes the responsibility of caring for all creation.

- Give thanks and praise to God for creation, especially for your own life and the lives of the people around you.
- Think of how you, your family, and your community can take better care of all creation. Pray that you fully develop your capacity to love, to know the truth, and to use your freedom wisely.

God established a covenant with us at the moment of our creation, and we keep this covenant by freely placing ourselves in God's hands and being responsive to God's invitation to live in communion with God and people.

- How do you use your freedom to respond to God's invitation?
- Think about the aspects of your life for which you most need God's wisdom to live in harmony and love. Put yourself in God's hands, and let God help and direct you.

▶ Genesis, chapters 1–2

---

watering all the surface of the ground— 7*† the LORD God formed man out of the clay of the ground and blew into his nostrils the breath of life, and so man became a living being.

8*† Then the LORD God planted a garden in Eden, in the east, and he placed there the man whom he had formed. 9* Out of the ground the LORD God made various trees grow that were delightful to look at and good for food, with the tree of life in the middle of the garden and the tree of the knowledge of good and bad.

10† A river rises in Eden to water the garden; beyond there it divides and becomes four branches. 11 The name of the first is the Pishon; it is the one that winds through the whole land of Havilah, where there is gold. 12 The gold of that land is excellent; bdellium and lapis lazuli are also there. 13* The name of the second river is the Gihon; it is the one that winds all through the land of Cush. 14 The name of the third river is the Tigris; it is the one that flows east of Asshur. The fourth river is the Euphrates.

15* The LORD God then took the man and settled him in the garden of Eden, to cultivate and care for it. 16* The LORD God gave man this order: "You are free to eat from any of the trees of the garden 17* except the tree of knowledge of good and bad. From that tree you shall not eat; the moment you eat from it you are surely doomed to die."

2, 7: God is portrayed as a potter molding man's body out of clay. There is a play on words in Hebrew between *adam* ("man") and *adama* ("ground"). *Being:* literally, "soul."

2, 8: *Eden:* used here as the name of a region in southern Mesopotamia; the term is derived from the Sumerian word *eden,* "fertile plain." A similar-sounding Hebrew word means "delight"; the *garden in Eden* could therefore be understood as the "garden of delight," so that, through the Greek version, it is now known also as "paradise," literally, a "pleasure park."

2, 10–14: *Rises:* in flood to overflow its banks. *Beyond there:* as one travels upstream. *Branches:* literally, "heads," i.e., upper courses.

Eden is near the head of the Persian Gulf, where the Tigris and the Euphrates join with two other streams to form a single river. *The land of Cush* here and in Gn 10, 8, is not Ethiopia (Nubia) as elsewhere, but the region of the Kassites east of Mesopotamia.

2, 7: Gn 3, 19; 18, 27; Tb 8, 6; Jb 34, 15; Pss 103, 14; 104, 29; Eccl 3, 20; 12, 7; Wis 7, 1; Sir 33, 10; 1 Cor 15, 45.
2, 8: Is 51, 3; Ez 31, 9.
2, 9: Gn 3, 22; Prv 3, 18; Rv 2, 7; 22, 2.14.
2, 13: Sir 24, 25.
2, 15: Sir 7, 15.
2, 16: Ps 104, 14.
2, 17: Gn 3, 2f; Rom 6, 23.

18* The LORD God said: "It is not good for the man to be alone. I will make a suitable partner for him." 19 So the LORD God formed out of the ground various wild animals and various birds of the air, and he brought them to the man to see what he would call them; whatever the man called each of them would be its name. 20 The man gave names to all the cattle, all the birds of the air, and all the wild animals; but none proved to be the suitable partner for the man.

21* So the LORD God cast a deep sleep on the man, and while he was asleep, he took out one of his ribs and closed up its place with flesh. 22 The LORD God then built up into a woman the rib that he had taken from the man. When he brought her to the man, 23† the man said:

"This one, at last, is bone of my bones
    and flesh of my flesh;
This one shall be called 'woman,'
    for out of 'her man' this one has
        been taken."

24*† That is why a man leaves his father and mother and clings to his wife, and the two of them become one body.

25 The man and his wife were both naked, yet they felt no shame.

The Fall of Man

3 ¹ Now the serpent was the most cunning of all the animals that the LORD God had made. The serpent asked the woman, "Did God really tell you not to eat from any of the trees in the garden?" ² The woman answered the serpent: "We may eat of the fruit of the trees in the garden; ³* it is only about the fruit of the tree in the middle of the garden that God said, 'You shall not eat it or even touch it, lest you die.' " ⁴* But the serpent said to the woman: "You certainly will not die! ⁵† No, God knows well that the moment you eat of it your eyes will be opened and you will be like gods who know what is good and what is bad." ⁶* The woman saw that the tree was good for food, pleasing to the eyes, and desirable for gaining wisdom. So she took some of its fruit and ate it; and she also gave some to her husband, who was with her, and he ate it. ⁷ Then the eyes of both of them were opened, and they realized that they were naked; so they sewed fig leaves together and made loincloths for themselves.

Catholic Connections

ORIGINAL SIN BREAKS OUR RELATIONSHIP WITH GOD

The story of Adam and Eve is about the human weakness for sinning and disobeying God. The serpent tells Adam and Eve they can be like God, and know good and evil. After disobeying God, they recognize that they are naked and feel shame. Their relationship of trust with God is broken. This story teaches that soon after men and women were created, sin entered human history and led to pain and suffering.

This reality—that every human person, beginning with our first ancestors, chooses to disobey God—the Catholic church calls original sin. Original sin is another way of saying that every person makes choices that separate him or her from God. We are born into this condition, which has been passed on from the beginning of the human race.

▸ Gn 3, 1–24

8*† When they heard the sound of the LORD God moving about in the garden at the breezy time of the day, the man and his wife hid themselves from the LORD God among the trees of the garden. ⁹ The LORD God then called to the man and asked him, "Where are you?" ¹⁰ He answered, "I heard you in the garden; but I was afraid, because I was naked, so I hid myself." ¹¹ Then he asked, "Who told you that you were naked? You have eaten, then, from the tree of which I had forbidden you to eat!" ¹² The man replied, "The woman whom you put here with

† 2, 23: There is a play on the similar-sounding Hebrew words *ishsha* ("woman") and *ishah* ("her man, her husband").
2, 24: *One body:* literally "one flesh"; classical Hebrew has no specific word for "body." The sacred writer stresses the fact that conjugal union is willed by God.
3, 5: *Like gods who know:* or "like God who knows."
3, 8: *The breezy time of the day:* literally "the wind of the day." On most days in Palestine a cooling breeze blows from the sea shortly before sunset.

* 2, 18: Tb 8, 6; Sir 36, 24;   Eph 5, 31.
1 Cor 11, 9; 1 Tm 2,   3, 3: Gn 2, 17; Rom 6, 23.
13.   3, 4f: Wis 2, 24; Sir 25, 14;
2, 21: Sir 17, 1; 1 Cor 11, 8f;   Is 14, 14; Jn 8, 44;
1 Tm 2, 13.   2 Cor 11, 3.
2, 24: Mt 19, 5; Mk 10, 7;   3, 6: Gn 3, 22; 1 Tm 2, 14.
1 Cor 7, 10f;   3, 8: Jer 23, 24.

me—she gave me fruit from the tree, and so I ate it." 13* The LORD God then asked the woman, "Why did you do such a thing?" The woman answered, "The serpent tricked me into it, so I ate it."

14* Then the LORD God said to the serpent:

> "Because you have done this, you shall
> 　be banned
> 　　from all the animals
> 　　and from all the wild creatures;
> On your belly shall you crawl,
> 　and dirt shall you eat
> 　　all the days of your life.
> 15*†I will put enmity between you and
> 　　the woman,
> 　and between your offspring and hers;
> He will strike at your head,
> 　while you strike at his heel."

16* To the woman he said:

> "I will intensify the pangs of
> 　your childbearing;
> 　in pain shall you bring forth children.
> Yet your urge shall be for your husband,
> 　and he shall be your master."

17* To the man he said: "Because you listened to your wife and ate from the tree of which I had forbidden you to eat,

> "Cursed be the ground because of you!
> 　In toil shall you eat its yield
> 　　all the days of your life.
> 18　Thorns and thistles shall it bring forth to you,
> 　as you eat of the plants of the field.
> 19* By the sweat of your face
> 　shall you get bread to eat,
> Until you return to the ground,
> 　from which you were taken;
> For you are dirt,
> 　and to dirt you shall return."

20† The man called his wife Eve, because she became the mother of all the living.

21 For the man and his wife the LORD God made leather garments, with which he clothed them. 22* Then the LORD God said: "See! The man has become like one of us, knowing what is good and what is bad! Therefore, he must not be allowed to put out his hand to take fruit from the tree of life also, and thus eat of it and live forever." 23 The LORD God therefore banished him from the garden of Eden, to till the ground from which he had been taken. 24† When he expelled the man, he settled him east of the garden of Eden; and he stationed the cherubim and the fiery revolving sword, to guard the way to the tree of life.

Cain and Abel

4 1† The man had relations with his wife Eve, and she conceived and bore Cain, saying, "I have produced a man with the help of the LORD." 2 Next she bore his brother Abel. Abel became a keeper of flocks, and Cain a tiller of the soil. 3 In the course of time Cain brought an offering to the LORD from the fruit of the soil, 4* while Abel, for his part, brought one of the best firstlings of his flock. The LORD looked with favor on Abel and his offering, 5 but on Cain and his offering he did not. Cain greatly resented this and was crestfallen. 6 So the LORD said to Cain: "Why are you so resentful and crestfallen? 7*† If you do well, you can hold up your head; but if not, sin is a demon lurking at the door: his urge is toward you, yet you can be his master."

8* Cain said to his brother Abel, "Let us go out in the field." When they were in the field, Cain attacked his brother Abel and killed him. 9 Then the LORD asked Cain, "Where is your brother Abel?" He answered, "I do not know. Am I my brother's keeper?" 10 The LORD then said: "What have you done! Listen: Your brother's blood cries out to me from the soil! 11* Therefore you shall be banned from the soil that opened its mouth to receive your brother's blood from your hand. 12 If you till the soil, it shall no longer give you its produce. You

---

3, 15: *He will strike . . . at his heel:* since the antecedent for *he* and *his* is the collective noun offspring, i.e., all the descendants of the woman, a more exact rendering of the sacred writer's words would be, "They will strike . . . at their heels." However, later theology saw in this passage more than unending hostility between snakes and men. The serpent was regarded as the devil (Wis 2, 24; Jn 8, 44; Rv 12, 9; 20, 2), whose eventual defeat seems implied in the contrast between *head* and *heel*. Because "the Son of God was revealed to destroy the works of the devil" (1 Jn 3, 8), the passage can be understood as the first promise of a Redeemer for fallen mankind. The woman's offspring then is primarily Jesus Christ.

3, 20: This verse seems to be out of place; it would fit better after v 24. The Hebrew name *hawwa* ("Eve") is related to the Hebrew word *hay* ("living").

3, 24: The above rendering is based on the ancient Greek version; that of the current Hebrew is, When he expelled the man, he settled east of the garden of Eden, the cherubim.

4, 1: The Hebrew name *qayin* ("Cain") and the term *qaniti* ("I have produced") present another play on words.

4, 7: *Demon lurking:* in Hebrew, *robes,* literally "croucher," is used here, like the similar Akkadian term *rabisu,* to designate a certain kind of evil spirit.

3, 13: 2 Cor 11, 3.
3, 14: Is 65, 25; Mi 7, 17; Rv 12, 9.
3, 15: Is 7, 14; 9, 5; Rom 16, 20; 1 Jn 3, 8; Rv 12, 17.
3, 16: 1 Cor 11, 3; Eph 5, 22f; 1 Tm 2, 12.
3, 17: Gn 5, 29; Rom 5, 12; 8, 20; Heb 6, 8.
3, 19: Gn 2, 7; Jb 10, 9; 34, 15; Pss 90, 3; 103, 14;

Eccl 3, 20; 12, 7; Wis 15, 8; Sir 10, 9; 17, 2; Rom 5, 12; 1 Cor 15, 21; Heb 9, 27.
3, 22: Gn 2, 9; Rv 22, 2.14.
4, 4: Ex 34, 19; Heb 11, 4.
4, 7: Sir 7, 1; Jude 11.
4, 8: Wis 10, 3; Mt 23, 35; Lk 11, 51; 1 Jn 3, 12; Jude 11.
4, 11: Dt 27, 24.

Brothers and Sisters

LIVE IT!

"Am I my brother's keeper?" (Gn 4, 9). With that famous question, Cain pretends that he does not know where his brother is. God does not answer Cain's question directly, but each of us knows the response. We are—each of us and all of us—responsible for one another: family, friends, and strangers. We are brothers and sisters because God has created us that way. We cannot avoid our obligation to watch out for one another.

Are there people in your life who need you to be a brother or sister to them? If so, commit yourself right now to reach out to them.

▸ Gn 4, 9

shall become a restless wanderer on the earth." ¹³ Cain said to the LORD: "My punishment is too great to bear. ¹⁴ Since you have now banished me from the soil, and I must avoid your presence and become a restless wanderer on the earth, anyone may kill me at sight." ¹⁵† "Not so!" the LORD said to him. "If anyone kills Cain, Cain shall be avenged sevenfold." So the LORD put a mark on Cain, lest anyone should kill him at sight. ¹⁶† Cain then left the LORD'S presence and settled in the land of Nod, east of Eden.

Descendants of Cain and Seth

¹⁷† Cain had relations with his wife, and she conceived and bore Enoch. Cain also became the founder of a city, which he named after his son Enoch. ¹⁸ To Enoch was born Irad, and Irad became the father of Mehujael; Mehujael became the father of Methusael, and Methusael became the father of Lamech. ¹⁹ Lamech took two wives; the name of the first was Adah, and the name of the second Zillah. ²⁰ Adah gave birth to Jabal, the ancestor of all who dwell in tents and keep cattle. ²¹ His brother's name was Jubal; he was the ancestor of all who play the lyre and the pipe. ²² Zillah, on her part, gave birth to Tubalcain, the ancestor of all who forge instruments of bronze and iron. The sister of Tubalcain was Naamah. ²³ Lamech said to his wives:

"Adah and Zillah, hear my voice;
    wives of Lamech, listen to my utterance:
I have killed a man for wounding me,
    a boy for bruising me.

24   If Cain is avenged sevenfold,
          then Lamech seventy-sevenfold."

²⁵† Adam again had relations with his wife, and she gave birth to a son whom she called Seth. "God has granted me more offspring in place of Abel,"

THE CYCLE OF VIOLENCE

Cain was a murderer. Some might say he deserved the death penalty. But in Gn 4, 15, God marks Cain so that he is protected from being killed. God seeks to stop the cycle of violence. Why kill someone to show that it is wrong to kill someone?

Think of a television show or movie with violent sequences that you have seen recently. What attitude did it portray toward violence? Often, violence in revenge is shown as justified, even satisfying. How does violence on television or in the movies affect your own attitude toward it? How might you respond to God's call to stop the cycle of violence?

▸ Gn 4, 15

4, 15: *A mark:* probably a tattoo. The use of tattooing for tribal marks has always been common among the nomads of the Near Eastern deserts.
4, 16: *The land of Nod:* not a definite geographic region. The term merely means "the land of nomads."
4, 17–22: In vv 12–16 Cain was presented as the archetype of nomadic peoples. The sacred author in this section follows another ancient tradition that makes Cain the prototype of sedentary peoples with higher material culture.
4, 25f: *Has granted:* Hebrew *shat,* a wordplay on the name *shet*

("Seth"). *Enosh:* in Hebrew, a synonym of *adam* ("man"). *At that time . . . name:* men began to call God by his personal name, Yahweh, rendered as "the Lord" in this version of the Bible. The ancient, so-called Yahwist source used here employs the name Yahweh long before the time of Moses. Another ancient source, the Elohist (from its use of the term *Elohim,* "God," instead of *Yahweh,* "Lord," for the pre-Mosaic period), makes Moses the first to use Yahweh as the proper name of Israel's God, previously known by other names as well; cf Ex 3, 13ff.

G
N

she said, "because Cain slew him." 26* To Seth, in turn, a son was born, and he named him Enosh.

At that time men began to invoke the LORD by name.

Generations: Adam to Noah

5 1*†This is the record of the descendants of Adam. When God created man, he made him in the likeness of God; 2 he created them male and female. When they were created, he blessed them and named them "man."

3* Adam was one hundred and thirty years old when he begot a son in his likeness, after his image; and he named him Seth.* 4 Adam lived eight hundred years after the birth of Seth, and he had other sons and daughters. 5 The whole lifetime of Adam was nine hundred and thirty years; then he died.

6 When Seth was one hundred and five years old, he became the father of Enosh. 7 Seth lived eight hundred and seven years after the birth of Enosh, and he had other sons and daughters. 8 The whole lifetime of Seth was nine hundred and twelve years; then he died.

9 When Enosh was ninety years old, he became the father of Kenan. 10 Enosh lived eight hundred and fifteen years after the birth of Kenan, and he had other sons and daughters. 11 The whole lifetime of Enosh was nine hundred and five years; then he died.

12 When Kenan was seventy years old, he became the father of Mahalalel. 13 Kenan lived eight hundred and forty years after the birth of Mahalalel, and he had other sons and daughters. 14 The whole lifetime of Kenan was nine hundred and ten years; then he died.

15 When Mahalalel was sixty-five years old, he became the father of Jared. 16 Mahalalel lived eight hundred and thirty years after the birth of Jared, and he had other sons and daughters. 17 The whole lifetime of Mahalalel was eight hundred and ninety-five years; then he died.

18 When Jared was one hundred and sixty-two years old, he became the father of Enoch. 19 Jared lived eight hundred years after the birth of Enoch, and he had other sons and daughters. 20 The whole lifetime of Jared was nine hundred and sixty-two years; then he died.

21 When Enoch was sixty-five years old, he became the father of Methuselah. 22 Enoch lived three hundred years after the birth of Methuselah, and had other sons and daughters. 23 The whole lifetime of Enoch was three hundred and sixty-five years. 24*† Then Enoch walked with God, and he was no longer here, for God took him.

25 When Methuselah was one hundred and eighty-seven years old, he became the father of Lamech. 26 Methuselah lived seven hundred and eighty-two years after the birth of Lamech, and he had other sons and daughters. 27 The whole lifetime of Methuselah was nine hundred and sixty-nine years; then he died.

28 When Lamech was one hundred and eighty-two years old, he begot a son 29*† and named him Noah, saying, "Out of the very ground that the LORD has put under a curse, this one shall bring us relief from our work and the toil of our hands." 30 Lamech lived five hundred and ninety-five years after the birth of Noah, and he had other sons and daughters. 31 The whole lifetime of Lamech was seven hundred and seventy-seven years; then he died.

32* When Noah was five hundred years old, he became the father of Shem, Ham and Japheth.

Origin of the Nephilim

6 1† When men began to multiply on earth and daughters were born to them, 2*† the sons of heaven saw how beautiful the daughters of man were, and so they took for their wives as many of them as they chose. 3† Then the LORD said: "My spirit shall not remain in man forever, since he is but flesh. His days shall comprise one hundred and twenty years."

5, 1–32: Although this chapter, with its highly schematic form, belongs to the relatively late "Priestly document," it is based on very ancient traditions. Together with Gn 11, 10–26, its primary purpose is to bridge the genealogical gap between Adam and Abraham. Adam's line is traced through Seth, but several names in the series are the same as, or similar to, certain names in Cain's line (Gn 4, 17ff). The long lifespans attributed to these ten antediluvian patriarchs have a symbolic rather than a historical value. Babylonian tradition also recorded ten kings with fantastically high ages who reigned successively before the flood.

5, 24: In place of the usual formula, *Then he died,* the change to *Enoch walked with God* clearly implies that he did not die, but like Elijah (2 Kgs 2, 11f) was taken alive to God's abode.

5, 29: There is a similarity in sound between the Hebrew word *noah,* "Noah," and the verbal phrase *yenahamenu,* "he will bring us relief"; this latter refers both to the curse put on the soil because of the fall of man (Gn 3, 17ff) and to Noah's success in agriculture, especially in raising grapes for wine (Gn 9, 20f).

6, 1–4: This is apparently a fragment of an old legend that had

borrowed much from ancient mythology. The sacred author incorporates it here, not only in order to account for the prehistoric giants of Palestine, whom the Israelites called *the Nephilim,* but also to introduce the story of the flood with a moral orientation—the constantly increasing wickedness of mankind.

6, 2: *The sons of heaven:* literally "the sons of the gods" or "the sons of God," i.e., the celestial beings of mythology.

6, 3: *My spirit:* the breath of life referred to in Gn 2, 7. *His days . . . years:* probably the time God would still let men live on earth before destroying them with the flood, rather than the maximum span of life God would allot to individual men in the future.

4, 26: 1 Chr 1, 1; Lk 3, 38.
5, 1: Gn 1, 27; Wis 2, 23;
   Sir 17, 1; 1 Cor 11, 7;
   Jas 3, 9.
5, 3: Gn 4, 25.
5, 3–32: 1 Chr 1, 1–4;
Lk 3, 36ff.
5, 24: Wis 4, 10f; Sir 44, 16;
   49, 14; Heb 11, 5.
5, 29: Gn 3, 17ff.
5, 32: Gn 6, 10; 10, 1.
6, 2: Mt 24, 38; Lk 17, 26f.

⁴*† At that time the Nephilim appeared on earth (as well as later), after the sons of heaven had intercourse with the daughters of man, who bore them sons. They were the heroes of old, the men of renown.

¹¹* In the eyes of God the earth was corrupt and full of lawlessness. ¹²* When God saw how corrupt the earth had become, since all mortals led depraved lives on earth, ¹³* he said to Noah: "I have decided to put an end to all mortals on earth; the

Sin Has Social Consequences

At the beginning of the Noah story, sin has continued to spread so that it has become an accepted part of society. The Great Flood, which wipes out a whole civilization, symbolizes the consequences of widespread sin. Later in Genesis, the story of the tower of Babel (11, 1–9) symbolizes another consequence of the institutionalized sin of disobedience and pride.

When sin becomes part of our social systems and our institutions, the church calls it social sin. Social sin is a result of personal sin, but it is bigger than any one person's choice. Examples of social sin are the unequal distribution of the world's wealth, the exploitation of workers by corporations, and discrimination based on race or gender. The good news is that God's saving power is greater than social sin! What are the effects of social sin in your community? in your country? in the world? How are Christians in your church or community organizing to stand against social sin?

▶ Gn 6, 1—9, 17

Warning of the Flood

⁵*† When the LORD saw how great was man's wickedness on earth, and how no desire that his heart conceived was ever anything but evil, ⁶ he regretted that he had made man on the earth, and his heart was grieved.

⁷ So the LORD said: "I will wipe out from the earth the men whom I have created, and not only the men, but also the beasts and the creeping things and the birds of the air, for I am sorry that I made them." ⁸ But Noah found favor with the LORD.

⁹* These are the descendants of Noah. Noah, a good man and blameless in that age, ¹⁰ for he walked with God, begot three sons: Shem, Ham and Japheth.

earth is full of lawlessness because of them. So I will destroy them and all life on earth.

Preparation for the Flood

¹⁴† "Make yourself an ark of gopherwood, put various compartments in it, and cover it inside and out with pitch. ¹⁵† This is how you shall build it: the length of the ark shall be three hundred cubits, its width fifty cubits, and its height thirty cubits. ¹⁶† Make an opening for daylight in the ark, and finish the ark a cubit above it. Put an entrance in the side of the ark, which you shall make with bottom, second and third decks. ¹⁷* I, on my part, am about to bring the flood [waters] on the earth, to destroy everywhere all creatures in which there is the breath

---

6, 4: *As well as later:* According to Nm 13, 33, when the Israelites invaded Palestine and found there the tall aboriginal Anakim, they likened them to the Nephilim; cf Dt 2, 10f. Perhaps the huge megalithic structures in Palestine were thought to have been built by a race of giants, whose superhuman strength was attributed to semidivine origin. *The heroes of old:* the legendary worthies of ancient mythology.

6, 5—8, 22: The story of the great flood here recorded is a composite narrative based on two separate sources interwoven into an intricate patchwork. To the Yahwist source, with some later editorial additions, are usually assigned 6, 5–8; 7, 1–5.7–10.12.16b.17b.22–23; 8, 2b–3a.6–12.13b.20–22. The other sections come from the "Priestly document." The combination of the two sources produced certain duplications (e.g., 6, 13–22 of the Yahwist source, beside 7, 1–5 of the Priestly source); also certain inconsistencies, such as the number of the various animals taken into the ark (6, 19f; 7, 14f of the Priestly source, beside 7, 2f of the Yahwist source), and the timetable of the flood (8, 3–5.13f of the Priestly source, beside 7, 4.10.12.17b; 8, 6.10.12 of the Yahwist source). Both biblical sources go back ultimately to an ancient Mesopotamian story of a

great flood, preserved in the eleventh tablet of the Gilgamesh Epic. The latter account, in some respects remarkably similar to the biblical account, is in others very different from it.

6, 14: *Gopherwood:* an unidentified wood not mentioned elsewhere; *gopher* is merely the Hebrew word for it.

6, 15: The dimensions of Noah's ark were approximately 440 x 73 x 44 feet, a foot and a half to the cubit. The ark of the Babylonian flood story was an exact cube, 120 cubits in length, width, and height.

6, 16: *Opening for daylight:* a conjectural rendering of the Hebrew word *sohar,* occurring only here. The reference is probably to an open space on all sides near the top of the ark to admit light and air. The ark also had a window or hatch, which could be opened and closed (Gn 8, 6).

6, 4: Wis 14, 6; Bar 3, 26.   6, 12: Ps 14, 2.
6, 5: Ps 14, 2f.   6, 13: Sir 40, 9f; 44, 17; Mt
6, 9: Wis 10, 4; Sir 44, 17.   24, 37ff.
6, 11: Jb 22, 15ff.   6, 17: Gn 7, 4.21; 2 Pt 2, 5.

of life; everything on earth shall perish. 18* But with you I will establish my covenant; you and your sons, your wife and your sons' wives, shall go into the ark. 19 Of all other living creatures you shall bring two into the ark, one male and one female, that you may keep them alive with you. 20 Of all kinds of birds, of all kinds of beasts, and of all kinds of creeping things, two of each shall come into the ark with you, to stay alive. 21 Moreover, you are to provide yourself with all the food that is to be eaten, and store it away, that it may serve as provisions for you and for them." 22 This Noah did; he carried out all the commands that God gave him.

7 1* Then the LORD said to Noah: "Go into the ark, you and all your household, for you alone in this age have I found to be truly just. 2 Of every clean animal, take with you seven pairs, a male and its mate; and of the unclean animals, one pair, a male and its mate; 3 likewise, of every clean bird of the air, seven pairs, a male and a female, and of all the unclean birds, one pair, a male and a female. Thus you will keep their issue alive over all the earth. 4* Seven days from now I will bring rain down on the earth for forty days and forty nights, and so I will wipe out from the surface of the earth every moving creature that I have made." 5 Noah did just as the LORD had commanded him.

The Great Flood

6 Noah was six hundred years old when the flood waters came upon the earth. 7* Together with his sons, his wife, and his sons' wives, Noah went into the ark because of the waters of the flood. 8 Of the clean animals and the unclean, of the birds, and of everything that creeps on the ground, 9* [two by two] male and female entered the ark with Noah, just as the LORD had commanded him. 10 As soon as the seven days were over, the waters of the flood came upon the earth.

11† In the six hundredth year of Noah's life, in the second month, on the seventeenth day of the month: it was on that day that

All the fountains of the great abyss burst forth,
and the floodgates of the sky were opened.

12 For forty days and forty nights heavy rain poured down on the earth.

13 On the precise day named, Noah and his sons Shem, Ham and Japheth, and Noah's wife, and the three wives of Noah's sons had entered the ark,

▶ Gn 6, 1—9, 17

?did you KNOW?

The Flood

The sin of Adam and Eve in the garden starts a disastrous trend in which each generation adds to sin in the world. This sin leads to the corruption of the world and the destruction of human beings. The Great Flood illustrates the ancient belief that God washed the world clean of this sinfulness and gave another chance to those who were faithful to God.

Other ancient cultures had stories about great floods. But in those stories, vindictive gods caused the floods for petty reasons. These gods had no real love for humanity. The Bible's Flood story is unique because it insists that God acted out of justice and in response to great evil.

God takes great care to save Noah and his family because they are faithful to God. After the Flood, God makes a covenant with Noah, promising never to destroy the earth by flood again—another unique element not found in the stories of other cultures.

14 together with every kind of wild beast, every kind of domestic animal, every kind of creeping thing of the earth, and every kind of bird. 15 Pairs of all creatures in which there was the breath of life entered the ark with Noah. 16 Those that entered were male and female, and of all species they came, as God had commanded Noah. Then the LORD shut him in.

17 The flood continued upon the earth for forty days. As the waters increased, they lifted the ark, so that it rose above the earth. 18 The swelling waters increased greatly, but the ark floated on the surface of the waters. 19 Higher and higher above the earth rose the waters, until all the highest mountains everywhere were submerged, 20 the crest rising fifteen cubits higher than the submerged mountains. 21* All creatures that stirred on earth perished: birds, cattle, wild animals, and all that swarmed on the earth, as well as all mankind. 22 Everything on dry

---

7, 11: *Abyss:* the subterranean ocean; see note on Gn 1, 2.

6, 18: Gn 9, 9; Wis 14, 6;
    Heb 11, 7; 1 Pt 3, 20.
7, 1: Wis 10, 4; Sir 44, 17;
    2 Pt 2, 5.
7, 4: Gn 6, 17; 2 Pt 2, 5.

7, 7: Wis 14, 6; 1 Pt 3, 20;
    2 Pt 2, 5.
7, 9: Gn 6, 19.
7, 21ff: Jb 22, 16; Mt 24, 39;
    Lk 17, 27; 2 Pt 3, 6.

8, 11

land with the faintest breath of life in its nostrils died out. ²³ The LORD wiped out every living thing on earth: man and cattle, the creeping things and the birds of the air; all were wiped out from the earth. Only Noah and those with him in the ark were left.

8 ⁷, ²⁴† The waters maintained their crest over the earth for one hundred and fifty days, ⁸, ¹ and then God remembered Noah and all the animals, wild and tame, that were with him in the ark. So God made a wind sweep over the earth, and the waters began to subside. ² The fountains of the abyss and the floodgates of the sky were closed, and the downpour from the sky was held back. ³ Gradually the waters receded from the earth. At the end of one hundred and fifty days, the waters had so diminished ⁴† that, in the seventh month, on the seventeenth day of the month, the ark came to rest on the mountains of Ararat. ⁵ The waters continued to diminish until the tenth month, and on the first day of the tenth month the tops of the mountains appeared.

⁶† At the end of forty days Noah opened the hatch he had made in the ark, ⁷ and he sent out a raven, to see if the waters had lessened on the earth. It flew back and forth until the waters dried off from the earth. ⁸ Then he sent out a dove, to see if the waters had lessened on the earth. ⁹ But the dove could find no place to alight and perch, and it returned to him in the ark, for there was water all over the earth. Putting out his hand, he caught the dove and drew it back to him inside the ark. ¹⁰ He wait-

ed seven days more and again sent the dove out from the ark. ¹¹ In the evening the dove came back to him, and there in its bill was a plucked-off olive leaf! So Noah knew that the waters had lessened on the earth. ¹² He waited still another seven days and then released the dove once more; and this time it did not come back.

¹³ In the six hundred and first year of Noah's life, in the first month, on the first day of the month, the water began to dry up on the earth. Noah then removed the covering of the ark and saw that the surface of the ground was drying up. ¹⁴ In the second month, on the twenty-seventh day of the month, the earth was dry.

¹⁵ Then God said to Noah: ¹⁶ "Go out of the ark, together with your wife and your sons and your sons' wives. ¹⁷* Bring out with you every living thing that is with you—all bodily creatures, be they

did you KNOW?

Water in the Bible

For the ancient Hebrews, while water often represented a source of life, it also represented forces of destruction over which God triumphs. In the story of Creation, God is portrayed as mastering the waters that represent chaos (Gn 1, 1–2) — God constructs the upper and lower firmaments to hold back the waters. At the time of the Great Flood, God releases the waters and they destroy life on the world. At the time of the Exodus, God will once again display the divine mastery of the waters, as will Jesus Christ later on.

birds or animals or creeping things of the earth—and let them abound on the earth, breeding and multiplying on it." ¹⁸ So Noah came out, together with his wife and his sons and his sons' wives; ¹⁹ and all the animals, wild and tame, all the birds, and all the creeping creatures of the earth left the ark, one kind after another.

---

† **7, 24:** This verse belongs to chapter 7 but its contents properly introduce chapter 8.
8, 4: *Ararat:* ancient Urartu, north of the Mesopotamian plain, part of modern Armenia.
8, 6: In the original Yahwist source, from which this verse is taken, the forty days refer to the full period of the flood itself (cf Gn

7, 4.17); in the present context, however, they seem to refer to a period following the date just given in v 5 from the Priestly source.

8, 17: Gn 1, 22.28.

20 Then Noah built an altar to the LORD, and choosing from every clean animal and every clean bird, he offered holocausts on the altar. 21*† When the LORD smelled the sweet odor, he said to himself: "Never again will I doom the earth because of man, since the desires of man's heart are evil from the start; nor will I ever again strike down all living beings, as I have done.

22* As long as the earth lasts,
    seedtime and harvest,
    cold and heat,
  Summer and winter,
    and day and night
    shall not cease."

Covenant with Noah

9 1* God blessed Noah and his sons and said to them: "Be fertile and multiply and fill the earth. 2 Dread fear of you shall come upon all the animals of the earth and all the birds of the air, upon all the creatures that move about on the ground and all the fishes of the sea; into your power they are delivered. 3*† Every creature that is alive shall be yours to eat; I give them all to you as I did the green plants. 4*† Only flesh with its lifeblood still in it you shall not eat. 5* For your own lifeblood, too, I will demand an accounting: from every animal I will demand it, and from man in regard to his fellow man I will demand an accounting for human life.

6*   If anyone sheds the blood of man,
    by man shall his blood be shed;
  For in the image of God
    has man been made.

7* Be fertile, then, and multiply; abound on earth and subdue it."

8 God said to Noah and to his sons with him: 9* "See, I am now establishing my covenant with you and your descendants after you 10 and with every living creature that was with you: all the birds, and the various tame and wild animals that were with you and came out of the ark. 11* I will establish my covenant with you, that never again shall all bodily creatures be destroyed by the waters of a flood; there shall not be another flood to devastate the earth." 12 God added: "This is the sign that I am giving for all ages to come, of the covenant between me and you and every living creature with you: 13* I set my bow in the clouds to serve as a sign of the covenant between me and the earth. 14 When I bring clouds over the earth, and the bow appears in the clouds, 15* I will recall the covenant I have made between me and you and all living beings, so that the waters shall never again become a flood to destroy all mortal beings. 16 As the bow appears in the clouds, I will see it and recall the everlasting covenant that I have established between God and all living beings—all mortal creatures that are on earth." 17 God told Noah: "This is the sign of the covenant I have established between me and all mortal creatures that are on earth."

PRAY IT

The Rainbow

What do you see when you see a rainbow? Do you see a multicolored arc caused by the refraction of sunlight through droplets of water? Or do you see a wonder of nature that causes you to stop and stare in awe? Something as remarkable as a rainbow can never be reduced to a scientific explanation. It's no wonder that the writer of Genesis used it as a symbol of God's covenant promise. When God and Israel see the rainbow in the clouds, they will recall their covenant together.

God of imagination and color, only you could come up with the idea of a rainbow! Rainstorm and sunshine, harmony and diversity, mercy and hope, promise and joy, wonder and awe. Are these inside me, the wondrous creation you delight in? Guide me to the rainbows in my life!

▶ Gn 9, 8–17

8, 21: *From the start:* literally "from his youth." It is uncertain whether this means from the beginning of the human race or from the early years of the individual.

9, 3: Antediluvian creatures, including man, are depicted as vegetarians (Gn 1, 29f), becoming carnivorous only after the flood.

9, 4: Because a living being dies when it loses most of its blood, the ancients regarded blood as the seat of life, and therefore as sacred. Although in itself the prohibition against eating meat with blood in it is comparable to the ritual laws of the Mosaic code, the Jews considered it binding on all men, because it was given by God to Noah, the new ancestor of all mankind; therefore the early Christian Church retained it for a time (Acts 15, 20.29).

8, 21: Sir 44, 18; Is 54, 9; Rom 7, 18.
8, 22: Jer 33, 20.25.
9, 1: Gn 1, 2. 28; 8, 17; Jas 3, 7.
9, 3: Gn 1, 29f; Dt 12, 15.
9, 4: Lv 7, 26f; 17, 4; Dt 12, 16.23; 1 Sm 14, 33; Acts 15, 20.
9, 5: Gn 4, 10f; Ex 21, 12.
9, 6: Gn 1, 26f; Lv 24, 17; Nm 35, 33; Jas 3, 9.
9, 7: Gn 1, 28; 8, 17; 9, 2.
9, 9: Gn 6, 18.
9, 11: Sir 44, 18; Is 54, 9.
9, 13: Sir 43, 12.
9, 15: Is 54, 9.

Noah and His Sons

18*† The sons of Noah who came out of the ark were Shem, Ham and Japheth. (Ham was the father of Canaan.) 19 These three were the sons of Noah, and from them the whole earth was peopled.

20 Now Noah, a man of the soil, was the first to plant a vineyard. 21* When he drank some of the wine, he became drunk and lay naked inside his tent. 22 Ham, the father of Canaan, saw his father's nakedness, and he told his two brothers outside about it. 23 Shem and Japheth, however, took a robe, and holding it on their backs, they walked backward and covered their father's nakedness; since their faces were turned the other way, they did not see their father's nakedness. 24 When Noah woke up from his drunkenness and learned what his youngest son had done to him, 25* he said:

"Cursed be Canaan!
The lowest of slaves
shall he be to his brothers."

26† He also said:

"Blessed be the LORD, the God of Shem!
Let Canaan be his slave.
27† May God expand Japheth,
so that he dwells among the tents
of Shem;
and let Canaan be his slave."

28 Noah lived three hundred and fifty years after the flood. 29 The whole lifetime of Noah was nine hundred and fifty years; then he died.

Table of the Nations

10 1† These are the descendants of Noah's sons, Shem, Ham and Japheth, to whom sons were born after the flood.

2*†The descendants of Japheth:
Gomer, Magog, Madai, Javan, Tubal,
Meshech and Tiras.*
3† The descendants of Gomer:
Ashkenaz, Riphath and Togarmah.
4† The descendants of Javan:
Elishah, Tarshish, the Kittim and
the Rodanim.

5 These are the descendants of Japheth, and from them sprang the maritime nations, in their respective lands—each with its own language—by their clans within their nations.

6† The descendants of Ham:
Cush, Mizraim, Put and Canaan.
7 The descendants of Cush:
Seba, Havilah, Sabtah, Raamah and Sabteca.
The descendants of Raamah:
Sheba and Dedan.

8† Cush became the father of Nimrod, who was the first potentate on earth. 9 He was a mighty hunter by the grace of the LORD; hence the saying, "Like Nimrod, a mighty hunter by the grace of the LORD." 10† The chief cities of his kingdom were Babylon, Erech and Accad, all of them in the land of Shinar. 11† From that land he went forth to Asshur, where he built Nineveh, Rehoboth-Ir and Calah, 12† as well as Resen, between Nineveh and Calah, the latter being the principal city.

9, 18–27: This story seems to be a composite of two earlier accounts; in the one, Ham was guilty, whereas, in the other, it was Canaan. One purpose of the story is to justify the Israelites' enslavement of the Canaanites because of certain indecent sexual practices in the Canaanite religion. Obviously the story offers no justification for enslaving African Negroes, even though Canaan is presented as a "son" of Ham because the land of Canaan belonged to Hamitic Egypt at the time of the Israelite invasion.
9, 26: *Blessed . . . Shem:* perhaps the text read originally, "Blessed of the LORD be Shem," which would be expected in the context.
9, 27: In the Hebrew text there is a play on the words *yapt* ("expand") and *yepet* ("Japheth").
10, 1–32: This chapter presents a remarkably good classification of the various peoples known to the ancient Israelites; it is theologically important in stressing the basic family unity of all men on earth. The relationship between the various peoples is based partly on linguistic, partly on geographic, and partly on political grounds *according to their . . . languages, . . . lands and nations:* (v 31). In general, *the descendants of Japheth* (vv 2–5) are the peoples of the Indo-European languages to the north and west of Mesopotamia and Syria; *the descendants of Ham* (vv 6–20) are the Hamitic-speaking peoples of northern Africa; and *the descendants of Shem* (vv 21–31) are the Semitic-speaking peoples of Mesopotamia, Syria and Arabia. But there are many exceptions to this rule; the Semitic-speaking peoples of Canaan, for instance, are considered descendants of Ham,

because at the time they were subject to Hamitic Egypt (vv 6.15–19). This chapter is a composite from the Yahwist source (vv 8–19.21. 24–30) of about the ninth century B.C., and the Priestly source (vv 1–7.20.22f.31f) of a few centuries later. That is why certain tribes of Arabia are listed under both Ham (v 7) and Shem (vv 26ff).
10, 2: *Gomer:* the Cimmerians; *Madai:* the Medes; *Javan:* the Greeks.
10, 3: *Ashkenaz:* the Scythians.
10, 4: *Elishah:* Cyprus; *the Kittim:* certain inhabitants of Cyprus; *the Rodanim:* the inhabitants of Rhodes.
10, 6: *Cush:* Biblical Ethiopia, modern Nubia; *Mizraim:* Egypt; *Put:* either Punt in East Africa or Libya.
10, 8: *Cush:* here, the Kassites; see note on Gn 2, 10–14. *Nimrod:* probably Tukulti-Ninurta I (thirteenth century B.C.), the first Assyrian conqueror of Babylonia and a famous city-builder at home.
10, 10: *Shinar:* ancient Sumer in southern Mesopotamia, mentioned also in Gn 11, 2; 14, 1.
10, 11: *Asshur:* Assyria. *Rehoboth-Ir:* literally "wide-streets city," was probably not the name of another city, but an epithet of Nineveh; cf Jon 3, 3.
10, 12: *Calah:* Assyrian Kalhu, the capital of Assyria in the ninth century B.C.

9, 18: Gn 5, 32; 10, 1.   10, 2–8: 1 Chr 1, 5–10.
9, 21: Lam 4, 21; Heb 2, 15.   10, 2: Ez 38, 2.
9, 25: Dt 27, 16; Wis 12, 11.

13* Mizraim became the father of the Ludim, the Anamim, the Lehabim, the Naphtuhim, 14† the Pathrusim, the Casluhim, and the Caphtorim from whom the Philistines sprang.

15† Canaan became the father of Sidon, his first-born, and of Heth; 16 also of the Jebusites, the Amorites, the Girgashites, 17 the Hivites, the Arkites, the Sinites, 18 the Arvadites, the Zemarites and the Hamathites. Afterward, the clans of the Canaanites spread out, 19† so that the Canaanite borders extended from Sidon all the way to Gerar, near Gaza, and all the way to Sodom, Gomorrah, Admah and Zeboiim, near Lasha.

20 These are the descendants of Ham, according to their clans and languages, by their lands and nations.

21 To Shem also, Japheth's oldest brother and the ancestor of all the children of Eber, sons were born.

22* The descendants of Shem:
Elam, Asshur, Arpachshad, Lud and Aram.
23   The descendants of Aram:
Uz, Hul, Gether and Mash.

24 Arpachshad became the father of Shelah, and Shelah became the father of Eber. 25† To Eber two sons were born: the name of the first was Peleg, for in his time the world was divided; and the name of his brother was Joktan.

26 Joktan became the father of Almodad, Sheleph, Hazarmaveth, Jerah, 27 Hadoram, Uzal, Diklah, 28 Obal, Abimael, Sheba 29 Ophir, Havilah and Jobab. All these were descendants of Joktan. 30 Their settlements extended all the way to Sephar, the eastern hill country.

31 These are the descendants of Shem, according to their clans and languages, by their lands and nations.

32 These are the groupings of Noah's sons, according to their origins and by their nations. From these the other nations of the earth branched out after the flood.

The Tower of Babel

11 1† The whole world spoke the same language, using the same words. 2† While men were migrating in the east, they came upon a valley in the land of Shinar and settled there. 3 They said to one another, "Come, let us mold bricks and harden them with fire." They used bricks for stone, and bitumen for mortar. 4† Then they said, "Come, let us build ourselves a city and a tower with its top in the sky, and so make a name for ourselves; otherwise we shall be scattered all over the earth."

5 The LORD came down to see the city and the tower that the men had built. 6 Then the LORD said: "If now, while they are one people, all speaking the same language, they have started to do this, nothing will later stop them from doing whatever they presume to do. 7 Let us then go down and there confuse their language, so that one will not understand what another says." 8 Thus the LORD scattered them from there all over the earth, and they stopped building the city. 9† That is why it was called Babel, because there the LORD confused the speech of all the world. It was from that place that he scattered them all over the earth.

The Line from Shem to Abraham

10*† This is the record of the descendants of Shem. When Shem was one hundred years old, he became the father of Arpachshad, two years after the flood. 11 Shem lived five hundred years after the birth of Arpachshad, and he had other sons and daughters.

12† When Arpachshad was thirty-five years old, he became the father of Shelah. 13 Arpachshad lived four hundred and three years after the birth of Shelah, and he had other sons and daughters.

14 When Shelah was thirty years old, he became the father of Eber. 15 Shelah lived four hundred and three years after the birth of Eber, and he had other sons and daughters.

16† When Eber was thirty-four years old, he became the father of Peleg. 17 Eber lived four hundred

---

10, 14: *The Pathrusim:* the people of upper (southern) Egypt; cf Is 11, 11; Jer 44, 1; Ez 29, 14; 30, 14. *Caphtorim:* Crete; for Caphtor as the place of origin of the Philistines, cf Dt 2, 23; Am 9, 7; Jer 47, 4.

10, 15: *Heth:* the biblical Hittites; see note on Gn 23; 3.

10, 19: *Lasha:* the reading of this name is uncertain; perhaps it should be "Bela"; cf Gn 14, 2.

10, 25: In the Hebrew text there is a play on the name *Peleg* and the word *niplega,* "was divided."

11, 1–9: This story, based on traditions about the temple towers or ziggurats of Babylonia, is used by the sacred writer primarily to illustrate man's increasing wickedness, shown here in his presumptuous effort to create an urban culture apart from God. The secondary motive in the story is to present an imaginative origin of the diversity of the languages among the various peoples inhabiting the earth, as well as an artificial explanation of the name "Babylon."

11, 2: *Shinar:* see note on Gn 10, 10.

11, 4: *Tower with its top in the sky:* a direct reference to the chief ziggurat of Babylon, the *E-sag-ila,* signifying "the house that raises high its head." Babylonian ziggurats were the earliest skyscrapers.

11, 9: *Babel:* the Hebrew form of the name "Babylon"; the native name, *Bab-ili,* means "gate of the gods." The Hebrew word *balil,* "he confused," has a similar sound. Apparently the name referred originally only to a certain part of the city, the district near the gate that led to the temple area.

11, 10–26: This section is a continuation of the genealogical record given in Gn 5, 1–32; see note there. Although the ages of the patriarchs in this list are much lower than those of the antediluvian patriarchs, they are still artificial and devoid of historical value. The ages given here are from the current Hebrew text; the Samaritan and Greek texts have divergent sets of numbers in most cases.

11, 12: The Greek text has a certain Kenan (cf Gn 5, 9f) between Arpachshad and Shelah. The text is followed in Lk 3, 36.

11, 16: *Eber:* the eponymous ancestor of the Hebrews, "descendants of Eber" (Gn 11, 21.24–30); see note on Gn 14, 13.

10, 13–18: 1 Chr 1, 11–16.   11, 10–26: 1 Chr 1, 24–27; Lk
10, 22–29: 1 Chr 1, 17–23.   3, 34ff.

A Barrier or a Bridge?

LIVE IT!

Language can be either a barrier or a bridge. Through our speech, we connect with other people. And we often hear it expressed that love, music, and a smile are universal languages. Yet, languages also separate, symbolizing differences between cultures and nations that can erupt in wars and other atrocities.

The story of the tower of Babel is an ancient explanation of why the separation between people, symbolized by different languages, occurs. The people ignore God's command to "fill the earth" (Gn 1, 28). Instead, they gather in one place to try to build a tower reaching to heaven, a sin of pride and arrogance. God confuses their language to foil their plan. It is not language but pride that separates us.

In the Acts of the Apostles, chapter 2, language serves as a bridge. The Holy Spirit enables the people from many different lands to hear the Apostles speaking in their own languages. The Spirit serves to unify us, no matter what earthly language we speak. Anyone who has attended a World Youth Day knows that when we live by the Spirit, we can rise above the differences of language and culture. The Good News is universal and unites us!

▶ Gn 11, 1–9

and thirty years after the birth of Peleg, and he had other sons and daughters.

¹⁸ When Peleg was thirty years old, he became the father of Reu. ¹⁹ Peleg lived two hundred and nine years after the birth of Reu, and he had other sons and daughters.

²⁰ When Reu was thirty-two years old, he became the father of Serug. ²¹ Reu lived two hundred and seven years after the birth of Serug, and he had other sons and daughters.

²² When Serug was thirty years old, he became the father of Nahor. ²³ Serug lived two hundred years after the birth of Nahor, and he had other sons and daughters.

²⁴ When Nahor was twenty-nine years old, he became the father of Terah. ²⁵ Nahor lived one hundred and nineteen years after the birth of Terah, and he had other sons and daughters.

²⁶* When Terah was seventy years old, he became the father of Abram, Nahor and Haran.

II: The Patriarch Abraham

Terah

²⁷ This is the record of the descendants of Terah. Terah became the father of Abram, Nahor and Haran, and Haran became the father of Lot. ²⁸† Haran died before his father Terah, in his native land, in Ur of the Chaldeans. ²⁹* Abram and Nahor took wives; the name of Abram's wife was Sarai, and the name of Nahor's wife was Milcah, daughter of Haran, the father of Milcah and Iscah. ³⁰ Sarai was barren; she had no child.

³¹*† Terah took his son Abram, his grandson Lot, son of Haran, and his daughter-in-law Sarai, the wife of his son Abram, and brought them out of Ur of the Chaldeans, to go to the land of Canaan. But when they reached Haran, they settled there. ³²† The lifetime of Terah was two hundred and five years; then Terah died in Haran.

Abram's Call and Migration

12 ¹* The LORD said to Abram: "Go forth from the land of your kinsfolk and from your father's house to a land that I will show you.

²* "I will make of you a great nation,
and I will bless you;
I will make your name great,
so that you will be a blessing.

11, 28: *Ur of the Chaldeans:* Ur was an extremely ancient city of the Sumerians (later, of the Babylonians) in southern Mesopotamia. The Greek text has "the land of the Chaldeans." In either case, the term *Chaldeans* is an anachronism, because the Chaldeans were not known to history until approximately a thousand years after Abraham's time.

11, 31: The Samaritan and Greek texts include Nahor and his wife in Terah's migration to Haran. Although this is probably due to scribal harmonization, Nahor's family actually did migrate to Haran; cf Gn 24, 10; 27, 43.

11, 32: Since Terah was seventy years old when his son Abraham was born (v 26), and Abraham was seventy-five when he left Haran

(Gn 12, 4), Terah lived in Haran for sixty years after Abraham's departure. According to the tradition in the Samaritan text, Terah died when he was one hundred and forty-five years old, therefore, in the same year in which Abraham left Haran. This is the tradition followed in St. Stephen's speech: Abraham left Haran "after his father died" (Acts 7, 4).

11, 26: Jos 24, 2; 1 Chr 1, 27.	**12, 1:** Acts 7, 3; Heb 11, 8.
11, 29: Gn 17, 15; 20, 12.	**12, 2:** Gn 17, 6; Sir 44, 20;
11, 31: Jos 24, 3; Neh 9, 7; Jdt	Rom 4, 17–22.
5, 6–9; Acts 7, 4.	

GN

3*†I will bless those who bless you
   and curse those who curse you.
All the communities of the earth
   shall find blessing in you."

4* Abram went as the LORD directed him, and Lot went with him. Abram was seventy-five years old when he left Haran. 5† Abram took his wife Sarai,

try east of Bethel, pitching his tent with Bethel to the west and Ai to the east. He built an altar there to the LORD and invoked the LORD by name. 9† Then Abram journeyed on by stages to the Negeb.

Abram and Sarai in Egypt

10* There was famine in the land; so Abram went down to Egypt to sojourn there, since the famine in

Introducing
▶ ABRAHAM AND SARAH

Abraham, whose name was originally Abram, is an important figure for three major world religions: Judaism, Christianity, and Islam. Abraham is regarded as the great example of faith in God. He first appears in Gn 11, 26. For many years, Abram lives in Haran in northern Mesopotamia (see map 1, "The World of the Patriarchs") with his wife, Sarai. God calls Abram and Sarai to leave their home, seals a covenant with them, and changes their names to Abraham and Sarah. God's covenant promises that they will be the parents "of a host of nations" (17, 5) and their descendants will be as numerous as the "stars of the sky" (22, 17).

Later, God requests that Abraham sacrifice his son Isaac. God stops him from going through with it, but Abraham's willingness to cooperate with God and his complete trust in God become the foundation for Israel's faith. Not surprisingly, in the Old Testament, when a prophet or teacher needed an example of someone with unwavering trust in God, Abraham was often cited.

In the New Testament, Abraham is revered as the first patriarch to enter into a covenant with God (see Mt 1, 1; Lk 16, 19–31) and the great pioneer of Israel's faith (Acts 7, 2–50; Rom 4, 1–25; Heb 7, 1–10).

▶ Gn 12, 1–25, 11

his brother's son Lot, all the possessions that they had accumulated, and the persons they had acquired in Haran, and they set out for the land of Canaan. When they came to the land of Canaan, 6 Abram passed through the land as far as the sacred place at Shechem, by the terebinth of Moreh. (The Canaanites were then in the land.)

7* The LORD appeared to Abram and said, "To your descendants I will give this land." So Abram built an altar there to the LORD who had appeared to him. 8 From there he moved on to the hill coun-

the land was severe. 11 When he was about to enter Egypt, he said to his wife Sarai: "I know well how beautiful a woman you are. 12 When the Egyptians see you, they will say, 'She is his wife'; then they will kill me, but let you live. 13*† Please say, therefore, that you are my sister, so that it may go well with me on your account and my life may be spared for your sake." 14 When Abram came to Egypt, the Egyptians saw how beautiful the woman was; 15 and when Pharaoh's courtiers saw her, they praised her to Pharaoh. So she was taken into Pharaoh's palace.

12, 3: *Shall find blessing in you:* the sense of the Hebrew expression is probably reflexive, "shall bless themselves through you" (i.e., in giving a blessing they shall say, "May you be as blessed as Abraham"), rather than passive, "shall be blessed in you." Since the term is understood in a passive sense in the New Testament (Acts 3, 25; Gal 3, 8), it is rendered here by a neutral expression that admits of both meanings. So also in the blessings given by God to Isaac (Gn 26, 4) and Jacob (Gn 28, 14).

12, 5: *Persons:* slaves and retainers that formed the social aggregate under the leadership of Abraham; cf Gn 14, 14.

12, 9: *The Negeb:* the semidesert land of southern Palestine.

12, 13: *You are my sister:* although Abraham's deceit may not be

fully defensible, his statement was at least a half-truth; Sarah was indeed his relative, called "a sister" in Hebrew; cf Gn 20, 12. Moreover, the ancient traditions on which this story and the parallel ones in Gn 20, 1–18 and 26, 6–11 are based, probably come from the Hurrian custom of wife-sister marriage. Among the Hurrians, with whom Abraham's clan lived in close contact at Haran, a man could adopt his wife as his sister and thus give her higher status.

12, 3: Gn 18, 18; 22, 18; Acts 3, 25; Gal 3, 8.	12, 7: Ex 33, 1; Dt 34, 4; Acts 7, 5.
12, 4f: Gn 11, 31; Jos 24, 3; Acts 7, 4.	12, 10: Gn 26, 1.
	12, 13: Gn 20, 12f; 26, 7.

16† On her account it went very well with Abram, and he received flocks and herds, male and female slaves, male and female asses, and camels.

17* But the LORD struck Pharaoh and his household with severe plagues because of Abram's wife Sarai. 18 Then Pharaoh summoned Abram and said to him: "How could you do this to me! Why didn't you tell me she was your wife? 19 Why did you say, 'She is my sister,' so that I took her for my wife? Here, then, is your wife. Take her and be gone!"

20 Then Pharaoh gave men orders concerning him, and they sent him on his way, with his wife and all that belonged to him.

Abram and Lot Part

13 1* From Egypt Abram went up to the Negeb with his wife and all that belonged to him, and Lot accompanied him. 2* Now Abram was very rich in livestock, silver and gold. 3 From the Negeb he traveled by stages toward Bethel, to the place between Bethel and Ai where his tent had formerly stood, 4* the site where he had first built the altar; and there he invoked the LORD by name.

5 Lot, who went with Abram, also had flocks and herds and tents, 6 so that the land could not support them if they stayed together; their possessions were so great that they could not dwell together. 7 There were quarrels between the herdsmen of Abram's livestock and those of Lot's. (At this time the Canaanites and the Perizzites were occupying the land.)

8 So Abram said to Lot: "Let there be no strife between you and me, or between your herdsmen and mine, for we are kinsmen. 9 Is not the whole land at your disposal? Please separate from me. If you prefer the left, I will go to the right; if you prefer the right, I will go to the left." 10 Lot looked about and saw how well watered the whole Jordan Plain was as far as Zoar, like the LORD's own garden, or like Egypt. (This was before the LORD had destroyed Sodom and Gomorrah.) 11 Lot, therefore, chose for himself the whole Jordan Plain and set out eastward. Thus they separated from each other; 12 Abram stayed in the land of Canaan, while Lot settled among the cities of the Plain, pitching his tents near Sodom. 13* Now the inhabitants of Sodom were very wicked in the sins they committed against the LORD.

14* After Lot had left, the LORD said to Abram: "Look about you, and from where you are, gaze to the north and south, east and west; 15* all the land that you see I will give to you and your descendants forever. 16* I will make your descendants like the dust of the earth; if anyone could count the dust of the earth, your descendants too might be counted. 17 Set forth and walk about in the land, through its length and breadth, for to you I will give it." 18* Abram moved his tents and went on to settle near the terebinth of Mamre, which is at Hebron. There he built an altar to the LORD.

The Four Kings

14 1† In the days of . . . , Amraphel king of Shinar, Arioch king of Ellasar, Chedorlaomer king of Elam, and Tidal king of Goiim 2 made war on Bera king of Sodom, Birsha king of Gomorrah, Shinab king of Admah, Shemeber king of Zeboiim, and the king of Bela (that is, Zoar). 3† All the latter kings joined forces in the Valley of Siddim (that is, the Salt Sea). 4 For twelve years they had been subject to Chedorlaomer, but in the thirteenth year they rebelled. 5† In the fourteenth year Chedorlaomer and the kings allied with him came and defeated the Rephaim in Ashteroth-karnaim, the Zuzim in Ham, the Emim in Shaveh-kiriathaim, 6* and the Horites in the hill country of Seir, as far as El-paran, close by the wilderness. 7 They then turned back and came to Enmishpat (that is, Kadesh), and they subdued the whole country both of the Amalekites and of the Amorites who dwelt in Hazazon-tamar. 8 Thereupon the king of Sodom, the king of Gomorrah, the king of Admah, the king of Zeboiim, and the king of Bela (that is, Zoar) marched out, and in the Valley of Siddim they went into battle against them: 9 against Chedorlaomer king of Elam, Tidal king of Goiim, Amraphel king of Shinar, and Arioch king of Ellasar—four kings against five. 10 Now the Valley of Siddim was full of bitumen pits; and as the kings of Sodom and Gomorrah fled, they fell into these, while the rest fled to the mountains. 11 The victors seized all the possessions and food supplies of Sodom and Gomorrah and then went their way, 12* taking with them Abram's nephew Lot, who had been living in Sodom, as well as his possessions.

12, 16: *Camels:* domesticated camels probably did not come into common use in the ancient Near East until the end of the 2nd millennium B.C. Thus the mention of camels at the time of the patriarchs (Gn 24, 11–64; 30, 43; 31, 17.34; 32, 8.16; 37, 25) is seemingly an anachronism.

14, 1: *In the days of . . . :* the personal name by which the event is dated has not been preserved.

14, 3: *The Salt Sea:* now known as the Dead Sea.

14, 5f: The five kings came from north to south through the land east of the Jordan.

12, 17: Ps 105, 14.
13, 1: Gn 12, 9.
13, 2: Ps 112, 1ff; Prv 10, 22.
13, 4: Gn 12, 8.
13, 13: Gn 18, 20; Ez 16, 49; 2 Pt 2, 6ff; Jude 7.
13, 14: Gn 28, 14.
13, 15: Gn 12, 7; Mt 5, 4; Lk 1, 55; Acts 7, 5; Gal 3, 16.
13, 16: Gn 22, 17; Nm 23, 10.
13, 18: Gn 14, 13.
14, 6: Dt 2, 12.
14, 12: Gn 13, 10ff.

13† A fugitive came and brought the news to Abram the Hebrew, who was camping at the terebinth of Mamre the Amorite, a kinsman of Eshcol and Aner; these were in league with Abram. 14 When Abram heard that his nephew had been captured, he mustered three hundred and eighteen of his retainers, born in his house, and went in pursuit as far as Dan. 15 He and his party deployed against them at night, defeated them, and pursued them as far as Hobah, which is north of Damascus. 16 He recovered all the possessions, besides bringing back his kinsman Lot and his possessions, along with the women and the other captives.

17 When Abram returned from his victory over Chedorlaomer and the kings who were allied with him, the king of Sodom went out to greet him in the Valley of Shaveh (that is, the King's Valley).

18*† Melchizedek, king of Salem, brought out bread and wine, and being a priest of God Most High, he blessed Abram with these words:

19† "Blessed be Abram by God Most High,
　　the creator of heaven and earth;
20† And blessed be God Most High,
　　who delivered your foes into your hand."

Then Abram gave him a tenth of everything.

21 The king of Sodom said to Abram, "Give me the people; the goods you may keep." 22† But Abram replied to the king of Sodom: "I have sworn to the LORD, God Most High, the creator of heaven and earth, 23 that I would not take so much as a thread or a sandal strap from anything that is yours, lest you should say, 'I made Abram rich.' 24 Nothing for me except what my servants have used up and the share that is due to the men who joined me— Aner, Eshcol and Mamre; let them take their share."

The Covenant with Abram

15 1 Some time after these events, this word of the LORD came to Abram in a vision:

"Fear not, Abram!
　I am your shield;
　I will make your reward very great."

2 But Abram said, "O Lord GOD, what good will your gifts be, if I keep on being childless and have as my heir the steward of my house, Eliezer?" 3 Abram continued, "See, you have given me no offspring, and so one of my servants will be my heir." 4* Then the word of the LORD came to him: "No, that one shall not be your heir; your own issue shall be your heir." 5* He took him outside and said, "Look up at the sky and count the stars, if you can. Just so," he added, "shall your descendants be." 6*† Abram put his faith in the LORD, who credited it to him as an act of righteousness.

Catholic Connections

BREAD AND WINE

Melchizedek, a king and priest, uses bread and wine in a ritual to bless Abram. Bread and wine served as an ancient symbol of nourishment and celebration. The sacrament of the Eucharist has its roots in rituals such as this one. See Heb 7, 1–10 for a New Testament interpretation of Melchizedek's importance.

▸ Gn 14, 17–20

---

†

14, 13: *Abram the Hebrew:* elsewhere in the Old Testament, until the last pre-Christian centuries, the term "Hebrew" is used only by non-Israelites, or by Israelites in speaking to foreigners, since it evidently had a disparaging connotation—something like "immigrant." The account in this chapter may, therefore, have been taken originally from a non-Israelite source, in which Abraham, a warlike sheik of Palestine, appears as a truly historical figure of profane history.

14, 18: *Salem:* traditionally identified with Jerusalem (Ps 76, 3), but the Hebrew text is not certain; instead of the present *melek shalem* ("king of Salem") the original may have been *melek shelomo* ("a king allied to him"). In Heb 7, 2, "king of Salem" is interpreted as "king of peace" (*shalom*).

14, 19: *God most High:* in Hebrew, *el-elyon.* In Canaanite texts, each element may occur separately as the name of a specific deity, or they may be applied together to a single deity, as is done here by the Canaanite priest Melchizedek. For the Israelites, *el* became a poetic synonym for *elohim* ("God"); *elyon* ("Most High") became one of the titles of their God Yahweh.

14, 20: *Abram gave him:* literally "he gave him"; but *Abram* is to be understood as the subject of the sentence, for the tithes were the tenth part assigned to priests; cf Heb 7, 4–10.

14, 22: Abraham uses the name of the Canaanite god *el-elyon* ("God, the Most High") in apposition to the name of his God, *yahweh* ("the LORD").

15, 6: Abraham's *faith* in God's promises was regarded as *an act of righteousness,* i.e., as expressing the "right" attitude of man toward God. In turn, God credited this to Abraham, i.e., gave him title to the fulfillment of God's promises. St. Paul (Rom 4, 1–25; Gal 3, 6–9) makes Abraham's faith a model for that of Christians.

14, 18: Ps 110, 4; Heb 5, 6.
　10; 7, 1.
15, 4: Gn 17, 16.
15, 5: Gn 22, 17; 28, 14;
　Ex 32, 13; Dt 1, 10;

Sir 44, 21; Rom 4, 18;
　Heb 11, 12.
15, 6: 1 Mc 2, 52; Rom 4,
　3.9.22; Gal 3, 6f; Jas
　2, 23.

G
N

⁷* He then said to him, "I am the LORD who brought you from Ur of the Chaldeans to give you this land as a possession." ⁸ "O Lord GOD," he asked, "how am I to know that I shall possess it?" ⁹*† He answered him, "Bring me a three-year-old heifer, a three-year-old she-goat, a three-year-old ram, a turtledove, and a young pigeon." ¹⁰ He brought him all these, split them in two, and placed each half opposite the other; but the birds he did not cut up. ¹¹ Birds of prey swooped down on the carcasses, but Abram stayed with them. ¹² As the sun was about to set, a trance fell upon Abram, and a deep, terrifying darkness enveloped him.

¹³* Then the LORD said to Abram: "Know for certain that your descendants shall be aliens in a land not their own, where they shall be enslaved and oppressed for four hundred years. ¹⁴* But I will bring judgment on the nation they must serve, and in the end they will depart with great wealth. ¹⁵ You, however, shall join your forefathers in peace; you shall be buried at a contented old age. ¹⁶*† In the fourth time-span the others shall come back here; the wickedness of the Amorites will not have reached its full measure until then."

¹⁷† When the sun had set and it was dark, there appeared a smoking brazier and a flaming torch, which passed between those pieces. ¹⁸*† It was on that occasion that the LORD made a covenant with Abram, saying: "To your descendants I give this land, from the Wadi of Egypt to the Great River [the Euphrates], ¹⁹* the land of the Kenites, the Kenizzites, the Kadmonites, ²⁰ the Hittites, the Perizzites, the Rephaim, ²¹ the Amorites, the Canaanites, the Girgashites, and the Jebusites."

Birth of Ishmael

16 ¹*† Abram's wife Sarai had borne him no children. She had, however, an Egyptian maidservant named Hagar. ²* Sarai said to Abram: "The LORD has kept me from bearing children. Have intercourse, then, with my maid; perhaps I shall have sons through her." Abram heeded Sarai's request. ³ Thus, after Abram had lived ten years in the land of Canaan, his wife Sarai took her maid, Hagar the Egyptian, and gave her to her husband Abram to be his concubine. ⁴* He had intercourse with her, and she became pregnant. When she became aware of her pregnancy, she looked on her mistress with disdain. ⁵* So Sarai said to Abram: "You are responsible for this outrage against me. I myself gave my maid to your embrace; but ever since she became aware of her pregnancy, she has been looking on me with disdain. May the LORD decide between

did you KNOW?

Fire

Fire appears frequently throughout the Old Testament, symbolizing two aspects of God: presence and holiness. Fire symbolizes a special presence of God in the sealing of the covenant with Abraham (Gn 15, 17), in the burning bush (Ex 3, 2), and in the pillar of fire leading Israel through the desert (Ex 13, 21). Fire also symbolizes God's holiness appearing to purge and purify those who deviate from God's ways, as in Sodom and Gomorrah (Gn 19, 24) and the seventh plague against Egypt (Ex 9, 23).

▸ Gn 15, 17

you and me!" ⁶ Abram told Sarai: "Your maid is in your power. Do to her whatever you please." Sarai then abused her so much that Hagar ran away from her.

⁷*† The LORD'S messenger found her by a spring in the wilderness, the spring on the road to Shur, ⁸ and he asked, "Hagar, maid of Sarai, where have you come from and where are you going?" She answered, "I am running away from my mistress, Sarai." ⁹ But the LORD'S messenger told her: "Go back to your mistress and submit to her abusive treatment. ¹⁰* I will make your descendants so numerous," added the LORD'S messenger, "that they

---

† **15, 9:** *Three-year-old:* ritually mature.
15, 16: *Time-span:* the Hebrew term *dor* is commonly rendered as "generation," but it may signify a period of varying length. Neither this passage nor the statement about the four hundred years has any value for determining how long the Israelites were in Egypt.
15, 17: *Brazier:* literally "oven"; a portable one is meant here. The smoke and fire represent God's presence. Although the text does not mention it, Abraham no doubt also walked between the split carcasses. For the meaning of this strange ceremony, see note on Jer 34, 18f.
15, 18: *Made a covenant:* literally "cut a covenant"; the expression derives from the ceremony of cutting the animals in two.

16, 1–6: Sarah's actions are all in keeping with the laws of the time, as known from ancient extra-biblical sources.
16, 7: *The LORD'S messenger:* a manifestation of God in human form; therefore in v 13 the messenger is identified with the Lord himself.

15, 7: Gn 11, 31; 12, 1; Ex 32, 13; Neh 9, 7f; Acts 7, 2f.
15, 9: Lv 1, 14.
15, 13: Ex 12, 40; Nm 20, 15; Jdt 5, 9f; Is 52, 4; Acts 13, 20; Gal 3, 17.
15, 14: Ex 3, 8.21f.
15, 16: 1 Kgs 21, 26.
15, 18: Ex 32, 13; Neh 9, 8; Ps 105, 11; Sir 44, 21.
15, 19f: Dt 7, 1.
16, 1: Gn 11, 30.
16, 2: Gn 21, 8f; Gal 4, 22.
16, 4: 1 Sm 1, 6; Prv 30, 23.
16, 5–16: Gn 21, 10–19.
16, 7: Ex 15, 22.
16, 10: Gn 17, 20; 21, 13.18; 25, 12–18.

LIVE IT!

Love and Jealousy

A love triangle in the Bible! The relationship between Abram, Sarai, and Hagar is shocking by Christian moral standards but would not have been unusual in their time. A patriarch like Abram would often have children by several wives, slaves, and concubines (something like mistresses who lived with the household). It's not surprising that such relationships would have fostered jealousy and tension. The conflict between Hagar and Sarai must have been fierce for Hagar to leave the security of Abram's household.

So, why does God's angel seek out Hagar and ask her to return to a place where she is likely to be mistreated? To answer this, we have to remember that the writer of Genesis was concerned more with explaining the rise of nations than with teaching a moral lesson. Hagar must return to bear her son, Ishmael, so that the Ishmaelites (descendants of Ishmael) have a clear connection to Abraham as their ancestor.

Today, we encourage victims of abuse and harassment to speak out and take action. When we encounter people who have been abused or harassed, we need to help them seek justice and set things right. Remember the larger message in Genesis—that every person is created in God's image and is to be treated with the utmost dignity and respect. Carrying out this message is our responsibility as brothers and sisters to one another.

▶ Gn 16, 1–16

will be too many to count. [11]† Besides," the LORD's messenger said to her:

"You are now pregnant and shall bear a son;
    you shall name him Ishmael,
For the LORD has heard you,
    God has answered you.

[12]* He shall be a wild ass of a man,
    his hand against everyone,
    and everyone's hand against him;
In opposition to all his kin
    shall he encamp."

[13]*† To the LORD who spoke to her she gave a name, saying, "You are the God of Vision"; she meant, "Have I really seen God and remained alive after my vision?" [14]† That is why the well is called Beer-lahai-roi. It is between Kadesh and Bered.

[15]* Hagar bore Abram a son, and Abram named the son whom Hagar bore him Ishmael. [16] Abram was eighty-six years old when Hagar bore him Ishmael.

Covenant of Circumcision

17 [1]*† When Abram was ninety-nine years old, the LORD appeared to him and said: "I am God the Almighty. Walk in my presence and be blameless. [2]* Between you and me I will establish my covenant, and I will multiply you exceedingly."

[3] When Abram prostrated himself, God continued to speak to him: [4]* "My covenant with you is this: you are to become the father of a host of nations. [5]*† No longer shall you be called Abram; your name shall be Abraham, for I am making you the father of a host of nations. [6] I will render you exceedingly fertile; I will make nations of you; kings shall stem from you. [7]* I will maintain my covenant with you and your descendants after you throughout the ages as an everlasting pact, to be your God and the God of your descendants after you. [8]* I will give to you and to your descendants after you the land in which you are now staying, the whole land of Canaan, as a permanent possession; and I will be their God."

16, 11: *Ishmael:* in Hebrew the name means "God has heard."
16, 13: *The God of Vision:* in Hebrew, *el-roi;* hence the name of the spring. *Remained alive:* for the ancient notion that a person died on seeing God, cf Gn 32, 31; Ex 20, 19; Dt 4, 33; Jgs 13, 22.
16, 14: *Beer-lahai-roi:* probably "the well of living sight," i.e., the well where one can see (God) and yet live.
17, 1: *The Almighty:* traditional but incorrect rendering of the divine title *shaddai,* of uncertain meaning.
17, 5: *Abram* and *Abraham* are merely two forms of the same name, both meaning, "the father is exalted"; another variant form is Abiram (Nm 16, 1; 1 Kgs 16, 34). The additional *-ha-* in the form

Abraham is explained by folk etymology as coming from *ab-hamon goyim,* "father of a host of nations."

16, 12: Gn 21, 20; 25, 18.
16, 13: Gn 24, 62.
16, 15: Gn 16, 2; Gal 4, 22.
17, 1: Gn 35, 11; Ex 6, 3.
17, 2: Gn 12, 2; 13, 16; Ex 32, 13.
17, 4: Sir 44, 21; Rom 4, 17.
17, 5: Neh 9, 7.
17, 7: Ps 105, 42; Lk 1, 72f; Gal 3, 16.
17, 8: Ex 32, 13; Dt 1, 8; 14, 2; Lk 1, 55; Acts 7, 5.

⁹ God also said to Abraham: "On your part, you and your descendants after you must keep my covenant throughout the ages. ¹⁰* This is my covenant with you and your descendants after you that you must keep: every male among you shall be circumcised. ¹¹* Circumcise the flesh of your foreskin, and that shall be the mark of the covenant between you and me. ¹²* Throughout the ages, every male among you, when he is eight days old, shall be circumcised, including houseborn slaves and those acquired with money from any foreigner who is not of your blood. ¹³ Yes, both the houseborn slaves and those acquired with money must be circumcised. Thus my covenant shall be in your flesh as an everlasting pact. ¹⁴ If a male is uncircumcised, that is, if the flesh of his foreskin has not been cut away, such a one shall be cut off from his people; he has broken my covenant."

¹⁵† God further said to Abraham: "As for your wife Sarai, do not call her Sarai; her name shall be Sarah. ¹⁶* I will bless her, and I will give you a son by her. Him also will I bless; he shall give rise to nations, and rulers of peoples shall issue from him." ¹⁷*† Abraham prostrated himself and laughed as he said to himself, "Can a child be born

did you KNOW?

Circumcision

Circumcision, the removal of the foreskin of the penis, was practiced by many peoples in the ancient world. In Israel, circumcision was performed shortly after birth. It symbolized that this person belonged to the people of God, and was required by the covenant that God made first with Abraham, then with Moses and all Israel. Today, most Jews continue circumcision as a religious practice, and other people may be circumcised for personal reasons.

In the early church, circumcision became the center of a controversy about whether Gentiles who wanted to become Christians had to first become Jews (Acts of the Apostles, chapter 15; Phil 3, 9).

▶ Gn 17, 9–14

Covenant

Covenant is a powerful word in the Bible, with deep religious significance because it expresses the intimate relationship between God and God's people. At its most basic level, a covenant is a promise by both parties involved to do certain things.

In the covenant God makes with Noah, God promises never to destroy the earth again, and Noah's family promises to fill the earth and subdue it (Gn 9, 1–17). In the covenant with Abraham, God promises that Abram's descendants will be numerous and become a great nation. In return, Abram and all the male members of his household and their male descendants must practice circumcision to mark that they belong to God (17, 1–27). In the Covenant made at Mount Sinai with Moses (Ex 19, 1–9) and the Hebrew people, God promises to give them the Promised Land. In return, they promise to follow the laws God gives to them.

As told by the author of Genesis, these covenants are always initiated by God, who wants to lead the people to a better way of life. But the people must respond to God's offer as a sign of their faith in God. The New Testament tells of a new and lasting Covenant for all people and for all time (2 Cor 3, 3; Gal 4, 21–31).

And so we, each of us, are part of these ancient promises. Like the many faithful people who have gone before us, we too are the descendants of Abraham and Sarah, believers in the one God and members of God's family. We too are heirs to a special, intimate relationship with the Holy One of Israel.

▶ Gn 17, 1–27

---

† 17, 15: Sarai and Sarah are variant forms of the same name, both meaning "princess."

17, 17: Laughed: yishaq, which is the Hebrew form of the name "Isaac"; other similar explanations of the name are given in Gn 18, 12 and 21, 6.

* 17, 10: Jn 7, 22; Acts 7, 8; Rom 4, 11.
17, 11: Sir 44, 21.
17, 12: Lv 12, 3; Lk 1, 59;
2, 21.
17, 16: Gn 18, 10; Gal 4, 23.
17, 17: Rom 4, 19; Heb 11, 11f.

GN

to a man who is a hundred years old? Or can Sarah give birth at ninety?" 18 Then Abraham said to God, "Let but Ishmael live on by your favor!" 19* God replied: "Nevertheless, your wife Sarah is to bear you a son, and you shall call him Isaac. I will maintain my covenant with him as an everlasting pact, to be his God and the God of his descendants after him. 20* As for Ishmael, I am heeding you: I hereby bless him. I will make him fertile and will multiply him exceedingly. He shall become the father of twelve chieftains, and I will make of him a great nation. 21* But my covenant I will maintain with Isaac, whom Sarah shall bear to you by this time next year." 22 When he had finished speaking with him, God departed from Abraham.

23 Then Abraham took his son Ishmael and all his slaves, whether born in his house or acquired with his money—every male among the members of Abraham's household—and he circumcised the flesh of their foreskins on that same day, as God had told him to do. 24* Abraham was ninety-nine years old when the flesh of his foreskin was circumcised, 25 and his son Ishmael was thirteen years old when the flesh of his foreskin was circumcised. 26 Thus, on that same day Abraham and his son Ishmael were circumcised; 27 and all the male members of his household, including the slaves born in his house or acquired with his money from foreigners, were circumcised with him.

Abraham's Visitors

18 1 The LORD appeared to Abraham by the terebinth of Mamre, as he sat in the entrance of his tent, while the day was growing hot. 2* Looking up, he saw three men standing nearby. When he saw them, he ran from the entrance of the tent to greet them; and bowing to the ground, 3† he said: "Sir, if I may ask you this favor, please do not go on past your servant. 4 Let some water be brought, that you may bathe your feet, and then rest yourselves under the tree. 5 Now that you have come this close to your servant, let me bring you a little food, that you may refresh yourselves; and af-

terward you may go on your way." "Very well," they replied, "do as you have said."

6† Abraham hastened into the tent and told Sarah, "Quick, three seahs of fine flour! Knead it and make rolls." 7 He ran to the herd, picked out a tender, choice steer, and gave it to a servant, who quickly prepared it. 8† Then he got some curds and milk, as well as the steer that had been prepared, and set these before them; and he waited on them under the tree while they ate.

9 "Where is your wife Sarah?" they asked him. "There in the tent," he replied. 10*† One of them said, "I will surely return to you about this time next year, and Sarah will then have a son." Sarah was listening at the entrance of the tent, just behind him. 11* Now Abraham and Sarah were old, advanced in years, and Sarah had stopped having her womanly periods. 12† So Sarah laughed to herself and said, "Now that I am so withered and my husband is so old, am I still to have sexual pleasure?" 13 But the LORD said to Abraham: "Why did Sarah laugh and say, 'Shall I really bear a child, old as I am?' 14* Is anything too marvelous for the LORD to do? At the appointed time, about this time next year, I will return to you, and Sarah will have a son." 15 Because she was afraid, Sarah dissembled, saying, "I didn't laugh." But he said, "Yes you did."

Abraham Intercedes for Sodom

16 The men set out from there and looked down toward Sodom; Abraham was walking with them, to see them on their way. 17 The LORD reflected: "Shall I hide from Abraham what I am about to do, 18* now that he is to become a great and populous nation, and all the nations of the earth are to find blessing in him? 19 Indeed, I have singled him out that he may direct his sons and his posterity to keep the way of the LORD by doing what is right and just, so that the LORD may carry into effect for Abraham the promises he made about him." 20*† Then the LORD said: "The outcry against Sodom and Gomorrah is so great, and their sin so grave, 21 that I must go down and see

---

† **18, 3:** Abraham addresses the leader of the group, whom he does not yet recognize as Yahweh; in the next two verses he speaks to all three men. The other two are later (Gn 19, 1) identified as messengers.

18, 6: *Three seahs:* one ephah, about half a bushel.

18, 8: *Curds:* a type of soft cheese or yoghurt.

18, 10: *One of them:* i.e., the Lord. Abraham now realizes this for the first time when he hears the prediction of a miraculous birth. *About this time next year:* literally "when the time becomes alive," i.e., at the time when birth is due after the period of gestation; the conception is understood as taking place soon after the prediction.

18, 12: *Sarah laughed:* see note on Gn 17, 17.

18, 20: Israelite tradition was unanimous in ascribing the destruction of Sodom and Gomorrah to the wickedness of these cities, but tradition varied in regard to the nature of this wickedness. Ac-

cording to the present account of the Yahwist, the sin of Sodom was homosexuality (Gn 19, 4f), which is therefore also known as sodomy; but according to Isaiah (1, 9f; 3, 9), it was a lack of social justice; Ezekiel (16, 46–51) described it as a disregard for the poor, whereas Jeremiah (23, 14) saw it as general immorality.

17, 19: Gn 11, 30; 21, 2; Ex 32, 13; Sir 44, 22.
17, 20: Gn 16, 10; 21, 13.18; 25, 12–16.
17, 21: Gn 18, 14; 21, 2; 26, 2–5; Rom 9, 7.
17, 24: Gn 17, 10; Rom 4, 11.
18, 2: Heb 13, 1f.
18, 10: Gn 17, 19; 21, 1;

2 Kgs 4, 16; Rom 9, 9.
18, 11: Gn 17, 17; Rom 4, 19; Heb 11, 11f.
18, 14: Mt 19, 26; Mk 10, 27; Lk 1, 37; 18, 27; Rom 4, 21.
18, 18: Lk 1, 55.
18, 20: Gn 19, 13; Is 3, 9; Lk 17, 28; Jude 7.

What's So Funny?

LIVE IT!

Laughter is not a word we usually associate with the Bible, and certainly not with the Old Testament. Most of the stories are serious, filled with accounts of sacrifice, battles, and the Covenant. But here is Sarah, an old woman, long past childbearing age. She overhears one of Abraham's mysterious guests tell him that in a year, he and Sarah will have a son (Gn 18, 10). How can she help but laugh? She and Abraham do produce, of course, a son called Isaac, whose Hebrew name, Yishaq, means "laughed." Sarah's cynical chuckles must have turned to joyful laughs at the birth of her beloved son. Laughter is a wonderful response to the gift of life and is a natural and often spontaneous response to God's presence within us and around us.

"Is anything too marvelous for the LORD to do?" (verse 14). We are all tempted to laugh at the notion that miracles can happen to us. As we grow in faith and open ourselves to God's goodness, our laughter will change from cynical laughter to joyful laughter.

▸ Gn 18, 9–15

---

whether or not their actions fully correspond to the cry against them that comes to me. I mean to find out."

22 While the two men walked on farther toward Sodom, the LORD remained standing before Abra-

Get Close to God

PRAY IT

Our prayers reveal what we believe about God and what we value. Abraham's bargaining for the inhabitants of Sodom and Gomorrah shows his faith, his care for others, and his closeness with God. Although he is humble, he deals with God as a friend whom he is not afraid to be honest with.

We too must be honest with God in our prayer. Too many Christians simply do not trust God enough to be completely themselves with God. They are afraid to share their doubts, anger, grief, and frustrations. But God is big enough to handle it all. Find a way in your prayer to share your innermost thoughts and feelings with God. For some people, journaling helps; others yell and shout aloud at the Lord. Remember that God's healing touch cannot enter our life until we are willing to share our deepest feelings.

▸ Gn 18, 22–33

ham. 23 Then Abraham drew nearer to him and said: "Will you sweep away the innocent with the guilty? 24 Suppose there were fifty innocent people in the city; would you wipe out the place, rather than spare it for the sake of the fifty innocent people within it? 25* Far be it from you to do such a thing, to make the innocent die with the guilty, so that the innocent and the guilty would be treated alike! Should not the judge of all the world act with justice?" 26 The LORD replied, "If I find fifty innocent people in the city of Sodom, I will spare the whole place for their sake." 27* Abraham spoke up again: "See how I am presuming to speak to my Lord, though I am but dust and ashes! 28 What if there are five less than fifty innocent people? Will you destroy the whole city because of those five?" "I will not destroy it," he answered, "if I find forty-five there." 29 But Abraham persisted, saying, "What if only forty are found there?" He replied, "I will forbear doing it for the sake of the forty." 30 Then he said, "Let not my Lord grow impatient if I go on. What if only thirty are found there?" He replied, "I will forbear doing it if I can find but thirty there." 31 Still he went on, "Since I have thus dared to speak to my Lord, what if there are no more than twenty?" "I will not destroy it," he answered, "for the sake of the twenty." 32* But he still persisted, "Please, let not my Lord grow angry if I speak up this last time. What if there are at least ten there?" "For the sake of those ten," he replied, "I will not destroy it."

33 The LORD departed as soon as he had finished speaking with Abraham, and Abraham returned home.

18, 25: Dt 32, 4; Jb 8, 3.20;   18, 27: Sir 10, 9; 17, 27.
      Wis 12, 15.   18, 32: Jer 5, 1; Ez 22, 30.

Destruction of Sodom and Gomorrah

19 [1] The two angels reached Sodom in the evening, as Lot was sitting at the gate of Sodom. When Lot saw them, he got up to greet them; and bowing down with his face to the ground, [2]*† he said, "Please, gentlemen, come aside into your servant's house for the night, and bathe your feet; you can get up early to continue your journey." But they replied, "No, we shall pass the night in the town square." [3] He urged them so strongly, however, that they turned aside to his place and entered his house. He prepared a meal for them, baking cakes without leaven, and they dined.

[4]* Before they went to bed, all the townsmen of Sodom, both young and old—all the people to the last man—closed in on the house. [5] They called to Lot and said to him, "Where are the men who came to your house tonight? Bring them out to us that we

against Lot, moving in closer to break down the door. [10] But his guests put out their hands, pulled Lot inside with them, and closed the door; [11]† at the same time they struck the men at the entrance of the house, one and all, with such a blinding light that they were utterly unable to reach the doorway.

[12]*† Then the angels said to Lot: "Who else belongs to you here? Your sons [sons-in-law] and your daughters and all who belong to you in the city—take them away from it! [13]* We are about to destroy this place, for the outcry reaching the LORD against those in the city is so great that he has sent us to destroy it." [14]† So Lot went out and spoke to his sons-in-law, who had contracted marriage with his daughters. "Get up and leave this place," he told them; "the LORD is about to destroy the city." But his sons-in-law thought he was joking.

LIVE IT!

Be Kind to Strangers

If our first gesture to outsiders were one of respect, kindness, and gracious hospitality, what might our world be like? The story of Sodom and Gomorrah shows us the results of disrespect, inhospitality, and the attempted abuse of strangers. Like Abraham, Lot is a wonderful host. But the people of Sodom want Lot's visitors for their own sexual pleasure. For the author of Genesis, this horrendous crime calls for the most severe punishment.

As children of God, it is our responsibility to extend our kindness to stranger and friend alike. So how are visitors or new students treated in your school? How are visitors treated in your home?

▸ Gn 19, 1–11

may have intimacies with them." [6] Lot went out to meet them at the entrance. When he had shut the door behind him, [7] he said, "I beg you, my brothers, not to do this wicked thing. [8] I have two daughters who have never had intercourse with men. Let me bring them out to you, and you may do to them as you please. But don't do anything to these men, for you know they have come under the shelter of my roof." [9]* They replied, "Stand back! This fellow," they sneered, "came here as an immigrant, and now he dares to give orders! We'll treat you worse than them!" With that, they pressed hard

[15] As dawn was breaking, the angels urged Lot on, saying, "On your way! Take with you your wife and your two daughters who are here, or you will be swept away in the punishment of the city." [16] When he hesitated, the men, by the LORD'S mercy, seized his hand and the hands of his wife and his two daughters and led them to safety outside the city. [17]* As soon as they had been brought outside, he was told: "Flee for your life! Don't look back or stop anywhere on the Plain. Get off to the hills at once, or you will be swept away." [18] "Oh, no, my lord!" replied Lot. [19] "You have already thought enough of

---

19, 2: *Gentlemen:* Lot does not yet know that the distinguished-looking men are God's messengers; cf Gn 18, 3.

19, 11: *Blinding light:* a preternatural flash that temporarily dazed the wicked men and revealed to Lot the true nature of his guests.

19, 12: Since Lot apparently had no *sons,* a glossator interpreted the term to mean *sons-in-law.*

19, 14: It is uncertain whether Lot's *sons-in-law* were fully married to his daughters or only "engaged" to them (Israelite "engagement" was the first part of the marriage ceremony), or even whether

the daughters involved were the same as, or different from, the two daughters who were still in their father's house.

19, 2: Wis 10, 6; Sir 16, 8; Ez 16, 50; Heb 13, 1f.
19, 4–9: Jgs 19, 22–25; Jude 7.
19, 9: Gn 13, 12; 2 Pt 2, 7f.
19, 12: 2 Pt 7, 9.
19, 13: Is 1, 7.9; Zep 2, 9; Lk 17, 29.
19, 17: Wis 10, 6.

your servant to do me the great kindness of intervening to save my life. But I cannot flee to the hills to keep the disaster from overtaking me, and so I shall die. 20† Look, this town ahead is near enough to escape to. It's only a small place. Let me flee there—it's a small place, isn't it?—that my life may be saved." 21 "Well, then," he replied, "I will also grant you the favor you now ask. I will not overthrow the town you speak of. 22* Hurry, escape there! I cannot do anything until you arrive there." That is why the town is called Zoar.

23* The sun was just rising over the earth as Lot arrived in Zoar; 24* at the same time the LORD rained down sulphurous fire upon Sodom and Gomorrah [from the LORD out of heaven]. 25*† He overthrew those cities and the whole Plain, together with the inhabitants of the cities and the produce of the soil. 26* But Lot's wife looked back, and she was turned into a pillar of salt.

27 Early the next morning Abraham went to the place where he had stood in the LORD's presence. 28*† As he looked down toward Sodom and Gomorrah and the whole region of the Plain, he saw dense smoke over the land rising like fumes from a furnace.

29 Thus it came to pass: when God destroyed the Cities of the Plain, he was mindful of Abraham by sending Lot away from the upheaval by which God overthrew the cities where Lot had been living.

Moabites and Ammonites

30† Since Lot was afraid to stay in Zoar, he and his two daughters went up from Zoar and settled in the hill country, where he lived with his two daughters in a cave. 31 The older one said to the younger: "Our father is getting old, and there is not a man on earth to unite with us as was the custom everywhere. 32 Come, let us ply our father with wine and then lie with him, that we may have offspring by our father." 33 So that night they plied their father with wine, and the older one went in and lay with her father; but he was not aware of her lying down or her getting up. 34 Next day the older one said to the younger: "Last night it was I who lay with my father. Let us ply him with wine again tonight, and

then you go in and lie with him, that we may both have offspring by our father." 35 So that night, too, they plied their father with wine, and then the younger one went in and lay with him; but again he was not aware of her lying down or her getting up.

36 Thus both of Lot's daughters became pregnant by their father. 37*† The older one gave birth to a son whom she named Moab, saying, "From my father." He is the ancestor of the Moabites of today. 38*† The younger one, too, gave birth to a son, and she named him Ammon, saying, "The son of my kin." He is the ancestor of the Ammonites of today.

Abraham at Gerar

20 1† Abraham journeyed on to the region of the Negeb, where he settled between Kadesh and Shur. While he stayed in Gerar, 2 he said of his wife Sarah, "She is my sister." So Abimelech, king of Gerar, sent and took Sarah. 3 But God came to Abimelech in a dream one night and said to him, "You are about to die because of the woman you have taken, for she has a husband." 4 Abimelech, who had not approached her, said: "O Lord, would you slay a man even though he is innocent? 5 He himself told me, 'She is my sister,' and she herself also stated, 'He is my brother.' I did it in good faith and with clean hands." 6 God answered him in the dream: "Yes, I know you did it in good faith. In fact, it was I who kept you from sinning against me; that is why I did not let you touch her. 7† Therefore, return the man's wife—as a spokesman he will intercede for you—that your life may be saved. If you do not return her, you can be sure that you and all who are yours will certainly die."

8 Early the next morning Abimelech called all his court officials and informed them of everything that had happened, and the men were horrified. 9 Then Abimelech summoned Abraham and said to him: "How could you do this to us! What wrong did I do to you that you should have brought such monstrous guilt on me and my kingdom? You have treated me in an intolerable way. 10 What were you afraid of," he asked him, "that you should have done such a thing?" 11 "I was afraid," answered

---

19, 20: *A small place:* the Hebrew word *misar,* literally "a little thing," has the same root consonants as the name of the town *Zoar* in v 22.

19, 25: *Overthrew:* the consistent use of this term, literally "turned upside down," to describe the destruction of the *Cities of the Plain* seems to imply that their upheaval (v 29) was caused primarily by an earthquake; this would naturally be accompanied by a disastrous fire, especially in a region containing bitumen (Gn 14, 10) and its accompanying gases.

19, 28f: From the height east of Hebron, Abraham could easily see the region at the southern end of the Dead Sea, where the *Cities of the Plain* were probably located.

19, 30–38: This Israelite tale about the origin of Israel's neighbors east of the Jordan and the Dead Sea was told partly to ridicule these racially related but rival nations and partly to give folk etymologies for their names.

19, 37: *From my father:* in Hebrew, *meabi,* similar in sound to the name "Moab."

19, 38: *The son of my kin:* in Hebrew, *ben-ammi,* similar in sound to the name "Ammonites."

20, 1–18: This story from the Elohist source (see note on Gn 4, 25) combines elements found in the two very similar but distinct stories of the Yahwist source in Gn 12, 10–20 and 26, 6–11.

20, 7: *Spokesman:* the Hebrew term *nabi* used here is regularly translated as "prophet," but it simply means "one who speaks on behalf of another," whether the latter is God, as in almost all cases, or another man, as in Ex 4, 16.

19, 22: Wis 10, 6.   Am 4, 11.
19, 23: Pss 9, 6; 11, 6; 107, 34.   19, 26: Wis 10, 7; Lk 17, 32.
19, 24: Wis 10, 7; Is 1, 9; 13, 19;   19, 28: Rv 9, 2; 14, 10f.
   Lam 4, 6; 17, 29; 2 Pt 2, 6.   19, 37: Dt 2, 9.
19, 25: Dt 29, 22; Jer 50, 40;   19, 38: Dt 2, 19.

Abraham, "because I thought there would surely be no fear of God in this place, and so they would kill me on account of my wife. 12* Besides, she is in truth my sister, but only my father's daughter, not my mother's; and so she became my wife. 13 When God sent me wandering from my father's house, I asked her: 'Would you do me this favor? In whatever place we come to, say that I am your brother.' "

14 Then Abimelech took flocks and herds and male and female slaves and gave them to Abraham; and after he restored his wife Sarah to him, 15 he said, "Here, my land lies at your disposal; settle wherever you please." 16† To Sarah he said: "See, I have given your brother a thousand shekels of silver. Let that serve you as a vindication before all who are with you; your honor has been preserved with everyone." 17 Abraham then interceded with God, and God restored health to Abimelech, that is, to his wife and his maidservants, so that they could bear children; 18 for God had tightly closed every womb in Abimelech's household on account of Abraham's wife Sarah.

Birth of Isaac

21 1* The LORD took note of Sarah as he had said he would; he did for her as he had promised. 2* Sarah became pregnant and bore Abraham a son in his old age, at the set time that God had stated. 3* Abraham gave the name Isaac to this son of his whom Sarah bore him. 4* When his son Isaac was eight days old, Abraham circumcised him, as God had commanded. 5 Abraham was a hundred years old when his son Isaac was born to him. 6* Sarah then said, "God has given me cause to laugh, and all who hear of it will laugh with me. 7 Who would have told Abraham," she added, "that Sarah would nurse children! Yet I have borne him a son in his old age." 8 Isaac grew, and on the day of the child's weaning Abraham held a great feast.

9† Sarah noticed the son whom Hagar the Egyptian had borne to Abraham playing with her son Isaac; 10* so she demanded of Abraham: "Drive out that slave and her son! No son of that slave is going to share the inheritance with my son Isaac!" 11 Abraham was greatly distressed, especially on account of his son Ishmael. 12* But God said to Abraham: "Do not be distressed about the boy or about your slave woman. Heed the demands of

Hagar's Rescue

Genesis 21, 9–21 is part 2 of the Hagar and Ishmael story begun in 16, 1–16. Once again, Hagar is the victim of Sarah's jealousy. But this time God does not send her back. Seemingly facing certain death, Hagar receives from God the ability to see the opportunity for life in front of her. This time the writer of Genesis makes the point that God rescues the abused and abandoned. Hagar and Ishmael survive, and from their descendants, a great people emerges.

Hagar's story reminds us that God wants to rescue us from oppression, injustice, and abuse. Often, we want to ask God to magically take these things away. But because God has given human beings free will, we cannot always be spared from the abuse and injustice of others. In your prayer, you can always ask God to rescue you, to give you the vision to see the healthy choices you can make to improve your situation. Do that right now if you are in an unjust or abusive situation.

▶ Gn 21, 9–21

Sarah, no matter what she is asking of you; for it is through Isaac that descendants shall bear your name. 13 As for the son of the slave woman, I will make a great nation of him also, since he too is your offspring."

14† Early the next morning Abraham got some bread and a skin of water and gave them to Hagar. Then, placing the child on her back, he sent her away. As she roamed aimlessly in the wilderness of Beer-sheba, 15 the water in the skin was used up. So she put the child down under a shrub, 16 and then went and sat down opposite him, about a bowshot away; for she said to herself, "Let me not watch to see the child die." As she sat opposite him, he be-

---

20, 16: *A thousand shekels of silver:* not a gift distinct from that of the animals and the slaves (v 14), but the monetary value of these.

21, 9–19: This story of Hagar's expulsion, in the Elohist source, is in general a duplicate of the one from the Yahwist source in Gn 16, 5–14; but the two stories differ greatly in detail.

21, 14: *Placing the child on her back:* the phrase is translated from an emended form of the Hebrew text. In the current faulty Hebrew text, Abraham put the bread and the waterskin on Hagar's back, while her son apparently walked beside her. This reading

seems to be a scribal attempt at harmonizing the present passage with the data of the Priestly source, in which Ishmael would have been at least fourteen years old when Isaac was born; compare Gn 16, 16 with 21, 5; cf 17, 25. But in the present Elohist story Ishmael is obviously a little boy, not much older than Isaac; cf vv 15, 18.

20, 12: Gn 12, 13.
21, 1: Gn 17, 19; 18, 10.
21, 2: Gal 4, 23; Heb 11, 11.
21, 3: Mt 1, 2; Lk 3, 34.
21, 4: Gn 17, 10ff; Acts 7, 8.
21, 6: Gn 17, 17.
21, 10: Jgs 11, 2; Gal 4, 30.
21, 12: Rom 9, 7; Heb 11, 18.

gan to cry. [17]* God heard the boy's cry, and God's messenger called to Hagar from heaven: "What is the matter, Hagar? Don't be afraid; God has heard the boy's cry in this plight of his. [18] Arise, lift up the boy and hold him by the hand; for I will make of him a great nation." [19] Then God opened her eyes, and she saw a well of water. She went and filled the skin with water, and then let the boy drink.

[20] God was with the boy as he grew up. He lived in the wilderness and became an expert bowman, [21] with his home in the wilderness of Paran. His mother got a wife for him from the land of Egypt.

The Pact at Beer-sheba

[22]† About that time Abimelech, accompanied by Phicol, the commander of his army, said to Abraham: "God is with you in everything you do. [23]† Therefore, swear to me by God at this place that you will not deal falsely with me or with my progeny and posterity, but will act as loyally toward me and the land in which you stay as I have acted toward you." [24] To this Abraham replied, "I so swear."

[25] Abraham, however, reproached Abimelech about a well that Abimelech's men had seized by force. [26] "I have no idea who did that," Abimelech replied. "In fact, you never told me about it, nor did I ever hear of it until now."

[27] Then Abraham took sheep and cattle and gave them to Abimelech and the two made a pact. [28] Abraham also set apart seven ewe lambs of the flock, [29] and Abimelech asked him, "What is the purpose of these seven ewe lambs that you have set apart?" [30] Abraham answered, "The seven ewe lambs you shall accept from me that thus I may have your acknowledgment that the well was dug by me." [31]† This is why the place is called Beer-sheba; the two of them took an oath there. [32] When they had thus made the pact in Beer-sheba, Abimelech, along with Phicol, the commander of his army, left and returned to the land of the Philistines.

[33]† Abraham planted a tamarisk at Beer-sheba, and there he invoked by name the LORD, God the Eternal. [34] Abraham resided in the land of the Philistines for many years.

The Testing of Abraham

22 [1]*† Some time after these events, God put Abraham to the test. He called to him, "Abraham!" "Ready!" he replied. [2]*† Then God said: "Take your son Isaac, your only one, whom you love, and go to the land of Moriah. There you shall offer him up as a holocaust on a height that I will point out to you." [3] Early the next morning Abraham saddled his donkey, took with him his son Isaac, and two of his servants as well, and with

PRAY IT

Ultimate Trust in God!

To us it seems horrible that God would ask Abraham to sacrifice his son Isaac. But this story is meant to be a sign of Abraham's complete trust in God. Ultimately, God prevented the sacrifice because God wanted not Isaac's death but Abraham's faith. Because of his willingness to respond to God's demand, Abraham is recognized as the father of our faith. Our trust in God should be as total as Abraham's trust was.

We probably won't ever be faced with the test of Abraham, but the story shows us the power of faith. Because of Abraham's faith in God's promise, Isaac lived and became the father of Jacob, whose twelve sons became the twelve tribes of Israel. In your prayer, reflect or journal on the following questions:

■ Because of your beliefs, have you ever had to give up someone or something that was precious to you?
■ How has your life been enriched as a result of your trust in God in a difficult situation?

▶ Gn 22, 1–19

---

†
21, 22: Here and in v 32 the Greek text has ". . . Abimelech, accompanied by Ahuzzath, his councilor, and Phicol . . ."; but this is probably a secondary harmonization with Gn 26, 26. Abimelech took Phicol with him in order to intimidate Abraham by a show of strength.

21, 23: *This place:* Beer-sheba (v 31). Abimelech had come from Gerar (Gn 20, 2), about thirty miles west of Beer-sheba.

21, 31: *Beer-sheba:* the Hebrew name really means "the well of the seven," i.e., the place where there are seven wells, alluded to in the episode of the *seven ewe lambs,* vv 28ff; but it can also be interpreted to mean "the well of the oath."

21, 33: *God the Eternal:* in Hebrew, *el olam,* perhaps the name

of the deity of the pre-Israelite sanctuary at Beer-sheba, but used by Abraham merely as a title of Yahweh; cf Is 40, 28.

22, 1: *God put Abraham to the test:* to prove the firmness of Abraham's faith in God's promise that through Isaac all the nations of the earth would find blessing; cf Gn 18, 10.18; 21, 12.

22, 2: *Only one:* uniquely precious, especially loved; therefore the same term is rendered in vv 12.16 as "beloved."

*

21, 17: Gn 16, 7.	**22, 2:** 2 Chr 3, 1; 1 Mc 2, 52;
22, 1: Sir 44, 20.	Heb 11, 17.

the wood that he had cut for the holocaust, set out for the place of which God had told him.

⁴ On the third day Abraham got sight of the place from afar. ⁵ Then he said to his servants: "Both of you stay here with the donkey, while the boy and I go on over yonder. We will worship and then come back to you." ⁶ Thereupon Abraham took the wood for the holocaust and laid it on his son Isaac's shoulders, while he himself carried the fire and the knife. ⁷ As the two walked on together, Isaac spoke

Chap. 22

to his father Abraham: "Father!" he said. "Yes, son," he replied. Isaac continued, "Here are the fire and the wood, but where is the sheep for the holocaust?" ⁸ "Son," Abraham answered, "God himself will provide the sheep for the holocaust." Then the two continued going forward.

⁹* When they came to the place of which God had told him, Abraham built an altar there and arranged the wood on it. Next he tied up his son Isaac, and put him on top of the wood on the altar. ¹⁰* Then he reached out and took the knife to slaughter his son. ¹¹ But the LORD's messenger called to him from heaven, "Abraham, Abraham!" "Yes, Lord," he answered. ¹²* "Do not lay your hand

on the boy," said the messenger. "Do not do the least thing to him. I know now how devoted you are to God, since you did not withhold from me your own beloved son." ¹³ As Abraham looked about, he spied a ram caught by its horns in the thicket. So he went and took the ram and offered it up as a holocaust in place of his son. ¹⁴† Abraham named the site Yahweh-yireh; hence people now say, "On the mountain the LORD will see."

¹⁵ Again the LORD's messenger called to Abraham from heaven ¹⁶* and said: "I swear by myself, declares the LORD, that because you acted as you did in not withholding from me your beloved son, ¹⁷* I will bless you abundantly and make your descendants as countless as the stars of the sky and the sands of the seashore; your descendants shall take possession of the gates of their enemies, ¹⁸* and in your descendants all the nations of the earth shall find blessing—all this because you obeyed my command."

¹⁹ Abraham then returned to his servants, and they set out together for Beer-sheba, where Abraham made his home.

Nahor's Descendants

²⁰† Some time afterward, the news came to Abraham: "Milcah too has borne sons, to your brother Nahor: ²¹ Uz, his first-born, his brother Buz, Kemuel (the father of Aram), ²² Chesed, Hazo, Pildash, Jidlaph and Bethuel." ²³ Bethuel became the father of Rebekah. These eight Milcah bore to Abraham's brother Nahor. ²⁴ His concubine, whose name was Reumah, also bore children: Tebah, Gaham, Tahash and Maacah.

Purchase of a Burial Place

23 ¹ The span of Sarah's life was one hundred and twenty-seven years. ² She died in Kiriath-arba (that is, Hebron) in the land of Canaan, and Abraham performed the customary mourning rites for her. ³† Then he left the side of his dead one and addressed the Hittites: ⁴*† "Although I am a resident alien among you, sell me from your holdings a piece of property for a burial ground, that I may bury my dead wife." ⁵ The Hittites answered Abraham: "Please, sir, ⁶ listen to us! You are an elect of God among us. Bury your

---

22, 14: *Yahweh-yireh:* a Hebrew expression meaning "the Lord will see"; the reference is to the words in v 8, "God himself will see to it."

22, 20–24: A list of Aramean tribes who lived to the east and northeast of Israel, twelve in number, like the twelve tribes of Israel (Gn 35, 23) and the twelve tribes of Ishmael (Gn 25, 12–16).

23, 3: *The Hittites:* a non-Semitic people in Canaan; their relationship to the well-known Hittites of Asia Minor is uncertain.

23, 4: *A resident alien:* literally "a sojourner and a settler," i.e., a long-term resident alien. Such a one would normally not have the right to own property. The importance of Abraham's purchase of the

field in Machpelah, which is worded in technical legal terms, lies in the fact that it gave his descendants their first, though small, land rights in the country that God had promised the patriarch they would one day inherit as their own. Abraham therefore insists on purchasing the field and not receiving it as a gift.

*

22, 9: Jas 2, 21.
22, 10: Wis 10, 5.
22, 12: Rom 8, 32; 1 Jn 4, 9.
22, 16f: Gn 15, 5; Ex 32, 13;
    Lk 1, 73; Rom 4, 13;
    Heb 6, 13f; 11, 12.

22, 17: Gn 24, 60.
22, 18: Gn 12, 3; 18, 18; 26,
    4; Sir 44, 21; Acts 3,
    25; Gal 3, 16.
23, 4: Gn 33, 19; Acts 7, 16;
    Heb 11, 9.

dead in the choicest of our burial sites. None of us would deny you his burial ground for the burial of your dead." 7 Abraham, however, began to bow low before the local citizens, the Hittites, 8 while he appealed to them: "If you will allow me room for burial of my dead, listen to me! Intercede for me with Ephron, son of Zohar, asking him 9 to sell me the cave of Machpelah that he owns; it is at the edge of his field. Let him sell it to me in your presence, at its full price, for a burial place."

10† Now Ephron was present with the Hittites. So Ephron the Hittite replied to Abraham in the hearing of the Hittites who sat on his town council: 11 "Please, sir, listen to me! I give you both the field and the cave in it; in the presence of my kinsmen I make this gift. Bury your dead!" 12 But Abraham, after bowing low before the local citizens, addressed Ephron in the hearing of these men: 13 "Ah, if only you would please listen to me! I will pay you the price of the field. Accept it from me, that I may bury my dead there." 14 Ephron replied to Abraham, "Please, 15† sir, listen to me! A piece of land worth four hundred shekels of silver—what is that between you and me, as long as you can bury your dead?" 16*† Abraham accepted Ephron's terms; he weighed out to him the silver that Ephron had stipulated in the hearing of the Hittites, four hundred shekels of silver at the current market value.

17* Thus Ephron's field in Machpelah, facing Mamre, together with its cave and all the trees anywhere within its limits, was conveyed 18 to Abraham by purchase in the presence of all the Hittites who sat on Ephron's town council. 19 After this transaction, Abraham buried his wife Sarah in the cave of the field of Machpelah, facing Mamre (that is, Hebron) in the land of Canaan. 20 Thus the field with its cave was transferred from the Hittites to Abraham as a burial place.

Isaac and Rebekah

24 1 Abraham had now reached a ripe old age, and the LORD had blessed him in every way. 2*† Abraham said to the senior servant of his household, who had charge of all his possessions: "Put your hand under my thigh, 3* and I will make you swear by the LORD, the God of heaven

and the God of earth, that you will not procure a wife for my son from the daughters of the Canaanites among whom I live, 4 but that you will go to my own land and to my kindred to get a wife for my son Isaac." 5 The servant asked him: "What if the woman is unwilling to follow me to this land? Should I then take your son back to the land from which you migrated?" 6 "Never take my son back there for any reason," Abraham told him. 7* "The LORD, the God of heaven, who took me from my father's house and the land of my kin, and who confirmed by oath the promise he then made to me, 'I will give this land to your descendants'—he will send his messenger before you, and you will obtain a wife for my son there. 8 If the woman is unwilling to follow you, you will be released from this oath. But never take my son back there!" 9 So the servant put his hand under the thigh of his master Abraham and swore to him in this undertaking.

10† The servant then took ten of his master's camels, and bearing all kinds of gifts from his master, he made his way to the city of Nahor in Aram Naharaim. 11 Near evening, at the time when women go out to draw water, he made the camels kneel by the well outside the city. 12† Then he prayed: "LORD, God of my master Abraham, let it turn out favorably for me today and thus deal graciously with my master Abraham. 13 While I stand here at the spring and the daughters of the townsmen are coming out to draw water, 14 if I say to a girl, 'Please lower your jug, that I may drink,' and she answers, 'Take a drink, and let me give water to your camels, too,' let her be the one whom you have decided upon for your servant Isaac. In this way I shall know that you have dealt graciously with my master."

15* He had scarcely finished these words when Rebekah (who was born to Bethuel, son of Milcah, the wife of Abraham's brother Nahor) came out with a jug on her shoulder. 16 The girl was very beautiful, a virgin, untouched by man. She went down to the spring and filled her jug. As she came up, 17 the servant ran toward her and said, "Please give me a sip of water from your jug." 18 "Take a drink, sir," she replied, and quickly lowering the jug onto her hand, she gave him a drink. 19 When she

---

23, 10: *Who sat on his town council:* probable meaning of the literal translation, "who came in at the gate of his city"; so also in v 18.

23, 15: *Four hundred shekels:* probably an exorbitant sum; Jeremiah (32, 9) paid only seventeen shekels for his field in Anathoth, though the Babylonian invasion no doubt helped to reduce the price.

23, 16: *The current market value:* the standard weight called a shekel varied according to time and place.

24, 2: *Put your hand under my thigh:* the symbolism of this act was apparently connected with the Hebrew concept of children issuing from their father's "thigh" (Gn 46, 26; Ex 1, 5). Perhaps the man who took such an oath was thought to bring the curse of sterility on himself if he did not fulfill his sworn promise. Jacob made Joseph

swear in the same way (Gn 47, 29). In both these instances, the oath was taken to carry out the last request of a man upon his death.

24, 10: *Nahor:* it is uncertain whether this is to be understood as the name of Abraham's brother (Gn 11, 27), Rebekah's grandfather (Gn 24, 15), or the city of the same name (as known from the Mari documents); *Aram Naharaim,* situated near Haran (Gn 11, 31) in northern Mesopotamia.

24, 12: *Let it turn out favorably for me:* let me have a favorable omen; cf end of v 14.

23, 16: Acts 7, 16.   14, 3; Tb 4, 12.
23, 17f: Gn 49, 29f.   24, 7: Gn 12, 7; Ex 6, 8; Tb
24, 2f: Gn 47, 29.   5, 17; Gal 3, 16.
24, 3: Gn 24, 37; 28, 1f; Jgs   24, 15: Gn 22, 23.

had let him drink his fill, she said, "I will draw water for your camels, too, until they have drunk their fill." 20 With that, she quickly emptied her jug into the drinking trough and ran back to the well to draw more water, until she had drawn enough for all the camels. 21 The man watched her the whole time, silently waiting to learn whether or not the LORD had made his errand successful. 22 When the camels had finished drinking, the man took out a gold ring weighing half a shekel, which he fastened on her nose, and two gold bracelets weighing ten shekels, which he put on her wrists. 23 Then he asked her: "Whose daughter are you? Tell me, please. And is there room in your father's house for us to spend the night?" 24 She answered: "I am the daughter of Bethuel the son of Milcah, whom she bore to Nahor. 25 There is plenty of straw and fodder at our place," she added, "and room to spend the night." 26 The man then bowed down in worship to the LORD, 27 saying: "Blessed be the LORD, the God of my master Abraham, who has not let his constant kindness toward my master fail. As for myself also, the LORD has led me straight to the house of my master's brother."

28 Then the girl ran off and told her mother's household about it. 29* Now Rebekah had a brother named Laban. 30 As soon as he saw the ring and the bracelets on his sister Rebekah and heard her words about what the man had said to her, Laban rushed outside to the man at the spring. When he reached him, he was still standing by the camels at the spring. 31 So he said to him: "Come, blessed of the LORD! Why are you staying outside when I have made the house ready for you, as well as a place for the camels?" 32 The man then went inside; and while the camels were being unloaded and provided with straw and fodder, water was brought to bathe his feet and the feet of the men who were with him. 33 But when the table was set for him, he said, "I will not eat until I have told my tale." "Do so," they replied.

34 "I am Abraham's servant," he began. 35 "The LORD has blessed my master so abundantly that he has become a wealthy man; he has given him flocks and herds, silver and gold, male and female slaves, and camels and asses. 36 My master's wife Sarah bore a son to my master in her old age, and he has given him everything he owns. 37 My master put me under oath, saying: 'You shall not procure a wife for my son among the daughters of the Canaanites in whose land I live; 38 instead, you shall go to my father's house, to my own relatives, to get a wife for my son.' 39 When I asked my master, 'What if the woman will not follow me?' 40* he replied: 'The LORD, in whose presence I have always walked, will send his messenger with you and make your errand successful, and so you will get a wife for my son

from my own kindred of my father's house. 41 Then you shall be released from my ban. If you visit my kindred and they refuse you, then, too, you shall be released from my ban.'

42 "When I came to the spring today, I prayed: 'LORD, God of my master Abraham, may it be your will to make successful the errand I am engaged on! 43 While I stand here at the spring, if I say to a young woman who comes out to draw water, Please give me a little water from your jug, 44 and she answers, Not only may you have a drink, but I will give water to your camels, too—let her be the woman whom the LORD has decided upon for my master's son.'

45 "I had scarcely finished saying this prayer to myself when Rebekah came out with a jug on her shoulder. After she went down to the spring and drew water, I said to her, 'Please let me have a drink.' 46 She quickly lowered the jug she was carrying and said, 'Take a drink, and let me bring water for your camels, too.' So I drank, and she watered the camels also. 47 When I asked her, 'Whose daughter are you?' she answered, 'The daughter of Bethuel, son of Nahor, born to Nahor by Milcah.' So I put the ring on her nose and the bracelets on her wrists. 48 Then I bowed down in worship to the LORD, blessing the LORD, the God of my master Abraham, who had led me on the right road to obtain the daughter of my master's kinsman for his son. 49 If, therefore, you have in mind to show true loyalty to my master, let me know; but if not, let me know that, too. I can then proceed accordingly."

50* Laban and his household said in reply: "This thing comes from the LORD; we can say nothing to you either for or against it. 51 Here is Rebekah, ready for you; take her with you, that she may become the wife of your master's son, as the LORD has said." 52 When Abraham's servant heard their answer, he bowed to the ground before the LORD. 53 Then he brought out objects of silver and gold and articles of clothing and presented them to Rebekah; he also gave costly presents to her brother and mother. 54* After he and the men with him had eaten and drunk, they spent the night there.

When they were up the next morning, he said, "Give me leave to return to my master." 55 Her brother and mother replied, "Let the girl stay with us a short while, say ten days; after that she may go." 56 But he said to them, "Do not detain me, now that the LORD has made my errand successful; let me go back to my master." 57 They answered, "Let us call the girl and see what she herself has to say about it." 58 So they called Rebekah and asked her, "Do you wish to go with this man?" She answered, "I do." 59 At this they allowed their sister Rebekah

24, 29: Gn 27, 43.   24, 50f: Tb 7, 12.
24, 40: Tb 5, 17; 10, 13.   24, 54: Tb 7, 14; 8, 20.

and her nurse to take leave, along with Abraham's servant and his men. [60]* Invoking a blessing on Rebekah, they said:

> "Sister, may you grow
> into thousands of myriads;
> And may your descendants gain possession
> of the gates of their enemies!"

[61] Then Rebekah and her maids started out; they mounted their camels and followed the man. So the servant took Rebekah and went on his way. [62]* Meanwhile Isaac had gone from Beer-lahai-roi and was living in the region of the Negeb. [63]† One day toward evening he went out . . . in the field, and as he looked around, he noticed that camels were approaching. [64] Rebekah, too, was looking about, and when she saw him, she alighted from her camel [65] and asked the servant, "Who is the man out there, walking through the fields toward us?" "That is my master," replied the servant. Then she covered herself with her veil.

[66] The servant recounted to Isaac all the things he had done. [67] Then Isaac took Rebekah into his tent; he married her, and thus she became his wife. In his love for her Isaac found solace after the death of his mother Sarah.

Abraham's Sons by Keturah

25 [1]*† Abraham married another wife, whose name was Keturah. [2] She bore him Zimran, Jokshan, Medan, Midian, Ishbak and Shuah. [3]* Jokshan became the father of Sheba and Dedan. The descendants of Dedan were the Asshurim, the Letushim, and the Leummim. [4] The descendants of Midian were Ephah, Epher, Hanoch, Abida and Eldaah. All of these were descendants of Keturah.

[5] Abraham deeded everything that he owned to his son Isaac. [6]† To his sons by concubinage, however, he made grants while he was still living, as he sent them away eastward, to the land of Kedem, away from his son Isaac.

Death of Abraham

[7] The whole span of Abraham's life was one hundred and seventy-five years. [8] Then he breathed his last, dying at a ripe old age, grown old after a full life; and he was taken to his kinsmen. [9]* His sons Isaac and Ishmael buried him in the cave of

did you KNOW?

Abraham's Descendants

God promised Hagar that her son Ishmael would be made "a great nation" (Gn 21, 18). The Old Testament lists twelve princely tribes that descended from Abraham's older son (Gn 25, 13–16), tribes traditionally associated with the people of ancient Edom. A much later Islamic tradition identifies Muhammad and his descendants—the Muslims—as "children of Ishmael."

Abraham's younger son, Isaac, was the father of Jacob. The Jewish people trace their lineage to Jacob and his twelve sons. Because Jesus was a Jew, Christians ultimately trace their ancestry through Jacob to Abraham as well.

Thus, three major world religions—Judaism, Christianity, and Islam—all see Abraham as their "father in faith."

▸ Gn 25, 12–18

Machpelah, in the field of Ephron, son of Zohar the Hittite, which faces Mamre, [10] the field that Abraham had bought from the Hittites; there he was buried next to his wife Sarah. [11] After the death of Abraham, God blessed his son Isaac, who made his home near Beer-lahai-roi.

Descendants of Ishmael

[12] These are the descendants of Abraham's son Ishmael, whom Hagar the Egyptian, Sarah's slave, bore to Abraham. [13]* These are the names of Ishmael's sons, listed in the order of their birth: Nebaioth (Ishmael's first-born), Kedar, Adbeel, Mibsam,* [14] Mishma, Dumah, Massa, [15] Hadad, Tema, Jetur, Naphish and Kedemah. [16]* These are the sons of Ishmael, their names by their villages and encampments; twelve chieftains of as many tribal groups.

[17] The span of Ishmael's life was one hundred and thirty-seven years. After he had breathed his

---

24, 63: *He went out:* the meaning of the Hebrew term that follows this is obscure.

25, 1–11: Though mentioned here, Abraham's marriage to a "concubine," or wife of secondary rank, and his death are not to be understood as happening chronologically after the events narrated in the preceding chapter.

25, 6: *The land of Kedem:* or "the country of the East," the region

inhabited by the Kedemites or Easterners (Gn 29, 1; Jgs 6, 3.33; Jb 1, 3; Is 11, 14). The names mentioned in vv 2ff, as far as they can be identified, are those of tribes in the Arabian desert.

24, 60: Gn 22, 17.   25, 9f: Gn 23, 3–20.
24, 62: Gn 16, 13f; 25, 11.   25, 13–16: 1 Chr 1, 29ff.
25, 1–4: 1 Chr 1, 32f.   25, 13: Is 60, 7.
25, 3: Is 21, 13.   25, 16: Gn 17, 20.

last and died, he was taken to his kinsmen. [18]*† The Ishmaelites ranged from Havilah-by-Shur, which is on the border of Egypt, all the way to Asshur; and each of them pitched camp in opposition to his various kinsmen.

Sibling Rivalry

I t is common for siblings to have conflict in their relationship, but with Jacob and Esau, the conflict becomes extreme. Follow their story in Genesis, chapters 27–28. 33.

For another story of extreme sibling rivalry, see 37, 12–36. Joseph's brothers (all sons of Jacob) are so jealous of him that they plot to kill him. But instead, he gets sold as a slave—and that turns out to be a great career move for him.

The story of the prodigal son in Lk 15, 11–32 is yet another example of sibling rivalry.

Do you have any brothers or sisters? If so, how do you treat them? Do you ever pray for them? Do you ever tell them that you care about them—even if they drive you crazy at times?

If you don't have any brothers or sisters, how about cousins, neighbors, or friends? All relationships get better with prayer and care.

▶ Gn 25, 19–34

III: The Patriarchs Isaac and Jacob

Birth of Esau and Jacob

[19] This is the family history of Isaac, son of Abraham; Abraham had begotten Isaac. [20]* Isaac was forty years old when he married Rebekah, the daughter of Bethuel the Aramean of Paddan-aram and the sister of Laban the Aramean. [21] Isaac entreated the LORD on behalf of his wife, since she was sterile. The LORD heard his entreaty, and Rebekah became pregnant. [22] But the children in her womb jostled each other so much that she exclaimed, "If this is to be so, what good will it do me!" She went to consult the LORD, [23]* and he answered her:

"Two nations are in your womb,
   two peoples are quarreling while still
      within you;
But one shall surpass the other,
   and the older shall serve the younger."

[24]* When the time of her delivery came, there were twins in her womb. [25]† The first to emerge was reddish, and his whole body was like a hairy mantle; so they named him Esau. [26]*† His brother came out next, gripping Esau's heel; so they named him Jacob. Isaac was sixty years old when they were born.

[27]* As the boys grew up, Esau became a skillful hunter, a man who lived in the open; whereas Jacob was a simple man, who kept to his tents. [28] Isaac preferred Esau, because he was fond of game; but Rebekah preferred Jacob. [29] Once, when Jacob was cooking a stew, Esau came in from the open, famished. [30]† He said to Jacob, "Let me gulp down some of that red stuff; I'm starving." (That is why he was called Edom.) [31]*† But Jacob replied, "First give me your birthright in exchange for it." [32] "Look," said Esau, "I'm on the point of dying. What good will any birthright do me?" [33]* But Jacob insisted, "Swear to me first!" So he sold Jacob his birthright under oath. [34] Jacob then gave him some bread and the lentil stew; and Esau ate, drank, got up, and went his way. Esau cared little for his birthright.

Isaac and Abimelech

26 [1]* There was a famine in the land (distinct from the earlier one that had occurred in the days of Abraham), and Isaac went

---

25, 18: *Pitched camp:* literally "fell"; the same Hebrew verb is used in Jgs 7, 12 in regard to the hostile encampment of Bedouin tribes. The present passage shows the fulfillment of the prediction contained in Gn 16, 12.

25, 25: *Reddish:* in Hebrew, *admoni,* a reference to Edom, another name for Esau (v 30; 36, 1). Edom, however, was really the name of the country south of Moab where the descendants of Esau lived. It was called the "red" country because of its reddish sandstone. *Hairy:* in Hebrew, *sear,* a reference to Seir, another name for Edom (Gn 36, 8). One might expect the text to say, "So they named him Seir"; but Esau (*esaw*) also means "hairy."

25, 26: *Esau's heel:* the Hebrew is *baaqeb esaw,* a reference to the name Jacob; cf Gn 27, 36. Probably, however, the name Jacob has no true etymological connection with the Hebrew word for

"heel" (*aqeb*), but is instead a shortened form of some such name as *yaaqob-el* ("may God protect").

25, 30: *Red stuff:* in Hebrew, *adom;* another play on the word "Edom," the "red" land.

25, 31: *Birthright:* the privilege that entitled the first-born son to a position of honor in the family and to a double share in the possessions inherited from the father.

25, 18: Gn 16, 12.
25, 20: Gn 24, 66.
25, 23: Gn 27, 29; Nm 24, 18;
   Mal 1, 2–5; Rom 9, 11f.
25, 24: Hos 12, 3.
25, 26: Mt 1, 2
25, 27: Gn 27, 6f.
25, 31: Dt 21, 17.
25, 33: Heb 12, 16.
26, 1–14: Gn 12, 10–20.

down to Abimelech, king of the Philistines in Gerar.* [2] The LORD appeared to him and said: "Do not go down to Egypt, but continue to camp wherever in this land I tell you. [3]* Stay in this land, and I will be with you and bless you; for to you and your descendants I will give all these lands, in fulfillment of the oath that I swore to your father Abraham. [4]* I will make your descendants as numerous as the stars in the sky and give them all these lands, and in your descendants all the nations of the earth shall find blessing— [5] this because Abraham obeyed me, keeping my mandate (my commandments, my ordinances and my instructions)."

[6]† So Isaac settled in Gerar. [7] When the men of the place asked questions about his wife, he answered, "She is my sister." He was afraid, if he called her his wife, the men of the place would kill him on account of Rebekah, since she was very beautiful. [8] But when he had been there for a long time, Abimelech, king of the Philistines, happened to look out of a window and was surprised to see Isaac fondling his wife Rebekah. [9] He called for Isaac and said: "She must certainly be your wife! How could you have said, 'She is my sister'?". Isaac replied, "I thought I might lose my life on her account." [10] "How could you do this to us!" exclaimed Abimelech. "It would have taken very little for one of the men to lie with your wife, and you would have thus brought guilt upon us!" [11] Abimelech therefore gave this warning to all his men: "Anyone who molests this man or his wife shall forthwith be put to death."

[12]† Isaac sowed a crop in that region and reaped a hundredfold the same year. Since the LORD blessed him, [13]* he became richer and richer all the time, until he was very wealthy indeed. [14] He acquired such flocks and herds, and so many work animals, that the Philistines became envious of him. ([15]* The Philistines had stopped up and filled with dirt all the wells that his father's servants had dug back in the days of his father Abraham.) [16] So Abimelech said to Isaac, "Go away from us; you have become far too numerous for us." [17] Isaac left there and made the Wadi Gerar his regular campsite. ([18] Isaac reopened the wells which his father's

servants had dug back in the days of his father Abraham and which the Philistines had stopped up after Abraham's death; he gave them the same names that his father had given them.) [19] But when Isaac's servants dug in the wadi and reached spring water in their well, [20]† the shepherds of Gerar quarreled with Isaac's servants, saying, "The water belongs to us!" So the well was called Esek, because they had challenged him there. [21]† Then they dug another well, and they quarreled over that one too; so it was called Sitnah. [22] When he had moved on from there, he dug still another well; but over this one they did not quarrel. It was called Rehoboth, because he said, "The LORD has now given us ample room, and we shall flourish in the land."

[23] From there Isaac went up to Beer-sheba. [24]* The same night the LORD appeared to him and said: "I am the God of your father Abraham. You have no need to fear, since I am with you. I will bless you and multiply your descendants for the sake of my servant Abraham." [25] So he built an altar there and invoked the LORD by name. After he had pitched his tent there, his servants began to dig a well nearby.

[26]* Abimelech had meanwhile come to him from Gerar, accompanied by Ahuzzath, his councilor, and Phicol, the general of his army. [27] Isaac asked them, "Why have you come to me, seeing that you hate me and have driven me away from you?" [28] They answered: "We are convinced that the LORD is with you, so we propose that there be a sworn agreement between our two sides—between you and us. Let us make a pact with you: [29] you shall not act unkindly toward us, just as we have not molested you, but have always acted kindly toward you and have let you depart in peace. Henceforth, 'The LORD's blessing be upon you!' " [30] Isaac then made a feast for them, and they ate and drank. [31] Early the next morning they exchanged oaths. Then Isaac bade them farewell, and they departed from him in peace.

[32] That same day Isaac's servants came and brought him news about the well they had been digging; they told him, "We have reached water!" [33]† He called it Shibah; hence the name of the city, Beer-sheba, to this day.

26, 6–11: The Yahwist's version of the wife-sister episode at Gerar; the Elohist's version (Gn 20, 1–18) is connected with Abraham and Sarah.

26, 12–33: The Yahwist's version of the story about the wells at Beer-sheba; again, the Elohist's version (Gn 21, 22f) is connected with Abraham. A redactor joined the two accounts by means of the parenthetical verses 15 and 18.

26, 20: *Esek:* "challenge."

26, 21: *Sitnah:* "opposition"; one might expect the text to be continued by some such words as "because they were in opposition there."

26, 33: *Shibah:* "seven," for the sake of a closer assonance with Beer-sheba; but the present version of the story says nothing about

there being seven wells there as implied in Gn 21, 28–31. The Greek version understood the Hebrew text more logically as *shebua,* "oath," in keeping with the present story.

26, 1: Gn 12, 1.	**26, 13f:** Jb 1, 3.
26, 3: Gn 12, 7; 15, 18; Ex 32, 13; Ps 105, 9; Sir 44, 22; Heb 11, 9.	**26, 15–24:** Gn 21, 25–31.
	26, 24: Gn 46, 3.
26, 4: Gn 12, 3; 22, 17f; 28, 14; Ex 32, 13.	**26, 26–33:** Gn 21, 22–31; Prv 16, 7.

34*† When Esau was forty years old, he married Judith, daughter of Beeri the Hittite, and Basemath, daughter of Elon the Hivite. 35 But they became a source of embitterment to Isaac and Rebekah.

Jacob's Deception

27 1† When Isaac was so old that his eyesight had failed him, he called his older son Esau and said to him, "Son!" "Yes, father!" he replied. 2 Isaac then said, "As you can see, I am so old that I may now die at any time. 3 Take your gear, therefore—your quiver and bow—and go out into the country to hunt some game for me. 4† With your catch prepare an appetizing dish for me, such as I like, and bring it to me to eat, so that I may give you my special blessing before I die."

carefully to what I tell you. 9 Go to the flock and get me two choice kids. With these I will prepare an appetizing dish for your father, such as he likes. 10 Then bring it to your father to eat, that he may bless you before he dies." 11* "But my brother Esau is a hairy man," said Jacob to his mother Rebekah, "and I am smooth-skinned! 12 Suppose my father feels me? He will think I am making sport of him, and I shall bring on myself a curse instead of a blessing." 13 His mother, however, replied: "Let any curse against you, son, fall on me! Just do as I say. Go and get me the kids."

14 So Jacob went and got them and brought them to his mother; and with them she prepared an appetizing dish, such as his father liked. 15 Rebekah then took the best clothes of her older son Esau that

Introducing ▶ JACOB

According to the Bible, Abraham was the father of Isaac, and Isaac was the father of Jacob, and Jacob was the father of twelve sons who became the leaders of the twelve tribes of Israel. Jacob, like his ancestors, participated in the covenant with God that promised a great land and many descendants. He is portrayed as a very human character with a wide range of emotions and actions, both good and bad. Jacob is a repentant brother, a kind father, and a successful herder, but he is also a trickster who steals his brother Esau's birthright and his father's blessing (Gn 25, 29–34; 27, 1–29). It is no wonder that Jacob's name means "supplanter" or "heel grabber."

In a dream, God renews the covenant promises to Jacob (28, 10–17), and in another dream (35, 9–15), God changes Jacob's name to Israel (Gn 32, 23–33). Jacob's descendants become known as the Israelites. His story reveals that God's blessing continues to work even through flawed human beings.

▶ Gn 25, 19—50, 14

5* Rebekah had been listening while Isaac was speaking to his son Esau. So when Esau went out into the country to hunt some game for his father, 6 Rebekah said to her son Jacob, "Listen! I overheard your father tell your brother Esau, 7 'Bring me some game and with it prepare an appetizing dish for me to eat, that I may give you my blessing with the LORD'S approval before I die.' 8 Now, son, listen

she had in the house, and gave them to her younger son Jacob to wear; 16 and with the skins of the kids she covered up his hands and the hairless parts of his neck. 17 Then she handed her son Jacob the appetizing dish and the bread she had prepared.

18 Bringing them to his father, Jacob said, "Father!" "Yes?" replied Isaac. "Which of my sons are you?" 19 Jacob answered his father: "I am Esau,

---

26, 34f: These verses from the Priestly source, which have no logical connection with the preceding stories, serve as an introduction to the following section on Esau's loss of his birthright by suggesting a motivation for this in Isaac's and Rebekah's dislike for Esau's Canaanite wives.

27, 1–45: What Jacob did in deceiving his father and thereby cheating Esau out of Isaac's deathbed blessing is condemned as blameworthy, not only by Hosea (12, 4) and Jeremiah (9, 3), but also, indirectly, by the Yahwist narrator of the present story, who makes the reader sympathize with Esau as the innocent victim of a cruel plot, and shows that Jacob and his mother, the instigator of the plot, paid

for it by a lifelong separation from each other. The story was told because it was part of the mystery of God's ways in salvation history—his use of weak, sinful men to achieve his own ultimate purpose.

27, 4: My special blessing: "the blessing of my soul." The same expression is used also in vv 19, 25, 31. In the context it must mean something like a solemn deathbed blessing, believed to be especially efficacious.

26, 34f: Gn 27, 46.   27, 11: Gn 25, 25.
27, 5: Gn 25, 28.

did you KNOW?

God's Surprising Choice

In most ancient cultures, including Israel's, the oldest son of the family was expected to inherit his father's property (the birthright) and authority (the blessing). In the story of Esau and Jacob, Jacob tricks Esau (the oldest son) out of his birthright (Gn 25, 29–34) and deceives his blind father into giving him the blessing (27, 1–29).

It is surprising that Genesis makes no comment on the morality of Jacob's actions. However, the story is not about morality but about God's justice: God is not bound by human expectations. Again and again in the Old Testament, God defies human rules by choosing the "little ones" for big responsibilities: Jacob, Joseph, Ruth, David, and Esther, for example. Even the Israelites themselves were an unlikely choice on God's part. Why didn't God choose a nation of great wealth and power instead of a group that was enslaved?

The story of Jacob and Esau reminds us that God does not bow to human rules, expectations, or plans. God's ways are often surprising! (For more on God's surprising choices, see reading plan 5, "The Justice of God.")

▶ Gn 27, 1–40

his blessing.) [24] Again he asked him, "Are you really my son Esau?" "Certainly," he replied. [25] Then Isaac said, "Serve me your game, son, that I may eat of it and then give you my blessing." Jacob served it to him, and Isaac ate; he brought him wine, and he drank. [26] Finally his father Isaac said to him, "Come closer, son, and kiss me." [27]* As Jacob went up and kissed him, Isaac smelled the fragrance of his clothes. With that, he blessed him, saying,

"Ah, the fragrance of my son
 is like the fragrance of a field
  that the LORD has blessed!

[28] "May God give to you
  of the dew of the heavens
 And of the fertility of the earth
  abundance of grain and wine.

[29]* "Let peoples serve you,
  and nations pay you homage;
 Be master of your brothers,
  and may your mother's sons bow down
   to you.

 Cursed be those who curse you,
  and blessed be those who bless you."

[30] Jacob had scarcely left his father, just after Isaac had finished blessing him, when his brother Esau came back from his hunt. [31] Then he too prepared an appetizing dish with his game, and bringing it to his father, he said, "Please, father, eat some of your son's game, that you may then give me your special blessing." [32] "Who are you?" his father Isaac asked him. "I am Esau," he replied, "your first-born son." [33] With that, Isaac was seized with a fit of uncontrollable trembling. "Who was it, then," he asked, "that hunted game and brought it to me? I finished eating it just before you came, and I blessed him. Now he must remain blessed!" [34] On hearing his father's words, Esau burst into loud, bitter sobbing. "Father, bless me too!" he begged. [35] When Isaac explained, "Your brother came here by a ruse and carried off your blessing," [36]*† Esau exclaimed, "He has been well named Jacob! He has now supplanted me twice! First he took away my birthright, and now he has taken away my blessing." Then he pleaded, "Haven't you saved a blessing for me?" [37] Isaac replied: "I have already appointed him your master, and I have assigned to him all his kinsmen as his slaves; besides, I have enriched him with

your first-born. I did as you told me. Please sit up and eat some of my game, so that you may give me your special blessing." [20] But Isaac asked, "How did you succeed so quickly, son?" He answered, "The LORD, your God, let things turn out well with me." [21] Isaac then said to Jacob, "Come closer, son, that I may feel you, to learn whether you really are my son Esau or not." [22] So Jacob moved up closer to his father. When Isaac felt him, he said, "Although the voice is Jacob's, the hands are Esau's." [23] (He failed to identify him because his hands were hairy, like those of his brother Esau; so in the end he gave him

---

27, 36: *He has now supplanted me:* in Hebrew, *wayyaqebeni,* a wordplay on the name Jacob, *yaaqob;* see Jer 9, 3 and note, as well as Gn 25, 26. There is also a play between the Hebrew words *bekora* ("birthright") and *beraka* ("blessing").

27, 27: Gn 22, 17f; Heb 11, 20.
27, 29: Gn 25, 23; 49, 8;

Nm 24, 9.
27, 36: Gn 25, 26. 29–34;
Hos 12, 4.

grain and wine. What then can I do for you, son?" ³⁸* But Esau urged his father, "Have you only that one blessing, father? Bless me too!" Isaac, however, made no reply; and Esau wept aloud. ³⁹* Finally Isaac spoke again and said to him:

"Ah, far from the fertile earth
    shall be your dwelling;
    far from the dew of the heavens above!
⁴⁰* "By your sword you shall live,
    and your brother you shall serve;
But when you become restive,
    you shall throw off his yoke from
        your neck."

⁴¹* Esau bore Jacob a grudge because of the blessing his father had given him. He said to himself, "When the time of mourning for my father comes, I will kill my brother Jacob." ⁴² When Rebekah got news of what her older son Esau had in mind, she called her younger son Jacob and said to him: "Listen! Your brother Esau intends to settle accounts with you by killing you. ⁴³ Therefore, son, do what I tell you: flee at once to my brother Laban in Haran, ⁴⁴ and stay with him a while until your brother's fury subsides ⁴⁵ [until your brother's anger against you subsides] and he forgets what you did to him. Then I will send for you and bring you back. Must I lose both of you in a single day?"

Jacob Sent to Laban

⁴⁶*† Rebekah said to Isaac: "I am disgusted with life because of the Hittite women. If Jacob also should marry a Hittite woman, a native of the land, like these women, what good would life be to me?"

28 ¹* Isaac therefore called Jacob, greeted him with a blessing, and charged him: "You shall not marry a Canaanite woman! ²* Go now to Paddan-aram, to the home of your mother's father Bethuel, and there choose a wife for yourself from among the daughters of your uncle Laban. ³ May God Almighty bless you and make you fertile, multiply you that you may become an assembly of

peoples. ⁴* May he extend to you and your descendants the blessing he gave to Abraham, so that you may gain possession of the land where you are staying, which he assigned to Abraham." ⁵* Then Isaac sent Jacob on his way; he went to Paddan-aram, to Laban, son of Bethuel, the Aramean, and brother of Rebekah, the mother of Jacob and Esau.

⁶ Esau noted that Isaac had blessed Jacob when he sent him to Paddan-aram to get himself a wife there, charging him, as he gave him his blessing, not to marry a Canaanite woman, ⁷ and that Jacob had obeyed his father and mother and gone to Paddan-aram. ⁸ Esau realized how displeasing the Canaanite women were to his father Isaac, ⁹* so he went to Ishmael, and in addition to the wives he had, married Mahalath, the daughter of Abraham's son Ishmael and sister of Nebaioth.

Jacob's Dream at Bethel

¹⁰ Jacob departed from Beer-sheba and proceeded toward Haran. ¹¹† When he came upon a certain shrine, as the sun had already set, he stopped there for the night. Taking one of the stones at the shrine, he put it under his head and lay down to sleep at that spot. ¹²*† Then he had a dream: a stairway rested on the ground, with its top reaching to the heavens; and God's messengers were going up and down on it. ¹³* And there was the LORD standing beside him and saying: "I, the LORD, am the God of your forefather Abraham and the God of Isaac; the land on which you are lying I will give to you and your descendants. ¹⁴* These shall be as plentiful as the dust of the earth, and through them you shall spread out east and west, north and south. In you and your descendants all the nations of the earth shall find blessing. ¹⁵* Know that I am with you; I will protect you wherever you go, and bring you back to this land. I will never leave you until I have done what I promised you."

¹⁶ When Jacob awoke from his sleep, he exclaimed, "Truly, the LORD is in this spot, although I did not know it!" ¹⁷† In solemn wonder he cried out: "How awesome is this shrine! This is nothing

---

† **27, 46—28, 9:** This section, which is from the Priestly source and a direct sequel of Gn 26, 34f, presents a different, though not contradictory, reason for Jacob's going to Paddan-aram: namely, to preserve racial purity among the chosen people. The account of Esau's marriages is given for the purpose of explaining the racial mixture of the Edomites, who were descended in part from tribes related to Israel, in part from older peoples in Edom called Hittites, Horites or Hivites, and in part from the Ishmaelite (Arabian) tribes who later invaded the region.
28, 11: *Shrine:* literally "place," often used specifically of a sacred site. Here the place was Bethel (v 19), a sacred site as early as the time of Abraham (Gn 12, 8).
28, 12: *Stairway:* in Hebrew, *sullam,* traditionally but inaccurately translated as "ladder." The corresponding verb, *salal,* means "to heap up" something, such as dirt for a highway or ramp. The imagery

in Jacob's dream is derived from the Babylonian ziggurat or temple tower, "with its top in the sky" (Gn 11, 4), and with brick steps leading up to a small temple at the top.
28, 17: *This:* the stone Jacob used as a headrest; cf v 22. *That:* the stairway Jacob saw in his dream.

---

*
27, 38: Heb 12, 17.
27, 39: Heb 11, 20.
27, 40: 2 Kgs 8, 20. 22;
    2 Chr 21, 8.
27, 41: Wis 10, 10; Ob 10.
27, 46: Gn 26, 34f.
28, 1: Gn 24, 3f; 26, 35.
28, 2: Gn 22, 22; 17, 1f.4f.
28, 4: Ex 32, 13.

28, 5: Jdt 8, 26.
28, 9: Gn 36, 2f.
28, 12: Jn 1, 51.
28, 13: Dt 1, 8; Mi 7, 28.
28, 14: Gn 12, 3; 13, 14f; 15,
    5f; 18, 18; 22, 17f; 26,
    4; Dt 19, 8; Sir 44, 21.
28, 15: Gn 31, 3.

Friendship with God

Just as Jacob is leaving his home and everything he knows, God establishes a personal relationship with him through a dream. In this relationship, God and Jacob interact personally, are accountable to each other, and trust each other. Jacob will need this relationship to help him through the tough times ahead. See Gn 32, 23–33 for further developments in Jacob's relationship with God.

God, I want to know your presence. Use my dreams and my waking thoughts, use my family, friends, and neighbors, use your holy word. Use them all to reach me. For I know your presence will sustain me on my most difficult journeys, as it did Jacob.

▸ Gn 28, 10–22

else but an abode of God, and that is the gateway to heaven!" ¹⁸*† Early the next morning Jacob took the stone that he had put under his head, set it up as a memorial stone, and poured oil on top of it. ¹⁹*† He called that site Bethel, whereas the former name of the town had been Luz.

²⁰ Jacob then made this vow: "If God remains with me, to protect me on this journey I am making and to give me enough bread to eat and clothing to wear, ²¹ and I come back safe to my father's house, the LORD shall be my God. ²² This stone that I have set up as a memorial stone shall be God's abode. Of everything you give me, I will faithfully return a tenth part to you."

Arrival in Haran

29 ¹*† After Jacob resumed his journey, he came to the land of the Easterners. ²* Looking about, he saw a well in the open coun-

try, with three droves of sheep huddled near it, for droves were watered from that well. A large stone covered the mouth of the well. ³ Only when all the shepherds were assembled there could they roll the stone away from the mouth of the well and water the flocks. Then they would put the stone back again over the mouth of the well.

⁴ Jacob said to them, "Friends, where are you from?" "We are from Haran," they replied. ⁵* Then he asked them, "Do you know Laban, son of Nahor?" "We do," they answered. ⁶ He inquired further, "Is he well?" "He is," they answered; "and here comes his daughter Rachel with his flock." ⁷ Then he said: "There is still much daylight left; it is hardly the time to bring the animals home. Why don't you water the flocks now, and then continue pasturing them?" ⁸ "We cannot," they replied, "until all the shepherds are here to roll the stone away from the mouth of the well; only then can we water the flocks."

⁹ While he was still talking with them, Rachel arrived with her father's sheep; she was the one who tended them. ¹⁰ As soon as Jacob saw Rachel, the daughter of his uncle Laban, with the sheep of his uncle Laban, he went up, rolled the stone away from the mouth of the well, and watered his uncle's sheep. ¹¹† Then Jacob kissed Rachel and burst into tears. ¹² He told her that he was her father's relative, Rebekah's son, and she ran to tell her father. ¹³ When Laban heard the news about his sister's son Jacob, he hurried out to meet him. After embracing and kissing him, he brought him to his house. Jacob then recounted to Laban all that had happened, ¹⁴† and Laban said to him, "You are indeed my flesh and blood."

Marriage to Leah and Rachel

After Jacob had stayed with him a full month, ¹⁵ Laban said to him: "Should you serve me for nothing just because you are a relative of mine? Tell me what your wages should be." ¹⁶ Now Laban had two daughters; the older was called Leah, the younger Rachel. ¹⁷† Leah had lovely eyes, but Rachel was well formed and beautiful. ¹⁸† Since Jacob had fallen in love with Rachel, he answered Laban, "I will serve you seven years for your

---

28, 18: *Memorial stone:* in Hebrew, *masseba,* a stone which might vary in shape and size, set upright and usually intended for some religious purpose. Since the custom of erecting such "sacred pillars" in Palestine went back to its pre-Israelite period, their pagan associations were often retained; therefore, later Israelite religion forbade their erection (Lv 26, 1; Dt 16, 22) and ordered the destruction of those that were associated with paganism (Ex 34, 31; Dt 12, 3).

28, 19: *Bethel:* i.e., "house of God"; the reference is to the abode of God in v 17.

29, 1: *Easterners:* see note on Gn 25, 6.

29, 11: *Burst into tears:* literally "raised his voice and wept," i.e., for joy.

29, 14: *Flesh and blood:* literally "bone and flesh," i.e., a close relative; on the Hebrew idiom, see Gn 2, 23.

29, 17: *Lovely eyes:* The adjective modifying *eyes* is often translated as "weak," but "lovely" is the more probable word.

29, 18: Jacob offers to render service (Jos 15, 16f; 1 Sm 17, 25; 18, 17) in lieu of the customary bridal price (Ex 22, 16f; Dt 22, 29).

28, 18: Gn 31, 13; 35, 14f.
28, 19: Gn 35, 6; 48, 3; Jos 18, 13; Jgs 1, 23; Hos 12, 4.

29, 1: Wis 10, 10.
29, 2: Gn 24, 11f.
29, 5: Tb 7, 4.

younger daughter Rachel." ¹⁹ Laban replied, "I prefer to give her to you rather than to an outsider. Stay with me." ²⁰* So Jacob served seven years for Rachel, yet they seemed to him but a few days because of his love for her.

²¹ Then Jacob said to Laban, "Give me my wife, that I may consummate my marriage with her, for

Jacob's Children

³¹ When the LORD saw that Leah was unloved, he made her fruitful, while Rachel remained barren. ³²*† Leah conceived and bore a son, and she named him Reuben; for she said, "It means, 'The LORD saw my misery; now my husband will love me.'" ³³† She conceived again and bore a son, and

When Lies Boomerang

Predictably, Jacob becomes upset when he finds out that he has been deceived by Laban (Gn 29, 25). Yet, the very reason Jacob is working for his uncle Laban is that he has fled from his brother Esau, whom he deceived several years ago (27, 1–40). Jacob's lies and deceit have boomeranged, so now he is the victim.

Somehow, our lies, gossip, and manipulation of others often come back to haunt us. So it was with Jacob. So it will be with us if we follow his example.

▸ Gn 29, 15–30

my term is now completed." ²² So Laban invited all the local inhabitants and gave a feast. ²³ At the nightfall he took his daughter Leah and brought her to Jacob, and Jacob consummated the marriage with her. ²⁴ (Laban assigned his slave girl Zilpah to his daughter Leah as her maidservant.) ²⁵† In the morning Jacob was amazed: it was Leah! So he cried out to Laban: "How could you do this to me! Was it not for Rachel that I served you? Why did you dupe me?" ²⁶ "It is not the custom in our country," Laban replied, "to marry off a younger daughter before an older one. ²⁷*† Finish the bridal week for this one, and then I will give you the other too, in return for another seven years of service with me."

²⁸ Jacob agreed. He finished the bridal week for Leah, and then Laban gave him his daughter Rachel in marriage. ²⁹ (Laban assigned his slave girl Bilhah to his daughter Rachel as her maidservant.) ³⁰* Jacob then consummated his marriage with Rachel also, and he loved her more than Leah. Thus he remained in Laban's service another seven years.

said, "It means, 'The LORD heard that I was unloved,' and therefore he has given me this one also"; so she named him Simeon. ³⁴† Again she conceived and bore a son, and she said, "Now at last my husband will become attached to me, since I have now borne him three sons"; that is why she named him Levi. ³⁵*† Once more she conceived and bore a son, and she said, "This time I will give grateful praise to the LORD"; therefore she named him Judah. Then she stopped bearing children.

30 ¹* When Rachel saw that she failed to bear children to Jacob, she became envious of her sister. She said to Jacob, "Give me children or I shall die!" ²* In anger Jacob retorted, "Can I take the place of God, who has denied you the fruit of the womb?" ³*† She replied, "Here is my maidservant Bilhah. Have intercourse with her, and let her give birth on my knees, so that I too may have offspring, at least through her." ⁴† So she gave him her maidservant Bilhah as a consort, and Jacob

---

29, 25: *Jacob was amazed:* he had not recognized Leah because a bride was veiled when she was brought to her bridegroom; cf Gn 24, 65.

29, 27: *The bridal week:* an ancient wedding lasted for seven days of festivities; cf Jgs 14, 12.

29, 32: *Reuben:* The literal meaning of the Hebrew name is "look, a son!" But in this case, as also with the names of all the other sons of Jacob, a symbolic rather than an etymological interpretation of the name is given, because the name and the persons were regarded as closely interrelated. The symbolic interpretation of Reuben's name, according to the Yahwist source, is based on the similar-sounding, *raa beonyi,* "he saw my misery." In the Elohist source, the name is explained by the similar-sounding *yeehabani,* "he will love me."

29, 33: *Simeon:* in popular etymology, related to *shama,* "he heard."

29, 34: *Levi:* related to *yillaweh,* "he will become attached."
29, 35: *Judah:* related to *odeh,* "I will give grateful praise."
30, 3: *On my knees:* in the ancient Near East, a father would take a newborn child in his lap to signify that he acknowledged it as his own; Rachel uses the ceremony in order to adopt the child and establish her legal rights to it.
30, 4: *Consort:* the Hebrew word normally means "wife," but here it refers to a wife of secondary rank, who did not have the full legal rights of an ordinary wife.

29, 20: Hos 12, 13.
29, 27: Hos 12, 13.
29, 30: Dt 21, 15ff.
29, 32: Gn 49, 3.
29, 35: Mt 1, 2; Lk 3, 33.
30, 1: Prv 30, 16.
30, 2: 2 Kgs 5, 7.
30, 3: Gn 16, 2ff.

GN

had intercourse with her. [5] When Bilhah conceived and bore a son, [6]† Rachel said, "God has vindicated me; indeed he has heeded my plea and given me a son." Therefore she named him Dan. [7] Rachel's maidservant Bilhah conceived again and bore a second son, [8]† and Rachel said, "I engaged in a fateful struggle with my sister, and I prevailed." So she named him Naphtali.

[9] When Leah saw that she had ceased to bear children, she gave her maidservant Zilpah to Jacob as a consort. [10] So Jacob had intercourse with Zilpah, and she conceived and bore a son. [11]† Leah then said, "What good luck!" So she named him Gad. [12] Then Leah's maidservant Zilpah bore a second son to Jacob; [13]† and Leah said, "What good fortune!"—meaning, "Women call me fortunate." So she named him Asher.

[14]† One day, during the wheat harvest, when Reuben was out in the field, he came upon some mandrakes which he brought home to his mother Leah. Rachel asked Leah, "Please let me have some of your son's mandrakes." [15] Leah replied, "Was it not enough for you to take away my husband, that you must now take my son's mandrakes too?" "Very well, then!" Rachel answered. "In exchange for your son's mandrakes, Jacob may lie with you tonight." [16] That evening, when Jacob came home from the fields, Leah went out to meet him. "You are now to come in with me," she told him, "because I have paid for you with my son's mandrakes." So that night he slept with her, [17] and God heard her prayer; she conceived and bore a fifth son to Jacob. [18]† Leah then said, "God has given me my reward for having let my husband have my maidservant"; so she named him Issachar. [19] Leah conceived again and bore a sixth son to Jacob; [20]† and she said, "God has brought me a precious gift. This time my husband will offer me presents, now that I have borne him six sons"; so she named him Zebulun. [21] Finally, she gave birth to a daughter, and she named her Dinah.

[22] Then God remembered Rachel; he heard her prayer and made her fruitful. [23]* She conceived and bore a son, and she said, "God has removed my disgrace." [24]† So she named him Joseph, meaning, "May the LORD add another son to this one for me!"

Jacob Outwits Laban

[25] After Rachel gave birth to Joseph, Jacob said to Laban: "Give me leave to go to my homeland. [26] Let me have my wives, for whom I served you, and my children, too, that I may depart. You know very well the service that I have rendered you." [27] Laban answered him: "If you will please. . . .

"I have learned through divination that it is because of you that God has blessed me. [28] So," he continued, "state what wages you want from me, and I will pay them." [29] Jacob replied: "You know what work I did for you and how well your livestock fared under my care; [30] the little you had before I came has grown into very much, since the LORD's blessings came upon you in my company. Therefore I should now do something for my own household as well." [31] "What should I pay you?" Laban asked. Jacob answered: "You do not have to pay me anything outright. I will again pasture and tend your flock, if you do this one thing for me: [32]† go through your whole flock today and remove from it every dark animal among the sheep and every spotted or speckled one among the goats. Only such animals shall be my wages. [33] In the future, whenever you check on these wages of mine, let my honesty testify against me: any animal in my possession that is not a speckled or spotted goat, or a dark sheep, got there by theft!" [34] "Very well," agreed Laban. "Let it be as you say."

[35]† That same day Laban removed the streaked and spotted he-goats and all the speckled and spotted she-goats, all those with some white on them, as well as the fully dark-colored sheep; these he left . . . in charge of his sons. [36] Then he put a three days' journey between himself and Jacob, while Jacob continued to pasture the rest of Laban's flock.

[37] Jacob, however, got some fresh shoots of

---

†

30, 6: *Dan:* explained by the term *dannanni,* "he has vindicated me."

30, 8: *Naphtali:* explained by the phrase *"naptule elohim niptalti,"* literally, "in a divine wrestling match I have wrestled," perhaps implying the concept of an ordeal; hence the above rendering, *I engaged in a fateful struggle.*

30, 11: *Gad:* explained by the Hebrew term *begad,* literally "in luck," i.e., *what good luck!*

30, 13: *Asher:* explained by the term *beoshri,* literally "in my good fortune," i.e., *what good fortune,* and by the term *ishsheruni,* "they call me fortunate."

30, 14: *Mandrakes:* an herb whose root was anciently thought to promote conception. The Hebrew word for mandrakes, *dudaim,* has erotic connotations, since it sounds like the words *daddayim* ("breasts") and *dodim* ("sexual pleasure").

30, 18: *Issachar:* explained by the terms, *sekari,* "my reward," and in v 16, *sakor sekartika,* literally "I have hired you," i.e., I have paid for you.

30, 20: *Zebulun:* related to the Akkadian word *zubullum,* "bridegroom's gift," is explained by the terms, *zebadani . . . zebed tob,* "he has brought me a precious gift," and *yizbeleni,* "he will offer me presents."

30, 24: *Joseph:* explained by the words *yosep,* "may he add," and in v 23, *asap,* "he has removed."

30, 32: *Dark . . . sheep . . . spotted or speckled . . . goats:* In the Near East the normal color of sheep is light gray, whereas that of goats is uniform dark brown or black. Ordinarily, therefore, Jacob would have received but few animals.

30, 35: By giving the abnormally colored animals to his sons, Laban not only deprived Jacob of his first small wages, but he also designed to prevent in this way the future breeding of such animals in the part of his flock entrusted to Jacob.

---

*

30, 23: Lk 1, 25.

poplar, almond and plane trees, and he made white stripes in them by peeling off the bark down to the white core of the shoots. 38 The rods that he had thus peeled he then set upright in the watering troughs, so that they would be in front of the animals that drank from the troughs. When the animals were in heat as they came to drink, 39† the goats mated by the rods, and so they brought forth streaked, speckled and spotted kids. 40 The sheep, on the other hand, Jacob kept apart, and he set these animals to face the streaked or fully dark-colored animals of Laban. Thus he produced special flocks of his own, which he did not put with Laban's flock. 41 Moreover, whenever the hardier animals were in heat, Jacob would set the rods in the troughs in full view of these animals, so that they mated by the rods; 42 but with the weaker animals he would not put the rods there. So the feeble animals would go to Laban, but the sturdy ones to Jacob. 43 Thus the man grew increasingly prosperous, and he came to own not only large flocks but also male and female servants and camels and asses.

Flight from Laban

31 1 Jacob learned that Laban's sons were saying, "Jacob has taken everything that belonged to our father, and he has accumulated all this wealth of his by using our father's property." 2 Jacob perceived, too, that Laban's attitude toward him was not what it had previously been. 3* Then the LORD said to Jacob, "Return to the land of your fathers, where you were born, and I will be with you."

4 So Jacob sent for Rachel and Leah to meet him where he was in the field with his flock. 5 There he said to them: "I have noticed that your father's attitude toward me is not as it was in the past; but the God of my father has been with me. 6 You well know what effort I put into serving your father; 7* yet your father cheated me and changed my wages time after time. God, however, did not let him do me any harm. 8† Whenever your father said, 'The speckled animals shall be your wages,' the en-

tire flock would bear speckled young; whenever he said, 'The streaked animals shall be your wages,' the entire flock would bear streaked young. 9 Thus God reclaimed your father's livestock and gave it to me. 10 Once, in the breeding season, I had a dream in which I saw mating he-goats that were streaked, speckled and mottled. 11 In the dream God's messenger called to me, 'Jacob!' 'Here!' I replied. 12 Then he said, 'Note well. All the he-goats in the flock, as they mate, are streaked, speckled and mottled, for I have seen all the things that Laban has been doing to you. 13* I am the God who appeared to you in Bethel, where you anointed a memorial stone and made a vow to me. Up, then! Leave this land and return to the land of your birth.'"

14 Rachel and Leah answered him: "Have we still an heir's portion in our father's house? 15† Are we not regarded by him as outsiders? He not only sold us; he has even used up the money that he got for us! 16* All the wealth that God reclaimed from our father really belongs to us and our children. Therefore, do just as God has told you." 17 Jacob proceeded to put his children and wives on camels, 18 and he drove off with all his livestock and all the property he had acquired in Paddan-aram, to go to his father Isaac in the land of Canaan.

19*† Now Laban had gone away to shear his sheep, and Rachel had meanwhile appropriated her father's household idols. 20† Jacob had hoodwinked Laban the Aramean by not telling him of his intended flight. 21 Thus he made his escape with all that he had. Once he was across the Euphrates, he headed for the highlands of Gilead.

22 On the third day, word came to Laban that Jacob had fled. 23† Taking his kinsmen with him, he pursued him for seven days until he caught up with him in the hill country of Gilead. 24* But that night God appeared to Laban the Aramean in a dream and warned him, "Take care not to threaten Jacob with any harm."

Jacob and Laban in Gilead

25 When Laban overtook Jacob, Jacob's tents were pitched in the highlands; Laban also pitched his

---

30, 39–42: Jacob's stratagem was based on the widespread notion among simple people that visual stimuli can have prenatal effects on the offspring of breeding animals. Thus, the rods on which Jacob had whittled stripes or bands or chevron marks were thought to cause the female goats that looked at them to bear kids with lighter-colored marks on their dark hair, while the gray ewes were thought to bear lambs with dark marks on them simply by visual cross-breeding with the dark goats.

31, 8–12: This Elohist account of the miraculous increase in Jacob's flock differs somewhat from the Yahwist account given in Gn 30, 32–42.

31, 15: *Outsiders:* literally "foreign women"; they lacked the favored legal status of native women. *Used up:* literally "eaten, consumed"; the bridal price that a man received for giving his daughter in marriage was legally reserved as her inalienable dowry.

31, 19: *Household idols:* in Hebrew, *teraphim,* figurines used in divination (Ez 21, 26; Zec 10, 2). Laban calls them his "gods" (v 30).

31, 20: *Hoodwinked:* literally "stolen the heart of," i.e., lulled the mind of. *Aramean:* The earliest extra-biblical references to the Arameans date from several centuries after the time of Jacob; to call Laban an *Aramean* and to have him speak Aramaic (v 47) would seem to be an anachronism.

31, 23: *For seven days:* literally "a way of seven days," a general term to designate a long distance; it would have taken a camel caravan many more days to travel from Haran to Gilead, the region east of the northern half of the Jordan.

31, 3: Gn 26, 3; 28, 15; 32, 10.
31, 7: Jdt 8, 26.
31, 13: Gn 28, 18.
31, 16: Wis 10, 10f.
31, 19: Gn 19, 34; 1 Sm 19, 13.
31, 24: Wis 10, 12.

tents there, on Mount Gilead. 26† "What do you mean," Laban demanded of Jacob, "by hoodwinking me and carrying off my daughters like war captives? 27 Why did you dupe me by stealing away secretly? You should have told me, and I would have sent you off with merry singing to the sound of tambourines and harps. 28 You did not even allow me a parting kiss to my daughters and grandchildren! What you have now done is a senseless thing. 29 I have it in my power to harm all of you; but last night the God of your father said to me, 'Take care not to threaten Jacob with any harm!' 30 Granted that you had to leave because you were desperately homesick for your father's house, why did you steal my gods?" 31 "I was frightened," Jacob replied to Laban, "at the thought that you might take your daughters away from me by force. 32 But as for your gods, the one you find them with shall not remain alive! If, with my kinsmen looking on, you identify anything here as belonging to you, take it." Jacob, of course, had no idea that Rachel had stolen the idols.

33 Laban then went in and searched Jacob's tent and Leah's tent, as well as the tents of the two maidservants; but he did not find the idols. Leaving Leah's tent, he went into Rachel's. 34* Now Rachel had taken the idols, put them inside a camel cushion, and seated herself upon them. When Laban had rummaged through the rest of her tent without finding them, 35 Rachel said to her father, "Let not my lord feel offended that I cannot rise in your presence; a woman's period is upon me." So, despite his search, he did not find his idols.

36 Jacob, now enraged, upbraided Laban. "What crime or offense have I committed," he demanded, "that you should hound me so fiercely? 37 Now that you have ransacked all my things, have you found a single object taken from your belongings? If so, produce it here before your kinsmen and mine, and let them decide between us two.

38 "In the twenty years that I was under you, no ewe or she-goat of yours ever miscarried, and I have never feasted on a ram of your flock. 39*† I never brought you an animal torn by wild beasts; I made good the loss myself. You held me responsible for

anything stolen by day or night. 40 How often the scorching heat ravaged me by day, and the frost by night, while sleep fled from my eyes! 41 Of the twenty years that I have now spent in your household, I slaved fourteen years for your two daughters and six years for your flock, while you changed my wages time after time. 42* If my ancestral God, the God of Abraham and the Awesome One of Isaac, had not been on my side, you would now have sent me away empty-handed. But God saw my plight and the fruits of my toil, and last night he gave judgment."

43† Laban replied to Jacob: "The women are mine, their children are mine, and the flocks are mine; everything you see belongs to me. But since these women are my daughters, I will now do something for them and for the children they have borne. 44 Come, then, we will make a pact; you and I; the LORD shall be a witness between us."

45* Then Jacob took a stone and set it up as a memorial stone. 46 Jacob said to his kinsmen, "Gather some stones." So they got some stones and made a mound; and they had a meal there at the mound. 47† Laban called it Jegar-sahadutha, but Jacob named it Galeed. 48 "This mound," said Laban, "shall be a witness from now on between you and me." That is why it was named Galeed— 49† and also Mizpah, for he said: "May the LORD keep watch between you and me when we are out of each other's sight. 50 If you mistreat my daughters, or take other wives besides my daughters, remember that even though no one else is about, God will be witness between you and me."

51 Laban said further to Jacob: "Here is this mound, and here is the memorial stone that I have set up between you and me. 52 This mound shall be witness, and this memorial stone shall be witness, that, with hostile intent, neither may I pass beyond this mound into your territory nor may you pass beyond it into mine. 53 May the God of Abraham and the god of Nahor [their ancestral deities] maintain justice between us!" Jacob took the oath by the Awesome One of Isaac. 54 He then offered a sacrifice on the mountain and invited his kinsmen to share in the meal. When they had eaten, they passed the night on the mountain.

---

†
31, 26: *War captives:* literally "women captured by the sword"; the women of a conquered people were treated as part of the victor's booty; cf 1 Sm 30, 2; 2 Kgs 5, 2.

31, 39: Laban's actions were contrary to the customs of the ancient Near East, as recorded in the Code of Hammurabi: "If in a sheepfold an act of god has occurred, or a lion has made a kill, the shepherd shall clear himself before the deity, and the owner of the fold must accept the loss" (par. 266); cf Ex 22, 12.

31, 43–54: In this account of the treaty between Laban and Jacob, the Yahwist and Elohist sources are closely interwoven. The *mound* or cairn of stones comes from the Yahwist source, the *memorial stone* or stele comes from the Elohist one.

31, 47: *Jegar-sahadutha:* an Aramaic term meaning "mound of witness." *Galeed:* in Hebrew, *galed,* with the same meaning; also offers an explanation of the regional name Gilead.

31, 49: *Mizpah:* a town in Gilead; cf Jgs. 10, 17; 11, 11.34; Hos 5, 1. The Hebrew name *mispa* ("lookout") is allied to *yisep yhwh* ("may the LORD keep watch"), and also echoes the word *masseba* ("memorial pillar").

31, 34: Gn 31, 19.   31, 42: Gn 19, 24.29.
31, 39: Ex 22, 12.   31, 45: Gn 28, 18; 35, 14.

32 [1] Early the next morning, Laban kissed his grandchildren and his daughters goodbye; then he set out on his journey back home, [2] while Jacob continued on his own way. Then God's messengers encountered Jacob. [3]† When he saw them he said, "This is God's encampment." So he named that place Mahanaim.

Embassy to Esau

[4]* Jacob sent messengers ahead to his brother Esau in the land of Seir, the country of Edom, [5] with this message: "Thus shall you say to my lord Esau: 'Your servant Jacob speaks as follows: I have been staying with Laban and have been detained there until now. [6] I own cattle, asses and sheep, as well as male and female servants. I am sending my lord this information in the hope of gaining your favor.' " [7] When the messengers returned to Jacob, they said, "We reached your brother Esau. He is now coming to meet you, accompanied by four hundred men."

[8] Jacob was very much frightened. In his anxiety, he divided the people who were with him, as well as his flocks, herds, and camels, into two camps. [9] "If Esau should attack and overwhelm one camp," he reasoned, "the remaining camp may still survive." [10]* Then he prayed, "O God of my father Abraham and God of my father Isaac! You told me, O LORD, 'Go back to the land of your birth, and I will be good to you.' [11] I am unworthy of all the acts of kindness that you have loyally performed for your servant: although I crossed the Jordan here with nothing but my staff, I have now grown into two companies. [12]* Save me, I pray, from the hand of my brother Esau! Otherwise I fear that when he comes he will strike me down and slay the mothers and children. [13] You yourself said, 'I will be very good to you, and I will make your descendants like the sands of the sea, which are too numerous to count.' "

[14] After passing the night there, Jacob selected from what he had with him the following presents for his brother Esau: [15] two hundred she-goats and twenty he-goats; two hundred ewes and twenty rams; [16] thirty milch camels and their young; forty cows and ten bulls; twenty she-asses and ten he-asses. [17] He put these animals in charge of his servants, in separate droves, and he told the servants, "Go on ahead of me, but keep a space between one drove and the next." [18] To the servant in the lead he gave this instruction: "When my brother Esau meets you, he may ask you, 'Whose man are you? Where are you going? To whom do these animals ahead of you belong?' [19] Then you shall answer, 'They belong to your brother Jacob, but they have been sent as a gift to my lord Esau; and Jacob himself is right behind us.' " [20] He gave similar instructions to the second servant and the third and to all the others who followed behind the droves, namely: "Thus and thus shall you say to Esau, when you reach him; [21] and be sure to add, 'Your servant Jacob is right behind us.' " For Jacob reasoned, "If I first appease him with gifts that precede me, then later, when I face him, perhaps he will forgive me." [22] So the gifts went on ahead of him, while he stayed that night in the camp.

Struggle with the Angel

[23] In the course of that night, however, Jacob arose, took his two wives, with the two maid-

Wrestling with God

Even after twenty years, Jacob is anxious about meeting Esau again. This time, Jacob uses his craftiness not to deceive Esau but to gain Esau's good graces. Then while on the way home, he has an amazing religious experience. Many Scripture scholars believe that the strange wrestling encounter is a symbol that Jacob has become a changed person. He finally realizes that in all his troubles, God was his true opponent.

Perhaps at times you have wrestled with yourself or with God. It is not so much that God is your opponent or that you are in a contest. It is the wrestling itself that matters. When you face the challenges, especially the big ones, you wrestle between the person you are now and the person God is calling you to be.

In your prayer, reflect or journal on the following questions:

■ When does it seem like God is trying to wrestle with you? What does it feel like?
■ Is God challenging you about something in your life right now?
■ What blessings might you gain in accepting God's challenge and changing your life?

▶ Gn 32, 23–33

32, 3: *Mahanaim:* a town in Gilead (Jos 13, 26.30; 21, 38; 2 Sm 2, 8; etc.). The Hebrew name means "two camps." There are other allusions to the name in vv 8.11.

32, 4: Gn 36, 6.   32, 12: Gn 28, 14; 48, 16; Ex
32, 10: Gn 31, 3.   32, 13; Heb 11, 12.

servants and his eleven children, and crossed the ford of the Jabbok. 24 After he had taken them across the stream and had brought over all his possessions, 25† Jacob was left there alone. Then some man wrestled with him until the break of dawn. 26* When the man saw that he could not prevail over him, he struck Jacob's hip at its socket, so that the hip socket was wrenched as they wrestled. 27 The man then said, "Let me go, for it is daybreak." But Jacob said, "I will not let you go until you bless me." 28* "What is your name?" the man asked. He answered, "Jacob." 29† Then the man said, "You shall no longer be spoken of as Jacob, but as Israel, because you have contended with divine and human beings and have prevailed." 30 Jacob then asked him, "Do tell me your name, please." He answered, "Why should you want to know my name?" With that, he bade him farewell. 31*† Jacob named the place Peniel, "Because I have seen God face to face," he said, "yet my life has been spared."

32 At sunrise, as he left Penuel, Jacob limped along because of his hip. 33 That is why, to this day, the Israelites do not eat the sciatic muscle that is on the hip socket, inasmuch as Jacob's hip socket was struck at the sciatic muscle.

Jacob and Esau Meet

33 1 Jacob looked up and saw Esau coming, accompanied by four hundred men. So he divided his children among Leah, Rachel and the two maidservants, 2 putting the maids and their children first, Leah and her children next, and Rachel and Joseph last. 3 He himself went on ahead of them, bowing to the ground seven times, until he reached his brother. 4 Esau ran to meet him, embraced him, and flinging himself on his neck, kissed him as he wept.

5 When Esau looked about, he saw the women and children. "Who are these with you?" he asked. Jacob answered, "They are the children whom God has graciously bestowed on your servant." 6 Then the maidservants and their children came forward and bowed low; 7 next, Leah and her children came forward and bowed low; lastly, Rachel and her children came forward and bowed low. 8 Then Esau asked, "What did you intend with all those droves that I encountered?" Jacob answered, "It was to gain my lord's favor." 9 "I have plenty," replied Esau; "you should keep what is yours, brother." 10 "No, I beg you!" said Jacob. "If you will do me the favor, please accept this gift from me, since to come into your presence is for me like coming into the presence of God, now that you have received me so kindly. 11 Do accept the present I have brought you; God has been generous toward me, and I have an abundance." Since he so urged him, Esau accepted.

12 Then Esau said, "Let us break camp and be on

Letting Go of the Past

LIVE IT!

Jacob is understandably apprehensive as he approaches his long-estranged twin brother. How will Esau react? But Esau, who was wronged by Jacob, runs to meet him and gives him a hug. All is forgiven, and the two are reconciled at last. This story is like the parable of the prodigal son in Lk 15, 11–32.

All of us have wronged others, especially the people we care about most. All of us have also experienced forgiveness. Nothing is quite like the freedom that comes with genuine forgiveness and reconciliation. A burden is lifted. A heavy heart is made lighter. A vengeful attitude is transformed into a feeling of inner peace and harmony. This is the work of God's grace. Forgiveness and reconciliation are powerful signs of the presence of God. We can almost feel the enormous sense of relief experienced by Jacob as he realizes his brother holds no grudge.

Does a relationship in your life need forgiveness and reconciliation? If so, what can you do to bring about healing in this relationship?

▶ Gn 33, 1–17

†

32, 25: *Some man:* a messenger of the Lord in human form, as is clear from vv 29ff.

32, 29: *Israel:* the first part of the Hebrew name *Yisrael* is given a popular explanation in the word *sarita,* "you contended"; the second part is the first syllable of *elohim,* "divine beings." The present incident, with a similar allusion to the name Israel, is referred to in Hos 12, 5, where the mysterious wrestler is explicitly called an angel.

32, 31: *Peniel:* a variant of the word Penuel (v 32), the name of a town on the north bank of the Jabbok in Gilead (Jgs 8, 8f.17; 1 Kgs 12, 25). The name is explained as meaning "the face of God," *peniel. Yet my life has been spared:* see note on Gn 16, 13.

32, 26: Hos 12, 4.   18, 31; 2 Kgs 17, 34.
32, 28: Gn 35, 10; 1 Kgs   **32, 31:** Jgs 13, 22.

GN

our way; I will travel alongside you." ¹³ But Jacob replied: "As my lord can see, the children are frail. Besides, I am encumbered with the flocks and herds, which now have sucklings; if overdriven for a single day, the whole flock will die. ¹⁴ Let my lord, then, go on ahead of me, while I proceed more slowly at the pace of the livestock before me and at the pace of my children, until I join my lord in Seir." ¹⁵ Esau replied, "Let me at least put at your disposal some of the men who are with me." But Jacob said, "For what reason? Please indulge me in this, my lord." ¹⁶ So on the same day that Esau began his journey back to Seir, ¹⁷† Jacob journeyed

The Rape of Dinah

34 ¹† Dinah, the daughter whom Leah had borne to Jacob, went out to visit some of the women of the land. ²† When Shechem, son of Hamor the Hivite, who was chief of the region, saw her, he seized her and lay with her by force. ³ Since he was strongly attracted to Dinah, daughter of Jacob, indeed was really in love with the girl, he endeavored to win her affection. ⁴ Shechem also asked his father Hamor, "Get me this girl for a wife."

⁵ Meanwhile, Jacob heard that Shechem had defiled his daughter Dinah; but since his sons were

No Way, Shechem!

A news article reported on the rape of a girl by a group of high school boys. The girl was dating one of the boys and went to a party where she became intoxicated. The boys decided to take advantage of her and one-by-one raped her. The next day, she told her parents what had happened, the police were contacted, and the boys were arrested. Many people were left wondering how this could have happened in their little town.

Rape is more about power than it is about sex. The story in Genesis, chapter 34, tells us of Shechem, a local prince, who rapes Dinah. Because of his power, he figured he could do what he wanted to her. But in the end, his life is taken.

The boys in the story above felt that they had the power to do what they wanted, but in the end, they were arrested and sentenced to serve time in a juvenile facility. We are to respect one another. Position or power does not give us the right to commit sexual violence. Rape and any other sexual abuse is an outrage to God.

▸ **Gn 34, 1–31**

to Succoth. There he built a home for himself and made booths for his livestock. That is why the place was called Succoth.

¹⁸* Having thus come from Paddan-aram, Jacob arrived safely at the city of Shechem, which is in the land of Canaan, and he encamped in sight of the city. ¹⁹*† The plot of ground on which he had pitched his tent he bought for a hundred pieces of bullion from the descendants of Hamor, the founder of Shechem. ²⁰* He set up a memorial stone there and invoked "El, the God of Israel."

out in the fields with his livestock, he held his peace until they came home. ⁶ Now Hamor, the father of Shechem, went out to discuss the matter with Jacob, ⁷* just as Jacob's sons were coming in from the fields. When they heard the news, the men were shocked and seethed with indignation. What Shechem had done was an outrage in Israel; such a thing could not be tolerated.

⁸ Hamor appealed to them, saying, "My son Shechem has his heart set on your daughter. Please give her to him in marriage. ⁹ Intermarry with us; give your daughters to us, and take our daughters

†
33, 17: *Succoth:* an important town near the confluence of the Jabbok and the Jordan (Jos 13, 27; Jgs 8, 5–16; 1 Kgs 7, 46). *Booths:* in Hebrew, *sukkot*, of the same sound as the name of the town.
33, 19: *Pieces of bullion:* in Hebrew, *kesita,* a monetary unit of which the value is now unknown. *Descendants of Hamor:* Hamorites, "the men of Hamor"; cf Jgs 9, 28. Hamor was regarded as the eponymous ancestor of the pre-Israelite inhabitants of Shechem.
34, 1–31: Behind the story of the rape of Dinah and the revenge of Jacob's sons on the men of the city of Shechem there probably lies

a dimly recollected historical event connected with an armed conflict between the earliest Israelite tribes invading central Canaan and the Hurrian inhabitants of the Shechem region.
34, 2: *Hivite:* The Greek text has "Horite"; the terms were apparently used indiscriminately to designate the Hurrian or other non-Semitic elements in Palestine.

33, 18: Gn 12, 6; Jn 4, 6.   33, 20: Jgs 6, 24.
33, 19: Jos 24, 32; Jn 4, 5;   34, 7: 2 Sm 13, 12.
     Acts 7, 16.

GN

for yourselves. ¹⁰ Thus you can live among us. The land is open before you; you can settle and move about freely in it, and acquire landed property here." ¹¹ Then Shechem, too, appealed to Dinah's father and brothers: "Do me this favor, and I will pay whatever you demand of me. ¹² No matter how high you set the bridal price, I will pay you whatever you ask; only give me the maiden in marriage."

Revenge of Jacob's Sons

¹³ Jacob's sons replied to Shechem and his father Hamor with guile, speaking as they did because their sister Dinah had been defiled. ¹⁴ "We could not do such a thing," they said, "as to give our sister to an uncircumcised man; that would be a disgrace for us. ¹⁵ We will agree with you only on this condition, that you become like us by having every male among you circumcised. ¹⁶ Then we will give you our daughters and take yours in marriage; we will settle among you and become one kindred people with you. ¹⁷ But if you do not comply with our terms regarding circumcision, we will take our daughter and go away."

¹⁸ Their proposal seemed fair to Hamor and his son Shechem. ¹⁹ The young man lost no time in acting in the matter, since he was deeply in love with Jacob's daughter. Moreover, he was more highly respected than anyone else in his clan. ²⁰ So Hamor and his son Shechem went to their town council and thus presented the matter to their fellow townsmen: ²¹ "These men are friendly toward us. Let them settle in the land and move about in it freely; there is ample room in the country for them. We can marry their daughters and give our daughters to them in marriage. ²² But the men will agree to live with us and form one kindred people with us only on this condition, that every male among us be circumcised as they themselves are. ²³ Would not the livestock they have acquired—all their animals—then be ours? Let us, therefore, give in to them, so that they may settle among us."

²⁴† All the able-bodied men of the town agreed with Hamor and his son Shechem, and all the males, including every able-bodied man in the community, were circumcised. ²⁵* On the third day, while they were still in pain, Dinah's full brothers Simeon and Levi, two of Jacob's sons, took their swords, advanced against the city without any trouble, and massacred all the males. ²⁶* After they had put Hamor and his son Shechem to the sword, they took Dinah from Shechem's house and left. ²⁷ Then the other sons of Jacob followed up the slaughter and sacked the city in reprisal for their sister Dinah's defilement. ²⁸ They seized their flocks, herds and asses, whatever was in the city and in the country around. ²⁹* They carried off all their wealth, their women, and their children, and took for loot whatever was in the houses.

³⁰ Jacob said to Simeon and Levi: "You have brought trouble upon me by making me loathsome to the inhabitants of the land, the Canaanites and the Perizzites. I have so few men that, if these people unite against me and attack me, I and my family will be wiped out." ³¹ But they retorted, "Should our sister have been treated like a harlot?"

Bethel Revisited

35 ¹* God said to Jacob: "Go up now to Bethel. Settle there and build an altar there to the God who appeared to you while you were fleeing from your brother Esau." ²† So Jacob told his family and all the others who were with him: "Get rid of the foreign gods that you have among you; then purify yourselves and put on fresh clothes. ³ We are now to go up to Bethel, and I will build an altar there to the God who answered me in my hour of distress and who has been with me wherever I have gone." ⁴† They therefore handed over to Jacob all the foreign gods in their possession and also the rings they had in their ears. ⁵ Then, as they set out, a terror from God fell upon the towns round about, so that no one pursued the sons of Jacob.

⁶* Thus Jacob and all the people who were with him arrived in Luz [that is, Bethel] in the land of Canaan. ⁷* There he built an altar and named the place Bethel, for it was there that God had revealed himself to him when he was fleeing from his brother.

⁸† Death came to Rebekah's nurse Deborah; she was buried under the oak below Bethel, and so it was called Allon-bacuth.

⁹ On Jacob's arrival from Paddan-aram, God appeared to him again and blessed him. ¹⁰* God said to him:

"You whose name is Jacob
   shall no longer be called Jacob,
   but Israel shall be your name."

34, 24: *Every able-bodied man in the community:* literally "all those who go out at the gate of the city," apparently meaning the men who go out to war. By temporarily crippling them through circumcision, Jacob's sons deprived the city of its defenders.

35, 2: *Foreign gods:* pagan images, including household idols (see note on Gn 31, 19), that Jacob's people brought with them from Paddan-aram.

35, 4: *Rings:* Earrings were often worn as amulets connected with pagan magic.

35, 8: This verse may have stood originally in some other context. Rebekah's nurse is spoken of without a name, in Gn 24, 59. *Allon-bacuth:* the Hebrew name means "oak of weeping."

34, 25: Gn 49, 6.
34, 26: Jdt 9, 2.
34, 29: Jdt 9, 3f.
35, 1: Gn 28, 12f.
35, 6: Gn 28, 19; Jos 18, 13;
Jgs 1, 22f.
35, 7: Gn 28, 12f.
35, 10: 1 Kgs 18, 31; 2 Kgs 17, 34.

GN

Thus he was named Israel. [11] God also said to him:

"I am God Almighty;
   be fruitful and multiply.
A nation, indeed an assembly of nations,
   shall stem from you,
   and kings shall issue from your loins.
[12]* The land I once gave
   to Abraham and Isaac
   I now give to you;
And to your descendants after you
   will I give this land."

[13] Then God departed from him. [14]* On the site where God had spoken with him, Jacob set up a memorial stone, and upon it he made a libation and poured out oil. [15] Jacob named the site Bethel, because God had spoken with him there.

Jacob's Family

[16] Then they departed from Bethel: but while they still had some distance to go on the way to Ephrath, Rachel began to be in labor and to suffer great distress. [17] When her pangs were most severe, her midwife said to her, "Have no fear! This time, too, you have a son." [18]† With her last breath—for she was at the point of death—she called him Ben-oni; his father, however, named him Benjamin. [19]*† Thus Rachel died; and she was buried on the road to Ephrath [that is, Bethlehem]. [20] Jacob set up a memorial stone on her grave, and the same monument marks Rachel's grave to this day.

[21] Israel moved on and pitched his tent beyond Migdal-eder. [22]* While Israel was encamped in that region, Reuben went and lay with Bilhah, his father's concubine. When Israel heard of it, he was greatly offended.

The sons of Jacob were now twelve. [23] The sons of Leah: Reuben, Jacob's first-born, Simeon, Levi, Judah, Issachar, and Zebulun; [24]† the sons of Rachel: Joseph and Benjamin; [25] the sons of Rachel's maid Bilhah: Dan and Naphtali; [26] the sons of Leah's maid Zilpah: Gad and Asher. These are the sons of Jacob who were born to him in Paddan-aram.

[27] Jacob went home to his father Isaac at Mamre, in Kiriath-arba [that is, Hebron], where Abraham and Isaac had stayed. [28] The lifetime of Isaac was one hundred and eighty years; [29] then he breathed his last. After a full life, he died as an old man and was taken to his kinsmen. His sons Esau and Jacob buried him.

Edomite Lists

36 [1] These are the descendants of Esau [that is, Edom]. [2]*† Esau took his wives from among the Canaanite women: Adah, daughter of Elon the Hittite; Oholibamah, granddaughter through Anah of Zibeon the Hivite; [3] and Basemath, daughter of Ishmael and sister of Nebaioth. [4]* Adah bore Eliphaz to Esau; Basemath bore Reuel; [5]* and Oholibamah bore Jeush, Jalam and Korah. These are the sons of Esau who were born to him in the land of Canaan.

[6]* Esau took his wives, his sons, his daughters, and all the members of his household, as well as his livestock comprising various animals and all the property he had acquired in the land of Canaan, and went to the land of Seir, out of the way of his brother Jacob. [7] Their possessions had become too great for them to dwell together, and the land in which they were staying could not support them because of their livestock. [8]* So Esau settled in the highlands of Seir. [Esau is Edom.] [9] These are the descendants of Esau, ancestor of the Edomites, in the highlands of Seir.

[10] These are the names of Esau's sons: Eliphaz, son of Esau's wife Adah; and Reuel, son of Esau's wife Basemath. [11]* The sons of Eliphaz were Teman, Omar, Zepho, Gatam and Kenaz. [12] (Esau's son Eliphaz had a concubine Timna, and she bore Amalek to Eliphaz.) These are the descendants of Esau's wife Adah. [13]* The sons of Reuel were Nahath, Zerah, Shammah and Mizzah. These are the descendants of Esau's wife Basemath. [14]* The descendants of Esau's wife Oholibamah—granddaughter through Anah of Zibeon—whom she bore to Esau were Jeush, Jalam and Korah.

[15] The following are the clans of Esau's descendants. The descendants of Eliphaz, Esau's first-born:

---

† **35, 18:** *Ben-oni:* means either "son of my vigor" or, more likely in the context, "son of affliction." *Benjamin:* "son of the right hand." This may be interpreted to signify a son who is his father's help and support, but more likely its original meaning was "southerner." In the Hebrew idiom, the south lies to one's right hand, and Benjamin was the southernmost of the Rachel tribes.

35, 19: *Bethlehem:* the gloss comes from a later tradition that identified the site with Bethlehem, also called Ephrath or Ephratha (Jos 15, 59; Ru 4, 11; Mi 5, 1). But Rachel's grave was actually near Ramah (Jer 31, 15), a few miles north of Jerusalem, in the territory of Benjamin (1 Sm 20, 2).

35, 24ff: Benjamin is here said to have been born in *Paddan-aram,* either because all twelve sons of Jacob are considered as a unit, or because the Priestly source, from which vv 23–29 are taken,

follows a tradition different from that of the Elohistic source found in vv 16–20.

36, 2–14: The names of Esau's wives and of their fathers given here differ considerably from their names cited from other old sources in Gn 26, 34 and 28, 9. *Zibeon the Hivite:* In v 20 he is called a *Horite;* see note on Gn 34, 2.

35, 12: Ex 32, 13; Heb 11, 9.
35, 14: Gn 28, 18; 31, 45.
35, 19: Gn 48, 7; 1 Sm 10, 2; Mi 5, 2.
35, 22: Gn 49, 4; 1 Chr 5, 1.
36, 2: Gn 26, 34.
36, 4: 1 Chr 1, 35.
36, 5: 1 Chr 1, 35.
36, 6: Gn 32, 4.
36, 8: Dt 2, 4f; Jos 24, 4.
36, 11f: 1 Chr 1, 36.
36, 13: 1 Chr 1, 37.
36, 14: 1 Chr 1, 35.

the clans of Teman, Omar, Zepho, Kenaz, 16 Korah, Gatam and Amalek. These are the clans of Eliphaz in the land of Edom; they are descended from Adah. 17 The descendants of Esau's son Reuel: the clans of Nahath, Zerah, Shammah and Mizzah. These are the clans of Reuel in the land of Edom; they are descended from Esau's wife Basemath. 18 The descendants of Esau's wife Oholibamah: the clans of Jeush, Jalam and Korah. These are the clans of Esau's wife Oholibamah, daughter of Anah. 19 Such are the descendants of Esau [that is, Edom] according to their clans.

20*† The following are the descendants of Seir the Horite, the original settlers in the land: Lotan, Shobal, Zibeon, Anah, 21 Dishon, Ezer and Dishan; they are the Horite clans descended from Seir, in the land of Edom. 22* Lotan's descendants were Hori and Hemam, and Lotan's sister was Timna. 23 Shobal's descendants were Alvan, Mahanath, Ebal, Shepho and Onam. 24 Zibeon's descendants were Aiah and Anah. (He is the Anah who found water in the desert while he was pasturing the asses of his father Zibeon.) 25 The descendants of Anah were Dishon and Oholibamah, daughter of Anah. 26 The descendants of Dishon were Hemdan, Eshban, Ithran and Cheran. 27 The descendants of Ezer were Bilhan, Zaavan and Akan. 28 The descendants of Dishan were Uz and Aran. 29 These are the Horite clans: the clans of Lotan, Shobal, Zibeon, Anah, 30 Dishon, Ezer and Dishan; they were the clans of the Horites, clan by clan, in the land of Seir.

31*† The following are the kings who reigned in the land of Edom before any king reigned over the Israelites. 32 Bela, son of Beor, became king in Edom; the name of his city was Dinhabah. 33 When Bela died, Jobab, son of Zerah, from Bozrah, succeeded him as king. 34 When Jobab died, Husham, from the land of the Temanites, succeeded him as king. He defeated the Midianites in the country of Moab; the name of his city was Avith. 35 When Husham died, Hadad, son of Bedad, succeeded him as king. 36 When Hadad died, Samlah, from Masrekah, succeeded him as king. 37 When Samlah died, Shaul, from Rehoboth-on-the-River, succeeded him as king. 38 When Shaul died, Baal-hanan, son of Achbor, succeeded him as king. 39 When Baal-hanan died, Hadar succeeded him as king; the name of his city was Pau. (His wife's name was Mehetabel; she was the daughter of Matred, son of Mezahab.)

40 The following are the names of the clans of Esau individually according to their subdivisions and localities: the clans of Timna, Alvah, Jetheth, 41 Oholibamah, Elah, Pinon, 42 Kenaz, Teman, Mibzar, 43 Magdiel and Iram. These are the clans of the Edomites, according to their settlements in their territorial holdings. [Esau was the father of the Edomites.]

IV: Joseph and His Brothers

Joseph Sold into Egypt

37 1 Jacob settled in the land where his father had stayed, the land of Canaan. 2 This is his family history. When Joseph was seventeen years old, he was tending the flocks with his brothers; he was an assistant to the sons of his father's wives Bilhah and Zilpah, and he brought his father bad reports about them.

3 Israel loved Joseph best of all his sons, for he was the child of his old age; and he had made him a long tunic. 4 When his brothers saw that their father loved him best of all his sons, they hated him so much that they would not even greet him.

5* Once Joseph had a dream, which he told to his brothers: 6 "Listen to this dream I had. 7 There we were, binding sheaves in the field, when suddenly my sheaf rose to an upright position, and your sheaves formed a ring around my sheaf and bowed down to it." 8* "Are you really going to make yourself king over us?" his brothers asked him. "Or impose your rule on us?" So they hated him all the more because of his talk about his dreams.

9 Then he had another dream, and this one, too, he told to his brothers. "I had another dream," he said; "this time, the sun and the moon and eleven stars were bowing down to me." 10 When he also told it to his father, his father reproved him. "What is the meaning of this dream of yours?" he asked. "Can it be that I and your mother and your brothers are to come and bow to the ground before you?" 11 So his brothers were wrought up against him but his father pondered the matter.

12 One day, when his brothers had gone to pasture their father's flocks at Shechem, 13 Israel said to Joseph, "Your brothers, you know, are tending our flocks at Shechem. Get ready; I will send you to them." "I am ready," Joseph answered. 14 "Go then," he replied; "see if all is well with your brothers and the flocks, and bring back word." So he sent him off from the valley of Hebron. When Joseph

36, 20: *Seir the Horite:* According to Dt 2, 12, the highlands of Seir were inhabited by Horites before they were occupied by the Edomites.
36, 31: *Before any king reigned over the Israelites:* obviously this statement was written after the time of Saul, Israel's first king.

36, 20f: 1 Chr 1, 38.   37, 5: Gn 42, 9.
36, 22–28: 1 Chr 1, 39–42.   37, 8: Gn 50, 17.
36, 31–43: 1 Chr 1, 45–54.

GN

reached Shechem, [15] a man met him as he was wandering about in the fields. "What are you looking for?" the man asked him. [16] "I am looking for my brothers," he answered. "Could you please tell me where they are tending the flocks?" [17] The man told him, "They have moved on from here; in fact,

him and threw him into the cistern, which was empty and dry.

[25]* They then sat down to their meal. Looking up, they saw a caravan of Ishmaelites coming from Gilead, their camels laden with gum, balm and resin to be taken down to Egypt. [26]* Judah said to

Introducing
▶ JOSEPH

The timeless power of Joseph's story is reaffirmed by the long and successful run of the Broadway play *Joseph and the Amazing Technicolor Dreamcoat*. (In other Bible versions, the "long tunic" in Gn 37, 3 is translated as a "coat of many colors.") The play is based on chapters 37–50 of Genesis, which contains one of the world's greatest stories of family, jealousy, betrayal, and forgiveness.

**   A son of Jacob and Rachel, Joseph carries to Egypt the divine promises of land and descendants, and eventually becomes the link with the story of Moses and the Exodus. As Jacob's favorite son, Joseph experiences the jealousy of his brothers, who sell him to Egyptian merchants. In Egypt, Joseph rises to power, becoming second in command to the pharaoh. Later, when Joseph's brothers come to Egypt looking for food, he forgives them and becomes reconciled with them.**

**   Joseph's story encourages us to forgive others, even when we have been unjustly treated by them. Whenever we have been greatly wronged, remembering Joseph will offer us hope and courage.**

**   ▶ Gn 37, 1—50, 26**

I heard them say, 'Let us go on to Dothan.'" So Joseph went after his brothers and caught up with them in Dothan. [18] They noticed him from a distance, and before he came up to them, they plotted to kill him. [19] They said to one another: "Here comes that master dreamer! [20]* Come on, let us kill him and throw him into one of the cisterns here; we could say that a wild beast devoured him. We shall then see what comes of his dreams."

   [21]† When Reuben heard this, he tried to save him from their hands, saying, "We must not take his life. [22]* Instead of shedding blood," he continued, "just throw him into that cistern there in the desert; but don't kill him outright." His purpose was to rescue him from their hands and restore him to his father. [23] So when Joseph came up to them, they stripped him of the long tunic he had on; [24] then they took

his brothers: "What is to be gained by killing our brother and concealing his blood? [27] Rather, let us sell him to these Ishmaelites, instead of doing away with him ourselves. After all, he is our brother, our own flesh." His brothers agreed. [28]*† They sold Joseph to the Ishmaelites for twenty pieces of silver. Some Midianite traders passed by, and they pulled Joseph up out of the cistern and took him to Egypt. [29] When Reuben went back to the cistern and saw that Joseph was not in it, he tore his clothes, [30] and returning to his brothers, he exclaimed: "The boy is gone! And I—where can I turn?" [31] They took Joseph's tunic, and after slaughtering a goat, dipped the tunic in its blood. [32] They then sent someone to bring the long tunic to their father, with the message: "We found this. See whether it is your son's tunic or not." [33]* He recognized it and exclaimed:

---

† **37, 21–36:** The chapter thus far is from the Yahwist source, as are also vv 25–28a. But vv 21–24 and 28b–36 are from the Elohist source. In the latter, Reuben tries to rescue Joseph, who is taken in Reuben's absence by certain Midianites; in the Yahwist source, it is Judah who saves Joseph's life by having him sold to certain Ishmaelites. Although the two variant forms in which the story was handed down in early oral tradition differ in these minor points, they agree on the essential fact that Joseph was brought as a slave into Egypt because of the jealousy of his brothers.

37, 28: *They sold Joseph . . . silver:* in the Hebrew text, these words occur between *out of the cistern* and *(they) took him to Egypt* at the end of the verse.

37, 20: Gn 44, 28.
37, 22: Gn 42, 22.
37, 25: Gn 43, 11.
37, 26: Jb 16, 18.

37, 28: Ps 105, 17; Wis 10, 13; Acts 7, 9.
37, 33: Gn 44, 28.

"My son's tunic! A wild beast has devoured him! Joseph has been torn to pieces!" 34 Then Jacob rent his clothes, put sackcloth on his loins, and mourned his son many days. 35* Though his sons and daughters tried to console him, he refused all consolation, saying, "No, I will go down mourning to my son in the nether world." Thus did his father lament him.

36* The Midianites, meanwhile, sold Joseph in Egypt to Potiphar, a courtier of Pharaoh and his chief steward.

Judah and Tamar

38 1† About that time Judah parted from his brothers and pitched his tent near a certain Adullamite named Hirah. 2* There he met the daughter of a Canaanite named Shua, married her, and had relations with her. 3 She conceived and bore a son, whom she named Er. 4 Again she conceived and bore a son, whom she named Onan. 5*† Then she bore still another son, whom she named Shelah. They were in Chezib when he was born.

6 Judah got a wife named Tamar for his first-born, Er. 7* But Er, Judah's first-born, greatly offended the LORD; so the LORD took his life. 8*† Then Judah said to Onan, "Unite with your brother's widow, in fulfillment of your duty as brother-in-law, and thus preserve your brother's line." 9 Onan, however, knew that the descendants would not be counted as his; so whenever he had relations with his brother's widow, he wasted his seed on the ground, to avoid contributing offspring for his brother. 10 What he did greatly offended the LORD, and the LORD took his life too. 11 Thereupon Judah said to his daughter-in-law Tamar, "Stay as a widow in your father's house until my son Shelah grows up"—for he feared that Shelah also might die like his brothers. So Tamar went to live in her father's house.

12 Years passed, and Judah's wife, the daughter of Shua, died. After Judah completed the period of mourning, he went up to Timnah for the shearing of his sheep, in company with his friend Hirah the Adullamite. 13 When Tamar was told that her father-in-law was on his way up to Timnah to shear his sheep, 14* she took off her widow's garb, veiled

did you KNOW?

Levirate Marriage

Why does Onan have to marry his dead brother's wife and have a son by her? One of the laws specified in Dt 25, 5–10 regulates what is called levirate marriage. *Levirate* means "brother-in-law." When a man's married brother dies without a son, that man is obligated to marry the wife who was left, and the first son whom she bears shall "continue the line of the deceased" (verse 6). This marriage practice seems to have developed in Israel for several reasons:

- A male child was needed to be heir to the dead man's property because women generally did not own property.
- The dead man's widow needed support and protection.
- A male heir ensured that the family property was kept within the immediate family.

▶ Gn 38, 8

her face by covering herself with a shawl, and sat down at the entrance to Enaim, which is on the way to Timnah; for she was aware that, although Shelah was now grown up, she had not been given to him in marriage. 15 When Judah saw her, he mistook her for a harlot, since she had covered her face. 16 So he went over to her at the roadside, and not realizing that she was his daughter-in-law, he said, "Come, let me have intercourse with you." She replied, "What will you pay me for letting you have intercourse with me?" 17 He answered, "I will send you a kid from the flock." "Very well," she said, "provided you leave a pledge until you send it." 18† Judah asked, "What pledge am I to give you?" She answered, "Your seal and cord, and the staff you carry." So he gave them to her and had intercourse

---

38, 1–30: This chapter, from the Yahwist source, has nothing to do with the Joseph story in which Judah is still living with his father and brothers. The sacred author inserted this independent account from the life of Judah at this place to mark the long lapse of time during which Joseph's family knew nothing of his life in Egypt. This is apparently a personalized history of the early days of the tribe of Judah, which interbred with several Canaanite clans, though some of these soon became extinct.

38, 5: *Chezib:* a variant form of Achzib (Jos 15, 44; Mi 1, 14), a town in the Judean Shephelah.

38, 8: *Preserve your brother's line:* literally, "raise up seed for your brother." The ancient Israelites regarded as very important their law of levirate, or "brother-in-law" marriage; see notes on Dt 25, 5;

Ru 2, 20. In the present story, it is primarily Onan's violation of this law, rather than the means he used to circumvent it, that brought on him God's displeasure (vv 9f).

38, 18: *Seal and cord:* the cylinder seal, through which a hole was bored lengthwise so that it could be worn from the neck by a cord, was a distinctive means of identification. Apparently a man's staff was also marked with his name (Nm 17, 16f) or other sign of identification.

37, 35: Gn 42, 38.
37, 36: Ps 105, 17.
38, 2: 1 Chr 2, 3.
38, 5: 1 Chr 4, 21.

38, 7: 1 Chr 2, 3.
38, 8: Dt 25, 5; Mt 22, 24;
　　Mk 12, 19; Lk 20, 28.
38, 14: Prv 7, 10.

GN

with her, and she conceived by him. [19] When she went away, she took off her shawl and put on her widow's garb again.

[20] Judah sent the kid by his friend the Adullamite to recover the pledge from the woman; but he could not find her. [21]† So he asked the men of the place, "Where is the temple prostitute, the one by the roadside in Enaim?" But they answered, "There has never been a temple prostitute here." [22] He went back to Judah and told him, "I could not find her; and besides, the men of the place said there was no temple prostitute there." [23] "Let her keep the things," Judah replied; "otherwise we shall become a laughingstock. After all, I did send her the kid, even though you were unable to find her."

[24] About three months later, Judah was told that his daughter-in-law Tamar had played the harlot and was then with child from her harlotry. "Bring her out," cried Judah; "she shall be burned." [25] But as they were bringing her out, she sent word to her father-in-law, "It is by the man to whom these things belong that I am with child. Please verify," she added, "whose seal and cord and whose staff these are." [26] Judah recognized them and said, "She is more in the right than I am, since I did not give her to my son Shelah." But he had no further relations with her.

[27]* When the time of her delivery came, she was found to have twins in her womb. [28] While she was giving birth, one infant put out his hand; and the midwife, taking a crimson thread, tied it on his hand, to note that this one came out first. [29]*† But as he withdrew his hand, his brother came out; and she said, "What a breach you have made for yourself!" So he was called Perez. [30]*† Afterward his brother came out; he was called Zerah.

Joseph's Temptation

39 [1]† When Joseph was taken down to Egypt, a certain Egyptian (Potiphar, a courtier of Pharaoh and his chief steward) bought him from the Ishmaelites who had brought him there. [2]* But since the LORD was with him, Joseph got on very well and was assigned to the household of his Egyptian master. [3] When his master saw that the LORD was with him and brought him success in

whatever he did, [4]* he took a liking to Joseph and made him his personal attendant; he put him in charge of his household and entrusted to him all his possessions. [5] From the moment that he put him in charge of his household and all his possessions, the LORD blessed the Egyptian's house for Joseph's sake; in fact, the LORD's blessing was on everything he owned, both inside the house and out. [6] Having left everything he owned in Joseph's charge, he gave no thought, with Joseph there, to anything but the food he ate.

Now Joseph was strikingly handsome in countenance and body. [7] After a time, his master's wife began to look fondly at him and said, "Lie with me." [8] But he refused. "As long as I am here," he told her, "my master does not concern himself with anything in the house, but has entrusted to me all he owns. [9] He wields no more authority in this house than I do, and he has withheld from me nothing but yourself, since you are his wife. How, then, could I commit so great a wrong and thus stand condemned before God?" [10]* Although she tried to entice him day after day, he would not agree to lie beside her, or even stay near her.

[11] One such day, when Joseph came into the house to do his work, and none of the household servants were then in the house, [12] she laid hold of him by his cloak, saying, "Lie with me!" But leaving the cloak in her hand, he got away from her and ran outside. [13] When she saw that he had left his cloak in her hand as he fled outside, [14] she screamed for her household servants and told them, "Look! My husband has brought in a Hebrew slave to make sport of us! He came in here to lie with me, but I cried out as loud as I could. [15] When he heard me scream for help, he left his cloak beside me and ran away outside."

[16] She kept the cloak with her until his master came home. [17] Then she told him the same story: "The Hebrew slave whom you brought here broke in on me, to make sport of me. [18] But when I screamed for help, he left his cloak beside me and fled outside." [19] As soon as the master heard his wife's story about how his slave had treated her, he became enraged. [20]* He seized Joseph and threw him into the jail where the royal prisoners were confined.

---

† **38, 21:** *Temple prostitute:* the Hebrew term *qedesha,* literally "consecrated woman," designates a woman who had ritual intercourse with men in pagan fertility rites; cf Dt 23, 18; Hos 4, 14, where the same Hebrew word is used. Hirah the Adullamite uses a word that refers to a higher social class than that designated by the term *zona,* common "harlot," used in vv 15.24.

38, 29: *He was called Perez:* the Hebrew word means "breach."

38, 30: *He was called Zerah:* a name connected here by popular etymology with a Hebrew verb for the red light of dawn, alluding apparently to the crimson thread.

39, 1: *(Potiphar . . . chief steward):* These words in the text serve to harmonize ch 39 from the Yahwist source, with Gn 37, 36, and

40, 1–23, from the Elohist. In the former, the Ishmaelites who bought Joseph from his brothers (Gn 37, 28) sold him to the unnamed "Egyptian master" of ch 39. In the latter, the Midianites who kidnaped Joseph (Gn 37, 28; 40, 15) sold him to Potiphar, Pharaoh's chief steward (Gn 37, 36), whose house was used as a royal prison (Gn 40, 2f).

---

*

38, 27: 1 Chr 2, 4.
38, 29: Rv 4, 12; Mt 1, 3; Lk 3, 33.
38, 30: Nm 26, 20; 1 Chr 2, 4; Mt 1, 3.
39, 2: 1 Sm 3, 19; 10, 7;

18, 14; 2 Sm 5, 10; 2 Kgs 18, 7; Acts 7, 9.
39, 4: Dn 1, 9.
39, 10: 1 Mc 2, 53.
39, 20: Ps 105, 18.

But even while he was in prison, [21]* the LORD remained with Joseph; he showed him kindness by making the chief jailer well-disposed toward him. [22] The chief jailer put Joseph in charge of all the prisoners in the jail, and everything that had to be done there was done under his management. [23] The chief jailer did not concern himself with anything at all that was in Joseph's charge, since the LORD was with him and brought success to all he did.

The Dreams Interpreted

40 [1] Some time afterward, the royal cupbearer and baker gave offense to their lord, the king of Egypt. [2] Pharaoh was angry with his two courtiers, the chief cupbearer and the chief baker, [3] and he put them in custody in the house of the chief steward (the same jail where Joseph was confined). [4] The chief steward assigned Joseph to them, and he became their attendant.

After they had been in custody for some time, [5] the cupbearer and the baker of the king of Egypt who were confined in the jail both had dreams on the same night, each dream with its own meaning. [6] When Joseph came to them in the morning, he noticed that they looked disturbed. [7] So he asked Pharaoh's courtiers who were with him in custody in his master's house, "Why do you look so sad today?" [8]* They answered him, "We have had dreams, but there is no one to interpret them for us." Joseph said to them, "Surely, interpretations come from God. Please tell the dreams to me."

[9] Then the chief cupbearer told Joseph his dream. "In my dream," he said, "I saw a vine in front of me, [10] and on the vine were three branches. It had barely budded when its blossoms came out, and its clusters ripened into grapes. [11] Pharaoh's cup was in my hand; so I took the grapes, pressed them out into his cup, and put it in Pharaoh's hand." [12] Joseph said to him: "This is what it means. The three branches are three days; [13]† within three days Pharaoh will lift up your head and restore you to your post. You will be handing Pharaoh his cup as you formerly used to do when you were his cupbearer. [14] So if you will still remember, when all is well with you, that I was here with you, please do me the favor of mentioning me to Pharaoh, to get me out of this place. [15] The truth is that I was kidnaped from the land of the Hebrews, and here I have not done anything for which I should have been put into a dungeon."

[16] When the chief baker saw that Joseph had given this favorable interpretation, he said to him: "I

too had a dream. In it I had three wicker baskets on my head; [17] in the top one were all kinds of bakery products for Pharaoh, but the birds were pecking at them out of the basket on my head." [18] Joseph said to him in reply: "This is what it means. The three baskets are three days; [19] within three days Pharaoh will lift up your head and have you impaled on a stake, and the birds will be pecking the flesh from your body."

[20] And in fact, on the third day, which was Pharaoh's birthday, when he gave a banquet to all his staff, with his courtiers around him, he lifted up the heads of the chief cupbearer and chief baker. [21] He restored the chief cupbearer to his office, so that he again handed the cup to Pharaoh; [22] but the chief baker he impaled—just as Joseph had told them in his interpretation. [23] Yet the chief cupbearer gave no thought to Joseph; he had forgotten him.

Pharaoh's Dream

41 [1] After a lapse of two years, Pharaoh had a dream. He saw himself standing by the Nile, [2] when up out of the Nile came seven cows, handsome and fat; they grazed in the reed grass. [3] Behind them seven other cows, ugly and gaunt, came up out of the Nile; and standing on the bank of the Nile beside the others, [4] the ugly, gaunt cows ate up the seven handsome, fat cows. Then Pharaoh woke up.

[5] He fell asleep again and had another dream. He saw seven ears of grain, fat and healthy, growing on a single stalk. [6] Behind them sprouted seven ears of grain, thin and blasted by the east wind; [7] and the seven thin ears swallowed up the seven fat, healthy ears. Then Pharaoh woke up, to find it was only a dream.

[8] Next morning his spirit was agitated. So he summoned all the magicians and sages of Egypt and recounted his dreams to them; but no one could interpret his dreams for him. [9] Then the chief cupbearer spoke up and said to Pharaoh: "On this occasion I am reminded of my negligence. [10] Once, when Pharaoh was angry, he put me and the chief baker in custody in the house of the chief steward. [11] Later, we both had dreams on the same night, and each of our dreams had its own meaning. [12]* There with us was a Hebrew youth, a slave of the chief steward; and when we told him our dreams, he interpreted them for us and explained for each of us the meaning of his dream. [13] And it turned out just as he had told us: I was restored to my post, but the other man was impaled."

40, 13: *Lift up your head:* signifying "pardon you." In v 19 "to lift up the head" means "to behead"; and finally, in v 20, the same expression means "to review the case (of someone)." Joseph couches his interpretation of the dreams in equivocal terms.

39, 21: Acts 7, 9f.   **41, 12:** Dn 1, 17.
40, 8: Gn 41, 16.

14* Pharaoh therefore had Joseph summoned, and they hurriedly brought him from the dungeon. After he shaved and changed his clothes, he came into Pharaoh's presence. 15 Pharaoh then said to him: "I had certain dreams that no one can interpret. But I hear it said of you that the moment you are told a dream you can interpret it." 16* "It is not I," Joseph replied to Pharaoh, "but God who will give Pharaoh the right answer."

17 Then Pharaoh said to Joseph: "In my dream, I was standing on the bank of the Nile, 18 when up from the Nile came seven cows, fat and well-formed; they grazed in the reed grass. 19 Behind them came seven other cows, scrawny, most ill-formed and gaunt. Never have I seen such ugly specimens as these in all the land of Egypt! 20 The gaunt, ugly cows ate up the first seven fat cows. 21 But when they had consumed them, no one could tell that they had done so, because they looked as ugly as before. Then I woke up. 22 In another dream, I saw seven ears of grain, fat and healthy, growing on a single stalk. 23 Behind them sprouted seven ears of grain, shriveled and thin and blasted by the east wind; 24 and the seven thin ears swallowed up the seven healthy ears. I have spoken to the magicians, but none of them can give me an explanation."

25 Joseph said to Pharaoh: "Both of Pharaoh's dreams have the same meaning. God has thus foretold to Pharaoh what he is about to do. 26 The seven healthy cows are seven years, and the seven healthy ears are seven years—the same in each dream. 27 So also, the seven thin, ugly cows that came up after them are seven years, as are the seven thin, wind-blasted ears; they are seven years of famine. 28 It is just as I told Pharaoh: God has revealed to Pharaoh what he is about to do. 29 Seven years of great abundance are now coming throughout the land of Egypt; 30 but these will be followed by seven years of famine, when all the abundance in the land of Egypt will be forgotten. When the famine has ravaged the land, 31 no trace of the abundance will be found in the land because of the famine that follows it—so utterly severe will that famine be. 32 That Pharaoh had the same dream twice means that the matter has been reaffirmed by God and that God will soon bring it about.

33 "Therefore, let Pharaoh seek out a wise and discerning man and put him in charge of the land of Egypt. 34 Pharaoh should also take action to appoint overseers, so as to regiment the land during the seven years of abundance. 35 They should hus-

did you KNOW?

Dreams

In the ancient world, belief in the reality and significance of dreams was widespread. The ancients believed that dreams and visions revealed messages, prophecies, and healing from their gods. Israel shared this view of the importance of dreams. Joseph is described as an interpreter of dreams, and this skill earns him Pharaoh's respect (Gn 41, 37–45), as well as his brothers' jealousy (37, 5–11).

In the Old Testament, the prophets are often referred to as seers because the word of God so often comes to them through dreams and visions. The focus, however, is always on the word of God and its meaning, not on the dream itself. In fact, God usually gives a character in the story the interpretation of the dream, which aims to lead the people to more faithful observance of the covenant. If the dream does not do this, it is to be considered a false dream. (See other references to dreams in Gn 28, 10–22; Dt 13, 2–6; Sir 34, 1–4; Jer 27, 9–10; 29, 8–9; Jl 3, 1; Zec 1, 8; Mt 1, 20; 2, 13.)

▸ Gn 37, 1–11; 40, 1—41, 36

band all the food of the coming good years, collecting the grain under Pharaoh's authority, to be stored in the towns for food. 36 This food will serve as a reserve for the country against the seven years of famine that are to follow in the land of Egypt, so that the land may not perish in the famine."

37* This advice pleased Pharaoh and all his officials. 38 "Could we find another like him," Pharaoh asked his officials, "a man so endowed with the spirit of God?" 39 So Pharaoh said to Joseph: "Since God has made all this known to you, no one can be as wise and discerning as you are. 40* You shall be in charge of my palace, and all my people shall dart at your command. Only in respect to the throne shall I outrank you. 41 Herewith," Pharaoh told Joseph, "I place you in charge of the whole land of Egypt." 42† With

---

† **41, 42**: *Signet ring*: a finger ring in which was set a stamp seal, different from the cylinder seal such as Judah wore; see note on Gn 38, 18. This is an authentic detail. By receiving Pharaoh's signet ring, Joseph was made vizier of Egypt (v 43); the vizier was known as "seal-bearer of the king of Lower Egypt." Another authentic detail is the *gold chain*, a symbol of high office in ancient Egypt.

* 41, 14: Ps 105, 20.   41, 40: Ps 105, 21; Wis 10,
41, 16: Gn 40, 8.   14; 1 Mc 2, 53; Acts 7,
41, 37: Acts 7, 10.   10.

that, Pharaoh took off his signet ring and put it on Joseph's finger. He had him dressed in robes of fine linen and put a gold chain about his neck. 43† He then had him ride in the chariot of his vizier, and they shouted "Abrek!" before him.

Thus was Joseph installed over the whole land of Egypt. 44 "I, Pharaoh, proclaim," he told Joseph, "that without your approval no one shall move hand or foot in all the land of Egypt." 45† Pharaoh also bestowed the name of Zaphenath-paneah on Joseph, and he gave him in marriage Asenath, the daughter of Potiphera, priest of Heliopolis. 46 Joseph was thirty years old when he entered the service of Pharaoh, king of Egypt.

After Joseph left Pharaoh's presence, he traveled throughout the land of Egypt. 47 During the seven years of plenty, when the land produced abundant crops, 48 he husbanded all the food of these years of plenty that the land of Egypt was enjoying and stored it in the towns, placing in each town the crops of the fields around it. 49 Joseph garnered grain in quantities like the sands of the sea, so vast that at last he stopped measuring it, for it was beyond measure.

50* Before the famine years set in, Joseph became the father of two sons, born to him by Asenath, daughter of Potiphera, priest of Heliopolis. 51† He named his first-born Manasseh, meaning, "God has made me forget entirely the sufferings I endured at the hands of my family"; 52† and the second he named Ephraim, meaning, "God has made me fruitful in the land of my affliction."

53 When the seven years of abundance enjoyed by the land of Egypt came to an end, 54* the seven years of famine set in, just as Joseph had predicted. Although there was famine in all the other countries, food was available throughout the land of Egypt. 55 When hunger came to be felt throughout the land of Egypt and the people cried to Pharaoh for bread, Pharaoh directed all the Egyptians to go to Joseph and do whatever he told them. 56 When the famine had spread throughout the land, Joseph opened all the cities that had grain and rationed it to the Egyptians, since the famine had gripped the land of Egypt. 57 In fact, all the world came to Joseph to obtain rations of grain, for famine had gripped the whole world.

The Brothers' First Journey to Egypt

42 1 When Jacob learned that grain rations were available in Egypt, he said to his sons: "Why do you keep gaping at one another? 2* I hear," he went on, "that rations of grain are available in Egypt. Go down there and buy some for us, that we may stay alive rather than die of hunger." 3 So ten of Joseph's brothers went down to buy an emergency supply of grain from Egypt. 4 It was only Joseph's full brother Benjamin that Jacob did not send with the rest, for he thought some disaster might befall him. 5* Thus, since there was famine in the land of Canaan also, the sons of Israel were among those who came to procure rations.

6* It was Joseph, as governor of the country, who dispensed the rations to all the people. When Joseph's brothers came and knelt down before him with their faces to the ground, 7 he recognized them as soon as he saw them. But he concealed his own identity from them and spoke sternly to them. "Where do you come from?" he asked them. They answered, "From the land of Canaan, to procure food."

8 When Joseph recognized his brothers, although they did not recognize him, 9*† he was reminded of the dreams he had about them. He said to them: "You are spies. You have come to see the nakedness of the land." 10 "No, my lord," they replied. "On the contrary, your servants have come to procure food. 11 All of us are sons of the same man. We are honest men; your servants have never been spies." 12 But he answered them: "Not so! You have come to see the nakedness of the land." 13* "We your servants," they said, "were twelve brothers, sons of a certain man in Canaan; but the youngest one is at present with our father, and the other one is gone." 14 "It is just as I said," Joseph persisted; "you are spies. 15 This is how you shall be tested: unless your youngest brother comes here, I swear by the life of Pharaoh that you shall not leave here. 16 So send one of your number to get your brother, while the rest of you stay here under arrest. Thus shall your words be tested for their truth; if they are untrue, as Pharaoh lives, you are spies!" 17 With that, he locked them up in the guardhouse for three days.

18 On the third day Joseph said to them: "Do this, and you shall live; for I am a God-fearing man. 19 If

---

41, 43: *Abrek:* apparently a cry of homage, though the word's derivation and actual meaning are uncertain.

41, 45: *Zaphenath-paneah:* a Hebrew transcription of an Egyptian name meaning "the god speaks and he (the new-born child) lives." *Asenath:* means "belonging to (the Egyptian goddess) Neith." *Potiphera:* means "he whom Ra (the Egyptian god) gave"; a shorter form of the same name was borne by Joseph's master (Gn 37, 36). *Heliopolis:* in Hebrew, *On,* a city seven miles northeast of modern Cairo, site of the chief temple of the sun god; it is mentioned also in v 50; Gn 46, 20; Ez 30, 17.

41, 51: *Manasseh:* allusion to this name is in the Hebrew expression, *nishshani,* "he made me forget."

41, 52: *Ephraim:* related to the Hebrew expression *hiphrani,* "(God) has made me fruitful."

42, 9.12: *The nakedness of the land:* the military weakness of the land, like human nakedness, should not be seen by strangers.

41, 50: Gn 46, 20; 48, 5.

41, 54: Ps 105, 16; Acts 7, 11.

42, 2: Acts 7, 12.

42, 5: Jdt 5, 10; Acts 7, 11.

42, 6: Ps 105, 21.

42, 9: Gn 37, 5.

42, 13: Gn 44, 20.

you have been honest, only one of your brothers need be confined in this prison, while the rest of you may go and take home provisions for your starving families. 20* But you must come back to me with your youngest brother. Your words will thus be verified, and you will not die." To this they agreed. 21* To one another, however, they said: "Alas, we are being punished because of our brother. We saw the anguish of his heart when he pleaded with us, yet we paid no heed; that is why this anguish has now come upon us." 22* "Didn't I tell you," broke in Reuben, "not to do wrong to the boy? But you wouldn't listen! Now comes the reckoning for his blood." 23 They did not know, of course, that Joseph understood what they said, since he spoke with them through an interpreter. 24 But turning away from them, he wept. When he was able to speak to them again, he had Simeon taken from them and bound before their eyes. 25 Then Joseph gave orders to have their containers filled with grain, their money replaced in each one's sack, and provisions given them for their journey. After this had been done for them, 26 they loaded their donkeys with the rations and departed.

27† At the night encampment, when one of them opened his bag to give his donkey some fodder, he was surprised to see his money in the mouth of his bag. 28 "My money has been returned!" he cried out to his brothers. "Here it is in my bag!" At that their hearts sank. Trembling, they asked one another, "What is this that God has done to us?"

29 When they got back to their father Jacob in the land of Canaan, they told him all that had happened to them. 30 "The man who is lord of the country," they said, "spoke to us sternly and put us in custody as if we were spying on the land. 31 But we said to him: 'We are honest men; we have never been spies. 32 There were twelve of us brothers, sons of the same father; but one is gone, and the youngest one is at present with our father in the land of Canaan.' 33 Then the man who is lord of the country said to us: 'This is how I shall know if you are honest men: leave one of your brothers with me, while the rest of you go home with rations for your starving families. 34 When you come back to me with your youngest brother, and I know that you are honest men and not spies, I will restore your brother to you, and you may move about freely in the land.' "

35 When they were emptying their sacks, there in each one's sack was his moneybag! At the sight of their moneybags, they and their father were dismayed. 36 Their father Jacob said to them: "Must you make me childless? Joseph is gone, and Simeon is gone, and now you would take away Benjamin! Why must such things always happen to me!" 37 Then Reuben told his father: "Put him in my care, and I will bring him back to you. You may kill my own two sons if I do not return him to you." 38* But Jacob replied: "My son shall not go down with you. Now that his full brother is dead, he is the only one left. If some disaster should befall him on the journey you must make, you would send my white head down to the nether world in grief."

The Second Journey to Egypt

43 1† Now the famine in the land grew more severe. 2 So when they had used up all the rations they had brought from Egypt, their father said to them, "Go back and procure us a little more food." 3* But Judah replied: "The man strictly warned us, 'You shall not appear in my presence unless your brother is with you.' 4 If you are willing to let our brother go with us, we will go down to procure food for you. 5* But if you are not willing, we will not go down, because the man told us, 'You shall not appear in my presence unless your brother is with you.' " 6 Israel demanded, "Why did you bring this trouble on me by telling the man that you had another brother?" 7 They answered: "The man kept asking about ourselves and our family: 'Is your father still living? Do you have another brother?' We had to answer his questions. How could we know that he would say, 'Bring your brother down here'?"

8* Then Judah urged his father Israel: "Let the boy go with me, that we may be off and on our way if you and we and our children are to keep from starving to death. 9* I myself will stand surety for him. You can hold me responsible for him. If I fail to bring him back, to set him in your presence, you can hold it against me forever. 10 Had we not dilly-dallied, we could have been there and back twice by now!"

11* Their father Israel then told them: "If it must be so, then do this: Put some of the land's best products in your baggage and take them down to the man as gifts: some balm and honey, gum and resin, and pistachios and almonds. 12 Also take extra money along, for you must return the amount

---
42, 27–28: These two verses are from the Yahwist source, whereas the rest of the chapter is from the Elohist source, in which the men find the money in their sacks (not "bags"—a different Hebrew word) only when they arrive home (v 35); cf Gn 43, 21.

43, 1–34: This chapter and the following one are from the Yahwist source, in which Judah, not Reuben as in the Elohist source, volunteers to go surety for Benjamin.

42, 20: Gn 43, 5.
42, 21: Gn 37, 18–27.
42, 22: Gn 37, 22.
42, 38: Gn 37, 35.
43, 3: Gn 44, 23.

43, 5: Gn 42, 20.
43, 8: Gn 42, 37.
43, 9: Gn 44, 32.
43, 11: Gn 45, 23.

that was put back in the mouths of your bags; it may have been a mistake. [13] Take your brother, too, and be off on your way back to the man. [14] May God Almighty dispose the man to be merciful toward you, so that he may let your other brother go, as well as Benjamin. As for me, if I am to suffer bereavement, I shall suffer it."

[15] So the men got the gifts, took double the amount of money with them, and, accompanied by Benjamin, were off on their way down to Egypt to present themselves to Joseph. [16] When Joseph saw Benjamin with them, he told his head steward, "Take these men into the house, and have an animal slaughtered and prepared, for they are to dine with me at noon." [17] Doing as Joseph had ordered, the steward conducted the men to Joseph's house. [18] But on being led to his house, they became apprehensive. "It must be," they thought, "on account of the money put back in our bags the first time, that we are taken inside; they want to use it as a pretext to attack us and take our donkeys and seize us as slaves." [19] So they went up to Joseph's head steward and talked to him at the entrance of the house. [20]* "If you please, sir," they said, "we came down here once before to procure food. [21]* But when we arrived at a night's encampment and opened our bags, there was each man's money in the mouth of his bag—our money in the full amount! We have now brought it back. [22] We have brought other money to procure food with. We do not know who put the first money in our bags." [23] "Be at ease," he replied; "you have no need to fear. Your God and the God of your father must have put treasures in your bags for you. As for your money, I received it." With that, he led Simeon out to them.

[24] The steward then brought the men inside Joseph's house. He gave them water to bathe their feet, and got fodder for their donkeys. [25] Then they set out their gifts to await Joseph's arrival at noon, for they had heard that they were to dine there. [26] When Joseph came home, they presented him with the gifts they had brought inside, while they bowed down before him to the ground. [27]* After inquiring how they were, he asked them, "And how is your aged father, of whom you spoke? Is he still in good health?" [28] "Your servant our father is thriving and still in good health," they said, as they bowed respectfully. [29]* When Joseph's eye fell on his full

brother Benjamin, he asked, "Is this your youngest brother, of whom you told me?" Then he said to him, "May God be gracious to you, my boy!" [30] With that, Joseph had to hurry out, for he was so overcome with affection for his brother that he was on the verge of tears. He went into a private room and wept there.

[31] After washing his face, he reappeared and, now in control of himself, gave the order, "Serve the meal." [32]† It was served separately to him, to the brothers, and to the Egyptians who partook of his board. (Egyptians may not eat with Hebrews; that is abhorrent to them.) [33] When they were seated by his directions according to their age, from the oldest to the youngest, they looked at one another in amazement; [34]† and as portions were brought to them from Joseph's table, Benjamin's portion was five times as large as anyone else's. So they drank freely and made merry with him.

Final Test

44

[1]† Then Joseph gave his head steward these instructions: "Fill the men's bags with as much food as they can carry, and put each man's money in the mouth of his bag. [2] In the mouth of the youngest one's bag put also my silver goblet, together with the money for his rations." The steward carried out Joseph's instructions. [3] At daybreak the men and their donkeys were sent off. [4] They had not gone far out of the city when Joseph said to his head steward: "Go at once after the men! When you overtake them, say to them, 'Why did you repay good with evil? Why did you steal the silver goblet from me? [5]† It is the very one from which my master drinks and which he uses for divination. What you have done is wrong.' "

[6] When the steward overtook them and repeated these words to them, [7] they remonstrated with him: "How can my lord say such things? Far be it from your servants to do such a thing! [8] We even brought back to you from the land of Canaan the money that we found in the mouths of our bags. Why, then, would we steal silver or gold from your master's house? [9] If any of your servants is found to have the goblet, he shall die, and as for the rest of us, we shall become my lord's slaves." [10] But he replied, "Even though it ought to be as you propose, only the one who is found to have it shall become my slave, and the rest of you shall be exonerated."

43, 32: *Separately to him:* that Joseph did not eat with the other Egyptians was apparently a matter of rank.

43, 34: *Five times as large as:* probably an idiomatic expression for "much larger than."

44, 1f: Replacement of the money in the men's bags is probably a redactional addition here, taken from the Yahwist account of the first visit. It is only the goblet in Benjamin's bag, not any replaced money, that plays a part in the rest of the chapter.

44, 5: *Divination:* seeking omens through liquids poured into a cup or bowl was a common practice in the ancient Near East; cf v 15. Even though divination was frowned on in later Israel (Lv 19, 31), it is in this place an authentic touch which the sacred author does not hesitate to ascribe to Joseph, the wisest man in Egypt.

43, 20: Gn 42, 3.
43, 21: Gn 42, 27f.
43, 27: Tb 7, 4.
43, 29: Gn 42, 13.

11 Then each of them eagerly lowered his bag to the ground and opened it; 12 and when a search was made, starting with the oldest and ending with the youngest, the goblet turned up in Benjamin's bag. 13 At this, they tore their clothes. Then, when each man had reloaded his donkey, they returned to the city.

14 As Judah and his brothers reentered Joseph's house, he was still there; so they flung themselves on the ground before him. 15 "How could you do such a thing?" Joseph asked them. "You should have known that such a man as I could discover by divination what happened." 16† Judah replied: "What can we say to my lord? How can we plead or how try to prove our innocence? God has uncovered your servants' guilt. Here we are, then, the slaves of my lord—the rest of us no less than the one in whose possession the goblet was found." 17 "Far be it from me to act thus!" said Joseph. "Only the one in whose possession the goblet was found shall become my slave; the rest of you may go back safe and sound to your father."

18 Judah then stepped up to him and said: "I beg you, my lord, let your servant speak earnestly to my lord, and do not become angry with your servant, for you are the equal of Pharaoh. 19† My lord asked your servants, 'Have you a father, or another brother?' 20* So we said to my lord, 'We have an aged father, and a young brother, the child of his old age. This one's full brother is dead, and since he is the only one by that mother who is left, his father dotes on him.' 21 Then you told your servants, 'Bring him down to me that my eyes may look on him.' 22 We replied to my lord, 'The boy cannot leave his father; his father would die if he were to leave him.' 23* But you told your servants, 'Unless your youngest brother comes back with you, you shall not come into my presence again.' 24 When we returned to your servant our father, we reported to him the words of my lord.

25 "Later, our father told us to come back and buy some food for the family. 26 So we reminded him, 'We cannot go down there; only if our youngest brother is with us can we go, for we may not see the man if our youngest brother is not with us.' 27 Then your servant our father said to us, 'As you know, my wife bore me two sons. 28* One of them, however, disappeared, and I had to conclude that he must

have been torn to pieces by wild beasts; I have not seen him since. 29 If you now take this one away from me, too, and some disaster befalls him, you will send my white head down to the nether world in grief.'

30 "If then the boy is not with us when I go back to your servant my father, whose very life is bound up with his, he will die as soon as he sees that the boy is missing; 31 and your servants will thus send the white head of our father down to the nether world in grief. 32* Besides, I, your servant, got the boy from his father by going surety for him, saying, 'If I fail to bring him back to you, father, you can hold it against me forever.' 33 Let me, your servant, therefore, remain in place of the boy as the slave of my lord, and let the boy go back with his brothers. 34 How could I go back to my father if the boy were not with me? I could not bear to see the anguish that would overcome my father."

The Truth Revealed

45 1 Joseph could no longer control himself in the presence of all his attendants, so he cried out, "Have everyone withdraw from me!" Thus no one else was about when he made himself known to his brothers. 2 But his sobs were so loud that the Egyptians heard him, and so the news reached Pharaoh's palace. 3* "I am Joseph," he said to his brothers. "Is my father still in good health?" But his brothers could give him no answer, so dumbfounded were they at him.

4 "Come closer to me," he told his brothers. When they had done so, he said: "I am your brother Joseph, whom you once sold into Egypt. 5* But now do not be distressed, and do not reproach yourselves for having sold me here. It was really for the sake of saving lives that God sent me here ahead of you. 6 For two years now the famine has been in the land, and for five more years tillage will yield no harvest. 7 God, therefore, sent me on ahead of you to ensure for you a remnant on earth and to save your lives in an extraordinary deliverance. 8† So it was not really you but God who had me come here; and he has made of me a father to Pharaoh, lord of all his household, and ruler over the whole land of Egypt.

9*† "Hurry back, then, to my father and tell him: 'Thus says your son Joseph: God has made me lord

---

44, 16: *Guilt:* in trying to do away with Joseph when he was young.
44, 19: *My lord . . . your servants:* such frequently repeated expressions in Judah's speech show the formal court style used by a subject in speaking to a high official.
45, 8: *Father to Pharaoh:* a term applied to a vizier in ancient Egypt.
45, 9–15: In these verses, as in Gn 46, 31—47, 5a, all from the Yahwist source, Joseph in his own name invites his father and broth-

ers to come to Egypt. Only after their arrival is Pharaoh informed of the fact. On the other hand, in 45, 16–20, from the Elohist source, it is Pharaoh himself who invites Joseph's kinsmen to migrate to his domain.

44, 20: Gn 42, 13.
44, 23: Gn 43, 3.
44, 28: Gn 37, 20.33.
44, 32: Gn 43, 9.

45, 3f: Acts 7, 13.
45, 5: Gn 50, 20; Sir 49, 15.
45, 9: Acts 7, 14.

LIVE IT!

God's Master Plan

After Joseph's tearful reconciliation with his brothers, he tells them that their past treatment of him enabled him to save them from the famine. Because he ended up in Egypt and rose to power, he can now invite them to stay as guests of the pharaoh.

Joseph realizes that good has come out of an evil act. He sees the events of his family's life as part of God's plan to preserve life and to make sure that the covenant continues. Joseph's insight does not justify what his brothers did, but it does help us realize that good can come out of a tragic event. It is often hard for us to understand why something bad is happening, but as time passes, we often gain perspective and insight. These are the rewards of trust and faith. Joseph remained faithful, despite many difficulties. Let us strive to do the same, assured that not even human sinfulness can thwart God's saving plans.

When have you experienced good things coming out of a bad situation? Has it ever seemed like God has upset part of your life, only to result in something better than you expected?

▶ Gn 45, 5–8

of all Egypt; come to me without delay. 10† You will settle in the region of Goshen, where you will be near me—you and your children and grandchildren, your flocks and herds, and everything that you own. 11 Since five years of famine still lie ahead, I will provide for you there, so that you and your family and all that are yours may not suffer want.' 12 Surely, you can see for yourselves, and Benjamin can see for himself, that it is I, Joseph, who am speaking to you. 13 Tell my father all about my high position in Egypt and what you have seen. But hurry and bring my father down here." 14 Thereupon he flung himself on the neck of his brother Benjamin and wept, and Benjamin wept in his arms. 15 Joseph then kissed all his brothers, crying over each of them; and only then were his brothers able to talk with him.

16 When the news reached Pharaoh's palace that Joseph's brothers had come, Pharaoh and his courtiers were pleased. 17 So Pharaoh told Joseph: "Say to your brothers: 'This is what you shall do: Load up your animals and go without delay to the land of Canaan. 18* There get your father and your families, and then come back here to me; I will assign you the best land in Egypt, where you will live off the fat of the land.' 19 Instruct them further: 'Do this. Take wagons from the land of Egypt for your children and your wives and to transport your father on your way back here. 20 Do not be concerned about your belongings, for the best in the whole land of Egypt shall be yours.' "

21 The sons of Israel acted accordingly. Joseph gave them the wagons, as Pharaoh had ordered, and he supplied them with provisions for the journey. 22 He also gave to each of them fresh clothing, but to Benjamin he gave three hundred shekels of silver and five sets of garments. 23 Moreover, what he sent to his father was ten jackasses loaded with the finest products of Egypt and ten jennies loaded with grain and bread and other provisions for his journey. 24 As he sent his brothers on their way, he told them, "Let there be no recriminations on the way."

25 So they left Egypt and made their way to their father Jacob in the land of Canaan. 26 When they told him, "Joseph is still alive—in fact, it is he who is ruler of all the land of Egypt," he was dumbfounded; he could not believe them. 27 But when they recounted to him all that Joseph had told them, and when he saw the wagons that Joseph had sent for his transport, the spirit of their father Jacob revived. 28 "It is enough," said Israel. "My son Joseph is still alive! I must go and see him before I die."

Migration to Egypt

46 1 Israel set out with all that was his. When he arrived at Beer-sheba, he offered sacrifices to the God of his father Isaac. 2 There God, speaking to Israel in a vision by night, called, "Jacob! Jacob!" "Here I am," he answered. 3† Then he said: "I am God, the God of your father. Do not be afraid to go down to Egypt, for there I

45, 10: *The region of Goshen:* modern Wadi Tumilat in the eastern part of the Nile Delta.
46, 3: *I am God:* more precisely according to the Hebrew text, "I am El." "El" is here a divine name, not the common noun "god."

45, 18: Acts 7, 14.

GN

will make you a great nation. ⁴ Not only will I go down to Egypt with you; I will also bring you back here, after Joseph has closed your eyes."

⁵ So Jacob departed from Beer-sheba, and the sons of Israel put their father and their wives and children on the wagons that Pharaoh had sent for his transport. ⁶* They took with them their livestock and the possessions they had acquired in the land of Canaan. Thus Jacob and all his descendants migrated to Egypt. ⁷ His sons and his grandsons, his daughters and his granddaughters—all his descendants—he took with him to Egypt.

⁸* These are the names of the Israelites, Jacob and his descendants, who migrated to Egypt.

Reuben, Jacob's first-born, ⁹*† and the sons of Reuben: Hanoch, Pallu, Hezron and Carmi. ¹⁰* The sons of Simeon: Nemuel, Jamin, Ohad, Jachin, Zohar, and Shaul, son of a Canaanite woman. ¹¹* The sons of Levi: Gershon, Kohath and Merari. ¹²* The sons of Judah: Er, Onan, Shelah, Perez and Zerah—but Er and Onan had died in the land of Canaan; and the sons of Perez were Hezron and Hamul. ¹³* The sons of Issachar: Tola, Puah, Jashub and Shimron. ¹⁴* The sons of Zebulun: Sered, Elon and Jahleel. ¹⁵ These were the sons whom Leah bore to Jacob in Paddan-aram, along with his daughter Dinah—thirty-three persons in all, male and female.

¹⁶* The sons of Gad: Zephon, Haggi, Shuni, Ezbon, Eri, Arod and Areli. ¹⁷* The sons of Asher: Imnah, Ishvah, Ishvi and Beriah, with their sister Serah; and the sons of Beriah: Heber and Malchiel. ¹⁸ These were the descendants of Zilpah, whom Laban had given to his daughter Leah; these she bore to Jacob—sixteen persons in all.

¹⁹ The sons of Jacob's wife Rachel: Joseph and Benjamin. ²⁰* In the land of Egypt Joseph became the father of Manasseh and Ephraim, whom Asenath, daughter of Potiphera, priest of Heliopolis, bore to him. ²¹* The sons of Benjamin: Bela, Becher, Ashbel, Gera, Naaman, Ahiram, Shupham, Hupham and Ard. ²² These were the sons whom Rachel bore to Jacob—fourteen persons in all.

²³* The sons of Dan: Hushim. ²⁴* The sons of Naphtali: Jahzeel, Guni, Jezer and Shillem. ²⁵ These were the sons of Bilhah, whom Laban had given to his daughter Rachel; these she bore to Jacob—seven persons in all.

²⁶* Jacob's people who migrated to Egypt—his direct descendants, not counting the wives of Jacob's sons—numbered sixty-six persons in all. ²⁷*† Together with Joseph's sons who were born to him in Egypt—two persons—all the people comprising Jacob's family who had come to Egypt amounted to seventy persons in all.

²⁸ Israel had sent Judah ahead to Joseph, so that he might meet him in Goshen. On his arrival in the region of Goshen, ²⁹ Joseph hitched the horses to his chariot and rode to meet his father Israel in Goshen. As soon as he saw him, he flung himself on his neck and wept a long time in his arms. ³⁰ And Israel said to Joseph, "At last I can die, now that I have seen for myself that Joseph is still alive."

³¹ Joseph then said to his brothers and his father's household: "I will go and inform Pharaoh, telling him: 'My brothers and my father's household, whose home is in the land of Canaan, have come to me. ³² The men are shepherds, having long been keepers of livestock; and they have brought with them their flocks and herds, as well as everything else they own.' ³³ So when Pharaoh summons you and asks what your occupation is, ³⁴ you must answer, 'We your servants, like our ancestors, have been keepers of livestock from the beginning until now,' in order that you may stay in the region of Goshen, since all shepherds are abhorrent to the Egyptians."

Settlement in Goshen

47 ¹ Joseph went and told Pharaoh, "My father and my brothers have come from the land of Canaan, with their flocks and herds and everything else they own; and they are now in the region of Goshen." ² He then presented to Pharaoh five of his brothers whom he had selected from their full number. ³ When Pharaoh asked them what their occupation was, they answered, "We, your servants, like our ancestors, are shepherds. ⁴* We have come," they continued, "in order to stay in this country, for there is no pasture for your servants' flocks in the land of Canaan, so severe has the famine been there. Please, therefore, let your servants settle in the region of Goshen." ⁵ Pharaoh said to Joseph, "They may settle in the region of Goshen; and if you know any of them to be quali-

---

46, 9–27: This genealogical list has here been inserted by a redactor who bases it on the clan lists (Nm 1, 5–50) at the time of Moses. Therefore it includes some of Jacob's grandchildren, who would hardly have been born when Joseph was still a relatively young man. The number *fourteen* (v 22) is based on a garbled version of the genealogical list.

46, 27: *Seventy persons:* either to be understood as a round number, or arrived at by including Jacob and Joseph with the preceding persons, who add up to sixty-eight.

46, 6: Ex 1, 1; Jos 24, 4; Jdt 5, 10; Acts 7, 15.
46, 8: Ex 1, 2.
46, 9: Ex 6, 14; Nm 26, 5; 1 Chr 5, 3.
46, 10: Ex 6, 15; Nm 26, 12; 1 Chr 4, 24.
46, 11: Ex 6, 16; Nm 3, 17; 26, 57; 1 Chr 6, 1.
46, 12: Gn 38, 3–10.29f; Nm 26, 19; Rv 4, 18–22; 1 Chr 2, 5.
46, 13: Nm 26, 23f; 1 Chr 7, 1.
46, 14: Nm 26, 26.
46, 16: Nm 26, 15f.
46, 17: Nm 26, 44; 1 Chr 7, 30f.
46, 20: Gn 41, 50; Nm 26, 28. 35.
46, 21: Nm 26, 38; 1 Chr 7, 6; 8, 1–4.
46, 23: Nm 26, 42.
46, 24: Nm 26, 48f; 1 Chr 7, 13.
46, 26: Ex 1, 5.
46, 27: Ex 1, 5; Dt 10, 22; Acts 7, 14.
47, 4: Ex 23, 9; Dt 23, 8.

fied, you may put them in charge of my own livestock."

Thus, when Jacob and his sons came to Joseph in
Egypt, and Pharaoh, king of Egypt, heard about it,
Pharaoh said to Joseph, "Now that your father and
brothers have come to you, 6 the land of Egypt is at
your disposal; settle your father and brothers in the
pick of the land." 7 Then Joseph brought his father
Jacob and presented him to Pharaoh. After Jacob
had paid his respects to Pharaoh, 8 Pharaoh asked
him, "How many years have you lived?" 9† Jacob
replied: "The years I have lived as a wayfarer
amount to a hundred and thirty. Few and hard have
been these years of my life, and they do not compare with the years that my ancestors lived as wayfarers." 10 Then Jacob bade Pharaoh farewell and
withdrew from his presence.

11† As Pharaoh had ordered, Joseph settled his
father and brothers and gave them holdings in
Egypt on the pick of the land, in the region of
Rameses. 12 And Joseph sustained his father and
brothers and his father's whole household, down to
the youngest, with food.

Joseph's Land Policy

13 Since there was no food in any country because of the extreme severity of the famine, and the
lands of Egypt and Canaan were languishing from
hunger, 14 Joseph gathered in, as payment for the
rations that were being dispensed, all the money
that was to be found in Egypt and Canaan, and he
put it in Pharaoh's palace. 15 When all the money
in Egypt and Canaan was spent, all the Egyptians
came to Joseph, pleading, "Give us food or we shall
perish under your eyes; for our money is gone."
16 "Since your money is gone," replied Joseph,
"give me your livestock, and I will sell you bread in
return for your livestock." 17 So they brought their
livestock to Joseph, and he sold them food in return for their horses, their flocks of sheep and
herds of cattle, and their donkeys. Thus he got
them through that year with bread in exchange for
all their livestock. 18 When that year ended, they
came to him in the following one and said: "We
cannot hide from my lord that, with our money
spent and our livestock made over to my lord,
there is nothing left to put at my lord's disposal except our bodies and our farm land. 19 Why should
we and our land perish before your very eyes? Take
us and our land in exchange for food, and we will
become Pharaoh's slaves and our land his property; only give us seed, that we may survive and not
perish, and that our land may not turn into
a waste."

20 Thus Joseph acquired all the farm land of
Egypt for Pharaoh, since with the famine too much
for them to bear, every Egyptian sold his field; so
the land passed over to Pharaoh, 21 and the people
were reduced to slavery, from one end of Egypt's territory to the other. 22 Only the priests' lands Joseph
did not take over. Since the priests had a fixed allowance from Pharaoh and lived off the allowance
Pharaoh had granted them, they did not have to sell
their land.

23 Joseph told the people: "Now that I have acquired you and your land for Pharaoh, here is your
seed for sowing the land. 24 But when the harvest is
in, you must give a fifth of it to Pharaoh, while you
keep four-fifths as seed for your fields, and as food
for yourselves and your families [and as food for
your children]." 25 "You have saved our lives!" they
answered. "We are grateful to my lord that we can
be Pharaoh's slaves." 26 Thus Joseph made it a law
for the land in Egypt, which is still in force, that a
fifth of its produce should go to Pharaoh. Only the
land of the priests did not pass over to Pharaoh.

Jacob Blesses Ephraim and Manasseh

27* Thus Israel settled in the land of Egypt, in the
region of Goshen. There they acquired property,
were fertile, and increased greatly. 28 Jacob lived in
the land of Egypt for seventeen years; the span of
his life came to a hundred and forty-seven years.
29 When the time approached for Israel to die, he
called his son Joseph and said to him: "If you really wish to please me, put your hand under my thigh
as a sign of your constant loyalty to me; do not let
me be buried in Egypt. 30* When I lie down with
my ancestors, have me taken out of Egypt and
buried in their burial place." 31† "I will do as you
say," he replied. But his father demanded, "Swear it
to me!" So Joseph swore to him. Then Israel bowed
at the head of the bed.

48 1 Some time afterward, Joseph was informed, "Your father is failing." So he
took along with him his two sons, Manasseh and
Ephraim. 2 When Jacob was told, "Your son Joseph
has come to you," he rallied his strength and sat up
in bed.

---

† **47, 9:** *Wayfarer . . . wayfarers:* man is merely a sojourner on
earth; cf Ps 39, 13.
47, 11: *The region of Rameses:* same as the region of Goshen; see
note on Gn 45, 10. The name Rameses, however, is an anachronism,
since this royal name did not come into use before the end of the
fourteenth century B.C., long after the time of Joseph.
47, 31: *Israel bowed at the head of the bed:* meaning perhaps

that he gave a nod of assent and appreciation as he lay on his bed.
By reading with different vowels the Hebrew word for "bed," the
Greek version translated it as "staff," and understood the phrase to
mean that he bowed in worship, leaning on the top of his staff; it is
thus quoted in Heb 11, 21.

47, 27: Ex 1, 7.   47, 30: Gn 50, 5.

3*† Jacob then said to Joseph: "God Almighty appeared to me at Luz in the land of Canaan, and blessing me, ⁴ he said, 'I will make you fertile and numerous and raise you into an assembly of tribes, and I will give this land to your descendants after you as a permanent possession.' ⁵ Your two sons, therefore, who were born to you in the land of Egypt before I joined you here, shall be mine; Ephraim and Manasseh shall be mine as much as Reuben and Simeon are mine. ⁶ Progeny born to you after them shall remain yours; but their heritage shall be recorded in the names of their two brothers. ⁷*† I do this because, when I was returning from Paddan, your mother Rachel died, to my sorrow, during the journey in Canaan, while we were still a short distance from Ephrath; and I buried her there on the way to Ephrath [that is, Bethlehem]."

⁸ When Israel saw Joseph's sons, he asked, "Who are these?" ⁹ "They are my sons," Joseph answered his father, "whom God has given me here." "Bring them to me," said his father, "that I may bless them." ¹⁰ (Now Israel's eyes were dim from age, and he could not see well.) When Joseph brought his sons close to him, he kissed and embraced them. ¹¹ Then Israel said to Joseph, "I never expected to see your face again, and now God has allowed me to see your descendants as well!"

¹² Joseph removed them from his father's knees and bowed down before him with his face to the ground. ¹³ Then Joseph took the two, Ephraim with his right hand, to Israel's left, and Manasseh with his left hand, to Israel's right, and led them to him. ¹⁴ But Israel, crossing his hands, put out his right hand and laid it on the head of Ephraim, although he was the younger, and his left hand on the head of Manasseh, although he was the first-born. ¹⁵* Then he blessed them with these words:

"May the God in whose ways
   my fathers Abraham and Isaac walked,
The God who has been my shepherd
   from my birth to this day,
¹⁶ The Angel who has delivered me from
   all harm,
   bless these boys
That in them my name be recalled,

and the names of my fathers, Abraham
   and Isaac,
And they may become teeming multitudes
   upon the earth!"

¹⁷ When Joseph saw that his father had laid his right hand on Ephraim's head, this seemed wrong to him; so he took hold of his father's hand, to remove it from Ephraim's head to Manasseh's, ¹⁸ saying, "That is not right, father; the other one is the first-born; lay your right hand on his head!" ¹⁹ But his father resisted. "I know it, son," he said, "I know. That one too shall become a tribe, and he too shall be great. Nevertheless, his younger brother shall surpass him, and his descendants shall become a multitude of nations." ²⁰* So when he blessed them that day and said, "By you shall the people of Israel pronounce blessings; may they say, 'God make you like Ephraim and Manasseh,'" he placed Ephraim before Manasseh.

²¹ Then Israel said to Joseph: "I am about to die. But God will be with you and will restore you to the land of your fathers. ²²*† As for me, I give to you, as to the one above his brothers, Shechem, which I captured from the Amorites with my sword and bow."

Jacob's Testament

49 ¹ Jacob called his sons and said: "Gather around, that I may tell you what is to happen to you in days to come.

² "Assemble and listen, sons of Jacob,
    listen to Israel, your father.

³ "You, Reuben, my first-born,
    my strength and the first fruit of
    my manhood,
    excelling in rank and excelling in power!
⁴* Unruly as water, you shall no longer excel,
    for you climbed into your father's bed
    and defiled my couch to my sorrow.

⁵† "Simeon and Levi, brothers indeed,
    weapons of violence are their knives.
⁶* Let not my soul enter their council,
    or my spirit be joined with their company;

48, 3: *Luz:* an older name of Bethel (Gn 28, 19).

48, 7: Since her early death prevented Rachel from bearing more than two sons, Jacob feels justified in treating her two grandsons as if they were her own offspring.

48, 22: Both the meaning of the Hebrew and the historical reference in this verse are obscure. By taking the Hebrew word for Shechem as a common noun meaning shoulder or mountain slope, some translators render the verse, "I give you one portion more than your brothers, which I captured . . ." The reference may be to the capture of Shechem by the sons of Jacob (Gn 34, 24–29). Shechem

lay near the border separating the tribal territory of Manasseh from that of Ephraim (Jos 16, 4–9; 17, 1f.7).

49, 5: *Knives:* if this is the meaning of the obscure Hebrew word here, the reference may be to the knives used in circumcising the men of Shechem (Gn 34, 24; cf Jos 5, 2).

48, 3f: Gn 28, 12–15; 35, 6.	**48, 22:** Jos 17, 14.17f; Jn 4, 5.
48, 7: Gn 35, 19.	**49, 4:** Gn 35, 22; 1 Chr 5, 1f.
48, 15: Heb 11, 21.	**49, 6:** Gn 34, 25.
48, 20: Heb 11, 21.	

American

Assemble and Hear!

Genesis 49, 1–2 is the first reading at Mass on the ninth day before Christmas. This is an important day for Filipino Catholics because it marks the beginning of Simbang Gabi, or Dawn Worship.

On the nine days before Christmas, people gather to celebrate Mass in the dark of the predawn—usually between four and five o'clock in the morning. Mass ends with chocolate and buns and socializing. In fact, this is such a popular custom that even people who don't come to Mass all year will make it for the nine Masses of Simbang Gabi! It is a special celebration of thankfulness for the gift of their Catholic faith.

This Philippine tradition is an example of a Catholic custom called a novena. A novena is a public or private prayer repeated nine times. It can be a prayer said every day for nine days, one day a week for nine weeks, one day a month for nine months, or in any other pattern of nine. Why not make up your own personal novena? Just think of a prayer in a form you find meaningful (journaling, singing, reading the Scriptures, or even praying silently), and repeat it once a day for nine days or once a week for nine weeks. Happy praying!

▸ **Gn 49, 1–2**

For in their fury they slew men,
    in their willfulness they maimed oxen.
7 Cursed be their fury so fierce,
    and their rage so cruel!
    I will scatter them in Jacob,
    disperse them throughout Israel.

8 "You, Judah, shall your brothers praise
    —your hand on the neck of your enemies;
    the sons of your father shall bow down
        to you.
9* Judah, like a lion's whelp,
    you have grown up on prey, my son.
    He crouches like a lion recumbent,
        the king of beasts—who would dare
        rouse him?
10† The scepter shall never depart from Judah,
    or the mace from between his legs,
    While tribute is brought to him,
    and he receives the people's homage.
11† He tethers his donkey to the vine,
    his purebred ass to the choicest stem.
    In wine he washes his garments,
    his robe in the blood of grapes.
12 His eyes are darker than wine,
    and his teeth are whiter than milk.

13 "Zebulun shall dwell by the seashore
    [This means a shore for ships],
    and his flank shall be based on Sidon.

14 "Issachar is a rawboned ass,
    crouching between the saddlebags.
15 When he saw how good a settled life was,
    and how pleasant the country,
    He bent his shoulder to the burden
    and became a toiling serf.

16† "Dan shall achieve justice for his kindred
    like any other tribe of Israel.
17 Let Dan be a serpent by the roadside,
    a horned viper by the path,
    That bites the horse's heel,
    so that the rider tumbles backward.

18 "[I long for your deliverance, O LORD!]

19† "Gad shall be raided by raiders,
    but he shall raid at their heels.

20 "Asher's produce is rich,
    and he shall furnish dainties for kings.

21 "Naphtali is a hind let loose,
    which brings forth lovely fawns.

---

† **49, 10:** *While tribute is brought to him:* this translation is based on a slight change in the Hebrew text, which, as it stands, would seem to mean, "until he comes to Shiloh." A somewhat different reading of the Hebrew text would be, "until he comes to whom it belongs." This last has been traditionally understood in a Messianic sense. In any case, the passage foretells the supremacy of the tribe of Judah, which found its fulfillment in the Davidic dynasty and ultimately in the Messianic Son of David, Jesus Christ.
49, 11: *In wine . . . the blood of grapes:* Judah's clothes are poet-

ically pictured as soaked with grape juice from trampling in the wine press, the rich vintage of his land; cf Is 63, 2.
49, 16: In Hebrew the verb for *achieve justice* is from the same root as the name Dan.
49, 19: In Hebrew there is a certain assonance between the name Gad and the words for "raided," "raiders" and "raid."

* 49, 9: 1 Chr 5, 2.

GN

22 "Joseph is a wild colt,
   a wild colt by a spring,
   a wild ass on a hillside.
23 Harrying and attacking,
   the archers opposed him;
24 But each one's bow remained stiff,
   as their arms were unsteady,
   By the power of the Mighty One of Jacob,
   because of the Shepherd, the Rock of Israel,
25† The God of your father, who helps you,
   God Almighty, who blesses you,
   With the blessings of the heavens above,
   the blessings of the abyss that
      crouches below,
   The blessings of breasts and womb,
26 the blessings of fresh grain and blossoms,
   The blessings of the everlasting mountains,
   the delights of the eternal hills.
   May they rest on the head of Joseph,
   on the brow of the prince among
      his brothers.

27 "Benjamin is a ravenous wolf;
   mornings he devours the prey,
   and evenings he distributes the spoils."

Farewell and Death

28 All these are the twelve tribes of Israel, and this is what their father said about them, as he bade them farewell and gave to each of them an appropriate message. 29 Then he gave them this charge: "Since I am about to be taken to my kindred, bury me with my fathers in the cave that lies in the field of Ephron the Hittite, 30* the cave in the field of Machpelah, facing on Mamre, in the land of Canaan, the field that Abraham bought from Ephron the Hittite for a burial ground. 31 There Abraham and his wife Sarah are buried, and so are Isaac and his wife Rebekah, and there, too, I buried Leah— 32 the field and the cave in it that had been purchased from the Hittites."

33 When Jacob had finished giving these instructions to his sons, he drew his feet into the bed, breathed his last, and was taken to his kindred.

Jacob's Funeral

50 1 Joseph threw himself on his father's face and wept over him as he kissed him. 2 Then he ordered the physicians in his service to embalm his father. When they embalmed Israel, 3 they spent forty days at it, for that is the full period of embalming; and the Egyptians mourned him for seventy days. 4 When that period of mourning was over, Joseph spoke to Pharaoh's courtiers. "Please do me this favor," he said, "and convey to Pharaoh this request of mine. 5* Since my father, at the point of death, made me promise on oath to bury him in the tomb that he had prepared for himself in the land of Canaan, may I go up there to bury my father and then come back?" 6 Pharaoh replied, "Go and bury your father, as he made you promise on oath."

7 So Joseph left to bury his father; and with him went all of Pharaoh's officials who were senior members of his court and all the other dignitaries of Egypt, 8 as well as Joseph's whole household, his brothers, and his father's household; only their children and their flocks and herds were left in the region of Goshen. 9 Chariots, too, and charioteers went up with him; it was a very large retinue.

10† When they arrived at Goren-ha-atad, which is beyond the Jordan, they held there a very great and solemn memorial service; and Joseph observed seven days of mourning for his father. 11 When the Canaanites who inhabited the land saw the mourning at Goren-ha-atad, they said, "This is a solemn funeral the Egyptians are having." That is why the place was named Abel-mizraim. It is beyond the Jordan.

12 Thus Jacob's sons did for him as he had instructed them. 13* They carried him to the land of Canaan and buried him in the cave in the field of Machpelah, facing on Mamre, the field that Abraham had bought for a burial ground from Ephron the Hittite.

14 After Joseph had buried his father he returned to Egypt, together with his brothers and all who had gone up with him for the burial of his father.

Plea for Forgiveness

15 Now that their father was dead, Joseph's brothers became fearful and thought, "Suppose Joseph has been nursing a grudge against us and now plans to pay us back in full for all the wrong we did him!" 16 So they approached Joseph and said: "Before your father died, he gave us these instructions: 17 'You shall say to Joseph, Jacob begs you to forgive the criminal wrongdoing of your

---

49, 25f: A very similar description of the agricultural riches of the tribal land of Joseph is given in Dt 33, 13–16.
50, 10f: *Goren-ha-atad:* "Threshing Floor of the Brambles." *Abel-mizraim:* although the name really means "watercourse of the Egyptians," it is understood here, by a play on the first part of the term, to mean "mourning of the Egyptians." The site has not been identified through either reading of the name. But it is difficult to see why the mourning rites should have been held in the land *beyond the Jordan*

when the burial was at Hebron. Perhaps an earlier form of the story placed the mourning rites beyond the Wadi of Egypt, the traditional boundary between Canaan and Egypt (Nm 34, 5; Jos 15, 4.47).

49, 30: Gn 23, 17.   50, 13: Gn 23, 16; Acts 7, 16.
50, 5: Gn 47, 30.

brothers, who treated you so cruelly." Please, therefore, forgive the crime that we, the servants of your father's God, committed." When they spoke these words to him, Joseph broke into tears. [18] Then his brothers proceeded to fling themselves down before him and said, "Let us be your slaves!" [19] But Joseph replied to them: "Have no fear. Can I take the place of God? [20]* Even though you meant harm to me, God meant it for good, to achieve his present end, the survival of many people. [21]* Therefore have no fear. I will provide for you and for your children." By thus speaking kindly to them, he reassured them.

[22] Joseph remained in Egypt, together with his father's family. He lived a hundred and ten years. [23]* He saw Ephraim's children to the third generation, and the children of Manasseh's son Machir were also born on Joseph's knees.

Death of Joseph

[24]* Joseph said to his brothers: "I am about to die. God will surely take care of you and lead you out of this land to the land that he promised on oath to Abraham, Isaac and Jacob." [25]* Then, putting the sons of Israel under oath, he continued, "When God thus takes care of you, you must bring my bones up with you from this place." [26]* Joseph died at the age of a hundred and ten. He was embalmed and laid to rest in a coffin in Egypt.

50, 20: Gn 45, 5; Sir 49, 15.   Heb 11, 22.
50, 21: Gn 47, 12.   50, 25: Ex 13, 19; Heb 11, 22.
50, 23: Nm 32, 39; Jos 17, 1.   50, 26: Sir 49, 15.
50, 24: Ex 3, 8; Jos 24, 32;

did you KNOW?

Israel's Ancestry

Although the Israelites descended from many different kin, the Book of Genesis traces their origins back to a series of common ancestors, which served to unite them as a people. Genesis tells the stories of those great ancestors, men and women called patriarchs and matriarchs, who were the founders of what later became the people of Israel. The twelve tribes of Israel are understood to be descendants from Jacob's twelve sons (see Jacob's last words in Genesis, chapter 49, for a description of those tribes). Twelve becomes an important number that comes up again and again in the Bible. For example, the twelve Apostles are Jesus' closest followers in the New Testament.

It can be confusing to remember who is related to whom, so here's a chart to keep everyone straight:

Hagar (Sarah's slave)
└─Ishmael
Abraham
└─Isaac
Sarah
    Rebekah
      ┌─Esau (Edom)
      └─Jacob (Israel)

Leah
┌─Reuben
├─Simeon
├─Levi
├─Judah
├─Issachar
├─Zebulun
└─Dinah
(only daughter)

Bilhah (Rachel's maid)
┌─Dan
└─Naphtali

Zilpah (Leah's maid)
┌─Gad
└─Asher

Rachel
┌─Joseph
└─Benjamin

┌─Ephraim
└─Manasseh

- Levi's tribe was set aside as priests and was not assigned land after the conquest of Canaan.
- Because Jacob adopted Joseph's sons Ephraim and Manasseh, Joseph is the father of two tribes.

Exodus

Click! Chains snap shut around your ankles. Crack! The tip of a whip whistles past your head. Bang! A door shuts, leaving you in darkness. These are the sounds of slavery, and they come as a surprise at the beginning of the Book of Exodus. What happened after the happy ending in Genesis? Like an action-packed drama, Exodus tells a story of deceit and broken promises, and of how God's miraculous interventions delivered the Israelites from their slavery in Egypt.

At a Glance

I. The Israelites in Egypt (1, 1—12, 36).

II. The Exodus from Egypt and the Journey to Sinai (12, 37—18, 27).

III. The Covenant at Mount Sinai (19, 1—24, 18).

IV. The Dwelling and Its Furnishings (25, 1—40, 38).

In-depth

The Book of Exodus is the story of Israel's liberation. Exodus literally means "departure," and this book's central story is of how God liberates the people from slavery in Egypt (an event called the Exodus). Its central character is Moses, who is chosen by God to become God's voice and the instrument of God's power. Exodus was written hundreds of years after these events, using oral traditions that described the origin of many of the Israelite's beliefs and religious rituals.

Exodus is divided into four main sections. The first two sections, chapters 1–18, begin with the Israelites enslaved in Egypt and prohibited from worshiping their God. Israel cries out to God, and God answers by sending Moses. When Pharaoh refuses to let the Israelites go, God sends ten devastating plagues, and Pharaoh finally gives in. Later, Pharaoh changes his mind and chases the Israelites, only to have his army destroyed after the Israelites' escape through the Red Sea. This section ends with the people wandering through the wilderness, sustained by food and water miraculously provided by God.

Quick Facts

Period Covered
sometime from 1500 to 1250 B.C.

Author
unknown author gathering oral traditions and stories from various tribal peoples

Themes
God liberates people from slavery and oppression. God sustains the Israelites in the wilderness. God forms a covenant marked by laws and rituals.

Sections three and four of Exodus, chapters 19–40, occur at Mount Sinai. There, God enters into a covenant with all the people. God's part of the Sinai Covenant is to guarantee continued protection. Israel's part is to be faithful to God alone, a faithfulness marked by special laws (chapters 20–23) and special worship (chapters 24–31) that unite them as a people. Exodus ends with Israel still encamped at Mount Sinai, struggling to become a people of the Covenant.

The stories and laws in Exodus are at the heart of both Jewish and Christian belief in a God who saves, a God of freedom. You cannot fully appreciate the meaning of Jesus' life, death, and Resurrection without knowing these stories.

Exodus

I: The Israelites In Egypt

Jacob's Descendants in Egypt

1 [1]† These are the names of the sons of Israel who, accompanied by their households, migrated with Jacob into Egypt: [2]† Reuben, Simeon, Levi and Judah; [3] Issachar, Zebulun and Benjamin; [4] Dan and Naphtali; Gad and Asher. [5]*† The total number of the direct descendants of Jacob was seventy. Joseph was already in Egypt.

[6]* Now Joseph and all his brothers and that whole generation died. [7] But the Israelites were fruitful and prolific. They became so numerous and strong that the land was filled with them.

The Oppression

[8]*† Then a new king, who knew nothing of Joseph, came to power in Egypt. [9] He said to his subjects, "Look how numerous and powerful the Israelite people are growing, more so than we ourselves! [10] Come, let us deal shrewdly with them to stop their increase; otherwise, in time of war they too may join our enemies to fight against us, and so leave our country."

[11]*† Accordingly, taskmasters were set over the Israelites to oppress them with forced labor. Thus they had to build for Pharaoh the supply cities of Pithom and Raamses. [12] Yet the more they were oppressed, the more they multiplied and spread. The Egyptians, then, dreaded the Israelites [13] and reduced them to cruel slavery, [14]† making life bitter for them with hard work in mortar and brick and all kinds of field work—the whole cruel fate of slaves.

Command to the Midwives

[15] The king of Egypt told the Hebrew midwives, one of whom was called Shiphrah and the other Puah, [16]† "When you act as midwives for the Hebrew women and see them giving birth, if it is a boy, kill him; but if it is a girl, she may live." [17] The midwives, however, feared God; they did not do as the king of Egypt had ordered them, but let the boys live. [18] So the king summoned the midwives and asked them, "Why have you acted thus, allowing the boys to live?" [19] The midwives answered Pharaoh, "The Hebrew women are not like the Egyptian women. They are robust and give birth before the

---

1, 1: *Sons of Israel:* here literally the first-generation sons of Jacob. Cf v 5. However, beginning with Ex 1, 7 the same Hebrew phrase refers to the more remote descendants of Jacob; hence, from there on, it is ordinarily rendered as "the Israelites." *Households:* the family in its fullest sense, including wives, children and servants.

1, 2: The sons of Jacob are listed here according to the respective mothers. Cf Gn 29; 31; 30, 20; 35, 16–26.

1, 5: *Direct descendants:* literally, persons coming from the loins of Jacob; hence, wives and servants are here excluded. Cf Gn 46, 26.

1, 8: *Who knew nothing of Joseph:* this king ignored the services that Joseph had rendered to Egypt.

1, 11: *Pharaoh:* not a personal name, but a title common to all the kings of Egypt.

1, 14: *Mortar:* either the wet clay with which the bricks were made, as in Na 3, 14, or the cement used between the bricks in building, as in Gn 11, 3.

1, 16: *And see them giving birth:* the Hebrew text is uncertain.

1, 5: Gn 46, 27; Dt 10, 22; Acts 7, 14.
1, 6: Gn 50, 26.
1, 8ff: Acts 7, 18.
1, 11: Dt 26, 6.

EX

Saving Lives

In the story of the birth of Moses, Pharaoh ordered the Egyptian midwives to kill all the male Israelite babies at birth. The midwives recognized such killing as an atrocity and refused to obey Pharaoh. Their actions might be considered civil disobedience against unjust laws.

Some people claim that the right to have an abortion is a just law. Aren't they right? Consider this incident: At a youth group gathering, abortion was discussed and a video was shown on how abortions are performed. One young man shared that although he did not believe in abortion, he used to believe exceptions could be made, such as in the case of rape or incest. After watching the video, he said he no longer believed such exceptions could be morally justified. A young woman said the video had convinced her that abortion was in the same moral category as serial murder. These young people, like the midwives in Exodus, recognized that all human life is sacred.

▸ Ex 1, 15–22

midwife arrives." 20 Therefore God dealt well with the midwives. The people, too, increased and grew strong. 21 And because the midwives feared God, he built up families for them. 22*† Pharaoh then commanded all his subjects, "Throw into the river every boy that is born to the Hebrews, but you may let all the girls live."

Birth and Adoption of Moses

2 1* Now a certain man of the house of Levi married a Levite woman, 2* who conceived and bore a son. Seeing that he was a goodly child, she hid him for three months. 3† When she could hide him no longer, she took a papyrus basket, daubed it with bitumen and pitch, and putting the child in it, placed it among the reeds on the river bank. 4 His sister stationed herself at a distance to find out what would happen to him.

5 Pharaoh's daughter came down to the river to bathe, while her maids walked along the river bank. Noticing the basket among the reeds, she sent her handmaid to fetch it. 6 On opening it, she looked, and lo, there was a baby boy, crying! She was moved with pity for him and said, "It is one of the Hebrews' children." 7 Then his sister asked Pharaoh's daughter, "Shall I go and call one of the Hebrew women to nurse the child for you?" 8 "Yes, do so," she answered. So the maiden went and called the child's own mother. 9 Pharaoh's daughter said

to her, "Take this child and nurse it for me, and I will repay you." The woman therefore took the child and nursed it. 10*† When the child grew, she brought him to Pharaoh's daughter, who adopted him as her son and called him Moses; for she said, "I drew him out of the water."

Moses' Flight to Midian

11*† On one occasion, after Moses had grown up, when he visited his kinsmen and witnessed their forced labor, he saw an Egyptian striking a Hebrew, one of his own kinsmen. 12 Looking about and seeing no one, he slew the Egyptian and hid him in the sand. 13 The next day he went out again, and now two Hebrews were fighting! So he asked the culprit, "Why are you striking your fellow Hebrew?" 14 But he replied, "Who has appointed you ruler and judge over us? Are you thinking of killing me as you killed the Egyptian?" Then Moses became afraid and thought, "The affair must certainly be known."

15* Pharaoh, too, heard of the affair and sought to put him to death. But Moses fled from him and stayed in the land of Midian. As he was seated there by a well, 16 seven daughters of a priest of Midian came to draw water and fill the troughs to water their father's flock. 17 But some shepherds came and drove them away. Then Moses got up and defended them and watered their flock. 18† When

1, 22: *The river:* the Nile, which was "the" river for the Egyptians.
2, 3: *Basket:* literally, "chest" or "ark"; the same Hebrew word is used in Gn 6, 14 for Noah's ark. Here, however, the chest was made of papyrus stalks.
2, 10: *When the child grew:* probably when he was weaned or a little later. *Moses:* in Hebrew, *Mosheh;* the Hebrew word for "draw out" is *mashah.* This explanation of the name is not intended as a scientific etymology but as a play on words. The name is probably derived from an Egyptian word for "has been born," referring the birth to a god thought to be its sponsor.

2, 11: *After Moses had grown up:* Acts 7, 23 indicates that this was after an interval of nearly forty years. Cf Ex 7, 7. *Striking:* probably in the sense of "flogging"; according to some, "slaying."
2, 18: *Reuel:* he was also called Jethro. Cf Ex 3, 1; 4, 18; 18, 1.

1, 22: Acts 7, 19.   2, 10: Acts 7, 21; Heb 11, 24.
2, 1: Ex 6, 20; Nm 26, 59.   2, 11–14: Acts 7, 23–28.
2, 2: Acts 7, 20; Heb 11, 23.   2, 15: Acts 7, 29; Heb 11, 27.

they returned to their father Reuel, he said to them, "How is it you have returned so soon today?" 19† They answered, "An Egyptian saved us from the interference of the shepherds. He even drew water for us and watered the flock!" 20 "Where is the man?" he asked his daughters. "Why did you leave him there? Invite him to have something to eat." 21 Moses agreed to live with him, and the man gave him his daughter Zipporah in marriage. 22*† She bore him a son, whom he named Gershom; for he said, "I am a stranger in a foreign land."

The Burning Bush

23* A long time passed, during which the king of Egypt died. Still the Israelites groaned and cried out because of their slavery. As their cry for release went up to God, 24* he heard their groaning and was mindful of his covenant with Abraham, Isaac and Jacob. 25 He saw the Israelites and knew. . . .

3 1† Meanwhile Moses was tending the flock of his father-in-law Jethro, the priest of Midian.

Leading the flock across the desert, he came to Horeb, the mountain of God. 2*† There an angel of the LORD appeared to him in fire flaming out of a bush. As he looked on, he was surprised to see that the bush, though on fire, was not consumed. 3 So Moses decided, "I must go over to look at this remarkable sight, and see why the bush is not burned."

The Call of Moses

4 When the LORD saw him coming over to look at it more closely, God called out to him from the bush, "Moses! Moses!" He answered, "Here I am." 5* God said, "Come no nearer! Remove the sandals from your feet, for the place where you stand is holy ground. 6*† I am the God of your father," he continued, "the God of Abraham, the God of Isaac, the God of Jacob." Moses hid his face, for he was afraid to look at God. 7 But the LORD said, "I have witnessed the affliction of my people in Egypt and have heard their cry of complaint against their slave drivers, so I know well what they are suffering.

Introducing ▶ MOSES

Moses is, without doubt, the most important character in the Pentateuch, if not the entire Old Testament. Struggling to find language to describe his greatness, Dt 34, 10 says, "Since then no prophet has arisen in Israel like Moses, whom the Lord knew face to face." Born to a couple from the tribe of Levi and raised as an Egyptian by the Pharaoh's daughter, Moses was perfectly suited to negotiate Israel's freedom from slavery in Egypt. In event after event, the author of Exodus shows us Moses' wonder-working power, his prophetic skill, and his intimacy with God.

    Despite all of Moses' great accomplishments, he never loses his humanness. He lacks confidence in his ability to speak (Ex 4, 10), he is angry and frustrated with his people (17, 4), and he bargains with God out of love for his people (32, 11–14). Moses, noble but also knowing sadness, is elegantly portrayed in the passage where he dies within sight of the Promised Land (Deuteronomy, chapter 34). These qualities paint a picture of someone whose perseverance and trust allowed God to work through him.

    A prophet is literally God's voice, and Moses was indeed God's voice, which shaped Israel to be a people of the Covenant. All other leaders and figures in the Old Testament are compared with Moses. In the New Testament, even Jesus is compared with Moses.

2, 19: *An Egyptian:* Moses was probably wearing Egyptian dress, or spoke Egyptian to Reuel's daughters.

2, 22: *Gershom:* the name is explained as if it came from the Hebrew word *ger,* "stranger," joined to the Hebrew word *sham,* "there." Some Greek and Latin manuscripts add here a passage taken from Ex 18, 4.

3, 1: *The mountain of God:* probably given this designation because of the divine apparitions which took place there, such as on this occasion and when the Israelites were there after the departure from Egypt.

3, 2: *An angel of the LORD:* the visual form under which God appeared and spoke to men is referred to indifferently in some Old Testament texts either as God's angel or as God himself. Cf Gn 16, 7.13; Ex 14, 19.24f; Nm 22, 22–35; Jgs 6, 11–18.

3, 6: The appearance of God caused fear of death, since it was believed that no one could see God and live; cf Gn 32, 30. *The God of Abraham . . . Jacob:* cited by Christ in proof of the resurrection since the patriarchs, long dead, live on in God who is the God of the living. Cf Mt 22, 32; Mk 12, 26; Lk 20, 37.

2, 22: Ex 18, 3.
2, 23: Ex 3, 7.9; Dt 26, 7.
2, 24: Ex 6, 5; Pss 105, 8f; 106, 44f.
3, 2–10: Acts 7, 30–35.
3, 5: Jos 5, 15.
3, 6: Ex 4, 5; Mt 22, 32; Mk 12, 36; Lk 20, 37.

Asian

American

Holy Ground

In many Asian cultures, before people enter a home, they remove their shoes. People do this before entering a mosque too. Perhaps you remove your shoes before entering your home as well. Removing one's shoes is a common sign of respect. Moses is commanded to remove his sandals in Ex 3, 5. Why? Because he is standing on holy ground. Why is the ground holy? Because God is present.

Moses is awestruck and humbled by his experience of God's presence. In today's multimedia culture, we are rarely awed by anything. Even the burning bush would be just another special effect. How can we regain our sense of awe at God's majesty? Some people experience it in nature, looking at a star-filled sky or the waves rolling in on the ocean. Others experience it in getting to know other people deeply. Still others find it in the amazing patterns that science reveals. The one common element to experiencing awe seems to be the ability to slow down, look closely, and appreciate what you discover.

So slow down, find your own holy ground, take your shoes off, and let God fill you with awe!

▶ Ex 3, 1–6

8*† Therefore I have come down to rescue them from the hands of the Egyptians and lead them out of that land into a good and spacious land, a land flowing with milk and honey, the country of the Canaanites, Hittites, Amorites, Perizzites, Hivites and Jebusites. 9 So indeed the cry of the Israelites has reached me, and I have truly noted that the Egyptians are oppressing them. 10 Come, now! I will send you to Pharaoh to lead my people, the Israelites, out of Egypt."

11† But Moses said to God, "Who am I that I should go to Pharaoh and lead the Israelites out of Egypt?" 12 He answered, "I will be with you; and this shall be your proof that it is I who have sent you: when you bring my people out of Egypt, you will worship God on this very mountain." 13 "But," said Moses to God, "when I go to the Israelites and say to them, 'The God of your fathers has sent me to you,' if they ask me, 'What is his name?' what am I to tell them?" 14† God replied, "I am who am."

▶ ▶ ▶ ▶ ▶ ▶ ▶ ▶ ▶ ▶

NATIVE AMERICAN

The Name of God

Many Native American peoples, such as the Lakota and the Sioux, have several names for God. Wakan-Tanka and Tun-ka-shi-la are still commonly used today. These words for God are often translated as Great Spirit.

This is a good translation because Wakan is a word that brings together the concepts of mystery, sacredness, holiness, awe, and inspiration. Tanka describes something that is great.

Tun-ka-shi-la is often used the same way as Wakan-Tanka, but its meaning is slightly different. Tun-ka-shi-la is often translated as Grandfather or Great Grandfather, but it means the "one who is the oldest, so old that nothing or no one is older." Tun-ka-shi-la is a name that reflects the Great Spirit as the source of all things, the one who has existed from the beginning.

▶ Ex 3, 13–15

 ▶ ▶ ▶ ▶ ▶ ▶ ▶ ▶ ▶ ▶

3, 8: *I have come down:* a figure of speech signifying an extraordinary divine intervention in human affairs. Cf Gn 11, 5.7. *Flowing with milk and honey:* an expression denoting agricultural prosperity, which seems to have been proverbial in its application to Palestine. Cf Ex 13, 5; Nm 13, 27; Jos 5, 6; Jer 11, 5; 32, 22; Ez 20, 6.15.

3, 11: *Who am I:* besides naturally shrinking from such a tremendous undertaking, Moses realized that, as a fugitive from Pharaoh, he could hardly hope to carry out a mission to him. Perhaps he also recalled that on one occasion even his own kinsmen questioned his authority. Cf Ex 2, 14.

3, 14: *I am who am:* apparently this utterance is the source of the word *Yahweh*, the proper personal name of the God of Israel. It is commonly explained in reference to God as the absolute and necessary Being. It may be understood of God as the Source of all

3, 8f: Gn 15, 19ff.

？did you KNOW?

God's Mysterious Name

"I am who am"—one possible translation of Yahweh from Ex 3, 14—seems more like a definition than a name. Some scholars have suggested Yahweh might be better translated "he causes to be what exists." In any case, the four Hebrew letters *YHWH* (or Yahweh in English) are difficult to translate. Over the centuries, the Jewish people stopped pronouncing the four letters out of reverence for God and replaced them with the word Adonai, meaning "my Lord." Most English translations of the Bible respect this long-standing tradition, translating the original *YHWH* as LORD. This mysterious name of God reminds us that no name or symbol can fully express who God is.

▸ Ex 3, 13–15

Then he added, "This is what you shall tell the Israelites: I AM sent me to you."

15* God spoke further to Moses, "Thus shall you say to the Israelites: The LORD, the God of your fathers, the God of Abraham, the God of Isaac, the God of Jacob, has sent me to you.

"This is my name forever;
this is my title for all generations.

16† "Go and assemble the elders of the Israelites, and tell them: The LORD, the God of your fathers, the God of Abraham, Isaac and Jacob, has appeared to me and said: I am concerned about you and about the way you are being treated in Egypt; 17 so I have decided to lead you up out of the misery of Egypt into the land of the Canaanites, Hittites, Amorites, Perizzites, Hivites and Jebusites, a land flowing with milk and honey.

18* "Thus they will heed your message. Then you and the elders of Israel shall go to the king of Egypt and say to him: The LORD, the God of the Hebrews,

has sent us word. Permit us, then, to go a three-days' journey in the desert, that we may offer sacrifice to the LORD, our God.

19 "Yet I know that the king of Egypt will not allow you to go unless he is forced. 20 I will stretch out my hand, therefore, and smite Egypt by doing all kinds of wondrous deeds there. After that he will send you away. 21 I will even make the Egyptians so well-disposed toward this people that, when you leave, you will not go empty-handed. 22*† Every woman shall ask her neighbor and her house guest for silver and gold articles and for clothing to put on your sons and daughters. Thus you will despoil the Egyptians."

Confirmation of Moses' Mission

4 1 "But," objected Moses, "suppose they will not believe me, nor listen to my plea? For they may say, 'The LORD did not appear to you.' " 2 The LORD therefore asked him, "What is that in your hand?" "A staff," he answered. 3* The LORD then said, "Throw it on the ground." When he threw it on the ground it was changed into a serpent, and Moses shied away from it. 4 "Now, put out your hand," the LORD said to him, "and take hold of its tail." So he put out his hand and laid hold of it, and it became a staff in his hand. 5 "This will take place so that they may believe," he continued, "that the LORD, the God of their fathers, the God of Abraham, the God of Isaac, the God of Jacob, did appear to you."

6 Again the LORD said to him, "Put your hand in your bosom." He put it in his bosom, and when he withdrew it, to his surprise his hand was leprous, like snow. 7 The LORD then said, "Now, put your hand back in your bosom." Moses put his hand back in his bosom, and when he withdrew it, to his surprise it was again like the rest of his body. 8 "If they will not believe you, nor heed the message of the first sign, they should believe the message of the second. 9* And if they will not believe even these two signs, nor heed your plea, take some water from the river and pour it on the dry land. The water you take from the river will become blood on the dry land."

Aaron's Office as Assistant

10* Moses, however, said to the LORD, "If you please, Lord, I have never been eloquent, neither in the past, nor recently, nor now that you have spoken to your servant; but I am slow of speech and

---

created beings. Out of reverence for this name, the term *Adonai*, "my Lord," was later used as a substitute. The word LORD in the present version represents this traditional usage. The word "Jehovah" arose from a false reading of this name as it is written in the current Hebrew text.
3, 16: *Elders:* the Israelite leaders, who were usually older men. They were representatives of the people.
3, 22: *Articles:* probably jewelry. *Despoil:* this was permissible,

that the Israelites might compensate themselves for their many years of servitude; besides, the Egyptians would give these things willingly, Cf Ex 12, 33–36.

3, 15: Ps 135, 13.   4, 3: Ex 7, 10.
3, 18: Ex 5, 3.   4, 9: Ex 7, 17.19f.
3, 22: 21f: Ex 11, 2f; 12, 35f.   4, 10: Ex 6, 12.

GOD SENDS PROPHETS TO LIBERATE HIS PEOPLE!

¡Dios envía profetas para liberar a su pueblo!

EX

HISPANIC

God responded to the cry of his people, choosing Moses as a prophet and commissioning him to lead the Israelites to freedom. Despite Moses' first doubts, with God's assistance, Moses became an effective and powerful leader. God would not let Moses' excuses stand in the way of God's mission of liberation.

Christians share in Jesus Christ's prophetic work as well. We too need to speak out against injustice and help the victims of oppression. Like the prophets before us, we can only succeed with God's help.

In our time, great spiritual leaders have risen up to lead people to freedom: Mohandas Gandhi, Martin Luther King Jr., Dorothy Day, Archbishop Oscar Romero, and Cesar Chavez are just a few. As in the case of Moses, God inspired these leaders to see their people experiencing injustice and to seek to liberate them from oppressive powers. You can be sure that these people also had their doubts and relied on God for their strength and hope.

■ Are you aware of any group that is being oppressed today? How might God be calling you to help?

■ Ask God for wisdom, strength, and help in your mission.

▶ Ex 4, 1–17

tongue." ¹¹ The LORD said to him, "Who gives one man speech and makes another deaf and dumb? Or who gives sight to one and makes another blind? Is it not I, the LORD? ¹² Go, then! It is I who will assist you in speaking and will teach you what you are to say." ¹³† Yet he insisted, "If you please, Lord, send someone else!" ¹⁴ Then the LORD became angry with Moses and said, "Have you not your brother, Aaron the Levite? I know that he is an eloquent speaker. Besides, he is now on his way to meet you. ¹⁵ When he sees you, his heart will be glad. You are to speak to him, then, and put the words in his mouth. I will assist both you and him in speaking and will teach the two of you what you are to do. ¹⁶*† He shall speak to the people for you: he shall be your spokesman, and you shall be as God to him. ¹⁷† Take this staff in your hand; with it you are to perform the signs."

Moses' Return to Egypt

¹⁸† After this Moses returned to his father-in-law Jethro and said to him, "Let me go back, please, to my kinsmen in Egypt, to see whether they are still living." Jethro replied, "Go in peace." ¹⁹* In Midian the LORD said to Moses, "Go back to Egypt, for all the men who sought your life are dead." ²⁰ So Moses took his wife and his sons, and started back to the land of Egypt, with them riding the ass. The staff of God he carried with him. ²¹† The LORD said to him, "On your return to Egypt, see that you perform before Pharaoh all the wonders I have put in your power. I will make him obstinate, however, so that he will not let the people go. ²²* So you shall say to Pharaoh: Thus says the LORD: Israel is my son, my first-born. ²³* Hence I tell you: Let my son go, that he may serve me. If you refuse to let him go, I warn you, I will kill your son, your first-born."

²⁴† On the journey, at a place where they spent the night, the Lord came upon Moses and would have killed him. ²⁵* But Zipporah took a piece of flint and cut off her son's foreskin and, touching his person, she said, "You are a spouse of blood to me." ²⁶ Then God let Moses go. At that time she said, "A spouse of blood," in regard to the circumcision.

4, 13: *Send someone else:* literally, "Send by means of him whom you will send," that is, "Send whom you will."

4, 16: *Spokesman:* literally, "mouth"; Aaron was to serve as a mouthpiece for Moses, as a prophet does for God; hence the relation between Moses and Aaron is compared to that between God and his prophet. Cf Ex 7, 1.

4, 17: *This staff:* probably the same as that of vv 2ff; but some understand it here of a new staff now given by God to Moses.

4, 18: Moses did not tell his father-in-law his main reason for returning to Egypt, but this secondary motive which he offered was also true.

4, 21: *Make him obstinate:* literally, "harden his heart." God permitted Pharaoh to be stubborn in his opposition to the departure of the Israelites. Cf Rom 9, 17f.

4, 24ff: Apparently God was angry with Moses for having failed to keep the divine command given to Abraham in Gn 17, 10ff. Moses' life is spared when his wife circumcises their son.

4, 16: 15f: Ex 7, 1.
   4, 19: Ex 2, 15.23.
   4, 22: Sir 36, 11.

4, 23: Ex 11, 5; 12, 29.
4, 25: Is 6, 2; 7, 20.

27 The LORD said to Aaron, "Go into the desert to meet Moses." So he went, and when they met at the mountain of God, Aaron kissed him. 28 Moses informed him of all the LORD had said in sending him, and of the various signs he had enjoined upon him. 29 Then Moses and Aaron went and assembled all the elders of the Israelites. 30 Aaron told them everything the LORD had said to Moses, and he performed the signs before the people. 31 The people believed, and when they heard that the LORD was concerned about them and had seen their affliction, they bowed down in worship.

Pharaoh's Obduracy

5 1 After that, Moses and Aaron went to Pharaoh and said, "Thus says the LORD, the God of Israel: Let my people go, that they may celebrate a feast to me in the desert." 2 Pharaoh answered, "Who is the LORD, that I should heed his plea to let Israel go? I do not know the LORD; even if I did, I would not let Israel go." 3* They replied, "The God of the Hebrews has sent us word. Let us go a three days' journey in the desert, that we may offer sacrifice to the LORD, our God; otherwise he will punish us with pestilence or the sword."

4 The king of Egypt answered them, "What do you mean, Moses and Aaron, by taking the people away from their work? Off to your labor! 5 Look how numerous the people of the land are already," continued Pharaoh, "and yet you would give them rest from their labor!"

6† That very day Pharaoh gave the taskmasters and foremen of the people this order: 7† "You shall no longer supply the people with straw for their brickmaking as you have previously done. Let them go and gather straw themselves! 8 Yet you shall levy upon them the same quota of bricks as they have previously made. Do not reduce it. They are lazy; that is why they are crying, 'Let us go to offer sacrifice to our God.' 9 Increase the work for the men, so that they keep their mind on it and pay no attention to lying words."

10 So the taskmasters and foremen of the people went out and told them, "Thus says Pharaoh: I will not provide you with straw. 11 Go and gather the straw yourselves, wherever you can find it. Yet there must not be the slightest reduction in your work." 12 The people, then, scattered throughout the land of Egypt to gather stubble for straw, 13 while the taskmasters kept driving them on, saying, "Finish your work, the same daily amount as when your straw was supplied."

Complaint of the Foremen

14 The foremen of the Israelites, whom the taskmasters of Pharaoh had placed over them, were beaten, and were asked, "Why have you not completed your prescribed amount of bricks yesterday and today, as before?"

15 Then the Israelite foremen came and made this appeal to Pharaoh: "Why do you treat your servants in this manner? 16 No straw is supplied to your servants, and still we are told to make bricks. Look how your servants are beaten! It is you who are at fault." 17 Pharaoh answered, "It is just because you are lazy that you keep saying, 'Let us go and offer sacrifice to the LORD.' 18 Off to work, then! Straw shall not be provided for you, but you must still deliver your quota of bricks."

19 The Israelite foremen knew they were in a sorry plight, having been told not to reduce the daily amount of bricks. 20 When, therefore, they left Pharaoh and came upon Moses and Aaron, who were waiting to meet them, 21 they said to them, "The LORD look upon you and judge! You have brought us into bad odor with Pharaoh and his servants and have put a sword in their hands to slay us."

Renewal of God's Promise

22 Moses again had recourse to the LORD and said, "Lord, why do you treat this people so badly? And why did you send me on such a mission? 23 Ever since I went to Pharaoh to speak in your name, he has maltreated this people of yours, and you have done nothing to rescue them."

6 1 Then the LORD answered Moses, "Now you shall see what I will do to Pharaoh. Forced by my mighty hand, he will send them away; compelled by my outstretched arm, he will drive them from his land."

2 God also said to Moses, "I am the LORD. 3* As God the Almighty I appeared to Abraham, Isaac and Jacob, but my name, LORD, I did not make known to them. 4* I also established my covenant with them, to give them the land of Canaan, the land in which they were living as aliens. 5* And now that I have heard the groaning of the Israelites, whom the Egyptians are treating as slaves, I am mindful of my covenant. 6 Therefore, say to the Israelites: I am the LORD. I will free you from the forced labor of the Egyptians and will deliver you from their slavery. I will rescue you by my outstretched arm and with mighty acts of judgment. 7* I will take you as my own people, and you shall

E
X

5, 6: *The taskmasters and foremen:* the former were higher officials and probably Egyptians; the latter were lower officials, chosen from the Israelites themselves. Cf v 14.

5, 7: Straw was mixed with the clay to give the sun-dried bricks greater consistency.

5, 3: Ex 3, 18.   6, 5: Ex 2, 24.
6, 3: Gn 17, 1; 35, 11.   6, 7: Lv 26, 12.
6, 4: Gn 15, 18; 17, 4–8.

Why Me?

Read Ex 5, 22–23. Can you imagine how Moses must have felt? He did what God told him to do, and things only got worse for the Israelites. But Moses was still able to talk to God, even if only to say, "Why did you send me?"

Thomas Merton, a famous Trappist monk and spiritual writer, knew that Christians sometimes feel like Moses did:

The Christian
must have the courage
to follow Christ.
The Christian
who is risen in Christ
must dare
to be like Christ:
he must dare
to follow conscience
even in unpopular causes.
He must, if necessary,
be able to disagree with the majority
and make decisions
that he knows
to be according to the Gospel
and teaching of Christ,
even when others
do not understand
why he is acting this way.
(*He Is Risen*, p. 22)

The next time you are feeling a little like Moses and wondering, Why me? try this prayer:

Faithful God, help me to trust in you during times of disappointment and disillusion. I want to believe you are working in ways I cannot see. Please help my disbelief. For I know that you will honor my best efforts and make things come out right in the end. Amen.

▸ Ex 5, 22–23

have me as your God. You will know that I, the LORD, am your God when I free you from the labor of the Egyptians 8 and bring you into the land which I swore to give to Abraham, Isaac and Jacob. I will give it to you as your own possession—I, the LORD!" 9 But when Moses told this to the Israelites, they would not listen to him because of their dejection and hard slavery.

10 Then the LORD said to Moses, 11 "Go and tell Pharaoh, king of Egypt, to let the Israelites leave his land." 12* But Moses protested to the LORD, "If the Israelites would not listen to me, how can it be that Pharaoh will listen to me, poor speaker that I am!" 13 Still, the LORD, to bring the Israelites out of Egypt, spoke to Moses and Aaron and gave them his orders regarding both the Israelites and Pharaoh, king of Egypt.

Genealogy of Moses and Aaron

14*† These are the heads of the ancestral houses. The sons of Reuben, the first-born of Israel, were Hanoch, Pallu, Hezron and Carmi; these are the clans of Reuben. 15* The sons of Simeon were Jemuel, Jamin, Ohad, Jachin, Zohar and Shaul, who was the son of a Canaanite woman; these are the clans of Simeon. 16* The names of the sons of Levi, in their genealogical order, are Gershon, Kohath and Merari. Levi lived one hundred and thirty-seven years. 17* The sons of Gershon, as heads of clans, were Libni and Shimei. 18* The sons of Kohath were Amram, Izhar, Hebron and Uzziel. Kohath lived one hundred and thirty-three years. 19* The sons of Merari were Mahli and Mushi. These are the clans of Levi in their genealogical order.

20*† Amram married his aunt Jochebed, who bore him Aaron, Moses and Miriam. Amram lived one hundred and thirty-seven years. 21 The sons of Izhar were Korah, Nepheg and Zichri. 22 The sons of Uzziel were Mishael, Elzaphan and Sithri. 23* Aaron married Amminadab's daughter, Elisheba, the sister of Nahshon; she bore him Nadab, Abihu, Eleazar and Ithamar. 24 The sons of Korah were Assir, Elkanah and Abiasaph. These are the clans of the Korahites. 25 Aaron's son, Eleazar, married one of Putiel's daughters, who bore him Phinehas. These are the heads of the ancestral clans of the Levites. 26 This is the Aaron and this the Moses to whom the LORD said, "Lead the Israelites from the land of Egypt, company by company." 27 These are the ones who spoke to Pharaoh, king of Egypt, to

---

6, 14: The purpose of the genealogy here is to give the line from which Moses and Aaron sprang. Reuben and Simeon are first mentioned because, as older brothers of Levi, their names occur before his in the genealogy.
6, 20: *His aunt:* more exactly, "his father's sister." Later on such a marriage was forbidden. Cf Lv 18, 12. Hence, the Greek and Latin versions render here, "his cousin."

6, 12: Ex 6, 30.   23, 7.
6, 14: Nm 26, 5f; 1 Chr 5, 3.   6, 18: Nm 3, 27; 1 Chr 6, 2.
6, 15: Nm 26, 12; 1 Chr 4,   18.
24.   6, 19: Nm 3, 20; 1 Chr 6, 19;
6, 16: Nm 3, 17; 1 Chr 6, 1.   23, 21.
16; 23, 6.   6, 20: Nm 26, 59.
6, 17: Nm 3, 21; 1 Chr 6, 17;   6, 23: Ru 4, 19f; 1 Chr 2, 10.

You Promised, God

The Israelite people had been slaves for so long, they were discouraged and did not believe Moses' liberating message in Ex 6, 1–9. Moses probably sounded crazy to them. The writer of Exodus reminds us of God's faithfulness to God's promises and that God's plans cannot be stopped by human weakness. We too may find it hard to believe in God's power in our life when we feel burdened and oppressed, especially over a long time.

In your prayer, reflect or journal on the following questions and suggestion:

- When do you find it hard to believe in God's promises?
- What people do you know who find it hard to accept God's power in their life?
- What barriers are keeping them from accepting God?
- Make up your own prayer expressing your desire to count on God's promises.

▸ Ex 6, 1–9

bring the Israelites out of Egypt—the same Moses and Aaron.

Moses and Aaron before Pharaoh

²⁸ On the day the LORD spoke to Moses in Egypt ²⁹ he said, "I am the LORD. Repeat to Pharaoh, king of Egypt, all that I tell you." ³⁰* But Moses protested to the LORD, "Since I am a poor speaker, how can it be that Pharaoh will listen to me?"

7 ¹*† The LORD answered him, "See! I have made you as God to Pharaoh, and Aaron your brother shall act as your prophet. ² You shall tell him all that I command you. In turn, your brother Aaron shall tell Pharaoh to let the Israelites leave his land. ³ Yet I will make Pharaoh so obstinate that, despite the many signs and wonders that I will work in the land of Egypt, ⁴ he will not listen to you. Therefore

I will lay my hand on Egypt and by great acts of judgment I will bring the hosts of my people, the Israelites, out of the land of Egypt, ⁵ so that the Egyptians may learn that I am the LORD, as I stretch out my hand against Egypt and lead the Israelites out of their midst."

⁶ Moses and Aaron did as the LORD had commanded them. ⁷ Moses was eighty years old and Aaron eighty-three when they spoke to Pharaoh.

The Staff Turned into a Snake

⁸ The LORD told Moses and Aaron, ⁹* "If Pharaoh demands that you work a sign or wonder, you shall say to Aaron: Take your staff and throw it down before Pharaoh, and it will be changed into a snake." ¹⁰ Then Moses and Aaron went to Pharaoh and did as the LORD had commanded. Aaron threw his staff down before Pharaoh and his servants, and it was changed into a snake. ¹¹* Pharaoh, in turn, summoned wise men and sorcerers, and they also, the magicians of Egypt, did likewise by their magic arts. ¹² Each one threw down his staff, and it was changed into a snake. But Aaron's staff swallowed their staffs. ¹³ Pharaoh, however, was obstinate and would not listen to them, just as the LORD had foretold.

First Plague: Water Turned into Blood

¹⁴† Then the LORD said to Moses, "Pharaoh is obdurate in refusing to let the people go. ¹⁵ Tomorrow morning, when he sets out for the water, go and present yourself by the river bank, holding in your hand the staff that turned into a serpent. ¹⁶ Say to him: The LORD, the God of the Hebrews, sent me to you with the message: Let my people go to worship me in the desert. But as yet you have not listened. ¹⁷* The LORD now says: This is how you shall know that I am the LORD. I will strike the water of the river with the staff I hold, and it shall be changed into blood. ¹⁸ The fish in the river shall die, and the river itself shall become so polluted that the Egyptians will be unable to drink its water."

¹⁹ The LORD then said to Moses, "Say to Aaron: Take your staff and stretch out your hand over the waters of Egypt—their streams and canals and pools, all their supplies of water—that they may become blood. Throughout the land of Egypt there shall be blood, even in the wooden pails and stone jars."

²⁰ Moses and Aaron did as the LORD had commanded. Aaron raised his staff and struck the

---

7, 1: Just as God had his prophets to speak to men in his name, so Moses had Aaron as his "prophet" to speak to Pharaoh. Cf Ex 4, 16.

7, 14: Most of the ten plagues of Egypt seem to be similar to certain natural phenomena of that country; but they are represented as

supernatural at least in their greater intensity and in their occurring exactly according to Moses' commands.

6, 30: Ex 6, 12.   **7, 11:** 2 Tm 3, 8.
7, 1: Ex 4, 15f.   **7, 17–21:** Ex 4, 9; Pss 78, 44;
7, 9: Ex 4, 3.   105, 29; Wis 11, 5–7.

waters of the river in full view of Pharaoh and his servants, and all the water of the river was changed into blood. 21 The fish in the river died, and the river itself became so polluted that the Egyptians could not drink its water. There was blood throughout the land of Egypt. 22 But the Egyptian magicians did the same by their magic arts. So Pharaoh remained obstinate and would not listen to Moses and Aaron, just as the LORD had foretold. 23 He turned away and went into his house, with no concern even for this. 24 All the Egyptians had to dig in the neighborhood of the river for drinking water, since they could not drink the river water.

Second Plague: the Frogs

25 Seven days passed after the LORD had struck the river. 26*† Then the LORD said to Moses, "Go to Pharaoh and tell him: Thus says the LORD: Let my people go to worship me. 27 If you refuse to let them go, I warn you, I will send a plague of frogs over all your territory. 28 The river will teem with frogs. They will come up into your palace and into your bedroom and onto your bed, into the houses of your servants, too, and your subjects, even into your ovens and your kneading bowls. 29 The frogs will swarm all over you and your subjects and your servants."

8 1 The LORD then told Moses, "Say to Aaron: Stretch out your hand and your staff over the streams and canals and pools, to make frogs overrun the land of Egypt." 2 Aaron stretched out his hand over the waters of Egypt, and the frogs came up and covered the land of Egypt. 3 But the magicians did the same by their magic arts. They, too, made frogs overrun the land of Egypt.

4 Then Pharaoh summoned Moses and Aaron and said, "Pray the LORD to remove the frogs from me and my subjects, and I will let the people go to offer sacrifice to the LORD." 5 Moses answered Pharaoh, "Do me the favor of appointing the time when I am to pray for you and your servants and your subjects, that the frogs may be taken away from you and your houses and be left only in the river." 6 "Tomorrow," said Pharaoh. Then Moses replied, "It shall be as you have said, so that you may learn that there is none like the LORD, our God. 7 The frogs shall leave you and your houses, your servants and your subjects; only in the river shall they be left."

8 After Moses and Aaron left Pharaoh's presence, Moses implored the LORD to fulfill the promise he had made to Pharaoh about the frogs; 9† and the LORD did as Moses had asked. The frogs in the houses and courtyards and fields died off. 10 Heaps and heaps of them were gathered up, and there was a stench in the land. 11 But when Pharaoh saw that there was a respite, he became obdurate and would not listen to them, just as the LORD had foretold.

Third Plague: the Gnats

12*† Thereupon the LORD said to Moses, "Tell Aaron to stretch out his staff and strike the dust of the earth, that it may be turned into gnats throughout the land of Egypt." 13 They did so. Aaron stretched out his hand, and with his staff he struck the dust of the earth, and gnats came upon man and beast. The dust of the earth was turned into gnats throughout the land of Egypt. 14* Though the magicians tried to bring forth gnats by their magic arts, they could not do so. As the gnats infested man and beast, 15† the magicians said to Pharaoh, "This is the finger of God." Yet Pharaoh remained obstinate and would not listen to them, just as the LORD had foretold.

Fourth Plague: the Flies

16 Again the LORD told Moses, "Early tomorrow morning present yourself to Pharaoh when he goes forth to the water, and say to him: Thus says the LORD: Let my people go to worship me. 17 If you will not let my people go, I warn you, I will loose swarms of flies upon you and your servants and your subjects and your houses. The houses of the Egyptians and the very ground on which they stand shall be filled with swarms of flies. 18 But on that day I will make an exception of the land of Goshen: there shall be no flies where my people dwell, that you may know that I am the LORD in the midst of the earth. 19 I will make this distinction between my people and your people. This sign shall take place tomorrow." 20* This the LORD did. Thick swarms of flies entered the house of Pharaoh and houses of his servants; throughout Egypt the land was infested with flies.

21 Then Pharaoh summoned Moses and Aaron and said to them, "Go and offer sacrifice to your God in this land." 22† But Moses replied, "It is not right to do so, for the sacrifices we offer to the LORD, our God, are an abomination to the Egyptians. If

---

† 7, 26—8, 28: This is Ex 8, 1–32 in the verse enumeration of the Vulgate.

8, 9: *Courtyards:* some render "farmhouses."

8, 12.17: *Gnats, flies:* it is uncertain what species of troublesome insects are here meant.

8, 15: *The finger of God:* understood by the magicians as the *staff* mentioned in Ex 8, 13. Cf Lk 11, 20.

8, 22: The Egyptians would fiercely resent the sacrifice of any animal they considered sacred. Certain animals were worshiped in Egypt, at least as the symbols of various deities.

7, 26–29: Pss 78, 45; 105, 30.   8, 20: Pss 78, 45; 105, 31;
8, 12f: Ps 105, 31.   Wis 16, 9.
8, 14: Wis 17, 7.

did you KNOW?

Plagues and the Crossing of the Red Sea

The writer of Exodus combines several versions of what happened in describing the ten plagues and the crossing of the Red Sea. Like in a fine tapestry, the different strands are carefully woven together to produce a suspenseful story. When Pharaoh refuses to let the Israelites go, God sends ten plagues to convince Pharaoh to cooperate. The first nine plagues are exaggerations of naturally occurring events. For example, Exodus says the first plague is the water of the Nile turning to blood. At times, silt and microbes pollute and redden the Nile, making the water undrinkable. The Israelite people see God at work in the timing of these natural events.

Finally, God must resort to drastic measures. For the tenth plague, God sends the angel of death to kill the first-born children of the Egyptians. Moses has the Israelites mark their doorposts with the blood of a lamb so that the angel of death "passes over" their homes. Pharaoh is now eager to get rid of the Israelites and releases them from service. They gladly begin their journey to God's Promised Land.

After the Israelites leave, Pharaoh regrets his decision and sends his army after them. As the Egyptians close in, the Israelites seem to be trapped at the marshlands by the Red Sea (see map 2, "The Exodus from Egypt"). Although the prose version of this situation in Exodus, chapter 14, and the poetic version in chapter 15 differ in many details, both stress that the Israelites are able to pass through a section of wetlands that were made nearly dry by a strong east wind. The chariot wheels of the Egyptians get stuck in the mud, and as the water returns, they drown. Again, it is the timing of God's help that enables the miraculous escape. God hears God's people and sets them free!

▸ Ex 7, 1—14, 31

before their very eyes we offer sacrifices which are an abomination to them, will not the Egyptians stone us? 23 We must go a three days' journey in the desert to offer sacrifice to the LORD, our God, as he commands us." 24 "Well, then," said Pharaoh, "I will let you go to offer sacrifice to the LORD, your God, in the desert, provided that you do not go too far away and that you pray for me." 25 Moses answered, "As soon as I leave your presence I will pray to the LORD that the flies may depart tomorrow from Pharaoh and his servants and his subjects. Pharaoh, however, must not play false again by refusing to let the people go to offer sacrifice to the LORD." 26 When Moses left Pharaoh's presence, he prayed to the LORD; 27 and the LORD did as Moses had asked. He removed the flies from Pharaoh and his servants and subjects. Not one remained. 28 But once more Pharaoh became obdurate and would not let the people go.

Fifth Plague: the Pestilence

9 1 Then the LORD said to Moses, "Go to Pharaoh and tell him: Thus says the LORD, the God of the Hebrews: Let my people go to worship me. 2 If you refuse to let them go and persist in holding them, 3 I warn you, the LORD will afflict all your livestock in the field—your horses, asses, camels, herds and flocks—with a very severe pestilence. 4 But the LORD will distinguish between the livestock of Israel and that of Egypt, so that none belonging to the Israelites will die." 5 And setting a definite time, the LORD added, "Tomorrow the LORD shall do this in the land." 6* And on the next day the LORD did so. All the livestock of the Egyptians died, but not one beast belonging to the Israelites. 7 But though Pharaoh's messengers informed him that not even one beast belonging to the Israelites had died, he still remained obdurate and would not let the people go.

Sixth Plague: the Boils

8 Then the LORD said to Moses and Aaron, "Take a double handful of soot from a furnace, and in the presence of Pharaoh let Moses scatter it toward the sky. 9 It will then turn into fine dust over the whole land of Egypt and cause festering boils on man and beast throughout the land."

10 So they took soot from a furnace and stood in the presence of Pharaoh. Moses scattered it toward the sky, and it caused festering boils on man and beast. 11 The magicians could not stand in Moses' presence, for there were boils on the magicians no less than on the rest of the Egyptians. 12 But the LORD made Pharaoh obstinate, and he would not

EX

listen to them, just as the LORD had foretold to Moses.

Seventh Plague: the Hail

¹³ Then the LORD told Moses, "Early tomorrow morning present yourself to Pharaoh and say to him: Thus says the LORD, the God of the Hebrews: Let my people go to worship me, ¹⁴ or this time I will hurl all my blows upon you and your servants and your subjects, that you may know that there is none like me anywhere on earth. ¹⁵ For by now I would have stretched out my hand and struck you and your subjects with such pestilence as would wipe you from the earth. ¹⁶*† But this is why I have spared you: to show you my power and to make my name resound throughout the earth! ¹⁷ Will you still block the way for my people by refusing to let them go? ¹⁸ I warn you, then, tomorrow at this hour I will rain down such fierce hail as there has never been in Egypt from the day the nation was founded up to the present. ¹⁹ Therefore, order all your livestock and whatever else you have in the open fields to be brought to a place of safety. Whatever man or beast remains in the fields and is not brought to shelter shall die when the hail comes upon them." ²⁰ Some of Pharaoh's servants feared the warning of the LORD and hurried their servants and livestock off to shelter. ²¹ Others, however, did not take the warning of the LORD to heart and left their servants and livestock in the fields.

²² The LORD then said to Moses, "Stretch out your hand toward the sky, that hail may fall upon the entire land of Egypt, on man and beast and every growing thing in the land of Egypt." ²³* When Moses stretched out his staff toward the sky, the LORD sent forth hail and peals of thunder. Lightning flashed toward the earth, and the LORD rained down hail upon the land of Egypt; ²⁴ and lightning constantly flashed through the hail, such fierce hail as had never been seen in the land since Egypt became a nation. ²⁵ It struck down every man and beast that was in the open throughout the land of Egypt; it beat down every growing thing and splintered every tree in the fields. ²⁶ Only in the land of Goshen, where the Israelites dwelt, was there no hail.

²⁷ Then Pharaoh summoned Moses and Aaron and said to them, "I have sinned again! The LORD is just; it is I and my subjects who are at fault. ²⁸ Pray to the LORD, for we have had enough of God's thunder and hail. Then I will let you go; you need stay no longer." ²⁹ Moses replied, "As soon as I leave the city I will extend my hands to the LORD; the thunder will cease, and there will be no more hail. Thus you shall learn that the earth is the LORD'S. ³⁰ But you and your servants, I know, do not yet fear the LORD God."

³¹ Now the flax and the barley were ruined, because the barley was in ear and the flax in bud. ³² But the wheat and the spelt were not ruined, for they grow later.

³³ When Moses had left Pharaoh's presence and had gone out of the city, he extended his hands to the LORD. Then the thunder and the hail ceased, and the rain no longer poured down upon the earth. ³⁴ But Pharaoh, seeing that the rain and hail and thunder had ceased, sinned again: he with his servants became obdurate, ³⁵ and in his obstinacy he would not let the Israelites go, as the LORD had foretold through Moses.

Eighth Plague: the Locusts

10 ¹ Then the LORD said to Moses, "Go to Pharaoh, for I have made him and his servants obdurate in order that I may perform these signs of mine among them ²* and that you may recount to your son and grandson how ruthlessly I dealt with the Egyptians and what signs I wrought among them, so that you may know that I am the LORD."

³ So Moses and Aaron went to Pharaoh and told him, "Thus says the LORD, the God of the Hebrews: How long will you refuse to submit to me? Let my people go to worship me. ⁴ If you refuse to let my people go, I warn you, tomorrow I will bring locusts into your country. ⁵ They shall cover the ground, so that the ground itself will not be visible. They shall eat up the remnant you saved unhurt from the hail, as well as all the foliage that has since sprouted in your fields. ⁶ They shall fill your houses and the houses of your servants and of all the Egyptians; such a sight your fathers or grandfathers have not seen from the day they first settled on this soil up to the present day." With that he turned and left Pharaoh.

⁷ But Pharaoh's servants said to him, "How long must he be a menace to us? Let the men go to worship the LORD, their God. Do you not yet realize that Egypt is being destroyed?" ⁸ So Moses and Aaron were brought back to Pharaoh, who said to them, "You may go and worship the LORD, your God. But how many of you will go?" ⁹ "Young and old must go with us," Moses answered, "our sons and daughters as well as our flocks and herds must accompany us. That is what a feast of the LORD

---

† **9, 16:** *To show you:* some ancient versions read, "to show through you." Cf Rom 9, 17.

* **9, 16:** Rom 9, 17.   **10, 2:** Dt 6, 20ff.
9, 23f: Pss 78, 47; 105, 32f.

means to us." [10]† "The LORD help you," Pharaoh replied, "if I ever let your little ones go with you! Clearly, you have some evil in mind. [11]† No, no! Just you men can go and worship the LORD. After all, that is what you want." With that they were driven from Pharaoh's presence.

[12]* The LORD then said to Moses, "Stretch out your hand over the land of Egypt, that locusts may swarm over it and eat up all the vegetation and whatever the hail has left." [13]† So Moses stretched out his staff over the land of Egypt, and the LORD sent an east wind blowing over the land all that day and all that night. At dawn the east wind brought the locusts. [14] They swarmed over the whole land of Egypt and settled down on every part of it. Never before had there been such a fierce swarm of locusts, nor will there ever be. [15] They covered the surface of the whole land, till it was black with them. They ate up all the vegetation in the land and the fruit of whatever trees the hail had spared. Nothing green was left on any tree or plant throughout the land of Egypt.

[16] Hastily Pharaoh summoned Moses and Aaron and said, "I have sinned against the LORD, your God, and against you. [17] But now, do forgive me my sin once more, and pray the LORD, your God, to take at least this deadly pest from me." [18] When Moses left the presence of Pharaoh, he prayed to the LORD, [19]† and the LORD changed the wind to a very strong west wind, which took up the locusts and hurled them into the Red Sea. But though not a single locust remained within the confines of Egypt, [20] the LORD made Pharaoh obstinate, and he would not let the Israelites go.

Ninth Plague: the Darkness

[21]† Then the LORD said to Moses, "Stretch out your hand toward the sky, that over the land of Egypt there may be such intense darkness that one can feel it." [22]* So Moses stretched out his hand toward the sky, and there was dense darkness throughout the land of Egypt for three days. [23] Men could not see one another, nor could they move from where they were, for three days. But all the Israelites had light where they dwelt.

[24] Pharaoh then summoned Moses and Aaron and said, "Go and worship the LORD. Your little

ones, too, may go with you. But your flocks and herds must remain." [25] Moses replied, "You must also grant us sacrifices and holocausts to offer up to the LORD, our God. [26] Hence, our livestock also must go with us. Not an animal must be left behind. Some of them we must sacrifice to the LORD, our God, but we ourselves shall not know which ones we must sacrifice to him until we arrive at the place itself." [27] But the LORD made Pharaoh obstinate, and he would not let them go. [28] "Leave my presence," Pharaoh said to him, "and see to it that you do not appear before me again! The day you appear before me you shall die!" [29] Moses replied, "Well said! I will never appear before you again."

Tenth Plague: the Death of the First-born

11 [1] Then the LORD told Moses, "One more plague will I bring upon Pharaoh and upon Egypt. After that he will let you depart. In fact, he will not merely let you go; he will drive you away. [2]* Instruct your people that every man is to ask his neighbor, and every woman her neighbor, for silver and gold articles and for clothing." [3] The LORD indeed made the Egyptians well-disposed toward the people; Moses himself was very highly regarded by Pharaoh's servants and the people in the land of Egypt.

[4]* Moses then said, "Thus says the LORD: At midnight I will go forth through Egypt. [5]* Every first-born in this land shall die, from the first-born of Pharaoh on the throne to the first-born of the slave-girl at the handmill, as well as all the first-born of the animals. [6] Then there shall be loud wailing throughout the land of Egypt, such as has never been, nor will ever be again. [7] But among the Israelites and their animals not even a dog shall growl, so that you may know how the LORD distinguishes between the Egyptians and the Israelites. [8]* All these servants of yours shall then come down to me, and prostrate before me, they shall beg me, 'Leave us, you and all your followers!' Only then will I depart." With that he left Pharaoh's presence in hot anger.

[9] The LORD said to Moses, "Pharaoh refuses to listen to you that my wonders may be multiplied in the land of Egypt." [10] Thus, although Moses and Aaron performed these various wonders in Pharaoh's

---

10, 10: *The LORD help you . . . :* literally, "May the LORD be with you in the same way as I let you . . ."; a sarcastic blessing intended as a curse.

10, 11: Pharaoh realized that if the men alone went they would have to return to their families. He suspected that the Hebrews had no intention of returning.

10, 13: *East wind:* coming across the desert from Arabia, the strong east wind brings Egypt the burning sirocco and, at times, locusts. Cf Ex 14, 21.

10, 19: *The Red Sea:* according to the traditional translation, but the Hebrew is literally, "the Reed Sea"; hence the Red Sea of Exodus

was probably a body of shallow water somewhat to the north of the present deep Red Sea.

10, 21: *Darkness:* at times a storm from the south, called the *khamsin,* blackens the sky of Egypt with sand from the Sahara; the dust in the air is then so thick that the darkness can, in a sense, "be felt."

10, 12ff: Pss 78, 46; 105, 34f.   11, 4: Ex 12, 12.
10, 22: Ps 105, 28.   11, 5f: Ex 12, 29f.
11, 2f: Ex 3, 21f; 12, 35f.   11, 8: Ex 12, 31ff.

presence, the LORD made Pharaoh obstinate, and he would not let the Israelites leave his land.

The Passover Ritual Prescribed

12 ¹ The LORD said to Moses and Aaron in the land of Egypt, ²*† "This month shall stand at the head of your calendar; you shall reckon it the first month of the year. ³ Tell the whole community of Israel: On the tenth of this month every one of your families must procure for itself a lamb, one apiece for each household. ⁴† If a family is too small for a whole lamb, it shall join the nearest household in procuring one and shall share in the lamb in proportion to the number of persons who partake of it. ⁵ The lamb must be a year-old male and without blemish. You may take it from either the sheep or the goats. ⁶ You shall keep it until the fourteenth day of this month, and then, with the whole assembly of Israel present, it shall be slaughtered during the evening twilight. ⁷ They shall take some of its blood and apply it to the two doorposts and the lintel of every house in which they partake of the lamb. ⁸ That same night they shall eat its roasted flesh with unleavened bread and bitter herbs. ⁹ It shall not be eaten raw or boiled, but roasted whole, with its head and shanks and inner organs. ¹⁰ None of it must be kept beyond the next morning; whatever is left over in the morning shall be burned up.

¹¹† "This is how you are to eat it: with your loins girt, sandals on your feet and your staff in hand, you shall eat like those who are in flight. It is the Passover of the LORD. ¹² For on this same night I will go through Egypt, striking down every first-born of the land, both man and beast, and executing judgment on all the gods of Egypt—I, the LORD! ¹³* But the blood will mark the houses where you are. Seeing the blood, I will pass over you; thus, when I strike the land of Egypt, no destructive blow will come upon you.

¹⁴ "This day shall be a memorial feast for you, which all your generations shall celebrate with pilgrimage to the LORD, as a perpetual institution. ¹⁵ For seven days you must eat unleavened bread. From the very first day you shall have your houses clear of all leaven. Whoever eats leavened bread from the first day to the seventh shall be cut off

from Israel. ¹⁶ On the first day you shall hold a sacred assembly, and likewise on the seventh. On these days you shall not do any sort of work, except to prepare the food that everyone needs.

¹⁷* "Keep, then, this custom of the unleavened bread. Since it was on this very day that I brought your ranks out of the land of Egypt, you must celebrate this day throughout your generations as a perpetual institution. ¹⁸ From the evening of the fourteenth day of the first month until the evening of the twenty-first day of this month you shall eat unleavened bread. ¹⁹ For seven days no leaven may be found in your houses. Anyone, be he a resident alien or a native, who eats leavened food shall be cut off from the community of Israel. ²⁰ Nothing leavened may you eat; wherever you dwell you may eat only unleavened bread."

Promulgation of the Passover

²¹ Moses called all the elders of Israel and said to them, "Go and procure lambs for your families, and slaughter them as Passover victims. ²²*† Then take a bunch of hyssop, and dipping it in the blood that is in the basin, sprinkle the lintel and the two doorposts with this blood. But none of you shall go outdoors until morning. ²³ For the LORD will go by, striking down the Egyptians. Seeing the blood on the lintel and the two doorposts, the LORD will pass over that door and not let the destroyer come into your houses to strike you down.

²⁴ "You shall observe this as a perpetual ordinance for yourselves and your descendants. ²⁵ Thus, you must also observe this rite when you have entered the land which the LORD will give you as he promised. ²⁶* When your children ask you, 'What does this rite of yours mean?' ²⁷ you shall reply, 'This is the Passover sacrifice of the LORD, who passed over the houses of the Israelites in Egypt; when he struck down the Egyptians, he spared our houses.' "

Then the people bowed down in worship, ²⁸ and the Israelites went and did as the LORD had commanded Moses and Aaron.

Death of the First-born

²⁹* At midnight the LORD slew every first-born in the land of Egypt, from the first-born of Pharaoh on

---

12, 2: *This month:* Abib, the month of "ripe grain." Cf Ex 13, 4; 23, 15; 34, 18; Dt 16, 1. It occurred near the vernal equinox, March-April. Later it was known by the Babylonian name of Nisan. Cf Neh 2, 1; Est 3, 7.

12, 4: *Share in the lamb:* probably, in the expenses of its purchase. Some explain, "reckon for the lamb the number of persons required to eat it." Cf Ex 12, 10.

12, 11: *Passover:* in Hebrew, *pesach*, in Aramaic, *pascha*. In the following verses the same root is used in the verb "to pass over." The word may be originally Egyptian, *pesach*, "the blow," i.e., the final plague which destroyed the Egyptian first-born.

12, 22: *Hyssop:* a plant with many woody branchlets that made a convenient sprinkler.

12, 2–20: Lv 23, 5–8; Nm 9,
          2–5; 28, 16ff; Dt 16,
          1–8.
12, 13: Heb 11, 28.
12, 17: Ex 13, 3.

12, 22f: Ex 12, 7.13.
12, 26f: Ex 13, 8.14; Dt 6, 20f.
12, 29f: Ex 11, 4ff; Pss 78, 51;
          105, 36; 136, 10; Wis
          18, 10–16.

?did you KNOW?

The Passover

"Why is this night so different from all other nights?" This question, asked by the youngest member of the family, is part of the Jewish celebration of the Passover celebration. Jewish people continue to celebrate the Passover today in fulfillment of Moses' command, "You shall observe this as a perpetual ordinance for yourselves and your descendants" (Ex 12, 24).

The Passover is celebrated around a meal including lamb and unleavened bread. The lamb recalls the Passover lamb whose blood was placed on the doorpost to protect the firstborn from the angel of death. The unleavened bread recalls the haste in which the people prepared to depart. Retelling the ancient story, generations of Jews have remembered that "night of nights" when the angel of death passed over the Israelites' houses and struck down the firstborn of the Egyptians. On that night, the people of God were finally released from slavery. Thus, Passover is a celebration of God's gift of freedom—a religious Independence Day, so to speak.

It was during the Passover celebration that Jesus had his farewell dinner (see Jn 13, 1), placing himself as the paschal sacrifice. Christians see Jesus as the new Passover; through his death and Resurrection, we are finally liberated from all bondage, including sin and death.

▶ Ex 12, 14–28

the throne to the first-born of the prisoner in the dungeon, as well as all the first-born of the animals. 30 Pharaoh arose in the night, he and all his servants and all the Egyptians; and there was loud wailing throughout Egypt, for there was not a house without its dead.

Permission To Depart

31 During the night Pharaoh summoned Moses and Aaron and said, "Leave my people at once, you and the Israelites with you! Go and worship the LORD as you said. 32 Take your flocks, too, and your herds, as you demanded, and begone; and you will be doing me a favor."

33 The Egyptians likewise urged the people on, to hasten their departure from the land; they thought that otherwise they would all die. 34 The people, therefore, took their dough before it was leavened, in their kneading bowls wrapped in their cloaks on their shoulders. 35* The Israelites did as Moses had commanded: they asked the Egyptians for articles of silver and gold and for clothing. 36 The LORD indeed had made the Egyptians so well-disposed toward the people that they let them have whatever they asked for. Thus did they despoil the Egyptians.

II: The Exodus From Egypt and the Journey to Sinai

Departure from Egypt

37* The Israelites set out from Rameses for Succoth, about six hundred thousand men on foot, not counting the children. 38† A crowd of mixed ancestry also went up with them, besides their livestock, very numerous flocks and herds. 39 Since the dough they had brought out of Egypt was not leavened, they baked it into unleavened loaves. They had been rushed out of Egypt and had no opportunity even to prepare food for the journey.

40*† The time the Israelites had stayed in Egypt was four hundred and thirty years. 41 At the end of four hundred and thirty years, all the hosts of the LORD left the land of Egypt on this very date. 42 This was a night of vigil for the LORD, as he led them out of the land of Egypt; so on this same night all the Israelites must keep a vigil for the LORD throughout their generations.

Passover Regulations

43 The LORD said to Moses and Aaron, "These are the regulations for the Passover. No foreigner may partake of it. 44 However, any slave who has been bought for money may partake of it, provided you have first circumcised him. 45 But no transient alien or hired servant may partake of it. 46*† It must be eaten in one and the same house; you may not take any of its flesh outside the house. You shall not

EX

12, 38: *Mixed ancestry:* half-Hebrew and half-Egyptian. Cf Nm 11, 4; Lv 24, 10f.

12, 40: *In Egypt:* according to some ancient sources, "in Canaan and Egypt," thus reckoning from the time of Abraham. Cf Gal 3, 17.

12, 46: *You shall not break any of its bones:* the application of these words to our Lord on the cross shows that the Paschal lamb

was a prophetic type of Christ, immolated to free men from the bondage of sin. Cf also 1 Cor 5, 7; 1 Pt 1, 19.

12, 35f: Ex 3, 21f; 11, 2f; Ps 105, 37f.
12, 37: Nm 33, 3ff.
12, 40: Gn 15, 13; Acts 7, 6; Gal 3, 17.
12, 46: Nm 9, 12; Jn 19, 36.

break any of its bones. [47] The whole community of Israel must keep this feast. [48]* If any aliens living among you wish to celebrate the Passover of the LORD, all the males among them must first be circumcised, and then they may join in its observance just like the natives. But no man who is uncircumcised may partake of it. [49] The law shall be the same for the resident alien as for the native."

[50] All the Israelites did just as the LORD had commanded Moses and Aaron. [51] On that same day the LORD brought the Israelites out of Egypt company by company.

Consecration of First-born

13 [1] The LORD spoke to Moses and said, [2]* "Consecrate to me every first-born that opens the womb among the Israelites, both of man and beast, for it belongs to me."

[3]* Moses said to the people, "Remember this day on which you came out of Egypt, that place of slavery. It was with a strong hand that the LORD brought you away. Nothing made with leaven must be eaten. [4] This day of your departure is in the month of Abib. [5] Therefore, it is in this month that you must celebrate this rite, after the LORD, your God, has brought you into the land of the Canaanites, Hittites, Amorites, Hivites and Jebusites, which he swore to your fathers he would give you, a land flowing with milk and honey. [6] For seven days you shall eat unleavened bread, and the seventh day shall also be a festival to the LORD. [7] Only unleavened bread may be eaten during the seven days; no leaven and nothing leavened may be found in all your territory. [8] On this day you shall explain to your son, 'This is because of what the LORD did for me when I came out of Egypt.' [9]* It shall be as a sign on your hand and as a reminder on your forehead; thus the law of the LORD will ever be on your lips, because with a strong hand the LORD brought you out of Egypt. [10] Therefore, you shall keep this prescribed rite at its appointed time from year to year.

[11] "When the LORD, your God, has brought you into the land of the Canaanites, which he swore to you and your fathers he would give you, [12]* you shall dedicate to the LORD every son that opens the womb; and all the male firstlings of your animals shall belong to the LORD. [13] Every first-born of an ass you shall redeem with a sheep. If you do not redeem it, you shall break its neck. Every first-born son you must redeem. [14] If your son should ask you later on, 'What does this mean?' you shall tell him, 'With a strong hand the LORD brought us out of Egypt, that place of slavery. [15] When Pharaoh stubbornly refused to let us go, the LORD killed every first-born in the land of Egypt, every first-born of man and of beast. That is why I sacrifice to the LORD everything of the male sex that opens the womb, and why I redeem every first-born of my sons.' [16]* Let this, then, be as a sign on your hand and as a pendant on your forehead: with a strong hand the LORD brought us out of Egypt."

Toward the Red Sea

[17]† Now, when Pharaoh let the people go, God did not lead them by way of the Philistines' land, though this was the nearest; for he thought, should the people see that they would have to fight, they might change their minds and return to Egypt. [18] Instead, he rerouted them toward the Red Sea by way of the desert road. In battle array the Israelites marched out of Egypt. [19]* Moses also took Joseph's bones along, for Joseph had made the Israelites swear solemnly that, when God should come to them, they would carry his bones away with them.

[20]* Setting out from Succoth, they camped at Etham near the edge of the desert.

[21]*† The Lord preceded them, in the daytime by means of a column of cloud to show them the way, and at night by means of a column of fire to give them light. Thus they could travel both day and night. [22] Neither the column of cloud by day nor the column of fire by night ever left its place in front of the people.

14 [1] Then the LORD said to Moses, [2]*† "Tell the Israelites to turn about and camp before Pi-hahiroth, between Migdol and the sea. You shall camp in front of Baal-zephon, just opposite, by the sea. [3] Pharaoh will then say, 'The Israelites are wandering about aimlessly in the land. The desert has closed in on them.' [4] Thus will I make Pharaoh so obstinate that he will pursue them. Then I will receive glory through Pharaoh and all his army, and the Egyptians will know that I am the LORD."

This the Israelites did. [5] When it was reported to the king of Egypt that the people had fled, Pharaoh

---

13, 17: *By way of the Philistines' land:* the most direct route from Egypt to Palestine, along the shore of the Mediterranean.

13, 21: *A column of cloud . . . a column of fire:* probably one and the same preternatural phenomenon, a central nucleus of fire surrounded by smoke; only at night was its luminous nature visible. Cf Ex 40, 38.

14, 2: These places have not been definitively identified. Even the relative position of *Pi-hahiroth* and *Baal-zephon* is not clear; perhaps the former was on the west shore of the sea, where the Israelites were, and the latter on the opposite shore.

12, 48: 47f: Nm 9, 14.
  13, 2: Ex 13, 12–15.
13, 3–10: Ex 12, 2–20.
  13, 9: Ex 13, 16; Dt 6, 8; 11, 18.
13, 12–15: Ex 13, 2; 22, 29f; 34, 19f; Nm 3, 12f; 8, 16; 18, 15; Dt 15, 19.
13, 16: Ex 13, 9.
13, 19: Gn 50, 25; Jos 24, 32.
13, 20: Nm 33, 6.
13, 21f: Ex 40, 38; Nm 9, 15–22; Dt 1, 33; Neh 9, 19; Pss 78, 14; 105, 39; Wis 10, 17.
14, 2: Nm 33, 7f.

GOD LIBERATES US FROM OPPRESSION!

Many centuries before Christ, the Israelites migrated to Egypt from Canaan, seeking food because of an extreme drought in their land. The Egyptians, taking advantage of the Israelites' need for food and shelter, set taskmasters to rule over them and made their lives bitter with hard service.

- Have you, your family, or your people ever experienced oppression through forced labor?
- Are you aware of situations in which people are being oppressed or exploited because of their immigrant status, their educational level, or their need for food and shelter?
- Pray for God's liberating power, and ask God to give you the strength to fight unjust situations and oppression.

The Israelite people groaned under their slavery and asked God for help. God responded to their plight and sent Moses to lead them into freedom. But they needed to overcome their fear of the unknown future and step out in trust. Their liberation was accomplished when they responded to God's initiative to free themselves from a life of bondage. To be free, we must first be willing to admit that we are enslaved to something.

- What types of oppression or pressures have taken away your freedom to live according to God's will?
- How can your community help young people to recognize when they are enslaved by social and peer pressures?
- Pray with Psalm 54 to ask for God's help in your struggle. Or pray with Psalm 146 to praise and thank God for liberation that you have experienced.

▶ Ex 14, 1–31

and his servants changed their minds about them. "What have we done!" they exclaimed. "Why, we have released Israel from our service!" 6 So Pharaoh made his chariots ready and mustered his soldiers— 7 six hundred first-class chariots and all the other chariots of Egypt, with warriors on them all. 8* So obstinate had the LORD made Pharaoh that he pursued the Israelites even while they were marching away in triumph. 9 The Egyptians, then, pursued them; Pharaoh's whole army, his horses, chariots and charioteers, caught up with them as they lay encamped by the sea, at Pi-hahiroth, in front of Baal-zephon.

Crossing of the Red Sea

10 Pharaoh was already near when the Israelites looked up and saw that the Egyptians were on the march in pursuit of them. In great fright they cried out to the LORD. 11 And they complained to Moses, "Were there no burial places in Egypt that you had to bring us out here to die in the desert? Why did you do this to us? Why did you bring us out of Egypt? 12 Did we not tell you this in Egypt, when we said, 'Leave us alone. Let us serve the Egyptians'? Far

better for us to be the slaves of the Egyptians than to die in the desert." 13 But Moses answered the people, "Fear not! Stand your ground, and you will see the victory the LORD will win for you today. These Egyptians whom you see today you will never see again. 14 The LORD himself will fight for you; you have only to keep still."

15 Then the LORD said to Moses, "Why are you crying out to me? Tell the Israelites to go forward. 16 And you, lift up your staff and, with hand outstretched over the sea, split the sea in two, that the Israelites may pass through it on dry land. 17 But I will make the Egyptians so obstinate that they will go in after them. Then I will receive glory through Pharaoh and all his army, his chariots and charioteers. 18 The Egyptians shall know that I am the LORD, when I receive glory through Pharaoh and his chariots and charioteers."

19 The angel of God, who had been leading Israel's camp, now moved and went around behind them. The column of cloud also, leaving the front,

14, 8: 5–8: Wis 19, 3; 1 Mc 4, 9.

bitter. Hence this place was called Marah. 24 As the people grumbled against Moses, saying, "What are we to drink?" 25* he appealed to the LORD, who pointed out to him a certain piece of wood. When he threw this into the water, the water became fresh.

It was here that the LORD, in making rules and regulations for them, put them to the test. 26* "If you really listen to the voice of the LORD, your God," he told them, "and do what is right in his eyes: if you heed his commandments and keep all his precepts, I will not afflict you with any of the diseases with which I afflicted the Egyptians; for I, the LORD, am your healer."

27* Then they came to Elim, where there were twelve springs of water and seventy palm trees, and they camped there near the water.

The Desert of Sin

16 1† Having set out from Elim, the whole Israelite community came into the desert of Sin, which is between Elim and Sinai, on the fifteenth day of the second month after their departure from the land of Egypt. 2 Here in the desert the

The Quail and Manna

4*† Then the LORD said to Moses, "I will now rain down bread from heaven for you. Each day the people are to go out and gather their daily portion; thus will I test them, to see whether they follow my instructions or not. 5 On the sixth day, however, when they prepare what they bring in, let it be twice as much as they gather on the other days." 6 So Moses and Aaron told all the Israelites, "At evening you will know that it was the LORD who brought you out of the land of Egypt; 7* and in the morning you will see the glory of the LORD, as he heeds your grumbling against him. But what are we that you should grumble against us? 8 When the LORD gives you flesh to eat in the evening," continued Moses, "and in the morning your fill of bread, as he heeds the grumbling you utter against him, what then are we? Your grumbling is not against us, but against the LORD."

9 Then Moses said to Aaron, "Tell the whole Israelite community: Present yourselves before the LORD, for he has heard your grumbling." 10 When Aaron announced this to the whole Israelite community, they turned toward the desert, and lo, the

Those Whiny Israelites   LIVE IT!

It's so easy to complain, isn't it? As soon as things aren't quite the way we would like, we start fussing and whining and grumbling. We have all done it. We are no different from the Israelites who, despite having just been miraculously delivered from slavery, start complaining after a few days in the wilderness. "Why," they ask, "would God lead us through the Red Sea only to let us die of hunger?"

Perspective. Faith. That's what it takes. Once we have been through a crisis or spent time in a place where people are truly poor and hungry, we gain a perspective on our own culture, on our own tendency to want everything just the way we like it and as soon as possible. The next time we hear ourselves complaining about something, let's pause and try to see a bigger picture, perhaps the one that God sees. Then we can ask ourselves, Is this really worth complaining about?

▶ Ex 16, 1–3

whole Israelite community grumbled against Moses and Aaron. 3 The Israelites said to them, "Would that we had died at the LORD'S hand in the land of Egypt, as we sat by our fleshpots and ate our fill of bread! But you had to lead us into this desert to make the whole community die of famine!"

glory of the LORD appeared in the cloud! 11 The LORD spoke to Moses and said, 12 "I have heard the grumbling of the Israelites. Tell them: In the evening twilight you shall eat flesh, and in the morning you shall have your fill of bread, so that you may know that I, the LORD, am your God."

16, 1: *On the fifteenth day of the second month:* just one full month after their departure from Egypt. Cf Ex 12, 2.51; Nm 33, 3f. They encamped in the desert of Sin on a Friday; the murmuring (vv 2f) occurred on the sabbath, the arrival of the quail (v 13) the evening before Sunday, followed by six mornings (vv 14–27) of collecting manna before the next sabbath.

16, 4: *Bread from heaven:* as a gift from God, the manna is said to come down from the sky. Cf Ps 78, 25; Wis 16, 20. Perhaps it was similar to a natural substance that is still found in small quantities on

the Sinai peninsula, but here it is, at least in part, clearly miraculous. Our Lord referred to the manna as a type of the Blessed Eucharist. Cf Jn 6, 32.49–52.

15, 25: Sir 38, 5.
15, 26: Dt 7, 15.
15, 27: Nm 33, 9.

16, 4: Pss 78, 24f; 105, 40;
    Jn 6, 31f; 1 Cor 10, 3.
16, 7: 6f; Ex 16, 12.

Asian American

Manna and Rice

Rice is the symbol of our life
We eat rice daily
There are different kinds of rice
But we are one
as the rice-eating community
Rice is the symbol of celebration
We express our joy of harvest with it
There are many sufferings in Asia
but we anticipate the time of cosmic
   celebration.

      (From Maren C. Tirabassi and
      Kathy Wonson Eddy, editors,
      Gifts of Many Cultures, p. 186)

This poem from Japan by Masao and
Fumiko Takenaka expresses their appreciation for rice, the most basic food
of the Japanese. It unites them as a
people and reminds them to be joyful.
In a similar way, Exodus tells how the
gift of manna united the Israelites and
gave them a reason for celebration
despite their many trials. What foods
unite you and your friends? family?
culture? What connections do you see
between manna, rice, and the Eucharist?

▶ Ex 16, 1–36

---

¹³* In the evening quail came up and covered the camp. In the morning a dew lay all about the camp, ¹⁴ and when the dew evaporated, there on the surface of the desert were fine flakes like hoarfrost on the ground. ¹⁵*† On seeing it, the Israelites asked one another, "What is this?" for they did not know what it was. But Moses told them, "This is the bread which the LORD has given you to eat.

Regulations Regarding the Manna

¹⁶ "Now, this is what the LORD has commanded. So gather it that everyone has enough to eat, an omer for each person, as many of you as there are, each man providing for those of his own tent." ¹⁷ The Israelites did so. Some gathered a large and some a small amount. ¹⁸*† But when they measured it out by the omer, he who had gathered a large amount did not have too much, and he who had gathered a small amount did not have too little. They so gathered that everyone had enough to eat. ¹⁹ Moses also told them, "Let no one keep any of it over until tomorrow morning." ²⁰ But they would not listen to him. When some kept a part of it over until the following morning, it became wormy and rotten. Therefore Moses was displeased with them.

²¹ Morning after morning they gathered it, till each had enough to eat; but when the sun grew hot, the manna melted away. ²² On the sixth day they gathered twice as much food, two omers for each person. When all the leaders of the community came and reported this to Moses, ²³ he told them, "That is what the LORD prescribed. Tomorrow is a day of complete rest, the sabbath, sacred to the LORD. You may either bake or boil the manna, as you please; but whatever is left put away and keep for the morrow." ²⁴ When they put it away for the morrow, as Moses commanded, it did not become rotten or wormy. ²⁵ Moses then said, "Eat it today, for today is the sabbath of the LORD. On this day you will not find any of it on the ground. ²⁶ On the other six days you can gather it, but on the seventh day, the sabbath, none of it will be there." ²⁷ Still, on the seventh day some of the people went out to gather it, although they did not find any. ²⁸ Then the LORD said to Moses, "How long will you refuse to keep my commandments and laws? ²⁹ Take note! The LORD has given you the sabbath. That is why on the sixth day he gives you food for two days. On the seventh day everyone is to stay home and no one is to go out." ³⁰ After that the people rested on the seventh day.

³¹*† The Israelites called this food manna. It was like coriander seed, but white, and it tasted like wafers made with honey.

³² Moses said, "This is what the LORD has commanded. Keep an omerful of manna for your descendants, that they may see what food I gave you to eat in the desert when I brought you out of the land of Egypt." ³³*† Moses then told Aaron, "Take an urn and put an omer of manna in it. Then place it before the LORD in safekeeping for your descendants."

---

† **16, 15:** *What is this:* the original *man hu* is thus rendered by the ancient versions, which understood the phrase as a popular etymology of the Hebrew word *man*, "manna"; some render, "This is manna."

16, 18: St. Paul cites this passage as an example of equitable sharing. Cf 2 Cor 8, 15.

16, 31: *Coriander seed:* small, round, aromatic seeds of bright brown color; the comparison, therefore, refers merely to the size and shape, not to the taste or color of the manna.

16, 33: *Urn:* according to the Greek translation, which is followed in Heb 9, 4, this was a golden vessel.

*
16, 13: Nm 11, 31; Ps 78, 27f.	**16, 31:** Nm 11, 7.
16, 15: Dt 8, 3.	**16, 33:** Heb 9, 4.
16, 18: 2 Cor 8, 15.	

34† So Aaron placed it in front of the commandments for safekeeping, as the LORD had commanded Moses.

35* The Israelites ate this manna for forty years, until they came to settled land; they ate manna until they reached the borders of Canaan. 36 [An omer is one tenth of an ephah.]

Water from the Rock

17 1* From the desert of Sin the whole Israelite community journeyed by stages, as the LORD directed, and encamped at Rephidim.

Here there was no water for the people to drink. 2* They quarreled, therefore, with Moses and said, "Give us water to drink." Moses replied, "Why do you quarrel with me? Why do you put the LORD to a test?" 3 Here, then, in their thirst for water, the people grumbled against Moses, saying, "Why did you ever make us leave Egypt? Was it just to have us die here of thirst with our children and our livestock?" 4 So Moses cried out to the LORD, "What shall I do with this people? A little more and they will stone me!" 5 The LORD answered Moses, "Go over there in front of the people, along with some of the elders of Israel, holding in your hand, as you go, the staff with which you struck the river. 6* I will be standing there in front of you on the rock in Horeb. Strike the rock, and the water will flow from it for the people to drink." This Moses did, in the presence of the elders of Israel. 7*† The place was called Massah and Meribah, because the Israelites quarreled there and tested the LORD, saying, "Is the LORD in our midst or not?"

Battle with Amalek

8*† At Rephidim, Amalek came and waged war against Israel. 9 Moses, therefore, said to Joshua, "Pick out certain men, and tomorrow go out and engage Amalek in battle. I will be standing on top of the hill with the staff of God in my hand." 10 So Joshua did as Moses told him: he engaged Amalek in battle after Moses had climbed to the top of the hill with Aaron and Hur. 11 As long as Moses kept his hands raised up, Israel had the better of the fight, but when he let his hands rest, Amalek had the better of the fight. 12 Moses' hands, however, grew tired; so they put a rock in place for him to sit on. Meanwhile Aaron and Hur supported his hands, one on one side and one on the other, so that his hands remained steady till sunset. 13 And Joshua mowed down Amalek and his people with the edge of the sword.

14* Then the LORD said to Moses, "Write this down in a document as something to be remembered, and recite it in the ears of Joshua. I will completely blot out the memory of Amalek from under the heavens." 15† Moses also built an altar there, which he called Yahweh-nissi; 16 for he said, "The LORD takes in hand his banner; the LORD will war against Amalek through the centuries."

Prayer in Support of Others

During the battle against Amalek, Moses' outstretched arms could be understood as a prayer of support for the Israelites. It was an effective prayer, too, because as long as he was able to maintain it, the Israelites were winning. When he could not maintain the prayer by himself, Aaron and Hur helped.

Prayer makes a difference. Research has shown that prayer helps people's emotional and physical health and healing, though it cannot explain why. Spiritual energy is a proven, powerful force.

Prayer doesn't even need words. To hold someone in prayer, just think of them and quietly take their pain or joy into your heart.

▸ Ex 17, 8–16

Meeting with Jethro

18 1 Now Moses' father-in-law Jethro, the priest of Midian, heard of all that God had done for Moses and for his people Israel: how the LORD had brought Israel out of Egypt. 2 So his father-in-law Jethro took along Zipporah, Moses' wife, whom Moses had sent back to him, 3* and her two sons. One of these was called Gershom; for he said, "I am a stranger in a foreign land." 4 The other

---

†
16, 34: *The commandments:* the two tablets of the ten commandments, which were kept in the ark. Cf Ex 25, 16.21f.

17, 7: *Massah . . . Meribah:* Hebrew words meaning respectively, "the (place of the) test," and, "the (place of the) quarreling."

17, 8: *Amalek:* the Amalekites were an aboriginal people of southern Palestine and the Sinai peninsula. Cf Nm 24, 20.

17, 15: *Yahweh-nissi:* meaning, "the LORD is my banner."

16, 35: Jos 5, 12.
17, 1: Nm 33, 12ff.
17, 2–7: Nm 20, 2–13.
17, 6: 5f; Dt 8, 15; Pss 78, 15f; 105, 41; Wis 11, 4; Is 43, 20; 48, 21.
17, 7: Ps 95, 8f.
17, 8: Dt 25, 17; 1 Sm 15, 2.
17, 14: Nm 24, 20; 1 Sm 15, 3.20.
18, 3: Ex 2, 22.

was called Eliezer; for he said, "My father's God is my helper; he has rescued me from Pharaoh's sword." 5 Together with Moses' wife and sons, then, his father-in-law Jethro came to him in the desert where he was encamped near the mountain of God, 6 and he sent word to Moses, "I, Jethro, your father-in-law, am coming to you, along with your wife and her two sons."

7 Moses went out to meet his father-in-law, bowed down before him, and kissed him. Having greeted each other, they went into the tent. 8 Moses then told his father-in-law of all that the LORD had done to Pharaoh and the Egyptians for the sake of Israel, and of all the hardships they had had to endure on their journey, and how the LORD had come to their rescue. 9 Jethro rejoiced over all the goodness that the LORD had shown Israel in rescuing them from the hands of the Egyptians. 10 "Blessed be the LORD," he said, "who has rescued his people from the hands of Pharaoh and the Egyptians. 11 Now I know that the LORD is a deity great beyond any other; for he took occasion of their being dealt with insolently to deliver the people from the power of the Egyptians." 12 Then Jethro, the father-in-law of Moses, brought a holocaust and other sac-

Why do you sit alone while all the people have to stand about you from morning till evening?" 15 Moses answered his father-in-law, "The people come to me to consult God. 16 Whenever they have a disagreement, they come to me to have me settle the matter between them and make known to them God's decisions and regulations."

17 "You are not acting wisely," his father-in-law replied. 18* "You will surely wear yourself out, and not only yourself but also these people with you. The task is too heavy for you; you cannot do it alone. 19 Now, listen to me, and I will give you some advice, that God may be with you. Act as the people's representative before God, bringing to him whatever they have to say. 20 Enlighten them in regard to the decisions and regulations, showing them how they are to live and what they are to do. 21* But you should also look among all the people for able and God-fearing men, trustworthy men who hate dishonest gain, and set them as officers over groups of thousands, of hundreds, of fifties, and of tens. 22 Let these men render decisions for the people in all ordinary cases. More important cases they should refer to you, but all the lesser cases they can settle themselves. Thus, your burden

Sharing Responsibility

Was Moses a workaholic (see Ex 18, 18)? Maybe he just found himself suddenly overwhelmed with too many responsibilities. Fortunately for Moses, he had a wise father-in-law who could see an alternative that Moses could not see—or maybe did not want to see.

Who in this story do you feel most like?
- Moses, surrounded by people clamoring for your attention
- Jethro, concerned about Moses but able to offer some advice
- one of the people, hoping that Moses has a few minutes to listen to your problem
- one of the trustworthy judges, chosen by Moses to make sure that the Israelites experience justice in all their day-to-day business

When leaders share responsibility, they are saying to other people, "I trust you, we're in this together, and you are needed." When you are in a leadership position, remember Jethro's advice to Moses and don't be a lone ranger; ask others to help!

▶ Ex 18, 13–26

rifices to God, and Aaron came with all the elders of Israel to participate with Moses' father-in-law in the meal before God.

Appointment of Minor Judges

13 The next day Moses sat in judgment for the people, who waited about him from morning until evening. 14 When his father-in-law saw all that he was doing for the people, he inquired, "What sort of thing is this that you are doing for the people?

will be lightened, since they will bear it with you. 23 If you do this, when God gives you orders you will be able to stand the strain, and all these people will go home satisfied."

24 Moses followed the advice of his father-in-law and did all that he had suggested. 25 He picked out able men from all Israel and put them in charge of

---

18, 18: Nm 11, 14.   18, 21.25: Dt 1, 15; 16, 18.

EX

the people as officers over groups of thousands, of hundreds, of fifties, and of tens. 26 They rendered decisions for the people in all ordinary cases. The more difficult cases they referred to Moses, but all the lesser cases they settled themselves. 27 Then Moses bade farewell to his father-in-law, who went off to his own country.

III: The Covenant at Mount Sinai

Arrival at Sinai

19 1* In the third month after their departure from the land of Egypt, on its first day, the Israelites came to the desert of Sinai. 2 After the journey from Rephidim to the desert of Sinai, they pitched camp.

While Israel was encamped here in front of the mountain, 3 Moses went up the mountain to God. Then the LORD called to him and said, "Thus shall you say to the house of Jacob; 4* tell the Israelites: You have seen for yourselves how I treated the Egyptians and how I bore you up on eagle wings and brought you here to myself. 5* Therefore, if you hearken to my voice and keep my covenant, you shall be my special possession, dearer to me than all other people, though all the earth is mine. 6*† You shall be to me a kingdom of priests, a holy nation. That is what you must tell the Israelites." 7 So Moses went and summoned the elders of the people. When he set before them all that the LORD had ordered him to tell them, 8 the people all answered together, "Everything the LORD has said, we will do." Then Moses brought back to the LORD the response of the people.

9* The LORD also told him, "I am coming to you in a dense cloud, so that when the people hear me speaking with you, they may always have faith in you also." When Moses, then, had reported to the LORD the response of the people, 10 the LORD added, "Go to the people and have them sanctify themselves today and tomorrow. Make them wash their garments 11 and be ready for the third day; for on the third day the LORD will come down on Mount Sinai before the eyes of all the people. 12* Set limits for the people all around the mountain, and tell them: Take care not to go up the mountain, or even to touch its base. If anyone touches the mountain he must be put to death.

13 No hand shall touch him; he must be stoned to death or killed with arrows. Such a one, man or beast, must not be allowed to live. Only when the ram's horn resounds may they go up to the mountain." 14 Then Moses came down from the mountain to the people and had them sanctify themselves and wash their garments. 15 He warned them, "Be ready for the third day. Have no intercourse with any woman."

The Great Theophany

16 On the morning of the third day there were peals of thunder and lightning, and a heavy cloud over the mountain, and a very loud trumpet blast, so that all the people in the camp trembled. 17* But Moses led the people out of the camp to meet God, and they stationed themselves at the foot of the mountain. 18 Mount Sinai was all wrapped in smoke, for the LORD came down upon it in fire. The smoke rose from it as though from a furnace, and the whole mountain trembled violently. 19 The trumpet blast grew louder and louder, while Moses was speaking and God answering him with thunder.

20 When the LORD came down to the top of Mount Sinai, he summoned Moses to the top of the mountain, and Moses went up to him. 21 Then the LORD told Moses, "Go down and warn the people not to break through toward the LORD in order to see him; otherwise many of them will be struck down. 22 The priests, too, who approach the LORD must sanctify themselves; else he will vent his anger upon them." 23 Moses said to the LORD, "The people cannot go up to Mount Sinai, for you yourself warned us to set limits around the mountain to make it sacred." 24 The LORD repeated, "Go down now! Then come up again along with Aaron. But the priests and the people must not break through to come up to the LORD; else he will vent his anger upon them." 25 So Moses went down to the people and told them this.

The Ten Commandments

20 1† Then God delivered all these commandments:

2* "I, the LORD, am your God, who brought you out of the land of Egypt, *that place of slavery. 3 You shall not have other gods besides me. 4* You shall not carve idols for yourselves in the shape of

---

19, 6: *Kingdom of priests:* inasmuch as the whole Israelite nation was consecrated to God in a special way, it formed a race of royal priests who participated in the liturgical sacrifices, even though the actual offering of the sacrifices was the exclusive prerogative of the Aaronic priesthood. The same condition exists in the New Dispensation as regards the whole Christian people and the Christian priesthood in the strict sense. Cf Is 61, 6; 1 Pt 2, 5.9.

20, 1–17: The precise division of these precepts into "ten commandments" is somewhat uncertain. Traditionally among Catholics

vv 1–6 are considered as only one commandment, and v 17 as two. Cf Dt 5, 6–21.

19, 1f: Nm 33, 15.	**19:17: 16ff:** Dt 4, 10ff.
19, 4: Dt 32, 11.	**20, 2–17:** Dt 5, 6–21.
19, 5: Dt 7, 6; 14, 2; 26, 18f; 32, 8f.	**20, 2:** Lv 26, 13; Ps 81, 10; Hos 13, 4.
19, 6: 1 Pt 2, 9.	**20, 4:** Ex 34, 17; Lv 26, 1; Dt 4, 15–19; 27, 15.
19, 9: Ex 20, 21; 24, 15–18.	
19, 12f: Ex 34, 3; Heb 12, 18f.	

?did you KNOW?

The Ten Commandments

The Covenant God made with the Is-raelites is often called the Sinai Covenant. The Ten Commandments are a handy summary of the Sinai Covenant—literally handy because they can be counted off on one's fingers. Because the Command-ments are short (so short that they are sometimes called the Ten Words) and most of them begin with a similar phrase ("You shall not"), they are easily commit-ted to memory. The ancient Israelites believed that everyone had to know and observe these basic rules if God's people were to live together in peace and securi-ty. Today, three major world religions—Jewish, Christian, and Islamic—continue to revere the Ten Commandments as ba-sic building blocks of human community.

For the ancient Israelites, the Ten Commandments covered specific behav-iors that made them different from the neighboring cultures. Over the centuries, Christians have applied the moral princi-ples of the Ten Commandments to many other moral questions. In fact, the *Cate-chism of the Catholic Church* presents the Ten Commandments as the structure for teaching about many moral issues. For Jesus' teaching on the Commandments, see Mt 5, 1—7, 29; 22, 34–40; Mk 12, 28–34.

▸ Ex 20, 1–17

7* "You shall not take the name of the LORD, your God, in vain. For the LORD will not leave un-punished him who takes his name in vain.

8 "Remember to keep holy the sabbath day. 9 Six days you may labor and do all your work, 10* but the seventh day is the sabbath of the LORD, your God. No work may be done then either by you, or your son or daughter, or your male or female slave, or your beast, or by the alien who lives with you. 11* In six days the LORD made the heavens and the earth, the sea and all that is in them; but on the seventh day he rested. That is why the LORD has blessed the sabbath day and made it holy.

12* "Honor your father and your mother, that you may have a long life in the land which the LORD, your God, is giving you.*

13* "You shall not kill.

14* "You shall not commit adultery.

15* "You shall not steal.

16* "You shall not bear false witness against your neighbor.

17* "You shall not covet your neighbor's house. You shall not covet your neighbor's wife, nor his male or female slave, nor his ox or ass, nor anything else that belongs to him."

The Fear of God

18* When the people witnessed the thunder and lightning, the trumpet blast and the mountain smoking, they all feared and trembled. So they took up a position much farther away 19 and said to Moses, "You speak to us, and we will listen; but let not God speak to us, or we shall die." 20 Moses an-swered the people, "Do not be afraid, for God has come to you only to test you and put his fear upon you, lest you should sin." 21 Still the people re-mained at a distance, while Moses approached the cloud where God was.

22 The LORD told Moses, "Thus shall you speak to the Israelites: You have seen for yourselves that I have spoken to you from heaven. 23* Do not make anything to rank with me; neither gods of silver nor gods of gold shall you make for yourselves.

24*† "An altar of earth you shall make for me, and upon it you shall sacrifice your holocausts and peace offerings, your sheep and your oxen. In what-ever place I choose for the remembrance of my name I will come to you and bless you. 25* If you make an altar of stone for me, do not build it of cut stone, for by putting a tool to it you desecrate it.

EX

anything in the sky above or on the earth below or in the waters beneath the earth; 5*† you shall not bow down before them or worship them. For I, the LORD, your God, am a jealous God, inflicting pun-ishment for their fathers' wickedness on the chil-dren of those who hate me, down to the third and fourth generation; 6 but bestowing mercy down to the thousandth generation, on the children of those who love me and keep my commandments.

---

†
20, 5: *Jealous:* demanding exclusive allegiance, such as a wife must have for her husband.
20, 24: *I choose for the remembrance of my name:* literally, "where I make my name to be remembered": at the sacred site where God wishes to be worshiped and his name revered.

*
20, 5: Ex 34, 7.14; Nm 14, 18; Dt 4, 24; 6, 15.
20, 7: Lv 19, 12; 24, 16.
20, 10: 8ff: Ex 23, 12; 31, 13–16;
34, 21; 35, 2; Lv 23, 3.
20, 11: Ex 31, 17; Gn 2, 2f.
20, 12–16: Mt 19, 18f; Mk 10, 19; Lk 18, 20; Rom 13, 9.
20, 12: Mt 15, 4; Mk 7, 10; Eph 6, 2f.
20, 13: Mt 5, 21.
20, 14: Lv 18, 20; 20, 10; Dt 22, 22; Mt 5, 27.
20, 15: Lv 19, 11.
20, 16: Ex 23, 1; Dt 19, 16ff; Prv 19, 5.9; 24, 28.
20, 17: Rom 7, 7.
20, 18–21: Dt 4, 11; 5, 22–27; 18, 16; Heb 12, 18f.
20, 23: Ex 20, 3f.
20, 24: Dt 12, 5.11; 14, 23; 16, 6.
20, 25: Dt 27, 5; Jos 8, 31.

The TEN Commandments

1 I, the LORD, am your God . . . You shall not have other gods besides me. **2** You shall not take the name of the LORD, your God, in vain. **3** Remember to keep holy the Sabbath day. **4** Honor your father and your mother. **5** You shall not kill. **6** You shall not commit adultery. **7** You shall not steal. **8** You shall not bear false witness against your neighbor. **9 & 10** You shall not covet your neighbor's house. You shall not covet your neighbor's wife . . . nor anything else that belongs to him.

20, 2–17

---

26 You shall not go up by steps to my altar, on which you must not be indecently uncovered.

Laws Regarding Slaves

21 **1†** "These are the rules you shall lay before them. **2*** When you purchase a Hebrew slave, he is to serve you for six years, but in the seventh year he shall be given his freedom without cost. **3** If he comes into service alone, he shall leave alone; if he comes with a wife, his wife shall leave with him. **4** But if his master gives him a wife and she bears him sons or daughters, the woman and her children shall remain the master's property and the man shall leave alone. **5** If, however, the slave declares, 'I am devoted to my master and my wife and children; I will not go free,' **6†** his master shall bring him to God and there, at the door or doorpost, he shall pierce his ear with an awl, thus keeping him as his slave forever.

7 "When a man sells his daughter as a slave, she

21, 1: *Rules:* judicial precedents to be used in settling questions of law and custom. This introductory phrase serves as the title of the following collection of civil and religious laws (chapters 21–23) which is called in Ex 24, 7, *the book of the covenant.*

21, 6: *To God:* to the sanctuary; or perhaps the phrase is to be rendered, "to the gods," in the sense of "to the judges." Cf Ps 82, 1.

Since the expression "to have an open ear" meant "to obey," a pierced ear lobe was an ancient symbol of obedience. Cf Ps 40, 7.

21, 2–6: Lv 25, 39ff; Dt 15, 12–18; Jer 34, 14.

shall not go free as male slaves do. ⁸† But if her master, who had destined her for himself, dislikes her, he shall let her be redeemed. He has no right to sell her to a foreigner, since he has broken faith with her. ⁹ If he destines her for his son, he shall treat her like a daughter. ¹⁰ If he takes another wife, he shall not withhold her food, her clothing, or her conjugal rights. ¹¹ If he does not grant her these three things, she shall be given her freedom absolutely, without cost to her.

Personal Injury

¹²* "Whoever strikes a man a mortal blow must be put to death. ¹³ He, however, who did not hunt a man down, but caused his death by an act of God, may flee to a place which I will set apart for this purpose. ¹⁴ But when a man kills another after mali-

²⁰ "When a man strikes his male or female slave with a rod so hard that the slave dies under his hand, he shall be punished. ²¹ If, however, the slave survives for a day or two, he is not to be punished, since the slave is his own property.

²²* "When men have a fight and hurt a pregnant woman, so that she suffers a miscarriage, but no further injury, the guilty one shall be fined as much as the woman's husband demands of him, and he shall pay in the presence of the judges. ²³† But if injury ensues, you shall give life for life, ²⁴ eye for eye, tooth for tooth, hand for hand, foot for foot, ²⁵ burn for burn, wound for wound, stripe for stripe.

²⁶ "When a man strikes his male or female slave in the eye and destroys the use of the eye, he shall let the slave go free in compensation for the eye. ²⁷ If he knocks out a tooth of his male or female

Living the Ten Commandments

LIVE IT!

God gave the Israelites the Ten Commandments, which united them and required from them certain attitudes and behaviors toward God and their fellow Israelites. Obedience to the Commandments became the sign of faithfulness to the Covenant with God. Later, the prophets again and again held the Israelites accountable for this Covenant, calling them to repent and reconcile with God when they disobeyed God's Law.

The Ten Comomandments continue to be the moral foundation for Jews and Christians today. How do you use them in making your moral decisions? How familiar are you with church teaching that applies the Ten Commandments today? Ask God for the understanding and the strength to keep God's Commandments, especially those that are the most difficult for you.

▶ Ex 20, 1–17

ciously scheming to do so, you must take him even from my altar and put him to death. ¹⁵ Whoever strikes his father or mother shall be put to death.

¹⁶* "A kidnaper, whether he sells his victim or still has him when caught, shall be put to death.

¹⁷* "Whoever curses his father or mother shall be put to death.

¹⁸ "When men quarrel and one strikes the other with a stone or with his fist, not mortally, but enough to put him in bed, ¹⁹ the one who struck the blow shall be acquitted, provided the other can get up and walk around with the help of his staff. Still, he must compensate him for his enforced idleness and provide for his complete cure.

slave, he shall let the slave go free in compensation for the tooth.

²⁸ "When an ox gores a man or a woman to death, the ox must be stoned; its flesh may not be eaten. The owner of the ox, however, shall go unpunished. ²⁹ But if an ox was previously in the habit of goring people and its owner, though warned, would not keep it in; should it then kill a man or a woman, not only must the ox be stoned, but its owner also must be put to death. ³⁰ If, however, a fine is imposed on him, he must pay in ransom for his life whatever amount is imposed on him. ³¹ This law applies if it is a boy or a girl that the ox gores. ³² But if it is a male or a female slave that it

---

21, 8: *Destined her:* intended her as a wife of second rank.

21, 23ff: This section is known as the *lex talionis,* the law of tit for tat. The purpose of this law was not merely the enforcement of rigorous justice, but also the prevention of greater penalties than would be just. Christ refers to this passage when he exhorts Christians to cede their lawful rights for the sake of charity. Cf Mt 5, 38ff.

21, 12ff: Lv 24, 17; Nm 35, 15–29; Dt 4, 41f; 19, 2–5.
21, 16: Dt 24, 7.

21, 17: Lv 20, 9; Prv 20, 20; Mt 15, 4; Mk 7, 10.
21, 22–25: Lv 24, 18–21; Dt 19, 21; Mt 5, 38.

gores, he must pay the owner of the slave thirty shekels of silver, and the ox must be stoned.

Property Damage

33 "When a man uncovers or digs a cistern and does not cover it over again, should an ox or an ass fall into it, 34 the owner of the cistern must make good by restoring the value of the animal to its owner; the dead animal, however, he may keep.

35 "When one man's ox hurts another's ox so badly that it dies, they shall sell the live ox and divide this money as well as the dead animal equally between them. 36 But if it was known that the ox was previously in the habit of goring and its owner would not keep it in, he must make full restitution, an ox for an ox; but the dead animal he may keep.

37*† "When a man steals an ox or a sheep and slaughters or sells it, he shall restore five oxen for the one ox, and four sheep for the one sheep.

22 1† "[If a thief is caught in the act of housebreaking and beaten to death, there is no bloodguilt involved. 2 But if after sunrise he is thus beaten, there is bloodguilt.] He must make full restitution. If he has nothing, he shall be sold to pay for his theft. 3 If what he stole is found alive in his possession, be it an ox, an ass or a sheep, he shall restore two animals for each one stolen.

4† "When a man is burning over a field or a vineyard, if he lets the fires spread so that it burns in another's field, he must make restitution with the best produce of his own field or vineyard. 5 If the fire spreads further, and catches on to thorn bushes, so that shocked grain or standing grain or the field itself is burned up, the one who started the fire must make full restitution.

Trusts and Loans

6 "When a man gives money or any article to another for safekeeping and it is stolen from the latter's house, the thief, if caught, must make twofold restitution. 7† If the thief is not caught, the owner of the house shall be brought to God, to swear that he himself did not lay hands on his neighbor's property. 8 In every question of dishonest appropriation, whether it be about an ox, or an ass, or a

sheep, or a garment, or anything else that has disappeared, where another claims that the thing is his, both parties shall present their case before God; the one whom God convicts must make two-fold restitution to the other.

9 "When a man gives an ass, or an ox, or a sheep, or any other animal to another for safekeeping, if it dies, or is maimed or snatched away, without anyone witnessing the fact, 10 the custodian shall swear by the LORD that he did not lay hands on his neighbor's property; the owner must accept the oath, and no restitution is to be made. 11 But if the custodian is really guilty of theft, he must make restitution to the owner. 12* If it has been killed by a wild beast, let him bring it as evidence, and he need not make restitution for the mangled animal.

13 "When a man borrows an animal from his neighbor, if it is maimed or dies while the owner is not present, the man must make restitution. 14 But if the owner is present, he need not make restitution. If it was hired, this was covered by the price of its hire.

Social Laws

15* "When a man seduces a virgin who is not betrothed, and lies with her, he shall pay her marriage price and marry her. 16† If her father refuses to give her to him, he must still pay him the customary marriage price for virgins.

17* "You shall not let a sorceress live.

18* "Anyone who lies with an animal shall be put to death.

19* "Whoever sacrifices to any god, except to the LORD alone, shall be doomed.

20* "You shall not molest or oppress an alien, for you were once aliens yourselves in the land of Egypt. 21 You shall not wrong any widow or orphan. 22 If ever you wrong them and they cry out to me, I will surely hear their cry. 23 My wrath will flare up, and I will kill you with the sword; then your own wives will be widows, and your children orphans.

24* "If you lend money to one of your poor neighbors among my people, you shall not act like an extortioner toward him by demanding interest from him. 25 If you take your neighbor's cloak as a pledge, you shall return it to him before sunset;

21, 37—22, 30: In the Vulgate, 22, 1–31.
22, 1f: *If a thief is caught:* this seems to be a fragment of what was once a longer law on housebreaking, which has been inserted here into the middle of a law on stealing animals. At night the householder would be justified in killing a burglar outright, but not so in the daytime, when the burglar could more easily be caught alive. *He must make full restitution:* this stood originally immediately after 21, 37.
22, 4: The Greek and Latin versions understood this verse as a prohibition against allowing one's cattle to graze in the field of another.

22, 7: *Brought to God:* see note on Ex 21, 6. Cf also Ex 22, 10.
22, 16: *The customary marriage price for virgins:* fifty shekels according to Dt 22, 29.

21, 37: 2 Sm 12, 6.	22, 20–23: Ex 23, 9; Lv 19, 33f;
22, 12: Gn 31, 39.	Dt 10, 18f; 24, 17f; 27,
22, 15f: Dt 22, 28f.	19; Zec 7, 10.
22, 17: Lv 19, 26.31; 20, 6.27;	22, 24–26: Lv 25, 35–38; Dt 23,
Dt 18, 10f.	19f; 24, 10–13; Ez 18,
22, 18: Lv 18, 23; Dt 27, 21.	7f.17f.
22, 19: Dt 13; 17, 2–7.	

LIVE IT!

Would You Do It?

"You shall not molest or oppress an alien. . . . You shall not wrong any widow or orphan" (Ex 22, 20–21). This section of the Sinai laws reminds the Israelites to take care of the poor and vulnerable in their midst. It reminds the Israelites not to become abusive like the Egyptians.

How can we care for poor people? Consider this story: Mike and Dave were spending some time in New York City. During a walk, they went by the train station, a place where many runaways and homeless people found refuge. They came across a young man hunched over with his back to the wall. His clothes were wet, and he was shivering. He was holding a cup, panhandling. Dave took out some change and threw it into the cup. Mike just stood and stared. Dave motioned to Mike to keep on moving, but Mike didn't move. Then, Mike did something that amazed Dave. He sat down and took off his shoes, an almost brand-new pair of insulated leather hiking boots he had received for Christmas. He motioned to the young homeless man to do the same. He took his boots and socks and put them on the young man. Mike put on the young man's old canvas sneakers, stood up, and walked away. Dave followed in silence.

▶ Ex 22, 20–26

E
X

---

26 for this cloak of his is the only covering he has for his body. What else has he to sleep in? If he cries out to me, I will hear him; for I am compassionate.

27*† "You shall not revile God, nor curse a prince of your people.

28 "You shall not delay the offering of your harvest and your press. You shall give me the first-born of your sons. 29* You must do the same with your oxen and your sheep; for seven days the firstling may stay with its mother, but on the eighth day you must give it to me.

30* "You shall be men sacred to me. Flesh torn to pieces in the field you shall not eat; throw it to the dogs.

23

1* "You shall not repeat a false report. Do not join the wicked in putting your hand, as an unjust witness, upon anyone. 2 Neither shall you allege the example of the many as an excuse for doing wrong, nor shall you, when testifying in a lawsuit, side with the many in perverting justice. 3* You shall not favor a poor man in his lawsuit.

4* "When you come upon your enemy's ox or ass going astray, see to it that it is returned to him. 5 When you notice the ass of one who hates you lying prostrate under its burden, by no means desert him; help him, rather, to raise it up.

6 "You shall not deny one of your needy fellow men his rights in his lawsuit. 7 You shall keep away from anything dishonest. The innocent and the just you shall not put to death, nor shall you acquit the guilty. 8* Never take a bribe, for a bribe blinds even the most clear-sighted and twists the words even of the just. 9* You shall not oppress an alien; you well know how it feels to be an alien, since you were once aliens yourselves in the land of Egypt.

Religious Laws

10* "For six years you may sow your land and gather in its produce. 11 But the seventh year you shall let the land lie untilled and unharvested, that the poor among you may eat of it and the beasts of the field may eat what the poor leave. So also shall you do in regard to your vineyard and your olive grove.

12* "For six days you may do your work, but on the seventh day you must rest, that your ox and your ass may also have rest, and that the son of your maidservant and the alien may be refreshed. 13 Give heed to all that I have told you.

"Never mention the name of any other god; it shall not be heard from your lips.

14*† "Three times a year you shall celebrate a pilgrim feast to me. 15† You shall keep the feast of Unleavened Bread. As I have commanded you, you

---

† **22, 27:** *God:* or perhaps "the gods," in the sense of "the judges," as the parallel with *a prince of your people* suggests.

23, 14: These three feasts are elsewhere called the Passover, Pentecost and Booths. Cf Ex 34, 18–26; Lv 23; Dt 16.

23, 15: *Appear before me:* the original expression was "see my face"; so also in several other places, as Ex 23, 17; 34, 23f; Dt 16, 16; 31, 11.

22, 27: Acts 23, 5.
22, 29: Ex 13, 2; 34, 19; Lv 22, 27; Dt 15, 19.
22, 30: Lv 7, 24; 17, 15; 22, 8.
23, 1f: Dt 19, 16ff.
23, 3: Lv 19, 15.
23, 4: Dt 22, 1ff.

23, 8: Dt 16, 19; 27, 25; Sir 20, 28.
23, 9: Ex 22, 21.
23, 10f: Lv 25, 3–7.
23, 12: Ex 20, 8.
23, 14–17: Ex 34, 18.22ff; Lv 23; Dt 16, 1–17.

must eat unleavened bread for seven days at the pre-scribed time in the month of Abib, for it was then that you came out of Egypt. No one shall appear before me empty-handed. ¹⁶ You shall also keep the feast of the grain harvest with the first of the crop that you have sown in the field; and finally, the feast at the fruit harvest at the end of the year, when you gather in the produce from the fields. ¹⁷ Thrice a year shall all your men appear before the LORD God.

¹⁸* "You shall not offer the blood of my sacrifice with leavened bread; nor shall the fat of my feast be kept overnight till the next day. ¹⁹† The choicest first fruits of your soil you shall bring to the house of the LORD, your God.

"You shall not boil a kid in its mother's milk.

Reward of Fidelity

²⁰* "See, I am sending an angel before you, to guard you on the way and bring you to the place I have prepared. ²¹† Be attentive to him and heed his voice. Do not rebel against him, for he will not for-give your sin. My authority resides in him. ²² If you heed his voice and carry out all I tell you, I will be an enemy to your enemies and a foe to your foes.

²³ "My angel will go before you and bring you to the Amorites, Hittites, Perizzites, Canaanites, Hivites and Jebusites; and I will wipe them out. ²⁴*† Therefore, you shall not bow down in worship before their gods, nor shall you make anything like them; rather, you must demolish them and smash their sacred pillars. ²⁵ The LORD, your God, you shall worship; then I will bless your food and drink, and I will remove all sickness from your midst; ²⁶ no woman in your land will be barren or miscar-ry; and I will give you a full span of life.

²⁷* "I will have the fear of me precede you, so that I will throw into panic every nation you reach. I will make all your enemies turn from you in flight, ²⁸† and ahead of you I will send hornets to drive the Hivites, Canaanites and Hittites out of your way. ²⁹ But not in one year will I drive them all out before you; else the land will become so desolate that the wild beasts will multiply against you. ³⁰ In-

stead, I will drive them out little by little before you, until you have grown numerous enough to take possession of the land. ³¹*† I will set your bound-aries from the Red Sea to the sea of the Philistines, and from the desert to the River; all who dwell in this land I will hand over to you to be driven out of your way. ³² You shall not make a covenant with them or their gods. ³³* They must not abide in your land, lest they make you sin against me by ensnar-ing you into worshiping their gods."

Ratification of the Covenant

24 ¹ Moses himself was told, "Come up to the LORD, you and Aaron, with Nadab, Abihu, and seventy of the elders of Israel. You shall all worship at some distance, ² but Moses alone is to come close to the LORD; the others shall not come too near, and the people shall not come up at all with Moses."

³* When Moses came to the people and related all the words and ordinances of the LORD, they all answered with one voice, "We will do everything that the LORD has told us." ⁴† Moses then wrote down all the words of the LORD and, rising early the next day, he erected at the foot of the mountain an altar and twelve pillars for the twelve tribes of Israel. ⁵ Then, having sent certain young men of the Israelites to offer holocausts and sacrifice young bulls as peace offerings to the LORD, ⁶ Moses took half of the blood and put it in large bowls; the other half he splashed on the altar. ⁷ Taking the book of the covenant, he read it aloud to the peo-ple, who answered, "All that the LORD has said, we will heed and do." ⁸* Then he took the blood and sprinkled it on the people, saying, "This is the blood of the covenant which the LORD has made with you in accordance with all these words of his."

⁹ Moses then went up with Aaron, Nadab, Abihu, and seventy elders of Israel, ¹⁰ and they beheld the God of Israel. Under his feet there appeared to be sapphire tilework, as clear as the sky itself. ¹¹† Yet he did not smite these chosen Israelites. After gaz-ing on God, they could still eat and drink.

23, 19: *Boil a kid in its mother's milk:* this was part of a Canaan-ite ritual; hence it is forbidden here as a pagan ceremony.

23, 21: *My authority resides in him:* literally, "My name is with-in him."

23, 24: *Make anything like them:* some render, "act according to their conduct." *Sacred pillars:* objects of religious veneration at Canaanite sanctuaries.

23, 28: *Hornets:* some understand this figuratively of various troublesome afflictions; others translate the Hebrew word as "lep-rosy." Cf Dt 7, 20; Jos 24, 12; Wis 12, 8.

23, 31: *The sea of the Philistines:* the Mediterranean. *The River:* the Euphrates. Only in the time of David and Solomon did the terri-tory of Israel come near to reaching such distant borders.

24, 4: *Pillars:* stone shafts or slabs, erected as symbols of the fact that each of the twelve tribes had entered into this covenant with

God; not idolatrous as in Ex 23, 24, although the same Hebrew word is used in both passages. See note on Gn 28, 18.

24, 11: *After gazing on God:* the ancients thought that the sight of God would bring instantaneous death. Cf Ex 33, 20; Gn 16, 13; 32, 31; Jgs 6, 22f; 13, 22. *Eat and drink:* partake of the sacrificial meal.

23, 18f: Ex 34, 25f.
23, 20: Ex 14, 19; 32, 34; 33, 2.
23, 24: 23f: Ex 34, 10–16; Nm 33, 51f; Dt 7, 24ff.
23, 27ff: Dt 2, 25; 7, 20ff.

23, 31: Gn 15, 18; Dt 11, 24; Jos 1, 4.
23, 32f: Ex 34, 12–16; Dt 7, 2ff.
24, 3: Ex 19, 8.
24, 8: 5ff: Heb 9, 18ff.

Sacrifice and the Eucharist

Sacrifice is defined as an offering made to God that becomes holy by being set apart, blessed, and burned or consumed. Just as food and gifts were brought to a king as a form of tribute and worship, so too in Israel animals were brought to God and sacrificed, their blood splattered on the altar, and their meat cooked and eaten as a form of worship that brought communion with God. The blood symbolized God's gift of life, and when the blessed sacrifice was eaten, communion occurred between God and people. In Exodus, chapter 24, when Israel is about to ratify the Covenant with God, Moses smears the blood of the animal on the altar to assert the Israelites' union with God through the observance of the Covenant.

In the New Testament, the language Jesus uses at his Last Supper seems to reflect this sacrificial understanding. Jesus shares bread and wine as his body and blood and speaks about a New Covenant that will be ratified by the giving of his body and the shedding of his blood. Even today, Catholics celebrating the Eucharist in Jesus' memory encounter the real presence of Jesus in the sacred food of bread and wine, recalling the New Covenant of love he established through giving his body and shedding his blood.

▸ **Ex 24, 1–8**

Moses on the Mountain

12* The LORD said to Moses, "Come up to me on the mountain and, while you are there, I will give you the stone tablets on which I have written the commandments intended for their instruction." 13 So Moses set out with Joshua, his aide, and went up to the mountain of God. 14 The elders, however, had been told by him, "Wait here for us until we return to you. Aaron and Hur are staying with you. If anyone has a complaint, let him refer the matter to them." 15 After Moses had gone up, a cloud covered the mountain. 16* The glory of the LORD settled upon Mount Sinai. The cloud covered it for six days, and on the seventh day he called to Moses from the midst of the cloud. 17* To the Israelites the glory of the LORD was seen as a consuming fire on the mountaintop. 18* But Moses passed into the midst of the cloud as he went up on the mountain; and there he stayed for forty days and forty nights.

IV: The Dwelling and Its Furnishings

Collection of Materials

25 1* This is what the LORD then said to Moses: 2 "Tell the Israelites to take up a collection for me. From every man you shall accept the contribution that his heart prompts him to give me. 3* These are the contributions you shall accept from them: gold, silver and bronze; 4 violet, purple and scarlet yarn; fine linen and goat hair; 5† rams' skins dyed red, and tahash skins; acacia wood; 6 oil for the light; spices for the anointing oil and for the fragrant incense; 7 onyx stones and other gems for mounting on the ephod and the breastpiece.

8* "They shall make a sanctuary for me, that I may dwell in their midst. 9* This Dwelling and all its furnishings you shall make exactly according to the pattern that I will now show you.

Plan of the Ark

10* "You shall make an ark of acacia wood, two and a half cubits long, one and a half cubits wide, and one and a half cubits high. 11 Plate it inside and outside with pure gold, and put a molding of gold around the top of it. 12 Cast four gold rings and fasten them on the four supports of the ark, two rings on one side and two on the opposite side. 13 Then make poles of acacia wood and plate them with gold. 14 These poles you are to put through the rings on the sides of the ark, for carrying it; 15 they must remain in the rings of the ark and never be withdrawn. 16 In the ark you are to put the commandments which I will give you.

17† "You shall then make a propitiatory of pure gold, two cubits and a half long, and one and a half cubits wide. 18† Make two cherubim of beaten gold

---

25, 5: *Tahash:* perhaps the name of a marine animal, such as the dugong or the porpoise. The Greek and Latin versions took it for the color hyacinth.

25, 17: *Propitiatory:* this traditional rendering of the Hebrew term, which may mean merely "cover," is derived from its connection with the ceremony of the Day of Atonement whereby God was rendered "propitious." Cf Lv 16, 14ff.

25, 18ff: *Cherubim:* probably in the form of human-headed winged lions. The cherubim over the ark formed the throne for the invisible Lord. Cf Ps 80, 2. For a more detailed description of the somewhat different cherubim in the temple of Solomon, see 1 Kgs 6, 23–28; 2 Chr 3, 10–13.

24, 12: Ex 31, 18; 32, 15f;	25, 3: Ex 35, 4–9.
Dt 5, 22.	25, 8f: Ex 26, 1–30; 36, 8–38.
24, 16: Sir 45, 4.	25, 9: Acts 7, 44.
24, 17: Ex 19, 18; Heb 12, 18.	25, 10–22: Ex 37, 1–9; Heb 9,
24, 18: Ex 34, 28; Dt 9, 9.	1–5.
25, 1–7: Ex 35, 4–9.20–29.	

EX

wood and plate with gold. ²⁹† Of pure gold you shall make its plates and cups, as well as its pitchers and bowls for pouring libations. ³⁰* On the table you shall always keep showbread set before me.

The Lampstand

³¹* "You shall make a lampstand of pure beaten gold—its shaft and branches—with its cups and knobs and petals springing directly from it. ³² Six branches are to extend from the sides of the lampstand, three branches on one side, and three on the other. ³³† On one branch there are to be three cups, shaped like almond blossoms, each with its knob and petals; on the opposite branch there are to be three cups, shaped like almond blossoms, each with its knob and petals; and so for the six branches that extend from the lampstand. ³⁴† On the shaft there are to be four cups, shaped like almond blossoms, with their knobs and petals, ³⁵ including a knob below each of the three pairs of branches that extend from the lampstand. ³⁶ Their knobs and branches shall so spring from it that the whole will form but a single piece of pure beaten gold. ³⁷*† You shall then make seven lamps for it and so set up the lamps that they shed their light on the space in front of the lampstand. ³⁸† These, as well as the trimming shears and trays, must be of pure gold. ³⁹ Use a talent of pure gold for the lampstand and all its appurtenances. ⁴⁰* See that you make them according to the pattern shown you on the mountain.

The Tent Cloth

26 ¹*† "The Dwelling itself you shall make out of sheets woven of fine linen twined and of violet, purple and scarlet yarn, with cherubim embroidered on them. ² The length of each shall be twenty-eight cubits, and the width four cubits; all the sheets shall be of the same size. ³ Five of the sheets are to be sewed together, edge to edge; and the same for the other five. ⁴ Make loops of violet yarn along the edge of the end sheet in one set, and the same along the edge of the end sheet in the other set. ⁵ There are to be fifty loops along the edge of the end sheet in the first set, and fifty loops

for the two ends of the propitiatory, ¹⁹ fastening them so that one cherub springs direct from each end. ²⁰ The cherubim shall have their wings spread out above, covering the propitiatory with them; they shall be turned toward each other, but with their faces looking toward the propitiatory. ²¹ This propitiatory you shall then place on top of the ark. In the ark itself you are to put the commandments which I will give you. ²² There I will meet you and there, from above the propitiatory, between the two cherubim on the ark of the commandments, I will tell you all the commands that I wish you to give the Israelites.

The Table

²³* "You shall also make a table of acacia wood, two cubits long, a cubit wide, and a cubit and a half high. ²⁴ Plate it with pure gold and make a molding of gold around it. ²⁵† Surround it with a frame, a handbreadth high, with a molding of gold around the frame. ²⁶ You shall also make four rings of gold for it and fasten them at the four corners, one at each leg, ²⁷ on two opposite sides of the frame as holders for the poles to carry the table. ²⁸ These poles for carrying the table you shall make of acacia

---

25, 25: *A frame:* probably placed near the bottom of the legs to keep them steady. The golden table of Herod's temple is pictured thus on the Arch of Titus.

25, 29f: The *plates* held the showbread, that is, the holy bread which was placed upon the table every sabbath as an offering to God, and was later eaten by the priests. The *cups* held the incense which was strewn upon the bread. Cf Lv 24, 5–9. The libation wine was poured from the *pitchers* into the *bowls*. All these vessels were kept on the golden table.

25, 33: In keeping with the arrangement of the ornaments on the shaft, the three sets of ornaments on each branch were probably so placed that one was at the top and the other two equally spaced along the length of the branch. *Knob:* the cup-shaped seed capsule at the base of a flower.

25, 34f: Of the four ornaments on the shaft, one was at the top and one was below each of the three sets of side branches.

25, 37: The lamps were probably shaped like small boats, with the wick at one end; the end with the wick was turned toward the front of the lampstand.

25, 38: *Trays:* small receptacles for the burnt-out wicks.

26, 1: *Sheets:* strips of tapestry, woven of white linen, the colored threads being used for the cherubim which were embroidered on them. These sheets were stretched across the top of the Dwelling to form a roof, their free ends hanging down inside the boards which formed walls.

25, 23–30: Ex 37, 10–16.   25, 37: Lv 24, 2ff; Nm 8, 2.
25, 30: Lv 24, 5ff.   25, 40: Heb 8, 5.
25, 31–40: Ex 37, 17–24.   26, 1–14: Ex 36, 8–19.

along the edge of the corresponding sheet in the second set, and so placed that the loops are directly opposite each other. ⁶ Then make fifty clasps of gold, with which to join the two sets of sheets, so that the Dwelling forms one whole.

⁷† "Also make sheets woven of goat hair, to be used as a tent covering over the Dwelling. ⁸ Eleven such sheets are to be made; the length of each shall be thirty cubits, and the width four cubits: all eleven sheets shall be of the same size. ⁹† Sew five of the sheets, edge to edge, into one set, and the other six sheets into another set. Use the sixth sheet double at the front of the tent. ¹⁰ Make fifty loops along the edge of the end sheet in one set, and fifty loops along the edge of the end sheet in the second set. ¹¹ Also make fifty bronze clasps and put them into the loops, to join the tent into one whole. ¹² There will be an extra half sheet of tent covering, which shall be allowed to hang down over the rear of the Dwelling. ¹³ Likewise, the sheets of the tent will have an extra cubit's length to be left hanging down on either side of the Dwelling to protect it. ¹⁴ Over the tent itself you shall make a covering of rams' skins dyed red, and above that, a covering of tahash skins.

The Wooden Walls

¹⁵* "You shall make boards of acacia wood as walls for the Dwelling. ¹⁶ The length of each board is to be ten cubits, and its width one and a half cubits. ¹⁷† Each board shall have two arms that shall serve to fasten the boards in line. In this way all the boards of the Dwelling are to be made. ¹⁸ Set up the boards of the Dwelling as follows: twenty boards on the south side, ¹⁹ with forty silver pedestals under the twenty boards, so that there are two pedestals under each board, at its two arms; ²⁰ twenty boards on the other side of the Dwelling, the north side, ²¹ with their forty silver pedestals, two under each board; ²² six boards for the rear of the Dwelling, to the west; ²³ and two boards for the corners at the rear of the Dwelling. ²⁴ These two shall be double at the bottom, and likewise double at the top, to the first ring. That is how both boards in the corners are to be made. ²⁵ Thus, there shall be in the rear eight boards, with their sixteen silver pedestals, two pedestals under each board. ²⁶ Also make bars of

acacia wood: five for the boards on one side of the Dwelling, ²⁷ five for those on the other side, and five for those at the rear, toward the west. ²⁸ The center bar, at the middle of the boards, shall reach across from end to end. ²⁹ Plate the boards with gold, and make gold rings on them as holders for the bars, which are also to be plated with gold. ³⁰ You shall erect the Dwelling according to the pattern shown you on the mountain.

The Veils

³¹* "You shall have a veil woven of violet, purple and scarlet yarn, and of fine linen twined, with cherubim embroidered on it.* ³²† It is to be hung on four gold-plated columns of acacia wood, which shall have hooks of gold and shall rest on four silver pedestals. ³³ Hang the veil from clasps. The ark of the commandments you shall bring inside, behind this veil which divides the holy place from the holy of holies. ³⁴ Set the propitiatory on the ark of the commandments in the holy of holies.

³⁵ "Outside the veil you shall place the table and the lampstand, the latter on the south side of the Dwelling, opposite the table, which is to be put on the north side. ³⁶† For the entrance of the tent make a variegated curtain of violet, purple and scarlet yarn and of fine linen twined. ³⁷ Make five columns of acacia wood for this curtain; have them plated with gold, with their hooks of gold; and cast five bronze pedestals for them.

The Altar of Holocausts

27 ¹* "You shall make an altar of acacia wood, on a square, five cubits long and five cubits wide; it shall be three cubits high. ² At the four corners there are to be horns, so made that they spring directly from the altar. You shall then plate it with bronze. ³ Make pots for removing the ashes, as well as shovels, basins, forks and fire pans, all of which shall be of bronze. ⁴† Make a grating of bronze network for it; this to have four bronze rings, one at each of its four corners. ⁵ Put it down around the altar, on the ground. This network is to be half as high as the altar. ⁶ You shall also make poles of acacia wood for the altar, and plate them with bronze. ⁷ These poles are to be put through the rings, so that they are on either side of the altar

---

26, 7: *Tent covering:* the cloth made of sheets of goat hair to cover the Dwelling.

26, 9: Half the width of the end strip was folded back at the front of the Dwelling, thus leaving another half-strip to hang down at the rear. Cf v 12.

26, 17: *Arms:* literally, "hands." According to some, they served as "tongue and groove" to mortise the boards together; according to others, they were pegs at the bottom of the boards and fitted into sockets in the pedestals.

26, 32: *Hooks:* probably placed near the tops of the columns, to hold the rope from which the veils and curtains hung.

26, 36: *Variegated:* without definite designs such as the cherubim on the inner veil.

27, 4: *Grating:* it is not clear whether this was flush with the altar or at some small distance from it; in the latter case the space between the altar and the grating would be filled with stones and serve as a platform around the altar, which would otherwise be too high for the priest to reach conveniently.

26, 15–30: Ex 36, 20–34.   26, 31–37: Ex 36, 35–38.
26, 31: 2 Chr 3, 14.   27, 1–8: Ex 38, 1–7.

when it is carried. ⁸† Make the altar itself in the form of a hollow box, just as it was shown you on the mountain.

Court of the Dwelling

⁹* "You shall also make a court for the Dwelling. On the south side the court shall have hangings a hundred cubits long, woven of fine linen twined, ¹⁰ with twenty columns and twenty pedestals of bronze; the hooks and bands on the columns shall be of silver. ¹¹ On the north side there shall be similar hangings, a hundred cubits long, with twenty columns and twenty pedestals of bronze; the hooks and bands on the columns shall be of silver. ¹² On the west side, across the width of the court, there shall be hangings, fifty cubits long, with ten columns and ten pedestals. ¹³ The width of the court on the east side shall be fifty cubits. ¹⁴ On one side there shall be hangings to the extent of fifteen cubits, with three columns and three pedestals; ¹⁵ on the other side there shall be hangings to the extent of fifteen cubits, with three columns and three pedestals.

¹⁶ "At the entrance of the court there shall be a variegated curtain, twenty cubits long, woven of violet, purple and scarlet yarn and of fine linen twined. It shall have four columns and four pedestals.

¹⁷ "All the columns around the court shall have bands and hooks of silver, and pedestals of bronze. ¹⁸ The enclosure of the court is to be one hundred cubits long, fifty cubits wide, and five cubits high. Fine linen twined must be used, and the pedestals must be of bronze. ¹⁹ All the fittings of the Dwelling, whatever be their use, as well as all its tent pegs and all the tent pegs of the court, must be of bronze.

Oil for the Lamps

²⁰* "You shall order the Israelites to bring you clear oil of crushed olives, to be used for the light, so that you may keep lamps burning regularly. ²¹ From evening to morning Aaron and his sons shall maintain them before the LORD in the meeting tent, outside the veil which hangs in front of the commandments. This shall be a perpetual ordinance for the Israelites throughout their generations.

The Priestly Vestments

28 ¹* "From among the Israelites have your brother Aaron, together with his sons Nadab, Abihu, Eleazar and Ithamar, brought to you, that they may be my priests. ² For the glorious adornment of your brother Aaron you shall have sacred vestments made. ³ Therefore, to the various expert workmen whom I have endowed with skill, you shall give instructions to make such vestments for Aaron as will set him apart for his sacred service as my priest. ⁴ These are the vestments they shall make: a breastpiece, an ephod, a robe, a brocaded tunic, a miter and a sash. In making these sacred vestments which your brother Aaron and his sons are to wear in serving as my priests, ⁵ they shall use gold, violet, purple and scarlet yarn and fine linen.

The Ephod and Breastpiece

⁶*† "The ephod they shall make of gold thread and of violet, purple and scarlet yarn, embroidered on cloth of fine linen twined. ⁷ It shall have a pair of shoulder straps joined to its two upper ends. ⁸ The embroidered belt on the ephod shall extend out from it and, like it, be made of gold thread, of violet, purple and scarlet yarn, and of fine linen twined.

⁹ "Get two onyx stones and engrave on them the names of the sons of Israel: ¹⁰ six of their names on one stone, and the other six on the other stone, in the order of their birth. ¹¹ As a gem-cutter engraves a seal, so shall you have the two stones engraved with the names of the sons of Israel and then mounted in gold filigree work. ¹² Set these two stones on the shoulder straps of the ephod as memorial stones of the sons of Israel. Thus Aaron shall bear their names on his shoulders as a reminder before the LORD. ¹³* Make filigree rosettes of gold, ¹⁴ as well as two chains of pure gold, twisted like cords, and fasten the cordlike chains to the filigree rosettes.

¹⁵*† "The breastpiece of decision you shall also have made, embroidered like the ephod with gold thread and violet, purple and scarlet yarn on cloth of fine linen twined. ¹⁶ It is to be square when folded double, a span high and a span wide. ¹⁷† On it you shall mount four rows of precious stones: in

---

† **27, 8:** *Hollow:* probably filled with earth or stones when in use. Cf Ex 20, 24f.

28, 6: *Ephod:* this Hebrew word is retained in the translation because it is the technical term for a peculiar piece of the priestly vestments, the exact nature of which is uncertain. It seems to have been a sort of apron that hung from the shoulders of the priest by *shoulder straps* (v 7) and was tied around his waist by the loose ends of the attached belt (v 8).

28, 15–30: *Breastpiece:* in shape like a modern altar burse, it was a pocketlike receptacle for holding the *Urim* and *Thummim* (v 30), and formed an integral part of the ephod, to which it was attached

by an elaborate system of rings and chains. Both the ephod and its breastpiece were made of brocaded linen.

28, 17–20: The translation of the Hebrew names of some of these gems is quite conjectural.

27, 9–19: Ex 38, 9–20.   Sir 45, 8–14.
27, 20f: Lv 24, 1–4.   28, 13f: Ex 28, 22.25;
28, 1–5: Ex 39, 1; Sir 45, 7.   39, 15.18.
28, 6–12: Ex 39, 2–7;   28, 15–21: Ex 39, 15–21.

the first row, a carnelian, a topaz and an emerald; 18 in the second row, a garnet, a sapphire and a beryl; 19 in the third row, a jacinth, an agate and an amethyst; 20 in the fourth row, a chrysolite, an onyx and a jasper. These stones are to be mounted in gold filigree work, 21 twelve of them to match the names of the sons of Israel, each stone engraved like a seal with the name of one of the twelve tribes.

22 "When the chains of pure gold, twisted like cords, have been made for the breastpiece, 23 you shall then make two rings of gold for it and fasten them to the two upper ends of the breastpiece. 24 The gold cords are then to be fastened to the two rings at the upper ends of the breastpiece, 25 the other two ends of the cords being fastened in front to the two filigree rosettes which are attached to the shoulder straps of the ephod. 26 Make two other rings of gold and put them on the two lower ends of the breastpiece, on its edge that faces the ephod. 27 Then make two more rings of gold and fasten them to the bottom of the shoulder straps next to where they join the ephod in front, just above its embroidered belt. 28 Violet ribbons shall bind the rings of the breastpiece to the rings of the ephod, so that the breastpiece will stay right above the embroidered belt of the ephod and not swing loose from it.

29 "Whenever Aaron enters the sanctuary, he will thus bear the names of the sons of Israel on the breastpiece of decision over his heart as a constant reminder before the LORD. 30*† In this breastpiece of decision you shall put the Urim and Thummim, that they may be over Aaron's heart whenever he enters the presence of the LORD. Thus he shall always bear the decisions for the Israelites over his heart in the LORD's presence.

Other Vestments

31* "The robe of the ephod you shall make entirely of violet material. 32 It shall have an opening for the head in the center, and around this opening there shall be a selvage, woven as at the opening of a shirt, to keep it from being torn. 33 All around the hem at the bottom you shall make pomegranates, woven of violet, purple and scarlet yarn and fine linen twined, with gold bells between them; 34 first a gold bell, then a pomegranate, and thus alternating all around the hem of the robe. 35 Aaron shall wear it when ministering, that its tinkling may be

heard as he enters and leaves the LORD's presence in the sanctuary; else he will die.

36 "You shall also make a plate of pure gold and engrave on it, as on a seal engraving, "Sacred to the LORD." 37* This plate is to be tied over the miter with a violet ribbon in such a way that it rests on the front of the miter, 38 over Aaron's forehead. Since Aaron bears whatever guilt the Israelites may incur in consecrating any of their sacred gifts, this plate must always be over his forehead, so that they may find favor with the LORD.

39* "The tunic of fine linen shall be brocaded. The miter shall be made of fine linen. The sash shall be of variegated work.

40 "Likewise, for the glorious adornment of Aaron's sons you shall have tunics and sashes and turbans made. 41† With these you shall clothe your brother Aaron and his sons. Anoint and ordain them, consecrating them as my priests. 42* You must also make linen drawers for them, to cover their naked flesh from their loins to their thighs. 43 Aaron and his sons shall wear them whenever they go into the meeting tent or approach the altar to minister in the sanctuary, lest they incur guilt and die. This shall be a perpetual ordinance for him and for his descendants.

Consecration of the Priests

29 1* "This is the rite you shall perform in consecrating them as my priests. Procure a young bull and two unblemished rams. 2 With fine wheat flour make unleavened cakes mixed with oil, and unleavened wafers spread with oil, 3 and put them in a basket. Take the basket of them along with the bullock and the two rams. 4 Aaron and his sons you shall also bring to the entrance of the meeting tent, and there wash them with water. 5 Take the vestments and clothe Aaron with the tunic, the robe of the ephod, the ephod itself, and the breastpiece, fastening the embroidered belt of the ephod around him. 6 Put the miter on his head, the sacred diadem on the miter. 7 Then take the anointing oil and anoint him with it, pouring it on his head. 8 Bring forward his sons also and clothe them with the tunics, 9* gird them with the sashes, and tie the turbans on them. Thus shall the priesthood be theirs by perpetual law, and thus shall you ordain Aaron and his sons.

28, 30: *Urim and Thummim:* both the meaning of these Hebrew words and the exact nature of the objects so designated are uncertain. They were apparently lots of some kind which were drawn or cast by the priest to ascertain God's decision in doubtful matters. Hence, the burse in which they were kept was called "the breastpiece of decision."

28, 41: *Ordain them:* literally, "fill their hands," a technical expression used solely for the installation of priests. The phrase proba-

bly originated in the custom of placing in the priests' hands the instruments or other symbols of the sacerdotal office.

28, 30: Lv 8, 8; Sir 45, 11.   **28, 39–43:** Ex 39, 27ff.
28, 31–35: Ex 39, 20ff; Lv 8, 9; Sir   **28, 42:** Ez 44, 18.
   45, 10.   **29, 1–8:** Lv 8, 1–9.
28, 37: Ex 39, 31; Lv 8, 9.   **29, 9:** Lv 8, 13.

Ordination Sacrifices

10* "Now bring forward the bullock in front of the meeting tent. There Aaron and his sons shall lay their hands on its head. 11 Then slaughter the bullock before the LORD, at the entrance of the meeting tent. 12 Take some of its blood and with your finger put it on the horns of the altar. All the rest of the blood you shall pour out at the base of the altar. 13 All the fat that covers its inner organs, as well as the lobe of its liver and its two kidneys, together with the fat that is on them, you shall take and burn on the altar. 14* But the flesh and hide and offal of the bullock you must burn up outside the camp, since this is a sin offering.

15 "Then take one of the rams, and after Aaron and his sons have laid their hands on its head, 16 slaughter it. The blood you shall take and splash on all the sides of the altar. 17 Cut the ram into pieces; its inner organs and shanks you shall first wash, and then put them with the pieces and with the head. 18 The entire ram shall then be burned on the altar, since it is a holocaust, a sweet-smelling oblation to the LORD.

19 "After this take the other ram, and when Aaron and his sons have laid their hands on its head, 20 slaughter it. Some of its blood you shall take and put on the tip of Aaron's right ear and on the tips of his sons' right ears and on the thumbs of their right hands and the great toes of their right feet. Splash the rest of the blood on all the sides of the altar. 21 Then take some of the blood that is on the altar, together with some of the anointing oil, and sprinkle this on Aaron and his vestments, as well as on his sons and their vestments, that his sons and their vestments may be sacred.

22† "Now, from this ram you shall take its fat: its fatty tail, the fat that covers its inner organs, the lobe of its liver, its two kidneys with the fat that is on them, and its right thigh, since this is the ordination ram; 23 then, out of the basket of unleavened food that you have set before the LORD, you shall take one of the loaves of bread, one of the cakes made with oil, and one of the wafers. 24† All these things you shall put into the hands of Aaron and his sons, so that they may wave them as a wave offering before the LORD. 25 After you have received them back from their hands, you shall burn them on top of the holocaust on the altar as a sweet-smelling oblation to the

LORD. 26 Finally, take the breast of Aaron's ordination ram and wave it as a wave offering before the LORD; this is to be your own portion.

27*† "Thus shall you set aside the breast of whatever wave offering is waved, as well as the thigh of whatever raised offering is raised up, whether this be the ordination ram or anything else belonging to Aaron or to his sons. 28 Such things are due to Aaron and his sons from the Israelites by a perpetual ordinance as a contribution. From their peace offerings, too, the Israelites shall make a contribution, their contribution to the LORD.

29* "The sacred vestments of Aaron shall be passed down to his descendants, that in them they may be anointed and ordained. 30 The descendant who succeeds him as priest and who is to enter the meeting tent to minister in the sanctuary shall be clothed with them for seven days.

31* "You shall take the flesh of the ordination ram and boil it in a holy place. 32 At the entrance of the meeting tent Aaron and his sons shall eat the flesh of the ram and the bread that is in the basket. 33 They themselves are to eat of these things by which atonement was made at their ordination and consecration; but no layman may eat of them, since they are sacred. 34 If some of the flesh of the ordination sacrifice or some of the bread remains over on the next day, this remnant must be burned up; it is not to be eaten, since it is sacred. 35* Carry out all these orders in regard to Aaron and his sons just as I have given them to you.

"Seven days you shall spend in ordaining them, 36*† sacrificing a bullock each day as a sin offering, to make atonement. Thus also shall you purge the altar in making atonement for it; you shall anoint it in order to consecrate it. 37 Seven days you shall spend in making atonement for the altar and in consecrating it. Then the altar will be most sacred, and whatever touches it will become sacred.

38*† "Now, this is what you shall offer on the altar: two yearling lambs as the sacrifice established for each day; 39 one lamb in the morning and the other lamb at the evening twilight. 40 With the first lamb there shall be a tenth of an ephah of fine flour mixed with a fourth of a hin of oil of crushed olives and, as its libation, a fourth of a hin of wine. 41 The other lamb you shall offer at the evening twilight, with the same cereal offering and libation as in the

---

†

29, 22: *Fatty tail:* the thick layer of fat surrounding the tails of sheep and rams bred in Palestine even today. It is regarded as a choice food. Cf Lv 3, 9.

29, 24–26: *Wave offering:* the portions of a peace offering, breast and right thigh, which the officiating priest moved to and fro (waved) in the presence of the Lord. They were reserved for Aaron and his sons.

29, 27–30: These verses are a parenthetical interruption of the ordination ritual; v 31 belongs logically immediately after v 26.

29, 36f: *Purge the altar:* the construction of an altar by profane

hands rendered it impure. The anointing and consecration of the altar purified it and made it sacred.

29, 38–42: A parenthesis inserted into the rubrics for consecrating the altar; v 43 belongs directly after v 37.

29, 10–26: Lv 8, 14–30.
  29, 14: Heb 13, 11.
  29, 27f: Lv 7, 31–34; 10, 14f;
        Nm 18, 18f; Dt 18, 3.
  29, 29: Nm 20, 26.28.

29, 31–34: Lv 8, 31f.
  29, 35: Lv 8, 36.
  29, 36f: Lv 8, 33ff.
  29, 38–42: Nm 28, 3–8.

morning. You shall offer this as a sweet-smelling oblation to the LORD. 42 Throughout your generations this established holocaust shall be offered before the LORD at the entrance of the meeting tent, where I will meet you and speak to you.

43* "There, at the altar, I will meet the Israelites; hence, it will be made sacred by my glory. 44 Thus I will consecrate the meeting tent and the altar, just as I also consecrate Aaron and his sons to be my priests. 45 I will dwell in the midst of the Israelites and will be their God. 46 They shall know that I, the LORD, am their God who brought them out of the land of Egypt, so that I, the LORD, their God, might dwell among them.

Altar of Incense

30 1* "For burning incense you shall make an altar of acacia wood, 2 with a square surface, a cubit long, a cubit wide, and two cubits high, with horns that spring directly from it. 3 Its grate on top, its walls on all four sides, and its horns you shall plate with pure gold. Put a gold molding around it. 4 Underneath the molding you shall put gold rings, two on one side and two on the opposite side, as holders for the poles used in carrying it. 5 Make the poles, too, of acacia wood and plate them with gold. 6* This altar you are to place in front of the veil that hangs before the ark of the commandments where I will meet you.

7 "On it Aaron shall burn fragrant incense. Morning after morning, when he prepares the lamps, 8 and again in the evening twilight, when he lights the lamps, he shall burn incense. Throughout your generations this shall be the established incense offering before the LORD. 9 On this altar you shall not offer up any profane incense, or any holocaust or cereal offering; nor shall you pour out a libation upon it. 10* Once a year Aaron shall perform the atonement rite on its horns. Throughout your generations this atonement is to be made once a year with the blood of the atoning sin offering. This altar is most sacred to the LORD."

Census Tax

11 The LORD also said to Moses, 12* "When you take a census of the Israelites who are to be registered, each one, as he is enrolled, shall give the LORD a forfeit for his life, so that no plague may come upon them for being registered. 13* Everyone who enters the registered group must pay a half-shekel, according to the standard of the sanctuary shekel, twenty gerahs to the shekel. This payment of a half-shekel is a contribution to the LORD. 14 Everyone of twenty years or more who enters the registered group must give this contribution to the LORD. 15 The rich need not give more, nor shall the poor give less, than a half-shekel in this contribution to the LORD to pay the forfeit for their lives. 16* When you receive this forfeit money from the Israelites, you shall donate it to the service of the meeting tent, that there it may be the Israelites' reminder, before the LORD, of the forfeit paid for their lives."

The Laver

17 The LORD said to Moses, 18* "For ablutions you shall make a bronze laver with a bronze base. Place it between the meeting tent and the altar, and put water in it. 19* Aaron and his sons shall use it in washing their hands and feet. 20 When they are about to enter the meeting tent, they must wash with water, lest they die. Likewise when they approach the altar in their ministry, to offer an oblation to the LORD, 21 they must wash their hands and feet, lest they die. This shall be a perpetual ordinance for him and his descendants throughout their generations."

The Anointing Oil

22 The LORD said to Moses, 23 "Take the finest spices: five hundred shekels of free-flowing myrrh; half that amount, that is, two hundred and fifty shekels, of fragrant cinnamon; two hundred and fifty shekels of fragrant cane; 24 five hundred shekels of cassia—all according to the standard of the sanctuary shekel; together with a hin of olive oil; 25* and blend them into sacred anointing oil, perfumed ointment expertly prepared. 26* With this sacred anointing oil you shall anoint the meeting tent and the ark of the commandments, 27 the table and all its appurtenances, the lampstand and its appurtenances, the altar of incense 28 and the altar of holocausts with all its appurtenances, and the laver with its base. 29 When you have consecrated them, they shall be most sacred; whatever touches them shall be sacred. 30* Aaron and his sons you shall also anoint and consecrate as my priests. 31 To the Israelites you shall say: As sacred anointing oil this shall belong to me throughout your generations. 32 It may not be used in any ordinary anointing of the body, nor may you make any other oil of a like mixture. It is sacred, and shall be treated as sacred by you. 33 Whoever prepares a perfume like this, or whoever puts any of this on a layman, shall be cut off from his kinsmen."

The Incense

34* The LORD told Moses, "Take these aromatic substances: storax and onycha and galbanum, these

---

29, 43: Ex 25, 22.
30, 1–5: Ex 37, 25–28.
30, 6: Ex 40, 26.
30, 10: Lv 16, 18.

30, 12: Nm 1, 2f; 26, 2.
30, 13: Mt 17, 24–27.
30, 16: Ex 38, 25.
30, 18: Ex 38, 8; 40, 7.30.

30, 19ff: Ex 40, 31f.
30, 25: Ex 37, 29.
30, 26–29: Ex 40, 9ff; Lv 8, 10;

Nm 7, 1.
30, 30: Ex 29, 7; Lv 8, 12.
30, 34ff: Ex 25, 6; 37, 29.

and pure frankincense in equal parts; [35] and blend them into incense. This fragrant powder, expertly prepared, is to be salted and so kept pure and sacred. [36] Grind some of it into fine dust and put this before the commandments in the meeting tent where I will meet you. This incense shall be treated as most sacred by you. [37] You may not make incense of a like mixture for yourselves; you must treat it as sacred to the LORD. [38] Whoever makes an incense like this for his own enjoyment of its fragrance, shall be cut off from his kinsmen."

Choice of Artisans

31 [1]* The LORD said to Moses, [2] "See, I have chosen Bezalel, son of Uri, son of Hur, of the tribe of Judah, [3] and I have filled him with a divine spirit of skill and understanding and knowledge in every craft: [4] in the production of embroidery, in making things of gold, silver or bronze, [5] in cutting and mounting precious stones, in carving wood, and in every other craft. [6] As his assistant I have appointed Oholiab, son of Ahisamach, of the tribe of Dan. I have also endowed all the experts with the necessary skill to make all the things I have ordered you to make: [7]* the meeting tent, the ark of the commandments with the propitiatory on top of it, all the furnishings of the tent, [8] the table with its appurtenances, the pure gold lampstand with all its appurtenances, the altar of incense, [9] the altar of holocausts with all its appurtenances, the laver with its base, [10]† the service cloths, the sacred vestments for Aaron the priest, the vestments for his sons in their ministry, [11] the anointing oil, and the fragrant incense for the sanctuary. All these things they shall make just as I have commanded you."

Sabbath Laws

[12]* The LORD said to Moses, [13] "You must also tell the Israelites: Take care to keep my sabbaths, for that is to be the token between you and me throughout the generations, to show that it is I, the LORD, who make you holy. [14] Therefore, you must keep the sabbath as something sacred. Whoever desecrates it shall be put to death. If anyone does work on that day, he must be rooted out of his people. [15] Six days there are for doing work, but the seventh day is the sabbath of complete rest, sacred to the LORD. Anyone who does work on the sabbath day shall be put to death. [16] So shall the Israelites observe the sabbath, keeping it throughout their generations as a perpetual covenant. [17] Between me and the Israelites it is to be an everlasting token; for in six days the LORD made the heavens and the earth, but on the seventh day he rested at his ease."

[18]* When the LORD had finished speaking to Moses on Mount Sinai, he gave him the two tablets of the commandments, the stone tablets inscribed by God's own finger.

The Golden Calf

32 [1]* When the people became aware of Moses' delay in coming down from the mountain, they gathered around Aaron and said to him, "Come, make us a god who will be our leader; as for the man Moses who brought us out of the land of Egypt, we do not know what has happened to him." [2] Aaron replied, "Have your wives and sons and daughters take off the golden earrings they are wearing, and bring them to me." [3] So all the people took off their earrings and brought them to Aaron, [4]* who accepted their offering, and fashioning this gold with a graving tool, made a molten calf. Then they cried out, "This is your God, O Israel, who brought you out of the land of Egypt." [5]† On seeing this, Aaron built an altar before the calf and proclaimed, "Tomorrow is a feast of the LORD." [6]* Early the next day the people offered holocausts and brought peace offerings. Then they sat down to eat and drink, and rose up to revel.

[7] With that, the LORD said to Moses, "Go down at once to your people, whom you brought out of the land of Egypt, for they have become depraved. [8]* They have soon turned aside from the way I pointed out to them, making for themselves a molten calf and worshiping it, sacrificing to it and crying out, 'This is your God, O Israel, who brought you out of the land of Egypt!' [9]* I see how stiffnecked this people is," continued the LORD to Moses. [10] "Let me alone, then, that my wrath may blaze up against them to consume them. Then I will make of you a great nation."

[11]* But Moses implored the LORD, his God, saying, "Why, O LORD, should your wrath blaze up against your own people, whom you brought out of the land of Egypt with such great power and with so strong a hand? [12] Why should the Egyptians say, 'With evil intent he brought them out, that he might kill them in the mountains and exterminate them from the face of the earth'? Let your blazing wrath die down; relent in punishing your people.

---

† **31, 10:** *The service cloths:* so the Greek. They were perhaps the colored cloths mentioned in Nm 4, 4–15.

32, 5: *The calf . . . a feast of the LORD:* from this it is clear that the golden calf was intended as an image, not of a false god, but of the LORD himself, his strength being symbolized by the strength of a young bull. The Israelites, however, had been forbidden to represent the Lord under any visible form. Cf Ex 20, 4.

31, 1–6: Ex 35, 30–35.
31, 7–11: Ex 35, 10–19.
31, 12–17: Ex 20, 8–11; 35, 1–3.
31, 18: Ex 24, 12; 32, 15f; Dt 5, 22.
32, 1: Ex 32, 23; Acts 7, 40.
32, 4: Ex 32, 8; 1 Kgs 12, 28.
32, 6: 1 Cor 10, 7.
32, 8: 7f: Dt 9, 12.16.
32, 9f: Dt 9, 13; Ps 106, 23.
32, 11f: Nm 14, 13ff; Dt 9, 28.

LIVE IT!

Caught Up in the Moment

Now that I think about it, it was a stupid thing to do. But it is so hard to be objective when you are caught up in the excitement of the moment. We had been waiting a long time for Moses—too long, it seems. We got bored and restless. You know how it is. Someone came up with the idea of the golden calf. It sounded like fun, something to pass the time and remind us of the old gods. And I have to admit, that calf did look pretty good!

I do feel sorry for Aaron. Moses saw what we had done and hurled the stone tablets to the ground in a fit of rage. Aaron tried to explain how it was, but Moses would hear none of it. He was upset. He had a right to be. There is no valid excuse for what we did. Aaron tried to pretend that the calf sort of formed itself, but it was a feeble excuse. We all knew it. And when we learned what was on the stone tablets, we knew we had done wrong. Moses had those tablets from the hands of God. This was to have been a solemn moment, followed by a great celebration. But instead, we had to face the wrath of Moses and pick up the shattered pieces of stone.

It is so easy to lose sight of what we are all about. It is so easy to do something stupid when we are bored and tired of waiting. And then, we wonder how we could have let ourselves get so far off track. It is too easy, isn't it? We are all too human at times.

No, I don't blame Moses for losing his temper. He had every right. We let him down. We let ourselves down. But most of all, we let God down.

▶ Ex 32, 1–35

13* Remember your servants Abraham, Isaac and Israel, and how you swore to them by your own self, saying, 'I will make your descendants as numerous as the stars in the sky; and all this land that I promised, I will give your descendants as their perpetual heritage.' " 14 So the LORD relented in the punishment he had threatened to inflict on his people.

15* Moses then turned and came down the mountain with the two tablets of the commandments in his hands, tablets that were written on both sides, front and back; 16* tablets that were made by God, having inscriptions on them that were engraved by God himself. 17 Now, when Joshua heard the noise of the people shouting, he said to Moses, "That sounds like a battle in the camp." 18 But Moses answered, "It does not sound like cries of victory, nor does it sound like cries of defeat; the sounds that I hear are cries of revelry." 19* As he drew near the camp, he saw the calf and the dancing. With that, Moses' wrath flared up, so that he threw the tablets down and broke them on the base of the mountain. 20*† Taking the calf they had made, he fused it in the fire and then ground it down to powder, which he scattered on the water and made the Israelites drink.

21 Moses asked Aaron, "What did this people ever do to you that you should lead them into so grave a sin?" Aaron replied, "Let not my lord be angry. 22 You know well enough how prone the people are to evil. 23 They said to me, 'Make us a god to be our leader; as for the man Moses who brought us out of the land of Egypt, we do not know what has happened to him.' 24 So I told them, 'Let anyone who has gold jewelry take it off.' They gave it to me, and I threw it into the fire, and this calf came out."

25 When Moses realized that, to the scornful joy of their foes, Aaron had let the people run wild, 26* he stood at the gate of the camp and cried, "Whoever is for the LORD, let him come to me!" All the Levites then rallied to him, 27† and he told them, "Thus says the LORD, the God of Israel: Put your sword on your hip, every one of you! Now go up and down the camp, from gate to gate, and slay your own kinsmen, your friends and neighbors!" 28 The Levites carried out the command of Moses, and that day there fell about three thousand of the people. 29† Then Moses said, "Today you have been dedicated to the LORD, for you were against your own sons and kinsmen, to bring a blessing upon yourselves this day."

32, 20: *The water:* the stream that flowed down Mount Sinai. Cf Dt 9, 21.
32, 27: *Slay your own kinsmen . . .:* those who were especially guilty of the idolatry.
32, 29: *Dedicated to the LORD:* because of their zeal for the true worship of the Lord, the Levites were chosen to be special ministers of the ritual service. However, the meaning of the Hebrew here is somewhat disputed.

32, 13: Gn 22, 16f.   32, 19: Dt 9, 16f.
32, 15: Dt 9, 15.   32, 20: Dt 9, 21.
32, 16: Ex 31, 18.   32, 26–29: Dt 33, 8f.

The Atonement

30* On the next day Moses said to the people, "You have committed a grave sin. I will go up to the LORD, then; perhaps I may be able to make atonement for your sin." 31 So Moses went back to the LORD and said, "Ah, this people has indeed committed a grave sin in making a god of gold for themselves! 32† If you would only forgive their sin! If you will not, then strike me out of the book that you have written." 33 The LORD answered, "Him only who has sinned against me will I strike out of my book. 34 Now, go and lead the people whither I have told you. My angel will go before you. When it is time for me to punish, I will punish them for their sin."

35 Thus the LORD smote the people for having had Aaron make the calf for them.

33 1* The LORD told Moses, "You and the people whom you have brought up from the land of Egypt, are to go up from here to the land which I swore to Abraham, Isaac and Jacob I would give to their descendants. 2* Driving out the Canaanites, Amorites, Hittites, Perizzites, Hivites and Jebusites, I will send an angel before you 3 to the land flowing with milk and honey. But I myself will not go up in your company, because you are a stiff-necked people; otherwise I might exterminate you on the way." 4 When the people heard this bad news, they went into mourning, and no one wore his ornaments.

5 The LORD said to Moses, "Tell the Israelites: You are a stiff-necked people. Were I to go up in your company even for a moment, I would exterminate you. Take off your ornaments, therefore; I will then see what I am to do with you." 6 So, from Mount Horeb onward, the Israelites laid aside their ornaments.

Moses' Intimacy with God

7*† The tent, which was called the meeting tent, Moses used to pitch at some distance away, outside the camp. Anyone who wished to consult the LORD would go to this meeting tent outside the camp. 8 Whenever Moses went out to the tent, the people would all rise and stand at the entrance of their own tents, watching Moses until he entered the tent. 9 As Moses entered the tent, the column of cloud would come down and stand at its entrance while the LORD spoke with Moses. 10 On seeing the column of cloud stand at the entrance of the tent, all the people would rise and worship at the entrance of their own tents. 11* The LORD used to speak to Moses face to face, as one man speaks to another. Moses would then return to the camp, but his young assistant, Joshua, son of Nun, would not move out of the tent.

12* Moses said to the LORD, "You, indeed, are telling me to lead this people on; but you have not let me know whom you will send with me. Yet you have said, 'You are my intimate friend,' and also, 'You have found favor with me.' 13 Now, if I have found favor with you, do let me know your ways so that, in knowing you, I may continue to find favor with you. Then, too, this nation is, after all, your own people." 14† "I myself," the LORD answered, "will go along, to give you rest." 15 Moses replied, "If you are not going yourself, do not make us go up from here. 16 For how can it be known that we, your people and I, have found favor with you, except by your going with us? Then we, your people and I, will be singled out from every other people on the earth." 17 The LORD said to Moses, "This request, too, which you have just made, I will carry out, because you have found favor with me and you are my intimate friend."

18 Then Moses said, "Do let me see your glory!" 19* He answered, "I will make all my beauty pass before you, and in your presence I will pronounce my name, 'LORD'; I who show favors to whom I will, I who grant mercy to whom I will. 20* But my face you cannot see, for no man sees me and still lives. 21 Here," continued the LORD, "is a place near me where you shall station yourself on the rock. 22 When my glory passes I will set you in the hollow of the rock and will cover you with my hand until I have passed by. 23† Then I will remove my hand, so that you may see my back; but my face is not to be seen."

Renewal of the Tablets

34 1* The LORD said to Moses, "Cut two stone tablets like the former, that I may write on them the commandments which were on the former tablets that you broke. 2 Get ready for tomorrow morning, when you are to go up Mount

---

32, 32: *The book that you have written:* the list of God's intimate friends. In a similar sense St. Paul wished to be anathema from Christ for the sake of his brethren. Cf Rom 9, 3.

33, 7–11: *The meeting tent* is mentioned here by anticipation; its actual construction is described in the following chapters.

33, 14: *I myself:* literally, "my face," that is, "my presence." *To give you rest:* in the Promised Land; some understand, "to put your mind at rest"; others, by a slight emendation in the text, render, "to lead you."

33, 23: *You may see my back:* man can see God's glory as reflected in creation, but his "face," that is, God as he is in himself, mortal man cannot behold. Cf 1 Cor 13, 12.

32, 30–34: Dt 9, 18ff.   Sir 45, 4–6.
   33, 1: Gn 12, 7.   33, 12: Ex 32, 34.
   33, 2: Ex 23, 23.   33, 19: Rom 9, 15.
   33, 7: Ex 29, 42f.   33, 20: Jn 1, 18; 1 Tm 6, 16.
   33, 11: Nm 12, 8; Dt 34, 10;   34, 1: Dt 10, 1f.

PRAY IT

God Passing By

How close can we get to God without actually seeing God's face? If anyone would know, it is Moses. His rather amazing encounter with God is recorded in Ex 33, 18–23.

We too can experience, as many saints and mystics have, a deep intimacy with God. It is significant that God and Moses most often met in nature. If you are lucky, you have a favorite outdoor spot. Perhaps it is a place where you can simply sit and ponder as you gaze at the scenery before you. Perhaps during a sunset on a lovely summer evening or while gazing at the sea or a flowing stream, you somehow connect with God. You may not actually see or feel the hand of God, but somehow you know that God is with you and you are catching a glimpse of God's glory. You feel yourself held in the palm of God's gracious hand. And sometimes, like Moses (see 34, 29), you are transformed by the power of God's presence.

Where do you most fully experience the presence of God?

▶ Ex 33, 18–23

Sinai and there present yourself to me on the top of the mountain. ³* No one shall come up with you, and no one is even to be seen on any part of the mountain; even the flocks and the herds are not to go grazing toward this mountain." ⁴ Moses then cut two stone tablets like the former, and early the next morning he went up Mount Sinai as the LORD had commanded him, taking along the two stone tablets.

⁵ Having come down in a cloud, the LORD stood with him there and proclaimed his name, "LORD." ⁶ Thus the LORD passed before him and cried out, "The LORD, the LORD, a merciful and gracious God, slow to anger and rich in kindness and fidelity,

⁷* continuing his kindness for a thousand generations, and forgiving wickedness and crime and sin; yet not declaring the guilty guiltless, but punishing children and grandchildren to the third and fourth generation for their fathers' wickedness!" ⁸ Moses at once bowed down to the ground in worship. ⁹ Then he said, "If I find favor with you, O LORD, do come along in our company. This is indeed a stiff-necked people; yet pardon our wickedness and sins, and receive us as your own."

Religious Laws

¹⁰ "Here, then," said the LORD, "is the covenant I will make. Before the eyes of all your people I will work such marvels as have never been wrought in any nation anywhere on earth, so that this people among whom you live may see how awe-inspiring are the deeds which I, the LORD, will do at your side. ¹¹* But you, on your part, must keep the commandments I am giving you today.

"I will drive out before you the Amorites, Canaanites, Hittites, Perizzites, Hivites, and Jebusites. ¹²* Take care, therefore, not to make a covenant with these inhabitants of the land that you are to enter; else they will become a snare among you. ¹³† Tear down their altars; smash their sacred pillars, and cut down their sacred poles. ¹⁴† You shall not worship any other god, for the LORD is 'the Jealous One'; a jealous God is he. ¹⁵ Do not make a covenant with the inhabitants of that land; else, when they render their wanton worship to their gods and sacrifice to them, one of them may invite you and you may partake of his sacrifice. ¹⁶ Neither shall you take their daughters as wives for your sons; otherwise, when their daughters render their wanton worship to their gods, they will make your sons do the same.

¹⁷* "You shall not make for yourselves molten gods.

¹⁸* "You shall keep the feast of Unleavened Bread. For seven days at the prescribed time in the month of Abib you are to eat unleavened bread, as I commanded you; for in the month of Abib you came out of Egypt.

¹⁹* "To me belongs every first-born male that opens the womb among all your livestock, whether in the herd or in the flock. ²⁰ The firstling of an ass you shall redeem with one of the flock; if you do not redeem it, you must break its neck. The first-born among your sons you shall redeem.

34, 13: *Sacred poles:* "Ashera" was the name of a Canaanite goddess. In her honor wooden poles (*asherot*) were erected, just as stone pillars (*massebot*) were erected in honor of the god Baal. Both were placed near the altar in a Canaanite shrine.

34, 14: *The LORD is 'the Jealous One':* see note on Ex 20, 5. Some, by a slight emendation, render, "The LORD is jealous for his name." Cf Ez 39, 25.

34, 3: Ex 19, 12f.21.
34, 7: 6f: Ex 20, 5f; Nm 14, 18; Dt 5, 9f; Jer 32, 18.
34, 11: Ex 13, 5; 33, 2.
34, 12–16: Ex 23, 32f; Dt 7, 1–5;
12, 2f.
34, 17: Lv 19, 4; 5, 8f.
34, 18: Ex 12, 15ff; 13, 3f.
34, 19f: Ex 13, 2.12f; 23, 15.

?did you KNOW?

Major Jewish Feasts

The joyful anticipation that we feel before a major holiday seems to be shared by people of all cultures and religious traditions. Certainly, the Israelites had that feeling before the three festivals described in Ex 34, 18–26 (and in 23, 14–17). They looked forward to them the way we might look forward to Christmas or Easter. These three feasts were called pilgrimage feasts because they required males to travel to the Temple in Jerusalem.

The *feast of Unleavened Bread*, which began on the day after Passover and lasted a week, marked the beginning of the barley harvest. This feast probably originated in a pre-Passover agricultural holiday. Originally, unleavened bread—bread made without yeast—was eaten during this week to symbolize a fresh start. Later, the feast was connected to the Passover celebration, and the custom of eating unleavened bread came to be seen as a reminder of the haste with which the people had left Egypt—before having time to leaven their bread.

The *feast of Weeks*, or Pentecost, began seven weeks after the barley harvest, to celebrate the start of the wheat harvest. Later, the feast of Weeks took on added significance. Because the Israelites had arrived at Mount Sinai in the third month after their departure from Egypt (19, 1), this weeklong feast came to be seen as a celebration of God's Covenant with Israel.

The third weeklong festival, *the feast of Booths*, was celebrated as the produce of the land was gathered. Much like our own Thanksgiving Day, it was a time set aside to thank God for the bounty of the earth. It is the most popular of the pilgrimage feasts. In Exodus, it is called the feast at the fruit harvest, and in other places, simply the festival (1 Kgs 8, 2).

▶ Ex 34, 18–26

"No one shall appear before me empty-handed. ²¹* "For six days you may work, but on the seventh day you shall rest; on that day you must rest even during the seasons of plowing and harvesting. ²²*† "You shall keep the feast of Weeks with the first of the wheat harvest; likewise, the feast at the fruit harvest at the close of the year. ²³ Three times a year all your men shall appear before the Lord, the LORD God of Israel. ²⁴ Since I will drive out the nations before you to give you a large territory, there will be no one to covet your land when you go up three times a year to appear before the LORD, your God. ²⁵ "You shall not offer me the blood of sacrifice with leavened bread, nor shall the sacrifice of the Passover feast be kept overnight for the next day. ²⁶* "The choicest first fruits of your soil you shall bring to the house of the LORD, your God.

"You shall not boil a kid in its mother's milk."

Radiance of Moses' Face

²⁷ Then the LORD said to Moses, "Write down these words, for in accordance with them I have made a covenant with you and with Israel." ²⁸* So Moses stayed there with the LORD for forty days and forty nights, without eating any food or drinking any water, and he wrote on the tablets the words of the covenant, the ten commandments.

²⁹ As Moses came down from Mount Sinai with the two tablets of the commandments in his hands, he did not know that the skin of his face had become radiant while he conversed with the LORD. ³⁰ When Aaron, then, and the other Israelites saw Moses and noticed how radiant the skin of his face had become, they were afraid to come near him. ³¹ Only after Moses called to them did Aaron and all the rulers of the community come back to him. Moses then spoke to them. ³² Later on, all the Israelites came up to him, and he enjoined on them all that the LORD had told him on Mount Sinai. ³³† When he finished speaking with them, he put a veil over his face. ³⁴* Whenever Moses entered the presence of the LORD to converse with him, he removed the veil until he came out again. On coming out, he would tell the Israelites all that had been

---

† **34, 22:** *Feast of Weeks:* the festival of thanksgiving for the harvest, celebrated seven weeks or fifty days after the beginning of the harvest. It was also called Pentecost (fiftieth) and coincided with the giving of the law on Mount Sinai, fifty days after the offering of the first fruits (Lv 23 10f; Dt 16, 9).

34, 33: *He put a veil over his face:* St. Paul sees in this a symbol of the failure of the Jews to recognize Jesus as the promised Messiah; the true spiritual meaning of the writings of Moses and the prophets is still veiled from the unbelieving Jews. Cf 2 Cor 3, 7–18.

34, 21: Ex 20, 9f.   **34, 28:** Ex 24, 18; Dt 9, 9.18;
34, 22f: Ex 23, 16f; Dt 16,   10, 2.4.
     10.13.16.   **34, 34:** 33f; 2 Cor 3, 13.16.
34, 26: 25f; Ex 23, 18f.

commanded. 35 Then the Israelites would see that the skin of Moses' face was radiant; so he would again put the veil over his face until he went in to converse with the LORD.

Sabbath Regulations

35 1* Moses assembled the whole Israelite community and said to them, "This is what the LORD has commanded to be done. 2 On six days work may be done, but the seventh day shall be sacred to you as the sabbath of complete rest to the LORD. Anyone who does work on that day shall be put to death. 3 You shall not even light a fire in any of your dwellings on the sabbath day."

Collection of Materials

4 Moses told the whole Israelite community, "This is what the LORD has commanded: 5* Take up among you a collection for the LORD. Everyone, as his heart prompts him, shall bring, as a contribution to the LORD, gold, silver and bronze; 6 violet, purple and scarlet yarn; fine linen and goat hair; 7 rams' skins dyed red, and tahash skins; acacia wood; 8 oil for the light; spices for the anointing oil and for the fragrant incense; 9 onyx stones and other gems for mounting on the ephod and on the breastpiece.

Call for Artisans

10* "Let every expert among you come and make all that the LORD has commanded: 11 the Dwelling, with its tent, its covering, its clasps, its boards, its bars, its columns and its pedestals; 12 the ark, with its poles, the propitiatory, and the curtain veil; 13 the table, with its poles and all its appurtenances, and the showbread; 14 the lampstand, with its appurtenances, the lamps, and the oil for the light; 15 the altar of incense, with its poles; the anointing oil, and the fragrant incense; the entrance curtain for the entrance of the Dwelling; 16 the altar of holocausts, with its bronze grating, its poles, and all its appurtenances; the laver, with its base; 17 the hangings of the court, with their columns and pedestals; the curtain for the entrance of the court; 18 the tent pegs for the Dwelling and for the court, with their ropes; 19 the service cloths for use in the sanctuary; the sacred vestments for Aaron, the priest, and the vestments worn by his sons in their ministry."

The Contribution

20 When the whole Israelite community left Moses' presence, 21 everyone, as his heart suggested and his spirit prompted, brought a contribution to the LORD for the construction of the meeting tent, for all its services, and for the sacred vestments. 22* Both the men and the women, all as their hearts prompted them, brought brooches, earrings, rings, necklaces and various other gold articles. Everyone who could presented an offering of gold to the LORD. 23 Everyone who happened to have violet, purple or scarlet yarn, fine linen or goat hair, rams' skins dyed red or tahash skins, brought them. 24 Whoever could make a contribution of silver or bronze offered it to the LORD; and everyone who happened to have acacia wood for any part of the work, brought it. 25 All the women who were expert spinners brought hand-spun violet, purple and scarlet yarn and fine linen thread. 26 All the women who possessed the skill, spun goat hair. 27 The princes brought onyx stones and other gems for mounting on the ephod and on the breastpiece; 28 as well as spices, and oil for the light, anointing oil, and fragrant incense. 29 Every Israelite man and woman brought to the LORD such voluntary offerings as they thought best, for the various kinds of work which the LORD had commanded Moses to have done.

The Artisans

30* Moses said to the Israelites, "See, the LORD has chosen Bezalel, son of Uri, son of Hur, of the tribe of Judah, 31 and has filled him with a divine spirit of skill and understanding and knowledge in every craft: 32 in the production of embroidery, in making things of gold, silver or bronze, 33 in cutting and mounting precious stones, in carving wood, and in every other craft. 34 He has also given both him and Oholiab, son of Ahisamach, of the tribe of Dan, the ability to teach others. 35 He has endowed them with skill to execute all types of work: engraving, embroidering, the making of variegated cloth of violet, purple and scarlet yarn and fine linen thread, weaving, and all other arts and crafts.

36 1* "Bezalel, therefore, will set to work with Oholiab and with all the experts whom the LORD has endowed with skill and understanding in knowing how to execute all the work for the service of the sanctuary, just as the LORD has commanded."

2 Moses then called Bezalel and Oholiab and all the other experts whom the LORD had endowed with skill, men whose hearts moved them to come and take part in the work. 3 They received from Moses all the contributions which the Israelites had brought for establishing the service of the sanctuary. Still, morning after morning the people continued to bring their voluntary offerings to Moses. 4 Thereupon the experts who were executing the

various kinds of work for the sanctuary, all left the work they were doing, 5 and told Moses, "The people are bringing much more than is needed to carry out the work which the LORD has commanded us to do." 6 Moses, therefore, ordered a proclamation to be made throughout the camp: "Let neither man nor woman make any more contributions for the sanctuary." So the people stopped bringing their offerings; 7 there was already enough at hand, in fact, more than enough, to complete the work to be done.

The Tent Cloth and Coverings

8* The various experts who were executing the work, made the Dwelling with its ten sheets woven of fine linen twined, having cherubim embroidered on them with violet, purple and scarlet yarn. 9 The length of each sheet was twenty-eight cubits, and the width four cubits; all the sheets were of the same size. 10 Five of the sheets were sewed together, edge to edge; and the same for the other five. 11 Loops of violet yarn were made along the edge of the end sheet in the first set, and the same along the edge of the end sheet in the second set. 12 Fifty loops were thus put on one inner sheet, and fifty loops on the inner sheet in the other set, with the loops directly opposite each other. 13 Then fifty clasps of gold were made, with which the sheets were joined so that the Dwelling formed one whole.

14 Sheets of goat hair were also woven as a tent over the Dwelling. Eleven such sheets were made. 15 The length of each sheet was thirty cubits and the width four cubits; all eleven sheets were of the same size. 16 Five of these sheets were sewed edge to edge into one set; and the other six sheets into another set. 17 Fifty loops were made along the edge of the end sheet in one set, and fifty loops along the edge of the corresponding sheet in the other set. 18 Fifty bronze clasps were made with which the tent was joined so that it formed one whole. 19 A covering for the tent was made of rams' skins dyed red, and above that, a covering of tahash skins.

The Boards

20* Boards of acacia wood were made as walls for the Dwelling. 21 The length of each board was ten cubits, and the width one and a half cubits. 22 Each board had two arms, fastening them in line. In this way all the boards of the Dwelling were made. 23 They were set up as follows: twenty boards on the south side, 24 with forty silver pedestals under the twenty boards, so that there were two pedestals under each board, at its two arms; 25 twenty boards on the other side of the Dwelling, the north side, 26 with their forty silver pedestals, two under each board; 27 six boards at the rear of the Dwelling, to the west; 28 and two boards at the corners in the rear of the Dwelling. 29 These were double at the bottom, and likewise double at the top, to the first ring. That is how both boards in the corners were made. 30 Thus, there were in the rear eight boards, with their sixteen silver pedestals, two pedestals under each board. 31 Bars of acacia wood were also made, five for the boards on one side of the Dwelling, 32 five for those on the other side, and five for those at the rear, to the west. 33 The center bar, at the middle of the boards, was made to reach across from end to end. 34 The boards were plated with gold, and gold rings were made on them as holders for the bars, which were also plated with gold.

The Veil

35* The veil was woven of violet, purple and scarlet yarn, and of fine linen twined, with cherubim embroidered on it. 36 Four gold-plated columns of acacia wood, with gold hooks, were made for it, and four silver pedestals were cast for them.

37 The curtain for the entrance of the tent was made of violet, purple and scarlet yarn, and of fine linen twined, woven in a variegated manner. 38 Its five columns, with their hooks as well as their capitals and bands, were plated with gold; their five pedestals were of bronze.

The Ark

37 1 Bezalel made the ark of acacia wood, two and a half cubits long, one and a half cubits wide, and one and a half cubits high. 2 The inside and outside were plated with gold, and a molding of gold was put around it. 3 Four gold rings were cast and put on its four supports, two rings for one side and two for the opposite side. 4 Poles of acacia wood were made and plated with gold; 5 these were put through the rings on the sides of the ark, for carrying it.

6 The propitiatory was made of pure gold, two and a half cubits long and one and a half cubits wide. 7 Two cherubim of beaten gold were made for the two ends of the propitiatory, 8 one cherub fastened at one end, the other at the other end, springing directly from the propitiatory at its two ends. 9* The cherubim had their wings spread out above, covering the propitiatory with them. They were turned toward each other, but with their faces looking toward the propitiatory.

The Table

10* The table was made of acacia wood, two cubits long, one cubit wide, and one and a half cubits

36, 8–19: Ex 26, 1–14.   37, 9: 1–9: Ex 25, 10–22.
36, 20–34: Ex 26, 15–29.   37, 10–16: Ex 25, 23–30.
36, 35–38: Ex 26, 31–37.

?did you KNOW?

The Ark of the Covenant

The ark of the Covenant, which Bezalel made in fulfillment of God's command, was a portable box in which the Israelites kept the tablets of the Law (see Dt 10, 1–5; 1 Kgs 8, 9) and possibly other sacred items. The large box was made of gold-plated wood, with four rings attached to its lower corners; through these rings, gold-plated poles were inserted for carrying the ark in procession. On top of the ark sat two golden angels facing each other, their wings touching over their heads.

The ark of the Covenant was a symbol of God's saving presence among the Israelites. It accompanied them during their forty years in the desert (Nm 10, 33–36) and was solemnly carried through the Jordan River when they entered the Promised Land (Jos 3, 1–17). Later, the Israelite soldiers took the ark into battle, invoking God's strength against their enemies (1 Sm 4, 1–11). After the ark was lost in battle to the Philistines, David retrieved it and brought it to Jerusalem (2 Sm 6, 1–23), where his son Solomon eventually enthroned it in the Temple, in the holy of holies (1 Kgs 8, 1–11). The ark remained there until the destruction of Jerusalem in 587 B.C., when it was lost to history.

▸ Ex 37, 1–9

high. 11 It was plated with pure gold, and a molding of gold was put around it. 12 A frame a handbreadth high was also put around it, with a molding of gold around the frame. 13 Four rings of gold were cast for it and fastened, one at each of the four corners. 14 The rings were alongside the frame as holders for the poles to carry the table. 15 These poles were made of acacia wood and plated with gold. 16 The vessels that were set on the table, its plates and cups, as well as its pitchers and bowls for pouring libations, were of pure gold.

The Lampstand

17* The lampstand was made of pure beaten gold—its shaft and branches as well as its cups and knobs and petals springing directly from it. 18 Six branches extended from its sides, three branches on one side and three on the other. 19 On one branch there were three cups, shaped like almond blossoms, each with its knob and petals; on the opposite branch there were three cups, shaped like almond blossoms, each with its knob and petals; and so for the six branches that extended from the lampstand. 20 On the shaft there were four cups, shaped like almond blossoms, with their knobs and petals, 21 including a knob below each of the three pairs of branches that extended from the lampstand. 22 The knobs and branches sprang so directly from it that the whole formed but a single piece of pure beaten gold. 23 Its seven lamps, as well as its trimming shears and trays, were made of pure gold. 24 A talent of pure gold was used for the lampstand and its various appurtenances.

The Altar of Incense

25* The altar of incense was made of acacia wood, on a square, a cubit long, a cubit wide, and two cubits high, having horns that sprang directly from it. 26 Its grate on top, its walls on all four sides, and its horns were plated with pure gold; and a molding of gold was put around it. 27 Underneath the molding gold rings were placed, two on one side and two on the opposite side, as holders for the poles to carry it. 28 The poles, too, were made of acacia wood and plated with gold.

29* The sacred anointing oil and the fragrant incense were prepared in their pure form by a perfumer.

The Altar of Holocausts

38 1* The altar of holocausts was made of acacia wood, on a square, five cubits long and five cubits wide; its height was three cubits. 2 At the four corners horns were made that sprang directly from the altar. The whole was plated with bronze. 3 All the utensils of the altar, the pots, shovels, basins, forks and fire pans, were likewise made of bronze. 4 A grating of bronze network was made for the altar and placed round it, on the ground, half as high as the altar itself. 5 Four rings were cast for the four corners of the bronze grating, as holders for the poles, 6 which were made of acacia wood and plated with bronze. 7 The poles were put through the rings on the sides of the altar for carrying it. The altar was made in the form of a hollow box.

37, 17–24: Ex 25, 31–39.   37, 29: Ex 30, 23ff.34ff.
37, 25–28: Ex 30, 1–5.   38, 1–7: Ex 27, 1–8; 2 Chr 1, 5.

EX

8*† The bronze laver, with its bronze base, was made from the mirrors of the women who served at the entrance of the meeting tent.

The Court

9* The court was made as follows. On the south side of the court there were hangings, woven of fine linen twined, a hundred cubits long, 10 with twenty columns and twenty pedestals of bronze, the hooks and bands of the columns being of silver. 11 On the north side there were similar hangings, one hundred cubits long, with twenty columns and twenty pedestals of bronze, the hooks and bands of the columns being of silver. 12 On the west side there were hangings, fifty cubits long, with ten columns and ten pedestals, the hooks and bands of the columns being of silver. 13 On the east side the court was fifty cubits long. 14 Toward one side there were hangings to the extent of fifteen cubits, with three columns and three pedestals; 15 toward the other side, beyond the entrance of the court, there were likewise hangings to the extent of fifteen cubits, with three columns and three pedestals. 16 The hangings on all sides of the court were woven of fine linen twined. 17 The pedestals of the columns were of bronze, while the hooks and bands of the columns were of silver; the capitals were silver-plated, and all the columns of the court were banded with silver.

18 At the entrance of the court there was a variegated curtain, woven of violet, purple and scarlet yarn and of fine linen twined, twenty cubits long and five cubits wide, in keeping with the hangings of the court. 19 There were four columns and four pedestals of bronze for it, while their hooks were of silver. 20 All the tent pegs for the Dwelling and for the court around it were of bronze.

Amount of Metal Used

21 The following is an account of the various amounts used on the Dwelling, the Dwelling of the commandments, drawn up at the command of Moses by the Levites under the direction of Ithamar, son of Aaron the priest. 22* However, it was Bezalel, son of Uri, son of Hur, of the tribe of Judah, who made all that the Lord commanded Moses, 23 and he was assisted by Oholiab, son of Ahisamach, of the tribe of Dan, who was an engraver, an embroiderer, and a weaver of variegated cloth of violet, purple and scarlet yarn and of fine linen.

24 All the gold used in the entire construction of the sanctuary, having previously been given as an offering, amounted to twenty-nine talents and seven hundred and thirty shekels, according to the standard of the sanctuary shekel. 25 The amount of the silver received from the community was one hundred talents and one thousand seven hundred and seventy-five shekels, according to the standard of the sanctuary shekel; 26* one bekah apiece, that is, a half-shekel apiece, according to the standard of the sanctuary shekel, was received from every man of twenty years or more who entered the registered group; the number of these was six hundred and three thousand five hundred and fifty men. 27 One hundred talents of silver were used for casting the pedestals of the sanctuary and the pedestals of the veil, one talent for each pedestal, or one hundred talents for the one hundred pedestals. 28 The remaining one thousand seven hundred and seventy-five shekels were used for making the hooks on the columns, for plating the capitals, and for banding them with silver. 29 The bronze, given as an offering, amounted to seventy talents and two thousand four hundred shekels. 30 With this were made the pedestals at the entrance of the meeting tent, the bronze altar with its bronze gratings and all the appurtenances of the altar, 31 the pedestals around the court, the pedestals at the entrance of the court, and all the tent pegs for the Dwelling and for the court around it.

The Vestments

39 1* With violet, purple and scarlet yarn were woven the service cloths for use in the sanctuary, as well as the sacred vestments for Aaron, as the LORD had commanded Moses.

2* The ephod was woven of gold thread and of violet, purple and scarlet yarn and of fine linen twined. 3 Gold was first hammered into gold leaf and then cut up into threads, which were woven with the violet, purple and scarlet yarn into an embroidered pattern on the fine linen. 4 Shoulder straps were made for it and joined to its two upper ends. 5 The embroidered belt on the ephod extended out from it, and like it, was made of gold thread, of violet, purple and scarlet yarn, and of fine linen twined, as the LORD had commanded Moses. 6 The onyx stones were prepared and mounted in gold filigree work; they were engraved like seal engravings with the names of the sons of Israel. 7 These stones were set on the shoulder straps of the ephod as memorial stones of the sons of Israel, just as the LORD had commanded Moses.

8* The breastpiece was embroidered like the ephod, with gold thread and violet, purple and scarlet yarn on cloth of fine linen twined. 9 It was

---

38, 8: The reflecting surface of ancient mirrors was usually of polished bronze. *The women who served:* cf 1 Sm 2, 22.

38, 8: Ex 30, 18–21.
38, 9–20: Ex 27, 9–19.
38, 22f: Ex 31, 2.6; 35, 30.34; 36, 1.
38, 26: Nm 1, 46.
39, 1: Ex 31, 10.
39, 2–10: Ex 28, 6–12.
39, 8–14: Ex 28, 15–21.

square and folded double, a span high and a span wide in its folded form. 10 Four rows of precious stones were mounted on it: in the first row a carnelian, a topaz and an emerald; 11 in the second row, a garnet, a sapphire and a beryl; 12 in the third row a jacinth, an agate and an amethyst; 13 in the fourth row a chrysolite, an onyx and a jasper. They were mounted in gold filigree work. 14 These stones were twelve, to match the names of the sons of Israel, and each stone was engraved like a seal with the name of one of the twelve tribes.

15* Chains of pure gold, twisted like cords, were made for the breastpiece, 16 together with two gold filigree rosettes and two gold rings. The two rings were fastened to the two upper ends of the breastpiece. 17 The two gold chains were then fastened to the two rings at the ends of the breastpiece. 18 The other two ends of the two chains were fastened in front to the two filigree rosettes, which were attached to the shoulder straps of the ephod. 19 Two other gold rings were made and put on the two lower ends of the breastpiece, on the edge facing the ephod. 20 Two more gold rings were made and fastened to the bottom of the two shoulder straps next to where they joined the ephod in front, just above its embroidered belt. 21 Violet ribbons bound the rings of the breastpiece to the rings of the ephod, so that the breastpiece stayed right above the embroidered belt of the ephod and did not swing loose from it. All this was just as the LORD had commanded Moses.

The Other Vestments

22 The robe of the ephod was woven entirely of violet yarn, 23 with an opening in its center like the opening of a shirt, with selvage around the opening to keep it from being torn. 24 At the hem of the robe pomegranates were made of violet, purple and scarlet yarn and of fine linen twined; 25 bells of pure gold were also made and put between the pomegranates all around the hem of the robe: 26 first a bell, then a pomegranate, and thus alternating all around the hem of the robe which was to be worn in performing the ministry—all this, just as the LORD had commanded Moses.

27* For Aaron and his sons there were also woven tunics of fine linen; 28 the miter of fine linen; the ornate turbans of fine linen; drawers of linen [of fine linen twined]; 29 and sashes of variegated work made of fine linen twined and of violet, purple and scarlet yarn, as the LORD had commanded Moses. 30* The plate of the sacred diadem was made of pure gold and inscribed, as on a seal engraving: "Sa-

cred to the LORD." 31 It was tied over the miter with a violet ribbon, as the LORD had commanded Moses.

Presentation of the Work to Moses

32 Thus the entire work of the Dwelling of the meeting tent was completed. The Israelites did the work just as the LORD had commanded Moses. 33 They then brought to Moses the Dwelling, the tent with all its appurtenances, the clasps, the boards, the bars, the columns, the pedestals, 34 the covering of rams' skins dyed red, the covering of tahash skins, the curtain veil; 35 the ark of the commandments with its poles, the propitiatory, 36 the table with all its appurtenances and the showbread, 37 the pure gold lampstand with its lamps set up on it and with all its appurtenances, the oil for the light, 38 the golden altar, the anointing oil, the fragrant incense; the curtain for the entrance of the tent, 39 the altar of bronze with its bronze grating, its poles and all its appurtenances, the laver with its base, 40 the hangings of the court with their columns and pedestals, the curtain for the entrance of the court with its ropes and tent pegs, all the equipment for the service of the Dwelling of the meeting tent; 41 the service cloths for use in the sanctuary, the sacred vestments for Aaron the priest, and the vestments to be worn by his sons in their ministry. 42 The Israelites had carried out all the work just as the LORD had commanded Moses. 43 So when Moses saw that all the work was done just as the LORD had commanded, he blessed them.

Erection of the Dwelling

40 1 Then the LORD said to Moses, 2*† "On the first day of the first month you shall erect the Dwelling of the meeting tent.* 3* Put the ark of the commandments in it, and screen off the ark with the veil. 4 Bring in the table and set it. Then bring in the lampstand and set up the lamps on it. 5 Put the golden altar of incense in front of the ark of the commandments, and hang the curtain at the entrance of the Dwelling. 6 Put the altar of holocausts in front of the entrance of the Dwelling of the meeting tent. 7 Place the laver between the meeting tent and the altar, and put water in it. 8 Set up the court round about, and put the curtain at the entrance of the court.

9* "Take the anointing oil and anoint the Dwelling and everything in it, consecrating it and all its furnishings, so that it will be sacred. 10 Anoint the altar of holocausts and all its appurtenances,

---

40, 2: *On the first day of the first month:* almost a year after the departure of the Israelites from Egypt. Cf v 17.

39, 15–21: Ex 28, 31–35.
39, 27ff: Ex 28, 39–42.
39, 30f: Ex 28, 36f.
40, 2–8: Ex 40, 16–33.

40, 2: Ex 26, 30.
40, 3ff: Ex 26, 33ff.
40, 9ff: Ex 30, 26–29.

American

Asian

Umbrellas, Arks, and Tents

Umbrellas offer protection from the sun or rain. In Asian cultures, servants would hold umbrellas over emperors and kings. Catholics in Indonesia have adapted this custom for their worship. Often, an umbrella is set up over the tabernacle. Umbrellas are held over a priest when he carries the Blessed Sacrament or over the statue of Jesus' Sacred Heart when it is carried in a procession. The umbrella has become a sign of reverence for something that symbolizes God's presence.

The ark of the Covenant was built to act like an umbrella, to protect and reverence the tablets of the Law (the Commandments). When the ark was not being carried, it rested in the tabernacle in the holy of holies, which was a special tent at the center of the Israelites' camp. The ark and the tent served the same practical purpose as an umbrella and had the same deeper meaning of reverencing God's presence.

The next time you use an umbrella, remember how umbrellas are used to show respect for that which is holy: the body of Christ, the Ten Commandments, and one of God's greatest creations, you!

▶ Ex 40, 1–15

consecrating it, so that it will be most sacred. 11 Likewise, anoint the laver with its base, and thus consecrate it.

12* "Then bring Aaron and his sons to the entrance of the meeting tent, and there wash them with water. 13 Clothe Aaron with the sacred vestments and anoint him, thus consecrating him as my priest. 14 Bring forward his sons also, and clothe them with the tunics. 15 As you have anointed their father, anoint them also as my priests. Thus, by being anointed, they shall receive a perpetual priesthood throughout all future generations."

16 Moses did exactly as the LORD had commanded him. 17 On the first day of the first month of the second year the Dwelling was erected. 18 It was Moses who erected the Dwelling. He placed its pedestals, set up its boards, put in its bars, and set up its columns. 19 He spread the tent over the Dwelling and put the covering on top of the tent, as the LORD had commanded him. 20* He took the commandments and put them in the ark; he placed poles alongside the ark and set the propitiatory upon it. 21 He brought the ark into the Dwelling and hung the curtain veil, thus screening off the ark of the commandments, as the LORD had commanded him. 22 He put the table in the meeting tent, on the north side of the Dwelling, outside the veil, 23* and arranged the bread on it before the LORD, as the LORD had commanded him. 24 He placed the lampstand in the meeting tent, opposite the table, on the south side of the Dwelling, 25 and he set up the lamps before the LORD, as the LORD had commanded him. 26 He placed the golden altar in the meeting tent, in front of the veil, 27 and on it he burned fragrant incense, as the LORD had commanded him. 28 He hung the curtain at the entrance of the Dwelling. 29 He put the altar of holocausts in front of the entrance of the Dwelling of the meeting tent, and offered holocausts and cereal offerings on it, as the LORD had commanded him. 30* He placed the laver between the meeting tent and the altar, and put water in it for washing. 31 Moses and Aaron and his sons used to wash their hands and feet there, 32 for they washed themselves whenever they went into the meeting tent or approached the altar, as the LORD commanded Moses. 33 Finally, he set up the court around the Dwelling and the altar and hung the curtain at the entrance of the court. Thus Moses finished all the work.

God's Presence in the Dwelling

34* Then the cloud covered the meeting tent, and the glory of the LORD filled the Dwelling. 35 Moses could not enter the meeting tent, because the cloud settled down upon it and the glory of the LORD filled the Dwelling. 36 Whenever the cloud rose from the Dwelling, the Israelites would set out on their journey. 37 But if the cloud did not lift, they would not go forward; only when it lifted did they go forward. 38 In the daytime the cloud of the LORD was seen over the Dwelling; whereas at night, fire was seen in the cloud by the whole house of Israel in all the stages of their journey.

40, 12–15: Ex 28, 41; 29, 4–9; Lv 8, 1–13.
40, 20ff: Ex 25, 16.21; 26, 33ff.
40, 23: Ex 25, 30.
40, 30ff: Ex 30, 18ff.
40, 34–38: Nm 9, 15–22.

When approaching a stop sign, come to a complete stop before proceeding." "You are not allowed to pass when a yellow line is on your side of the road." Sometime soon you will be given a book to learn these rules of driving—unless you have already had the pleasure! These laws may be a pain to memorize, but without them driving would be chaos. The Book of Leviticus has a similar function. It is primarily a list of laws, rules, and instructions to ensure holiness and order in worship and the people's way of life.

At a Glance

I. Ritual of Sacrifices (chapters 1—7).

II. Ceremony of Ordination (chapters 8—10).

III. Laws regarding Legal Purity (chapters 11—16).

IV. Code of Legal Holiness (chapters 17—26).

V. Redemption of Offerings (chapter 27).

In-depth

Leviticus, the third book of the Pentateuch, or Torah, is named after the tribe of Levi, whose male members were designated priests in Israel. It was their responsibility to conduct appropriate worship of God. For that reason, the book has often been referred to as the Torah (Law) of the Priests.

Most Scripture scholars believe that the laws and regulations in Leviticus developed over hundreds of years after the people entered the Promised Land. The book was composed at a time when the priests were struggling to unify Israel as it lay in ruins from its Babylonian conquerers. They wished to gather the various traditions and regulations that governed Israel's way of life. The author of Leviticus, referred to as the Priestly writer, writes as if these gathered traditions and regulations were given by God to Moses at Mount Sinai as part of the original Law. The author wishes to show that these laws are an extension of the Sinai Covenant.

If the goal of Israel's existence is to "be holy, because I [the Lord] am holy" (Lv 11, 45), then the Book of Leviticus records how holiness becomes part of every aspect of Israel's existence. Chapters 17–26 are described as the Code of Legal Holiness. The words on love of neighbor in 19, 18 are quoted several times in the New Testament. The purpose of Leviticus is to call Israel to follow the Law, and thus become a holy people and make its land a suitable place for God to dwell.

The customs and rites in Jesus' time are observances of the laws in Leviticus. Many of those customs and rites were left behind as Christianity emerged as a distinct religion.

Quick Facts

Period Covered
after the Exodus, during the Israelites' encampment at Mount Sinai

Author
the Priestly writer writing after the Babylonian Exile

Theme
to teach the way of holiness through observance of the Law and religious ritual

Leviticus

I: Ritual of Sacrifices

Holocausts

1 ¹ The LORD called Moses, and from the meeting tent gave him this message: ²*† "Speak to the Israelites and tell them: When any one of you wishes to bring an animal offering to the LORD, such an offering must be from the herd or from the flock.

³*† "If his holocaust offering is from the herd, it must be a male without blemish. To find favor with the LORD, he shall bring it to the entrance of the meeting tent ⁴* and there lay his hand on the head of the holocaust, so that it may be acceptable to make atonement for him. ⁵* He shall then slaughter the bull before the LORD, but Aaron's sons, the priests, shall offer up its blood by splashing it on the sides of the altar which is at the entrance of the meeting tent. ⁶ Then he shall skin the holocaust and cut it up into pieces. ⁷ After Aaron's sons, the priests, have put some burning embers on the altar and laid some wood on them, ⁸ they shall lay the pieces of meat, together with the head and the suet, on top of the wood and embers on the altar. ⁹* The inner organs and the shanks, however, the offerer shall first wash with water. The priest shall then burn the whole offering on the altar as a holocaust, a sweet-smelling oblation to the LORD.

¹⁰ "If his holocaust offering is from the flock, that is, a sheep or a goat, he must bring a male without blemish. ¹¹ This he shall slaughter before the LORD at the north side of the altar. Then Aaron's sons, the priests, shall splash its blood on the sides of the altar. ¹² When the offerer has cut it up into pieces, the priest shall lay these, together with the head and suet, on top of the wood and the fire on the altar. ¹³ The inner organs and the shanks, however, the offerer shall first wash with water. The priest shall offer them up and then burn the whole offering on the altar as a holocaust, a sweet-smelling oblation to the LORD.

¹⁴* "If he offers a bird as a holocaust to the LORD, he shall choose a turtledove or a pigeon as his offering. ¹⁵* Having brought it to the altar where it is to be burned, the priest shall snap its head loose and squeeze out its blood against the side of the altar. ¹⁶ Its crop and feathers shall be removed and thrown on the ash heap at the east side of the altar. ¹⁷ Then, having split the bird down the middle

---

1, 2: *From the herd or from the flock:* the only animals which could be used as sacrificial victims were either of the bovine class (bulls, cows and calves) or the ovine class (sheep and lambs, goats and kids). Excluded, therefore, were not only all wild animals, but also such "unclean" domestic animals as the camel and the ass. See note on Lv 11, 1ff.

1, 3: *Holocaust:* from the Greek word meaning "wholly burned," this is the technical term for the special type of sacrifice in which an entire animal except its hide was consumed in the fire on the altar. The primary purpose of this complete gift was to render glory and praise to God.

1, 2: Lv 22, 18.19.
1, 3: Ex 12, 5.
1, 4: Lv 3, 2.8.13; 4, 15; 8, 14.22; 16, 21; Ex 29, 10.15.
1, 5: Lv 3, 8.
1, 9: Lv 3, 5.16; Ex 29, 18.
1, 14: Lv 5, 7; 12, 8; Lk 2, 24.
1, 15: Lv 5, 8.

without separating the halves, the priest shall burn it on the altar, over the wood on the fire, as a holocaust, a sweet-smelling oblation to the LORD.

Cereal Offerings

2 1* "When anyone wishes to bring a cereal offering to the LORD, his offering must consist of fine flour. He shall pour oil on it and put frankincense over it. 2*† When he has brought it to Aaron's sons, the priests, one of them shall take a handful of this fine flour and oil, together with all the frankincense, and this he shall burn on the altar as a token offering, a sweet-smelling oblation to the LORD. 3* The rest of the cereal offering belongs to Aaron and his sons. It is a most sacred oblation to the LORD.

4 "When the cereal offering you present is baked in an oven, it must be in the form of unleavened cakes made of fine flour mixed with oil, or of unleavened wafers spread with oil. 5* If you present a cereal offering that is fried on a griddle, it must be of fine flour mixed with oil and unleavened. 6 Such a cereal offering must be broken into pieces, and oil must be poured over it. 7 If you present a cereal offering that is prepared in a pot, it must be of fine flour, deep-fried in oil. 8 A cereal offering that is made in any of these ways you shall bring to the LORD, offering it to the priest, who shall take it to the altar. 9 Its token offering the priest shall then lift from the cereal offering and burn on the altar as a sweet-smelling oblation to the LORD. 10 The rest of the cereal offering belongs to Aaron and his sons. It is a most sacred oblation to the LORD.

11* "Every cereal offering that you present to the LORD shall be unleavened, for you shall not burn any leaven or honey as an oblation to the LORD. 12 Such you may indeed present to the LORD in the offering of first fruits, but they are not to be placed on the altar for a pleasing odor. 13*† However, every cereal offering that you present to the LORD shall be seasoned with salt. Do not let the salt of the covenant of your God be lacking from your cereal offering. On every offering you shall offer salt.

14 "If you present a cereal offering of first fruits to the LORD, you shall offer it in the form of fresh grits of new ears of grain, roasted by fire. 15 On this cereal offering you shall put oil and frankincense. 16 For its token offering the priest shall then burn

---

? did you KNOW?

The Covenant Laws

Even though Christians are not bound by the Jewish religion—see the Letters to the Hebrews and to the Romans—the laws in Leviticus help us understand the meaning of life for the Israelites. These laws developed out of their experience of striving to be faithful to God and were interpreted and taught by the priests of the tribe of Levi.

The purity laws may seem the strangest to us today. They defined who or what was pure—that is, free from contamination—and therefore acceptable to God. They included laws on sickness, especially leprosy, because physical disease was understood as a symptom of sin or spiritual contamination. Purity laws also covered food, animals, bodily discharges, and corpses.

Other laws described proper relationships between people. These laws reflected more the intentions of the heart. Later, the prophets and Jesus would emphasize that impurity comes from the heart, not from something outside the person (Mk 7, 1–23). Other laws regulated priestly ministry, and still others regulated social institutions. Nothing was left to chance. The laws of the Covenant made it clear that God was present in every aspect of the people's lives.

---

some of the grits and oil, together with all the frankincense, as an oblation to the LORD.

Peace Offerings

3 1*† "If someone in presenting a peace offering makes his offering from the herd, he may offer before the LORD either a male or a female animal, but it must be without blemish. 2* He shall lay his hand on the head of his offering, and then

---

†

   2, 2: *Token offering:* literally, "reminder." Instead of burning the whole cereal offering, they burned only this part of it on the altar; it thus corresponded to the fat of the peace offering. See note on Lv 3, 1.

   2, 13: *The salt of the covenant of your God:* the partaking in common of salt by those seated together at table was an ancient symbol of friendship and alliance. Cf Mk 9, 49 and Col 4, 6; and see note on Nm 18, 19.

   3, 1: *Peace offering:* thus the ancient versions have rendered the Hebrew word, which perhaps means more exactly, "fulfillment sac-

rifice," offered up in fulfillment of a vow. Cf Prv 7, 14. Its characteristic feature was the sacred banquet at which the offerer and his guests partook of the meat of the sacrificed animal. Cf Lv 7, 11–21.

*

2, 1: Nm 15, 4.	Mk 8, 15; Lk 12, 1;
2, 2: Lv 6, 15.	1 Cor 5, 7; Gal 5, 9.
2, 3: Lv 7, 9f; Sir 7, 31;	2, 13: Ez 43, 24.
1 Cor 9, 13.	3, 1: Lv 22, 21.
2, 5: 1 Chr 23, 29.	3, 2: Lv 1, 4.
2, 11: Lv 6, 16f; Mt 16, 12;	

slaughter it at the entrance of the meeting tent; but Aaron's sons, the priests, shall splash its blood on the sides of the altar. 3* From the peace offering he shall offer as an oblation to the LORD the fatty membrane over the inner organs, and all the fat that adheres to them, 4† as well as the two kidneys, with the fat on them near the loins, and the lobe of the liver, which he shall sever above the kidneys. 5* All this Aaron's sons shall then burn on the altar with the holocaust, on the wood over the fire, as a sweet-smelling oblation to the LORD.

6 "If the peace offering he presents to the LORD is from the flock, he may offer either a male or a female animal, but it must be without blemish. 7 If he presents a lamb as his offering, he shall bring it before the LORD, 8 and after laying his hand on the head of his offering, he shall slaughter it before the meeting tent; but Aaron's sons shall splash its blood on the sides of the altar. 9*† As an oblation to the LORD he shall present the fat of the peace offering: the whole fatty tail, which he must sever close to the spine, the fatty membrane over the inner organs, and all the fat that adheres to them, 10 as well as the two kidneys, with the fat on them near the loins, and the lobe of the liver, which he must sever above the kidneys. 11 All this the priest shall burn on the altar as the food of the LORD's oblation.

12 "If he presents a goat, he shall bring it before the LORD, 13 and after laying his hand on its head, he shall slaughter it before the meeting tent; but Aaron's sons shall splash its blood on the sides of the altar. 14 From it he shall offer as an oblation to the LORD the fatty membrane over the inner organs, and all the fat that adheres to them, 15 as well as the two kidneys, with the fat on them near the loins, and the lobe of the liver, which he must sever above the kidneys. 16 All this the priest shall burn on the altar as the food of the sweet-smelling oblation. All the fat belongs to the LORD. 17*† This shall be a perpetual ordinance for your descendants wherever they may dwell. You shall not partake of any fat or any blood."

Sin Offerings: For Priests

4 ¹ The LORD said to Moses, 2*† "Tell the Israelites: When a person inadvertently commits a sin against some command of the LORD by doing one of the forbidden things, 3*† if it is the anointed priest who thus sins and thereby makes the people also become guilty, he shall present to the LORD a young, unblemished bull as a sin offering for the sin he committed. 4* Bringing the bullock to the entrance of the meeting tent, before the LORD, he shall lay his hand on its head and slaughter it before the LORD. 5 The anointed priest shall then take some of the bullock's blood and bring it into the meeting tent, 6* where, dipping his finger in the blood, he shall sprinkle it seven times before the LORD, toward the veil of the sanctuary. 7* The priest shall also put some of the blood on the horns of the altar of fragrant incense which is before the

PRAY IT
Sin Offering

The sin-offering laws probably seem strange to you. Because of Jesus' sacrifice, Christians have never had to make sin offerings. But they do serve an important role in understanding what Jesus' death and Resurrection mean for our own sin and salvation.

The Israelites understood that sin affects not only the sinner but also those whose lives the sinner touches. They understood sin as incurring a debt that must be repaid. The sinner made a guilt offering to atone for the sin.

Isaiah said that God made the life of the suffering servant a guilt offering for those who were too far into debt to repay (Is 53, 10). At the Last Supper, Jesus told the Apostles, "This is my blood . . . which will be shed on behalf of many for the forgiveness of sins" (Mt 26, 28). Jesus became our sin offering to take on the debt of our sin. In prayerful thanks for this great gift, read Eph 1, 3–14.

▸ Lv 4, 1—5, 26

3, 4: *The lobe of the liver:* some render, "the fatty covering of the liver."

3, 9: *The whole fatty tail:* see note on Ex 29, 22.

3, 17: *Any fat:* only the fat mentioned in vv 9f.14f is meant; other fat could be eaten by the Israelites.

4, 2: *A sin:* not necessarily a moral fault; included are all the cases of ritual uncleanness which people necessarily incurred in certain unavoidable circumstances.

4, 3: *The anointed priest:* his violation of the ceremonial law brought a sort of collective guilt on all the people whom he represented before God. *Sin offering:* more exactly, "sacrifice for remitting sin"; sin is here understood as explained above.

3, 3: Ex 29, 13.22.	22–29.
3, 5: Lv 6, 12.	4, 3: Heb 7, 27.
3, 9: Lv 9, 19.	4, 4: Lv 1, 3f.
3, 17: Lv 17, 10–14; Gn 9, 4;	4, 6: Lv 8, 11.
Dt 12, 16.23; 15, 23.	4, 7: Lv 8, 15; 9, 9; 16, 18;
4, 2: Lv 5, 15.17; Nm 15,	Ex 29, 12.

LORD in the meeting tent. The rest of the bullock's blood he shall pour out at the base of the altar of holocausts which is at the entrance of the meeting tent. 8 From the sin-offering bullock he shall remove all the fat: the fatty membrane over the inner organs, and all the fat that adheres to them, 9 as well as the two kidneys, with the fat on them near the loins, and the lobe of the liver, which he must sever above the kidneys. 10 This is the same as is removed from the ox of the peace offering; and the priest shall burn it on the altar of holocausts. 11* The hide of the bullock and all its flesh, with its head, legs, inner organs and offal, 12 in short, the whole bullock, shall be brought outside the camp to a clean place where the ashes are deposited and there be burned up in a wood fire. At the place of the ash heap, there it must be burned.

For the Community

13* "If the whole community of Israel inadvertently and without even being aware of it does something that the LORD has forbidden and thus makes itself guilty, 14 should it later on become known that the sin was committed, the community shall present a young bull as a sin offering. They shall bring it before the meeting tent, 15* and here, before the LORD, the elders of the community shall lay their hands on the bullock's head. When the bullock has been slaughtered before the LORD, 16 the anointed priest shall bring some of its blood into the meeting tent, 17 and dipping his finger in the blood, he shall sprinkle it seven times before the LORD, toward the veil. 18 He shall also put some of the blood on the horns of the altar of fragrant incense which is before the LORD in the meeting tent. The rest of the blood he shall pour out at the base of the altar of holocausts which is at the entrance of the meeting tent. 19 All of its fat he shall take from it and burn on the altar, 20 doing with this bullock just as he did with the other sin-offering bullock. Thus the priest shall make atonement for them, and they will be forgiven. 21 This bullock must also be brought outside the camp and burned, just as has been prescribed for the other one. This is the sin offering for the community.

For the Princes

22 "Should a prince commit a sin inadvertently by doing one of the things which are forbidden by some commandment of the LORD, his God, and thus become guilty, 23 if later on he learns of the sin he committed, he shall bring as his offering an unblemished male goat. 24 Having laid his hands on

its head, he shall slaughter the goat as a sin offering before the LORD, in the place where the holocausts are slaughtered. 25 The priest shall then take some of the blood of the sin offering on his finger and put it on the horns of the altar of holocausts. The rest of the blood he shall pour out at the base of this altar. 26* All of the fat he shall burn on the altar like the fat of the peace offering. Thus the priest shall make atonement for the prince's sin, and it will be forgiven.

For Private Persons

27* "If a private person commits a sin inadvertently by doing one of the things which are forbidden by the commandments of the LORD, and thus becomes guilty, 28 should he later on learn of the sin he committed, he shall bring an unblemished she-goat as the offering for his sin. 29* Having laid his hand on the head of the sin offering, he shall slaughter it at the place of the holocausts. 30 The priest shall then take some of its blood on his finger and put it on the horns of the altar of holocausts. The rest of the blood he shall pour out at the base of the altar. 31* All the fat shall be removed, just as the fat is removed from the peace offering, and the priest shall burn it on the altar for an odor pleasing to the LORD. Thus the priest shall make atonement for him, and he will be forgiven.

32 "If, however, for his sin offering he presents a lamb, he shall bring an unblemished female. 33 Having laid his hand on its head, he shall slaughter this sin offering in the place where the holocausts are slaughtered. 34 The priest shall then take some of the blood of the sin offering on his finger and put it on the horns of the altar of holocausts. The rest of the blood he shall pour out at the base of the altar. 35* All the fat shall be removed, just as the fat is removed from the peace-offering lamb, and the priest shall burn it on the altar with the other oblations of the LORD. Thus the priest shall make atonement for the man's sin, and it will be forgiven.

For Special Cases

5 1* "If any person refuses to give the information which, as a witness of something he has seen or learned, he has been adjured to give, and thus commits a sin and has guilt to bear; 2* or if someone, without being aware of it, touches any unclean thing, as the carcass of an unclean wild animal, or that of an unclean domestic animal, or that of an unclean swarming creature, and thus becomes unclean and guilty; 3 or if someone, without being

4, 11: Lv 8, 17; 9, 11; Ex 29,
    14; Nm 19, 5.
4, 13: Lv 5, 2–4; Nm 15, 24–26.

4, 15: Lv 1, 4.
4, 26: Lv 3, 3–5.
4, 27: Nm 15, 27.

4, 29: Lv 1, 4.
4, 31: Lv 1, 9; 3, 3–5.
4, 35: Lv 3, 9.

5, 1: Prv 29, 24.
5, 2: Lv 11, 24.31.39; 12;
    13; 15.

aware of it, touches some human uncleanness, whatever kind of uncleanness this may be, and then recognizes his guilt; 4* or if someone, without being aware of it, rashly utters an oath to do good or evil, such as men are accustomed to utter rashly, and then recognizes that he is guilty of such an oath; 5* then whoever is guilty in any of these cases shall confess the sin he has incurred, 6 and as his sin offering for the sin he has committed he shall bring to the LORD a female animal from the flock, a ewe lamb or a she-goat. The priest shall then make atonement for his sin.

7* "If, however, he cannot afford an animal of the flock, he shall bring to the LORD as the sin offering for his sin two turtledoves or two pigeons, one for a sin offering and the other for a holocaust. 8* He shall bring them to the priest, who shall offer the one for the sin offering first. Snapping its head loose at the neck, yet without breaking it off completely, 9* he shall sprinkle some of the blood of the sin offering against the side of the altar. The rest of the blood shall be squeezed out against the base of the altar. Such is the offering for sin. 10 The other bird shall be offered as a holocaust in the usual way. Thus the priest shall make atonement for the sin the man committed, and it will be forgiven.

11 "If he is unable to afford even two turtledoves or two pigeons, he shall present as a sin offering for his sin one tenth of an ephah of fine flour. He shall not put oil or frankincense on it, because it is a sin offering. 12 When he has brought it to the priest, the latter shall take a handful of this flour as a token offering, and this he shall burn as a sin offering on the altar with the other oblations of the LORD. 13* Thus the priest shall make atonement for the sin that the man committed in any of the above cases, and it will be forgiven. The rest of the flour, like the cereal offerings, shall belong to the priest."

Guilt Offerings

14 The LORD said to Moses, 15† "If someone commits a sin by inadvertently cheating in the LORD's sacred dues, he shall bring to the LORD as his guilt offering an unblemished ram from the flock, valued at two silver shekels according to the standard of the sanctuary shekel. 16* He shall also restore what he has sinfully withheld from the sanctuary, adding to it a fifth of its value. This is to be given to the priest, who shall then make atonement for

him with the guilt-offering ram, and he will be forgiven.

17*† "If someone, without being aware of it, commits such a sin by doing one of the things which are forbidden by some commandment of the LORD, that he incurs guilt for which he must answer, 18 he shall bring as a guilt offering to the priest an unblemished ram of the flock of the established value. The priest shall then make atonement for the fault which was unwittingly committed, and it will be forgiven. 19 Such is the offering for guilt; the penalty of the guilt must be paid to the LORD."

20 The LORD said to Moses, 21 "If someone commits a sin of dishonesty against the LORD by denying his neighbor a deposit or a pledge for a stolen article, or by otherwise retaining his neighbor's goods unjustly, 22 or if, having found a lost article, he denies the fact and swears falsely about it with any of the sinful oaths that men make in such cases, 23 he shall therefore, since he has incurred guilt by his sin, restore the thing that was stolen or unjustly retained by him or the deposit left with him or the lost article he found 24 or whatever else he swore falsely about; on the day of his guilt offering he shall make full restitution of the thing itself, and in addition, give the owner one fifth of its value. 25 As his guilt offering he shall bring to the LORD an unblemished ram of the flock of the established value. When he has presented this as his guilt offering to the priest, 26 the latter shall make atonement for him before the LORD, and he will be forgiven whatever guilt he may have incurred."

The Daily Holocaust

6 1 The LORD said to Moses, 2† "Give Aaron and his sons the following command: This is the ritual for holocausts. The holocaust is to remain on the hearth of the altar all night until the next morning, and the fire is to be kept burning on the altar. 3 The priest, clothed in his linen robe and wearing linen drawers on his body, shall take away the ashes to which the fire has reduced the holocaust on the altar, and lay them at the side of the altar. 4 Then, having taken off these garments and put on other garments, he shall carry the ashes to a clean place outside the camp. 5 The fire on the altar is to be kept burning; it must not go out. Every morning the priest shall put firewood on it. On this he shall lay out the holocaust and burn the fat of the peace

---

5, 15: *Cheating:* not offering the full amount in tithes, first fruits, etc. *Guilt offering:* its characteristic was a certain additional penalty imposed as reparation for the injustice involved in the fault which was atoned for by this sacrifice. However, in certain passages, e.g., Lv 14, 12f; Nm 6, 12; Ezr 10, 19, the term "guilt offering" is used for more important cases of "sin offerings" where no apparent injustice is involved.
5, 17: *Without being aware of it:* the case naturally presupposes that later on the offender learns of his mistake. Cf Lv 4, 13f.

6, 2: *Ritual:* literally, "law, instruction." Here, and in the following paragraphs, are given additional prescriptions for various kinds of sacrifices which were, in part, treated of in the preceding chapters.

5, 4: Jgs 11, 30f; 1 Sm 14, 24; Mk 6, 23; Acts 23, 12.	5, 8: Lv 1, 15.17.
	5, 9: Lv 1, 15.
	5, 13: Lv 4, 26.35.
5, 5: Lv 26, 40; Nm 5, 7.	5, 16: Lv 22, 14.
5, 7: Lv 12, 8; Lk 2, 24.	5, 17: Lv 4, 2.

offerings. 6 The fire is to be kept burning continuously on the altar; it must not go out.

Daily Cereal Offering

7 "This is the ritual of the cereal offering. One of Aaron's sons shall first present it before the LORD, in front of the altar. 8 Then he shall take from it a handful of its fine flour and oil, together with all the frankincense that is on it, and this he shall burn on the altar as its token offering, a sweet-smelling oblation to the LORD. 9 The rest of it Aaron and his sons may eat; but it must be eaten in the form of unleavened cakes and in a sacred place: in the court of the meeting tent they shall eat it. 10 It shall not be baked with leaven. I have given it to them as their portion from the oblations of the LORD; it is most sacred, like the sin offering and the guilt offering. 11 All the male descendants of Aaron may partake of it as their rightful share in the oblations of the LORD perpetually throughout your generations. Whatever touches the oblations becomes sacred."

12† The LORD said to Moses, 13 "This is the offering that Aaron and his sons shall present to the LORD [on the day he is anointed]: one tenth of an ephah of fine flour for the established cereal offering, half in the morning and half in the evening. 14 It shall be well kneaded and fried in oil on a griddle when you bring it in. Having broken the offering into pieces, you shall present it as a sweet-smelling oblation to the LORD. 15 Aaron's descendant who succeeds him as the anointed priest shall do likewise. This is a perpetual ordinance: for the Lord the whole offering shall be burned. 16 Every cereal offering of a priest shall be a whole burnt offering; it may not be eaten."

Sin Offerings

17 The LORD said to Moses, 18* "Tell Aaron and his sons: This is the ritual for sin offerings. At the place where holocausts are slaughtered, there also, before the LORD, shall the sin offering be slaughtered. It is most sacred. 19* The priest who presents the sin offering may partake of it; but it must be eaten in a sacred place, in the court of the meeting tent. 20 Whatever touches its flesh shall become sacred. If any of its blood is spilled on a garment, the stained part must be washed in a sacred place. 21* A clay vessel in which it has been cooked shall thereafter be broken; if it is cooked in a bronze vessel, this shall be scoured afterward and rinsed with water. 22* All the males of the priestly line may partake of the sin offering, since it is most sacred. 23* But no one may partake of any sin offering of which some blood has been brought into the meeting tent to make atonement in the sanctuary; such an offering must be burned up in the fire.

Guilt Offerings

7 1 "This is the ritual for guilt offerings, which are most sacred. 2* At the place where the holocausts are slaughtered, there also shall the guilt offering be slaughtered. Its blood shall be splashed on the sides of the altar. 3* All of its fat shall be taken from it and offered up: the fatty tail, the fatty membrane over the inner organs, 4 as well as the two kidneys with the fat on them near the loins, and the lobe of the liver, which must be severed above the kidneys. 5 All this the priest shall burn on the altar as an oblation to the LORD. This is the guilt offering. 6* All the males of the priestly line may partake of it; but it must be eaten in a sacred place, since it is most sacred.

7 "Because the sin offering and the guilt offering are alike, both having the same ritual, the guilt offering likewise belongs to the priest who makes atonement with it. 8 Similarly, the priest who offers a holocaust for someone may keep for himself the hide of the holocaust that he has offered. 9* Also, every cereal offering that is baked in an oven or deep-fried in a pot or fried on a griddle shall belong to the priest who offers it, 10* whereas all cereal offerings that are offered up dry or mixed with oil shall belong to all of Aaron's sons without distinction.

Peace Offerings

11 "This is the ritual for the peace offerings that are presented to the LORD. 12 When anyone makes a peace offering in thanksgiving, together with his thanksgiving sacrifice he shall offer unleavened cakes mixed with oil, unleavened wafers spread with oil, and cakes made of fine flour mixed with oil and well kneaded. 13† His offering shall also include loaves of leavened bread along with the victim of his peace offering for thanksgiving. 14 From each of his offerings he shall present one portion as a contribution to the LORD; this shall belong to the priest who splashes the blood of the peace offering.

6, 12–16: This is another law about the daily or "established" cereal offering. It differs in some respects from the preceding law (vv 7–11) and also from the law in Ex 29, 38–42. Hence, the words *on the day he is anointed* were probably added by some later scribe in order to avoid the difficulty of harmonizing this law with the other two laws on the same matter.

7, 13: *Leavened bread:* these loaves were not burned on the altar (cf Lv 2, 11), but were eaten at the "communion" meal which followed the sacrifice. See note on Lv 3, 1.

6, 18: Lv 7, 2.
6, 19: Lv 10, 17.
6, 21: Lv 11, 33; 15, 12.
6, 22: Lv 7, 6; Nm 18, 10.
6, 23: Lv 4, 5; Heb 13, 11.
7, 2: Lv 6, 18.
7, 3–5: Lv 3, 4.9f.14–16; 4, 8f.
7, 6: Lv 6, 22.
7, 9: Lv 2, 3–10; Nm 18, 9; Ez 44, 29.
7, 10: Lv 2, 14f.

15* "The flesh of the thanksgiving sacrifice shall be eaten on the day it is offered; none of it may be kept till the next day. 16 However, if the sacrifice is a votive or a free-will offering, it should indeed be eaten on the day the sacrifice is offered, but what is left over may be eaten on the next day. 17 Should any flesh from the sacrifice be left over on the third day, it must be burned up in the fire. 18 If, therefore, any of the flesh of the peace offering is eaten on the third day, it shall not win favor for him nor shall it be reckoned to his credit; rather, it shall be considered as refuse, and anyone who eats of it shall have his guilt to bear. 19 Should the flesh touch anything unclean, it may not be eaten, but shall be burned up in the fire.

"All who are clean may partake of this flesh. 20 If, however, someone while in a state of uncleanness eats any of the flesh of a peace offering belonging to the LORD, that person shall be cut off from his people. 21 Likewise, if someone touches anything unclean, whether the uncleanness be of human or of animal origin or from some loathsome crawling creature, and then eats of a peace offering belonging to the LORD, that person, too, shall be cut off from his people."

Prohibition against Blood and Fat

22 The LORD said to Moses, 23*† "Tell the Israelites: You shall not eat the fat of any ox or sheep or goat. 24* Although the fat of an animal that has died a natural death or has been killed by wild beasts may be put to any other use, you may not eat it. 25 If anyone eats the fat of an animal from which an oblation is made to the LORD, such a one shall be cut off from his people. 26 Wherever you dwell, you shall not partake of any blood, be it of bird or of animal. 27* Every person who partakes of any blood shall be cut off from his people."

The Portions for Priests

28 The LORD said to Moses, 29 "Tell the Israelites: He who presents a peace offering to the LORD shall bring a part of it as his special offering to him, 30† carrying in with his own hands the oblations to the LORD. The fat is to be brought in, together with the breast, which is to be waved as a wave offering before the LORD. 31* The priest shall burn the fat on the altar, but the breast belongs to Aaron and his

sons. 32 Moreover, from your peace offering you shall give to the priest the right leg as a raised offering. 33 The descendant of Aaron who offers up the blood and fat of the peace offering shall have the right leg as his portion, 34* for from the peace offerings of the Israelites I have taken the breast that is waved and the leg that is raised up, and I have given them to Aaron, the priest, and to his sons by a perpetual ordinance as a contribution from the Israelites."

35† This is the priestly share from the oblations of the LORD, allotted to Aaron and his sons on the day he called them to be the priests of the LORD; 36 on the day he anointed them the LORD ordered the Israelites to give them this share by a perpetual ordinance throughout their generations.

37 This is the ritual for holocausts, cereal offerings, sin offerings, guilt offerings, [ordination offerings] and peace offerings, 38 which the LORD enjoined on Moses at Mount Sinai at the time when he commanded the Israelites in the wilderness of Sinai to bring their offerings to the LORD.

II: Ceremony of Ordination

Ordination of Aaron and His Sons

8 1*† The LORD said to Moses, 2† "Take Aaron and his sons, together with the vestments, the anointing oil, the bullock for a sin offering, the two rams, and the basket of unleavened food. 3 Then assemble the whole community at the entrance of the meeting tent." 4 And Moses did as the LORD had commanded. When the community had assembled at the entrance of the meeting tent, 5 Moses told them what the LORD had ordered to be done. 6* Bringing forward Aaron and his sons, he first washed them with water. 7* Then he put the tunic on Aaron, girded him with the sash, clothed him with the robe, placed the ephod on him, and girded him with the embroidered belt of the ephod, fastening it around him. 8*† He then set the breastpiece on him, with the Urim and Thummim in it, 9* and put the miter on his head, attaching the gold plate, the sacred diadem, over the front of the miter, at his forehead, as the LORD had commanded him to do.

10* Taking the anointing oil, Moses anointed and consecrated the Dwelling, with all that was in it.

7, 23: *The fat:* only the particular portions specified in Lv 3, 9f. 14f are meant. *Ox or sheep or goat:* such animals as could be sacrificed; the fat of other clean animals could be eaten.

7, 30–34: *A wave offering . . . a raised offering:* these ceremonies are described in Ex 29, 24–28. The Hebrew word for "raised offering" is also rendered, in certain contexts, as "contribution."

7, 35: *The priestly share:* literally, "the anointed part."

8, 1–9.21: Though presented in the form of a narrative, this description of Aaron's ordination was intended to serve as a guide for all future ordinations.

8, 2: *The vestments,* etc.: already described in Ex 28–29.
8, 8: *The Urim and Thummim:* see note on Ex 28, 30.

7, 15–18: Lv 19, 6f.
7, 23: Lv 3, 17.
7, 24: Lv 22, 8.
7, 27: Lv 17, 10.
7, 31: Lv 3, 11.16.
7, 34: Ex 29, 27f.

8, 1–36: cf Ex 29.
8, 6f: Ex 40, 12f.
8, 7ff: Sir 45, 8–13.
8, 8: Ex 28, 30.
8, 9: Ex 28, 36.
8, 10: Ex 30, 26.

11 Then he sprinkled some of this oil seven times on the altar, and anointed the altar, with all its appurtenances, and the laver, with its base, thus consecrating them. 12* He also poured some of the anointing oil on Aaron's head, thus consecrating him. 13 Moses likewise brought forward Aaron's sons, clothed them with tunics, girded them with sashes, and put turbans on them, as the LORD had commanded him to do.

Ordination Sacrifices

14 When he had brought forward the bullock for a sin offering, Aaron and his sons laid their hands on its head. 15* Then Moses slaughtered it, and taking some of its blood, with his finger he put it on the horns around the altar, thus purifying the altar. He also made atonement for the altar by pouring out the blood at its base when he consecrated it. 16* Taking all the fat that was over the inner organs, as well as the lobe of the liver and the two kidneys with their fat, Moses burned them on the altar. 17 The bullock, however, with its hide and flesh and offal he burned in the fire outside the camp, as the LORD had commanded him to do.

18 He next brought forward the holocaust ram, and Aaron and his sons laid their hands on its head. 19 When he had slaughtered it, Moses splashed its blood on all sides of the altar. 20 After cutting up the ram into pieces, he burned the head, the cut-up pieces and the suet; 21 then, having washed the inner organs and the shanks with water, he also burned these remaining parts of the ram on the altar as a holocaust, a sweet-smelling oblation to the LORD, as the LORD had commanded him to do.

22 Then he brought forward the second ram, the ordination ram, and Aaron and his sons laid their hands on its head. 23* When he had slaughtered it, Moses took some of its blood and put it on the tip of Aaron's right ear, on the thumb of his right hand, and on the big toe of his right foot. 24 Moses had the sons of Aaron also come forward, and he put some of the blood on the tips of their right ears, on the thumbs of their right hands, and on the big toes of their right feet. The rest of the blood he splashed on the sides of the altar. 25 He then took the fat: the fatty tail and all the fat over the inner organs, the lobe of the liver and the two kidneys with their fat, and likewise the right leg; 26 from the basket of unleavened food that was set before the LORD he took one unleavened cake, one loaf of bread made with oil, and one wafer; these he placed on top of the portions of fat and the right leg. 27 He then put all these things into the hands of Aaron and his sons, whom he had wave them as a wave offering before the LORD. 28 When he had received them back, Moses burned them with the holocaust on the altar as the ordination offering, a sweet-smelling oblation to the LORD. 29 He then took the breast and waved it as a wave offering before the LORD; this was Moses' own portion of the ordination ram. All this was in keeping with the LORD's command to Moses. 30 Taking some of the anointing oil and some of the blood that was on the altar, Moses sprinkled with it Aaron and his vestments, as well as his sons and their vestments, thus consecrating both Aaron and his vestments and his sons and their vestments.

31 Finally, Moses said to Aaron and his sons, "Boil the flesh at the entrance of the meeting tent, and there eat it with the bread that is in the basket of the ordination offering, in keeping with the command I have received: 'Aaron and his sons shall eat of it.' 32 What is left over of the flesh and the bread you shall burn up in the fire. 33 Moreover, you are not to depart from the entrance of the meeting tent for seven days, until the days of your ordination are completed; for your ordination is to last for seven days. 34† The LORD has commanded that what has been done today be done to make atonement for you. 35 Hence you must remain at the entrance of the meeting tent day and night for seven days, carrying out the prescriptions of the LORD; otherwise you shall die; for this is the command I have received." 36 So Aaron and his sons did all that the LORD had commanded through Moses.

Octave of the Ordination

9 1 On the eighth day Moses summoned Aaron and his sons, together with the elders of Israel, 2 and said to Aaron, "Take a calf for a sin offering and a ram for a holocaust, both without blemish, and offer them before the LORD. 3 Tell the elders of Israel, too: Take a he-goat for a sin offering, a calf and a lamb, both unblemished yearlings, for a holocaust, 4 and an ox and a ram for a peace offering, to sacrifice them before the LORD, along with a cereal offering mixed with oil; for today the LORD will reveal himself to you." 5 So they brought what Moses had ordered. When the whole community had come forward and stood before the LORD, 6 Moses said, "This is what the LORD orders you to do, that the glory of the LORD may be revealed to

---

8, 34: The sense is not quite clear. Either the verse gives merely the reason why God ordered this ceremony, or it contains God's command that the same ceremony be used in all future ordinations, or it decrees a repetition of the entire ceremony on each of the seven days. At least a sin offering for atonement was made on each of these days. Cf Ex 29, 29–36.

8, 12: Sir 45, 15.
8, 15: Lv 4, 7; Heb 9, 22.
8, 16f: Lv 3, 4; 4, 8–11.
8, 23: Lv 14, 14.

you. [7] Come up to the altar," Moses then told Aaron, "and offer your sin offering and your holocaust in atonement for yourself and for your family; then present the offering of the people in atonement for them, as the LORD has commanded."

[8] Going up to the altar, Aaron first slaughtered the calf that was his own sin offering. [9] When his sons presented the blood to him, he dipped his finger in the blood and put it on the horns of the altar. The rest of the blood he poured out at the base of the altar. [10] He then burned on the altar the fat, the kidneys and the lobe of the liver that were taken from the sin offering, as the LORD had commanded Moses; [11] but the flesh and the hide he burned up in the fire outside the camp. [12] Then Aaron slaughtered his holocaust. When his sons brought him the blood, he splashed it on all sides of the altar. [13] They then brought him the pieces and the head of the holocaust, and he burned them on the altar. [14] Having washed the inner organs and the shanks, he burned these also with the holocaust on the altar.

[15] Thereupon he had the people's offering brought up. Taking the goat that was for the people's sin offering, he slaughtered it and offered it up for sin as before. [16] Then he brought forward the holocaust, other than the morning holocaust, and offered it in the usual manner. [17] He then presented the cereal offering; taking a handful of it, he burned it on the altar. [18] Finally he slaughtered the ox and the ram, the peace offering of the people. When his sons brought him the blood, Aaron splashed it on all sides of the altar. [19]* The portions of fat from the ox and from the ram, the fatty tail, the fatty membrane over the inner organs, the two kidneys, with the fat that is on them, and the lobe of the liver, [20] he placed on top of the breasts and burned them on the altar, [21]* having first waved the breasts and the right legs as a wave offering before the LORD, in keeping with the LORD's command to Moses.

Revelation of the Lord's Glory

[22] Aaron then raised his hands over the people and blessed them. When he came down from offering the sin offering and holocaust and peace offering, [23]* Moses and Aaron went into the meeting tent. On coming out they again blessed the people. Then the glory of the LORD was revealed to all the people. [24]* Fire came forth from the LORD's presence and consumed the holocaust and the remnants of the fat on the altar. Seeing this, all the people cried out and fell prostrate.

Nadab and Abihu

10 [1]*† During this time Aaron's sons Nadab and Abihu took their censers and, strewing incense on the fire they had put in them, they offered up before the LORD profane fire, such as he had not authorized. [2]*† Fire therefore came forth from the LORD's presence and consumed them, so that they died in his presence. [3]*† Moses then said to Aaron, "This is as the LORD said:

> Through those who approach me I will
>   manifest my sacredness;
> In the sight of all the people I will reveal
>   my glory."

But Aaron said nothing. [4] Then Moses summoned Mishael and Elzaphan, the sons of Aaron's uncle Uzziel, with the order, "Come, remove your kinsmen from the sanctuary and carry them to a place outside the camp." [5]† So they went in and took them, in their tunics, outside the camp, as Moses had commanded.

Conduct of the Priests

[6]*† Moses said to Aaron and his sons Eleazar and Ithamar, "Do not bare your heads or tear your garments, lest you bring not only death on yourselves but God's wrath also on the whole community. Your kinsmen, the rest of the house of Israel, shall mourn for those whom the LORD's fire has smitten; [7] but do not you go beyond the entry of the meeting tent, else you shall die; for the anointing oil of the LORD is upon you." So they did as Moses told them.

[8] The LORD said to Aaron, [9]* "When you are to go to the meeting tent, you and your sons are forbidden under pain of death, by a perpetual ordinance throughout your generations, to drink any wine or strong drink. [10]* You must be able to distinguish between what is sacred and what is profane, between what is clean and what is unclean; [11]* you must teach the Israelites all the laws that the LORD has given them through Moses."

10, 1: *Nadab and Abihu:* the older sons of Aaron. Cf Ex 6, 23f.

10, 2: *Fire:* perhaps after the manner of lightning.

10, 3: *I will manifest my sacredness:* the presence of God is so sacred that it strikes dead those who approach him without the proper holiness. Cf Nm 20, 13; Ez 28, 22.

10, 5: *In their tunics:* they were buried just as they were, with no shroud or funeral solemnities.

10, 6: *Bare your heads:* go without the customary head covering, as a sign of mourning. Some interpreters, however, understand it as the cutting off of one's hair, which ordinarily all the Israelites, men as well as women, let grow long. Cf Is 15, 2; Jer 7, 29. Still others understand the verb to mean "to let one's hair hang loose and wild." Cf Lv 13, 45; 21, 10, where the same phrase is used.

9, 19f: Lv 3, 3ff.
9, 21: Lv 7, 31f.
9, 23: Nm 6, 23–26.
9, 24: 1 Kgs 18, 38; 2 Chr 7, 1.
10, 1: Lv 16, 1; Nm 3, 4; 26, 61; 1 Chr 24, 2.
10, 2: Nm 16, 35.
10, 3: Lv 21, 17.21.
10, 6: Lv 21, 10.
10, 9: Ez 44, 21.
10, 10: Lv 11, 47; 20, 25; Ez 22, 26; 44, 23.
10, 11: Sir 45, 16.

L
V

The Eating of the Priestly Portions

12* Moses said to Aaron and his surviving sons, Eleazar and Ithamar, "Take the cereal offering left over from the oblations of the LORD, and eat it beside the altar in the form of unleavened cakes. Since it is most sacred, 13 you must eat it in a sacred place. This is your due from the oblations of the LORD, and that of your sons; such is the command I have received. 14* With your sons and daughters you shall also eat the breast of the wave offering and the leg of the raised offering, in a clean place; for these have been assigned to you and your children as your due from the peace offerings of the Israelites. 15 The leg of the raised offering and the breast of the wave offering shall first be brought in with the oblations, the fatty portions, that are to be waved as a wave offering before the LORD. Then they shall belong to you and your children by a perpetual ordinance, as the LORD has commanded."

16† When Moses inquired about the goat of the sin offering, he discovered that it had all been burned. So he was angry with the surviving sons of Aaron, Eleazar and Ithamar, and said, 17* "Why did you not eat the sin offering in the sacred place, since it is most sacred? It has been given to you that you might bear the guilt of the community and make atonement for them before the LORD. 18 If its blood was not brought into the inmost part of the sanctuary, you should certainly have eaten the offering in the sanctuary, in keeping with the command I had received." 19 Aaron answered Moses, "Even though they presented their sin offering and holocaust before the LORD today, yet this misfortune has befallen me. Had I then eaten of the sin offering today, would it have been pleasing to the LORD?" 20 On hearing this, Moses was satisfied.

III: Laws Regarding Legal Purity

Clean and Unclean Food

11 1† The LORD said to Moses and Aaron, 2 "Speak to the Israelites and tell them: Of all land animals these are the ones you may eat: 3 any animal that has hoofs you may eat, provided it is cloven-footed and chews the cud. 4 But you shall not eat any of the following that only chew the cud or only have hoofs: the camel, which indeed chews the cud, but does not have hoofs and is

?did you KNOW?

The Israelite Diet

The diet of the ancient Israelites consisted mainly of breads, cereals, fruits, vegetables, and dairy products. Meat was served only on special occasions because it was expensive. A typical family meal was made up of barley or wheat bread, grapes, figs, olive oil, beans, cucumbers, onions, and cheese. On festive occasions, beef or lamb might grace the table as well.

The laws in Leviticus, chapter 11, contain many restrictions regarding the eating of animals. The reasons for these restrictions are not clear, although many scholars believe that one purpose was to keep the Israelites from consuming animals used in pagan worship (for example, the pig offered in Babylonian services). Hygiene was likely another consideration.

The basic "meat laws" were as follows:

- **Of the larger animals, those that chewed their cud and had split hooves could be eaten. Therefore, lamb was acceptable, but pork was not.**
- **Sea creatures only with both fins and scales could be eaten. Thus, catfish and eels were to be avoided.**
- **Eagles, vultures, buzzards, and many other birds were excluded from the table.**
- **Rodents, reptiles, and insects (except locusts and grasshoppers) were spurned altogether.**

The blood from all animals had to be drained completely before cooking because blood was seen as the life force and therefore as belonging to God alone. In addition, it was unlawful to touch or eat any animal found dead; contact with any dead body made one impure.

▸ **Lv 11, 1–47**

10, 16–19: *Eleazar and Ithamar* burned the entire goat of the sin offering (Lv 9, 15) instead of eating it in a sacred place (Lv 6, 19) to bear the guilt of the community. Aaron defends this action of his sons against Moses' displeasure by implying that they did not have sufficient sanctity to eat the flesh of the victim and thus perform the expiation of the people. They themselves still labored under the blow of the divine anger which struck their brothers Nadab and Abihu.

11, 1ff: These distinctions between edible and inedible meats

were probably based on traditional ideas of hygiene, but they are here given a moral, religious basis: the inedible varieties are classified as "unclean" to remind the Israelites that they are to be a pure and holy people, dedicated to the Lord.

10, 12: Lv 6, 16.   10, 17: Lv 6, 18f.
10, 14f: Lv 7, 34.

therefore unclean for you; [5]† the rock badger, which indeed chews the cud, but does not have hoofs and is therefore unclean for you; [6] the hare, which indeed chews the cud, but does not have hoofs and is therefore unclean for you; and the pig, [7] which does indeed have hoofs and is cloven-footed, but does not chew the cud and is therefore unclean for you. [8] Their flesh you shall not eat, and their dead bodies you shall not touch; they are unclean for you.

[9] "Of the various creatures that live in the water, you may eat the following: whatever in the seas or in river waters has both fins and scales you may eat. [10] But of the various creatures that crawl or swim in the water, whether in the sea or in the rivers, all those that lack either fins or scales are loathsome for you, [11] and you shall treat them as loathsome. Their flesh you shall not eat, and their dead bodies you shall loathe. [12] Every water creature that lacks fins or scales is loathsome for you.

[13]† "Of the birds, these you shall loathe and, as loathsome, they shall not be eaten: the eagle, the vulture, the osprey, [14] the kite, the various species of falcons, [15] the various species of crows, [16] the ostrich, the nightjar, the gull, the various species of hawks, [17] the owl, the cormorant, the screech owl, [18] the barn owl, the desert owl, the buzzard, [19]† the stork, the various species of herons, the hoopoe, and the bat.

[20] "The various winged insects that walk on all fours are loathsome for you. [21] But of the various winged insects that walk on all fours you may eat those that have jointed legs for leaping on the ground; [22]† hence of these you may eat the following: the various kinds of locusts, the various kinds of grasshoppers, the various kinds of katydids, and the various kinds of crickets. [23] All other winged insects that have four legs are loathsome for you.

[24]† "Such is the uncleanness that you contract, that everyone who touches their dead bodies shall be unclean until evening, [25] and everyone who picks up any part of their dead bodies shall wash his garments and be unclean until evening. [26]† All hoofed animals that are not cloven-footed or do not chew the cud are unclean for you; everyone who touches them becomes unclean. [27]† Of the various quadrupeds, all those that walk on paws are unclean for you; everyone who touches their dead bodies shall be unclean until evening, [28] and everyone who picks up their dead bodies shall wash his garments and be unclean until evening. Such is their uncleanness for you.

[29] "Of the creatures that swarm on the ground, the following are unclean for you: the rat, the mouse, the various kinds of lizards, [30] the gecko, the chameleon, the agama, the skink, and the mole. [31] Among the various swarming creatures, these are unclean for you. Everyone who touches them when they are dead shall be unclean until evening. [32] Everything on which one of them falls when dead becomes unclean. Any such article that men use, whether it be an article of wood, cloth, leather or goat hair, must be put in water and remain unclean until evening, when it again becomes clean. [33] Should any of these creatures fall into a clay vessel, everything in it becomes unclean, and the vessel itself you must break. [34] Any solid food that was in contact with water, and any liquid that men drink, in any such vessel become unclean. [35] Any object on which one of their dead bodies falls, becomes unclean; if it is an oven or a jar-stand, this must be broken to pieces; they are unclean and shall be treated as unclean by you. [36]† However, a spring or a cistern for collecting water remains clean; but whoever touches the dead body becomes unclean. [37] Any sort of cultivated grain remains clean even though one of their dead bodies falls on it; [38] but if the grain has become moistened, it becomes unclean when one of these falls on it.

[39] "When one of the animals that you could otherwise eat, dies of itself, anyone who touches its dead body shall be unclean until evening; [40]* and anyone who eats of its dead body shall wash his garments and be unclean until evening; so also, anyone who removes its dead body shall wash his garments and be unclean until evening.

[41] "All the creatures that swarm on the ground are loathsome and shall not be eaten. [42] Whether it crawls on its belly, goes on all fours, or has many legs, you shall eat no swarming creature: they are loathsome. [43]* Do not make yourselves loathsome or unclean with any swarming creature through be-

---

† **11, 5f:** According to modern zoology, *the rock badger* (hyrax Syriacus) is classified as an ungulate, and *the hare* as a rodent; neither is a ruminant. They appear to chew their food as the true ruminants do, and it is upon this appearance that the classification in the text is based.

11, 13–19.30: The identification of the various Hebrew names for these birds and reptiles is in many cases uncertain.

11, 19: *The bat:* actually a mammal, but listed here with the birds because of its wings.

11, 22: The Hebrew distinguishes four classes of edible locust-like insects, but the difference between them is quite uncertain. Cf Mt 3, 4.

11, 24–28: This paragraph sharpens the prohibition against unclean animals: not only is their meat unfit for food, but contact with their dead bodies makes a person ritually unclean.

11, 26: *All hoofed animals that are not cloven-footed:* such as the horse and the ass.

11, 27: *All those that walk on paws:* such as dogs and cats.

11, 36: *Whoever touches the dead body:* to remove the dead insect from the water supply.

11, 40: Lv 17, 15; 22, 8.   11, 43f: Lv 20, 25f.

ing contaminated by them. ⁴⁴* For I, the LORD, am your God; and you shall make and keep yourselves holy, because I am holy. You shall not make yourselves unclean, then, by any swarming creature that crawls on the ground. ⁴⁵ Since I, the LORD, brought you up from the land of Egypt that I might be your God, you shall be holy, because I am holy.

⁴⁶ "This is the law for animals and birds and for all the creatures that move about in the water or swarm on the ground, ⁴⁷* that you may distinguish between the clean and the unclean, between creatures that may be eaten and those that may not be eaten."

Uncleanness of Childbirth

12 ¹ The LORD said to Moses, ²*† "Tell the Israelites: When a woman has conceived and gives birth to a boy, she shall be unclean for seven days, with the same uncleanness as at her menstrual period. ³* On the eighth day, the flesh of the boy's foreskin shall be circumcised, ⁴ and then she shall spend thirty-three days more in becoming purified of her blood; she shall not touch anything sacred nor enter the sanctuary till the days of her purification are fulfilled. ⁵ If she gives birth to a girl, for fourteen days she shall be as unclean as at her

NATIVE AMERICAN

A Mother's Prayer at Childbirth

Sun, moon, stars,
you that move in the heavens,
hear this mother!
A new life has come among you.
Make its path smooth that it may reach
the brow of the first hill.

Winds, clouds, rain, mist,
all that move in the air,
hear this mother!
A new life has come among you.
Make its path smooth that it may reach
the brow of the second hill.

Hills, valleys, rivers, lakes, trees, grasses,
all of the earth,
hear this mother!
A new life has come among you.
Make its path smooth that it may reach
the brow of the third hill.

Birds that fly in the air,
animals that dwell in the forest,
insects that creep in the grasses and burrow
　　in the ground,
hear this mother!
A new life has come among you.
Make its path smooth that it may reach
the brow of the fourth hill.

All the heavens, air and earth,
hear this mother!
A new life has come among you.
Make its path smooth—then shall it travel
　　beyond the four hills!

*(From Suzanne Slesin and
Emily Gwathmey, compilers, Amen, n.p.)*

Like the Israelites, with their purification ritual described in Leviticus, chapter 12, most cultures have rituals and prayers associated with childbirth. In this mother's prayer of the Omaha tribe, the four hills refer to the four parts of human life—childhood, youth, adulthood, and old age. What a wonderful reminder that life is a journey and that all creation is invited to celebrate new life.

▶ Lv 12, 1–8

12, 2f: The uncleanness of the woman was more serious during the first period, the seven days after the birth of a boy or the fourteen days after the birth of a girl; only during this period would the rules given in Lv 15, 19–24 apply.

11, 44: Lv 19, 2; 20, 7.26;
　　Mt 5, 48; 1 Pt 1, 16.
11, 47: Lv 10, 10.

12, 2: Lv 15, 19.
12, 3: Gn 17, 12; Jn 7, 22.

menstruation, after which she shall spend sixty-six days in becoming purified of her blood.

6*"When the days of her purification for a son or for a daughter are fulfilled, she shall bring to the priest at the entrance of the meeting tent a yearling lamb for a holocaust and a pigeon or a turtledove for a sin offering. 7 The priest shall offer them up before the LORD to make atonement for her, and thus she will be clean again after her flow of blood. Such is the law for the woman who gives birth to a boy or a girl child. 8*† If, however, she cannot afford a lamb, she may take two turtledoves or two pigeons, the one for a holocaust and the other for a sin offering. The priest shall make atonement for her, and thus she will again be clean."

Leprosy

13 1 The LORD said to Moses and Aaron, 2*† "If someone has on his skin a scab or pustule or blotch which appears to be the sore of leprosy, he shall be brought to Aaron, the priest, or to one of the priests among his descendants, 3 who shall examine the sore on his skin. If the hair on the sore has turned white and the sore itself shows that it has penetrated below the skin, it is indeed the sore of leprosy; the priest, on seeing this, shall declare the man unclean. 4 If, however, the blotch on the skin is white, but does not seem to have penetrated below the skin, nor has the hair turned white, the priest shall quarantine the stricken man for seven days. 5 On the seventh day the priest shall again examine him. If he judges that the sore has remained unchanged and has not spread on the skin, the priest shall quarantine him for another seven days, 6 and once more examine him on the seventh day. If the sore is now dying out and has not spread on the skin, the priest shall declare the man clean; it was merely eczema. The man shall wash his garments and so become clean. 7 But if, after he has shown himself to the priest to be declared clean, the eczema spreads at all on his skin, he shall once more show himself to the priest. 8 Should the priest, on examining it, find that the eczema has indeed spread on the skin, he shall declare the man unclean; it is leprosy.

9 "When someone is stricken with leprosy, he shall be brought to the priest. 10 Should the priest, on examining him, find that there is a white scab on the skin which has turned the hair white and that there is raw flesh in it, 11 it is skin leprosy that

has long developed. The priest shall declare the man unclean without first quarantining him, since he is certainly unclean. 12† If leprosy breaks out on the skin and, as far as the priest can see, covers all the skin of the stricken man from head to foot, 13 should the priest then, on examining him, find that the leprosy does cover his whole body, he shall declare the stricken man clean; since it has all turned white, the man is clean. 14 But as soon as raw flesh appears on him, he is unclean; 15 on observing the raw flesh, the priest shall declare him unclean, because raw flesh is unclean; it is leprosy. 16 If, however, the raw flesh again turns white, he shall return to the priest; 17 should the latter, on examining him, find that the sore has indeed turned white, he shall declare the stricken man clean, and thus he will be clean.

18 "If a man who had a boil on his skin which later healed, 19 should now in the place of the boil have a white scab or a pink blotch, he shall show himself to the priest. 20 If the latter, on examination, sees that it is deeper than the skin and that the hair has turned white, he shall declare the man unclean: it is the sore of leprosy that has broken out in the boil. 21 But if the priest, on examining him, finds that there is no white hair in it and that it is not deeper than the skin and is already dying out, the priest shall quarantine him for seven days. 22 If it has then spread on the skin, the priest shall declare him unclean; the man is stricken. 23 But if the blotch remains in its place without spreading, it is merely the scar of the boil; the priest shall therefore declare him clean.

24 "If a man had a burn on his skin, and the proud flesh of the burn now becomes a pink or a white blotch, 25 the priest shall examine it. If the hair has turned white on the blotch and this seems to have penetrated below the skin, it is leprosy that has broken out in the burn; the priest shall therefore declare him unclean and stricken with leprosy. 26 But if the priest, on examining it, finds that there is no white hair on the blotch and that this is not deeper than the skin and is already dying out, the priest shall quarantine him for seven days. 27 Should the priest, when examining it on the seventh day, find that it has spread at all on the skin, he shall declare the man unclean and stricken with leprosy. 28 But if the blotch remains in its place without spreading on the skin and is already dying out, it is merely the scab of the burn; the priest shall

---

12, 8: Forty days after the birth of Jesus, his Virgin Mother made this offering of the poor (Lk 2, 22.24); since the holocaust was offered in thanksgiving for the birth of the child, this was most fittingly offered by Mary. However, because of her miraculous delivery, she was not really obliged to make the sin offering of purification.
13, 2ff: Various kinds of skin blemishes are treated here which were not contagious but simply disqualified their subjects from association with others, especially in public worship, until they were

declared ritually clean. The Hebrew term used does not refer to Hansen's disease, currently called leprosy.
13, 12ff: *If leprosy breaks out on the skin:* the symptoms described here point to a form of skin disease which is merely on the surface and therefore easily cured.

12, 6: Lk 2, 22.   13, 2: Dt 24, 8.
12, 8: Lv 1, 14; Lk 2, 24.

therefore declare the man clean, since it is only the scar of the burn.

29 "When a man or a woman has a sore on the head or cheek, 30† should the priest, on examining it, find that the sore has penetrated below the skin and that there is fine yellow hair on it, the priest shall declare the person unclean, for this is scall, a leprous disease of the head or cheek. 31 But if the priest, on examining the scall sore, finds that it has not penetrated below the skin, though the hair on it may not be black, the priest shall quarantine the person with scall sore for seven days, 32 and on the seventh day again examine the sore. If the scall has not spread and has no yellow hair on it and does not seem to have penetrated below the skin, 33 the man shall shave himself, but not on the diseased spot. Then the priest shall quarantine him for another seven days. 34 If the priest, when examining the scall on the seventh day, finds that it has not spread on the skin and that it has not penetrated below the skin, he shall declare the man clean; the latter shall wash his garments, and thus he will be clean. 35 But if the scall spreads at all on his skin after he has been declared clean, 36 the priest shall again examine it. If the scall has indeed spread on the skin, he need not look for yellow hair; the man is surely unclean. 37 If, however, he judges that the scall has remained in its place and that black hair has grown on it, the disease has been healed; the man is clean, and the priest shall declare him clean.

38 "When the skin of a man or a woman is spotted with white blotches, 39† the priest shall make an examination. If the blotches on the skin are white and already dying out, it is only tetter that has broken out on the skin, and the person therefore is clean.

40 "When a man loses the hair of his head, he is not unclean merely because of his bald crown. 41 So too, if he loses the hair on the front of his head, he is not unclean merely because of his bald forehead. 42 But when there is a pink sore on his bald crown or bald forehead, it is leprosy that is breaking out there. 43 The priest shall examine him; and if the scab on the sore of the bald spot has the same pink appearance as that of skin leprosy of the fleshy part of the body, 44 the man is leprous and unclean, and the priest shall declare him unclean by reason of the sore on his head.

45 "The one who bears the sore of leprosy shall keep his garments rent and his head bare, and shall muffle his beard; he shall cry out, 'Unclean, unclean!' 46* As long as the sore is on him he shall declare himself unclean, since he is in fact unclean.

He shall dwell apart, making his abode outside the camp.

Leprosy of Clothes

47† "When a leprous infection is on a garment of wool or of linen, 48 or on woven or knitted material of linen or wool, or on a hide or anything made of leather, 49 if the infection on the garment or hide, or on the woven or knitted material, or on any leather article is greenish or reddish, the thing is indeed infected with leprosy and must be shown to the priest. 50 Having examined the infection, the priest shall quarantine the infected article for seven days.

51 "On the seventh day the priest shall again examine the infection. If it has spread on the garment, or on the woven or knitted material, or on the leather, whatever be its use, the infection is malignant leprosy, and the article is unclean. 52 He shall therefore burn up the garment, or the woven or knitted material of wool or linen, or the leather article, whatever it may be, which is infected; since it has malignant leprosy, it must be destroyed by fire. 53 But if the priest, on examining the infection, finds that it has not spread on the garment, or on the woven or knitted material, or on the leather article, 54 he shall give orders to have the infected article washed and then quarantined for another seven days.

55 "Then the priest shall again examine the infected article after it has been washed. If the infection has not changed its appearance, even though it may not have spread, the article is unclean and shall be destroyed by fire. 56 But if the priest, on examining the infection, finds that it is dying out after the washing, he shall tear the infected part out of the garment, or the leather, or the woven or knitted material. 57 If, however, the infection again appears on the garment, or on the woven or knitted material, or on the leather article, it is still virulent and the thing infected shall be destroyed by fire. 58 But if, after the washing, the infection has left the garment, or the woven or knitted material, or the leather article, the thing shall be washed a second time, and thus it will be clean. 59* This is the law for leprous infection on a garment of wool or linen, or on woven or knitted material, or on any leather article, to determine whether it is clean or unclean."

Purification after Leprosy

14 1 The LORD said to Moses, 2* "This is the law for the victim of leprosy at the time of his purification. He shall be brought to the

---

13, 30: *Scall:* a scabby or scaly eruption of the scalp. According to some, "ringworm."

13, 39: *Tetter:* vitiligo, a harmless form of skin disease.

13, 47: *A leprous infection:* some mold or fungus growth resembling human leprosy.

13, 46: Nm 5, 2; 12, 14f;   **14, 2:** Mt 8, 4; Mk 1, 44;
        2 Kgs 15, 5; Lk 17, 12.   Lk 5, 14.
13, 59: Lv 14, 54.

priest, [3] who is to go outside the camp to examine him. If the priest finds that the sore of leprosy has healed in the leper, [4]† he shall order the man who is to be purified, to get two live, clean birds, as well as some cedar wood, scarlet yarn, and hyssop. [5]† The priest shall then order him to slay one of the birds over an earthen vessel with spring water in it. [6] Taking the living bird with the cedar wood, the scarlet yarn and the hyssop, the priest shall dip them all in the blood of the bird that was slain over the spring water, [7] and then sprinkle seven times the man to be purified from his leprosy. When he has thus purified him, he shall let the living bird fly away over the countryside. [8] The man being purified shall then wash his garments and shave off all his hair and bathe in water; only when he is thus made clean may he come inside the camp; but he shall still remain outside his tent for seven days. [9] On the seventh day he shall again shave off all the hair of his head, his beard, his eyebrows, and any other hair he may have, and also wash his garments and bathe his body in water; and so he will be clean.

Purification Sacrifices

[10] "On the eighth day he shall take two unblemished male lambs, one unblemished yearling ewe lamb, three tenths of an ephah of fine flour mixed with oil for a cereal offering, and one log of oil. [11] The priest who performs the purification ceremony shall place the man who is being purified, as well as all these offerings, before the LORD at the entrance of the meeting tent. [12] Taking one of the male lambs, the priest shall present it as a guilt offering, along with the log of oil, waving them as a wave offering before the LORD. [13] (This lamb he shall slaughter in the sacred place where the sin offering and the holocaust are slaughtered; because, like the sin offering, the guilt offering belongs to the priest and is most sacred.) [14]* Then the priest shall take some of the blood of the guilt offering and put it on the tip of the man's right ear, the thumb of his right hand, and the big toe of his right foot. [15] The priest shall also take the log of oil and pour some of it into the palm of his own left hand; [16] then, dipping his right forefinger in it, he shall sprinkle it seven times before the LORD. [17] Of the oil left in his hand the priest shall put some on the tip of the man's right ear, the thumb of his right hand, and the big toe of his right foot, over the blood of the guilt offering. [18] The rest of the oil in his hand the priest shall put on the head of the man being

purified. Thus shall the priest make atonement for him before the LORD. [19] Only after he has offered the sin offering in atonement for the man's uncleanness shall the priest slaughter the holocaust [20] and offer it, together with the cereal offering, on the altar before the LORD. When the priest has thus made atonement for him, the man will be clean.

Poor Leper's Sacrifice

[21] "If a man is poor and cannot afford so much, he shall take one male lamb for a guilt offering, to be used as a wave offering in atonement for himself, one tenth of an ephah of fine flour mixed with oil for a cereal offering, a log of oil, [22]† and two turtledoves or pigeons, which he can more easily afford, the one as a sin offering and the other as a holocaust. [23] On the eighth day of his purification he shall bring them to the priest, at the entrance of the meeting tent before the LORD. [24] Taking the guilt-offering lamb, along with the log of oil, the priest shall wave them as a wave offering before the LORD. [25] When he has slaughtered the guilt-offering lamb, he shall take some of its blood, and put it on the tip of the right ear of the man being purified, on the thumb of his right hand, and on the big toe of his right foot. [26] The priest shall then pour some of the oil into the palm of his own left hand [27] and with his right forefinger sprinkle it seven times before the LORD. [28] Some of the oil in his hand the priest shall also put on the tip of the man's right ear, the thumb of his right hand, and the big toe of his right foot, over the blood of the guilt offering. [29] The rest of the oil in his hand the priest shall put on the man's head. Thus shall he make atonement for him before the LORD. [30] Then, of the turtledoves or pigeons, such as the man can afford, [31] the priest shall offer up one as a sin offering and the other as a holocaust, along with the cereal offering. Thus shall the priest make atonement before the LORD for the man who is to be purified. [32] This is the law for one afflicted with leprosy who has insufficient means for his purification."

Leprosy of Houses

[33] The LORD said to Moses and Aaron, [34] "When you come into the land of Canaan, which I am giving you to possess, if I put a leprous infection on any house of the land you occupy, [35] the owner of the house shall come and report to the priest, 'It looks to me as if my house were infected.' [36] The priest shall then order the house to be cleared out before he goes in to examine the infection, lest

---

14, 4: *Scarlet yarn:* probably used for tying the hyssop sprig to the cedar branchlet.
14, 5: *Spring water:* literally, "living water," taken from some source of running water, not from a cistern.

14, 22: *Two turtledoves:* substitutes for the two additional lambs, similar to the offering of a poor woman after childbirth. Cf Lv 12, 8.

14, 14: Lv 8, 23f.

everything in the house become unclean. Only after this is he to go in to examine the house. [37] If the priest, on examining it, finds that the infection on the walls of the house consists of greenish or reddish depressions which seem to go deeper than the surface of the wall, [38] he shall close the door of the house behind him and quarantine the house for seven days. [39] On the seventh day the priest shall return to examine the house again. If he finds that the infection has spread on the walls, [40] he shall order the infected stones to be pulled out and cast in an unclean place outside the city. [41] The whole inside of the house shall then be scraped, and the mortar that has been scraped off shall be dumped in an unclean place outside the city. [42] Then new stones shall be brought and put in the place of the old stones, and new mortar shall be made and plastered on the house.

[43] "If the infection breaks out once more after the stones have been pulled out and the house has been scraped and replastered, [44] the priest shall come again; and if he finds that the infection has spread in the house, it is corrosive leprosy, and the house is unclean. [45] It shall be pulled down, and all its stones, beams and mortar shall be hauled away to an unclean place outside the city. [46] Whoever enters a house while it is quarantined shall be unclean until evening. [47] Whoever sleeps or eats in such a house shall also wash his garments. [48] If the priest finds, when he comes to examine the house, that the infection has in fact not spread after the plastering, he shall declare the house clean, since the infection has been healed. [49] To purify the house, he shall take two birds, as well as cedar wood, scarlet yarn, and hyssop. [50] One of the birds he shall slay over an earthen vessel with spring water in it. [51] Then, taking the cedar wood, the hyssop and the scarlet yarn, together with the living bird, he shall dip them all in the blood of the slain bird and the spring water, and sprinkle the house seven times. [52] Thus shall he purify the house with the bird's blood and the spring water, along with the living bird, the cedar wood, the hyssop, and the scarlet yarn. [53] He shall then let the living bird fly away over the countryside outside the city. When he has thus made atonement for it, the house will be clean.

[54] "This is the law for every kind of human leprosy and scall, [55]* for leprosy of garments and houses, [56] as well as for scabs, pustules and blotches, [57] so that it may be manifest when there is a state of uncleanness and when a state of cleanness. This is the law for leprosy."

Personal Uncleanness

15 [1] The LORD said to Moses and Aaron, [2]* "Speak to the Israelites and tell them:

Every man who is afflicted with a chronic flow from his private parts is thereby unclean. [3] Such is his uncleanness from this flow that it makes no difference whether the flow drains off or is blocked up; his uncleanness remains. [4] Any bed on which the man afflicted with the flow lies, is unclean, and any piece of furniture on which he sits, is unclean. [5] Anyone who touches his bed shall wash his garments, bathe in water, and be unclean until evening. [6] Whoever sits on a piece of furniture on which the afflicted man was sitting, shall wash his garments, bathe in water, and be unclean until evening. [7] Whoever touches the body of the afflicted man shall wash his garments, bathe in water, and be unclean until evening. [8] If the afflicted man spits on a clean man, the latter shall wash his garments, bathe in water, and be unclean until evening. [9] Any saddle on which the afflicted man rides, is unclean. [10] Whoever touches anything that was under him shall be unclean until evening; whoever lifts up any such thing shall wash his garments, bathe in water, and be unclean until evening. [11] Anyone whom the afflicted man touches with unrinsed hands shall wash his garments, bathe in water, and be unclean until evening. [12] Earthenware touched by the afflicted man shall be broken; and every wooden article shall be rinsed with water.

[13] "When a man who has been afflicted with a flow becomes free of his affliction, he shall wait seven days for his purification. Then he shall wash his garments and bathe his body in fresh water, and so he will be clean. [14] On the eighth day he shall take two turtledoves or two pigeons, and going before the LORD, to the entrance of the meeting tent, he shall give them to the priest, [15] who shall offer them up, the one as a sin offering and the other as a holocaust. Thus shall the priest make atonement before the LORD for the man's flow.

[16] "When a man has an emission of seed, he shall bathe his whole body in water and be unclean until evening. [17] Any piece of cloth or leather with seed on it shall be washed with water and be unclean until evening.

[18] "If a man lies carnally with a woman, they shall both bathe in water and be unclean until evening.

[19]* "When a woman has her menstrual flow, she shall be in a state of impurity for seven days. Anyone who touches her shall be unclean until evening. [20] Anything on which she lies or sits during her impurity shall be unclean. [21] Anyone who touches her bed shall wash his garments, bathe in water, and be unclean until evening. [22] Whoever touches any article of furniture on which she was

L
V

did you KNOW?

Monthly Periods

Not every woman suffers pain and swelling as part of her menstrual cycle. But many do. Imagine the life of women in Old Testament days. No sanitary supplies, just strips of cloth. Not much privacy. Not much sympathy from men. No understanding of human biology. Just the monthly flow of blood and the trouble and discomfort of dealing with it.

And on top of the discomfort, women were seen as unclean during their menstrual period. How unfair! How uncaring! How did this unclean concept in Lv 15, 19–33 develop, anyway? It probably had to do with blood's being a powerful sign of life. To the ancient Israelites, the loss of blood may have symbolized illness and death.

Thankfully, we do not apply all the Mosaic laws to our life today. We have grown in our understanding of human biology and of human dignity. Let's never stop growing.

▶ **Lv 15, 19–33**

sitting, shall wash his garments, bathe in water, and be unclean until evening. 23† But if she is on the bed or on the seat when he touches it, he shall be unclean until evening. 24* If a man dares to lie with her, he contracts her impurity and shall be unclean for seven days; every bed on which he then lies also becomes unclean.

25* "When a woman is afflicted with a flow of blood for several days outside her menstrual period, or when her flow continues beyond the ordinary period, as long as she suffers this unclean flow she shall be unclean, just as during her menstrual period. 26 Any bed on which she lies during such a flow becomes unclean, as it would during her menstruation, and any article of furniture on which she

sits becomes unclean just as during her menstruation. 27 Anyone who touches them becomes unclean; he shall wash his garments, bathe in water, and be unclean until evening.

28 "If she becomes freed from her affliction, she shall wait seven days, and only then is she to be purified. 29 On the eighth day she shall take two turtledoves or two pigeons and bring them to the priest at the entrance of the meeting tent. 30 The priest shall offer up one of them as a sin offering and the other as a holocaust. Thus shall the priest make atonement before the LORD for her unclean flow.

31 "You shall warn the Israelites of their uncleanness, lest by defiling my Dwelling, which is in their midst, their uncleanness be the cause of their death.

32 "This is the law for the man who is afflicted with a chronic flow, or who has an emission of seed, and thereby becomes unclean; 33 as well as for the woman who has her menstrual period, or who is afflicted with a chronic flow; the law for male and female; and also for the man who lies with an unclean woman."

The Day of Atonement

16 1 After the death of Aaron's two sons, who died when they approached the LORD's presence, the LORD spoke to Moses 2*† and said to him, "Tell your brother Aaron that he is not to come whenever he pleases into the sanctuary, inside the veil, in front of the propitiatory on the ark; otherwise, when I reveal myself in a cloud above the propitiatory, he will die. 3 Only in this way may Aaron enter the sanctuary. He shall bring a young bullock for a sin offering and a ram for a holocaust. 4 He shall wear the sacred linen tunic, with the linen drawers next his flesh, gird himself with the linen sash and put on the linen miter. But since these vestments are sacred, he shall not put them on until he has first bathed his body in water. 5* From the Israelite community he shall receive two male goats for a sin offering and one ram for a holocaust.

6 "Aaron shall bring in the bullock, his sin offering to atone for himself and for his household. 7 Taking the two male goats, and setting them before the LORD at the entrance of the meeting tent, 8† he shall cast lots to determine which one is for the LORD and which for Azazel. 9 The goat that is determined by lot for the LORD, Aaron shall bring

---

15, 23: What is added to the legislation by this verse is uncertain in both the Hebrew and the Greek.

16, 2: *The sanctuary, inside the veil:* the innermost part of the sanctuary, known also as "the holy of holies." Cf Ex 26, 33f. Here the high priest was allowed to enter only once a year, on Yom Kippur, the Day of Atonement. In Heb 9, 3–12 this ceremony is applied to Christ's single act of Redemption, whereby he won for us an everlasting atonement. *Propitiatory:* see note on Ex 25, 17.

16, 8: *Azazel:* perhaps a name for Satan, used only in this chapter. The ancient versions translated this word as "the escaping goat," whence the English word "scapegoat."

15, 24: Lv 18, 19.   16, 2: Heb 9, 6–12.
15, 25: Mt 9, 20; Mk 5, 25;   16, 5: Nm 29, 11.
　　　　Lk 8, 43.

in and offer up as a sin offering. [10] But the goat determined by lot for Azazel he shall set alive before the LORD, so that with it he may make atonement by sending it off to Azazel in the desert.

[11] "Thus shall Aaron offer up the bullock, his sin offering, to atone for himself and for his family. When he has slaughtered it, [12] he shall take a censer full of glowing embers from the altar before the LORD, as well as a double handfull of finely ground fragrant incense, and bringing them inside the veil, [13]† there before the LORD he shall put incense on the fire, so that a cloud of incense may cover the propitiatory over the commandments; else he will die. [14]* Taking some of the bullock's blood, he shall sprinkle it with his finger on the fore part of the propitiatory and likewise sprinkle some of the blood with his finger seven times in front of the propitiatory.

[15]* "Then he shall slaughter the people's sin-offering goat, and bringing its blood inside the veil, he shall do with it as he did with the bullock's blood, sprinkling it on the propitiatory and before it. [16] Thus he shall make atonement for the sanctuary because of all the sinful defilements and faults of the Israelites. He shall do the same for the meeting tent, which is set up among them in the midst

of their uncleanness. [17] No one else may be in the meeting tent from the time he enters the sanctuary to make atonement until he departs. When he has made atonement for himself and his household, as well as for the whole Israelite community, [18]* he shall come out to the altar before the LORD and make atonement for it also. Taking some of the bullock's and the goat's blood, he shall put it on the horns around the altar, [19] and with his finger sprinkle some of the blood on it seven times. Thus he shall render it clean and holy, purged of the defilements of the Israelites.

The Scapegoat

[20] "When he has completed the atonement rite for the sanctuary, the meeting tent and the altar, Aaron shall bring forward the live goat. [21]* Laying both hands on its head, he shall confess over it all the sinful faults and transgressions of the Israelites, and so put them on the goat's head. He shall then have it led into the desert by an attendant. [22]* Since the goat is to carry off their iniquities to an isolated region, it must be sent away into the desert.

[23]† "After Aaron has again gone into the meeting tent, he shall strip off and leave in the sanctuary the linen vestments he had put on when he entered

L
V

The Scapegoat

What an interesting tradition! In the Israelite ritual described in Lv 16, 20–21, the leader symbolically transfers all the people's sins onto a goat and drives it away. It is a liberating act that allows a fresh start.

But today, the idea of a scapegoat conveys oppression rather than freedom. A person becomes the scapegoat when other people blame him or her for their problems. Here is an example:

Suppose you are on a soccer team that expects this week's game to be easy, so no one works hard at practice. On game day, the score is tied near the end of the game. Your team is already thinking about going home when the other team scores a goal and wins the game. Everyone gets mad at the goalie for not preventing the goal. The goalie is the scapegoat, but everyone should share in the fault for the loss because they did not practice well or play their best.

- **Have you ever been the scapegoat for someone else's problems? If so, how did that feel? What did you do?**
- **Have you ever scapegoated someone else when you were partly to blame for some situation? What happened? How will you prevent scapegoating in the future?**

▸ **Lv 16, 20–21**

16, 13: *Else he will die:* the smoke is to conceal the resplendent majesty of God, the sight of which would strike any man dead.

16, 23: This verse is best read after v 25. According to later Jewish practice the high priest again went into the holy of holies to remove the censer.

16, 14: Heb 9, 13.25.
16, 15: Heb 5, 1; 6, 19.
16, 18: Ex 30, 12.

16, 21: Is 53, 6; 2 Cor 5, 21.
16, 22: Is 53, 11.12; Jn 1, 29; 1 Pt 2, 24.

there. ²⁴ After bathing his body with water in a sacred place, he shall put on his vestments, and then come out and offer his own and the people's holocaust, in atonement for himself and for the people, ²⁵ and also burn the fat of the sin offering on the altar.

²⁶ "The man who has led away the goat for Azazel shall wash his garments and bathe his body in water; only then may he enter the camp. ²⁷* The sin-offering bullock and goat whose blood was brought into the sanctuary to make atonement, shall be taken outside the camp, where their hides and flesh and offal shall be burned up in the fire. ²⁸ The one who burns them shall wash his garments and bathe his body in water; only then may he enter the camp.

The Fast

²⁹*† "This shall be an everlasting ordinance for you: on the tenth day of the seventh month every one of you, whether a native or a resident alien, shall mortify himself and shall do no work. ³⁰ Since on this day atonement is made for you to make you clean, so that you may be cleansed of all your sins before the LORD, ³¹ by everlasting ordinance it shall be a most solemn sabbath for you, on which you must mortify yourselves.

³² "This atonement is to be made by the priest who has been anointed and ordained to the priesthood in succession to his father. He shall wear the linen garments, the sacred vestments, ³³ and make atonement for the sacred sanctuary, the meeting tent and the altar, as well as for the priests and all the people of the community. ³⁴* This, then, shall be an everlasting ordinance for you: once a year atonement shall be made for all the sins of the Israelites."

Thus was it done, as the LORD had commanded Moses.

IV: Code of Legal Holiness

Sacredness of Blood

17 ¹ The LORD said to Moses, ² "Speak to Aaron and his sons, as well as to all the Israelites, and tell them: This is what the LORD has commanded. ³† Any Israelite who slaughters an ox or a sheep or a goat, whether in the camp or outside of it, ⁴ without first bringing it to the entrance of the meeting tent to present it as an offering to the LORD in front of his Dwelling, shall be judged guilty of bloodshed; and for this, such a man shall be cut off from among his people. ⁵ Therefore, such sacrifices as they used to offer up in the open field the Israelites shall henceforth offer to the LORD, bringing them to the priest at the entrance of the meeting tent and sacrificing them there as peace offerings to the LORD. ⁶ The priest shall splash the blood on the altar of the LORD at the entrance of the meeting tent and there burn the fat for an odor pleasing to the LORD. ⁷* No longer shall they offer their sacrifices to the satyrs to whom they used to render their wanton worship. This shall be an everlasting ordinance for them and their descendants.

⁸ "Tell them, therefore: Anyone, whether of the house of Israel or of the aliens residing among them, who offers a holocaust or sacrifice ⁹ without bringing it to the entrance of the meeting tent to offer it to the LORD, shall be cut off from his kinsmen. ¹⁰* And if anyone, whether of the house of Israel or of the aliens residing among them, partakes of any blood, I will set myself against that one who partakes of blood and will cut him off from among his people. ¹¹*† Since the life of a living body is in its blood, I have made you put it on the altar, so that atonement may thereby be made for your own lives, because it is the blood, as the seat of life, that makes atonement. ¹² That is why I have told the Israelites: No one among you, not even a resident alien, may partake of blood.

¹³ "Anyone hunting, whether of the Israelites or of the aliens residing among them, who catches an animal or a bird that may be eaten, shall pour out its blood and cover it with earth. ¹⁴* Since the life of every living body is its blood, I have told the Israelites: You shall not partake of the blood of any meat. Since the life of every living body is its blood, anyone who partakes of it shall be cut off.

¹⁵* Everyone, whether a native or an alien, who eats of an animal that died of itself or was killed by a wild beast, shall wash his garments, bathe in water, and be unclean until evening, and then he will be clean. ¹⁶ If he does not wash or does not bathe his body, he shall have the guilt to bear."

16, 29: *Mortify himself:* literally, "afflict his soul"; traditionally understood by the Jews as signifying abstinence from all food. This is the only fast day prescribed in the Mosaic law.

17, 3ff: The ancients considered blood the seat and sign of life, and therefore something sacred, even in animals. Cf Gn 9, 4f. Hence, even the ordinary butchering of an animal for meat was looked upon as having a sacrificial character, so that it should be performed at the sanctuary. This law, however, could not be carried out without great difficulty when the Israelites were scattered throughout Palestine, and so was modified in Dt 12, 20ff.

17, 11: *That atonement may thereby be made for your own lives:* hence, the sacrifice of an animal was a symbolic act which substi-

tuted the victim's life for the life of the offerer, who thus acknowledged that he deserved God's punishments for his sins. This idea of sacrifice is applied in Heb 9–10 to the death of Christ, inasmuch as "without the shedding of blood there is no forgiveness" (Heb 9, 22).

16, 27: Heb 13, 11.
16, 29: Lv 23, 27.32; Nm 29, 7.
16, 34: Heb 9, 7.25.
17, 7: Ex 34, 15; Dt 32, 17; 2 Chr 11, 15; 1 Cor

10, 20.
17, 10: Lv 3, 17.
17, 11: Gn 9, 4.
17, 14: Lv 7, 26f.
17, 15: Lv 11, 39f; 22, 8.

The Sanctity of Sex

18 [1] The LORD said to Moses, [2] "Speak to the Israelites and tell them: I, the LORD, am your God. [3] You shall not do as they do in the land of Egypt, where you once lived, nor shall you do as they do in the land of Canaan, where I am bringing you; do not conform to their customs. [4] My decrees you shall carry out, and my statutes you shall take care to follow. I, the LORD, am your God. [5]* Keep, then, my statutes and decrees, for the man who carries them out will find life through them. I am the LORD.

[6]† "None of you shall approach a close relative to have sexual intercourse with her. I am the LORD. [7]* You shall not disgrace your father by having intercourse with your mother. Besides, since she is your own mother, you shall not have intercourse with her. [8]* You shall not have intercourse with your father's wife, for that would be a disgrace to your father. [9] You shall not have intercourse with your sister, your father's daughter or your mother's daughter, whether she was born in your own household or born elsewhere. [10] You shall not have intercourse with your son's daughter or with your daughter's daughter, for that would be a disgrace to your own family. [11] You shall not have intercourse with the daughter whom your father's wife bore to him, since she, too, is your sister. [12]* You shall not have intercourse with your father's sister, since she is your father's relative. [13] You shall not have intercourse with your mother's sister, since she is your mother's relative. [14]* You shall not disgrace your father's brother by being intimate with his wife, since she, too, is your aunt. [15] You shall not have intercourse with your daughter-in-law; she is your son's wife, and therefore you shall not disgrace her. [16]*† You shall not have intercourse with your brother's wife, for that would be a disgrace to your brother. [17] You shall not have intercourse with a woman and also with her daughter, nor shall you marry and have intercourse with her son's daughter or her daughter's daughter; this would be shameful, because they are related to her. [18] While your wife is still living you shall not marry her sister as her rival; for thus you would disgrace your first wife.

[19] "You shall not approach a woman to have intercourse with her while she is unclean from menstruation. [20] You shall not have carnal relations

---

A Very Special Gift

LIVE IT!

The laws about sexual relations in Leviticus, chapter 18, are another example of how holiness extended to all aspects of life for the Israelites. The people had experienced the sexual promiscuity of other cultures (see Genesis, chapter 19). To become a great nation, the children of God, they had to abandon unhealthy and unholy sexual practices and follow God's way.

Young people today also receive many confusing cultural messages about when it is okay to have sex. In movies, television, and music, sex happens all the time between unmarried people, with no consequences. But the church, parents, and teachers are saying to wait until marriage. What is a person to believe?

Think about this: Suppose you are receiving a special gift for Christmas. The gift has been wrapped up and then hidden until Christmas Day. How would it feel if you discovered the present and opened it before Christmas? You probably would initially feel some excitement and pleasure in opening the gift. But the special meaning of opening it on the right day would be lost—for both you and the one presenting it to you.

Sex is a wonderful gift from God, meant for that day when you say, "I do," to someone you are committed to for life. You can only appreciate the full beauty of the gift when it is shared in marriage. God wants us to wait, so it will be as special as it is meant to be.

▸ Lv 18, 1–30

---

† **18, 6–18:** These laws are formulated as directed to the male Israelites only, but naturally the same norms of consanguinity and affinity would apply to the women as well. Marriage, as well as casual intercourse, is here forbidden between men and women of the specified degrees of relationship.
18, 16: *With your brother's wife:* it was the violation of this law which aroused the wrath of John the Baptist against Herod Antipas. Cf Mk 6, 18. An exception to this law is made in Dt 25, 5.

* 18, 5: Gal 3, 12.　　　　　18, 12f: Lv 20, 19.
18, 7–16: Lv 20, 11–21.　　18, 14: Lv 20, 20.
18, 8: Dt 23, 1; 27, 20;　　18, 16: Lv 20, 21; Mt 14, 3f;
　　1 Cor 5, 1.　　　　　　　　　Mk 6, 18.

with your neighbor's wife, defiling yourself with her. [21]*† You shall not offer any of your offspring to be immolated to Molech, thus profaning the name of your God. I am the LORD. [22]* You shall not lie with a male as with a woman; such a thing is an abomination. [23]* You shall not have carnal relations with an animal, defiling yourself with it; nor shall a woman set herself in front of an animal to mate with it; such things are abhorrent.

[24] "Do not defile yourselves by any of these things by which the nations whom I am driving out of your way have defiled themselves. [25] Because their land has become defiled, I am punishing it for its wickedness, by making it vomit out its inhabitants. [26] You, however, whether natives or resident aliens, must keep my statutes and decrees forbidding all such abominations [27] by which the previous inhabitants defiled the land; [28] otherwise the land will vomit you out also for having defiled it, just as it vomited out the nations before you. [29] Everyone who does any of these abominations shall be cut off from among his people. [30]* Heed my charge, then, not to defile yourselves by observing the abominable customs that have been observed before you. I, the LORD, am your God."

Various Rules of Conduct

19 [1] The LORD said to Moses, [2]* "Speak to the whole Israelite community and tell them: Be holy, for I, the LORD, your God, am holy. [3]* Revere your mother and father, and keep my sabbaths. I, the LORD, am your God.

[4]* "Do not turn aside to idols, nor make molten gods for yourselves. I, the LORD, am your God.

[5] "When you sacrifice your peace offering to the LORD, if you wish it to be acceptable, [6] it must be eaten on the very day of your sacrifice or on the following day. Whatever is left over until the third day shall be burned up in the fire. [7]* If any of it is eaten on the third day, the sacrifice will be unacceptable as refuse; [8] whoever eats of it then shall pay the penalty for having profaned what is sacred to the LORD. Such a one shall be cut off from his people.

[9]* "When you reap the harvest of your land, you shall not be so thorough that you reap the field to its very edge, nor shall you glean the stray ears of grain. [10] Likewise, you shall not pick your vineyard bare, nor gather up the grapes that have fallen. These things you shall leave for the poor and the alien. I, the LORD, am your God.

[11]* "You shall not steal. You shall not lie or speak falsely to one another. [12]* You shall not swear falsely by my name, thus profaning the name of your God. I am the LORD.

[13]* "You shall not defraud or rob your neighbor. You shall not withhold overnight the wages of your day laborer. [14] You shall not curse the deaf, or put a stumbling block in front of the blind, but you shall fear your God. I am the LORD.

[15]* "You shall not act dishonestly in rendering judgment. Show neither partiality to the weak nor deference to the mighty, but judge your fellow men justly. [16] You shall not go about spreading slander among your kinsmen; nor shall you stand by idly when your neighbor's life is at stake. I am the LORD.

[17]* "You shall not bear hatred for your brother in your heart. Though you may have to reprove your fellow man, do not incur sin because of him. [18]*† Take no revenge and cherish no grudge against your fellow countrymen. You shall love your neighbor as yourself. I am the LORD.

[19] "Keep my statutes: do not breed any of your domestic animals with others of a different species; do not sow a field of yours with two different kinds of seed; and do not put on a garment woven with two different kinds of thread.

[20]† "If a man has carnal relations with a female slave who has already been living with another man but has not yet been redeemed or given her freedom, they shall be punished but not put to death, because she is not free. [21] The man, moreover, shall bring to the entrance of the meeting tent a ram as his guilt offering to the LORD. [22] With this ram the priest shall make atonement before the LORD for the sin he has committed, and it will be forgiven him.

[23]† "When you come into the land and plant any fruit tree there, first look upon its fruit as if it were uncircumcised. For three years, while its fruit remains uncircumcised, it may not be eaten. [24] In the

---

18, 21: *Immolated to Molech:* the reference is to the Canaanite custom of sacrificing children to the god Molech. The little victims were first slain and then cremated. Cf Ez 16, 20ff; 20, 26.31; 23, 37.

19, 18: *You shall love your neighbor as yourself:* cited by our Lord as the second of the two most important commandments of God. Cf Mt 22, 39; Mk 12, 31. Although in the present context the word "neighbor" is restricted to "fellow countrymen," in Lk 10, 29–37 Christ extends its meaning to embrace all men, even enemies. Cf also Mt 5, 43ff.

19, 20ff: This law seems out of its proper context here; perhaps it stood originally after Lv 20, 12. *Female slave . . . given her freedom:* reference is to the case treated of in Ex 21, 7–11.

19, 23ff: *Uncircumcised:* by analogy with a newborn boy, the newly planted tree was considered impure until "circumcised" by offering to the Lord all the fruit it bore in the fourth year.

18, 21: Lv 20, 2–5; Dt 18, 10; 2 Kgs 16, 3; 21, 6.
18, 22: Lv 20, 13; Rom 1, 27; 1 Cor 6, 9f.
18, 23: Lv 20, 15f; Ex 22, 18.
18, 30: Lv 20, 23; Dt 18, 9.
19, 2: Lv 11, 44; Mt 5, 48; 1 Pt 1, 16.
19, 3: Ex 20, 12.
19, 4: Lv 26, 1; Ex 20, 3–5; 34, 17; Dt 27, 15.
19, 7: Lv 7, 18.
19, 9: Lv 23, 22; Dt 24, 19ff.
19, 11: Ex 20, 15f.
19, 12: Ex 20, 7; Mt 5, 33.
19, 13: Dt 24, 14f.
19, 15: Ex 23, 2f; Dt 1, 17; 16, 19; Ps 82, 2; Prv 24, 23.
19, 17: Mt 18, 15; Lk 17, 3; Gal 6, 1; 1 Jn 3, 14.
19, 18: Mt 5, 43; 19, 19; 22, 39; Mk 12, 31; Rom 13, 9; Gal 5, 14; Jas 2, 8.

You Shall Be Holy

As the Israelites' image of God developed, so did their sense of how they needed to live as God's people. As God's chosen people, they felt called to behave according to God's plan for them by keeping themselves pure as individuals and as a community. The laws in the Book of Leviticus are examples of how they lived out the call to be holy. For them, holiness was not just for the Sabbath or the Temple, but for every day and everything.

Think about the choices you make in the following areas. How do your choices help you to be holy as God is holy?

- what you eat
- what you watch
- what you wear
- what you buy
- what you listen to
- how you relate to other people

▸ Leviticus, chapters 19–20

fourth year, however, all of its fruit shall be sacred to the LORD as a thanksgiving feast to him. 25 Not until the fifth year may you eat its fruit. Thus it will continue its yield for you. I, the LORD, am your God.

26* "Do not eat meat with the blood still in it. Do not practice divination or soothsaying. 27*† Do not clip your hair at the temples, nor trim the edges of your beard. 28 Do not lacerate your bodies for the dead, and do not tattoo yourselves. I am the LORD.

29 "You shall not degrade your daughter by making a prostitute of her; else the land will become corrupt and full of lewdness. 30* Keep my sabbaths, and reverence my sanctuary. I am the LORD.

31* "Do not go to mediums or consult fortune-tellers, for you will be defiled by them. I, the LORD, am your God.

32 "Stand up in the presence of the aged, and show respect for the old; thus shall you fear your God. I am the LORD.

33* "When an alien resides with you in your land, do not molest him. 34* You shall treat the

alien who resides with you no differently than the natives born among you; have the same love for him as for yourself; for you too were once aliens in the land of Egypt. I, the LORD, am your God.

35 "Do not act dishonestly in using measures of length or weight or capacity. 36* You shall have a true scale and true weights, an honest ephah and an honest hin. I, the LORD, am your God, who brought you out of the land of Egypt. 37 Be careful, then, to observe all my statutes and decrees. I am the LORD."

Penalties for Various Sins

20 1 The LORD said to Moses, 2* "Tell the Israelites: Anyone, whether an Israelite or an alien residing in Israel, who gives any of his offspring to Molech shall be put to death. Let his fellow citizens stone him. 3* I myself will turn against such a man and cut him off from the body of his people; for in giving his offspring to Molech, he has defiled my sanctuary and profaned my holy name. 4 Even if his fellow citizens connive at such a man's crime of giving his offspring to Molech, and fail to put him to death, 5 I myself will set my face against that man and his family and will cut off from their people both him and all who join him in his wanton worship of Molech. 6* Should anyone turn to mediums and fortune-tellers and follow their wanton ways, I will turn against such a one and cut him off from his people. 7* Sanctify yourselves, then, and be holy; for I, the LORD, your God, am holy. 8 Be careful, therefore, to observe what I, the LORD, who make you holy, have prescribed.

9* "Anyone who curses his father or mother shall be put to death; since he has cursed his father or mother, he has forfeited his life. 10* If a man commits adultery with his neighbor's wife, both the adulterer and the adulteress shall be put to death. 11* If a man disgraces his father by lying with his father's wife, both the man and his stepmother shall be put to death; they have forfeited their lives. 12* If a man lies with his daughter-in-law, both of them shall be put to death; since they have committed an abhorrent deed, they have forfeited their lives. 13* If a man lies with a male as with a woman, both of them shall be put to death for their abominable deed; they have forfeited their lives. 14* If a man marries a woman and her mother also, the man and the two women as well shall be burned to death for their shameful conduct, so that such shamefulness may not be found among you. 15* If a man has carnal relations with an animal, the man

† 19, 27: See note on Lv 21, 5.

19, 26: Lv 3, 17; Dt 18, 10; 2 Kgs 17, 17; 21, 6; 2 Chr 33, 6.
19, 27: Lv 21, 5.
19, 30: Lv 26, 2; Ex 20, 8.
19, 31: Lv 20, 6.27; Dt 18, 11; Is 8, 19.
19, 33: Ex 22, 20; 23, 9; Jer 22, 3; Mal 3, 5.
19, 34: Dt 10, 19.

19, 36: Dt 25, 13.15; Prv 11, 1; 16, 11; 20, 10; Ez 45, 10.
20, 2: Lv 18, 21.
20, 3: Ez 23, 39.
20, 6: Lv 19, 31.
20, 7: Lv 11, 44; 19, 2; 1 Pt 1, 16.
20, 9: Ex 21, 17; Prv 20, 20;
Mt 15, 4; Mk 7, 10.
20, 10: Lv 18, 20; Dt 22, 22; Jn 8, 5.
20, 11: Lv 18, 7f.
20, 12: Lv 18, 15.
20, 13: Lv 18, 22.
20, 14: Lv 18, 17; Dt 27, 23.
20, 15: Ex 22, 18; Dt 27, 21.

shall be put to death, and the animal shall be slain. ¹⁶* If a woman goes up to any animal to mate with it, the woman and the animal shall be slain; let them both be put to death; their lives are forfeit. ¹⁷* If a man consummates marriage with his sister or his half-sister, they shall be publicly cut off from their people for this shameful deed; the man shall pay the penalty of having had intercourse with his own sister. ¹⁸* If a man lies in sexual intercourse with a woman during her menstrual period, both of them shall be cut off from their people, because they have laid bare the flowing fountain of her blood. ¹⁹* You shall not have intercourse with your mother's sister or your father's sister; whoever does so shall pay the penalty of incest. ²⁰ If a man disgraces his uncle by having intercourse with his uncle's wife, the man and his aunt shall pay the penalty by dying childless. ²¹ If a man marries his brother's wife and thus disgraces his brother, they shall be childless because of this incest.

²² "Be careful to observe all my statutes and all my decrees; otherwise the land where I am bringing you to dwell will vomit you out. ²³* Do not conform, therefore, to the customs of the nations whom I am driving out of your way, because all these things that they have done have filled me with disgust for them. ²⁴* But to you I have said: Their land shall be your possession, a land flowing with milk and honey. I am giving it to you as your own, I, the LORD, your God, who have set you apart from the other nations. ²⁵* You, too, must set apart, then, the clean animals from the unclean, and the clean birds from the unclean, so that you may not be contaminated with the uncleanness of any beast or bird or of any swarming creature in the land that I have set apart for you. ²⁶* To me, therefore, you shall be sacred; for I, the LORD, am sacred, I, who have set you apart from the other nations to be my own.

²⁷*† "A man or a woman who acts as a medium or fortune-teller shall be put to death by stoning; they have no one but themselves to blame for their death."

Sanctity of the Priesthood

21 ¹*† The LORD said to Moses, "Speak to Aaron's sons, the priests, and tell them: None of you shall make himself unclean for any dead person among his people, ² except for his nearest relatives, his mother or father, his son or daughter, his brother ³ or his maiden sister, who is of his own family while she remains unmarried; for these he may make himself unclean. ⁴ But for a sister who has married out of his family he shall not make himself unclean; this would be a profanation.

⁵*† "The priests shall not make bare the crown of the head, nor shave the edges of the beard, nor lacerate the body. ⁶† To their God they shall be sacred, and not profane his name; since they offer up the oblations of the LORD, the food of their God, they must be holy.

⁷* "A priest shall not marry a woman who has been a prostitute or has lost her honor, nor a woman who has been divorced by her husband; for the priest is sacred to his God. ⁸ Honor him as sacred who offers up the food of your God; treat him as sacred, because I, the LORD, who have consecrated him, am sacred.

⁹ "A priest's daughter who loses her honor by committing fornication and thereby dishonors her father also, shall be burned to death.

¹⁰† "The most exalted of the priests, upon whose head the anointing oil has been poured and who has been ordained to wear the special vestments, shall not bare his head or rend his garments, ¹¹ nor shall he go near any dead person. Not even for his father or mother may he thus become unclean ¹²* or leave the sanctuary; otherwise he will profane the sanctuary of his God, for with the anointing oil upon him, he is dedicated to his God, to me, the LORD.

¹³ "The priest shall marry a virgin. ¹⁴* Not a widow or a woman who has been divorced or a woman who has lost her honor as a prostitute, but a virgin, taken from his own people, shall he marry; ¹⁵ otherwise he will have base offspring among his people. I, the LORD, have made him sacred."

Irregularities

¹⁶ The LORD said to Moses, ¹⁷ "Speak to Aaron and tell him: None of your descendants, of whatever generation, who has any defect shall come forward to offer up the food of his God. ¹⁸ Therefore, he who has any of the following defects may not come forward: he who is blind, or lame, or who has any disfigurement or malformation, ¹⁹ or a crippled foot or hand, ²⁰ or who is humpbacked or weakly

---

† **20, 27:** This verse is best read immediately after v 6.

21, 1: *Unclean for any dead person:* by preparing the corpse for burial. Cf Nm 6, 6; 19, 11–19.

21, 5: Such mourning customs of the Canaanites were forbidden to all the Israelites, but especially to the priests. Cf Lv 19, 27f.

21, 6: *Sacred:* the same Hebrew word has both the active meaning of "holy," that is, keeping oneself free from profane impurities, and the passive meaning of "sacred," that is, set apart from what is profane and therefore treated with religious reverence.

21, 10: *Bare his head:* see note on Lv 10, 6.

* 20, 16: Lv 18, 23.
20, 17: Lv 18, 9; Dt 27, 22.
20, 18: Lv 18, 19.
20, 19: Lv 18, 12f.
20, 23: Lv 18, 30.
20, 24: Ex 3, 8.17; 6, 8.
20, 25: Lv 11, 2–47; Dt 14, 4–20.
20, 26: Lv 11, 44; Ex 19, 6;

1 Pt 1, 16.
20, 27: Lv 19, 31; Ex 22, 17; Dt 18, 11.
21, 1: Ez 44, 25.
21, 5: Ez 44, 20.
21, 7: Ez 44, 22.
21, 12: Lv 10, 7.
21, 14: Ez 44, 22.

or walleyed, or who is afflicted with eczema, ring-worm or hernia. 21 No descendant of Aaron the priest who has any such defect may draw near to of-fer up the oblations of the LORD; on account of his defect he may not draw near to offer up the food of his God. 22 He may, however, partake of the food of his God: of what is most sacred as well as of what is sacred. 23 Only, he may not approach the veil nor go up to the altar on account of his defect; he shall not profane these things that are sacred to me, for it is I, the LORD, who make them sacred."

24 Moses, therefore, told this to Aaron and his sons and to all the Israelites.

Sacrificial Banquets

22 1 The LORD said to Moses, 2 "Tell Aaron and his sons to respect the sacred offer-ings which the Israelites consecrate to me; else they will profane my holy name. I am the LORD.

3 "Tell them: If any one of you, or of your de-scendants in any future generation, dares, while he is in a state of uncleanness, to draw near the sacred offerings which the Israelites consecrate to the LORD, such a one shall be cut off from my presence. I am the LORD.

4* "No descendant of Aaron who is stricken with leprosy, or who suffers from a flow, may eat of these sacred offerings, unless he again becomes clean. Moreover, if anyone touches a person who has become unclean by contact with a corpse, or if any-one has had an emission of seed, 5* or if anyone touches any swarming creature or any man whose uncleanness, of whatever kind it may be, is conta-gious, 6* the one who touches such as these shall be unclean until evening and may not eat of the sacred portions until he has first bathed his body in water; 7 then, when the sun sets, he again becomes clean. Only then may he eat of the sacred offerings, which are his food. 8* He shall not make himself unclean by eating of any animal that has died of itself or has been killed by wild beasts. I am the LORD.

9 "They shall keep my charge and not do wrong in this matter; else they will die for their profana-tion. I am the LORD who have consecrated them.

10* "Neither a lay person nor a priest's tenant or hired servant may eat of any sacred offering. 11 But a slave whom a priest acquires by purchase or who is born in his house may eat of his food. 12 A priest's daughter who is married to a layman may not eat of the sacred contributions. 13 But if a priest's daughter is widowed or divorced and, hav-ing no children, returns to her father's house, she may then eat of her father's food as in her youth.

No layman, however, may eat of it. 14* If such a one eats of a sacred offering through inadvertence, he shall make restitution to the priest for the sacred offering, with an increment of one fifth of the amount. 15* The sacred offerings which the Israelites contribute to the LORD the priests shall not allow to be profaned 16 nor in the eating of the sacred offer-ing shall they bring down guilt that must be pun-ished; it is I, the LORD, who make them sacred."

Unacceptable Victims

17 The LORD said to Moses, 18 "Speak to Aaron and his sons and to all the Israelites, and tell them: When anyone of the house of Israel, or any alien re-siding in Israel, who wishes to offer a sacrifice, brings a holocaust as a votive offering or as a free-will offering to the LORD, 19* if it is to be accept-able, the ox or sheep or goat that he offers must be an unblemished male. 20* You shall not offer one that has any defect, for such a one would not be ac-ceptable for you. 21* When anyone presents a peace offering to the LORD from the herd or the flock in fulfillment of a vow, or as a free-will offering, if it is to find acceptance, it must be unblemished; it shall not have any defect. 22 One that is blind or crippled or maimed, or one that has a running sore or mange or ringworm, you shall not offer to the LORD; do not put such an animal on the altar as an oblation to the LORD. 23 An ox or a sheep that is in any way ill-proportioned or stunted you may in-deed present as a free-will offering, but it will not be acceptable as a votive offering. 24 One that has its testicles bruised or crushed or torn out or cut off you shall not offer to the LORD. You shall neither do this in your own land 25* nor receive from a for-eigner any such animals to offer up as the food of your God; since they are deformed or defective, they will not be acceptable for you."

26 The LORD said to Moses, 27* "When an ox or a lamb or a goat is born, it shall remain with its mother for seven days; only from the eighth day on-ward will it be acceptable, to be offered as an obla-tion to the LORD. 28 You shall not slaughter an ox or a sheep on one and the same day with its young. 29 Whenever you offer a thanksgiving sacrifice to the LORD, so offer it that it may be acceptable for you; 30* it must, therefore, be eaten on the same day; none of it shall be left over until the next day. I am the LORD.

31 "Be careful to observe the commandments which I, the LORD, give you, 32 and do not profane my holy name; in the midst of the Israelites I, the LORD, must be held as sacred. It is I who made you

22, 4: Lv 7, 20; 15, 16.   Ez 44, 31.
22, 5: Lv 11, 24.43.
22, 6: Heb 10, 22.   22, 10: 1 Sm 21, 6; Mt 12, 4.
22, 8: Lv 17, 15; Dt 14, 21;   22, 14: Lv 5, 16; 27, 13.15.
                                 19.

22, 15: Lv 19, 8; Nm 18, 32.   22, 21: Lv 3, 1.6.
22, 19: Lv 1, 3.10.   22, 25: Mal 1, 14.
22, 20: Dt 15, 21; 17, 1; Mal   22, 27: Ex 22, 29.
   1, 8.14.   22, 30: Lv 7, 15.

sacred [33] and led you out of the land of Egypt, that I, the LORD, might be your God."

Holy Days

23 [1] The LORD said to Moses, [2] "Speak to the Israelites and tell them: The following are the festivals of the LORD, my feast days, which you shall celebrate with a sacred assembly.

[3]* "For six days work may be done; but the seventh day is the sabbath rest, a day for sacred assembly, on which you shall do no work. The sabbath shall belong to the LORD wherever you dwell.

Passover

[4]* "These, then, are the festivals of the LORD which you shall celebrate at their proper time with a sacred assembly. [5]* The Passover of the LORD falls on the fourteenth day of the first month, at the evening twilight. [6]* The fifteenth day of this month is the LORD's feast of Unleavened Bread. For seven days you shall eat unleavened bread. [7]* On the first of these days you shall hold a sacred assembly and do no sort of work. [8] On each of the seven days you shall offer an oblation to the LORD. Then on the seventh day you shall again hold a sacred assembly and do no sort of work."

[9] The LORD said to Moses, [10] "Speak to the Israelites and tell them: When you come into the land which I am giving you, and reap your harvest, you shall bring a sheaf of the first fruits of your harvest to the priest, [11]† who shall wave the sheaf before the LORD that it may be acceptable for you. On the day after the sabbath the priest shall do this. [12] On this day, when your sheaf is waved, you shall offer to the LORD for a holocaust an unblemished yearling lamb. [13] Its cereal offering shall be two tenths of an ephah of fine flour mixed with oil, as a sweet-smelling oblation to the LORD; and its libation shall be a fourth of a hin of wine. [14]† Until this day, when you bring your God this offering, you shall not eat any bread or roasted grain or fresh kernels. This shall be a perpetual statute for you and your descendants wherever you dwell.

Pentecost

[15]* "Beginning with the day after the sabbath, the day on which you bring the wave-offering sheaf, you shall count seven full weeks, [16]*† and then on the day after the seventh week, the fiftieth day, you shall present the new cereal offering to the LORD. [17] For the wave offering of your first fruits to the LORD, you shall bring with you from wherever you live two loaves of bread made of two tenths of an ephah of fine flour and baked with leaven. [18] Besides the bread, you shall offer to the LORD a holocaust of seven unblemished yearling lambs, one young bull, and two rams, along with their cereal offering and libations, as a sweet-smelling oblation to the LORD. [19]* One male goat shall be sacrificed as a sin offering, and two yearling lambs as a peace offering. [20] The priest shall wave the bread of the first fruits and the two lambs as a wave offering before the LORD; these shall be sacred to the LORD and belong to the priest. [21] On this same day you shall by proclamation have a sacred assembly, and no sort of work may be done. This shall be a perpetual statute for you and your descendants wherever you dwell.

[22] "When you reap the harvest of your land, you shall not be so thorough that you reap the field to its very edge, nor shall you glean the stray ears of your grain. These things you shall leave for the poor and the alien. I, the LORD, am your God."

New Year's Day

[23] The LORD said to Moses, [24] "Tell the Israelites: On the first day of the seventh month you shall keep a sabbath rest, with a sacred assembly and with the trumpet blasts as a reminder; [25] you shall then do no sort of work, and you shall offer an oblation to the LORD."

The Day of Atonement

[26]* The LORD said to Moses, [27]* "The tenth of this seventh month is the Day of Atonement, when you shall hold a sacred assembly and mortify yourselves and offer an oblation to the LORD. [28] On this day you shall not do any work, because it is the Day of Atonement, when atonement is made for you before the LORD, your God. [29] Anyone who does not mortify himself on this day shall be cut off from his people; [30] and if anyone does any work on this day, I will remove him from the midst of his people. [31] This is a perpetual statute for you and your descendants wherever you dwell: you shall do no work, [32] but shall keep a sabbath of complete rest and mortify yourselves. Beginning on the evening

---

† **23, 11:** *The sabbath:* according to the Jewish tradition this was the feast day itself, the fifteenth of Nisan, which was a special day of rest. Cf v 7. However, some understand here the Saturday of the Passover week, or even the Saturday following it; cf Jn 19, 31.

23, 14: *Any bread:* made from the new grain. The harvest had first to be sanctified for man's use by this offering to God.

23, 16: *The fiftieth:* from the Greek word for this we have the name "Pentecost." Cf 2 Mc 12, 31; Acts 2, 1. It was also called "the feast of the Seven Weeks," or simply "the feast of Weeks" (Nm 28, 26; Dt 16, 10; Tb 2, 1). *The new cereal offering:* of flour made from the new grain. Pentecost was the thanksgiving feast at the end of the grain harvest, which began after Passover. Later tradition made it a commemoration of the giving of the law at Sinai.

*	
23, 3: Ex 20, 8–11; 23, 12; 31, 14f; 34, 21; Dt 5, 12–15; Lk 13, 14.	**23, 7:** Ex 12, 15; Nm 28, 18.25.
23, 4: Ex 23, 14–19.	**23, 15:** Ex 34, 22; Nm 28, 26; Dt 16, 9.
23, 5: Nm 9, 2f; 28, 16.	**23, 16:** Acts 2, 1.
23, 6: Ex 12, 18; 13, 3.10; 23, 15; 34, 18.	**23, 19:** Nm 28, 30.
	23, 26: Lv 25, 9.
	23, 27: Lv 16, 29f; Nm 29, 7.

Asian American

Korean Festival Customs

In preparation for the Lunar New Year (in January or February) and for the Moon Festival (a feast of thanksgiving in August), Korean families follow some traditional customs. These customs are similar to those of the Israelite festivals described in Leviticus, chapter 23.

In Korea, the day before each feast is used for purification. People take ceremonial baths symbolizing the total cleansing of their body, their spirit, and their attitudes. The baths wash away meanness, carelessness, and other faults. The people also wear new clothes and often get a new haircut.

Before sunrise on the day of the feast, the people bow before a table holding name cards of their ancestors. They use incense, pour out wine, and pray to their ancestors, asking for their intercession and help. Family members pray silently for all their individual and family needs. During the day, families visit the homes of their extended family. During these visits, prayer ritual is often repeated.

After a day of visiting, families return home for a feast of the best food and drink possible. The sharing of food is the most significant part of the meal. Neighbors exchange portions of food with one another and bring food to poor families. Families set food on a small table near the door as an offering of thanks to the Creator and sprinkle rice on the ground around their house in gratitude for the crops.

▶ Lv 23, 4–44

LORD's feast of Booths, which shall continue for seven days. 35 On the first day there shall be a sacred assembly, and you shall do no sort of work. 36 For seven days you shall offer an oblation to the LORD, and on the eighth day you shall again hold a sacred assembly and offer an oblation to the LORD. On that solemn closing you shall do no sort of work.

37 "These, therefore, are the festivals of the LORD on which you shall proclaim a sacred assembly, and offer as an oblation to the LORD holocausts and cereal offerings, sacrifices and libations, as prescribed for each day, 38 in addition to those of the LORD's sabbaths, your donations, your various votive offerings and the free-will offerings that you present to the LORD.

39* "On the fifteenth day, then, of the seventh month, when you have gathered in the produce of the land, you shall celebrate a pilgrim feast of the LORD for a whole week. The first and the eighth day shall be days of complete rest. 40† On the first day you shall gather foliage from majestic trees, branches of palms and boughs of myrtles and of valley poplars, and then for a week you shall make merry before the LORD, your God. 41* By perpetual statute for you and your descendants you shall keep this pilgrim feast of the LORD for one whole week in the seventh month of the year. 42 During this week every native Israelite among you shall dwell in booths, 43* that your descendants may realize that, when I led the Israelites out of the land of Egypt, I made them dwell in booths. I, the LORD, am your God."

44 Thus did Moses announce to the Israelites the festivals of the LORD.

The Sanctuary Light

24 1 The LORD said to Moses, 2* "Order the Israelites to bring you clear oil of crushed olives for the light, so that you may keep lamps burning regularly. 3 In the meeting tent, outside the veil that hangs in front of the commandments, Aaron shall set up the lamps to burn before the LORD regularly, from evening till morning. Thus, by

---

† **23, 34:** *Feast of Booths:* the joyful observance of the vintage and fruit harvest. Cf Dt 16, 13. During the seven days of the feast the Israelites camped in booths of branches erected on the roofs of their houses or in the streets in commemoration of their wanderings in the desert, where they dwelt in booths.
23, 40: *Foliage:* literally, "fruit," but here probably used in the general sense of "produce, growth." These branches were used for constructing the "booths" or huts in which the people lived during the feast. Cf Neh 8, 15. However, from about the time of Christ on, the Jews have understood this of "fruit" in the strict sense; hence, branches of lemons and oranges were carried with the other branches in joyous procession.

of the ninth of the month, you shall keep this sabbath of yours from evening to evening."

The Feast of Booths

33 The LORD said to Moses, 34*† "Tell the Israelites: The fifteenth day of this seventh month is the

23, 34: Nm 29, 12; Dt 16, 13;   23, 41: Nm 29, 12–38.
          2 Mc 1, 9.18; Jn 7, 2.   23, 43: Dt 31, 10–13.
23, 39: Ex 23, 16; Dt 16, 13.   24, 2: Ex 27, 20f.

a perpetual statute for you and your descendants, 4* the lamps shall be set up on the pure gold lampstand, to burn regularly before the LORD.

The Showbread

5* "You shall take fine flour and bake it into twelve cakes, using two tenths of an ephah of flour for each cake. 6 These you shall place in two piles, six in each pile, on the pure gold table before the LORD. 7 On each pile put some pure frankincense, which shall serve as an oblation to the LORD, a token offering for the bread. 8* Regularly on each sabbath day this bread shall be set out afresh before the LORD, offered on the part of the Israelites by an everlasting agreement. 9 It shall belong to Aaron and his sons, who must eat it in a sacred place, since, as something most sacred among the various oblations to the LORD, it is his by perpetual right."

Punishment of Blasphemy

10 Among the Israelites there was a man born of an Israelite mother (Shelomith, daughter of Dibri, of the tribe of Dan) and an Egyptian father. 11 This man quarreled publicly with another Israelite and cursed and blasphemed the LORD'S name. So the people brought him to Moses, 12 who kept him in custody till a decision from the LORD should settle the case for them. 13 The LORD then said to Moses, 14 "Take the blasphemer outside the camp, and when all who heard him have laid their hands on his head, let the whole community stone him. 15 Tell the Israelites: Anyone who curses his God shall bear the penalty of his sin; 16* whoever blasphemes the name of the LORD shall be put to death. The whole community shall stone him; alien and native alike must be put to death for blaspheming the LORD'S name.

17* "Whoever takes the life of any human being shall be put to death; 18* whoever takes the life of an animal shall make restitution of another animal. A life for a life! 19 Anyone who inflicts an injury on his neighbor shall receive the same in return. 20* Limb for limb, eye for eye, tooth for tooth! The same injury that a man gives another shall be inflicted on him in return. 21 Whoever slays an animal shall make restitution, but whoever slays a man shall be put to death. 22* You shall have but one rule, for alien and native alike. I, the LORD, am your God."

23* When Moses told this to the Israelites, they took the blasphemer outside the camp and stoned him; they carried out the command that the LORD had given Moses.

The Sabbatical Year

25 1 The LORD said to Moses on Mount Sinai, 2 "Speak to the Israelites and tell them: When you enter the land that I am giving you, let the land, too, keep a sabbath for the LORD. 3* For six years you may sow your field, and for six years prune your vineyard, gathering in their produce. 4* But during the seventh year the land shall have a complete rest, a sabbath for the LORD, when you may neither sow your field nor prune your vineyard. 5† The aftergrowth of your harvest you shall not reap, nor shall you pick the grapes of your untrimmed vines in this year of sabbath rest for the land. 6 While the land has its sabbath, all its produce will be food equally for you yourself and for your male and female slaves, for your hired help and the tenants who live with you, 7 and likewise for your livestock and for the wild animals on your land.

The Jubilee Year

8 "Seven weeks of years shall you count—seven times seven years—so that the seven cycles amount to forty-nine years. 9 Then, on the tenth day of the seventh month let the trumpet resound; on this, the Day of Atonement, the trumpet blast shall re-echo throughout your land. 10*† This fiftieth year you shall make sacred by proclaiming liberty in the land for all its inhabitants. It shall be a jubilee for you, when every one of you shall return to his own property, every one to his own family estate. 11 In this fiftieth year, your year of jubilee, you shall not sow, nor shall you reap the aftergrowth or pick the grapes from the untrimmed vines. 12 Since this is the jubilee, which shall be sacred for you, you may not eat of its produce, except as taken directly from the field.

13 "In this year of jubilee, then, every one of you shall return to his own property. 14 Therefore, when you sell any land to your neighbor or buy any from him, do not deal unfairly. 15* On the basis of the number of years since the last jubilee shall you purchase the land from him; and so also, on the basis of the number of years for crops, shall he sell it to you. 16 When the years are many, the price shall be

---

† **25, 5ff:** As long as the produce of the sabbatical year remains on the field, it remains available to everyone; cf v 12. In Ex 23, 10f the poor and the wild beasts that have no other source of nourishment are alone mentioned.

25, 10: *Fiftieth year:* to arrive at this number, the preceding year of jubilee is included in the count, and therefore this is more exactly the forty-ninth year, the seventh sabbatical year. *Liberty:* Israelite slaves were set free (v 50) and landed property was returned to its original owner (v 13): two important laws for preserving the social and economic equilibrium. *Jubilee:* derived from the Hebrew word *yobel,* "ram's horn," which was blown on this occasion.

24, 4: Ex 25, 31.
24, 5: Ex 25, 30; 1 Kgs 7, 48;
  2 Chr 4, 19; 13, 11;
  Heb 9, 2.
24, 8: 1 Chr 9, 32.
24, 16: 1 Kgs 21, 10.13; Mt
  26, 65f; Jn 10, 33.
24, 17: Gn 9, 5f; Ex 21, 12;
  Nm 35, 31; Dt 19, 11f.
24, 18: Ex 21, 33f.

24, 20: Dt 19, 21; Mt 5, 38.
24, 22: Lv 19, 34; Ex 12, 49;
  46, 17; Lk 4, 19.
24, 23: Acts 7, 57f.
25, 3: Ex 23, 10f.
25, 4: 1 Mc 6, 49.53.
25, 10: Nm 36, 4; Is 61, 2; Ez
  46, 17; Lk 4, 19.
25, 15: Lv 27, 18.23.

7 x 7 + 1 = Jubilee!

In the Bible, seven is a special number. Just as the seventh day of the week was set aside as a day of rest in ancient Israel, so the seventh year was set aside as a year of rest for the land. Fields were to remain uncultivated during the seventh year; whatever fruits or grains grew on their own were to be left for the poor. The "sabbatical year" was a reminder to the people that the land actually belonged to God, not to them.

Seven may be a special number, but seven times seven plus one is very special. The fiftieth year—the year after seven times seven years—was declared the Jubilee year, and God's Law demanded some very special things to happen. The people were to take a year of vacation from their normal routine. This meant no planting for a farmer, no lending for a banker, and no big sales for a merchant. Why this break? Because God wanted the Jubilee year to be a time when everyone started over with a clean slate. During the Jubilee, all land was to be returned to its original owners, and all Israelite slaves were to be set free. Debts were to be forgiven and justly settled. The year of Jubilee was like the reset button on a computer, stopping everything and returning it to its original setting. It was a check against the unjust distribution of property and wealth.

The Catholic church has continued the custom of celebrating the fiftieth year, especially when it marks the end of a century. Faithful to its Jewish roots, the church sees the Jubilee year as a special time for renewal. In preparation for a Jubilee year, it asks individuals and communities to commit themselves to following Jesus more faithfully.

▶ Leviticus, chapter 25

18 "Observe my precepts and be careful to keep my regulations, for then you will dwell securely in the land. 19* The land will yield its fruit and you will have food in abundance, so that you may live there without worry. 20* Therefore, do not say, 'What shall we eat in the seventh year, if we do not then sow or reap our crop?' 21 I will bestow such blessings on you in the sixth year that there will then be crop enough for three years. 22* When you sow in the eighth year, you will continue to eat from the old crop; and even into the ninth year, when the crop comes in, you will still have the old to eat from.

Redemption of Property

23* "The land shall not be sold in perpetuity; for the land is mine, and you are but aliens who have become my tenants. 24 Therefore, in every part of the country that you occupy, you must permit the land to be redeemed. 25* When one of your countrymen is reduced to poverty and has to sell some of his property, his closest relative, who has the right to redeem it, may go and buy back what his kinsman has sold. 26 If, however, the man has no relative to redeem his land, but later on acquires sufficient means to buy it back in his own name, 27 he shall make a deduction from the price in proportion to the number of years since the sale, and then pay back the balance to the one to whom he sold it, so that he may thus regain his own property. 28* But if he does not acquire sufficient means to buy back his land, what he has sold shall remain in the possession of the purchaser until the jubilee, when it must be released and returned to its original owner.

29 "When someone sells a dwelling in a walled town, he has the right to buy it back during the time of one full year from its sale. 30 But if such a house in a walled town has not been redeemed at the end of a full year, it shall belong in perpetuity to the purchaser and his descendants; nor shall it be released in the jubilee. 31 However, houses in villages that are not encircled by walls shall be considered as belonging to the surrounding farm land; they may be redeemed at any time, and in the jubilee they must be released.

32 "In levitical cities the Levites shall always have the right to redeem the town houses that are their property. 33 Any town house of the Levites in their cities that had been sold and not redeemed, shall be released in the jubilee; for the town houses of the Levites are their hereditary property in the midst of

so much the more; when the years are few, the price shall be so much the less. For it is really the number of crops that he sells you. 17 Do not deal unfairly, then; but stand in fear of your God. I, the LORD, am your God.

25, 19: Lv 26, 5.
25, 20: Mt 6, 25.31; Lk 12, 22.29.
25, 22: Lv 26, 10.
25, 23: 1 Pt 2, 11.
25, 25: Ru 2, 20; 4, 4.6; Jer 32, 7f.
25, 28: Lv 27, 24.

the Israelites. 34* Moreover, the pasture land belonging to their cities shall not be sold at all; it must always remain their hereditary property.

35* "When one of your fellow countrymen is reduced to poverty and is unable to hold out beside you, extend to him the privileges of an alien or a tenant, so that he may continue to live with you. 36 Do not exact interest from your countryman either in money or in kind, but out of fear of God let him live with you. 37* You are to lend him neither money at interest nor food at a profit. 38 I, the LORD, am your God, who brought you out of the land of Egypt to give you the land of Canaan and to be your God.

39* "When, then, your countryman becomes so impoverished beside you that he sells you his services, do not make him work as a slave. 40 Rather, let him be like a hired servant or like your tenant, working with you until the jubilee year, 41 when he, together with his children, shall be released from your service and return to his kindred and to the property of his ancestors. 42 Since those whom I brought out of the land of Egypt are servants of mine, they shall not be sold as slaves to any man. 43 Do not lord it over them harshly, but stand in fear of your God.

44 "Slaves, male and female, you may indeed possess, provided you buy them from among the neighboring nations. 45 You may also buy them from among the aliens who reside with you and from their children who are born and reared in your land. Such slaves you may own as chattels, 46* and leave to your sons as their hereditary property, making them perpetual slaves. But you shall not lord it harshly over any of the Israelites, your kinsmen.

47 "When one of your countrymen is reduced to such poverty that he sells himself to a wealthy alien who has a permanent or a temporary residence among you, or to one of the descendants of an immigrant family, 48 even after he has thus sold his services he still has the right of redemption; he may be redeemed by one of his own brothers, 49 or by his uncle or cousin, or by some other relative or fellow clansman; or, if he acquires the means, he may redeem himself. 50 With his purchaser he shall compute the years from the sale to the jubilee, distributing the sale price over these years as though he had been hired as a day laborer. 51 The more such years there are, the more of the sale price he shall pay back as ransom; 52 the fewer years there are left

before the jubilee year, the more he has to his credit; in proportion to his years of service shall he pay his ransom. 53 The alien shall treat him as a servant hired on an annual basis, and he shall not lord it over him harshly under your very eyes. 54* If he is not thus redeemed, he shall nevertheless be released, together with his children, in the jubilee year. 55 For to me the Israelites belong as servants; they are servants of mine, because I brought them out of the land of Egypt, I, the LORD, your God.

The Reward of Obedience

26

1* "Do not make false gods for yourselves. You shall not erect an idol or a sacred pillar for yourselves, nor shall you set up a stone figure for worship in your land; for I, the LORD, am your God. 2* Keep my sabbaths, and reverence my sanctuary. I am the LORD.

3† "If you live in accordance with my precepts and are careful to observe my commandments, 4* I will give you rain in due season, so that the land will bear its crops, and the trees their fruit; 5 your threshing will last till vintage time, and your vintage till the time for sowing, and you will have food to eat in abundance, so that you may dwell securely in your land. 6 I will establish peace in the land, that you may lie down to rest without anxiety. I will rid the country of ravenous beasts, and keep the sword of war from sweeping across your land. 7 You will rout your enemies and lay them low with your sword. 8 Five of you will put a hundred of your foes to flight, and a hundred of you will chase ten thousand of them, till they are cut down by your sword. 9 I will look with favor upon you, and make you fruitful and numerous, as I carry out my covenant with you. 10* So much of the old crops will you have stored up for food that you will have to discard them to make room for the new. 11* I will set my Dwelling among you, and will not disdain you. 12 Ever present in your midst, I will be your God, and you will be my people; 13 for it is I, the LORD, your God, who brought you out of the land of the Egyptians and freed you from their slavery, breaking the yoke they had laid upon you and letting you walk erect.

Punishment of Disobedience

14 "But if you do not heed me and do not keep all these commandments, 15 if you reject my precepts and spurn my decrees, refusing to obey all my commandments and breaking my covenant, 16 then I, in

---

† **26, 3–45:** Since God's covenant was with the Israelite nation as a whole, these promises and threats are made primarily to the entire community. The rewards and punishments are of a temporal nature because the community as such exists only here on earth, not in the hereafter.

25, 34: Nm 35, 3.
25, 35: Dt 15, 7.8.
25, 37: Dt 23, 19.
25, 39: 1 Kgs 9, 22.
25, 46: Is 14, 1f.
25, 54: Ex 21, 2f.
26, 1: Lv 19, 4; Ex 20, 4;

Nm 33, 52; Dt 5, 8.
26, 2: Ex 20, 8.
26, 4: Ps 85, 13.
26, 10: Lv 25, 22.
26, 11f: Ex 29, 45; Ez 39, 26ff;
2 Cor 6, 16.

turn, will give you your deserts. I will punish you with terrible woes—with wasting and fever to dim the eyes and sap the life. You will sow your seed in vain, for your enemies will consume the crop. 17* I will turn against you, till you are beaten down before your enemies and lorded over by your foes. You will take to flight though no one pursues you.

18 "If even after this you do not obey me, I will increase the chastisement for your sins sevenfold, 19 to break your haughty confidence. I will make the sky above you as hard as iron, and your soil as hard as bronze, 20 so that your strength will be spent in vain; your land will bear no crops, and its trees no fruit.

21 "If then you become defiant in your unwillingness to obey me, I will multiply my blows another sevenfold, as your sins deserve. 22 I will unleash the wild beasts against you, to rob you of your children and wipe out your livestock, till your population dwindles away and your roads become deserted.

23 "If, with all this, you still refuse to be chastened by me and continue to defy me, 24* I, too, will defy you and will smite you for your sins seven times harder than before. 25 I will make the sword, the avenger of my covenant, sweep over you. Though you then huddle together in your walled cities, I will send in pestilence among you, till you are forced to surrender to the enemy. 26* And as I cut off your supply of bread, ten women will need but one oven for baking all the bread they dole out to you in rations—not enough food to still your hunger.

27 "If, despite all this, you still persist in disobeying and defying me, 28 I, also, will meet you with fiery defiance and will chastise you with sevenfold fiercer punishment for your sins, 29*† till you begin to eat the flesh of your own sons and daughters. 30* I will demolish your high places, overthrow your incense stands, and cast your corpses on those of your idols. In my abhorrence of you, 31 I will lay waste your cities and devastate your sanctuaries, refusing to accept your sweet-smelling offerings. 32* So devastated will I leave the land that your very enemies who come to live there will stand aghast at the sight of it. 33* You yourselves I will scatter among the nations at the point of my drawn sword, leaving your countryside desolate and your cities deserted. 34* Then shall the land retrieve its lost sabbaths during all the time it lies waste, while you are in the land of your enemies; then shall the land

have rest and make up for its sabbaths 35 during all the time that it lies desolate, enjoying the rest that you would not let it have on the sabbaths when you lived there.

36 "Those of you who survive in the lands of their enemies I will make so fainthearted that, if leaves rustle behind them, they will flee headlong, as if from the sword, though no one pursues them; 37 stumbling over one another as if to escape a weapon, while no one is after them—so helpless will you be to take a stand against your foes! 38 You will be lost among the Gentiles, swallowed up in your enemies' country. 39* Those of you who survive in the lands of their enemies will waste away for their own and their fathers' guilt.

40 "Thus they will have to confess that they and their fathers were guilty of having rebelled against me and of having defied me, 41 so that I, too, had to defy them and bring them into their enemies' land. Then, when their uncircumcised hearts are humbled and they make amends for their guilt, 42* I will remember my covenant with Jacob, my covenant with Isaac, and my covenant with Abraham; and of the land, too, I will be mindful. 43 But the land must first be rid of them, that in its desolation it may make up its lost sabbaths, and that they, too, may make good the debt of their guilt for having spurned my precepts and abhorred my statutes. 44 Yet even so, even while they are in their enemies' land, I will not reject or spurn them, lest, by wiping them out, I make void my covenant with them; for I, the Lord, am their God. 45* I will remember them because of the covenant I made with their forefathers, whom I brought out of the land of Egypt under the very eyes of the Gentiles, that I, the Lord, might be their God."

46† These are the precepts, decrees and laws which the Lord had Moses promulgate on Mount Sinai in the pact between himself and the Israelites.

V: Redemption of Offerings

Redemption of Votive Offerings

27 1 The Lord said to Moses, 2 "Speak to the Israelites and tell them: When anyone fulfills a vow of offering one or more persons to the Lord, who are to be ransomed at a fixed sum of money, 3 for persons between the ages of twenty and sixty, the fixed sum, in sanctuary shekels, shall be fifty silver shekels for a man, 4 and thirty shekels

L
V

---

†

26, 29: *Eat the flesh of your own sons and daughters:* extreme famine in cities under siege often forced their inhabitants to such dire means of subsistence. Cf Dt 28, 53; Jer 19, 9; Ez 5, 10; 2 Kgs 6, 28f.

26, 46: The Book of Leviticus seems originally to have ended here; the following chapter is an appendix.

26, 17: Dt 28, 25.
26, 24f: Jer 2, 30;
     Ez 5, 17; 14, 17.
26, 26: Is 9, 19; Ez 4, 16; 5,
     16; 14, 13; Mi 6, 14.
26, 29: Is 9, 18.
26, 30: 2 Chr 14, 5; 34, 3.4.7;
     Ez 6, 3–6.
26, 32: 1 Kgs 9, 8; Jer 9, 11;

18, 16; 19, 8; 25, 18;
     Ez 5, 15.
26, 33: Jer 9, 16; Zec 7, 14.
26, 34: Lv 25, 2; 2 Chr 36, 21.
26, 39: Ez 4, 17; 24, 23; 33,
     10.
26, 42: Ex 6, 5; 2 Kgs 13, 23;
     Ps 106, 45; Ez 16, 60.
26, 45: Ex 12, 51.

for a woman; [5] for persons between the ages of five and twenty, the fixed sum shall be twenty shekels for a youth, and ten for a maiden; [6] for persons between the ages of one month and five years, the fixed sum shall be five silver shekels for a boy, and three for a girl; [7] for persons of sixty or more, the fixed sum shall be fifteen shekels for a man, and ten for a woman. [8] However, if the one who took the vow is too poor to meet the fixed sum, the person must be set before the priest, who shall determine the sum for his ransom in keeping with the means of the one who made the vow.

[9] "If the offering vowed to the LORD is an animal that may be sacrificed, every such animal, when vowed to the LORD, becomes sacred. [10] The offerer shall not present a substitute for it by exchanging either a better for a worse one or a worse for a better one. If he attempts to offer one animal in place of another, both the original and its substitute shall be treated as sacred. [11] If the animal vowed to the LORD is unclean and therefore unfit for sacrifice, it must be set before the priest, [12]† who shall determine its value in keeping with its good or bad qualities, and the value set by the priest shall stand. [13]* If the offerer wishes to redeem the animal, he shall pay one fifth more than this valuation.

[14] "When someone dedicates his house as sacred to the LORD, the priest shall determine its value in keeping with its good or bad points, and the value set by the priest shall stand. [15] If the one who dedicated his house wishes to redeem it, he shall pay one fifth more than the price thus established, and then it will again be his.

[16] "If the object which someone dedicates to the LORD is a piece of his hereditary land, its valuation shall be made according to the amount of seed required to sow it, the acreage sown with a homer of barley seed being valued at fifty silver shekels. [17] If the dedication of a field is made at the beginning of a jubilee period, the full valuation shall hold; [18]* but if it is some time after this, the priest shall estimate its money value according to the number of years left until the next jubilee year, with a corresponding rebate on the valuation. [19] If the one who dedicated his field wishes to redeem it, he shall pay one fifth more than the price thus established, and so reclaim it. [20] If, instead of redeeming such a field, he sells it to someone else, it may no longer be redeemed; [21] but at the jubilee it shall be released as sacred to the LORD; like a field that is doomed, it shall become priestly property.

[22] "If the field that some man dedicates to the LORD is one he had purchased and not a part of his hereditary property, [23] the priest shall compute its value in proportion to the number of years until the next jubilee, and on the same day the price thus established shall be given as sacred to the LORD; [24]* at the jubilee, however, the field shall revert to the hereditary owner of this land from whom it had been purchased.

[25] "Every valuation shall be made according to the standard of the sanctuary shekel. There are twenty gerahs to the shekel.

Offerings Not To Be Redeemed

[26]* "Note that a first-born animal, which as such already belongs to the LORD, may not be dedicated by vow to him. If it is an ox or a sheep, it shall be ceded to the LORD; [27]† but if it is an unclean animal, it may be redeemed by paying one fifth more than its fixed value. If it is not redeemed, it shall be sold at its fixed value.

[28]* "Note, also, that any one of his possessions which a man vows as doomed to the LORD, whether it is a human being or an animal or a hereditary field, shall be neither sold nor ransomed; everything that is thus doomed becomes most sacred to the LORD. [29]† All human beings that are doomed lose the right to be redeemed; they must be put to death.

[30]* "All tithes of the land, whether in grain from the fields or in fruit from the trees, belong to the LORD, as sacred to him. [31] If someone wishes to buy back any of his tithes, he shall pay one fifth more than their value. [32] The tithes of the herd and the flock shall be determined by ceding to the LORD as sacred every tenth animal as they are counted by the herdsman's rod. [33] It shall not matter whether good ones or bad ones are thus chosen, and no exchange may be made. If any exchange is attempted, both the original animal and its substitute shall be treated as sacred, without the right of being bought back."

[34] These are the commandments which the LORD gave Moses on Mount Sinai for the Israelites.

27, 12: *Determine its value:* fix the price at which the animal may be sold to someone else. Only the original owner must pay the twenty percent tax, as a penalty for buying back what he had vowed to God. So also for houses and fields that are vowed to the Lord, as treated of in the following verses. The money from the sale or from the redemption of such vowed property naturally goes to the sanctuary.

27, 27: *An unclean animal:* such as the first-born of an ass, which was unfit for sacrifice. According to Ex 13, 13; 34, 20, a first-born ass was to be redeemed by offering a sheep in its stead, or was to have its neck broken. The present law is probably a later modification of the earlier one.

27, 29: *All human beings that are doomed:* according to some interpreters, this signifies the idolatrous Canaanites, who were doomed to destruction by divine authority; according to others, this drastic law was enacted for the purpose of discouraging private persons from rashly vowing their slaves or other dependents as offerings to God. Cf Ex 22, 19; Dt 13, 13–19.

27, 13: Lv 22, 14.
27, 18: Lv 25, 15f.
27, 24: Lv 25, 10.28.41.
27, 26: Ex 13, 2.
27, 28: 1 Sm 15, 21.
27, 30: Nm 18, 21.24;
2 Chr 31, 5f.12; Mal 3, 8.10.

Sound the trumpet, beat the drum, we are going to war! The call to arms brings out the best and the worst in people—courage and cowardice, love and hate, hope and fear. The Book of Numbers records the varied experiences of the Israelites as they prepare for the armed conquest of the Promised Land. But most important, it tells of God's insistence that they maintain their purity and holiness to be worthy recipients of God's promises.

At a Glance

I. Preparation for the Departure from Sinai (1, 1—10, 10).

II. From Sinai to the Plains of Moab (10, 11—22, 1).

III. On the Plains of Moab (22, 2—36, 13).

In-depth

Although the Book of Numbers is named for the two censuses mentioned in it (chapters 1 and 26), the book's original Hebrew name, meaning "in the desert," describes it better. Numbers picks up the story of the Israelites where Exodus leaves off. The first section begins with a census at Mount Sinai to determine who is eligible for military service. As the people prepare to enter the Promised Land, their leaders review the laws and regulations with them.

In the second section, the Israelites begin their journey to the Promised Land. Unfortunately, they have not learned to put their faith in God, and their journey is marked by grumbling, rebellion, and even idolatry. When the first army refuses to enter the Promised Land because of reports that it is inhabited by a race of giants (Nm 13, 33), God decrees that none of the older generation who left Egypt shall enter the Promised Land. So, the Israelites begin their desert wandering, which lasts thirty-eight years (see map 2, "The Exodus from Egypt").

The third section of Numbers paints a more hopeful picture. The people of the new generation are faithful and obedient as they prepare to enter the Land. They experience victory against the Midianites (chapter 31) and conquer the land east of the Jordan (chapter 32). The God who liberated their ancestors from Egypt, sustained and led them through the wilderness with Moses, is the same God who now makes ready to fulfill the promise of the Land to Israel.

Numbers was written by priestly scribes hundreds of years after these events, after the people had lost the Promised Land to the Babylonians. They fully appreciated the gift of the Land only after they had lost it. For the Israelites in the Babylonian Exile, Numbers portrayed the hopeful, grateful, and faithful hearts required of those whom God blesses.

Quick Facts

Period Covered
the thirty-eight years of wandering in the desert after the Exodus

Authors
priestly scribes writing during the Babylonian Exile (587–538 B.C.)

Theme
Faithfulness and gratefulness to God are necessary for Israel to obtain the Promised Land.

The Book of *Numbers*

Numbers

Chap. 31

I: Preparation for the Departure from Sinai

The Census

1 ¹ In the year following that of the Israelites' departure from the land of Egypt, on the first day of the second month, the LORD said to Moses in the meeting tent in the desert of Sinai: ²*† "Take a census of the whole community of the Israelites, by clans and ancestral houses, registering each male individually. ³ You and Aaron shall enroll in companies all the men in Israel of twenty years or more who are fit for military service.

Moses' Assistants

⁴ "To assist you there shall be a man from each tribe, the head of his ancestral house. ⁵* These are the names of those who are to assist you:

from Reuben: Elizur, son of Shedeur;
⁶ from Simeon: Shelumiel, son of Zurishaddai;
⁷ from Judah: Nahshon, son of Amminadab;
⁸ from Issachar: Nethanel, son of Zuar;
⁹ from Zebulun: Eliab, son of Helon;
¹⁰ from Ephraim: Elishama, son of Ammihud,
     and from Manasseh: Gamaliel, son of Pedahzur,
     for the descendants of Joseph;

¹¹ from Benjamin: Abidan, son of Gideoni;
¹² from Dan: Ahiezer, son of Ammishaddai;
¹³ from Asher: Pagiel, son of Ochran;
¹⁴ from Gad: Eliasaph, son of Reuel;
¹⁵ from Naphtali: Ahira, son of Enan."

¹⁶*† These were councilors of the community, princes of their ancestral tribes, chiefs of the troops of Israel. ¹⁷ So Moses and Aaron took these men who had been designated, ¹⁸ and assembled the whole community on the first day of the second month. Every man of twenty years or more then declared his name and lineage according to clan and ancestral house, ¹⁹ as the LORD had commanded Moses.

Count of the Twelve Tribes

This is their census as taken in the desert of Sinai ²⁰ Of the descendants of Reuben, the first-born of Israel, registered by lineage in clans and ancestral houses: when all the males of twenty years or more who were fit for military service were polled, ²¹ forty-six thousand five hundred were enrolled in the tribe of Reuben

²² Of the descendants of Simeon, registered by lineage in clans and ancestral houses: when all the males of twenty years or more who were fit for mil-

---

1, 2: All Israel was divided into tribes, each tribe into clans, and each clan into ancestral houses.
1, 16: *Troops:* literally "thousands"; this division of the Israelites, with its subdivisions of "hundreds, fifties and tens," was primarily for military and judicial purposes. Cf Ex 18, 21: 2 Sm 18, 1.

1, 2f: Nm 14, 29; 26, 2–51. **1, 16:** Ex 18, 21.25.
1, 5–15: Nm 10, 14–27.

itary service were polled, 23 fifty-nine thousand three hundred were enrolled in the tribe of Simeon.

24 Of the descendants of Gad, registered by lineage in clans and ancestral houses: when all the males of twenty years or more who were fit for military service were polled, 25 forty-five thousand six hundred and fifty were enrolled in the tribe of Gad.

26 Of the descendants of Judah, registered by lineage in clans and ancestral houses: when all the males of twenty years or more who were fit for military service were polled, 27 seventy-four thousand six hundred were enrolled in the tribe of Judah.

28 Of the descendants of Issachar, registered by lineage in clans and ancestral houses: when all the males of twenty years or more who were fit for military service were polled, 29 fifty-four thousand four hundred were enrolled in the tribe of Issachar.

30 Of the descendants of Zebulun, registered by lineage in clans and ancestral houses: when all the males of twenty years or more who were fit for military service were polled, 31 fifty-seven thousand four hundred were enrolled in the tribe of Zebulun.

32 Of the descendants of Joseph—

Of the descendants of Ephraim, registered by lineage in clans and ancestral houses: when all the males of twenty years or more who were fit for military service were polled, 33 forty thousand five hundred were enrolled in the tribe of Ephraim.

34 Of the descendants of Manasseh, registered by lineage in clans and ancestral houses: when all the males of twenty years or more who were fit for military service were polled, 35 thirty-two thousand two hundred were enrolled in the tribe of Manasseh.

36 Of the descendants of Benjamin, registered by lineage in clans and ancestral houses: when all the males of twenty years or more who were fit for military service were polled, 37 thirty-five thousand four hundred were enrolled in the tribe of Benjamin.

38 Of the descendants of Dan, registered by lineage in clans and ancestral houses: when all the males of twenty years or more who were fit for military service were polled, 39 sixty-two thousand seven hundred were enrolled in the tribe of Dan.

40 Of the descendants of Asher, registered by lineage in clans and ancestral houses: when all the males of twenty years or more who were fit for military service were polled, 41 forty-one thousand five hundred were enrolled in the tribe of Asher.

42 Of the descendants of Naphtali, registered by lineage in clans and ancestral houses: when all the

males of twenty years or more who were fit for military service were polled, 43 fifty-three thousand four hundred were enrolled in the tribe of Naphtali.

44 It was these who were registered, each according to his ancestral house, in the census taken by Moses and Aaron and the twelve princes of Israel. 45 The total number of the Israelites of twenty years or more who were fit for military service, registered by ancestral houses, 46 was six hundred and three thousand five hundred and fifty.

Levites Omitted in the Census

47*† The Levites, however, were not registered by ancestral tribe with the others. 48 For the LORD had told Moses, 49 "The tribe of Levi alone you shall not enroll nor include in the census along with the other Israelites. 50* You are to give the Levites charge of the Dwelling of the commandments with all its equipment and all that belongs to it. It is they who shall carry the Dwelling with all its equipment and who shall be its ministers. They shall therefore camp around the Dwelling. 51* When the Dwelling is to move on, the Levites shall take it down; when the Dwelling is to be pitched, it is the Levites who shall set it up. Any layman who comes near it shall be put to death. 52* While the other Israelites shall camp by companies, each in his own division of the camp, 53* the Levites shall camp around the Dwelling of the commandments. Otherwise God's wrath will strike the Israelite community. The Levites, then, shall have charge of the Dwelling of the commandments." 54 All this the Israelites fulfilled as the LORD had commanded Moses.

Arrangement of the Tribes

2 1 The LORD said to Moses and Aaron: 2* "The Israelites shall camp, each in his own division, under the ensigns of their ancestral houses. They shall camp around the meeting tent, but at some distance from it.

3† "Encamped on the east side, toward the sunrise, shall be the divisional camp of Judah, arranged in companies. [The prince of the Judahites was Nahshon, son of Amminadab, 4 and his soldiers amounted in the census to seventy-four thousand six hundred.] 5 With Judah shall camp the tribe of Issachar [their prince was Nethanel, son of Zuar, 6 and his soldiers amounted in the census to fifty-four thousand four hundred] 7 and the tribe of Zebulun. [Their prince was Eliab, son of Helon, 8 and his soldiers amounted in the census to fifty-seven thousand four hundred. 9 The total number

---

1, 47: The Levites were not enrolled in this census, which was principally for military purposes, but a separate census was made of them. Cf Nm 3, 15f.39.

2, 3–31: A similar arrangement of the tribes around the central sanctuary in the ideal Israelite state is given in Ez 48.

1, 47: Nm 2, 33; 3, 14–39; 26, 57–62.
1, 50: Nm 3, 7f; 4, 2–49; 1 Chr 6, 48.
1, 51: Nm 3, 10.38; 18, 7;
2 Sm 6, 6f; 1 Chr 13, 10.
1, 52: Nm 2, 2.34.
1, 53: Nm 3, 7f.38; 8, 19; 18, 4f.
2, 2: Nm 1, 52.

did you KNOW?

Holy War

The Book of Numbers begins with a census of "all the men in Israel of twenty years or more who are fit for miliary service" (1, 3). The people of Israel are preparing to take over the land God had promised to them, the Chosen People. This is no ordinary war but a holy war, a war that they believe is divinely inspired, even a war God commands. In 31, 2, God says to Moses, "Avenge the Israelites on the Midianites." The Israelites go on to kill every Midianite except for the young girls who are virgins.

How are we to understand this? Does God really order the killing of innocent people? To answer this, let's first remember that the writers of the Bible were influenced by their own cultural background and understanding of God. Three main things were probably on the mind of the writer of Numbers. First, the early Israelites viewed God as a warrior god fighting for them. Second, they believed the Canaanites were a wicked and idolatrous people who deserved punishment. And finally, they believed the Midianites deserved special punishment because they had led the Israelites into idolatry and sin at Shittim (see 25, 1–5).

Holy wars are dangerous. Throughout history, people have committed atrocities in the name of God. Christians must interpret the Old Testament in the light of Jesus' teachings in the New Testament. And Jesus clearly taught about a God of mercy and love, not a God of war and vengeance. This is one area where the New Testament teaching replaces an earlier Old Testament understanding. Holy wars have no place in the lives of Christians.

of those registered by companies in the camp of Judah was one hundred and eighty-six thousand four hundred.] These shall be first on the march.

10 "On the south side shall be the divisional camp of Reuben, arranged in companies. [Their prince was Elizur, son of Shedeur, 11 and his soldiers amounted in the census to forty-six thousand five hundred.] 12 Beside them shall camp the tribe of Simeon [their prince was Shelumiel, son of Zurishaddai, 13 and his soldiers amounted in the census to fifty-nine thousand three hundred] 14 and next the tribe of Gad. [Their prince was Eliasaph, son of Reuel, 15 and his soldiers amounted in the census to forty-five thousand six hundred and fifty. 16 The total number of those registered by companies in the camp of Reuben was one hundred and fifty-one thousand four hundred and fifty.] These shall be second on the march.

17 "Then the meeting tent and the camp of the Levites shall set out in the middle of the line. As in camp, so also on the march, every man shall be in his proper place, with his own division.

18 "On the west side shall be the divisional camp of Ephraim, arranged in companies. [Their prince was Elishama, son of Ammihud, 19 and his soldiers amounted in the census to forty thousand five hundred.] 20 Beside them shall camp the tribe of Manasseh [their prince was Gamaliel, son of Pedahzur, 21 and his soldiers amounted in the census to thirty-two thousand two hundred] 22 and the tribe of Benjamin. [Their prince was Abidan, son of Gideoni, 23 and his soldiers amounted in the census to thirty-five thousand four hundred. 24 The total number of those registered by companies in the camp of Ephraim was one hundred and eight thousand one hundred.] These shall be third on the march.

25 "On the north side shall be the divisional camp of Dan, arranged in companies. [Their prince was Ahiezer, son of Ammishaddai, 26 and his soldiers amounted in the census to sixty-two thousand seven hundred.] 27 Beside them shall camp the tribe of Asher [their prince was Pagiel, son of Ochran, 28 and his soldiers amounted in the census to forty-one thousand five hundred] 29 and next the tribe of Naphtali. [Their prince was Ahira, son of Enan, 30 and his soldiers amounted in the census to fifty-three thousand four hundred. 31 The total number of those registered by companies in the camp of Dan was one hundred and fifty-seven thousand six hundred.] These shall be the last of the divisions on the march."

32* This was the census of the Israelites taken by ancestral houses. The total number of those registered by companies in the camps was six hundred and three thousand five hundred and fifty. 33 The Levites, however, were not registered with the other Israelites, for so the LORD had commanded Moses. 34 The Israelites did just as the LORD had commanded Moses; both in camp and on the march they were in their own divisions, every man according to his clan and his ancestral house.

2, 32–33: Nm 1, 46–49.

The Sons of Aaron

3 ¹ The following were the descendants of Aaron and Moses at the time that the LORD spoke to Moses on Mount Sinai. ²* The sons of Aaron were Nadab his first-born, Abihu, Eleazar, and Ithamar. ³ These are the names of the sons of Aaron, the anointed priests who were ordained to exercise the priesthood. ⁴* But when Nadab and Abihu offered profane fire before the LORD in the desert of Sinai, they met death in the presence of the LORD, and left no sons. Thereafter only Eleazar and Ithamar performed the priestly functions under the direction of their father Aaron.

Levites in Place of the First-born

⁵ Now the LORD said to Moses: ⁶* "Summon the tribe of Levi and present them to Aaron the priest, as his assistants. ⁷* They shall discharge his obligations and those of the whole community before the meeting tent by serving at the Dwelling. ⁸ They shall have custody of all the furnishings of the meeting tent and discharge the duties of the Israelites in the service of the Dwelling. ⁹* You shall give the Levites to Aaron and his sons; they have been set aside from among the Israelites as dedicated to me. ¹⁰* But only Aaron and his descendants shall you appoint to have charge of the priestly functions. Any layman who comes near shall be put to death."

¹¹ The LORD said to Moses, ¹²* "It is I who have chosen the Levites from the Israelites in place of every first-born that opens the womb among the Israelites. The Levites, therefore, are mine, ¹³ because every first-born is mine. When I slew all the first-born in the land of Egypt, I made all the first-born in Israel sacred to me, both of man and of beast. They belong to me; I am the LORD."

Census of the Levites

¹⁴ The LORD said to Moses in the desert of Sinai, ¹⁵* "Take a census of the Levites by ancestral houses and clans, registering every male of a month or more." ¹⁶ Moses, therefore, took their census in accordance with the command the LORD had given him.

¹⁷* The sons of Levi were named Gershon, Kohath and Merari. ¹⁸ The descendants of Gershon, by clans, were named Libni and Shimei. ¹⁹ The descendants of Kohath, by clans, were Amram, Izhar, Hebron and Uzziel. ²⁰ The descendants of Merari, by clans, were Mahli and Mushi. These were the clans of the Levites by ancestral houses.

Duties of the Levitical Clans

²¹ To Gershon belonged the clan of the Libnites and the clan of the Shimeites; these were the clans of the Gershonites. ²² When all their males of a month or more were registered, they numbered seven thousand five hundred. ²³ The clans of the Gershonites camped behind the Dwelling, to the west. ²⁴ The prince of their ancestral house was Eliasaph, son of Lael. ²⁵*† At the meeting tent they had charge of whatever pertained to the Dwelling, the tent and its covering, the curtain at the entrance of the meeting tent, ²⁶ the hangings of the court, the curtain at the entrance of the court enclosing both the Dwelling and the altar, and the ropes.

²⁷ To Kohath belonged the clans of the Amramites, the Izharites, the Hebronites, and the Uzzielites; these were the clans of the Kohathites. ²⁸ When all their males of a month or more were registered, they numbered eight thousand three hundred. They had charge of the sanctuary. ²⁹ The clans of the Kohathites camped at the south side of the Dwelling. ³⁰ The prince of their ancestral house was Elizaphan, son of Uzziel. ³¹† They had charge of whatever pertained to the ark, the table, the lampstand, the altars, the utensils with which the ministry of the sanctuary was exercised, and the veil. ³² The chief prince of the Levites, however, was Eleazar, son of Aaron the priest; he was supervisor over those who had charge of the sanctuary.

³³ To Merari belonged the clans of the Mahlites and the Mushites; these were the clans of Merari. ³⁴ When all their males of a month or more were registered, they numbered six thousand two hundred. ³⁵ The prince of the ancestral house of the clans of Merari was Zuriel, son of Abihail. They camped at the north side of the Dwelling. ³⁶† The Merarites were charged with the care of whatever pertained to the boards of the Dwelling, its bars, columns, pedestals, and all its fittings, ³⁷ as well as the columns of the surrounding court with their pedestals, pegs and ropes.

³⁸ East of the Dwelling, that is, in front of the

---

† **3, 25f:** The Gershonites had two wagons for transporting these things; cf Nm 7, 7. For a description of the Dwelling, see Ex 26, 1–6; the tent, Ex 26, 7–13; its covering, Ex 26, 14; the curtain at the entrance, Ex 26, 36; the hangings of the court, Ex 27, 9–15; the curtain at the entrance of the court, Ex 27, 16; the ropes of the Dwelling, Ex 35, 18.

3, 31: The Kohathites had to carry these sacred objects on their shoulders; cf Nm 7, 9. For a description of the ark, see Ex 25, 10–22; the table, Ex 25, 23–30; the lampstand, Ex 25, 31–40; the altars, Ex 27, 1–8; 30, 1–10.

3, 36f: The Merarites had four wagons for transporting this heavy material; cf Nm 7, 8. For a description of the boards, bars, etc., of the Dwelling, see Ex 26, 15–30; the columns, pedestals, etc., of the court, Ex 27, 9–19.

*
3, 2: Ex 6, 23.	**3, 12f:** Nm 3, 41; 8, 16f;
3, 4: Nm 26, 61; Lv 10, 1f;	Ex 13, 2.12.15.
1 Chr 24, 2.	**3, 15:** Nm 3, 39; 26, 62.
3, 6: Nm 18, 2.	**3, 17–20:** Nm 26, 57; Gn 46, 11;
3, 7: Nm 8, 24.	Ex 6, 16–19; 1 Chr 6,
3, 9: Nm 8, 19.	1f.16–19.
3, 10: Nm 1, 51; 18, 7.	**3, 25–26:** Ex 26, 7.14.36; 36, 14.

meeting tent, toward the sunrise, were camped Moses and Aaron and the latter's sons. They discharged the obligations of the sanctuary for the Israelites. Any layman who came near was to be put to death.

[39] The total number of male Levites a month old or more whom Moses had registered by clans in keeping with the LORD'S command, was twenty-two thousand.

Census and Ransom of First-born

[40] The LORD then said to Moses, "Take a census of all the first-born males of the Israelites a month old or more, and compute their total number. [41] Then assign the Levites to me, the LORD, in place of all the first-born of the Israelites, as well as their cattle in place of all the first-born among the cattle of the Israelites." [42] So Moses took a census of all the first-born of the Israelites, as the LORD had commanded him. [43] When all the first-born males of a month or more were registered, they numbered twenty-two thousand two hundred and seventy-three.

[44] The LORD said to Moses: [45] "Take the Levites in place of all the first-born of the Israelites, and the Levites' cattle in place of their cattle, that the Levites may belong to me. I am the LORD. [46] As ransom for the two hundred and seventy-three first-born of the Israelites who outnumber the Levites, [47]* you shall take five shekels for each individual, according to the standard of the sanctuary shekel, twenty gerahs to the shekel. [48] Give this silver to Aaron and his sons as ransom for the extra number." [49] So Moses took the silver as ransom from those who were left when the rest had been redeemed by the Levites. [50] From the first-born of the Israelites he received in silver one thousand three hundred and sixty-five shekels according to the sanctuary standard. [51] He then gave this ransom silver to Aaron and his sons, as the LORD had commanded him.

Duties Further Defined

4 [1] The LORD said to Moses and Aaron: [2] "Among the Levites take a total of the Kohathites, by clans and ancestral houses, all the men of the Kohathites [3]*† between thirty and fifty years of age; these are to undertake obligatory tasks in the meeting tent.

[4] "The service of the Kohathites in the meeting tent concerns the most sacred objects. [5]† In breaking camp, Aaron and his sons shall go in and take down the screening curtain and cover the ark of the commandments with it. [6] Over these they shall put a cover of tahash skin, and on top of this spread an all-violet cloth. They shall then put the poles in place. [7] On the table of the Presence they shall spread a violet cloth and put on it the plates and cups, as well as the bowls and pitchers for libations; the established bread offering shall remain on the table. [8] Over these they shall spread a scarlet cloth and cover all this with tahash skin. They shall then put the poles in place. [9] They shall use a violet cloth to cover the lampstand with its lamps, trimming shears, and trays, as well as the various containers of oil from which it is supplied. [10] The lampstand with all its utensils they shall then enclose in a covering of tahash skin, and place on a litter. [11]† Over the golden altar they shall spread a violet cloth, and cover this also with a covering of tahash skin. They shall then put the poles in place. [12] Taking the utensils of the sanctuary service, they shall wrap them all in violet cloth and cover them with tahash skin. They shall then place them on a litter. [13]† After cleansing the altar of its ashes, they shall spread a purple cloth over it. [14]† On this they shall put all the utensils with which it is served: the fire pans, forks, shovels, basins, and all the utensils of the altar. They shall then spread a covering of tahash skin over this, and put the poles in place.

[15]* "Only after Aaron and his sons have finished covering the sacred objects and all their utensils on breaking camp, shall the Kohathites enter to carry them. But they shall not touch the sacred objects; if they do they will die. These, then, are the objects in the meeting tent that the Kohathites shall carry.

[16] "Eleazar, son of Aaron the priest, shall be in charge of the oil for the light, the fragrant incense, the established cereal offering, and the anointing oil. He shall be in charge of the whole Dwelling with all the sacred objects and utensils that are in it."

[17] The LORD said to Moses and Aaron: [18] "Do not let the group of Kohathite clans perish from the body of the Levites. [19] That they may live and not die when they approach the most sacred objects, this is what you shall do for them: Aaron and his sons shall go in and assign to each of them his task and what he must carry; [20]* but the Kohathites shall not go in to look upon the sacred objects, even for an instant; if they do, they will die."

[21] The LORD said to Moses, [22] "Take a total

---

† **4, 3:** *Thirty:* at a later period the Levites began to serve when they were twenty-five (Nm 8, 24) or even only twenty years old (1 Chr 23, 24.27; 2 Chr 31, 17; Ezr 3, 8; but cf 1 Chr 23, 3).
4, 5: *The screening curtain:* the veil between the inner and the outer rooms of the sanctuary. Cf Ex 26, 31–33.
4, 11: *The golden altar:* the altar of incense. Cf Ex 30, 1–6.
4, 13: *The altar:* the bronze altar of holocausts. Cf Ex 27, 1–8.

4, 14: *Forks:* used in turning over the sacrificed animal on the fire of the altar. *Basins:* to receive the sacrificial blood; cf Zec 9, 15.

3, 47: Nm 18, 16; Ex 30, 13; Lv 27, 25; Ez 45, 12.
4, 3: Nm 8, 24; 1 Chr 23, 24–27.
4, 15: 2 Sm 6, 6f; 1 Chr 13, 9f.
4, 20: 1 Sm 6, 19.

among the Gershonites also, by ancestral houses and clans, 23 of all the men between thirty and fifty years of age; these are to undertake obligatory tasks in the meeting tent. 24 This is the task of the clans of the Gershonites, what they must do and what they must carry: 25 they shall carry the sheets of the Dwelling, the meeting tent with its covering and the outer wrapping of tahash skin, the curtain at the entrance of the meeting tent, 26 the hangings of the court, the curtain at the entrance of the court that encloses both the Dwelling and the altar, together with their ropes and all other objects necessary in their use. Whatever is to be done with these things shall be their task. 27 The service of the Gershonites shall be entirely under the direction of Aaron and his sons, with regard to what they must do and what they must carry; you shall make each man of them responsible for what he is to carry. 28 This, then, is the task of the Gershonites in the meeting tent; and they shall be under the supervision of Ithamar, son of Aaron the priest.

29 "Among the Merarites, too, you shall enroll by clans and ancestral houses 30 all their men between thirty and fifty years of age; these are to undertake obligatory tasks in the meeting tent. 31* This is what they shall be responsible for carrying, all the years of their service in the meeting tent: the boards of the Dwelling with its bars, columns and pedestals, 32 and the columns of the surrounding court with their pedestals, pegs and ropes. You shall designate for each man of them all the objects connected with his service, which he shall be responsible for carrying. 33 This, then, is the task of the clans of the Merarites during all their service in the meeting tent under the supervision of Ithamar, son of Aaron the priest."

Number of Adult Levites

34 So Moses and Aaron and the princes of the community made a registration among the Kohathites, by clans and ancestral houses, 35 of all the men between thirty and fifty years of age. These were to undertake obligatory tasks in the meeting tent; 36 as registered by clans, they numbered two thousand seven hundred and fifty. 37 Such was the census of all the men of the Kohathite clans who were to serve in the meeting tent, which Moses took, together with Aaron, as the LORD bade him.

38 The registration was then made among the Gershonites, by clans and ancestral houses, 39 of all the men between thirty and fifty years of age. These were to undertake obligatory tasks in the meeting tent; 40 as registered by clans and ancestral houses, they numbered two thousand six hundred and thirty. 41 Such was the census of all the men of the Gershonite clans who were to serve in the meeting tent, which Moses took, together with Aaron, at the LORD's bidding.

42 Then the registration was made among the Merarites, by clans and ancestral houses, 43 of all the men from thirty up to fifty years of age. These were to undertake obligatory tasks in the meeting tent; 44 as registered by clans, they numbered three thousand two hundred. 45 Such was the census of the men of the Merarite clans which Moses took, together with Aaron, as the LORD bade him.

46 Therefore, when Moses and Aaron and the Israelite princes had completed the registration among the Levites, by clans and ancestral houses, 47 of all the men between thirty and fifty years of age who were to undertake tasks of service or transport of the meeting tent, 48 the total number registered was eight thousand five hundred and eighty. 49 According to the LORD's bidding to Moses, they gave them their individual assignments for service and for transport; so the LORD had commanded Moses.

The Unclean Expelled

5 1 The LORD said to Moses: 2*† "Order the Israelites to expel from camp every leper, and everyone suffering from a discharge, and everyone who has become unclean by contact with a corpse. 3* Male and female alike, you shall compel them to go out of the camp; they are not to defile the camp in which I dwell." 4 The Israelites obeyed the command that the LORD had given Moses; they expelled them from the camp.

Unjust Possession

5† The LORD said to Moses, 6* "Tell the Israelites: If a man (or woman) commits a fault against his fellow man and wrongs him, thus breaking faith with the LORD, 7 he shall confess the wrong he has done, restore his ill-gotten goods in full, and in addition give one fifth of their value to the one he has wronged. 8† However, if the latter has no next of kin to whom restoration of the ill-gotten goods can

---

5, 2: For the laws regarding victims of leprosy, see Lv 13–14; those suffering from a discharge, Lv 15; the unclean by contact with a corpse, Nm 19, 11–22; Lv 21, 1–4.

5, 5–10: The basic law on unjust possession is given in Lv 5, 14–26. The new item here concerns the case where the injured party has died and left no heirs, in which case the restitution must be made to the priest.

5, 8: Next of kin: literally, "redeemer," a technical term denoting

the nearest relative, upon whom devolved the obligation of "redeeming" the family property, in order to keep it within the family. Cf Lv 25, 25; Ru 4, 1–6.

4, 31: Nm 3, 36f.   **5, 3:** Nm 35, 34.
  5, 2: Nm 19, 11.13; Lv 13,   **5, 6ff:** Lv 5, 21–25.
    46; 21, 1; 22, 4.

be made, the goods to be restored shall be the LORD'S and shall fall to the priest; this is apart from the atonement ram with which the priest makes amends for the guilty man. [9]* Likewise, every sacred contribution that the Israelites are bound to make shall fall to the priest. [10]* Each Israelite man may dispose of his own sacred contributions; they become the property of the priest to whom he gives them."

Ordeal for a Suspected Adulteress

[11] The LORD said to Moses, [12] "Speak to the Israelites and tell them: If a man's wife goes astray and becomes unfaithful to him [13]* by having intercourse with another man, though her husband has not sufficient evidence of the fact, so that her impurity remains unproved for lack of a witness who might have caught her in the act; [14] or if a man is overcome by a feeling of jealousy that makes him suspect his wife, whether she was actually impure or not: [15] he shall bring his wife to the priest and shall take along as an offering for her a tenth of an ephah of barley meal. However, he shall not pour oil on it nor put frankincense over it, since it is a cereal offering of jealousy, a cereal offering for an appeal in a question of guilt.

[16] "The priest shall first have the woman come forward and stand before the LORD. [17]*† In an earthen vessel he shall meanwhile put some holy water, as well as some dust that he has taken from the floor of the Dwelling. [18]† Then, as the woman stands before the LORD, the priest shall uncover her head and place in her hands the cereal offering of her appeal, that is, the cereal offering of jealousy, while he himself shall hold the bitter water that brings a curse. [19] Then he shall adjure the woman, saying to her, 'If no other man has had intercourse with you, and you have not gone astray by impurity while under the authority of your husband, be immune to the curse brought by this bitter water. [20] But if you have gone astray while under the authority of your husband and have acted impurely by letting a man other than your husband have intercourse with you'— [21]† so shall the priest adjure the woman with this oath of imprecation—'may the

LORD make you an example of malediction and imprecation among your people by causing your thighs to waste away and your belly to swell! [22]*† May this water, then, that brings a curse, enter your body to make your belly swell and your thighs waste away!' And the woman shall say, 'Amen, amen!' [23] The priest shall put these imprecations in writing and shall then wash them off into the bitter water, [24] which he is to have the woman drink, so that it may go into her with all its bitter curse. [25] But first he shall take the cereal offering of jealousy from the woman's hand, and having waved this offering before the LORD, shall put it near the altar, [26]* where he shall take a handful of the cereal offering as its token offering and burn it on the altar. Only then shall he have the woman drink the water. [27] Once she has done so, if she has been impure and unfaithful to her husband, this bitter water that brings a curse will go into her, and her belly will swell and her thighs will waste away, so that she will become an example of imprecation among her people. [28] If, however, the woman has not defiled herself, but is still pure, she will be immune and will still be able to bear children.

[29] "This, then, is the law for jealousy: When a woman goes astray while under the authority of her husband and acts impurely, [30] or when such a feeling of jealousy comes over a man that he becomes suspicious of his wife, he shall have her stand before the LORD, and the priest shall apply this law in full to her. [31]† The man shall be free from guilt, but the woman shall bear such guilt as she may have."

Laws Concerning Nazirites

6 [1] The LORD said to Moses: [2]† "Speak to the Israelites and tell them: When a man (or a woman) solemnly takes the nazirite vow to dedicate himself to the LORD, [3]* he shall abstain from wine and strong drink; he may neither drink wine vinegar, other vinegar, or any kind of grape juice, nor eat either fresh or dried grapes. [4] As long as he is a nazirite he shall not eat anything of the produce of the vine; not even unripe grapes or grapeskins. [5]* While he is under the nazirite vow, no razor shall touch his hair. Until the period of his dedication to

---

5, 17: *Holy water:* water from the laver that stood in the court of the Dwelling.

5, 18: *Appeal:* by which she invokes the Lord and refers her case to his decision.

5, 21: *An example of malediction and imprecation:* the woman's name would be used in curses and oaths to invoke a similar misfortune on another person or on oneself. Cf Is 65, 15; Jer 29, 22.

5, 22: *Amen:* a Hebrew word meaning, "certainly, truly," used to give assent to a statement, a curse, a blessing, a prayer, or the like; in this sense of "so be it," the Christian liturgy also uses it after prayers and blessings.

5, 31: *Free from guilt:* by fulfilling his obligation of obtaining a decision in the matter.

6, 1ff: *Nazirite:* from the Hebrew word *nazir,* meaning "set apart

as sacred, dedicated, vowed." The nazirite vow could be either for a limited period or for life. Those bound by this vow had to abstain from all the products of the grapevine, from cutting or shaving their hair, and from contact with a corpse. They were regarded as men of God like the prophets; cf Am 2, 11f. Examples of lifelong nazirites were Samson (Jgs 13, 4f.7; 16, 17), Samuel (1 Sm 1, 11), and John the Baptizer (Lk 1, 15). At the time of Christ the practice of taking the nazirite vow for a limited period seems to have been quite common, even among the early Christians; cf Acts 18, 18; 21, 23f.26.

5, 9: Dt 18, 3f; Ex 44, 29f.   **5, 26:** Lv 5, 12.
5, 10: Lv 10, 12–15.   **6, 3f:** Jgs 13, 7.14.
5, 13: Lv 18, 20; Jn 8, 4.   **6, 5:** Jgs 13, 5; 16, 17; 1 Sm
5, 17: Nm 19, 17.   1, 11.
5, 22: Ps 109, 18.

the LORD is over, he shall be sacred, and shall let the hair of his head grow freely. [6]* As long as he is dedicated to the LORD, he shall not enter where a dead person is. [7] Not even for his father or mother, his sister or brother, should they die, may he become unclean, since his head bears his dedication to God. [8] As long as he is a nazirite he is sacred to the LORD.

[9] "If someone dies very suddenly in his presence, so that his dedicated head becomes unclean, he shall shave his head on the day of his purification, that is, on the seventh day. [10] On the eighth day he shall bring two turtledoves or two pigeons to the priest at the entrance of the meeting tent. [11] The priest shall offer up the one as a sin offering and the other as a holocaust, thus making atonement for him for the sin he has committed by reason of the dead person. On the same day he shall reconsecrate his head [12] and begin anew the period of his dedication to the LORD as a nazirite, bringing a yearling lamb as a guilt offering. The previous period is not valid, because his dedicated head became unclean.

[13]* "This is the ritual for the nazirite: On the day he completes the period of his dedication he shall go to the entrance of the meeting tent, [14] bringing as his offering to the LORD one unblemished yearling lamb for a holocaust, one unblemished yearling ewe lamb for a sin offering, one unblemished ram as a peace offering, along with their cereal offerings and libations, [15] and a basket of unleavened cakes of fine flour mixed with oil and of unleavened wafers spread with oil. [16] The priest shall present them before the LORD, and shall offer up the sin offering and the holocaust for him. [17] He shall then offer up the ram as a peace offering to the LORD, with its cereal offering and libation, and the basket of unleavened cakes. [18]* Then at the entrance of the meeting tent the nazirite shall shave his dedicated head, collect the hair, and put it in the fire that is under the peace offering. [19] After the nazirite has shaved off his dedicated hair, the priest shall take a boiled shoulder of the ram, as well as one unleavened cake and one unleavened wafer from the basket, and shall place them in the hands of the nazirite. [20] The priest shall then wave them as a wave offering before the LORD. They become sacred and shall belong to the priest, along with the breast of the wave offering and the leg of the raised offering. Only after this may the nazirite drink wine.

[21] "This, then, is the law for the nazirite; this is the offering to the LORD which is included in his vow of dedication apart from anything else which his means may allow. Thus shall he carry out the law of his dedication in keeping with the vow he has taken."

The Priestly Blessing

[22] The LORD said to Moses: [23] "Speak to Aaron and his sons and tell them: This is how you shall bless the Israelites. Say to them:

[24]   The LORD bless you and keep you!
[25]†   The LORD let his face shine upon you, and be gracious to you!
[26]†   The LORD look upon you kindly and give you peace!

[27] So shall they invoke my name upon the Israelites, and I will bless them."

God Bless You

A very old blessing in Nm 6, 22–27 (some of which is repeated in Ps 4, 7 and 67, 1) was not originally a Christian blessing, but its three parts remind us of Christian blessings calling on the Trinity.

This blessing is a good one for special occasions. You could write it on a card for a birthday, Mother's Day or Father's Day, a wedding anniversary, or any other special event. Or you could use it to make a poster or an engraving for a first Communion, a wedding, or a confirmation.

If this blessing sounds familiar, maybe it's because on New Year's Day (the feast of Mary, mother of God), we hear it as the first reading. It's the perfect way to start the new year.

▸ Nm 6, 22–27

Offerings of Princes

7 [1]* Now, when Moses had completed the erection of the Dwelling and had anointed and consecrated it with all its equipment (as well as the altar with all its equipment), [2] an offering was made by the princes of Israel, who were heads of ancestral houses; the same princes of the tribes who supervised the census. [3] The offering they brought

---

†
6, 25: *Let his face shine:* a Hebrew idiom for "smile."
6, 26: *Peace:* the Hebrew word includes the idea of "prosperity, happiness."

*
6, 6: Nm 19, 11.16; Lv 21, 11.
6, 13: Acts 21, 24.26.
6, 18: Acts 18, 18; 21, 24.
7, 1: Ex 40, 17.

before the LORD consisted of six baggage wagons and twelve oxen, that is, a wagon for every two princes, and an ox for every prince. These they presented as their offering before the Dwelling.

4 The LORD then said to Moses, 5 "Accept their offering, that these things may be put to use in the service of the meeting tent. Assign them to the Levites, to each group in proportion to its duties." 6 So Moses accepted the wagons and oxen, and assigned them to the Levites. 7* He gave two wagons and four oxen to the Gershonites in proportion to their duties, 8 and four wagons and eight oxen to the Merarites in proportion to their duties, under the supervision of Ithamar, son of Aaron the priest. 9* He gave none to the Kohathites, because they had to carry on their shoulders the sacred objects which were their charge.

10* For the dedication of the altar also, the princes brought offerings before the altar on the day it was anointed. 11 But the LORD said to Moses, "Let one prince a day present his offering for the dedication of the altar."

12† The one who presented his offering on the first day was Nahshon, son of Amminadab, prince of the tribe of Judah. 13 His offering consisted of one silver plate weighing a hundred and thirty shekels according to the sanctuary standard and one silver basin weighing seventy shekels, both filled with fine flour mixed with oil for a cereal offering; 14 one gold cup of ten shekels' weight filled with incense; 15 one young bull, one ram, and one yearling lamb for a holocaust; 16 one goat for a sin offering; 17 and two oxen, five rams, five goats, and five yearling lambs for a peace offering. This was the offering of Nahshon, son of Amminadab.

18 On the second day Nethanel, son of Zuar, prince of Issachar, made his offering. 19 He presented as his offering one silver plate weighing a hundred and thirty shekels according to the sanctuary standard and one silver basin weighing seventy shekels, both filled with fine flour mixed with oil for a cereal offering; 20 one gold cup of ten shekels' weight filled with incense; 21 one young bull, one ram, and one yearling lamb for a holocaust; 22 one goat for a sin offering; 23 and two oxen, five rams, five goats, and five yearling lambs for a peace offering. This was the offering of Nethanel, son of Zuar.

24 On the third day it was the turn of Eliab, son of Helon, prince of the Zebulunites. 25 His offering consisted of one silver plate weighing a hundred and thirty shekels according to the sanctuary standard and one silver basin weighing seventy shekels, both filled with fine flour mixed with oil for a ce-

real offering; 26 one gold cup of ten shekels' weight filled with incense; 27 one young bull, one ram, and one yearling lamb for a holocaust; 28 one goat for a sin offering; 29 and two oxen, five rams, five goats, and five yearling lambs for a peace offering. This was the offering of Eliab, son of Helon.

30 On the fourth day it was the turn of Elizur, son of Shedeur, prince of the Reubenites. 31 His offering consisted of one silver plate weighing a hundred and thirty shekels according to the sanctuary standard and one silver basin weighing seventy shekels, both filled with fine flour mixed with oil for a cereal offering; 32 one gold cup of ten shekels' weight filled with incense; 33 one young bull, one ram, and one yearling lamb for a holocaust; 34 one goat for a sin offering; 35 and two oxen, five rams, five goats, and five yearling lambs for a peace offering. This was the offering of Elizur, son of Shedeur.

36 On the fifth day it was the turn of Shelumiel, son of Zurishaddai, prince of the Simeonites. 37 His offering consisted of one silver plate weighing a hundred and thirty shekels according to the sanctuary standard and one silver basin weighing seventy shekels, both filled with fine flour mixed with oil for a cereal offering; 38 one gold cup of ten shekels' weight filled with incense; 39 one young bull, one ram, and one yearling lamb for a holocaust; 40 one goat for a sin offering; 41 and two oxen, five rams, five goats, and five yearling lambs for a peace offering. This was the offering of Shelumiel, son of Zurishaddai.

42 On the sixth day it was the turn of Eliasaph, son of Reuel, prince of the Gadites. 43 His offering consisted of one silver plate weighing a hundred and thirty shekels according to the sanctuary standard and one silver basin weighing seventy shekels, both filled with fine flour mixed with oil for a cereal offering; 44 one gold cup of ten shekels' weight filled with incense; 45 one young bull, one ram, and one yearling lamb for a holocaust; 46 one goat for a sin offering; 47 and two oxen, five rams, five goats, and five yearling lambs for a peace offering. This was the offering of Eliasaph, son of Reuel.

48 On the seventh day it was the turn of Elishama, son of Ammihud, prince of the Ephraimites. 49 His offering consisted of one silver plate weighing a hundred and thirty shekels according to the sanctuary standard and one silver basin weighing seventy shekels, both filled with fine flour mixed with oil for a cereal offering; 50 one gold cup of ten shekels' weight filled with incense; 51 one young bull, one ram, and one yearling lamb for a holocaust; 52 one goat for a sin offering; 53 and two oxen, five rams, five goats, and five yearling lambs

---

† **7, 12–88:** The repetitious account of the same offerings brought by each of the twelve tribal princes and the summary of them are characteristic of an official registration.

7, 7f: Nm 4, 24–33.   7, 10: Nm 7, 84.
7, 9: Nm 3, 31; 4, 4–15.

for a peace offering. This was the offering of Elishama, son of Ammihud.

⁵⁴ On the eighth day it was the turn of Gamaliel, son of Pedahzur, prince of the Manassehites. ⁵⁵ His offering consisted of one silver plate weighing a hundred and thirty shekels according to the sanctuary standard and one silver basin weighing seventy shekels, both filled with fine flour mixed with oil for a cereal offering; ⁵⁶ one gold cup of ten shekels' weight filled with incense; ⁵⁷ one young bull, one ram, and one yearling lamb for a holocaust; ⁵⁸ one goat for a sin offering; ⁵⁹ and two oxen, five rams, five goats, and five yearling lambs for a peace offering. This was the offering of Gamaliel, son of Pedahzur.

⁶⁰ On the ninth day it was the turn of Abidan, son of Gideoni, prince of the Benjaminites. ⁶¹ His offering consisted of one silver plate weighing a hundred and thirty shekels according to the sanctuary standard and one silver basin weighing seventy shekels, both filled with fine flour mixed with oil for a cereal offering; ⁶² one gold cup of ten shekels' weight filled with incense; ⁶³ one young bull, one ram, and one yearling lamb for a holocaust; ⁶⁴ one goat for a sin offering; ⁶⁵ and two oxen, five rams, five goats, and five yearling lambs for a peace offering. This was the offering of Abidan, son of Gideoni.

⁶⁶ On the tenth day it was the turn of Ahiezer, son of Ammishaddai, prince of the Danites. ⁶⁷ His offering consisted of one silver plate weighing a hundred and thirty shekels according to the sanctuary standard and one silver basin weighing seventy shekels, both filled with fine flour mixed with oil for a cereal offering; ⁶⁸ one gold cup of ten shekels' weight filled with incense; ⁶⁹ one young bull, one ram, and one yearling lamb for a holocaust; ⁷⁰ one goat for a sin offering; ⁷¹ and two oxen, five rams, five goats, and five yearling lambs for a peace offering. This was the offering of Ahiezer, son of Ammishaddai.

⁷² On the eleventh day it was the turn of Pagiel, son of Ochran, prince of the Asherites. ⁷³ His offering consisted of one silver plate weighing a hundred and thirty shekels according to the sanctuary standard and one silver basin weighing seventy shekels, both filled with fine flour mixed with oil for a cereal offering; ⁷⁴ one gold cup of ten shekels' weight filled with incense; ⁷⁵ one young bull, one ram, and one yearling lamb for a holocaust; ⁷⁶ one goat for a sin offering; ⁷⁷ and two oxen, five rams, five goats, and five yearling lambs for a peace offering. This was the offering of Pagiel, son of Ochran.

⁷⁸ On the twelfth day it was the turn of Ahira, son of Enan, prince of the Naphtalites. ⁷⁹ His offering consisted of one silver plate weighing a hundred and thirty shekels according to the sanctuary standard and one silver basin weighing seventy shekels, both filled with fine flour mixed with oil for a cereal offering; ⁸⁰ one gold cup of ten shekels' weight filled with incense; ⁸¹ one young bull, one ram, and one yearling lamb for a holocaust; ⁸² one goat for a sin offering; ⁸³ and two oxen, five rams, five goats, and five yearling lambs for a peace offering. This was the offering of Ahira, son of Enan.

⁸⁴ These were the offerings for the dedication of the altar, given by the princes of Israel on the occasion of its anointing: twelve silver plates, twelve silver basins, and twelve gold cups. ⁸⁵ Each silver plate weighed a hundred and thirty shekels, and each silver basin seventy, so that all the silver of these vessels amounted to two thousand four hundred shekels, according to the sanctuary standard. ⁸⁶ The twelve gold cups that were filled with incense weighed ten shekels apiece, according to the sanctuary standard, so that all the gold of the cups amounted to one hundred and twenty shekels. ⁸⁷ The animals for the holocausts were, in all, twelve young bulls, twelve rams, and twelve yearling lambs, with their cereal offerings; those for the sin offerings were twelve goats. ⁸⁸ The animals for the peace offerings were, in all, twenty-four oxen, sixty rams, sixty goats, and sixty yearling lambs. These, then, were the offerings for the dedication of the altar after it was anointed.

The Voice

⁸⁹* When Moses entered the meeting tent to speak with him, he heard the voice addressing him from above the propitiatory on the ark of the commandments, from between the two cherubim; and it spoke to him. . . .

The Lamps Set Up

8 ¹ The LORD spoke to Moses, and said, ²* "Give Aaron this command: When you set up the seven lamps, have them throw their light toward the front of the lampstand." ³ Aaron did so, setting up the lamps to face toward the front of the lampstand, just as the LORD had commanded Moses. ⁴* The lampstand was made of beaten gold in both its shaft and its branches, according to the pattern which the LORD had shown Moses.

Purification of the Levites

⁵ The LORD said to Moses: ⁶† "Take the Levites from among the Israelites and purify them. ⁷† This is what

---

8, 6: *Purify them:* in the language of the Pentateuch only the priests were "consecrated," that is, made sacred or set aside for the Lord, in an elaborate ceremony described in Ex 29; Lv 8. The Levites were merely "purified," that is, made ritually clean for their special work.

8, 7: *Water of remission:* literally, "water of sin," that is, for the remission of sin.

7, 89: Ex 25, 22.   8, 4: Ex 25, 31.40.
8, 2: Ex 25, 37.

you shall do to them to purify them. Sprinkle them with the water of remission; then have them shave their whole bodies and wash their clothes, and so purify themselves. 8 They shall take a young bull, along with its cereal offering of fine flour mixed with oil; you shall take another young bull for a sin offering. 9 Then have the Levites come forward in front of the meeting tent, where you shall assemble also the whole community of the Israelites. 10 While the Levites are present before the LORD, the Israelites shall lay their hands upon them. 11 Let Aaron then offer the Levites before the LORD as a wave offering from the Israelites, thus devoting them to the service of the LORD. 12 The Levites in turn shall lay their hands on the heads of the bullocks, which shall then be immolated, the one as a sin offering and the other as a holocaust to the LORD, in atonement for the Levites. 13 Thus, then, shall you have the Levites stand before Aaron and his sons, to be offered as a wave offering to the LORD; 14* and thus shall you set aside the Levites from the rest of the Israelites, that they may be mine.

15 "Only then shall the Levites enter upon their service in the meeting tent. You shall purify them and offer them as a wave offering; 16* because they, among the Israelites, are strictly dedicated to me; I have taken them for myself in place of every first-born that opens the womb among the Israelites. 17* Indeed, all the first-born among the Israelites, both of man and of beast, belong to me; I consecrated them to myself on the day I slew all the first-born in the land of Egypt. 18 But in place of all the first-born Israelites I have taken the Levites; 19* and I have given these dedicated Israelites to Aaron and his sons to discharge the duties of the Israelites in the meeting tent and to make atonement for them, so that no plague may strike among the Israelites should they come near the sanctuary."

20 Thus, then, did Moses and Aaron and the whole community of the Israelites deal with the Levites, carrying out exactly the command which the LORD had given Moses concerning them. 21† When the Levites had cleansed themselves of sin and washed their clothes, Aaron offered them as a wave offering before the LORD, and made atonement for them to purify them. 22 Only then did they enter upon their service in the meeting tent under the supervision of Aaron and his sons. The command which the LORD had given Moses concerning the Levites was carried out.

Age Limits for Levitical Service

23 The LORD said to Moses: 24* "This is the rule for the Levites. Each from his twenty-fifth year onward shall perform the required service in the meeting tent. 25 When he is fifty years old, he shall retire from the required service and work no longer. 26 His service with his fellow Levites shall consist in sharing their responsibilities in the meeting tent, but he shall not do the work. This, then, is how you are to regulate the duties of the Levites."

Second Passover

9 1 In the first month of the year following their departure from the land of Egypt, the LORD said to Moses in the desert of Sinai, 2 "Tell the Israelites to celebrate the Passover at the prescribed time. 3* The evening twilight of the fourteenth day of this month is the prescribed time when you shall celebrate it, observing all its rules and regulations." 4 Moses, therefore, told the Israelites to celebrate the Passover. 5 And they did so, celebrating the Passover in the desert of Sinai during the evening twilight of the fourteenth day of the first month, just as the LORD had commanded Moses.

6 There were some, however, who were unclean because of a human corpse and so could not keep the Passover that day. These men came up to Moses and Aaron that same day 7 and said, "Although we are unclean because of a corpse, why should we be deprived of presenting the LORD'S offering at its proper time along with the other Israelites?" 8 Moses answered them, "Wait until I learn what the LORD will command in your regard."

9 The LORD then said to Moses: 10 "Speak to the Israelites and say: If any one of you or of your descendants is unclean because of a corpse, or if he is absent on a journey, he may still keep the LORD'S Passover. 11* But he shall keep it in the second month, during the evening twilight of the fourteenth day of that month, eating it with unleavened bread and bitter herbs, 12* and not leaving any of it over till morning, nor breaking any of its bones, but observing all the rules of the Passover. 13 However, anyone who is clean and not away on a journey, who yet fails to keep the Passover, shall be cut off from his people, because he did not present the LORD'S offering at the prescribed time. That man shall bear the consequences of his sin.

14*† "If an alien who lives among you wishes to keep the LORD'S Passover, he too shall observe the

† 8, 21: Cleansed themselves of sin: by having the "water of remission" sprinkled on them as prescribed in v 7.
9, 14: An alien: this passage presupposes that he is already circumcised as prescribed in Ex 12, 48.

8, 14: Nm 3, 45.
8, 16: Nm 3, 12.45.
8, 17: Nm 3, 13; 13, 2; Lk 2, 23.
8, 19: Nm 3, 9f.

8, 24: Nm 4, 3.23.
9, 3: Ex 12, 6; Lv 23, 5.
9, 11: 2 Chr 30, 2–15.
9, 12: Ex 12, 46; Jn 19, 36.
9, 14: Ex 12, 48f.

rules and regulations for the Passover. You shall have the same law for the resident alien as for the native of the land."

The Fiery Cloud

15*† On the day when the Dwelling was erected, the cloud covered the Dwelling, the tent of the commandments; but from evening until morning it took on the appearance of fire over the Dwelling. 16 It was always so: during the day the Dwelling was covered by the cloud, which at night had the appearance of fire. 17* Whenever the cloud rose from the tent, the Israelites would break camp; wherever the cloud came to rest, they would pitch camp. 18* At the bidding of the LORD the Israelites moved on, and at his bidding they encamped. As long as the cloud stayed over the Dwelling, they remained in camp.

19 Even when the cloud tarried many days over the Dwelling, the Israelites obeyed the LORD and would not move on; 20 yet sometimes the cloud was over the Dwelling only for a few days. It was at the bidding of the LORD that they stayed in camp, and it was at his bidding that they departed. 21 Sometimes the cloud remained there only from evening until morning; and when it rose in the morning, they would depart. Or if the cloud lifted during the day, or even at night, they would then set out. 22 Whether the cloud tarried over the Dwelling for two days or for a month or longer, the Israelites remained in camp and did not depart; but when it lifted, they moved on. 23 Thus, it was always at the bidding of the LORD that they encamped, and at his bidding that they set out; ever heeding the charge of the LORD, as he had bidden them through Moses.

The Silver Trumpets

10 1 The LORD said to Moses: 2 "Make two trumpets of beaten silver, which you shall use in assembling the community and in breaking camp. 3 When both are blown, the whole community shall gather round you at the entrance of the meeting tent; 4 but when one of them is blown, only the princes, the chiefs of the troops of Israel, shall gather round you. 5 When you sound the first alarm, those encamped on the east side shall set out; 6 when you sound the second alarm, those encamped on the south side shall set out; when you sound the third alarm, those encamped on the west side shall set out; when you sound the fourth alarm, those encamped on the north side shall set out. Thus shall the alarm be sounded for

them to depart. 7 But in calling forth an assembly you are to blow an ordinary blast, without sounding the alarm.

8 "It is the sons of Aaron, the priests, who shall blow the trumpets; and the use of them is prescribed by perpetual statute for you and your descendants. 9* When in your own land you go to war against an enemy that is attacking you, you shall sound the alarm on the trumpets, and the LORD, your God, will remember you and save you from your foes. 10*† On your days of celebration, your festivals, and your new-moon feasts, you shall blow the trumpets over your holocausts and your peace offerings; this will serve as a reminder of you before your God. I, the LORD, am your God."

II: From Sinai to the Plains of Moab

Departure from Sinai

11 In the second year, on the twentieth day of the second month, the cloud rose from the Dwelling of the commandments. 12 The Israelites moved on from the desert of Sinai by stages, until the cloud came to rest in the desert of Paran.

13 The first time that they broke camp at the bidding of the LORD through Moses, 14* the camp of the Judahites, under its own standard and arranged in companies, was the first to set out. Nahshon, son of Amminadab, was over their host, 15 and Nethanel, son of Zuar, over the host of the tribe of Issachar, 16 and Eliab, son of Helon, over the host of the tribe of Zebulun. 17 Then, after the Dwelling was dismantled, the clans of Gershon and Merari set out, carrying the Dwelling. 18 The camp of the Reubenites, under its own standard and arranged in companies, was the next to set out, with Elizur, son of Shedeur, over their host, 19 and Shelumiel, son of Zurishaddai, over the host of the tribe of Simeon, 20 and Eliasaph, son of Reuel, over the host of the tribe of Gad. 21 The clan of Kohath then set out, carrying the sacred objects for the Dwelling, which was to be erected before their arrival. 22 The camp of the Ephraimites next set out, under its own standard and arranged in companies, with Elishama, son of Ammihud, over their host, 23 and Gamaliel, son of Pedahzur, over the host of the tribe of Manasseh, 24 and Abidan, son of Gideoni, over the host of the tribe of Benjamin. 25 Finally, as rear guard for all the camps, the camp of the Danites set out, under its own standard and arranged in companies, with Ahiezer, son of Amishaddai, over their host, 26 and

---

9, 15: *The cloud:* already mentioned at the departure from Egypt; cf Ex 13, 21f.

10, 10: *Days of celebration:* special holidays, such as the occasion of a victory. *Festivals:* the great annual feasts of the Passover, Pentecost and Booths described in Lv 23; Nm 28–29.

9, 15: Ex 13, 21.
9, 17: Wis 18, 3.
9, 18: 1 Cor 10, 1.
10, 9: 2 Chr 13, 14.

10, 10: Nm 29, 1; 2 Chr 29, 26ff.
10, 14ff: Nm 2, 3.5.7.

Pagiel, son of Ochran, over the host of the tribe of Asher, 27 and Ahira, son of Enan, over the host of the tribe of Naphtali. 28 This was the order of departure for the Israelites, company by company.

Hobab as Guide

As they were setting out, 29 Moses said to his brother-in-law Hobab, son of Reuel the Midianite, "We are setting out for the place which the LORD has promised to give us. Come with us, and we will be generous toward you, for the LORD has promised prosperity to Israel." 30† But he answered, "No, I will not come. I am going instead to my own country and to my own kindred." 31 Moses said, "Please, do not leave us; you know where we can camp in the desert, and you will serve as eyes for us. 32 If you come with us, we will share with you the prosperity the LORD will bestow on us."

Into the Desert

33*† They moved on from the mountain of the LORD, a three days' journey, and the ark of the covenant of the LORD which was to seek out their resting place went the three days' journey with them. 34 And when they set out from camp, the cloud of the LORD was over them by day.

35 Whenever the ark set out, Moses would say,

"Arise, O LORD, that your enemies may
be scattered,
and those who hate you may flee
before you."

36 And when it came to rest, he would say,

"Return, O LORD, you who ride upon
the clouds,
to the troops of Israel."

Discontent of the People

11 1* Now the people complained in the hearing of the LORD; and when he heard it his wrath flared up so that the fire of the LORD burned among them and consumed the outskirts of the camp. 2 But when the people cried out to Moses, he prayed to the LORD and the fire died out. 3† Hence that place was called Taberah, because there the fire of the LORD burned among them.

4* The foreign elements among them were so greedy for meat that even the Israelites lamented

again, "Would that we had meat for food! 5 We remember the fish we used to eat without cost in Egypt, and the cucumbers, the melons, the leeks, the onions, and the garlic. 6* But now we are famished; we see nothing before us but this manna."

7*† Manna was like coriander seed and had the appearance of bdellium. 8 When they had gone about and gathered it up, the people would grind it between millstones or pound it in a mortar, then cook it in a pot and make it into loaves, which tasted like cakes made with oil. 9* At night, when the dew fell upon the camp, the manna also fell.

10 When Moses heard the people, family after family, crying at the entrance of their tents, so that the LORD became very angry, he was grieved. 11 "Why do you treat your servant so badly?" Moses asked the LORD. "Why are you so displeased with me that you burden me with all this people? 12 Was it I who conceived all this people? or was it I who gave them birth, that you tell me to carry them at my bosom, like a foster father carrying an infant, to the land you have promised under oath to their fathers? 13 Where can I get meat to give to all this people? For they are crying to me, 'Give us meat for our food.' 14 I cannot carry all this people by myself, for they are too heavy for me. 15 If this is the way you will deal with me, then please do me the favor of killing me at once, so that I need no longer face this distress."

The Seventy Elders

16 Then the LORD said to Moses, "Assemble for me seventy of the elders of Israel, men you know for true elders and authorities among the people, and bring them to the meeting tent. When they are in place beside you, 17 I will come down and speak with you there. I will also take some of the spirit that is on you and will bestow it on them, that they may share the burden of the people with you. You will then not have to bear it by yourself.

18 "To the people, however, you shall say: Sanctify yourselves for tomorrow, when you shall have meat to eat. For in the hearing of the LORD you have cried, 'Would that we had meat for food! Oh, how well off we were in Egypt!' Therefore the LORD will give you meat for food, 19 and you will eat it, not for one day, or two days, or five, or ten, or twenty days, 20 but for a whole month—until it comes out of your very nostrils and becomes loathsome to you. For you have spurned the LORD who is in your

---

10, 30ff: Hobab wished to be coaxed before granting the favor. From Jgs 1, 16 it seems probable that he did accede to Moses' request.

10, 33: *The mountain of the LORD*: Sinai (Horeb), elsewhere always called "the mountain of God."

11, 3: *Taberah*: means "the burning."

11, 7: *Coriander seed*: see note on Ex 16, 31. Bdellium: a trans-

parent, amber-colored gum resin, which is also mentioned in Gn 2, 12.

10, 33: Dt 1, 33.	11, 7f: Ex 16, 14f.31; Ps 78,
11, 1: Dt 9, 22.	24; Wis 16, 20; Jn
11, 4: Ps 78, 18.	6, 31.
11, 6: 5f: Nm 21, 5; Ex 16, 3;	11, 9: Ex 16, 14f.
Acts 7, 39.	

midst, and in his presence you have wailed, 'Why did we ever leave Egypt?' "

²¹ But Moses said, "The people around me include six hundred thousand soldiers; yet you say, 'I will give them meat to eat for a whole month.' ²² Can enough sheep and cattle be slaughtered for them? If all the fish of the sea were caught for them, would they have enough?" ²³ The LORD answered Moses, "Is this beyond the LORD's reach? You shall see now whether or not what I have promised you takes place."

The Spirit on the Elders

²⁴ So Moses went out and told the people what the LORD had said. Gathering seventy elders of the people, he had them stand around the tent. ²⁵† The LORD then came down in the cloud and spoke to him. Taking some of the spirit that was on Moses, he bestowed it on the seventy elders; and as the spirit came to rest on them, they prophesied. ²⁶ Now two men, one named Eldad and the other Medad, were not in the gathering but had been left in the camp. They too had been on the list, but had not gone out to the tent; yet the spirit came to rest on them also, and they prophesied in the camp. ²⁷ So, when a young man quickly told Moses, "Eldad and Medad are prophesying in the camp," ²⁸ Joshua, son on Nun, who from his youth had been Moses' aide, said, "Moses, my lord, stop them." ²⁹ But Moses answered him, "Are you jealous for my sake? Would that all the people of the LORD were prophets! Would that the LORD might bestow his spirit on them all!" ³⁰ Then Moses retired to the camp, along with the elders of Israel.

The Quail

³¹*† There arose a wind sent by the LORD, that drove in quail from the sea and brought them down over the camp site at a height of two cubits from the ground for the distance of a day's journey all around the camp. ³²*† All that day, all night, and all the next day the people gathered in the quail. Even the one who got the least gathered ten homers of them. Then they spread them out all around the

camp. ³³ But while the meat was still between their teeth, before it could be consumed, the LORD's wrath flared up against the people, and he struck them with a very great plague. ³⁴† So that place was named Kibroth-hattaavah, because it was there that the greedy people were buried.

³⁵ From Kibroth-hattaavah the people set out for Hazeroth.

Jealousy of Aaron and Miriam

12 While they were in Hazeroth, ¹† Miriam and Aaron spoke against Moses on the pretext of the marriage he had contracted with a Cushite woman. ²† They complained, "Is it through Moses alone that the LORD speaks? Does he not speak through us also?" And the LORD heard this ³* Now, Moses himself was by far the meekest man on the face of the earth. ⁴ So at once the LORD said to Moses and Aaron and Miriam, "Come out, you three, to the meeting tent." And the three of them went. ⁵ Then the LORD came down in the column of cloud, and standing at the entrance of the tent, called Aaron and Miriam. When both came forward, ⁶ he said, "Now listen to the words of the LORD:

Should there be a prophet among you,
   in visions will I reveal myself to him,
   in dreams will I speak to him;
⁷* Not so with my servant Moses!
   Throughout my house he bears my trust:
⁸*   face to face I speak to him,
   plainly and not in riddles.
The presence of the LORD he beholds.

Why, then, did you not fear to speak against my servant Moses?"

Miriam's Leprosy

⁹ So angry was the LORD against them that when he departed, ¹⁰*† and the cloud withdrew from the tent, there was Miriam, a snow-white leper! When Aaron turned and saw her a leper, ¹¹ "Ah, my lord!" he said to Moses, "please do not charge us with the

---

11, 25: *They prophesied:* in the sense, not of foretelling the future, but of speaking in enraptured enthusiasm. Such manifestations of mystic exaltation occurred in the early days of Hebrew prophecy (1 Sm 10, 10ff; 19, 20ff) and in the first years of the Church (Acts 2, 6–11.17; 19, 6; 1 Cor 12–14).
11, 31: *At a height of two cubits from the ground:* exhausted by the storm, the quail could take but short, low flights, so that they were easily captured. To give food to the hungry people, God may have used the natural phenomenon of the annual migration of quail across the Sinai Peninsula. In the spring large flocks of these birds cross the Gulf of Aqabah flying toward the west; in the fall they fly back eastward from the Mediterranean. The sea mentioned here probably refers to the former body of water.
11, 32: *They spread them out:* to cure by drying.
11, 34: *Kibroth-hattaavah:* means "graves of greed."

12, 1: *Cushite woman:* apparently Zipporah, the Midianitess, is meant; cf Ex 2, 21. Perhaps the term is used here merely in the sense of "despised foreigner."
12, 2: The real reason for Miriam's quarrel with her brother Moses was her jealousy of his superior position; his Cushite wife served only as an occasion for the dispute. Aaron merely followed his sister in her rebellion; hence she alone was punished.
12, 10: *A snow-white leper:* afflicted with "white leprosy," a skin disease that generally is not serious or of long duration. Cf Lv 13, 3–6.

11, 31: Ps 78, 26ff.
11, 32f: Nm 78, 26–31; 1 Cor
   10, 6–7.
12, 3: Sir 45, 1f.

12, 7: Sir 45, 3; Heb 3, 2.5.
12, 8: Ex 33, 11; Dt 34, 10.
12, 10: Dt 24, 9.

The Jealousy of Miriam and Aaron

Miriam. I don't know, Aaron. Sometimes Moses really gets to me. He seems to forget that we're all in this together.

Aaron. Yes, we are God's chosen people. All of us, not just Moses. And, of course, he married outside the fold. A Cushite, of all people.

Miriam. It really is a scandal. He is the self-appointed leader of our people, and yet he is not even married to an Israelite woman. That just doesn't sit well with our people.

Aaron. And he can be so aloof. I know he has a special connection with God, and I know it isn't easy being a leader. But he always seems to set himself apart, acting like he's better than the rest of us.

Miriam. What bothers me most is that Moses assumes that God speaks only through him.

Aaron. Yes, it's as if the rest of us have no role to play. What if I receive a revelation from God? Will Moses respond the same way we are expected to whenever he speaks? I doubt it!

Miriam. So do I. He pretends to be humble and to speak for God. I'm tired of it. We need to have a voice also.

Jealousy is like a dangerous cancer, growing until it affects your whole outlook on life (see what happens to Miriam in Nm 12, 9–10). What happens inside of you when you feel jealous? How does jealousy affect your attitudes toward other people?

▸ **Numbers, chapter 12**

sin that we have foolishly committed! [12] Let her not thus be like the stillborn babe that comes forth from its mother's womb with its flesh half consumed." [13] Then Moses cried to the LORD, "Please, not this! Pray, heal her!" [14] But the LORD answered Moses, "Suppose her father had spit in her face, would she not hide in shame for seven days? Let her be confined outside the camp for seven days; only then may she be brought back." [15] So Miriam was confined outside the camp for seven days, and the people did not start out again until she was brought back.

[16] After that the people set out from Hazeroth and encamped in the desert of Paran.

The Twelve Scouts

13 [1] The LORD said to Moses, [2] "Send men to reconnoiter the land of Canaan, which I am giving the Israelites. You shall send one man from each ancestral tribe, all of them princes." [3]* So Moses dispatched them from the desert of Paran, as the LORD had ordered. All of them were leaders among the Israelites; [4] by name they were:

Shammua, son of Zaccur, of the tribe
　　of Reuben;

[5] Shaphat, son of Hori, of the tribe of Simeon;
[6] Caleb, son of Jephunneh, of the tribe of Judah;
[7] Igal [son of Joseph] of the tribe of Issachar;
[10] Gaddiel, son of Sodi, of the tribe of Zebulun;
[11] Gaddi, son of Susi, of the tribe of Manasseh, for
　　the Josephites, with
[8] Hoshea, son of Nun, of the tribe of Ephraim;
[9] Palti, son of Raphu, of the tribe of Benjamin;
[12] Ammiel, son of Gemalli, of the tribe of Dan;
[13] Sethur, son of Michael, of the tribe of Asher;
[14] Nahbi, son of Vophsi, of the tribe of Naphtali;
[15] Geuel, son of Machi, of the tribe of Gad.

[16]† These are the names of the men whom Moses sent out to reconnoiter the land. But Hoshea, son of Nun, Moses called Joshua.

[17] In sending them to reconnoiter the land of Canaan, Moses said to them, "Go up here in the Negeb, up into the highlands, [18] and see what kind of land it is. Are the people living there strong or weak, few or many? [19] Is the country in which they live good or bad? Are the towns in which they dwell open or fortified? [20] Is the soil fertile or barren, wooded or clear? And do your best to get some of the fruit of the land." It was then the season for early grapes.

---

† **13, 16:** *Joshua:* in Hebrew, "Jehoshua," which was later modified to "Jeshua," the Hebrew pronunciation of the name "Jesus." Hoshea and Joshua are variants of one original name meaning "the LORD saves." Cf Mt 1, 21.

* 13, 3–33: Dt 1, 22–28.

²¹† So they went up and reconnoitered the land from the desert of Zin as far as where Rehob adjoins Labo of Hamath. ²²*† Going up by way of the Negeb, they reached Hebron, where Ahiman, Sheshai and Talmai, descendants of the Anakim, were living. [Hebron had been built seven years before Zoan in Egypt.] ²³† They also reached the Wadi Eshcol, where they cut down a branch with a single cluster of grapes on it, which two of them carried on a pole, as well as some pomegranates and figs. ²⁴* It was because of the cluster the Israelites cut there that they called the place Wadi Eshcol.

Their Return

²⁵ After reconnoitering the land for forty days they returned, ²⁶* met Moses and Aaron and the whole community of the Israelites in the desert of Paran at Kadesh, made a report to them all, and showed them the fruit of the country. ²⁷ They told Moses: "We went into the land to which you sent us. It does indeed flow with milk and honey, and here is its fruit. ²⁸* However, the people who are living in the land are fierce, and the towns are fortified and very strong. Besides, we saw descendants of the Anakim there. ²⁹ Amalekites live in the region of the Negeb; Hittites, Jebusites and Amorites dwell in the highlands, and Canaanites along the seacoast and the banks of the Jordan."

³⁰ Caleb, however, to quiet the people toward Moses, said, "We ought to go up and seize the land, for we can certainly do so." ³¹ But the men who had gone up with him said, "We cannot attack these people; they are too strong for us." ³²* So they spread discouraging reports among the Israelites about the land they had scouted, saying, "The land that we explored is a country that consumes its inhabitants. And all the people we saw there are huge men, ³³*† veritable giants [the Anakim were a race of giants]; we felt like mere grasshoppers, and so we must have seemed to them."

Threats of Revolt

14 ¹ At this, the whole community broke out with loud cries, and even in the night the people wailed. ²* All the Israelites grumbled against Moses and Aaron, the whole community saying to them, "Would that we had died in the land of Egypt, or that here in the desert we were dead! ³ Why is the LORD bringing us into this land only to have us fall by the sword? Our wives and little ones will be taken as booty. Would it not be better for us to return to Egypt?" ⁴ So they said to one another, "Let us appoint a leader and go back to Egypt."

⁵ But Moses and Aaron fell prostrate before the whole assembled community of the Israelites; ⁶ while Joshua, son of Nun, and Caleb, son of Jephunneh, who had been in the party that scouted the land, tore their garments ⁷* and said to the whole community of the Israelites, "The country which we went through and explored is a fine, rich land. ⁸ If the LORD is pleased with us, he will bring us in and give us that land, a land flowing with milk and honey. ⁹*† But do not rebel against the LORD! You need not be afraid of the people of that land; they are but food for us! Their defense has left them, but the LORD is with us. Therefore, do not be afraid of them." ¹⁰ In answer, the whole community threatened to stone them.

The Lord's Sentence

But then the glory of the LORD appeared at the meeting tent to all the Israelites. ¹¹* And the LORD said to Moses, "How long will this people spurn me? How long will they refuse to believe in me, despite all the signs I have performed among them? ¹²* I will strike them with pestilence and wipe them out. Then I will make of you a nation greater and mightier than they."

¹³* But Moses said to the LORD: "Are the Egyptians to hear of this? For by your power you brought out this people from among them. ¹⁴* And are they to tell of it to the inhabitants of this land? It has been heard that you, O LORD, are in the midst of this people; you, LORD, who plainly reveal yourself! Your cloud stands over them, and you go before them by day in a column of cloud and by night in a column of fire. ¹⁵ If now you slay this whole people, the nations who have heard such reports of you will say, ¹⁶* 'The LORD was not able to bring this people into the land he swore to give them;

13, 21: *The desert of Zin:* north of Paran and southwest of the Dead Sea. It is quite distinct from "the desert of Sin" near the border of Egypt (Ex 16, 1; 17, 1; Nm 33, 11). *Labo of Hamath:* a town near Riblah (Jer 39, 5f) at the southern border of Hamath, an independent kingdom in southern Syria. David's conquests extended as far as Hamath (2 Sm 8, 9ff), and Labo thus formed the northern border of the ideal extent of Israel's possessions (Nm 34, 7ff; Ez 47, 15; 48, 1). Some commentators think that this verse is a later addition to the text; cf Dt 1, 24.

13, 22.28: *Anakim:* an aboriginal race in southern Palestine, largely absorbed by the Canaanites before the Israelite invasion. Either because of their tall stature or because of the massive stone structures left by them the Israelites regarded them as giants.

13, 23: *Eshcol:* means "cluster."

13, 33: *Giants:* in Hebrew, "nephilim." Cf Gn 6, 4.

14, 9: *They are but food for us:* that is, "we can easily consume and destroy them." This is the answer to the pessimistic report that this land "consumes its inhabitants" (Nm 13, 32).

13, 22: Jos 11, 21f.
13, 24: Nm 32, 9; Dt 1, 24f.
13, 26f: Ex 3, 8.17.
13, 28f: Dt 9, 1f.
13, 32: Nm 32, 9; Jos 14, 8.
13, 33: Dt 2, 10.
14, 2: Ex 16, 3; Ps 106, 25.
14, 7f: Dt 1, 25.
14, 9: Dt 7, 18.
14, 11: Ps 78, 22.32.
14, 12: Ex 32, 10.
14, 13–16: Ex 32, 12; Dt 9, 26ff; Ps 106, 23.
14, 14: Ex 13, 21; Jos 2, 9f.
14, 16: Ex 32, 12; Dt 9, 28.

that is why he slaughtered them in the desert.' [17] Now then, let the power of my Lord be displayed in its greatness, even as you have said, [18]* 'The LORD is slow to anger and rich in kindness, forgiving wickedness and crime; yet not declaring the guilty guiltless, but punishing children to the third and fourth generation for their fathers' wickedness.' [19]* Pardon, then, the wickedness of this people in keeping with your great kindness, even as you have forgiven them from Egypt until now."

[20] The LORD answered: "I pardon them as you have asked. [21] Yet, by my life and the LORD's glory that fills the whole earth, [22]* of all the men who have seen my glory and the signs I worked in Egypt and in the desert, and who nevertheless have put me to the test ten times already and have failed to heed my voice, [23] not one shall see the land which I promised on oath to their fathers. None of these who have spurned me shall see it. [24]* But because my servant Caleb has a different spirit and follows me unreservedly, I will bring him into the land where he has just been, and his descendants shall possess it. [25]† But now, since the Amalekites and Canaanites are living in the valleys, turn away tomorrow and set out in the desert on the Red Sea road."

[26] The LORD also said to Moses and Aaron: [27]* "How long will this wicked community grumble against me? I have heard the grumblings of the Israelites against me. [28]† Tell them: By my life, says the LORD, I will do to you just what I have heard you say. [29]* Here in the desert shall your dead bodies fall. Of all your men of twenty years or more, registered in the census, who grumbled against me, [30] not one shall enter the land where I solemnly swore to settle you, except Caleb, son of Jephunneh, and Joshua, son of Nun. [31]* Your little ones, however, who you said would be taken as booty, I will bring in, and they shall appreciate the land you spurned. [32] But as for you, your bodies shall fall here in the desert, [33]* here where your children must wander for forty years, suffering for your faithlessness, till the last of you lies dead in the desert. [34] Forty days you spent in scouting the land; forty years shall you suffer for your crimes: one year for each day. Thus you will realize what it means to oppose me. [35] I, the LORD, have sworn to do this to all

this wicked community that conspired against me: here in the desert they shall die to the last man."

[36]* And so it happened to the men whom Moses had sent to reconnoiter the land and who on returning had set the whole community grumbling against him by spreading discouraging reports about the land; [37] these men who had given out the bad report about the land were struck down by the LORD and died. [38]* Of all the men who had gone to reconnoiter the land, only Joshua, son of Nun, and Caleb, son of Jephunneh, survived.

Unsuccessful Invasion

[39] When Moses repeated these words to all the Israelites, the people felt great remorse. [40]* Early the next morning they started up into the foothills, saying, "Here we are, ready to go up to the place that the LORD spoke of: for we were indeed doing wrong." [41] But Moses said, "Why are you again disobeying the LORD's orders? This cannot succeed. [42]* Do not go up, because the LORD is not in your midst; if you go, you will be beaten down before your enemies. [43] For there the Amalekites and Canaanites face you, and you will fall by the sword. You have turned back from following the LORD; therefore the LORD will not be with you."

[44]* Yet they dared to go up into the foothills, even though neither the ark of the covenant of the LORD nor Moses left the camp. [45]† And the Amalekites and Canaanites who dwelt in that hill country came down and defeated them, beating them back as far as Hormah.

Secondary Offerings

15 [1] The LORD said to Moses, [2]† "Give the Israelites these instructions: When you have entered the land that I will give you for your homesteads, [3] if you make to the LORD a sweet-smelling oblation from the herd or from the flock, in holocaust, in fulfillment of a vow, or as a freewill offering, or for one of your festivals, [4] whoever does so shall also present to the LORD a cereal offering consisting of a tenth of an ephah of fine flour mixed with a fourth of a hin of oil, [5] as well as a libation of a fourth of a hin of wine, with each lamb sacrificed in holocaust or otherwise. [6] With each sacrifice of a ram you shall present a cereal offering

---

14, 25: *The valleys:* the low-lying plains in the Negeb and along the seacoast and in the Jordan depression as well as the higher valleys in the mountains farther north; cf Nm 14, 45.

14, 28f: God punished the malcontents by giving them their wish; cf v 2. Their lack of faith and of confidence in God is cited in 1 Cor 10, 10, and Heb 3, 12–18, as a warning for Christians.

14, 45: *Hormah:* one of the Canaanite royal cities in southern Judea (Jos 12, 14), known at this time as "Zephath"; the origin of the later name is told in Nm 21, 3; Jgs 1, 17.

15, 2–16: These laws on sacrifice are complementary to those of Lv 1–3. Since the food of the Israelites consisted not only of meat but

also of bread, oil and wine, so, besides the animal oblations, they offered flour, wine and oil in sacrifice to the Lord.

14, 18: Ex 20, 5; 34, 6f; Pss 103, 8; 145, 8.
14, 19: Ps 78, 38.
14, 22f: Dt 1, 35.
14, 24: Jos 14, 8f.
14, 27: Ex 16, 7.12.
14, 29: Dt 1, 35; Heb 3, 17.
14, 31: Dt 1, 39.
14, 33f: Nm 13, 26; 32, 13; Ps 95, 10; Ez 4, 6.
14, 36f: Nm 13, 17.32f; 1 Cor 10, 10.
14, 38: Nm 26, 65.
14, 40: Nm 13, 18; Dt 1, 42.
14, 42: Dt 1, 42.
14, 44: Dt 1, 43.

of two tenths of an ephah of fine flour mixed with a third of a hin of oil, 7 and a libation of a third of a hin of wine, thus making a sweet-smelling offering to the LORD. 8 When you sacrifice an ox as a holocaust, or in fulfillment of a vow, or as a peace offering to the LORD, 9 with it you shall present a cereal offering of three tenths of an ephah of fine flour mixed with half a hin of oil, 10 and a libation of half a hin of wine, as a sweet-smelling oblation to the LORD. 11 The same is to be done for each ox, ram, lamb or goat. 12 Whatever the number you offer, do the same for each of them.

13 "All the native-born shall make these offerings in the same way, whenever they present a sweet-smelling oblation to the LORD. 14 Likewise, in any future generation, any alien residing with you permanently or for a time, who presents a sweet-smelling oblation to the LORD, shall do as you do. 15 There is but one rule for you and for the resident alien, a perpetual rule for all your descendants. Before the LORD you and the alien are alike, 16 with the same law and the same application of it for the alien residing among you as for yourselves."

17 The LORD said to Moses, 18 "Speak to the Israelites and tell them: When you enter the land into which I will bring you 19 and begin to eat of the food of that land, you shall offer the LORD a contribution 20*† consisting of a cake of your first batch of dough. You shall offer it just as you offer a contribution from the threshing floor. 21 Throughout your generations you shall give a contribution to the LORD from your first batch of dough.

Sin Offerings

22*† "When through inadvertence you fail to carry out any of these commandments which the LORD gives to Moses, 23 and through Moses to you, from the time the LORD first issues the commandment down through your generations: 24 if the community itself unwittingly becomes guilty of the fault of inadvertence, the whole community shall offer the holocaust of one young bull as a sweet-smelling oblation pleasing to the LORD, along with its prescribed cereal offering and libation, as well as one he-goat as a sin offering. 25* Then the priest shall make atonement for the whole Israelite community; thus they will be forgiven the inadvertence for

which they have brought their holocaust as an oblation to the LORD. 26 Not only the whole Israelite community, but also the aliens residing among you, shall be forgiven, since the fault of inadvertence affects all the people.

27* "However, if it is an individual who sins inadvertently, he shall bring a yearling she-goat as a sin offering, 28 and the priest shall make atonement before the LORD for him who sinned inadvertently; when atonement has been made for him, he will be forgiven. 29 You shall have but one law for him who sins inadvertently, whether he be a native Israelite or an alien residing with you.

30* "But anyone who sins defiantly, whether he be a native or an alien, insults the LORD, and shall be cut off from among his people. 31* Since he has despised the word of the LORD and has broken his commandment, he must be cut off. He has only himself to blame."

The Sabbath-breaker

32 While the Israelites were in the desert, a man was discovered gathering wood on the sabbath day. 33 Those who caught him at it brought him to Moses and Aaron and the whole assembly. 34*† But they kept him in custody, for there was no clear decision as to what should be done with him. 35 Then the LORD said to Moses, "This man shall be put to death; let the whole community stone him outside the camp." 36 So the whole community led him outside the camp and stoned him to death, as the LORD had commanded Moses.

Tassels on the Cloak

37 The LORD said to Moses, 38*† "Speak to the Israelites and tell them that they and their descendants must put tassels on the corners of their garments, fastening each corner tassel with a violet cord. 39 When you use these tassels, let the sight of them remind you to keep all the commandments of the LORD, without going wantonly astray after the desires of your hearts and eyes. 40 Thus you will remember to keep all my commandments and be holy to your God. 41* I, the LORD, am your God who, as God, brought you out of Egypt that I, the LORD, may be your God."

---

† **15, 20:** *Dough:* some render, "barley grits." This word is used elsewhere only in Ez 44, 30 and Neh 10, 33; a related Hebrew word is used in Lv 2, 14.

15, 22ff: Although no moral guilt is incurred by an inadvertent violation of God's commandments, the sanctity of the law can require some reparation even for such violations.

15, 34: *No clear decision:* they already knew that a willful violation of the sabbath was a capital offense, but they did not yet know how the death penalty was to be inflicted.

15, 38: *Tassels:* at the time of Christ these tassels were worn by all pious Jews, including our Lord (Mt 9, 20f; Mk 6, 56); the Pharisees wore very large ones in ostentation of their zeal for the law (Mt 23, 5).

15, 20: 19–20: Ez 44, 30.
15, 22f: Lv 4, 13f.
15, 25: Lv 4, 20.
15, 27f: Lv 4, 27f.
15, 30: Dt 17, 12.
15, 31: Prv 13, 13.
15, 34: Lv 24, 12.
15, 38: Dt 22, 12.
15, 41: Lv 22, 32f.

Rebellion of Korah

16 ¹ † Korah, son of Izhar, son of Kohath, son of Levi, [and Dathan and Abiram, sons of Eliab, son of Pallu, son of Reuben] took ² two hundred and fifty Israelites who were leaders in the community, members of the council and men of note. They stood before Moses, ³* and held an assembly against Moses and Aaron, to whom they said, "Enough from you! The whole community, all of them, are holy; the LORD is in their midst. Why then should you set yourselves over the LORD's congregation?"

⁴ When Moses heard this, he fell prostrate. ⁵ Then he said to Korah and to all his band, "May the LORD make known tomorrow morning who belongs to him and who is the holy one and whom he will have draw near to him! Whom he chooses, he will have draw near him. ⁶ Do this: take your censers [Korah and all his band] ⁷ and put fire in them and place incense in them before the LORD tomorrow. He whom the LORD then chooses is the holy one. Enough from you Levites!"

⁸ Moses also said to Korah, "Listen to me, you Levites! ⁹* Is it too little for you that the God of Israel has singled you out from the community of Israel, to have you draw near him for the service of the LORD's Dwelling and to stand before the community to minister for them? ¹⁰ He has allowed you and your kinsmen, the descendants of Levi, to approach him, and yet you now seek the priesthood too. ¹¹ It is therefore against the LORD that you and all your band are conspiring. For what has Aaron done that you should grumble against him?"

Rebellion of Dathan and Abiram

¹²† Moses summoned Dathan and Abiram, sons of Eliab, but they answered, "We will not go. ¹³ Are you not satisfied with having led us here away from a land flowing with milk and honey, to make us perish in the desert, that you must now lord it over us? ¹⁴† Far from bringing us to a land flowing with milk and honey, or giving us fields and vineyards for our inheritance, will you also gouge out our eyes? No, we will not go."

¹⁵* Then Moses became very angry and said to the LORD, "Pay no heed to their offering. I have never taken a single ass from them, nor have I wronged any one of them."

Korah

¹⁶ Moses said to Korah, "You and all your band shall appear before the LORD tomorrow—you and they and Aaron too. ¹⁷ Then each of your two hundred and fifty followers shall take his own censer, put incense in it, and offer it to the LORD; and you and Aaron, each with his own censer, shall do the same." ¹⁸ So they all took their censers, and laying incense on the fire they had put in them, they took their stand by the entrance of the meeting tent along with Moses and Aaron. ¹⁹ Then, when Korah had assembled all his band against them at the entrance of the meeting tent, the glory of the LORD appeared to the entire community, ²⁰ and the LORD said to Moses and Aaron, ²¹ "Stand apart from this band, that I may consume them at once." ²² But they fell prostrate and cried out, "O God, God of the spirits of all mankind, will one man's sin make you angry with the whole community?" ²³ The LORD answered Moses, ²⁴ "Speak to the community and tell them: Withdraw from the space around the Dwelling" [of Korah, Dathan and Abiram].

Punishment of Dathan and Abiram

²⁵† Moses, followed by the elders of Israel, arose and went to Dathan and Abiram. ²⁶ Then he warned the community, "Keep away from the tents of these wicked men and do not touch anything that is theirs: otherwise you too will be swept away because of all their sins." ²⁷ When Dathan and Abiram had come out and were standing at the entrances of their tents with their wives and sons and little ones, ²⁸ Moses said, "This is how you shall know that it was the LORD who sent me to do all I have done, and that it was not I who planned it: ²⁹ if these men die an ordinary death, merely suffering the fate common to all mankind, then it was not the LORD who sent me. ³⁰ But if the LORD does something entirely new, and the ground opens its mouth and swallows them alive down into the nether world, with all belonging to them, then you will know that these men have defied the LORD." ³¹* No sooner had he finished saying all this than

---

† **16, 1ff:** The evidence seems to show that there were two distinct rebellions: one of Korah and his band (Nm 27, 3) and the other of Dathan and Abiram (Dt 11, 6); cf Ps 106. The present account combines both events into one narrative; but even here it is rather easy to separate the two, once certain proper names (vv 1.6.24.32.35) have been identified as glosses. The rebellion of the Reubenites, Dathan and Abiram, was of a political nature, against Moses alone as the civil leader; these rebels were punished by being swallowed alive in an earthquake. The rebellion of Korah was of a religious nature, against the religious leadership of both Moses and Aaron; about two hundred and fifty malcontents joined Korah's band; they were punished by fire. The parts of the present section which refer to the rebellion of Dathan and Abiram are vv 12–15 and vv 25–34 of chapter 16; the rest of chapter 16 and all of chapter 17 concern the rebellion of Korah.

16, 12: *We will not go:* to appear before Moses' tribunal.

16, 14: *Gouge out our eyes:* blind us to the real state of affairs.

16, 25: Since Dathan and Abiram had refused to go to Moses (vv 12ff), he, with the elders as witnesses, was obliged to go to their tent.

16, 3: Ps 106, 16ff; Sir 45, 19; 1 Cor 10, 10.
16, 9: Dt 10, 8.
16, 15: 1 Sm 12, 3.
16, 31ff: Nm 26, 10; Lv 10, 2; Dt 11, 6; Ps 106, 7f.

the ground beneath them split open, 32 and the earth opened its mouth and swallowed them and their families [and all of Korah's men] and all their possessions. 33 They went down alive to the nether world with all belonging to them; the earth closed over them, and they perished from the community. 34 But all the Israelites near them fled at their shrieks, saying, "The earth might swallow us too!"

Punishment of Korah

35† So they withdrew from the space around the Dwelling [of Korah, Dathan and Abiram]. And fire from the LORD came forth which consumed the two hundred and fifty men who were offering the incense.

17 1 The LORD said to Moses, 2 "Tell Eleazar, son of Aaron the priest, to remove the censers from the embers; and scatter the fire some distance away, 3† for these sinners have consecrated the censers at the cost of their lives. Have them hammered into plates to cover the altar, because in being presented before the LORD they have become sacred. In this way they shall serve as a sign to the Israelites." 4 So Eleazar the priest had the bronze censers of those burned during the offering hammered into a covering for the altar, 5 in keeping with the orders which the LORD had given him through Moses. This cover was to be a reminder to the Israelites that no layman, no one who was not a descendant of Aaron, should approach the altar to offer incense before the LORD, lest he meet the fate of Korah and his band.

6 The next day the whole Israelite community grumbled against Moses and Aaron, saying, "It is you who have slain the LORD's people." 7 But while the community was deliberating against them, Moses and Aaron turned toward the meeting tent, and the cloud now covered it and the glory of the LORD appeared. 8 Then Moses and Aaron came to the front of the meeting tent, 9 and the LORD said to Moses and Aaron, 10 "Depart from this community, that I may consume them at once." But they fell prostrate.

11* Then Moses said to Aaron, "Take your censer, put fire from the altar in it, lay incense on it, and bring it quickly to the community to make atonement for them; for wrath has come forth from the

LORD and the blow is falling." 12 Obeying the orders of Moses, Aaron took his censer and ran in among the community, where the blow was already falling on the people. Then, as he offered the incense and made atonement for the people, 13 standing there between the living and the dead, the scourge was checked. 14 Yet fourteen thousand seven hundred died from the scourge, in addition to those who died because of Korah. 15 When the scourge had been checked, Aaron returned to Moses at the entrance of the meeting tent.

Aaron's Staff

16 The LORD now said to Moses, 17† "Speak to the Israelites and get one staff from them for each ancestral house, twelve staffs in all, one from each of their tribal princes. Mark each man's name on his staff; 18† and mark Aaron's name on Levi's staff, for the head of Levi's ancestral house shall also have a staff. 19 Then lay them down in the meeting tent, in front of the commandments, where I meet you. 20 There the staff of the man of my choice shall sprout. Thus will I suppress from my presence the Israelites' grumbling against you."

21 So Moses spoke to the Israelites, and their princes gave him staffs, twelve in all, one from each tribal prince; and Aaron's staff was with them. 22 Then Moses laid the staffs down before the LORD in the tent of the commandments. 23 The next day, when Moses entered the tent, Aaron's staff, representing the house of Levi, had sprouted and put forth not only shoots, but blossoms as well, and even bore ripe almonds! 24 Moses thereupon brought out all the staffs from the LORD's presence to the Israelites. After each prince identified his own staff and took it, 25 the LORD said to Moses, "Put back Aaron's staff in front of the commandments, to be kept there as a warning to the rebellious, so that their grumbling may cease before me; if it does not, they will die." 26 And Moses did as the LORD had commanded him.

Charge of the Sacred Things

27† Then the Israelites cried out to Moses, "We are perishing; we are lost, we are all lost! 28 Every time anyone approaches the Dwelling of the LORD, he dies! Are we to perish to the last man?"

16, 35: This verse continues v 24; the first sentence is transposed from v 27.

17, 3: Whatever was brought into intimate contact with something sacred shared in its sacredness. See note on Nm 19, 20.

17, 17: The staff was not merely an article of practical use, but also a symbol of authority; cf Gn 49, 10; Nm 24, 17; Jer 48, 17. Hence, the staff of a leader of a tribe was considered the emblem of his tribe; in fact, certain Hebrew words for "staff" also means "tribe." Perhaps for this reason, to avoid confusion, the author here uses the term "ancestral house" instead of the ordinary word for "tribe."

17, 18: *Levi's staff:* it is not clear whether this is considered as one

of the twelve mentioned in the preceding verse, or as a thirteenth staff. Sometimes Levi is reckoned as one of the twelve tribes (e.g., Dt 27, 12f), but more often the number twelve is arrived at by counting the two sub-tribes of Joseph, i.e., Ephraim and Manasseh, as distinct tribes. In this passage also it seems probable that the tribe of Levi is considered apart from the other twelve.

17, 27f: Logically these two verses belong immediately after Nm 16, 35.

17, 11: Wis 18, 20f.

18 ¹ † The LORD said to Aaron, "You and your sons as well as the other members of your ancestral house shall be responsible for the sanctuary; but the responsibility of the priesthood shall rest on you and your sons alone. ²† Bring with you also your other kinsmen of the tribe of Levi, your ancestral tribe, as your associates and assistants, while you and your sons are in front of the tent of the commandments. ³ They shall look after your persons and the whole tent; however, they shall not come near the sacred vessels or the altar, lest both they and you die. ⁴† As your associates they shall have charge of all the work connected with the meeting tent. But no layman shall come near you. ⁵ You shall have charge of the sanctuary and of the altar, that wrath may not fall again upon the Israelites.

⁶* "Remember, it is I who have taken your kinsmen, the Levites, from the body of the Israelites; they are a gift to you, dedicated to the LORD for the service of the meeting tent. ⁷*† But only you and your sons are to have charge of performing the priestly functions in whatever concerns the altar and the room within the veil. I give you the priesthood as a gift. Any layman who draws near shall be put to death."

The Priests' Share of the Sacrifices

⁸*† The LORD said to Aaron, "I myself have given you charge of the contributions made to me in the various sacred offerings of the Israelites; by perpetual ordinance I have assigned them to you and to your sons as your priestly share. ⁹ You shall have the right to share in the oblations that are most sacred, in whatever they offer me as cereal offerings or sin offerings or guilt offerings; these shares shall accrue to you and to your sons. ¹⁰ In eating them you shall treat them as most sacred; every male among you may partake of them. As sacred, they belong to you.

¹¹*† "You shall also have what is removed from the gift in every wave offering of the Israelites; by perpetual ordinance I have assigned it to you and to your sons and daughters. All in your family who are clean may partake of it. ¹²* I have also as-signed to you all the best of the new oil and of the new wine and grain that they give to the LORD as their first fruits; ¹³ and likewise, of whatever grows on their land, the first products that they bring in to the LORD shall be yours; all of your family who are clean may partake of them. ¹⁴† Whatever is doomed in Israel shall be yours. ¹⁵* Every living thing that opens the womb, whether of man or of beast, such as are to be offered to the LORD, shall be yours; but you must let the first-born of man, as well as of unclean animals, be redeemed. ¹⁶ The ransom for a boy is to be paid when he is a month old; it is fixed at five silver shekels according to the sanctuary standard, twenty gerahs to the shekel. ¹⁷ But the first-born of cattle, sheep or goats shall not be redeemed; they are sacred. Their blood you must splash on the altar and their fat you must burn as a sweet-smelling oblation to the LORD. ¹⁸* Their meat, however, shall be yours, just as the breast and the right leg of the wave offering belong to you. ¹⁹† By perpetual ordinance I have assigned to you and to your sons and daughters all the contributions from the sacred gifts which the Israelites make to the LORD; this is an inviolable covenant to last forever before the LORD, for you and for your descendants." ²⁰*† Then the LORD said to Aaron, "You shall not have any heritage in the land of the Israelites nor hold any portion among them; I will be your portion and your heritage among them.

Tithes Due the Levites

²¹* "To the Levites, however, I hereby assign all tithes in Israel as their heritage in recompense for the service they perform in the meeting tent. ²² The Israelites may no longer approach the meeting tent; else they will incur guilt deserving death. ²³ Only the Levites are to perform the service of the meeting tent, and they alone shall be held responsible; this is a perpetual ordinance for all your generations. The Levites, therefore, shall not have any heritage among the Israelites, ²⁴ for I have assigned to them as their heritage the tithes which the Israelites give as a contribution to the LORD. That is why I have or-

---

18, 1ff: This law, which kept unqualified persons from contact with sacred things, is the answer to the Israelites' cry in Nm 17, 28. It is followed by other laws concerning priests and Levites.

18, 2: *Associates:* in Hebrew this word alludes to the popular etymology of the name "Levi." Cf Gn 29, 34.

18, 4: *Layman:* here, "one who is not a Levite"; in v 7, "one who is not a priest."

18, 7: *Veil:* the outer veil, or "curtain," is probably meant.

18, 8ff: Two classes of offerings are here distinguished: the most sacred offering, which only the male members of the priestly families could eat (vv 8ff), and the other offerings, which even the women of the priestly families could eat (vv 11–19).

18, 11: *Wave offering:* this included the breast and right leg (v 18), the shoulder of the peace offering (Lv 7, 30–34), and portions of the nazirite sacrifice (Nm 6, 19f).

18, 14: *Doomed:* in Hebrew, *herem,* which means here "set aside from profane use and made sacred to the Lord." Cf Lv 27, 21.28.

18, 19: *An inviolable covenant:* literally, "a covenant of salt." Cf 2 Chr 13, 5. The reference may perhaps be to the preservative power of salt (cf Mt 5, 13); but more likely the phrase refers to the custom of partaking of the same salt in common to render a contract unbreakable. See note on Lv 2, 13.

18, 20: The priests and Levites were forbidden to own hereditary land such as the other Israelites possessed; therefore in the allotment of the land they were not to receive any portion of it. Certain cities, however, were assigned to them for their residence; cf Nm 35, 1–8.

18, 6: Nm 3, 9; 8, 19.
18, 7: Nm 3, 10.
18, 8: Nm 5, 9.
18, 11: Ex 29, 27f; Lv 7, 34; 10, 14.
18, 12f: Dt 18, 4; 26, 2.
18, 15: Ex 13, 2.
18, 18: Lv 7, 31–34.
18, 20: Dt 10, 9; 18, 1f; Jos 13, 33; Ez 44, 28.
18, 21: Heb 7, 5.

dered that they are not to have any heritage among the Israelites."

Tithes Paid by the Levites

25 The LORD said to Moses, 26 "Give the Levites these instructions: When you receive from the Israelites the tithes I have assigned you from them as your heritage, you are to make a contribution from them to the LORD, a tithe of the tithes; 27 and your contribution will be credited to you as if it were grain from the threshing floor or new wine from the press. 28 Thus you too shall make a contribution from all the tithes you receive from the Israelites, handing over to Aaron the priest the part to be contributed to the LORD. 29 From all the gifts that you receive, and from the best parts, you are to consecrate to the LORD your own full contribution.

30 "Tell them also: Once you have made your contribution from the best part, the rest of the tithes will be credited to you Levites as if it were produce of the threshing floor or of the wine press. 31 Your families, as well as you, may eat them anywhere, since they are your recompense for service at the meeting tent. 32 You will incur no guilt so long as you make a contribution of the best part. Do not profane the sacred gifts of the Israelites and so bring death on yourselves."

Ashes of the Red Heifer

19 1 The LORD said to Moses and Aaron: 2 "This is the regulation which the law of the LORD prescribes. Tell the Israelites to procure for you a red heifer that is free from every blemish and defect and on which no yoke has ever been laid. 3† This is to be given to Eleazar the priest, to be led outside the camp and slaughtered in his presence. 4† Eleazar the priest shall take some of its blood on his finger and sprinkle it seven times toward the front of the meeting tent. 5 Then the heifer shall be burned in his sight, with its hide and flesh, its blood and offal; 6 and the priest shall take some cedar wood, hyssop and scarlet yarn and throw them into the fire in which the heifer is being burned. 7 The priest shall then wash his garments and bathe his body in water. He remains unclean until the evening, and only afterward may he return to the camp. 8 Likewise, he who burned the heifer shall wash his garments, bathe his body in water, and be unclean until evening. 9 Finally, a man who

is clean shall gather up the ashes of the heifer and deposit them in a clean place outside the camp. There they are to be kept for preparing lustral water for the Israelite community. The heifer is a sin offering. 10 He who has gathered up the ashes of the heifer shall also wash his garments and be unclean until evening. This is a perpetual ordinance, both for the Israelites and for the aliens residing among them.

Use of the Ashes

11 "Whoever touches the dead body of any human being shall be unclean for seven days; 12 he shall purify himself with the water on the third and on the seventh day, and then he will be clean again. But if he fails to purify himself on the third and on the seventh day, he will not become clean. 13* Everyone who fails to purify himself after touching the body of any deceased person, defiles the Dwelling of the LORD and shall be cut off from Israel. Since the lustral water has not been splashed over him, he remains unclean: his uncleanness still clings to him.

14 "This is the law: When a man dies in a tent, everyone who enters the tent, as well as everyone already in it, shall be unclean for seven days; 15 likewise, every vessel that is open, or with its lid unfastened, shall be unclean. 16 Moreover, everyone who in the open country touches a dead person, whether he was slain by the sword or died naturally, or who touches a human bone or a grave, shall be unclean for seven days. 17† For anyone who is thus unclean, ashes from the sin offering shall be put in a vessel, and spring water shall be poured on them. 18 Then a man who is clean shall take some hyssop, dip it in this water, and sprinkle it on the tent and on all the vessels and persons that were in it, or on him who touched a bone, a slain person or other dead body, or a grave. 19 The clean man shall sprinkle the unclean on the third and on the seventh day; thus purified on the seventh day, he shall wash his garments and bathe his body in water, and in the evening he will be clean again. 20† Any unclean man who fails to have himself purified shall be cut off from the community, because he defiles the sanctuary of the LORD. As long as the lustral water has not been splashed over him, he remains unclean. 21 This shall be a perpetual ordinance for you.

19, 3: *Outside the camp:* several Fathers of the Church saw in this a prefiguring of the sacrificial death of Christ outside the walls of Jerusalem; cf Jn 19, 20; Heb 13, 12; in the purifying water, into which the ashes of the red heifer were put, they saw a type of the water of Baptism.

19, 4: *Toward the front of the meeting tent:* since the tabernacle faced the east (Ex 26, 15–30), the killing of the heifer took place east of the camp; in later times it was done on the Mount of Olives, east of the Temple.

19, 17ff: "If . . . the sprinkled ashes of a heifer sanctify the unclean unto the cleansing of the flesh, how much more will the blood of Christ . . . cleanse your conscience from dead works?" (Heb 9, 13f).

19, 20: Ritual uncleanness is, as it were, contagious; so also sacredness; see note on Nm 17, 3.

19, 13: Lv 15, 31.

"One who sprinkles the lustral water shall wash his garments, and anyone who comes in contact with this water shall be unclean until evening. [22] Moreover, whatever the unclean person touches becomes unclean itself, and anyone who touches it becomes unclean until evening."

Death of Miriam

20 [1] † The whole Israelite community arrived in the desert of Zin in the first month, and the people settled at Kadesh. It was here that Miriam died, and here that she was buried.

Water Famine at Kadesh

[2] As the community had no water, they held a council against Moses and Aaron. [3] The people contended with Moses, exclaiming, "Would that we too had perished with our kinsmen in the LORD's presence! [4] Why have you brought the LORD's community into this desert where we and our livestock are dying? [5] Why did you lead us out of Egypt, only to bring us to this wretched place which has neither grain nor figs nor vines nor pomegranates? Here there is not even water to drink!" [6] But Moses and Aaron went away from the assembly to the entrance of the meeting tent, where they fell prostrate.

Sin of Moses and Aaron

Then the glory of the LORD appeared to them, [7] and the LORD said to Moses, [8] "Take the staff and assemble the community, you and your brother Aaron, and in their presence order the rock to yield its waters. From the rock you shall bring forth water for the community and their livestock to drink." [9] So Moses took the staff from its place before the LORD, as he was ordered. [10]* He and Aaron assembled the community in front of the rock, where he said to them, "Listen to me, you rebels! Are we to bring water for you out of this rock?" [11]*† Then, raising his hand, Moses struck the rock twice with his staff, and water gushed out in abundance for the community and their livestock to drink. [12]† But the LORD said to Moses and Aaron, "Because you were not faithful to me in showing forth my sanctity be-

fore the Israelites, you shall not lead this community into the land I will give them."
[13]* These are the waters of Meribah, where the Israelites contended against the LORD, and where he revealed his sanctity among them.

Edom's Refusal

[14]† From Kadesh Moses sent men to the king of Edom with the message: "Your brother Israel has this to say: You know of all the hardships that have befallen us, [15] how our fathers went down to Egypt, where we stayed a long time, how the Egyptians maltreated us and our fathers, [16]* and how, when we cried to the LORD, he heard our cry and sent an angel who led us out of Egypt. Now here we are at the town of Kadesh at the edge of your territory. [17]† Kindly let us pass through your country. We will not cross any fields or vineyards, nor drink any well water, but we will go straight along the royal road without turning to the right or to the left, until we have passed through your territory."
[18] But Edom answered him, "You shall not pass through here; if you do, I will advance against you with the sword." [19] The Israelites insisted, "We want only to go up along the highway. If we or our livestock drink any of your water, we will pay for it. Surely there is no harm in merely letting us march through." [20]* But Edom still said, "No, you shall not pass through," and advanced against them with a large and heavily armed force. [21] Therefore, since Edom refused to let them pass through their territory, Israel detoured around them.

Death of Aaron

[22]*† Setting out from Kadesh, the whole Israelite community came to Mount Hor. [23] There at Mount Hor, on the border of the land of Edom, the LORD said to Moses and Aaron, [24] "Aaron is about to be taken to his people; he shall not enter the land I am giving to the Israelites, because you both rebelled against my commandment at the waters of Meribah. [25]* Take Aaron and his son Eleazar and bring them up on Mount Hor. [26] Then strip Aaron of his garments and put them on his son Eleazar; for there Aaron shall be taken in death."

20, 1: *The first month:* we would expect the mention also of the day and of the year (after the exodus) when this took place; cf similar dates in Nm 1, 1; 10, 11; 33, 38; Dt 1, 3. Here the full date seems to have been lost. Probably the Israelites arrived in Kadesh in the third year after the exodus. Cf Dt 1, 46. *The desert of Zin:* a barren region with a few good oases, southwest of the Dead Sea. See note on Nm 13, 21.
20, 11: *Twice:* perhaps because he had not sufficient faith to work the miracle with the first blow. Cf v 12.
20, 12f: The sin of Moses and Aaron consisted in doubting God's mercy toward the ever-rebellious people. *In showing forth my sanctity:* God's sacred power and glory: an allusion to the name of the place, Kadesh, which means "sanctified, sacred." Meribah means "contention." Cf Ex 17, 7.
20, 14: *Your brother Israel:* the Edomites were descended from

Esau, the brother of Jacob. Their country, to the southeast of the Dead Sea, was also known as Seir; cf Gn 25, 24ff; 36, 1.8f.
20, 17: *The royal road:* an important highway, running north and south along the plateau east of the Dead Sea. In ancient times it was much used by caravans and armies; later it was improved by the Romans, and large stretches of it are still clearly recognizable.
20, 22: *Mount Hor:* not definitively identified, but probably to be sought in the vicinity of Kadesh. According to Dt 10, 6, Aaron died at Moserah (cf "Moseroth" in Nm 33, 30f), which is apparently the name of the region in which Mount Hor is situated.

20, 10: Ex 17, 5f.
20, 11: Ps 78, 15f; Wis 11, 4;
    1 Cor 10, 4.
20, 13: Nm 27, 14; Ex 17, 7.
20, 16: Ex 2, 23.
20, 20: Jgs 11, 17.
20, 22: 21f; Nm 33, 37.
20, 25f: Dt 32, 50.

²⁷ Moses did as the LORD commanded. When they had climbed Mount Hor in view of the whole community, ²⁸* Moses stripped Aaron of his garments and put them on his son Eleazar. Then Aaron died there on top of the mountain. When Moses and Eleazar came down from the mountain, ²⁹ all the community understood that Aaron had passed away; and for thirty days the whole house of Israel mourned him.

Victory over Arad

21 ¹ *† When the Canaanite king of Arad, who lived in the Negeb, heard that the Israelites were coming along the way of Atharim, he engaged them in battle and took some of them captive. ²* Israel then made this vow to the LORD: "If you deliver this people into my hand, I will doom their cities." ³*† Later, when the LORD heeded Israel's prayer and delivered up the Canaanites, they doomed them and their cities. Hence that place was named Hormah.

The Bronze Serpent

⁴ From Mount Hor they set out on the Red Sea road, to bypass the land of Edom. But with their patience worn out by the journey, ⁵*† the people complained against God and Moses, "Why have you brought us up from Egypt to die in this desert, where there is no food or water? We are disgusted with this wretched food!"

⁶*† In punishment the LORD sent among the people saraph serpents, which bit the people so that many of them died. ⁷ Then the people came to Moses and said, "We have sinned in complaining against the LORD and you. Pray the LORD to take the serpents from us." So Moses prayed for the people, ⁸† and the LORD said to Moses, "Make a saraph and mount it on a pole, and if anyone who has been bitten looks at it, he will recover." ⁹*† Moses accordingly made a bronze serpent and mounted it on a pole, and whenever anyone who had been bitten by a serpent looked at the bronze serpent, he recovered.

Chap. 21

Journey around Moab

¹⁰* The Israelites moved on and encamped in Oboth. ¹¹† Setting out from Oboth, they encamped in Iye-abarim in the desert fronting Moab on the east. ¹² Setting out from there, they encamped in the Wadi Zered. ¹³ Setting out from there, they encamped on the other side of the Arnon, in the desert that extends from the territory of the Amorites; for the Arnon forms Moab's boundary with the Amorites. ¹⁴† Hence it is said in the "Book of the Wars of the LORD":

"Waheb in Suphah and the wadies,
¹⁵   Arnon and the wadi gorges
That reach back toward the site of Ar
    and slant to the border of Moab."

¹⁶† From there they went to Beer, where there was the well of which the LORD said to Moses, "Bring the people together, and I will give them water." ¹⁷ Then it was that Israel sang this song:

"Spring up, O well!—so sing to it—
¹⁸   The well that the princes sank,

21, 1–3: The account of this episode seems to be a later insertion here, for Nm 21, 4, belongs logically immediately after Nm 20, 29. Perhaps this is the same event as that mentioned in Jgs 1, 16f.
21, 3: *Hormah:* related to the Hebrew word *herem,* meaning "doomed." See notes on Nm 14, 45; 18, 14.
21, 5: *This wretched food:* apparently the manna is meant.
21, 6: *Saraph:* the Hebrew name for a certain species of venomous snakes; the word probably signifies "the fiery one," these snakes being so called from the burning effect of their poisonous bite.
21, 8: *If anyone who has been bitten looks at it, he will recover:* "and as Moses lifted up the serpent in the desert, even so must the Son of Man be lifted up, that those who believe in him may not perish, but may have life everlasting" (Jn 3, 14f).
21, 9: King Hezekiah, in his efforts to abolish idolatry, "smashed the bronze serpent which Moses had made" (2 Kgs 18, 4).

21, 11: *Iye-abarim:* probably means "the ruins in the Abarim (Mountains)." See note on Nm 27, 12.
21, 14: *The "Book of the Wars of the LORD":* an ancient collection of Israelite songs, now lost. *Waheb in Suphah:* since neither place is mentioned elsewhere, it is quite uncertain whether these dubious Hebrew words are even to be considered as place names; some Hebrew words apparently lost must have preceded this phrase.
21, 16: *Beer:* means a well.

20, 28: Nm 33, 38.   21, 6: Dt 8, 15; Wis 16, 5;
21, 1: Nm 33, 40.   1 Cor 10, 9.
21, 2: Jos 6, 17; Jgs 1, 17.   21, 9: Wis 16, 6f.10; Jn 3,
21, 5: Nm 14, 45.   14f.
21, 5: Nm 11, 6; Ex 16, 3.   21, 10: Nm 33, 43f.

that the nobles of the people dug,
with their scepters and their staffs."

From Beer they went to Mattanah, 19 from Mattanah to Nahaliel, from Nahaliel to Bamoth, 20† from Bamoth to the cleft in the plateau of Moab at the headland of Pisgah that overlooks Jeshimon.

Victory over Sihon

21 Now Israel sent men to Sihon, king of the Amorites, with the message, 22 "Let us pass through your country. We will not turn aside into any field or vineyard, nor will we drink any well water, but we will go straight along the royal road until we have passed through your territory." 23* Sihon, however, would not let Israel pass through his territory, but mustered all his forces and advanced into the desert against Israel. When he reached Jahaz, he engaged Israel in battle. 24 But Israel defeated him at the point of the sword, and took possession of his land from the Arnon to the Jabbok and as far as the country of the Ammonites, whose boundary was at Jazer. 25* Israel seized all the towns here and settled in these towns of the Amorites, in Heshbon and all its dependencies. 26 Now Heshbon was the capital of Sihon, king of the Amorites, who had fought against the former king of Moab and had seized all his land from Jazer to the Arnon. 27 That is why the poets say:

"Come to Heshbon, let it be rebuilt,
  let Sihon's capital be firmly constructed.
28 For fire went forth from Heshbon
  and a blaze from the city of Sihon;
It consumed the cities of Moab
  and swallowed up the high places of
    the Arnon.
29† Woe to you, O Moab!
  You are ruined, O people of Chemosh!
He let his sons become fugitives
  and his daughters be taken captive
  by the Amorite king Sihon.
30 Their plowland is ruined from Heshbon
    to Dibon;
  Ar is laid waste; fires blaze as far as Medeba."

31 When Israel had settled in the land of the Amorites, 32 Moses sent spies to Jazer; Israel then captured it with its dependencies and dispossessed the Amorites who were there.

Victory over Og

33* Then they turned and went up along the road to Bashan. But Og, king of Bashan, advanced against them with all his people to give battle at Edrei. 34* The LORD, however, said to Moses, "Do not be afraid of him; for into your hand I will deliver him with all his people and his land. Do to him as you did to Sihon, king of the Amorites, who lived in Heshbon." 35 So they struck him down with his sons and all his people, until not a survivor was left to him, and they took possession of his land.

22 1† Then the Israelites moved on and encamped in the plains of Moab on the other side of the Jericho stretch of the Jordan.

III: On the Plains of Moab

Balaam Summoned

2 Now Balak, son of Zippor, saw all that Israel did to the Amorites. 3 Indeed, Moab feared the Israelites greatly because of their numbers, and detested them. 4 So Moab said to the elders of Midian, "Soon this horde will devour all the country around us as an ox devours the grass of the field." And Balak, Zippor's son, who was king of Moab at that time, 5 sent messengers to Balaam, son of Beor, at Pethor on the Euphrates, in the land of the Amawites, summoning him with these words, "A people has come here from Egypt who now cover the face of the earth and are settling down opposite us! 6† Please come and curse this people for us; they are stronger than we are. We may then be able to defeat them and drive them out of the country. For I know that whoever you bless is blessed and whoever you curse is cursed." 7 Then the elders of Moab and of Midian left with the divination fee in hand and went to Balaam. When they had given him Balak's message, 8 he said to them in reply, "Stay here overnight, and I will give you whatever answer the LORD gives me." So the princes of Moab lodged with Balaam.

9 Then God came to Balaam and said, "Who are these men visiting you?" 10 Balaam answered God, "Balak, son of Zippor, king of Moab, sent me the

---

21, 20: *Jeshimon:* "the wasteland"; in 1 Sm 23, 19.24, and 26, 1.3, this is the desert of Judah, on the western side of the Dead Sea, but here and in Nm 23, 28, it seems to refer to the southern end of the Jordan valley where Beth-jeshimoth was situated.

21, 29: *Chemosh:* the chief god of the Moabites, and mentioned as such in the famous inscription of Mesha, king of Moab, who was the contemporary of the dynasty of Omri in Israel. Cf 1 Kgs 11, 7.33; 2 Kgs 23, 13; Jer 48, 7.13.

22, 1: *The plains of Moab:* the lowlands to the northeast of the Dead Sea, between the Jordan and the foothills below Mount Nebo.

Here the Israelites remained until they crossed the Jordan, as told in Jos 1–4. Jericho lay to the west of the Jordan.

22, 6: *Curse this people for us:* Balak believed that if Balaam forecast an evil omen for Israel, this evil would come to pass, as if by magic. Balaam was a soothsayer or foreteller; cf Jos 13, 22.

21, 23: Dt 2, 32; Jgs 11, 20.   21, 33: Dt 3, 1ff.
21, 25f: Jos 21, 39; Jgs 11, 26.   21, 34: Ps 136, 17ff.

message: [11] 'This people that came here from Egypt now cover the face of the earth. Please come and lay a curse on them for us; we may then be able to give them battle and drive them out.' " [12] But God said to Balaam, "Do not go with them and do not curse this people, for they are blessed." [13] The next morning Balaam arose and told the princes of Balak, "Go back to your own country, for the LORD has refused to let me go with you." [14] So the princes of Moab went back to Balak with the report, "Balaam refused to come with us."

Second Appeal to Balaam

[15] Balak again sent princes, who were more numerous and more distinguished than the others. [16] On coming to Balaam they told him, "This is what Balak, son of Zippor, has to say: Please do not refuse to come to me. [17] I will reward you very handsomely and will do anything you ask of me. Please come and lay a curse on this people for me." [18]* But Balaam replied to Balak's officials, "Even if Balak gave me his house full of silver and gold, I could not do anything, small or great, contrary to the command of the LORD, my God. [19] But, you too shall stay here overnight, till I learn what else the LORD may tell me."

[20] That night God came to Balaam and said to him, "If these men have come to summon you, you may go with them; yet only on the condition that you do exactly as I tell you." [21] So the next morning when Balaam arose, he saddled his ass, and went off with the princes of Moab.

The Talking Ass

[22]† But now the anger of God flared up at him for going, and the angel of the LORD stationed himself on the road to hinder him as he was riding along on his ass, accompanied by two of his servants. [23] When the ass saw the angel of the LORD standing on the road with sword drawn, she turned off the road and went into the field, and Balaam had to beat her to bring her back on the road. [24] Then the angel of the LORD took his stand in a narrow lane between vineyards with a stone wall on each side. [25] When the ass saw the angel of the LORD there, she shrank against the wall; and since she squeezed Balaam's leg against it, he beat her again. [26] The angel of the LORD then went ahead, and stopped next in a passage so narrow that there was no room to move either to the right or to the left. [27] When the ass saw the angel of the LORD

PRAY IT

The Talking Donkey

Balaam is an interesting biblical character. He is not an Israelite and seems to be a sort of prophet for hire. Balak, the king of Moab, hires him to prophesy against Israel. But Balaam, hearing a message from God through his "ass" or donkey, instead of cursing the Israelites, blesses them four times. Even though the Israelites were unfaithful, God continues to be with them, to bless them.

Balaam is a sign of the universal character of God's call, and the donkey is a symbol of the poor and oppressed. The complaining and whining donkey represents those who usually are not heard but are given a voice through the prophets.

This story gives us two insights into prayer. First, if God can use a donkey to talk to Balaam, God can use anything to talk to us. God speaks to us in many ways—through our experiences, the Scriptures, poetry and music, our relationship with nature, and more. Are we paying attention? Second, God wants us to hear the often unheard voice of the poor and oppressed. Do you hear God's voice expressed through them?

▶ Nm 22, 22–35

there, she cowered under Balaam. So, in anger, he again beat the ass with his stick.

[28]* But now the LORD opened the mouth of the ass, and she asked Balaam, "What have I done to you that you should beat me these three times?" [29] "You have acted so willfully against me," said Balaam to the ass, "that if I but had a sword at hand, I would kill you here and now." [30] But the ass said to Balaam, "Am I not your own beast, and have you not always ridden upon me until now? Have I been in the habit of treating you this way before?" "No," replied Balaam.

[31] Then the LORD removed the veil from Balaam's eyes, so that he too saw the angel of the

---

22, 22: *The anger of God flared up:* not merely because Balaam was going to Balak, for he had God's permission for the journey (v 20), but perhaps because he was tempted by avarice to curse Israel against God's command. "They have followed the way of Balaam, son of Bosor, who loved the wages of wrongdoing" (2 Pt 2, 15); "abandoned themselves to Balaam's error for the sake of gain" (Jude 11). Cf v 32 and compare Ex 4, 18–26.

22, 18: Nm 24, 13.　　　　**22, 28:** Nm 2 Pt 2, 16.

LORD standing on the road with sword drawn; and he fell on his knees and bowed to the ground. [32] But the angel of the LORD said to him, "Why have you beaten your ass these three times? It is I who have come armed to hinder you because this rash journey of yours is directly opposed to me. [33] When the ass saw me, she turned away from me these three times. If she had not turned away from me, I would have killed you; her I would have spared." [34] Then Balaam said to the angel of the LORD, "I have sinned. Yet I did not know that you stood against me to oppose my journey. Since it has displeased you, I will go back home." [35] But the angel of the LORD said to Balaam, "Go with the men; but you may say only what I tell you." So Balaam went on with the princes of Balak.

[36] When Balak heard that Balaam was coming, he went out to meet him at the boundary city Ir-Moab on the Arnon at the end of the Moabite territory. [37] And he said to Balaam, "I sent an urgent summons to you! Why did you not come to me? Did you think I could not reward you?" [38] Balaam answered him, "Well, I have come to you after all. But what power have I to say anything? I can speak only what God puts in my mouth." [39] Then Balaam went with Balak, and they came to Kiriath-huzoth. [40] Here Balak slaughtered oxen and sheep, and sent portions to Balaam and to the princes who were with him.

The First Oracle

[41] The next morning Balak took Balaam up on Bamoth-baal, and from there he saw some of the clans.

23

[1] Then Balaam said to Balak, "Build me seven altars, and prepare seven bullocks and seven rams for me here." [2] So he did as Balaam had ordered, offering a bullock and a ram on each altar. And Balak said to him, "I have erected the seven altars, and have offered a bullock and a ram on each." [3] Balaam then said to him, "Stand here by your holocaust while I go over there. Perhaps the LORD will meet me, and then I will tell you whatever he lets me see." He went out on the barren height, [4] and God met him. [5] When he had put an utterance in Balaam's mouth, the LORD said to him, "Go back to Balak, and speak accordingly." [6] So he went back to Balak, who was still standing by his

holocaust together with all the princes of Moab. [7]*† Then Balaam gave voice to his oracle:

> From Aram has Balak brought me here,
>   Moab's king, from the Eastern Mountains:
> "Come and lay a curse for me on Jacob,
>   come and denounce Israel."
> [8]   How can I curse whom God has not cursed?
>   How denounce whom the LORD has
>   not denounced?
> [9]† For from the top of the crags I see him,
>   from the heights I behold him.
> Here is a people that lives apart
>   and does not reckon itself among
>   the nations.
> [10]† Who has ever counted the dust of Jacob,
>   or numbered Israel's wind-borne particles?
> May I die the death of the just,
>   may my descendants be as many as theirs!

[11] "What have you done to me?" cried Balak to Balaam. "It was to curse my foes that I brought you here; instead, you have even blessed them." [12] Balaam replied, "Is it not what the LORD puts in my mouth that I must repeat with care?"

The Second Oracle

[13]† Then Balak said to him, "Please come with me to another place from which you can see only some and not all of them, and from there curse them for me." [14] So he brought him to the lookout field on the top of Pisgah, where he built seven altars and offered a bullock and a ram on each of them. [15] Balaam then said to Balak, "Stand here by your holocaust, while I seek a meeting over there." [16] Then the LORD met Balaam, and having put an utterance in his mouth, he said to him, "Go back to Balak, and speak accordingly." [17] So he went back to Balak, who was still standing by his holocaust together with the princes of Moab. When Balak asked him, "What did the LORD say?" [18] Balaam gave voice to his oracle:

> Be aroused, O Balak, and hearken;
>   give ear to my testimony, O son of Zippor!
> [19]   God is not man that he should speak falsely,
>   nor human, that he should change
>   his mind.
> Is he one to speak and not act,

23, 7: *Aram:* the ancient name of the region later known as Syria. *The Eastern Mountains:* the low ranges in the Syrian desert near the Euphrates and Balaam's town of Pethor; cf Nm 22, 5.
  23, 9: *A people that lives apart:* Israel, as the chosen people of God, occupied a unique place among the nations, from which they kept themselves aloof.
  23, 10: *The dust of Jacob . . . Israel's wind-borne particles:* the Israelites will be as numerous as dust in a desert sandstorm. *May I . . .*

as many as theirs: a formula by which Balaam swears he is speaking the truth; he sees the reward of virtue in having numerous descendants.
  23, 13: *To another place:* Balak thought that if Balaam would view Israel from a different site, he could forecast a different kind of omen.

to decree and not fulfill?
20 It is a blessing I have been given
    to pronounce;
    a blessing which I cannot restrain.
21† Misfortune is not observed in Jacob,
    nor misery seen in Israel.
The LORD, his God, is with him;
    with him is the triumph of his King.
22*† It is God who brought him out of Egypt,
    a wild bull of towering might.
23 No, there is no sorcery against Jacob,
    nor omen against Israel.
It shall yet be said of Jacob,
    and of Israel, "Behold what God
      has wrought!"
24* Here is a people that springs up like a lioness,
    and stalks forth like a lion;
It rests not till it has devoured its prey
    and has drunk the blood of the slain.

25 "Even though you cannot curse them," said Balak to Balaam, "at least do not bless them." 26 But Balaam answered Balak, "Did I not warn you that I must do all that the LORD tells me?"

The Third Oracle

27 Then Balak said to Balaam, "Come, let me bring you to another place; perhaps God will approve of your cursing them for me from there." 28 So he took Balaam to the top of Peor, that overlooks Jeshimon. 29 Balaam then said to him, "Here build me seven altars; and here prepare for me seven bullocks and seven rams." 30 And Balak did as Balaam had ordered, offering a bullock and a ram on each altar.

24   1 Balaam, however, perceiving that the LORD was pleased to bless Israel, did not go aside as before to seek omens, but turned his gaze toward the desert. 2 When he raised his eyes and saw Israel encamped, tribe by tribe, the spirit of God came upon him, 3 and he gave voice to his oracle:

The utterance of Balaam, son of Beor,
    the utterance of the man whose eye is true,
4 The utterance of one who hears what
      God says,
    and knows what the Most High knows,

Of one who sees what the Almighty sees,
    enraptured, and with eyes unveiled:
5 How goodly are your tents, O Jacob;
    your encampments, O Israel!
6 They are like gardens beside a stream,
    like the cedars planted by the LORD.
7 His wells shall yield free-flowing waters,
    he shall have the sea within reach;
His king shall rise higher than. . . .
    and his royalty shall be exalted.
8* It is God who brought him out of Egypt,
    a wild bull of towering might.
He shall devour the nations like grass,
    their bones he shall strip bare.
9* He lies crouching like a lion,
    or like a lioness; who shall arouse him?
Blessed is he who blesses you,
    and cursed is he who curses you!

10*† Balak beat his palms together in a blaze of anger at Balaam and said to him, "It was to curse my foes that I summoned you here; yet three times now you have even blessed them instead! 11 Be off at once, then, to your home. I promised to reward you richly, but the LORD has withheld the reward from you!" 12 Balaam replied to Balak, "Did I not warn the very messengers whom you sent to me, 13* 'Even if Balak gave me his house full of silver and gold, I could not of my own accord do anything, good or evil, contrary to the command of the LORD'? Whatever the LORD says I must repeat.

The Fourth Oracle

14 "But now that I am about to go to my own people, let me first warn you what this people will do to your people in the days to come." 15 Then Balaam gave voice to his oracle:

The utterance of Balaam, son of Beor,
    the utterance of the man whose eye is true,
16 The utterance of one who hears what
      God says,
    and knows what the Most High knows,
Of one who sees what the Almighty sees,
    enraptured and with eyes unveiled.
17*† I see him, though not now;
    I behold him, though not near:
A star shall advance from Jacob,
    and a staff shall rise from Israel,

---

† **23, 21:** *Misfortune . . . misery:* Balaam admits that he is unable to predict any evils for Israel.
    23, 22: *A wild bull of towering might:* the reference is to Israel, rather than to God.
    24, 10: *Balak beat his palms:* a sign of disclaiming any responsibility for paying the promised reward.
    24, 17: *A star . . . a staff:* many of the Fathers have understood this as a Messianic prophecy, although it is not referred to anywhere in the New Testament; in this sense the star is Christ himself, just as

he is the staff from Israel; cf Is 11, 1. But it is doubtful whether this passage is to be connected with the "star of the Magi" in Mt 2, 1–12. *The Shuthites:* mentioned in other documents of this period as nomads on the borded of Palestine.

23, 22: Nm 24, 8.	27, 29; 49, 9.
23, 24: Nm 24, 9; Gn 49, 9.	24, 10: Nm 23, 11.
24, 8: Nm 23, 22.	24, 13: Nm 22, 18.
24, 9: Nm 23, 24; Gn 12, 3;	24, 17: 2 Sm 8, 2.

That shall smite the brows of Moab,
and the skulls of all the Shuthites,
18 Till Edom is dispossessed,
and no fugitive is left in Seir.
Israel shall do valiantly,
19 and Jacob shall overcome his foes.

20*†Upon seeing Amalek, Balaam gave voice to his oracle:

First of the peoples was Amalek,
but his end is to perish forever.

21† Upon seeing the Kenites, he gave voice to his oracle:

Your abode is enduring, O smith,
and your nest is set on a cliff;
22 Yet destined for burning—
even as I watch—are your inhabitants.

23† Upon seeing . . . he gave voice to his oracle:

Alas, who shall survive of Ishmael,
24 to deliver his people from the hands of
the Kittim?
When they have conquered Asshur and
conquered Eber,
He too shall perish forever.

25 Then Balaam set out on his journey home; and Balak also went his way.

Worship of Baal of Peor

25 1 *† While Israel was living at Shittim, the people degraded themselves by having illicit relations with the Moabite women. 2* These then invited the people to the sacrifices of their god, and the people ate of the sacrifices and worshiped their god. 3* When Israel thus submitted to the rites of Baal of Peor, the LORD's anger flared up against Israel, 4*† and he said to Moses, "Gather all the leaders of the people, and hold a public execution of the guilty ones before the LORD, that his blazing wrath may be turned away from Israel." 5 So Moses told the Israelite judges, "Each of you shall kill those of his men who have submitted to the rites of Baal of Peor."

Zeal of Phinehas

6† Yet a certain Israelite came and brought in a Midianite woman to his clansmen in the view of Moses and of the whole Israelite community, while they were weeping at the entrance of the meeting tent. 7* When Phinehas, son of Eleazar, son of Aaron the priest, saw this, he left the assembly, and taking a lance in hand, 8 followed the Israelite into his retreat where he pierced the pair of them, the Israelite and the woman. Thus the slaughter of Israelites was checked; 9 but only after twenty-four thousand had died.

10 Then the LORD said to Moses, 11† "Phinehas, son of Eleazar, son of Aaron the priest, has turned my anger from the Israelites by his zeal for my honor among them; that is why I did not put an end to the Israelites for the offense to my honor. 12* Announce, therefore, that I hereby give him my pledge of friendship, 13 which shall be for him and for his descendants after him the pledge of an everlasting priesthood, because he was zealous on behalf of his God and thus made amends for the Israelites."

14† The Israelite slain with the Midianite woman was Zimri, son of Salu, prince of an ancestral house of the Simeonites. 15 The slain Midianite woman was Cozbi, daughter of Zur, who was head of a clan, an ancestral house, in Midian.

Vengeance on the Midianites

16† The LORD then said to Moses, 17* "Treat the Midianites as enemies and crush them, 18 for they have been your enemies by their wily dealings with you as regards Peor and as regards their kinswoman Cozbi, the daughter of the Midianite prince, who was killed at the time of the slaughter because of Peor."

24, 20: *First:* literally "the beginning." Amalek was an aboriginal people in Palestine and therefore considered as of great antiquity. There is a deliberate contrast here between the words first and end.

24, 21: The Kenites lived in high strongholds in the mountains of southern Palestine and the Sinai Peninsula, and were skilled in working the various metals found in their territory. Their name is connected, at least by popular etymology, with the Hebrew word for "smith"; of similar sound is the Hebrew word for "nest"—hence the play on words in the present passage.

24, 23f: The translation of this short oracle is based on a reconstructed text and is rather uncertain. *Ishmael:* the survival of Ishmael is indicated in Gn 17, 20; 21, 13.18.

25, 1: *Shittim:* the full name was Abel-shittim, a locality at the foot of the mountains in the northeastern corner of the plains of Moab (Nm 33, 49). *Illicit relations:* perhaps as part of the licentious worship of Baal of Peor.

25, 4: *Hold a public execution:* the same phrase occurs in 2 Sm 21, 6–14, where the context shows that at least a part of the penalty consisted in being denied honorable burial. In both passages, dismemberment as a punishment for the breaking of covenant pledges is a current understanding of the phrase.

25, 6: *Midianite woman:* at this time the Midianites were leagued with the Moabites in opposing Israel; cf Nm 22, 4.7. Balaam had induced both the Midianites (Nm 31, 16) and the Moabites (Rv 2, 14) to lure the Israelites to the obscene rites of Baal of Peor. *They were weeping:* on account of the plague that had struck them; cf v 8.

25, 11: *For my honor:* by taking vengeance on those who had made Baal of Peor a rival of the Lord.

25, 14f: The nobility of the slain couple is mentioned in order to stress the courage of Phinehas in punishing them. The zeal of Phinehas became proverbial; cf Ps 106, 30; Sir 45, 23; 1 Mc 2, 26.54.

25, 16ff: The account of the execution of this command is given in Nm 31, 1–18.

24, 20: Ex 17, 14; 1 Sm 15, 3.
25, 1: Nm 31, 16.
25, 2: Ex 34, 15f.
25, 3: Ps 106, 28; Hos 9, 10.
25, 4: Dt 4, 3.

25, 7: Ps 106, 30.
25, 12f: Sir 45, 23f; Ps 106, 31;
1 Mc 2, 26.54.
25, 17f: Nm 31, 2–12.

The Second Census

26 [19]† After the slaughter [1] the LORD said to Moses and Eleazar, son of Aaron the priest, [2]* "Take a census, by ancestral houses, throughout the community of the Israelites of all those of twenty years or more who are fit for military service in Israel." [3] So on the plains of Moab along the Jericho stretch of the Jordan, Moses and the priest Eleazar registered [4] those of twenty years or more, as the LORD had commanded Moses.

The Israelites who came out of the land of Egypt were as follows:

[5]* Of Reuben, the first-born of Israel, the Reubenites by clans were: through Hanoch the clan of the Hanochites, through Pallu the clan of the Palluites, [6] through Hezron the clan of the Hezronites, through Carmi the clan of the Carmites. [7] These were the clans of the Reubenites, of whom forty-three thousand seven hundred and thirty men were registered.

[8] From Pallu descended Eliab, [9]* and the descendants of Eliab were Dathan and Abiram —the same Dathan and Abiram, councilors of the community, who revolted against Moses and Aaron [like Korah's band when it rebelled against the LORD]. [10] The earth opened its mouth and swallowed them as a warning [Korah too and the band that died when the fire consumed two hundred and fifty men. [11] The descendants of Korah, however, did not die out].

[12]† The Simeonites by clans were: through Nemuel the clan of the Nemuelites, through Jamin the clan of the Jaminites, through Jachin the clan of the Jachinites, [13] through Sohar the clan of the Soharites, through Shaul the clan of the Shaulites. [14] These were the clans of the Simeonites, of whom twenty-two thousand two hundred men were registered.

[15] The Gadites by clans were: through Zephon the clan of the Zephonites, through Haggi the clan of the Haggites, through Shuni the clan of the Shunites, [16] through Ozni the clan of the Oznites, through Eri the clan of the Erites, [17] through Arod the clan of the Arodites, through Areli the clan of the Arelites. [18] These were the clans of the Gadites, of whom forty thousand five hundred men were registered.

[19]* The sons of Judah who died in the land of Canaan were Er and Onan. [20] The Judahites by clans were: through Shelah the clan of the Shelahites, through Perez the clan of the Perezites, through Zerah the clan of the Zerahites. [21] The Perezites were: through Hezron the clan of the Hezronites, through Hamul the clan of the Hamulites. [22] These were the clans of Judah, of whom seventy-six thousand five hundred men were registered.

[23] The Issacharites by clans were: through Tola the clan of the Tolaites, through Puvah the clan of the Puvahites, [24] through Jashub the clan of the Jashubites, through Shimron the clan of the Shimronites. [25] These were the clans of Issachar, of whom sixty-four thousand three hundred men were registered.

[26] The Zebulunites by clans were: through Sered the clan of the Seredites, through Elon the clan of the Elonites, through Jahleel the clan of the Jahleelites. [27] These were the clans of the Zebulunites, of whom sixty thousand five hundred men were registered.

[28] The sons of Joseph were Manasseh and Ephraim. [29] The Manassehites by clans were: through Machir the clan of the Machirites, through Gilead, a descendant of Machir, the clan of the Gileadites. [30] The Gileadites were: through Abiezer the clan of the Abiezrites, through Helek the clan of the Helekites, [31] through Asriel the clan of the Asrielites, through Shechem the clan of the Shechemites, [32] through Shemida the clan of the Shemidaites, through Hepher the clan of the Hepherites. [33]* Zelophehad, son of Hepher, had no sons, but only daughters, whose names were Mahlah, Noah, Hoglah, Milcah and Tirzah. [34] These were the clans of Manasseh, of whom fifty-two thousand seven hundred men were registered.

[35] The Ephraimites by clans were: through Shuthelah the clan of the Shuthelahites, through Becher the clan of the Bechrites, through Tahan the clan of the Tahanites. [36] The Shuthelahites were: through Eran the clan of the Eranites. [37] These were the clans of the Ephraimites, of whom thirty-two thousand five hundred men were registered.

These were the descendants of Joseph by clans.

[38] The Benjaminites by clans were: through Bela the clan of the Belaites, through Ashbel the clan of the Ashbelites, through Ahiram the clan of the Ahiramites, [39] through Shupham the clan of the Shuphamites, through Hupham the clan of the Huphamites. [40] The descendants of Bela were Arad and Naaman: through Arad the clan of the Aradites, through Naaman the clan of the Naamanites. [41] These were the Benjaminites by clans, of whom forty-five thousand six hundred men were registered.

26, 19: This is the last verse of Ch 25.
26, 12: *Nemuel:* so also in Gn 46, 10; 1 Chr 4, 24. In Ex 6, 15, the same man is called "Jemuel"; it is uncertain which form is correct.

26, 2: Nm 1, 2f.
26, 5f: 1 Chr 5, 3.
26, 9f: Nm 16, 1.32.
26, 19: Gn 38, 7.10; 46, 12;

1 Chr 2, 3.
26, 33: Nm 27, 1; 36, 11;
Jos 17, 3.

N
M

⁴² The Danites by clans were: through Shuham the clan of the Shuhamites. These were the clans of Dan, ⁴³ of whom sixty-four thousand four hundred men were registered.

⁴⁴ The Asherites by clans were: through Imnah the clan of the Imnites, through Ishvi the clan of the Ishvites, through Beriah the clan of the Beriites, ⁴⁵ through Heber the clan of the Heberites, through Malchiel the clan of the Malchielites. ⁴⁶ The name of Asher's daughter was Serah. ⁴⁷ These were the clans of Asher, of whom fifty-three thousand four hundred men were registered.

⁴⁸ The Naphtalites by clans were: through Jahzeel the clan of the Jahzeelites, through Guni the clan of the Gunites, ⁴⁹ through Jezer the clan of the Jezerites, through Shillem the clan of the Shillemites. ⁵⁰ These were the clans of Naphtali, of whom forty-five thousand four hundred men were registered.

⁵¹ These six hundred and one thousand seven hundred and thirty were the Israelites who were registered.

Allotment of the Land

⁵²† The LORD said to Moses, ⁵³* "Among these groups the land shall be divided as their heritage in keeping with the number of individuals in each group. ⁵⁴* To a large group you shall assign a large heritage, to a small group a small heritage, each group receiving its heritage in proportion to the number of men registered in it. ⁵⁵ But the land shall be divided by lot, as the heritage of the various ancestral tribes. ⁵⁶ As the lot falls shall each group, large or small, be assigned its heritage."

Census of the Levites

⁵⁷ The Levites registered by clans were: through Gershon the clan of the Gershonites, through Kohath the clan of the Kohathites, through Merari the clan of the Merarites. ⁵⁸ These also were clans of Levi: the clan of the Libnites, the clan of the Hebronites, the clan of the Mahlites, the clan of the Mushites, the clan of the Korahites.

Among the descendants of Kohath was Amram, ⁵⁹ whose wife was named Jochebed. She also was of the tribe of Levi, born to the tribe in Egypt. To Amram she bore Aaron and Moses and their sister Miriam. ⁶⁰ To Aaron were born Nadab and Abihu,

Eleazar and Ithamar. ⁶¹ But Nadab and Abihu died when they offered profane fire before the LORD.

⁶²* The total number of male Levites one month or more of age, who were registered, was twenty-three thousand. They were not registered with the other Israelites, however, for no heritage was given them among the Israelites.

⁶³ These, then, were the men registered by Moses and the priest Eleazar in the census of the Israelites taken on the plains of Moab along the Jericho stretch of the Jordan. ⁶⁴ Among them there was not a man of those who had been registered by Moses and the priest Aaron in the census of the Israelites taken in the desert of Sinai. ⁶⁵* For the LORD had told them that they would surely die in the desert, and not one of them was left except Caleb, son of Jephunneh, and Joshua, son of Nun.

Zelophehad's Daughters

27 ¹* Zelophehad, son of Hepher, son of Gilead, son of Machir, son of Manasseh, son of Joseph, had daughters named Mahlah, Noah, Hoglah, Milcah and Tirzah. They came forward, ² and standing in the presence of Moses, the priest Eleazar, the princes, and the whole community at the entrance of the meeting tent, said: ³† "Our father died in the desert. Although he did not join those who banded together against the LORD [in Korah's band], he died for his own sin without leaving any sons. ⁴ But why should our father's name be withdrawn from his clan merely because he had no son? Let us, therefore, have property among our father's kinsmen."

Laws Concerning Heiresses

⁵† When Moses laid their case before the LORD, ⁶ the LORD said to him, ⁷ "The plea of Zelophehad's daughters is just; you shall give them hereditary property among their father's kinsmen, letting their father's heritage pass on to them. ⁸ Therefore, tell the Israelites: If a man dies without leaving a son, you shall let his heritage pass on to his daughter; ⁹ if he has no daughter, you shall give his heritage to his brothers; ¹⁰ if he has no brothers, you shall give his heritage to his father's brothers; ¹¹* if his father had no brothers, you shall give his heritage to his nearest relative in his

---

[†] **26, 52–56:** The division of Canaan among the various tribes and clans and families was determined partly by the size of each group and partly by lot. Perhaps the lots determined the respective locality of each tribal land and the section reserved for each clan, while the relative size of the allotted locality and section depended on the numerical strength of each group. The Hebrews considered the outcome of the drawing of lots as an expression of God's will; cf Acts 1, 23–26.

27, 3: *He did not join . . . against the LORD:* had he done so, he and his heirs could have rightly been deprived of the privilege of receiving a portion in the Promised Land.

27, 5–11: The purpose of this law, as also that of the related laws in Nm 36, 2–10 (heiresses to marry within the same tribe), Dt 25, 5–10 (levirate marriage), and Lv 25, 10 (return of property in the jubilee year), was to keep the landed property within the proper domain of each tribe.

*

26, 53: Jos 11, 23.   **26, 65:** Nm 14, 22ff.29.
26, 54: Nm 33, 54; 35, 8.   **27, 1:** Nm 26, 33; Jos 17, 3.
26, 62: Nm 3, 39.   **27, 11:** Jer 32, 6–9.

clan, who shall then take possession of it." This is the legal norm for the Israelites, as the LORD commanded Moses.

Joshua To Succeed Moses

12*† The LORD said to Moses, "Go up here into the Abarim Mountains and view the land that I am giving to the Israelites. 13* When you have viewed it, you too shall be taken to your people, as was your brother Aaron, 14* because in the rebellion of the community in the desert of Zin you both rebelled against my order to manifest my sanctity to them by means of the water." [This is the water of Meribah of Kadesh in the desert of Zin.]

15 Then Moses said to the LORD, 16† "May the LORD, the God of the spirits of all mankind, set over the community a man 17 who shall act as their leader in all things, to guide them in all their actions; that the LORD's community may not be like sheep without a shepherd." 18*† And the LORD replied to Moses, "Take Joshua, son of Nun, a man of spirit, and lay your hand upon him. 19 Have him stand in the presence of the priest Eleazar and of the whole community, and commission him before their eyes. 20 Invest him with some of your own dignity, that the whole Israelite community may obey him. 21† He shall present himself to the priest Eleazar, to have him seek out for him the decisions of the Urim in the LORD's presence; and as he directs, Joshua, all the Israelites with him, and the community as a whole shall perform all their actions."

22 Moses did as the LORD had commanded him. Taking Joshua and having him stand in the presence of the priest Eleazar and of the whole community, 23 he laid his hands on him and gave him his commission, as the LORD had directed through Moses.

General Sacrifices

28 1 The LORD said to Moses, 2 "Give the Israelites this commandment: At the times I have appointed, you shall be careful to present to me the food offerings that are offered to me as sweet-smelling oblations.

Each Morning and Evening

3*† "You shall tell them therefore: This is the oblation which you shall offer to the LORD: two unblemished yearling lambs each day as the established holocaust, 4 offering one lamb in the morning and the other during the evening twilight, 5† each with a cereal offering of one tenth of an ephah of fine flour mixed with a fourth of a hin of oil of crushed olives. 6 This is the established holocaust that was offered at Mount Sinai as a sweet-smelling oblation to the LORD. 7† And as the libation for the first lamb, you shall pour out to the LORD in the sanctuary a fourth of a hin of wine. 8 The other lamb, to be offered during the evening twilight, you shall offer with the same cereal offering and the same libation as in the morning, as a sweet-smelling oblation to the LORD.

On the Sabbath

9 "On the sabbath day you shall offer two unblemished yearling lambs, with their cereal offering, two tenths of an ephah of fine flour mixed with oil, and with their libations. 10 Each sabbath there shall be the sabbath holocaust in addition to the established holocaust and its libation.

At the New Moon Feast

11† "On the first of each month you shall offer as a holocaust to the LORD two bullocks, one ram, and seven unblemished yearling lambs, 12 with three tenths of an ephah of fine flour mixed with oil as the cereal offering for each bullock, two tenths of an ephah of fine flour mixed with oil as the cereal offering for the ram, 13 and one tenth of an ephah of fine flour mixed with oil as the cereal offering for each lamb, that the holocaust may be a sweet-smelling oblation to the LORD. 14 Their libations shall be half a hin of wine for each bullock, a third of a hin for the ram, and a fourth of a hin for each lamb. This is the new moon holocaust for every new moon of the year. 15 Moreover, one goat shall be sacrificed as a sin offering to the LORD. These are to be offered in addition to the established holocaust and its libation.

27, 12: *The Abarim Mountains:* the range on the eastern side of the Dead Sea.

27, 16: *The God of the spirits of all mankind:* the sense is either that God knows the character and abilities of all men and therefore knows best whom to appoint (cf Acts 1, 24), or, more probably, that God is Master of life and death and therefore can call Moses from this world whenever he wishes; cf the same phrase in Nm 16, 22, where "spirit" evidently means "the life principle."

27, 18: *A man of spirit:* literally, "a man in whom there is spirit": one who has the qualities of a good leader—courage, prudence, and strength of will. Cf Gn 41, 38; Dt 34, 9.

27, 21: *The Urim:* certain sacred objects which the Hebrew priests employed to ascertain the divine will, probably by obtaining a positive or negative answer to a given question. The full expression was "the Urim and Thummim"; cf Ex 28, 30; Lv 8, 8; Dt 33, 8; Ezr

2, 63; Neh 7, 65. Joshua was ordinarily not to receive direct revelations from God as Moses had received them.

28, 3: *The established holocaust:* "the tamid holocaust," the technical term for the daily sacrifice.

28, 5: *Oil of crushed olives:* this oil, made in a mortar, was purer and more expensive than oil extracted in the olive press.

28, 7: *In the sanctuary:* according to Sir 50, 15, it was at the base of the altar.

28, 11: *On the first of each month:* literally, "at the new moons"; beginning on the evening when the crescent of the new moon first appeared.

27, 12: Dt 3, 27; 32, 49; 34, 1.   27, 18: Dt 34, 9.
27, 13f: Nm 20, 12.24.   28, 3–8: Ex 29, 38–42.
27, 14: Dt 32, 51.

At the Passover

[16]*† "On the fourteenth day of the first month falls the Passover of the LORD, [17] and the fifteenth day of this month is the pilgrimage feast. For seven days unleavened bread is to be eaten. [18]* On the first of these days you shall hold a sacred assembly, and do no sort of work. [19] As an oblation you shall offer a holocaust to the LORD, which shall consist of two bullocks, one ram, and seven yearling lambs that you are sure are unblemished, [20] with their cereal offerings of fine flour mixed with oil, offering three tenths of an ephah for each bullock, two tenths for the ram, [21] and one tenth for each of the seven lambs; [22] and offer one goat as a sin offering in atonement for yourselves. [23] These offerings you shall make in addition to the established morning holocaust: [24] you shall make exactly the same offerings each day for seven days as food offerings, in addition to the established holocaust with its libation, for a sweet-smelling oblation to the LORD. [25]* On the seventh day you shall hold a sacred assembly, and do no sort of work.

At Pentecost

[26]*† "On the day of first fruits, on your feast of Weeks, when you present to the LORD the new cereal offering, you shall hold a sacred assembly, and do no sort of work. [27] You shall offer as a sweet-smelling holocaust to the LORD two bullocks, one ram, and seven yearling lambs that you are sure are unblemished, [28] with their cereal offerings of fine flour mixed with oil; offering three tenths of an ephah for each bullock, two tenths of the seven lambs; [29] and one tenth for each of the seven lambs. [30] Moreover, one goat shall be offered as a sin offering in atonement for yourselves. [31] You shall make these offerings, together with their libations, in addition to the established holocaust with its cereal offering.

On New Year's Day

29 [1]*† "On the first day of the seventh month you shall hold a sacred assembly, and do no sort of work; it shall be a day on which you sound the trumpet. [2] You shall offer as a sweet-smelling holocaust to the LORD one bullock, one ram, and seven unblemished yearling lambs, [3] with

did you KNOW?

Other Jewish Feasts

In chapter 29 of Numbers, we find the instructions for two more Jewish festivals. (For other Jewish festivals, see Ex 34, 18–26.) The festival of trumpets is a fall celebration prescribed for "the first day of the seventh month" (Nm 29, 1). This day of rest, marked by trumpet blasts and sacrifices, came to be called Rosh Hashanah (head of the year), the beginning of the Jewish New Year.

On the tenth day of the seventh month, the Israelites celebrated the Day of Atonement (Yom Kippur). On this solemn day of penance and fasting, the high priest laid the sins of the people on a so-called scapegoat (see Lv 16, 20–21), then ran the beast into the wilderness, thus symbolically purifying the nation.

▶ Nm 29, 1–11

their cereal offerings of fine flour mixed with oil; offering three tenths of an ephah for the bullock, two tenths for the ram, [4] and one tenth for each of the seven lambs. [5] Moreover, one goat shall be offered as a sin offering in atonement for yourselves. [6] These are to be offered in addition to the ordinary new moon holocaust with its cereal offering, and in addition to the established holocaust with its cereal offering, together with the libations prescribed for them, as a sweet-smelling oblation to the LORD.

On the Day of Atonement

[7]*† "On the tenth day of this seventh month you shall hold a sacred assembly, and mortify yourselves, and do no sort of work. [8] You shall offer as a sweet-smelling holocaust to the LORD one bullock, one ram, and seven yearling lambs that you are sure are unblemished, [9] with their cereal offerings of

---

† **28, 16:** *On the fourteenth day:* toward evening at the end of this day; cf Ex 12, 6.18.

28, 26: *The day of first fruits:* a unique term for this feast, which is usually called "the feast of Weeks"; it was celebrated as a thanksgiving for the wheat harvest seven weeks after the barley harvest (Passover). In the time of Christ it was commonly known by the Greek word "Pentecost," that is, "fiftieth" (day after the Passover); see note on Lv 23, 16.

29, 1: *The first day of the seventh month:* (about September-October) is now the Jewish New Year's Day. In the older calendar the year began with the first of Nisan (March-April); cf Ex 12, 2.

29, 7: *The tenth day of this seventh month:* the Day of Atonement. *Mortify yourselves:* literally, "afflict your souls," that is, with fasting.

28, 16: Ex 12, 18; Lv 23, 5; Dt 16, 1.
28, 18: Ex 12, 16; Lv 23, 7.
28, 25: Ex 12, 16; 13, 6;
Lv 23, 8.
28, 26: Ex 34, 22.
29, 1: Nm 10, 10; Lv 23, 24.
29, 7: Lv 16, 29; 23, 27f.32.

fine flour mixed with oil; offering three tenths of an ephah for the bullock, two tenths for the ram, [10] and one tenth for each of the seven lambs. [11]† Moreover, one goat shall be sacrificed as a sin offering. These are to be offered in addition to the atonement sin offering, the established holocaust with its cereal offering, and their libations.

On the Feast of Booths

[12]*† "On the fifteenth day of the seventh month you shall hold a sacred assembly, and do no sort of work; then, for seven days following, you shall celebrate a pilgrimage feast to the LORD. [13]† You shall offer as a sweet-smelling holocaust to the LORD thirteen bullocks, two rams, and fourteen yearling lambs that are unblemished, [14] with their cereal offerings of fine flour mixed with oil; offering three tenths of an ephah for each of the thirteen bullocks, two tenths for each of the two rams, [15] and one tenth for each of the fourteen lambs. [16] Moreover, one goat shall be sacrificed as a sin offering. These are to be offered in addition to the established holocaust with its cereal offering and libation.

[17] "On the second day you shall offer twelve bullocks, two rams, and fourteen unblemished yearling lambs, [18] with their cereal offerings and libations as prescribed for the bullocks, rams and lambs in proportion to their number, [19] as well as one goat for a sin offering, besides the established holocaust with its cereal offering and libation.

[20] "On the third day you shall offer eleven bullocks, two rams, and fourteen unblemished yearling lambs, [21] with their cereal offerings and libations as prescribed for the bullocks, rams and lambs in proportion to their number, [22] as well as one goat for a sin offering, besides the established holocaust with its cereal offering and libation.

[23] "On the fourth day you shall offer ten bullocks, two rams, and fourteen unblemished yearling lambs, [24] with their cereal offerings and libations as prescribed for the bullocks, rams and lambs in proportion to their number, [25] as well as one goat for a sin offering, besides the established holocaust with its cereal offering and libation.

[26] "On the fifth day you shall offer nine bullocks, two rams, and fourteen unblemished yearling lambs, [27]* with their cereal offerings and libations as prescribed for the bullocks, rams and lambs in

proportion to their number, [28] as well as one goat for a sin offering, besides the established holocaust with its cereal offering and libation.

[29] "On the sixth day you shall offer eight bullocks, two rams, and fourteen unblemished yearling lambs, [30] with their cereal offerings and libations as prescribed for the bullocks, rams and lambs in proportion to their number, [31] as well as one goat for a sin offering, besides the established holocaust with its cereal offering and libation.

[32] "On the seventh day you shall offer seven bullocks, two rams, and fourteen unblemished yearling lambs, [33] with their cereal offerings and libations as prescribed for the bullocks, rams and lambs in proportion to their number, [34] as well as one goat for a sin offering, besides the established holocaust with its cereal offering and libation.

[35]*† "On the eighth day you shall hold a solemn meeting, and do no sort of work. [36] You shall offer up in holocaust as a sweet-smelling oblation to the LORD one bullock, one ram, and seven unblemished yearling lambs, [37] with their cereal offerings and libations as prescribed for the bullocks, rams and lambs in proportion to their number, [38] as well as one goat for a sin offering, besides the established holocaust with its cereal offering and libation.

[39] "These are the offerings you shall make to the LORD on your festivals, besides whatever holocausts, cereal offerings, libations, and peace offerings you present as your votive or free-will offerings."

30

[1] Moses then gave the Israelites these instructions, just as the LORD had ordered him.

Validity and Annulment of Vows

[2] Moses said to the heads of the Israelite tribes, "This is what the LORD has commanded: [3]*† When a man makes a vow to the LORD or binds himself under oath to a pledge of abstinence, he shall not violate his word, but must fulfill exactly the promise he has uttered.

[4] "When a woman, while still a maiden in her father's house, makes a vow to the LORD, or binds herself to a pledge, [5] if her father learns of her vow or the pledge to which she bound herself and says nothing to her about it, then any vow or any pledge

---

29, 11: *The atonement sin offering:* the bullock prescribed in Lv 16, 11f.

29, 12: This feast of Booths celebrating the vintage harvest was the most popular of all and therefore had the most elaborate ritual. See note on Lv 23, 34.

29, 13: *Thirteen bullocks:* the number of bullocks sacrificed before the octave day was seventy, arranged on a descending scale so that the number on the seventh day was the sacred number seven.

29, 35: *A solemn meeting:* the Hebrew word is the technical term for the closing celebration of the three major feasts of the Passover,

Pentecost and Booths, or of other special feasts that lasted for a week. Cf Lv 23, 36; Dt 16, 8; 2 Chr 7, 9; Neh 8, 18.

30, 3: *A vow . . . a pledge:* here the former signifies the doing of some positive good deed, in particular the offering of some sacrifice; the latter signifies the abstaining from some otherwise licit action or pleasure; cf v 14.

---

*

29, 12: Lv 23, 34f.   29, 35: Lv 23, 36; Jn 7, 37.
29, 27: Nm 29, 30.37.   30, 3: Dt 23, 22; Eccl 5, 3f.

did you KNOW?

Making a Vow

Vow.

Such a simple word, really. Three letters. One syllable. But its simplicity masks its meaning. If a word's length were directly related to its significance, then *vow* would have to become a long word indeed. It is a heavy word, one that we use sparingly. We tend to associate it with marriage or the life commitment of religious priests, sisters, and brothers. Vows can be public or private, solumn or simple.

From a faith perspective, a person making a vow is making a deep, binding promise before God. A vow cannot really be captured on paper. A vow must be lived out. It must be internalized. It is the foundation for a life choice. For we know, deep in our heart, that God is part of our vows.

The Israelites also took vows seriously. Numbers, chapter 30, is devoted to laws about vows. The laws were sexist by our standards. For example, a father or a husband could veto a woman's vows. Such laws were deemed acceptable in the Israelites' patriarchal society, but they are not in ours.

▸ **Nm 30, 2–6**

she has made remains valid. 6 But if on the day he learns of it her father expresses to her his disapproval, then any vow or any pledge she has made becomes null and void; and the LORD releases her from it, since her father has expressed to her his disapproval.

7 "If she marries while under a vow or under a rash pledge to which she bound herself, 8 and her husband learns of it, yet says nothing to her that day about it, then the vow or pledge she had made remains valid. 9 But if on the day he learns of it her husband expresses to her his disapproval, he thereby annuls the vow she had made or the rash pledge

to which she had bound herself, and the LORD releases her from it. 10 The vow of a widow or of a divorced woman, or any pledge to which such a woman binds herself, is valid.

11† "If it is in her husband's house that she makes a vow or binds herself under oath to a pledge, 12 and her husband learns of it yet says nothing to express to him his disapproval, then any vow or any pledge she has made remains valid. 13 But if on the day he learns of them her husband annuls them, then whatever she has expressly promised in her vow or in her pledge becomes null and void; since her husband has annulled them, the LORD releases her from them.

14 "Any vow or any pledge that she makes under oath to mortify herself, her husband can either allow to remain valid or render null and void. 15 But if her husband, day after day, says nothing at all to her about them, he thereby allows as valid any vow or any pledge she has made; he has allowed them to remain valid, because on the day he learned of them he said nothing to her about them. 16† If, however, he countermands them some time after he first learned of them, he is responsible for her guilt."

17 These are the statutes which the LORD prescribed through Moses concerning the relationship between a husband and his wife, as well as between a father and his daughter while she is still a maiden in her father's house.

Extermination of the Midianites

31 1† The LORD said to Moses, 2 "Avenge the Israelites on the Midianites, and then you shall be taken to your people." 3 So Moses told the people, "Select men from your midst and arm them for war, to attack the Midianites and execute the LORD's vengeance on them. 4 From each of the tribes of Israel you shall send a band of one thousand men to war." 5 From the clans of Israel, therefore, a thousand men of each tribe were levied, so that there were twelve thousand men armed for war. 6 Moses sent them out on the campaign, a thousand from each tribe, with Phinehas, son of Eleazar, the priest for the campaign, who had with him the sacred vessels and the trumpets for sounding the alarm. 7 They waged war against the Midianites, as the LORD had commanded Moses, and killed every male among them. 8† Besides those slain in battle, they killed the five Midianite kings: Evi, Rekem, Zur, Hur and Reba; and they also executed Balaam, son of Beor, with the sword. 9 But the Israelites kept

---

the women of the Midianites with their little ones as captives, and all their herds and flocks and wealth as spoil, 10 while they set on fire all the towns where they had settled and all their encampments. 11 Then they took all the booty, with the people and beasts they had captured, and brought the captives, together with the spoils and booty, 12 to Moses and the priest Eleazar and to the Israelite community at their camp on the plains of Moab, along the Jericho stretch of the Jordan.

Treatment of the Captives

13 When Moses and the priest Eleazar, with all the princes of the community, went outside the camp to meet them, 14 Moses became angry with the officers of the army, the clan and company commanders, who were returning from combat. 15 "So you have spared all the women!" he exclaimed. 16* "Why, they are the very ones who on Balaam's advice prompted the unfaithfulness of the Israelites toward the LORD in the Peor affair, which began the slaughter of the LORD's community. 17† Slay, therefore, every male child and every woman who has had intercourse with a man. 18 But you may spare and keep for yourselves all girls who had no intercourse with a man.

Purification after Combat

19 "Moreover, you shall stay outside the camp for seven days, and those of you who have slain anyone or touched anyone slain in battle shall purify yourselves on the third and on the seventh day. This applies both to you and to your captives. 20 You shall also purify every article of cloth, leather, goats' hair, or wood."

21 Eleazar the priest told the soldiers who had returned from combat: "This is what the law, as prescribed by the LORD to Moses, ordains: 22 Whatever can stand fire, such as gold, silver, bronze, iron, tin and lead, 23† you shall put into the fire, that it may become clean; however, it must also be purified with lustral water. But whatever cannot stand fire you shall put into the water. 24 On the seventh day you shall wash your clothes, and then you will again be clean. After that you may enter the camp."

Division of the Booty

25 The LORD said to Moses: 26 "With the help of the priest Eleazar and of the heads of the ancestral houses, count up all the human captives and the beasts that have been taken; 27† then divide them evenly, giving half to those who took active part in the war by going out to combat, and half to the rest of the community. 28 You shall levy a tax for the LORD on the warriors who went out to combat: one out of every five hundred persons, oxen, asses and sheep 29 in their half of the spoil you shall turn over to the priest Eleazar as a contribution to the LORD. 30 From the Israelites' half you shall take one out of every fifty persons, and the same from the different beasts, oxen, asses and sheep, and give them to the Levites, who have charge of the LORD's Dwelling." 31 So Moses and the priest Eleazar did this, as the LORD had commanded Moses.

Amount of Booty

32 This booty, what was left of the loot which the soldiers had taken, amounted to six hundred and seventy-five thousand sheep, 33 seventy-two thousand oxen, 34 sixty-one thousand asses, 35 and thirty-two thousand girls who were still virgins.

36 The half that fell to those who had gone out to combat was: three hundred and thirty-seven thousand five hundred sheep, 37 of which six hundred and seventy-five fell as tax to the LORD; 38 thirty-six thousand oxen, of which seventy-two fell as tax to the LORD; 39 thirty thousand five hundred asses, of which sixty-one fell as tax to the LORD; 40 and sixteen thousand persons, of whom thirty-two fell as tax to the LORD. 41 The taxes contributed to the LORD, Moses gave to the priest Eleazar, as the LORD had commanded him.

42 The half for the other Israelites, which fell to the community when Moses had taken it from the soldiers, was: 43 three hundred and thirty-seven thousand five hundred sheep, 44 thirty-six thousand oxen, 45 thirty thousand five hundred asses, 46 and sixteen thousand persons. 47 From this, the Israelites' share, Moses, as the LORD had ordered, took one out of every fifty, both of persons and of beasts, and gave them to the Levites, who had charge of the LORD's Dwelling.

Gifts of the Officers

48 Then the officers who had been clan and company commanders of the army came up to Moses 49 and said to him, "Your servants have counted up the soldiers under our command, and not one is

---

31, 17: There are later references to Midian in Jgs 6–8; 1 Kgs 11, 18; Is 60, 6. The present raid was only against those Midianites who were dwelling at this time near the encampment of the Israelites.

31, 23: *Lustral water:* water mixed with the ashes of the red heifer as prescribed in Nm 19, 9.

31, 27: *Divide them evenly:* for a similar division of the booty into two equal parts, between those who engaged in the fray and those who stayed with the baggage, cf 1 Sm 30, 24. But note that here the tax on the booty of the non-combatants is ten times as much as that on the soldier's booty.

31, 16: 2 Pt 2, 15; Rv 2, 14.

missing. [50]† So, to make atonement for ourselves before the LORD, each of us will bring as an offering to the LORD some gold article he has picked up, such as an anklet, a bracelet, a ring, an earring, or a necklace." [51] Moses and the priest Eleazar accepted this gold from them, all of it in well-wrought articles. [52] The gold that they gave as a contribution to the LORD amounted in all to sixteen thousand seven hundred and fifty shekels. This was from the clan and company commanders; [53] what the common soldiers had looted each one kept for himself. [54] Moses, then, and the priest Eleazar accepted the gold from the clan and company commanders, and put it in the meeting tent as a memorial for the Israelites before the LORD.

Request of Gad and Reuben

32 [1]† Now the Reubenites and Gadites had a very large number of livestock. Noticing that the land of Jazer and of Gilead was grazing country, [2] they came to Moses and the priest Eleazar and to the princes of the community and said, [3]† "The region of Ataroth, Dibon, Jazer, Nimrah, Heshbon, Elealeh, Sebam, Nebo and Baal-meon, [4] which the LORD has laid low before the community of Israel, is grazing country. Now, since your servants have livestock," [5] they continued, "if we find favor with you, let this land be given to your servants as their property. Do not make us cross the Jordan."

Moses' Rebuke

[6] But Moses answered the Gadites and Reubenites: "Are your kinsmen, then, to engage in war, while you remain here? [7] Why do you wish to discourage the Israelites from crossing to the land the LORD has given them? [8]* That is just what your fathers did when I sent them from Kadesh-barnea to reconnoiter the land. [9] They went up to the Wadi Eshcol and reconnoitered the land, then so discouraged the Israelites that they would not enter the land the LORD had given them. [10]* At that time the wrath of the LORD flared up, and he swore, [11] 'Because they have not followed me unreservedly, none of these men of twenty years or more who have come up from Egypt shall ever see this country I promised under oath to Abraham and Isaac

and Jacob, [12]*† except the Kenizzite Caleb, son of Jephunneh, and Joshua, son of Nun, who have followed the LORD unreservedly.' [13] So in his anger with the Israelites the LORD made them wander in the desert forty years, until the whole generation that had done evil in the sight of the LORD had died out. [14] And now here you are, a brood of sinners, rising up in your fathers' place to add still more to the LORD's blazing wrath against the Israelites. [15] If you turn away from following him, he will make them stay still longer in the desert, and so you will bring about the ruin of this whole nation."

Counter Proposal

[16] But they were insistent with him: "We wish only to build sheepfolds here for our flocks, and towns for our families; [17]* but we ourselves will march as troops in the van of the Israelites, until we have led them to their destination. Meanwhile our families can remain here in the fortified towns, safe from attack by the natives. [18] We will not return to our homes until every one of the Israelites has taken possession of his heritage, [19]* and will not claim any heritage with them once we cross the Jordan, so long as we receive a heritage for ourselves on this eastern side of the Jordan."

Agreement Reached

[20]† Moses said to them in reply: "If you keep your word to march as troops in the LORD's vanguard [21] and to cross the Jordan in full force before the LORD until he has driven his enemies out of his way [22]* and the land is subdued before him, then you may return here, quit of every obligation to the LORD and to Israel, and this region shall be your possession before the LORD. [23] But if you do not do this, you will sin against the LORD, and you can be sure that you will not escape the consequences of your sin. [24] Build the towns, then, for your families, and the folds for your flocks, but also fulfill your express promise."

[25] The Gadites and Reubenites answered Moses, "Your servants will do as you command, my lord. [26]* While our wives and children, our herds and other livestock remain in the towns of Gilead, [27] all your servants will go across as armed troops to battle before the LORD, just as your lordship says."

---

† **31, 50:** The precise nature and use of some of these articles of gold is not certain.

32, 1: *Gilead:* the name of the western part of the plateau east of the Jordan, sometimes signifying the whole region from the Yarmuk to the Jordan, sometimes only the northern part of this region, and sometimes, as here, only its southern part. Jazer lay to the east of southern Gilead.

32, 3: The places named in this verse, as well as the additional ones given in vv 34–38, were all in the former kingdom of Sihon, that is, in the region between the Jabbok and the Arnon. Cf Nm 21, 23f; Jos 13, 19–21.24–27.

32, 12: *Kenizzite:* a member of the clan of Kenaz, which, according to Gn 36, 11.15.42, was Edomitic; hence, although Caleb belonged to the tribe of Judah (Nm 13, 6; 34, 19), he must have had Edomite blood in his veins; cf also Jos 14, 6.14.

32, 20ff: Since the ark of the Lord was borne into battle with the Israelite army, the vanguard was said to march before the Lord.

32, 8f: Nm 13, 31ff; Dt 1, 22.　　**32, 19:** Jos 13, 8.
32, 10f: Dt 1, 34f.　　**32, 22:** Jos 1, 15.
32, 12: Nm 14, 24; Dt 1, 36.　　**32, 26:** Jos 1, 14.
32, 17: Jos 4, 12f.

28 Moses, therefore, gave this order in their regard to the priest Eleazar, to Joshua, son of Nun, and to the heads of the ancestral tribes of the Israelites: 29 "If all the Gadites and Reubenites cross the Jordan with you as combat troops before the LORD, you shall give them Gilead as their property when the land has been subdued before you. 30 But if they will not go across with you as combat troops before the LORD, you shall bring their wives and children and livestock across before you into Canaan, and they shall have their property with you in the land of Canaan."

31 To this the Gadites and Reubenites replied, "We will do what the LORD has commanded us, your servants. 32 We ourselves will go across into the land of Canaan as troops before the LORD, but we will retain our hereditary property on this side of the Jordan." 33*† So Moses gave them [the Gadites and Reubenites, as well as half the tribe of Manasseh, son of Joseph, the kingdom of Sihon, king of the Amorites, and the kingdom of Og, king of Bashan,] the land with its towns and the districts that surrounded them.

34 The Gadites rebuilt the fortified towns of Dibon, Ataroth, Aroer, 35 Atroth-shophan, Jazer, Jogbehah, 36 Beth-nimrah and Beth-haran, and they built sheepfolds. 37 The Reubenites rebuilt Heshbon, Elealeh, Kiriathaim, 38† Nebo, Baal-meon [names to be changed!], and Sibmah. These towns, which they rebuilt, they called by their old names.

Other Conquests

39 The descendants of Machir, son of Manasseh, invaded Gilead and captured it, driving out the Amorites who were there. 40* [Moses gave Gilead to Machir, son of Manasseh, and he settled there.] 41* Jair, a Manassehite clan, campaigned against the tent villages, captured them and called them Havvoth-jair. 42 Nobah also campaigned against Kenath, captured it with its dependencies and called it Nobah after his own name.

Stages on the Journey

33

1 † The following are the stages by which the Israelites journeyed up by companies from the land of Egypt under the guidance of Moses and Aaron. 2 By the LORD'S command Moses recorded the starting places of the various stages. The starting places of the successive stages were:

3† They set out from Rameses in the first month,
    on the fifteenth day of the first month.
On the Passover morrow the Israelites
    went forth
in triumph, in view of all Egypt,
4* While the Egyptians buried their first-born
    all of whom the LORD had struck down;
on their gods, too, the LORD
    executed judgments.

From Egypt to Sinai

5 Setting out from Rameses, the Israelites camped at Succoth. 6 Setting out from Succoth, they camped at Etham near the edge of the desert. 7* Setting out from Etham, they turned back to Pi-hahiroth, which is opposite Baal-zephon, and they camped opposite Migdol. 8* Setting out from Pi-hahiroth, they crossed over through the sea into the desert, and after a three days' journey in the desert of Etham, they camped at Marah. 9* Setting out from Marah, they came to Elim, where there were twelve springs of water and seventy palm trees, and they camped there. 10 Setting out from Elim, they camped beside the Red Sea. 11 Setting out from the Red Sea, they camped in the desert of Sin. 12 Setting out from the desert of Sin, they camped at Dophkah. 13 Setting out from Dophkah, they camped at Alush. 14* Setting out from Alush, they camped at Rephidim, where there was no water for the people to drink. 15* Setting out from Rephidim, they camped in the desert of Sinai.

From Sinai to Kadesh

16 Setting out from the desert of Sinai, they camped at Kibroth-hattaavah. 17* Setting out from Kibroth-hattaavah, they camped at Hazeroth. 18 Setting out from Hazeroth, they camped at Rithmah. 19 Setting out from Rithmah, they camped at Rimmon-perez. 20 Setting out from Rimmon-perez, they camped at Libnah. 21 Setting out

---

32, 33: The preceding is concerned solely with the two tribes of Gad and Reuben and with the land of the former kingdom of Sihon; hence it seems probable that the sudden reference here to the half-tribe of Manasseh and to their territory in Bashan, the former kingdom of Og, is a later addition to the text.

32, 38: The phrase in brackets is a gloss, warning the reader either to change the order of the preceding names, or, more probably, to read some other word, such as bosheth, "shame," for Baal. *They called by their old names:* literally, "they called by their names" (see Textual Notes); however, some understand the current Hebrew text to mean, "they called by new names."

33, 1ff: This list of camping sites was drawn up by Moses, as v 2 expressly states. However, in its present form it probably includes some glosses. Moreover, a comparison with the more detailed accounts of the journey as given elsewhere shows that this is not complete. It records just forty camping sites, not counting the starting place, Rameses, and the terminus, the plains of Moab. This number, which corresponds exactly to the forty years of wandering in the desert, is probably a schematic device. Besides, it seems that in its present form the order of some of these names has been disturbed. Several names listed here are not recorded elsewhere.

33, 3f: These two verses were probably borrowed from some ancient song celebrating the exodus from Egypt.

32, 33: Dt 3, 12; 29, 7; Jos 12,
    6; 13, 8.
32, 40: Dt 3, 15.
32, 41: Dt 3, 14.
33, 4f: Ex 12, 12.29.37.
33, 7: Ex 14, 2.

33, 8: Ex 15, 22.
33, 9: Ex 15, 27.
33, 14: Ex 17, 1.
33, 15: Ex 19, 2.
33, 17f: Nm 11, 34f.

N
M

from Libnah, they camped at Rissah. 22 Setting out from Rissah, they camped at Kehelathah. 23 Setting out from Kehelathah, they camped at Mount Shepher. 24 Setting out from Mount Shepher, they camped at Haradah. 25 Setting out from Haradah, they camped at Makheloth. 26 Setting out from Makheloth, they camped at Tahath. 27 Setting out from Tahath, they camped at Terah. 28 Setting out from Terah, they camped at Mithkah. 29 Setting out from Mithkah, they camped at Hashmonah. 30† Setting out from Hashmonah,—

From Mount Hor to Ezion-geber

They camped at Moseroth. 31 Setting out from Moseroth, they camped at Bene-jaakan. 32 Setting out from Bene-jaakan, they camped at Mount Gidgad. 33 Setting out from Mount Gidgad, they camped at Jotbathah. 34 Setting out from Jotbathah, they camped at Abronah. 35 Setting out from Abronah, they camped at Ezion-geber. 36* Setting out from Ezion-geber,—

From Kadesh to Mount Hor

They camped in the desert of Zin, at Kadesh. 37 Setting out from Kadesh, they camped at Mount Hor on the border of the land of Edom. 38* [Aaron the priest ascended Mount Hor at the LORD's command, and there he died in the fortieth year from the departure of the Israelites from the land of Egypt, on the first day of the fifth month. 39 Aaron was a hundred and twenty-three years old when he died on Mount Hor. 40† Now, when the Canaanite king of Arad, who lived in the Negeb in the land of Canaan, heard that the Israelites were coming. . . .] 41 Setting out from Mount Hor,—

From Ezion-geber to the Plains of Moab

† They camped at Zalmonah. 42 Setting out from Zalmonah, they camped at Punon. 43 Setting out from Punon, they camped at Oboth. 44 Setting out from Oboth, they camped at Iye-abarim on the border of Moab. 45 Setting out from Iye-abarim, they camped at Dibon-gad. 46 Setting out from Dibon-gad, they camped at Almon-diblathaim. 47 Setting out from Almon-diblathaim, they camped in the Abarim Mountains opposite Nebo. 48 Setting out from the Abarim Mountains, they camped on the plains of Moab along the Jericho stretch of the Jordan. 49 Their camp along the Jordan on the plains of Moab extended from Beth-jeshimoth to Abel-shittim.

Conquest and Division of Canaan

50 The LORD spoke to Moses on the plains of Moab beside the Jericho stretch of the Jordan and said to him: 51 "Tell the Israelites: When you go across the Jordan into the land of Canaan, 52* drive out all the inhabitants of the land before you; destroy all their stone figures and molten images, and demolish all their high places.

53 "You shall take possession of the land and settle in it, for I have given you the land as your property. 54* You shall apportion the land among yourselves by lot, clan by clan, assigning a large heritage to a large group and a small heritage to a small group. Wherever anyone's lot falls, there shall his property be within the heritage of his ancestral tribe.

55* "But if you do not drive out the inhabitants of the land before you, those whom you allow to remain will become as barbs in your eyes and thorns in your sides, and they will harass you in the country where you live, 56 and I will treat you as I had intended to treat them."

The Boundaries

34 1 The LORD said to Moses, 2 "Give the Israelites this order: When you enter the land of Canaan, this is the territory that shall fall to you as your heritage—the land of Canaan with its boundaries:

3* "Your southern boundary shall be at the desert of Zin along the border of Edom; on the east it shall begin at the end of the Salt Sea, 4* and turning south of the Akrabbim Pass, it shall cross Zin, and extend south of Kadesh-barnea to Hazar-addar; thence it shall cross to Azmon, 5* and turning from Azmon to the Wadi of Egypt, shall terminate at the Sea.

6† "For your western boundary you shall have the Great Sea with its coast; this shall be your western boundary.

7† "The following shall be your boundary on the north: from the Great Sea you shall draw a line to Mount Hor, 8 and shall continue it from Mount Hor to Labo in the land of Hamath, with the boundary extending through Zedad. 9 Thence the boundary shall reach to Ziphron and termi-

---

† **33, 30–36:** Moseroth is mentioned in Dt 10, 6 (in the form of "Moserah"), as the place where Aaron died. It must therefore have been close to Mount Hor; cf Nm 20, 22ff. It seems very probable that the section vv 36b–41a stood originally immediately after v 30a.
33, 40: The verse begins the same account of the victory over Arad as is given in Nm 21, 1ff, where it also follows the account of Aaron's death.
33, 41b–49: It seems that this section stood originally immediately after v 36a.

34, 6: *The Great Sea:* the Mediterranean.
34, 7f: *Mount Hor:* different from the one where Aaron died; cf Nm 20, 22; 33, 37f.

33, 36f: Nm 20, 1.22.
33, 38: Nm 20, 25; Dt 32, 50.
33, 52: Ex 23, 31; 34, 1; Dt 7, 5; 12, 3.
33, 54: Nm 26, 53ff.
33, 55: Jos 23, 13; Jgs 2, 3.
34, 3: Jos 15, 1f.
34, 4: Jos 15, 3.
34, 5: Jos 15, 4.

nate at Hazar-enan. This shall be your northern boundary.

10 "For your eastern boundary you shall draw a line from Hazar-enan to Shepham. 11 From Shepham the boundary shall go down to Ar-Baal, east of Ain, and descending further, shall strike the ridge on the east side of the Sea of Chinnereth; 12 thence the boundary shall continue along the Jordan and terminate with the Salt Sea.

"This is the land that shall be yours, with the boundaries that surround it."

13 Moses also gave this order to the Israelites: "This is the land, to be apportioned among you by lot, which the LORD has commanded to be given to the nine and one half tribes. 14 For all the ancestral houses of the tribe of Reuben, and the ancestral houses of the tribe of Gad, as well as half of the tribe of Manasseh, have already received their heritage; 15 these two and one half tribes have received their heritage on the eastern side of the Jericho stretch of the Jordan, toward the sunrise."

Supervisors of the Allotment

16 The LORD said to Moses, 17 "These are the names of the men who shall apportion the land among you: Eleazar the priest, and Joshua, son of Nun, 18* and one prince from each of the tribes whom you shall designate for this task. 19 These shall be as follows:

from the tribe of Judah: Caleb, son of Jephunneh;
20 from the tribe of Simeon: Samuel, son of Ammihud;
21 from the tribe of Benjamin: Elidad, son of Chislon;
22 from the tribe of Dan: Bukki, son of Jogli;
23 from the tribe of Manasseh: Hanniel, son of Ephod; and
24 from the tribe of Ephraim: Kemuel, son of Shiphtan, for the descendants of Joseph;
25 from the tribe of Zebulun: Elizaphan, son of Parnach;
26 from the tribe of Issachar: Paltiel, son of Azzan;
27 from the tribe of Asher: Ahihud, son of Shelomi;
28 from the tribe of Naphtali: Pedahel, son of Ammihud."

29 These are they whom the LORD commanded to assign the Israelites their heritage in the land of Canaan.

Cities for the Levites

35 1 The LORD gave these instructions to Moses on the plains of Moab beside the Jericho stretch of the Jordan: 2* "Tell the Israelites that out of their hereditary property they shall give the Levites cities for homes, as well as pasture lands around the cities. 3 The cities shall serve them to dwell in, and the pasture lands shall serve their herds and flocks and other animals. 4 The pasture lands of the cities to be assigned the Levites shall extend a thousand cubits from the city walls in each direction. 5 Thus you shall measure out two thousand cubits outside the city along each side—east, south, west and north—with the city lying in the center. This shall serve them as the pasture lands of their cities.

6* "Now these are the cities you shall give to the Levites: the six cities of asylum which you must establish as places where a homicide can take refuge, and in addition forty-two other cities— 7 a total of forty-eight cities with their pasture lands to be assigned the Levites. 8† In assigning the cities from the property of the Israelites, take more from a larger group and fewer from a smaller one, so that each group will cede cities to the Levites in proportion to its own heritage."

Cities of Asylum

9 The LORD said to Moses, 10 "Tell the Israelites: When you go across the Jordan into the land of Canaan, 11* select for yourselves cities to serve as cities of asylum, where a homicide who has killed someone unintentionally may take refuge. 12† These cities shall serve you as places of asylum from the avenger of blood, so that a homicide shall not be put to death unless he is first tried before the community. 13 Six cities of asylum shall you assign: 14 three beyond the Jordan, and three in the land of Canaan. 15 These six cities of asylum shall serve not only the Israelites but all the resident or transient aliens among them, so that anyone who has killed another unintentionally may take refuge there.

Murder and Manslaughter

16*† "If a man strikes another with an iron instrument and causes his death, he is a murderer and shall be put to death. 17 If a man strikes another with a death-dealing stone in his hand and causes his death, he is a murderer and shall be put to death. 18 If a man strikes another with a death-dealing club in his hand and causes his death, he is a murderer

---

35, 8: This provision was hardly observed in the actual assignment of the levitical cities as narrated in Jos 21.

35, 12: *The avenger of blood:* one of the close relatives of the slain (2 Sm 14, 7) who, as executor of public justice, had the right and duty to take the life of the murderer; cf Dt 19, 6. 12; Jos 20, 3. 5.9.

35, 16–25: Here, as also in Dt 19, 1–13, there is a casuistic development of the original law as stated in Ex 21, 12ff.

34, 18: Nm 1, 4.   **35, 11:** 10ff: Dt 19, 2; Jos 20, 2ff.
35, 2: Jos 14, 3f; 21, 2.   **35, 16:** Ex 21, 12; Lv 24, 17.
35, 6: Dt 4, 41f; Jos 20, 2.

and shall be put to death. [19] The avenger of blood may execute the murderer, putting him to death on sight.

[20]* "If a man pushes another out of hatred, or after lying in wait for him throws something at him, and causes his death, [21] or if he strikes another out of enmity and causes his death, he shall be put to death as a murderer. The avenger of blood may execute the murderer on sight.

[22]* "However, if a man pushes another accidentally and not out of enmity, or if without lying in wait for him he throws some object at him, [23] or without seeing him throws a death-dealing stone which strikes him and causes his death, although he was not his enemy nor seeking to harm him: [24] then the community, deciding the case between the slayer and the avenger of blood in accordance with these norms, [25]* shall free the homicide from the avenger of blood and shall remand him to the city of asylum where he took refuge; and he shall stay there until the death of the high priest who has been anointed with sacred oil. [26] If the homicide of his own accord leaves the bounds of the city of asylum where he has taken refuge, [27] and the avenger of blood finds him beyond these bounds and kills him, the avenger incurs no blood-guilt; [28] the homicide was bound to stay in his city of asylum until the death of the high priest. Only after the death of the high priest may the homicide return to his own district.

[29] "These shall be norms for you and all your descendants, wherever you live, for rendering judgment.

Witnesses

[30]* "Whenever someone kills another, the evidence of witnesses is required for the execution of the murderer. The evidence of a single witness is not sufficient for putting a person to death.

No Indemnity

[31] "You shall not accept indemnity in place of the life of a murderer who deserves the death penalty; he must be put to death. [32] Nor shall you accept indemnity to allow a refugee to leave his city of asylum and again dwell elsewhere in the land before the death of the high priest. [33] You shall not desecrate the land where you live. Since bloodshed desecrates the land, the land can have no atonement for the blood shed on it except through the blood of him who shed it. [34]* Do not defile the land in which you live and in the midst of which I dwell; for I am the LORD who dwells in the midst of the Israelites."

Property of Heiresses

36 [1] The heads of the ancestral houses in the clan of descendants of Gilead, son of Machir, son of Manasseh—one of the Josephite clans—came up and laid this plea before Moses and the priest Eleazar and before the princes who were the heads of the ancestral houses of the other Israelites. [2]* They said: "The LORD commanded you, my lord, to apportion the land by lot among the Israelites; and you, my lord, were also commanded by the LORD to give the heritage of our kinsman Zelophehad to his daughters. [3] But if they marry into one of the other Israelite tribes, their heritage will be withdrawn from our ancestral heritage and will be added to that of the tribe into which they marry; thus the heritage that fell to us by lot will be diminished. [4]† When the Israelites celebrate the jubilee year, the heritage of these women will be permanently added to that of the tribe into which they marry and will be withdrawn from that of our ancestral tribe."

[5]† So Moses gave this regulation to the Israelites according to the instructions of the LORD: "The tribe of the Josephites are right in what they say. [6] This is what the LORD commands with regard to the daughters of Zelophehad: They may marry anyone they please, provided they marry into a clan of their ancestral tribe, [7] so that no heritage of the Israelites will pass from one tribe to another, but all the Israelites will retain their own ancestral heritage. [8] Therefore, every daughter who inherits property in any of the Israelite tribes shall marry someone belonging to a clan of her own ancestral tribe, in order that all the Israelites may remain in possession of their own ancestral heritage. [9] Thus, no heritage can pass from one tribe to another, but all the Israelite tribes will retain their own ancestral heritage."

[10] The daughters of Zelophehad obeyed the command which the LORD had given to Moses. [11] Mahlah, Tirzah, Hoglah, Milcah and Noah, Zelophehad's daughters, married relatives on their father's side [12] within the clans of the descendants of Manasseh, son of Joseph; hence their heritage remained in the tribe of their father's clan.

Conclusion

[13] These are the commandments and decisions which the LORD prescribed for the Israelites through Moses, on the plains of Moab beside the Jericho stretch of the Jordan.

36, 4: Before the jubilee year various circumstances, such as divorce, could make such property revert to its original tribal owners; but in the jubilee year it became irrevocably attached to its new owners.

36, 5–9: This is a supplement to the law given in Nm 27, 5–11.

35, 20: Ex 21, 14; Dt 19, 11.
35, 22: Jos 20, 3.
35, 25: Jos 20, 6.
35, 30: Dt 17, 6; 19, 15; Jn 8, 17; 2 Cor 13, 1;

1 Tm 5, 19.
35, 34: Ex 29, 45.
36, 2: Nm 26, 55; 27, 6; Jos 17, 3f.

I magine this touching scene: You are standing at the bedside of your aging grandparent with all your cousins and family members. Your grandfather or grandmother begins to speak, sharing stories about the lessons he or she has learned from life. You listen to the familiar stories as if for the first time, and you are awed by the wisdom and love they contain. This is the scene Deuteronomy sets up—Moses is like the wise, aging grandparent, sharing his instructions and encouragement before dying.

At a Glance

I. Historical Review and Exhortation (1, 1—4, 43).

II. God and His Covenant (4, 44—11, 32).

III. Exposition of the Law (12, 1—26, 19).

IV. Final Words of Moses (27, 1—34, 12).

In-depth

The word Deuteronomy means "second law" in Greek. The first Law given on Mount Sinai was proposed by God to guide Israel in its wilderness journey. Written at a time when Israel was settled in the Promised Land and in need of religious reformation, Deuteronomy is a "second Law," adapted to the new situation of a people that needs to be reminded of its Covenant with God.

Deuteronomy has four divisions:

- In the first section (1, 1—4, 43), Moses addresses Israel by reviewing its history since Mount Horeb (Deuteronomy's term for Mount Sinai). Moses calls Israel to faithfulness and loyalty.

- In the second section (4, 44—11, 32), Moses reviews the Ten Commandments and the essence of the Law. He reminds the Israelites of the rewards for obeying and the consequences of disobeying the Law.

- In the third section (chapters 12–26), the most important section of Deuteronomy, Moses spells out a law to shape and govern the Israelites' new life as they settle in the Land.

- Finally, in the fourth section (chapters 27–34), Moses gives his last will and testament, offers a final blessing, and dies. His death is portrayed as the "sealing" of the second Law.

More than anything else, Deuteronomy stresses Israel as one people, with one God, one sanctuary, and now one land. These elements not only make Israel a unique people but bind it together in unity and solidarity. The Land of Promise now becomes a symbol of God's blessing and favor, the fulfillment of God's promises in the Covenant.

Quick Facts

Period Covered
just before the Israelites enter the Promised Land

Authors
scribes from the eighth century B.C. adapting the earlier Covenant Law to Israel's changing situation

Theme
the importance of the Covenant, the total commitment required by God's law

The Book of *Deuteronomy*

Deuteronomy

I: Historical Review and Exhortation

Introduction

1 [1]† These are the words which Moses spoke to all Israel beyond the Jordan [in the desert, in the Arabah, opposite Suph, between Paran and Tophel, Laban, Hazeroth and Dizahab; [2] it is a journey of eleven days from Horeb to Kadesh-barnea by way of the highlands of Seir].

[3] In the fortieth year, on the first day of the eleventh month, Moses spoke to the Israelites all the commands that the LORD had given him in their regard. [4]* After he had defeated Sihon, king of the Amorites, who lived in Heshbon, and Og, king of Bashan, who lived in Ashtaroth and in Edrei, [5] Moses began to explain the law in the land of Moab beyond the Jordan, as follows:

Departure from Horeb

[6] "The LORD, our God, said to us at Horeb, 'You have stayed long enough at this mountain. [7]*† Leave here and go to the hill country of the Amorites and to all the surrounding regions, the land of the Canaanites in the Arabah, the mountains, the foothills, the Negeb and the seacoast; to Lebanon, and as far as the Great River [the Euphrates]. [8]* I have given that land over to you. Go now and occupy the land I swore to your fathers, Abraham, Isaac and Jacob, I would give to them and to their descendants.'

Appointment of Elders

[9]† "At that time I said to you, 'Alone, I am unable to carry you. [10]* The LORD, your God, has so multiplied you that you are now as numerous as the stars in the sky. [11] May the LORD, the God of your fathers, increase you a thousand times over, and bless you as he promised! [12] But how can I alone bear the crushing burden that you are, along with your bickering? [13]* Choose wise, intelligent and experienced men from each of your tribes, that I may appoint them as your leaders.' [14] You answered me, 'We agree to do as you have proposed.' [15] So I took outstanding men of your tribes, wise and experienced, and made them your leaders as officials over thousands, over hundreds, over fifties and over tens, and other tribal officers. [16]* I charged your judges at that time, 'Listen to complaints among your kinsmen, and administer true justice to both parties even if one of them is an alien. [17] In rendering judg-

---

† **1, 1:** The local setting of all these discourses is in the land of Moab beyond the Jordan (cf v 5), also known as the plains of Moab (Nm 36, 13).
1, 7: The Amorites and the Canaanites formed the principal part of the pre-Israelite population of Palestine. *The foothills:* the hills on the western slope of the Judean mountain range. *The Arabah:* the valley of the Jordan and the depression south of the Dead Sea. *The Negeb:* the arid land in southern Palestine.

1, 9: *Carry you:* cf v 31.

* ———————————
1, 4: Dt 3, 2; Nm 21, 21–35.
1, 7: Nm 13, 29.
1, 8: Gn 12, 7; 15, 18; 17, 7f; 28, 13f.
1, 10: Dt 10, 22; Gn 15, 5.
1, 13ff: Ex 18, 21–25.
1, 16f: Ex 18, 26; 2 Chr 19, 6f; Prv 24, 23; Jn 7, 24; Jas 2, 9.

ment, do not consider who a person is; give ear to the lowly and to the great alike, fearing no man, for judgment is God's. Refer to me any case that is too hard for you and I will hear it.' 18 Thereupon I gave you all the commands you were to fulfill.

The Twelve Scouts

19* "Then, in obedience to the command of the LORD, our God, we set out from Horeb and journeyed through the whole desert, vast and fearful as you have seen, in the direction of the hill country of the Amorites. We had reached Kadesh-barnea 20 when I said to you, 'You have come to the hill country of the Amorites, which the LORD, our God, is giving us. 21 The LORD, your God, has given this land over to you. Go up and occupy it, as the LORD, the God of your fathers, commands you. Do not fear or lose heart.' 22* Then all of you came up to me and said, 'Let us send men ahead to reconnoiter the land for us and report to us on the road we must follow and the cities we must take.' 23 Agreeing with the proposal, I chose twelve men from your number, one from each tribe. 24 They set out into the hill country as far as the Wadi Eshcol, and explored it. 25 Then, taking along some of the fruit of the land, they brought it down to us and reported, 'The land which the LORD, our God, gives us is good.'

Threats of Revolt

26* "But you refused to go up, and after defying the command of the LORD, your God, 27*† you set to murmuring in your tents, 'Out of hatred for us the LORD has brought us up out of the land of Egypt, to deliver us into the hands of the Amorites and destroy us. 28* What shall we meet with up there? Our kinsmen have made us fainthearted by reporting that the people are stronger and taller than we, and their cities are large and fortified to the sky; besides, they saw the Anakim there.'

29 "But I said to you, 'Have no dread or fear of them. 30 The LORD, your God, who goes before you, will himself fight for you, just as he took your part before your very eyes in Egypt, 31 as well as in the desert, where you saw how the LORD, your God, carried you, as a man carries his child, all along your journey until you arrived at this place.' 32 Despite this, you would not trust the LORD, your God, 33* who journeys before you to find you a resting place—by day in the cloud, and by night in the fire, to show the way you must go. 34 When the LORD

heard your words, he was angry; 35* and he swore, 'Not one man of this evil generation shall look upon the good land I swore to give to your fathers, 36† except Caleb, son of Jephunneh; he shall see it. For to him and to his sons I will give the land he trod upon, because he has followed the LORD unreservedly.'

37* "The LORD was angered against me also on your account, and said, 'Not even you shall enter there, 38* but your aide Joshua, son of Nun, shall enter. Encourage him, for he is to give Israel its heritage. 39* Your little ones, who you said would become booty, and your children, who as yet do not know good from bad—they shall enter; to them I will give it, and they shall occupy it. 40 But as for yourselves: turn about and proceed into the desert on the Red Sea road.'

Unsuccessful Invasion

41* "In reply you said to me, 'We have sinned against the LORD. We will go up ourselves and fight, just as the LORD, our God, commanded us.' And each of you girded on his weapons, making light of going up into the hill country. 42 But the LORD said to me, 'Warn them: Do not go up and fight, lest you be beaten down before your enemies, for I will not be in your midst.' 43 I gave you this warning but you would not listen. In defiance of the LORD'S command you arrogantly marched off into the hill country. 44 Then the Amorites living there came out against you and, like bees, chased you, cutting you down in Seir as far as Hormah. 45 On your return you wept before the LORD, but he did not listen to your cry or give ear to you. 46 That is why you had to stay as long as you did at Kadesh.

Northward along Edom

2 1* "When we did turn and proceed into the desert on the Red Sea road, as the LORD had commanded me, we circled around the highlands of Seir for a long time. 2 Finally the LORD said to me, 3 'You have wandered round these highlands long enough; turn and go north. 4 Give this order to the people: You are now about to pass through the territory of your kinsmen, the descendants of Esau, who live in Seir. Though they are afraid of you, be very careful 5 not to come in conflict with them, for I will not give you so much as a foot of their land, since I have already given Esau possession of the highlands of Seir. 6 You shall purchase from them

---

†
1, 27: *In your tents:* among yourselves.
1, 36: *Except Caleb:* Joshua also was allowed to enter, but he is not referred to here because special mention is made of him in v 38 as the successor of Moses.

1, 19: Dt 8, 15; 32, 10.   **1, 26:** Dt 9, 23.
1, 22–28: Nm 13, 2–34.   **1, 27:** Dt 9, 28; Nm 14, 1–4;

Ps 106, 25.   Nm 20, 12.
1, 28: Dt 9, 1f.   **1, 38:** Dt 31, 3.7; Nm 27,
1, 33: Ex 13, 21; Nm 10, 33f;   18ff; 34, 17.
   14, 14.   **1, 39f:** Nm 14, 31.
1, 35: 34ff; Nm 14, 22f.28–38; Jos   **1, 41–45:** Nm 14, 40.42–45.
   14, 9.   **2, 1:** Dt 1, 40; Nm 14, 25;
1, 37: Dt 4, 21; 34, 4;   21, 4.

with silver the food you eat and the well water you drink. [7]* The LORD, your God, has blessed you in all your undertakings; he has been concerned about your journey through this vast desert. It is now forty years that he has been with you, and you have never been in want.'

Along Moab

[8]* "Then we left behind us the Arabah route, Elath, Ezion-geber, and Seir, where our kinsmen, the descendants of Esau, live; and we went on toward the desert of Moab. [9]* And the LORD said to me, 'Do not show hostility to the Moabites or engage them in battle, for I will not give you possession of any of their land, since I have given Ar to the descendants of Lot as their own. [10]* [Formerly the Emim lived there, a people strong and numerous and tall like the Anakim; [11] like them they were considered Rephaim. It was the Moabites who called them Emim. [12]* In Seir, however, the former inhabitants were the Horites; the descendants of Esau dispossessed them, clearing them out of the way and taking their place, just as the Israelites have done in the land of their heritage which the LORD has given them.] [13]* Get ready, then, to cross the Wadi Zered.' So we crossed it. [14]* Thirty-eight years had elapsed between our departure from Kadesh-barnea and that crossing; in the meantime the whole generation of soldiers had perished from the camp, as the LORD had sworn they should. [15] For it was the LORD's hand that was against them, till he wiped them out of the camp completely.

Along Ammon

[16] "When at length death had put an end to all the soldiers among the people, [17] the LORD said to me, [18] 'You are now about to leave Ar and the territory of Moab behind. [19]* As you come opposite the Ammonites, do not show hostility or come in conflict with them, for I will not give you possession of any land of the Ammonites, since I have given it to the descendants of Lot as their own. [20] [This also was considered a country of the Rephaim from its former inhabitants, whom the Ammonites called Zamzummim, [21] a people strong and numerous and tall like the Anakim. But these, too, the LORD cleared out of the way for the Ammonites, who ousted them and took their place. [22] He had done the same for the descendants of Esau, who dwell in

Seir, by clearing the Horites out of their way, so that the descendants of Esau have taken their place down to the present. [23]† So also the Caphtorim, migrating from Caphtor, cleared away the Avvim, who once dwelt in villages as far as Gaza, and took their place.]

Defeat of Sihon

[24]* " 'Advance now across the Wadi Arnon. I now deliver into your hands Sihon, the Amorite king of Heshbon, and his land. Begin the occupation; engage him in battle. [25] This day I will begin to put a fear and dread of you into every nation under the heavens, so that at the mention of your name they will quake and tremble before you.'

[26] "So I sent messengers from the desert of Kedemoth to Sihon, king of Heshbon, with this offer of peace: [27] 'Let me pass through your country by the highway; I will go along it without turning aside to the right or to the left. [28] For the food I eat which you will supply, and for the water you give me to drink, you shall be paid in silver. Only let me march through, [29]* as the descendants of Esau who dwell in Seir and the Moabites who dwell in Ar have done, until I cross the Jordan into the land which the LORD, our God, is about to give us.' [30] But Sihon, king of Heshbon, refused to let us pass through his land, because the LORD, your God, made him stubborn in mind and obstinate in heart that he might deliver him up to you, as indeed he has now done.

[31] "Then the LORD said to me, 'Now that I have already begun to hand over to you Sihon and his land, begin the actual occupation.' [32] So Sihon and all his people advanced against us to join battle at Jahaz; [33]* but since the LORD, our God, had delivered him to us, we defeated him and his sons and all his people. [34]*† At that time we seized all his cities and doomed them all, with their men, women and children; we left no survivor. [35] Our only booty was the livestock and the loot of the captured cities. [36]* From Aroer on the edge of the Wadi Arnon and from the city in the wadi itself, as far as Gilead, no city was too well fortified for us to whom the LORD had delivered them up. [37]* However, in obedience to the command of the LORD, our God, you did not encroach upon any of the Ammonite land, neither the region bordering on the Wadi Jabbok, nor the cities of the highlands.

2, 23: *The Caphtorim:* members of one of the groups of sea peoples who invaded the coast of Egypt and the southern part of Palestine about 1200 B.C. *Caphtor:* the ancient name of the island of Crete. Cf Am 9, 7.
2, 34: *Doomed:* see notes on Nm 18, 14; 21, 3.

2, 7: Dt 8, 2ff.
2, 8: Jgs 11, 18.
2, 9: Gn 19, 36f.
2, 10: Dt 1, 28.
2, 12: Gn 36, 20f.
2, 13: Nm 21, 12.
2, 14: Nm 14, 29.33.35.
2, 19: Gn 19, 38.
2, 24: Nm 21, 13; Jgs 11, 19–22.
2, 29: Dt 2, 5.8f; Jgs 11, 17.
2, 33: Dt 29, 7; Nm 21, 23–32.
2, 34: Dt 3, 6; 29, 7f.
2, 36: Dt 3, 12; Jos 13, 9.16; Jgs 11, 26.
2, 37: Nm 21, 24; Jos 12, 2.

Defeat of Og

3 1* "Then we turned and proceeded toward Bashan. But Og, king of Bashan, advanced against us with all his people to give battle at Edrei. 2* The LORD, however, said to me, 'Do not be afraid of him, for I have delivered him into your hand with all his people and his land. Do to him as you did to Sihon, king of the Amorites, who lived in Heshbon.' 3 And thus the LORD, our God, delivered into our hands Og, king of Bashan, with all his people. We defeated him so completely that we left him no survivor. 4 At that time we captured all his cities, none of them eluding our grasp, the whole region of Argob, the kingdom of Og in Bashan: sixty cities in all, 5 to say nothing of the great number of unwalled towns. All the cities were fortified with high walls and gates and bars. 6* As we had done to Sihon, king of Heshbon, so also here we doomed all the cities, with their men, women and children; 7 but all the livestock and the loot of each city we took as booty for ourselves.

8 "And so at that time we took from the two kings of the Amorites beyond the Jordan the territory from the Wadi Arnon to Mount Hermon 9 [which is called Sirion by the Sidonians and Senir by the Amorites], 10 comprising all the cities of the plateau and all Gilead and all the cities of the kingdom of Og in Bashan including Salecah and Edrei. 11† [Og, king of Bashan, was the last remaining survivor of the Rephaim. He had a bed of iron, nine regular cubits long and four wide, which is still preserved in Rabbah of the Ammonites.]

Allotment of the Conquered Lands

12* "When we occupied the land at that time, I gave Reuben and Gad the territory from Aroer, on the edge of the Wadi Arnon, halfway up into the highlands of Gilead, with the cities therein. 13 The rest of Gilead and all of Bashan, the kingdom of Og, the whole Argob region, I gave to the half-tribe of Manasseh. [All this region of Bashan was once called a land of the Rephaim. 14* Jair, a Manassehite clan, took all the region of Argob as far as the border of the Geshurites and Maacathites, and called it after his own name Bashan Havvoth-jair, the name it bears today.] 15 To Machir I gave Gilead, 16 and to Reuben and Gad the territory from Gilead to the Wadi Arnon—including the wadi bed and its banks—and to the Wadi Jabbok, which is the border of the Ammonites, 17* as well as the Arabah with the Jordan and its eastern banks from Chin-

nereth to the Salt Sea of the Arabah, under the slopes of Pisgah.

18*† "At that time I charged them as follows: 'The LORD, your God, has given you this land as your own. But all you troops equipped for battle must cross over in the vanguard of your brother Israelites. 19* Only your wives and children, as well as your livestock, of which I know you have a large number, shall remain behind in the towns I have given you, 20* until the LORD has settled your kinsmen as well, and they too possess the land which the LORD, your God, will give them on the other side of the Jordan. Then you may all return to the possessions I have given you.'

21 "It was then that I instructed Joshua, 'Your eyes have seen all that the LORD, your God, has done to both these kings; so, too, will the LORD do to all the kingdoms which you will encounter over there. 22 Fear them not, for the LORD, your God, will fight for you.'

Refusal to Moses

23 "And it was then that I besought the LORD, 24 'O Lord GOD, you have begun to show to your servant your greatness and might. For what god in heaven or on earth can perform deeds as mighty as yours? 25 Ah, let me cross over and see this good land beyond the Jordan, this fine hill country, and the Lebanon!' 26* But the LORD was angry with me on your account and would not hear me. 'Enough!' the LORD said to me. 'Speak to me no more of this. 27* Go up to the top of Pisgah and look out to the west, and to the north, and to the south, and to the east. Look well, for you shall not cross this Jordan. 28* Commission Joshua, and encourage and strengthen him, for he shall cross at the head of this people and shall put them in possession of the land you are to see.' 29 This was while we were in the ravine opposite Beth-peor.

Advantages of Fidelity

4 1 "Now, Israel, hear the statutes and decrees which I am teaching you to observe, that you may live, and may enter in and take possession of the land which the LORD, the God of your fathers, is giving you 2* In your observance of the commandments of the LORD, your God, which I enjoin upon you, you shall not add to what I command you nor subtract from it 3* You have seen with your own eyes what the LORD did at Baal-peor: the LORD, your God, destroyed from your midst everyone that

---

3, 11: *Bed of iron:* some translate, "a sarcophagus of basalt."
3, 18: *I charged them:* the words which follow were spoken to the men of Reuben and Gad (cf Nm 32).

3, 1: Dt 29, 6; Nm 21, 33.
3, 2f: Nm 21, 34f.
3, 6: Ps 135, 10ff.
3, 12f: Nm 32, 29.32f;

Jos 13, 8.29.
3, 14: Nm 32, 41; Jos 13, 11. 13.
3, 17: Dt 4, 49; Jos 12, 3.
3, 18: Jos 1, 14; 4, 12.
3, 19: Nm 32, 1.4; Jos 1, 14.
3, 20: Jos 22, 4.

3, 26: Dt 4, 21.
3, 27: Dt 34, 4; Nm 27, 12f.
3, 28: Dt 1, 38; 31, 7; Nm 27, 22f.
4, 2: Dt 13, 1.
4, 3: Nm 25, 3–9.

followed the Baal of Peor; [4] but you, who clung to the LORD, your God, are all alive today [5] Therefore, I teach you the statutes and decrees as the LORD, my God, has commanded me, that you may observe them in the land you are entering to occupy [6] Observe them carefully, for thus will you give evidence of your wisdom and intelligence to the nations, who will hear of all these statutes and say, 'This great nation is truly a wise and intelligent people' [7]* For what great nation is there that has gods so close to it as the Lord, our God, is to us whenever we call upon him? [8] Or what great nation has statutes and decrees that are as just as this whole law which I am setting before you today?

Revelation at Horeb

[9]* "However, take care and be earnestly on your guard not to forget the things which your own eyes have seen, nor let them slip from your memory as long as you live, but teach them to your children and to your children's children: [10]*† There was the day on which you stood before the LORD, your God, at Horeb, and he said to me, 'Assemble the people for me; I will have them hear my words, that they may learn to fear me as long as they live in the land and may so teach their children.' [11]* You came near and stood at the foot of the mountain, which blazed to the very sky with fire and was enveloped in a dense black cloud. [12]* Then the LORD spoke to you from the midst of the fire. You heard the sound of the words, but saw no form; there was only a voice. [13] He proclaimed to you his covenant, which he commanded you to keep: the ten commandments, which he wrote on two tablets of stone. [14] The LORD charged me at that time to teach you the statutes and decrees which you are to observe over in the land you will occupy.

Danger of Idolatry

[15]* "You saw no form at all on the day the LORD spoke to you at Horeb from the midst of the fire. Be strictly on your guard, therefore, [16]* not to degrade yourselves by fashioning an idol to represent any figure, whether it be the form of a man or of a woman, [17] of any animal on the earth or of any bird that flies in the sky, [18] of anything that crawls on the ground or of any fish in the waters under the earth. [19]* And when you look up to the heavens and behold the sun or the moon or any star among the heavenly hosts, do not be led astray into adoring them and serving them. These the LORD, your God, has let fall to the lot of all other nations under the heavens; [20]*† but you he has taken and led out of that iron foundry, Egypt, that you might be his very own people, as you are today. [21]* Since the LORD was angered against me on your account and swore that I should not cross the Jordan nor enter the good land which he is giving you as a heritage, [22]* I myself shall die in this country without crossing the Jordan; but you will cross over and take possession of that good land. [23]* Take heed, therefore, lest, forgetting the covenant which the LORD, your God, has made with you, you fashion for yourselves against his command an idol in any form whatsoever. [24] For the LORD, your God, is a consuming fire, a jealous God.

God's Fidelity

[25]† "When you have children and grandchildren, and have grown old in the land, should you then degrade yourselves by fashioning an idol in any form and by this evil done in his sight provoke the LORD, your God, [26] I call heaven and earth this day to witness against you, that you shall all quickly perish from the land which you will occupy when you cross the Jordan. You shall not live in it for any length of time but shall be promptly wiped out. [27]* The LORD will scatter you among the nations, and there shall remain but a handful of you among the nations to which the LORD will lead you. [28]* There you shall serve gods fashioned by the hands of man out of wood and stone, gods which can neither see nor hear, neither eat nor smell. [29]* Yet there too you shall seek the LORD, your God; and you shall indeed find him when you search after him with your whole heart and your whole soul. [30] In your distress, when all these things shall have come upon you, you shall finally return to the LORD, your God, and heed his voice. [31]* Since the LORD, your God, is a merciful God, he will not abandon and destroy you, nor forget the covenant which under oath he made with your fathers.

Proofs of God's Love

[32] "Ask now of the days of old, before your time, ever since God created man upon the earth; ask from one end of the sky to the other: Did anything

---

4, 10: Beginning here and continuing on for several verses (at least to the end of v 14) is the "reminiscence," the account of the things that the Israelites should recall and teach their children.
4, 20: Egypt is called an *iron foundry,* or furnace for smelting iron, because God allowed the Israelites to be afflicted there for the sake of their spiritual purification; the same expression for Egypt occurs also in 1 Kgs 8, 51; Jer 11, 4; compare the expression, "the furnace of affliction," in Is 48, 10.
4, 25: *Grown old:* Israel will lose the freshness of its youthful fervor.

4, 7: 2 Sm 7, 23.
4, 9: Dt 11, 19; Ps 78, 3–6.
4, 10: Heb 12, 18f.
4, 11: Ex 19, 17f.
4, 12: Dt 4, 33.36; 5, 4.
4, 15: Ex 24, 12; 31, 18; 34, 28.
4, 16: Dt 5, 8; Ex 20, 4.
4, 19: Dt 17, 3; Jb 31, 26ff.
4, 20: 1 Kgs 8, 51; Jer 11, 4.
4, 21: Dt 1, 37; 3, 26.
4, 22: Dt 3, 27.
4, 23: Dt 4, 16.
4, 27f: Dt 28, 36.62.64.
4, 28: Ps 135, 15ff; Is 44, 9.
4, 29: Jer 29, 13.
4, 31: Dt 31, 8.

so great ever happen before? Was it ever heard of? 33* Did a people ever hear the voice of God speaking from the midst of fire, as you did, and live? 34*† Or did any god venture to go and take a nation for himself from the midst of another nation, by testings, by signs and wonders, by war, with his strong hand and outstretched arm, and by great terrors, all of which the LORD, your God, did for you in Egypt before your very eyes? 35 All this you were allowed to see that you might know the LORD is God and there is no other. 36 Out of the heavens he let you hear his voice to discipline you; on earth he let you see his great fire, and you heard him speaking out of the fire. 37 For love of your fathers he chose their descendants and personally led you out of Egypt by his great power, 38 driving out of your way nations greater and mightier than you, so as to bring you in and to make their land your heritage, as it is today. 39* This is why you must now know, and fix in your heart, that the LORD is God in the heavens above and on earth below, and that there is no other. 40* You must keep his statutes and commandments which I enjoin on you today, that you and your children after you may prosper, and that you may have long life on the land which the LORD, your God, is giving you forever."

Cities of Refuge

41* Then Moses set apart three cities in the region east of the Jordan, 42 that a homicide might take refuge there if he unwittingly killed his neighbor to whom he had previously borne no malice, and that he might save his life by fleeing to one of these cities: 43 Bezer in the desert, in the region of the plateau, for the Reubenites; Ramoth in Gilead for the Gadites; and Golan in Bashan for the Manassehites.

II: God and His Covenant

Introduction

44 This is the law which Moses set before the Israelites. 45 These are the ordinances, statutes and decrees which he proclaimed to them when they had come out of Egypt 46 and were beyond the Jordan in the ravine opposite Beth-peor, in the land of Sihon, king of the Amorites, who dwelt in Heshbon and whom Moses and the Israelites defeated after

coming out of Egypt. 47 They occupied his land and the land of Og, king of Bashan, as well—the land of these two kings of the Amorites in the region east of the Jordan: 48† from Aroer on the edge of the Wadi Arnon to Mount Sion (that is, Hermon) 49* and all the Arabah east of the Jordan, as far as the Arabah Sea under the slopes of Pisgah.

The Covenant at Horeb

5 1 Moses summoned all Israel and said to them, "Hear, O Israel, the statutes and decrees which I proclaim in your hearing this day, that you may learn them and take care to observe them. 2* The LORD, our God, made a covenant with us at Horeb; 3 not with our fathers did he make this covenant, but with us, all of us who are alive here this day. 4 The LORD spoke with you face to face on the mountain from the midst of the fire. 5* Since you were afraid of the fire and would not go up the mountain, I stood between the LORD and you at that time, to announce to you these words of the LORD:

The Decalogue

6* 'I, the LORD, am your God, who brought you out of the land of Egypt,* that place of slavery. 7* You shall not have other gods besides me. 8* You shall not carve idols for yourselves in the shape of anything in the sky above or on the earth below or in the waters beneath the earth; 9*† you shall not bow down before them or worship them. For I, the LORD, your God, am a jealous God, inflicting punishments for their fathers' wickedness on the children of those who hate me, down to the third and fourth generation 10* but bestowing mercy, down to the thousandth generation, on the children of those who love me and keep my commandments.

11* 'You shall not take the name of the LORD, your God, in vain. For the LORD will not leave unpunished him who takes his name in vain.

12 'Take care to keep holy the sabbath day as the LORD, your God, commanded you. 13 Six days you may labor and do all your work; 14* but the seventh day is the sabbath of the LORD, your God. No work may be done then, whether by you, or your son or daughter, or your male or female slave, or your ox or ass or any of your beasts, or the alien who lives with you. Your male and female slave should rest as

---

4, 34: *Testings:* the demonstrations of God's power as in the ten great plagues of Egypt; cf Dt 7, 19; 29, 2.

4, 48: *Sion:* another name for Mount Hermon, besides those mentioned in Dt 3, 9.

5, 9f: God does not punish us for another's sins, but because of the solidarity of human society, the good or evil deeds of one generation may make their effects felt even in later generations. Yet note how God's mercy allows the good effects of virtue to last much longer than the bad effects of vice: a thousand generations compared to three or four.

4, 33: Dt 4, 36; 5, 24.26; Ex 20, 19.
4, 34: Dt 7, 19; 26, 8; 29, 2; Ex 7, 3; 15, 3–10; Jer 32, 21.
4, 39: Dt 4, 35.
4, 40: Dt 6, 2f; 12, 28.
4, 41ff: Dt 19, 2–13; Nm 35, 6–29; Jos 20, 8; 21, 27.36f; 1 Chr 6, 71. 80.
4, 49: Dt 3, 17.

5, 2: Dt 28, 69.
5, 5: Ex 24, 2.
5, 6–21: Ex 20, 2–17.
5, 6: Ps 81, 11.
5, 7: Ps 81, 10.
5, 8: Dt 27, 15; Lv 26, 1; Ps 97, 7.
5, 9: Ex 34, 14.
5, 10: Dt 7, 9; Ex 20, 6.
5, 11: Mt 5, 33.
5, 14: Gn 2, 2; Ex 20, 8; 23, 12; Heb 4, 4.

NATIVE AMERICAN

The Lakota Code

See how similar these guidelines from a Native American tribal code are to the Ten Commandments (Dt 5, 1–21), not to mention our own civil laws, school policies, and even family rules. What can we learn from them?

- Love one another.
- Pity orphan children. Be kind to them because they are poor; feed them and clothe them.
- Do not kill one another.
- Do not steal anything from anyone, especially from your own people.
- Do not tell lies to anyone, or lie about anyone.
- Respect your brothers and sisters. Do not marry in your own family.
- The ability to make good speech is a great gift from their maker, owner of all things, to the people. This is why you should not talk badly about anyone. Bad talk can hurt one's family or everyday life.
- Never quarrel among one another. Be good to others and always be friendly to whomever you meet, wherever you meet them.
- Do not brag about yourself, or try to hurt another's feelings. The generous person is the one who is respected.

   (Ron Zeilinger, *Sacred Ground*, pp. 74–75)

▶ Dt 5, 1–21

you do. 15* For remember that you too were once slaves in Egypt, and the LORD, your God, brought you from there with his strong hand and outstretched arm. That is why the LORD, your God, has commanded you to observe the sabbath day.

16* 'Honor your father and your mother, as the LORD, your God, has commanded you, that you may have a long life and prosperity in the land which the LORD, your God, is giving you.

17* 'You shall not kill.

18 'You shall not commit adultery.

19 'You shall not steal.

20 'You shall not bear dishonest witness against your neighbor.

21 'You shall not covet your neighbor's wife.

'You shall not desire your neighbor's house or field, nor his male or female slave, nor his ox or ass, nor anything that belongs to him.'

Moses as Mediator

22 "These words, and nothing more, the LORD spoke with a loud voice to your entire assembly on the mountain from the midst of the fire and the dense cloud. He wrote them upon two tablets of stone and gave them to me. 23 But when you heard the voice from the midst of the darkness, while the mountain was ablaze with fire, you came to me in the person of all your tribal heads and elders, 24* and said, 'The LORD, our God, has indeed let us see his glory and his majesty! We have heard his voice from the midst of the fire and have found out today that a man can still live after God has spoken with him. 25* But why should we die now? Surely this great fire will consume us. If we hear the voice of the LORD, our God, any more, we shall die. 26 For what mortal has heard, as we have, the voice of the living God speaking from the midst of fire, and survived? 27* Go closer, you, and hear all that the LORD, our God, will say, and then tell us what the LORD, our God, tells you; we will listen and obey.'

28* "The LORD heard your words as you were speaking to me and said to me, 'I have heard the words these people have spoken to you, which are all well said. 29 Would that they might always be of such a mind, to fear me and to keep all my commandments! Then they and their descendants would prosper forever. 30 Go, tell them to return to their tents. 31 Then you wait here near me and I will give you all the commandments, the statutes and decrees you must teach them, that they may observe them in the land which I am giving them to possess.'

32 "Be careful, therefore, to do as the LORD, your God, has commanded you, not turning aside to the right or to the left, 33* but following exactly the way prescribed for you by the LORD, your God, that you may live and prosper, and may have long life in the land which you are to occupy.

6 [1]* "These then are the commandments, the statutes and decrees which the LORD, your God, has ordered that you be taught to observe in the land into which you are crossing for conquest, [2]* so that you and your son and your grandson may fear the LORD, your God, and keep, throughout the days of your lives, all his statutes and commandments which I enjoin on you, and thus have long life. [3] Hear then, Israel, and be careful to observe them, that you may grow and prosper the more, in keeping with the promise of the LORD, the God of your fathers, to give you a land flowing with milk and honey.

The Great Commandment

[4]*† "Hear, O Israel! The LORD is our God, the LORD alone! [5]* Therefore, you shall love the LORD, your God, with all your heart, and with all your soul, and with all your strength. [6] Take to heart these words which I enjoin on you today. [7]* Drill them into your children. Speak of them at home and abroad, whether you are busy or at rest. [8]*† Bind them at your wrist as a sign and let them be as a pendant on your forehead. [9]* Write them on the doorposts of your houses and on your gates.

Fidelity in Prosperity

[10]* "When the LORD, your God, brings you into the land which he swore to your fathers, Abraham, Isaac and Jacob, that he would give you, a land with fine, large cities that you did not build, [11] with houses full of goods of all sorts that you did not garner, with cisterns that you did not dig, with vineyards and olive groves that you did not plant; and when, therefore, you eat your fill, [12]* take care not to forget the LORD, who brought you out of the land of Egypt, that place of slavery. [13]*† The LORD, your God, shall you fear; him shall you serve, and by his name shall you swear. [14] You shall not follow other gods, such as those of the surrounding nations, [15]* lest the wrath of the LORD, your God, flare up against you and he destroy you from the face of the land; for the LORD, your God, who is in your midst, is a jealous God. [16]* "You shall not put the LORD, your God, to the test, as you did at Massah. [17] But keep the commandments of the LORD, your God, and the ordinances and statutes he has enjoined on you. [18] Do

what is right and good in the sight of the LORD, that you may, according to his word, prosper, and may enter in and possess the good land which the LORD promised on oath to your fathers, [19]* thrusting all your enemies out of your way.

Instruction to Children

[20]* "Later on, when your son asks you what these ordinances, statutes and decrees mean which the

The Shema: Putting God First

Deuteronomy 6, 4 is the most famous declaration of faith in the Old Testament: "Hear, O Israel! The LORD is our God, the LORD alone!" This short verse, part of a prayer called the Shema, is uttered daily by faithful Jews. It has been so important that the commands of verses 8–9 often have been interpreted literally. The Pharisees of Jesus' day, for example, wore miniature copies of the prayer on their bodies and attached other copies to their doorposts. Orthodox Jews today continue this tradition. Keeping the law of God is a privilege—something to be "worn" with pride!

The Shema reminds Jewish people to put God first and to love God with all their heart, soul, and might. Think about someone who seems to carry God in their heart all the time. Are they lost and frustrated? Do they seem angry and hate filled? Chances are they seem more relaxed and sure of themselves than most people do. Having God in your sights at all times will help in more ways than you could ever imagine!

▸ Dt 6, 4–9

6, 4f: This passage contains the basic principle of the whole Mosaic law, the keynote of the Book of Deuteronomy: since the Lord alone is God, we must love him with an undivided heart. Christ cited these words as "the greatest and the first commandment," embracing in itself the whole law of God (Mt 22, 37f and parallels).

6, 8: *Bind them . . . as a sign:* these injunctions were probably meant merely in a figurative sense; cf Ex 13, 9.16. However, the later Jews understood them literally, and tied on their wrists and foreheads "phylacteries," boxes containing strips of parchment on which the words were inscribed; cf Mt 23, 5.

6, 13: *Him shall you serve:* here, to "serve" God means especially

to "worship" him; in this sense it is quoted by our Lord (Mt 4, 10) as an argument against worshiping the devil.

6, 1: Dt 4, 1; 5, 31; 12, 1.
6, 2: Dt 4, 40; 5, 29; 10, 12f.
6, 4: Mk 12, 29.
6, 5: Dt 10, 12; 11, 13; Mt 22, 37; Mk 12, 30; Lk 10, 27.
6, 7: 6f: Dt 4, 9; 11, 18; 32, 46.
6, 8: Dt 11, 18; Ex 13, 9. 16; Mt 23, 5.
6, 9: Dt 11, 20.
6, 10f: Jos 24, 13.
6, 12: Dt 5, 6.
6, 13: Dt 10, 20; Mt 4, 10; Lk 4, 8.
6, 15: 14f: Dt 8, 19; 11, 16.28.
6, 16: Nm 20, 1–13.
6, 19: Ex 23, 27; 34, 11.
6, 20: Ex 12, 26; 13, 14.

LORD, our God, has enjoined on you, ²¹* you shall say to your son, 'We were once slaves of Pharaoh in Egypt, but the LORD brought us out of Egypt with his strong hand ²² and wrought before our eyes signs and wonders, great and dire, against Egypt and against Pharaoh and his whole house. ²³ He brought us from there to lead us into the land he promised on oath to our fathers, and to give it to us. ²⁴ Therefore, the LORD commanded us to observe all these statutes in fear of the LORD, our God, that we may always have as prosperous and happy a life as we have today; ²⁵ and our justice before the LORD, our God, is to consist in carefully observing all these commandments he has enjoined on us.'

Destruction of Pagans

7 ¹* "When the LORD, your God, brings you into the land which you are to enter and occupy, and dislodges great nations before you—the Hittites, Girgashites, Amorites, Canaanites, Perizzites, Hivites and Jebusites: seven nations more numerous and powerful than you— ²* and when the LORD, your God, delivers them up to you and you defeat them, you shall doom them. Make no covenant with them and show them no mercy. ³* You shall not intermarry with them, neither giving your daughters to their sons nor taking their daughters for your sons. ⁴ For they would turn your sons from following me to serving other gods, and then the wrath of the LORD would flare up against you and quickly destroy you.

⁵*† "But this is how you must deal with them: Tear down their altars, smash their sacred pillars, chop down their sacred poles, and destroy their idols by fire. ⁶* For you are a people sacred to the LORD, your God; he has chosen you from all the nations on the face of the earth to be a people peculiarly his own. ⁷ It was not because you are the largest of all nations that the LORD set his heart on you and chose you, for you are really the smallest of all nations. ⁸ It was because the LORD loved you and because of his fidelity to the oath he had sworn to your fathers, that he brought you out with his strong hand from the place of slavery, and ransomed you from the hand of Pharaoh, king of Egypt. ⁹* Understand, then, that the LORD, your God, is God indeed, the faithful God who keeps his merciful covenant down to the thousandth generation toward those who love him and keep his commandments, ¹⁰ but who repays with destruction the person who hates him; he does not dally with such a one, but makes him personally pay for it. ¹¹ You

shall therefore carefully observe the commandments, the statutes and the decrees which I enjoin on you today.

Blessings of Obedience

¹²* "As your reward for heeding these decrees and observing them carefully, the LORD, your God, will keep with you the merciful covenant which he promised on oath to your fathers. ¹³* He will love and bless and multiply you; he will bless the fruit of your womb and the produce of your soil, your grain and wine and oil, the issue of your herds and the young of your flocks, in the land which he swore to your fathers he would give you. ¹⁴ You will be blessed above all peoples; no man or woman among you shall be childless nor shall your livestock be barren. ¹⁵ The LORD will remove all sickness from you; he will not afflict you with any of the malignant diseases that you know from Egypt, but will leave them with all your enemies.

¹⁶ "You shall consume all the nations which the LORD, your God, will deliver up to you. You are not to look on them with pity, lest you be ensnared into serving their gods. ¹⁷* Perhaps you will say to yourselves, 'These nations are greater than we. How can we dispossess them?' ¹⁸ But do not be afraid of them. Rather, call to mind what the LORD, your God, did to Pharaoh and to all Egypt: ¹⁹* the great testings which your own eyes have seen, the signs and wonders, his strong hand and outstretched arm with which the LORD, your God, brought you out. The same also will he do to all the nations of whom you are now afraid. ²⁰* Moreover, the LORD, your God, will send hornets among them, until the survivors who have hidden from you are destroyed. ²¹ Therefore, do not be terrified by them, for the LORD, your God, who is in your midst, is a great and awesome God. ²²* He will dislodge these nations before you little by little. You cannot exterminate them all at once, lest the wild beasts become too numerous for you. ²³* The LORD, your God, will deliver them up to you and will rout them utterly until they are annihilated. ²⁴* He will deliver their kings into your hand, that you may make their names perish from under the heavens. No man will be able to stand up against you, till you have put an end to them. ²⁵ The images of their gods you shall destroy by fire. Do not covet the silver or gold on them, nor take it for yourselves, lest you be ensnared by it; for it is an abomination to the LORD, your God. ²⁶ You shall not bring any abominable thing into your house, lest you be doomed

---

† 7, 5: *Sacred pillars . . . poles:* see note on Ex 34, 13.

6, 21: Ex 20, 2.
7, 1: Ex 23, 23; 33, 2.
7, 2: Ex 34, 12.

7, 3f: Ex 34, 16; 1 Kgs 11, 1f.
7, 5: Dt 12, 3; Ex 34, 13.
7, 6: Dt 14, 2; 26, 18;

Ex 19, 6.
7, 9f: Dt 5, 9f.
7, 12–16: Dt 28, 1–14; Ex 23,
    22–26; Lv 26, 3–13.
7, 13: Dt 30, 9.
7, 17f: Dt 1, 28ff.

7, 19: Dt 4, 34.
7, 20: Ex 23, 28ff.
7, 22: Ex 23, 29f.
7, 23: Dt 7, 2.
7, 24: Dt 11, 25.

with it; loathe and abhor it utterly as a thing that is doomed.

God's Care

8 ¹* "Be careful to observe all the commandments I enjoin on you today, that you may live and increase, and may enter in and possess the land which the LORD promised on oath to your fathers. ²* Remember how for forty years now the LORD, your God, has directed all your journeying in the desert, so as to test you by affliction and find out whether or not it was your intention to keep his commandments. ³*† He therefore let you be afflicted with hunger, and then fed you with manna, a food unknown to you and your fathers, in order to show you that not by bread alone does man live, but by every word that comes forth from the mouth of the LORD. ⁴* The clothing did not fall from you in tatters, nor did your feet swell these forty years. ⁵ So you must realize that the LORD, your God, disciplines you even as a man disciplines his son.

Danger of Prosperity

⁶ "Therefore, keep the commandments of the LORD, your God, by walking in his ways and fearing him. ⁷* For the LORD, your God, is bringing you into a good country, a land with streams of water, with springs and fountains welling up in the hills and valleys, ⁸ a land of wheat and barley, of vines and fig trees and pomegranates, of olive trees and of honey, ⁹ a land where you can eat bread without stint and where you will lack nothing, a land whose stones contain iron and in whose hills you can mine copper. ¹⁰ But when you have eaten your fill, you must bless the LORD, your God, for the good country he has given you. ¹¹ Be careful not to forget the LORD, your God, by neglecting his commandments and decrees and statutes which I enjoin on you today: ¹² lest, when you have eaten your fill,

AFRICAN AMERICAN   The Principle of *Ujima*

Decades before the Civil War, the Underground Railroad helped thousands of African slaves find their way to freedom. The Underground Railroad was not a real railroad but a loose network of antislavery northerners—mostly African Americans—who helped escaped slaves reach safety in the free states or Canada. People called conductors guided groups of fugitive slaves through isolated areas at night so they wouldn't be spotted. Others opened their homes and farms to give them safe places to stay during the day. It was dangerous work because professional slave catchers and local officials were always looking for escaped slaves to return for financial rewards.

    The Underground Railroad is just one example of what can be accomplished through the Kwanzaa principle of *ujima* (see "Kwanzaa as a Way of Life," Dt 10, 12–22), which is collective work and responsibility. Our African American ancestors in this country worked together bravely for the common good. Many members of the Underground Railroad were former slaves themselves and took responsibility for freeing others as they themselves had been freed. Today, we need young people with the same sense of responsibility and the willingness to work together in order to free others from poverty, violence, and addiction.

    Martin Luther King Jr. did this. In his last speech, he said to you and me: "I've been to the Mountain top and I've seen the Promised Land. I may not get there with you, but I want you to know that we as a people will get to the Promised Land." He knew that he would not live to see his people freed from prejudice and discrimination. But he spent his whole life working with others toward that goal.

    The author of Deuteronomy wrote long after Moses' time. Many of the Chosen People had indeed become wealthy, so he used Moses' authority to remind them of how they had gotten to where they were. Their ancestors—escaped, impoverished slaves—trusted in God and worked together over a long time to bring prosperity to the nation. This is the mentality we too must cultivate in order to bring success to ourselves and our people.

▸ Dt 8, 11–18

---

† **8, 3:** *Not by bread alone, etc.:* quoted by our Lord in Mt 4, 4. The sense is: God takes care of those who love him even when natural means seem to fail them.

8, 1: Dt 4, 1; 6, 1.
8, 2: Dt 2, 7; 29, 4; Am 2, 10.
8, 3: Ex 16, 12–15.35; Nm
8, 4: Dt 29, 4; Neh 9, 21.
8, 7: Dt 11, 10ff.
11, 6–9: Mt 4, 4; Lk 4, 4.

and have built fine houses and lived in them, [13] and have increased your herds and flocks, your silver and gold, and all your property, [14] you then become haughty of heart and unmindful of the LORD, your God, who brought you out of the land of Egypt, that place of slavery; [15]* who guided you through the vast and terrible desert with its saraph serpents and scorpions, its parched and waterless ground; who brought forth water for you from the flinty rock [16] and fed you in the desert with manna, a food unknown to your fathers, that he might afflict you and test you, but also make you prosperous in the end. [17]* Otherwise, you might say to yourselves, 'It is my own power and the strength of my own hand that has obtained for me this wealth.' [18] Remember then, it is the LORD, your God, who gives you the power to acquire wealth, by fulfilling, as he has now done, the covenant which he swore to your fathers. [19]* But if you forget the LORD, your God, and follow other gods, serving and worshiping them, I forewarn you this day that you will perish utterly. [20] Like the nations which the LORD destroys before you, so shall you too perish for not heeding the voice of the LORD, your God.

Unmerited Success

9 [1]* "Hear, O Israel! You are now about to cross the Jordan to enter in and dispossess nations greater and stronger than yourselves, having large cities fortified to the sky, [2]* the Anakim, a people great and tall. You know of them and have heard it said of them, 'Who can stand up against the Anakim?' [3]* Understand, then, today that it is the LORD, your God, who will cross over before you as a consuming fire; he it is who will reduce them to nothing and subdue them before you, so that you can drive them out and destroy them quickly, as the LORD promised you. [4]* After the LORD, your God, has thrust them out of your way, do not say to yourselves, 'It is because of my merits that the LORD has brought me in to possess this land'; for it is really because of the wickedness of these nations that the LORD is driving them out before you. [5] No, it is not because of your merits or the integrity of your heart that you are going in to take possession of their land; but the LORD, your God, is driving these nations out before you on account of their wickedness and in order to keep the promise which he made on oath to your fathers, Abraham, Isaac and Jacob. [6] Understand this, therefore: it is not because of your merits that the LORD, your God, is giving you this good land to possess, for you are a stiff-necked people.

The Golden Calf

[7]* "Bear in mind and do not forget how you angered the LORD, your God, in the desert. From the day you left the land of Egypt until you arrived in this place, you have been rebellious toward the LORD. [8]* At Horeb you so provoked the LORD that he was angry enough to destroy you, [9]* when I had gone up the mountain to receive the stone tablets of the covenant which the LORD made with you. Meanwhile I stayed on the mountain forty days and forty nights without eating or drinking, [10]* till the LORD gave me the two tablets of stone inscribed, by God's own finger, with a copy of all the words that the LORD spoke to you on the mountain from the midst of the fire on the day of the assembly. [11] Then, at the end of the forty days and forty nights, when the LORD had given me the two stone tablets of the covenant, [12]* he said to me, 'Go down from here now, quickly, for your people whom you have brought out of Egypt have become depraved; they have already turned aside from the way I pointed out to them and have made for themselves a molten idol. [13] I have seen now how stiff-necked this people is,' the LORD said to me. [14] 'Let me be, that I may destroy them and blot out their name from under the heavens. I will then make of you a nation mightier and greater than they.'

[15]* "When I had come down again from the blazing, fiery mountain, with the two tablets of the covenant in both my hands, [16] I saw how you had sinned against the LORD, your God: you had already turned aside from the way which the LORD had pointed out to you by making for yourselves a molten calf! [17]* Raising the two tablets with both hands I threw them from me and broke them before your eyes. [18]* Then, as before, I lay prostrate before the LORD for forty days and forty nights without eating or drinking, because of all the sin you had committed in the sight of the LORD and the evil you had done to provoke him. [19]* For I dreaded the fierce anger of the LORD against you: his wrath would destroy you. Yet once again the LORD listened to me. [20] With Aaron, too, the LORD was deeply angry, and would have killed him had I not prayed for him also at that time. [21]* Then, taking the calf, the sinful object you had made, and fusing it with fire, I ground it down to powder as fine as dust, which I threw into the wadi that went down the mountainside.

[22]* "At Taberah, at Massah, and at Kibrothhattaavah likewise, you provoked the LORD to anger. [23]* And when he sent you up from Kadesh-

8, 15: Wis 11, 4.
8, 17: Dt 9, 4.
8, 19: Dt 4, 25f; 30, 18.
9, 1: Dt 1, 28; 4, 38.
9, 2: Nm 13, 33.

9, 3: Dt 31, 3; Ex 23, 27.
9, 4: Dt 8, 17.
9, 7: Dt 31, 27; Ex 14, 11; Nm 14, 11.
9, 8: Ex 32, 4; Ps 106, 19.

9, 9: Ex 24, 12.18; 34, 28.
9, 10: Ex 31, 18.
9, 12ff: Ex 32, 7–10.
9, 15: Ex 32, 15.
9, 17: 16f: Ex 32, 19.

9, 18: Ex 32, 31; 34, 28.
9, 19: Dt 10, 10; Ex 32, 10.
9, 21: Ex 32, 20.
9, 22: Ex 17, 7; Nm 11, 1ff.34.
9, 23: Nm 14, 1–4; Ps 106, 24f.

barnea to take possession of the land he was giving you, you rebelled against this command of the LORD, your God, and would not trust or obey him. 24 Ever since I have known you, you have been rebels against the LORD.

25 "Those forty days, then, and forty nights, I lay prostrate before the LORD, because he had threatened to destroy you. 26 This was my prayer to him: O Lord GOD, destroy not your people, the heritage which your majesty has ransomed and brought out of Egypt with your strong hand. 27 Remember your servants, Abraham, Isaac and Jacob. Look not upon the stubbornness of this people nor upon their wickedness and sin, 28* lest the people from whose land you have brought us say, 'The LORD was not able to bring them into the land he promised them'; or 'Out of hatred for them he brought them out to slay them in the desert.' 29* They are, after all, your people and your heritage, whom you have brought out by your great power and with your outstretched arm.

10 1* "At that time the LORD said to me, 'Cut two tablets of stone like the former; then come up the mountain to me. Also make an ark of wood. 2 I will write upon the tablets the commandments that were on the former tablets that you broke, and you shall place them in the ark.' 3* So I made an ark of acacia wood, and cut two tablets of stone like the former, and went up the mountain carrying the two tablets. 4* The LORD then wrote on them, as he had written before, the ten commandments which he spoke to you on the mountain from the midst of the fire on the day of the assembly. After the LORD had given them to me, 5* I turned and came down the mountain, and placed the tablets in the ark I had made. There they have remained, in keeping with the command the LORD gave me.

6* [The Israelites set out from Beeroth Benejaakan for Moserah, where Aaron died and was buried, his son Eleazar succeeding him in the priestly office. 7* From there they set out for Gudgodah, and from Gudgodah for Jotbathah, a region where there is water in the wadies.]

8* "At that time the LORD set apart the tribe of Levi to carry the ark of the covenant of the LORD, to be in attendance before the LORD and minister to

him, and to give blessings in his name, as they have done to this day. 9* For this reason, Levi has no share in the heritage with his brothers; the LORD himself is his heritage, as the LORD, your God, has told him.

10 "After I had spent these other forty days and forty nights on the mountain, and the LORD had once again heard me and decided not to destroy you, 11* he said to me, 'Go now and set out at the head of your people, that they may enter in and occupy the land which I swore to their fathers I would give them.'

The Lord's Majesty

12* "And now, Israel, what does the LORD, your God, ask of you but to fear the LORD, your God, and follow his ways exactly, to love and serve the LORD, your God, with all your heart and all your soul, 13 to keep the commandments and statutes of the LORD which I enjoin on you today for your own good? 14*† Think! The heavens, even the highest heavens, belong to the LORD, your God, as well as the earth and everything on it. 15* Yet in his love for your fathers the LORD was so attached to them as to choose you, their descendants, in preference to all other peoples, as indeed he has now done. 16† Circumcise your hearts, therefore, and be no longer stiff-necked. 17* For the LORD, your God, is the God of gods, the LORD of lords, the great God, mighty and awesome, who has no favorites, accepts no bribes; 18 who executes justice for the orphan and the widow, and befriends the alien, feeding and clothing him. 19* So you too must befriend the alien, for you were once aliens yourselves in the land of Egypt. 20* The LORD, your God, shall you fear, and him shall you serve; hold fast to him and swear by his name. 21 He is your glory, he, your God, who has done for you those great and terrible things which your own eyes have seen. 22* Your ancestors went down to Egypt seventy strong, and now the LORD, your God, has made you as numerous as the stars of the sky.

The Wonders of the Lord

11 1 "Love the LORD, your God, therefore, and always heed his charge: his statutes, decrees and commandments. 2 It is not your children, who have not known it from experience, but

---

10, 14: *Even the highest heavens:* literally, "and the heavens of the heavens"; compare the phrase, "the third heaven," in 2 Cor 12, 2.

10, 16: *Circumcise your hearts:* cf Dt 30, 6; Jer 4, 4; Rom 2, 29. The "uncircumcised heart" (Lv 26, 41; Jer 9, 25; Ez 44, 7.9) is closed and unreceptive to divine grace and guidance, just as "uncircumcised ears" (Jer 6, 10) are closed to sound, and "uncircumcised lips" (Ex 6, 12.30) do not open well in speech.

9, 28: Nm 14, 14ff.   10, 1: Ex 34, 1.
9, 29: Dt 4, 20; Ex 6, 6f.   10, 3: Ex 34, 4.

10, 4: Ex 20, 1–17; 34, 28.
10, 5: Ex 40, 20; 1 Kgs 8, 9.
10, 6: Nm 33, 31.
10, 7: Nm 33, 32f.
10, 8: Nm 3; 6; 23–27;
  16, 9.
10, 9: Nm 18, 20.
10, 11: Ex 32, 34; 33, 1.
10, 12: Dt 6, 2.5.
10, 14: Neh 9, 6.

10, 15: Dt 7, 6ff.
10, 17: 2 Chr 19, 7; Jb 34, 19;
  Wis 6, 7; Acts 10, 34;
  Rom 2, 11; Gal 2, 6.
10, 19: Ex 22, 21; 23, 9; Lv
  19, 33f.
10, 20: Dt 6, 13; Mt 4, 10; Lk
  4, 8.
10, 22: Gn 46, 27; Ex 1, 5;
  Acts 7, 14.

AFRICAN AMERICAN
Kwanzaa as a Way of Life

The heart of the Law is love, our love for God and God's love for us. We express that love through the values we live out. Conflicts occur when the way we rank our values comes into conflict with the way someone else ranks their values.

For example: You may place a value on completing all your schoolwork, studying, and excelling in school. Another person sitting near you in class may not place the same high value on school. The two of you may come into conflict because this person disrupts the class and makes it difficult for you to understand what the teacher is explaining.

This is why a universal value system is important. It is why the Book of Deuteronomy has laws on everything from worship to sanitation. These laws gave the Israelites a common value system.

Kwanzaa is the name of a value system accepted by many African peoples. It was developed by Maulana Karenga after studying many different cultures throughout Africa. In 1965, he codified the unifying aspects of each of these cultures into the seven principles of Kwanzaa (also known as the Nguzo Saba). The seven principles are written in Swahili (an African trade and business language) and speak to the holistic development of the individual, family, community, nation, and race. Kwanzaa is celebrated from 26 December to 1 January. It is good that more and more African Americans are celebrating it each year, but these principles must be fully put into practice year-round as a way of life.

Kwanzaa is not a religion or a religious holiday, but it can strengthen the faith that you already practice. Look up the Bible passages listed with the following Kwanzaa principles to learn more about each one:

1. *umoja* (unity): Psalm 133; I Cor 12, 12–26
2. *kujichagulia* (self-determination): Jdt 8, 9–36
3. *ujima* (collective work and responsibility): Dt 8, 11–18
4. *ujamaa* (cooperative economics): Mt 16, 25
5. *nia* (purpose): Rom 8, 28
6. *kuumba* (creativity): Mt 25, 14–30
7. *imani* (faith): Gal 6, 9

▶ Dt 10, 12–22

DT

you yourselves who must now understand the discipline of the LORD, your God; his majesty, his strong hand and outstretched arm; ³* the signs and deeds he wrought among the Egyptians, on Pharaoh, king of Egypt, and on all his land; ⁴* what he did to the Egyptian army and to their horses and chariots, engulfing them in the water of the Red Sea as they pursued you, and bringing ruin upon them even to this day; ⁵ what he did for you in the desert until you arrived in this place; ⁶* and what he did to the Reubenites Dathan and Abiram, sons of Eliab, when the ground opened its mouth and swallowed them up out of the midst of Israel, with their families and tents and every living thing that belonged to them. ⁷ With your own eyes you have seen all these great deeds that the LORD has done. ⁸ Keep all the commandments, then, which I enjoin on you today, that you may be strong enough to en-

ter in and take possession of the land into which you are crossing, ⁹ and that you may have long life on the land which the LORD swore to your fathers he would give to them and their descendants, a land flowing with milk and honey.

The Gift of Rain

¹⁰ "For the land which you are to enter and occupy is not like the land of Egypt from which you have come, where you would sow your seed and then water it by hand, as in a vegetable garden. ¹¹* No, the land into which you are crossing for conquest is a land of hills and valleys that drinks in rain from the heavens, ¹² a land which the LORD,

---

11, 3: Dt 6, 22; Ps 78, 42–51.
11, 4: Ex 14, 26ff; 15, 9; Pss 78, 53; 106, 11.
11, 6: Nm 16, 31ff.
11, 11f: Dt 8, 7.

your God, looks after; his eyes are upon it continually from the beginning of the year to the end. 13*† If, then, you truly heed my commandments which I enjoin on you today, loving and serving the LORD, your God, with all your heart and all your soul, 14† I will give the seasonal rain to your land, the early rain and the late rain, that you may have your grain, wine and oil to gather in; 15* and I will bring forth grass in your fields for your animals. Thus you may eat your fill. 16* But be careful lest your heart be so lured away that you serve other gods and worship them. 17 For then the wrath of the LORD will flare up against you and he will close up the heavens, so that no rain will fall, and the soil will not yield its crops, and you will soon perish from the good land he is giving you.

Reward of Fidelity

18* "Therefore, take these words of mine into your heart and soul. Bind them at your wrist as a sign, and let them be a pendant on your forehead. 19 Teach them to your children, speaking of them at home and abroad, whether you are busy or at rest. 20 And write them on the doorposts of your houses and on your gates, 21 so that, as long as the heavens are above the earth, you and your children may live on in the land which the LORD swore to your fathers he would give them.

22 "For if you are careful to observe all these commandments I enjoin on you, loving the LORD, your God, and following his ways exactly, and holding fast to him, 23* the LORD will drive all these nations out of your way, and you will dispossess nations greater and mightier than yourselves. 24*† Every place where you set foot shall be yours: from the desert and from Lebanon, from the Euphrates River to the Western Sea, shall be your territory. 25* None shall stand up against you; the LORD, your God, will spread the fear and dread of you through any land where you set foot, as he promised you.

A Blessing and a Curse

26* "I set before you here, this day, a blessing and a curse: 27 a blessing for obeying the commandments of the LORD, your God, which I enjoin on you today; 28 a curse if you do not obey the commandments of the LORD, your God, but turn aside

from the way I ordain for you today, to follow other gods, whom you have not known. 29*† When the LORD, your God, brings you into the land which you are to enter and occupy, then you shall pronounce the blessing on Mount Gerizim, the curse on Mount Ebal. 30 [Are they not beyond the Jordan, on the other side of the western road in the country of the Canaanites who live in the Arabah, opposite the Gilgal beside the terebinth of Moreh?] 31 For you are about to cross the Jordan to enter and occupy the land which the LORD, your God, is giving you. When therefore, you take possession of it and settle there, 32 be careful to observe all the statutes and decrees that I set before you today.

III: Exposition of the Law

One Sanctuary

12 1 "These are the statutes and decrees which you must be careful to observe in the land which the LORD, the God of your fathers, has given you to occupy, as long as you live on its soil. 2* Destroy without fail every place on the high mountains, on the hills, and under every leafy tree where the nations you are to dispossess worship their gods. 3 Tear down their altars, smash their sacred pillars, destroy by fire their sacred poles, and shatter the idols of their gods, that you may stamp out the remembrance of them in any such place.

4 "That is not how you are to worship the LORD, your God. 5* Instead, you shall resort to the place which the LORD, your God, chooses out of all your tribes and designates as his dwelling 6 and there you shall bring your holocausts and sacrifices, your tithes and personal contributions, your votive and freewill offerings, and the firstlings of your herds and flocks. 7 There, too, before the LORD, your God, you and your families shall eat and make merry over all your undertakings, because the LORD, your God, has blessed you. 8 You shall not do as we are now doing; here, everyone does what seems right to himself, 9 since you have not yet reached your resting place, the heritage which the LORD, your God, will give you. 10 But after you have crossed the Jordan and dwell in the land which the LORD, your God, is giving you as a heritage, when he has given you rest from all your enemies round about and

D
T

11, 13ff: As often in the Prophets, the discourse passes into the words of God himself. Cf Dt 7, 4; 17, 3; 28, 20; 29, 4f.

11, 14: *The early rain:* the rains which begin in October or November and continue intermittently throughout the winter. *The late rain:* the heavy showers of March and April. In Palestine the crops are sown in the autumn and reaped in the spring.

11, 24: *The Western Sea:* the Mediterranean.

11, 29: *You shall pronounce the blessing . . . the curse:* for the full ceremony, see chapters 27 and 28. *Gerizim . . . Ebal:* adjacent mountains in Samaria with a deep ravine between them. Their summits command an excellent view of the entire country.

11, 13f: Dt 10, 12; Lv 26, 4.
11, 15: Ps 104, 14.
11, 16f: Dt 4, 25f; 6, 14.
11, 18–21: Dt 6, 6–9.
11, 23: Dt 7, 1; 9, 1.
11, 24: Ex 23, 31.
11, 25: Dt 2, 25; 7, 24; Ex 23, 27.

11, 26ff: Dt 28, 2–45; 30, 1. 15.19.
11, 29: Dt 27, 12f.
12, 2f: Dt 7, 5; Ex 23, 24; 34, 13.
12, 5–7.11f: Dt 14, 22–26; 15, 19f; 16, 2.10f.14f; 26, 2.

you live there in security, [11] then to the place which the LORD, your God, chooses as the dwelling place for his name you shall bring all the offerings I command you: your holocausts and sacrifices, your tithes and personal contributions, and every special offering you have vowed to the LORD. [12] You shall make merry before the LORD, your God, with your sons and daughters, your male and female slaves, as well as with the Levite who belongs to your community but has no share of his own in your heritage. [13] Take care not to offer up your holocausts in any place you fancy, [14] but offer them up in the place which the LORD chooses from among your tribes; there you shall make whatever offerings I enjoin upon you.

Profane and Sacred Meals

[15] "However, in any of your communities you may slaughter and eat to your heart's desire as much meat as the LORD, your God, has blessed you with; and the unclean as well as the clean may eat it, as they do the gazelle or the deer. [16]* Only, you shall not partake of the blood, but must pour it out on the ground like water. [17] Moreover, you shall not, in your own communities, partake of your tithe of grain or wine or oil, of the first-born of your herd or flock, of any offering you have vowed, of your freewill offerings, or of your personal contributions. [18] These you must eat before the LORD, your God, in the place he chooses, along with your son and daughter, your male and female slave, and the Levite who belongs to your community; and there, before the LORD, you shall make merry over all your undertakings. [19]* Take care, also, that you do not neglect the Levite as long as you live in the land.

[20]*† "After the LORD, your God, has enlarged your territory, as he promised you, when you wish meat for food, you may eat it at will, to your heart's desire; [21] and if the place which the LORD, your God, chooses for the abode of his name is too far, you may slaughter in the manner I have told you any of your herd or flock that the LORD has given you, and eat it to your heart's desire in your own community. [22] You may eat it as you would the gazelle or the deer: the unclean and the clean eating it alike. [23] But make sure that you do not partake of the blood; for blood is life, and you shall not consume this seat of life with the flesh. [24] Do not partake of the blood, therefore, but pour it out on the

ground like water. [25] Abstain from it, that you and your children after you may prosper for doing what is right in the sight of the LORD. [26] However, any sacred gifts or votive offerings that you may have, you shall bring with you to the place which the LORD chooses, [27]* and there you must offer both the flesh and the blood of your holocausts on the altar of the LORD, your God; of your other sacrifices the blood indeed must be poured out against the altar of the LORD, your God, but their flesh may be eaten. [28] Be careful to heed all these commandments I enjoin on you, that you and your descendants may always prosper for doing what is good and right in the sight of the LORD, your God.

Pagan Rites

[29] "When the LORD, your God, removes the nations from your way as you advance to dispossess them, be on your guard! Otherwise, once they have been wiped out before you and you have replaced them and are settled in their land, [30] you will be lured into following them. Do not inquire regarding their gods, 'How did these nations worship their gods? I, too, would do the same.' [31]* You shall not thus worship the LORD, your God, because they offered to their gods every abomination that the LORD detests, even burning their sons and daughters to their gods.

Penalties for Idolatry

13 [1] "Every command that I enjoin on you, you shall be careful to observe, neither adding to it nor subtracting from it.

[2]† "If there arises among you a prophet or a dreamer who promises you a sign or wonder, [3] urging you to follow other gods, whom you have not known, and to serve them: even though the sign or wonder he has foretold you comes to pass, [4] pay no attention to the words of that prophet or that dreamer; for the LORD, your God, is testing you to learn whether you really love him with all your heart and with all your soul. [5] The LORD, your God, shall you follow, and him shall you fear; his commandment shall you observe, and his voice shall you heed, serving him and holding fast to him alone. [6]* But that prophet or that dreamer shall be put to death, because, in order to lead you astray from the way which the LORD, your God, has directed you to take, he has preached apostasy from the LORD, your God, who brought you out of the land of Egypt and

---

† **12, 20:** *Meat for food:* as on special feasts. Meat was not eaten every day in Israel, even by the wealthy.

13, 2.4.6: *Dreamer:* a false prophet who pretended to have received revelations from God in his dreams; cf Jer 23, 25–32; Zec 10, 2. But dreams could also be a channel of true prophecy (Nm 12, 6; Jl 3, 1) and of genuine revelations (Gn 20, 3.6; 31, 10.24; 37, 5.9; Mt 1, 20; 2, 12f.19; etc.)

12, **16:** Dt 15, 23; Gn 9, 4; Lv 3, 17.

12, **19:** Dt 14, 27.

12, **20:** Dt 19, 8; Gn 28, 14;

Ex 34, 24.

12, **27:** Lv 17, 11.

12, **31:** Lv 18, 21, Jer 7, 31.

13, **6–10.14:** Dt 6, 14; 17, 2–7.

ransomed you from that place of slavery. Thus shall you purge the evil from your midst.

7 "If your own full brother, or your son or daughter, or your beloved wife, or your intimate friend, entices you secretly to serve other gods, whom you and your fathers have not known, 8 gods of any other nation, near at hand or far away, from one end of the earth to the other: 9 do not yield to him or listen to him, nor look with pity upon him, to spare or shield him, 10 but kill him. Your hand shall be the first raised to slay him; the rest of the people shall join in with you. 11 You shall stone him to death, because he sought to lead you astray from the LORD, your God, who brought you out of the land of Egypt, that place of slavery. 12 And all Israel, hearing of it, shall fear and never again do such evil as this in your midst.

13 "If, in any of the cities which the LORD, your God, gives you to dwell in, you hear it said 14 that certain scoundrels have sprung up among you and have led astray the inhabitants of their city to serve other gods whom you have not known, 15 you must inquire carefully into the matter and investigate it thoroughly. If you find that it is true and an established fact that this abomination has been committed in your midst, 16* you shall put the inhabitants of that city to the sword, dooming the city and all life that is in it, even its cattle, to the sword. 17 Having heaped up all its spoils in the middle of its square, you shall burn the city with all its spoils as a whole burnt offering to the LORD, your God. Let it be a heap of ruins forever, never to be rebuilt. 18 You shall not retain anything that is doomed, that the blazing wrath of the LORD may die down and he may show you mercy and in his mercy for you may multiply you as he promised your fathers on oath; 19 because you have heeded the voice of the LORD, your God, keeping all his commandments which I enjoin on you today, doing what is right in his sight.

Pagan Mourning Rites

14 1* "You are children of the LORD, your God. You shall not gash yourselves nor shave the hair above your foreheads for the dead. 2* For you are a people sacred to the LORD, your God, who has chosen you from all the nations on the face of the earth to be a people peculiarly his own.

Clean and Unclean Animals

3* "You shall not eat any abominable thing. 4* These are the animals you may eat: the ox, the

sheep, the goat, 5† the red deer, the gazelle, the roe deer, the ibex, the addax, the oryx, and the mountain sheep. 6 Any animal that has hoofs you may eat, provided it is cloven-footed and chews the cud. 7 But you shall not eat any of the following that only chew the cud or only have cloven hoofs: the camel, the hare and the rock badger, which indeed chew the cud, but do not have hoofs and are therefore unclean for you; 8* and the pig, which indeed has hoofs and is cloven-footed, but does not chew the cud and is therefore unclean for you. Their flesh you shall not eat, and their dead bodies you shall not touch.

14, 3–21

9 "Of the various creatures that live in the water, whatever has both fins and scales you may eat, 10 but all those that lack either fins or scales you shall not eat; they are unclean for you.

11 "You may eat all clean birds. 12 But you shall not eat any of the following: the eagle, the vulture, the osprey, 13 the various kites and falcons, 14 all the various species of crows, 15 the ostrich, the nightjar, the gull, the various species of hawks, 16 the owl, the screech owl, the ibis, 17 the desert owl, the buzzard, the cormorant, 18 the stork, the various species of herons, the hoopoe, and the bat. 19† All winged insects, too, are unclean for you and shall not be eaten. 20 But you may eat any clean winged creatures.

21*† "You must not eat any animal that has died

14, 5: *The gazelle, the addax, the oryx:* species of antelopes. *The ibex:* a species of wild goat.

14, 19f: The apparent contradiction is to be resolved in the light of Lv 11, 20–23; the unclean winged insects are those that walk on the ground; the clean winged creatures are those that leap on the ground, such as certain species of locusts.

14, 21: *Boil a kid in its mother's milk:* see note on Ex 23, 19.

13, 16f: Jos 6, 18.24; 7, 26; 8, 28.
14, 1: Lv 19, 28.
14, 2: Dt 7, 6.
14, 3: Ez 4, 14; Acts 10, 14.
14, 4–20: Lv 11, 2–23.
14, 8: Lv 11, 26.
14, 21: Ex 22, 30; 23, 19; 34, 26.

D
T

of itself, for you are a people sacred to the LORD, your God. But you may give it to an alien who belongs to your community, and he may eat it, or you may sell it to a foreigner.

"You shall not boil a kid in its mother's milk.

Tithes

22* "Each year you shall tithe all the produce that grows in the field you have sown; 23* then in the place which the LORD, your God, chooses as the dwelling place of his name you shall eat in his presence your tithe of the grain, wine and oil, as well as the firstlings of your herd and flock, that you may learn always to fear the LORD, your God. 24† If, however, the journey is too much for you and you are not able to bring your tithe, because the place which the LORD, your God, chooses for the abode of his name is too far for you, considering how the LORD has blessed you, 25 you may exchange the tithe for money and, with the purse of money in hand, go to the place which the LORD, your God, chooses. 26 You may then exchange the money for whatever you desire, oxen or sheep, wine or strong drink, or anything else you would enjoy, and there before the LORD, your God, you shall partake of it and make merry with your family. 27* But do not neglect the Levite who belongs to your community, for he has no share in the heritage with you.

28 "At the end of every third year you shall bring out all the tithes of your produce for that year and deposit them in community stores, 29* that the Levite who has no share in the heritage with you, and also the alien, the orphan and the widow who belong to your community, may come and eat their fill; so that the LORD, your God, may bless you in all that you undertake.

Debts and the Poor

15 1*† "At the end of every seven-year period you shall have a relaxation of debts, 2 which shall be observed as follows. Every creditor shall relax his claim on what he has loaned his neighbor; he must not press his neighbor, his kinsman, because a relaxation in honor of the LORD has been proclaimed. 3* You may press a foreigner, but you shall relax the claim on your kinsman for what

is yours. 4 Nay, more! since the LORD, your God, will bless you abundantly in the land he will give you to occupy as your heritage, there should be no one of you in need. 5 If you but heed the voice of the LORD, your God, and carefully observe all these commandments which I enjoin on you today, 6* you will lend to many nations, and borrow from none; you will rule over many nations, and none will rule over you, since the LORD, your God, will bless you as he promised. 7 If one of your kinsmen in any community is in need in the land which the LORD, your God, is giving you, you shall not harden your heart nor close your hand to him in his need. 8* Instead, you shall open your hand to him and freely lend him enough to meet his need. 9 Be on your guard lest, entertaining the mean thought that the seventh year, the year of relaxation, is near, you grudge help to your needy kinsman and give him nothing; else he will cry to the LORD against you and you will be held guilty. 10 When you give to him, give freely and not with ill will; for the LORD, your God, will bless you for this in all your works and undertakings. 11*† The needy will never be lacking in the land; that is why I command you to open your hand to your poor and needy kinsman in your country.

Hebrew Slaves

12* "If your kinsman, a Hebrew man or woman, sells himself to you, he is to serve you for six years, but in the seventh year you shall dismiss him from your service, a free man. 13 When you do so, you shall not send him away empty-handed, 14 but shall weight him down with gifts from your flock and threshing floor and wine press, in proportion to the blessing the LORD, your God, has bestowed on you. 15* For remember that you too were once slaves in the land of Egypt, and the LORD, your God, ransomed you. That is why I am giving you this command today. 16 If, however, he tells you that he does not wish to leave you, because he is devoted to you and your household, since he fares well with you, 17*† you shall take an awl and thrust it through his ear into the door, and he shall then be your slave forever. Your female slave, also, you shall treat in the same way. 18 You must not be reluctant to let your slave go free, since the service he has given you

---

14, 24: *Considering how the LORD has blessed you:* should the Israelite farmer be blessed with an abundant harvest, a tenth of this would be too much to transport for a great distance.

15, 1: *At the end of every seven-year period:* in every seventh, or sabbatical, year. Cf Dt 15, 9; 31, 10; and compare Jer 34, 14 with Dt 15, 12. *A relaxation of debts:* it is uncertain whether a full cancellation of debts is meant, or merely a suspension of payment on them or on their interest among the Israelites. Cf Ex 23, 11 where the same Hebrew root is used of a field that is "let lie fallow" in the sabbatical year.

15, 11: *The needy will never be lacking:* compare the words of Christ, "The poor you have always with you" (Mt 26, 11).

15, 17: *His ear:* cf Ex 21, 6 and the note there.

14, 22: Lv 27, 30.
14, 23f: Dt 12, 5ff.
14, 27: Dt 12, 12.19.
14, 29: 28f: Dt 26, 12.
15, 1: Neh 10, 31.
15, 3: Dt 23, 20.
15, 6: Dt 28, 12f.
15, 8: Lv 25, 35; Sir 29, 1f;
Mt 5, 42.
15, 11: Dt 15, 8; Sir 29, 12.
15, 12: Ex 21, 2; Jer 34, 14.
15, 15: Dt 5, 15.
15, 17: 16f: Ex 21, 5f.

for six years was worth twice a hired man's salary; then also the LORD, your God, will bless you in everything you do.

Firstlings

19* "You shall consecrate to the LORD, your God, all the male firstlings of your herd and of your flock. You shall not work the firstlings of your cattle, nor shear the firstlings of your flock. 20* Year after year you and your family shall eat them before the LORD, your God, in the place he chooses. 21 If, however, a firstling is lame or blind or has any other serious defect, you shall not sacrifice it to the LORD, your God, 22 but in your own communities you may eat it, the unclean and the clean eating it alike, as you would a gazelle or a deer. 23* Only, you shall not partake of its blood, which must be poured out on the ground like water.

Feast of the Passover

16 1*† "Observe the month of Abib by keeping the Passover of the LORD, your God, since it was in the month of Abib that he brought you by night out of Egypt. 2 You shall offer the Passover sacrifice from your flock or your herd to the LORD, your God, in the place which he chooses as the dwelling place of his name. 3* You shall not eat leavened bread with it. For seven days you shall eat with it only unleavened bread, the bread of affliction, that you may remember as long as you live the day of your departure from the land of Egypt; for in frightened haste you left the land of Egypt. 4 Nothing leavened may be found in all your territory for seven days, and none of the meat which you sacrificed on the evening of the first day shall be kept overnight for the next day.

5 "You may not sacrifice the Passover in any of the communities which the LORD, your God, gives you; 6 only at the place which he chooses as the dwelling place of his name, and in the evening at sunset, on the anniversary of your departure from Egypt, shall you sacrifice the Passover. 7 You shall cook and eat it at the place the LORD, your God, chooses; then in the morning you may return to your tents. 8 For six days you shall eat unleavened bread, and on the seventh there shall be a solemn meeting in honor of the LORD, your God; on that day you shall not do any sort of work.

Feast of Weeks

9* "You shall count off seven weeks, computing them from the day when the sickle is first put to the standing grain. 10† You shall then keep the feast of Weeks in honor of the LORD, your God, and the measure of your own freewill offering shall be in proportion to the blessing the LORD, your God, has bestowed on you. 11* In the place which the LORD, your God, chooses as the dwelling place of his name, you shall make merry in his presence together with your son and daughter, your male and female slave, and the Levite who belongs to your community, as well as the alien, the orphan and the widow among you. 12 Remember that you too were once slaves in Egypt, and carry out these statutes carefully.

Feast of Booths

13*† "You shall celebrate the feast of Booths for seven days, when you have gathered in the produce from your threshing floor and wine press. 14* You shall make merry at your feast, together with your son and daughter, your male and female slave, and also the Levite, the alien, the orphan and the widow who belong to your community. 15 For seven days you shall celebrate this pilgrim feast in honor of the LORD, your God, in the place which he chooses; since the LORD, your God, has blessed you in all your crops and in all your undertakings, you shall do naught but make merry.

16* "Three times a year, then, every male among you shall appear before the LORD, your God, in the place which he chooses: at the feast of Unleavened Bread, at the feast of Weeks, and at the feast of Booths. No one shall appear before the LORD empty-handed, 17 but each of you with as much as he can give, in proportion to the blessings which the LORD, your God, has bestowed on you.

Judges

18 "You shall appoint judges and officials throughout your tribes to administer true justice for the people in all the communities which the LORD, your God, is giving you. 19* You shall not distort justice; you must be impartial. You shall not take a bribe; for a bribe blinds the eyes even of the wise and twists the words even of the just. 20 Justice and justice alone shall be your aim, that you may have life and may possess the land which the LORD, your God, is giving you.

16, 1: *Abib:* "ear of grain, ripe grain," the name of the month in which the barley harvest fell, corresponding to our March and April; at a later period this month received the Babylonian name of "Nisan."

16, 10: *Feast of Weeks:* later known more commonly as "Pentecost."

16, 13: See note on Lv 23, 34.

15, 19: Ex 13, 11.
15, 20: Dt 14, 23.
15, 23: 21ff: Dt 12, 15f; Lv 22, 20.
16, 1–8: Ex 12, 2–20; 23, 15;
    Nm 28, 16ff.24f.
16, 3f: Ex 13, 6f; 34, 18.
16, 9–12: Lv 23, 15–21.

16, 11: Dt 12, 5.7.12.18.
16, 13–15: Ex 23, 16; Lv 23,
    34–43; Nm 29, 12–38.
16, 14: Dt 16, 11.
16, 16: Ex 23, 14f.17; 34, 23;
    2 Chr 8, 13.
16, 19: Dt 1, 17; Ex 23, 8.

D
T

Pagan Worship

21*† "You shall not plant a sacred pole of any kind of wood beside the altar of the LORD, your God, which you will build; 22† nor shall you erect a sacred pillar, such as the LORD, your God, detests.

17 1* "You shall not sacrifice to the LORD, your God, from the herd or from the flock an animal with any serious defect; that would be an abomination to the LORD, your God.

2* "If there is found among you, in any one of the communities which the LORD, your God, gives you, a man or a woman who does evil in the sight of the LORD, your God, and transgresses his covenant, 3* by serving other gods, or by worshiping the sun or the moon or any of the host of the sky, against my command; 4 and if, on being informed of it, you find by careful investigation that it is true and an established fact that this abomination has been committed in Israel: 5† you shall bring the man (or woman) who has done the evil deed out to your city gates and stone him to death. 6* The testimony of two or three witnesses is required for putting a person to death; no one shall be put to death on the testimony of only one witness. 7* At the execution, the witnesses are to be the first to raise their hands against him; afterward all the people are to join in. Thus shall you purge the evil from your midst.

Judges

8 "If in your own community there is a case at issue which proves too complicated for you to decide, in a matter of bloodshed or of civil rights or of personal injury, you shall then go up to the place which the LORD, your God, chooses, 9* to the levitical priests or to the judge who is in office at that time. They shall study the case and then hand down to you their decision. 10 According to this decision that they give you in the place which the LORD chooses, you shall act, being careful to do exactly as they direct. 11 You shall carry out the directions they give you and the verdict they pronounce for you, without turning aside to the right or to the left from the decision they hand down to you. 12† Any man who has the insolence to refuse to listen to the priest who officiates there in the ministry of the LORD, your God, or to the judge, shall die. Thus

shall you purge the evil from your midst. 13 And all the people, on hearing of it, shall fear, and never again be so insolent.

?did you KNOW?

The Torah

The Hebrew word Torah means "instruction" or "teaching," and only over time has come to mean "the Law." Torah refers most fundamentally to the Law that was recorded as given by God to Moses on Mount Sinai. As the people of Israel lived the Torah, it became equated with their very life and existence. It was the key for their organization as a people and gave consistency to their struggle to live their Covenant with God.

Jewish people refer to the first five books of the Bible (the Pentateuch) as the Torah because those books contain the Law and instruction on how to live it. The other books of the Old Testament are also strongly connected to the Torah. The historical books record how the people and their kings kept the Torah or disobeyed it. When they obeyed, they were blessed with happiness, health, and prosperity. When they disobeyed, they were punished with barrenness, destruction, and death. The prophets in the prophetic books call the people to faithfulness to the Law. They condemn idolatry and injustice and call the people to live the spirit of the Torah.

What law are Christians called to live by? For a hint, see the Letter of Paul to the Galatians and the Letter of James.

▶ Dt 17, 8–11

16, 21—17, 7: This section seems to be out of its proper place, since it interrupts the natural sequence of the laws for the judges (Dt 16, 18–20 and 17, 8–13). It probably belongs to the similar section, Dt 12, 29—14, 2.
16, 22: 21f: *Sacred pole . . . sacred pillar;* see note on Ex 34, 13.
17, 5: *Out to your city gates:* outside the gates in an unclean place; cf Lv 24, 14; Nm 15, 36; Acts 7, 58; Heb 13, 12.
17, 12: *The priest:* the high priest; *the judge:* a layman. The for-

mer presided over the court in cases which directly concerned religion, the latter in cases of a more secular nature; cf 2 Chr 19, 8–11.

16, 21: 1 Kgs 14, 15; 2 Chr 33, 3.	**17, 6:** Dt 19, 15; Nm 35, 30; Mt 18, 16; Jn 8, 17; 2 Cor 13, 1.
17, 1: Lv 22, 20.	
17, 2–7: Dt 13, 6–15.	**17, 7:** Dt 13, 10.
17, 3: Dt 4, 19.	**17, 9:** Dt 21, 5; 2 Chr 19, 8.

DT

The King

14* "When you have come into the land which the LORD, your God, is giving you, and have occupied it and settled in it, should you then decide to have a king over you like all the surrounding nations, 15* you shall set that man over you as your king whom the LORD, your God, chooses. He whom you set over you as king must be your kinsman; a foreigner, who is no kin of yours, you may not set over you. 16*† But he shall not have a great number of horses; nor shall he make his people go back again to Egypt to acquire them, against the LORD's warning that you must never go back that way again. 17* Neither shall he have a great number of wives, lest his heart be estranged, nor shall he accumulate a vast amount of silver and gold. 18* When he is enthroned in his kingdom, he shall have a copy of this law made from the scroll that is in the custody of the levitical priests. 19 He shall keep it with him and read it all the days of his life that he may learn to fear the LORD, his God, and to heed and fulfill all the words of this law and these statutes. 20 Let him not become estranged from his countrymen through pride, nor turn aside to the right or to the left from these commandments. Then he and his descendants will enjoy a long reign in Israel.

Priests

18 1* "The whole priestly tribe of Levi shall have no share in the heritage with Israel; they shall live on the oblations of the LORD and the portions due to him. 2 Levi shall have no heritage among his brothers; the LORD himself is his heritage, as he has told him. 3 The priests shall have a right to the following things from the people: from those who are offering a sacrifice, whether the victim is from the herd or from the flock, the priest shall receive the shoulder, the jowls and the stomach. 4* You shall also give him the first fruits of your grain and wine and oil, as well as the first fruits of the shearing of your flock; 5 for the LORD, your God, has chosen him and his sons out of all your tribes to be always in attendance to minister in the name of the LORD.

6 "When a Levite goes from one of your communities anywhere in Israel in which he ordinarily resides, to visit, as his heart may desire, the place which the LORD chooses, 7 he may minister there in the name of the LORD, his God, like all his fellow Levites who are in attendance there before the LORD. 8 He shall then receive the same portions to eat as the rest, along with his monetary offerings and heirlooms.

Prophets

9* "When you come into the land which the LORD, your God, is giving you, you shall not learn to imitate the abominations of the peoples there. 10*† Let there not be found among you anyone who immolates his son or daughter in the fire, nor a fortune-teller, soothsayer, charmer, diviner, 11 or caster of spells, nor one who consults ghosts and spirits or seeks oracles from the dead. 12* Anyone who does such things is an abomination to the LORD, and because of such abominations the LORD, your God, is driving these nations out of your way. 13 You, however, must be altogether sincere toward the LORD, your God. 14 Though these nations whom you are to dispossess listen to their soothsayers and fortune-tellers, the LORD, your God, will not permit you to do so.

15*† "A prophet like me will the LORD, your God, raise up for you from among your own kinsmen; to him you shall listen. 16* This is exactly what you requested of the LORD, your God, at Horeb on the day of the assembly, when you said, 'Let us not again hear the voice of the LORD, our God, nor see this great fire any more, lest we die.' 17 And the LORD said to me, 'This was well said. 18 I will raise up for them a prophet like you from among their kinsmen, and will put my words into his mouth; he shall tell them all that I command him. 19* If any man will not listen to my words which he speaks in my name, I myself will make him answer for it. 20* But if a prophet presumes to speak in my name an oracle that I have not commanded him to speak, or speaks in the name of other gods, he shall die.'

17, 16: *Horses:* chariotry for war. *The LORD's warning:* the same warning is also referred to in Dt 28, 68, although it is not mentioned explicitly elsewhere in the Pentateuch. We know from other sources that Egypt used to export war horses to Palestine. The danger envisioned here is that some king might make Israel a vassal of Egypt for the sake of such military aid.

18, 10f: *Immolates his son or daughter in the fire:* to Molech. See note on Lv 18, 21. Such human sacrifices are classed here with other pagan superstitions because they were believed to possess magical powers for averting a calamity; cf 2 Kgs 3, 27. Three other forms of superstition are listed here: augury (by a fortune-teller, a soothsayer or a diviner); black magic (by a charmer . . . or caster of spells); and necromancy (by one who consults ghosts and spirits or seeks oracles from the dead).

18, 15: *A prophet like me:* from the context (opposition to the pagan soothsayers) it seems that Moses is referring in general to all

the true prophets who were to succeed him. But since Christ is the Great Prophet in whom the prophetic office finds its fulfillment and completion, this passage was understood in a special Messianic sense both by the Jews (Jn 6, 14; 7, 40) and by the Apostles (Acts 3, 22; 7, 37).

17, 14: 1 Sm 8, 5.19f.
17, 15: 1 Sm 9, 16; 10, 24; 16, 12.
17, 16: Dt 28, 68; 1 Kgs 4, 26; 10, 26.
17, 17: 1 Kgs 11; 3f; Neh 13, 26.
17, 18: Dt 31, 9.26.
18, 1: Nm 18, 8f. 20–24; 1 Cor 9, 13.
18, 4: Nm 18, 12; 2 Chr 31, 5.
18, 9: Dt 12, 29ff; Lv 18, 26–30.
18, 10f: Lv 18, 21; 19, 31; 20, 27; 1 Sm 28, 7; 2 Kgs 17, 17; 21, 6.
18, 12: Dt 9, 4.
18, 15: Jn 1, 45; 6, 14; Acts 3, 22; 7, 37.
18, 16: Ex 20, 19.
18, 19: Acts 3, 23.
18, 20.22: Dt 13, 2ff.

DT

21 "If you say to yourselves, 'How can we recognize an oracle which the LORD has spoken?', 22 know that, even though a prophet speaks in the name of the LORD, if his oracle is not fulfilled or verified, it is an oracle which the LORD did not speak. The prophet has spoken it presumptuously, and you shall have no fear of him.

Cities of Refuge

19 1 "When the LORD, your God, removes the nations whose land he is giving you, and you have taken their place and are settled in their cities and houses, 2*† you shall set apart three cities in the land which the LORD, your God, is giving you to occupy. 3 You shall thereby divide into three regions the land which the LORD, your God, will give you as a heritage, and so arrange the routes that every homicide will be able to find a refuge.

4* "It is in the following case that a homicide may take refuge in such a place to save his life: when someone unwittingly kills his neighbor to whom he had previously borne no malice. 5 For example, if he goes with his neighbor to a forest to cut wood, and as he swings his ax to fell a tree, its head flies off the handle and hits his neighbor a mortal blow, he may take refuge in one of these cities to save his life. 6† Should the distance be too great, the avenger of blood may in the heat of his anger pursue the homicide and overtake him and strike him dead, even though he does not merit death since he had previously borne the slain man no malice. 7 That is why I order you to set apart three cities.

8* "But if the LORD, your God, enlarges your territory, as he swore to your fathers, and gives you all the land he promised your fathers he would give 9 in the event that you carefully observe all these commandments which I enjoin on you today, loving the LORD, your God, and ever walking in his ways: then add three cities to these three. 10 Thus, in the land which the LORD, your God, is giving you as a heritage, innocent blood will not be shed and you will not become guilty of bloodshed.

11* "However, if someone lies in wait for his neighbor out of hatred for him, and rising up against him, strikes him mortally, and then takes refuge in one of these cities, 12 the elders of his own city shall send for him and have him taken from there, and shall hand him over to be slain by the avenger of blood. 13 Do not look on him with pity,

but purge from Israel the stain of shedding innocent blood, that you may prosper.

Removal of Landmarks

14* "You shall not move your neighbor's landmarks erected by your forefathers in the heritage you receive in the land which the LORD, your God, is giving you to occupy.

False Witnesses

15* "One witness alone shall not take the stand against a man in regard to any crime or any offense of which he may be guilty; a judicial fact shall be established only on the testimony of two or three witnesses.

16 "If an unjust witness takes the stand against a man to accuse him of a defection from the law, 17* the two parties in the dispute shall appear before the LORD in the presence of the priests or judges in office at that time; 18 and if after a thorough investigation the judges find that the witness is a false witness and has accused his kinsman falsely, 19* you shall do to him as he planned to do to his kinsman. Thus shall you purge the evil from your midst. 20 The rest, on hearing of it, shall fear, and never again do a thing so evil among you. 21* Do not look on such a man with pity. Life for life, eye for eye, tooth for tooth, hand for hand, and foot for foot!

Courage in War

20 1 "When you go out to war against your enemies and you see horses and chariots and an army greater than your own, do not be afraid of them, for the LORD, your God, who brought you up from the land of Egypt, will be with you.

2 "When you are about to go into battle, the priest shall come forward and say to the soldiers: 3 'Hear, O Israel! Today you are going into battle against your enemies. Be not weakhearted or afraid; be neither alarmed nor frightened by them. 4* For it is the LORD, your God, who goes with you to fight for you against your enemies and give you victory.'

5* "Then the officials shall say to the soldiers, 'Is there anyone who has built a new house and not yet had the housewarming? Let him return home, lest he die in battle and another dedicate it. 6 Is there anyone who has planted a vineyard and never

---

19, 2: *Set apart three cities:* the Israelites were to have at least six cities of refuge, three in the land east of the Jordan and three in the land of Canaan west of the Jordan (Nm 35, 9–34); but since the three cities east of the Jordan had now been appointed (Dt 4, 41–43), reference is made here only to the three west of the Jordan. The execution of this command is narrated in Jos 20.
19, 6: *The avenger of blood:* see note on Nm 35, 12.

19, 2: Dt 4, 41ff; Ex 21, 13; Nm 35, 10–15; Jos 20, 2.8.
19, 4: Dt 4, 42; Nm 35, 15; Jos 20, 3.5.
19, 8: Gn 15, 18–21; 28, 14; Ex 23, 31; 34, 24.
19, 11ff: Ex 21, 12.14; Nm 35, 20f.
19, 14: Dt 27, 17; Prv 23, 10; Hos 5, 10.
19, 15: Dt 17, 6; Nm 35, 30; Mt 18, 16; Jn 8, 17; 2 Cor 13, 1.
19, 17: Dt 17, 8f.
19, 19: 18f: Dn 13, 61f.
19, 21: Ex 21, 23f; Lv 24, 20; Mt 5, 38.
20, 4: Dt 1, 30; 3, 22; Jos 23, 10.
20, 5ff: 1 Mc 3, 56.

DT

Facing Life's Battles

LIVE IT!

What are the wars in your life? Where do you experience conflict and lack of peace? We all hope that we will not face war in armed conflict. But in a sense, war is around us in the conflicts of everyday life.

We have fights with family and friends. We battle the pressures of society and our peers. We are at odds with the future. Deuteronomy 20, 1 tells us that we are not to fear times of war because our God is with us and will be our strength.

When we face conflict, our faith will be tested, but we must hold strong and true to what God tells us. If we let our heart be filled with God, the wars that we face will become opportunities for God's love to triumph.

What conflicts do you encounter these days? Do you sense God is with you in these conflicts? If so, how? Pray for peace-filled ways to resolve conflict.

▶ Dt 20, 1

---

yet enjoyed its fruits? Let him return home, lest he die in battle and another enjoy its fruits in his stead. 7* Is there anyone who has betrothed a woman and not yet taken her as his wife? Let him return home, lest he die in battle and another take her to wife.' 8* In fine, the officials shall say to the soldiers, 'Is there anyone who is afraid and weakhearted? Let him return home, lest he make his fellows as fainthearted as himself.'

9 "When the officials have finished speaking to the soldiers, military officers shall be appointed over the army.

Cities of the Enemy

10 "When you march up to attack a city, first offer it terms of peace. 11 If it agrees to your terms of peace and opens its gates to you, all the people to be found in it shall serve you in forced labor. 12 But if it refuses to make peace with you and instead offers you battle, lay siege to it, 13 and when the LORD, your God, delivers it into your hand, put every male in it to the sword; 14* but the women and children and livestock and all else in it that is worth plundering you may take as your booty, and you may use this plunder of your enemies which the LORD, your God, has given you.

15 "That is how you shall deal with any city at a considerable distance from you, which does not belong to the peoples of this land. 16 But in the cities of those nations which the LORD, your God, is

giving you as your heritage, you shall not leave a single soul alive. 17* You must doom them all—the Hittites, Amorites, Canaanites, Perizzites, Hivites and Jebusites —as the LORD, your God, has commanded you, 18 lest they teach you to make any such abominable offerings as they make to their gods, and you thus sin against the LORD, your God.

Trees of a Besieged City

19 "When you are at war with a city and have to lay siege to it for a long time before you capture it, you shall not destroy its trees by putting an ax to them. You may eat their fruit, but you must not cut down the trees. After all, are the trees of the field men, that they should be included in your siege? 20 However, those trees which you know are not fruit trees you may destroy, cutting them down to build siegeworks with which to reduce the city that is resisting you.

Expiation of Untraced Murder

21 1† "If the corpse of a slain man is found lying in the open on the land which the LORD, your God, is giving you to occupy, and it is not known who killed him, 2 your elders and judges shall go out and measure the distances to the cities that are in the neighborhood of the corpse. 3 When it is established which city is nearest the corpse, the elders of that city shall take a heifer that has never been put to work as a draft animal under a yoke, 4† and

---

† **21, 1–9:** This paragraph is best read immediately after Dt 19, 21. The slain man may not necessarily have been murdered; he may have been killed by a wild beast. But the blood of the slain cries out to God from the soil where it was shed; cf Gn 4, 10. Therefore a religious ceremony of propitiation is here prescribed in order to avert God's anger on the community.

21, 4: *They shall cut the heifer's throat there in the wadi:* its blood is to be carried away by the stream, signifying thereby the removal of

the human blood from the soil. This is not a sacrifice but a symbolic action; the priests are present merely as official witnesses.

20, 7: Dt 24, 5.   Jos 22, 8.
20, 8: Jgs 7, 3.   **20, 17:** 16f: Dt 7, 1f; Jos 10, 40;
20, 14: 13f: Nm 31, 7.9.11;   11, 14.

D
T

bringing it down to a wadi with an ever-flowing stream at a place that has not been plowed or sown, they shall cut the heifer's throat there in the wadi. [5]* The priests, the descendants of Levi, shall also be present, for the LORD, your God, has chosen them to minister to him and to give blessings in his name, and every case of dispute or violence must be settled by their decision. [6]† Then all the elders of that city nearest the corpse shall wash their hands over the heifer whose throat was cut in the wadi, [7]† and shall declare, 'Our hands did not shed this blood, and our eyes did not see the deed. [8] Absolve, O LORD, your people Israel, whom you have ransomed, and let not the guilt of shedding innocent blood remain in the midst of your people Israel.' Thus they shall be absolved from the guilt of bloodshed, [9] and you shall purge from your midst the guilt of innocent blood, that you may prosper for doing what is right in the sight of the LORD.

Marriage with a Female Captive

[10] "When you go out to war against your enemies and the LORD, your God, delivers them into your hand, so that you take captives, [11] if you see a comely woman among the captives and become so enamored of her that you wish to have her as wife, [12]† you may take her home to your house. But before she may live there, she must shave her head and pare her nails [13] and lay aside her captive's garb. After she has mourned her father and mother for a full month, you may have relations with her, and you shall be her husband and she shall be your wife. [14] However, if later on you lose your liking for her, you shall give her her freedom, if she wishes it; but you shall not sell her or enslave her, since she was married to you under compulsion.

Rights of the First-born

[15] "If a man with two wives loves one and dislikes the other; and if both bear him sons, but the first-born is of her whom he dislikes: [16] when he comes to bequeath his property to his sons he may not consider as his first-born the son of the wife he loves, in preference to his true first-born, the son of the wife whom he dislikes. [17] On the contrary, he shall recognize as his first-born the son of her whom he dislikes, giving him a double share of whatever he happens to own, since he is the first fruits of his manhood, and to him belong the rights of the first-born.

The Incorrigible Son

[18] "If a man has a stubborn and unruly son who will not listen to his father or mother, and will not obey them even though they chastise him, [19]† his father and mother shall have him apprehended and brought out to the elders at the gate of his home city, [20] where they shall say to those city elders, 'This son of ours is a stubborn and unruly fellow who will not listen to us; he is a glutton and a drunkard.' [21] Then all his fellow citizens shall stone him to death. Thus shall you purge the evil from your midst, and all Israel, on hearing of it, shall fear.

Corpse of a Criminal

[22]† "If a man guilty of a capital offense is put to death and his corpse hung on a tree, [23]*† it shall not remain on the tree overnight. You shall bury it the same day; otherwise, since God's curse rests on him who hangs on a tree, you will defile the land which the LORD, your God, is giving you as an inheritance.

Care for Lost Animals

22 [1]* "You shall not see your kinsman's ox or sheep driven astray without showing concern about it; see to it that it is returned to your kinsman. [2] If this kinsman does not live near you, or you do not know who he may be, take it to your own place and keep it with you until he claims it; then give it back to him. [3] You shall do the same with his ass, or his garment, or anything else which your kinsman loses and you happen to find; you may not be unconcerned about them. [4] You shall not see your kinsman's ass or ox foundering on the road without showing concern about it; see to it that you help him lift it up.

Various Precepts

[5] "A woman shall not wear an article proper to a man, nor shall a man put on a woman's dress; for anyone who does such things is an abomination to the LORD, your God.

21, 6: *Wash their hands:* a symbolic gesture in protestation of one's own innocence when human blood is unjustly shed; cf Mt 27, 24.

21, 7: *This blood:* the blood of the slain man as symbolized by the heifer's blood.

21, 12f: *Shave her head . . . :* these symbolic actions are meant to signify the purification of the woman from her pagan defilement or perhaps the end of her period of mourning for her previous husband.

21, 19: *The gate:* in the city walls. This open space served as the forum for the administration of justice. Cf Dt 22, 15; 25, 7; Ru 4, 1f.11; Is 29, 21; Am 5, 10.12.15.

21, 22: *Hung on a tree:* some understand, "impaled on a stake." In any case the hanging or impaling was not the means used to execute the criminal; he was first put to death by the ordinary means, stoning, and his corpse was then exposed on high as a salutary warning for others. Cf Jos 8, 29; 10, 26; 1 Sm 31, 10; 2 Sm 21, 9.

21, 23: *God's curse rests on him who hangs on a tree:* St. Paul quotes these words in Gal 3, 13, where he applies them to the crucified Savior, who "redeemed us from the curse of the law, becoming a curse for us."

21, 5: Dt 19, 17.　　　　**22, 1–4:** Ex 23, 4f.
21, 23: Gal 3, 13.

6 "If, while walking along, you chance upon a bird's nest with young birds or eggs in it, in any tree or on the ground, and the mother bird is sitting on them, you shall not take away the mother bird along with her brood; 7 you shall let her go, although you may take her brood away. It is thus that you shall have prosperity and a long life.

8 "When you build a new house, put a parapet around the roof; otherwise, if someone falls off, you will bring blood-guilt upon your house.

9*† "You shall not sow your vineyard with two different kinds of seed; if you do, its produce shall become forfeit, both the crop you have sown and the yield of the vineyard. 10 You shall not plow with an ox and an ass harnessed together. 11 You shall not wear cloth of two different kinds of thread, wool and linen, woven together.

12*† "You shall put twisted cords on the four corners of the cloak that you wrap around you.

Crimes against Marriage

13 "If a man, after marrying a woman and having relations with her, comes to dislike her, 14 and makes monstrous charges against her and defames her by saying, 'I married this woman, but when I first had relations with her I did not find her a virgin,' 15† the father and mother of the girl shall take the evidence of her virginity and bring it to the elders at the city gate. 16 There the father of the girl shall say to the elders, 'I gave my daughter to this man in marriage, but he has come to dislike her, 17 and now brings monstrous charges against her, saying: I did not find your daughter a virgin. But here is the evidence of my daughter's virginity!' And they shall spread out the cloth before the elders of the city. 18† Then these city elders shall take the man and chastise him, 19 besides fining him one hundred silver shekels, which they shall give to the girl's father, because the man defamed a virgin in Israel. Moreover, she shall remain his wife, and he may not divorce her as long as he lives.

20 "But if this charge is true, and evidence of the girl's virginity is not found, 21 they shall bring the girl to the entrance of her father's house and there her townsmen shall stone her to death, because she committed a crime against Israel by her unchasteness in her father's house. Thus shall you purge the evil from your midst.

22* "If a man is discovered having relations with a woman who is married to another, both the man

and the woman with whom he has had relations shall die. Thus shall you purge the evil from your midst.

23† "If within the city a man comes upon a maiden who is betrothed, and has relations with her, 24 you shall bring them both out to the gate of the city and there stone them to death: the girl because she did not cry out for help though she was in the city, and the man because he violated his neighbor's wife. Thus shall you purge the evil from your midst.

25 "If, however, it is in the open fields that a man comes upon such a betrothed maiden, seizes her and has relations with her, the man alone shall die. 26 You shall do nothing to the maiden, since she is not guilty of a capital offense. This case is like that of a man who rises up against his neighbor and murders him: 27 it was in the open fields that he came upon her, and though the betrothed maiden may have cried out for help, there was no one to come to her aid.

28* "If a man comes upon a maiden that is not betrothed, takes her and has relations with her, and their deed is discovered, 29 the man who had relations with her shall pay the girl's father fifty silver shekels and take her as his wife, because he has deflowered her. Moreover, he may not divorce her as long as he lives.

23

1† "A man shall not marry his father's wife, nor shall he dishonor his father's bed.

Membership in the Community

2 "No one whose testicles have been crushed or whose penis has been cut off, may be admitted into the community of the Lord. 3 No child of an incestuous union may be admitted into the community of the LORD, nor any descendant of his even to the tenth generation. 4* No Ammonite or Moabite may ever be admitted into the community of the LORD, nor any descendants of theirs even to the tenth generation, 5* because they would not succor you with food and water on your journey after you left Egypt, and because Moab hired Balaam, son of Beor, from Pethor in Aram Naharaim, to curse you; 6 though the LORD, your God, would not listen to Balaam and turned his curse into a blessing for you, because he loves you. 7 Never promote their peace and prosperity as long as you live. 8* But do not abhor the Edomite, since he is your brother, nor the

---

22, 9: *Become forfeit:* to the sanctuary; cf Lv 19, 19; Jos 6, 19.

22, 12: *Twisted cords:* referred to as "tassels" on "violet cords" in Nm 15, 38. See note there.

22, 15: *The evidence of her virginity:* the bridal garment or sheet stained with a little blood from the first nuptial relations.

22, 18: *Chastise him:* flog him, as prescribed in Dt 25, 1–3.

22, 23: *A maiden who is betrothed:* a girl who is married but not

yet brought to her husband's home and whose marriage is therefore still unconsummated.

23, 1: *Father's wife:* stepmother. *Dishonor:* cf Dt 27, 20.

22, 9: Dt 9,11, Lv 19, 19.   23, 4: Neh 13, 1f.
22, 12: Nm 15, 38; Mt 23, 5.   23, 5: Nm 24, 10.
22, 22: Lv 20, 10; Jn 8, 4f.   23, 8: Gn 25, 24ff.
22, 28f: Ex 22, 16.

Egyptian, since you were an alien in his country. [9] Children born to them may in the third generation be admitted into the community of the LORD.

Cleanliness in Camp

[10] "When you are in camp during an expedition against your enemies, you shall keep yourselves from everything offensive. [11] If one of you becomes unclean because of a nocturnal emission, he shall go outside the camp, and not return until, [12] toward evening, he has bathed in water; then, when the sun has set, he may come back into the camp. [13] Outside the camp you shall have a place set aside to be used as a latrine. [14] You shall also keep a trowel in your equipment and with it, when you go outside to ease nature, you shall first dig a hole and afterward cover up your excrement. [15] Since the LORD, your God, journeys along within your camp to defend you and to put your enemies at your mercy, your camp must be holy; otherwise, if he sees anything indecent in your midst, he will leave your company.

Various Precepts

[16] "You shall not hand over to his master a slave who has taken refuge from him with you. [17]† Let him live with you wherever he chooses, in any one of your communities that pleases him. Do not molest him.

[18]*† "There shall be no temple harlot among the Israelite women, nor a temple prostitute among the Israelite men. [19] You shall not offer a harlot's fee or a dog's price as any kind of votive offering in the house of the LORD, your God; both these things are an abomination to the LORD, your God.

[20]* "You shall not demand interest from your countrymen on a loan of money or of food or of anything else on which interest is usually demanded. [21] You may demand interest from a foreigner, but not from your countryman, so that the LORD, your God, may bless you in all your undertakings on the land you are to enter and occupy.

[22] "When you make a vow to the LORD, your God, you shall not delay in fulfilling it; otherwise you will be held guilty, for the LORD, your God, is strict in requiring it of you. [23] Should you refrain from making a vow, you will not be held guilty. [24] But you must keep your solemn word and fulfill the votive offering you have freely promised to the LORD.

[25] "When you go through your neighbor's vineyard, you may eat as many of his grapes as you wish, but do not put them in your basket. [26] When you go through your neighbor's grainfield, you may pluck some of the ears with your hand, but do not put a sickle to your neighbor's grain.

Marriage Laws

24 [1]† "When a man, after marrying a woman and having relations with her, is later displeased with her because he finds in her something indecent, and therefore he writes out a bill of divorce and hands it to her, thus dismissing her from his house: [2] if on leaving his house she goes and becomes the wife of another man, [3] and the second husband, too, comes to dislike her and dismisses her from his house by handing her a written bill of divorce; [4] or if this second man who has married her, dies; then her former husband, who dismissed her, may not again take her as his wife after she has become defiled. That would be an abomination before the LORD, and you shall not bring such guilt upon the land which the LORD, your God, is giving you as a heritage.

[5]* "When a man is newly wed, he need not go out on a military expedition, nor shall any public duty be imposed on him. He shall be exempt for one year for the sake of his family, to bring joy to the wife he has married.

Justice, Equity, and Charity

[6]† "No one shall take a hand mill or even its upper stone as a pledge for debt, for he would be taking the debtor's sustenance as a pledge.

[7]* "If any man is caught kidnaping a fellow Israelite in order to enslave him and sell him, the kidnaper shall be put to death. Thus shall you purge the evil from your midst.

[8]* "In an attack of leprosy you shall be careful to observe exactly and to carry out all the directions of

---

23, 17: *In any one of your communities:* from this it would seem that the slave in question is a fugitive from a foreign country.

23, 18f: The pagans believed that they could enter into special relationship with their gods and goddesses by having sexual relations with the pagan priests and priestesses who prostituted themselves for this purpose. The money paid for this was considered a sort of votive offering made to the pagan sanctuary. Such abominations were naturally forbidden in Israel. *A dog's price:* the money paid the pagan priest for his indecent service.

24, 1–4: This law is directly concerned only with forbidding divorced couples to remarry each other, and indirectly with checking hasty divorces, by demanding sufficient cause and certain legal formalities. Divorce itself is taken for granted and tolerated as an existing custom whose evils this law seeks to lessen. Cf Dt 22, 19.29; Mal

2, 14ff. Christ gave the authentic interpretation of this law: "Moses, by reason of the hardness of your heart, permitted you to put away your wives; but it was not so from the beginning" (Mt 19, 8f).

24, 1: *Something indecent:* a rather indefinite phrase, meaning perhaps "immodest conduct." At the time of Christ the rabbis differed in opinion concerning the sufficient grounds for divorce; cf Mt 19, 3.

24, 6: Since the Israelites ground their grain into flour only in sufficient quantity for their current need, to deprive a debtor of his hand mill was virtually equivalent to condemning him to starve to death.

23, 18: 1 Kgs 14, 24; 22, 46;
    2 Kgs 23, 7.
23, 20: Ex 22, 25; Lv 25, 37;
    Lk 6, 34f.

24, 5: Dt 20, 7.
24, 7: Ex 21, 16.
24, 8: Lv 13, 1–14.

the levitical priests. Take care to act in accordance with the instructions I have given them. [9]* Remember what the LORD, your God, did to Miriam on the journey after you left Egypt.

[10]† "When you make a loan of any kind to your neighbor, you shall not enter his house to receive a pledge from him, [11] but shall wait outside until the man to whom you are making the loan brings his pledge outside to you. [12] If he is a poor man, you shall not sleep in the mantle he gives as a pledge, [13]* but shall return it to him at sunset that he himself may sleep in it. Then he will bless you, and it will be a good deed of yours before the LORD, your God.

[14] "You shall not defraud a poor and needy hired servant, whether he be one of your own countrymen or one of the aliens who live in your communities. [15]* You shall pay him each day's wages before sundown on the day itself, since he is poor and looks forward to them. Otherwise he will cry to the LORD against you, and you will be held guilty.

[16]* "Fathers shall not be put to death for their children, nor children for their fathers; only for his own guilt shall a man be put to death.

[17]* "You shall not violate the rights of the alien or of the orphan, nor take the clothing of a widow as a pledge. [18] For, remember, you were once slaves in Egypt, and the LORD, your God, ransomed you from there; that is why I command you to observe this rule.

[19]* "When you reap the harvest in your field and overlook a sheaf there, you shall not go back to get it; let it be for the alien, the orphan or the widow, that the LORD, your God, may bless you in all your undertakings. [20] When you knock down the fruit of your olive trees, you shall not go over the branches a second time; let what remains be for the alien, the orphan and the widow. [21] When you pick your grapes, you shall not go over the vineyard a second time; let what remains be for the alien, the orphan, and the widow. [22] For remember that you were once slaves in Egypt; that is why I command you to observe this rule.

25 [1] "When men have a dispute and bring it to court, and a decision is handed down to them acquitting the innocent party and condemning the guilty party, [2] if the latter deserves

?did you KNOW?

The Poor, the Strangers, the Widows, and the Orphans

One remarkable aspect of Israel's Covenant was the command to care for the poor, the "aliens" or strangers, the widows, and the orphans. These four groups were the outsiders in ancient Israel because they fell outside Israel's socioeconomic system. The poor often had no means to sustain themselves. Strangers were not part of Israel's tribal organization. Widows depended on the charity of others. Orphans were destitute because they had no family to help them survive.

God provides a reason why Israel must care for the poor and oppressed. Just as the Israelites were enslaved in Egypt— when they were poor, oppressed, orphans in a foreign land—and God responded to their cry for help, so they must care for the poor, oppressed, forgotten, and marginalized in their midst. Can this be any less true for us today?

▶ Dt 24, 10–21

stripes, the judge shall have him lie down and in his presence receive the number of stripes his guilt deserves. [3]*† Forty stripes may be given him, but no more; lest, if he were beaten with more stripes than these, your kinsman should be looked upon as disgraced because of the severity of the beating.

[4]*† "You shall not muzzle an ox when it is treading out grain.

Levirate Marriage

[5]*† "When brothers live together and one of them dies without a son, the widow of the deceased

---

24, 10f: The debtor had the right to select the pledge that the creditor demanded as a guarantee for his loan.

25, 3: *Forty stripes:* a relatively mild punishment in ancient times. Later Jewish practice limited the number to thirty-nine; cf 2 Cor 11, 24.

25, 4: St Paul argues from this verse that a laborer has the right to live on the fruits of his labor; cf 1 Cor 9, 9; 1 Tm 5, 18.

25, 5: *When brothers live together:* when relatives of the same clan, though married, hold their property in common. It was only in this case that the present law was to be observed, since one of its

purposes was to keep the property of the deceased within the same clan. Such a marriage of a widow with her brother-in-law is known as a "levirate" marriage from the Latin word *levir*, meaning "a husband's brother."

24, 9: Nm 12, 10–15.
24, 13: Ex 22, 26.
24, 15: 14f: Lv 19, 13; Tb 4, 15; Sir 34, 25f; Jer 22, 13.
24, 16: 2 Kgs 14, 6; 2 Chr 25, 4; Ez 18, 20.
24, 17: Ex 22, 22; 23, 9.
24, 19ff: Lv 19, 9f; 23, 22.
25, 3: 2 Cor 11, 24.
25, 4: 1 Cor 9, 9; 1 Tm 5, 18.
25, 5: Mt 22, 24; Mk 12, 19; Lk 20, 28.

shall not marry anyone outside the family; but her husband's brother shall go to her and perform the duty of a brother-in-law by marrying her. 6* The first-born son she bears shall continue the line of the deceased brother, that his name may not be blotted out from Israel. 7 If, however, a man does not care to marry his brother's wife, she shall go up to the elders at the gate and declare, 'My brother-in-law does not intend to perform his duty toward me and refuses to perpetuate his brother's name in Israel.' 8 Thereupon the elders of his city shall summon him and admonish him. If he persists in saying, 'I am not willing to marry her,' 9† his sister-in-law, in the presence of the elders, shall go up to him and strip his sandal from his foot and spit in his face, saying publicly, 'This is how one should be treated who will not build up his brother's family!' 10 And his lineage shall be spoken of in Israel as 'the family of the man stripped of his sandal.'

Various Precepts

11 "When two men are fighting and the wife of one intervenes to save her husband from the blows of his opponent, if she stretches out her hand and seizes the latter by his private parts, 12 you shall chop off her hand without pity.

13* "You shall not keep two differing weights in your bag, one large and the other small; 14 nor shall you keep two different measures in your house, one large and the other small. 15 But use a true and just weight, and a true and just measure, that you may have a long life on the land which the LORD, your God, is giving you. 16 Everyone who is dishonest in any of these matters is an abomination to the LORD, your God.

17*† "Bear in mind what Amalek did to you on the journey after you left Egypt, 18 how without fear of any god he harassed you along the way, weak and weary as you were, and cut off at the rear all those who lagged behind. 19* Therefore, when the LORD, your God, gives you rest from all your enemies round about in the land which he is giving you to occupy as your heritage, you shall blot out the memory of Amalek from under the heavens. Do not forget!

Thanksgiving for the Harvest

26 1 "When you have come into the land which the LORD, your God, is giving you as a heritage, and have occupied it and settled in it, 2* you shall take some first fruits of the various products of the soil which you harvest from the land which the LORD, your God, gives you, and putting them in a basket, you shall go to the place which the LORD, your God, chooses for the dwelling place of his name. 3 There you shall go to the priest in office at that time and say to him, 'Today I acknowledge to the LORD, my God, that I have indeed come into the land which he swore to our fathers he would give us.' 4 The priest shall then receive the basket from you and shall set it in front of the altar of the LORD, your God. 5*† Then you shall declare before the LORD, your God, 'My father was a wandering Aramean who went down to Egypt with a small household and lived there as an alien. But there he became a nation great, strong and numerous. 6* When the Egyptians maltreated and oppressed us, imposing hard labor upon us, 7 we cried to the LORD, the God of our fathers, and he heard our cry and saw our affliction, our toil and our oppression. 8* He brought us out of Egypt with his strong hand and outstretched arm, with terrifying power, with signs and wonders; 9* and bringing us into this country, he gave us this land flowing with milk and honey. 10 Therefore, I have now brought you the first fruits of the products of the soil which you, O LORD, have given me.' And having set them before the LORD, your God, you shall bow down in his presence. 11* Then you and your family, together with the Levite and the aliens who live among you, shall make merry over all these good things which the LORD, your God, has given you.

Prayer with the Tithes

12*† "When you have finished setting aside all the tithes of your produce in the third year, the year of the tithes, and you have given them to the Levite, the alien, the orphan and the widow, that they may eat their fill in your own community, 13† you shall declare before the LORD, your God, 'I have purged my house of the sacred portion and I have given it to the Levite, the alien, the orphan and the widow,

---

25, 9f: The penalty decreed for a man who refuses to comply with this law of family loyalty is public disgrace (the widow is to spit in his face) and the curse of poverty; sandals were proverbially a man's cheapest possession (cf Am 2, 6; 8, 6), and therefore "a man without sandals" was the poorest of the poor. Some commentators, however, connect this symbolic act with the ceremony mentioned in Ru 4, 7f.

25, 17–19: This attack on Israel by Amalek is not mentioned elsewhere in the Old Testament, although it probably was connected with the battle mentioned in Ex 17, 8. A campaign against Amalek was carried out by Saul; cf 1 Sm 15.

26, 5: *Aramean:* either in reference to the origin of the patriarchs from Aram Naharaim (cf Gn 24, 10; 25, 20; 28, 5; 31, 20.24), or

merely in the sense of "nomad," in the same way as "Arab" was later used; cf Jer 3, 2.

26, 12: *And you have given them to the Levite . . . :* as prescribed in Dt 14, 28f.

25, 6–9: Ru 4, 5–10.
25, 13ff: Lv 19, 35f; Prv 16, 11;
  Ez 45, 10; Ml 6, 11.
25, 17: Ex 17, 8.
25, 19: Ex 17, 14; 1 Sm 15, 2f.
26, 2: Ex 23, 19; 34, 26.
26, 5: Gn 46, 6f; Acts 7, 14f.

26, 6f: Ex 1, 8–22; 2, 23ff; 3,
  9; Nm 20, 15f.
26, 8: Ex 12, 51.
26, 9: Ex 3, 8.
26, 11: Dt 12, 7.12.
26, 12: Dt 14, 28f.

just as you have commanded me. In this I have not broken or forgotten any of your commandments: ¹⁴† I have not eaten any of the tithe as a mourner; I have not brought any of it out as one unclean; I have not offered any of it to the dead. I have thus hearkened to the voice of the LORD, my God, doing just as you have commanded me. ¹⁵ Look down, then, from heaven, your holy abode, and bless your people Israel and the soil you have given us in the land flowing with milk and honey which you promised on oath to our fathers.'

The Covenant

¹⁶ "This day the LORD, your God, commands you to observe these statutes and decrees. Be careful, then, to observe them with all your heart and with all your soul. ¹⁷* Today you are making this agreement with the LORD: he is to be your God and you are to walk in his ways and observe his statutes, commandments and decrees, and to hearken to his voice. ¹⁸* And today the LORD is making this agreement with you: you are to be a people peculiarly his own, as he promised you; and provided you keep all his commandments, ¹⁹ he will then raise you high in praise and renown and glory above all other nations he has made, and you will be a people sacred to the LORD, your God, as he promised."

IV: Final Words of Moses

Ceremonies

27 ¹ Then Moses, with the elders of Israel, gave the people this order: "Keep all these commandments which I enjoin on you today. ² On the day you cross the Jordan into the land which the LORD, your God, is giving you, set up some large stones and coat them with plaster. ³* Also write on them, at the time you cross, all the words of this law, that you may thus enter into the land flowing with milk and honey, which the LORD, your God, and the God of your fathers, is giving you as he promised you. ⁴ When, moreover, you have crossed the Jordan, besides setting up on Mount Ebal these stones concerning which I command you today, and coating them with plaster, ⁵* you shall also build to the LORD, your God, an altar made of stones that no iron tool has touched. ⁶ You shall make this altar of the LORD, your God, with undressed stones, and shall offer on it holocausts to the LORD, your God. ⁷ You shall also sacrifice peace

offerings and eat them there, making merry before the LORD, your God. ⁸† On the stones you shall inscribe all the words of this law very clearly."

⁹* Moses, with the levitical priests, then said to all Israel: "Be silent, O Israel, and listen! This day you have become the people of the LORD, your God. ¹⁰ You shall therefore hearken to the voice of the LORD, your God, and keep his commandments and statutes which I enjoin on you today."

¹¹ That same day Moses gave the people this order: ¹²* "When you cross the Jordan, Simeon, Levi, Judah, Issachar, Joseph and Benjamin shall stand on Mount Gerizim to pronounce blessings over the people, ¹³ while Reuben, Gad, Asher, Zebulun, Dan and Naphtali shall stand on Mount Ebal to pronounce curses.

The Twelve Curses

¹⁴ "The Levites shall proclaim aloud to all the men of Israel: ¹⁵*† 'Cursed be the man who makes a carved or molten idol —an abomination to the LORD, the product of a craftsman's hands—and sets it up in secret!' And all the people shall answer, 'Amen!'

¹⁶* 'Cursed be he who dishonors his father or his mother!' And all the people shall answer, 'Amen!'

¹⁷* 'Cursed be he who moves his neighbor's landmarks!' And all the people shall answer, 'Amen!'

¹⁸* 'Cursed be he who misleads a blind man on his way!' And all the people shall answer, 'Amen!'

¹⁹* 'Cursed be he who violates the rights of the alien, the orphan or the widow!' And all the people shall answer, 'Amen!'

²⁰* 'Cursed be he who has relations with his father's wife, for he dishonors his father's bed!' And all the people shall answer, 'Amen!'

²¹* 'Cursed be he who has relations with any animal!' And all the people shall answer, 'Amen!'

²²* 'Cursed be he who has relations with his sister or his half-sister!' And all the people shall answer, 'Amen!'

²³* 'Cursed be he who has relations with his mother-in-law!' And all the people shall answer, 'Amen!'

²⁴* 'Cursed be he who slays his neighbor in secret!' And all the people shall answer, 'Amen!'

²⁵ 'Cursed be he who accepts payment for slaying an innocent man!' And all the people shall answer, 'Amen!'

26, 14: These are allusions to pagan religious practices.
27, 8: *On the stones:* cf vv 3f; not the stones of the altar.
27, 15–26: *Amen:* see note on Nm 5, 22.

26, 17: Ex 24, 7.
26, 18f: Dt 7, 6; 14, 2; 28, 1; Ex 19, 5.
27, 3: Jos 8, 32.
27, 5: Ex 20, 25; Jos 8, 31.
27, 9: Dt 26, 17ff.
27, 12f: Dt 11, 29; Jos 8, 33f.
27, 15: Ex 20, 4.23; Lv 19, 4; Wis 14, 8.
27, 16: Dt 21, 18–21; Ex 21, 17; Lv 20, 9.
27, 17: Dt 19, 14.
27, 18: Lv 19, 14.
27, 19: Dt 24, 17; Ex 22, 21f.
27, 20: Dt 22; 23, 1; Lv 18, 8; 20, 11.
27, 21: Ex 22, 18; Lv 18, 23; 20, 15.
27, 22: Lv 18, 9; 20, 17.
27, 23: Lv 18, 17; 20, 14.
27, 24: Ex 20, 13; 21, 12; Nm 35, 20f.

26* 'Cursed be he who fails to fulfill any of the provisions of this law!' And all the people shall answer, 'Amen!'

Blessings for Obedience

28 †1* "Thus, then, shall it be:* if you continue to heed the voice of the LORD, your God, and are careful to observe all his commandments which I enjoin on you today, the LORD, your God, will raise you high above all the nations of the earth.* 2 When you hearken to the voice of the LORD, your God, all these blessings will come upon you and overwhelm you:

3   "May you be blessed in the city,
          and blessed in the country!
4*   "Blessed be the fruit of your womb,
          the produce of your soil and the offspring
          of your livestock,
          the issue of your herds and the young of
          your flocks!
5   "Blessed be your grain bin and your
          kneading bowl!
6†   "May you be blessed in your coming in,
          and blessed in your going out!

Victory and Prosperity

7† "The LORD will beat down before you the enemies that rise up against you; though they come out against you from but one direction, they will flee before you in seven. 8 The LORD will affirm his blessing upon you, on your barns and on all your undertakings, blessing you in the land that the LORD, your God, gives you. 9* Provided that you keep the commandments of the LORD, your God, and walk in his ways, he will establish you as a people sacred to himself, as he swore to you; 10*† so that, when all the nations of the earth see you bearing the name of the LORD, they will stand in awe of you. 11 The LORD will increase in more than goodly measure the fruit of your womb, the offspring of your livestock, and the produce of your soil, in the land which he swore to your fathers he would give you. 12* The LORD will open up for you his rich treasure house of the heavens, to give your land rain in due season, blessing all your undertakings, so that you will lend to many nations and borrow from none. 13† The LORD will make you the head,

not the tail, and you will always mount higher and not decline, as long as you obey the commandments of the LORD, your God, which I order you today to observe carefully; 14 not turning aside to the right or to the left from any of the commandments which I now give you, in order to follow other gods and serve them.

HAIL MARY

Catholic Connections

Deuteronomy 28, 4 might sound familiar to you. These words, also found in Lk 1, 42, are part of a prayer called the Hail Mary. In this passage, Moses reminds the Israelites that they shall be blessed because of their obedience, and Mary is the ultimate example of the blessings that come from obedience to God's will.

▸ Dt 28, 1–6

Curses for Disobedience

15* "But if you do not hearken to the voice of the LORD, your God, and are not careful to observe all his commandments which I enjoin on you today, all these curses shall come upon you and overwhelm you:

16   "May you be cursed in the city,
          and cursed in the country!

17   "Cursed be your grain bin and your
          kneading bowl!

28, 1–69: This chapter would read better immediately after chapter 26.

28, 6: *In your coming in . . . in your going out:* at the beginning and end of every action, or in all actions in general.

28, 7.25: *From but one direction . . . in seven:* in one compact mass, contrasted with many scattered groups.

28, 10: *You bearing the name of the LORD:* literally, "The LORD's name is called over you," an expression signifying ownership and protection. Cf 2 Sm 12, 28; 1 Kgs 8, 43; Is 4, 1; 63, 19; Jer 7, 10f; 14, 9; 15, 16; 25, 29; Am 9, 12.

28, 13: *The head, not the tail:* in the honorable position as leader. Cf Is 9, 14; 19, 15.

27, 26: Gal 3, 10.
28, 1–68: Lv 26, 1–45.
28, 1–14: Dt 7, 12–16.
28, 1: Dt 26, 19.
28, 4: Dt 7, 13; 30.9.

28, 9: Dt 26, 18; Ex 19, 5f.
28, 10: Dt 2, 25; 11, 25.
28, 12: Dt 15, 6.
28, 15: Bar 1, 20; Dn 9, 11; Mal 2, 2.

¹⁸ "Cursed be the fruit of your womb,
   the produce of your soil and the offspring
      of your livestock,
   the issue of your herds and the young of
      your flocks!

¹⁹ "May you be cursed in your coming in,
   and cursed in your going out!

Sickness and Defeat

²⁰ "The LORD will put a curse on you, defeat and frustration in every enterprise you undertake, until you are speedily destroyed and perish for the evil you have done in forsaking me. ²¹ The LORD will bring a pestilence upon you that will persist until he has exterminated you from the land you are entering to occupy. ²² The LORD will strike you with wasting and fever, with scorching, fiery drought, with blight and searing wind, that will plague you until you perish. ²³* The sky over your heads will be like bronze and the earth under your feet like iron. ²⁴ For rain the LORD will give your land powdery dust, which will come down upon you from the sky until you are destroyed. ²⁵* The LORD will let you be beaten down before your enemies; though you advance against them from one direction, you will flee before them in seven, so that you will become a terrifying example to all the kingdoms of the earth. ²⁶ Your carcasses will become food for all the birds of the air and for the beasts of the field, with no one to frighten them off. ²⁷* The LORD will strike you with Egyptian boils and with tumors, eczema and the itch, until you cannot be cured. ²⁸ And the LORD will strike you with madness, blindness and panic, ²⁹ so that even at midday you will grope like a blind man in the dark, unable to find your way.

Despoilment

"You will be oppressed and robbed continually, with no one to come to your aid. ³⁰ Though you betroth a wife, another man will have her. Though you build a house, you will not live in it. Though you plant a vineyard, you will not enjoy its fruits. ³¹ Your ox will be slaughtered before your eyes, and you will not eat of its flesh. Your ass will be stolen in your presence, but you will not recover it. Your flocks will be given to your enemies, with no one to come to your aid. ³² Your sons and daughters will be given to a foreign nation while you look on and grieve for them in constant helplessness. ³³ A peo-

ple whom you do not know will consume the fruit of your soil and of all your labor, and you will be oppressed and crushed at all times without surcease, ³⁴ until you are driven mad by what your eyes must look upon. ³⁵† The LORD will strike you with malignant boils of which you cannot be cured, on your knees and legs, and from the soles of your feet to the crown of your head.

Exile

³⁶* "The LORD will bring you, and your king whom you have set over you, to a nation which you and your fathers have not known, and there you will serve strange gods of wood and stone, ³⁷ and will call forth amazement, reproach and barbed scorn from all the nations to which the LORD will lead you.

Fruitless Labors

³⁸* "Though you spend much seed on your field, you will harvest but little, for the locusts will devour the crop. ³⁹* Though you plant and cultivate vineyards, you will not drink or store up the wine, for the grubs will eat the vines clean. ⁴⁰* Though you have olive trees throughout your country, you will have no oil for ointment, for your olives will drop off unripe. ⁴¹* Though you beget sons and daughters, they will not remain with you, but will go into captivity. ⁴² Buzzing insects will infest all your trees and the crops of your soil. ⁴³ The alien residing among you will rise higher and higher above you, while you sink lower and lower. ⁴⁴ He will lend to you, not you to him. He will become the head, you the tail.

⁴⁵ "All these curses will come upon you, pursuing you and overwhelming you, until you are destroyed, because you would not hearken to the voice of the LORD, your God, nor keep the commandments and statutes he gave you. ⁴⁶† They will light on you and your descendants as a sign and a wonder for all time. ⁴⁷ Since you would not serve the LORD, your God, with joy and gratitude for abundance of every kind, ⁴⁸ therefore in hunger and thirst, in nakedness and utter poverty, you will serve the enemies whom the LORD will send against you. He will put an iron yoke on your neck, until he destroys you.

Invasion and Siege

⁴⁹* "The LORD will raise up against you a nation from afar, from the end of the earth, that swoops

---

† **28, 35:** This verse is best read with v 27.
28, 46: *A sign and a wonder:* an ominous example, attracting attention; cf Dt 29, 21–28.

* **28, 23:** 22f: Lv 26, 19.
28, 25: Lv 26, 17.37.
28, 27: Ex 9, 9ff.
28, 36: 1 Kgs 9, 7ff; 2 Chr 7, 20ff; 33, 11; 36, 6.20.
28, 38: Ml 6, 15; Hg 1, 6.
28, 39: Zep 1, 13.
28, 40: Mi 6, 15.
28, 41: Lam 1, 5.
28, 49–52: Jer 5, 15ff; Bar 4, 15f.

down like an eagle, a nation whose tongue you do not understand, 50 a nation of stern visage, that shows neither respect for the aged nor pity for the young. 51 They will consume the offspring of your livestock and the produce of your soil, until you are destroyed; they will leave you no grain or wine or oil, no issue of your herds or young of your flocks, until they have brought about your ruin. 52 They will besiege you in each of your communities, until the great, unscalable walls you trust in come tumbling down all over your land. They will so besiege you in every community throughout the land which the LORD, your God, has given you, 53* that in the distress of the siege to which your enemy subjects you, you will eat the fruit of your womb, the flesh of your own sons and daughters whom the LORD, your God, has given you. 54 The most refined and fastidious man among you will begrudge his brother and his beloved wife and his surviving children 55 any share in the flesh of his children that he himself is using for food when nothing else is left him in the straits of the siege to which your enemy will subject you in all your communities. 56 The most refined and delicate woman among you, so delicate and refined that she would not venture to set the sole of her foot on the ground, will begrudge her beloved husband and her son and daughter 57 the afterbirth that issues from her womb and the infant she brings forth when she secretly uses them for food for want of anything else, in the straits of the siege to which your enemy will subject you in your communities.

Plagues

58 "If you are not careful to observe every word of the law which is written in this book, and to revere the glorious and awesome name of the LORD, your God, 59 he will smite you and your descendants with severe and constant blows, malignant and lasting maladies. 60*† He will again afflict you with all the diseases of Egypt which you dread, and they will persist among you. 61 Should there be any kind of sickness or calamity not mentioned in this book of the law, that too the LORD will bring upon you until you are destroyed. 62* Of you who were numerous as the stars in the sky, only a few will be left, because you would not hearken to the voice of the LORD, your God.

Exile

63* "Just as the LORD once took delight in making you grow and prosper, so will he now take delight in ruining and destroying you, and you will be plucked out of the land you are now entering to occupy. 64* The LORD will scatter you among all the nations from one end of the earth to the other, and there you will serve strange gods of wood and stone, such as you and your fathers have not known. 65† Among these nations you will find no repose, not a foot of ground to stand upon, for there the LORD will give you an anguished heart and wasted eyes and a dismayed spirit. 66 You will live in constant suspense and stand in dread both day and night, never sure of your existence. 67 In the morning you will say, 'Would that it were evening!' and in the evening you will say, 'Would that it were morning!' for the dread that your heart must feel and the sight that your eyes must see. 68*† The LORD will send you back in galleys to Egypt, to the region I told you that you were never to see again; and there you will offer yourselves for sale to your enemies as male and female slaves, but there will be no buyer."

69 These are the words of the covenant which the LORD ordered Moses to make with the Israelites in the land of Moab, in addition to the covenant which he made with them at Horeb.

Past Favors Recalled

29 1 Moses summoned all Israel and said to them, "You have seen all that the LORD did in the land of Egypt before your very eyes to Pharaoh and all his servants and to all his land; 2* the great testings your own eyes have seen, and those great signs and wonders. 3† But not even at the present day has the LORD yet given you a mind to understand, or eyes to see, or ears to hear. 4* 'I led you for forty years in the desert. Your clothes did not fall from you in tatters nor your sandals from your feet; 5 bread was not your food, nor wine or beer your drink. Thus you should know that I, the LORD, am your God.' 6* When we came to this place, Sihon, king of Heshbon, and Og, king of Bashan, came out to engage us in battle, but we defeated them 7* and took over their land, which we then gave as a heritage to the Reubenites, Gadites, and half the tribe of Manasseh. 8 Keep the terms of this covenant, therefore, and

D
T

28, 60: *He will again afflict you with all the diseases of Egypt:* such as the Lord had promised to remove from his people; cf Dt 7, 15.

28, 65: *Wasted eyes:* worn out and disappointed in their longing gaze.

28, 68: *In galleys:* in the ships of the Phoenician slave traders (Ez 27, 13; Jl 4, 6; Am 1, 9), who also dealt with Egypt (Is 23, 3).

29, 3: *Eyes to see . . . ears to hear:* with inner, spiritual discernment. Cf Mt 13, 43.

28, 53: Lv 26, 29; 2 Kgs 6, 28f; Jer 19, 9; Lam 4, 10; Bar 2.3.
28, 60: Dt 28, 27.
28, 62: Dt 1, 10; Jer 42, 2.
28, 63: Dt 30, 9.
28, 64: Lv 26, 33.

28, 68: Hos 8, 13; 9, 3.
29, 2: Dt 4, 34; Ex 19, 4.
29, 4: Dt 8, 2.4.
29, 6: Dt 2, 24.32; 3, 1; Nm 21, 33ff.
29, 7: Dt 3, 16; Nm 32, 33.

fulfill them, that you may succeed in whatever you do.

All Israel Bound to the Covenant

9 "You are all now standing before the LORD, your God—your chiefs and judges, your elders and officials, and all of the men of Israel, 10 together with your wives and children and the aliens who live in your camp, down to those who hew wood and draw water for you— 11† that you may enter into the covenant of the LORD, your God, which he concluded with you today under this sanction of a curse; 12 so that he may now establish you as his people and he may be your God, as he promised you and as he swore to your fathers Abraham, Isaac and Jacob. 13 But it is not with you alone that I am making this covenant, under this sanction of a curse; 14† it is just as much with those who are not here among us today as it is with those of us who are now here present before the LORD, our God.

Warning against Idolatry

15 "You know in what surroundings we lived in the land of Egypt and what we passed by in the nations we traversed, 16 and you saw the loathsome idols of wood and stone, of gold and silver, that they possess. 17 Let there be, then, no man or woman, no clan or tribe among you, who would now turn away their hearts from the LORD, our God, to go and serve these pagan gods! Let there be no root that would bear such poison and wormwood among you! 18† If any such person, upon hearing the words of this curse, should beguile himself into thinking that he can safely persist in his stubbornness of heart, as though to sweep away both the watered soil and the parched ground, 19 the LORD will never consent to pardon him. Instead, the LORD's wrath and jealousy will flare up against that man, and every curse mentioned in this book will alight on him. The LORD will blot out his name from under the heavens 20 and will single him out from all the tribes of Israel for doom, in keeping with all the curses of the covenant inscribed in this book of the law.

Punishment for Infidelity

21 "Future generations, your own descendants who will rise up after you, as well as the foreigners who will come here from far-off lands, when they see the calamities of this land and the ills with which the LORD has smitten it— 22* all its soil being nothing but sulphur and salt, a burnt-out waste, unsown and unfruitful, without a blade of grass, destroyed like Sodom and Gomorrah, Admah and Zeboiim, which the LORD overthrew in his furious wrath— 23* they and all the nations will ask, 'Why has the LORD dealt thus with this land? Why this fierce outburst of wrath?' 24 And the answer will be, 'Because they forsook the covenant which the LORD, the God of their fathers, had made with them when he brought them out of the land of Egypt, 25 and they went and served other gods and adored them, gods whom they did not know and whom he had not let fall to their lot: 26 that is why the LORD was angry with this land and brought on it all the imprecations listed in this book; 27* in his furious wrath and tremendous anger the LORD uprooted them from their soil and cast them out into a strange land, where they are today.' 28† [Both what is still hidden and what has already been revealed concern us and our descendants forever, that we may carry out all the words of this law.]

Mercy for the Repentant

30 1* "When all these things which I have set before you, the blessings and the curses, are fulfilled in you, and from among whatever nations the LORD, your God, may have dispersed you, you ponder them in your heart: 2* then, provided that you and your children return to the LORD, your God, and heed his voice with all your heart and all your soul, just as I now command you, 3 the LORD, your God, will change your lot; and taking pity on you, he will again gather you from all the nations wherein he has scattered you. 4 Though you may have been driven to the farthest corner of the world, even from there will the LORD, your God, gather you; even from there will he bring you back. 5 The LORD, your God, will then bring you into the land which your fathers once occupied, that you too may occupy it, and he will make you more prosperous and numerous than your fathers. 6*† The LORD, your God, will circumcise your hearts and the hearts of your descendants, that you may love the LORD, your God, with all your heart and all your soul, and so may live. 7 But all those curses the LORD, your God, will assign to your enemies and the foes who persecuted you. 8 You, however, must

---

29, 11: *Sanction of a curse:* the present pact binds under penalty of the curses mentioned in this book. Cf v 20.

29, 14: *Not here among us:* this includes their descendants.

29, 18: *To sweep away both the watered soil and the parched ground:* apparently a proverb signifying that such an unfaithful Israelite will cause God to punish the good with the wicked, to root out the good plants growing in irrigated soil, together with the worthless plants growing in the dry ground.

29, 28: *What is still hidden:* the events of the future. *What has al-*

ready been revealed: God's law and the punishments in store for those who break it. Leave the future to God; our business is to keep his law.

30, 6: *Circumcise your hearts:* see note on Dt 10, 16.

29, 22: Gn 14, 10f; 19, 24f.
29, 23f: 1 Kgs 9, 8f; Jer 22, 8f.
29, 27: Dn 9, 11–14.
30, 1: Dt 11, 26ff.
30, 2f: Neh 1, 9.
30, 6: Dt 6, 5.

again heed the LORD's voice and carry out all his commandments which I now enjoin on you. [9]* Then the LORD, your God, will increase in more than goodly measure the returns from all your labors, the fruit of your womb, the offspring of your livestock, and the produce of your soil; for the LORD, your God, will again take delight in your prosperity, even as he took delight in your fathers', [10] if only you heed the voice of the LORD, your God, and keep his commandments and statutes that are written in this book of the law, when you return to the LORD, your God, with all your heart and all your soul.

God's Command Clear

[11]† "For this command which I enjoin on you today is not too mysterious and remote for you. [12] It is not up in the sky, that you should say, 'Who will go up in the sky to get it for us and tell us of it, that we may carry it out?' [13] Nor is it across the sea, that you should say, 'Who will cross the sea to get it for us and tell us of it, that we may carry it out?' [14]† No, it is something very near to you, already in your mouths and in your hearts; you have only to carry it out.

The Choice before Israel

[15] "Here, then, I have today set before you life and prosperity, death and doom. [16] If you obey the commandments of the LORD, your God, which I enjoin on you today, loving him, and walking in his ways, and keeping his commandments, statutes and decrees, you will live and grow numerous, and the LORD, your God, will bless you in the land you are entering to occupy. [17] If, however, you turn away your hearts and will not listen, but are led astray and adore and serve other gods, [18] I tell you now that you will certainly perish; you will not have a long life on the land which you are crossing the Jordan to enter and occupy. [19]* I call heaven and earth today to witness against you: I have set before you life and death, the blessing and the curse.* Choose life, then, that you and your descendants may live, [20] by loving the LORD, your God, heeding his voice, and holding fast to him. For that will mean life for you, a long life for you to live on the land which the LORD swore he would give to your fathers Abraham, Isaac and Jacob."

Choose Life then, that you and your descendants may LIVE

The Lord's Leadership

31 [1] When Moses had finished speaking these words to all Israel, [2]* he said to them, "I am now one hundred and twenty years old and am no longer able to move about freely; besides, the LORD has told me that I shall not cross this Jordan. [3]* It is the LORD your God, who will cross before you; he will destroy these nations before you, that you may supplant them. [It is Joshua who will cross before you, as the LORD promised.] [4]* The LORD will deal with them just as he dealt with Sihon and Og, the kings of the Amorites whom he destroyed, and with their country. [5]* When, therefore, the LORD delivers them up to you, you must deal with them exactly as I have ordered you. [6]* Be brave and steadfast; have no fear or dread of them, for it is the LORD, your God, who marches with you; he will never fail you or forsake you."

Call of Joshua

[7]* Then Moses summoned Joshua and in the presence of all Israel said to him, "Be brave and steadfast, for you must bring this people into the land which the LORD swore to their fathers he would give them; you must put them in possession of their heritage. [8] It is the LORD who marches before you; he will be with you and will never fail you or forsake you. So do not fear or be dismayed."

30, 11–14: God has revealed his will so clearly that ignorance of his law can be no excuse. St Paul in Rom 10, 6–10, applies these words to the ease with which we can come to faith and salvation in Christ.

30, 14: *In your mouths:* that you may readily talk about it; cf Dt 6, 7; 11, 19. *And in your hearts:* that you may easily remember it; cf Dt 6, 6; 11, 18.

30, 9: Dt 28, 11.
30, 19: Dt 4, 26.
30, 19: Dt 11, 26ff; 28, 2.15.
31, 2: Dt 34, 7; Nm 20, 12.
31, 3: Dt 9, 3.
31, 4: Nm 21, 21–35.
31, 5: Dt 7, 2.
31, 6: Dt 20, 3f.
31, 7f: Jos 1, 6f.9.

The Reading of the Law

9 When Moses had written down this law, he entrusted it to the levitical priests who carry the ark of the covenant of the LORD, and to all the elders of Israel, 10*† giving them this order: "On the feast of Booths, at the prescribed time in the year of relaxation which comes at the end of every seven-year period, 11† when all Israel goes to appear before the LORD, your God, in the place which he chooses, you shall read this law aloud in the presence of all Israel. 12 Assemble the people—men, women and children, as well as the aliens who live in your communities—that they may hear it and learn it, and so fear the LORD, your God, and carefully observe all the words of this law. 13 Their children also, who do not know it yet, must hear it and learn it, that they too may fear the LORD, your God, as long as you live on the land which you will cross the Jordan to occupy."

Commission of Joshua

14† The LORD said to Moses, "The time is now approaching for you to die. Summon Joshua, and present yourselves at the meeting tent that I may

HISPANICS LIVE THE HISTORY OF SALVATION!

As Moses did, Hispanics express their faith in the Lord of history:

Lord, you who are the Lord of all,
we, the Hispanic people of the United States,
conscious of being a people with its own identity,
born of common roots,
cultural traditions, language, and faith,
and in diversity united,
direct this prayer to you.

Lord and master of history,
we, a people, as we experience the same hungers and hurts,
make a preferential option for the poor,
and we stand in solidarity with this suffering humanity.

From your creative womb, we have been born;
we are your family, your believing people.
In this moment of grace, we feel ourselves called
to a "prophetic mission";
working together and participating in community,
we speak in your name to church and society.

Raised up as a people, intent on being authors
of our own history,
we walk with hope and in a progressive process.
Together we contribute to the coming of
the Kingdom of God here and now,
struggling to establish the new society, with an economy, relationships, and values
based on the love and the justice of your Son, Jesus Christ.

We ask this in company with Mary,
the mother of all believers.
Amen.

*(Secretariat for Hispanic Affairs, **Prophetic Voices**, p. 23)*

31, 10: *The year of relaxation:* cf Dt 15, 1ff and the note there.
31, 11ff: Reading the law not only instructed the people but also consoled them by the assurance of the divine goodness.
31, 14f.23: V 23 is best read immediately after v 15; perhaps the original order was vv 7–8.14–15.23.

31, 10f: Dt 16, 13ff.

give him his commission." So Moses and Joshua went and presented themselves at the meeting tent. [15] And the LORD appeared at the tent in a column of cloud, which stood still at the entrance of the tent.

A Command to Moses

[16]* The LORD said to Moses, "Soon you will be at rest with your fathers, and then this people will take to rendering wanton worship to the strange gods among whom they will live in the land they are about to enter. They will forsake me and break the covenant which I have made with them. [17] At that time my anger will flare up against them; I will forsake them and hide my face from them, so that they will become a prey to be devoured, and many evils and troubles will befall them. At that time they will indeed say, 'Is it not because our God is not among us that these evils have befallen us?' [18] Yet I will be hiding my face from them at that time only because of all the evil they have done in turning to other gods. [19]* Write out this song, then, for yourselves. Teach it to the Israelites and have them recite it, so that this song may be a witness for me against the Israelites. [20] For when I have brought them into the land flowing with milk and honey which I promised on oath to their fathers, and they have eaten their fill and grown fat, if they turn to other gods and serve them, despising me and breaking my covenant; [21] then, when many evils and troubles befall them, this song, which their descendants will not have forgotten to recite, will bear witness against them. For I know what they are inclined to do even at the present time, before I have brought them into the land which I promised on oath to their fathers." [22] So Moses wrote this song that same day, and he taught it to the Israelites.

Commission of Joshua

[23]* Then the LORD commissioned Joshua, son of Nun, and said to him, "Be brave and steadfast, for it is you who must bring the Israelites into the land which I promised them on oath. I myself will be with you."

The Law Placed in the Ark

[24] When Moses had finished writing out on a scroll the words of the law in their entirety, [25]* he gave the Levites who carry the ark of the covenant of the LORD this order: [26] "Take this scroll of the law

and put it beside the ark of the covenant of the LORD, your God, that there it may be a witness against you. [27] For I already know how rebellious and stiff-necked you will be. Why, even now, while I am alive among you, you have been rebels against the LORD! How much more, then, after I am dead! [28]* Therefore, assemble all your tribal elders and your officials before me, that I may speak these words for them to hear, and so may call heaven and earth to witness against them. [29]* For I know that after my death you are sure to become corrupt and to turn aside from the way along which I directed you, so that evil will befall you in some future age because you have done evil in the LORD'S sight, and provoked him by your deeds."

The Song of Moses

[30] Then Moses recited the words of this song from beginning to end, for the whole assembly of Israel to hear:

A

32 [1]† Give ear, O heavens, while I speak;
let the earth hearken to the words of my mouth!

[2] May my instruction soak in like the rain,
and my discourse permeate like the dew,
Like a downpour upon the grass,
like a shower upon the crops:

[3] For I will sing the LORD'S renown.
Oh, proclaim the greatness of our God!

[4]* The Rock—how faultless are his deeds,
how right all his ways!
A faithful God, without deceit,
how just and upright he is!

[5]* Yet basely has he been treated by his degenerate children,
a perverse and crooked race!

[6]* Is the LORD to be thus repaid by you,
O stupid and foolish people?
Is he not your father who created you?
Has he not made you and established you?

[7]* Think back on the days of old,
reflect on the years of age upon age.
Ask your father and he will inform you,
ask your elders and they will tell you:

---

† **32, 1–43:** In the style of the great prophets, the speaker is often God himself. The whole song is a poetic sermon, having for its theme God's benefits to Israel (vv 1–14) and Israel's ingratitude and idolatry in turning to the gods of the pagans, which sins will be punished by the pagans themselves (vv 15–29); in turn, the foolish pride of the pagans will be punished, and the Lord's honor will be vindicated (vv 30–43).

31, 16: Jgs 2, 12.17.
31, 19: Dt 31, 21; 32, 1–43.
31, 23: Dt 31, 7f; Jos 1, 5ff.
31, 25: 24f; Dt 31, 9.
31, 28: Dt 32, 1–43.
31, 29: Jgs 2, 19.

32, 4: Ps 92, 15; Rv 15, 3.
32, 5: Dt 31, 29; Ps 78, 8; Lk 9, 41.
32, 6: Ex 4, 22; Is 63, 16; 64, 8; Jer 31, 9.
32, 7: Dt 4, 32; Ps 44, 2.

8*†When the Most High assigned the nations
　　　　their heritage,
　　　when he parceled out the descendants
　　　　of Adam,
　　He set up the boundaries of the peoples
　　　after the number of the sons of God;
9* While the LORD's own portion was Jacob,
　　　his hereditary share was Israel.

10* He found them in a wilderness,
　　　a wasteland of howling desert.
　　He shielded them and cared for them,
　　　guarding them as the apple of his eye.

11* As an eagle incites its nestlings forth
　　　by hovering over its brood,
　　So he spread his wings to receive them
　　　and bore them up on his pinions.
12 The LORD alone was their leader,
　　　no strange god was with him.
13† He had them ride triumphant over the
　　　　summits of the land
　　　and live off the products of its fields,
　　Giving them honey to suck from its rocks
　　　and olive oil from its hard, stony ground;

14† Butter from its cows and milk from its
　　　　sheep,
　　　with the fat of its lambs and rams;
　　Its Bashan bulls and its goats,
　　　with the cream of its finest wheat;
　　and the foaming blood of its grapes
　　　you drank.

B

15*†[So Jacob ate his fill,]
　　　the darling grew fat and frisky;
　　　you became fat and gross and gorged.
　　They spurned the God who made them
　　　and scorned their saving Rock.
16* They provoked him with strange gods
　　　and angered him with abominable idols.

17 They offered sacrifice to demons, to
　　　　"no-gods,"
　　　to gods whom they had not known before,
　　To newcomers just arrived,
　　　of whom their fathers had never stood
　　　in awe.

18* You were unmindful of the Rock that
　　　　begot you,
　　　You forgot the God who gave you birth.
19 When the LORD saw this, he was filled
　　　with loathing
　　　and anger toward his sons and daughters.
20* "I will hide my face from them," he said,
　　　"and see what will then become
　　　　of them.
　　What a fickle race they are,
　　　sons with no loyalty in them!
21* "Since they have provoked me with their
　　　　'no god'
　　　and angered me with their vain idols,
　　I will provoke them with a 'no-people';
　　　with a foolish nation I will anger them.

22* "For by my wrath a fire is enkindled
　　　that shall rage to the depths of
　　　　the netherworld,
　　Consuming the earth with its yield,
　　　and licking with flames the roots of
　　　　the mountains.
23 I will spend on them woe upon woe
　　　and exhaust all my arrows against them:

24 "Emaciating hunger and consuming fever
　　　and bitter pestilence,
　　And the teeth of wild beasts I will send
　　　　among them,
　　　with the venom of reptiles gliding in
　　　　the dust.

25* "Snatched away by the sword in the street
　　　and by sheer terror at home
　　Shall be the youth and the maiden alike,
　　　the nursing babe as well as the hoary old
　　　　man.

26 "I would have said, 'I will make an end
　　　　of them
　　　and blot out their name from
　　　　men's memories,'
27 Had I not feared the insolence of
　　　　their enemies,
　　　feared that these foes would
　　　　mistakenly boast,
　　'Our own hand won the victory;
　　　the LORD had nothing to do with it.'"

D
T

32, 8: *The sons of God:* the angels; cf Jb 1, 6; 2, 1; 38, 7; Ps
89, 7f. Here the various nations are portrayed as having their respective guardian angels. Cf Dn 10, 20f; 12, 1.
32, 13: *The land:* Canaan.
32, 14: *Bashan:* a fertile grazing land east of the Jordan, famous
for its strong cattle. Cf Ps 22, 13; Ez 39, 18; Am 4, 1.
32, 15: *The darling:* a probable meaning of the Hebrew word
yeshurun, a term of endearment for "Israel." Cf Dt 33, 5.26; Is 44, 2.

32, 8: Gn 10, 1–32; Acts 17,
　　26.
32, 9: Ex 19, 5; Ps 33, 12.
32, 10: Dt 8, 15; Jer 2, 6;
　　Zec 2, 8.
32, 11: Ex 19, 4.
32, 15: Dt 31, 20.
32, 16: Nm 25, 2f; Ps 78, 58.
32, 18: Jer 2, 32.
32, 20: Dt 31, 17.
32, 21: Rom 10, 19.
32, 22: Lam 4, 11.
32, 25: Lv 26, 25.

28† For they are a people devoid of reason,
    having no understanding.
29 If they had insight they would realize
      what happened,
    they would understand their future and say,

C

30 "How could one man rout a thousand,
    or two men put ten thousand to flight,
    Unless it was because their Rock sold them
    and the LORD delivered them up?"
31 Indeed, their "rock" is not like our Rock,
    and our foes are under condemnation.

32 They are a branch of Sodom's vine-stock,
    from the vineyards of Gomorrah.
    Poisonous are their grapes
    and bitter their clusters.
33 Their wine is the venom of dragons
    and the cruel poison of cobras.

34 "Is not this preserved in my treasury,
    sealed up in my storehouse,
35 Against the day of vengeance and requital,
    against the time they lose their footing?"
    Close at hand is the day of their disaster,
    and their doom is rushing upon them!

36*† Surely, the LORD shall do justice for
      his people;
    on his servants he shall have pity.
    When he sees their strength failing,
    and their protected and unprotected alike
      disappearing,

37* He will say, "Where are their gods
    whom they relied on as their 'rock'?
38 Let those who ate the fat of your sacrifices
    and drank the wine of your libations
    Rise up now and help you!
    Let them be your protection!

39* "Learn then that I, I alone, am God,
    and there is no god besides me.
    It is I who bring both death and life,
    I who inflict wounds and heal them,
    and from my hand there is no rescue.

40 "To the heavens I raise my hand and swear:
    As surely as I live forever,

41 I will sharpen my flashing sword,
    and my hand shall lay hold of my quiver.

"With vengeance I will repay my foes
    and requite those who hate me.
42 I will make my arrows drunk with blood,
    and my sword shall gorge itself with flesh—
    With the blood of the slain and the captured,
    Flesh from the heads of the enemy leaders."

43 Exult with him, you heavens,
    glorify him, all you angels of God;
    For he avenges the blood of his servants
    and purges his people's land.

44 So Moses, together with Joshua, son of Nun, went and recited all the words of this song for the people to hear.

Final Appeal

45 When Moses had finished speaking all these words to all Israel, 46* he said, "Take to heart all the warning which I have now given you and which you must impress on your children, that you may carry out carefully every word of this law. 47 For this is no trivial matter for you; rather, it means your very life, since it is by this means that you are to enjoy a long life on the land which you will cross the Jordan to occupy."

Moses to View Canaan

48 On that very day the LORD said to Moses, 49* "Go up on Mount Nebo, here in the Abarim Mountains [it is in the land of Moab facing Jericho], and view the land of Canaan, which I am giving to the Israelites as their possession. 50* Then you shall die on the mountain you have climbed, and shall be taken to your people, just as your brother Aaron died on Mount Hor and there was taken to his people; 51* because both of you broke faith with me among the Israelites at the waters of Meribath-kadesh in the desert of Zin by failing to manifest my sanctity among the Israelites. 52* You may indeed view the land at a distance, but you shall not enter that land which I am giving to the Israelites."

Blessing upon the Tribes

33

1 This is the blessing which Moses, the man of God, pronounced upon the Israelites before he died. 2*† He said:

32, 28–35: The reference is to the pagan nations, not to Israel.
32, 36: *Their protected and unprotected:* the meaning of the Hebrew is uncertain; according to some, the idea is "slaves and freemen."
33, 2–5.26–29: These verses seem to form an independent hymn describing, in the form of a theophany, the conquest of Canaan. The first section of this hymn (vv 2–5) serves here as an introduction to the various "blessings"; the second section (vv 26–29), as their conclusion.

32, 36: 2 Mc 7, 6.
32, 37f: Jgs 10, 14; Jer 2, 28.
32, 39: Dt 4, 35; Tb 13, 2; Wis 16, 13.
32, 46: Dt 4, 9.
32, 49: Nm 27, 12; 33, 47f.
32, 50: Nm 20, 24ff.28; 27, 13; 33, 38.
32, 51: Nm 20, 12; 27, 14.
32, 52: Dt 3, 27; 34, 4.
33, 2: Ex 19, 18.20; Jgs 5, 4f.

DT

"The LORD came from Sinai
    and dawned on his people from Seir;
He shone forth from Mount Paran
    and advanced from Meribath-kadesh,
While at his right hand a fire blazed forth
    and his wrath devastated the nations.
³† But all his holy ones were in his hand;
    they followed at his feet
    and he bore them up on his pinions.
⁴* A law he gave to us;
    he made the community of Jacob his
        domain,
⁵†   and he became king of his darling,
When the chiefs of the people assembled
    and the tribes of Israel came together.
⁶*† "May Reuben live and not die out,
    but let his men be few."
⁷*† The following is for Judah. He said:
"The LORD hears the cry of Judah;
    you will bring him to his people.
His own hands defend his cause
    and you will be his help against his foes."

⁸*† Of Levi he said:
"To Levi belong your Thummim,
    to the man of your favor your Urim;
For you put him to the test at Massah
    and you contended with him at the waters
        of Meribah.
⁹† He said of his father, 'I regard him not';
    his brothers he would not acknowledge,
    and his own children he refused
        to recognize.
Thus the Levites keep your words,
    and your covenant they uphold.
¹⁰* They promulgate your decisions to Jacob
    and your law to Israel.
They bring the smoke of sacrifice to
       your nostrils,
    and burnt offerings to your altar.
¹¹ Bless, O LORD, his possessions
    and accept the ministry of his hands.
Break the backs of his adversaries
    and of his foes, that they may not rise."

¹²* Of Benjamin he said:
"Benjamin is the beloved of the LORD,
    who shelters him all the day,
    while he abides securely at his breast."

¹³* Of Joseph he said:
"Blessed by the LORD is his land
    with the best of the skies above
    and of the abyss crouching beneath;
¹⁴ With the best of the produce of the year,
    and the choicest sheaves of the months;
¹⁵ With the finest gifts of the age-old
       mountains
    and the best from the timeless hills;
¹⁶† With the best of the earth and its fullness,
    and the favor of him who dwells in
       the bush.
These shall come upon the head of Joseph
    and upon the brow of the prince among
       his brothers,
¹⁷ The majestic bull, his father's first-born,
    whose horns are those of the wild ox
With which to gore the nations,
    even those at the ends of the earth."
[These are the myriads of Ephraim,
    and these the thousands of Manasseh.]

¹⁸* Of Zebulun he said:
"Rejoice, O Zebulun, in your pursuits,
    and you, Issachar, in your tents!
¹⁹† You who invite the tribes to the mountains
    where feasts are duly held,
Because you suck up the abundance of
       the seas
    and the hidden treasures of the sand."

²⁰* Of Gad he said:
"Blessed be he who has made Gad so vast!
    He lies there like a lion
    that has seized the arm and head of
       the prey.
²¹*† He saw that the best should be his
    when the princely portion was assigned,
    while the heads of the people were gathered.

33, 3: *His holy ones were in his hand:* the Israelites were protected by the Lord.

33, 5.26: *The darling:* see note on Dt 32, 15.

33, 6: In keeping with the other blessings, probably this verse was once introduced by the phrase, "Of Reuben he said." It is to be noted that there is no blessing here for Simeon.

33, 7: *Bring him to his people:* this probably refers to the isolated position of the tribe of Judah during the conquest of the Promised Land (cf Jgs 1, 17–19); according to some commentators the reference is to the divided kingdom.

33, 8: *Thummim . . . Urim:* see note on Ex 28, 30.

33, 9: The reference is probably to the Levites' slaughter of their brethren after the affair of the golden calf in the desert; cf Ex 32, 27–29.

33, 16: *Him who dwells in the bush:* a title given to the Lord because of his appearance to Moses in the burning bush; cf Ex 3.

33, 19: *The abundance of the seas:* perhaps the wealth that

comes from sea-borne trade or from fishing. *The hidden treasures of the sand:* possibly an allusion to the valuable purple dye extracted from certain marine shells found on the coast of northern Palestine.

33, 21: *The princely portion:* Moses gave the tribe of Gad their land on the east of the Jordan only on condition that they would help the other tribes conquer the land west of the river; cf Nm 32; Jos 22.

33, 4: Jn 1, 17; 7, 19.	**33, 13–17:** Gn 49, 22–26.
33, 6: Gn 49, 3f.	**33, 18f:** Gn 49, 13ff.
33, 7: Gn 49, 8–12.	**33, 20f:** Gn 49, 19.
33, 8: Gn 49, 5; Ex 17, 7; 28,	**33, 21:** Nm 32, 1.5.16–19.
30; Nm 20, 13.	31f; Jos 1, 12–15;
33, 10: Ex 30, 7f.	1 Chr 5, 18–22.
33, 12: Gn 49, 27.	

D
T

He carried out the justice of the LORD
and his decrees respecting Israel."

22*†Of Dan he said:
"Dan is a lion's whelp,
that springs forth from Bashan!"

23*†Of Naphtali he said:
"Naphtali is enriched with favors
and filled with the blessings of the LORD;
The lake and south of it are his possession!"

24*†Of Asher he said:
"More blessed than the other sons
be Asher!
May he be the favorite among his brothers,
as the oil of his olive trees runs over
his feet!

25   May your bolts be of iron and bronze;
may your strength endure through all
your days!"

26   "There is no god like the God of the
darling,
who rides the heavens in his power,
and rides the skies in his majesty;

27   He spread out the primeval tent;
he extended the ancient canopy.
He drove the enemy out of your way
and the Amorite he destroyed.

28*   Israel has dwelt securely,
and the fountain of Jacob has
been undisturbed.
In a land of grain and wine,
where the heavens drip with dew.

29*   How fortunate you are, O Israel!
Where else is a nation victorious in
the LORD?
The LORD is your saving shield,
and his sword is your glory.
Your enemies fawn upon you,
as you stride upon their heights."

Death and Burial of Moses

34 ¹* Then Moses went up from the plains
of Moab to Mount Nebo, the headland
of Pisgah which faces Jericho, and the LORD
showed him all the land—Gilead, and as far as
Dan, ² all Naphtali, the land of Ephraim and
Manasseh, all the land of Judah as far as the Western Sea, ³ the Negeb, the circuit of the Jordan with
the lowlands at Jericho, city of palms, and as far
as Zoar. ⁴* The LORD then said to him, "This is the
land which I swore to Abraham, Isaac and Jacob
that I would give to their descendants. I have let
you feast your eyes upon it, but you shall not
cross over." ⁵* So there, in the land of Moab,
Moses, the servant of the LORD, died as the LORD
had said; ⁶ and he was buried in the ravine opposite Beth-peor in the land of Moab, but to this day
no one knows the place of his burial. ⁷* Moses
was one hundred and twenty years old when he
died, yet his eyes were undimmed and his vigor
unabated. ⁸ For thirty days the Israelites wept for
Moses in the plains of Moab, till they had completed the period of grief and mourning
for Moses.

⁹* Now Joshua, son of Nun, was filled with the

MOSES' DEATH

Why did Moses die on the brink of entering
the Promised Land? This question has disturbed many generations of believers. The one
who received God's call to lead the Israelites
out of slavery; who amazed Pharaoh with
wonders and called down plagues on Egypt;
who opened the Red Sea and received the
tablets of the Law on Mount Sinai—this great
leader did not get to enjoy the success of his
work (Nm 20, 12)! Deuteronomy 34, 1–6 simply tells us that Moses died on Mount Nebo
and that his burial place was forgotten.

But consider this: By the time Deuteronomy was written, Moses had become a legendary figure. Many of the details of his life
had been forgotten. Perhaps it is fitting that
Moses' story ends as it began: shrouded in
mystery, tragedy, and hope. What hope? The
hope for another prophet like Moses (18, 15)
that remained alive and strong in the
Israelites' hearts.

▶ Deuteronomy, chapter 34

†

33, 22: The sense is, "May he leap up like a lion of Bashan"; the heavily wooded hills of Bashan were notorious for their lions, but the tribe of Dan was not settled in this region.

33, 23: *The lake:* the Lake of Gennesaret on which the land of this tribe bordered.

33, 24: The land of the tribe of Asher was covered with olive groves.

33, 22: Gn 49, 16f.
33, 23: Gn 49, 21; Jos 19, 32–39.
33, 24f: Gn 49, 20.
33, 28: Gn 27, 28.
33, 29: Dt 4, 7f.
34, 1: Dt 3, 27.

34, 4: Dt 3, 27; 32, 52; Gn 12, 7; 15, 18.
34, 5: Dt 32, 50.
34, 7: Dt 31, 2.
34, 9: Nm 27, 18.23; Jos 1, 17.

DT

spirit of wisdom, since Moses had laid his hands upon him; and so the Israelites gave him their obedience, thus carrying out the LORD's command to Moses.

10* Since then no prophet has arisen in Israel like Moses, whom the LORD knew face to face.

11* He had no equal in all the signs and wonders the LORD sent him to perform in the land of Egypt against Pharaoh and all his servants and against all his land, 12 and for the might and the terrifying power that Moses exhibited in the sight of all Israel.

34, 10: Ex 33, 11.   34, 11: Dt 4, 34.

Introduction to the

Historical
Books

Have you ever noticed that many older people enjoy telling stories about the past? Sometimes, it seems that their past experiences are more real to them than present-day events. Those of us who are younger may get tired of hearing about the "good old days." Still, a lot is to be gained from listening carefully to the memories of our elders. The sixteen historical books of the Old Testament, like the voices of respected elders, tell the stories of God at work in ancient Israel. In reading these stories, we can see more clearly how God works in today's world.

In-depth

THE HISTORICAL BOOKS RECOUNT THE PERIOD of Israelite history from 1250 to 100 B.C. In those books, we read about the following events:

- the Israelites' settlement in the Promised Land and their struggle to protect themselves from their enemies (the Books of Joshua and Judges)
- the rise of a united kingdom under David (1 and 2 Samuel, 1 Kings)
- the division of the kingdom into northern and southern kingdoms, and the various kings and prophets of each, until the fall of Jerusalem in 587 B.C. (1 and 2 Kings, 1 and 2 Chronicles)
- the return from Exile and the rebuilding of the nation (Ezra and Nehemiah)
- the Jewish resistance to Greek domination in the second century before Christ (1 and 2 Maccabees)

In addition, the books contain three "novels" about the human challenge to trust God in difficult times (Tobit, Judith, and Esther).

The historical books of the Old Testament are not like the history books that we read in school. Those who write history books today generally try to report the facts with little interpretation. "Let the events speak for themselves," they say. However, those who wrote the historical books of the Old Testament had a different purpose: "Let us tell you what the events *mean in the light of our faith in God."* Thus, the history contained in these books is often called sacred history because it reveals God's message and God's purpose in history.

Scripture scholars find evidence of two general groups shaping the final form of the historical books. The first group is called the Deuteronomic school of writers because it was responsible for the highly influential Book of Deuteronomy. This group also wrote Joshua, Judges, 1 and 2 Samuel, and 1 and 2 Kings. The Deuteronomists were convinced that God rewarded the good and punished the wicked in this world. Thus, you will find in these books a repeated pattern of (1) God's offer of love, (2) the people's faithlessness and sin, (3) God's just punishment, (4) the people's repentance and cry for help, (5) God's forgiveness and mercy, and (6) the people's repeated sin.

The second group (or person), sometimes called the Chronicler, is responsible for 1 and 2 Chronicles, and probably Ezra and Nehemiah. The Chronicler still emphasized that God rewards the faithful and punishes the unfaithful, but the measurement for what is faithful had changed. Instead of emphasizing faithfulness to the Sinai Covenant, the Chronicler emphasized faithfulness to proper worship, particularly worship at the Temple in Jerusalem. The Chronicler wrote after the destruction of the northern and southern kingdoms, to nurture the faith of a small community trying to rebuild itself.

Some of the religious truths you will learn from reading these books are as follows:

- God is not removed from the affairs of this world, but cares deeply about what is happening in human history.
- People are happier when they follow the law of God than when they turn away from the Law.
- All human beings, from the beginning of history, are joined in a common struggle to find sense and meaning in the ups and downs of life.

As you read these books, remember that the authors' understanding of God is not the same as Jesus' understanding. Although not denying the truths about God taught by these books, Christians have a larger context for understanding God's unconditional love and unlimited mercy: Jesus' teaching in the New Testament.

Other Background

- **The Book of Ruth was not originally one of the historical books. It was written later than the books it is now sandwiched between.**

- **The Books of 1 and 2 Chronicles review the same historical period as 1 and 2 Samuel and 1 and 2 Kings.**

- **Tobit, Judith, and Esther are fictional works that use history only as a backdrop. Their purpose is to encourage fidelity to God's law in hard times.**

- **Tobit, Judith, 1 and 2 Maccabees, and parts of Esther are not found in every translation of the Old Testament and are not contained in many Protestant Bibles. See "The Case of the Missing Books," near Tb 1, 16.**

When you were young, did you ask to hear your favorite book over and over again? Do you remember feeling secure because you knew how the story would turn out? Often, familiar stories appeal to us because of their simple justice: evil is punished, and good is rewarded. The author of the Book of Joshua applies this simple justice to the conquest of the Promised Land: those who follow God are rewarded, and those who do not are destroyed.

At a Glance

I. Conquest of Canaan
(1, 1—12, 24).

II. Division of the Land
(13, 1—21, 45).

III. Return of the Transjordan Tribes and Joshua's Farewell
(22, 1—24, 33).

In-depth

The Book of Joshua is named after the Israelite hero who succeeds Moses and leads the people in their takeover of the Promised Land. At the beginning of the book, Joshua promises the Israelites that they will conquer the land of Canaan and make it their own if they are faithful to the Covenant of Moses. They respond with enthusiasm, "We will obey you as completely as we obeyed Moses" (1, 16). The author describes how by remaining true to the Commandments of God, the various Israelite tribes, under Joshua's leadership, take over the land and settle in it with their families and livestock (see map 2, "The Exodus from Egypt").

Today, biblical scholars doubt that the conquest of the Promised Land by the twelve tribes of Israel was as complete and easy as it is written in Joshua. Archaeologists have found evidence that Canaanites continued to live in the area after the "conquest." The historical memories preserved in the book were reshaped by the author to emphasize an important lesson of faith: God would preserve the Israelites on their land as long as they obeyed the Commandments.

The belief in the triumph of good and the punishment of evil is at the heart of the Book of Joshua. Like Judges, 1 and 2 Samuel, and 1 and 2 Kings, the Book of Joshua is inspired by the Book of Deuteronomy, which insists that God rewards the just and punishes the wicked in this world (see Dt 30, 15–20). The Book of Joshua challenges us to remember that God is our surest hope in all the ups and downs of history.

Quick Facts

Period Covered
after the desert wandering, from about 1250 to 1200 B.C.

Author
unknown, from the Deuteronomic tradition, writing in the seventh or sixth century B.C.

Themes
Israel's conquest of the Promised Land, the triumph of good and the punishment of evil

Of Note
The name Jesus is the Greek form of Joshua, which means "God saves."

The Book of Joshua

Joshua

I: Conquest of Canaan

Divine Promise of Assistance

1 ¹ After Moses, the servant of the LORD, had died, the LORD said to Moses' aid Joshua, son of Nun: ² "My servant Moses is dead. So prepare to cross the Jordan here, with all the people, into the land I will give the Israelites. ³ As I promised Moses, I will deliver to you every place where you set foot. ⁴*† Your domain is to be all the land of the Hittites, from the desert and from Lebanon east to the great river Euphrates and west to the Great Sea. ⁵* No one can withstand you while you live. I will be with you as I was with Moses: I will not leave you nor forsake you. ⁶ Be firm and steadfast, so that you may give this people possession of the land which I swore to their fathers I would give them. ⁷ Above all, be firm and steadfast, taking care to observe the entire law which my servant Moses enjoined on you. Do not swerve from it either to the right or to the left, that you may succeed wherever you go. ⁸ Keep this book of the law on your lips. Recite it by day and by night, that you may observe carefully all that is written in it; then you will successfully attain your goal. ⁹* I command you: be firm and steadfast! Do not fear nor be dismayed, for the LORD, your God, is with you wherever you go."

¹⁰ So Joshua commanded the officers of the people: ¹¹* "Go through the camp and instruct the people, 'Prepare your provisions, for three days from now you shall cross the Jordan here, to march in and take possession of the land which the LORD, your God, is giving you.' "

The Transjordan Tribes

¹² Joshua reminded the Reubenites, the Gadites, and the half-tribe of Manasseh: ¹³ "Remember what Moses, the servant of the LORD, commanded you when he said, 'The LORD, your God, will permit you to settle in this land.' ¹⁴* Your wives, your children, and your livestock shall remain in the land Moses gave you here beyond the Jordan. But all the warriors among you must cross over armed ahead of your kinsmen and you must help them ¹⁵* until the LORD has settled your kinsmen, and they like you possess the land which the LORD, your God, is giving them. Afterward you may return and occupy your own land, which Moses, the servant of the LORD, has given you east of the Jordan." ¹⁶ "We will do all you have commanded us," they answered Joshua, "and we will go wherever you send us. We will obey you as completely as we obeyed Moses. ¹⁷ But may the LORD, your God, be with you as he was with Moses. ¹⁸ If anyone rebels against your orders and does not obey every command you give him, he shall be put to death. But be firm and steadfast."

1, 4: The ideal frontiers are given: in the south the desert of Sinai, in the north the Lebanon range, in the east the Euphrates, and in the west the Great Sea, the Mediterranean.

1, 4: 3f: Jos 14, 9; Gn 15, 18; Dt 11, 24.
1, 5: Dt 31, 8; Heb 13, 5.
1, 9: 7f: Dt 31, 7f.
1, 11: Dt 11, 31.
1, 14: Nm 32, 26.
1, 15: Jos 22, 4; Dt 3, 20.

Be Not Afraid

"Be firm and steadfast! Do not fear nor be dismayed, for the LORD, your God, is with you wherever you go" (Jos 1, 9).

Living proof:

Saint Joan of Arc was a humble, uneducated peasant maiden from fifteenth-century France. Inspired by saintly voices, she overcame numerous obstacles to lead the French troops into battle against British invaders.

Saint Thomas More, a distinguished scholar and lawyer, refused to approve King Henry VIII's divorce and remarriage and establishment of the Church of England.

Dorothy Day, twentieth-century American cofounder of the Catholic Worker Movement, challenged all Christians to serve poor and homeless people and dedicated her life to nonviolence.

Archbishop Oscar Romero of El Salvador was shot while saying Mass in 1980 because he dared to speak against the military groups that were terrorizing and killing the poor people of his diocese.

These four people, along with many others, have taken to heart God's words to Joshua. If you are not familiar with their stories, take time to learn more about these Catholic heroes.

▶ Jos 1, 5–9

Spies Saved by Rahab

2 ¹*† Then Joshua, son of Nun, secretly sent out two spies from Shittim, saying, "Go, reconnoiter the land and Jericho." When the two reached Jericho, they went into the house of a harlot named Rahab, where they lodged. ² But a report was brought to the king of Jericho that some Israelites had come there that night to spy out the land. ³ So the king of Jericho sent Rahab the order, "Put out the visitors who have entered your house, for they have come to spy out the entire land." ⁴* The woman had taken the two men and hidden them, so she said, "True, the men you speak of came to me, but I did not know where they came from. ⁵ At dark, when it was time for the gate to be shut, they left, and I do not know where they went. You will have to pursue them immediately to overtake them." ⁶† Now, she had led them to the roof, and hidden them among her stalks of flax spread out there. ⁷ But the pursuers set out along the way to the fords of the Jordan, and once they had left, the gate was shut.

⁸† Before the spies fell asleep, Rahab came to them on the roof ⁹* and said: "I know that the LORD has given you the land, that a dread of you has come upon us, and that all the inhabitants of the land are overcome with fear of you. ¹⁰* For we have heard how the LORD dried up the waters of the Red Sea before you when you came out of Egypt, and how you dealt with Sihon and Og, the two kings of the Amorites beyond the Jordan, whom you doomed to destruction. ¹¹* At these reports, we are disheartened; everyone is discouraged because of you, since the LORD, your God, is God in heaven above and on earth below. ¹²* Now then, swear to me by the LORD that, since I am showing kindness to you, you in turn will show kindness to my family; and give me an unmistakable token ¹³ that you are to spare my father and mother, brothers and sisters, and all their kin, and save us from death." ¹⁴ "We pledge our lives for yours," the men answered her. "If you do not betray this errand of ours, we will be faithful in showing kindness to you when the LORD gives us the land."

¹⁵† Then she let them down through the window with a rope; for she lived in a house built into the city wall. ¹⁶ "Go up into the hill country," she sug-

---

2, 1: *Harlot:* this is the regular equivalent of the Hebrew word, but perhaps it is used here of Rahab in the broader sense of a woman who kept a public house. Joshua's spies hoped to remain undetected at such an inn.

2, 6: *Stalks of flax spread out:* to dry in the sun, after they had been soaked in water, according to the ancient process of preparing flax for linen-making. In the Near East the flax harvest occurs near the time of the feast of the Passover (Jos 4, 19; 5, 10); cf Ex 9, 31.

2, 8–11: Rahab's faith and good works are praised in the New Testament; cf Heb 11, 31; Jas 2, 25.

2, 15: *A house built into the city wall:* such houses, which used the city wall for their own inner walls, have been found at ancient sites. The upper story of Rahab's house was evidently higher than the city wall. It was through the window of such a house that St. Paul escaped from Damascus; cf Acts 9, 25; 2 Cor 11, 33.

2, 1: Mt 1, 5; Jas 2, 25.   Nm 21, 23–26.33ff.
2, 4: Jos 6, 17.   **2, 11:** Dt 4, 39.
2, 9: Ex 15, 15f; 23, 27.   **2, 12:** Jos 2, 18; 6, 23.25.
2, 10: Jos 4, 23; Ex 14, 21;

A Prayer Against Prejudice

Creator of diverse people, the Israelites united themselves with Rahab, someone outside their group, and trusted her. Lead me to be open to befriending those who are different from me so that I may learn to trust them as well.

Forgive my friends and me for every time we have looked at someone different and considered them to be of lesser quality. Forgive us for each time we have talked about certain people as if we were superior. Forgive our cliques that look down on others and won't associate with them. And help us forgive those who have looked down on us. Amen.

▶ Joshua, chapter 2

Joshua, "The LORD has delivered all this land into our power; indeed, all the inhabitants of the land are overcome with fear of us."

Preparations for Crossing the Jordan

3 ¹* Early the next morning, Joshua moved with all the Israelites from Shittim to the Jordan, where they lodged before crossing over. ² Three days later the officers went through the camp ³ and issued these instructions to the people: "When you see the ark of the covenant of the LORD, your God, which the levitical priests will carry, you must also break camp and follow it, ⁴ that you may know the way to take, for you have not gone over this road before. But let there be a space of two thousand cubits between you and the ark. Do not come nearer to it." ⁵ Joshua also said to the people, "Sanctify yourselves, for tomorrow the LORD will perform wonders among you." ⁶ And he directed the priests to take up the ark of the covenant and go on ahead of the people; and they did so.

⁷* Then the LORD said to Joshua, "Today I will begin to exalt you in the sight of all Israel, that they may know I am with you, as I was with Moses. ⁸ Now command the priests carrying the ark of the covenant to come to a halt in the Jordan when they reach the edge of the waters."

⁹ So Joshua said to the Israelites, "Come here and listen to the words of the LORD, your God." ¹⁰* He continued: "This is how you will know that there is a living God in your midst, who at your approach will dispossess the Canaanites, Hittites, Hivites, Perizzites, Girgashites, Amorites and Jebusites. ¹¹ The ark of the covenant of the LORD of the whole earth will precede you into the Jordan. ¹²* [Now choose twelve men, one from each of the tribes of Israel.] ¹³ When the soles of the feet of the priests carrying the ark of the LORD, the Lord of the whole earth, touch the water of the Jordan, it will cease to flow; for the water flowing down from upstream will halt in a solid bank."

The Crossing Begun

¹⁴ The people struck their tents to cross Jordan, with the priests carrying the ark of the covenant ahead of them. ¹⁵† No sooner had these priestly bearers of the ark waded into the waters at the edge of the Jordan, which overflows all its banks during the entire season of the harvest, ¹⁶*† than

---

gested to them, "that your pursuers may not find you. Hide there for three days, until they return; then you may proceed on your way." ¹⁷ The men answered her, "This is how we will fulfill the oath you made us take: ¹⁸ When we come into the land, tie this scarlet cord in the window through which you are letting us down; and gather your father and mother, your brothers and all your family into your house. ¹⁹ Should any of them pass outside the doors of your house, he will be responsible for his own death, and we shall be guiltless. But we shall be responsible if anyone in the house with you is harmed. ²⁰ If, however, you betray this errand of ours, we shall be quit of the oath you have made us take." ²¹ "Let it be as you say," she replied, and bade them farewell. When they were gone, she tied the scarlet cord in the window.

²² They went up into the hills, where they stayed three days until their pursuers, who had sought them all along the road without finding them, returned. ²³ Then the two came back down from the hills, crossed the Jordan to Joshua, son of Nun, and reported all that had befallen them. ²⁴ They assured

---

3, 15: *Season of the harvest:* toward the end of March and the beginning of April, when the grain and other crops that grew during the rainy season of winter were reaped. The crossing took place "on the tenth day of the first month" of the Hebrew year, which began with the first new moon after the spring equinox; cf Jos 4, 19. At this time of the year the Jordan would be swollen as a result of the winter rains and the melting snow of Mount Hermon.
3, 16: The sudden damming of the river could have been caused by a landslide, as has happened on other occasions. The miraculous

character of this event would not thereby be removed because God, who foretold it (Jos 3, 13), also caused it to take place at precisely the right moment (Jos 3, 15), whether or not he used natural forces to accomplish his will.

3, 1: Jos 2, 1.   **3, 12:** Jos 4, 2.4.
3, 7: Jos 1, 5; 4, 14.   **3, 16:** Ps 114, 3.
3, 10: Ex 33, 2; Dt 7, 1.

the waters flowing from upstream halted, backing up in a solid mass for a very great distance indeed, from Adam, a city in the direction of Zarethan; while those flowing downstream toward the Salt Sea of the Arabah disappeared entirely. Thus the people crossed over opposite Jericho. 17* While all Israel crossed over on dry ground, the priests carrying the ark of the covenant of the LORD remained motionless on dry ground in the bed of the Jordan until the whole nation had completed the passage.

Memorial Stones

4 1 After the entire nation had crossed the Jordan, the LORD said to Joshua, 2* "Choose twelve men from the people, one from each tribe, 3* and instruct them to take up twelve stones from this spot in the bed of the Jordan where the priests have been standing motionless. Carry them over with you, and place them where you are to stay tonight."

4 Summoning the twelve men whom he had selected from among the Israelites, one from each tribe, 5 Joshua said to them: "Go to the bed of the Jordan in front of the ark of the LORD, your God; lift to your shoulders one stone apiece, so that they will equal in number the tribes of the Israelites. 6 In the future, these are to be a sign among you. When your children ask you what these stones mean to you, 7* you shall answer them, 'The waters of the Jordan ceased to flow before the ark of the covenant of the LORD when it crossed the Jordan.' Thus these stones are to serve as a perpetual memorial to the Israelites." 8 The twelve Israelites did as Joshua had commanded: they took up as many stones from the bed of the Jordan as there were tribes of the Israelites, and carried them along to the camp site, where they placed them, according to the LORD's direction. 9 Joshua also had twelve stones set up in the bed of the Jordan on the spot where the priests stood who were carrying the ark of the covenant. They are there to this day.

10† The priests carrying the ark remained in the bed of the Jordan until everything had been done that the LORD had commanded Joshua to tell the people. The people crossed over quickly, 11 and when all had reached the other side, the ark of the LORD, borne by the priests, also crossed to its place in front of them. 12* The Reubenites, Gadites, and half-tribe of Manasseh, armed, marched in the vanguard of the Israelites, as Moses had ordered. 13 About forty thousand troops equipped for battle passed over before the LORD to the plains of Jericho.

14* That day the LORD exalted Joshua in the sight of all Israel, and thenceforth during his whole life they respected him as they had respected Moses.

15 Then the LORD said to Joshua, 16* "Command the priests carrying the ark of the commandments to come up from the Jordan." 17 Joshua did so, 18 and when the priests carrying the ark of the covenant of the LORD had come up from the bed of the Jordan, as the soles of their feet regained the dry ground, the waters of the Jordan resumed their course and as before overflowed all its banks.

19 The people came up from the Jordan on the tenth day of the first month, and camped in Gilgal on the eastern limits of Jericho. 20 At Gilgal Joshua set up the twelve stones which had been taken from the Jordan, 21 saying to the Israelites, "In the future, when the children among you ask their fathers what these stones mean, 22 you shall inform them, 'Israel crossed the Jordan here on dry ground.' 23* For the LORD, your God, dried up the waters of the Jordan in front of you until you crossed over, just as the LORD, your God, had done at the Red Sea, which he dried up in front of us until we crossed over; 24 in order that all the peoples of the earth may learn that the hand of the LORD is mighty, and that you may fear the LORD, your God, forever."

Rites at Gilgal

5 1 When all the kings of Amorites to the west of the Jordan and all the kings of the Canaanites by the sea heard that the LORD had dried up the waters of the Jordan before the Israelites until they crossed over, they were disheartened and lost courage at their approach.

2 On this occasion the LORD said to Joshua, "Make flint knives and circumcise the Israelite nation for the second time." 3† So Joshua made flint knives and circumcised the Israelites at Gibeath-haaraloth, 4* under these circumstances: Of all the people who came out of Egypt, every man of military age had died in the desert during the journey after they left Egypt. 5 Though all the men who came out were circumcised, none of those born in the desert during the journey after the departure from Egypt were circumcised. 6* Now the Israelites had wandered forty years in the desert, until all the warriors among the people that came forth from Egypt died off because they had not obeyed the command of the LORD. For the LORD swore* that he would not let them see the land flowing

---

4, 10–18: After the digression about the two sets of memorial stones, the author resumes the narrative by briefly repeating the story of the crossing, which he had already told in Jos 3, 14–17.
5, 3: *Gibeath-haaraloth:* "Hill of the Foreskins."

3, 17: Jos 4, 7.22.
4, 2: Jos 3, 12.
4, 3: Jos 3, 13; 4, 8f; Dt 27, 2.
4, 7: Jos 3, 13.16.
4, 12: Dt 3, 18.
4, 14: Jos 3, 7.
4, 16: Jos 3, 6.
4, 23: Ex 14, 21.
5, 4: Nm 14, 29; 26, 64f; Dt 2, 16; Ps 106, 26;
1 Cor 10, 5.
5, 6: Nm 14, 29.
5, 6: Heb 3, 11.17.

with milk and honey which he had promised their fathers he would give us. 7* It was the children whom he raised up in their stead whom Joshua circumcised, for these were yet with foreskins, not having been circumcised on the journey. 8 When the rite had been performed, the whole nation remained in camp where they were, until they recovered. 9*† Then the LORD said to Joshua, "Today I have removed the reproach of Egypt from you." Therefore the place is called Gilgal to the present day.

10*† While the Israelites were encamped at Gilgal on the plains of Jericho, they celebrated the Passover on the evening of the fourteenth of the month. 11 On the day after the Passover they ate of the produce of the land in the form of unleavened cakes and parched grain. On that same day 12* after the Passover on which they ate of the produce of the land, the manna ceased. No longer was there manna for the Israelites, who that year ate of the yield of the land of Canaan.

Siege at Jericho

13*† While Joshua was near Jericho, he raised his eyes and saw one who stood facing him, drawn sword in hand. Joshua went up to him and asked, "Are you one of us or of our enemies?" 14 He replied, "Neither. I am the captain of the host of the LORD and I have just arrived." Then Joshua fell prostrate to the ground in worship, and said to him, "What has my lord to say to his servant?" 15* The captain of the host of the LORD replied to Joshua, "Remove your sandals from your feet, for the place on which you are standing is holy." And Joshua obeyed.

6 1 Now Jericho was in a state of siege because of the presence of the Israelites, so that no one left or entered. 2 And to Joshua the LORD said, "I have delivered Jericho and its king into your power. 3 Have all the soldiers circle the city, marching once around it. Do this for six days, 4* with seven priests carrying ram's horns ahead of the ark. On the seventh day march around the city seven times, and have the priests blow the horns. 5 When they give a long blast on the ram's horns and you hear that signal, all the people shall shout aloud. The

wall of the city will collapse, and they will be able to make a frontal attack."

6 Summoning the priests, Joshua, son of Nun, then ordered them to take up the ark of the covenant with seven of the priests carrying ram's horns in front of the ark of the LORD. 7 And he ordered the people to proceed in a circle around the city, with the picked troops marching ahead of the ark of the LORD. 8 At this order they proceeded, with the seven priests who carried the ram's horns before the LORD blowing their horns, and the ark of the covenant of the LORD following them. 9 In front of the priests with the horns marched the picked troops; the rear guard followed the ark, and the blowing of horns was kept up continually as they marched. 10 But the people had been commanded by Joshua not to shout or make any noise or outcry until he gave the word: only then were they to shout. 11 So he had the ark of the LORD circle the city, going once around it, after which they returned to camp for the night.

12 Early the next morning, Joshua had the priests take up the ark of the LORD. 13 The seven priests bearing the ram's horns marched in front of the ark of the LORD, blowing their horns. Ahead of these marched the picked troops, while the rear guard followed the ark of the LORD, and the blowing of horns was kept up continually. 14 On this second day they again marched around the city once before returning to camp; and for six days in all they did the same.

15 On the seventh day, beginning at daybreak, they marched around the city seven times in the same manner; on that day only did they march around the city seven times. 16 The seventh time around, the priests blew the horns and Joshua said to the people, "Now shout, for the LORD has given you the city 17* and everything in it. It is under the LORD's ban. Only the harlot Rahab and all who are in the house with her are to be spared, because she hid the messengers we sent. 18*† But be careful not to take, in your greed, anything that is under the ban; else you will bring upon the camp of Israel this ban and the misery of it. 19 All silver and gold, and the articles of bronze or iron, are sacred to the LORD. They shall be put in the treasury of the LORD."

5, 9: *The place is called Gilgal:* by popular etymology, because of the similarity of sound with the Hebrew word *gallothi,* "I have removed." Gilgal probably means "(the place of) the circle of standing stones." Cf Jos 4, 4–8.

5, 10: *The month:* the first month of the year, later called Nisan; see note on Jos 3, 15. The crossing of the Jordan occurred, therefore, about the same time of the year as did the equally miraculous crossing of the Red Sea; cf Ex 12–14.

5, 13—6, 26: The account of the siege of Jericho embraces: (1) the command of the Lord, through his angel, to Joshua (Jos 5, 13—6, 5); (2) Joshua's instructions to the Israelites, with a brief summary of how these orders were carried out (Jos 6, 6–11); (3) a description of the

action on each of the first six days (Jos 6, 12–14); (4) the events on the seventh day (Jos 6, 15–26).

6, 18: *That is under the ban:* that is doomed to destruction; see notes on Lv 27, 29; Nm 18, 14; 21, 3.

5, 7: Dt 1, 39.	**5, 15:** Ex 3, 5; Acts 7, 33.
5, 9: Jos 4, 19.	**6, 4:** Nm 10, 8f.
5, 10: Ex 12, 6; Lv 23, 5; Nm 9, 3–5.	**6, 17:** Jos 2, 4; Dt 20, 17; Heb 11, 31.
5, 12: Ex 16, 35.	**6, 18:** Jos 7, 12.25; Dt 13, 18.
5, 13: Ex 23, 20.	

The Fall of Jericho

20*† As the horns blew, the people began to shout. When they heard the signal horn, they raised a tremendous shout. The wall collapsed, and the people stormed the city in a frontal attack and took it. 21* They observed the ban by putting to the sword all living creatures in the city: men and women, young and old, as well as oxen, sheep and asses.

22* Joshua directed the two men who had spied out the land, "Go into the harlot's house and bring out the woman with all her kin, as you swore to her you would do." 23* The spies entered and brought out Rahab, with her father, mother, brothers, and all her kin. Her entire family they led forth and placed them outside the camp of Israel. 24* The city itself they burned with all that was in it, except the silver, gold, and articles of bronze and iron, which were placed in the treasury of the house of the LORD. 25† Because Rahab the harlot had hidden the messengers whom Joshua had sent to reconnoiter Jericho, Joshua spared her with her family and all her kin, who continue in the midst of Israel to this day.

26*† On that occasion Joshua imposed the oath: Cursed before the LORD be the man who attempts to rebuild this city, Jericho. He shall lose his first-born when he lays its foundation, and he shall lose his youngest son when he sets up its gates.

27* Thus the LORD was with Joshua so that his fame spread throughout the land.

Defeat at Ai

7 1* But the Israelites violated the ban; Achan, son of Carmi, son of Zerah, son of Zara of the tribe of Judah, took goods that were under the ban, and the anger of the LORD flared up against the Israelites.

2 Joshua next sent men from Jericho to Ai, which is near Bethel on its eastern side, with instructions to go up and reconnoiter the land. When they had explored Ai, 3 they returned to Joshua and advised, "Do not send all the people up; if only about two or three thousand go up, they can overcome Ai. The enemy there are few; you need not call for an effort from all the people." 4 About three thousand of the people made the attack, but they were defeated by those at Ai, 5 who killed some thirty-six of them. They pressed them back across the clearing in front of the city gate till they broke ranks, and defeated them finally on the descent, so that the confidence of the people melted away like water.

6 Joshua, together with the elders of Israel, rent his garments and lay prostrate before the ark of the LORD until evening; and they threw dust on their heads. 7 "Alas, O Lord GOD," Joshua prayed, "why did you ever allow this people to pass over the Jordan, delivering us into the power of the Amorites, that they might destroy us? Would that we had been content to dwell on the other side of the Jordan. 8 Pray, Lord, what can I say, now that Israel has turned its back to its enemies? 9 When the Canaanites and the other inhabitants of the land hear of it, they will close in around us and efface our name from the earth. What will you do for your great name?"

10 The LORD replied to Joshua: "Stand up. Why are you lying prostrate? 11* Israel has sinned: they have violated the covenant which I enjoined on them. They have stealthily taken goods subject to the ban, and have deceitfully put them in their baggage. 12* If the Israelites cannot stand up to their enemies, but must turn their back to them, it is because they are under the ban. I will not remain with you unless you remove from among you whoever has incurred the ban. 13* Rise, sanctify the people. Tell them to sanctify themselves before tomorrow, for the LORD, the God of Israel, says: You are under the ban, O Israel. You cannot stand up to your enemies until you remove from among you whoever has incurred the ban. 14 In the morning you must present yourselves by tribes. The tribe which the LORD designates shall come forward by clans; the clan which the LORD designates shall come forward by families; the family which the LORD designates shall come forward one by one. 15 He who is designated as having incurred the ban shall be destroyed by fire, with all that is his, because he has violated the covenant of the LORD and has committed a shameful crime in Israel."

Achan's Guilt and Punishment

16† Early the next morning Joshua had Israel come forward by tribes, and the tribe of Judah was

---

6, 20: *The wall collapsed:* by the miraculous intervention of God. The blowing of the horns and the shouting of the people were a customary feature of ancient warfare, here intended by God as a test of the people's obedience and of their faith in his promise; cf Heb 11, 30.

6, 25: From Mt 1, 5, we learn that Rahab married Salmon of the tribe of Judah and thus became the great-great-grandmother of David, Christ's ancestor; cf Ru 4, 18–22.

6, 26: *He shall lose his first-born . . . its gates:* this curse was fulfilled when Hiel rebuilt Jericho as a fortified city during the reign of Ahab, king of Israel, cf 1 Kgs 16, 34. Till then Jericho was merely an unwalled village; cf Jos 18, 12.21; Jgs 3, 13; 2 Sm 10, 5.

7, 16ff: *Was designated:* probably by means of the Urim and Thummim; cf 1 Sm 14, 38–42. See note on Ex 28, 30.

6, 20: 2 Mc 12, 15; Heb 11, 30.	**6, 27:** Jos 1, 5.
6, 21: Dt 7, 2.	**7, 1:** Jos 6, 18; 22, 20; 1 Chr 2, 7.
6, 22: Jos 2, 14.	**7, 11:** Jos 6, 17–19.
6, 23: Jos 2, 13; Heb 11, 31.	**7, 12:** Jos 6, 18.
6, 24: Jos 8, 2.	**7, 13:** Jos 3, 5; Lv 20, 7; 1 Sm 16, 5.
6, 26: 1 Kgs 16, 34.	

designated. 17* Then he had the clans of Judah come forward, and the clan of Zerah was designated. He had the clan of Zerah come forward by families, and Zabdi was designated. 18 Finally he had that family come forward one by one, and Achan, son of Carmi, son of Zabdi, son of Zerah of the tribe of Judah, was designated. 19 Joshua said to Achan, "My son, give to the LORD, the God of Israel, glory and honor by telling me what you have done; do not hide it from me." 20 Achan answered Joshua, "I have indeed sinned against the LORD, the God of Israel. This is what I have done: 21 Among the spoils, I saw a beautiful Babylonian mantle, two hundred shekels of silver, and a bar of gold fifty shekels in weight; in my greed I took them. They are now hidden in the ground inside my tent, with the silver underneath." 22 The messengers whom Joshua sent hastened to the tent and found them hidden there, with the silver underneath. 23 They took them from the tent, brought them to Joshua and all the Israelites, and spread them out before the LORD.

24 Then Joshua and all Israel took Achan, son of Zerah, with the silver, the mantle, and the bar of gold, and with his sons and daughters, his ox, his ass and his sheep, his tent, and all his possessions, and led them off to the Valley of Achor. 25* Joshua said, "The LORD bring upon you today the misery with which you have afflicted us!" And all Israel stoned him to death 26*† and piled a great heap of stones over him, which remains to the present day. Then the anger of the LORD relented. That is why the place is called the Valley of Achor to this day.

Capture of Ai

8 1* The LORD then said to Joshua, "Do not be afraid or dismayed. Take all the army with you and prepare to attack Ai. I have delivered the king of Ai into your power, with his people, city, and land. 2* Do to Ai and its king what you did to Jericho and its king; except that you may take its spoil and livestock as booty. Set an ambush behind the city." 3† So Joshua and all the soldiers prepared to attack Ai. Picking out thirty thousand warriors, Joshua sent them off by night 4 with these orders: "See that you ambush the city from the rear, at no great distance; then all of you be on the watch. 5 The rest of the people and I will come up to the city, and when they make a sortie against us as they did the last time, we will flee from them. 6 They will keep coming out after us until we have drawn them

away from the city, for they will think we are fleeing from them as we did the last time. When this occurs, 7 rise from ambush and take possession of the city, which the LORD, your God, will deliver into your power. 8 When you have taken the city, set it afire in obedience to the LORD'S command. These are my orders to you." 9 Then Joshua sent them away. They went to the place of ambush, taking up their position to the west of Ai, toward Bethel. Joshua, however, spent that night in the plain.

10 Early the next morning Joshua mustered the army and went up to Ai at its head, with the elders of Israel. 11 When all the troops he led were drawn up in position before the city, they pitched camp north of Ai, on the other side of the ravine. 12 [He took about five thousand men and set them in ambush between Bethel and Ai, west of the city.] 13 Thus the people took up their stations, with the main body north of the city and the ambush west of it, and Joshua waited overnight among his troops. 14 The king of Ai saw this, and he and all his army came out very early in the morning to engage Israel in battle at the descent toward the Arabah, not knowing that there was an ambush behind the city. 15 Joshua and the main body of the Israelites fled in seeming defeat toward the desert, 16 till the last of the soldiers in the city had been called out to pursue them. 17 Since they were drawn away from the city, with every man engaged in this pursuit of Joshua and the Israelites, not a soldier remained in Ai [or Bethel], and the city was open and unprotected.

18 Then the LORD directed Joshua, "Stretch out the javelin in your hand toward Ai, for I will deliver it into your power." Joshua stretched out the javelin in his hand toward the city, 19 and as soon as he did so, the men in ambush rose from their post, rushed in, captured the city, and immediately set it on fire. 20 By the time the men of Ai looked back, the smoke from the city was already sky-high. Escape in any direction was impossible, because the Israelites retreating toward the desert now turned on their pursuers; 21 for when Joshua and the main body of Israelites saw that the city had been taken from ambush and was going up in smoke, they struck back at the men of Ai. 22* Since those in the city came out to intercept them, the men of Ai were hemmed in by Israelites on either side, who cut them down without any fugitives or survivors 23 except the king, whom they took alive and brought to Joshua.

7, 26: *Achor:* "misery, affliction." The reference is to the saying of Joshua in v 25, with an allusion also to the similar-sounding name of Achan.

8, 3: *Thirty thousand warriors:* this figure of the Hebrew text, which seems extremely high, may be due to a copyist's error; some manuscripts of the Septuagint have "three thousand," which is the

---

number of the whole army in the first, unsuccessful attack (Jos 7, 4); the variant reading in v 12 mentions "five thousand."

7, 17: Nm 26, 20.   **8, 1:** Jos 2, 24.
7, 25: Jos 6, 18; 22, 20;   **8, 2:** Jos 6, 21.24; Dt 20,
    1 Chr 2, 7.   14.
7, 26: Jos 8, 29.   **8, 22:** Dt 7, 2.

24 All the inhabitants of Ai who had pursued the Israelites into the desert were slain by the sword there in the open, down to the last man. Then all Israel returned and put to the sword those inside the city. 25 There fell that day a total of twelve thousand men and women, the entire population of Ai. 26* Joshua kept the javelin in his hand stretched out until he had fulfilled the doom on all the inhabitants of Ai. 27 However, the Israelites took for themselves as booty the livestock and the spoil of that city, according to the command of the LORD issued to Joshua. 28* Then Joshua destroyed the place by fire, reducing it to an everlasting mound of ruins, as it remains today. 29* He had the king of Ai hanged on a tree until evening; then at sunset Joshua ordered the body removed from the tree and cast at the entrance of the city gate, where a great heap of stones was piled up over it, which remains to the present day.

Altar on Mount Ebal

30† Later Joshua built an altar to the LORD, the God of Israel, on Mount Ebal, 31* of unhewn stones on which no iron tool had been used, in keeping with the command to the Israelites of Moses, the servant of the LORD, as recorded in the book of the law. On this altar they offered holocausts and peace offerings to the LORD. 32* There, in the presence of the Israelites, Joshua inscribed upon the stones a copy of the law written by Moses. 33* And all Israel, stranger and native alike, with their elders, officers and judges, stood on either side of the ark facing the levitical priests who were carrying the ark of the covenant of the LORD. Half of them were facing Mount Gerizim and half Mount Ebal, thus carrying out the instructions of Moses, the servant of the LORD, for the blessing of the people of Israel on this first occasion. 34* Then were read aloud all the words of the law, the blessings and the curses, exactly as written in the book of the law. 35* Every single word that Moses had commanded, Joshua read aloud to the entire community, including the women and children, and the strangers who had accompanied Israel.

Confederacy against Israel

9 1* When the news reached the kings west of the Jordan, in the mountain regions and in the foothills, and all along the coast of the Great Sea as far as Lebanon: Hittites, Amorites, Canaanites, Perizzites, Hivites and Jebusites, 2 they all

Catholic Connections

THE IMPORTANCE OF ALTARS

As soon as the Israelites were able, they built an altar in the Promised Land and renewed their Covenant with God. The altar was a visible sign of the constant need for rededication and renewal.

The altar is an important symbol for Catholics. Catholics gather around the altar to remember and celebrate Jesus' sacrificial death, his Resurrection, and our new Covenant with God. And we gather around the altar to share a meal. We remember the story of our faith, and we are joined together as a community of faith.

The next time you are in church, look at the altar and think about all the other altars in Catholic churches around the world. Think about all the other people who are celebrating the Mass even as you sit there. Think about all the people, beginning with Jesus and the Apostles, who have celebrated their Christian faith around an altar. You are united with them just as surely as the Israelite people were united with one another at Mount Ebal.

▸ Jos 8, 30–35

formed an alliance to launch a common attack against Joshua and Israel.

The Gibeonite Deception

3* On learning what Joshua had done to Jericho and Ai, the inhabitants of Gibeon 4 put into effect a device of their own. They chose provisions for a journey, making use of old sacks for their asses, and old wineskins, torn and mended. 5 They wore old,

---

8, 30–35: These ceremonies were prescribed in Dt 11, 29, and Dt 27, 2–26. See notes on those passages.

8, 26: Ex 17, 11ff.
8, 28: Dt 13, 16.
8, 29: Jos 10, 26f; Dt 21, 22f; Jn 19, 31.

8, 31: Ex 20, 24f; Dt 27, 5f.
8, 32: Dt 27, 2.8.
8, 33: Jos 3, 3; Dt 11, 27; 27, 12; 31, 9.12.
8, 34: Dt 28, 2–68; 30, 19;

31, 11; Neh 8, 2f.
8, 35: Dt 31, 12.
9, 1: Jos 3, 10; Ex 3, 8.17; 23, 23; Dt 1, 7.
9, 3: Jos 6, 21.24; 11, 19.

patched sandals and shabby garments; and all the bread they took was dry and crumbly. 6* Thus they journeyed to Joshua in the camp at Gilgal, where they said to him and to the men of Israel, "We have come from a distant land to propose that you make an alliance with us." 7† But the men of Israel replied to the Hivites, "You may be living in land that is ours. How, then, can we make an alliance with you?" 8 But they answered Joshua, "We are your servants." Then Joshua asked them, "Who are you? Where do you come from?" 9* They answered him, "Your servants have come from a far-off land, because of the fame of the LORD, your God. For we have heard reports of all that he did in Egypt 10* and all that he did to the two kings of the Amorites beyond the Jordan, Sihon, king of Heshbon, and Og, king of Bashan, who lived in Ashtaroth. 11 So our elders and all the inhabitants of our country said to us, 'Take along provisions for the journey and go to meet them. Say to them: We are your servants; we propose that you make an alliance with us.' 12 This bread of ours was still warm when we brought it from home as provisions the day we left to come to you, but now it is dry and crumbled. 13 Here are our wineskins, which were new when we filled them, but now they are torn. Look at our garments and sandals, which are worn out from the very long journey." 14* Then the Israelite princes partook of their provisions, without seeking the advice of the LORD. 15* So Joshua made an alliance with them and entered into an agreement to spare them, which the princes of the community sealed with an oath.

Gibeonites Made Vassals

16 Three days after the agreement was entered into, the Israelites learned that these people were from nearby, and would be living in Israel. 17 The third day on the road, the Israelites came to their cities of Gibeon, Chephirah, Beeroth and Kiriathjearim, 18 but did not attack them, because the princes of the community had sworn to them by the LORD, the God of Israel. When the entire community grumbled against the princes, 19 these all remonstrated with the people, "We have sworn to them by the LORD, the God of Israel, and so we cannot harm them. 20 Let us therefore spare their lives and so deal with them that we shall not be pun-

ished for the oath we have sworn to them." 21† Thus the princes recommended that they be let live, as hewers of wood and drawers of water for the entire community; and the community did as the princes advised them.

22 Joshua summoned the Gibeonites and said to them, "Why did you lie to us and say that you lived at a great distance from us, when you will be living in our very midst? 23 For this are you accursed: every one of you shall always be a slave [hewers of wood and drawers of water] for the house of my God." 24* They answered Joshua, "Your servants were fully informed of how the LORD, your God, commanded his servant Moses that you be given the entire land and that all its inhabitants be destroyed before you. Since, therefore, at your advance, we were in great fear for our lives, we acted as we did. 25 And now that we are in your power, do with us what you think fit and right." 26† Joshua did what he had decided: while he saved them from being killed by the Israelites, 27* at the same time he made them, as they still are, hewers of wood and drawers of water for the community and for the altar of the LORD, in the place of the LORD's choice.

The Siege of Gibeon

10 1* Now Adonizedek, king of Jerusalem, heard that, in the capture and destruction of Ai, Joshua had done to that city and its king as he had done to Jericho and its king. He heard also that the inhabitants of Gibeon had made their peace with Israel, remaining among them, 2 and that there was great fear abroad, because Gibeon was large enough for a royal city, larger even than the city of Ai, and all its men were brave. 3 So Adonizedek, king of Jerusalem, sent for Hoham, king of Hebron, Piram, king of Jarmuth, Japhia, king of Lachish, and Debir, king of Eglon, 4* to come to his aid for an attack on Gibeon, since it had concluded peace with Joshua and the Israelites. 5† The five Amorite kings, of Jerusalem, Hebron, Jarmuth, Lachish and Eglon, united all their forces and marched against Gibeon, where they took up siege positions. 6* Thereupon, the men of Gibeon sent an appeal to Joshua in his camp at Gilgal: "Do not abandon your servants. Come up here quickly and save us. Help us, because all the Amorite kings of the mountain country have joined forces against us."

9, 7: *The Hivites:* apparently the Gibeonites belonged to this larger ethnic group (cf also Jos 11, 19), although in 2 Sm 21, 2 they are classed as Amorites; both groups are listed among the seven nations in Canaan whom the Israelites were to exterminate; cf Dt 7, 1f.

9, 21: *Hewers of wood and drawers of water:* proverbial terms for the lowest social class in the Israelite community; cf Dt 29, 10f.

9, 26f: Later on, Saul violated the immunity of the Gibeonites, but David vindicated it; cf 2 Sm 21, 1–9.

10, 5: *Hebron . . . Eglon:* these four cities were to the south and southwest of Jerusalem.

9, 6: Ex 23, 32; Dt 7, 2.
9, 9: Jos 2, 10.
9, 10: Nm 21, 25.33.
9, 14: Nm 27, 21.
9, 15: Jos 11, 19; 2 Sm 21, 2.
9, 24: Ex 23, 27f; Dt 7, 1f.
9, 27: Dt 12, 5.
10, 1: Jos 9, 15; 6, 21.24; 8, 26–29.
10, 4: Jos 9, 15.
10, 6: Jos 9, 6.

Joshua's Victory

[7] So Joshua marched up from Gilgal with his picked troops and the rest of his soldiers. [8] Meanwhile the LORD said to Joshua, "Do not fear them, for I have delivered them into your power. Not one of them will be able to withstand you." [9] And when Joshua made his surprise attack upon them after an all-night march from Gilgal, [10] the LORD threw them into disorder before him. The Israelites inflicted a great slaughter on them at Gibeon and pursued them down the Beth-horon slope, harassing them as far as Azekah and Makkedah.

[11]*† While they fled before Israel along the descent from Beth-horon, the LORD hurled great stones from the sky above them all the way to Azekah, killing many. More died from these hailstones than the Israelites slew with the sword. [12] On this day, when the LORD delivered up the Amorites to the Israelites,

Joshua prayed to the LORD,
and said in the presence of Israel:
Stand still, O sun, at Gibeon,
O moon, in the valley of Aijalon!
[13]*†And the sun stood still,
and the moon stayed,
while the nation took vengeance on
its foes.

Is this not recorded in the Book of Jashar? The sun halted in the middle of the sky; not for a whole day did it resume its swift course. [14] Never before or since was there a day like this, when the LORD obeyed the voice of a man; for the LORD fought for Israel. [15] [Then Joshua and all Israel returned to the camp at Gilgal.]

Execution of Amorite Kings

[16] Meanwhile the five kings who had fled, hid in a cave at Makkedah. [17] When Joshua was told that the five kings had been discovered hiding in a cave at Makkedah, [18] he said, "Roll large stones to the mouth of the cave and post men over it to guard them. [19] But do not remain there yourselves. Pursue your enemies, and harry them in the rear. Do not allow them to escape to their cities, for the LORD, your God, has delivered them into your power."

[20] Once Joshua and the Israelites had finally inflicted the last blows in this very great slaughter,

and the survivors had escaped from them into the fortified cities, [21] all the army returned safely to Joshua and the camp at Makkedah, no man uttering a sound against the Israelites. [22] Then Joshua said, "Open the mouth of the cave and bring out those five kings to me." [23] Obediently, they brought out to him from the cave the five kings, of Jerusalem, Hebron, Jarmuth, Lachish and Eglon. [24] When they had done so, Joshua summoned all the men of Israel and said to the commanders of the soldiers who had marched with him, "Come forward and put your feet on the necks of these kings." They came forward and put their feet upon their necks. [25] Then Joshua said to them, "Do not be afraid or dismayed, be firm and steadfast. This is what the LORD will do to all the enemies against whom you fight." [26]* Thereupon Joshua struck and killed them, and hanged them on five trees, where they remained hanging until evening. [27] At sunset they were removed from the trees at the command of Joshua and cast into the cave where they had hidden; over the mouth of the cave large stones were placed, which remain until this very day.

Conquest of Southern Canaan

[28]* Makkedah, too, Joshua captured and put to the sword at that time. He fulfilled the doom on the city, on its king, and on every person in it, leaving no survivors. Thus he did to the king of Makkedah what he had done to the king of Jericho. [29] Joshua then passed on with all Israel from Makkedah to Libnah, which he attacked. [30] Libnah also, with its king, the LORD delivered into the power of Israel. He put it to the sword with every person there, leaving no survivors. Thus he did to its king what he had done to the king of Jericho. [31] Joshua next passed on with all Israel from Libnah to Lachish, where they set up a camp during the attack. [32] The LORD delivered Lachish into the power of Israel, so that on the second day Joshua captured it and put it to the sword with every person in it, just as he had done to Libnah. [33] At that time Horam, king of Gezer, came up to help Lachish, but Joshua defeated him and his people, leaving him no survivors. [34] From Lachish, Joshua passed on with all Israel to Eglon; encamping near it, they attacked it [35] and captured it the same day, putting it to the sword. He fulfilled the doom that day on every person in it, just as he had done at Lachish. [36] From Eglon,

---

10, 11: *Great stones from the sky:* the hailstones mentioned in the next sentence.

10, 13: *Is this not recorded:* the reference is to the preceding, poetic passage. Evidently the Book of Jashar, like the Book of the Wars of the LORD (Nm 21, 14), recounted in epic style the exploits of Israel's early heroes. *The sun halted:* though it is widely supposed that this passage describes in popular language and according to external appearances a miraculous lengthening of the day, it is equally probable that Joshua's prayer was rather for an abrupt obscuration of

the sun, which would impede his enemies in their flight homeward and also prevent them from rallying their forces; this request would have been answered by the hailstorm (cf Sir 46, 5) and by a darkness relieved only twenty-four hours later, well into the next day.

10, 11: Jb 38, 22.   10, 26f: Jos 8, 29; Dt 21, 22f.
10, 13: Sir 46, 4; Is 28, 21;   10, 28: Jos 6, 21.
Heb 3, 11.

Joshua went up with all Israel to Hebron, which they attacked ³⁷ and captured. They put it to the sword with its king, all its towns, and every person there, leaving no survivors, just as Joshua had done to Eglon. He fulfilled the doom on it and on every person there. ³⁸ Then Joshua and all Israel turned back to Debir and attacked it, ³⁹ capturing it with its king and all its towns. They put them to the sword and fulfilled the doom on every person there, leaving no survivors. Thus was done to Debir and its king what had been done to Hebron, as well as to Libnah and its king.

⁴⁰* Joshua conquered the entire country; the mountain regions, the Negeb, the foothills, and the mountain slopes, with all their kings. He left no survivors, but fulfilled the doom on all who lived there, just as the LORD, the God of Israel, had commanded. ⁴¹† Joshua conquered from Kadesh-barnea to Gaza, and all the land of Goshen to Gibeon. ⁴² All these kings and their lands Joshua captured in a single campaign, for the LORD, the God of Israel, fought for Israel. ⁴³ Thereupon Joshua with all Israel returned to the camp at Gilgal.

Northern Confederacy

11 ¹† When Jabin, king of Hazor, learned of this, he sent a message to Jobab, king of Madon, to the king of Shimron, to the king of Achshaph, ²* and to the northern kings in the mountain regions and in the Arabah near Chinneroth, in the foothills, and in Naphath-dor to the west. ³ These were Canaanites to the east and west, Amorites, Hittites, Perizzites and Jebusites in the mountain regions, and Hivites at the foot of Hermon in the land of Mizpah. ⁴ They came out with all their troops, an army numerous as the sands on the seashore, and with a multitude of horses and chariots. ⁵† All these kings joined forces and marched to the waters of Merom, where they encamped together to fight against Israel.

⁶ The LORD said to Joshua, "Do not fear them, for by this time tomorrow I will stretch them slain before Israel. You must hamstring their horses and burn their chariots." ⁷ Joshua with his whole army came upon them at the waters of Merom in a surprise attack. ⁸* The LORD delivered them into the power of the Israelites, who defeated them and pursued them to Greater Sidon, to Misrephoth-maim, and eastward to the valley of Mizpeh. They struck them all down, leaving no survivors. ⁹ Joshua did to them as the LORD had commanded: he hamstrung their horses and burned their chariots.

Conquest of Northern Canaan

¹⁰ At that time Joshua, turning back, captured Hazor and slew its king with the sword; for Hazor formerly was the chief of all those kingdoms. ¹¹ He also fulfilled the doom by putting every person there to the sword, till none was left alive. Hazor itself he burned. ¹²* Joshua thus captured all those kings with their cities and put them to the sword, fulfilling the doom on them, as Moses, the servant of the LORD, had commanded. ¹³ However, Israel did not destroy by fire any of the cities built on raised sites, except Hazor, which Joshua burned. ¹⁴ The Israelites took all the spoil and livestock of these cities as their booty; but the people they put to the sword, until they had exterminated the last of them, leaving none alive. ¹⁵* As the LORD had commanded his servant Moses, so Moses commanded Joshua, and Joshua acted accordingly. He left nothing undone that the LORD had commanded Moses should be done.

Survey of the Conquest

¹⁶* So Joshua captured all this land: the mountain regions, the entire Negeb, all the land of Goshen, the foothills, the Arabah, as well as the mountain regions and foothills of Israel, ¹⁷* from Mount Halak that rises toward Seir as far as Baal-gad in the Lebanon valley at the foot of Mount Hermon. All their kings he captured and put to death. ¹⁸ Joshua waged war against all these kings for a long time. ¹⁹* With the exception of the Hivites who lived in Gibeon, no city made peace with the Israelites; all were taken in battle. ²⁰* For it was the design of the LORD to encourage them to wage war against Israel, that they might be doomed to destruction and thus receive no mercy, but be exterminated, as the LORD had commanded Moses.

²¹*† At that time Joshua penetrated the mountain regions and exterminated the Anakim in Hebron, Debir, Anab, the entire mountain region of

---

10, 41: *Goshen:* a town and its surrounding district at the southern end of the Judean mountains (cf Jos 11, 16; 15, 51); not to be confused with the land of Goshen in northeastern Egypt (Gen 45, 10), although in the current Hebrew Bible both names are spelled the same.

11, 1ff: *Hazor, Madon, Shimron, and Chinneroth:* cities and their surrounding districts in eastern Galilee. *Achshaph and Naphath-dor:* southwest of Galilee. *The mountain regions:* in central and northern Galilee.

11, 5: *The waters of Merom:* a stream in central Galilee that flows southeast to water the fertile Arabah, or plain of Chinneroth on the western shore of the lake of Gennesaret.

11, 21ff: Most of the land assigned to the tribe of Judah was not conquered by it till the early period of the Judges. See note on Jgs 1, 1–36.

10, 40: Dt 20, 16f.
11, 2: Jos 12, 3; Jgs 1, 27.
11, 8: Jos 13, 6.
11, 12: Dt 7, 2; 20, 16f.
11, 15: Dt 7, 2.
11, 16: Jos 10, 41; 12, 8.

11, 17: Jos 12, 7; Dt 7, 24.
11, 19: Jos 9, 3.7.15.
11, 20: Dt 2, 30; 20, 16f.
11, 21: Jos 15, 13f; Nm 13, 22; Dt 1, 28.

Judah, and the entire mountain region of Israel. Joshua fulfilled the doom on them and on their cities, 22 so that no Anakim were left in the land of the Israelites. However, some survived in Gaza, in Gath, and in Ashdod. 23*† Thus Joshua captured the whole country, just as the LORD had foretold to Moses. Joshua gave it to Israel as their heritage, apportioning it among the tribes. And the land enjoyed peace.

Lists of Conquered Kings

12 †1 The kings of the land east of the Jordan, from the River Arnon to Mount Hermon, including all the eastern section of the Arabah, whom the Israelites conquered and whose lands they occupied, were: 2* First, Sihon, king of the Amorites, who lived in Heshbon. His domain extended from Aroer, which is on the bank of the Wadi Arnon, to include the wadi itself, and the land northward through half of Gilead to the Wadi Jabbok, 3* as well as the Arabah from the eastern side of the Sea of Chinnereth, as far south as the eastern side of the Salt Sea of the Arabah in the direction of Beth-jeshimoth, to a point under the slopes of Pisgah. 4* Secondly, Og, king of Bashan, a survivor of the Rephaim, who lived at Ashtaroth and Edrei. 5 He ruled over Mount Hermon, Salecah, and all Bashan as far as the boundary of the Geshurites and Maacathites, and over half of Gilead as far as the territory of Sihon, king of Heshbon. 6* After Moses, the servant of the LORD, and the Israelites conquered them, he assigned their land to the Reubenites, the Gadites, and the half-tribe of Manasseh, as their property.

7 This is a list of the kings whom Joshua and the Israelites conquered west of the Jordan and whose land, from Baal-gad in the Lebanon valley to Mount Halak which rises toward Seir, Joshua apportioned to the tribes of Israel. 8 It included the mountain regions and foothills, the Arabah, the slopes, the desert, and the Negeb, belonging to the Hittites, Amorites, Canaanites, Perizzites, Hivites and Jebusites. 9* They were the kings of Jericho, Ai (which is near Bethel), 10 Jerusalem, Hebron, 11* Jarmuth, Lachish, 12* Eglon, Gezer, 13* Debir, Geder, 14 Hormah, Arad, 15* Libnah, Adullam, 16* Makkedah, Bethel, 17* Tappuah, Hepher, 18* Aphek, Lasharon, 19* Madon, Hazor, 20* Shimron, Achshaph, 21* Taanach, Megiddo, 22* Kedesh, Jokneam (at Carmel),

did you KNOW?
The Conquest of Canaan

A strong parallel connects the beginning of the story of Joshua—the crossing of the Jordan River, God's direction and protection of the Israelites (symbolized by the ark), and the renewal of the Covenant at Mount Ebal—and the events of the Exodus from Egypt. The parallel reinforces how the conquest of Canaan was part of God's continued liberation of the Chosen People and a key moment in the history of Israel.

As the Israelites moved in on the Promised Land, the Canaanites were one of several groups of people that the Israelites had to deal with. Joshua 12, 8 also mentions Hittites, Amorites, Perizzites, Hivites, and Jebusites. But the Canaanites seemed to be the dominant inhabitants. They were primarily an agricultural society and believed that their gods, called baals, controlled the rains, the seasons, and the fertility of the soil. For the Israelites, God was revealed as the only God over all creation and history.

The conquest of the Canaanites through violence might make you wonder what the Israelites believed about God. Basically, they believed the Canaanite baals were an offense against God. Because the Canaanites would not change, the Israelites felt justified in killing them and taking their land. (See "Holy War," near Nm 2, 1.) Later, Christians would not be able to justify such actions because of Jesus' teaching that everyone is loved by God and that we must love even our enemies. But at the time Joshua was written, God and God's plan for humanity had not yet been fully revealed.

▶ Joshua, chapter 12

11, 23: *The land enjoyed peace:* of a limited and temporary nature. Many of the individual tribes had still to fight against the remaining Canaanites; cf Jos 15, 13–17; 17, 12f. This verse forms the conclusion to the first part of the book. Cf note on Jos 12, 1–24.

12, 1–24: This chapter, inserted between the two principal parts of the book (chapters 1–11 and 13–21), resembles the lists of conquered cities which are inscribed on monuments of the Egyptian and Assyrian monarchs. Perhaps it was copied here from some such public Israelite record.

11, 23: Jos 14, 1–19, 51; Nm 34, 2–12.
12, 2–5: Nm 21, 21–26.33ff.
  12, 3: Jos 13, 20.
  12, 4: Jos 13, 11f.
  12, 6: Nm 32, 33; Dt 3, 12f.
  12, 9: Jos 6, 2; 8, 23.
12, 11: 10f. Jos 10, 23.
  12, 12: Jos 10, 23.33.

12, 13: Jos 10, 38f; 15, 36.
12, 15: Jos 10, 29f; 15, 35.
12, 16: Jos 8, 17; 10, 28.
12, 17: Jos 15, 34.
12, 18: Jos 15, 53.
12, 19: Jos 11, 1.10.
12, 20: Jos 11, 1.
12, 21: Jos 17, 11.
12, 22: Jos 19, 37.

23* and Dor (in Naphath-dor), the foreign king at Gilgal, 24 and the king of Tirzah, thirty-one kings in all.

II: Division of the Land

Division of Land Commanded

13 1* When Joshua was old and advanced in years, the LORD said to him: "Though now you are old and advanced in years, a very large part of the land still remains to be conquered. 2† This additional land includes all Geshur and all the districts of the Philistines 3* (from the stream adjoining Egypt to the boundary of Ekron in the north is reckoned Canaanite territory, though held by the five lords of the Philistines in Gaza, Ashdod, Ashkelon, Gath and Ekron); also where the Avvim are in the south; 4 all the land of the Canaanites from Mearah of the Sidonians to Aphek, and the boundaries of the Amorites; 5 and the Gebalite territory; and all the Lebanon on the east, from Baal-gad at the foot of Mount Hermon to Labo in the land of Hamath. 6* At the advance of the Israelites I will drive out all the Sidonian inhabitants of the mountain regions between Lebanon and Misrephoth-maim; at least include these areas in the division of the Israelite heritage, just as I have commanded you. 7 Now, therefore, apportion among the nine tribes and the half-tribe of Manasseh the land which is to be their heritage."

The Eastern Tribes

8* Now the other half of the tribe of Manasseh, as well as the Reubenites and Gadites, had received their heritage which Moses, the servant of the LORD, had given them east of the Jordan: 9 from Aroer on the bank of the Wadi Arnon and the city in the wadi itself, through the tableland of Medeba and Dibon, 10 with the rest of the cities of Sihon, king of the Amorites, who reigned in Heshbon, to the boundary of the Ammonites; 11 also Gilead and the territory of the Geshurites and Maacathites, all Mount Hermon, and all Bashan as far as Salecah, 12 the entire kingdom in Bashan of Og, a survivor of the Rephaim, who reigned at Ashtaroth and Edrei. Though Moses conquered and occupied these territories, 13 the Israelites did not dislodge the Geshurites and Maacathites, so that Geshur and Maacath survive in the midst of Israel to this day. 14* However, to the tribe of Levi Moses assigned no heritage since, as the LORD had promised them, the LORD, the God of Israel, is their heritage.

Reuben

15* What Moses gave to the Reubenite clans:* 16 Their territory reached from Aroer, on the bank of the Wadi Arnon, and the city in the wadi itself, through the tableland about Medeba, 17 to include Heshbon and all its towns which are on the tableland, Dibon, Bamoth-baal, Beth-baal-meon, 18 Jahaz, Kedemoth, Mephaath, 19 Kiriathaim, Sibmah, Zereth-shahar on the knoll within the valley, 20 Beth-peor, the slopes of Pisgah, Beth-jeshimoth, 21* and the other cities of the tableland and, generally, of the kingdom of Sihon. This Amorite king, who reigned in Heshbon, Moses had killed, with his vassals, the princes of Midian, who were settled in the land: Evi, Rekem, Zur, Hur and Reba; 22* and among their slain followers the Israelites put to the sword also the soothsayer Balaam, son of Beor. 23 The boundary of the Reubenites was the bank of the Jordan. These cities and their villages were the heritage of the clans of the Reubenites.

Gad

24* What Moses gave to the Gadite clans: 25 Their territory included Jazer, all the cities of Gilead, and half the land of the Ammonites as far as Aroer, toward Rabbah 26 (that is, from Heshbon to Ramath-mizpeh and Betonim, and from Mahanaim to the boundary of Lodebar); 27 and in the Jordan valley: Beth-haram, Beth-nimrah, Succoth, Zaphon, the other part of the kingdom of Sihon, king of Heshbon, with the bank of the Jordan to the southeastern tip of the Sea of Chinnereth. 28 These cities and their villages were the heritage of the clans of the Gadites.

Manasseh

29* What Moses gave to the clans of the half-tribe of Manasseh: 30* Their territory included Mahanaim, all of Bashan, the entire kingdom of Og, king of Bashan, and all the villages of Jair, which are sixty cities in Bashan. 31 Half of Gilead, with Ashtaroth and Edrei, once the royal cities of Og in Bashan, fell to the descendants of Machir, son of Manasseh, for half the clans descended from Machir.

32 These are the portions which Moses gave when he was in the plains of Moab, beyond the Jordan

---

13, 2: *Geshur:* not to be confused with the large Aramaean district of the same name in Bashan (vv 11–13; Dt 3, 14); here it is a region to the south of the Philistine country, since vv 2–5 list the unconquered lands along the coast from south to north; cf also 1 Sm 27, 8.

12, 23: Jos 11, 2.
13, 1: Jos 23, 1.
13, 3: Jgs 3, 3.
13, 6: Jos 11, 8.
13, 8: Jos 12, 6; Nm 32, 33.
13, 14: Jos 14, 3f; Nm 18, 20–24.
13, 15–31: Dt 3, 12–17.

13, 15–23: Nm 21, 25–31; 32, 37f.
13, 21: Nm 21, 24; 31, 8; Dt 3, 10.
13, 22: Nm 31, 8.
13, 24–28: Nm 32, 34ff.
13, 29–31: Nm 32, 39ff.
13, 30: Nm 32, 41.

east of Jericho. [33]* However, Moses gave no heritage to the tribe of Levi, since the LORD himself, the God of Israel, is their heritage, as he promised.

The Western Tribes

14 [1]* Here follow the portions which the Israelites received in the land of Canaan. Eleazar the priest, Joshua, son of Nun, and the heads of families in the tribes of the Israelites determined [2]* their heritage by lot, in accordance with the instructions the LORD had given through Moses concerning the remaining nine and a half tribes. [3]* For to two and a half tribes Moses had already given a heritage beyond the Jordan; and though the Levites were given no heritage among the tribes, [4]* the descendants of Joseph formed two tribes, Manasseh and Ephraim. The Levites themselves received no share of the land except cities to live in, with their pasture lands for the cattle and flocks. [5] Thus, in apportioning the land, did the Israelites carry out the instructions of the LORD to Moses.

Caleb's Portion

[6]* When the Judahites came up to Joshua in Gilgal, the Kenizzite Caleb, son of Jephunneh, said to him: "You know what the LORD said to the man of God, Moses, about you and me in Kadesh-barnea. [7]* I was forty years old when the servant of the LORD, Moses, sent me from Kadesh-barnea to reconnoiter the land; and I brought back to him a conscientious report. [8]* My fellow scouts who went up with me discouraged the people, but I was completely loyal to the LORD, my God. [9] On that occasion Moses swore this oath, 'The land where you have set foot shall become your heritage and that of your descendants forever, because you have been completely loyal to the LORD, my God.' [10]* Now, as he promised, the LORD has preserved me while Israel was journeying through the desert, for the forty-five years since the LORD spoke thus to Moses; and although I am now eighty-five years old, [11]* I am still as strong today as I was the day Moses sent me forth, with no less vigor whether for war or for ordinary tasks. [12]* Give me, therefore, this mountain region which the LORD promised me that day, as you yourself heard. True, the Anakim are there, with large fortified cities, but if the LORD is with me

I shall be able to drive them out, as the LORD promised." [13]* Joshua blessed Caleb, son of Jephunneh, and gave him Hebron as his heritage. [14] Therefore Hebron remains the heritage of the Kenizzite Caleb, son of Jephunneh, to the present day, because he was completely loyal to the LORD, the God of Israel. [15]* Hebron was formerly called Kiriath-arba, for Arba, the greatest among the Anakim. And the land enjoyed peace.

Boundaries of Judah

15 [1]* The lot for the clans of the Judahite tribe fell in the extreme south toward the boundary of Edom, the desert of Zin in the Negeb. [2]* The boundary there ran from the bay that forms the southern end of the Salt Sea, [3] southward below the pass of Akrabbim, across through Zin, up to a point south of Kadesh-barnea, across to Hezron, and up to Addar; from there, looping around Karka, [4] it crossed to Azmon and then joined the Wadi of Egypt before coming out at the sea. [This is your southern boundary.] [5] The eastern boundary was the Salt Sea as far as the mouth of the Jordan.

[6]* The northern boundary climbed from the bay where the Jordan meets the sea, up to Beth-hoglah, and ran north of Beth-arabah, up to Eben-Bohan-ben-Reuben. [7]* Thence it climbed to Debir, north of the vale of Achor, in the direction of the Gilgal that faces the pass of Adummim, on the south side of the wadi; from there it crossed to the waters of En-shemesh and emerged at En-rogel. [8]*† Climbing again to the Valley of Ben-Hinnom on the southern flank of the Jebusites [that is, Jerusalem], the boundary rose to the top of the mountain at the northern end of the Valley of Rephaim, which bounds the Valley of Hinnom on the west. [9]* From the top of the mountain it ran to the fountain of waters of Nephtoah, extended to the cities of Mount Ephron, and continued to Baalah, or Kiriath-jearim. [10] From Baalah the boundary curved westward to Mount Seir and passed north of the ridge of Mount Jearim (that is, Chesalon); thence it descended to Beth-shemesh, and ran across to Timnah. [11] It then extended along the northern flank of Ekron, continued through Shikkeron, and across to Mount Baalah, thence to include Jabneel, before it came out at the sea. [12] The western boundary was the Great Sea and its coast. This was the complete boundary of the clans of the Judahites.

---

† **15, 8:** *The Valley of Ben-hinnom:* the southern limit of Jerusalem. Ben-hinnom means "son of Hinnom." The place was also called Valley of Hinnom, in Hebrew *ge-hinnom,* whence the word "Gehenna" is derived.

13, 33: Jos 18, 7; Nm 18, 20.
14, 1: Jos 17, 4; 21, 1; Nm 34, 17f.
14, 2: Nm 26, 55; 33, 54; 34, 13.
14, 3: Jos 13, 8.14.33.

14, 4: Jos 21, 3–40; Gn 48, 5.
14, 6: Nm 14, 24.30; 32, 12; Dt 1, 36.38.
14, 7: Nm 14, 6–9.
14, 8: Nm 13, 31ff; 14, 24; 32, 12; Dt 1, 36.
14, 10: Nm 14, 30.
14, 11: Sir 46, 1ff.
14, 12: Jos 11, 21.

14, 13: Jos 10, 36f; 15, 13–19; 21, 11f.
14, 15: Jgs 1, 10.
15, 1: Nm 34, 3.
15, 2–4: Nm 34, 3ff.
15, 6: Jos 18, 18f.22.
15, 7: Jos 7, 26; 18, 16ff; 2 Sm 17, 17.
15, 8: Jos 18, 16.
15, 9: Jos 18, 15.

Conquest by Caleb

13* As the LORD had commanded, Joshua gave Caleb, son of Jephunneh,* a portion among the Judahites, namely, Kiriath-arba (Arba was the father of Anak), that is, Hebron. 14* And Caleb drove out from there the three Anakim, the descendants of Anak: Sheshai, Ahiman and Talmai. 15* From there he marched up against the inhabitants of Debir, which was formerly called Kiriath-sepher. 16 Caleb said, "I will give my daughter Achsah in marriage to the one who attacks Kiriath-sepher and captures it." 17† Othniel, son of Caleb's brother Kenaz, captured it, and so Caleb gave him his daughter Achsah in marriage. 18 On the day of her marriage to Othniel, she induced him to ask her father for some land. Then, as she alighted from the ass, Caleb asked her, "What is troubling you?" 19 She answered, "Give me an additional gift! Since you have assigned to me land in the Negeb, give me also pools of water." So he gave her the upper and the lower pools.

Cities of Judah

20† This is the heritage of the clans of the tribe of Judahites: 21 The cities of the tribe of the Judahites in the extreme southern district toward Edom were: Kabzeel, Eder, Jagur, 22 Kinah, Dimonah, Adadah, 23 Kedesh, Hazor and Ithnan; 24 Ziph, Telem, Bealoth, 25 Hazor-hadattah, and Kerioth-hezron (that is, Hazor); 26 Amam, Shema, Moladah, 27 Hazar-gaddah, Heshmon, Beth-pelet, 28 Hazar-shual, Beer-sheba, and Biziothiah, 29 Baalah, Iim, Ezem, 30 Eltolad, Chesil, Hormah, 31* Ziklag, Madmannah, Sansannah, 32 Lebaoth, Shilhim and En-rimmon; a total of twenty-nine cities with their villages.

33† In the foothills: Eshtaol, Zorah, Ashnah, 34 Zanoah, Engannim, Tappuah, Enam, 35 Jarmuth, Adullam, Socoh, Azekah, 36 Shaaraim, Adithaim, Gederah, and Gederothaim; fourteen cities and their villages. 37 Zenan, Hadashah, Migdal-gad, 38 Dilean, Mizpeh, Joktheel, 39 Lachish, Bozkath, Eglon, 40 Cabbon, Lahmam, Chitlish, 41 Gederoth, Beth-dagon, Naamah and Makkedah; sixteen cities and their villages. 42 Libnah, Ether, Ashan, 43 Iphtah, Ashnah, Nezib, 44 Keilah, Achzib and Mareshah; nine cities and their villages. 45 Ekron and its

towns and villages; 46 from Ekron to the sea, all the towns that lie alongside Ashdod and their villages; 47 Ashdod and its towns and villages; Gaza and its towns and villages, as far as the Wadi of Egypt and the coast of the Great Sea.

48 In the mountain regions: Shamir, Jattir, Socoh, 49 Dannah, Kiriath-sannah (that is, Debir), 50 Anab, Eshtemoh, Anim, 51 Goshen, Holon and Giloh; eleven cities and their villages. 52 Arab, Dumah, Eshan, 53 Janim, Beth-tappuah, Aphekah, 54 Humtah, Kiriath-arba (that is, Hebron), and Zior; nine cities and their villages. 55 Maon, Carmel, Ziph, Juttah, 56 Jezreel, Jokdeam, Zanoah, 57 Kain, Gibbeah and Timnah; ten cities and their villages. 58 Halhul, Beth-zur, Gedor, 59 Maarath, Beth-anoth and Eltekon; six cities and their villages. Tekoa, Ephrathah (that is, Bethlehem), Peor, Etam, Kulom, Tatam, Zores, Karim, Gallim, Bether and Manoko; eleven cities and their villages. 60* Kiriath-baal (that is, Kiriath-jearim) and Rabbah: two cities and their villages.

61† In the desert: Beth-arabah, Middin, Secacah, 62 Nibshan, Ir-hamelah and En-gedi; six cities and their villages. 63* [But the Jebusites who lived in Jerusalem the Judahites could not drive out; so the Jebusites dwell in Jerusalem beside the Judahites to the present day.]

The Joseph Tribes

16 1† The lot that fell to the Josephites extended from the Jordan at Jericho to the waters of Jericho east of the desert; then the boundary went up from Jericho to the heights at Bethel. 2 Leaving Bethel for Luz, it crossed the ridge to the border of the Archites at Ataroth, 3* and descended westward to the border of the Japhletites, to that of Lower Beth-horon, and to Gezer, ending thence at the sea.

Ephraim

4 Within the heritage of Manasseh and Ephraim, sons of Joseph, 5*† the dividing line for the heritage of the clans of the Ephraimites ran from east of Ataroth-addar to Upper Beth-horon 6* and thence to the sea. From Michmethath on the north,

---

15, 17–19: The story of Othniel is told again in Jgs 1, 13–15; cf also Jgs 3, 9–11.
15, 20–62: This elaborate list of the cities of Judah was probably taken from a document made originally for administrative purposes; the cities are divided into four provincial districts, some of which have further subdivisions. For similar lists of the cities of Judah, cf Jos 19, 2–7; 1 Chr 4, 28–32; Neh 11, 25–30. This list has suffered in transmission, so that the totals given in vv 32 and 36 are not exact, and some of the names are probably misspelled; many of the cities cannot be identified.
15, 33: In the foothills: see note on Dt 1, 7.
15, 61: In the desert: in the Jordan rift near the Dead Sea.
16, 1–17.18: The boundaries and cities of Judah, the most important tribe, having been given, the land of the next most important

group, the two Josephite tribes of Ephraim and Manasseh, is now described, though it was separated from Judah by the territories of Benjamin (Jos 18, 11–20) and Dan (Jos 19, 40–48).
16, 1–3: This line formed the southern boundary of Ephraim and the northern boundaries of Benjamin and of Dan.
16, 5: The dividing line: separating Ephraim from Manasseh. Ephraim's northern border (v 5) is given in an east-to-west direction; its eastern border (v 6f) in a north-to-south direction.

15, 13–19: Jgs 1, 10–15.   15, 60: Jos 18, 14.
15, 13: Jos 14, 13ff.   15, 63: Jgs 1, 21; 2 Sm 5, 6.
15, 14: Nm 13, 22; Jgs 1, 20.   16, 3: Jos 10, 10.33.
15, 15: Jos 10, 38.   16, 5: Jos 18, 13.
15, 31: 1 Sm 27, 6.   16, 6: Jos 17, 7.

their boundary curved eastward around Taanath-shiloh, and continued east of it to Janoah; 7 from there it descended to Ataroth and Naarah, and skirting Jericho, it ended at the Jordan. 8* From Tappuah the boundary ran westward to the Wadi Kanah and ended at the sea. This was the heritage of the clans of the Ephraimites, 9* including the villages that belonged to each city set aside for the Ephraimites within the territory of the Manassehites. 10* But they did not drive out the Canaanites living in Gezer, who live on within Ephraim to the present day, though they have been impressed as laborers.

Manasseh

17 1* Now as for the lot that fell to the tribe of Manasseh as the first-born of Joseph: since his eldest son, Machir, the father of Gilead, was a warrior, who had already obtained Gilead and Bashan, 2* the allotment was now made to the other descendants of Manasseh, the clans of Abiezer, Helek, Asriel, Shechem, Hepher and Shemida, the other male children of Manasseh, son of Joseph.

3* Furthermore, Zelophehad, son of Hepher, son of Gilead, son of Machir, son of Manasseh, had had no sons, but only daughters, whose names were Mahlah, Noah, Hoglah, Milcah, and Tirzah. 4* These presented themselves to Eleazar the priest, to Joshua, son of Nun, and to the princes, saying, "The LORD commanded Moses to give us a heritage among our kinsmen." So in obedience to the command of the LORD a heritage was given to each of them among their father's kinsmen. 5* Thus ten shares fell to Manasseh apart from the land of Gilead and Bashan beyond the Jordan, 6 since these female descendants of Manasseh received each a portion among his sons. The land of Gilead fell to the rest of the Manassehites.

7† Manasseh bordered on Asher. From Michmethath, near Shechem, another boundary ran southward to include the natives of En-Tappuah, 8 because the district of Tappuah belonged to Manasseh, although Tappuah itself was an Ephraimite city on the border of Manasseh. 9* This same boundary continued down to the Wadi Kanah. The cities that belonged to Ephraim from among the cities of Manasseh were those to the south of the wadi; thus the territory of Manasseh ran north of the wadi and ended at the sea. 10 The land on the south belonged to Ephraim and that on the north to Manasseh; with the sea as their common boundary, they reached Asher on the north and Issachar on the east.

11* Moreover, in Issachar and in Asher Manasseh was awarded Beth-shean* and its towns, Ibleam and its towns, Dor and its towns and the natives there, Endor and its towns and natives, Taanach and its towns and natives, and Megiddo and its towns and natives [the third is Naphath-dor]. 12 Since the Manassehites could not conquer these cities, the Canaanites persisted in this region. 13 When the Israelites grew stronger they impressed the Canaanites as laborers, but they did not drive them out.

Protest of Joseph Tribes

14* The descendants of Joseph said to Joshua, "Why have you given us only one lot and one share as our heritage? Our people are too many, because of the extent to which the LORD has blessed us." 15 Joshua answered them, "If you are too many, go up to the forest and clear out a place for yourselves there in the land of the Perizzites and Rephaim, since the mountain regions of Ephraim are so narrow." 16* For the Josephites said, "Our mountain regions are not enough for us; on the other hand, the Canaanites living in the valley region all have iron chariots, in particular those in Beth-shean and its towns, and those in the valley of Jezreel." 17 Joshua therefore said to Ephraim and Manasseh, the house of Joseph, "You are a numerous people and very strong. You shall have not merely one share, 18 for the mountain region which is now forest shall be yours when you clear it. Its adjacent land shall also be yours if, despite their strength and iron chariots, you drive out the Canaanites."

18 1* After they had subdued the land, the whole community of the Israelites assembled at Shiloh, where they set up the meeting tent.

The Seven Remaining Portions

2 Seven tribes among the Israelites had not yet received their heritage. 3 Joshua therefore said to the Israelites, "How much longer will you put off taking steps to possess the land which the LORD, the God of your fathers, has given you? 4 Choose three men from each of your tribes; I will commission them to begin a survey of the land, which they shall describe

17, 7: *Manasseh bordered on Asher:* only at the extreme northwestern section of Manasseh's territory. The boundary given in the following sentences (vv 7–10) is a more detailed description of the one already mentioned in Jos 16, 5ff, as separating Manasseh from Ephraim.

16, 8: Jos 17, 7.
16, 9: Jos 17, 9.
16, 10: Jgs 1, 29.
17, 1: Gn 41, 51; 46, 20; 48, 18; 50, 23; Nm 26, 29; Dt 3, 13.15.
17, 2: Nm 26, 29–32.
17, 3: Nm 26, 33; 27, 1; 36, 2.
17, 4: Nm 27, 6f; 36, 2.
17, 5: Jos 13, 30f.
17, 9: Jos 16, 8f.
17, 11: 1 Chr 7, 29.
17, 11ff: Jgs 1, 27f.
17, 14: Jos 16, 4; Gn 48, 19f.22.
17, 16: Jgs 6, 33.
18, 1: Jos 19, 51.

for purposes of inheritance. When they return to me, [5]* you shall divide it into seven parts. Judah is to retain its territory in the south, and the house of Joseph its territory in the north. [6] You shall bring here to me the description of the land in seven sections. I will then cast lots for you here before the LORD, our God. [7]* For the Levites have no share among you, because the priesthood of the LORD is their heritage; while Gad, Reuben, and the half-tribe of Manasseh have already received the heritage east of the Jordan which Moses, the servant of the LORD, gave them."

[8] When those who were to map out the land were ready for the journey, Joshua instructed them to survey the land, prepare a description of it, and return to him; then he would cast lots for them there before the LORD in Shiloh. [9] So they went through the land, listed its cities in writing in seven sections, and returned to Joshua in the camp at Shiloh. [10] Joshua then divided up the land for the Israelites into their separate shares, casting lots for them before the LORD in Shiloh.

Benjamin

[11] One lot fell to the clans of the tribe of Benjaminites. The territory allotted them lay between the descendants of Judah and those of Joseph. [12]*† Their northern boundary began at the Jordan and went over the northern flank of Jericho, up westward into the mountains, till it reached the desert of Beth-aven. [13]* From there it crossed over to the southern flank of Luz (that is, Bethel). Then it ran down to Ataroth-addar, on the mountaintop south of Lower Beth-horon. [14] For the western border, the boundary line swung south from the mountaintop opposite Beth-horon till it reached Kiriath-baal (that is, Kiriath-jearim), which city belonged to the Judahites. This was the western boundary. [15] The southern boundary began at the limits of Kiriath-jearim and projected to the spring at Nephtoah. [16]* It went down to the edge of the mountain on the north of the Valley of Rephaim, where it faces the Valley of Ben-hinnom; and continuing down the Valley of Hinnom along the southern flank of the Jebusites, reached En-rogel. [17] Inclining to the north, it extended to En-shemesh, and thence to Geliloth, opposite the pass of Adummim. Then it dropped to Eben-Bohan-ben-Reuben, [18]* across the northern flank of the Arabah

overlook, down into the Arabah. [19] From there the boundary continued across the northern flank of Beth-hoglah and extended to the northern tip of the Salt Sea, at the southern end of the Jordan. This was the southern boundary. [20] The Jordan bounded it on the east. This was how the heritage of the clans of the Benjaminites was bounded on all sides.

[21] Now the cities belonging to the clans of the tribe of the Benjaminites were: Jericho, Beth-hoglah, Emek-keziz, [22] Beth-arabah, Zemaraim, Bethel, [23] Avvim, Parah, Ophra, [24] Chephar-ammoni, Ophni and Geba; twelve cities and their villages. [25] Also Gibeon, Ramah, Beeroth, [26] Mizpeh, Chephirah, Mozah, [27] Rekem, Irpeel, Taralah, [28] Zela, Haeleph, the Jebusite city (that is, Jerusalem), Gibeah and Kiriath; fourteen cities and their villages. This was the heritage of the clans of Benjaminites.

Simeon

19 [1] The second lot fell to Simeon. The heritage of the clans of the tribe of Simeonites lay within that of the Judahites. [2]* For their heritage they received Beer-sheba, Shema, Moladah, [3] Hazar-shual, Balah, Ezem, [4] Eltolad, Bethul, Hormah, [5] Ziklag, Bethmar-caboth, Hazar-susah, [6] Beth-lebaoth and Sharuhen; thirteen cities and their villages. [7] Also En-rimmon, Ether and Ashan; four cities and their villages, [8] besides all the villages around these cities as far as Baalath-beer (that is, Ramoth-negeb). This was the heritage of the clans of the tribe of the Simeonites. [9] This heritage of the Simeonites was within the confines of the Judahites; for since the portion of the latter was too large for them, the Simeonites obtained their heritage within it.

Zebulun

[10]† The third lot fell to the clans of the Zebulunites. The limit of their heritage was at Sarid. [11] Their boundary went up west . . . and through Mareal, reaching Dabbesheth and the wadi that is near Jokneam. [12] From Sarid eastward it ran to the district of Chisloth-tabor, on to Daberath, and up to Japhia. [13] From there it continued eastward to Gath-hepher and to Eth-kazin, extended to Rimmon, and turned to Neah. [14] Skirting north of Hannathon, the boundary ended at the valley of Iphtahel. [15] Thus, with Kattath, Nahalal, Shimron,

---

18, 12–20: Benjamin's northern boundary (vv 12f) corresponded to part of the southern boundary of Ephraim (Jos 16, 1f). Their western border (v 14) was the eastern border of Dan (cf Jos 19, 40–47). Their southern boundary (vv 15–19) corresponded to part of the northern boundary of Judah (Jos 15, 6–9).

19, 10–16: Zebulun's territory was in the central section of the Plain of Esdraelon and of southern Galilee; it was bounded on the south by Manasseh, on the southeast by Issachar, on the northeast and north by Naphtali, and on the west by Asher. The site of the later

city of Nazareth was within its borders. Bethlehem of Zebulun was, of course, distinct from the city of the same name in Judah. *Twelve cities:* apparently seven of the names are missing from v 15, unless some of the places mentioned in vv 12–14 are to be included in the number.

18, 5: Jos 15, 1—17, 18.	**28,** 19.
18, 7: Jos 13, 8.33.	**18, 16:** Jos 15, 7f.
18, 12: Jos 16, 1.	**18, 18:** Jos 15, 6.
18, 13: Jos 16, 2f.5; Gn	**19, 2–8:** 1 Chr 4, 28–33.

JOS

Idalah and Bethlehem, there were twelve cities and their villages [16] to comprise the heritage of the clans of the Zebulunites.

Issachar

[17]† The fourth lot fell to Issachar. The territory of the clans of the Issacharites [18] included Jezreel, Chesulloth, Shunem, [19] Hapharaim, Shion, Anaharath, [20] Rabbith, Kishion, Ebez, [21] Remeth, Engannim, En-haddah and Beth-pazzez. [22] The boundary reached Tabor, Shahazumah and Bethshemesh, ending at the Jordan. These sixteen cities and their villages [23] were the heritage of the clans of the Issacharites.

Asher

[24]† The fifth lot fell to the clans of the tribe of the Asherites. [25] Their territory include Helkath, Hali, Beten, Achshaph, [26] Allammelech, Amad and Mishal, and reached Carmel on the west, and Shihor-libnath. [27] In the other direction, it ran eastward of Beth-dagon, reached Zebulun and the valley of Iphtahel; then north of Beth-emek and Neiel, it extended to Cabul, [28]* Mishal, Abdon, Rehob, Hammon and Kanah, near Greater Sidon. [29] Then the boundary turned back to Ramah and to the fortress city of Tyre; thence it cut back to Hosah and ended at the sea. Thus, with Mahalab, Achzib, [30] Ummah, Acco, Aphek and Rehob, there were twenty-two cities and their villages [31] to comprise the heritage of the clans of the tribe of the Asherites.

Naphtali

[32]† The sixth lot fell to the Naphtalites. The boundary of the clans of the Naphtalites [33] extended from Heleph, from the oak at Zaanannim to Lakkum, including Adami-nekeb and Jabneel, and ended at the Jordan. [34] In the opposite direction, westerly, it ran through Aznoth-tabor and from there extended to Hukkok; it touched Zebulun on the south, Asher on the west, and the Jordan on the east. [35] The fortified cities were Ziddim, Zer, Hammath, Rakkath, Chinnereth, [36] Adamah, Ramah, Hazor, [37] Kedesh, Edrei, En-hazor, [38]* Yiron, Migdal-el, Horem, Beth-anath and Beth-shemesh; nineteen cities and their villages, [39] to comprise the heritage of the clans of the tribe of the Naphtalites.

Dan

[40]† The seventh lot fell to the clans of the tribe of Danites. [41] Their heritage was the territory of Zorah, Eshtaol, Ir-shemesh, [42]* Shaalabbin, Aijalon, Ithlah, [43] Elon, Timnah, Ekron, [44] Eltekoh, Gibbethon, Baalath, [45] Jehud, Bene-berak, Gath-rimmon, [46] Me-jarkon and Rakkon, with the coast at Joppa. [47]*† But the territory of the Danites was too small for them; so the Danites marched up and attacked Leshem, which they captured and put to the sword. Once they had taken possession of Leshem, they renamed the settlement after their ancestor Dan. [48] These cities and their villages were the heritage of the clans of the tribe of the Danites.

Joshua's City

[49] When the last of them had received the portions of the land they were to inherit, the Israelites assigned a heritage in their midst to Joshua, son of Nun. [50]* In obedience to the command of the LORD, they gave him the city which he requested, Timnah-serah in the mountain region of Ephraim. He rebuilt the city and made it his home.

[51] These are the final portions into which Eleazar the priest, Joshua, son of Nun, and the heads of families in the tribes of the Israelites divided the land by lot in the presence of the LORD, at the door of the meeting tent in Shiloh.

Cities of Asylum

20 [1]† The LORD said to Joshua: [2]* "Tell the Israelites to designate the cities of which I spoke to them through Moses, [3] to which one guilty of accidental and unintended homicide may flee for asylum from the avenger of blood. [4] To one of these cities the killer shall flee, and standing at the entrance of the city gate, he shall plead his case before the elders, who must receive him and assign him a place in which to live among them. [5] Though the avenger of blood pursues him, they are not to deliver up the homicide who slew his fellow man unintentionally and not out of previous hatred. [6]* Once he has stood judgment before the community, he shall live on in that city till the death of the high priest who is in office at the time. Then the killer may go back home to his own city from which he fled."

---

† **19, 17–23:** Issachar's land was on the eastern watershed of the Plain of Esdraelon, but also included the southeastern end of the Galilean mountains. It was surrounded by Manasseh on the south and east, by Naphtali on the north, and by Zebulun on the west. Jezreel (v 18) dominated the plain to which it gave its name, the later form of which was Esdraelon.

19, 24–31: Asher inherited the western slope of the Galilean hills as far as the sea, with Manasseh to the south, Zebulun and Naphtali to the east, and Phoenicia to the north.

19, 32–39: Naphtali received eastern Galilee; Asher was to the west and Zebulun and Issachar were to the south, while the upper Jordan and Mount Hermon formed the eastern border. Part of the

tribe of Dan later on occupied the northern extremity of Naphtali's lands, at the sources of the Jordan (v 47).

19, 40–46: The original territory of Dan was a small enclave between Judah, Benjamin, Ephraim and the Philistines.

19, 47: *Leshem:* called Laish in Jgs 18, where the story of the migration of the Danites is told at greater length.

20, 1–9: The laws concerning the cities of refuge are given in Nm 35, 9–28; Dt 19, 1–13; see notes on Nm 35, 16–25; Dt 19, 2.

*
19, 28f: Jgs 1, 31.	19, 50: Jos 24, 30; Jgs 2, 9.
19, 38: Jgs 1, 33.	20, 2: Ex 21, 13; Nm 35, 10–14;
19, 42: Jgs 1, 35.	Dt 4, 41–43; 19, 2–9.
19, 47: Jgs 18, 27–29.	20, 6: Nm 35, 12.24f.

List of Cities

7* So they set apart Kedesh in Galilee in the mountain region of Naphtali, Shechem in the mountain region of Ephraim, and Kiriath-arba (that is, Hebron) in the mountain region of Judah. 8* And beyond the Jordan east of Jericho they designated Bezer on the open tableland in the tribe of Reuben, Ramoth in Gilead in the tribe of Gad, and Golan in Bashan in the tribe of Manasseh. 9* These were the designated cities to which any Israelite or stranger living among them who had killed a person accidentally might flee to escape death at the hand of the avenger of blood, until he could appear before the community.

Levitical Cities

21 1*† The heads of the Levite families came up to Eleazar the priest, to Joshua, son of Nun, and to the heads of families of the other tribes of the Israelites 2* at Shiloh in the land of Canaan, and said to them, "The LORD commanded, through Moses, that cities be given us to dwell in, with pasture lands for our livestock." 3 Out of their own heritage, in obedience to this command of the LORD, the Israelites gave the Levites the following cities with their pasture lands.

4 When the first lot among the Levites fell to the clans of the Kohathites, the descendants of Aaron the priest obtained thirteen cities by lot from the tribes of Judah, Simeon and Benjamin. 5 The rest of the Kohathites obtained ten cities by lot from the clans of the tribe of Ephraim, from the tribe of Dan, and from the half-tribe of Manasseh. 6 The Gershonites obtained thirteen cities by lot from the clans of the tribe of Issachar, from the tribe of Asher, from the tribe of Naphtali, and from the half-tribe of Manasseh. 7 The clans of the Merarites obtained twelve cities from the tribes of Reuben, Gad and Zebulun. 8* These cities with their pasture lands the Israelites allotted to the Levites in obedience to the LORD'S command through Moses.

Cities of the Priests

9* From the tribes of the Judahites and Simeonites they designated the following cities, 10 and assigned them to the descendants of Aaron in the Kohathite clan of the Levites, since the first lot fell to them: 11 first, Kiriath-arba (Arba was the father of Anak), that is, Hebron, in the mountain region of Judah, with the adjacent pasture lands, 12* al-

though the open country and villages belonging to the city had been given to Caleb, son of Jephunneh, as his property. 13 Thus to the descendants of Aaron the priest were given the city of asylum for homicides at Hebron, with its pasture lands; also, Libnah with its pasture lands, 14 Jattir with its pasture lands, Eshtemoa with its pasture lands, 15 Holon with its pasture lands, Debir with its pasture lands, 16 Ashan with its pasture lands, Juttah with its pasture lands, and Beth-shemesh with its pasture lands: nine cities from the two tribes mentioned. 17 From the tribe of Benjamin they obtained the four cities of Gibeon with its pasture lands, Geba with its pasture lands, 18* Anathoth with its pasture lands, and Almon with its pasture lands. 19 These cities which with their pasture lands belonged to the priestly descendants of Aaron, were thirteen in all.

Cities of the Other Kohathites

20* The rest of the Kohathite clans among the Levites obtained by lot, from the tribe of Ephraim, four cities. 21 They were assigned, with its pasture lands, the city of asylum for homicides at Shechem in the mountain region of Ephraim; also Gezer with its pasture lands, 22 Kibzaim with its pasture lands, and Beth-horon with its pasture lands. 23 From the tribe of Dan they obtained the four cities of Elteke with its pasture lands, Gibbethon with its pasture lands, 24 Aijalon with its pasture lands, and Gath-rimmon with its pasture lands; 25 and from the half-tribe of Manasseh the two cities of Taanach with its pasture lands and Ibleam with its pasture lands. 26 These cities which with their pasture lands belonged to the rest of the Kohathite clans were ten in all.

Cities of the Gershonites

27* The Gershonite clan of the Levites received from the half-tribe of Manasseh two cities: the city of asylum for homicides at Golan with its pasture lands; and also Beth-Astharoth with its pasture lands. 28 From the tribe of Issachar they obtained the four cities of Kishion with its pasture lands, Daberath with its pasture lands, 29 Jarmuth with its pasture lands, and En-gannim with its pasture lands; 30 from the tribe of Asher, the four cities of Mishal with its pasture lands, Abdon with its pasture lands, 31 Helkath with its pasture lands, and Rehob with its pasture lands; 32 and from the tribe

---

† **21, 1:** The order to establish special cities for the Levites is given in Nm 35, 1–8. The forty-eight cities listed here were hardly the exclusive possession of the Levites; at least the more important of them, such as Hebron, Shechem and Ramoth in Gilead, were certainly peopled for the most part by the tribe in whose territory they were situated. But in all these cities the Levites had special property rights which they did not possess in other cities; cf Lv 25, 32ff.

20, 7: Jos 15, 13; 19, 37; 21, 21.
20, 8: Jos 21, 27.36f.
20, 9: Nm 35, 15.
21, 1: Ex 6, 16–19; Nm 3, 17–20.
21, 2: Nm 35, 2.
21, 8: Nm 35, 2.
21, 9–19: 1 Chr 6, 54–60.
21, 12: Jos 14, 14; 15, 13.
21, 18: Jer 1, 1.
21, 20–26: 1 Chr 6, 66–70.
21, 27–33: 1 Chr 6, 71–76.

of Naphtali, three cities: the city of asylum for homicides at Kedesh in Galilee, with its pasture lands; also Hammath with its pasture lands, and Rakkath with its pasture lands. 33 These cities which with their pasture lands belonged to the Gershonite clans were thirteen in all.

Cities of the Merarites

34* The Merarite clans, the last of the Levites, received from the tribe of Zebulun the four cities of Jokneam with its pasture lands, Kartah with its pasture lands, 35 Rimmon with its pasture lands, and Nahalal with its pasture lands; 36 also, across the Jordan, from the tribe of Reuben, four cities: the city of asylum for homicides at Bezer with its pasture lands, Jahaz with its pasture lands, 37 Kedemoth with its pasture lands, and Mephaath with its pasture lands; 38 and from the tribe of Gad a total of four cities: the city of asylum for homicides at Ramoth in Gilead with its pasture lands, also Mahanaim with its pasture lands, 39 Heshbon with its pasture lands, and Jazer with its pasture lands. 40 The cities which were allotted to the Merarite clans, the last of the Levites, were therefore twelve in all.

41* Thus the total number of cities within the territory of the Israelites which, with their pasture lands, belonged to the Levites, was forty-eight. 42 With each and every one of these cities went the pasture lands round about it.

43* And so the LORD gave Israel all the land he had sworn to their fathers he would give them. Once they had conquered and occupied it, 44 the LORD gave them peace on every side, just as he had promised their fathers. Not one of their enemies could withstand them; the LORD brought all their enemies under their power. 45* Not a single promise that the LORD made to the house of Israel was broken; every one was fulfilled.

III: Return of the Transjordan Tribes and Joshua's Farewell

The Eastern Tribes Dismissed

22 1 At that time Joshua summoned the Reubenites, the Gadites, and the half-tribe of Manasseh 2* and said to them: "You have done all that Moses, the servant of the LORD, commanded you, and have obeyed every command I gave you. 3 For many years now you have not once abandoned your kinsmen, but have faithfully carried out the commands of the LORD, your God. 4* Since, therefore, the LORD, your God, has settled your kinsmen as he promised them, you may now return to your tents beyond the Jordan; to your own land, where Moses, the servant of the LORD, gave you. 5* But be very careful to observe the precept and law which Moses, the servant of the LORD, enjoined upon you: love the LORD, your God; follow him faithfully; keep his commandments; remain loyal to him; and serve him with your whole heart and soul." 6 Joshua then blessed them and sent them away to their own tents.

7* (For, to half the tribe of Manasseh Moses had assigned land in Bashan; and to the other half Joshua had given a portion along with their kinsmen west of the Jordan.) What Joshua said to them when he sent them off to their tents with his blessing was, 8* "Now that you are returning to your own tents with great wealth, with very numerous livestock, with silver, gold, bronze and iron, and with a very large supply of clothing, divide these spoils of your enemies with your kinsmen there." 9* So the Reubenites, the Gadites, and the half-tribe of Manasseh left the other Israelites at Shiloh in the land of Canaan and returned to the land of Gilead, their own property, which they had received according to the LORD'S command through Moses.

The Altar beside the Jordan

10 When the Reubenites, the Gadites, and the half-tribe of Manasseh came to the region of the Jordan in the land of Canaan, they built there at the Jordan a conspicuously large altar. 11*† The other Israelites heard the report that the Reubenites, the Gadites, and the half-tribe of Manasseh had built an altar in the region of the Jordan facing the land of Canaan, across from them, 12† and therefore they assembled their whole community at Shiloh to declare war on them.

Accusation of the Western Tribes

13* First, however, they sent to the Reubenites, the Gadites, and the half-tribe of Manasseh in the

---

† **22, 11:** In the region of the Jordan facing the land of Canaan: on the eastern side of the Jordan valley. The river itself formed the boundary between these eastern tribes and the rest of the tribes who lived in what was formerly Canaan—though the term Canaan could also be used of both sides of the Jordan valley (cf v 10). The Transjordan tribes naturally built their altar in their own territory.

22, 12: To declare war on them: the western Israelites considered this altar, which seemed to violate the customary unity of the sanctuary (cf Lv 17, 1–9; Dt 12, 4–14), as a sign of secession and dangerous to national unity. The motives for the war were political as well as religious.

21, 34–38: 1 Chr 6, 77–81.
21, 41: Nm 35, 7.
21, 43: Gn 12, 7; 13, 15; 15, 18; 26, 3; 28, 4.13.
21, 45: Jos 23, 14f.
22, 2: Jos 1, 16f; Nm 32, 20ff; Dt 3, 18ff.
22, 4: Jos 1, 13; 13, 8; Nm 32, 33.
22, 5: Dt 6, 5f.17; 10, 12; 11, 1.13.22.
22, 7: Jos 17, 5.
22, 8: Nm 31, 27.
22, 9: Jos 18, 1; Nm 32, 1.26.29.
22, 11: Dt 13, 13ff.
22, 13: Ex 6, 25; Sir 45, 28.

A Prayer for Understanding

When the Israelite tribes located east of the Jordan build a large altar to worship God, the Israelite tribes who settled west of the Jordan become concerned. They think that by building more altars, the tribes to the east are compromising their belief in one God. Some are ready to go to war over this issue. But maintaining unity among the tribes is also important. So, the western tribes wisely send Phinehas and others to insist on the importance of one place of worship. Listening to the eastern tribes, Phinehas understands their good intentions, and war is avoided.

Think about times when you have jumped to conclusions about other people's actions. Then say the following prayer:

God of love and wisdom, a misunderstanding almost led to war among the Israelites. Help me to avoid jumping to conclusions about the actions of others. Help me to listen and understand their intentions, as Phinehas did. And let me be gracious in recognizing when I am wrong. Amen.

▸ Jos 22, 13–20

---

land of Gilead an embassy consisting of Phinehas, son of Eleazar the priest, [14] and ten princes, one from every tribe of Israel, each one being both prince and military leader of his ancestral house. [15] When these came to the Reubenites, the Gadites, and the half-tribe of Manasseh in the land of Gilead, they said to them: [16*] "The whole community of the LORD sends this message: What act of treachery is this you have committed against the God of Israel? You have seceded from the LORD this

day, and rebelled against him by building an altar of your own! [17*] For the sin of Peor, a plague came upon the community of the LORD. [18] We are still not free of that; must you now add to it? You are rebelling against the LORD today and by tomorrow he will be angry with the whole community of Israel! [19*†] If you consider the land you now possess unclean, cross over to the land the LORD possesses, where the Dwelling of the LORD stands, and share that with us. But do not rebel against the LORD, nor involve us in rebellion, by building an altar of your own in addition to the altar of the LORD, our God. [20*†] When Achan, son of Zerah, violated the ban, did not wrath fall upon the entire community of Israel? Though he was but a single man, he did not perish alone for his guilt!"

Reply of the Eastern Tribes

[21] The Reubenites, the Gadites, and the half-tribe of Manasseh replied to the military leaders of the Israelites: "The LORD is the God of gods. [22†] The LORD, the God of gods, knows and Israel shall know. If now we have acted out of rebellion or treachery against the LORD, our God, [23] and if we have built an altar of our own to secede from the LORD, or to offer holocausts, grain offerings or peace offerings upon it, the LORD himself will exact the penalty. [24] We did it rather out of our anxious concern lest in the future your children should say to our children: 'What have you to do with the LORD, the God of Israel? [25] For the LORD has placed the Jordan as a boundary between you and us. You descendants of Reuben and Gad have no share in the LORD.' Thus your children would prevent ours from revering the LORD. [26] So we decided to guard our interests by building this altar of our own: not for holocausts or for sacrifices, [27*] but as evidence for you on behalf of ourselves and our descendants, that we have the right to worship the LORD in his presence with our holocausts, sacrifices, and peace offerings. Now in the future your children cannot say to our children, 'You have no share in the LORD.' [28†] Our thought was, that if in the future they should speak thus to us or to our descendants, we could answer: 'Look at the model of the altar of the LORD which our fathers made, not for holocausts or for sacrifices, but to witness between you and us.' [29] Far be it from us to rebel against the LORD or to

---

†
22, 19: *Unclean:* not sanctified by the Dwelling of the Lord.

22, 20: *Achan . . . did not perish alone:* his guilt caused the failure of the first attack on Ai (Jos 7, 4–23); this fact is adduced as an argument for the solidarity and mutual responsibility of all the Israelites.

22, 22: *The LORD, the God of gods:* the Hebrew, which cannot be adequately rendered in English here, adds to the divine name Yahweh ("the LORD") two synonymous words for "God," *el* and *elohim.* The repetition of these three sacred words adds force to the protestations of fidelity and innocence.

22, 28: *To witness:* far from being destined to form a rival sanctuary, the model of the altar was intended by the eastern tribes solely as a means of teaching their children to be faithful to the one true sanctuary beyond the Jordan.

22, 16: Lv 17, 8f.
22, 17: Nm 25, 3f; Dt 4, 3.
22, 19: Jos 18, 1.
22, 20: Jos 7, 1.5.
22, 27: Dt 12, 5f.17f.

secede now from the LORD by building an altar for holocaust, grain offering, or sacrifice in addition to the altar of the LORD, our God, which stands before his Dwelling."

30 When Phinehas the priest and the princes of the community, the military leaders of the Israelites, heard what the Reubenites, the Gadites and the Manassehites had to say, they were satisfied. 31 Phinehas, son of Eleazar the priest, said to the Reubenites, the Gadites and the Manassehites, "Now we know that the LORD is with us. Since you have not committed this act of treachery against the LORD, you have kept the Israelites free from punishment by the LORD."

32 Phinehas, son of Eleazar the priest, and the princes returned from the Reubenites and the Gadites in the land of Gilead to the Israelites in the land of Canaan, and reported the matter to them. 33 The report satisfied the Israelites, who blessed God and decided against declaring war on the Reubenites and Gadites or ravaging the land they occupied.

34† The Reubenites and the Gadites gave the altar its name as a witness among them that the LORD is God.

Joshua's Final Plea

23 1* Many years later, after the LORD had given the Israelites rest from all their enemies round about them, and when Joshua was old and advanced in years, 2 he summoned all Israel (including their elders, leaders, judges and officers) and said to them: "I am old and advanced in years. 3 You have seen all that the LORD, your God, has done for you against all these nations; for it has been the LORD, your God, himself who fought for you. 4* Bear in mind that I have apportioned among your tribes as their heritage the nations that survive [as well as those I destroyed] between the Jordan and the Great Sea in the west. 5 The LORD, your God, will drive them out and dislodge them at your approach, so that you will take possession of their land as the LORD, your God, promised you. 6* Therefore strive hard to observe and carry out all that is written in the book of the law of Moses, not straying from it in any way, 7* or mingling with these nations while they survive among you. You must not invoke their gods, or swear by them, or serve them, or worship them, 8 but you must remain loyal to the LORD, your God, as you have been

to this day. 9 At your approach the LORD has driven out large and strong nations, and to this day no one has withstood you. 10* One of you puts to flight a thousand, because it is the LORD, your God, himself who fights for you, as he promised you. 11 Take great care, however, to love the LORD, your God. 12* For if you ever abandon him and ally yourselves with the remnant of these nations while they survive among you, by intermarrying and intermingling with them, 13 know for certain that the LORD, your God, will no longer drive these nations out of your way. Instead they will be a snare and a trap for you, a scourge for your sides and thorns for your eyes, until you perish from this good land which the LORD, your God, has given you.

14† "Today, as you see, I am going the way of all men. So now acknowledge with your whole heart and soul that not one of all the promises the LORD, your God, made to you has remained unfulfilled. Every promise has been fulfilled for you, with not one single exception. 15*† But just as every promise the LORD, your God, made to you has been fulfilled for you, so will he fulfill every threat, even so far as to exterminate you from this good land which the LORD, your God, has given you. 16 If you transgress the covenant of the LORD, your God, which he enjoined on you, serve other gods and worship them, the anger of the LORD will flare up against you and you will quickly perish from the good land which he has given you."

Reminder of the Divine Goodness

24 1 Joshua gathered together all the tribes of Israel at Shechem, summoning their elders, their leaders, their judges and their officers. When they stood in ranks before God, 2*† Joshua addressed all the people: "Thus says the LORD, the God of Israel: In times past your fathers, down to Terah, father of Abraham and Nahor, dwelt beyond the River and served other gods. 3* But I brought your father Abraham from the region beyond the River and led him through the entire land of Canaan. I made his descendants numerous, and gave him Isaac. 4* To Isaac I gave Jacob and Esau. To Esau I assigned the mountain region of Seir in which to settle, while Jacob and his children went down to Egypt.

5* "Then I sent Moses and Aaron, and smote Egypt with the prodigies which I wrought in her midst. 6* Afterward I led you out of Egypt, and

---

22, 34: The name of this altar was the Hebrew word for "witness," c ed.

23, 14: *Going the way of all men:* drawing near to death, the inevitable goal of all; cf 1 Kgs 2, 1f.

23, 15: *Every threat:* mentioned especially in Dt 28, 15–68.

24, 2: *Beyond the River:* east of the Euphrates; cf Gn 11, 28–31.

23, 1: Jos 13, 1.
23, 4: Jos 13, 2–7; 14, 2; 18, 10; Ps 78, 55.
23, 6: Jos 1, 7.
23, 7: Dt 7, 2ff.
23, 10: Ex 14, 14; Lv 26, 8; Dt 3, 22.
23, 12: Ex 34, 16; Dt 7, 3.
23, 15: Lv 26, 14–39; Dt 28, 15–68.
24, 2: Gn 11, 26. 31; 31, 53.
24, 3: Gn 12, 1; Acts 7, 2–4.
24, 4: Gn 25, 24ff; 36, 8; 46, 1.6; Acts 7, 15.
24, 5: Ex 3, 10; 7, 14—12, 30.
24, 6: Ex 12, 37.51; 14, 9.

LIVING THE COVENANT TODAY!

Some people think the Israelites were completely unified and without differences, but nothing could be further from the truth. Joshua 24, 1 tells how Joshua summoned the leaders of the twelve tribes to present themselves before God. In this gathering, they embraced their common faith in God and renewed the Covenant of Sinai, setting aside their differences and political struggles.

The twelve tribes were not unlike schools and neighborhoods in many parts of this country where young people gather in clubs, cliques, and even gangs, oftentimes dividing themselves by ethnic group or social class. Such division frequently leads to turf issues, conflict, and even violence.

Imagine if all the people in your school and neighborhood could come together, as the tribes did in Joshua's time, and embrace a common identity before God. Imagine the unity and strength you would have to help one another face life's challenges!

■ **What can you do to foster this type of vision in your school and neighborhood? With whom can you start to share this vision so that it becomes a reality?**

■ **Pray for the courage and ability you need to be God's instrument of unity, love, and peace.**

▶ Jos 24, 1–28

---

when you reached the sea, the Egyptians pursued your fathers to the Red Sea with chariots and horsemen. 7* Because they cried out to the LORD, he put darkness between your people and the Egyptians, upon whom he brought the sea so that it engulfed them. After you witnessed what I did to Egypt, and dwelt a long time in the desert, 8* I brought you into the land of the Amorites who lived east of the Jordan. They fought against you, but I delivered them into your power. You took possession of their land, and I destroyed them [the two kings of the Amorites] before you. 9* Then Balak, son of Zippor, king of Moab, prepared to war against Israel. He summoned Balaam, son of Beor, to curse you; 10* but I would not listen to Balaam. On the contrary, he had to bless you, and I saved you from him. 11* Once you crossed the Jordan and came to Jericho, the men of Jericho fought against you, but I delivered them also into your power. 12* † And I sent the hornets ahead of you which drove them [the Amorites, Perizzites, Canaanites, Hittites, Girgashites, Hivites and Jebusites] out of your way; it was not your sword or your bow.

13* "I gave you a land which you had not tilled and cities which you had not built, to dwell in; you have eaten of vineyards and olive groves which you did not plant.

14* "Now, therefore, fear the LORD and serve him completely and sincerely. Cast out the gods your fathers served beyond the River and in Egypt, and serve the LORD. 15* † If it does not please you to serve the LORD, decide today whom you will serve, the gods your fathers served beyond the River or the gods of the Amorites in whose country you are dwelling. As for me and my household, we will serve the LORD."

Renewal of the Covenant

16 But the people answered, "Far be it from us to forsake the LORD for the service of other gods. 17 For it was the LORD, our God, who brought us and our fathers up out of the land of Egypt, out of a state of slavery. He performed those great miracles before our very eyes and protected us along our entire journey and among all the peoples through whom we passed. 18 At our approach the LORD drove out [all the peoples, including] the Amorites who dwelt in the land. Therefore we also will serve the LORD, for he is our God."

19* † Joshua in turn said to the people, "You may not be able to serve the LORD, for he is a holy God;

24, 12: *The hornets:* see note on Ex 23, 28.
24, 15: *The gods your fathers served:* Abraham's ancestors were polytheists.
24, 19: *You may not be able:* fidelity to God's service is not easy, and therefore those who take such solemn obligations on themselves must be ever vigilant against human weakness.

24, 7: Ex 14, 10.20.27f.
24, 8: Nm 21, 21–35.
24, 9: Nm 22, 2–5.
24, 10: Nm 23, 1—24, 25.
24, 11: Jos 3, 14; 6, 1.
24, 12: Jos 11, 20; Ex 23, 28; Dt 7, 20.
24, 13: Dt 6, 10f.
24, 14: Dt 10, 12; 1 Sm 7, 3; 12, 24; Tb 14, 9.
24, 15: Dt 30, 15–19.
24, 19: Ex 20, 5; 23, 21; 34, 14; Lv 19, 2.

Fear the LORD
and serve him
completely
and
sincerely

24, 14

ised Joshua, "We will serve the LORD, our God, and obey his voice."

25 So Joshua made a covenant with the people that day and made statutes and ordinances for them at Shechem, 26* which he recorded in the book of the law of God. Then he took a large stone and set it up there under the oak that was in the sanctuary of the LORD. 27* And Joshua said to all the people, "This stone shall be our witness, for it has heard all the words which the LORD spoke to us. It shall be a witness against you, should you wish to deny your God." 28* Then Joshua dismissed the people, each to his own heritage.

Death of Joshua

29* After these events, Joshua, son of Nun, servant of the LORD, died at the age of a hundred and ten. 30* He was buried within the limits of his heritage at Timnath-serah in the mountain region of Ephraim north of Mount Gaash. 31 Israel served the LORD during the entire lifetime of Joshua and that of the elders who outlived Joshua and knew all that the LORD had done for Israel. 32*† The bones of Joseph, which the Israelites had brought up from Egypt, were buried in Shechem in the plot of ground Jacob had bought from the sons of Hamor, father of Shechem, for a hundred pieces of money. This was a heritage of the descendants of Joseph. 33* When Eleazar, son of Aaron, also died, he was buried on the hill which had been given to his son Phinehas in the mountain region of Ephraim.

he is a jealous God who will not forgive your transgressions or your sins. 20 If, after the good he has done for you, you forsake the LORD and serve strange gods, he will do evil to you and destroy you."

21 But the people answered Joshua, "We will still serve the LORD." 22 Joshua therefore said to the people, "You are your own witnesses that you have chosen to serve the LORD." They replied, "We are, indeed!" 23 "Now, therefore, put away the strange gods that are among you and turn your hearts to the LORD, the God of Israel." 24 Then the people prom-

---

†
24, 32: *The bones of Joseph:* the mummified body of Joseph (Gn 50, 25f), which the Israelites took with them as they left Egypt (Ex 13, 19), was fittingly buried at the ancient city of Shechem, near the border between the two Josephite tribes of Ephraim and Manasseh.

24, 26: Gn 28, 18; 31, 45; Jgs 9, 6.
24, 27: Gn 31, 48.52; Dt 31, 19.21.26.
24, 28: Jgs 2, 6.
24, 29ff: Jgs 2, 7ff.
24, 30: Jos 19, 50; Jgs 2, 9.
24, 32: Gn 33, 19; 50, 24; Ex 13, 19.
24, 33: Jos 22, 13.

"**M**om and Dad treat me like such a child." "I can't get a job without experience, but how can I get experience if I can't get a job?" The teenage years often feel like an in-between time, when young people pass from being children to becoming adults who must take responsibility for their own life. This time of transition holds many challenges. In some ways, the Book of Judges is about Israel's "teenage years." It tells about the difficulties faced by God's people in an in-between time: the two hundred years between the conquest of Canaan under Joshua and the establishment of the kingdom of Israel under Saul.

At a Glance

I. Palestine after the Death of Joshua (1, 1—3, 6).

II. Stories of the Judges (3, 7—16, 31).

III. The Tribes of Dan and Benjamin in the Days of the Judges (17, 1—21, 25).

In-depth

In the Book of Judges, the twelve tribes of Israel face two especially difficult challenges: how to live peacefully with one another and how to withstand the attacks of foreign armies. God answers the Israelites' prayers for help by raising up extraordinary men and women to lead the tribes. These famous leaders—Gideon, Deborah, Samson, and nine others—are called judges, but they aren't judges in courtrooms wearing black robes. They are local elders and military heroes who are chosen by God's spirit to lead the Israelites in times of crisis.

The pattern that we observed in the Book of Joshua also appears in the Book of Judges: when the people obey God's laws, they thrive; when they are disobedient, they suffer and need to be rescued by a leader raised up by God's spirit. The stories in Judges probably began as regional tales about local heroes. As they were collected and edited by the author of Judges, they became national stories influenced by the message of Deuteronomy: faithfulness to God is the only road to personal and tribal security.

Judges reminds us that the challenges of life, especially in the in-between times, are best handled through prayer and reliance on God. God can be trusted to lead us through all difficulties, both great and small.

Quick Facts

Period Covered

from 1220 to 1000 B.C.

Author

The book was put into final form by an unknown person from the Deuteronomic school, sometime during the Israelite monarchy.

Themes

God raises up mighty heroes to protect the people. God works even through flawed heroes.

Judges

Chap. 5

I: Palestine after the Death of Joshua

Pagan Survivors in Palestine

1 [1]*† After the death of Joshua the Israelites consulted the LORD, asking, "Who shall be first among us to attack the Canaanites and to do battle with them?" [2] The LORD answered, "Judah shall attack: I have delivered the land into his power." [3] Judah then said to his brother Simeon, "Come up with me into the territory allotted to me, and let us engage the Canaanites in battle. I will likewise accompany you into the territory allotted to you." So Simeon went with him.

[4] When the forces of Judah attacked, the LORD delivered the Canaanites and Perizzites into their power, and they slew ten thousand of them in Bezek. [5] It was in Bezek that they came upon Adonibezek and fought against him. When they defeated the Canaanites and Perizzites, [6] Adonibezek fled. They set out in pursuit, and when they caught him, cut off his thumbs and his big toes. [7] At this Adonibezek said, "Seventy kings, with their thumbs and big toes cut off, used to pick up scraps under my table. As I have done, so has God repaid me."

He was brought to Jerusalem, and there he died. [8] [The Judahites fought against Jerusalem and captured it, putting it to the sword; then they destroyed the city by fire.]

[9]* Afterward the Judahites went down to fight against the Canaanites who lived in the mountain region, in the Negeb, and in the foothills, [10]* Judah also marched against the Canaanites who dwelt in Hebron, which was formerly called Kiriath-arba, and defeated Sheshai, Ahiman and Talmai.* [11] From there they marched against the inhabitants of Debir, which was formerly called Kiriath-sepher. [12] And Caleb said, "I will give my daughter Achsah in marriage to the one who attacks Kiriath-sepher and captures it." [13]* Othniel, son of Caleb's younger brother Kenaz, captured it; so Caleb gave him his daughter Achsah in marriage. [14] On the day of her marriage to Othniel she induced him to ask her father for some land. Then, as she alighted from the ass, Caleb asked her, "What is troubling you?" [15] "Give me an additional gift," she answered. "Since you have assigned land in the Negeb to me, give me also pools of water." So Caleb gave her the upper and the lower pool. [16]*† The descendants of

---

† **1, 1–36:** This chapter summarizes events most of which occurred shortly after the death of Joshua. Perhaps because they were planned and inaugurated by him, they are also attributed to him in the last half of the preceding book (Jos 14–22).
1, 16: *Moses' father-in-law:* Reuel; cf Nm 10, 29–32 and note. *City of palms:* Jericho (cf Dt 34, 3), or a town in the Negeb.

1, 1: Jgs 20, 18; Nm 27, 21.
1, 9: Jos 10, 40; 11, 16; 12, 8.
1, 10: Jos 15, 13–19.
1, 10: Nm 13, 22; Jos 14, 15.
1, 13: Jgs 3, 9.
1, 16: Jgs 4, 11; Nm 10, 29–32.

Water in the Desert

Caleb's daughter, Achsah, asks for Gulloth-mayim (Jgs 1, 15) as her wedding present. Gulloth-mayim means "basins of water," and presumably, she was asking for a place with springs of fresh water. Achsah's new home will be in the desert, and she knows that her family will need water. She's not afraid to ask for what she needs.

In your prayer, reflect or journal on the following questions:

- What parts of your life are like a barren desert, that is, dry and lifeless?
- What could act as a spring for these parts of your life, bringing new life to them? Be bold in asking God to bring that new life.

▶ Jgs 1, 14–15

the Kenite, Moses' father-in-law, came up with the Judahites from the city of palms to the desert at Arad [which is in the Negeb]. But they later left and settled among the Amalekites.

17* Judah then went with his brother Simeon, and they defeated the Canaanites who dwelt in Zephath. After having doomed the city to destruction, they renamed it Hormah. 18* Judah, however, did not occupy Gaza with its territory, Ashkelon with its territory, or Ekron with its territory. 19* Since the LORD was with Judah, he gained possession of the mountain region. Yet he could not dislodge those who lived on the plain, because they had iron chariots. 20* As Moses had commanded, Hebron was given to Caleb, who then drove from it the three sons of Anak.

21*† The Benjaminites did not dislodge the Jebusites who dwelt in Jerusalem, with the result that the Jebusites live in Jerusalem beside the Benjaminites to the present day.

22 The house of Joseph, too, marched up against Bethel, and the LORD was with them. 23* The house of Joseph had a reconnaissance made of Bethel,

which formerly was called Luz. 24 The scouts saw a man coming out of the city and said to him, "Show us a way into the city, and we will spare you." 25 He showed them a way into the city, which they then put to the sword; but they let the man and his whole clan go free. 26 He then went to the land of the Hittites, where he built a city and called it Luz, as it is still called.

27* Manasseh did not take possession of Beth-shean with its towns or of Taanach with its towns. Neither did he dislodge the inhabitants of Dor and its towns, those of Ibleam and its towns, or those of Megiddo and its towns. The Canaanites kept their hold in this district. 28 When the Israelites grew stronger, they impressed the Canaanites as laborers, but did not drive them out. 29* Similarly, the Ephraimites did not drive out the Canaanites living in Gezer, and so the Canaanites live in Gezer in their midst.

30 Zebulun did not dislodge the inhabitants of Kitron or those of Nahalol; the Canaanites live among them, but have become forced laborers.

31* Nor did Asher drive out the inhabitants of Acco or those of Sidon, or take possession of Mahaleb, Achzib, Helbah, Aphik or Rehob. 32 The Asherites live among the Canaanite natives of the land, whom they have not dislodged.

33* Naphtali did not drive out the inhabitants of Beth-shemesh or those of Beth-anath, and so they live among the Canaanite natives of the land. However, the inhabitants of Beth-shemesh and Beth-anath have become forced laborers for them.

34* The Amorites hemmed in the Danites in the mountain region, not permitting them to go down into the plain. 35 The Amorites had a firm hold in Harheres, Aijalon and Shaalbim, but as the house of Joseph gained the upper hand, they were impressed as laborers.

36 The territory of the Amorites extended from the Akrabbim pass to Sela and beyond.

Infidelities of the Israelites

2 1* An angel of the LORD went up from Gilgal to Bochim and said, "It was I who brought you up from Egypt and led you into the land which I promised on oath to your fathers. I said that I would never break my covenant with you, 2* but that you were not to make a pact with the inhabitants of this land, and you were to pull down their altars. Yet you have not obeyed me. What did you

---

1, 21: According to Jos 18, 16, Jerusalem was assigned to the tribe of Benjamin. But it was not actually taken from the Jebusites until David captured it (2 Sm 5, 6–9) and made it his capital, outside the tribal organization.

1, 17: Nm 21, 3.
1, 18: Jos 11, 22.
1, 19: Jos 17, 16ff.
1, 20: Jos 14, 9.13; 15, 14.
1, 21: Jos 15, 63.
1, 23: Gn 28, 19; 35, 6; 48, 3; Jos 18, 13.
1, 27f: Jos 17, 11ff.
1, 29: Jos 16, 10.
1, 31f: Jos 19, 24–31.
1, 33: Jos 19, 32–39.
1, 34: Jos 19, 47f.
2, 1ff: Jgs 6, 8ff.
2, 2: Ex 34, 12f.15; Dt 7, 2.5; 21, 2f.

mean by this? ³* For now I tell you, I will not clear them out of your way; they shall oppose you and their gods shall become a snare for you."

⁴ When the angel of the LORD had made these threats to all the Israelites, the people wept aloud; ⁵† and so that place came to be called Bochim. They offered sacrifice there to the LORD.

⁶* When Joshua dismissed the people, each Israelite went to take possession of his own hereditary land. ⁷ The people served the LORD during the entire lifetime of Joshua, and of those elders who outlived Joshua and who had seen all the great work which the LORD had done for Israel. ⁸ Joshua, son of Nun, the servant of the LORD, was a hundred and ten years old when he died; ⁹* and they buried him within the borders of his heritage at Timnathheres in the mountain region of Ephraim north of Mount Gaash.

¹⁰ But once the rest of that generation were gathered to their fathers, and a later generation arose that did not know the LORD, or what he had done for Israel, ¹¹*† the Israelites offended the LORD by serving the Baals. ¹² Abandoning the LORD, the God of their fathers, who had led them out of the land of Egypt, they followed the other gods of the various nations around them, and by their worship of these gods provoked the LORD.

¹³† Because they had thus abandoned him and served Baal and the Ashtaroth, ¹⁴ the anger of the LORD flared up against Israel, and he delivered them over to plunderers who despoiled them. He allowed them to fall into the power of their enemies round about whom they were no longer able to withstand. ¹⁵* Whatever they undertook, the LORD turned into disaster for them, as in his warning he had sworn he would do, till they were in great distress. ¹⁶ Even when the LORD raised up judges to deliver them from the power of their despoilers, ¹⁷ they did not listen to their judges, but abandoned themselves to the worship of other gods. They were quick to stray from the way their fathers had taken, and did not follow their example of obedience to the commandments of the LORD. ¹⁸ Whenever the LORD raised up judges for them, he would be with the judge and save them from the power of their enemies as long as the judge lived; it was thus the LORD took pity on their distressful cries of affliction under their oppressors. ¹⁹* But when the judge died, they would relapse and do worse than their fathers, following other gods in service and worship, relinquishing none of their evil practices or stubborn conduct.

²⁰* In his anger toward Israel the LORD said, "Inasmuch as this nation has violated my covenant which I enjoined on their fathers, and has disobeyed me, ²¹ I for my part will not clear away for them any more of the nations which Joshua left when he died." ²² Through these nations the Israelites were to be made to prove whether or not

LIVE IT!

Obeying Authority

Have you ever decided to disobey your parents, your teachers, or maybe a boss at work? What were the consequences? Disobedience to legitimate authority tends to bring about bad consequences. Just read Jgs 2, 10–15. The people turned from God, and their separation from God led to defeat at the hands of their enemies.
God places parents, teachers, and other authority figures in our life to protect and support us. Their love and caring are an extension of God's love and caring. From their vantage point, they often see a bigger picture than we do. When we disobey their reasonable requests, we build walls between them and us, preventing God's love from reaching us. On the other hand, obedience leads to more trust, responsibility, and freedom. Of course, as Jesus himself showed us, no one is obligated to obey requests or directions that are abusive, demeaning, or immoral.
So, the next time you are having a problem with a person in authority, ask yourself, "Might obedience in this situation somehow bring me closer to God?"

▶ Jgs 2, 10–15

†

2, 5: *Bochim:* the Hebrew word for "weepers."
2, 11: *Baals:* the chief god of the Canaanites and the Phoenicians was called "Baal," a word meaning "lord." He was honored by various titles, hence the plural form here, equivalent to "the pagan gods."
2, 13: *Ashtaroth:* the Canaanite Phoenician goddess of love and

fertility was Astarte. The plural form used here refers to her various titles and images and is equivalent to "goddesses."

2, 3: Nm 33, 55; Jos 23, 13.
2, 6–9: Jos 24, 28–31.
2, 9: Jos 19, 50.
2, 11.14: Jgs 3, 7f; 4, 1f; 6, 1;

10, 6f; 13, 1.
2, 15: Dt 28, 15–68.
2, 19: Jgs 3, 12; 4, 1; 6, 1; 8, 33.
2, 20f: Jos 23, 16.

they would keep to the way of the LORD and continue in it as their fathers had done; 23 therefore the LORD allowed them to remain instead of expelling them immediately, or delivering them into the power of Israel.

3 1 The following are the nations which the LORD allowed to remain, so that through them he might try all those Israelites who had no experience of the battles with Canaan 2 [just to instruct, by training them in battle, those generations only of the Israelites who would not have had that previous experience]: 3*† the five lords of the Philistines; and all the Canaanites, the Sidonians, and the Hivites who dwell in the mountain region of Lebanon between Baal-hermon and the entrance to Hamath. 4 These served to put Israel to the test, to determine whether they would obey the commandments the LORD had enjoined on their fathers through Moses. 5 Besides, the Israelites were living among the Canaanites, Hittites, Amorites, Perizzites, Hivites and Jebusites. 6 In fact, they took their daughters in marriage, and gave their own daughters to their sons in marriage, and served their gods.

II: Stories of the Judges

Othniel

7*† Because the Israelites had offended the LORD by forgetting the LORD, their God, and serving the Baals and the Asherahs, 8 the anger of the LORD flared up against them, and he allowed them to fall into the power of Cushan-rishathaim, king of Aram Naharaim, whom they served for eight years. 9 But when the Israelites cried out to the LORD, he raised up for them a savior, Othniel, son of Caleb's younger brother Kenaz, who rescued them. 10* The spirit of the LORD came upon him, and he judged Israel. When he went out to war, the LORD delivered Cushan-rishathaim, king of Aram, into his power, so that he made him subject. 11* The land then was at rest for forty years, until Othniel, son of Kenaz, died.

Ehud

12 Again the Israelites offended the LORD, who because of this offense strengthened Eglon, king of Moab, against Israel. 13 In alliance with the Ammonites and Amalekites, he attacked and defeated Israel, taking possession of the city of palms. 14 The Israelites then served Eglon, king of Moab, for eighteen years.

15 But when the Israelites cried out to the LORD, he raised up for them a savior, the Benjaminite Ehud, son of Gera, who was left-handed. It was by him that the Israelites sent their tribute to Eglon, king of Moab. 16 Ehud made himself a two-edged dagger a foot long, and wore it under his clothes over his right thigh. 17 He presented the tribute to Eglon, king of Moab, who was very fat, 18 and after the presentation went off with the tribute bearers. 19 He returned, however, from where the idols are, near Gilgal, and said, "I have a private message for you, O king." And the king said, "Silence!" Then when all his attendants had left his presence, 20 and Ehud went in to him where he sat alone in his cool upper room, Ehud said, "I have a message from God for you." So the king rose from his chair, 21 and then Ehud with his left hand drew the dagger from his right thigh, and thrust it into Eglon's belly. 22 The hilt also went in after the blade, and the fat closed over the blade because he did not withdraw the dagger from his body.

23 Then Ehud went out into the hall, shutting the doors of the upper room on him and locking them. 24 When Ehud had left and the servants came, they saw that the doors of the upper room were locked, and thought, "He must be easing himself in the cool chamber." 25 They waited until they finally grew suspicious. Since he did not open the doors of the upper room, they took the key and opened them. There on the floor, dead, lay their lord!

26 During their delay Ehud made good his escape and, passing the idols, took refuge in Seirah. 27 On his arrival he sounded the horn in the mountain region of Ephraim, and the Israelites went down from the mountains with him as their leader. 28* "Follow me," he said to them, "for the LORD has delivered your enemies the Moabites into your power." So they followed him down and seized the fords of the Jordan leading to Moab, permitting no one to cross. 29 On that occasion they slew about ten thousand Moabites, all of them strong and valiant men. Not a man escaped. 30 Thus was Moab brought under the power of Israel at that time; and the land had rest for eighty years.

Shamgar

31 After him there was Shamgar, son of Anath, who slew six hundred Philistines with an oxgoad. He, too, rescued Israel.

3, 3: *The Philistines:* non-Semitic invaders, who gave their name to all Palestine, although they occupied only its southwestern plains. Their confederation embraced the five leading cities of Gaza, Ashkelon, Ashdod, Gath and Ekron.

3, 7: *Asherahs:* elsewhere rendered "sacred poles." See note on Ex 34, 13 and on Dt 7, 5. Here the word seems to mean "goddesses."

3, 3: Jos 13, 2–6.
3, 7: Jgs 2, 11ff.
3, 10: Jgs 6, 34; 11, 29; 13,
25; 14, 6.19; 15, 14.
3, 11: Jgs 5, 31; 8, 28.
3, 28: Jgs 4, 7.14; 7, 9.15.

Deborah and Barak

4 ¹ After Ehud's death, however, the Israelites again offended the LORD. ²* So the LORD allowed them to fall into the power of the Canaanite king, Jabin, who reigned in Hazor. The general of his army was Sisera, who dwelt in Harosheth-ha-goiim. ³ But the Israelites cried out to the LORD; for with his nine hundred iron chariots he sorely oppressed the Israelites for twenty years.

⁴ At this time the prophetess Deborah, wife of Lappidoth, was judging Israel. ⁵ She used to sit under Deborah's palm tree, situated between Ramah

Wartime Women

I n Judges, chapter 4, Deborah, a judge and prophet, rallies Barak and the Israelites to war, and Jael, another woman (who is not an Israelite), delivers the final blow to the enemy's commander, Sisera. In chapter 5, Deborah leads the victory celebration with an elaborate prayer-song that is probably one of the oldest texts in the Bible (see also Exodus, chapter 15).

In the Bible, women are often innocent victims of war. Usually, they do not do the fighting but are raped, killed, or widowed. Is Jael's violence the answer to this abuse? Is Jael a hero? Or is she still a victim of war, forced to make a violent choice in order to survive in a violent world? The writer of the Book of Judges gives no judgment on her actions.

When we are no longer victims, but have become people who abuse others, has the situation really improved? Or are we just doing to others what we would never want done to ourselves? In light of Jesus' teachings, these are important questions to ask. Let us pray:

God of love, please deliver us from being both victims of violence and agents of violence. Amen.

▸ Judges, chapter 4

and Bethel in the mountain region of Ephraim, and there the Israelites came up to her for judgment. ⁶* She sent and summoned Barak, son of Abinoam, from Kedesh of Naphtali. "This is what the LORD, the God of Israel, commands," she said to him; "go, march on Mount Tabor, and take with you ten thousand Naphtalites and Zebulunites. ⁷* I will lead Sisera, the general of Jabin's army, out to you at the Wadi Kishon, together with his chariots and troops, and will deliver them into your power." ⁸ But Barak answered her, "If you come with me, I will go; if you do not come with me, I will not go." ⁹ "I will certainly go with you," she replied, "but you shall not gain the glory in the expedition on which you are setting out, for the LORD will have Sisera fall into the power of a woman." So Deborah joined Barak and journeyed with him to Kedesh.

¹⁰* Barak summoned Zebulun and Naphtali to Kedesh, and ten thousand men followed him. Deborah also went up with him. ¹¹*† Now the Kenite Heber had detached himself from his own people, the descendants of Hobab, Moses' brother-in-law, and had pitched his tent by the terebinth of Zaanannim, which was near Kedesh.

¹² It was reported to Sisera that Barak, son of Abinoam, had gone up to Mount Tabor. ¹³ So Sisera assembled from Harosheth-ha-goiim at the Wadi Kishon all nine hundred of his iron chariots and all his forces. ¹⁴ Deborah then said to Barak, "Be off, for this is the day on which the LORD has delivered Sisera into your power. The LORD marches before you." So Barak went down Mount Tabor, followed by his ten thousand men. ¹⁵* And the LORD put Sisera and all his chariots and all his forces to rout before Barak. Sisera himself dismounted from his chariot and fled on foot. ¹⁶ Barak, however, pursued the chariots and the army as far as Harosheth-ha-goiim. The entire army of Sisera fell beneath the sword, not even one man surviving.

¹⁷† Sisera, in the meantime, had fled on foot to the tent of Jael, wife of the Kenite Heber, since Jabin, king of Hazor, and the family of the Kenite Heber were at peace with one another. ¹⁸ Jael went out to meet Sisera and said to him, "Come in, my lord, come in with me; do not be afraid." So he went into her tent, and she covered him with a rug. ¹⁹* He said to her, "Please give me a little water to drink. I am thirsty." But she opened a jug of milk for him to drink, and then covered him over. ²⁰ "Stand at the entrance of the tent," he said to her. "If anyone comes and asks, 'Is there someone here?' say, 'No!' "

4, 11: Most of the Kenites occupied a district in the southern part of Judah (Jgs 1, 16). A group of them, however, had detached themselves and settled in lower Galilee.

4, 17–22: It is to be noted that the sacred author merely records the fact of the murder of Sisera. We must not construe this as approval of Jael's action.

4, 2: Jos 11, 1.10; Ps 83, 10; 1 Sm 12, 9.
4, 6: Heb 11, 32.
4, 7: Jgs 5, 21; Ps 83, 10.
4, 10: Jgs 5, 18.
4, 11: Nm 10, 29.
4, 15: Ps 83, 10.
4, 19: Jgs 5, 25.

LIVE IT!

The Battle Within

Although the story of Deborah is inspiring, partly because so few women leaders are portrayed in the Bible, it is also a story of war and violence. The Book of Judges records one battle after another. It is wearying to read of so much fighting, and of rejoicing over someone's having a tent peg pounded into their head.

We need to keep our perspective here and understand that the way the Israelites viewed life at that time was simple: If they were victorious, God was with them. If they were defeated, God had been offended and had turned away from them.

What can we learn from this story? It teaches that God never turns away from us. The real victories to celebrate are the personal battles we win each day as we strive to become more faithful to God. Jesus calls us to make peace rather than war. Our greatest enemy is often within, as we strive to be the person God wants us to be, whether our name is Deborah or Joshua, Jennifer or Carlos.

What battle is going on inside you today? What choice in this battle leads to greater faithfulness to God?

▶ Judges, chapter 4

21* Instead Jael, wife of Heber, got a tent peg and took a mallet in her hand. While Sisera was sound asleep, she stealthily approached him and drove the peg through his temple down into the ground, so that he perished in death. 22 Then when Barak came in pursuit of Sisera, Jael went out to meet him and said to him, "Come, I will show you the man you seek." So he went in with her, and there lay Sisera dead, with the tent peg through his temple.

23 Thus on that day God humbled the Canaanite king, Jabin, before the Israelites; 24 their power weighed ever heavier upon him, till at length they destroyed the Canaanite king, Jabin.

Canticle of Deborah

5 1 On that day Deborah [and Barak, son of Abinoam] sang this song:

2† Of chiefs who took the lead in Israel,
　　of noble deeds by the people who bless
　　　　the LORD,
3 　Hear, O kings! Give ear, O princes!
　　I to the LORD will sing my song,
　　　my hymn to the LORD, the God of Israel.

4 　O LORD, when you went out from Seir,
　　when you marched from the land of Edom,
　The earth quaked and the heavens
　　　were shaken,

while the clouds sent down showers.
5* Mountains trembled
　　in the presence of the LORD, the One
　　　　of Sinai,
　　in the presence of the LORD, the God of
　　　　Israel.*

6* In the days of Shamgar, son of Anath,
　　in the days of slavery caravans ceased;
Those who traveled the roads
　　went by roundabout paths.
7 Gone was freedom beyond the walls
　　gone indeed from Israel.

When I, Deborah, rose,
　　when I rose, a mother in Israel,
8† New gods were their choice;
　　then the war was at their gates.
Not a shield could be seen, nor a lance,
　　among forty thousand in Israel!

9 　My heart is with the leaders of Israel,
　　nobles of the people who bless the LORD;
10 They who ride on white asses,
　　seated on saddlecloths as they go their way;
11 Sing of them to the strains of the harpers at
　　　the wells,
　　where men recount the just deeds of
　　　　the LORD,

---

† **5, 2–31:** This canticle is an excellent example of early Hebrew poetry, even though some of its verses are now obscure.

5, 8: *New gods:* pagan deities; cf Dt 32, 16–18. God punished the idolatry of the Israelites by leaving them relatively unarmed before the attacks of their enemies, who had better weapons, made of iron; cf 1 Sm 13, 19–22.

* 4, 21: Jgs 5, 26.
5, 5: Dt 33, 2; 2 Sm 22, 8;
　　Pss 18, 8; 68, 9.

5, 5: Ex 19, 16; Dt 4, 11; Ps
　　97, 5.
5, 6: Jgs 3, 31.

his just deeds that brought freedom
  to Israel.

12 Awake, awake, Deborah!
  awake, awake, strike up a song.
  Strength! arise, Barak,
  make despoilers your spoil, son
    of Abinoam.
13 Then down came the fugitives with
    the mighty,
  the people of the LORD came down for me
    as warriors.

14† From Ephraim, princes were in the valley;
  behind you was Benjamin, among
    your troops.
  From Machir came down commanders,
  from Zebulun wielders of the
    marshal's staff.

15* With Deborah were the princes of Issachar;
  Barak, too, was in the valley, his
    course unchecked.

  Among the clans of Reuben
  great were the searchings of heart.
16 Why do you stay beside your hearths
  listening to the lowing of the herds?
  Among the clans of Reuben
  great were the searchings of heart!

17 Gilead, beyond the Jordan, rests;
  why does Dan spend his time in ships?
  Asher, who dwells along the shore,
  is resting in his coves.
18* Zebulun is the people defying death;
  Naphtali, too, on the open heights!

19* The kings came and fought;
  then they fought, those kings of Canaan,
  At Taanach by the waters of Megiddo;
  no silver booty did they take.
20*†From the heavens the stars, too, fought;
  from their courses they fought against Sisera.

21* The Wadi Kishon swept them away;
  a wadi . . . , the Kishon.
22 Then the hoofs of the horses pounded,
  with the dashing, dashing of his steeds.

23† "Curse Meroz," says the LORD,
  "hurl a curse at its inhabitants!
  For they came not to my help,
  as warriors to the help of the LORD."

24* Blessed among women be Jael,
  blessed among tent-dwelling women.
25* He asked for water, she gave him milk;
  in a princely bowl she offered curds.
26 With her left hand she reached for the peg,
  with her right, for the workman's mallet.

  She hammered Sisera, crushed his head;
  she smashed, stove in his temple.
27 At her feet he sank down, fell, lay still;
  down at her feet he sank and fell;
  where he sank down, there he fell, slain.

28 From the window peered down and wailed
  the mother of Sisera, from the lattice:
  "Why is his chariot so long in coming?
  why are the hoofbeats of his
    chariots delayed?"
29 The wisest of her princesses answers her,
  and she, too, keeps answering herself:
30 "They must be dividing the spoil they took:
  there must be a damsel or two for
    each man,
  Spoils of dyed cloth as Sisera's spoil,
  an ornate shawl or two for me in the spoil."

31* May all your enemies perish thus, O LORD!
  but your friends be as the sun rising in
    its might!

And the land was at rest for forty years.

The Call of Gideon

6 [1] The Israelites offended the LORD, who there-fore delivered them into the power of Midian for seven years, [2] so that Midian held Israel subject. For fear of Midian the Israelites established the fire signals on the mountains, the caves for refuge, and the strongholds. [3]* And it used to be that when the Israelites had completed their sowing, Midian, Amalek and the Kedemites would come up, [4] en-camp opposite them, and destroy the produce of the land as far as the outskirts of Gaza, leaving no sustenance in Israel, nor sheep, oxen or asses. [5] For

---

5, 14–22: Praise for the tribes which formed the Israelite league against Sisera: Ephraim, Benjamin, Manasseh (represented by Machir), Zebulun, Issachar, and Naphtali (led by Barak), The tribes of Reuben, Gad (Gilead), Dan, and Asher are chided for their lack of co-operation. The more distant tribes of Judah and Simeon are not mentioned.

5, 20f: It would seem that nature aided the Hebrews in some way. Perhaps the torrential rains swelled the waters of Kishon, which then overwhelmed the Canaanites.

5, 23: Meroz: an unknown locality in which Hebrews probably resided, since its inhabitants are cursed for their failure to proffer aid.

5, 15: Jgs 4, 14.
5, 18: Jgs 4, 10.
5, 19: Jgs 1, 27; Jos 17, 11.
5, 20: Jgs 4, 15; Jos 10, 14.
5, 21: Jgs 4, 7.13.
5, 24: Jgs 4, 17; Jdt 13, 17;
  Lk 1, 28.42.
5, 25f: Jgs 4, 19.21.
5, 31: Ps 83, 10–19.
6, 3f: Jgs 7, 12; Dt 28, 30ff.

they would come up with their livestock, and their tents would become as numerous as locusts; and neither they nor their camels could be numbered, when they came into the land to lay it waste. 6 Thus was Israel reduced to misery by Midian, and so the Israelites cried out to the LORD.

7 When Israel cried out to the LORD because of Midian, 8* he sent a prophet to the Israelites who said to them, "The LORD, the God of Israel, says: I led you up from Egypt; I brought you out of the place of slavery. 9 I rescued you from the power of Egypt and of all your other oppressors. I drove them out before you and gave you their land. 10 And I said to you: I, the LORD, am your God; you shall not venerate the gods of the Amorites in whose land you are dwelling. But you did not obey me."

11 Then the angel of the LORD came and sat under the terebinth in Ophrah that belonged to Joash the Abiezrite. While his son Gideon was beating out wheat in the wine press to save it from the Midianites, 12 the angel of the LORD appeared to him and said, "The LORD is with you, O champion!" 13 "My LORD," Gideon said to him, "if the LORD is with us, why has all this happened to us? Where are his wondrous deeds of which our fathers told us when they said, 'Did not the LORD bring us up from Egypt?' For now the LORD has abandoned us and has delivered us into the power of Midian." 14 The LORD turned to him and said, "Go with the strength you have and save Israel from the power of Midian. It is I who send you." 15 But he answered him, "Please, my lord, how can I save Israel? My family is the meanest in Manasseh, and I am the most insignificant in my father's house." 16 "I shall be with you," the LORD said to him, "and you will cut down Midian to the last man." 17 He answered him, "If I find favor with you, give me a sign that you are speaking with me. 18 Do not depart from here, I pray you, until I come back to you and bring out my offering and set it before you." He answered, "I will await your return."

19 So Gideon went off and prepared a kid and an ephah of flour in the form of unleavened cakes. Putting the meat in a basket and the broth in a pot, he brought them out to him under the terebinth and presented them. 20* The angel of God said to him, "Take the meat and unleavened cakes and lay them on this rock; then pour out the broth." When he had done so, 21 the angel of the LORD stretched out the tip of the staff he held, and touched the meat and unleavened cakes. Thereupon a fire came up from the rock which consumed the meat and unleavened cakes, and the angel of the LORD disappeared from sight. 22* Gideon, now aware that it had been the angel of the LORD, said, "Alas, Lord, GOD, that I have seen the angel of the LORD face to face!" 23 The LORD answered him, "Be calm, do not fear. You shall not die." 24† So Gideon built there an altar to the LORD and called it Yahweh-shalom. To this day it is still in Ophrah of the Abiezrites.

25† That same night the LORD said to him, "Take the seven-year-old spare bullock and destroy your father's altar to Baal and cut down the sacred pole that is by it. 26 You shall build, instead, the proper kind of altar to the LORD, your God, on top of this stronghold. Then take the spare bullock and offer it as a holocaust on the wood from the sacred pole you have cut down." 27 So Gideon took ten of his servants and did as the LORD had commanded him. But through fear of his family and of the townspeople, he would not do it by day, but did it at night. 28 Early the next morning the townspeople found that the altar of Baal had been destroyed, the sacred pole near it cut down, and the spare bullock offered on the altar that was built. 29 They asked one another, "Who did this?" Their inquiry led them to the conclusion that Gideon, son of Joash, had done it. 30 So the townspeople said to Joash, "Bring out your son that he may die, for he has destroyed the altar of Baal and has cut down the sacred pole that was near it." 31 But Joash replied to all who were standing around him, "Do you intend to act in Baal's stead, or be his champion? If anyone acts for him, he shall be put to death by morning. If he whose altar has been destroyed is a god, let him act for himself!" 32*† So on that day Gideon was called Jerubbaal, because of the words, "Let Baal take action against him, since he destroyed his altar."

33 Then all Midian and Amalek and the Kedemites mustered and crossed over into the valley of Jezreel, where they encamped. 34 The spirit of the LORD enveloped Gideon; he blew the horn that summoned Abiezer to follow him. 35 He sent messengers, too, throughout Manasseh, which also obeyed his summons; through Asher, Zebulun and Naphtali, likewise, he sent messengers and these tribes advanced to meet the others. 36 Gideon said to God, "If indeed you are going to save Israel through me, as you promised, 37 I am putting this woolen fleece on the threshing floor. If dew comes on the fleece alone, while all the ground is dry, I shall know that you will save Israel through me, as you promised." 38 That is what took place. Early the next morning he wrung the dew from the fleece,

JGS

6, 24: *Yahweh-shalom:* Hebrew for "the LORD is peace," a reference to the LORD's words, "Be calm," literally, "Peace be to you!"

6, 25: *The sacred pole:* see note on Ex 34, 13.

6, 32: *Jerubbaal:* similar in sound to the Hebrew words meaning, "Let Baal take action."

6, 8ff: Jgs 2, 1f; 10, 11–14.
6, 20: Jgs 13, 19.
6, 22f: Gn 32, 31;

Dt 5, 24ff.
6, 32: 1 Sm 12, 11.

PRAY IT

Trusting God

The true test of love is loving without testing.

Gideon keeps testing God; he cannot bring himself to believe God's promises. Judges, chapters 6–8, gives a full picture of this hero who never quite understands what loving God is all about. Even after his victory, and his words of devotion to God, he makes a gold idol (Jgs 8, 22–28).

Most people are tempted to test God in some way: "God, I'll know you are there for me if I get this job." Fortunately, God is big enough to accept our testing. Just do not expect God to answer every request—at least not exactly the way you would like God to answer it.

How do you test God? Is your prayer more trusting than Gideon's prayer? The next time you feel anxious or afraid, use one of these Scripture passages for your prayer: Psalm 25; Psalm 27; John, chapter 14; 1 Jn 4, 7–21. Challenge yourself to trust God without testing.

▸ Jgs 6, 36–40

squeezing out of it a bowlful of water. 39 Gideon then said to God, "Do not be angry with me if I speak once more. Let me make just one more test with the fleece. Let the fleece alone be dry, but let there be dew on all the ground." 40 That night God did so; the fleece alone was dry, but there was dew on all the ground.

Defeat of Midian

7 1* Early the next morning Jerubbaal (that is, Gideon) encamped by En-harod with all his soldiers. The camp of Midian was in the valley north of Gibeath-hammoreh. 2 The LORD said to Gideon, "You have too many soldiers with you for me to deliver Midian into their power, lest Israel vaunt itself against me and say, 'My own power brought me the victory.' 3* Now proclaim to all the soldiers, 'If anyone is afraid or fearful, let him

leave.' " When Gideon put them to this test on the mountain, twenty-two thousand of the soldiers left, but ten thousand remained. 4 The LORD said to Gideon, "There are still too many soldiers. Lead them down to the water and I will test them for you there. If I tell you that a certain man is to go with you, he must go with you. But no one is to go if I tell you he must not." 5† When Gideon led the soldiers down to the water, the LORD said to him, "You shall set to one side everyone who laps up the water as a dog does with its tongue; to the other, everyone who kneels down to drink." 6 Those who lapped up the water raised to their mouths by hand numbered three hundred, but all the rest of the soldiers knelt down to drink the water. 7 The LORD said to Gideon, "By means of the three hundred who lapped up the water I will save you and will deliver Midian into your power. So let all the other soldiers go home." 8 Their horns, and such supplies as the soldiers had with them, were taken up, and Gideon ordered the rest of the Israelites to their tents, but kept the three hundred men. Now the camp of Midian was beneath him in the valley.

9 That night the LORD said to Gideon, "Go, descend on the camp, for I have delivered it up to you. 10 If you are afraid to attack, go down to the camp with your aide Purah. 11 When you hear what they are saying, you will have the courage to descend on the camp." So he went down with his aide Purah to the outposts of the camp. 12 The Midianites, Amalekites, and all the Kedemites lay in the valley, as numerous as locusts. Nor could their camels be counted, for these were as many as the sands on the seashore. 13† When Gideon arrived, one man was telling another about a dream. "I had a dream," he said, "that a round loaf of barley bread was rolling into the camp of Midian. It came to our tent and struck it, and as it fell it turned the tent upside down." 14 "This can only be the sword of the Israelite Gideon, son of Joash," the other replied. "God has delivered Midian and all the camp into his power." 15 When Gideon heard the description and explanation of the dream, he prostrated himself. Then returning to the camp of Israel, he said, "Arise, for the LORD has delivered the camp of Midian into your power."

16 He divided the three hundred men into three companies, and provided them all with horns and with empty jars and torches inside the jars. 17 "Watch me and follow my lead," he told them. "I shall go to the edge of the camp, and as I do, you

---

7, 5: The Lord desired not numerous but reliable soldiers. Those who drank from their hands were alert, standing ready to resist attack, whereas the others were careless and undependable. The cowardly soldiers had already been dismissed (v 3); cf Dt 20, 8.
7, 13: The barley loaf represents the agricultural Hebrews while

the tent refers to the nomadic Midianites. The overthrow of the tent indicates the victory of the Hebrews over their Midianite oppressors.

7, 1: Jgs 6, 32.   7, 3: Dt 20, 8.

must do also. [18] When I and those with me blow horns, you too must blow horns all around the camp and cry out, 'For the LORD and for Gideon!' " [19]† So Gideon and the hundred men who were with him came to the edge of the camp at the beginning of the middle watch, just after the posting of the guards. They blew the horns and broke the jars they were holding. [20] All three companies blew horns and broke their jars. They held the torches in their left hands, and in their right the horns they were blowing, and cried out, "A sword for the LORD and Gideon!" [21] They all remained standing in place around the camp, while the whole camp fell to running and shouting and fleeing. [22]* But the three hundred men kept blowing the horns, and throughout the camp the LORD set the sword of one against another. The army fled as far as Beth-shittah in the direction of Zarethan, near the border of Abel-meholah at Tabbath.

[23] The Israelites were called to arms from Naphtali, from Asher, and from all Manasseh, and they pursued Midian. [24] Gideon also sent messengers throughout the mountain region of Ephraim to say, "Go down to confront Midian, and seize the water courses against them as far as Beth-barah, as well as the Jordan." So all the Ephraimites were called to arms, and they seized the water courses as far as Beth-barah, and the Jordan as well. [25]* They captured the two princes of Midian, Oreb and Zeeb, killing Oreb at the rock of Oreb and Zeeb at the wine press of Zeeb. Then they pursued Midian and carried the heads of Oreb and Zeeb to Gideon beyond the Jordan.

8 [1] But the Ephraimites said to him, "What have you done to us, not calling us when you went to fight against Midian?" And they quarreled bitterly with him. [2]* "What have I accomplished now in comparison with you?" he answered them. "Is not the gleaning of Ephraim better than the vintage of Abiezer? [3] Into your power God delivered the princes of Midian, Oreb and Zeeb. What have I been able to do in comparison with you?" When he said this, their anger against him subsided.

[4] When Gideon reached the Jordan and crossed it with his three hundred men, they were exhausted and famished. [5] So he said to the men of Succoth, "Will you give my followers some loaves of bread? They are exhausted, and I am pursuing Zebah and Zalmunna, kings of Midian." [6]† But the princes of Succoth replied, "Are the hands of Zebah and Zal-

munna already in your possession, that we should give food to your army?" [7] Gideon said, "Very well; when the LORD has delivered Zebah and Zalmunna into my power, I will grind your flesh in with the thorns and briers of the desert." [8] He went up from there to Penuel and made the same request of them, but the men of Penuel answered him as had the men of Succoth. [9] So to the men of Penuel, too, he said, "When I return in triumph, I will demolish this tower."

[10] Now Zebah and Zalmunna were in Karkor with their force of about fifteen thousand men; these were all who were left of the whole Kedemite army, a hundred and twenty thousand swordsmen having fallen. [11] Gideon went up by the route of the nomads east of Nobah and Jogbehah, and attacked the camp when it felt secure. [12] Zebah and Zalmunna fled. He pursued them and took the two kings of Midian, Zebah and Zalmunna, captive, throwing the entire army into panic.

[13] Then Gideon, son of Joash, returned from battle by the pass of Heres. [14] He captured a young man of Succoth, who upon being questioned listed for him the seventy-seven princes and elders of Succoth. [15] So he went to the men of Succoth and said, "Here are Zebah and Zalmunna, with whom you taunted me, 'Are the hands of Zebah and Zalmunna already in your possession, that we should give food to your weary followers?' " [16] He took the elders of the city, and thorns and briers of the desert, and ground these men of Succoth into them. [17] He also demolished the tower of Penuel and slew the men of the city.

[18] Then he said to Zebah and Zalmunna, "Where now are the men you killed at Tabor?" "They all resembled you," they replied. "They appeared to be princes." [19] "They were my brothers, my mother's sons," he said. "As the LORD lives, if you had spared their lives, I should not kill you." [20] Then he said to his first-born, Jether, "Go, kill them." Since Jether was still a boy, he was afraid and did not draw his sword. [21] Zebah and Zalmunna said, "Come, kill us yourself, for a man's strength is like the man." So Gideon stepped forward and killed Zebah and Zalmunna. He also took the crescents that were on the necks of their camels.

[22] The Israelites then said to Gideon, "Rule over us—you, your son, and your son's son—for you rescued us from the power of Midian." [23] But Gideon answered them, "I will not rule over you, nor shall my son rule over you. The LORD must rule over you."

7, 19: *At the beginning of the middle watch:* about two hours before midnight. The ancient Hebrews divided the night into three watches of about four hours each. At the beginning of a watch the sentinels were changed.

8, 6: *Are the hands . . . in your possession . . . ?:* i.e., can you already boast of victory? The hands as well as the heads of slain

enemies were cut off and counted as trophies; cf 2 Sm 4, 8; 2 Kgs 10, 7f; and the Ugaritic Anath Epic, V AB, II 10ff.

7, 22f: Ps 83, 10; Is 9, 4.   Is 10, 26.
7, 25: Jgs 8, 3; Ps 83, 12;   8, 2: Jgs 6, 34.

JGS

24† Gideon went on to say, "I should like to make a request of you. Will each of you give me a ring from his booty?" (For being Ishmaelites, the enemy had gold rings.) 25 "We will gladly give them," they replied, and spread out a cloak into which everyone threw a ring from his booty. 26 The gold rings that he requested weighed seventeen hundred gold shekels, in addition to the crescents and pendants, the purple garments worn by the kings of Midian, and the trappings that were on the necks of their camels. 27 Gideon made an ephod out of the gold and placed it in his city Ophrah. However, all Israel paid idolatrous homage to it there, and caused the ruin of Gideon and his family.

28 Thus was Midian brought into subjection by the Israelites; no longer did they hold their heads high. And the land had rest for forty years, during the lifetime of Gideon.

Gideon's Son Abimelech

29 Then Jerubbaal, son of Joash, went back home to stay. 30* Now Gideon had seventy sons, his direct descendants, for he had many wives. 31† His concubine who lived in Shechem also bore him a son, whom he named Abimelech. 32 At a good old age Gideon, son of Joash, died and was buried in the tomb of his father Joash in Ophrah of the Abiezrites. 33† But after Gideon was dead, the Israelites again abandoned themselves to the Baals, making Baal of Berith their god 34 and forgetting the LORD, their God, who had delivered them from the power of their enemies all around them. 35 Nor were they grateful to the family of Jerubbaal [Gideon] for all the good he had done for Israel.

9 1* Abimelech, son of Jerubbaal, went to his mother's kinsmen in Shechem, and said to them and to the whole clan to which his mother's family belonged, 2 "Put this question to all the citizens of Shechem: 'Which is better for you: that seventy men, or all Jerubbaal's sons, rule over you, or that one man rule over you?' You must remember that I am your own flesh and bone." 3 When his mother's kin repeated these words to them on his behalf, all the citizens of Shechem sympathized with Abimelech, thinking, "He is our kinsman." 4 They also gave him seventy silver shekels from the temple of Baal of Berith, with which Abimelech hired shiftless men and ruffians as his followers.

5 He then went to his ancestral house in Ophrah, and slew his brothers, the seventy sons of Jerubbaal, on one stone. Only the youngest son of Jerubbaal, Jotham, escaped, for he was hidden. 6 Then all the citizens of Shechem and all Beth-millo came together and proceeded to make Abimelech king by the terebinth at the memorial pillar in Shechem.

7 When this was reported to him, Jotham went to the top of Mount Gerizim, and standing there, cried out to them in a loud voice: "Hear me, citizens of Shechem, that God may then hear you! 8* Once the trees went to anoint a king over themselves. So they said to the olive tree, 'Reign over us.' 9† But the olive tree answered them, 'Must I give up my rich oil, whereby men and gods are honored, and go to wave over the trees?' 10 Then the trees said to the fig tree, 'Come; you reign over us!' 11 But the fig tree answered them, 'Must I give up my sweetness and my good fruit, and go to wave over the trees?'

8, 24: *Ishmaelites:* here as in Gn 37, 25–28, the designation is not ethnic; it refers rather to their status as nomads.

8, 31: *Concubine:* a wife of secondary rank.

8, 33: *Baal of Berith:* one of the titles of Baal as worshiped by the Canaanites of Shechem, meaning "the lord of the covenant."

9, 9: *Whereby men and gods are honored:* oil was used in the worship both of the true God and of false gods; it was prescribed in

the worship of Yahweh (Lv 2, 1.6.15; 24, 2). It was also used to consecrate prophets, priests and kings (Ex 30, 25.30; 1 Sm 10, 1; 16, 13).

8, 30: Jgs 9, 2.5.   9, 8: Jgs 8, 22f.
9, 1: Jgs 8, 31.

12 Then the trees said to the vine, 'Come you, and reign over us.' 13† But the vine answered them, 'Must I give up my wine that cheers gods and men, and go to wave over the trees?' 14 Then all the trees said to the buckthorn, 'Come; you reign over us!' 15 But the buckthorn replied to the trees, 'If you wish to anoint me king over you in good faith, come and take refuge in my shadow. Otherwise, let fire come from the buckthorn and devour the cedars of Lebanon.'

16† "Now then, if you have acted in good faith and honorably in appointing Abimelech your king, if you have dealt well with Jerubbaal and with his family, and if you have treated him as he deserved— 17 for my father fought for you at the risk of his life when he saved you from the power of Midian; 18* but you have risen against his family this day and have killed his seventy sons upon one stone, and have made Abimelech, the son of his handmaid, king over the citizens of Shechem, because he is your kinsman— 19 if, then, you have acted in good faith and with honor toward Jerubbaal and his family this day, rejoice in Abimelech and may he in turn rejoice in you. 20 But if not, let fire come forth from Abimelech to devour the citizens of Shechem and Beth-millo, and let fire come forth from the citizens and from Beth-millo to devour Abimelech." 21 Then Jotham took flight to Beer, where he remained for fear of his brother Abimelech.

22 When Abimelech had ruled Israel for three years, 23 God put bad feelings between Abimelech and the citizens of Shechem, who rebelled against Abimelech. 24 This was to repay the violence done to the seventy sons of Jerubbaal and to avenge their blood upon their brother Abimelech, who killed them, and upon the citizens of Shechem, who encouraged him to kill his brothers. 25 The citizens of Shechem then set men in ambush for him on the mountaintops, and these robbed all who passed them on the road. But it was reported to Abimelech.

26 Now Gaal, son of Ebed, came over to Shechem with his kinsmen. The citizens of Shechem put their trust in him, 27 and went out into the fields, harvested their grapes and trod them out. Then they held a festival and went to the temple of their god, where they ate and drank and cursed Abimelech. 28* Gaal, son of Ebed, said, "Who is Abimelech? And why should we of Shechem serve him? Were not the son of Jerubbaal and his lieutenant Zebul once subject to the men of Hamor, father of Shechem? Why should we serve him? 29 Would that this people were entrusted to my command! I would depose Abimelech. I would say to Abimelech, 'Get a larger army and come out!' "

30 At the news of what Gaal, son of Ebed, had said, Zebul, the ruler of the city, was angry 31 and sent messengers to Abimelech in Arumah with the information: "Gaal, son of Ebed, and his kinsmen have come to Shechem and are stirring up the city against you. 32 Now rouse yourself; set an ambush tonight in the fields, you and the men who are with you. 33 Promptly at sunrise tomorrow morning, make a raid on the city. When he and his followers come out against you, deal with him as best you can."

34 During the night Abimelech advanced with all his soldiers and set up an ambush for Shechem in four companies. 35 Gaal, son of Ebed, went out and stood at the entrance of the city gate. When Abimelech and his soldiers rose from their place of ambush, 36 Gaal saw them and said to Zebul, "There are men coming down from the hilltops!" But Zebul answered him, "You see the shadow of the hills as men." 37 But Gaal went on to say, "Men are coming down from the region of Tabbur-Haares, and one company is coming by way of Elon-Meonenim." 38 Zebul said to him, "Where now is the boast you uttered, 'Who is Abimelech that we should serve him?' Are these not the men for whom you expressed contempt? Go out now and fight with them." 39 So Gaal went out at the head of the citizens of Shechem and fought against Abimelech. 40 But Abimelech routed him, and he fled before him; and many fell slain right up to the entrance of the gate. 41 Abimelech returned to Arumah, but Zebul drove Gaal and his kinsmen from Shechem, which they had occupied.

42 The next day, when the people were taking the field, it was reported to Abimelech, 43 who divided the men he had into three companies, and set up an ambush in the fields. He watched till he saw the people leave the city, and then rose against them for the attack. 44 Abimelech and the company with him dashed in and stood by the entrance of the city gate, while the other two companies rushed upon all who were in the field and attacked them. 45† That entire day Abimelech fought against the city, and captured it. He then killed its inhabitants and demolished the city, sowing the site with salt.

46 When they heard of this, all the citizens of Migdal-shechem went into the crypt of the temple

---

9, 13: *Cheers gods:* wine was used in the libations both of the Temple of Jerusalem and of pagan temples.
9, 16: Just as the noble trees refused the honor of royalty and were made subject to a mean plant, so did Abimelech of less noble birth than the seventy sons of Gideon now tyrannize over the people.

9, 45: *Sowing the site with salt:* a severe measure, which was a symbol of desolation, and even more, since it actually rendered the ground barren and useless.

*
9, 18: Jgs 8, 31.   9, 28: Gn 34, 2.6.

of El-berith. [47] It was reported to Abimelech that all the citizens of Migdal-shechem were gathered together. [48] So he went up Mount Zalmon with all his soldiers, took his ax in his hand, and cut down some brushwood. This he lifted to his shoulder, then said to the men with him, "Hurry! Do just as you have seen me do." [49] So all the men likewise cut down brushwood, and following Abimelech, placed it against the crypt. Then they set the crypt on fire over their heads, so that every one of the citizens of Migdal-shechem, about a thousand men and women, perished.

[50] Abimelech proceeded to Thebez, which he invested and captured. [51] Now there was a strong tower in the middle of the city, and all the men and women, in a word all the citizens of the city, fled there, shutting themselves in and going up to the roof of the tower. [52] Abimelech came up to the tower and fought against it, advancing to the very entrance of the tower to set it on fire. [53]* But a certain woman cast the upper part of a millstone down on Abimelech's head, and it fractured his skull. [54]* He immediately called his armor-bearer and said to him, "Draw your sword and dispatch me, lest they say of me that a woman killed me." So his attendant ran him through and he died. [55] When the Israelites saw that Abimelech was dead, they all left for their homes.

[56] Thus did God requite the evil Abimelech had done to his father in killing his seventy brothers. [57] God also brought all their wickedness home to the Shechemites, for the curse of Jotham, son of Jerubbaal, overtook them.

Tola

10 [1] After Abimelech there rose to save Israel the Issacharite Tola, son of Puah, son of Dodo, a resident of Shamir in the mountain region of Ephraim. [2] When he had judged Israel twenty-three years, he died and was buried in Shamir.

Jair

[3] Jair the Gileadite came after him and judged Israel twenty-two years. [4]*† He had thirty sons who rode on thirty saddle-asses and possessed thirty cities in the land of Gilead; these are called Havvoth-jair to the present day. [5] Jair died and was buried in Kamon.

Oppression by the Ammonites

[6] The Israelites again offended the LORD, serving the Baals and Ashtaroths, the gods of Aram, the gods of Sidon, the gods of Moab, the gods of the Ammonites, and the gods of the Philistines. Since they had abandoned the LORD and would not serve him, [7] the LORD became angry with Israel and allowed them to fall into the power of [the Philistines and] the Ammonites. [8] For eighteen years they afflicted and oppressed the Israelites in Bashan, and all the Israelites in the Amorite land beyond the Jordan in Gilead. [9] The Ammonites also crossed the Jordan to fight against Judah, Benjamin, and the house of Ephraim, so that Israel was in great distress.

[10] Then the Israelites cried out to the LORD, "We have sinned against you; we have forsaken our God and have served the Baals." [11]* The LORD answered the Israelites: "Did not the Egyptians, the Amorites,*

PRAY IT

The Effects of Sin

Once again, the Israelites lapse into sin and worship other gods (Jgs 10, 6). Once again, they cry out to God to save them (verse 10). Did they think their sins would have no effect on their lives?

Listen to these words from Pope John Paul II:

There is no sin, not even the most intimate and secret one, the most strictly individual one, that exclusively concerns the person committing it. With greater or lesser violence, with greater or lesser harm, every sin has repercussions on the . . . whole human family.

Have you done anything today that brought harm to you or others? Have you used your gifts and talents as God intended them to be used? Have you neglected an opportunity to share God's love with another person?

LORD, you know all things. Look on me with love and hear my prayer. Forgive my sins and give me strength to turn away from the lure of sin. Help me to be more generous in serving you and my neighbor. Help me to be a true follower of your Son, Jesus. Amen.

▶ Jgs 10, 10–16

10, 4: *Saddle-asses:* a sign of rank and wealth; cf Jgs 5, 10; 12, 14.

9, 53: 2 Sm 11, 21.   10, 11–14: Jgs 2, 1ff; 6, 8ff.
9, 54: 1 Sm 31, 4; 1 Chr 10, 4.   10, 11: Nm 21, 21–32.
10, 4: Dt 3, 14.

the Ammonites, the Philistines, ¹²* the Sidonians, the Amalekites, and the Midianites oppress you? Yet when you cried out to me, and I saved you from their grasp, ¹³ you still forsook me and worshiped other gods. Therefore I will save you no more. ¹⁴ Go and cry out to the gods you have chosen; let them save you now that you are in distress." ¹⁵ But the Israelites said to the LORD, "We have sinned. Do to us whatever you please. Only save us this day." ¹⁶ And they cast out the foreign gods from their midst and served the LORD, so that he grieved over the misery of Israel.

¹⁷* The Ammonites had gathered for war and encamped in Gilead, while the Israelites assembled and encamped in Mizpah. ¹⁸* And among the people the princes of Gilead said to one another, "The one who begins the war against the Ammonites shall be leader of all the inhabitants of Gilead."

Jephthah

11 ¹ There was a chieftain, the Gileadite Jephthah, born to Gilead of a harlot. ² Gilead's wife had also borne him sons, and on growing up the sons of the wife had driven Jephthah away, saying to him, "You shall inherit nothing in our family, for you are the son of another woman." ³ So Jephthah had fled from his brothers and had taken up residence in the land of Tob. A rabble had joined company with him, and went out with him on raids.

⁴ Some time later, the Ammonites warred on Israel. ⁵ When this occurred the elders of Gilead went to bring Jephthah from the land of Tob. ⁶ "Come," they said to Jephthah, "be our commander that we may be able to fight the Ammonites." ⁷ "Are you not the ones who hated me and drove me from my father's house?" Jephthah replied to the elders of Gilead. "Why do you come to me now, when you are in distress?" ⁸ The elders of Gilead said to Jephthah, "In any case, we have now come back to you; if you go with us to fight against the Ammonites, you shall be the leader of all of us who dwell in Gilead." ⁹ Jephthah answered the elders of Gilead, "If you bring me back to fight against the Ammonites and the LORD delivers them up to me, I shall be your leader." ¹⁰ The elders of Gilead said to Jephthah, "The LORD is witness between us that we will do as you say."

¹¹* So Jephthah went with the elders of Gilead, and the people made him their leader and commander. In Mizpah, Jephthah settled all his affairs before the LORD. ¹² Then he sent messengers to the king of the Ammonites to say, "What have you against me that you come to fight with me in my land?" ¹³* He answered the messengers of Jephthah, "Israel took away my land from the Arnon to the Jabbok and the Jordan when they came up from Egypt. Now restore the same peaceably."

¹⁴ Again Jephthah sent messengers to the king of the Ammonites, ¹⁵* saying to him, "This is what Jephthah says: Israel did not take the land of Moab or the land of the Ammonites. ¹⁶ For when they came up from Egypt, Israel went through the desert to the Red Sea and came to Kadesh. ¹⁷* Israel then sent messengers to the king of Edom saying, 'Let me pass through your land.' But the king of Edom did not give consent. They also sent to the king of Moab, but he too was unwilling. So Israel remained in Kadesh. ¹⁸* Then they went through the desert, and by-passing the land of Edom and the land of Moab, went east of the land of Moab and encamped across the Arnon. Thus they did not go through the territory of Moab, for the Arnon is the boundary of Moab. ¹⁹* Then Israel sent messengers to Sihon, king of the Amorites, king of Heshbon. Israel said to him, 'Let me pass through your land to my own place.' ²⁰ But Sihon refused to let Israel pass through his territory. On the contrary, he gathered all his soldiers, who encamped at Jahaz and fought Israel. ²¹ But the LORD, the God of Israel, delivered Sihon and all his men into the power of Israel, who defeated them and occupied all the land of the Amorites dwelling in that region, ²² the whole territory from the Arnon to the Jabbok, from the desert to the Jordan. ²³ If now the LORD, the God of Israel, has cleared the Amorites out of the way of his people, are you to dislodge Israel? ²⁴*† Should you not possess that which your god Chemosh gave you to possess, and should we not possess all that the LORD, our God, has cleared out for us? ²⁵* Again, are you any better than Balak, son of Zippor, king of Moab? Did he ever quarrel with Israel, or did he war against them ²⁶* when Israel occupied Heshbon and its villages, Aroer and its villages, and all the cities on the banks of the Arnon? Three hundred years have passed; why did you not recover them during that time? ²⁷ I have not sinned against you, but you wrong me by warring against me. Let the LORD, who is judge, decide this day between the Israelites and the Ammonites!" ²⁸ But the king of the

J
G
S

11, 24: *Chemosh:* the chief god of the Moabites—not of the Ammonites, whose leading deity was called Molech or Milcom; cf Nm 21, 29; 1 Kgs 11, 7; 2 Kgs 23, 13. The error is probably due to an ancient copyist. Jephthah argues from the viewpoint of his adversaries, the Ammonites, that they were entitled to all the land they had conquered with the aid of their god. It does not necessarily follow that Jephthah himself believed in the actual existence of this pagan god.

10, 12: Jgs 6, 3.
10, 17: Jgs 11, 29.
10, 18: Jgs 11, 5–11.
11, 11: Jgs 10, 18.
11, 13: Nm 21, 13.24ff.
11, 15: Dt 2, 9.19.
11, 17: Nm 20, 1.14.18–21; Dt 1, 46.

11, 18: Nm 21, 4.11.13; 22, 36; Dt 2, 8.
11, 19–22: Nm 21, 21–26; Dt 2, 26–36.
11, 24: Nm 21, 29; 1 Kgs 11, 7.
11, 25: Nm 22, 2; Jos 24, 9; Mi 6, 5.
11, 26: Nm 21, 25; Dt 2, 36.

Ammonites paid no heed to the message Jephthah sent him.

Jephthah's Vow

²⁹ The spirit of the LORD came upon Jephthah. He passed through Gilead and Manasseh, and through Mizpah-Gilead as well, and from there he went on to the Ammonites. ³⁰† Jephthah made a vow to the LORD. "If you deliver the Ammonites into my power," he said, ³¹ "whoever comes out of the doors of my house to meet me when I return in triumph from the Ammonites shall belong to the LORD. I shall offer him up as a holocaust."

³² Jephthah then went on to the Ammonites to fight against them, and the LORD delivered them into his power, ³³ so that he inflicted a severe defeat on them, from Aroer to the approach of Minnith (twenty cities in all) and as far as Abel-keramim. Thus were the Ammonites brought into subjection by the Israelites. ³⁴ When Jephthah returned to his house in Mizpah, it was his daughter who came forth, playing the tambourines and dancing. She was an only child: he had neither son nor daughter besides her. ³⁵* When he saw her, he rent his garments and said, "Alas, daughter, you have struck me down and brought calamity upon me. For I have made a vow to the LORD and I cannot retract." ³⁶ "Father," she replied, "you have made a vow to the LORD. Do with me as you have vowed, because the LORD has wrought vengeance for you on your enemies the Ammonites." ³⁷† Then she said to her father, "Let me have this favor. Spare me for two months, that I may go off down the mountains to mourn my virginity with my companions." ³⁸ "Go," he replied, and sent her away for two months. So she departed with her companions and mourned her virginity on the mountains. ³⁹ At the end of the two months she returned to her father, who did to her as he had vowed. She had not been intimate with man. It then became a custom in Israel ⁴⁰ for Israelite women to go yearly to mourn the daughter of Jephthah the Gileadite for four days of the year.

The Shibboleth Incident

12 ¹* The men of Ephraim gathered together and crossed over to Zaphon. They said to Jephthah, "Why do you go on to fight with the Ammonites without calling us to go with you? We will burn your house over you." ² Jephthah answered them, "My soldiers and I were engaged in a critical contest with the Ammonites. I summoned you, but you did not rescue me from their power. ³ When I saw that you would not effect a rescue, I took my life in my own hand and went on to the Ammonites, and the LORD delivered them into my power. Why, then, do you come up against me this day to fight with me?"

⁴ Then Jephthah called together all the men of Gilead and fought against Ephraim, whom they defeated; for the Ephraimites had said, "You of Gilead are Ephraimite fugitives in territory belonging to Ephraim and Manasseh." ⁵ The Gileadites took the fords of the Jordan toward Ephraim. When any of the fleeing Ephraimites said, "Let me pass," the men of Gilead would say to him, "Are you an Ephraimite?" If he answered, "No!" ⁶† they would ask him to say "Shibboleth." If he said "Sibboleth," not being able to give the proper pronunciation, they would seize him and kill him at the fords of the Jordan. Thus forty-two thousand Ephraimites fell at that time.

⁷ After having judged Israel for six years, Jephthah the Gileadite died and was buried in his city in Gilead.

Ibzan

⁸ After him Ibzan of Bethlehem judged Israel. ⁹ He had thirty sons. He also had thirty daughters married outside the family, and he brought in as wives for his sons thirty young women from outside the family. After having judged Israel for seven years, ¹⁰ Ibzan died and was buried in Bethlehem.

Elon

¹¹ After him the Zebulunite Elon judged Israel. When he had judged Israel for ten years, ¹² the Zebulunite Elon died and was buried in Elon in the land of Zebulun.

Abdon

¹³ After him the Pirathonite Abdon, son of Hillel, judged Israel. ¹⁴ He had forty sons and thirty grandsons who rode on seventy saddle-asses. After having judged Israel for eight years, ¹⁵ the Pirathonite Abdon, son of Hillel, died and was buried in Pirathon in the land of Ephraim on the mountain of the Amalekites.

11, 30–40: The text clearly implies that Jephthah vowed a human sacrifice, according to the custom of his pagan neighbors; cf 2 Kgs 3, 27. The inspired author merely records the fact; he does not approve of the action.

11, 37: *Mourn my virginity:* to bear children was woman's greatest pride; to be childless was regarded as a great misfortune. Hence Jephthah's daughter asks permission to mourn the fact that she will be put to death before she can bear children.

12, 6: *Shibboleth:* "an ear of grain." But this Hebrew word can also mean "flood water" as in Ps 69, 3.16. Apparently the Gileadites engaged the Ephraimites in conversation about the "flood water" of the Jordan. Differences in enunciating the initial sibilant of the Hebrew word betrayed different tribal affinities.

11, 35: Nm 30, 3.   **12, 1:** Jgs 8, 1.

The Birth of Samson

13 ¹* The Israelites again offended the LORD, who therefore delivered them into the power of the Philistines for forty years.

² There was a certain man from Zorah, of the clan of the Danites, whose name was Manoah. His wife was barren and had borne no children. ³* An angel of the LORD appeared to the woman and said to her, "Though you are barren and have had no children, yet you will conceive and bear a son. ⁴ Now, then, be careful to take no wine or strong drink and to eat nothing unclean. ⁵*† As for the son you will conceive and bear, no razor shall touch his head, for this boy is to be consecrated to God from the womb. It is he who will begin the deliverance of Israel from the power of the Philistines."

in the field. Since her husband Manoah was not with her, ¹⁰ the woman ran in haste and told her husband. "The man who came to me the other day has appeared to me," she said to him; ¹¹ so Manoah got up and followed his wife. When he reached the man, he said to him, "Are you the one who spoke to my wife?" "Yes," he answered. ¹² Then Manoah asked, "Now, when that which you say comes true, what are we expected to do for the boy?" ¹³ The angel of the LORD answered Manoah, "Your wife is to abstain from all the things of which I spoke to her. ¹⁴ She must not eat anything that comes from the vine, nor take wine or strong drink, nor eat anything unclean. Let her observe all that I have commanded her." ¹⁵ Then Manoah said to the angel of the LORD, "Can we persuade you to stay, while we

Introducing ▶ SAMSON

The story of Samson in Judges, chapters 13–16, is one of the most well known in the Bible. Most of us know Samson for his great feats of strength, such as killing a lion bare-handed and slaying a thousand men with the jawbone of a donkey. But did you also know that Samson's birth was announced by an angel and that the Book of Judges says "the spirit of the LORD stirred him" more often for Samson than for any other judge? Samson was a nazirite as well as a judge. Nazirites took vows to abstain from alcohol, avoid contact with dead bodies, and refrain from cutting their hair.

Like many of the other judges, Samson was a flawed hero. He broke all his nazirite vows, was controlled by lust, and used his great strength for personal revenge. Despite these flaws, God chose to use Samson. Samson paid for his sins, but ultimately, his tragic death brought victory over the Philistines. Once again, God's purposes were accomplished, even through a flawed and sinful human being.

⁶ The woman went and told her husband, "A man of God came to me; he had the appearance of an angel of God, terrible indeed. I did not ask him where he came from, nor did he tell me his name. ⁷ But he said to me, 'You will be with child and will bear a son. So take neither wine nor strong drink, and eat nothing unclean. For the boy shall be consecrated to God from the womb, until the day of his death.' " ⁸ Manoah then prayed to the LORD. "O LORD, I beseech you," he said, "may the man of God whom you sent, return to us to teach us what to do for the boy who will be born."

⁹ God heard the prayer of Manoah, and the angel of God came again to the woman as she was sitting

prepare a kid for you?" ¹⁶ But the angel of the LORD answered Manoah, "Although you press me, I will not partake of your food. But if you will, you may offer a holocaust to the LORD." Not knowing that it was the angel of the LORD, ¹⁷ Manoah said to him, "What is your name, that we may honor you when your words come true?" ¹⁸*† The angel of the LORD answered him, "Why do you ask my name, which is mysterious?" ¹⁹* Then Manoah took the kid with a cereal offering and offered it on the rock to the LORD, whose works are mysteries. While Manoah and his wife were looking on, ²⁰ as the flame rose to the sky from the altar, the angel of the LORD ascended in the flame of the altar. When Manoah and

---

13, 5: *Consecrated:* In Hebrew, *nazir.* Samson therefore was for life to be under the nazirite vow, which obliged him to abstain from drinking wine or having his hair cut; cf Nm 6, 2–8.

13, 18: *Mysterious:* incomprehensible, above human understanding. Hence, the angel speaks in the name of the Lord himself, to whom Manoah at once offers a sacrifice.

13, 1: Jgs 10, 6.   **13, 18:** Gn 32, 29.
13, 3f: 1 Sm 1, 20; Lk 1, 31.   **13, 19f:** Jgs 6, 19ff.
13, 5: Nm 6, 5.

his wife saw this, they fell prostrate to the ground; [21] but the angel of the LORD was seen no more by Manoah and his wife. Then Manoah, realizing that it was the angel of the LORD, [22]* said to his wife, "We will certainly die, for we have seen God." [23] But his wife pointed out to him, "If the LORD had meant to kill us, he would not have accepted a holocaust and cereal offering from our hands! Nor would he have let us see all this just now, or hear what we have heard."

[24]* The woman bore a son and named him Samson. The boy grew up and the LORD blessed him; [25] the spirit of the LORD first stirred him in Mahaneh-dan, which is between Zorah and Eshtaol.

Marriage of Samson

14 [1]† Samson went down to Timnah and saw there one of the Philistine women. [2] On his return he told his father and mother, "There is a Philistine woman I saw in Timnah whom I wish you to get as a wife for me." [3] His father and mother said to him, "Can you find no wife among your kinsfolk or among all our people, that you must go and take a wife from the uncircumcised Philistines?" But Samson answered his father, "Get her for me, for she pleases me." [4]* Now his father and mother did not know that this had been brought about by the LORD, who was providing an opportunity against the Philistines; for at that time they had dominion over Israel.

[5]† So Samson went down to Timnah with his father and mother. When they had come to the vineyards of Timnah, a young lion came roaring to meet him. [6] But the spirit of the LORD came upon Samson, and although he had no weapons, he tore the lion in pieces as one tears a kid. [7] However, on the journey to speak for the woman, he did not mention to his father or mother what he had done. [8] Later, when he returned to marry the woman who pleased him, he stepped aside to look at the remains of the lion and found a swarm of bees and honey in the lion's carcass. [9] So he scooped the honey out into his palms and ate it as he went along. When he came to his father and mother, he gave them some to eat, without telling them that he had scooped the honey from the lion's carcass. [10] His father also went down to the woman, and Samson gave a banquet there, since it was customary for the young men to do this. [11]† When they

met him, they brought thirty men to be his companions. [12] Samson said to them, "Let me propose a riddle to you. If within the seven days of the feast you solve it for me successfully, I will give you thirty linen tunics and thirty sets of garments. [13] But if you cannot answer it for me, you must give me thirty tunics and thirty sets of garments." "Propose your riddle," they responded; "we will listen to it." [14] So he said to them,

> "Out of the eater came forth food,
>   and out of the strong came forth sweetness."

After three days' failure to answer the riddle, [15] they said on the fourth day to Samson's wife, "Coax your husband to answer the riddle for us, or we will burn you and your family. Did you invite us here to reduce us to poverty?" [16] At Samson's side, his wife wept and said, "You must hate me; you do not love me, for you have proposed a riddle to my countrymen, but have not told me the answer." He said to her, "If I have not told it even to my father or my mother, must I tell it to you?" [17] But she wept beside him during the seven days the feast lasted. On the seventh day, since she importuned him, he told her the answer, and she explained the riddle to her countrymen.

[18] On the seventh day, before the sun set, the men of the city said to him,

> "What is sweeter than honey,
>   and what is stronger than a lion?"

He replied to them,

> "If you had not plowed with my heifer,
>   you would not have solved my riddle."

[19] The spirit of the LORD came upon him, and he went down to Ashkelon, where he killed thirty of their men and despoiled them; he gave their garments to those who had answered the riddle. Then he went off to his own family in anger, [20]* and Samson's wife was married to the one who had been best man at his wedding.

Samson Defeats the Philistines

15 [1] After some time, in the season of the wheat harvest, Samson visited his wife,

---

14, 1–3: Marriages were arranged by the parents of the bridegroom as well as of the bride; cf Gn 24, 2–8; 34, 3–6. The Mosaic law specified only seven pagan nations, not including the Philistines, in the prohibition against mixed marriages; cf Dt 7, 1–4. But national and religious sentiment was against any marriage with a non-Israelite; cf Gn 28, 1f; 1 Kgs 11, 1–10.

14, 5ff: Although Samson was accompanied by his parents on the journey to Timnah, v 7 implies that he was not near them when he tore the lion in pieces.

14, 11: *Companions:* known at a later period as "the friends of the bridegroom" (1 Mc 9, 39; Mk 2, 19), the best man and his fellows. Here they are Philistines (v 16), appointed by the family of the bride, who would also have several bridesmaids; cf Mt 25, 1–13.

13, 22: 21f; Jgs 6, 22f.	14, 4: Jgs 15, 11.
13, 24: Heb 11, 32.	14, 20: Jgs 15, 2.6.

bringing a kid. But when he said, "Let me be with my wife in private," her father would not let him enter, ² saying, "I thought it certain you wished to repudiate her; so I gave her to your best man. Her younger sister is more beautiful than she; you may have her instead." ³ Samson said to them, "This time the Philistines cannot blame me if I harm them." ⁴ So Samson left and caught three hundred foxes. Turning them tail to tail, he tied between each pair of tails one of the torches he had at hand. ⁵ He then kindled the torches and set the foxes loose in the standing grain of the Philistines, thus burning both the shocks and the standing grain, and the vineyards and olive orchards as well.

⁶* When the Philistines asked who had done this, they were told, "Samson, the son-in-law of the Timnite, because his wife was taken and given to his best man." So the Philistines went up and destroyed her and her family by fire. ⁷ Samson said to them, "If this is how you act, I will not stop until I have taken revenge on you." ⁸ And with repeated blows, he inflicted a great slaughter on them. Then he went down and remained in a cavern of the cliff of Etam.

⁹ The Philistines went up and, from a camp in Judah, deployed against Lehi. ¹⁰ When the men of Judah asked, "Why have you come up against us?" they answered, "To take Samson prisoner; to do to him as he has done to us." ¹¹ Three thousand men of Judah went down to the cavern in the cliff of Etam and said to Samson, "Do you not know that the Philistines are our rulers? Why, then, have you done this to us?" He answered them, "As they have done to me, so have I done to them." ¹² They said to him, "We have come to take you prisoner, to deliver you over to the Philistines." Samson said to them, "Swear to me that you will not kill me yourselves." ¹³* "No," they replied, "we will certainly not kill you but will only bind you and deliver you over to them." So they bound him with two new ropes and brought him up from the cliff. ¹⁴ When he reached Lehi, and the Philistines came shouting to meet him, the spirit of the LORD came upon him: the ropes around his arms became as flax that is consumed by fire and his bonds melted away from his hands. ¹⁵ Near him was the fresh jawbone of an ass; he reached out, grasped it, and with it killed a thousand men. ¹⁶ Then Samson said,

"With the jawbone of an ass
   I have piled them in a heap;
With the jawbone of an ass
   I have slain a thousand men."

¹⁷† As he finished speaking he threw the jawbone from him; and so that place was named Ramath-lehi. ¹⁸ Being very thirsty, he cried to the LORD and said, "You have granted this great victory by the hand of your servant. Must I now die of thirst or fall into the hands of the uncircumcised?" ¹⁹† Then God split the cavity in Lehi, and water issued from it, which Samson drank till his spirit returned and he revived. Hence that spring in Lehi is called En-hakkore to this day.

²⁰* Samson judged Israel for twenty years in the days of the Philistines.

16 ¹ Once Samson went to Gaza, where he saw a harlot and visited her. ² Informed that Samson had come there, the men of Gaza surrounded him with an ambush at the city gate all night long. And all the night they waited, saying, "Tomorrow morning we will kill him." ³ Samson rested there until midnight. Then he rose, seized the doors of the city gate and the two gateposts, and tore them loose, bar and all. He hoisted them on his shoulders and carried them to the top of the ridge opposite Hebron.

Samson and Delilah

⁴ After that he fell in love with a woman in the Wadi Sorek whose name was Delilah. ⁵ The lords of the Philistines came to her and said, "Beguile him and find out the secret of his great strength, and how we may overcome and bind him so as to keep him helpless. We will each give you eleven hundred shekels of silver."

⁶ So Delilah said to Samson, "Tell me the secret of your great strength and how you may be bound so as to be kept helpless." ⁷ "If they bind me with seven fresh bowstrings which have not dried," Samson answered her, "I shall be as weak as any other man." ⁸ So the lords of the Philistines brought her seven fresh bowstrings which had not dried, and she bound him with them. ⁹* She had men lying in wait in the chamber and so she said to him, "The Philistines are upon you, Samson!" But he snapped the strings as a thread of tow is severed by a whiff of flame; and the secret of his strength remained unknown.

¹⁰ Delilah said to Samson, "You have mocked me and told me lies. Now tell me how you may be bound." ¹¹* "If they bind me tight with new ropes, with which no work has been done," he answered her, "I shall be as weak as any other man." ¹² So Delilah took new ropes and bound him with them. Then she said to him, "The Philistines are upon

---

15, 17: *Ramath-lehi:* "heights of the jawbone."
15, 19: *En-hakkore:* "the spring of him who cries out," an allusion to Samson's cry in v 18.

15, 6: Jgs 14, 20.   16, 9: Jgs 15, 14.
15, 13: Jgs 16, 11f.   16, 11: Jgs 15, 13.
15, 20: Jgs 16, 31.

LIVE IT!

Manipulation

You'd think that Samson would catch on, wouldn't you? Delilah tries to coax from Samson the secret of his strength. By the third attempt, it seems rather obvious that she wants to betray him to the Philistines. Nonetheless, Samson finally is pestered into revealing his secret, and Delilah uses the information to betray him.

Have you ever had a confidence betrayed? Have you ever trusted someone with a secret only to discover later that your secret is out? It makes it that much harder to trust again, to be open and to share yourself with another. When the person who betrays your confidence is someone you love, the betrayal is even more painful.

We need to do some soul-searching here. Ask yourself: Am I the kind of person who can be trusted with someone's secret? Have I ever betrayed a confidence?

It is easier than we like to think to be like Delilah—abusing the trust built up in a relationship and manipulating another person, even someone we care deeply about. We need to resolve to be people of integrity, who would never betray a confidence for personal gain.

▶ Jgs 16, 4–22

you, Samson!" For there were men lying in wait in the chamber. But he snapped them off his arms like thread.

13 Delilah said to Samson again, "Up to now you have mocked me and told me lies. Tell me how you may be bound." He said to her, "If you weave my seven locks of hair into the web and fasten them with the pin, I shall be as weak as any other man." 14 So while he slept, Delilah wove his seven locks of hair into the web, and fastened them in with the pin. Then she said, "The Philistines are upon you, Samson!" Awakening from his sleep, he pulled out both the weaver's pin and the web.

15 Then she said to him, "How can you say that you love me when you do not confide in me? Three times already you have mocked me, and not told me the secret of your great strength!" 16 She importuned him continually and vexed him with her complaints till he was deathly weary of them. 17* So he took her completely into his confidence and told her, "No razor has touched my head, for I have been consecrated to God from my mother's womb. If I am shaved, my strength will leave me, and I shall be as weak as any other man!" 18 When Delilah saw that he had taken her completely into his confidence, she summoned the lords of the Philistines, saying, "Come up this time, for he has opened his heart to me." So the lords of the Philistines came and brought up the money with them. 19 She had him sleep on her lap, and called for a man who shaved off his seven locks of hair. Then she began to mistreat him, for his strength had left

him. 20 When she said, "The Philistines are upon you, Samson!", and he woke from his sleep, he thought he could make good his escape as he had done time and again, for he did not realize that the LORD had left him. 21 But the Philistines seized him and gouged out his eyes. Then they brought him down to Gaza and bound him with bronze fetters, and he was put to grinding in the prison. 22 But the hair of his head began to grow as soon as it was shaved off.

The Death of Samson

23*† The lords of the Philistines assembled to offer a great sacrifice to their god Dagon and to make merry. They said,

"Our god has delivered into our power
    Samson our enemy."

25 When their spirits were high, they said, "Call Samson that he may amuse us." So they called Samson from the prison, and he played the buffoon before them. 24 When the people saw him, they praised their god. For they said,

"Our god has delivered into our power
    our enemy, the ravager of our land,
    the one who has multiplied our slain."

Then they stationed him between the columns. 26 Samson said to the attendant who was holding his hand, "Put me where I may touch the columns

---

† **16, 23:** Dagon was originally a Mesopotamian deity, whom the Philistines came to worship as their own god of grain.

* 16, 17: Jgs 13, 5.   16, 23: 1 Sm 5, 2–5.

that support the temple and may rest against them." ²⁷ The temple was full of men and women: all the lords of the Philistines were there, and from the roof about three thousand men and women looked on as Samson provided amusement. ²⁸ Samson cried out to the LORD and said, "O Lord GOD, remember me! Strengthen me, O God, this last time that for my two eyes I may avenge myself once and for all on the Philistines." ²⁹ Samson grasped the two middle columns on which the temple rested and braced himself against them, one at his right hand, the other at his left. ³⁰ And Samson said, "Let me die with the Philistines!" He pushed hard, and the temple fell upon the lords and all the people who were in it. Those he killed at his death were more than those he had killed during his lifetime.

³¹* All his family and kinsmen went down and bore him up for burial in the grave of his father Manoah between Zorah and Eshtaol. He had judged Israel for twenty years.

16, 28–31

III: The Tribes of Dan and Benjamin in the Days of the Judges

Micah and the Levite

17 ¹ There was a man in the mountain region of Ephraim whose name was Micah. ² He said to his mother, "The eleven hundred

shekels of silver over which you pronounced a curse in my hearing when they were taken from you, are in my possession. It was I who took them; so now I will restore them to you." ³*† When he restored the eleven hundred shekels of silver to his mother, she took two hundred of them and gave them to the silversmith, who made of them a carved idol overlaid with silver. ⁴ Then his mother said, "May the LORD bless my son! I have consecrated the silver to the LORD as my gift in favor of my son, by making a carved idol overlaid with silver." It remained in the house of Micah. ⁵* Thus the layman Micah had a sanctuary. He also made an ephod and household idols, and consecrated one of his sons, who became his priest. ⁶* In those days there was no king in Israel; everyone did what he thought best.

⁷ There was a young Levite who had resided within the tribe of Judah at Bethlehem of Judah. ⁸ From that city he set out to find another place of residence. On his journey he came to the house of Micah in the mountain region of Ephraim. ⁹ Micah said to him, "Where do you come from?" He answered him, "I am a Levite from Bethlehem in Judah, and am on my way to find some other place of residence." ¹⁰* "Stay with me," Micah said to him. "Be father and priest to me, and I will give you ten silver shekels a year, a set of garments, and your food." ¹¹ So the young Levite decided to stay with the man, to whom he became as one of his own sons. ¹²† Micah consecrated the young Levite, who became his priest, remaining in his house. ¹³ Therefore Micah said, "Now I know that the LORD will prosper me, since the Levite has become my priest."

Migration of the Danites

18 ¹*† At that time there was no king in Israel. Moreover the tribe of Danites were in search of a district to dwell in, for up to that time they had received no heritage among the tribes of Israel.

² So the Danites sent from their clan a detail of five valiant men of Zorah and Eshtaol, to reconnoiter the land and scout it. With their instructions to go and scout the land, they traveled as far as the house of Micah in the mountain region of Ephraim, where they passed the night. ³*† Near the house of Micah, they recognized the voice of the young Levite and turned in that direction. "Who brought you here and what are you doing here?" they asked him. "What is your interest here?" ⁴* "This is how

---

17, 3: *Idol:* an image, not of a pagan god, but of the Lord. The Mosaic law forbade the making of an image even of the true God.

17, 12f: According to Nm 18, 1–7 only those Levites who were descended from Aaron could be consecrated as priests.

18, 1: The tribe of Dan had been assigned a territory with definite limits in central Palestine. However they were unable to gain possession of the better portion of their land (Jgs 1, 34). So they now seek territory elsewhere in Palestine.

18, 3: *Recognized the voice:* perhaps they noticed the peculiar pronunciation of his south Hebrew dialect.

16, 31: Jgs 15, 20.
17, 3: Ex 20, 4; Lv 19, 4.
17, 5: Jgs 18, 14.17.
17, 6: Jgs 18, 1; 21, 25.
17, 10: Jgs 18, 19.
18, 1: Jos 19, 40–48.
18, 3: Jgs 17, 7.
18, 4: Jgs 17, 10.

Micah treats me," he replied to them. "He pays me a salary and I am his priest." 5 They said to him, "Consult God, that we may know whether the undertaking we are engaged in will succeed." 6 The priest said to them, "Go and prosper: the LORD is favorable to the undertaking you are engaged in."

7 So the five men went on and came to Laish. They saw that the people dwelling there lived securely after the manner of the Sidonians, quiet and trusting, with no lack of any natural resources. They were distant from the Sidonians and had no contact with other people. 8 When the five returned to their kinsmen in Zorah and Eshtaol and were asked for a report, 9 they replied, "Come, let us attack them, for we have seen the land and it is very good. Are you going to hesitate? Do not be slothful about beginning your expedition to possess the land. 10 Those against whom you go are a trusting people, and the land is ample. God has indeed given it into your power: a place where no natural resource is lacking."

11 So six hundred men of the clan of the Danites, fully armed with weapons of war, set out from where they were in Zorah and Eshtaol, 12* and camped in Judah, up near Kiriath-jearim; hence to this day the place, which lies west of Kiriath-jearim, is called Mahaneh-dan.

13 From there they went on to the mountain region of Ephraim and came to the house of Micah. 14* The five men who had gone to reconnoiter the land of Laish said to their kinsmen, "Do you know that in these houses there are an ephod, household idols, and a carved idol overlaid with silver? Now decide what you must do!" 15 So turning in that direction, they went to the house of the young Levite at the home of Micah and greeted him. 16 The six hundred men girt with weapons of war, who were Danites, stood by the entrance of the gate, and the priest stood there also. 17 Meanwhile the five men who had gone to reconnoiter the land went up and entered the house of Micah. 18 When they had gone in and taken the ephod, the household idols, and the carved idol overlaid with silver, the priest said to them, "What are you doing?" 19* They said to him, "Be still: put your hand over your mouth. Come with us and be our father and priest. Is it better for you to be priest for the family of one man or to be priest for a tribe and a clan in Israel?" 20 The priest, agreeing, took the ephod, household idols, and carved idol and went off in the midst of the band. 21 As they turned to depart, they placed their little ones, their livestock, and their goods at the head of the column.

22 The Danites had already gone some distance, when those in the houses near that of Micah took up arms and overtook them. 23 They called to the Danites, who turned about and said to Micah, "What do you want, that you have taken up arms?" 24 "You have taken my god, which I made, and have gone off with my priest as well," he answered. "What is left for me? How, then, can you ask me what I want?" 25 The Danites said to him, "Let us hear no further sound from you, lest fierce men fall upon you and you and your family lose your lives." 26 The Danites then went on their way, and Micah, seeing that they were stronger than he, returned home.

27 Having taken what Micah had made, and the priest he had had, they attacked Laish, a quiet and trusting people; they put them to the sword and destroyed their city by fire. 28 No one came to their aid, since the city was far from Sidon and they had no contact with other people. The Danites then rebuilt the city, which was in the valley that belongs to Beth-rehob, and lived there. 29 They named it Dan after their ancestor Dan, son of Israel. However, the name of the city was formerly Laish. 30† The Danites set up the carved idol for themselves, and Jonathan, son of Gershom, son of Moses, and his descendants were priests for the tribe of the Danites until the time of the captivity of the land. 31 They maintained the carved idol Micah had made as long as the house of God was in Shiloh.

The Levite from Ephraim

19 1* At that time, when there was no king in Israel, there was a Levite residing in remote parts of the mountain region of Ephraim who had taken for himself a concubine from Bethlehem of Judah. 2 His concubine was unfaithful to him and left him for her father's house in Bethlehem of Judah, where she stayed for some four months. 3 Her husband then set out with his servant and a pair of asses, and went after her to forgive her and take her back. She brought him into her father's house, and on seeing him, the girl's father joyfully made him welcome. 4 He was detained by the girl's father, and so he spent three days with this father-in-law of his, eating and drinking and passing the night there. 5† On the fourth day they rose early in the morning and he prepared to go. But the girl's father said to his son-in-law, "Fortify yourself with a little food; you can go later on." 6 So they stayed and the two men ate and drank together. Then the girl's father said to the husband, "Why not decide to

---

18, 30: *Until . . . land:* about the year 734 B.C., when the Assyrian emperor Tiglath-pileser III subjected northern Palestine.

19, 5–9: Such importuning of guests to prolong their stay at the home of their host is characteristic of Oriental hospitality.

18, 12: Jgs 13, 25.   **18, 19:** Jgs 17, 10.
18, 14: Jgs 17, 4f.   **19, 1:** Jgs 17, 6.

spend the night here and enjoy yourself?" 7 The man still made a move to go, but when his father-in-law pressed him he went back and spent the night there.

8 On the fifth morning he rose early to depart, but the girl's father said, "Fortify yourself and tarry until the afternoon." When he and his father-in-law had eaten, 9 and the husband was ready to go with his concubine and servant, the girl's father said to him, "It is already growing dusk. Stay for the night. See, the day is coming to an end. Spend the night here and enjoy yourself. Early tomorrow you can start your journey home." 10 The man, however, refused to stay another night; he and his concubine set out with a pair of saddled asses, and traveled till they came opposite Jebus, which is Jerusalem. 11 Since they were near Jebus with the day far gone, the servant said to his master, "Come, let us turn off to this city of the Jebusites and spend the night in it." 12* But his master said to him, "We will not turn off to a city of foreigners, who are not Israelites, but will go on to Gibeah. 13* Come," he said to his servant, "let us make for some other place, either Gibeah or Ramah, to spend the night." 14 So they continued on their way till the sun set on them when they were abreast of Gibeah of Benjamin.

15*† There they turned off to enter Gibeah for the night. The man waited in the public square of the city he had entered, but no one offered them the shelter of his home for the night. 16 In the evening, however, an old man came from his work in the field; he was from the mountain region of Ephraim, though he lived among the Benjaminite townspeople of Gibeah. 17 When he noticed the traveler in the public square of the city, the old man asked where he was going, and whence he had come. 18 He said to him, "We are traveling from Bethlehem of Judah far up into the mountain region of Ephraim, where I belong. I have been to Bethlehem of Judah and am now going back home; but no one has offered us the shelter of his house. 19 We have straw and fodder for our asses, and bread and wine for the woman and myself and for our servant; there is nothing else we need." 20 "You are welcome," the old man said to him, "but let me provide for all your needs, and do not spend the night in the public square." 21* So he led them to his house and provided fodder for the asses. Then they washed their feet, and ate and drank.

The Outrage at Gibeah

22*† While they were enjoying themselves, the men of the city, who were corrupt, surrounded the house and beat on the door. They said to the old man whose house it was, "Bring out your guest, that we may abuse him." 23 The owner of the house went out to them and said, "No, my brothers; do not be so wicked. Since this man is my guest, do not commit this crime. 24 Rather let me bring out my maiden daughter or his concubine. Ravish them, or do whatever you want with them; but against the man you must not commit this wanton crime." 25 When the men would not listen to his host, the husband seized his concubine and thrust her outside to them. They had relations with her and abused her all night until the following dawn, when they let her go. 26 Then at daybreak the woman came and collapsed at the entrance of the house in which her husband was a guest, where she lay until the morning. 27 When her husband rose that day and opened the door of the house to start out again on his journey, there lay the woman, his concubine, at the entrance of the house with her hands on the threshold. 28 He said to her, "Come, let us go"; but there was no answer. So the man placed her on an ass and started out again for home.

29† On reaching home, he took a knife to the body of his concubine, cut her into twelve pieces, and sent them throughout the territory of Israel. 30* Everyone who saw this said, "Nothing like this has been done or seen from the day the Israelites came up from the land of Egypt to this day. Take note of it, and state what you propose to do."

Assembly of Israelites

20 1† So all the Israelites came out as one man: from Dan to Beer-sheba, and from the land of Gilead, the community was gathered to the LORD at Mizpah. 2 The leaders of all the people and all the tribesmen of Israel, four hundred thousand foot soldiers who were swordsmen, presented themselves in the assembly of the people of God. 3 Meanwhile, the Benjaminites heard that the Israelites had gone up to Mizpah. The Israelites asked to be told how the crime had taken place, 4* and the Levite, the husband of the murdered woman, testified: "My concubine and I went into Gibeah of Benjamin for the night. 5* But the citizens of Gibeah

---

19, 15: Private hospitality was the customary means of providing comfort to travelers where public facilities were so rare.

19, 22: *Who were corrupt:* literally "sons of Belial," indicating extreme perversion; cf Gn 19, 4–8. This crime and its punishment made the name Gibeah proverbial as a place of shameful wickedness; cf Hos 9, 9; 10, 9.

19, 29: A drastic means for arousing the tribes to avenge the unheard of crime of the Benjaminites.

20, 1: *From Dan to Beer-sheba:* from north to south. *The land of Gilead:* all the territory east of the Jordan.

19, 12: Jgs 1, 21.
19, 13: Jos 18, 25.
19, 15: Jgs 20, 4.
19, 21: Gn 18, 4; 24, 32; 43, 24.
19, 22–25: Gn 19, 4–9.
19, 30: Hos 9, 9; 10, 9.
20, 4: Jgs 19, 14f.
20, 5: Jgs 19, 22–27.

rose up against me by night and surrounded the house in which I was. Me they attempted to kill, and my concubine they abused so that she died. 6* So I took my concubine and cut her up and sent her through every part of the territory of Israel, because of the monstrous crime they had committed in Israel. 7*† Now that you are all here, O Israelites, state what you propose to do." 8 All the people rose as one man to say, "None of us is to leave for his tent or return to his home. 9 Now as for Gibeah, this is what we will do: We will proceed against it by lot, 10 taking from all the tribes of Israel ten men for every hundred, a hundred for every thousand, a thousand for every ten thousand, and procuring supplies for the soldiers who will go to deal fully and suitably with Gibeah of Benjamin for the crime it committed in Israel."

11 When, therefore, all the men of Israel without exception were leagued together against the city, 12† the tribes of Israel sent men throughout the tribe of Benjamin to say, "What is this evil which has occurred among you? 13 Now give up these corrupt men of Gibeah, that we may put them to death and thus purge the evil from Israel." But the Benjaminites refused to accede to the demand of their brothers, the Israelites. 14 Instead, the Benjaminites assembled from their other cities to Gibeah, to do battle with the Israelites. 15 The number of the Benjaminite swordsmen from the other cities on that occasion was twenty-six thousand, in addition to the inhabitants of Gibeah. 16 Included in this total were seven hundred picked men who were left-handed, every one of them able to sling a stone at a hair without missing. 17 Meanwhile the other Israelites who, without Benjamin, mustered four hundred thousand swordsmen ready for battle, 18*† moved on to Bethel and consulted God. When the Israelites asked who should go first in the attack on the Benjaminites, the LORD said, "Judah shall go first." 19 The next day the Israelites advanced on Gibeah with their forces.

War with Benjamin

20 On the day the Israelites drew up in battle array at Gibeah for the combat with Benjamin, 21 the Benjaminites came out of the city and felled twenty-two thousand men of Israel. 23 Then the Israelites went up and wept before the LORD until evening.

"Shall I again engage my brother Benjamin in battle?" they asked the LORD; and the LORD answered that they should. 22 But though the Israelite soldiers took courage and again drew up for combat in the same place as on the previous day, 24 when they met the Benjaminites for the second time, 25 once again the Benjaminites who came out of Gibeah against them felled eighteen thousand Israelites, all of them swordsmen. 26 So the entire Israelite army went up to Bethel, where they wept and remained fasting before the LORD until evening of that day, besides offering holocausts and peace offerings before the LORD. 27* When the Israelites consulted the LORD (for the ark of the covenant of God was there in those days, 28 and Phinehas, son of Eleazar, son of Aaron, was ministering to him in those days), and asked, "Shall I go out again to battle with Benjamin, my brother, or shall I desist?" the LORD said, "Attack! for tomorrow I will deliver him into your power." 29*† So Israel set men in ambush around Gibeah.

30 The Israelites went up against the Benjaminites for the third time and formed their line of battle at Gibeah as on other occasions. 31 The Benjaminites went out to meet them, and in the beginning they killed off about thirty of the Israelite soldiers in the open field, just as on the other occasions. 32 Therefore the Benjaminites thought, "We are defeating them as before"; not realizing that disaster was about to overtake them. The Israelites, however, had planned the flight so as to draw them away from the city onto the highways. They were drawn away from the city onto the highways, of which the one led to Bethel, the other to Gibeon. 33 And then all the men of Israel rose from their places. They reformed their ranks at Baal-tamar, and the Israelites in ambush rushed from their place west of Gibeah, 34 ten thousand picked men from all Israel, and advanced against the city itself. In a fierce battle, 35 the LORD defeated Benjamin before Israel; and on that day the Israelites killed twenty-five thousand one hundred men of Benjamin, all of them swordsmen.

36 To the Benjaminites it had looked as though the enemy were defeated, for the men of Israel gave ground to Benjamin, trusting in the ambush they had set at Gibeah. 37 But then the men in ambush made a sudden dash into Gibeah, overran it, and put the whole city to the sword. 38 Now, the other

---

20, 7: The Israelites were asked to decide at once what action to take concerning this crime; cf 2 Sm 16, 20. The Levite undoubtedly addressed the tribal heads who would speak in behalf of the multitude.

20, 12: Before the crime at Gibeah was punished, the Benjaminites were invited to join their brethren, the Israelites, in punishing the crime. Since they failed to respond, special messengers were sent asking them to deliver up the guilty ones. They replied by gathering their forces for combat.

20, 18: *Judah shall go first:* the same response as in Jgs 1, 1f, but without the assurance of immediate success. Only after the Israelites

were punished at the hands of the Benjaminites for their own grossness, and had performed penance, did they succeed in punishing the latter for their part in the crime of rape and murder, by gaining the victory over them.

20, 29–46: This stratagem proved more useful to the Israelites than force, as in the siege of Ai (Jos 8, 3–21). In the parallel accounts the first (vv 29–35) is a summary of the second (vv 36–46).

20, 6: Jgs 19, 29.
20, 7: Jgs 19, 30.
20, 18: Jgs 1, 1f.

20, 27: 1 Sm 4, 3f.
20, 29–46: Jos 8, 4–24.

Israelites had agreed with the men in ambush on a smoke signal they were to send up from the city. [39] And though the men of Benjamin had begun by killing off some thirty of the men of Israel, under the impression that they were defeating them as surely as in the earlier fighting, the Israelites wheeled about to resist [40] as the smoke of the signal column began to rise up from the city. It was when Benjamin looked back and saw the whole city in flames against the sky [41] that the men of Israel wheeled about. Therefore the men of Benjamin were thrown into confusion, for they realized the disaster that had overtaken them. [42] They retreated before the men of Israel in the direction of the desert, with the fight being pressed against them. In their very midst, meanwhile, those who had been in the city were spreading destruction. [43] The men of Benjamin had been surrounded, and were now pursued to a point east of Gibeah, [44] while eighteen thousand of them fell, warriors to a man. [45]* The rest turned and fled through the desert to the rock Rimmon. But on the highways the Israelites picked off five thousand men among them, and chasing them up to Gidom, killed another two thousand of them there. [46] Those of Benjamin who fell on that day were in all twenty-five thousand swordsmen, warriors to a man. [47] But six hundred others who turned and fled through the desert reached the rock Rimmon, where they remained for four months.

[48] The men of Israel withdrew through the territory of the Benjaminites, putting to the sword the inhabitants of the cities, the livestock, and all they chanced upon. Moreover they destroyed by fire all the cities they came upon.

Wives for the Survivors

21 [1]† Now the men of Israel had sworn at Mizpah that none of them would give his daughter in marriage to anyone from Benjamin. [2]* So the people went to Bethel and remained there before God until evening, raising their voices in bitter lament. [3] They said, "LORD, God of Israel, why has it come to pass in Israel that today one tribe of Israel should be lacking?" [4] Early the next day the people built an altar there and offered holocausts and peace offerings. [5]* Then the Israelites asked, "Are there any among all the tribes of Israel who did not come up to the LORD for the assembly?" For they had taken a solemn oath that anyone who did not go up to the LORD at Mizpah should be put to death without fail.

[6]† The Israelites were disconsolate over their brother Benjamin and said, "Today one of the tribes of Israel has been cut off. [7] What can we do about wives for the survivors, since we have sworn by the LORD not to give them any of our daughters in marriage?" [8] And when they asked whether anyone among the tribes of Israel had not come up to the LORD in Mizpah, they found that none of the men of Jabesh-gilead had come to the encampment for the assembly. [9] A roll call of the army established that none of the inhabitants of that city were present. [10] The community, therefore, sent twelve thousand warriors with orders to go to Jabesh-gilead and put those who lived there to the sword, including the women and children. [11]*† They were told to include under the ban all males and every woman who was not still a virgin. [12] Finding among the inhabitants of Jabesh-gilead four hundred young virgins, who had had no relations with men, they brought them to the camp at Shiloh in the land of Canaan. [13]* Then the whole community sent a message to the Benjaminites at the rock Rimmon, offering them peace. [14] When Benjamin returned at that time, they gave them as wives the women of Jabesh-gilead whom they had spared; but these proved to be not enough for them.

[15]† The people were still disconsolate over Benjamin because the LORD had made a breach among the tribes of Israel. [16] And the elders of the community said, "What shall we do for wives for the survivors? For every woman in Benjamin has been put to death." [17] They said, "Those of Benjamin who survive must have heirs, else one of the Israelite tribes will be wiped out. [18]† Yet we cannot give them any of our daughters in marriage, because the Israelites have sworn, 'Cursed be he who gives a woman to Benjamin!'" [19] Then they thought of the yearly feast of the LORD at Shiloh, north of Bethel, east of the highway that goes up from Bethel to Shechem, and south of Lebonah. [20] And they instructed the Benjaminites, "Go and lie in wait in the vineyards. [21] When you see the girls of Shiloh come out to do their dancing, leave the vineyards and each of you seize one of the girls of Shiloh for a wife, and go to the land of Benjamin. [22] When their fathers or their brothers come to complain to us, we

---

21, 1–3: The anger of the Israelites led them to destroy their brethren, the Benjaminites. Having realized their goal, however, they were soon filled with dismay, and sought to restore the tribe they had all but exterminated.

21, 6–9: This account is summarized in the parallel passage in vv 2–5.

21, 11: *Under the ban:* see note on Nm 21, 3.

21, 15: *Had made a breach:* what is here attributed to God was in reality the free and deliberate act of the Israelites and happened only by the permissive will of God. The ancients attributed to the first primary cause what is more directly due to secondary causes.

21, 18: Regardless of the serious consequences of their vow, the Israelites considered themselves obliged to fulfill it; cf Jgs 11, 31. 35f.39.

20, 45: Jgs 21, 13.
21, 2: Jgs 20, 26.
21, 5: Jgs 20, 8ff.

21, 11: Nm 31, 17.
21, 13: Jgs 20, 47.

shall say to them, 'Release them to us as a kindness, since we did not take a woman apiece in the war. Had you yourselves given them these wives, you would now be guilty.' "

23 The Benjaminites did this; they carried off a wife for each of them from their raid on the dancers, and went back to their own territory, where they rebuilt and occupied the cities. 24 Also at that time the Israelites dispersed; each of them left for his own heritage in his own clan and tribe.

25*† In those days there was no king in Israel; everyone did what he thought best.

21, 25: Cf Jgs 17, 6; 18, 1; 19, 1. The verse gives the reason why the lawlessness of the period of judges, and the events described herein, were possible.

21, 25: Jgs 17, 6; 18, 1; 19, 1.

Tracing one's family tree has become a popular pastime. People comb through courthouse files, study old tombstones in search of names and dates, and write to churches in foreign countries looking for baptismal and marriage records. In learning about our ancestors, we gain a better sense of our place in history and who we should be in light of that history. Ruth is a beautiful story of love and loyalty about one of Israel's ancestors. The story helps God's people understand who they are and how they should live.

At a Glance

I. **Naomi in Moab** (chapter 1).

II. **The Meeting** (chapters 2–3).

III. **Boaz Marries Ruth** (chapter 4).

In-depth

The Book of Ruth offers a surprising revelation about the family tree of King David: Ruth, King David's great-grandmother, was a foreigner, born and reared in the land of Moab. The Book of Ruth was written long after the death of her famous great-grandson, but it seems to preserve an accurate memory: King David was of mixed ancestry. Many Israelites were probably shocked that God worked through a member of an enemy tribe to advance the divine plan.

The Book of Ruth is sandwiched between Judges and 1 Samuel because its events take place during the time of the judges. It teaches some extremely important lessons:

■ Ruth was faithful to Naomi, her mother-in-law, even though she was of a different race and different faith. Ruth challenged the ancient Israelites, who tended to view foreigners with suspicion and to see nothing good in their enemies.

■ If God's plan included a Moabite woman among David's ancestors, then God's love and favor must extend beyond the boundaries of Israel. After the Exile, when Jewish marriages to foreigners were outlawed, the little Book of Ruth presented a huge challenge!

■ God works through the faithfulness of ordinary people living ordinary lives. No kings, wars, or dramatic miracles appear in the Book of Ruth.

The Book of Ruth is action packed and full of dialog; it is a dramatic story like the Books of Judith and Tobit. Some of the traditions of ancient Israel may seem strange to us today, but we can still gain a deeper understanding of ourselves and our faith by reading the story of King David's great-grandmother.

Quick Facts

Period Covered
sometime from 1200 to 1000 B.C.

Author
unknown, probably writing sometime during the monarchy (1000–800 B.C.)

Themes
God's plan includes non-Israelites. God works through ordinary people.

Ruth

Naomi in Moab

1 ¹† Once in the time of the judges there was a famine in the land; so a man from Bethlehem of Judah departed with his wife and two sons to reside on the plateau of Moab. ² The man was named Elimelech, his wife Naomi, and his sons Mahlon and Chilion; they were Ephrathites from Bethlehem of Judah. Some time after their arrival on the Moabite plateau, ³ Elimelech, the husband of Naomi, died, and she was left with her two sons, ⁴ who married Moabite women, one named Orpah, the other Ruth. When they had lived there about ten years, ⁵ both Mahlon and Chilion died also, and the woman was left with neither her two sons nor her husband. ⁶ She then made ready to go back from the plateau of Moab because word reached her there that the LORD had visited his people and given them food.

⁷ She and her two daughters-in-law left the place where they had been living. Then as they were on the road back to the land of Judah, ⁸† Naomi said to her two daughters-in-law, "Go back, each of you, to your mother's house! May the LORD be kind to you as you were to the departed and to me! ⁹ May the LORD grant each of you a husband and a home in which you will find rest." She kissed them goodby, but they wept with loud sobs, ¹⁰ and told her they would return with her to her people. ¹¹† "Go back, my daughters!" said Naomi. "Why should you come with me? Have I other sons in my womb who may become your husbands? ¹² Go back, daughters! Go, for I am too old to marry again. And even if I could offer any hopes, or if tonight I had a husband or had borne sons, ¹³ would you then wait and deprive yourselves of husbands until those sons grew up? No, my daughters! my lot is too bitter for you, because the LORD has extended his hand against me." ¹⁴ Again they sobbed aloud and wept; and Orpah kissed her mother-in-law good-by, but Ruth stayed with her.

¹⁵ "See now!" she said, "your sister-in-law has gone back to her people and her god. Go back after your sister-in-law!" ¹⁶† But Ruth said, "Do not ask me to abandon or forsake you! for wherever you go I will go, wherever you lodge I will lodge, your people shall be my people, and your God my God.

1, 1f: *In the time of the judges:* three generations before the end of the period of Judges; cf Ru 4, 21f. *Bethlehem of Judah:* to distinguish it from the town of the same name in the tribe of Zebulun (Jos 19, 15). *Ephrathites from Bethlehem:* belonging to a Judean clan which settled in Bethlehem; cf 1 Sm 17, 12; 1 Chr 2, 50f; 4, 4.

1, 8: *Mother's house:* the women's part of the dwelling; cf Jgs 4, 17; Song 3, 4.

1, 11: *Have I other sons . . . husbands?:* Naomi insisted that her daughters-in-law remain in their own country only for the sake of posterity. If she had had other sons, the levirate law would have obliged them to marry the widows of her deceased sons to perpetuate the names of the deceased; cf Gn 38, 8; Dt 25, 5f.

1, 16f: An example of heroic fidelity and piety. Ruth's decision, confirmed with an oath, to adhere to her mother-in-law impelled her to abandon her country and its pagan worship.

17 Wherever you die I will die, and there be buried. May the LORD do so and so to me, and more besides, if aught but death separates me from you!" 18 Naomi then ceased to urge her, for she saw she was determined to go with her.

The Return to Bethlehem

19 So they went on together till they reached Bethlehem. On their arrival there, the whole city was astir over them, and the women asked, "Can this be Naomi?" 20*† But she said to them, "Do not call me Naomi. Call me Mara, for the Almighty has made it very bitter for me. 21 I went away with an abundance, but the LORD has brought me back destitute. Why should you call me Naomi, since the LORD has pronounced against me and the Almighty has brought evil upon me?" 22† Thus it was that Naomi returned with the Moabite daughter-in-law, Ruth, who accompanied her back from the plateau of Moab. They arrived in Bethlehem at the beginning of the barley harvest.

4† Boaz himself came from Bethlehem and said to the harvesters, "The LORD be with you!" and they replied, "The LORD bless you!" 5 Boaz asked the overseer of his harvesters, "Whose girl is this?" 6* The overseer of the harvesters answered, "She is the Moabite girl who returned from the plateau of Moab with Naomi. 7 She asked leave to gather the gleanings into sheaves after the harvesters; and ever since she came this morning she has remained here until now, with scarcely a moment's rest."

8 Boaz said to Ruth, "Listen, my daughter! Do not go to glean in anyone else's field; you are not to leave here. Stay here with my women servants. 9 Watch to see which field is to be harvested, and follow them; I have commanded the young men to do you no harm. When you are thirsty, you may go and drink from the vessels the young men have filled." 10 Casting herself prostrate upon the ground, she said to him, "Why should I, a foreigner, be favored with your notice?" 11* Boaz answered her: "I have had a complete account of what you

Bill

LIVE IT!

Bill is a special person. He is different looking. Most people walk by Bill and ignore him. But the people who have looked beyond Bill's appearance have discovered one of the most beautiful people they will ever come to know.

Many people who have gotten to know Bill feel that they have found someone who is close to God. They have discovered a person who brings out the best in themselves.

In the same way, Ruth easily could have been overlooked by Boaz as just another poor person scavenging in his fields. Boaz took the opportunity to get to know her and found someone with inspiring faith and loyalty. God can be found in the ones who are forgotten. Reach out to them, and you might find God too.

▶ **Ru 2, 1–16**

The Meeting

2 1* Naomi had a prominent kinsman named Boaz, of the clan of her husband Elimelech. 2*† Ruth the Moabite said to Naomi, "Let me go and glean ears of grain in the field of anyone who will allow me that favor." Naomi said to her, "Go, my daughter," 3 and she went. The field she entered to glean after the harvesters happened to be the section belonging to Boaz of the clan of Elimelech.

have done for your mother-in-law after your husband's death; you have left your father and your mother and the land of your birth, and have come to a people whom you did not know previously. 12 May the LORD reward what you have done! May you receive a full reward from the LORD, the God of Israel, under whose wings you have come for refuge." 13 She said, "May I prove worthy of your kindness, my lord: you have comforted me, your

---

1, 20f: *Naomi:* means "amiable" or "pleasant," suggesting God's favor toward her. *The Almighty has brought evil upon me:* the ancients regarded adversity as a punishment from God for personal sin, as if good and evil were always repaid in a temporal and material manner.

1, 22: *Barley harvest:* early April. This circumstance favored the events of the narrative that follow.

2, 2: *Let me go and glean . . . grain:* even the poor, the widow, the

stranger, and the orphan had a right to glean at harvest time; cf Lv 19, 9f, 23, 22; Dt 24, 19–22.

2, 4: *The LORD be with you:* courtesy and religious feeling characterize the salutations of the Hebrews. This greeting is used in the Christian liturgy.

1, 20: Ex 15, 23.
2, 1: Ru 3, 2.12; 4, 21;
       Mt 1, 5.
2, 2: Dt 24, 19.
2, 6: Ru 1, 22.
2, 11: Ru 1, 14–17.

servant, with your consoling words; would indeed that I were a servant of yours!" 14 At mealtime Boaz said to her, "Come here and have some food; dip your bread in the sauce." Then as she sat near the reapers, he handed her some roasted grain and she ate her fill and had some left over. 15 She rose to glean, and Boaz instructed his servants to let her glean among the sheaves themselves without scolding her, 16 and even to let drop some handfuls and leave them for her to glean without being rebuked.

17 She gleaned in the field until evening, and when she beat out what she had gleaned it came to about an ephah of barley, 18 which she took into the city and showed to her mother-in-law. Next she brought out and gave her what she had left over from lunch. 19 So her mother-in-law said to her, "Where did you glean today? Where did you go to work? May he who took notice of you be blessed!" Then she told her mother-in-law with whom she had worked. "The man at whose place I worked today is named Boaz," she said. 20*† "May he be blessed by the LORD, who is ever merciful to the living and to the dead," Naomi exclaimed to her daughter-in-law; and she continued, "He is a relative of ours, one of our next of kin." 21 "He even told me," added Ruth the Moabite, "that I should stay with his servants until they complete his entire harvest." 22 "You would do well, my dear,"

Naomi rejoined, "to go out with his servants; for in someone else's field you might be insulted." 23 So she stayed gleaning with the servants of Boaz until the end of the barley and wheat harvests.

Ruth Again Presents Herself

3 When she was back with her mother-in-law, 1 Naomi said to her, "My daughter, I must seek a home for you that will please you. 2* Now is not Boaz, with whose servants you were, a relative of ours? This evening he will be winnowing barley at the threshing floor. 3 So bathe and anoint yourself; then put on your best attire and go down to the threshing floor. Do not make yourself known to the man before he has finished eating and drinking. 4† But when he lies down, take note of the place where he does so. Then go, uncover a place at his feet, and lie down. He will tell you what to do." 5 "I will do whatever you advise," Ruth replied. 6 So she went down to the threshing floor and did just as her mother-in-law had instructed her.

7 Boaz ate and drank to his heart's content. Then when he went and lay down at the edge of the sheaves, she stole up, uncovered a place at his feet, and lay down. 8 In the middle of the night, however, the man gave a start and turned around to find a woman lying at his feet. 9† He asked, "Who are

SERVICE TO THE POOR AND THE COMMUNITY!

The story of Ruth was a challenge to the Israelites' tendency to distrust foreigners. It is also an example of how service to the poor was an integral part of Israel's society. For in the story, Boaz, a wealthy and respected person, both provides for the poor and looks beyond the differences of race and faith to marry Ruth. Boaz's goal is to do God's will. His marriage to Ruth ensures that Naomi's land is redeemed and that she will have descendants to claim the land. Ruth's faithfulness and Boaz's integrity serve to gradually restore Naomi's hope in God's care.

In the New Testament, it becomes even clearer that God makes no distinctions between people of different races and cultures. And Jesus teaches that caring for the poor is one of the requirements for being God's people.

■ How do you treat people of different races, and how much is service to poor people a part of your life?
■ Pray that you can follow Ruth and Boaz's example and be an instrument of faith, hope, and justice for people in need.

---

† **2, 20:** *One of our next of kin:* literally "our redeemer," a near relative of the same clan who had the right and duty to restore the land which an impoverished kinsman had alienated (Lv 25, 25–28), and to marry the widow of a relative who had died without male offspring so as to raise up posterity to his name (Dt 25, 5–10).

3, 4: *Uncover a place at his feet . . . :* confident of the virtue

of Ruth and Boaz, Naomi advises this unusual expedient to her daughter-in-law for the purpose of introducing her claim.

3, 9: *Spread the corner of your cloak over me:* be my protector by marrying me according to the duty of a near kinsman; cf Dt 25, 5; Ez 16, 8.

2, 20: Ru 3, 9.   **3, 2:** Ru 1.

you?" And she replied, "I am your servant Ruth. Spread the corner of your cloak over me, for you are my next of kin." 10* He said, "May the LORD bless you, my daughter! You have been even more loyal now than before in not going after the young men, whether poor or rich. 11 So be assured, daughter, I will do for you whatever you say; all my townspeople know you for a worthy woman. 12*† Now, though indeed I am closely related to you, you have another relative still closer. 13* Stay as you are for tonight, and tomorrow, if he wishes to claim you, good! let him do so. But if he does not wish to claim you, as the LORD lives, I will claim you myself. Lie there until morning." 14 So she lay at his feet until morning, but rose before men could recognize one another. Boaz said, "Let it not be known that this woman came to the threshing floor." 15* Then he said to her, "Take off your cloak and hold it out." When she did so, he poured out six measures of barley, helped her lift the bundle, and left for the city.

16 Ruth went home to her mother-in-law, who asked, "How have you fared, my daughter?" So she told her all the man had done for her, 17 and concluded, "He gave me these six measures of barley because he did not wish me to come back to my mother-in-law empty-handed!" 18 Naomi then said, "Wait here, my daughter, until you learn what happens, for the man will not rest, but will settle the matter today."

Boaz Marries Ruth

4 1*† Boaz went and took a seat at the gate; and when he saw the closer relative of whom he had spoken come along, he called to him by name, "Come and sit beside me!" And he did so. 2† Then Boaz picked out ten of the elders of the city and asked them to sit nearby. When they had done this, 3 he said to the near relative: "Naomi, who has come back from the Moabite plateau, is putting up for sale the piece of land that belonged to our kinsman Elimelech. 4*† So I thought I would inform you, bidding you before those here present, including the elders of my people, to put in your claim for it if you wish to acquire it as next of kin. But if you do not wish to claim it, tell me so, that I may be guided accordingly, for no one has a prior claim to

yours, and mine is next." He answered, "I will put in my claim."

5*† Boaz continued, "Once you acquire the field from Naomi, you must take also Ruth the Moabite, the widow of the late heir, and raise up a family for the departed on his estate." 6 The near relative replied, "I cannot exercise my claim lest I depreciate my own estate. Put in a claim yourself in my stead, for I cannot exercise my claim." 7† Now it used to be the custom in Israel that, to make binding a contract of redemption or exchange, one party would take off his sandal and give it to the other. This was the form of attestation in Israel. 8 So the near relative, in saying to Boaz, "Acquire it for yourself," drew off his sandal. 9 Boaz then said to the elders and to all the people, "You are witnesses today that I have acquired from Naomi all the holdings of Elimelech, Chilion and Mahlon. 10 I also take Ruth the Moabite, the widow of Mahlon, as my wife, in

PRAY IT

Wherever You Go

R uth is under no obligation to leave her homeland and go to Israel with her mother-in-law, very likely facing a life of poverty. But her loyalty is rewarded, and she finds new life among God's people.

After reading Ruth's story, reflect on these questions:

- What do you find inspiring in Ruth's story?
- Who are you faithful to?
- What would have to be present in a relationship for you to have the kind of loyalty Ruth showed to Naomi?
- Can you make Ruth's words to Naomi your prayer to God?

Where you lead, I will follow; where you direct me, I will live; your people shall be my family; and you shall always be my God. (Adapted from Ru 1, 16)

3, 12: *Relative still closer:* who had a prior right and duty to marry Ruth.

4, 1: *Took a seat at the gate:* i.e., of the city, where business affairs were settled.

4, 2: *Ten of the elders:* to serve as judges in legal matters as well as witnesses of the settlement of business affairs; cf Dt 25, 7–9.

4, 4: Poverty had obliged Naomi to sell the land of her deceased husband. The law permitted the nearest kinsman to redeem the land and thus preserve the family patrimony; cf Lv 25, 25.

4, 5f: The heir of Elimelech's field had died without children (Ru 1, 5). The nearest of kin could now redeem the land but he must also take Ruth, the widow of the late heir, to wife to perpetuate the fam-

ily of the deceased; cf Dt 25, 5f. The first male child of such a marriage would be the legal son of Mahlon and grandson of Elimelech.

4, 7: *Take off his sandal . . . :* by this act the near relative renounced his legal right, both to the field of Elimelech and to the marriage with Ruth. The custom mentioned in Dt 25, 6 is somewhat different.

3, 10: Dt 25, 5.   4, 1: Ru 3, 12.
3, 12: Ru 4, 1.   4, 4: Lv 25, 25.
3, 13: Ru 4, 5; Dt 25, 5.   4, 5: Ru 3, 13; Dt 25, 5.
3, 15: Ru 2, 17.

R
U

order to raise up a family for her late husband on his estate, so that the name of the departed may not perish among his kinsmen and fellow citizens. Do you witness this today?" [11]* All those at the gate, including the elders, said, "We do so. May the LORD make this wife come into your house like Rachel and Leah, who between them built up the house of Israel. May you do well in Ephrathah and win fame in Bethlehem. [12]*† With the offspring the LORD will give you from this girl, may your house become like the house of Perez, whom Tamar bore to Judah."

[13] Boaz took Ruth. When they came together as man and wife, the LORD enabled her to conceive and she bore a son. [14] Then the women said to Naomi, "Blessed is the LORD who has not failed to provide you today with an heir! May he become fa-

mous in Israel! [15] He will be your comfort and the support of your old age, for his mother is the daughter-in-law who loves you. She is worth more to you than seven sons!" [16]† Naomi took the child, placed him on her lap, and became his nurse. [17]*† And the neighbor women gave him his name, at the news that a grandson had been born to Naomi. They called him Obed. He was the father of Jesse, the father of David.

[18]* These are the descendants of Perez: Perez was the father of Hezron,* [19] Hezron was the father of Ram, Ram was the father of Amminadab, [20]* Amminadab was the father of Nahshon, Nahshon was the father of Salmon, [21] Salmon was the father of Boaz, Boaz was the father of Obed, [22]* Obed was the father of Jesse, and Jesse became the father of David.

4, 12: *Perez, whom Tamar bore to Judah:* the right which Judah unwittingly satisfied for his daughter-in-law Tamar (Gn 38), Boaz willingly rendered to Ruth.

4, 16: *Placed him on her lap:* took him as her own; cf Gn 30, 3; 48, 12; Nm 11, 12.

4, 17: *The father of Jesse, the father of David:* indicating the place of Obed, Jesse and David in the line of Judah and the ancestry of Christ, the Messiah; cf Mt 1, 5f.

4, 11: Gn 29, 31—30, 24;
      35, 19.
4, 12: Gn 38, 29.
4, 17: Lk 1, 58.
4, 18–22: 1 Chr 2, 4–15;

Mt 1, 3–6.
4, 18: Gn 46, 12; 1 Chr 4, 1.
4, 20: Ex 6, 23; Nm 1, 7.
4, 22: 1 Sm 16, 10–13.

An ongoing national debate these days involves, on the one side, those who want more laws to protect workers, poor people, and the environment, and on the other side, those who want fewer laws and less government. The First Book of Samuel reflects a similar tension in Israel as the days of the judges come to an end and the first kings make their appearance. This period of Israelite history is filled with mighty struggles and colorful personalities, including a king who gradually loses his sanity and the shining hero who replaces him.

At a Glance

I. History of the Last Judges, Eli and Samuel (1, 1—7, 17).

II. Establishment of the Monarchy in Israel (8, 1—12, 25).

III. Saul and David (13, 1—31, 13).

In-depth

This book is named after Samuel, the last of the judges and a reluctant king-maker. Samuel, a prophet anointed to speak God's word to the nation, represents one way of governing. God works through the prophet's words to remind the people of Israel to be faithful to the terms of the Covenant. A second way of governing is represented by Saul, the first king anointed by Samuel to rule over the whole nation. God works through the king's laws and regulations to ensure that the people of Israel are faithful to the terms of the Covenant. In 1 Samuel, the former way of governing the Israelite nation gradually gives way to the latter, with an obvious gain and an obvious loss for the people.

When kings begin to rule Israel in place of judges and prophets, the people gain a more structured way of life and develop a greater national identity. These changes also make them stronger in facing threats from other nations. But at the same time, the people lose a great deal of personal freedom and independence. They are taxed and even forced into labor to support the king's government and building plans. Echoes of this debate on governing styles can be found throughout 1 Samuel (see "Doublets," near 9, 1).

Israel's kings were understood as being chosen by God and as being responsible for God's interests. First Samuel clearly emphasizes that the success of kings depends on their obedience to God's law. First Samuel reminds us that final authority in human affairs rests in no human being, but in God alone. Human systems are never perfect, but must constantly be reviewed and renewed.

Quick Facts

Period Covered
approximately 1080 to 1040 B.C.

Author
unknown, from the Deuteronomic tradition, probably using ancient court records and hero stories

Theme
tension between the need for a king and the people's reliance on God

Of Note
First and Second Samuel, originally one book, were made into two books when they were translated from Hebrew into Greek.

The First Book of *Samuel*

1 Samuel

I: History of the Last Judges, Eli and Samuel

Elkanah and His Family at Shiloh

1 ¹* There was a certain man from Ramathaim, Elkanah by name, a Zuphite from the hill country of Ephraim. He was the son of Jeroham, son of Elihu, son of Tohu, son of Zuph, an Ephraimite. ² He had two wives, one named Hannah, the other Peninnah; Peninnah had children, but Hannah was childless. ³* This man regularly went on pilgrimage from his city to worship the LORD of hosts and to sacrifice to him at Shiloh, where the two sons of Eli, Hophni and Phinehas, were ministering as priests of the LORD. ⁴ When the day came for Elkanah to offer sacrifice, he used to give a portion each to his wife Peninnah and to all her sons and daughters, ⁵* but a double portion to Hannah because he loved her, though the LORD had made her barren. ⁶* Her rival, to upset her, turned it into a constant reproach to her that the LORD had left her barren. ⁷ This went on year after year; each time they made their pilgrimage to the sanctuary of the LORD, Peninnah would approach her, and Hannah would weep and refuse to eat. ⁸* Her husband Elkanah used to ask her: "Hannah, why do you weep, and why do you refuse to eat? Why do you grieve? Am I not more to you than ten sons?"

Hannah's Prayer

⁹ Hannah rose after one such meal at Shiloh, and presented herself before the LORD; at the time, Eli the priest was sitting on a chair near the doorpost of the LORD'S temple. ¹⁰ In her bitterness she prayed to the LORD, weeping copiously, ¹¹*† and she made a vow, promising: "O LORD of hosts, if you look with pity on the misery of your handmaid, if you remember me and do not forget me, if you give your handmaid a male child, I will give him to the LORD for as long as he lives; neither wine nor liquor shall he drink, and no razor shall ever touch his head." ¹² As she remained long at prayer before the LORD, Eli watched her mouth, ¹³ for Hannah was praying silently; though her lips were moving, her voice could not be heard. Eli, thinking her drunk, ¹⁴ said to her, "How long will you make a drunken show of yourself? Sober up from your wine!" ¹⁵ "It isn't that, my lord," Hannah answered. "I am an unhappy woman. I have had neither wine nor liquor; I was only pouring out my troubles to the LORD. ¹⁶ Do not think your handmaid a ne'er-do-well; my prayer has been prompted by my deep sorrow and misery." ¹⁷ Eli said, "Go in peace, and may the God of Israel grant you what you have asked of him." ¹⁸ She replied, "Think kindly of your maidservant," and left. She went to her quarters, ate and drank with her husband, and no longer appeared down-

---

1, 11: *Give him to the LORD:* some ancient texts call Samuel a *nazir* in this context; see note on Nm 6, 1ff.

1, 1: 1 Chr 6, 19f.
1, 3: Ex 23, 14–17; 34, 23; Dt 16, 16; Jgs 21, 19.
1, 5: Dt 21, 15ff.
1, 6: Gn 16, 4f.
1, 8: Ru 4, 15.
1, 11: Nm 6, 1–5; Jgs 13, 2–5; 16, 17; Lk 1, 15.

cast. [19] Early the next morning they worshiped before the LORD, and then returned to their home in Ramah.

Hannah Bears a Son

When Elkanah had relations with his wife Hannah, the LORD remembered her. [20]† She conceived, and at the end of her term bore a son whom she called Samuel, since she had asked the LORD for him. [21] The next time her husband Elkanah was going up with the rest of his household to offer the customary sacrifice to the LORD and to fulfill his vows, [22] Hannah did not go, explaining to her husband, "Once the child is weaned, I will take him to appear before the LORD and to remain there forever; I will offer him as a perpetual nazirite." [23] Her husband Elkanah answered her: "Do what you think best; wait until you have weaned him. Only, may the LORD bring your resolve to fulfillment!" And so she remained at home and nursed her son until she had weaned him.

Samuel Is Offered to God

[24]† Once he was weaned, she brought him up with her, along with a three-year-old bull, an ephah of flour, and a skin of wine, and presented him at the temple of the LORD in Shiloh. [25] After the boy's father had sacrificed the young bull, Hannah, his mother, approached Eli [26] and said: "Pardon, my lord! As you live, my lord, I am the woman who stood near you here, praying to the LORD. [27] I prayed for this child, and the LORD granted my request. [28] Now I, in turn, give him to the LORD; as long as he lives, he shall be dedicated to the LORD." She left him there; [1]† and as she worshiped the LORD, she said:

2 [1]* "My heart exults in the LORD,
my horn† is exalted in my God.
I have swallowed up my enemies;
I rejoice in my victory.
[2]* There is no Holy One like the LORD;
there is no Rock like our God.

[3]*† "Speak boastfully no longer,
nor let arrogance issue from your mouths.

For an all-knowing God is the LORD,
a God who judges deeds.
[4]* The bows of the mighty are broken,
while the tottering gird on strength.
[5] The well-fed hire themselves out for bread,
while the hungry batten on spoil.
The barren wife bears seven sons,
while the mother of many languishes.
[6]* "The LORD puts to death and gives life;
he casts down to the nether world;
he raises up again.
[7] The LORD makes poor and makes rich,
he humbles, he also exalts.
[8]* He raises the needy from the dust;
from the ash heap he lifts up the poor,
To seat them with nobles
and make a glorious throne their heritage.
He gives to the vower his vow,
and blesses the sleep of the just.

"For the pillars of the earth are the LORD's,
and he has set the world upon them.

Prayers of Strong and Holy Women

Compare Hannah's prayer in 1 Sm 2, 1–10 to Mary's prayer in Lk 1, 46–55. Notice the joy, the confident faith in God's way, and the understanding that God will raise up those who are hungry, poor, and in need. Notice also how God will deal with the proud, the powerful, and the rich, especially in Mary's prayer. These holy women identify in their lives and in their prayers the bigger picture of what God is all about.

What strong and holy women in your life keep you in their prayers?

▶ 1 Sm 2, 1–10

1, 20: *Since she had asked:* this explanation would be more directly appropriate for the name Saul, which means "asked"; Samuel means "name of God."

1, 24: *An ephah:* a little more than a bushel.

1, 1: *And . . . said:* this belongs to ch 2.

2, 1–10: A hymn attributed to Hannah, the mother of Samuel, as her thanksgiving to God because she has borne a son despite her previous sterility. She praises God as the helper of the weak (1ff), who casts down the mighty and raises up the lowly (3ff), and who alone is the source of true strength (8ff); the hymn ends with a prayer for the king (v 10). This canticle has several points of resemblance with our Lady's Magnificat.

2, 1: *Horn:* the symbol of strength; cf Pss 18, 3; 75, 5; 89, 18; 112, 9.

2, 3: *Speak . . . mouths:* addressed to the enemies mentioned in v 1.

2, 1: Dt 33, 17; 2 Sm 22, 3; Ps 18, 2; Is 61, 10; Lk 1, 47.69.
2, 2: 2 Sm 22, 3; Ps 18, 2.
2, 3: Ps 75, 4.
2, 4: Is 40, 29.
2, 6: Dt 32, 39; Tb 4, 19; Jb 5, 11; Ps 30, 4; Wis 16, 13; Lk 1, 52.
2, 8: Jb 9, 6; 38, 6; Pss 104, 5; 121, 3.

9   He will guard the footsteps of his
     faithful ones,
     but the wicked shall perish in the darkness.
     For not by strength does man prevail;
10*   the LORD's foes shall be shattered.
     The Most High in heaven thunders;
     the LORD judges the ends of the earth.
     Now may he give strength to his king
     and exalt the horn of his anointed!"

11 When Elkanah returned home to Ramah, the child remained in the service of the LORD under the priest Eli.

Wickedness of Eli's Sons

12 Now the sons of Eli were wicked; they had respect neither for the LORD 13* nor for the priests' duties toward the people. When someone offered a sacrifice, the priest's servant would come with a three-pronged fork, while the meat was still boiling, 14 and would thrust it into the basin, kettle, caldron, or pot. Whatever the fork brought up, the priest would keep. That is how all the Israelites were treated who came to the sanctuary at Shiloh. 15 In fact, even before the fat was burned, the priest's servant would come and say to the man offering the sacrifice, "Give me some meat to roast for the priest. He will not accept boiled meat from you, only raw meat." 16* And if the man protested to him, "Let the fat be burned first as is the custom, then take whatever you wish," he would reply, "No, give it to me now, or else I will take it by force." 17 Thus the young men sinned grievously in the presence of the LORD; they treated the offerings to the LORD with disdain.

The LORD Rewards Hannah

18† Meanwhile the boy Samuel, girt with a linen apron, was serving in the presence of the LORD. 19 His mother used to make a little garment for him, which she would bring him each time she went up with her husband to offer the customary sacrifice. 20 And Eli would bless Elkanah and his wife, as they were leaving for home. He would say, "May the LORD repay you with children from this woman for the gift she has made to the LORD!" 21* The LORD favored Hannah so that she conceived

and gave birth to three more sons and two daughters, while young Samuel grew up in the service of the LORD.

Eli's Futile Rebuke

22† When Eli was very old, he heard repeatedly how his sons were treating all Israel [and that they were having relations with the women serving at the entry of the meeting tent.] 23 So he said to them: "Why are you doing such things? 24 No, my sons, you must not do these things! It is not a good report that I hear the people of the LORD spreading about you. 25 If a man sins against another man, one can intercede for him with the LORD; but if a man sins against the LORD, who can intercede for him?" But they disregarded their father's warning, since the LORD had decided on their death. 26* Meanwhile, young Samuel was growing in stature and in worth in the estimation of the LORD and of men.

Doom of Eli's House

27† A man of God came to Eli and said to him: "This is what the LORD says: 'I went so far as to reveal myself to your father's family when they were in Egypt as slaves to the house of Pharaoh. 28*† I chose them out of all the tribes of Israel to be my priests, to go up to my altar, to burn incense, and to wear the ephod before me; and I assigned all the oblations of the Israelites to your father's family. 29 Why do you keep a greedy eye on my sacrifices and on the offerings which I have prescribed? And why do you honor your sons in preference to me, fattening yourselves with the choicest part of every offering of my people Israel?' 30* This, therefore, is the oracle of the LORD, the God of Israel: 'I said in the past that your family and your father's family should minister in my presence forever. But now,' the LORD declares, 'away with this! for I will honor those who honor me, but those who spurn me shall be accursed. 31 Yes, the time is coming when I will break your strength and the strength of your father's family, so that no man in your family shall reach old age. 32 You shall witness as a disappointed rival all the benefits enjoyed by Israel, but there shall never be an old man in your family. 33 I will permit some of your family to remain at my altar, to wear

---

† 2, 18: *Linen apron:* called in Hebrew "ephod," but not the same as the high priest's ephod (Ex 28, 6–14) or the ephod used in divination (v 28). Samuel wore a simple apron such as was worn by the priests (1 Sm 22, 18), and on one occasion also by David (2 Sm 6, 14).
     2, 22: The bracketed words, which recall Ex 38, 8, are a gloss in the received text; they are lacking in the oldest Greek translation, and in a Hebrew manuscript from Qumran.
     2, 27–36: These verses propose the punishment of Eli from a point of view contemporary with the reform of Josiah (2 Kgs 23, 9; cf v 36); they hint at the events recorded in 1 Sm 22, 18–23 and 1 Kgs 2, 27. The older story of this divine warning is that in 1 Sm 3, 11–14.

2, 28: *Ephod:* a portable container, presumably of cloth, for the lots used in ritual consultation of God during the days of the Judges (Jgs 17, 5; 18, 14–15) and down into the time of David (1 Sm 14, 3ff; 23, 6ff; 30, 7f). The ephod of the high priest described in Ex 28, 6ff becomes a garment upon which a breastpiece of decision symbolizes, but no longer serves for, such consultation. The Exodus text codifies a later form of the tradition.

2, 10: Ps 98, 9.	2, 26: Lk 2, 52.
2, 13–15: Ex 29, 27f; Lv 7,	2, 28: 1 Sm 23, 9; 30, 7f; Jgs
29–36; Dt 18, 3.	17, 5.
2, 16: Lv 3, 3ff.	2, 30f: 2 Sm 22, 26; 1 Kgs 2,
2, 21: 1 Sm 3, 19.	27; Ps 18, 25.

out their eyes in consuming greed; but the rest of the men of your family shall die by the sword. 34* You shall have a sign in what will happen to your two sons, Hophni and Phinehas: both shall die on the same day. 35 I will choose a faithful priest who shall do what I have in heart and mind. I will establish a lasting house for him which shall function in the presence of my anointed forever. 36* Then whoever is left of your family will come to grovel before him for a piece of silver or a loaf of bread, and will say: Appoint me, I beg you, to a priestly function, that I may have a morsel of bread to eat.' "

Revelation to Samuel

3 1† During the time young Samuel was minister to the LORD under Eli, a revelation of the LORD was uncommon and vision infrequent. 2 One day Eli was asleep in his usual place. His eyes had lately grown so weak that he could not see. 3* The lamp of God was not yet extinguished, and Samuel was sleeping in the temple of the LORD where the ark of God was. 4 The LORD called to Samuel, who answered, "Here I am." 5 He ran to Eli and said, "Here I am. You called me." "I did not call you," Eli said. "Go back to sleep." So he went back to sleep. 6 Again the LORD called Samuel, who rose and went to Eli. "Here I am," he said. "You called me." But he answered, "I did not call you, my son. Go back to sleep."

7 At that time Samuel was not familiar with the LORD, because the LORD had not revealed anything to him as yet. 8 The LORD called Samuel again, for the third time. Getting up and going to Eli, he said, "Here I am. You called me." Then Eli understood that the LORD was calling the youth. 9 So he said to Samuel, "Go to sleep, and if you are called, reply, 'Speak, LORD, for your servant is listening.' " When Samuel went to sleep in his place, 10 the LORD came and revealed his presence, calling out as before, "Samuel, Samuel!" Samuel answered, "Speak, for your servant is listening." 11 The LORD said to Samuel: "I am about to do something in Israel that will cause the ears of everyone who hears it to ring. 12 On that day I will carry out in full against Eli everything I threatened against his family. 13* I announce to him that I am condemning his family once and for all, because of this crime: though he knew his sons were blaspheming God, he did not reprove them. 14 Therefore, I swear to the family of Eli that no sacrifice or offering will ever expiate its crime." 15 Samuel then slept until morning, when he got up early and opened the doors of the temple

of the LORD. He feared to tell Eli the vision, 16 but Eli called to him, "Samuel, my son!" He replied, "Here I am." 17† Then Eli asked, "What did he say to you? Hide nothing from me! May God do thus and so to you if you hide a single thing he told you." 18 So Samuel told him everything, and held nothing back. Eli answered, "He is the LORD. He will do what he judges best."

Samuel Acknowledged as Prophet

19* Samuel grew up, and the LORD was with him, not permitting any word of his to be without effect. 20* Thus all Israel from Dan to Beer-sheba came to know that Samuel was an accredited prophet of the LORD. 21 The LORD continued to appear at Shiloh; he manifested himself to Samuel at Shiloh through his word, 1† and Samuel spoke to all Israel.

Eli Teaches Samuel How to Pray

Eli taught Samuel to listen to God's voice with a simple sentence: "Speak, LORD, for your servant is listening" (1 Sm 3, 9). Let's look at that sentence as a prayer:

"Speak, LORD . . ." This is an invitation. It shows openness and readiness. It shows your recognition of God: "You are the Almighty, and I am ready to hear what you have to say."

". . . for your servant . . ." This shows humility. It is a recognition of yourself: "I am your servant. It is my desire to do what you want. My life's purpose is to serve you."

". . . is listening." This demonstrates your response: "I am not going to ignore you. I am not going to daydream or just pretend to pay attention. I will take in your message, and it will become part of me."

▶ I Sm 3, 1–19

3, 1: *Uncommon:* prophetic communications from God were almost unknown.
3, 17: *May God do thus and so to you:* the Biblical writers avoid repeating for us the specific terms of a curse as the speaker would have uttered it.

3, 1: *And . . . Israel:* this belongs to ch 4.

2, 34: 1 Sm 4, 11.
2, 36: 2 Kgs 23, 9.
3, 3: Ex 25, 22; 27, 20f; Lv 24, 2.4; 2 Chr 13, 11.
3, 13: 1 Sm 2, 27–36.
3, 19: 1 Sm 2, 21.
3, 20: Jgs 20, 1.

Defeat of the Israelites

4 At that time, the Philistines gathered for an attack on Israel. Israel went out to engage them in battle and camped at Ebenezer, while the Philistines camped at Aphek. 2 The Philistines then drew up in battle formation against Israel. After a fierce struggle Israel was defeated by the Philistines, who slew about four thousand men on the battlefield. 3 When the troops retired to the camp, the elders of Israel said, "Why has the LORD permitted us to be defeated today by the Philistines? Let us fetch the ark of the LORD from Shiloh that it may go into battle among us and save us from the grasp of our enemies."

Loss of the Ark

4*† So the people sent to Shiloh and brought from there the ark of the LORD of hosts, who is enthroned upon the cherubim. The two sons of Eli, Hophni and Phinehas, were with the ark of God. 5 When the ark of the LORD arrived in the camp, all Israel shouted so loudly that the earth resounded. 6 The Philistines, hearing the noise of shouting, asked, "What can this loud shouting in the camp of the Hebrews mean?" On learning that the ark of the LORD had come into the camp, 7 the Philistines were frightened. They said, "Gods have come to their camp." They said also, "Woe to us! This has never happened before. 8† Woe to us! Who can deliver us from the power of these mighty gods? These are the gods that struck the Egyptians with various plagues and with pestilence. 9 Take courage and be manly, Philistines; otherwise you will become slaves to the Hebrews, as they were your slaves. So fight manfully!" 10* The Philistines fought and Israel was defeated; every man fled to his own tent. It was a disastrous defeat, in which Israel lost thirty thousand foot soldiers. 11* The ark of God was captured, and Eli's two sons, Hophni and Phinehas, were among the dead.

Death of Eli

12* A Benjaminite fled from the battlefield and reached Shiloh that same day, with his clothes torn and his head covered with dirt. 13 When he arrived, Eli was sitting in his chair beside the gate, watching the road, for he was troubled at heart about the ark of God. The man, however, went into the city to divulge his news, which put the whole city in an uproar. 14 Hearing the outcry of the men standing near him, Eli inquired, "What does this commotion mean?" 15 (Eli was ninety-eight years old, and his eyes would not focus, so that he could not see.) 16 The man quickly came up to Eli and said, "It is I who have come from the battlefield; I fled from there today." He asked, "What happened, my son?" 17 And the messenger answered: "Israel fled from the Philistines; in fact, the troops suffered heavy losses. Your two sons, Hophni and Phinehas, are among the dead, and the ark of God has been captured." 18 At this mention of the ark of God, Eli fell backward from his chair into the gateway; since he was an old man and heavy, he died of a broken neck. He had judged Israel for forty years.

19 His daughter-in-law, the wife of Phinehas, was with child and at the point of giving birth. When she heard the news concerning the capture of the ark and the deaths of her father-in-law and her husband, she was seized with the pangs of labor, and gave birth. 20* She was about to die when the women standing around her said to her, "Never fear! You have given birth to a son." Yet she neither answered nor paid any attention. 21 [She named the child Ichabod, saying, "Gone is the glory from Israel," with reference to the capture of the ark of God and to her father-in-law and her husband.] 22* She said, "Gone is the glory from Israel," because the ark of God had been captured.

The Ark in the Temple of Dagon

5 1* The Philistines, having captured the ark of God, transferred it from Ebenezer to Ashdod. 2 They then took the ark of God and brought it into the temple of Dagon, placing it beside Dagon. 3 When the people of Ashdod rose early the next morning, Dagon was lying prone on the ground before the ark of the LORD. So they picked Dagon up and replaced him. 4 But the next morning early, when they arose, Dagon lay prone on the ground before the ark of the LORD, his head and hands broken off and lying on the threshold, his trunk alone intact. 5 For this reason, neither the priests of Dagon nor any others who enter the temple of Dagon tread on the threshold of Dagon in Ashdod to this very day; they always step over it.

The Ark Is Carried About

6*† Now the LORD dealt severely with the people of Ashdod. He ravaged and afflicted the city and its

---

4, 4: *Enthroned upon the cherubim:* this title of the Lord seems to have originated in the sanctuary at Shiloh; it represents the divine Majesty as seated upon a throne on which he can be borne through the heavens by winged creatures somewhat as in the visions of Ez 1 and 10.

4, 8: *These mighty gods:* the Philistines, who were polytheists, are represented as supposing the Israelites honored several gods.

5, 6: *Hemorrhoids . . . mice:* a double calamity fell upon them—

a plague of mice or rats, and a severe epidemic of pestilential tumors, probably the bubonic plague.

4, 4: Ex 25, 22.	35, 16ff.
4, 10: Ps 78, 61.	4, 22: Ps 78, 61.
4, 11: 1 Sm 2, 34.	5, 1–5: Jgs 16, 23–30; Is 45,
4, 12: Jos 7, 6; 2 Sm 1, 2; Jer	5f.20f.
7, 12.	5, 6: Ps 78, 66.
4, 20: 1 Sm 14, 3; Gn	

vicinity with hemorrhoids; he brought upon the city a great and deadly plague of mice that swarmed in their ships and overran their fields. 7 On seeing how matters stood, the men of Ashdod decided, "The ark of the God of Israel must not remain with us, for he is handling us and our god Dagon severely." 8 So they summoned all the Philistine lords and inquired of them, "What shall we do with the ark of the God of Israel?" The men of Gath replied, "Let them move the ark of the God of Israel on to us." 9 So they moved the ark of the God of Israel to Gath! But after it had been brought there, the LORD threw the city into utter turmoil: he afflicted its inhabitants, young and old, and hemorrhoids broke out on them. 10 The ark of God was next sent to Ekron; but as it entered that city, the people there cried out, "Why have they brought the ark of the God of Israel here to kill us and our kindred?" 11 Then they, too, sent a summons to all the Philistine lords and pleaded: "Send away the ark of the God of Israel. Let it return to its own place, that it may not kill us and our kindred." A deadly panic had seized the whole city, since the hand of God had been very heavy upon it. 12 Those who escaped death were afflicted with hemorrhoids, and the outcry from the city went up to the heavens.

The Ark To Be Returned

6 1 The ark of the LORD had been in the land of the Philistines seven months 2 when they summoned priests and fortune-tellers to ask, "What shall we do with the ark of the LORD? Tell us what we should send back with it." 3† They replied: "If you intend to send away the ark of the God of Israel, you must not send it alone, but must, by all means, make amends to him through a guilt offering. Then you will be healed, and will learn why he continues to afflict you." 4 When asked further, "What guilt offering should be our amends to him?", they replied:

"Five golden hemorrhoids and five golden mice to correspond to the number of Philistine lords, since the same plague has struck all of you and your lords. 5 Therefore, make images of the hemorrhoids and of the mice that are infesting your land and give them as a tribute to the God of Israel. Perhaps then he will cease to afflict you, your gods, and your land. 6* Why should you become stubborn, as the Egyptians and Pharaoh were stubborn? Was it not after he had dealt ruthlessly with them that the Israelites were released and departed? 7* So now set to work and make a new cart. Then take two milch cows that have not borne the yoke; hitch them to the cart, but drive their calves indoors away from them. 8 You shall next take the ark of the LORD and place it on the cart, putting in a box beside it the golden articles that you are offering, as amends for your guilt. Start it on its way, and let it go. 9 Then watch! If it goes up to Beth-shemesh along the route to his own territory, he has brought this great calamity upon us; if not, we will know it was not he who struck us, but that an accident happened to us."

The Ark in Beth-shemesh

10 They acted upon this advice. Taking two milch cows, they hitched them to the cart but shut up their calves indoors. 11 Then they placed the ark of the LORD on the cart, along with the box containing the golden mice and the images of the hemorrhoids. 12 The cows went straight for the route to Beth-shemesh and continued along this road, mooing as they went, without turning right or left. The Philistine lords followed them as far as the border of Beth-shemesh. 13 The people of Beth-shemesh were harvesting the wheat in the valley. When they looked up and spied the ark, they greeted it with rejoicing. 14* The cart came to the field of Joshua the Beth-shemite and stopped there. At a large stone in the field, the wood of the cart was split up and the cows were offered as a holocaust to the LORD. 15 The Levites, meanwhile, had taken down the ark of God and the box beside it, in which the golden articles were, and had placed them on the great stone. The men of Beth-shemesh also offered other holocausts and sacrifices to the LORD that day. 16 After witnessing this, the five Philistine lords returned to Ekron the same day.

Guilt Offering

17 The golden hemorrhoids the Philistines sent back as a guilt offering to the LORD were as follows: one for Ashdod, one for Gaza, one for Ashkelon, one for Gath, and one for Ekron. 18 The golden mice, however, corresponded to the number of all the cities of the Philistines belonging to the five lords, including fortified cities and open villages. The large stone on which the ark of the LORD was placed is still in the field of Joshua the Beth-shemite at the present time.

Penalty for Irreverence

19 The descendants of Jeconiah did not join in the celebration with the inhabitants of Beth-shemesh when they greeted the ark of the LORD, and seventy of them were struck down. The people

---

6, 3: *A guilt offering:* a propitiatory offering customary after unwitting transgression of the ordinances of God regarding holy things or property rights; cf Lv 6, 1ff.

6, 6: Ex 7, 14; 8, 15; 9, 34.   2 Sm 6, 3.
6, 7: Nm 19, 2; Dt 21, 3;   6, 14: 2 Sm 24, 21ff.

went into mourning at this great calamity with which the LORD had afflicted them. 20 The men of Beth-shemesh asked, "Who can stand in the presence of this Holy One? To whom shall he go from us?" 21 They then sent messengers to the inhabitants of Kiriath-jearim, saying, "The Philistines have returned the ark of the LORD; come down and get it."

7 1 So the inhabitants of Kiriath-jearim came for the ark of the LORD and brought it into the house of Abinadab on the hill, appointing his son Eleazar as guardian of the ark of the LORD.

Religious Reform

2 From the day the ark came to rest in Kiriath-jearim a long time, twenty years, elapsed, and the whole Israelite population turned to the LORD. 3* Samuel said to them: "If you wish with your whole heart to return to the LORD, put away your foreign gods and your Ashtaroth, devote yourselves to the LORD, and worship him alone. Then he will deliver you from the power of the Philistines." 4 So the Israelites put away their Baals and Ashtaroth, and worshiped the LORD alone. 5* Samuel then gave orders, "Gather all Israel to Mizpah, that I may pray to the LORD for you." 6*† When they were gathered at Mizpah, they drew water and poured it out on the ground before the LORD, and they fasted that day, confessing, "We have sinned against the LORD." It was at Mizpah that Samuel began to judge the Israelites.

Rout of the Philistines

7 When the Philistines heard that the Israelites had gathered at Mizpah, their lords went up against Israel. Hearing this, the Israelites became afraid of the Philistines 8* and said to Samuel, "Implore the LORD our God unceasingly for us, to save us from the clutches of the Philistines." 9* Samuel therefore took an unweaned lamb and offered it entire as a holocaust to the LORD. He implored the LORD for Israel, and the LORD heard him. 10 While Samuel was offering the holocaust, the Philistines advanced to join battle with Israel. That day, however, the LORD thundered loudly against the Philistines, and threw them into such confusion that they were defeated by Israel. 11 Thereupon the Israelites sallied

forth from Mizpah and pursued the Philistines, harrying them down beyond Beth-car. 12† Samuel then took a stone and placed it between Mizpah and Jeshanah; he named it Ebenezer, explaining, "To this point has the LORD helped us." 13* Thus were the Philistines subdued, never again to enter the territory of Israel, for the LORD was severe with them as long as Samuel lived. 14 The cities from Ekron to Gath which the Philistines had taken from Israel were restored to them. Israel also freed the territory of these cities from the dominion of the Philistines. Moreover there was peace between Israel and the Amorites.

15 Samuel judged Israel as long as he lived. 16 He made a yearly journey, passing through Bethel, Gilgal and Mizpah and judging Israel at each of these sanctuaries. 17* Then he used to return to Ramah, for that was his home. There, too, he judged Israel and built an altar to the LORD.

II: Establishment of the Monarchy in Israel

Request for a King

8 †1 In his old age Samuel appointed his sons judges over Israel. 2 His first-born was named Joel, his second son, Abijah; they judged at Beer-sheba. 3* His sons did not follow his example but sought illicit gain and accepted bribes, perverting justice. 4 Therefore all the elders of Israel came in a body to Samuel at Ramah 5* and said to him, "Now that you are old, and your sons do not follow your example, appoint a king over us, as other nations have, to judge us."

God Grants the Request

6 Samuel was displeased when they asked for a king to judge them. He prayed to the LORD, however, 7* who said in answer: "Grant the people's every request. It is not you they reject, they are rejecting me as their king. 8 As they have treated me constantly from the day I brought them up from Egypt to this day, deserting me and worshiping strange gods, so do they treat you too. 9 Now grant their request; but at the same time, warn them solemnly and inform them of the rights of the king who will rule them."

7, 6: *Poured it out on the ground:* for the symbolism, cf 2 Sm 14, 14.

7, 12: *Ebenezer:* or *eben ha-ezer,* means "stone of help."

8, 1: From this chapter on, the First Book of Samuel gives us two and sometimes three viewpoints on most of the events with which it is concerned, such as the appointment of Saul as king, the reasons for his downfall, his relationship with David, even the circumstances of Saul's death (1 Sm 31; 2 Sm 1). The choice of Saul as king is seen, in ch 8, followed by 10, 17–27 and ch 12, as motivated by the people's defection from the proper service of God; this later editorial approach incorporates not only narratives with which it is consistent,

but also early traditions (9, 1–10.16; ch 11) which portray the events and their motivation quite differently.

7, 3: 1 Sm 12, 10.20.24; Jos 24, 23; Jgs 6, 6–10; 10, 10–16.

7, 5: 1 Sm 10, 17; Jgs 20, 1.

7, 6: Jgs 20, 26; Ps 22, 14; Lam 2, 19.

7, 8: Ex 17, 9–13.

7, 9f: 2 Sm 22, 14f; Sir 46, 16ff.

7, 13: Jgs 3, 30; 8, 28; 11, 33.

7, 17: 1 Sm 9, 12; 14, 35.

8, 3: Ex 23, 8; Dt 16, 19; Prv 17, 23.

8, 5f: Dt 17, 14f; Hos 13, 10; Acts 13, 21.

8, 7f: 1 Sm 12, 1.12f; Jgs 8, 22f; 10, 13; 1 Kgs 9, 9.

The Rights of a King

10 Samuel delivered the message of the LORD in full to those who were asking him for a king. 11* He told them: "The rights of the king who will rule you will be as follows: He will take your sons and assign them to his chariots and horses, and they will run before his chariot. 12* He will also appoint from among them his commanders of groups of a thousand and of a hundred soldiers. He will set them to do his plowing and his harvesting, and to make his implements of war and the equipment of his chariots. 13 He will use your daughters as ointment-makers, as cooks, and as bakers. 14* He will take the best of your fields, vineyards, and olive groves, and give them to his officials. 15 He will tithe your crops and your vineyards, and give the revenue to his eunuchs and his slaves. 16 He will take your male and female servants, as well as your best oxen and your asses, and use them to do his work. 17* He will tithe your flocks and you yourselves will become his slaves. 18 When this takes place, you will complain against the king whom you have chosen, but on that day the LORD will not answer you."

Persistent Demand

19* The people, however, refused to listen to Samuel's warning and said, "Not so! There must be a king over us. 20 We too must be like other nations, with a king to rule us and to lead us in warfare and fight our battles." 21 When Samuel had listened to all the people had to say, he repeated it to the LORD, 22† who then said to him, "Grant their request and appoint a king to rule them." Samuel thereupon said to the men of Israel, "Each of you go to his own city."

9 1* There was a stalwart man from Benjamin named Kish, who was the son of Abiel, son of Zeror, son of Becorath, son of Aphiah, a Benjaminite. 2* He had a son named Saul, who was a handsome young man. There was no other Israelite handsomer than Saul; he stood head and shoulders above the people.

The Lost Asses

3 Now the asses of Saul's father, Kish, had wandered off. Kish said to his son Saul, "Take one of the servants with you and go out and hunt for the asses." 4 Accordingly they went through the hill country of Ephraim, and through the land of Shalishah. Not finding them there, they continued through the land of Shaalim without success. They also went through the land of Benjamin, but they failed to find the animals. 5 When they came to the land of Zuph, Saul said to the servant who was with him, "Come, let us turn back, lest my father forget about the asses and become anxious about us." 6 The servant replied, "Listen! There is a man of God in this city, a man held in high esteem; all that he says is sure to come true. Let us go there now! Perhaps he can tell us how to accomplish our errand." 7* But Saul said to his servant, "If we go, what can we offer the man? There is no bread in our bags, and we have no present to give the man of God. What have we?" 8† Again the servant answered Saul, "I have a quarter of a silver shekel. If I give that to the man of God, he will tell us our way." 10 Saul then said to his servant, "Well said! Come on, let us go!" And they went to the city where the man of God lived.

Quest for Samuel's Aid

11* As they were going up the ascent to the city, they met some girls coming out to draw water and inquired of them, "Is the seer in town?" 9*† (In former times in Israel, anyone who sent to consult God used to say, "Come, let us go to the seer." For he who is now called prophet was formerly called

did you KNOW?

Doublets

Often, more than one version of a story is recorded in the Bible. Genesis has two stories of the Creation (1, 1—2, 4; 2, 4–25). The First Book of Samuel has two different attitudes toward the request to have a king in Israel. Compare the anti-king passages of 8, 10–22 and 10, 17–19 with the pro-king passages of 9, 15–16 and chapter 11. Most likely, the difference of opinion comes from different parts of Israel. The Bible often combines two versions of a story, called doublets, to allow consideration of both sides of an issue.

9, 8: *A quarter of a silver shekel:* about a tenth of an ounce of silver.

9, 9: This verse is a later explanation of the term *seer,* first used in the text in 1 Sm 9, 11.

8, 11: 1 Sm 10, 25; Dt 17, 14–20; 1 Kgs 12.
8, 12: 2 Sm 15, 1; 1 Kgs 1, 5.
8, 14: 1 Sm 22, 7; 1 Kgs 21, 1–24; Ez 46, 18.
8, 17: 1 Kgs 12, 4.
8, 19: 1 Sm 10, 19.
9, 1: 1 Sm 14, 51; 1 Chr 8, 33.
9, 2: 1 Sm 10, 23.
9, 7f: Nm 22, 7; 1 Kgs 14, 3; 2 Kgs 4, 42; 5, 15; 8, 8f.
9, 11: Gn 24, 11ff; Ex 2, 16.
9, 9: Sir 46, 15.

seer.) 12*† The girls answered, "Yes, there—straight ahead. Hurry now; just today he came to the city, because the people have a sacrifice today on the high place. 13 When you enter the city, you may reach him before he goes up to the high place to eat. The people will not eat until he arrives; only after he blesses the sacrifice will the invited guests eat. Go up immediately, for you should find him right now."

Samuel's Revelation about Saul

14 So they went up to the city. As they entered it, Samuel was coming toward them on his way to the high place. 15* The day before Saul's arrival, the LORD had given Samuel the revelation: 16* "At this time tomorrow I will send you a man from the land of Benjamin whom you are to anoint as commander of my people Israel. He shall save my people from the clutches of the Philistines, for I have witnessed their misery and accepted their cry for help." 17 When Samuel caught sight of Saul, the LORD assured him, "This is the man of whom I told you; he is to govern my people." 18 Saul met Samuel in the gateway and said, "Please tell me where the seer lives." 19 Samuel answered Saul: "I am the seer. Go up ahead of me to the high place and eat with me today. In the morning, before dismissing you, I will tell you whatever you wish. 20 As for the asses you lost three days ago, do not worry about them, for they have been found. Whom does Israel desire ardently if not you and your father's family?" 21* Saul replied: "Am I not a Benjaminite, of one of the smallest tribes of Israel, and is not my clan the least among the clans of the tribe of Benjamin? Why say such things to me?"

22 Samuel then took Saul and his servant and brought them to the room, where he placed them at the head of the guests, of whom there were about thirty. 23 He said to the cook, "Bring the portion I gave you and told you to put aside." 24† So the cook took up the leg and what went with it, and placed it before Saul. Samuel said: "This is a reserved portion that has been set before you. Eat, for it was kept for you until your arrival; I explained that I was inviting

some guests." Thus Saul dined with Samuel that day. 25 When they came down from the high place into the city, a mattress was spread for Saul on the roof, 26 and he slept there.

Saul's Anointing

At daybreak Samuel called to Saul on the roof, "Get up, and I will start you on your journey." Saul rose, and he and Samuel went outside the city together. 27 As they were approaching the edge of the town, Samuel said to Saul, "Tell the servant to go on ahead of us, but stay here yourself for the moment, that I may give you a message from God."

10 1* Then, from a flask he had with him, Samuel poured oil on Saul's head; he also kissed him, saying: "The LORD anoints you commander over his heritage. You are to govern the LORD's people Israel, and to save them from the grasp of their enemies roundabout.

"This will be the sign for you that the LORD has anointed you commander over his heritage: 2*† When you leave me today, you will meet two men near Rachel's tomb at Zelzah in the territory of Benjamin, who will say to you, 'The asses you went to look for have been found. Your father is no longer worried about the asses, but is anxious about you and says, What shall I do about my son?' 3 Farther on, when you arrive at the terebinth of Tabor, you will be met by three men going up to God at Bethel; one will be bringing three kids, another three loaves of bread, and the third a skin of wine. 4 They will greet you and offer you two wave offerings of bread, which you will take from them. 5*† After that you will come to Gibeath-elohim, where there is a garrison of the Philistines. As you enter that city, you will meet a band of prophets, in a prophetic state, coming down from the high place preceded by lyres, tambourines, flutes and harps. 6* The spirit of the LORD will rush upon you, and you will join them in their prophetic state and will be changed into another man. 7 When you see these signs fulfilled, do whatever you judge feasible, because God is with you. 8*† Now go down ahead of

---

† 9, 12: *On the high place:* the local sanctuary on the top of a hill, where the sacrifice was offered and the sacrificial meal eaten.

9, 24: *And what went with it:* a slight change would give "and the fatty tail" as perhaps the original reading. Sheep in the Near East are exceptionally fat-tailed, and such a portion would be thought a special delicacy by the Hebrews. However, the ritual legislation as we know it (Lv 3, 9) would require that the fat tail be burned on the altar. If this general rule was later than the time of Samuel, the present text may have been retouched so as not to seem to contravene it. A Qumran text has "the festive (leg)" here.

10, 2: Here, as in Jer 31, 15, Rachel's tomb is placed north of Jerusalem. Later tradition understood Gn 35, 19f in the sense given by Mt 2, 16ff, and placed the tomb at Bethlehem, farther south.

10, 5: *A garrison of the Philistines:* the Hebrew word for "garrison" has been explained alternatively to mean a pillar erected to mark the Philistine occupation, or an inspector or officer for the col-

lection of taxes. *In a prophetic state:* in an ecstatic condition due to strong feelings of religious enthusiasm induced by a communal observance, possibly accompanied by music and dancing.

10, 8: By inserting this verse, with its seven days, an editor has prepared for one narrative of the rejection of Saul (1 Sm 13, 8–15) in the very context of Saul's anointing.

9, 12: 1 Sm 7, 17; 16, 2.5; 20, 6.29; Dt 12, 13; 1 Kgs 3, 2.4.
9, 15: Acts 13, 21.
9, 16: 1 Sm 10, 1.
9, 21: 1 Sm 15, 17.
10, 1: 1 Sm 9, 16f; 24, 7; Jgs 9, 9; 1 Kgs 1, 39;

Acts 13, 21.
10, 2: Jer 31, 15; Mk 14, 13.
10, 5f: 1 Sm 13, 3; 16, 13; 19, 20f.
10, 6: 1 Sm 11, 6; 16, 13; Jgs 14, 6.19; 15, 14; 2 Kgs 3, 15.
10, 8: 1 Sm 13, 8; Lv 3, 1.

me to Gilgal, for I shall come down to you, to offer holocausts and to sacrifice peace offerings. Wait seven days until I come to you; I shall then tell you what you must do."

Fulfillment of the Signs

⁹ As Saul turned to leave Samuel, God gave him another heart. That very day all these signs came to pass. . . . ¹⁰*† When they were going from there to Gibeah, a band of prophets met him, and the spirit of God rushed upon him, so that he joined them in their prophetic state. ¹¹* When all who had known him previously saw him in a prophetic state among the prophets, they said to one another, "What has happened to the son of Kish? Is Saul also among the prophets?" ¹² And someone from that district added, "And who is their father?" Thus the proverb arose, "Is Saul also among the prophets?" ¹³ When he came out of the prophetic state, he went home.

Silence about the Kingship

¹⁴ Saul's uncle inquired of him and his servant, "Where have you been?" Saul replied, "To look for the asses. When we could not find them, we went to Samuel." ¹⁵ Then Saul's uncle said, "Tell me, then, what Samuel said to you." ¹⁶ Saul said to his uncle, "He assured us that the asses had been found." But he mentioned nothing to him of what Samuel had said about the kingship.

Saul Chosen King by Lot

¹⁷* Samuel called the people together to the LORD at Mizpah ¹⁸* and addressed the Israelites: "Thus says the LORD, the God of Israel, 'It was I who brought Israel up from Egypt and delivered you from the power of the Egyptians and from the power of all the kingdoms that oppressed you.' ¹⁹* But today you have rejected your God, who delivers you from all your evils and calamities, by saying to him, 'Not so, but you must appoint a king over us.' Now, therefore, take your stand before the LORD according to tribes and families." ²⁰ So Samuel had all the tribes of Israel come forward, and the tribe of Benjamin was chosen. ²¹ Next he had the tribe of Benjamin come forward in clans, and the clan of Matri was chosen, and finally Saul, son of Kish, was chosen. But they looked for him in vain. ²²* Again they consulted the LORD, "Has he come here?" The LORD

answered, "He is hiding among the baggage." ²³* They ran to bring him from there; and when he stood among the people, he was head and shoulders above all the crowd. ²⁴* Samuel said to all the people, "Do you see the man whom the LORD has chosen? There is none like him among all the people!" Then all the people shouted, "Long live the king!"

²⁵*† Samuel next explained to the people the law of royalty and wrote it in a book, which he placed in the presence of the LORD. This done, Samuel dismissed the people, each to his own place. ²⁶ Saul also went home to Gibeah, accompanied by warriors whose hearts the LORD had touched. ²⁷* But certain worthless men said, "How can this fellow save us?" They despised him and brought him no present.

Defeat of the Ammonites

11 ¹*† About a month later, Nahash the Ammonite went up and laid siege to Jabesh-gilead. All the men of Jabesh begged Nahash, "Make a treaty with us, and we will be your subjects." ² But Nahash the Ammonite replied, "This is my condition for a treaty with you: I must gouge out every man's right eye, that I may thus bring ignominy on all Israel." ³ The elders of Jabesh said to him: "Give us seven days to send messengers throughout the territory of Israel. If no one rescues us, we will surrender to you." ⁴ When the messengers arrived at Gibeah of Saul, they related the news to the people, all of whom wept aloud. ⁵ Just then Saul came in from the field, behind his oxen. "Why are the people weeping?" he asked. The message of the inhabitants of Jabesh was repeated to him. ⁶* As he listened to this report, the spirit of God rushed upon him and he became very angry. ⁷* Taking a yoke of oxen, he cut them into pieces, which he sent throughout the territory of Israel by couriers with the message, "If anyone does not come out to follow Saul [and Samuel], the same as this will be done to his oxen!" In dread of the LORD, the people turned out to a man. ⁸ When he reviewed them in Bezek, there were three hundred thousand Israelites and seventy thousand Judahites.

⁹ To the messengers who had come he said, "Tell the inhabitants of Jabesh-gilead that tomorrow, while the sun is hot, they will be rescued." The messengers came and reported this to the inhabitants of

---

10, 10: The story has here been abridged by omitting the fulfillment of the first two signs given by Samuel (1 Sm 10, 2ff).

10, 25: *The law of royalty:* the charter defining the rights of the king.

11, 1: *About a month later:* there is ancient evidence for a longer introduction to this campaign. The time indication here may refer to its earlier stages rather than to the events of ch 10.

10, 10: 1 Sm 19, 20–24; Nm 11, 25.
10, 11: 1 Sm 19, 24.
10, 17: 1 Sm 7, 5.
10, 18: Ex 20, 2; Lv 11, 45; 25, 38; Nm 15, 41; Dt 5, 6; Jgs 6, 8f.
10, 19: 1 Sm 8, 19.
10, 22: 1 Sm 30, 24.

10, 23: 1 Sm 9, 2; 16, 7.
10, 24: 2 Sm 16, 16; 1 Kgs 1, 25; 2 Kgs 11, 12.
10, 25: 1 Sm 8, 11; Dt 17, 14–20.
10, 27: 1 Sm 11, 12.
11, 1: 1 Sm 12, 12; 31, 11.
11, 6: 1 Sm 16, 13; Jgs 14, 6.19.
11, 7: 1 Kgs 11, 30; 2 Kgs 13, 18.

Jabesh, who were jubilant, [10] and said to Nahash, "Tomorrow we will surrender to you, and you may do whatever you please with us." [11] On the appointed day, Saul arranged his troops in three companies and invaded the camp during the dawn watch. They slaughtered Ammonites until the heat of the day; by then the survivors were so scattered that no two were left together.

Saul Accepted as King

[12]*† The people then said to Samuel: "Who questioned whether Saul should rule over us? Hand over the men and we will put them to death." [13]* But Saul broke in to say, "No man is to be put to death this day, for today the LORD has saved Israel." [14] Samuel said to the people, "Come, let us go to Gilgal to inaugurate the kingdom there." [15] So all the people went to Gilgal, where, in the presence of the LORD, they made Saul king. They also sacrificed peace offerings there before the LORD, and Saul and all the Israelites celebrated the occasion with great joy.

Samuel's Integrity

12 [1]* Samuel addressed all Israel: "I have granted your request in every respect," he said. "I have set a king over you [2] and now the king is your leader. As for me, I am old and gray, and have sons among you. I have lived with you from my youth to the present day. [3]* Here I stand! Answer me in the presence of the LORD and of his anointed. Whose ox have I taken? Whose ass have I taken? Whom have I cheated? Whom have I oppressed? From whom have I accepted a bribe and overlooked his guilt? I will make restitution to you." [4] They replied, "You have neither cheated us, nor oppressed us, nor accepted anything from anyone." [5] So he said to them, "The LORD is witness against you this day, and his anointed as well, that you have found nothing in my possession." "He is witness," they agreed.

Samuel Upbraids the People

[6]* Continuing, Samuel said to the people: "The LORD is witness, who appointed Moses and Aaron, and who brought your fathers up from the land of Egypt. [7] Now, therefore, take your stand, and I shall arraign you before the LORD, and shall recount for you all the acts of mercy the LORD has done for you and your fathers. [8]* When Jacob and his sons went to Egypt and the Egyptians oppressed them, your fathers appealed to the LORD, who sent Moses and Aaron to bring them out of Egypt, and he gave them this place to live in. [9]* But they forgot the LORD their God; and he allowed them to fall into the clutches of Sisera, the captain of the army of Jabin, king of Hazor, into the grasp of the Philistines, and into the grip of the king of Moab, who made war against them. [10]* Each time they appealed to the LORD and said, 'We have sinned in forsaking the LORD and worshiping Baals and Ashtaroth; but deliver us now from the power of our enemies, and we will worship you.' [11]* Accordingly, the LORD sent Jerubbaal, Barak, Jephthah, and Samuel; he delivered you from the power of your enemies on every side, so that you were able to live in security. [12]* Yet, when you saw Nahash, king of the Ammonites, advancing against you, you said to me, 'Not so, but a king must rule us,' even though the LORD your God is your king.

Warnings for People and King

[13]* "Now you have the king you want, a king the LORD has given you. [14] If you fear the LORD and worship him, if you are obedient to him and do not rebel against the LORD'S command, if both you and the king who rules you follow the LORD your God—well and good. [15] But if you do not obey the LORD and if you rebel against his command, the LORD will deal severely with you and your king, and destroy you. [16] Now then, stand ready to witness the great marvel the LORD is about to accomplish before your eyes. [17]* Are we not in the harvest time for wheat? Yet I shall call to the LORD, and he will send thunder and rain. Thus you will see and understand how greatly the LORD is displeased that you have asked for a king." [18] Samuel then called to the LORD, and the LORD sent thunder and rain that day.

Assistance Promised

As a result, all the people dreaded the LORD and Samuel. [19] They said to Samuel, "Pray to the LORD your God for us, your servants, that we may not die for having added to all our other sins the evil of asking for a king." [20] "Do not fear," Samuel answered them. "It is true you have committed all this evil; still, you must not turn from the LORD, but must worship him with your whole heart. [21]* Do not turn to meaningless idols which can

---

11, 12–14: With these verses, an editor has harmonized the account of the acknowledgment of Saul as king at Mizpah (1 Sm 10, 17–24) with the public acclamation at Gilgal (1 Sm 11, 15) after the defeat of the Ammonites (1 Sm 11, 1–11). The Greek text of 1 Sm 11, 15 reads "and Samuel anointed Saul as king," instead of they made Saul king.

11, 12: 1 Sm 10, 27.
11, 13: 2 Sm 19, 23.
12, 1: 1 Sm 8, 7.9.22.
12, 3: Ex 20, 17; 23, 8; Nm 16, 15; Dt 16, 19; Sir 46, 19.
12, 6: Mi 6, 4.
12, 8: Gn 46, 5; Ex 1, 11; 2, 23ff.
12, 9: Jgs 3, 12ff; 4, 2f; 10, 7;

13, 1.
12, 10: 1 Sm 7, 3f.
12, 11: Jgs 6, 14.32; 11, 1.
12, 12: 1 Sm 8, 6f.19; 11, 1f; Jgs 8, 23.
12, 13: 1 Sm 8, 7.
12, 17: Ex 9, 23.28ff; 1 Kgs 18, 1.
12, 21: Dt 32, 37ff.

neither profit nor save; they are nothing. 22* For the sake of his own great name the LORD will not abandon his people, since the LORD himself chose to make you his people. 23* As for me, far be it from me to sin against the LORD by ceasing to pray for you and to teach you the good and right way. 24 But you must fear the LORD and worship him faithfully with your whole heart; keep in mind the great things he has done among you. 25 If instead you continue to do evil, both you and your king shall perish."

III: Saul and David

13 1† [Saul was . . . years old when he became king and he reigned . . . (two) years over Israel.]

Saul Offers Sacrifice

2 Saul chose three thousand men of Israel, of whom two thousand remained with him in Michmash and in the hill country of Bethel, and one thousand were with Jonathan in Gibeah of Benjamin. He sent the rest of the people back to their tents. 3*† Now Jonathan overcame the Philistine garrison which was in Gibeah, and the Philistines got word of it. Then Saul sounded the horn throughout the land, with a proclamation, "Let the Hebrews hear!" 4 Thus all Israel learned that Saul had overcome the garrison of the Philistines and that Israel had brought disgrace upon the Philistines; and the soldiers were called up to Saul in Gilgal. 5 The Philistines also assembled for battle, with three thousand chariots, six thousand horsemen, and foot soldiers as numerous as the sands of the seashore. Moving up against Israel, they encamped in Michmash, east of Beth-aven. 6* Some Israelites, aware of the danger and of the difficult situation, hid themselves in caves, in thickets, among rocks, in caverns, and in cisterns, 7† and other Hebrews passed over the Jordan into the land of Gad and Gilead. Saul, however, held out at Gilgal, although all his followers were seized with fear. 8* He waited seven days—the time Samuel had determined. When Samuel did not arrive at Gilgal, the men began to slip away from Saul. 9 He then said, "Bring me the holocaust and peace offerings," and he offered up the holocaust.

King Saul Reproved

10 He had just finished this offering when Samuel arrived. Saul went out to greet him, 11 and Samuel asked him, "What have you done?" Saul replied: "When I saw that the men were slipping away from me, since you had not come by the specified time, and with the Philistines assembled at Michmash, 12 I said to myself, 'Now the Philistines will come down against me at Gilgal, and I have not yet sought the LORD's blessing.' So in my anxiety I offered up the holocaust." 13 Samuel's response was: "You have been foolish! Had you kept the command the LORD your God gave you, the LORD would now establish your kingship in Israel as lasting; 14* but as things are, your kingdom shall not endure. The LORD has sought out a man after his own heart and has appointed him commander of his people, because you broke the LORD's command."

Philistine Invasion

15* Then Samuel set out from Gilgal and went his own way; but the rest of the people went up after Saul to meet the soldiers, going from Gilgal to Gibeah of Benjamin. Saul then numbered the soldiers he had with him, who were about six hundred. 16 Saul, his son Jonathan, and the soldiers they had with them were now occupying Geba of Benjamin, and the Philistines were encamped at Michmash. 17* Meanwhile, raiders left the camp of the Philistines in three bands. One band took the Ophrah road toward the district of Shual; 18 another turned in the direction of Beth-horon; and the third took the road for Geba that overlooks the Valley of the Hyenas toward the desert.

Disarmament of Israel

19* Not a single smith was to be found in the whole land of Israel, for the Philistines had said, "Otherwise the Hebrews will make swords or spears." 20 All Israel, therefore, had to go down to the Philistines to sharpen their plowshares, mattocks, axes, and sickles. 21 The price for the plowshares and mattocks was two-thirds of a shekel, and a third of a shekel for sharpening the axes and for setting the ox-goads. 22 And so on the day of battle neither sword nor spear could be found in the possession

---

13, 1: A formula like that of 2 Sm 5, 4 was introduced here at some time; but the age of Saul when he became king remains a blank, and the two years assigned for his reign in the received text cannot be correct. Tradition (Acts 13, 21) offers the round number, "forty years."

13, 3–4: *The Philistine garrison:* see note on 1 Sm 10, 5. *Let the Hebrews hear:* a different reading of these verses, based on the Greek, would yield: "And the Philistines heard that the Hebrews (or: the slaves) had revolted. Saul in the meantime sounded the trumpet throughout all the land (v 4), and all Israel heard that Saul. . . .'"

13, 7–15: These verses, like 1 Sm 10, 8, anticipate the rejection of Saul; a different occasion and motivation for this are given in ch 15, resumed in 1 Sm 28, 17f.

12, 22: Jer 14, 21; Ex 20, 9; Dn 3, 34.
12, 23: Ex 32, 11.
13, 3: 1 Sm 14, 1–15; Jgs 3, 27; 6, 34; 2 Sm 20, 1f.
13, 6: 1 Sm 14, 22.
13, 8: 1 Sm 10, 8.
13, 14: 1 Sm 25, 30; 2 Sm 7, 15f; Ps 78, 70; Acts 13, 22.
13, 15: 1 Sm 14, 2.
13, 17: 1 Sm 14, 15.
13, 19: Jgs 5, 8.

of any of the soldiers with Saul or Jonathan. Only Saul and his son Jonathan had them.

Jonathan's Exploit

23* An outpost of the Philistines had pushed forward to the pass of Michmash.

14 1* One day Jonathan, son of Saul, said to his armor-bearer, "Come, let us go over to the Philistine outpost on the other side." But he did not inform his father. 2 (Saul's command post was under the pomegranate tree near the threshing floor on the outskirts of Geba; those with him numbered about six hundred men. 3* Ahijah, son of Ahitub, brother of Ichabod, who was the son of Phinehas, son of Eli, the priest of the LORD at Shiloh, was wearing the ephod.) Nor did the soldiers know that Jonathan had gone. 4 Flanking the ravine through which Jonathan intended to get over to the Philistine outpost there was a rocky crag on each side, one called Bozez, the other Seneh. 5 One crag was to the north, toward Michmash, the other to the south, toward Geba. 6* Jonathan said to his armor-bearer: "Come, let us go over to that outpost of the uncircumcised. Perhaps the LORD will help us, because it is no more difficult for the LORD to grant victory through a few than through many." 7 His armor-bearer replied, "Do whatever you are inclined to do; I will match your resolve." 8 Jonathan continued: "We shall go over to those men and show ourselves to them. 9 If they say to us, 'Stay there until we can come to you,' we shall stop where we are; we shall not go up to them. 10 But if they say, 'Come up to us,' we shall go up, because the LORD has delivered them into our grasp. That will be our sign." 11 Accordingly, the two of them appeared before the outpost of the Philistines, who said, "Look, some Hebrews are coming out of the holes where they have been hiding." 12 The men of the outpost called to Jonathan and his armor-bearer. "Come up here," they said, "and we will teach you a lesson." So Jonathan said to his armor-bearer, "Climb up after me, for the LORD has delivered them into the grasp of Israel." 13 Jonathan clambered up with his armor-bearer behind him; as the Philistines turned to flee him, he cut them down, and his armor-bearer followed him and finished them off. 14 In this first exploit Jonathan and his armor-bearer slew about twenty men within half a furlong. 15 Then panic spread to the army and to the countryside, and all the soldiers, including the outpost and the raiding parties, were terror-stricken. The earth also shook, so that the panic was beyond human endurance.

Rout of the Philistines

16 The lookouts of Saul in Geba of Benjamin saw that the enemy camp had scattered and were running about in all directions. 17 Saul said to those around him, "Count the troops and find out if any of us are missing." When they had investigated, they found Jonathan and his armor-bearer missing. 18† Saul then said to Ahijah, "Bring the ephod here." (Ahijah was wearing the ephod in front of the Israelites at that time.) 19 While Saul was speaking to the priest, the tumult in the Philistine camp kept increasing. So he said to the priest, "Withdraw your hand." 20* And Saul and all his men shouted and rushed into the fight, where the Philistines, wholly confused, were thrusting swords at one another. 21* In addition, the Hebrews who had previously sided with the Philistines and had gone up with them to the camp, turned to join the Israelites under Saul and Jonathan. 22* Likewise, all the Israelites who were hiding in the hill country of Ephraim, on hearing that the Philistines were fleeing, pursued them in the rout. 23 Thus the LORD saved Israel that day.

Saul's Oath

† The battle continued past Beth-horon; 24 the whole people, about ten thousand combatants, were with Saul, and there was scattered fighting in every town in the hill country of Ephraim And Saul swore a very rash oath that day, putting the people under this ban: "Cursed be the man who takes food before evening, before I am able to avenge myself on my enemies" So none of the people tasted food 25 Indeed, there was a honeycomb lying on the ground, 26 and when the soldiers came to the comb the swarm had left it; yet no one would raise a hand to his mouth from it, because the people feared the oath

Violation of the Oath

27 Jonathan, who had not heard that his father had put the people under oath, thrust out the end of the staff he was holding and dipped it into the honey. Then he raised it to his mouth and his eyes lit up. 28 At this one of the soldiers spoke up: "Your

---

14, 18: *Ephod:* to be used in consulting God; see note on v 41, and that on 1 Sm 2, 28, above.

14, 23: *Past Beth-horon:* this is a textual correction influenced by 1 Sm 13, 18; the received Hebrew text refers to Bethel (Beth-aven), but the effect of the victory would seem to have been that the main ridge of mountains in the territories of Benjamin and Ephraim was cleared of Philistines.

13, 23: 1 Sm 14, 15.
14, 1: 1 Sm 13, 3.
14, 3: 1 Sm 2, 28; 4, 21; 14, 18; 23, 9; 30, 7.
14, 6: 1 Sm 17, 26.36.47; Sir

39, 18; 1 Mc 3, 19.
14, 20: Jgs 7, 22.
14, 21: 1 Sm 29, 4.
14, 22: 1 Sm 13, 6.

father put the people under a strict oath, saying, 'Cursed be the man who takes food this day!' As a result the people are weak." 29 Jonathan replied: "My father brings trouble to the land. Look how bright my eyes are from this small taste of honey I have had. 30 What is more, if the people had eaten freely today of their enemy's booty when they came across it, would not the slaughter of the Philistines by now have been the greater for it?"

Use of Flesh with Blood Forbidden

31 After the Philistines were routed that day from Michmash to Aijalon, the people were completely exhausted. 32* So they pounced upon the spoil and took sheep, oxen and calves, slaughtering them on the ground and eating the flesh with blood. 33 Informed that the people were sinning against the LORD by eating the flesh with blood, Saul said: "You have broken faith. Roll a large stone here for me." 34 He continued: "Mingle with the people and tell each of them to bring his ox or his sheep to me. Slaughter it here and then eat, but you must not sin against the LORD by eating the flesh with blood." So everyone brought to the LORD whatever ox he had seized, and they slaughtered them there; 35* and Saul built an altar to the LORD—this was the first time he built an altar to the LORD.

Jonathan in Danger of Death

36 Then Saul said, "Let us go down in pursuit of the Philistines by night, to plunder among them until daybreak and to kill them all off." They replied, "Do what you think best." But the priest said, "Let us consult God." 37* So Saul inquired of God: "Shall I go down in pursuit of the Philistines? Will you deliver them into the power of Israel?" But he received no answer on this occasion. 38 Saul then said, "Come here, all officers of the army. We must investigate and find out how this sin was committed today. 39 As the LORD lives who has given victory to Israel, even if my son Jonathan has committed it, he shall surely die!" But none of the people answered him. 40* So he said to all Israel, "Stand on one side, and I and my son Jonathan will stand on the other." The people responded, "Do what you think best." 41*† And Saul said to the LORD, the God of Israel: "Why did you not answer your servant this time? If the blame for this resides in me or my son Jonathan, LORD, God of Israel, respond

with Urim; but if this guilt is in your people Israel, respond with Thummim." Jonathan and Saul were designated, and the people went free. 42 Saul then said, "Cast lots between me and my son Jonathan." And Jonathan was designated. 43 Saul said to Jonathan, "Tell me what you have done." Jonathan replied, "I only tasted a little honey from the end of the staff I was holding. Am I to die for this?" 44* Saul said, "May God do thus and so to me if you do not indeed die, Jonathan!"

Rescue of Jonathan

45*† But the army said to Saul: "Is Jonathan to die, though it was he who brought Israel this great victory? This must not be! As the LORD lives, not a single hair of his head shall fall to the ground, for God was with him in what he did today!" Thus the soldiers were able to rescue Jonathan from death. 46 After that Saul gave up the pursuit of the Philistines, who returned to their own territory.

Wars and Victories

47* After taking over the kingship of Israel, Saul waged war on all their surrounding enemies— Moab, the Ammonites, Aram, Beth-rehob, the king of Zobah, and the Philistines. Wherever he turned, he was successful 48 and fought bravely. He defeated Amalek and delivered Israel from the hands of those who were plundering them.

Saul's Family

49*† The sons of Saul were Jonathan, Ishvi, and Malchishua; his two daughters were named, the elder, Merob, and the younger, Michal. 50 Saul's wife, who was named Ahinoam, was the daughter of Ahimaaz. The name of his general was Abner, son of Saul's uncle, Ner; 51* Kish, Saul's father, and Ner, Abner's father, were sons of Abiel.

52 An unremitting war was waged against the Philistines during Saul's lifetime. When Saul saw any strong or brave man, he took him into his service.

15 1 Samuel said to Saul: "It was I the LORD sent to anoint you king over his people Israel. Now, therefore, listen to the message of the LORD. 2* This is what the LORD of hosts has to say: 'I will punish what Amalek did to Israel when he barred his way as he was coming up from Egypt.

14, 41: The *Urim* and *Thummim,* or sacred lots, were a device for ascertaining the will of God; they ceased to be used after the time of David. The material and the shape of these objects, and the manner in which they were used, are unknown. They gave a "yes" or "no" answer to specific questions.

14, 45: *Rescue:* the Hebrew word used is that for the "redemption" of the first-born (Ex 13, 13ff).

14, 49: *Ishvi:* known also as Ishbaal, in 2 Sm 2, 8 and elsewhere. The name may once have read "Ishyo" here.

14, 32: 1 Sm 15, 19.21; Lv 3, 17; 7, 26f; 17, 10–14; Acts 15, 20.29.
14, 35: 1 Sm 7, 17; Jgs 6, 24.
14, 37: 1 Sm 28, 6.15.
14, 40: Jos 7, 13ff.
14, 41: 1 Sm 28, 6; Ex 28, 30; Dt 33, 8.
14, 44: 1 Sm 3, 17; Ru 1, 17.
14, 45: 2 Sm 14, 11; 1 Kgs 1, 52.
14, 47: 2 Sm 1, 22; 8, 2–5.
14, 49: 1 Sm 18, 20.25; 31, 2; 1 Chr 8, 33; 9, 39; 10, 2.
14, 51: 1 Sm 9, 1.
15, 2: Ex 17, 8–10.16; Dt 25, 17ff.

3*† Go, now, attack Amalek, and deal with him and all that he has under the ban. Do not spare him, but kill men and women, children and infants, oxen and sheep, camels and asses.' "

Disobedience of Saul

4† Saul alerted the soldiers, and at Telaim reviewed two hundred thousand foot soldiers and ten thousand men of Judah. 5 Saul went to the city of Amalek, and after setting an ambush in the wadi, 6* warned the Kenites: "Come! Leave Amalek and withdraw, that I may not have to destroy you with them, for you were kind to the Israelites when they came up from Egypt." After the Kenites left, 7* Saul routed Amalek from Havilah to the approaches of Shur, on the frontier of Egypt. 8 He took Agag, king of Amalek, alive, but on the rest of the people he put into effect the ban of destruction by the sword. 9 He and his troops spared Agag and the best of the fat sheep and oxen, and the lambs. They refused to carry out the doom on anything that was worthwhile, dooming only what was worthless and of no account.

Saul Is Reproved

10 Then the LORD spoke to Samuel: 11† "I regret having made Saul king, for he has turned from me and has not kept my command." At this Samuel grew angry and cried out to the LORD all night. 12 Early in the morning he went to meet Saul, but was informed that Saul had gone to Carmel, where he erected a trophy in his own honor, and that on his return he had passed on and gone down to Gilgal. 13 When Samuel came to him, Saul greeted him: "The LORD bless you! I have kept the command of the LORD." 14 But Samuel asked, "What, then, is the meaning of this bleating of sheep that comes to my ears, and the lowing of oxen that I hear?" 15 Saul replied: "They were brought from Amalek. The men spared the best sheep and oxen to sacrifice to the LORD, your God; but we have carried out the ban on the rest." 16 Samuel said to Saul: "Stop! Let me tell you what the LORD said to me last night." "Speak!" he replied. 17* Samuel then said: "Though little in your own esteem, are you not leader of the tribes of Israel? The LORD anointed you king of Israel 18* and sent you on a mission, saying, 'Go and put the sinful Amalekites under a ban of destruction. Fight against them until you have exterminated them.' 19* Why then have you disobeyed the LORD? You have pounced on the spoil, thus displeasing the LORD." 20 Saul answered Samuel: "I did indeed obey the LORD and fulfill the mission on which the LORD sent me. I have brought back Agag, and I have destroyed Amalek under the ban. 21* But from the spoil the men took sheep and oxen, the best of what had been banned, to sacrifice to the LORD their God in Gilgal." 22*† But Samuel said:

"Does the LORD so delight in holocausts
and sacrifices

Power and Corruption

Power corrupts. We have often heard that phrase. And in 1 Sm 15, 22–23, we have a vivid example. King Saul once again has decided to take matters in his own hands and goes against the word of the LORD. He seems to assume that his role as king exempts him from obedience to God. But Samuel reminds Saul that he has assumed way too much. No king, no president, no prime minster is above the law. Especially when that Law comes from God.

Have you ever been in a position of leadership and been tempted to abuse your privileges?

▶ **1 Sm 15, 22–23**

---

† **15, 3:** *Under the ban:* in such wars of extermination, all things (men, cities, beasts, etc.) were to be blotted out; nothing could be reserved for private use. The interpretation of God's will here attributed to Samuel is in keeping with the abhorrent practices of blood revenge prevalent among pastoral, seminomadic peoples such as the Hebrews had recently been. The slaughter of the innocent has never been in conformity with the will of God.

15, 4: The numbers here are not realistic; compare 1 Sm 14, 24 above.

15, 11: *I regret:* God manifests "regret" when, offended by men, he takes away his benefits, graces and favors. It is not God, but men, who change, to their own detriment.

15, 22: Samuel is disapproving, not of sacrifices in general, but of merely external sacrifices offered in defiance of God's commandment and without heartfelt obedience.

*
15, 3: 1 Sm 27, 8; 30, 17; Ex 17, 16; Nm 24, 20.
15, 6: Nm 24, 21.
15, 7: 1 Sm 27, 8.
15, 17: 1 Sm 9, 21.
15, 18: 1 Sm 28, 18.
15, 19: 14, 32.
15, 21: Lv 27, 28.
15, 22: Prv 21, 3; Hos 6, 6; Am 5, 21–25; Zec 10, 2; Mt 9, 13; 12, 7; Heb 10, 9.

as in obedience to the command of
   the LORD?
Obedience is better than sacrifice,
   and submission than the fat of rams.
23 For a sin like divination is rebellion,
   and presumption is the crime of idolatry.
Because you have rejected the command of
   the LORD,
   he, too, has rejected you as ruler."

Saul Asks Forgiveness

24* Saul replied to Samuel: "I have sinned, for I have disobeyed the command of the LORD and your instructions. In my fear of the people, I did what they said. 25 Now forgive my sin, and return with me, that I may worship the LORD." 26* But Samuel said to Saul, "I will not return with you, because you rejected the command of the LORD and the LORD rejects you as king of Israel." 27* As Samuel turned to go, Saul seized a loose end of his mantle, and it tore off. 28* So Samuel said to him: "The LORD has torn the kingdom of Israel from you this day, and has given it to a neighbor of yours, who is better than you. 29* The Glory of Israel neither retracts nor repents, for he is not man that he should repent." 30 But he answered: "I have sinned, yet honor me now before the elders of my people and before Israel. Return with me that I may worship

the LORD your God." 31 And so Samuel returned with him, and Saul worshiped the LORD.

Agag Is Cut Down

32 Afterward Samuel commanded, "Bring Agag, king of Amalek, to me." Agag came to him struggling and saying, "So it is bitter death!" 33* And Samuel said,

"As your sword has made women childless,
   so shall your mother be childless
     among women."

Then he cut Agag down before the LORD in Gilgal.

34 Samuel departed for Ramah, while Saul went up to his home in Gibeah of Saul. 35* Never again, as long as he lived, did Samuel see Saul. Yet he grieved over Saul, because the LORD regretted having made him king of Israel.

Samuel Sent to Bethlehem

16 1*† The LORD said to Samuel: "How long will you grieve for Saul, whom I have rejected as king of Israel? Fill your horn with oil, and be on your way. I am sending you to Jesse of Bethlehem, for I have chosen my king from among his sons." 2 But Samuel replied: "How can I go? Saul will hear of it and kill me." To this the LORD answered: "Take a heifer along and say, 'I have come to sacrifice to the LORD.' 3 Invite Jesse to the sacrifice, and I myself will tell you what to do; you are to anoint for me the one I point out to you."

4 Samuel did as the LORD had commanded him. When he entered Bethlehem, the elders of the city came trembling to meet him and inquired, "Is your visit peaceful, O seer?" 5* He replied: "Yes! I have come to sacrifice to the LORD. So cleanse yourselves and join me today for the banquet." He also had Jesse and his sons cleanse themselves and invited them to the sacrifice. 6 As they came, he looked at Eliab and thought, "Surely the LORD's anointed is here before him." 7* But the LORD said to Samuel: "Do not judge from his appearance or from his lofty stature, because I have rejected him. Not as man sees does God see, because man sees the appearance but the LORD looks into the heart." 8* Then Jesse called Abinadab and presented him before Samuel, who said, "The LORD has not chosen him." 9 Next Jesse presented Shammah, but Samuel said, "The LORD has not chosen this one either."

But the LORD said to Samuel: "Do not judge from his appearance or from his lofty stature, because I have rejected him. Not as man sees does God see, because man sees the *appearance,* but the **LORD** looks into the *heart.*

16, 7

---

† **16, 1:** The anointing here prepared for is unknown to David's brother Eliab in the next chapter (1 Sm 17, 28), and David is twice anointed after Saul's death (2 Sm 2, 4; 5, 3).

*

15, 24: 1 Sm 26, 21.
15, 26: 1 Kgs 11, 11.30f.
15, 27: 1 Sm 24, 6.
15, 28: 1 Sm 28, 17; 2 Sm 7, 15f.

15, 29: Nm 23, 19.
15, 33: Ex 21, 23.
15, 35: Gn 6, 6.
16, 1: 1 Kgs 1, 39; Ru 4,
  17–22; 1 Chr 11, 3;
  Is 11, 1; Lk 2, 4.
16, 5: 1 Sm 9, 12f; 20, 26; Ex

19, 10; Jb 1, 5.
16, 7: 1 Sm 10, 23f; 1 Chr
  28, 9; Prv 15, 11; Jer
  17, 10; 20, 12; Lk 16,
  15; Acts 1, 24.
16, 8ff: 1 Sm 17, 12f; 1 Chr 2,
  13ff.

10 In the same way Jesse presented seven sons before Samuel, but Samuel said to Jesse, "The LORD has not chosen any one of these." 11* Then Samuel asked Jesse, "Are these all the sons you have?" Jesse replied, "There is still the youngest, who is tending the sheep." Samuel said to Jesse, "Send for him; we will not begin the sacrificial banquet until he arrives here." 12* Jesse sent and had the young man brought to them. He was ruddy, a youth handsome to behold and making a splendid appearance. The LORD said, "There—anoint him, for this is he!" 13* Then Samuel, with the horn of oil in hand, anointed him in the midst of his brothers; and from that day on, the spirit of the LORD rushed upon David. When Samuel took his leave, he went to Ramah.

Saul's Spirit of Melancholy

14*† The spirit of the LORD had departed from Saul, and he was tormented by an evil spirit sent by the LORD. 15 So the servants of Saul said to him: "Please! An evil spirit from God is tormenting you. 16 If your lordship will order it, we, your servants here in attendance on you, will look for a man skilled in playing the harp. When the evil spirit from God comes over you, he will play and you will feel better." 17 Saul then told his servants, "Find me a skillful harpist and bring him to me." 18*† A servant spoke up to say: "I have observed that one of the sons of Jesse of Bethlehem is a skillful harpist. He is also a stalwart soldier, besides being an able speaker, and handsome. Moreover, the LORD is with him."

David Made Armor-Bearer

19 Accordingly, Saul dispatched messengers to ask Jesse to send him his son David, who was with the flock. 20* Then Jesse took five loaves of bread, a skin of wine, and a kid, and sent them to Saul by his son David. 21* Thus David came to Saul and entered his service. Saul became very fond of him, made him his armor-bearer, 22 and sent Jesse the message, "Allow David to remain in my service, for he meets with my approval." 23 Whenever the spirit from God seized Saul, David would take the harp and play, and Saul would be relieved and feel better, for the evil spirit would leave him.

The Challenge of Goliath

17 1 The Philistines rallied their forces for battle at Socoh in Judah and camped between Socoh and Azekah at Ephes-dammim. 2 Saul and the Israelites also gathered and camped in the Vale of the Terebinth, drawing up their battle line to meet the Philistines. 3 The Philistines were stationed on one hill and the Israelites on an opposite hill, with a valley between them.

4 A champion named Goliath of Gath came out from the Philistine camp; he was six and a half feet tall. 5 He had a bronze helmet on his head and wore a bronze corselet of scale armor weighing five thousand shekels, 6† and bronze greaves, and had a bronze scimitar slung from a baldric. 7*† The shaft of his javelin was like a weaver's heddle-bar, and its iron head weighed six hundred shekels. His shield-bearer went before him. 8 He stood and shouted to the ranks of Israel: "Why come out in battle formation? I am a Philistine, and you are Saul's servants. Choose one of your men, and have him come down to me. 9 If he beats me in combat and kills me, we will be your vassals; but if I beat him and kill him, you shall be our vassals and serve us." 10 The Philistine continued: "I defy the ranks of Israel today.

---

†
16, 14: *An evil spirit sent by the LORD:* the Lord permitted Saul to be tormented with violent fits of rage.

16, 18: Of the two traditions which describe the coming of David into Saul's service, the oldest Greek translation retains only the one comprised in 1 Sm 16, 14–23; 17, 1–11.32–54. This effort at consistency is not in accord with the character of the rest of the book; see note on 1 Sm 8, 1. Though square brackets are used in this edition to indicate the passages lacking in the oldest translation, this is meant only to help the reader follow one account at a time. Both are equally a part of the inspired text, as are also the various amplifications and retouchings of the narrative given within brackets in chs 18 and 19.

17, 6: *Scimitar:* the Hebrew word for this is rather rare, and the nature of the weapon was in doubt until recent years. It is not the same as the sword of v 45.

17, 7: *Six hundred shekels:* over 15 pounds.

16, 11: 1 Sm 17, 15.28.34;
 2 Sm 7, 8.
16, 12: 1 Sm 9, 2.
16, 13: 1 Sm 10, 6; 11, 6; Jgs
 3, 10; 9, 9; Sir 46, 13.
16, 14: 1 Sm 18, 10f.

16, 18: 2 Sm 17, 8.
16, 20: 1 Sm 9, 7f; 10, 4.27;
 16, 1; 17, 27ff.
16, 21: 1 Sm 18, 2.
17, 7: 2 Sm 21, 19; 1 Chr 11,
 23; 20, 5.

Give me a man and let us fight together." [11] Saul and all the men of Israel, when they heard this challenge of the Philistine, were dismayed and terror-stricken.

David Comes to the Camp

[12]*† [David was the son of an Ephrathite named Jesse, who was from Bethlehem in Judah. He had eight sons, and in the days of Saul was old and well on in years. [13] The three oldest sons of Jesse had followed Saul to war; these three sons who had gone off to war were named, the first-born Eliab, the second son Abinadab, and the third Shammah. [14] David was the youngest. While the three oldest had joined Saul, [15]* David would go and come from Saul to tend his father's sheep at Bethlehem.

some token from them. [19] Saul, and they, and all Israel are fighting against the Philistines in the Vale of the Terebinth." [20]* Early the next morning, having left the flock with a shepherd, David set out on his errand, as Jesse had commanded him. He reached the barricade of the camp just as the army, on their way to the battleground, were shouting their battle cry. [21] The Israelites and the Philistines drew up opposite each other in battle array. [22]* David entrusted what he had brought to the keeper of the baggage and hastened to the battle line where he greeted his brothers. [23] While he was talking with them, the Philistine champion, by name Goliath of Gath, came up from the ranks of the Philistines and spoke as before, and David listened. [24] When the Israelites saw the man, they all retreated before him,

Introducing ►**DAVID**

Who cannot love David? This shepherd-turned-king is one of the great tragic heroes of the Old Testament. David, whose name means "beloved," was the successor to Saul and the second king (1000–961 B.C.) of the new nation formed out of the twelve tribes of Israel. The youngest son of Jesse of the tribe of Judah, David was a member of Saul's court as a young man. Later, when Saul disappointed God, Samuel the prophet anointed David as Saul's successor. After Saul was killed, David established the neutral city of Jerusalem as his capital (see map 3, "The Kingdom Years"). He moved the ark of the LORD there, making this city the new religious center of Israel. Jerusalem is also known as the City of David.

David was a successful warrior, a capable king, and a gifted poet, having himself written some of the Psalms. He was also capable of great sin. His affair with Bathsheba seemed to lead to a string of violence and betrayal affecting his whole family. One of his sons, Absalom, even inspired a revolt against David. But through it all, David was passionately in love with God. God recognized this and promised David that someone from his house would sit upon the throne in Israel.

When Israel was destroyed and its kings taken prisoners, the people developed a hope that another anointed one, a messiah from the house of David, would rise up and lead Israel in God's ways once again. It is this hope for the Davidic messiah that is fulfilled by Jesus in the New Testament.

[16] [Meanwhile the Philistine came forward and took his stand morning and evening for forty days.

[17] [Now Jesse said to his son David: "Take this ephah of roasted grain and these ten loaves for your brothers, and bring them quickly to your brothers in the camp. [18] Also take these ten cheeses for the field officer. Greet your brothers and bring home

very much afraid. [25]* The Israelites had been saying: "Do you see this man coming up? He comes up to insult Israel. If anyone should kill him, the king would give him great wealth, and his daughter as well, and would grant exemption to his father's family in Israel." [26]* David now said to the men standing by: "What will be done for the man who

---

17, 12–31: An alternative account of how David came to undertake the combat with the Philistine is here inserted; it is continued in 1 Sm 17, 55—18, 6. See note on 1 Sm 16, 18.

17, 12: 1 Sm 16, 1.10; Ru 1, 2.
17, 15: 1 Sm 18, 2; 2 Sm 7, 8.
17, 20: 1 Sm 26, 5.
17, 22: 1 Sm 25, 13.

17, 25: 1 Sm 18, 17; Jos 15, 16.
17, 26: 1 Sm 18, 25; Jgs 15, 18; 2 Kgs 19, 4; Is 37, 4.

kills this Philistine and frees Israel of the disgrace? Who is this uncircumcised Philistine in any case, that he should insult the armies of the living God?" 27 They repeated the same words to him and said, "That is how the man who kills him will be rewarded." 28 When Eliab, his oldest brother, heard him speaking with the men, he grew angry with David and said: "Why did you come down? With whom have you left those sheep in the desert meanwhile? I know your arrogance and your evil intent. You came down to enjoy the battle!" 29 David replied, "What have I done now?—I was only talking." 30 Yet he turned from him to another and asked the same question; and everyone gave him

37* David continued: "The LORD, who delivered me from the claws of the lion and the bear, will also keep me safe from the clutches of this Philistine." Saul answered David, "Go! the LORD will be with you."

Preparation for the Encounter

38 Then Saul clothed David in his own tunic, putting a bronze helmet on his head and arming him with a coat of mail. 39 David also girded himself with Saul's sword over the tunic. He walked with difficulty, however, since he had never tried armor before. He said to Saul, "I cannot go in these, because I have never tried them before." So

❓ Taking On Goliath

David makes it look so easy. A slingshot, a stone, a skillful aim, and it is all over. Goliath is dead, and the Israelites win the day. It is a story that gives hope to anyone who has ever been bullied or harassed.

    A David lives in each of us, and plenty of Goliaths are out there ready to defeat us. The Goliaths we encounter can include peer pressure, an addiction, an abusive situation, or simply self-doubt. We may feel overpowered by these Goliaths, sure that they are too big for us to handle. But they are not! Those of us who believe in God, as David did, know that we are not alone. As followers of Jesus, we rely not on violence but on love and the support of the Christian community to defeat the Goliaths in our life. We can make David's story our own.

    Identify a Goliath in your life right now and journal about it. What stepping-stone can you take in defeating it?

▸ **1 Samuel, chapter 17**

the same answer as before. 31 The words that David had spoken were overheard and reported to Saul, who sent for him.]

David Fights Goliath

32 Then David spoke to Saul: "Let your majesty not lose courage. I am at your service to go and fight this Philistine." 33 But Saul answered David, "You cannot go up against this Philistine and fight with him, for you are only a youth, while he has been a warrior from his youth." 34* Then David told Saul: "Your servant used to tend his father's sheep, and whenever a lion or bear came to carry off a sheep from the flock, 35 I would go after it and attack it and rescue the prey from its mouth. If it attacked me, I would seize it by the jaw, strike it, and kill it. 36 Your servant has killed both a lion and a bear, and this uncircumcised Philistine will be as one of them, because he has insulted the armies of the living God."

he took them off. 40 Then, staff in hand, David selected five smooth stones from the wadi and put them in the pocket of his shepherd's bag. With his sling also ready to hand, he approached the Philistine.

David's Victory

41 With his shield-bearer marching before him, the Philistine also advanced closer and closer to David. 42 When he had sized David up, and seen that he was youthful, and ruddy, and handsome in appearance, he held him in contempt. 43 The Philistine said to David, "Am I a dog that you come against me with a staff?" Then the Philistine cursed David by his gods 44* and said to him, "Come here to me, and I will leave your flesh for the birds of the air and the beasts of the field." 45 David answered him: "You come against me with sword and spear and scimitar, but I come against you in the name of

the LORD of hosts, the God of the armies of Israel that you have insulted. ⁴⁶ Today the LORD shall deliver you into my hand; I will strike you down and cut off your head. This very day I will leave your corpse and the corpses of the Philistine army for the birds of the air and the beasts of the field; thus the whole land shall learn that Israel has a God. ⁴⁷* All this multitude, too, shall learn that it is not by sword or spear that the LORD saves. For the battle is the LORD'S, and he shall deliver you into our hands."

⁴⁸ The Philistine then moved to meet David at close quarters, while David ran quickly toward the battle line in the direction of the Philistine. ⁴⁹ David put his hand into the bag and took out a stone, hurled it with the sling, and struck the Philistine on the forehead. The stone embedded itself in his brow, and he fell prostrate on the ground. ⁵⁰* [Thus David overcame the Philistine with sling and stone; he struck the Philistine mortally, and did it without a sword.] ⁵¹* Then David ran and stood over him; with the Philistine's own sword [which he drew from its sheath] he dispatched him and cut off his head.

Flight of the Philistines

When they saw that their hero was dead, the Philistines took to flight. ⁵² Then the men of Israel and Judah, with loud shouts, went in pursuit of the Philistines to the approaches of Gath and to the gates of Ekron, and Philistines fell wounded along the road from Shaaraim as far as Gath and Ekron. ⁵³ On their return from the pursuit of the Philistines, the Israelites looted their camp. ⁵⁴*† David took the head of the Philistine and brought it to Jerusalem; but he kept Goliath's armor in his own tent.

David Presented to Saul

⁵⁵ [When Saul saw David go out to meet the Philistine, he asked his general Abner, "Abner, whose son is that youth?" Abner replied, "As truly as your majesty is alive, I have no idea." ⁵⁶ And the king said, "Find out whose son the lad is." ⁵⁷ So when David returned from slaying the Philistine, Abner took him and presented him to Saul. David was still holding the Philistine's head. ⁵⁸ Saul then asked him, "Whose son are you, young man?" David replied, "I am the son of your servant Jesse of Bethlehem."

David and Jonathan

18 ¹* [By the time David finished speaking with Saul, Jonathan had become as fond of David as if his life depended on him; he loved him as he loved himself. ²* Saul laid claim to David that day and did not allow him to return to his father's house. ³ And Jonathan entered into a bond with David, because he loved him as himself. ⁴* Jonathan divested himself of the mantle he was wearing and gave it to David, along with his military dress, and his sword, his bow and his belt. ⁵ David then carried out successfully every mission on which Saul sent him. So Saul put him in charge of his soldiers, and this was agreeable to the whole army, even to Saul's own officers.]

Saul's Jealousy

⁶* At the approach of Saul and David (on David's return after slaying the Philistine), women came out from each of the cities of Israel to meet King Saul, singing and dancing, with tambourines, joyful songs, and sistrums. ⁷* The women played and sang:

"Saul has slain his thousands,
    and David his ten thousands."

⁸ Saul was very angry and resentful of the song, for he thought: "They give David ten thousands, but only thousands to me. All that remains for him is the kingship." ⁹ [And from that day on, Saul was jealous of David.

¹⁰* [The next day an evil spirit from God came over Saul, and he raged in his house. David was in attendance, playing the harp as at other times, while Saul was holding his spear. ¹¹ Saul poised the spear, thinking to nail David to the wall, but twice David escaped him.] ¹² Saul then began to fear David, [because the LORD was with him, but had departed from Saul himself.] ¹³ Accordingly, Saul removed him from his presence by appointing him a field officer. So David led the people on their military expeditions, ¹⁴ and prospered in all his enterprises, for the LORD was with him. ¹⁵ Seeing how successful he was, Saul conceived a fear of David; ¹⁶* on the other hand, all Israel and Judah loved him, since he led them on their expeditions.

¹⁷* [Saul said to David, "There is my older daughter, Merob, whom I will give you in marriage if you become my champion and fight the battles of

---

† **17, 54:** At the time supposed by this narrative, Jerusalem was still Jebusite, and David had no military tent of his own; the verse is a later gloss.

17, 47: 1 Sm 14, 6; Ps 33, 16. **17, 51:** 1 Sm 21, 10.
17, 50: Sir 47, 4; 1 Mc 4, 30. **17, 54:** 1 Sm 31, 9.

18, 1: 1 Sm 19, 1–7; 20, 17; 23, 16; 2 Sm 1, 26; 9, 1.
18, 2: 1 Sm 16, 21; 17, 15.
18, 4: 2 Sm 1, 22.
18, 6: Ex 15, 20f; Jgs 11, 34; Jdt 15, 12.
18, 7: 1 Sm 21, 12; 29, 5; Sir 47, 6f.
18, 10f: 1 Sm 16, 14; 19, 9f; 20, 33; 22, 6; 26, 8.
18, 16: 2 Sm 5, 2.
18, 17: 1 Sm 14, 49; 17, 25.

the LORD." Saul had in mind, "I shall not touch him; let the Philistines strike him." 18 But David answered Saul: "Who am I? And who are my kin or my father's clan in Israel that I should become the king's son-in-law?" 19* However, when it was time for Saul's daughter Merob to be given to David, she was given in marriage to Adriel the Meholathite instead.]

20* Now Saul's daughter Michal loved David, and it was reported to Saul, who was pleased at this, 21 for he thought, "I will offer her to him to become a snare for him, so that the Philistines may strike him." [Thus for the second time Saul said to David, "You shall become my son-in-law today."] 22 Saul then ordered his servants to speak to David privately and to say: "The king is fond of you, and all his officers love you. You should become the king's son-in-law." 23 But when Saul's servants mentioned this to David, he said: "Do you think it easy to become the king's son-in-law? I am poor and insignificant." 24 When his servants reported to him the nature of David's answer, 25* Saul commanded them to say this to David: "The king desires no other price for the bride than the foreskins of one hundred Philistines, that he may thus take vengeance on his enemies." Saul intended in this way to bring about David's death through the Philistines. 26 When the servants reported this offer to David, he was pleased with the prospect of becoming the king's son-in-law. [Before the year was up,] 27 David made preparations and sallied forth with his men and slew two hundred Philistines. He brought back their foreskins and counted them out before the king, that he might thus become the king's son-in-law. So Saul gave him his daughter Michal in marriage. 28 Saul thus came to recognize that the LORD was with David; besides, his own daughter Michal loved David. 29 Therefore Saul feared David all the more [and was his enemy ever after].

30 [The Philistine chiefs continued to make forays, but each time they took the field, David was more successful against them than any other of Saul's officers, and as a result acquired great fame.]

Persecution of David

19 1* Saul discussed his intention of killing David with his son Jonathan and with all his servants. But Saul's son Jonathan, who was very fond of David, 2 told him: "My father Saul is trying to kill you. Therefore, please be on your guard tomorrow morning; get out of sight and remain in hiding. 3 I, however, will go out and stand beside my father in the countryside where you are, and will speak to him about you. If I learn anything, I will let you know."

4 Jonathan then spoke well of David to his father Saul, saying to him: "Let not your majesty sin against his servant David, for he has committed no offense against you, but has helped you very much by his deeds. 5* When he took his life in his hands and slew the Philistine, and the LORD brought about a great victory for all Israel through him, you were glad to see it. Why, then, should you become guilty of shedding innocent blood by killing David without cause?" 6 Saul heeded Jonathan's plea and swore, "As the LORD lives, he shall not be killed." 7 So Jonathan summoned David and repeated the whole conversation to him. Jonathan then brought David to Saul, and David served him as before.

8 When war broke out again, David went out to fight against the Philistines and inflicted a great defeat upon them, putting them to flight. 9* Then an evil spirit from the LORD came upon Saul as he was sitting in his house with spear in hand and David was playing the harp nearby. 10 Saul tried to nail David to the wall with the spear, but David eluded Saul, so that the spear struck only the wall, and David got away safe.

11† The same night, Saul sent messengers to David's house to guard it, that he might kill him in the morning. David's wife Michal informed him, "Unless you save yourself tonight, tomorrow you will be killed." 12* Then Michal let David down through a window, and he made his escape in safety. 13* Michal took the household idol and laid it in the bed, putting a net of goat's hair at its head and covering it with a spread. 14 When Saul sent messengers to arrest David, she said, "He is sick." 15 Saul, however, sent the messengers back to see David and commanded them, "Bring him up to me in the bed, that I may kill him." 16 But when the messengers entered, they found the household idol in the bed, with the net of goat's hair at its head. 17 Saul therefore asked Michal: "Why did you play this trick on me? You have helped my enemy to get away!" Michal answered Saul: "He threatened me, 'Let me go or I will kill you.'"

David and Samuel in Ramah

18 Thus David got safely away; he went to Samuel in Ramah, informing him of all that Saul had done to him. Then he and Samuel went to stay in the

---

19, 11: This story in all probability originally followed 1 Sm 18, 29, placing the episode of David's escape on the night of his marriage with Michal.

18, 19: 1 Sm 21, 8; 24, 16.
18, 20: 1 Sm 14, 49; 25, 44; 26, 23; 2 Sm 3, 13.
18, 25: 1 Sm 17, 26; Gn 34, 12.
19, 1: 1 Sm 18, 1; 20, 1ff.
19, 5: Dt 19, 10; Ps 119, 109.
19, 9f: 1 Sm 16, 14; 18, 10f.
19, 12: Jos 2, 15; Acts 9, 25; 2 Cor 11, 33.
19, 13: Gn 31, 19; Jos 17, 5; 18, 14.18.20.

sheds. [19] When Saul was told that David was in the sheds near Ramah, [20]* he sent messengers to arrest David. But when they saw the band of prophets, presided over by Samuel, in a prophetic frenzy, they too fell into the prophetic state. [21] Informed of this, Saul sent other messengers, who also fell into the prophetic state. For the third time Saul sent messengers, but they too fell into the prophetic state.

Saul among the Prophets

[22] Saul then went to Ramah himself. Arriving at the cistern of the threshing floor on the bare hilltop, he inquired, "Where are Samuel and David?", and was told, "At the sheds near Ramah." [23] As he set out from the hilltop toward the sheds, the spirit of God came upon him also, and he continued on in a prophetic condition until he reached the spot. At the sheds near Ramah [24]* he, too, stripped himself of his garments and he, too, remained in the prophetic state in the presence of Samuel; all that day and night he lay naked. That is why they say, "Is Saul also among the prophets?"

David Consults with Jonathan

20 [1]* David fled from the sheds near Ramah, and went to Jonathan. "What have I done?" he asked him. "What crime or what offense does your father hold against me that he seeks my life?" [2] Jonathan answered him: "Heaven forbid that you should die! My father does nothing, great or small, without disclosing it to me. Why, then, should my father conceal this from me? This cannot be so!" [3] But David replied: "Your father is well aware that I am favored with your friendship, so he has decided, 'Jonathan must not know of this lest he be grieved.' Nevertheless, as the LORD lives and as you live, there is but a step between me and death." [4] Jonathan then said to David, "I will do whatever you wish." [5]* David answered: "Tomorrow is the new moon, when I should in fact dine with the king. Let me go and hide in the open country until evening. [6] If it turns out that your father misses me, say, 'David urged me to let him go on short notice to his city Bethlehem, because his whole clan is holding its seasonal sacrifice there.' [7] If he says, 'Very well,' your servant is safe. But if he becomes quite angry, you can be sure he has planned some harm. [8]* Do this kindness for your servant because of the LORD'S bond between us, into which you brought me: if I am guilty, kill me yourself! Why should you give me up to your father?" [9] But Jonathan an-

swered: "Not I! If ever I find out that my father is determined to inflict injury upon you, I will certainly let you know." [10] David then asked Jonathan, "Who will tell me if your father gives you a harsh answer?"

Mutual Agreement

[11] [Jonathan replied to David, "Come, let us go out into the field." When they were out in the open country together, [12] Jonathan said to David: "As the LORD, the God of Israel, lives, I will sound out my father about this time tomorrow. Whether he is well disposed toward David or not, I will send you the information. [13]* Should it please my father to bring any injury upon you, may the LORD do thus and so to Jonathan if I do not apprise you of it and send you on your way in peace. May the LORD be with you even as he was with my father. [14] Only this: if I am still alive, may you show me the kindness of the LORD. But if I die, [15] never withdraw your kindness from my house. And when the LORD exterminates all the enemies of David from the surface of the earth, [16] the name of Jonathan must never be allowed by the family of David to die out from among you, or the LORD will make you answer for it." [17] And in his love for David, Jonathan renewed his oath to him, because he loved him as his very self.]

[18] Jonathan then said to him: "Tomorrow is the new moon; and you will be missed, since your place will be vacant. [19]* On the following day you will be missed all the more. Go to the spot where you hid on the other occasion and wait near the mound there. [20] On the third day of the month I will shoot arrows, as though aiming at a target. [21] I will then send my attendant to go and recover the arrows. If in fact I say to him, 'Look, the arrow is this side of you; pick it up,' come, for you are safe. As the LORD lives, there will be nothing to fear. [22] But if I say to the boy, 'Look, the arrow is beyond you,' go, for the LORD sends you away. [23] However, in the matter which you and I have discussed, the LORD shall be between you and me forever." [24] So David hid in the open country.

On the day of the new moon, when the king sat at table to dine, [25] taking his usual place against the wall, Jonathan sat facing him, while Abner sat at the king's side, and David's place was vacant. [26]*† Saul, however, said nothing that day, for he thought, "He must have become unclean by accident, and not yet have been cleansed." [27] On the next day, the second

---

20, 26: The meal on the first day of the month would have religious overtones, and a ritual impurity (Lv 15, 16; Dt 23, 10ff) would bar David from sharing in it.

19, 20: 1 Sm 10, 5f.10; Nm 11, 25.
19, 24: 1 Sm 10, 10ff.
20, 1: 1 Sm 19, 1–7.11–17.
20, 5: Nm 10, 10; 28, 11–15.
20, 8f: 1 Sm 23, 17f.

20, 13–16: 1 Sm 24, 22f; 2 Sm 9, 1–13; 21, 7.
20, 19: 1 Sm 19, 1–7.
20, 26: 1 Sm 16, 5; Lv 7, 20f; 15, 1ff.

Friends Forever

David and Jonathan have one of the most touching stories of friendship in the Bible. In 1 Sm 18, 1–4, Jonathan makes a special covenant with David. In chapter 20, their deep love leads them to risk their lives for each other. Saul, the king and Jonathan's father, is acting like a madman. He is insanely jealous of David and wants him dead.

Yet, Jonathan and David bring God into their relationship. This gives them the wisdom to see what is right and do it. When they have to part (see 20, 41–42), they weep and kiss and remind each other of their vows.

Not many teenagers deal with situations as drastic as this, but tension with parents over your choice of friends can be common. Parents may not understand why you like a person whom they dislike. It can leave you with a sense of being stuck in the middle.

Your response should be like David and Jonathan's, keeping God part of all your relationships. Each friendship then becomes a living prayer, and God will guide you through conflicts and help you make good decisions.

▸ 1 Samuel, chapter 20

day of the month, David's place was vacant. Saul inquired of his son Jonathan, "Why has the son of Jesse not come to table yesterday or today?" 28 Jonathan answered Saul: "David urgently asked me to let him go to his city, Bethlehem. 29 'Please let me go,' he begged, 'for we are to have a clan sacrifice in our city, and my brothers insist on my presence. Now, therefore, if you think well of me, give me leave to visit my brothers.' That is why he has not come to the king's table." 30 But Saul was extremely angry with Jonathan and said to him: "Son of a rebellious woman, do I not know that, to your own shame and to the disclosure of your mother's shame, you are the companion of Jesse's son? 31* Why, as long as the son of Jesse lives upon the earth, you cannot make good your claim to the kingship! So send for him, and bring him to me, for

he is doomed." 32 But Jonathan asked his father Saul: "Why should he die? What has he done?" 33* At this Saul brandished his spear to strike him, and thus Jonathan learned that his father was resolved to kill David. 34 Jonathan sprang up from the table in great anger and took no food that second day of the month, for he was grieved on David's account, since his father had railed against him.

Jonathan's Farewell

35 The next morning Jonathan went out into the field with a little boy for his appointment with David. 36 There he said to the boy, "Run and fetch the arrow." And as the boy ran, he shot an arrow beyond him in the direction of the city. 37 When the boy made for the spot where Jonathan had shot the arrow, Jonathan called after him, "The arrow is farther on!" 38 Again he called to his lad, "Hurry, be quick, don't delay!" Jonathan's boy picked up the arrow and brought it to his master. 39 The boy knew nothing; only Jonathan and David knew what was meant. 40 Then Jonathan gave his weapons to this boy of his and said to him, "Go, take them to the city." 41 When the boy had left, David rose from beside the mound and prostrated himself on the ground three times before Jonathan in homage. They kissed each other and wept aloud together. 42* At length Jonathan said to David, "Go in peace, in keeping with what we two have sworn by the name of the LORD: 'The LORD shall be between you and me, and between your posterity and mine forever.'"

21

1 Then David departed on his way, while Jonathan went back into the city.

The Holy Bread

2* David went to Ahimelech, the priest of Nob, who came trembling to meet him and asked, "Why are you alone? Is there no one with you?" 3 David answered the priest: "The king gave me a commission and told me to let no one know anything about the business on which he sent me or the commission he gave me. For that reason I have arranged a meeting place with my men. 4* Now what have you on hand? Give me five loaves, or whatever you can find." 5† But the priest replied to David, "I have no ordinary bread on hand, only holy bread; if the men have abstained from women, you may eat some of that." 6 David answered the

---

21, 5f: *From women:* the high priest, willing to distribute the holy bread to David and his men, requires that they be free from ritual uncleanness, associated in Old Testament times (Lv 15, 18) with the marriage act. David's answer supposes the discipline of a military campaign under the conditions of "holy war" (Dt 23, 10).

20, 31: 2 Sm 12, 5.
20, 33: 1 Sm 18, 11.
20, 42: 2 Sm 9, 1; 21, 7.
21, 2: Is 10, 32; Mk 2, 26.
21, 4: Lv 24, 5.9.

priest: "We have indeed been segregated from women as on previous occasions. Whenever I go on a journey, all the young men are consecrated—even for a secular journey. All the more so today, when they are consecrated at arms!" 7* So the priest gave him holy bread, for no other bread was on hand except the showbread which had been removed from the LORD's presence and replaced by fresh bread when it was taken away. 8 One of Saul's servants was there that day, detained before the LORD; his name was Doeg the Edomite, and he was Saul's chief henchman.

The Sword of Goliath

9 David then asked Ahimelech: "Do you have a spear or a sword on hand? I brought along neither my sword nor my weapons, because the king's business was urgent." 10* The priest replied: "The sword of Goliath the Philistine, whom you killed in the Vale of the Terebinth, is here [wrapped in a mantle] behind an ephod. If you wish to take that, take it; there is no sword here except that one." David said: "There is none to match it. Give it to me!"

David a Fugitive

11* That same day David took to flight from Saul, going to Achish, king of Gath. 12* But the servants of Achish said, "Is this not David, the king of the land? During their dances do they not sing,

'Saul has slain his thousands,
 but David his ten thousands'?"

13 David took note of these remarks and became very much afraid of Achish, king of Gath. 14 So, as they watched, he feigned insanity and acted like a madman in their hands, drumming on the doors of the gate and drooling onto his beard. 15 Finally Achish said to his servants: "You see the man is mad. Why did you bring him to me? 16 Do I not have enough madmen, that you bring in this one to carry on in my presence? Should this fellow come into my house?"

22 1* David left Gath and escaped to the cave of Adullam. When his brothers and the rest of his family heard about it, they came down to him there. 2 He was joined by all those who were in difficulties or in debt, or who were embittered, and he became their leader. About four hundred men were with him.

3 From there David went to Mizpeh of Moab and said to the king of Moab, "Let my father and mother stay with you, until I learn what God will do for me." 4† He left them with the king of Moab, and they stayed with him as long as David remained in the refuge.

5 But the prophet Gad said to David: "Do not remain in the refuge. Leave, and go to the land of Judah." And so David left and went to the forest of Hereth.

Doeg Betrays Ahimelech

6* Now Saul heard that David and his men had been located. At the time he was sitting in Gibeah under a tamarisk tree on the high place, holding his spear, while all his servants were standing by. 7* So he said to them: "Listen, men of Benjamin! Will the son of Jesse give all of you fields and vineyards? Will he make each of you an officer over a thousand or a hundred men, 8 that you have all conspired against me and no one tells me that my son has made an agreement with the son of Jesse? None of you shows sympathy for me or discloses to me that my son has stirred up my servant to be an enemy against me, as is the case today." 9* Then Doeg the Edomite, who was standing with the officers of Saul, spoke up: "I saw the son of Jesse come to Ahimelech, son of Ahitub, in Nob. 10 He consulted the LORD for him and gave him supplies, and the sword of Goliath the Philistine as well."

Slaughter of the Priests

11 At this the king sent a summons to Ahimelech the priest, son of Ahitub, and to all his family who were priests in Nob; and they all came to the king. 12 Then Saul said, "Listen, son of Ahitub!" He replied, "Yes, my lord." 13 Saul asked him, "Why did you conspire against me with the son of Jesse by giving him food and a sword and by consulting God for him, that he might rebel against me and become my enemy, as is the case today?" 14 Ahimelech answered the king: "And who among all your servants is as loyal as David, the king's son-in-law, captain of your bodyguard, and honored in your own house? 15 Is this the first time I have consulted God for him? No indeed! Let not the king accuse his servant or anyone in my family of such a thing. Your servant knows nothing at all, great or small, about the whole matter." 16 But the king said, "You shall die, Ahimelech, with all your family." 17* The king then commanded his henchmen standing by:

22, 4–5: *Refuge:* seemingly connected with the cave complex spoken of in v 1.

21, 7: 1 Sm 22, 9; Lv 24,   5–9: Mt 12, 3f; Mk 2,

26; Lk 6, 3ff.
21, 10: 1 Sm 17, 51.54.
21, 11: 1 Sm 27, 2; 29, 5.
21, 12: 1 Sm 18, 7; 29, 5.
22, 1: 2 Sm 23, 13; Ps 63;

Mi 1, 15.
22, 6: Ps 52.
22, 7: 1 Sm 8, 14.
22, 9f: 1 Sm 21, 2–10.
22, 17: 1 Sm 2, 31.33; 21, 7.

"Make the rounds and kill the priests of the LORD, for they assisted David. They knew he was a fugitive and yet failed to inform me." But the king's servants refused to lift a hand to strike the priests of the LORD.

[18] The king therefore commanded Doeg, "You make the rounds and kill the priests!" So Doeg the Edomite went from one to the next and killed the priests himself, slaying on that day eighty-five who wore the linen ephod. [19] Saul also put the priestly city of Nob to the sword, including men and women, children and infants, and oxen, asses and sheep.

Abiathar Escapes

[20]* One son of Ahimelech, son of Ahitub, named Abiathar, escaped and fled to David. [21] When Abiathar told David that Saul had slain the priests of the LORD, [22] David said to him: "I knew that day, when Doeg the Edomite was there, that he would surely tell Saul. I am responsible for the death of all your family. [23] Stay with me. Fear nothing; he that seeks your life must seek my life also. You are under my protection."

Keilah Liberated

23 [1]* David received information that the Philistines were attacking Keilah and plundering the threshing floors. [2]* So he consulted the LORD, inquiring, "Shall I go and defeat these Philistines?" The LORD answered, "Go, for you will defeat the Philistines and rescue Keilah." [3] But David's men said to him: "We are afraid here in Judah. How much more so if we go to Keilah against the forces of the Philistines!" [4] Again David consulted the LORD, who answered, "Go down to Keilah, for I will deliver the Philistines into your power." [5] David then went with his men to Keilah and fought with the Philistines. He drove off their cattle and inflicted a severe defeat on them, and thus rescued the inhabitants of Keilah.

[6]* Abiathar, son of Ahimelech, who had fled to David, went down with David to Keilah, taking the ephod with him.

Flight from Keilah

[7] When Saul was told that David had entered Keilah, he said: "God has put him in my grip. Now he has shut himself in, for he has entered a city with gates and bars." [8] Saul then called all the people to war, in order to go down to Keilah and besiege David and his men. [9]* When David found out that Saul was planning to harm him, he said to the priest Abiathar, "Bring forward the ephod."

[10] David then said: "O LORD God of Israel, your servant has heard a report that Saul plans to come to Keilah, to destroy the city on my account. [11] Will they hand me over? And now: will Saul come down as your servant has heard? O LORD God of Israel, tell your servant." The LORD answered, "He will come down." [12] David then asked, "Will the citizens of Keilah deliver me and my men into the grasp of Saul?" And the LORD answered, "Yes." [13] So David and his men, about six hundred in number, left Keilah and wandered from place to place. When Saul was informed that David had escaped from Keilah, he abandoned the expedition.

David and Jonathan in Horesh

[14] David now lived in the refuges in the desert, or in the barren hill country near Ziph. Though Saul sought him continually, the LORD did not deliver David into his grasp. [15] David was apprehensive because Saul had come out to seek his life; but while he was at Horesh in the barrens near Ziph, [16]* Saul's son, Jonathan, came down there to David and strengthened his resolve in the LORD. [17] He said to him: "Have no fear, my father Saul shall not lay a hand to you. You shall be king of Israel and I shall be second to you. Even my father Saul knows this." [18]* They made a joint agreement before the LORD in Horesh, where David remained, while Jonathan returned to his home.

Treachery of the Ziphites

[19]* Some of the Ziphites went up to Saul in Gibeah and said, "David is hiding among us, now in the refuges, and again at Horesh, or on the hill of Hachilah, south of the wasteland. [20] Therefore, whenever the king wishes to come down, let him do so. It will be our task to deliver him into the king's grasp." [21]* Saul replied: "The LORD bless you for your sympathy toward me. [22] Go now and make sure once more! Take note of the place where he sets foot" (for he thought, perhaps they are playing some trick on me). [23] "Look around and learn in which of all the various hiding places he is holding out. Then come back to me with sure information, and I will go with you. If he is in the region, I will search him out among all the families of Judah." [24]* So they went off to Ziph ahead of Saul. At this time David and his men were in the desert below Maon, in the Arabah south of the wasteland.

Escape from Saul

[25] When Saul and his men came looking for him, David got word of it and went down to the

---

22, 20: 1 Sm 23, 6; 30, 7;
   1 Kgs 2, 28f.
23, 1: Jos 15, 44.

23, 2: 1 Sm 28, 6.
23, 6: 1 Sm 22, 20; 30, 7.
23, 9: 1 Sm 2, 28.

23, 16: 1 Sm 18, 1.
23, 18: 1 Sm 18, 3; 20, 8.
23, 19: 1 Sm 26, 1–3; Ps 54.

23, 21: 2 Sm 2, 5.
23, 24: 1 Sm 25, 2.

gorge in the desert below Maon. Saul heard of this and pursued David into the desert below Maon. [26] As Saul moved along one rim of the gorge, David and his men took to the other. David was in anxious flight to escape Saul, and Saul and his men were attempting to outflank David and his men in order to capture them, [27] when a messenger came to Saul, saying, "Come quickly, because the Philistines have invaded the land." [28] Saul interrupted his pursuit of David and went to meet the Philistines. This is how that place came to be called the Gorge of Divisions.

David Spares Saul

24 [1] David then went up from there and stayed in the refuges behind Engedi. [2] And when Saul returned from the pursuit of the Philistines, he was told that David was in the desert near Engedi. [3] So Saul took three thousand picked men from all Israel and went in search of David and his men in the direction of the wild goat crags. [4]* When he came to the sheepfolds along the way, he found a cave, which he entered to ease nature. David and his men were occupying the inmost recesses of the cave.

[5] David's servants said to him, "This is the day of which the LORD said to you, 'I will deliver your enemy into your grasp; do with him as you see fit.' " So David moved up and stealthily cut off an end of Saul's mantle. [6]* Afterward, however, David regretted that he had cut off an end of Saul's mantle. [7]* He said to his men, "The LORD forbid that I should do such a thing to my master, the LORD's anointed, as to lay a hand on him, for he is the LORD's anointed." [8] With these words David restrained his men and would not permit them to attack Saul. Saul then left the cave and went on his way. [9] David also stepped out of the cave, calling to Saul, "My lord the king!" When Saul looked back, David bowed to the ground in homage [10] and asked Saul: "Why do you listen to those who say, 'David is trying to harm you'? [11] You see for yourself today that the LORD just now delivered you into my grasp in the cave. I had some thought of killing you, but I took pity on you instead. I decided, 'I will not raise a hand against my lord, for he is the LORD's anointed and a father to me.' [12]* Look here at this end of your mantle which I hold. Since I cut off an end of your mantle and did not kill you, see and be convinced that I plan no harm and no rebellion. I have done you no wrong, though you are hunting me down to take my life. [13] The LORD will judge between me and you, and the LORD will exact justice from you in my case. I shall not touch you. [14] The old

proverb says, 'From the wicked comes forth wickedness.' So I will take no action against you. [15] Against whom are you on campaign, O king of Israel? Whom are you pursuing? A dead dog, or a single flea! [16]* The LORD will be the judge; he will decide between me and you. May he see this, and take my part, and grant me justice beyond your reach!"

did you KNOW?

The LORD's Anointed

Israelite kings and prophets were anointed with oil to symbolize the powerful spirit of God that was present to them as they fulfilled their important role. The Hebrew word *mashiah*, translated in 1 Sm 24, 7 as "anointed [one]," is the root of the English word *messiah*. Often applied to kings in the Old Testament, this title was attached in the second century B.C. to the one "like David" who was expected to come (see Dn 9, 25). *Mashiah* translated into Greek is *christos*, which became the title given to Jesus by his followers: Jesus, the Christ; Jesus, the anointed one; Jesus, the Messiah.

Saul's Remorse

[17] When David finished saying these things to Saul, Saul answered, "Is that your voice, my son David?" And he wept aloud. [18] Saul then said to David: "You are in the right rather than I; you have treated me generously, while I have done you harm. [19] Great is the generosity you showed me today, when the LORD delivered me into your grasp and you did not kill me. [20] For if a man meets his enemy, does he send him away unharmed? May the LORD reward you generously for what you have done this day. [21]* And now, since I know that you shall surely be king and that sovereignty over Israel shall come into your possession, [22]* swear to me by the LORD that you will not destroy my descendants and that you will not blot out my name and family." [23] David gave Saul his oath and Saul returned home, while David and his men went up to the refuge.

24, 4: Ps 57.
24, 6: 1 Sm 15, 27.
24, 7: 1 Sm 10, 1; 31, 4;
2 Sm 1, 14.
24, 12: Rom 12, 19.
24, 16: 1 Sm 18, 19.31; 26,
19; Pss 35, 1ff; 43, 1.
24, 21: 1 Sm 26, 25.
24, 22: 2 Sm 9, 1ff.

Death of Samuel

25 [1]* Samuel died, and all Israel gathered to mourn him; they buried him at his home in Ramah.

Nabal and Abigail

[2]* Then David went down to the desert of Maon. There was a man of Maon who had property in Carmel; he was very wealthy, owning three thousand sheep and a thousand goats. At this time he was present for the shearing of his flock in Carmel. [3]* The man was named Nabal, his wife, Abigail. The woman was intelligent and attractive, but Nabal himself, a Calebite, was harsh and ungenerous in his behavior. [4] When David heard in the desert that Nabal was shearing his flock, [5] he sent ten young men, instructing them: "Go up to Carmel. Pay Nabal a visit and greet him in my name. [6] Say to him, 'Peace be with you, my brother, and with your family, and with all who belong to you. [7] I have just heard that shearers are with you. Now, when your shepherds were with us, we did them no injury, neither did they miss anything all the while they were in Carmel. [8] Ask your servants and they will tell you so. Look kindly on these young men, since we come at a festival time. Please give your servants and your son David whatever you can manage.' "

[9] When David's young men arrived, they delivered this message fully to Nabal in David's name, and then waited. [10] But Nabal answered the servants of David: "Who is David? Who is the son of Jesse? Nowadays there are many servants who run away from their masters. [11] Must I take my bread, my wine, my meat that I have slaughtered for my own shearers, and give them to men who come from I know not where?" [12] So David's young men retraced their steps and on their return reported to him all that had been said. [13] Thereupon David said to his men, "Let everyone gird on his sword." And so everyone, David included, girded on his sword. About four hundred men went up after David, while two hundred remained with the baggage.

[14] But Nabal's wife Abigail was informed of this by one of the servants, who said: "David sent messengers from the desert to greet our master, but he flew at them screaming. [15] Yet these men were very good to us. We were done no injury, neither did we miss anything all the while we were living among them during our stay in the open country. [16] For us

they were like a rampart night and day the whole time we were pasturing the sheep near them. [17] Now, see what you can do, for you must realize that otherwise evil is in store for our master and for his whole family. He is so mean that no one can talk to him." [18] Abigail quickly got together two hundred loaves, two skins of wine, five dressed sheep, five seahs of roasted grain, a hundred cakes of pressed raisins, and two hundred cakes of pressed figs, and loaded them on asses. [19] She then said to her servants, "Go on ahead; I will follow you." But she did not tell her husband Nabal.

[20] As she came down through a mountain defile riding on an ass, David and his men were also coming down from the opposite direction. When she met them, [21] David had just been saying: "Indeed, it was in vain that I guarded all this man's possessions in the desert, so that he missed nothing. He has repaid good with evil. [22]* May God do thus and so to David, if by morning I leave a single male alive among all those who belong to him." [23] As soon as Abigail saw David, she dismounted quickly from the ass and, falling prostrate on the ground before David, did him homage. [24] As she fell at his feet she said:

"My lord, let the blame be mine. Please let your handmaid speak to you, and listen to the words of your handmaid. [25]† Let not my lord pay attention to that worthless man Nabal, for he is just like his name. Fool is his name, and he acts the fool. I, your handmaid, did not see the young men whom my lord sent. [26]† Now, therefore, my lord, as the LORD lives, and as you live, it is the LORD who has kept you from shedding blood and from avenging yourself personally. May your enemies and those who seek to harm my lord become as Nabal! [27] Accept this present, then, which your maidservant has brought for my lord, and let it be given to the young men who follow my lord. [28] Please forgive the transgression of your handmaid, for the LORD shall certainly establish a lasting dynasty for my lord, because your lordship is fighting the battles of the LORD, and there is no evil to be found in you your whole life long. [29]*† If anyone rises to pursue you and to seek your life, may the life of my lord be bound in the bundle of the living in the care of the LORD your God; but may he hurl out the lives of your enemies as from the hollow of a sling. [30]* And when the LORD carries out for my lord the promise of success he has made concerning you, and ap-

---

†
25, 25: *Fool is his name:* Nabal in Hebrew means "a fool."
25, 26: Abigail anticipates that some misfortune will shortly overtake Nabal, as in fact it does (vv 37–38).
25, 29: *The bundle of the living:* the figure is perhaps taken from the practice of tying up valuables in a kerchief or bag for safekeeping. Abigail desires that David enjoy permanent peace and security, but that his enemies be subject to constant agitation and humiliation

like a stone whirled about, cast out of the sling, and thereafter disregarded.

*
25, 1: 1 Sm 28, 3; Sir 46, 13–20.	**25, 22:** 1 Kgs 16, 11; 21, 21; 2 Kgs 9, 8.
25, 2: 1 Sm 23, 24; Jos 15, 55.	**25, 29:** Ps 69, 28.
25, 3: 1 Sm 27, 3; Jos 14, 6; 1 Chr 2, 42.45.	**25, 30:** 1 Sm 13, 14; 2 Sm 3, 10.

points you as commander over Israel, [31] you shall not have this as a qualm or burden on your conscience, my lord, for having shed innocent blood or for having avenged yourself personally. When the LORD confers this benefit on your lordship, remember your handmaid." [32] David said to Abigail: "Blessed be the LORD, the God of Israel, who sent you to meet me today. [33] Blessed be your good judgment and blessed be you yourself, who this day have prevented me from shedding blood and from avenging myself personally. [34] Otherwise, as the LORD, the God of Israel, lives, who has restrained me from harming you, if you had not come so promptly to meet me, by dawn Nabal would not have had a single man or boy left alive." [35] David then took from her what she had brought him and said to her: "Go up to your home in peace! See, I have granted your request as a personal favor."

Nabal's Death

[36] When Abigail came to Nabal, there was a drinking party in his house like that of a king, and Nabal was merry because he was very drunk. So she told him nothing at all before daybreak the next morning. [37] But then, when Nabal had become sober, his wife told him what had happened. At this his courage died within him, and he became like a stone. [38] About ten days later the LORD struck him and he died. [39] On hearing that Nabal was dead, David said: "Blessed be the LORD, who has requited the insult I received at the hand of Nabal, and who restrained his servant from doing evil, but has punished Nabal for his own evil deeds."

David Marries Abigail and Ahinoam

David then sent a proposal of marriage to Abigail. [40] When David's servants came to Abigail in Carmel, they said to her, "David has sent us to you that he may take you as his wife." [41] Rising and bowing to the ground, she answered, "Your handmaid would become a slave to wash the feet of my lord's servants." [42] She got up immediately, mounted an ass, and followed David's messengers, with her five maids following in attendance upon her. She became his wife, [43]* and David also married Ahinoam of Jezreel. Thus both of them were his wives; but Saul gave David's wife Michal, Saul's own daughter, to Palti, son of Laish, who was from Gallim.*

Saul's Life Again Spared

26 [1] Men from Ziph came to Saul in Gibeah, reporting that David was hiding on the hill of Hachilah at the edge of the wasteland. [2] So Saul went off down to the desert of Ziph with three thousand picked men of Israel, to search for David in the desert of Ziph. [3] Saul camped beside the road on the hill of Hachilah, at the edge of the wasteland. David, who was living in the desert, saw that Saul had come into the desert after him [4] and sent out scouts, who confirmed Saul's arrival. [5]* David himself then went to the place where Saul was encamped and examined the spot where Saul and Abner, son of Ner, the general, had their sleeping quarters. Saul's were within the barricade, and all his soldiers were camped around him. [6]* David asked Ahimelech the Hittite, and Abishai, son of Zeruiah and brother of Joab, "Who will go down into the camp with me to Saul?" Abishai replied, "I will." [7] So David and Abishai went among Saul's soldiers by night and found Saul lying asleep within the barricade, with his spear thrust into the ground at his head and Abner and his men sleeping around him.

[8]* Abishai whispered to David: "God has delivered your enemy into your grasp this day. Let me nail him to the ground with one thrust of the spear; I will not need a second thrust!" [9] But David said to Abishai, "Do not harm him, for who can lay hands on the LORD'S anointed and remain unpunished? [10] As the LORD lives," David continued, "it must be the LORD himself who will strike him, whether the time comes for him to die, or he goes out and perishes in battle. [11] But the LORD forbid that I touch his anointed! Now take the spear which is at his head and the water jug, and let us be on our way." [12] So David took the spear and the water jug from their place at Saul's head, and they got away without anyone's seeing or knowing or awakening. All remained asleep, because the LORD had put them into a deep slumber.

David Taunts Abner

[13] Going across to an opposite slope, David stood on a remote hilltop at a great distance from Abner, son of Ner, and the troops. [14] He then shouted, "Will you not answer, Abner?" And Abner answered, "Who is it that calls me?" [15] David said to Abner: "Are you not a man whose like does not exist in Israel? Why, then, have you not guarded your lord the king when one of his subjects went to kill the king, your lord? [16] This is no creditable service you have performed. As the LORD lives, you people deserve death because you have not guarded your lord, the LORD'S anointed. Go, look: where are the king's spear and the water jug that was at his head?"

Saul Admits His Guilt

[17] Saul recognized David's voice and asked, "Is that your voice, my son David?" David answered,

---

25, 43: 1 Sm 27, 3.
25, 43: 1 Sm 18, 20; 27, 3;

30, 5; 2 Sm 3, 2.13ff;
1 Chr 3, 1.

26, 1f: 1 Sm 23, 19f; Ps 54.
26, 5: 1 Sm 17, 20.

26, 6: 1 Chr 2, 16.
26, 8: 1 Sm 18, 11; 19, 10.

"Yes, my lord the king." [18] He continued: "Why does my lord pursue his servant? What have I done? What evil do I plan? [19]*† Please, now, let my lord the king listen to the words of his servant. If the LORD has incited you against me, let an offering appease him; but if men, may they be cursed before the LORD, because they have exiled me so that this day I have no share in the LORD'S inheritance, but am told: 'Go, serve other gods!' [20] Do not let my blood flow to the ground far from the presence of the LORD. For the king of Israel has come out to seek a single flea as if he were hunting partridge in the mountains." [21] Then Saul said: "I have done wrong. Come back, my son David, I will not harm you again, because you have held my life precious today. Indeed, I have been a fool and have made a serious mistake." [22] But David answered: "Here is the king's spear. Let an attendant come over to get it. [23]* The LORD will reward each man for his justice and faithfulness. Today, though the LORD delivered you into my grasp, I would not harm the LORD'S anointed. [24] As I valued your life highly today, so may the LORD value my life highly and deliver me from all difficulties." [25]* Then Saul said to David: "Blessed are you, my son David! You shall certainly succeed in whatever you undertake." David went his way, and Saul returned to his home.

Refuge among Philistines

27 [1] But David said to himself: "I shall perish some day at the hand of Saul. I have no choice but to escape to the land of the Philistines; then Saul will give up his continuous search for me throughout the land of Israel, and I shall be out of his reach." [2]* Accordingly, David departed with his six hundred men and went over to Achish, son of Maoch, king of Gath. [3]* David and his men lived in Gath with Achish; each one had his family, and David had his two wives, Ahinoam from Jezreel and Abigail, the widow of Nabal from Carmel. [4] When Saul was told that David had fled to Gath, he no longer searched for him.

In Ziklag

[5] David said to Achish: "If I meet with your approval, let me have a place to live in one of the country towns. Why should your servant live with you in the royal city?" [6]*† That same day Achish gave him Ziklag, which has, therefore, belonged to

the kings of Judah up to the present time. [7]* In all, David lived a year and four months in the country of the Philistines.

Raids on Israel's Foes

[8]* David and his men went up and made raids on the Geshurites, Girzites, and Amalekites—peoples living in the land between Telam, on the approach to Shur, and the land of Egypt. [9] In attacking the land David would not leave a man or woman alive, but would carry off sheep, oxen, asses, camels, and clothes. On his return he brought these to Achish, [10]* who asked, "Whom did you raid this time?" And David answered, "The Negeb of Judah," or "The Negeb of Jarahmeel," or "The Negeb of the Kenites." [11] But David would not leave a man or woman alive to be brought to Gath, fearing that they would betray him by saying, "This is what David did." This was his custom as long as he lived in the country of the Philistines. [12] And Achish trusted David, thinking, "He must certainly be detested by his people Israel. I shall have him as my vassal forever."

28 [1] In those days the Philistines mustered their military forces to fight against Israel. So Achish said to David, "You realize, of course, that you and your men must go out on campaign with me to Jezreel." [2] David answered Achish, "Good! Now you shall learn what your servant can do." Then Achish said to David, "I shall appoint you my permanent bodyguard."

[3]* Now Samuel had died and, after being mourned by all Israel, was buried in his city, Ramah. Meanwhile Saul had driven mediums and fortune-tellers out of the land.

Saul in Dismay

[4] The Philistine levies advanced to Shunem and encamped. Saul, too, mustered all Israel; they camped on Gilboa. [5] When Saul saw the camp of the Philistines, he was dismayed and lost heart completely. [6]* He therefore consulted the LORD; but the LORD gave no answer, whether in dreams or by the Urim or through prophets. [7]* Then Saul said to his servants, "Find me a woman who is a medium, to whom I can go to seek counsel through her." His servants answered him, "There is a woman in Endor who is a medium."

26, 19: *The LORD's inheritance:* the land of Israel (Dt 32, 8f), under the Lord's special protection, where he could be freely worshiped.

27, 6: *Has . . . belonged to the kings of Judah:* as a personal holding, outside the system of tribal lands; Jerusalem, when taken by David, had a similar status (2 Sm 5, 7–9).

26, 19: 1 Sm 24, 16.
26, 23: 1 Sm 18, 20.
26, 25: 1 Sm 24, 21.
27, 2: 1 Sm 21, 11–16.
27, 3: 1 Sm 25, 3.44; 30, 3ff;
   2 Sm 2, 3.
27, 6: 1 Sm 30, 1.
27, 7: 1 Sm 29, 3.
27, 8: 1 Sm 15, 3.7.

27, 10: 1 Sm 30, 14.29; 1 Chr
   2, 9.25.42.
28, 1: 1 Sm 25, 1; Sir 46, 20.
28, 6: 1 Sm 14, 37.41; Ex 28,
   30; Lv 8, 8.
28, 7: Lv 19, 31; 20, 27; Dt
   18, 10ff; 1 Chr 10,
   13f; Acts 16, 16.

The Witch of Endor

8* So he disguised himself, putting on other clothes, and set out with two companions. They came to the woman by night, and Saul said to her, "Tell my fortune through a ghost; conjure up for me the one I ask you to." 9 But the woman answered him, "You are surely aware of what Saul has done, in driving the mediums and fortune-tellers out of the land. Why, then, are you laying snares for my life, to have me killed?" 10 But Saul swore to her by the LORD, "As the LORD lives, you shall incur no blame for this." 11 Then the woman asked him, "Whom do you want me to conjure up?" and he answered, "Samuel."

Samuel Appears

12† When the woman saw Samuel, she shrieked at the top of her voice and said to Saul, "Why have you deceived me? You are Saul!" 13 But the king said to her, "Have no fear. What do you see?" The woman answered Saul, "I see a preternatural being rising from the earth." 14 "What does he look like?" asked Saul. And she replied, "It is an old man who is rising, clothed in a mantle." Saul knew that it was Samuel, and so he bowed face to the ground in homage.

Saul's Doom

15* Samuel then said to Saul, "Why do you disturb me by conjuring me up?" Saul replied: "I am in great straits, for the Philistines are waging war against me and God has abandoned me. Since he no longer answers me through prophets or in dreams, I have called you to tell me what I should do." 16* To this Samuel said: "But why do you ask me, if the LORD has abandoned you and is with your neighbor? 17 The LORD has done to you what he foretold through me: he has torn the kingdom from your grasp and has given it to your neighbor David. 18* "Because you disobeyed the LORD'S directive and would not carry out his fierce anger against Amalek, the LORD has done this to you today. 19* Moreover, the LORD will deliver Israel, and you as well, into the clutches of the Philistines. By tomorrow you and your sons will be with me, and the LORD will have delivered the army of Israel into the hands of the Philistines."

Saul's Despair

20 Immediately Saul fell full length on the ground, for he was badly shaken by Samuel's message. Moreover, he had no bodily strength left, since he had eaten nothing all that day and night. 21 Then the woman came to Saul, and seeing that he was quite terror-stricken, said to him: "Remember, your maidservant obeyed you: I took my life in my hands and fulfilled the request you made of me. 22 Now you, in turn, please listen to your maidservant. Let me set something before you to eat, so that you may have strength when you go on your way." 23 But he refused, saying, "I will not eat." However, when his servants joined the woman in urging him, he listened to their entreaties, got up from the ground, and sat on a couch. 24 The woman had a stall-fed calf in the house, which she now quickly slaughtered. Then taking flour, she kneaded it and baked unleavened bread. 25 She set the meal before Saul and his servants, and they ate. Then they stood up and left the same night.

David's Aid Rejected

29 1* Now the Philistines had mustered all their forces in Aphek, and the Israelites were encamped at the spring of Harod near Jezreel. 2 As the Philistine lords were marching their groups of a hundred and a thousand, David and his men were marching in the rear guard with Achish. 3* The Philistine chiefs asked, "What are those Hebrews doing here?" And Achish answered them: "Why, that is David, the officer of Saul, king of Israel. He has been with me now for a year or two, and I have no fault to find with him from the day he came over to me until the present." 4* But the Philistine chiefs were angered at this and said to him: "Send that man back! Let him return to the place you picked out for him. He must not go down into battle with us, lest during the battle he become our enemy. For how else can he win back his master's favor, if not with the heads of these men of ours? 5* Is this not the David of whom they sing during their dances,

'Saul has slain his thousands,
    but David his ten thousands'?"

6 So Achish summoned David and said to him: "As the LORD lives, you are honest, and I should be

---

28, 12: Human beings cannot communicate at will with the souls of the dead. God may, however, permit a departed soul to appear to the living and even to disclose things unknown to them. Saul's own prohibition of necromancy and divination (v 3) was in keeping with the consistent teaching of the Old Testament. If we are to credit the reality of the apparition to Saul, it was due, not to the summons of the witch, but to God's will; the woman merely furnished the occasion.

28, 8: 1 Kgs 14, 2.   Sir 46, 20.
28, 15: Sir 46, 20.
28, 16: 1 Sm 15, 27f.   29, 1: 1 Sm 4, 1.
28, 18: 1 Sm 15, 18f.26.   29, 3: 1 Sm 27, 7.
28, 19: 1 Sm 31, 2–6;   29, 4: 1 Chr 12, 19f.
                                  29, 5: 1 Sm 18, 6f; 21, 11.

pleased to have you active with me in the camp, for I have found nothing wrong with you from the day of your arrival to this day. But you are not welcome to the lords. ⁷ Withdraw peaceably, now, and do nothing that might displease the Philistine lords." ⁸ But David said to Achish: "What have I done? Or what have you against your servant from the first day I have been with you to this day, that I cannot go to fight against the enemies of my lord the king?" ⁹ "You know," Achish answered David, "that you are acceptable to me. But the Philistine chiefs have determined you are not to go up with us to battle. ¹⁰ So the first thing tomorrow, you and your lord's servants who came with you, go to the place I picked out for you. Do not decide to take umbrage at this; you are as acceptable to me as an angel of God. But make an early morning start, as soon as it grows light, and be on your way." ¹¹ So David and his men left early in the morning to return to the land of the Philistines. The Philistines, however, went on up to Jezreel.

Ziklag in Ruins

30 ¹* Before David and his men reached Ziklag on the third day, the Amalekites had raided the Negeb and Ziklag, had stormed the city, and had set it on fire. ² They had taken captive the women and all who were in the city, young and old, killing no one; they had carried them off when they left. ³ David and his men arrived at the city to find it burned to the ground and their wives, sons and daughters taken captive. ⁴ Then David and those who were with him wept aloud until they could weep no more. ⁵* David's two wives, Ahinoam of Jezreel and Abigail, the widow of Nabal from Carmel, had also been carried off with the rest. ⁶ Now David found himself in great difficulty, for the men spoke of stoning him, so bitter were they over the fate of their sons and daughters. But with renewed trust in the LORD his God, ⁷* David said to Abiathar, the priest, son of Ahimelech, "Bring me the ephod!" When Abiathar brought him the ephod, ⁸ David inquired of the LORD, "Shall I pursue these raiders? Can I overtake them?" The LORD answered him, "Go in pursuit, for you shall surely overtake them and effect a rescue."

Raid of the Amalekites

⁹ So David went off with his six hundred men and came as far as the Wadi Besor, where those who were to remain behind halted. ¹⁰ David continued the pursuit with four hundred men, but two hundred were too exhausted to cross the Wadi Besor

and remained behind. ¹¹ An Egyptian was found in the open country and brought to David. He was provided with food, which he ate, and given water to drink; ¹² a cake of pressed figs and two cakes of pressed raisins were also offered to him. When he had eaten, he revived; he had not taken food nor drunk water for three days and three nights. ¹³ Then David asked him, "To whom do you belong, and where do you come from?" He replied: "I am an Egyptian, the slave of an Amalekite. My master abandoned me because I fell sick three days ago today. ¹⁴* We raided the Negeb of the Cherethites, the territory of Judah, and the Negeb of Caleb; and we set Ziklag on fire." ¹⁵ David then asked him, "Will you lead me down to this raiding party?" He answered, "Swear to me by God that you will not kill me or deliver me to my master, and I will lead you to the raiding party." ¹⁶ He did lead them, and there were the Amalekites scattered all over the ground, eating, drinking, and in a festive mood because of all the rich booty they had taken from the land of the Philistines and from the land of Judah.

The Booty Recovered

¹⁷* From dawn to sundown David attacked them, putting them under the ban so that none escaped except four hundred young men, who mounted their camels and fled. ¹⁸ David recovered everything the Amalekites had taken, and rescued his two wives. ¹⁹ Nothing was missing, small or great, booty or sons or daughters, of all that the Amalekites had taken. David brought back everything. ²⁰ Moreover, David took all the sheep and oxen, and as they drove them before him, they shouted, "This is David's spoil."

Division of the Spoils

²¹ When David came to the two hundred men who had been too exhausted to follow him, and whom he had left behind at the Wadi Besor, they came out to meet David and the men with him. On nearing them David greeted them. ²² But all the stingy and worthless men among those who had accompanied David spoke up to say, "Since they did not accompany us, we will not give them anything from the booty, except to each man his wife and children. Let them take those along and be on their way." ²³ But David said: "You must not do this, my brothers, after what the LORD has given us. He has protected us and delivered into our grip the band that came against us. ²⁴* Who could agree with this proposal of yours? Rather, the share of the one who goes down to battle and that of the one who re-

30, 1: 1 Sm 27, 6.10; 1 Chr 12, 21.
30, 5: 1 Sm 25, 42; 27, 3; 30, 5.
30, 7f: 1 Sm 2, 28; 23, 6; Ex 28, 30.
30, 14: 1 Sm 27, 10;
Ez 25, 16.
30, 17: 1 Sm 15, 3; Jos 6, 17;
Jgs 7, 12.
30, 24: 1 Sm 17, 22; 25, 13.

Suicide Is Not an Answer

LIVE IT!

In 1 Sm 31, 4, Saul commits suicide out of fear of what his enemies would do to him. His death leaves a gap for the Israelites, and David, Saul's enemy, deeply mourns his death in 2 Samuel, chapter 1.

A popular newspaper advice columnist printed a letter from someone who was writing to share a thought on suicide. He had decided that his life was not worth living anymore and planned to kill himself. The moment before he was about to do it, he thought about who would find him, and then he stopped. He realized that he couldn't put someone through the pain and suffering of finding him dead from suicide. Because he thought of another, he no longer looked at his life as hopeless.

No life is worthless! No pain is invincible! No matter how overwhelming your struggles and challenges seem, there are people who can help you, and people who could not bear to lose you. Seek God for help, seek others for help—suicide is never a solution!

For more on suicide, see "Judas's Suicide," Mt 27, 3–10.

▸ 1 Sm 31, 1–6

mains with the baggage shall be the same; they shall share alike." 25* And from that day forward he made it a law and a custom in Israel, as it still is today.

David's Gifts to Judah

26 When David came to Ziklag, he sent part of the spoil to the elders of Judah, city by city, saying, "This is a gift to you from the spoil of the enemies of the LORD": 27 to those in Bethel, to those in Ramoth-negeb, to those in Jattir, 28 to those in Aroer, to those in Siphmoth, to those in Eshtemoa, 29* to those in Racal, to those in the Jerahmeelite cities, to those in the Kenite cities, 30 to those in Hormah, to those in Borashan, to those in Athach, 31 to those in Hebron, and to all the places frequented by David and his men.

Death of Saul and His Sons

31 1* As they pressed their attack on Israel, with the Israelites fleeing before them and falling mortally wounded on Mount Gilboa, 2* the Philistines pursued Saul and his sons closely, and slew Jonathan, Abinadab, and Malchishua, sons of Saul. 3 The battle raged around Saul, and the archers hit him; he was pierced through the abdomen. 4* Then Saul said to his armor-bearer, "Draw your sword and run me through, lest these uncircumcised come and make sport of me." But

his armor-bearer, badly frightened, refused to do it. So Saul took his own sword and fell upon it. 5*† When the armor-bearer saw that Saul was dead, he too fell upon his sword and died with him. 6 Thus Saul, his three sons, and his armor-bearer died together on that same day.

7 When the Israelites on the slope of the valley and those along the Jordan saw that the men of Israel had fled and that Saul and his sons were dead, they too abandoned their cities and fled. Then the Philistines came and lived in those cities.

8 The day after the battle the Philistines came to strip the slain, and found Saul and his three sons lying on Mount Gilboa. 9* They cut off Saul's head and stripped him of his armor, and then sent the good news throughout the land of the Philistines to their idols and to the people. 10 They put his armor in the temple of Astarte, but impaled his body on the wall of Beth-shan.

Burial of Saul

11* When the inhabitants of Jabesh-gilead heard what the Philistines had done to Saul, 12† all their warriors set out, and after marching throughout the night, removed the bodies of Saul and his sons from the wall of Beth-shan, and brought them to Jabesh, where they cremated them. 13 Then they took their bones and buried them under the tamarisk tree in Jabesh, and fasted for seven days.

31, 5: This report of the suicidal act of Saul is presented as a part of his downfall, to be judged accordingly.

31, 12: *Cremated them:* cremation was not normally practiced in Israel, though it was known in the country from pre-Israelite times.

30, 25: Nm 31, 27.
30, 29: 1 Sm 27, 10.
31, 1–13: 1 Chr 10, 1–12; 2 Sm 1, 1–16; 4, 4.
31, 2: 1 Sm 14, 49; 28, 19; 1 Chr 10, 2f.
31, 4: 1 Sm 24, 7; Jgs 9, 54;
1 Chr 10, 4.
31, 5: 1 Sm 10, 1; 26, 9; 2 Mc 14, 42.
31, 9: 1 Sm 17, 54; 2 Sm 1, 20; 2 Mc 15, 35.
31, 11ff: 1 Sm 11, 1–11; 2 Sm 2, 4–7.

Politician Guilty of Taking Foreign Bribes!" "Minister Accused of Sexual Misconduct!" "Athlete Arrested on Drug Charges!" Sometimes it seems as if the news is filled with one scandal after another. "What's happening in the world today?" we may ask in despair. "Are there no honest, decent people left?" After reading 2 Samuel, you will realize that scandals among the rich and powerful are nothing new. But somehow, God's will is accomplished despite human sin.

At a Glance

David Mourns Saul's Death (1, 1—2, 7).

IV. The Reign of David (2, 8—20, 25).

V. Appendixes (21, 1—24, 25).

In-depth

The main character in 2 Samuel is King David, whom we already met in 1 Samuel. The youngest of Jesse's sons, David is secretly anointed to succeed King Saul; he kills Goliath, plays music in Saul's court, and is befriended by the king's son Jonathan. At the beginning of 2 Samuel, when David takes the throne and quickly extends Israel's boundaries in every direction, everything looks hopeful for the nation.

As 2 Samuel continues, however, we discover that this hero is far from perfect: he sleeps with Bathsheba, the wife of one of his soldiers, and then tries to deceive the man when Bathsheba reports that she is pregnant. Later, he has the soldier killed and takes Bathsheba as his own. Soon, several tragedies befall his family and further bad decisions hurt his reign, leaving us with a mixed picture of the second king of Israel. Was David a great saint or a great sinner?

It was through David that God established a new Covenant with the people of Israel (7, 1–17). This fact is underlined in a memorable way when David, after completing his own magnificent palace, declares that he will build a house for God. But God does not want a temple; God wishes to maintain a covenantal relationship with the people of Israel through all history: "Your throne shall stand firm forever" (verse 16).

Although a talented military leader and a powerful ruler, King David shared our broken human nature. The author of 2 Samuel reminds us that even the great and the mighty stand in need of God's help and mercy; even they must keep God's Covenant. Because of David's reliance on God, he became a symbol of the ideal king and of the future messiah. David's greatness—and our own—comes from a willing reliance on God.

Quick Facts

Period Covered
from 1000 to 961 B.C.

Author
same as for 1 Samuel

Theme
David's rise to power and his fall into sin

Of Note
Samuel does not appear in this book, although it carries his name.

2 Samuel

Report of Saul's Death

1 1* After the death of Saul, David returned from his defeat of the Amalekites and spent two days in Ziklag. 2 On the third day a man came from Saul's camp, with his clothes torn and dirt on his head. Going to David, he fell to the ground in homage. 3 David asked him, "Where do you come from?" He replied, "I have escaped from the Israelite camp." 4 "Tell me what happened," David bade him. He answered that the soldiers had fled the battle and that many of them had fallen and were dead, among them Saul and his son Jonathan. 5 Then David said to the youth who was reporting to him, "How do you know that Saul and his son Jonathan are dead?" 6* The youthful informant replied: "It was by chance that I found myself on Mount Gilboa and saw Saul leaning on his spear, with chariots and horsemen closing in on him. 7 He turned around and, seeing me, called me to him. When I said, 'Here I am,' 8 he asked me, 'Who are you?' and I replied, 'An Amalekite.' 9 Then he said to me, 'Stand up to me, please, and finish me off, for I am in great suffering, yet fully alive.' 10 So I stood up to him and dispatched him, for I knew that he could not survive his wound. I removed the crown from his head and the armlet from his arm and brought them here to my lord."

11* David seized his garments and rent them, and all the men who were with him did likewise. 12* They mourned and wept and fasted until evening for Saul and his son Jonathan, and for the soldiers of the LORD of the clans of Israel, because they had fallen by the sword. 13 Then David said to the young man who had brought him the information, "Where are you from?" He replied, "I am the son of an Amalekite immigrant." 14* David said to him, "How is it that you were not afraid to put forth your hand to desecrate the LORD's anointed?" 15 David then called one of the attendants and said to him, "Come, strike him down"; and the youth struck him a mortal blow. 16 Meanwhile David said to him, "You are responsible for your own death, for you testified against yourself when you said, 'I dispatched the LORD's anointed.'"

Elegy for Saul and Jonathan

17 Then David chanted this elegy for Saul and his son Jonathan, 18* which is recorded in the Book of Jashar to be taught to the Judahites. He sang:

19   "Alas! the glory of Israel, Saul,
            slain upon your heights;
        how can the warriors have fallen!

20*   "Tell it not in Gath,

1, 1: 1 Sm 30, 17–20; 31, 1-13.
1, 6–10: 2 Sm 4, 10; 1 Sm 31,
1–4; 1 Chr 10, 1–4.
1, 11: 2 Sm 13, 31.
1, 12: 1 Sm 31, 13.
1, 14: 1 Sm 10, 1; 24, 7; Ps 105, 15.
1, 18: Jos 10, 13.
1, 20: Jgs 16, 23; 1 Sm 31, 9; Mi 1, 10.

herald it not in the streets of Ashkelon,
Lest the Philistine maidens rejoice,
   lest the daughters of the strangers exult!
21*†Mountains of Gilboa,
   may there be neither dew nor rain
      upon you,
   nor upsurgings of the deeps!
Upon you lie begrimed the warriors' shields,
   the shield of Saul, no longer anointed
      with oil.

22* "From the blood of the slain,
   from the bodies of the valiant,
The bow of Jonathan did not turn back,
   or the sword of Saul return unstained.
23 Saul and Jonathan, beloved and cherished,
   separated neither in life nor in death,
   swifter than eagles, stronger than lions!
24 Women of Israel, weep over Saul,
   who clothed you in scarlet and in finery,
   who decked your attire with ornaments
      of gold.

25 "How can the warriors have fallen—
   in the thick of the battle,
   slain upon your heights!
26* "I grieve for you, Jonathan my brother!
   most dear have you been to me;
More precious have I held love for you
   than love for women.

27 "How can the warriors have fallen,
   the weapons of war have perished!"

David Anointed King

2 ¹ After this David inquired of the LORD, "Shall I go up into one of the cities of Judah?" The LORD replied to him, "Yes." Then David asked, "Where shall I go?" He replied, "To Hebron." ²* So David went up there accompanied by his two wives, Ahinoam of Jezreel and Abigail, the widow of Nabal of Carmel. ³ David also brought up his men with their families, and they dwelt in the cities near Hebron. ⁴* Then the men of Judah came there and anointed David king of the Judahites.

A report reached David that the men of Jabesh-gilead had buried Saul. ⁵ So David sent messengers to the men of Jabesh-gilead and said to them: "May you be blessed by the LORD for having done this kindness to your lord Saul in burying him. ⁶ And now may the LORD be kind and faithful to you. I,

did you KNOW?

David the Musician

David's song of mourning for Saul and Jonathan is another example of David's many talents. The Bible speaks in several places about David's ability as a musician and songwriter. One tradition says that he wrote all the Psalms, but no proof of this exists. His legendary reputation probably became exaggerated over the years to include many things only remotely related to his life.

▸ 2 Sm 1, 19–27

too, will be generous to you for having done this. ⁷ Take courage, therefore, and prove yourselves valiant men, for though your lord Saul is dead, the Judahites have anointed me their king."

IV: The Reign of David

Ishbaal King of Israel

⁸* Abner, son of Ner, Saul's general, took Ishbaal, son of Saul, and brought him over to Mahanaim, ⁹ where he made him king over Gilead, the Ashurites, Jezreel, Ephraim, Benjamin, and the rest of Israel. ¹⁰ Ishbaal, son of Saul, was forty years old when he became king over Israel, and he reigned for two years. The Judahites alone followed David. ¹¹* In all, David spent seven years and six months in Hebron as king of the Judahites.

Combat near Gibeon

¹² Now Abner, son of Ner, and the servants of Ishbaal, Saul's son, left Mahanaim for Gibeon. ¹³ Joab, son of Zeruiah, and David's servants also set out and met them at the pool of Gibeon. And they sat down, one group on one side of the pool and the other on the opposite side. ¹⁴ Then Abner said to Joab, "Let the young men rise and perform for us." Joab replied, "All right!" ¹⁵ So they rose and were counted off: twelve of the Benjaminites of Ishbaal, son of Saul, and twelve of David's servants. ¹⁶† Then each one grasped his opponent's head and

---

1, 21: *Upsurgings of the deeps:* this reading attempts to recover from an unintelligible Hebrew phrase the poetic parallel to dew and rain. The sense would be a wish that the mountain should have neither moisture from above nor water from springs or wells.
2, 16: The nature of this gruesome game is not clear, and the place name is variously given in the older texts.

1, 21: Gn 27, 28.
1, 22: 1 Sm 14, 47.
1, 26: 1 Sm 18, 1; 1 Mc 9,
   21.
2, 2: 1 Sm 25, 42f.
2, 4: 1 Sm 31, 11ff.
2, 8: 1 Sm 14, 50.
2, 11: 2 Sm 5, 5; 1 Kgs 2, 11.

thrust his sword into his opponent's side, and all fell down together. And so that place, which is in Gideon, was named the Field of the Sides.

Death of Asahel

¹⁷ After a very fierce battle that day, Abner and the men of Israel were defeated by David's servants. ¹⁸* The three sons of Zeruiah were there—Joab, Abishai, and Asahel. Asahel, who was as fleet of foot as a gazelle in the open field, ¹⁹* set out after Abner, turning neither right nor left in his pursuit. ²⁰ Abner turned around and said, "Is that you, Asahel?" He replied, "Yes." ²¹ Abner said to him, "Turn right or left; seize one of the young men and take what you can strip from him." But Asahel would not desist from his pursuit. ²²* Once more Abner said to Asahel: "Stop pursuing me! Why must I strike you to the ground? How could I face your brother Joab?" ²³ Still he refused to stop. So Abner struck him in the abdomen with the heel of his javelin, and the weapon protruded from his back. He fell there and died on the spot. And all who came to the place where Asahel had fallen and died, came to a halt. ²⁴ Joab and Abishai, however, continued the pursuit of Abner. The sun had gone down when they came to the hill of Ammah which lies east of the valley toward the desert near Geba.

Truce between Joab and Abner

²⁵ Here the Benjaminites rallied around Abner, forming a single group, and made a stand on the hilltop. ²⁶ Then Abner called to Joab and said: "Must the sword destroy to the utmost? Do you not know that afterward there will be bitterness? How much longer will you refrain from ordering the people to stop the pursuit of their brothers?" ²⁷ Joab replied, "As God lives, if you had not spoken, the soldiers would not have been withdrawn from the pursuit of their brothers until morning." ²⁸ Joab then sounded the horn, and all the soldiers came to a halt, pursuing Israel no farther and fighting no more. ²⁹ Abner and his men marched all night long through the Arabah, crossed the Jordan, marched all through the morning, and came to Mahanaim. ³⁰ Joab, after interrupting the pursuit of Abner, assembled all the men. Besides Asahel, nineteen other servants of David were missing. ³¹ But David's servants had fatally wounded three hundred and sixty men of Benjamin, followers of Abner. ³² They took up Asahel and buried him in his father's tomb in Bethlehem. Joab and his men made an all-night march, and dawn found them in Hebron.

3 ¹ There followed a long war between the house of Saul and that of David, in which David grew stronger, but the house of Saul weaker.

Sons Born in Hebron

²* Sons were born to David in Hebron: his firstborn, Amnon, of Ahinoam from Jezreel; ³* the second, Chileab, of Abigail the widow of Nabal of Carmel; the third, Absalom, son of Maacah the daughter of Talmai, king of Geshur; ⁴* the fourth, Adonijah, son of Haggith; the fifth, Shephatiah, son of Abital; ⁵ and the sixth, Ithream, of David's wife Eglah. These were born to David in Hebron.

Ishbaal and Abner Quarrel

⁶ During the war between the house of Saul and of David, Abner was gaining power in the house of Saul. ⁷* Now Saul had had a concubine, Rizpah, the daughter of Aiah. And Ishbaal, son of Saul, said to Abner, "Why have you been intimate with my father's concubine?" ⁸ Enraged at the words of Ishbaal, Abner said, "Am I a dog's head in Judah? At present I am doing a kindness to the house of your father Saul, to his brothers and his friends, by keeping you out of David's clutches; yet this day you charge me with a crime involving a woman! ⁹* May God do thus and so to Abner if I do not carry out for David what the LORD swore to him— ¹⁰* that is, take away the kingdom from the house of Saul and establish the throne of David over Israel and over Judah from Dan to Beer-sheba." ¹¹ In his fear of Abner, Ishbaal was no longer able to say a word to him.

Abner and David Reconciled

¹² Then Abner sent messengers to David in Telam, where he was at the moment, to say, "Make an agreement with me, and I will aid you by bringing all Israel over to you." ¹³* He replied, "Very well, I will make an agreement with you. But one thing I require of you. You must not appear before me unless you bring back Michal, Saul's daughter, when you come to present yourself to me." ¹⁴ At the same time David sent messengers to Ishbaal, son of Saul, to say, "Give me my wife Michal, whom I espoused by paying a hundred Philistine foreskins." ¹⁵* Ishbaal sent for her and took her away from her husband Paltiel, son of Laish, ¹⁶ who followed her weeping as far as Bahurim. But Abner said to him, "Go back!" And he turned back.

¹⁷ Abner then said in discussion with the elders of Israel: "For a long time you have been seeking David as your king. ¹⁸ Now take action, for the

---

2, 18: 2 Sm 23, 24, 1 Chr 2, 16.
2, 19: 1 Chr 27, 7.
2, 22: 2 Sm 3, 27f.30.
3, 2–5: 1 Chr 3, 14.
3, 3: 2 Sm 13, 37; 15, 8.

3, 4: 1 Kgs 1, 5.
3, 7: 2 Sm 21, 8ff.
3, 9: Ru 1, 17.
3, 10: 2 Sm 5, 2; 1 Sm 25, 30.
3, 13: 1 Sm 18, 20–27.
3, 15: 1 Sm 25, 44.

LORD has said of David, 'By my servant David I will save my people Israel from the grasp of the Philistines and from the grasp of all their enemies.'" ¹⁹ Abner also spoke personally to Benjamin, and then went to make his own report to David in Hebron concerning all that would be agreeable to Israel and to the whole house of Benjamin. ²⁰ When Abner, accompanied by twenty men, came to David in Hebron, David prepared a feast for Abner and for the men who were with him. ²¹ Then Abner said to David, "I will now go to assemble all Israel for my lord the king, that they may make an agreement with you; you will then be king over all whom you wish to rule." So David bade Abner farewell, and he went away in peace.

Death of Abner

²² Just then David's servants and Joab were coming in from an expedition, bringing much plunder with them. Abner, having been dismissed by David, was no longer with him in Hebron but had gone his way in peace. ²³ When Joab and the whole force he had with him arrived, he was informed, "Abner, son of Ner, came to David; he has been sent on his way in peace." ²⁴ So Joab went to the king and said: "What have you done? Abner came to you. Why did you let him go peacefully on his way? ²⁵ Are you not aware that Abner came to deceive you and to learn the ins and outs of all that you are doing?" ²⁶ Joab then left David, and without David's knowledge sent messengers after Abner, who brought him back from the cistern of Sirah. ²⁷* When Abner returned to Hebron, Joab took him aside within the city gate as though to speak with him privately. There he stabbed him in the abdomen, and he died in revenge for the killing of Joab's brother Asahel. ²⁸* Later David heard of it and said: "Before the LORD, I and my kingdom are forever innocent. ²⁹ May the full responsibility for the death of Abner, son of Ner, be laid to Joab and to all his family. May the men of Joab's family never be without one suffering from a discharge, or a leper, or one unmanly, one falling by the sword, or one in need of bread!" ³⁰ [Joab and his brother Abishai had lain in wait for Abner because he killed their brother Asahel in battle at Gibeon.]

David Mourns Abner

³¹* Then David said to Joab and to all the people who were with him, "Rend your garments, gird yourselves with sackcloth, and mourn over Abner." King David himself followed the bier. ³² When they had buried Abner in Hebron, the king wept aloud at the grave of Abner, and the people also wept. ³³ And the king sang this elegy over Abner:

"Would Abner have died like a fool?
³⁴   Your hands were not bound with chains,
        nor your feet placed in fetters;
     As men fall before the wicked, you fell."

And all the people continued to weep for him. ³⁵* Then they went to console David with food while it was still day. But David swore, "May God do thus and so to me if I eat bread or anything else before sunset." ³⁶ All the people noted this with approval, just as they were pleased with everything that the king did. ³⁷ So on that day all the people and all Israel came to know that the king had no part in the killing of Abner, son of Ner. ³⁸ The king then said to his servants: "You must recognize that a great general has fallen today in Israel. ³⁹* Although I am the anointed king, I am weak this day, and these men, the sons of Zeruiah, are too ruthless for me. May the LORD requite the evildoer in accordance with his evil deed."

Death of Ishbaal

4 ¹ When Ishbaal, son of Saul, heard that Abner had died in Hebron, he ceased to resist and all Israel was alarmed. ²* Ishbaal, son of Saul, had two company leaders named Baanah and Rechab, sons of Rimmon the Beerothite, of the tribe of Benjamin. [Beeroth, too, was ascribed to Benjamin: ³* the Beerothites fled to Gittaim, where they have been resident aliens to this day. ⁴*† Jonathan, son of Saul, had a son named Meribbaal with crippled feet. He was five years old when the news about Saul and Jonathan came from Jezreel, and his nurse took him up and fled. But in their hasty flight, he fell and became lame.] ⁵ The sons of Rimmon the Beerothite, Rechab and Baanah, came into the house of Ishbaal during the heat of the day, while he was taking his siesta. ⁶ The portress of the house had dozed off while sifting wheat, and was asleep. So Rechab and his brother Baanah slipped past ⁷ and entered the house while Ishbaal was lying asleep in his bedroom. They struck and killed him, and cut off his head. Then, taking the head, they traveled on the Arabah road all night long.

The Murder Avenged

⁸ They brought the head of Ishbaal to David in Hebron and said to the king: "This is the head of

---

4, 4: Saul's grandson *Meribbaal* is the subject of ch 9 below. The text of this verse may owe its present place to the fact that pre-Christian copies of the Books of Samuel tended to confuse his name with that of his uncle Ishbaal, Saul's son and successor, a principal figure in chapters 2–4.

3, 27: 1 Kgs 2, 5.32.
3, 28.30: 2 Sm 2, 22f.
3, 31: 2 Sm 21, 10.
3, 35: Ru 1, 17.

3, 39: Ps 28, 4; Is 3, 11.
4, 2: 2 Sm 9, 3; Jos 9, 17f.
4, 3: Jos 18, 25.
4, 4: 2 Sm 9, 3; 19, 25.

Ishbaal, son of your enemy Saul, who sought your life. Thus has the LORD this day avenged my lord the king on Saul and his posterity." 9 But David replied to Rechab and his brother Baanah, sons of Rimmon the Beerothite: "As the LORD lives, who rescued me from all difficulty, 10* in Ziklag I seized and put to death the man who informed me of Saul's death, thinking himself the bearer of good news for which I ought to give him a reward. 11 How much more now, when wicked men have slain an innocent man in bed at home, must I hold you responsible for his death and destroy you from the earth!" 12* So at a command from David, the young men killed them and cut off their hands and feet, hanging them up near the pool in Hebron. But he took the head of Ishbaal and buried it in Abner's grave in Hebron.

David King of Israel

5 1* All the tribes of Israel came to David in Hebron and said: "Here we are, your bone and your flesh. 2* In days past, when Saul was our king, it was you who led the Israelites out and brought them back. And the LORD said to you, 'You shall shepherd my people Israel and shall be commander of Israel.'" 3 When all the elders of Israel came to David in Hebron, King David made an agreement with them there before the LORD, and they anointed him king of Israel. 4 David was thirty years old when he became king, and he reigned for forty years: 5* seven years and six months in Hebron over Judah, and thirty-three years in Jerusalem over all Israel and Judah.

Capture of Zion

6*† Then the king and his men set out for Jerusalem against the Jebusites who inhabited the region. David was told, "You cannot enter here: the blind and the lame will drive you away!" which was their way of saying, "David cannot enter here."* 7 But David did take the stronghold of Zion, which is the City of David. 8* On that day David said: "All who wish to attack the Jebusites must strike at them through the water shaft. The lame and the blind shall be the personal enemies of David." That is why it is said, "The blind and the lame shall not en-

ter the palace." 9* David then dwelt in the stronghold, which was called the City of David; he built up the area from Millo to the palace. 10* David grew steadily more powerful, for the LORD of hosts was with him. 11* Hiram, king of Tyre, sent ambassadors to David; he furnished cedar wood, as well as carpenters and masons, who built a palace for David.* 12 And David knew that the LORD had established him as king of Israel and had exalted his rule for the sake of his people Israel.

David's Family in Jerusalem

13* David took more concubines and wives in Jerusalem after he had come from Hebron, and more sons and daughters were born to him in Jerusalem. 14 These are the names of those who were born to him in Jerusalem: Shammua, Shobab, Nathan, Solomon, 15 Ibhar, Elishua, Nepheg, Japhia, 16 Elishama, Baaliada, and Eliphelet.

Rout of the Philistines

17† When the Philistines heard that David had been anointed king of Israel, they all took the field in search of him. On hearing this, David went down to the refuge. 18† The Philistines came and overran the valley of Rephaim. 19 David inquired of the LORD, "Shall I attack the Philistines—will you deliver them into my grip?" The LORD replied to David, "Attack, for I will surely deliver the Philistines into your grip." 20† David then went to Baal-perazim, where he defeated them. He said, "The LORD has scattered my enemies before me like waters that have broken free." That is why the place is called Baal-perazim. 21 They abandoned their gods there, and David and his men carried them away. 22 But the Philistines came up again and overran the valley of Rephaim. 23 So David inquired of the LORD, who replied: "You must not attack frontally, but circle their rear and meet them before the mastic trees. 24† When you hear a sound of marching in the tops of the mastic trees, act decisively, for the LORD will have gone forth before you to attack the camp of the Philistines." 25 David obeyed the LORD's command and routed the Philistines from Gibeon as far as Gezer.

5, 6–12: David's most important military exploit, the taking of Jerusalem, is here presented before his battles with the Philistines, vv 17–25, which were earlier in time. The sense of vv 6 and 8 is in doubt.

5, 17: *Refuge:* probably near Adullam (1 Sm 22, 1–5).

5, 18–25: The successive defeats of the Philistines in the valley of Rephaim southwest of Jerusalem had the effect of blocking their access to the mountain ridge near Gibeon, and confining them to their holdings on the coast and in the foothills beyond Gezer to the west and south.

5, 20: *Baal-perazim:* means approximately "the lord of scatterings."

5, 24: *Sound of marching:* the wind in the treetops suggestive of the Lord's footsteps.

4, 10: 2 Sm 1, 6–10.14.16.
4, 12: Dt 21, 22f; 1 Sm 31, 10.
5, 1ff: 1 Chr 11, 1ff.
5, 2: 2 Sm 3, 10; Dt 17, 15; 1 Sm 18, 16.
5, 5: 2 Sm 2, 11; 1 Kgs 2, 11; 1 Chr 3, 4.
5, 6–10: 1 Chr 11, 4–9.
5, 6: Jos 15, 63; Jgs 1,
19. 21; Is 29, 3.
5, 8: Lv 21, 18; Mt 21, 14f.
5, 9: 1 Kgs 3, 1; 11, 27.
5, 10: Pss 78, 70ff.89; 132, 13.
5, 11–25: 1 Chr 14, 1–16.
5, 11f: 1 Kgs 5, 15; 1 Chr 14, 1f.
5, 13–16: 1 Chr 3, 5–8; 14, 3–7.

The Ark Brought to Jerusalem

6 [1]* David again assembled all the picked men of Israel, thirty thousand in number. [2]* Then David and all the people who were with him set out for Baala of Judah to bring up from there the ark of God, which bears the name of the LORD of hosts enthroned above the cherubim. [3]* The ark of God was placed on a new cart and taken away from the house of Abinadab on the hill. Uzzah and Ahio, sons of Abinadab, guided the cart, [4] with Ahio walking before it, [5]* while David and all the Israelites made merry before the LORD with all their strength, with singing and with citharas, harps, tambourines, sistrums and cymbals. [6] When they came to the threshing floor of Nodan, Uzzah reached out his hand to the ark of God and steadied it, for the oxen were making it tip. [7] But the LORD was angry with Uzzah; God struck him on that spot, and he died there before God. [8]* David was disturbed because the LORD had vented his anger on Uzzah. (The place has been called Perez-uzzah down to the present day.) [9] David feared the LORD that day and said, "How can the ark of the LORD come to me?" [10] So David would not have the ark of the LORD brought to him in the City of David, but diverted it to the house of Obed-edom the Gittite.

[11]* The ark of the LORD remained in the house of Obed-edom the Gittite for three months, and the LORD blessed Obed-edom and his whole house. [12]* When it was reported to King David that the LORD had blessed the family of Obed-edom and all that belonged to him, David went to bring up the ark of God from the house of Obed-edom into the City of David amid festivities. [13] As soon as the bearers of the ark of the LORD had advanced six steps, he sacrificed an ox and a fatling. [14]* Then David, girt with a linen apron, came dancing before the LORD with abandon, [15] as he and all the Israelites were bringing up the ark of the LORD with shouts of joy and to the sound of the horn. [16] As the ark of the LORD was entering the City of David, Saul's daughter Michal looked down through the window and saw King David leaping and dancing before the LORD, and she despised him in her heart. [17]* The ark of the LORD was brought in and set in its place within the tent David had pitched for it. Then David offered holocausts and peace offerings before the LORD. [18] When he finished making these offerings, he blessed the people in the name of the LORD of hosts. [19] He then distributed among all the people, to each man and each woman in the entire multitude of Israel, a loaf of bread, a cut of roast meat, and a raisin cake. With this, all the people left for their homes.

[20]* When David returned to bless his own family, Saul's daughter Michal came out to meet him and said, "How the king of Israel has honored himself today, exposing himself to the view of the slave girls of his followers, as a commoner might do!" [21]* But David replied to Michal: "I was dancing before the LORD. As the LORD lives, who preferred me to your father and his whole family when he appointed me commander of the LORD's people, Israel, not only will I make merry before the LORD,

The Dance of Life

LIVE IT!

It's a party! How else could we describe the festivities surrounding the triumphant bringing of the ark of the LORD into Jerusalem? And King David is leading the way, dancing before the LORD "with abandon" (2 Sm 6, 14). What a scene that must have been! What a wonderfully uninhibited way for David to express his great joy at escorting the ark into the city he has made his own.

So often we attend religious rituals as mere observers, much like Michal, David's wife, being critical and uninvolved. David shows us the true way to celebrate—with singing and dancing and eating. We need to celebrate together the presence of the LORD in our life! Here, David is our role model. Let us sing the song in our heart, and dance to the music God has planted within us.

How can we do a better job of celebrating the LORD in our life? Are we observers or participants in the dance of life?

▶ 2 Sm 6, 11–19

6, 1–11: 1 Chr 13, 1–14.
   6, 2: Ex 25, 10; Jos 15, 9; Ps 132, 8ff; 1 Chr 1, 4.
   6, 3: 1 Sm 4, 3f; 6, 7f; 7, 1;

Dn 3, 55.
   6, 5: Pss 68, 25f; 150, 3.5.
   6, 8: 1 Kgs 8, 1.
   6, 11: 1 Chr 26, 4.

6, 12–23: 1 Chr 15, 1–29; Ps 24, 7–10.
   6, 14: 1 Sm 2, 18.
   6, 17ff: Lv 1, 1–17; 3, 1–17;

1 Chr 16, 1ff.
   6, 20: 1 Chr 16, 43.
   6, 21: 1 Sm 13, 14; 15, 28.

22 but I will demean myself even more. I will be lowly in your esteem, but in the esteem of the slave girls you spoke of I will be honored." 23 And so Saul's daughter Michal was childless to the day of her death.

David's Concern for the Ark

7 1* When King David was settled in his palace, and the LORD had given him rest from his enemies on every side,* 2* he said to Nathan the prophet, "Here I am living in a house of cedar, while the ark of God dwells in a tent!" 3* Nathan answered the king, "Go, do whatever you have in mind, for the LORD is with you." 4 But that night the LORD spoke to Nathan and said: 5* "Go, tell my servant David, 'Thus says the LORD: Should you build me a house to dwell in? 6 I have not dwelt in a house from the day on which I led the Israelites out of Egypt to the present, but I have been going about in a tent under cloth. 7 In all my wanderings everywhere among the Israelites, did I ever utter a word to any one of the judges whom I charged to tend my people Israel, to ask: Why have you not built me a house of cedar?'

The LORD's Promises

8*† "Now then, speak thus to my servant David, 'The LORD of hosts has this to say: It was I who took you from the pasture and from the care of the flock to be commander of my people Israel. 9* I have been with you wherever you went, and I have destroyed all your enemies before you. And I will make you famous like the great ones of the earth. 10 I will fix a place for my people Israel; I will plant them so that they may dwell in their place without further disturbance. Neither shall the wicked continue to afflict them as they did of old, 11* since the time I first appointed judges over my people Israel. I will give you rest from all your enemies. The LORD also reveals to you that he will establish a house for you. 12* And when your time comes and you rest with your ancestors, I will raise up your heir after you, sprung from your loins, and I will make his kingdom firm. 13 It is he who shall build a house for my name. And I will make his royal throne firm forever. 14 I will be a father to him, and he shall be a son to me. And if he does wrong, I will correct him with the rod of men and with human chastisements; 15* but I will not withdraw my favor from him as I withdrew it from your predecessor Saul, whom I removed from my presence. 16* Your house and your kingdom shall endure forever before me; your throne shall stand firm forever.' " 17 Nathan reported all these words and this entire vision to David.

King David's Prayer

18* Then King David went in and sat before the LORD and said, "Who am I, Lord GOD, and who are the members of my house, that you have brought

David Praises God

Then King David went in and sat before the LORD, and said, "Who am I, Lord GOD, and who are the members of my house, that you have brought me to this point?" (2 Sm 7, 18). When was the last time you brought yourself before God, like King David, simply to offer praise for all God has done for you?

It is easy for us to feel too busy to take time for God. Then, we complain and get frustrated because God does not seem to be around, giving our life direction. Taking quiet moments to place ourselves in humility before our God and to praise God for the good we experience is important.

Find a quiet place, take just fifteen minutes. No radio, no television, no book. Think of all the positive and happy things in your life, and in your own words, say, "Thank you, God, for caring for me and the people I love!"

▸ 2 Sm 7, 18–29

7, 8–16: The prophecy to David contained in these verses is cited again, in poetic form, in Ps 89, 20–38, and alluded to in Ps 132. The promise regarding the people of Israel, vv 10–11, is a part of the promise to David at least as old as the composition of this chapter of Samuel, where it is anticipated in vv 6–7, and alluded to in David's thanksgiving, vv 23–24; it applies to the people an expression used of David in Ps 89, 23. The prophecy to David is the basis for Jewish expectation of a messiah, son of David, which Jesus Christ fulfilled in a transcendent way; cf Acts 2, 30; Heb 1, 5.

7, 1–29: 1 Chr 17, 1–27.
7, 1: 1 Kgs 5, 4.
7, 2: Dt 12, 10; 25, 19.
7, 3: Ps 132, 1–5.
7, 5: 1 Kgs 5, 17; 8, 16.27; 1 Chr 22, 8; 28, 3; Is 66, 1; Acts 7, 48.
7, 8: 1 Sm 16, 13; 17, 15–20; Ps 78, 70f; Am 7, 14.
7, 9: Ps 89, 27.
7, 11: 2 Sm 23, 5; 1 Kgs 2, 4–24.

7, 12ff: 1 Kgs 5, 19; 8, 19; 1 Chr 22, 10; 2 Chr 7, 18; Ps 89, 5.27f.30. 37f; Lk 1, 32;
Heb 1, 5.
7, 15: 2 Sm 23, 5; 1 Sm 13, 14; 15, 26.28; 2 Kgs 19, 34; 1 Chr 17, 11–14; Ps 89, 34.
7, 16: 2 Sm 23, 5; Dn 2, 45; 1 Mc 2, 57; Mk 11, 10; Lk 1, 32f; Heb 1, 8.
7, 18: 1 Chr 17, 16.

me to this point? ¹⁹† Yet even this you see as too little, Lord GOD; you have also spoken of the house of your servant for a long time to come: this too you have shown to man, Lord GOD! ²⁰ What more can David say to you? You know your servant, Lord GOD! ²¹ For your servant's sake and as you have had at heart, you have brought about this entire magnificent disclosure to your servant. ²²* And so—

"Great are you, Lord GOD! There is none like you and there is no God but you, just as we have heard it told. ²³* What other nation on earth is there like your people Israel, which God has led, redeeming it as his people; so that you have made yourself renowned by doing this magnificent deed, and by doing awe-inspiring things as you have cleared nations and their gods out of the way of your people, which you redeemed for yourself from Egypt? ²⁴* You have established for yourself your people Israel as yours forever, and you, LORD, have become their God. ²⁵ And now, LORD God, confirm for all time the prophecy you have made concerning your servant and his house, and do as you have promised. ²⁶ Your name will be forever great, when men say, 'The LORD of hosts is God of Israel,' and the house of your servant David stands firm before you. ²⁷ It is you, LORD of hosts, God of Israel, who said in a revelation to your servant, 'I will build a house for you.' Therefore your servant now finds the courage to make this prayer to you. ²⁸* And now, Lord GOD, you are God and your words are truth; you have made this generous promise to your servant. ²⁹ Do, then, bless the house of your servant that it may be before you forever; for you, Lord GOD, have promised, and by your blessing the house of your servant shall be blessed forever."

Summary of David's Wars

8 ¹*† After this David attacked the Philistines and conquered them, wresting . . . from the Philistines. ²† He also defeated Moab and then measured them with a line, making them lie down on the ground. He told off two lengths of line for execution, and a full length to be spared. Thus the Moabites became tributary to David. ³* Next David defeated Hadadezer, son of Rehob, king of Zobah, when he went to reestablish his dominion at the Euphrates River.* ⁴* David captured from him one thousand seven hundred horsemen and twenty thousand foot soldiers. And he hamstrung all the chariot horses, preserving only enough for a hundred chariots. ⁵ When the Arameans of Damascus came to the aid of Hadadezer, king of Zobah, David slew twenty-two thousand of them. ⁶ David then placed garrisons in Aram of Damascus, and the Arameans became subjects, tributary to David. The LORD brought David victory in all his undertakings. ⁷ David also took away the golden shields used by Hadadezer's servants and brought them to Jerusalem. [These Shishak, king of Egypt, took away when he came to Jerusalem in the days of Rehoboam, son of Solomon.] ⁸ From Tebah and Berothai, towns of Hadadezer, King David removed a very large quantity of bronze. ⁹ When Toi, king of Hamath, heard that David had defeated all the forces of Hadadezer, ¹⁰ he sent his son Hadoram to King David to greet him and to congratulate him for his victory over Hadadezer in battle, because Toi had been in many battles with Hadadezer. Hadoram also brought with him articles of silver, gold, and bronze. ¹¹ These, too, King David consecrated to the LORD, together with the silver and gold he had taken from every nation he had conquered: ¹² from Edom and Moab, from the Ammonites, from the Philistines, from the Amalekites, and from the plunder of Hadadezer, son of Rehob, king of Zobah.

¹³*† On his return, David became famous for having slain eighteen thousand Edomites in the Salt Valley; ¹⁴ after which he placed garrisons in Edom. Thus all the Edomites became David's subjects, and the LORD brought David victory in all his undertakings.

David's Officials

¹⁵* David reigned over all Israel, judging and administering justice to all his people. ¹⁶ Joab, son of Zeruiah, was in command of the army. Jehoshaphat, son of Ahilud, was chancellor. ¹⁷ Zadok, son of Ahitub, and Ahimelech, son of Abiathar, were priests. Shawsha was scribe. ¹⁸* Benaiah, son of Jehoiada, was in command of the Cherethites and Pelethites. And David's sons were priests.

---

†
7, 19: *This too you have shown to man:* the text as transmitted has, rather, "and this is instruction for (or: the law of) mankind." The author of Chronicles (1 Chr 17, 17) saw approximately the same phrase, which he endeavored to fit into the context in a quite different sense. The above is conjectural; cf Dt 5, 24.

8, 1: *Wresting . . . :* the Hebrew text here gives "the bridle of the cubit"; 1 Chr 18, 1 understood "Gath and its dependent villages"; others implausibly read "dominion of the capital city."

8, 2: *Two lengths . . . a full length:* usually taken to mean that two-thirds of them were executed; but it could mean that two-thirds were spared, if the line was used full length in their case but doubled on itself to make "two lines" for those to be put to death.

8, 13: *On his return:* possibly to Jerusalem, after the revolt of Absalom, a circumstance which this catalogue of victories would avoid mentioning. 1 Chr 18, 13 attributes the defeat of the Edomites to Abishai.

*
7, 22: Ex 15, 11; Is 45, 5.	11, 23.
7, 23: Dt 4, 7.34.	8, 4: Jos 11, 6. 9.
7, 24f: Ex 6, 7; Dt 7, 6; 26,	8, 13: 2 Kgs 14, 7.
17; 29, 12.	8, 15–18: 2 Sm 20, 23–26; 1 Kgs
7, 28: Nm 23, 19; Jn 17, 17.	4, 1–6; 1 Chr 18,
8, 1–18: 1 Chr 18, 1–17.	14–17.
8, 3–8: 2 Sm 10, 15–19.	8, 18: 2 Sm 15, 18; 20, 7.23;
8, 3: 2 Sm 10, 6; 1 Kgs	23, 20.

David and Meribbaal

9 [1]* David asked, "Is there any survivor of Saul's house to whom I may show kindness for the sake of Jonathan?" [2]* Now there was a servant of the family of Saul named Ziba. He was summoned to David, and the king asked him, "Are you Ziba?" He replied, "Your servant." [3]* Then the king inquired, "Is there any survivor of Saul's house to whom I may show God's kindness?" Ziba answered the king, "There is still Jonathan's son, whose feet are crippled." [4]* The king said to him, "Where is he?" and Ziba answered, "He is in the house of Machir, son of Ammiel, in Lodebar." [5] So King David sent for him and had him brought from the house of Machir, son of Ammiel, in Lodebar. [6] When Meribbaal, son of Jonathan, son of Saul, came to David, he fell prostrate in homage. David said, "Meribbaal," and he answered, "Your servant." [7] "Fear not," David said to him, "I will surely be kind to you for the sake of your father Jonathan. I will restore to you all the lands of your grandfather Saul, and you shall always eat at my table." [8]* Bowing low, he answered, "What is your servant that you should pay attention to a dead dog like me?" [9] The king then called Ziba, Saul's attendant, and said to him: "I am giving your lord's son all that belonged to Saul and to all his family. [10] You and your sons and servants must till the land for him. You shall bring in the produce, which shall be food for your lord's family to eat. But Meribbaal, your lord's son, shall always eat at my table." Ziba, who had fifteen sons and twenty servants, [11]* said to the king, "Your servant shall do just as my lord the king has commanded him." And so Meribbaal ate at David's table like one of the king's sons. [12]* Meribbaal had a young son whose name was Mica; and all the tenants of Ziba's family worked for Meribbaal. [13]* But Meribbaal lived in Jerusalem, because he always ate at the king's table. He was lame in both feet.

Insult of the Ammonites

10 [1]*† Some time later the king of the Ammonites died, and his son Hanun succeeded him as king. [2] David thought, "I will be kind to Hanun, son of Nahash, as his father was kind to me." So David sent his servants with condolences to Hanun for the loss of his father. But when David's servants entered the country of the Ammonites, [3] the Ammonite princes said to their lord Hanun: "Do you think that David is honoring your father by sending men with condolences? Is it not rather to explore the city, to spy on it, and to overthrow it, that David has sent his messengers to you?" [4]* Hanun, therefore, seized David's servants and, after shaving off half their beards and cutting away the lower halves of their garments at the buttocks, sent them away. [5] When he was told of it, King David sent out word to them, since the men were quite ashamed. "Stay in Jericho until your beards grow," he said, "and then come back."

Ammonites Defeated

[6]*† In view of the offense they had given to David, the Ammonites sent for and hired twenty thousand Aramean foot soldiers from Beth-rehob and Zobah, as well as the king of Maacah with one thousand men, and twelve thousand men from Tob. [7]* On learning this, David sent out Joab with the entire levy of trained soldiers. [8] The Ammonites came out and drew up in battle formation at the entrance of their city gate, while the Arameans of Zobah and Rehob and the men of Tob and Maacah remained apart in the open country. [9] When Joab saw the battle lines drawn up against him, both front and rear, he made a selection from all the picked troops of Israel and arrayed them against the Arameans. [10] He placed the rest of the soldiers under the command of his brother Abishai, who arrayed them against the Ammonites. [11] Joab said, "If the Arameans are stronger than I, you shall help me. But if the Ammonites are stronger than you, I will come to help you. [12] Be brave; let us prove our valor for the sake of our people and the cities of our God; the LORD will do what he judges best." [13] When Joab and the soldiers who were with him approached the Arameans for battle, they fled before him. [14] The Ammonites, seeing that the Arameans had fled, also fled from Abishai and withdrew into the city. Joab then ceased his attack on the Ammonites and returned to Jerusalem.

Arameans Defeated

[15]* Then the Arameans responded to their defeat by Israel with a full mustering of troops; [16] Hadadezer sent for and enlisted Arameans from beyond the Euphrates. They came to Helam, with Shobach, general of Hadadezer's army, at their head. [17] On receiving this news, David assembled all Israel, crossed the Jordan, and went to Helam. The Arameans drew up in formation against David and

2
S
M

10, 1: *Some time later:* early in the reign of David, since Hanun's father had been ruling in Ammon at the beginning of Saul's reign (1 Sm 11) and Solomon was as yet unborn (2 Sm 11, 1; 12, 24).

10, 6–9: A Hebrew text from Qumran (4Q Sam^a) comes closer in these verses to what is given in 1 Chr 19, 6–9. The scene of the conflict is more likely Rabbath-Ammon, with Josephus (Ant., vii, 123), than Madeba, as in 1 Chronicles; compare ch 11.

9, 1: 2 Sm 21, 7; 1 Sm 18, 1–4; 20, 8ff.15f.42.
9, 2: 2 Sm 16, 1–4; 19, 27.
9, 3: 2 Sm 4, 4.
9, 4: 2 Sm 17, 27.
9, 8: 1 Sm 24, 15.
9, 11: 2 Sm 19, 29.
9, 12: 1 Chr 8, 34.
9, 13: 2 Sm 21, 7.
10, 1–19: 1 Chr 19, 1–19.
10, 4: Is 20, 4.
10, 6: 2 Sm 8, 3; 1 Sm 14, 47.
10, 7: 2 Sm 11, 1.
10, 15–19: 2 Sm 8, 3–8; 1 Chr 9, 16–19.

fought with him. ¹⁸ But the Arameans gave way before Israel, and David's men killed seven hundred charioteers and forty thousand of the Aramean foot soldiers. Shobach, general of the army, was struck down and died on the field. ¹⁹ All of Hadadezer's vassal kings, in view of their defeat by Israel, then made peace with the Israelites and became their subjects. And the Arameans were afraid to give further aid to the Ammonites.

David's Sin

11 ¹*† At the turn of the year, when kings go out on campaign, David sent out Joab along with his officers and the army of Israel, and they ravaged the Ammonites and besieged Rabbah. David, however, remained in Jerusalem. ² One evening David rose from his siesta and strolled

⁷ When he came, David questioned him about Joab, the soldiers, and how the war was going, and Uriah answered that all was well. ⁸ David then said to Uriah, "Go down to your house and bathe your feet." Uriah left the palace, and a portion was sent out after him from the king's table. ⁹ But Uriah slept at the entrance of the royal palace with the other officers of his lord, and did not go down to his own house. ¹⁰ David was told that Uriah had not gone home. So he said to Uriah, "Have you not come from a journey? Why, then, did you not go down to your house?" ¹¹* Uriah answered David, "The ark and Israel and Judah are lodged in tents, and my lord Joab and your majesty's servants are encamped in the open field. Can I go home to eat and to drink and to sleep with my wife? As the LORD lives and as you live, I will do no such thing." ¹² Then David

Lust and Its Consequences

What the king wants, the king gets.

That seems to be the message of 2 Sm 11, 1–5. We are spared many of the details about the encounter between David and Bathsheba, but we do know this: Bathsheba is married to Uriah, so David has coveted another man's wife and committed adultery. When Bathsheba becomes pregnant, David attempts to deceive Uriah into thinking the baby is Uriah's, by bringing him home to have sex with Bathsheba. But Uriah refuses to do so because he and his comrades are in the midst of a war. Finally, David arranges for Uriah to be murdered in battle.

In one brief episode, David has broken four commandments. He has given in to lust, and it has led him into a situation that will affect his family, his kingship, and the whole nation of Israel.

It is so easy to give in to temptation, especially lust, because it can be so alluring, and because we generally fail to think beyond the moment. A dangerous thing.

Take a few moments to reflect on how you deal with your own sexual desires and temptations.

▸ 2 Sm 11, 1–5

about on the roof of the palace. From the roof he saw a woman bathing, who was very beautiful. ³* David had inquiries made about the woman and was told, "She is Bathsheba, daughter of Eliam, and wife of [Joab's armor-bearer] Uriah the Hittite." ⁴* Then David sent messengers and took her. When she came to him, he had relations with her, at a time when she was just purified after her monthly period. She then returned to her house. ⁵ But the woman had conceived, and sent the information to David, "I am with child."

⁶ David therefore sent a message to Joab, "Send me Uriah the Hittite." So Joab sent Uriah to David.

said to Uriah, "Stay here today also, I shall dismiss you tomorrow." So Uriah remained in Jerusalem that day. On the day following, ¹³ David summoned him, and he ate and drank with David, who made him drunk. But in the evening he went out to sleep on his bed among his lord's servants, and did not go down to his home. ¹⁴ The next morning David wrote a letter to Joab which he sent by Uriah. ¹⁵ In it he directed: "Place Uriah up front, where the fighting is fierce. Then pull back and leave him to be struck down dead." ¹⁶ So while Joab was besieging the city, he assigned Uriah to a place where he knew the defenders were strong. ¹⁷ When the men

---

11, 1: *At the turn of the year:* in the spring.

11, 1: 2 Sm 10, 7; 1 Chr 20, 1.   11, 4: Lv 15, 19.
11, 3: 2 Sm 23, 39.   11, 11: 1 Sm 4, 3f.

of the city made a sortie against Joab, some officers of David's army fell, and among them Uriah the Hittite died.

¹⁸ Then Joab sent David a report of all the details of the battle, ¹⁹ instructing the messenger, "When you have finished giving the king all the details of the battle, ²⁰ the king may become angry and say to you: 'Why did you go near the city to fight? Did you not know that they would shoot from the wall above? ²¹* Who killed Abimelech, son of Jerubbaal? Was it not a woman who threw a millstone down on him from the wall above, so that he died in Thebez? Why did you go near the wall?' Then you in turn shall say, 'Your servant Uriah the Hittite is also dead.' " ²²† The messenger set out, and on his arrival he relayed to David all the details as Joab had instructed him. ²³ He told David: "The men had us at a disadvantage and came out into the open against us, but we pushed them back to the entrance of the city gate. ²⁴ Then the archers shot at your servants from the wall above, and some of the king's servants died, among them your servant Uriah." ²⁵ David said to the messenger: "This is what you shall convey to Joab: 'Do not be chagrined at this, for the sword devours now here and now there. Strengthen your attack on the city and destroy it.' Encourage him."

²⁶ When the wife of Uriah heard that her husband had died, she mourned her lord. ²⁷ But once the mourning was over, David sent for her and brought her into his house. She became his wife and bore him a son. But the LORD was displeased with what David had done.

Nathan's Parable

12 ¹*† The LORD sent Nathan to David, and when he came to him, he said: "Judge this case for me! In a certain town there were two men, one rich, the other poor. ² The rich man had flocks and herds in great numbers. ³ But the poor man had nothing at all except one little ewe lamb that he had bought. He nourished her, and she grew up with him and his children. She shared the little food he had and drank from his cup and slept in his bosom. She was like a daughter to him. ⁴ Now, the rich man received a visitor, but he would not take from his own flocks and herds to prepare a meal for the wayfarer who had come to him. Instead he took the poor man's ewe lamb and made a meal of it for his visitor." ⁵ David grew very angry with that man and said to Nathan: "As the LORD lives, the man who has done this merits death! ⁶* He shall restore the ewe lamb fourfold because he has done this and has had no pity."

David's Punishment

⁷* Then Nathan said to David: "You are the man! Thus says the LORD God of Israel: 'I anointed you king of Israel. I rescued you from the hand of Saul. ⁸ I gave you your lord's house and your lord's wives

The Power of a Good Story

A story can be a powerful thing. Jesus knew the power of stories, so he often responded to questions by telling a story.

The prophet Nathan also knew the power of stories. His challenge was to force David to come to grips with what he had done with Bathsheba and Uriah. In 2 Samuel, Nathan cleverly creates a story in which David is to assume his familiar role as judge. David hears the case and is furious at the actions of the rich man in it, declaring that he should die for what he has done. Then, with four words, Nathan turns David's world upside down:

"You are the man!" (12, 7).

What can David say? He just condemned himself, and he knows it. Nathan has cleverly forced him into a moment of truth. You may want to read Psalm 51, which poetically records David's confession.

Yes, a story can be a powerful thing. Just ask Nathan. Or David. Or Jesus.

▶ 2 Sm 12, 1–12

11, 22: After this verse, the Greek text, which is here the older form, has David, angry with Joab, repeat exactly the questions Joab had foreseen in vv 20ff. In v 24 of our oldest Greek text, the messenger specifies that about eighteen men were killed.
12, 1–4: This utterance of Nathan is in regular lines in Hebrew, resembling English blank verse.

11, 21: Jgs 9, 50–54.
12, 1: Sir 47, 1.
12, 6: Ex 21, 37; Lk 19, 8.
12, 7: 1 Sm 16, 13.

for your own. I gave you the house of Israel and of Judah. And if this were not enough, I could count up for you still more. 9 Why have you spurned the LORD and done evil in his sight? You have cut down Uriah the Hittite with the sword; you took his wife as your own, and him you killed with the sword of the Ammonites. 10* Now, therefore, the sword shall never depart from your house, because you have despised me and have taken the wife of Uriah to be your wife.' 11* Thus says the LORD: 'I will bring evil upon you out of your own house. I will take your wives while you live to see it, and will give them to your neighbor. He shall lie with your wives in broad daylight. 12 You have done this deed in secret, but I will bring it about in the presence of all Israel, and with the sun looking down.' "

David's Repentance

13* Then David said to Nathan, "I have sinned against the LORD." Nathan answered David: "The LORD on his part has forgiven your sin: you shall not die. 14 But since you have utterly spurned the LORD by this deed, the child born to you must surely die." 15 Then Nathan returned to his house.

The LORD struck the child that the wife of Uriah had borne to David, and it became desperately ill. 16 David besought God for the child. He kept a fast, retiring for the night to lie on the ground clothed in sackcloth. 17 The elders of his house stood beside him urging him to rise from the ground; but he would not, nor would he take food with them. 18 On the seventh day, the child died. David's servants, however, were afraid to tell him that the child was dead, for they said: "When the child was alive, we spoke to him, but he would not listen to what we said. How can we tell him the child is dead? He may do some harm!" 19 But David noticed his servants whispering among themselves and realized that the child was dead. He asked his servants, "Is the child dead?" They replied, "Yes, he is." 20 Rising from the ground, David washed and anointed himself, and changed his clothes. Then he went to the house of the LORD and worshiped. He returned to his own house, where at his request food was set before him, and he ate. 21 His servants said to him: "What is this you are doing? While the child was living, you fasted and wept and kept vigil; now that the child is dead, you rise and take food." 22 He replied: "While the child was living, I fasted and wept, thinking, 'Perhaps the LORD will grant me the child's life.' 23* But now he is dead. Why should I fast? Can I bring him back again? I shall go to him,

but he will not return to me." 24 Then David comforted his wife Bathsheba. He went and slept with her; and she conceived and bore him a son, who was named Solomon. The LORD loved him 25 and sent the prophet Nathan to name him Jedidiah, on behalf of the LORD.

Ammonite War Ends

26* Joab fought against Rabbah of the Ammonites and captured this royal city. 27 He sent messengers to David with the word: "I have fought against Rabbah and have taken the water-city. 28 Therefore, assemble the rest of the soldiers, join the siege against the city and capture it, lest it be I that capture the city and it be credited to me." 29 So David assembled the rest of the soldiers and went to Rabbah. When he had fought against it and captured it, 30† he took the crown from Milcom's head. It weighed a talent, of gold and precious stones; it was placed on David's head. He brought out immense booty from the city, 31 and also led away the inhabitants, whom he assigned to work with saws, iron picks, and iron axes, or put to work at the brickmold. This is what he did to all the Ammonite cities. David and all the soldiers then returned to Jerusalem.

The Crime of Amnon

13 1* Some time later the following incident occurred. David's son Absalom had a beautiful sister named Tamar, and David's son Amnon loved her. 2 He was in such straits over his sister Tamar that he became sick; since she was a virgin, Amnon thought it impossible to carry out his designs toward her. 3* Now Amnon had a friend named Jonadab, son of David's brother Shimeah, who was very clever. 4 He asked him, "Prince, why are you so dejected morning after morning? Why not tell me?" So Amnon said to him, "I am in love with Tamar, my brother Absalom's sister." 5 Then Jonadab replied, "Lie down on your bed and pretend to be sick. When your father comes to visit you, say to him, 'Please let my sister Tamar come and encourage me to take food. If she prepares something appetizing in my presence, for me to see, I will eat it from her hand.' " 6 So Amnon lay down and pretended to be sick. When the king came to visit him, Amnon said to the king, "Please let my sister Tamar come and prepare some fried cakes before my eyes, that I may take nourishment from her hand."

7 David then sent home a message to Tamar,

12, 30: *Weighed a talent:* since this would be more than 75 pounds, some commentators picture the idol's crown as displaying a single precious stone of large size, which David took to wear; but the text does not say this.

12, 10: 2 Sm 13, 28f; 18, 14.   12, 23: Jb 7, 9.
12, 11: 2 Sm 16, 11.22.   12, 26–31: 1 Chr 20, 1–3.
12, 13: 1 Kgs 21, 29; Pss 32,   13, 1: 2 Sm 3, 2f; 1 Chr 3, 9.
   5; 50, 6; Sir 47, 11.   13, 3: 1 Sm 21, 21.

"Please go to the house of your brother Amnon and prepare some nourishment for him." [8] Tamar went to the house of her brother Amnon, who was in bed. Taking dough and kneading it, she twisted it into cakes before his eyes and fried the cakes. [9] Then she took the pan and set out the cakes before him. But Amnon would not eat; he said, "Have everyone leave me." When they had all left him, [10] Amnon said to Tamar, "Bring the nourishment into the bedroom, that I may have it from your hand." So Tamar picked up the cakes she had prepared and brought them to her brother Amnon in the bedroom. [11] But when she brought them to him to eat, he seized her and said to her, "Come! Lie with me, my sister!" [12]* But she answered him, "No, my brother! Do not shame me! That is an intolerable crime in Israel. Do not commit this insensate deed. [13]* Where would I take my shame? And you would be a discredited man in Israel. So please, speak to the king; he will not keep me from you."

[14] Not heeding her plea, he overpowered her; he shamed her and had relations with her. [15] Then Amnon conceived an intense hatred for her, which far surpassed the love he had had for her. "Get up and leave," he said to her. [16] She replied, "No, brother, because to drive me out would be far worse than the first injury you have done me." He would not listen to her, [17] but called the youth who was his attendant and said, "Put her outside, away from me, and bar the door after her." [18] Now she had on a long tunic, for that is how maiden princesses dressed in olden days. When his attendant put her out and barred the door after her, [19] Tamar put ashes on her head and tore the long tunic in which she was clothed. Then, putting her hands to her head, she went away crying loudly. [20] Her brother Absalom said to her: "Has your brother Amnon been with you? Be still now, my sister; he is your brother. Do not take this affair to heart." But Tamar remained grief-stricken and forlorn in the house of her brother Absalom. [21] King David, who got word of the whole affair, became very angry. He did not, however, spark the resentment of his son Amnon, whom he favored because he was his first-born. [22] Absalom, moreover, said nothing at all to Amnon, although he hated him for having shamed his sister Tamar.

Absalom's Plot

[23] After a period of two years Absalom had shearers in Baal-hazor near Ephraim, and he invited all the princes. [24] Absalom went to the king and said:

"Your servant is having shearers. Please, your majesty, come with all your retainers to your servant." [25] But the king said to Absalom, "No, my son, all of us should not go lest we be a burden to you." And though Absalom urged him, he refused to go and began to bid him goodbye. [26] Absalom then said, "If you will not come yourself, please let my brother Amnon come to us." The king asked him, "Why should he go to you?" [27] At Absalom's urging, however, he sent Amnon and all the other princes with him. Absalom prepared a banquet fit for royalty. [28]* But he had instructed his servants: "Now watch! When Amnon is merry with wine and I say to you, 'Kill Amnon,' put him to death. Do not be afraid, for it is I who order you to do it. Be resolute and act manfully."

Death of Amnon

[29] When the servants did to Amnon as Absalom had commanded, all the other princes rose, mounted their mules, and fled. [30] While they were still on the road, a report reached David that Absalom had killed all the princes and that not one of them had survived. [31]* The king stood up, rent his garments, and then lay on the ground. All his servants standing by him also rent their garments. [32] But Jonadab, son of David's brother Shimeah, spoke up: "Let not my lord think that all the young princes have been killed! Amnon alone is dead, for Absalom was determined on this ever since Amnon shamed his sister Tamar. [33] So let not my lord the king put faith in the report that all the princes are dead. Amnon alone is dead." [34] Meanwhile, Absalom had taken flight. Then the servant on watch looked about and saw a large group coming down the slope from the direction of Bahurim. He came in and reported this, telling the king that he had seen some men coming down the mountainside from the direction of Bahurim. [35] So Jonadab said to the king: "There! The princes have come. It is as your servant said." [36] No sooner had he finished speaking than the princes came in, weeping aloud. The king, too, and all his servants wept very bitterly. [37]* But Absalom, who had taken flight, went to Talmai, son of Ammihud, king of Geshur, [38] and stayed in Geshur for three years.

Efforts for Absalom's Return

[39] The king continued during all that time to mourn over his son; but his longing reached out for Absalom as he became reconciled to the death of Amnon.

13, 12: Lv 18, 9; 20, 17; Dt   13, 28f: 2 Sm 12, 10.
      27, 22.   13, 31: 2 Sm 1, 11.
13, 13: Gn 34, 7.   13, 37: 2 Sm 3, 3; 15, 8.

14

¹ When Joab, son of Zeruiah, observed how the king felt toward Absalom, ² he sent to Tekoa and brought from there a gifted woman, to whom he said: "Pretend to be in mourning. Put on mourning apparel and do not anoint yourself with oil, that you may appear to be a woman who has been long in mourning for a departed one. ³ Then go to the king and speak to him in this manner." And Joab instructed her what to say.

⁴ So the woman of Tekoa went to the king and fell prostrate to the ground in homage, saying, "Help, your majesty!" ⁵* The king said to her, "What do you want?" She replied: "Alas, I am a widow; my husband is dead. ⁶ Your servant had two sons, who quarreled in the field. There being no one to part them, one of them struck his brother and killed him. ⁷*† Then the whole clan confronted your servant and demanded: 'Give up the one who killed his brother. We must put him to death for the life of his brother whom he has slain; we must extinguish the heir also.' Thus they will quench my remaining hope and leave my husband neither name nor posterity upon the earth." ⁸ The king then said to the woman: "Go home. I will issue a command on your behalf." ⁹ The woman of Tekoa answered him, "Let me and my family be to blame, my lord king; you and your throne are innocent." ¹⁰ Then the king said, "If anyone says a word to you, have him brought to me, and he shall not touch you again." ¹¹ But she went on to say, "Please, your majesty, keep in mind the LORD your God, that the avenger of blood may not go too far in destruction and that my son may not be done away with." He replied, "As the LORD lives, not a hair of your son shall fall to the ground."

¹² The woman continued, "Please let your servant say still another word to my lord the king." He replied, "Speak." ¹³ So the woman said: "Why, then, do you think of this same kind of thing against the people of God? In pronouncing as he has, the king shows himself guilty, for not bringing back his own banished son. ¹⁴*† We must indeed die; we are then like water that is poured out on the ground and cannot be gathered up. Yet, though God does not bring back life, he does take thought how not to banish anyone from him. ¹⁵ And now, if I have presumed to speak of this matter to your majesty, it is because the people have given me cause to fear. And so your servant thought: 'Let me speak to the king. Perhaps he will grant the petition of his maid-servant. ¹⁶ For the king must surely consent to free his servant from the grasp of one who would seek to destroy me and my son as well from God's inheritance.' " ¹⁷*† And the woman concluded: "Let the word of my lord the king provide a resting place; indeed, my lord the king is like an angel of God, evaluating good and bad. The LORD your God be with you."

¹⁸ The king answered the woman, "Now do not conceal from me anything I may ask you!" The woman said, "Let my lord the king speak." ¹⁹ So the king asked, "Is Joab involved with you in all this?" And the woman answered: "As you live, my lord the king, it is just as your majesty has said, and not otherwise. It was your servant Joab who instructed me and told your servant all these things she was to say. ²⁰ Your servant Joab did this to come at the issue in a roundabout way. But my lord is as wise as an angel of God, so that he knows all things on earth."

Absalom's Return

²¹ Then the king said to Joab: "I hereby grant this request. Go, therefore, and bring back young Absalom." ²² Falling prostrate to the ground in homage and blessing the king, Joab said, "This day I know that I am in good favor with you, my lord the king, since the king has granted the request of his servant." ²³ Joab then went off to Geshur and brought Absalom to Jerusalem. ²⁴ But the king said, "Let him go to his own house; he shall not appear before me." So Absalom went off to his house and did not appear before the king.

²⁵ In all Israel there was not a man who could so be praised for his beauty as Absalom, who was without blemish from the sole of his foot to the crown of his head. ²⁶ When he shaved his head—which he used to do at the end of every year, because his hair became too heavy for him—the hair weighed two hundred shekels according to the royal standard. ²⁷* Absalom had three sons born to him, besides a daughter named Tamar, who was a beautiful woman.

Absalom Is Pardoned

²⁸ Absalom lived in Jerusalem for two years without appearing before the king. ²⁹ Then he summoned Joab to send him to the king, but Joab would not come to him. Although he summoned him a second time, Joab refused to come. ³⁰* He therefore instructed his servants: "You see Joab's field

---

14, 7: *Hope:* literally, "glowing coal." The image is similar to that of the lighted lamp, e.g., Ps 89, 17, to keep alive the ancestral name.

14, 14: *How not to banish:* a possible allusion to the religious institution of cities of refuge for involuntary murderers; see Nm 35, 9–15.

14, 17: *A resting place:* cf Ps 95, 11; Heb 3, 7—4, 11. The reference here is to a return home for Absalom to Israel.

14, 5f: 2 Kgs 6, 26f.
14, 7: Nm 35, 19.
14, 14: Jb 7, 9; 14, 7–12; Ps 88, 5.11ff.
14, 17.20: 1 Sm 29, 9.
14, 27: 2 Sm 18, 18.
14, 30: Jgs 15, 4f.

that borders mine, on which he has barley. Go, set it on fire." And so Absalom's servants set the field on fire. Joab's farmhands came to him with torn garments and reported to him what had been done. [31] At this, Joab went to Absalom in his house and asked him, "Why have your servants set my field on fire?" [32] Absalom answered Joab: "I was summoning you to come here, that I may send you to the king to say: 'Why did I come back from Geshur? I would be better off if I were still there!' Now, let me appear before the king. If I am guilty, let him put me to death." [33] Joab went to the king and reported this. The king then called Absalom, who came to him and in homage fell on his face to the ground before the king. Then the king kissed him.

Absalom's Plot

15 [1]* After this Absalom provided himself with chariots, horses, and fifty henchmen. [2] Moreover, Absalom used to rise early and stand alongside the road leading to the gate. If someone had a lawsuit to be decided by the king, Absalom would call to him and say, "From what city are you?" And when he replied, "Your servant is of such and such a tribe of Israel," [3] Absalom would say to him, "Your suit is good and just, but there is no one to hear you in the king's name." [4] And he would continue: "If only I could be appointed judge in the land! Then everyone who has a lawsuit to be decided might come to me and I would render him justice." [5] Whenever a man approached him to show homage, he would extend his hand, hold him, and kiss him. [6] By behaving in this way toward all the Israelites who came to the king for judgment, Absalom was stealing away the loyalties of the men of Israel.

Conspiracy in Hebron

[7] After a period of four years, Absalom said to the king: "Allow me to go to Hebron and fulfill a vow I made to the LORD. [8]* For while living in Geshur in Aram, your servant made this vow: 'If the LORD ever brings me back to Jerusalem, I will worship him in Hebron.'" [9] The king wished him a safe journey, and he went off to Hebron. [10] Then Absalom sent spies throughout the tribes of Israel to say, "When you hear the sound of the horn, declare Absalom king in Hebron." [11] Two hundred men had accompanied Absalom from Jerusalem. They had been invited and went in good faith, knowing nothing of the plan. [12]* Absalom also sent to Ahithophel the Gilonite, David's counselor, an invitation to come from his town, Giloh, for the sacrifices he was about to offer. So the conspiracy gained

strength, and the people with Absalom increased in numbers.

David Flees Jerusalem

[13]* An informant came to David with the report, "The Israelites have transferred their loyalty to Absalom." [14] At this, David said to all his servants who were with him in Jerusalem: "Up! Let us take flight, or none of us will escape from Absalom. Leave quickly, lest he hurry and overtake us, then visit disaster upon us and put the city to the sword." [15] The king's officers answered him, "Your servants are ready, whatever our lord the king chooses to do." [16]* Then the king set out, accompanied by his entire household, except for ten concubines whom he left behind to take care of the palace. [17] As the king left the city, with all his officers accompanying him, they halted opposite the ascent of the Mount of Olives, at a distance, [18]* while the whole army marched past him.

David and Ittai

As all the Cherethites and Pelethites, and the six hundred men of Gath who had accompanied him from that city, were passing in review before the king, [19] he said to Ittai the Gittite: "Why should you also go with us? Go back and stay with the king, for you are a foreigner and you, too, are an exile from your own country. [20] You came only yesterday, and shall I have you wander about with us today, wherever I have to go? Return and take your brothers with you, and may the LORD be kind and faithful to you." [21]* But Ittai answered the king, "As the LORD lives, and as my lord the king lives, your servant shall be wherever my lord the king may be, whether for death or for life." [22] So the king said to Ittai, "Go, then, march on." And Ittai the Gittite, with all his men and all the dependents that were with him, marched on. [23] Everyone in the countryside wept aloud as the last of the soldiers went by, and the king crossed the Kidron Valley with all the soldiers moving on ahead of him by way of the Mount of Olives, toward the desert.

David and the Priests

[24] Zadok, too [with all the Levite bearers of the ark of the covenant of God], and Abiathar brought the ark of God to a halt until the soldiers had marched out of the city. [25] Then the king said to Zadok: "Take the ark of God back to the city. If I find favor with the LORD, he will bring me back and permit me to see it and its lodging. [26]* But if he should say, 'I am not pleased with you,' I am ready; let him do to me as he sees fit." [27] The king also said

---

15, 1: 1 Sm 8, 11; 1 Kgs 1, 5.   15, 12: 2 Sm 16, 23.   15, 16: 2 Sm 16, 21f; 20, 3.   15, 21: Ru 1, 16.
15, 8: 2 Sm 3, 3; 13, 37.   15, 13: Ps 3.   15, 18: 2 Sm 8, 18.   15, 26: 2 Sm 16, 10.

to the priest Zadok: "See to it that you and Abiathar return to the city in peace, and both your sons with you, your own son Ahimaaz, and Abiathar's son Jonathan. 28 Remember, I shall be waiting at the fords near the desert until I receive information from you." 29 So Zadok and Abiathar took the ark of God back to Jerusalem and remained there.

30* As David went up the Mount of Olives, he wept without ceasing. His head was covered, and he was walking barefoot. All those who were with him also had their heads covered and were weeping as they went. 31* When David was informed that Ahithophel was among the conspirators with Absalom, he said, "O LORD, turn the counsel of Ahithophel to folly!"

David and Hushai

32* When David reached the top, where men used to worship God, Hushai the Archite was there to meet him, with rent garments and dirt upon his head. 33 David said to him: "If you come with me, you will be a burden to me. 34* But if you return to the city and say to Absalom, 'Let me be your servant, O king; I was formerly your father's servant, but now I will be yours,' you will undo for me the counsel of Ahithophel. 35 You will have the priests Zadok and Abiathar there with you. If you hear anything from the royal palace, you shall report it to the priests Zadok and Abiathar, 36 who have there with them both Zadok's son Ahimaaz and Abiathar's son Jonathan. Through them you shall send on to me whatever you hear." 37 So David's friend Hushai went into the city of Jerusalem as Absalom was about to enter it.

David and Ziba

16 1* David had gone a little beyond the top when Ziba, the servant of Meribbaal, met him with saddled asses laden with two hundred loaves of bread, an ephah of cakes of pressed raisins, an ephah of summer fruits, and a skin of wine. 2 The king said to Ziba, "What do you plan to do with these?" Ziba replied: "The asses are for the king's household to ride on. The bread and summer fruits are for your servants to eat, and the wine for those to drink who are weary in the desert." 3* Then the king said, "And where is your lord's son?" Ziba answered the king, "He is staying in Jerusalem, for he said, 'Now the Israelites will restore to me my father's kingdom.'" 4* The king therefore said to Ziba, "So! Everything Meribbaal had is yours."

Then Ziba said: "I pay you homage, my lord the king. May I find favor with you!"

David and Shimei

5* As David was approaching Bahurim, a man named Shimei, the son of Gera of the same clan as Saul's family, was coming out of the place, cursing as he came. 6 He threw stones at David and at all the king's officers, even though all the soldiers, including the royal guard, were on David's right and on his left. 7 Shimei was saying as he cursed: "Away, away, you murderous and wicked man! 8† The LORD has requited you for all the bloodshed in the family of Saul, in whose stead you became king, and the LORD has given over the kingdom to your son Absalom. And now you suffer ruin because you are a murderer." 9* Abishai, son of Zeruiah, said to the king: "Why should this dead dog curse my lord the king? Let me go over, please, and lop off his head." 10* But the king replied: "What business is it of mine or of yours, sons of Zeruiah, that he curses? Suppose the LORD has told him to curse David; who then will dare to say, 'Why are you doing this?'" 11* Then the king said to Abishai and to all his servants: "If my own son, who came forth from my loins, is seeking my life, how much more might this Benjaminite do so? Let him alone and let him curse, for the LORD has told him to. 12 Perhaps the LORD will look upon my affliction and make it up to me with benefits for the curses he is uttering this day." 13* David and his men continued on the road, while Shimei kept abreast of them on the hillside, all the while cursing and throwing stones and dirt as he went. 14 The king and all the soldiers with him arrived at the Jordan tired out, and stopped there for a rest.

Absalom's Counselors

15 In the meantime Absalom, accompanied by Ahithophel, entered Jerusalem with all the Israelites. 16* When David's friend Hushai the Archite came to Absalom, he said to him: "Long live the king! Long live the king!" 17 But Absalom asked Hushai: "Is this your devotion to your friend? Why did you not go with your friend?" 18 Hushai replied to Absalom: "On the contrary, I am his whom the LORD and all this people and all Israel have chosen, and with him I will stay. 19* Furthermore, as I was in attendance upon your father, so will I be before you. Whom should I serve, if not his son?" 20 Then Absalom said to Ahithophel, "Offer your counsel

---

16, 8: *Bloodshed . . . Saul:* refers to the episode recounted in 2 Sm 21, 1–14.

15, 30: 2 Sm 19, 5; Mi 1, 8.
15, 31: 2 Sm 16, 23; 17, 14. 23.

15, 32: 2 Sm 16, 16.
15, 34: 2 Sm 16, 19.
16, 1: 2 Sm 4, 4; 9, 1–13;

19, 18.25.
16, 3: 2 Sm 19, 26f.
16, 4: 2 Sm 19, 30.
16, 5: 2 Sm 3, 16; 19, 17. 22f; 1 Kgs 2, 8.
16, 9: 2 Sm 19, 23.29; 1 Sm

24, 15; 26, 6.
16, 10: 2 Sm 15, 25f; 19, 23.
16, 11: 2 Sm 12, 11.
16, 13: 2 Sm 19, 19–24.
16, 16: 2 Sm 15, 32–37.
16, 19: 2 Sm 15, 34.

on what we should do." 21* Ahithophel replied to Absalom: "Have relations with your father's concubines, whom he left behind to take care of the palace. When all Israel hears how odious you have made yourself to your father, all your partisans will take courage." 22* So a tent was pitched on the roof for Absalom, and he visited his father's concubines in view of all Israel.

Counsel of Ahithophel

23* Now the counsel given by Ahithophel at that time was as though one had sought divine revelation. Such was all his counsel both to David and to Absalom.

17 1 Ahithophel went on to say to Absalom: "Please let me choose twelve thousand men, and be off in pursuit of David tonight. 2 If I come upon him when he is weary and discouraged, I shall cause him to panic. When all the people with him flee, I shall strike down the king alone. 3 Then I can bring back the rest of the people to you, as a bride returns to her husband. It is the death of only one man you are seeking; then all the people will be at peace." 4 This plan was agreeable to Absalom and to all the elders of Israel.

Counsel of Hushai

5 Then Absalom said, "Now call Hushai the Archite also; let us hear what he too has to say." 6 When Hushai came to Absalom, Absalom said to him: "This is what Ahithophel proposed. Shall we follow his proposal? If not, speak up." 7 Hushai replied to Absalom, "This time Ahithophel has not given good counsel." 8* And he went on to say: "You know that your father and his men are warriors, and that they are as fierce as a bear in the wild robbed of her cubs. Moreover, since your father is skilled in warfare, he will not spend the night with the people. 9 Even now he lies hidden in one of the caves or in some other place. And if some of our soldiers should fall at the first attack, whoever hears of it will say, 'Absalom's followers have been slaughtered.' 10 Then even the brave man with the heart of a lion will lose courage. For all Israel knows that your father is a warrior and that those who are with him are brave.

11 "This is what I counsel: Let all Israel from Dan to Beer-sheba, who are as numerous as the sands by the sea, be called up for combat; and go with them yourself. 12 We can then attack him wherever we find him, settling down upon him as dew alights on the ground. None shall survive—neither he nor any

of his followers. 13 And if he retires into a city, all Israel shall bring ropes to that city and we can drag it into the gorge, so that not even a pebble of it can be found." 14* Then Absalom and all the Israelites pronounced the counsel of Hushai the Archite better than that of Ahithophel. For the LORD had decided to undo Ahithophel's good counsel, in order thus to bring Absalom to ruin.

David Told of the Plan

15 Then Hushai said to the priests Zadok and Abiathar: "This is the counsel Ahithophel gave Absalom and the elders of Israel, and this is what I counseled. 16 So send a warning to David immediately, not to spend the night at the fords near the desert, but to cross over without fail. Otherwise the king and all the people with him will be destroyed." 17 Now Jonathan and Ahimaaz were staying at En-rogel, since they could not risk being seen entering the city. A maidservant was to come with information for them, and they in turn were to go and report to King David. 18 But an attendant saw them and informed Absalom. They sped on their way and reached the house of a man in Bahurim who had a cistern in his courtyard. They let themselves down into this, 19 and the housewife took the cover and spread it over the cistern, strewing ground grain on the cover so that nothing could be noticed. 20 When Absalom's servants came to the woman at the house, they asked, "Where are Ahimaaz and Jonathan?" The woman replied, "They went by a short while ago toward the water." They searched, but found no one, and so returned to Jerusalem. 21 As soon as they left, Ahimaaz and Jonathan came up out of the cistern and went on to inform King David. They said to him: "Leave! Cross the water at once, for Ahithophel has given the following counsel in regard to you." 22 So David and all his people moved on and crossed the Jordan. By daybreak, there was no one left who had not crossed.

23* When Ahithophel saw that his counsel was not acted upon, he saddled his ass and departed, going to his home in his own city. Then, having left orders concerning his family, he hanged himself. And so he died and was buried in his father's tomb.

24 Now David had gone to Mahanaim when Absalom crossed the Jordan accompanied by all the Israelites. 25* Absalom had put Amasa in command of the army in Joab's place. Amasa was the son of an Ishmaelite named Ithra, who had married Abigail, daughter of Jesse and sister of Joab's mother Zeruiah. 26 Israel and Absalom encamped in the territory of Gilead.

16, 21: 2 Sm 15, 16; 20, 3.
16, 22: 2 Sm 12, 11f.
16, 23: 2 Sm 15, 12.31; 17, 23.
17, 8: Hos 13, 8.
17, 14: 2 Sm 15, 31.
17, 23: 2 Sm 15, 31; 16, 23.
17, 25: 2 Sm 19, 14; 20, 4–13.

27* When David came to Mahanaim, Shobi, son of Nahash from Rabbah of the Ammonites, Machir, son of Ammiel from Lodebar, and Barzillai, the Gileadite from Rogelim, 28* brought couches, coverlets, basins and earthenware, as well as wheat, barley, flour, roasted grain, beans, lentils, 29 honey, butter and cheese from the flocks and herds, for David and those who were with him to eat; for they said, "The people have been hungry and tired and thirsty in the desert."

Preparation for Battle

18 1 After mustering the troops he had with him, David placed officers in command of groups of a thousand and groups of a hundred. 2 David then put a third part of the soldiers under Joab's command, a third under command of Abishai, son of Zeruiah and brother of Joab, and a third under command of Ittai the Gittite. The king then said to the soldiers, "I intend to go out with you myself." 3 But they replied: "You must not come out with us. For if we should flee, we shall not count; even if half of us should die, we shall not count. You are equal to ten thousand of us. Therefore it is better that we have you to help us from the city." 4 So the king said to them, "I will do what you think best"; and he stood by the gate as all the soldiers marched out in units of a hundred and of a thousand. 5 But the king gave this command to Joab, Abishai and Ittai: "Be gentle with young Absalom for my sake." All the soldiers heard the king instruct the various leaders with regard to Absalom.

Defeat of Absalom

6 David's army then took the field against Israel, and a battle was fought in the forest near Mahanaim. 7 The forces of Israel were defeated by David's servants, and the casualties there that day were heavy—twenty thousand men. 8 The battle spread out over that entire region, and the thickets consumed more combatants that day than did the sword.

Death of Absalom

9 Absalom unexpectedly came up against David's servants. He was mounted on a mule, and, as the mule passed under the branches of a large terebinth, his hair caught fast in the tree. He hung between heaven and earth while the mule he had been riding ran off. 10 Someone saw this and reported to Joab that he had seen Absalom hanging from a terebinth. 11 Joab said to his informant: "If you saw him, why did you not strike him to the ground on the spot? Then it would have been my

duty to give you fifty pieces of silver and a belt." 12 But the man replied to Joab: "Even if I already held a thousand pieces of silver in my two hands, I would not harm the king's son, for the king charged you and Abishai and Ittai in our hearing to protect the youth Absalom for his sake. 13 Had I been disloyal and killed him, the whole matter would have come to the attention of the king, and you would stand aloof." 14* Joab replied, "I will not waste time with you in this way." And taking three pikes in hand, he thrust for the heart of Absalom, still hanging from the tree alive. 15 Next, ten of Joab's young armor-bearers closed in on Absalom, and killed him with further blows. 16* Joab then sounded the horn, and the soldiers turned back from the pursuit of the Israelites, because Joab called on them to halt. 17* Absalom was taken up and cast into a deep pit in the forest, and a very large mound of stones was erected over him. And all the Israelites fled to their own tents.

18* During his lifetime Absalom had taken a pillar and erected it for himself in the King's Valley, for he said, "I have no son to perpetuate my name." The pillar which he named for himself is called Yad-abshalom to the present day.

David Told of Absalom's Death

19 Then Ahimaaz, son of Zadok, said, "Let me run to take the good news to the king that the LORD has set him free from the grasp of his enemies." 20 But Joab said to him: "You are not the man to bring the news today. On some other day you may take the good news, but today you would not be bringing good news, for in fact the king's son is dead." 21 Then Joab said to a Cushite, "Go, tell the king what you have seen." The Cushite bowed to Joab and sped away. 22 But Ahimaaz, son of Zadok, said to Joab again, "Come what may, permit me also to run after the Cushite." Joab replied: "Why do you want to run, my son? You will receive no reward." 23 But he insisted, "Come what may, I want to run." Joab said to him, "Very well." Ahimaaz sped off by way of the Jordan plain and outran the Cushite.

24 Now David was sitting between the two gates, and a lookout mounted to the roof of the gate above the city wall, where he looked about and saw a man running all alone. 25 The lookout shouted to inform the king, who said, "If he is alone, he has good news to report." As he kept coming nearer, 26 the lookout spied another runner. From his place atop the gate he cried out, "There is another man running by himself." And the king responded, "He, too, is bringing good news." 27* Then the lookout

said, "I notice that the first one runs like Ahimaaz, son of Zadok." The king replied, "He is a good man; he comes with good news." 28 Then Ahimaaz called out and greeted the king. With face to the ground he paid homage to the king and said, "Blessed be the LORD your God, who has delivered up the men who rebelled against my lord the king." 29 But the king asked, "Is the youth Absalom safe?" And Ahimaaz replied, "I saw a great disturbance when the king's servant Joab sent your servant on, but I do not know what it was." 30 The king said, "Step aside and remain in attendance here." So he stepped aside and remained there. 31 When the Cushite came in, he said, "Let my lord the king receive the good news that this day the LORD has taken your part, freeing you from the grasp of all who rebelled against you." 32 But the king asked the Cushite, "Is young Absalom safe?" The Cushite replied, "May the enemies of my lord the king and all who rebel against you with evil intent be as that young man!"

19 1 The king was shaken, and went up to the room over the city gate to weep. He said as he wept, "My son Absalom! My son, my son Absalom! If only I had died instead of you, Absalom, my son, my son!"

Joab Reproves David

2 Joab was told that the king was weeping and mourning for Absalom; 3 and that day's victory was turned into mourning for the whole army when they heard that the king was grieving for his son. 4 The soldiers stole into the city that day like men shamed by flight in battle. 5* Meanwhile the king covered his face and cried out in a loud voice, "My son Absalom! Absalom! My son, my son!" 6 Then Joab went to his residence and said: "Though they saved your life and your sons' and daughters' lives, also the lives of your wives and those of your concubines, you have put all your servants to shame today 7 by loving those who hate you and hating those who love you. For you have shown today that officers and servants mean nothing to you. Indeed I am now certain that if Absalom were alive today and all of us dead, you would think that more suitable. 8 Now then, get up! Go out and speak kindly

Surviving Grief

It is a cold winter day when the state trooper comes to the door with the news that James Washington has just lost his son in an automobile accident. James falls to the ground in utter pain. Michael was just sixteen years old. James weeps as the trooper helps him up; the young officer begins to cry as he thinks of his own son, just three years of age.

There is no greater loss for parents than the death of a child. In 2 Sm 19, 1, King David is devastated by the death of his son Absalom, despite Absalom's betrayal. There is no easy answer or explanation when someone we love dies. How could God allow this? It is too hard to understand. What helps is to allow ourselves to mourn like David and to place ourselves into God's healing hands.

Life continues. Joab challenges David not to forget the people who have served him faithfully and count on his leadership (verses 6–8). In our grief, we must not forget the family and friends who grieve with us. We need them, and they need us to heal the pain of loss.

▶ 2 Sm 19, 1–9

to your servants. I swear by the LORD that if you do not go out, not a single man will remain with you overnight, and this will be a far greater disaster for you than any that has afflicted you from your youth until now." 9 So the king stepped out and sat at the gate. When all the people were informed that the king was sitting at the gate, they came into his presence.

The Reconciliation

Now the Israelites had fled to their separate tents, 10 but throughout the tribes of Israel all the people were arguing among themselves, saying to one another: "The king delivered us from the clutches of our enemies, and it was he who rescued us from the grip of the Philistines. But now he has fled from the country before Absalom, 11 and Absalom, whom we anointed over us, died in battle. Why, then, should you remain silent about restoring the king to his palace." When the talk of all Israel reached the king, 12 David sent word to the priests Zadok and Abiathar: "Say to the elders of Judah: 'Why should you be last to restore the king to his palace? 13 You are my brothers, you are my bone and flesh. Why should you be last to restore the king?' 14* Also say to Amasa: 'Are you not my bone and flesh? May God do thus and so to me, if you do not become my general permanently in place of Joab.' " 15 He won over all the Judahites as one man, and so they summoned the king to return, with all his servants.

David and Shimei

16 When the king, on his return, reached the Jordan, Judah had come to Gilgal to meet him and to escort him across the Jordan. 17* Shimei, son of Gera, the Benjaminite from Bahurim, hurried down with the Judahites to meet King David, 18* accompanied by a thousand men from Benjamin. Ziba, too, the servant of the house of Saul, accompanied by his fifteen sons and twenty servants, hastened to the Jordan before the king. 19* They crossed over the ford to bring the king's household over and to do whatever he wished. When Shimei, son of Gera, crossed the Jordan, he fell down before the king 20 and said to him: "May my lord not hold me guilty, and may he not remember and take to heart the wrong that your servant did the day my lord the king left Jerusalem. 21 For your servant knows that he has done wrong. Yet realize that I have been the first of the whole house of Joseph to come down today to meet my lord the king." 22 But Abishai, son

of Zeruiah, countered: "Shimei must be put to death for this. He cursed the LORD's anointed." 23* David replied: "What has come between you and me, sons of Zeruiah, that you would create enmity for me this day? Should anyone die today in Israel? Am I not aware that today I am king of Israel?" 24 Then the king said to Shimei, "You shall not die." And the king gave him his oath.

David and Meribbaal

25 Meribbaal, son of Saul, also went down to meet the king. He had not washed his feet nor trimmed his mustache nor washed his clothes from the day the king left until he returned safely. 26* When he came from Jerusalem to meet the king, the king asked him, "Why did you not go with me, Meribbaal?" 27* He replied: "My lord the king, my servant betrayed me. For your servant, who is lame, said to him, 'Saddle the ass for me, that I may ride on it and go with the king.' 28 But he slandered your servant before my lord the king. But my lord the king is like an angel of God. Do what you judge best. 29* For though my father's entire house deserved only death from my lord the king, yet you placed your servant among the guests at your table. What right do I still have to make further appeal to the king?" 30* But the king said to him: "Why do you go on talking? I say, 'You and Ziba shall divide the property.' " 31 Meribbaal answered the king, "Indeed let him have it all, now that my lord the king has returned safely to his palace."

David and Barzillai

32* Barzillai the Gileadite also came down from Rogelim and escorted the king to the Jordan for his crossing, taking leave of him there. 33 It was Barzillai, a very old man of eighty and very wealthy besides, who had provisioned the king during his stay in Mahanaim. 34 The king said to Barzillai, "Cross over with me, and I will provide for your old age as my guest in Jerusalem." 35 But Barzillai answered the king: "How much longer have I to live, that I should go up to Jerusalem with the king? 36 I am now eighty years old. Can I distinguish between good and bad? Can your servant taste what he eats and drinks, or still appreciate the voices of singers and songstresses? Why should your servant be any further burden to my lord the king? 37 In escorting the king across the Jordan, your servant is doing little enough! Why should the king give me this reward? 38 Please let your servant go back to die in his own city by the tomb of his father and mother. Here

19, 14: 2 Sm 17, 25; 20, 4.
19, 17: 2 Sm 16, 5–13.
19, 18: 2 Sm 16, 1–4; 19, 25–31.
19, 19ff: 2 Sm 16, 13; Ex 22, 27; 1 Kgs 2, 8.
19, 23: 2 Sm 16, 9f; 1 Sm 11, 13; 1 Kgs 2, 8.38.46.
19, 26: 2 Sm 16, 3.
19, 27: 2 Sm 9, 2–13; Dt 21, 12f.
19, 29: 2 Sm 9, 9ff.
19, 30: 2 Sm 16, 4.
19, 32: 2 Sm 17, 27ff; 1 Kgs 2, 7; Ezr 2, 61.

is your servant Chimham. Let him cross over with my lord the king. Do for him whatever you will." ³⁹ Then the king said to him, "Chimham shall come over with me, and I will do for him as you would wish. And anything else you would like me to do for you, I will do." ⁴⁰ Then all the people crossed over the Jordan, but the king remained; he kissed Barzillai and bade him Godspeed as he returned to his own district. ⁴¹ Finally the king crossed over to Gilgal, accompanied by Chimham.

Israel and Judah Quarrel

All the people of Judah and half of the people of Israel had escorted the king across. ⁴² But all these Israelites began coming to the king and saying, "Why did our brothers the Judahites steal you away and escort the king and his household across the Jordan, along with all David's men?" ⁴³ All the Judahites replied to the men of Israel: "Because the king is our relative. Why are you angry over this affair? Have we had anything to eat at the king's expense? Or have portions from his table been given to us?" ⁴⁴* The Israelites answered the Judahites: "We have ten shares in the king. Also, we are the first-born rather than you. Why do you slight us? Were we not first to speak of restoring the king?" Then the Judahites in turn spoke even more fiercely than the Israelites.

Sheba's Rebellion

20 ¹* Now a rebellious individual from Benjamin named Sheba, the son of Bichri, happened to be there. He sounded the horn and cried out,

> "We have no portion in David,
>   nor any share in the son of Jesse.
> Every man to his tent, O Israel!"

² So all the Israelites left David for Sheba, son of Bichri. But from the Jordan to Jerusalem the Judahites remained loyal to their king. ³* When King David came to his palace in Jerusalem, he took the ten concubines whom he had left behind to take care of the palace and placed them in confinement. He provided for them, but had no further relations with them. And so they remained in confinement to the day of their death, lifelong widows.

Amasa's Death

⁴* Then the king said to Amasa: "Summon the Judahites for me within three days. Then present

yourself here." ⁵ Accordingly Amasa set out to summon Judah, but delayed beyond the time set for him by David. ⁶ Then David said to Abishai: "Sheba, son of Bichri, may now do us more harm than Absalom did. Take your lord's servants and pursue him, lest he find fortified cities and take shelter while we look on." ⁷* So Joab and the Cherethites and Pelethites and all the warriors marched out behind Abishai from Jerusalem to campaign in pursuit of Sheba, son of Bichri. ⁸*† They were at the great stone in Gibeon when Amasa met them. Now Joab had a belt over his tunic, from which was slung, in its sheath near his thigh, a sword that could be drawn with a downward movement. ⁹ And Joab asked Amasa, "How are you, my brother?" With his right hand Joab held Amasa's beard as if to kiss him. ¹⁰* And since Amasa was not on his guard against the sword in Joab's other hand, Joab stabbed him in the abdomen with it, so that his entrails burst forth to the ground, and he died without receiving a second thrust. Then Joab and his brother Abishai pursued Sheba, son of Bichri. ¹¹ One of Joab's attendants stood by Amasa and said, "Let him who favors Joab and is for David follow Joab." ¹² Amasa lay covered with blood in the middle of the highroad, and the man noticed that all the soldiers were stopping. So he removed Amasa from the road to the field and placed a garment over him, because all who came up to him were stopping. ¹³ When he had been removed from the road, everyone went on after Joab in pursuit of Sheba, son of Bichri.

Joab Pursues Sheba

¹⁴ Sheba passed through all the tribes of Israel to Abel Beth-maacah. Then all the Bichrites assembled and they too entered the city after him. ¹⁵ So David's servants came and besieged him in Abel Beth-maacah. They threw up a mound against the city, and all the soldiers who were with Joab began battering the wall to throw it down. ¹⁶ Then a wise woman from the city stood on the outworks and called out, "Listen, listen! Tell Joab to come here, that I may speak with him." ¹⁷ When Joab had come near her, the woman said, "Are you Joab?" And he replied, "Yes." She said to him, "Listen to what your maidservant has to say." He replied, "I am listening." ¹⁸*† Then she went on to say: "There is an ancient saying, 'Let them ask if they will in Abel ¹⁹ or in Dan whether loyalty is finished or ended in Israel.' You are seeking to beat down a city that is a mother in Israel. Why do you wish to destroy

—
20, 8: The text of this verse is quite uncertain.
20, 18f: The proverbial expression here has been poorly transmitted, and its sense is doubtful.

19, 44: 1 Kgs 11, 31.
20, 1: 1 Kgs 12, 16.
20, 3: 2 Sm 15, 16; 16, 20ff.
20, 4: 2 Sm 17, 25; 19, 14.
20, 7: 2 Sm 8, 18.
20, 8: 2 Sm 2, 13.
20, 10: 1 Kgs 2, 5.
20, 18: Gn 49, 16.

the inheritance of the LORD?" 20 Joab answered, "Not at all, not at all! I do not wish to destroy or to ruin anything. 21 That is not the case at all. A man named Sheba, son of Bichri, from the hill country of Ephraim has rebelled against King David. Surrender him alone, and I will withdraw from the city." Then the woman said to Joab, "His head shall be thrown to you across the wall." 22 She went to all the people with her advice, and they cut off the head of Sheba, son of Bichri, and threw it out to Joab. He then sounded the horn, and they scattered from the city to their own tents, while Joab returned to Jerusalem to the king.

David's Officials

23* Joab was in command of the whole army of Israel. Banaiah, son of Jehoiada, was in command of the Cherethites and Pelethites. 24 Adoram was in charge of the forced labor. Jehoshaphat, son of Ahilud, was the chancellor. 25* Shawsha was the scribe. Zadok and Abiathar were priests. 26 Ira the Jairite was also David's priest.

V: Appendixes

Gibeonite Vengeance

21 1* During David's reign there was a famine for three successive years. David had recourse to the LORD, who said, "There is bloodguilt on Saul and his family because he put the Gibeonites to death." 2* So the king called the Gibeonites and spoke to them. (Now the Gibeonites were not Israelites, but survivors of the Amorites; and although the Israelites had given them their oath, Saul had attempted to kill them off in his zeal for the men of Israel and Judah.) 3 David said to the Gibeonites, "What must I do for you and how must I make atonement, that you may bless the inheritance of the LORD?" 4 The Gibeonites answered him, "We have no claim against Saul and his house for silver or gold, nor is it our place to put any man to death in Israel." Then he said, "I will do for you whatever you propose." 5 They said to the king, "As for the man who was exterminating us and who intended to destroy us that we might have no place in all the territory of Israel, 6 let seven men from among his descendants be given to us, that we may dismember them before the LORD in Gibeon, on the LORD's mountain." The king replied, "I will give them up." 7* The king, however, spared Meribbaal, son of Jonathan, son of Saul, because of the LORD's oath that formed a bond between David and

Saul's son Jonathan. 8* But the king took Armoni and Meribbaal, the two sons that Aiah's daughter Rizpah had borne to Saul, and the five sons of Saul's daughter Merob that she had borne to Adriel, son of Barzillai the Meholathite, 9 and surrendered them to the Gibeonites. They then dismembered them on the mountain before the LORD. The seven fell at the one time; they were put to death during the first days of the harvest—that is, at the beginning of the barley harvest.

10* Then Rizpah, Aiah's daughter, took sackcloth and spread it out for herself on the rock from the beginning of the harvest until rain came down on them from the sky, fending off the birds of the sky from settling on them by day, and the wild animals by night. 11 When David was informed of what Rizpah, Aiah's daughter, the concubine of Saul, had done, 12* he went and obtained the bones of Saul and of his son Jonathan from the citizens of Jabesh-gilead, who had carried them off secretly from the public square of Beth-shan, where the Philistines had hanged them at the time they killed Saul on Gilboa. 13 When he had brought up from there the bones of Saul and of his son Jonathan, the bones of those who had been dismembered were also gathered up. 14* Then the bones of Saul and of his son Jonathan were buried in the tomb of his father Kish at Zela in the territory of Benjamin. After all that the king commanded had been carried out, God granted relief to the land.

Exploits in Philistine Wars

15 There was another battle between the Philistines and Israel. David went down with his servants and fought the Philistines, but David grew tired. 16 Dadu, one of the Rephaim, whose bronze spear weighed three hundred shekels, was about to take him captive. Dadu was girt with a new sword and planned to kill David, 17* but Abishai, son of Zeruiah, came to his assistance and struck and killed the Philistine. Then David's men swore to him, "You must not go out to battle with us again, lest you quench the lamp of Israel."

18* After this there was another battle with the Philistines in Gob. On that occasion Sibbecai, from Husha, killed Saph, one of the Rephaim.* 19* There was another battle with the Philistines in Gob, in which Elhanan, son of Jair from Bethlehem, killed Goliath of Gath, who had a spear with a shaft like a weaver's heddle-bar. 20 There was another battle at Gath in which there was a man of large stature with six fingers on each hand and six toes on each foot—

20, 23: 2 Sm 8, 16ff; 23, 20.
20, 25: 2 Sm 8, 17f.
21, 1: 2 Sm 24, 13.
21, 2: Jos 9, 3–27.

21, 7: 2 Sm 9, 13; 1 Sm 18, 3; 20, 8ff.15f.42.
21, 8: 2 Sm 3, 7.
21, 10: 2 Sm 3, 31; 12, 16.

21, 12: 1 Sm 31, 10–13.
21, 14: 2 Sm 24, 25.
21, 17: 1 Kgs 11, 36; 15, 4; 2 Kgs 8, 19.

21, 18–22: 1 Chr 20, 4–8.
21, 18: 2 Sm 23, 27.
21, 19f: 1 Sm 17, 4.7.

twenty-four in all. He too was one of the Rephaim. ²¹* And when he insulted Israel, Jonathan, son of David's brother Shimei, killed him. ²² These four were Rephaim in Gath, and they fell at the hands of David and his servants.

Song of Thanksgiving

22 ¹*† David sang the words of this song to the LORD when the LORD had rescued him from the grasp of all his enemies and from the hand of Saul. ²* This is what he sang:

A

I

"O LORD, my rock, my fortress, my deliverer,
³*†   my God, my rock of refuge!
My shield, the horn of my salvation,
  my stronghold, my refuge,
  my savior, from violence you keep
  me safe.
⁴ 'Praised be the LORD,' I exclaim,
  and I am safe from my enemies.

II

⁵† "The breakers of death surged round
    about me,
  the floods of perdition overwhelmed me;
⁶ The cords of the nether world enmeshed me,
  the snares of death overtook me.
⁷† In my distress I called upon the LORD
  and cried out to my God;
From his temple he heard my voice,
  and my cry reached his ears.

III

⁸† "The earth swayed and quaked;
  the foundations of the heavens trembled
  and shook when his wrath flared up.
⁹ Smoke rose from his nostrils,
  and a devouring fire from his mouth;
  he kindled coals into flame.
¹⁰* He inclined the heavens and came down,
  with dark clouds under his feet.

¹¹*†He mounted a cherub and flew,
  borne on the wings of the wind.

The Lord Is My Rock

Build on the rock! What exactly does that mean? Have you ever watched a house being built? One of the first things that a contractor does is level the ground and put in a foundation. Upon the foundation, the structure begins to grow. A solid foundation will enable that house to stand for many years.

The same goes for our life, both personally and communally. What is your foundation—the rock—that your life is built on? In 2 Sm 22, 2, King David says to the LORD, "[You are] my rock, my fortress, my deliverer." David built his life on the rock and foundation of the LORD. As a result, he found refuge in times of fear. It was this rock that saved David and the people of Israel from the hands of their enemies. Because of David's reliance on God, his kingdom is seen by later generations of Jews as the ideal kingdom for Israel.

You too can find this same refuge, this same saving grace. Starting today, build your life with the Lord as your foundation (see Mt 7, 24–27). The next time you face a battle, be it drugs or envy or anger or lust, *stand on the rock!*

▸ 2 Sm 22, 1–4

---

† **22, 1–51:** This song of thanksgiving is also given, with a few small variants, in Ps 18. In both places it is attributed to David. Two main sections can be distinguished. In the first part, after an introductory stanza of praise to God (2–4), David describes the peril he was in (5–7), and then poetically depicts, under the form of a theophany, God's intervention in his behalf (8–20), concluding with an acknowledgment of God's justice (21–31). In the second part, God is praised for having prepared the psalmist for war (32–35), given him victory over his enemies (36–39), whom he put to flight (40–43), and bestowed on him dominion over many peoples (44–46). The entire song ends with paean of grateful praise (47–51).

22, 3: *The horn of my salvation:* my strong savior. The horn, the dreadful weapon of an enraged bull, was a symbol of strength; cf Lk 1, 69.

22, 5f: These verses are to be understood figuratively.

22, 7: *His temple:* his heavenly abode.

22, 8ff: God's intervention is graphically portrayed under the figures of an earthquake (vv 8.16) and a thunderstorm (vv 9–15); cf Jgs 5, 4f; Pss 29; 97, 2–6; Hb 3.

22, 11: *He mounted a cherub:* since God makes the winds his messengers, or "angels" (Ps 104, 4), he is spoken of poetically as riding on the clouds, or on the angelic creatures called "cherubim." His earthly throne above the ark of the covenant was likewise associated with two winged cherubim; cf Ex 37, 7ff. In both senses the Lord is enthroned upon the cherubim; cf Pss 79, 2; 99, 1.

21, 21: 2 Sm 13, 3.   22, 3: 1 Sm 2, 1f.
22, 1: Ps 18, 1.   22, 10: Ps 144, 5.
22, 2–51: Ps 18, 3–51.   22, 11: Ex 25, 18.

12 He made darkness the shelter about him,
with spattering rain and thickening clouds.
13 From the brightness of his presence
coals were kindled to flame.

14 "The LORD thundered from heaven;
the Most High gave forth his voice.
15* He sent forth arrows to put them to flight;
he flashed lightning and routed them.
16 Then the wellsprings of the sea appeared,
the foundations of the earth were laid bare,
At the rebuke of the LORD,
at the blast of the wind of his wrath.

17* "He reached out from on high and
grasped me;
he drew me out of the deep waters.
18 He rescued me from my mighty enemy,
from my foes, who were too powerful
for me.
19 They attacked me on my day of calamity,
but the LORD came to my support.
20 He set me free in the open,
and rescued me, because he loves me.

IV

21 "The LORD rewarded me according to
my justice;
according to the cleanness of my hands he
requited me.
22 For I kept the ways of the LORD
and was not disloyal to my God.
23 For his ordinances were all present to me,
and his statutes I put not from me;
24 But I was wholehearted toward him,
and I was on my guard against guilt.
25 And the LORD requited me according to
my justice,
according to my innocence in his sight.

26*† "Toward the faithful you are faithful;
toward the wholehearted you
are wholehearted;
27 Toward the sincere you are sincere;
but toward the crooked you are astute.
28 You save lowly people,
though on the lofty your eyes look down.
29† You are my lamp, O LORD!
O my God, you brighten the darkness
about me.

30 For with your aid I run against an
armed band,
and by the help of my God I leap over
a wall.
31* God's way is unerring;
the promise of the LORD is fire-tried;
he is a shield to all who take refuge
in him."

B

I

32 "For who is God except the LORD?
Who is a rock save our God?
33 The God who girded me with strength
and kept my way unerring;
34† Who made my feet swift as those of hinds
and set me on the heights;
35 Who trained my hands for war
till my arms could bend a bow of brass.

II

36 "You have given me your saving shield,
and your help has made me great.
37 You made room for my steps;
unwavering was my stride.
38 I pursued my enemies and destroyed them,
nor did I turn again till I made an end
of them.
39 I smote them and they did not rise;
they fell beneath my feet.

III

40 "You girded me with strength for war;
you subdued my adversaries beneath me.
41 My enemies you put to flight before me
and those who hated me I destroyed.
42 They cried for help—but no one saved them;
to the LORD—but he answered them not.
43 I ground them fine as the dust of the earth;
like the mud in the streets I trampled
them down.

IV

44 "You rescued me from the strife of my people;
you made me head over nations.
A people I had not known became my slaves;
45 as soon as they heard me, they obeyed.
46 The foreigners fawned and cringed before me;
they staggered forth from their fortresses."

---

† **22, 26f:** Men are treated by God in the same way they treat him and their fellow men.
22, 29: *My lamp:* a figure of life and happiness; cf 1 Kgs 11, 36.
22, 34: *The heights:* a natural stronghold safe from attack; cf Ps 62, 3; Hb 3, 19.

* 22, **15:** Ps 144, 6.   22, **26f:** 1 Sm 2, 30.
22, **17:** Ps 144, 7.   22, **31:** Prv 30, 5.

C

47 "The LORD live! And blessed be my Rock!
   Extolled be my God, Rock of my salvation.
48 O God, who granted me vengeance,
   who made peoples subject to me
49 and helped me escape from my enemies,
   Above my adversaries you exalt me
   and from the violent man you rescue me.
50* Therefore will I proclaim you, O LORD, among
   the nations,
   and I will sing praise to your name,
51 You who gave great victories to your king
   and showed kindness to your anointed,
   to David and his posterity forever."

The Last Words of David

23 ¹*† These are the last words of David:
   "The utterance of David, son of Jesse;
   the utterance of the man God raised up,
   Anointed of the God of Jacob,
   favorite of the Mighty One of Israel.
2* The spirit of the LORD spoke through me;
   his word was on my tongue.
3* The God of Israel spoke;
   of me the Rock of Israel said,
   'He that rules over men in justice,
   that rules in the fear of God,
4* Is like the morning light at sunrise
   on a cloudless morning,
   making the greensward sparkle after rain.'
5* Is not my house firm before God?
   He has made an eternal covenant with me,
   set forth in detail and secured.
   Will he not bring to fruition
   all my salvation and my every desire?
6* But the wicked are all like thorns to be
   cast away;
   they cannot be taken up by hand.
7 He who wishes to touch them
   must arm himself with iron and the shaft
   of a spear,
   and they must be consumed by fire."

David's Warriors

8*† These are the names of David's warriors. Ish-baal, son of Hachamoni, was the first of the Three. It was he who brandished his battle-ax over eight hundred slain in a single encounter. 9* Next to him, among the Three warriors, was Eleazar, son of Dodo the Ahohite. He was with David at Ephesdammim when the Philistines assembled there for battle. The Israelites had retreated, 10 but he stood his ground and fought the Philistines until his hand grew tired and became cramped, holding fast to the sword. The LORD brought about a great victory on that day; the soldiers turned back after Eleazar, but only to strip the slain. 11* Next to him was Shammah, son of Agee the Hararite. The Philistines had assembled at Lehi, where there was a plot of land full of lentils. When the soldiers fled from the Philistines, 12 he took his stand in the middle of the plot and defended it. He slew the Philistines, and the LORD brought about a great victory. Such were the deeds of the Three warriors.

13* During the harvest three of the Thirty went down to David in the cave of Adullam, while a Philistine clan was encamped in the Vale of Rephaim. 14 At that time David was in the refuge, and there was a garrison of Philistines in Bethlehem. 15 Now David had a strong craving and said, "Oh, that someone would give me a drink of water from the cistern that is by the gate of Bethlehem!" 16 So the Three warriors broke through the Philistine camp and drew water from the cistern that is by the gate of Bethlehem. But when they brought it to David he refused to drink it, and instead poured it out to the LORD, 17 saying: "The LORD forbid that I do this! Can I drink the blood of these men who went at the risk of their lives?" So he refused to drink it.

18 Abishai, brother of Joab, son of Zeruiah, was at the head of the Thirty. It was he who brandished his spear over three hundred slain. He was listed among the Thirty 19 and commanded greater respect than the Thirty, becoming their leader. However, he did not attain to the Three.

20* Benaiah, son of Jehoiada, a stalwart from Kabzeel, was a man of great achievements. It was he who slew the two lions in Moab. He also went down and killed the lion in the cistern at the time of the snow. 21 It was he, too, who slew an Egyptian of large stature. Although the Egyptian was armed with a spear, he went against him with a club and wrested the spear from the Egyptian's hand, then killed him with his own spear. 22 Such were the deeds performed by Benaiah, son of Jehoiada. He

---

† **23, 1–7:** The text of this short composition in the spirit of the wisdom writers (Prv 30, 1–6) is difficult in places; it views David's career in retrospect.

23, 8ff: There are thirty-seven warriors in all mentioned in this list. First there are the Three warriors most noted for singlehanded exploits (vv 8–12). Then comes the story of a daring adventure by three unnamed members of the larger group (vv 13–17). Next come the commanders of the king's bodyguard, Abishai (vv 18–19) and Benaiah (vv 20–23), with whom must be counted Asahel (v 24) and Joab (vv 18.24.37), and finally the group of the Thirty (vv 24–39).

* **22, 50:** Ps 22, 23; Rom 15, 9.
23, 1: 1 Kgs 2, 3–9; Sir 47, 8.
23, 2: Is 59, 21; Jer 1, 9.
23, 3: Ps 72, 1–4.
23, 4: Jgs 5, 31; Ps 72, 6.
23, 5: 2 Sm 7, 11.15f; Ps 89, 30; Is 55, 3.
23, 6: Dt 13, 14.
23, 8–39: 1 Chr 11, 41; 27, 1–15.
23, 9: 1 Sm 17, 1.
23, 11: Jgs 15, 9.
23, 13: 1 Sm 22, 1; Mi 1, 15.
23, 20: 2 Sm 8, 18; 20, 23; Jgs 14, 6; 1 Kgs 2, 29f.

was listed among the Thirty warriors ²³* and commanded greater respect than the Thirty. However, he did not attain to the Three. David put him in command of his bodyguard. ²⁴*† Asahel, brother of Joab. . . .

Among the Thirty were: Elhanan, son of Dodo, from Bethlehem; ²⁵ Shammah from En-harod; Elika from En-harod; ²⁶ Helez from Beth-pelet; Ira, son of Ikkesh, from Tekoa; ²⁷* Abiezer from Anathoth; Sibbekai from Hushah; ²⁸ Zalmon from Ahoh; Maharai from Netophah; ²⁹ Heled, son of Baanath, from Netophah; Ittai, son of Ribai, from Gibeah of the Benjaminites; ³⁰ Benaiah from Pirathon; Hiddai from Nahale-gaash; ³¹ Abibaal from Beth-arabah; Azmaveth from Bahurim; ³² Eliahba from Shaalbon; Jashen the Gunite; Jonathan, ³³ son of Shammah the Hararite; Ahiam, son of Sharar the Hararite; ³⁴ Eliphelet, son of Ahasbai, from Beth-maacah; Eliam, son of Ahithophel, from Gilo; ³⁵ Hezrai from Carmel; Paarai the Arbite; ³⁶ Igal, son of Nathan, from Zobah; Bani the Gadite; ³⁷ Zelek the Ammonite; Naharai from Beeroth, armor-bearer of Joab, son of Zeruiah; ³⁸ Ira from Jattir; Gareb from Jattir; ³⁹* Uriah the Hittite—thirty-seven in all.

Census of the People

24 ¹*† The LORD's anger against Israel flared again, and he incited David against the Israelites by prompting him to number Israel and Judah. ² Accordingly the king said to Joab and the leaders of the army who were with him, "Tour all the tribes in Israel from Dan to Beer-sheba and register the people, that I may know their number." ³ But Joab said to the king: "May the LORD your God increase the number of people a hundredfold for your royal majesty to see it with his own eyes. But why does it please my lord the king to order a thing of this kind?" ⁴ The king, however, overruled Joab and the leaders of the army, so they left the king's presence in order to register the people of Israel. ⁵ Crossing the Jordan, they began near Aroer, south of the city in the wadi, and went in the direction of Gad, toward Jazer. ⁶ They continued on to Gilead and to the district below Mount Hermon. Then they proceeded to Dan; from there they turned toward Sidon, ⁷ going to the fortress of Tyre and to all the cities of the Hivites and Canaanites, and ending up at Beer-sheba in the Negeb of Judah.

⁸ Thus they toured the whole country, reaching Jerusalem again after nine months and twenty days. ⁹ Joab then reported to the king the number of people registered: in Israel, eight hundred thousand men fit for military service; in Judah, five hundred thousand.

The Pestilence

¹⁰*† Afterward, however, David regretted having numbered the people, and said to the LORD: "I have sinned grievously in what I have done. But now, LORD, forgive the guilt of your servant, for I have been very foolish." ¹¹ When David rose in the morning, the LORD had spoken to the prophet Gad, David's seer, saying: ¹² "Go and say to David, 'This is what the LORD says: I offer you three alternatives; choose one of them, and I will inflict it on you.' " ¹³* Gad then went to David to inform him. He asked: "Do you want a three years' famine to come upon your land, or to flee from your enemy three months while he pursues you, or to have a three days' pestilence in your land? Now consider and decide what I must reply to him who sent me." ¹⁴ David answered Gad: "I am in very serious difficulty. Let us fall by the hand of God, for he is most merciful; but let me not fall by the hand of man." ¹⁵ Thus David chose the pestilence. Now it was the time of the wheat harvest when the plague broke out among the people. [The LORD then sent a pestilence over Israel from morning until the time appointed, and seventy thousand of the people from Dan to Beer-sheba died.] ¹⁶* But when the angel stretched forth his hand toward Jerusalem to destroy it, the LORD regretted the calamity and said to the angel causing the destruction among the people, "Enough now! Stay your hand." The angel of the LORD was then standing at the threshing floor of Araunah the Jebusite. ¹⁷† When David saw the angel who was striking the people, he said to the LORD: "It is I who have sinned; it is I, the shepherd, who have done wrong. But these are sheep; what have they done? Punish me and my kindred."

Sacrifice of Atonement

¹⁸ On the same day Gad went to David and said to him, "Go up and build an altar to the LORD on the threshing floor of Araunah the Jebusite." ¹⁹ Following Gad's bidding, David went up as the LORD had commanded. ²⁰ Now Araunah looked down

---

23, 24: A more complete notice about Asahel, who died early in his career (2 Sm 2, 16–23), is to be presumed lost at this point. Elhanan is the first of the Thirty.

24, 1ff: This story was probably joined at one time to 2 Sm 21, 1–14.

24, 10: The narrative supposes that since the people belonged to the Lord rather than to the king, only the Lord should know their exact number.

24, 17: Before this verse a Qumran manuscript (4Q Samᵃ) gives the fuller text of 1 Chr 21, 16, an alternative to the words "When David saw the angel who was striking the people."

23, 23: 1 Sm 22, 14.
23, 24: 2 Sm 2, 18–23.
23, 27: 2 Sm 21, 18.
23, 39: 2 Sm 11, 3f.
24, 1–25: 1 Chr 21, 1–27.
24, 10: 1 Sm 24, 6;
    1 Chr 21, 7.
24, 13: 2 Sm 24, 1.
24, 16: Ex 12, 23; 2 Kgs 19,
    35.

and noticed the king and his servants coming toward him while he was threshing wheat. So he went out and paid homage to the king, with face to the ground. 21 Then Araunah asked, "Why does my lord the king come to his servant?" David replied, "To buy the threshing floor from you, to build an altar to the LORD, that the plague may be checked among the people." 22* But Araunah said to David: "Let my lord the king take and offer up whatever he may wish. Here are oxen for holocausts, and threshing sledges and the yokes of the oxen for wood. 23 All this does Araunah give to the king." Araunah then said to the king, "May the LORD your God accept your offering." 24 The king, however, replied to Araunah, "No, I must pay you for it, for I cannot offer to the LORD my God holocausts that cost nothing." So David bought the threshing floor and the oxen for fifty silver shekels. 25 Then David built an altar there to the LORD, and offered holocausts and peace offerings. The LORD granted relief to the country, and the plague was checked in Israel.

24, 22f: 1 Sm 6, 14; 1 Kgs 19, 21.

The ancient Egyptians had an advanced civilization, yet today, the remains of their handiwork lie buried under centuries of sand. The great Roman Empire spanned the Western world at the time of Jesus, yet today, only scattered ruins testify to its existence. The same is true of the glorious but short-lived Israelite kingdom. The Books of 1 and 2 Kings trace its tragic collapse from the glories of Solomon's Temple to the Babylonian Exile.

At a Glance

I. The Reign of Solomon (1 Kgs 1, 1—11, 43).

II. Judah and Israel to the Time of Ahab (1 Kgs 12, 1—16, 34).

III. Stories of the Prophets (1 Kgs 17, 1—22, 54).

I. The Kingdoms of Israel and Judah (2 Kgs 1, 1—17, 41).

II. The Kingdom of Judah after 721 B.C. (2 Kgs 18, 1—25, 30).

In-depth

If the kingships of Saul and David could be described as the spring and summer of the Israelite kingdom, the Books of 1 and 2 Kings describe its fall and winter. The beginning of 1 Kings covers the glorious late summer under King Solomon. Solomon accumulated great riches, constructed a beautiful Temple, and built Jerusalem into a city rivaling any other center of power. But the summer was quickly over at Solomon's death, when the kingdom was split in two (see map 3, "The Kingdom Years"). The northern kingdom, called Israel, and the southern kingdom, called Judah, were ruled by a succession of kings, most of whom proved to be weak and sinful leaders. Their incompetence had disastrous consequences: the two kingdoms fell to foreign powers. Israel fell to the Assyrians in 722 B.C., and Judah to the Babylonians in 587 B.C.

The sorrow that we hear in 1 and 2 Kings is accompanied by a clear explanation: the people have fallen because of their wickedness and the wickedness of their leaders. Not surprisingly, the author of 1 and 2 Kings fashioned the history of God's people into a kind of morality tale, emphasizing the importance of faithfulness to the Covenant and the Law.

Of special interest in these books is the appearance of the classical prophet. Unlike the prophets of other lands, who were mere tools in the ruler's hand, the great prophets of Israel and Judah, like Elijah and Elisha, often directly opposed royal decisions and actions. Their job was not to pamper the ruler's pride, but to speak God's word clearly and boldly.

As we read about the terrible crises that the kingdoms of Judah and Israel faced, we can reflect on one of the basic truths of human history: Apart from God there is no hope. Only one thing remains as history passes: God's promise.

Quick Facts

Period Covered
from 961 to 587 B.C.

Author
unknown, from the Deuteronomic tradition, writing after the fall of Jerusalem

Theme
the history of Israel's and Judah's kings from Solomon until the fall of Jerusalem

Of Note
The two books of Kings were originally one book.

1 Kings

10, 23

I: The Reign of Solomon

1 ¹ When King David was old and advanced in years, though they spread covers over him he could not keep warm. ² His servants therefore said to him, "Let a young virgin be sought to attend you, lord king, and to nurse you. If she sleeps with your royal majesty, you will be kept warm." ³ So they sought for a beautiful girl throughout the territory of Israel, and found Abishag the Shunamite, whom they brought to the king. ⁴ The maiden, who was very beautiful, nursed the king and cared for him, but the king did not have relations with her.

Ambition of Adonijah

⁵ Adonijah, son of Haggith, began to display his ambition to be king. He acquired chariots, drivers, and fifty henchmen. ⁶ Yet his father never rebuked him or asked why he was doing this. Adonijah was also very handsome, and next in age to Absalom by the same mother. ⁷ He conferred with Joab, son of Zeruiah, and with Abiathar the priest, and they supported him. ⁸ However, Zadok the priest, Benaiah, son of Jehoiada, Nathan the prophet, and Shimei and his companions, the pick of David's army, did not side with Adonijah. ⁹† When he slaughtered sheep, oxen, and fatlings at the stone Zoheleth,

near En-rogel, Adonijah invited all his brothers, the king's sons, and all the royal officials of Judah. ¹⁰ But he did not invite the prophet Nathan, or Benaiah, or the pick of the army, or his brother Solomon.

Solomon Proclaimed King

¹¹ Then Nathan said to Bathsheba, Solomon's mother: "Have you not heard that Adonijah, son of Haggith, has become king without the knowledge of our lord David? ¹² Come now, let me advise you so that you may save your life and that of your son Solomon. ¹³ Go, visit King David, and say to him, 'Did you not, lord king, swear to your handmaid: Your son Solomon shall be king after me and shall sit upon my throne? Why, then, has Adonijah become king?' ¹⁴ And while you are still there speaking to the king, I will come in after you and confirm what you have said."

¹⁵ So Bathsheba visited the king in his room, while Abishag the Shunamite was attending him because of his advanced age. ¹⁶ Bathsheba bowed in homage to the king, who said to her, "What do you wish?" ¹⁷ She answered him: "My lord, you swore to me your handmaid by the LORD, your God, that my son Solomon should reign after you and sit upon your throne. ¹⁸ But now Adonijah has become

---

1, 9: *En-rogel:* the modern Job's Well southeast of Jerusalem. It marked the ancient boundary between the tribes of Benjamin and

Judah (Jos 15, 7; 18, 16). Here David's men sought information about Absalom's revolt (2 Sm 17, 17).

king, and you, my lord king, do not know it. [19] He has slaughtered oxen, fatlings, and sheep in great numbers; he has invited all the king's sons, Abiathar the priest, and Joab, the general of the army, but not your servant Solomon. [20]† Now, my lord king, all Israel is waiting for you to make known to them who is to sit on the throne after your royal majesty. [21] If this is not done, when my lord the king sleeps with his fathers, I and my son Solomon will be considered criminals."

[22] While she was still speaking to the king, the prophet Nathan came in. [23] When he had been announced, the prophet entered the king's presence and, bowing to the floor, did him homage. [24] Then Nathan said: "Have you decided, my lord king, that Adonijah is to reign after you and sit on your throne? [25] He went down today and slaughtered oxen, fatlings, and sheep in great numbers; he invited all the king's sons, the commanders of the army, and Abiathar the priest, and they are eating and drinking in his company and saying, 'Long live King Adonijah!' [26] But me, your servant, he did not invite; nor Zadok the priest, nor Benaiah, son of Jehoiada, nor your servant Solomon. [27] Was this done by my royal master's order without my being told who was to succeed to your majesty's kingly throne?"

[28] King David answered, "Call Bathsheba here." When she re-entered the king's presence and stood before him, [29] the king swore, "As the LORD lives, who has delivered me from all distress, [30] this very day I will fulfill the oath I swore to you by the LORD, the God of Israel, that your son Solomon should reign after me and should sit upon my throne in my place." [31] Bowing to the floor in homage to the king, Bathsheba said, "May my lord, King David, live forever!" [32] Then King David summoned Zadok the priest, Nathan the prophet, and Benaiah, son of Jehoiada. When they had entered the king's presence, [33] he said to them: "Take with you the royal attendants. Mount my son Solomon upon my own mule and escort him down to Gihon. [34] There Zadok the priest and Nathan the prophet are to anoint him king of Israel, and you shall blow the horn and cry, 'Long live King Solomon!' [35] When you come back in his train, he is to go in and sit upon my throne and reign in my place. I designate him ruler of Israel and of Judah." [36] In answer to the king, Benaiah, son of Jehoiada, said: "So be it! May the LORD, the God of my lord the king, so decree! [37] As the LORD has been with your royal majesty, so may he be with Solomon, and exalt his throne even more than that of my lord, King David!"

[38]† So Zadok the priest, Nathan the prophet, Benaiah, son of Jehoiada, and the Cherethites and Pelethites went down, and mounting Solomon on King David's mule, escorted him to Gihon. [39] Then Zadok the priest took the horn of oil from the tent

Introducing ▶ SOLOMON

Solomon was one of the sons of David and Bathsheba. He ruled for forty years after King David died, and he was the third and last king to rule over the united kingdom of Israel.

There is an old saying that often, our personal strengths are our greatest weaknesses. This is true of Solomon. He was a tremendous organizer, an able ruler, a clever politician, and a great builder—it was during his reign that the first Temple was built in Jerusalem. To fulfill these great accomplishments, however, Solomon taxed his people heavily, married foreign women to seal political alliances with other nations, and used forced labor to complete his building projects. These things offended God and made Solomon unpopular with the people of Israel.

When Solomon died, ten of the original twelve tribes from the northern part of Israel left the kingdom owing to these harsh practices and set up their own kingdom. Israel never again existed as a united kingdom ruled by an Israelite king. The author of Kings attributes this more to Solomon's acceptance of other gods near the end of his life than to his political mistakes.

---

† **1, 20:** At this time, neither law nor the right of primogeniture, but the will of the ruling monarch, determined succession to the throne.
1, 38: *Cherethites and Pelethites:* mercenaries in David's body-guard. They became part of his retinue after he defeated the Philistines and established himself in Jerusalem; cf 2 Sm 8, 18; 15, 18; 20, 23.

and anointed Solomon. They blew the horn and all the people shouted, "Long live King Solomon!" [40] Then all the people went up after him, playing flutes and rejoicing so much as to split open the earth with their shouting.

[41] Adonijah and all the guests who were with him heard it, just as they ended their banquet. When Joab heard the sound of the horn, he asked, "What does this uproar in the city mean?" [42] As he was speaking, Jonathan, son of Abiathar the priest, arrived. "Come," said Adonijah, "you are a man of worth and must bring good news." [43] "On the contrary!" Jonathan answered him. "Our lord, King David, has made Solomon king. [44] The king sent with him Zadok the priest, Nathan the prophet, Benaiah, son of Jehoiada, and the Cherethites and Pelethites, and they mounted him upon the king's own mule. [45] Zadok the priest and Nathan the prophet anointed him king at Gihon, and they went up from there rejoicing, so that the city is in an uproar. That is the noise you heard. [46] Besides, Solomon took his seat on the royal throne, [47] and the king's servants went in and paid their respects to our lord, King David, saying, 'May God make Solomon more famous than you and exalt his throne more than your own!' And the king in his bed worshiped God, [48] and this is what he said: 'Blessed be the LORD, the God of Israel, who has this day seated one of my sons upon my throne, so that I see it with my own eyes.' "

[49] All the guests of Adonijah left in terror, each going his own way. [50]† Adonijah, in fear of Solomon, also left; he went and seized the horns of the altar. [51] It was reported to Solomon that Adonijah, in his fear of King Solomon, had seized the horns of the altar and said, "Let King Solomon first swear that he will not kill me, his servant, with the sword." [52] Solomon answered, "If he proves himself worthy, not a hair shall fall from his head. But if he is found guilty of crime, he shall die." [53] King Solomon sent to have him brought down from the altar, and he came and paid homage to the king. Solomon then said to him, "Go to your home."

David's Last Instructions and Death

2 [1]† When the time of David's death drew near, he gave these instructions to his son Solomon: [2] "I am going the way of all mankind. Take courage and be a man. [3]* Keep the mandate of the LORD, your God, following his ways and observing his statutes, commands, ordinances, and decrees as they are written in the law of Moses, that you may succeed in whatever you do, wherever you turn, [4]* and the LORD may fulfill the promise he made on my behalf when he said, 'If your sons so conduct themselves that they remain faithful to me with their whole heart and with their whole soul, you shall always have someone of your line on the throne of Israel.' [5]* You yourself know what Joab, son of Zeruiah, did to me when he slew the two generals of Israel's armies, Abner, son of Ner, and Amasa, son of Jether. He took revenge for the blood of war in a time of peace, and put blood shed without provocation on the belt about my waist and on the sandal on my foot. [6] Act with the wisdom you possess; you must not allow him to go down to the grave in peaceful old age.

[7]* "But be kind to the sons of Barzillai the Gileadite, and have them eat at your table. For they received me kindly when I was fleeing your brother Absalom.

[8]* "You also have with you Shimei, son of Gera, the Benjaminite of Bahurim, who cursed me balefully when I was going to Mahanaim. Because he came down to meet me at the Jordan, I swore to him by the LORD that I would not put him to the sword. [9] But you must not let him go unpunished. You are a prudent man and will know how to deal with him to send down his hoary head in blood to the grave."

[10]* David rested with his ancestors and was buried in the City of David. [11]* The length of David's reign over Israel was forty years: he reigned seven years in Hebron and thirty-three years in Jerusalem.

The Kingdom Made Secure

[12] When Solomon was seated on the throne of his father David, with his sovereignty firmly established, [13] Adonijah, son of Haggith, went to Bathsheba, the mother of Solomon. "Do you come as a friend?" she asked. "Yes," he answered, [14] and added, "I have something to say to you." She replied, "Say it." [15] So he said: "You know that the kingdom was mine, and all Israel expected me to be king. But the kingdom escaped me and became my brother's, for the LORD gave it to him. [16] But now there is one favor I would ask of you. Do not refuse

1
K
G
S

1, 50: *Horns of the altar:* the protuberances on each of the four corners of the altar were surrounded with a special degree of holiness (Ex 27, 2; 29, 12), and constituted a place of asylum for transgressors of the law (Ex 21, 13f; 1 Kgs 2, 28).

2, 1–6.8–9: Solomon is expected to remove from his father's family the imputation of blood guilt brought upon it by Joab in the unwarranted killings of Abner (2 Sm 3, 27–29) and Amasa (2 Sm 19, 9–10); and likewise to punish Shimei for his curse, the effects of which David had pledged himself not to avenge in person (2 Sm 19, 21–23). The standards of morality presumed in these verses are far from the Christian ones.

2, 3: Dt 17, 19.
2, 4: 2 Sm 7, 11–16; Ps 132, 11f.
2, 5: 2 Sm 3, 27; 20, 10.
2, 7: 2 Sm 19, 33ff.
2, 8: 2 Sm 16, 5; 19, 19.
2, 10: Acts 2, 29.
2, 11: 1 Chr 29, 27.

me." And she said, "Speak on." [17†] He said, "Please ask King Solomon, who will not refuse you, to give me Abishag the Shunamite for my wife." [18] "Very well," replied Bathsheba, "I will speak to the king for you."

[19] Then Bathsheba went to King Solomon to speak to him for Adonijah, and the king stood up to meet her and paid her homage. Then he sat down upon his throne, and a throne was provided for the king's mother, who sat at his right. [20] "There is one small favor I would ask of you," she said. "Do not refuse me." "Ask it, my mother," the king said to her, "for I will not refuse you." [21] So she said, "Let Abishag the Shunamite be given to your brother Adonijah for his wife." [22] "And why do you ask Abishag the Shunamite for Adonijah?" King Solomon answered his mother. "Ask the kingdom for him as well, for he is my elder brother and has with him Abiathar the priest and Joab, son of Zeruiah." [23] And King Solomon swore by the LORD: "May God do thus and so to me, and more besides, if Adonijah has not proposed this at the cost of his life. [24] And now, as the LORD lives, who has seated me firmly on the throne of my father David and made of me a dynasty as he promised, this day shall Adonijah be put to death." [25] Then King Solomon sent Benaiah, son of Jehoiada, who struck him dead.

[26] The king said to Abiathar the priest: "Go to your land in Anathoth. Though you deserve to die, I will not put you to death this time, because you carried the ark of the Lord GOD before my father David and shared in all the hardships my father endured." [27*] So Solomon deposed Abiathar from his office of priest of the LORD, thus fulfilling the prophecy which the LORD had made in Shiloh about the house of Eli.

[28] When the news came to Joab, who had sided with Adonijah, though not with Absalom, he fled to the tent of the LORD and seized the horns of the altar. [29] King Solomon was told that Joab had fled to the tent of the LORD and was at the altar. He sent Benaiah, son of Jehoiada, with the order, "Go, strike him down." [30] Benaiah went to the tent of the LORD and said to him, "The king says, 'Come out.' " But he answered, "No! I will die here." Benaiah reported to the king, "This is what Joab said to me in reply." [31] The king answered him: "Do as he has said. Strike him down and bury him, and you will remove from me and from my family the blood which Joab shed without provocation. [32*] The

LORD will hold him responsible for his own blood, because he struck down two men better and more just than himself, and slew them with the sword without my father David's knowledge: Abner, son of Ner, general of Israel's army, and Amasa, son of Jether, general of Judah's army. [33] Joab and his descendants shall be responsible forever for their blood. But there shall be the peace of the LORD forever for David, and his descendants, and his house, and his throne." [34] Benaiah, son of Jehoiada, went back, struck him down and killed him; he was buried in his house in the desert. [35] The king appointed Benaiah, son of Jehoiada, over the army in his place, and put Zadok the priest in place of Abiathar.

[36] Then the king summoned Shimei and said to him: "Build yourself a house in Jerusalem and live there. Do not go anywhere else. [37] For if you leave, and cross the Kidron Valley, be certain you shall die without fail. You shall be responsible for your own blood." [38] Shimei answered the king: "I accept. Your servant will do just as the king's majesty has said." So Shimei stayed in Jerusalem for a long time. [39] But three years later, two of Shimei's servants ran away to Achish, son of Maacah, king of Gath, and Shimei was informed that his servants were in Gath. [40] So Shimei rose, saddled his ass, and went to Achish in Gath in search of his servants, whom he brought back. [41] When Solomon was informed that Shimei had gone from Jerusalem to Gath, and had returned, [42] the king summoned Shimei and said to him: "Did I not have you swear by the LORD to your clear understanding of my warning that, if you left and went anywhere else, you should die without fail? And you answered, 'I accept and obey.' [43] Why, then, have you not kept the oath of the LORD and the command that I gave you?" [44] And the king said to Shimei: "You know in your heart the evil that you did to my father David. Now the LORD requites you for your own wickedness. [45] But King Solomon shall be blessed, and David's throne shall endure before the LORD forever." [46] The king then gave the order to Benaiah, son of Jehoiada, who struck him dead as he left.

Wisdom of Solomon

3 [1*] With the royal power firmly in his grasp, Solomon allied himself by marriage with Pharaoh, king of Egypt. The daughter of Pharaoh, whom he married, he brought to the City of David, until he should finish building his palace, and the temple of the LORD, and the wall around Jerusalem.

2, 17.22–25: Abishag had been the concubine of King David (1 Kgs 1, 4). His successor, Solomon, inherited his father's harem. When Adonijah requested Abishag as his wife, he was subtly undermining the security of Solomon's throne and exposing himself to the suspicion of insurrection that would cost him his life; cf 2 Sm 3, 6–11; 16, 22.

2, 27: 1 Sm 2, 31.   3, 1: 1 Kgs 7, 8; 2 Chr 1, 1.
2, 32: 2 Sm 3, 27; 20, 10.

2 However, the people were sacrificing on the high places, for up to that time no temple had been built to the name of the LORD. 3 Solomon loved the LORD, and obeyed the statutes of his father David; yet he offered sacrifice and burned incense on the high places.

4 The king went to Gibeon to sacrifice there, because that was the most renowned high place. Upon its altar Solomon offered a thousand holocausts. 5 In Gibeon the LORD appeared to Solomon in a dream at night. God said, "Ask something of me and I will give it to you." 6 Solomon answered: "You have shown great favor to your servant, my father David, because he behaved faithfully toward you, with justice and an upright heart; and you have continued this great favor toward him, even today, seating a son of his on his throne. 7 O LORD, my God, you have made me, your servant, king to

GOD, GIVE ME WISDOM!

At the beginning of his reign, Solomon asked God for wisdom to govern his people. Under the advice of the prophet Nathan, Solomon became a great king. His failure came later because he betrayed God by accepting other gods and exploiting his people with work and taxes to build his magnificent royal city of Jerusalem.

Whenever you are in a leadership position, remember that you must use the power or authority you have in service to God and God's people; never use it to exploit others or for your own selfishness.

■ Ask God for the wisdom necessary to discern how to respond to the needs of people you lead.
■ Examine your leadership style frequently to see if you remain faithful to God's call to be a servant of those in need.

▶ 1 Kgs 3, 4–15

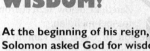

A Wise Heart

A famous prayer, often called the Peace Prayer, by Saint Francis of Assisi (A.D. 1181–1226), contains the line "LORD, grant that I may not so much seek to be . . . understood, as to understand."

It is almost as if Saint Francis is echoing the prayer of King Solomon, who lived two thousand years before him. The request is the same. Both men ask God to give them the gift of a wise heart—the ability to see things as God sees them.

What a difference wisdom can make in our life. What a wonderful thing to pray for. What a blessing to increase the amount of wisdom in our world. What inspiring examples we have in the prayers of Solomon a millennium before Jesus, and of Francis a millennium after.

Let us ask God daily for a wise heart.

▶ 1 Kgs 3, 9

succeed my father David; but I am a mere youth, not knowing at all how to act. 8 I serve you in the midst of the people whom you have chosen, a people so vast that it cannot be numbered or counted. 9* Give your servant, therefore, an understanding heart to judge your people and to distinguish right from wrong. For who is able to govern this vast people of yours?"

10 The LORD was pleased that Solomon made this request. 11 So God said to him: "Because you have asked for this—not for a long life for yourself, nor for riches, nor for the life of your enemies, but for understanding so that you may know what is right— 12 I do as you requested. I give you a heart so wise and understanding that there has never been anyone like you up to now, and after you there will come no one to equal you. 13* In addition, I give you what you have not asked for, such riches and glory that among kings there is not your like. 14 And if you follow me by keeping my statutes and commandments, as your father David did, I will give you a long life."

15 When Solomon awoke from his dream, he went to Jerusalem, stood before the ark of the covenant of the LORD, offered holocausts and peace offerings, and gave a banquet for all his servants.

1 KGS

3, 9: 2 Chr 1, 10.   3, 13: Wis 7, 11; Mt 6, 29.

Solomon's Judgment

16 Later, two harlots came to the king and stood before him. 17 One woman said: "By your leave, my lord, this woman and I live in the same house, and I gave birth in the house while she was present. 18 On the third day after I gave birth, this woman also gave birth. We were alone in the house; there was no one there but us two. 19 This woman's son died during the night; she smothered him by lying on him. 20 Later that night she got up and took my son from my side, as I, your handmaid, was sleeping. Then she laid him in her bosom, after she had laid her dead child in my bosom. 21 I rose in the morning to nurse my child, and I found him dead. But when I examined him in the morning light, I saw it was not the son whom I had borne."

22 The other woman answered, "It is not so! The living one is my son, the dead one is yours." But the first kept saying, "No, the dead one is your child, the living one is mine!" Thus they argued before the king.

23 Then the king said: "One woman claims, 'This, the living one, is my child, and the dead one is yours.' The other answers, 'No! The dead one is your child; the living one is mine.' " 24 The king continued, "Get me a sword." When they brought the sword before him, 25 he said, "Cut the living child in two, and give half to one woman and half to the other." 26 The woman whose son it was, in the anguish she felt for it, said to the king, "Please, my lord, give her the living child—please do not kill it!" The other, however, said, "It shall be neither mine nor yours. Divide it!" 27 The king then answered, "Give the first one the living child! By no means kill it, for she is the mother."

28 When all Israel heard the judgment the king had given, they were in awe of him, because they saw that the king had in him the wisdom of God for giving judgment.

Chief Officers of the Kingdom

4 1 Solomon was king over all Israel, 2 and these were the officials he had in his service:

Azariah, son of Zadok, priest;
3 Elihoreph and Ahijah, sons of Shisha, scribes; Jehoshaphat, son of Ahilud, chancellor;
4 [Benaiah, son of Jehoiada, commander of the army;
Zadok and Abiathar, priests;]
5 Azariah, son of Nathan, chief of the commissaries;

Zabud, son of Nathan, companion to the king;
6 Ahishar, major-domo of the palace; and Adoniram, son of Abda, superintendent of the forced labor.

Solomon's Royal State

7† Solomon had twelve commissaries for all Israel who supplied food for the king and his household, each having to provide for one month in the year. 8 Their names were:

the son of Hur in the hill country of Ephraim;
9 the son of Deker in Makaz, Shaalbim, Bethshemesh, Elon and Beth-hanan;
10 the son of Hesed in Arubboth, as well as in Socoh and the whole region of Hepher;
11 the son of Abinadab, who was married to Solomon's daughter Taphath, in all the Naphath-dor;
12 Baana, son of Ahilud, in Taanach and Megiddo, and beyond Jokmeam, and in all Beth-shean, and in the country around Zarethan below Jezreel from Beth-shean to Abel-meholah;
13 the son of Geber in Ramoth-Gilead, having charge of the villages of Jair, son of Manasseh, in Gilead; and of the district of Argob in Bashan—sixty large walled cities with gates barred with bronze;
14 Ahinadab, son of Iddo, in Mahanaim;
15 Ahimaaz, who was married to Basemath, another daughter of Solomon, in Naphtali;
16 Baana, son of Hushai, in Asher and along the rocky coast;
17 Jehoshaphat, son of Paruah, in Issachar;
18 Shimei, son of Ela, in Benjamin;
19† Geber, son of Uri, in the land of Gilead, the land of Sihon, king of the Amorites, and of Og, king of Bashan.

There was one prefect besides, in the king's own land.

5 7 These commissaries, one for each month, provided food for King Solomon and for all the guests at the royal table. They left nothing unprovided. 8 For the chariot horses and draft animals also, each brought his quota of barley and straw to the required place.

20† Judah and Israel were as numerous as the sands by the sea; they ate and drank and made

---

4, 7–19: The administration of the kingdom thus initiated by Solomon continued in its main features for the duration of the monarchy in Israel and Judah.
4, 19: One prefect . . . in the king's own land: the royal territory

of Judah had its own peculiar administration different from that of the twelve districts which had to supply the king and his household with a month's provisions of food each year (v 7).
5, 20: This verse belongs to ch 4.

AFRICAN AMERICAN

How Excellent

The First Book of Kings says, "Solomon surpassed all the Cedemites and all the Egyptians in wisdom" (5, 10).

This should be a source of pride for young African Americans. The people of Egypt and of the East are dark-skinned people. Ancient southern Egypt actually included the country of modern Ethiopia. The people in these countries must have been well known for their wisdom in order for the biblical author to use them in a comparison with Solomon. African Americans can praise God for their African ancestors: the wise, black people from Egypt and the East.

▸ 1 Kgs 5, 10

merry. ¹* Solomon ruled over all the kingdoms from the River to the land of the Philistines, down to the border of Egypt; they paid Solomon tribute and were his vassals as long as he lived.

² Solomon's supplies for each day were thirty kors of fine flour, sixty kors of meal; ³ ten fatted oxen, twenty pasture-fed oxen, and a hundred sheep, not counting harts, gazelles, roebucks, and fatted fowl.

⁴ He ruled over all the land west of the Euphrates, from Tiphsah to Gaza, and over all its kings, and he had peace on all his borders round about. ⁵ Thus Judah and Israel lived in security, every man under his vine or under his fig tree from Dan to Beersheba, as long as Solomon lived.

⁶* Solomon had four thousand stalls for his twelve thousand chariot horses.

⁹* Moreover, God gave Solomon wisdom and exceptional understanding and knowledge, as vast as the sand on the seashore. ¹⁰ Solomon surpassed all the Cedemites and all the Egyptians in wisdom. ¹¹ He was wiser than all other men—than Ethan the Ezrahite, or Heman, Chalcol, and Darda, the musicians—and his fame spread throughout the neighboring nations. ¹²* Solomon also uttered three thousand proverbs, and his songs numbered a

thousand and five. ¹³ He discussed plants, from the cedar on Lebanon to the hyssop growing out of the wall, and he spoke about beasts, birds, reptiles, and fishes. ¹⁴ Men came to hear Solomon's wisdom from all nations, sent by all the kings of the earth who had heard of his wisdom.

Preparations for the Temple

¹⁵ When Hiram, king of Tyre, heard that Solomon had been anointed king in place of his father, he sent an embassy to him; for Hiram had always been David's friend. ¹⁶ Solomon sent back this message to Hiram: ¹⁷ "You know that my father David, because of the enemies surrounding him on all sides, could not build a temple in honor of the LORD, his God, until such a time as the LORD should put these enemies under the soles of his feet. ¹⁸ But now the LORD, my God, has given me peace on all sides. There is no enemy or threat of danger. ¹⁹* So I propose to build a temple in honor of the LORD, my God, as the LORD predicted to my father David when he said: 'It is your son whom I will put upon your throne in your place who shall build the temple in my honor.' ²⁰ Give orders, then, to have cedars from the Lebanon cut down for me. My servants shall accompany yours, since you know that there is no one among us who is skilled in cutting timber like the Sidonians, and I will pay you whatever you say for your servants' salary."

²¹ When he had heard the words of Solomon, Hiram was pleased and said, "Blessed be the LORD this day, who has given David a wise son to rule this numerous people." ²² Hiram then sent word to Solomon, "I agree to the proposal you sent me, and I will provide all the cedars and fir trees you wish. ²³ My servants shall bring them down from the Lebanon to the sea, and I will arrange them into rafts in the sea and bring them wherever you say. There I will break up the rafts, and you shall take the lumber. You, for your part, shall furnish the provisions I desire for my household."

²⁴ So Hiram continued to provide Solomon with all the cedars and fir trees he wished; ²⁵ while Solomon every year gave Hiram twenty thousand kors of wheat to provide for his household, and twenty thousand measures of pure oil. ²⁶ The LORD, moreover, gave Solomon wisdom as he promised him, and there was peace between Hiram and Solomon, since they were parties to a treaty.

²⁷ King Solomon conscripted thirty thousand workmen from all Israel. ²⁸ He sent them to the Lebanon each month in relays of ten thousand, so that they spent one month in the Lebanon and two

5, 1: Sir 47, 15f; 2 Chr　　　5, 12: 1 Kgs 3, 12.
　9, 26.　　　　　　　　　　5, 19: 2 Sm 7, 13; 1 Chr
5, 6: 2 Chr 9, 25f.　　　　　　22, 10.
5, 9–14: Sir 47, 16f.

months at home. Adoniram was in charge of the draft. 29 Solomon had seventy thousand carriers and eighty thousand stonecutters in the mountain, 30 in addition to three thousand three hundred overseers, answerable to Solomon's prefects for the work, directing the people engaged in the work. 31 By order of the king, fine, large blocks were quarried to give the temple a foundation of hewn stone. 32 Solomon's and Hiram's builders, along with the Gebalites, hewed them out, and prepared the wood and stones for building the temple.

Building of the Temple

6 1*† In the four hundred and eightieth year from the departure of the Israelites from the land of Egypt, in the fourth year of Solomon's reign over Israel, in the month of Ziv, which is the second month, the construction of the temple of the LORD was begun.

2 The temple which King Solomon built for the LORD was sixty cubits long, twenty wide, and twenty-five high. 3 The porch in front of the temple was twenty cubits from side to side, along the width of the nave, and ten cubits deep in front of the temple. 4 Splayed windows with trellises were made for the temple, 5 and adjoining the wall of the temple, which enclosed the nave and the sanctuary, an annex of several stories was built. 6 Its lowest story was five cubits wide, the middle one six cubits wide, the third seven cubits wide, because there were offsets along the outside of the temple so that the beams would not be fastened into the walls of the temple. 7 (The temple was built of stone dressed at the quarry, so that no hammer, axe, or iron tool was to be heard in the temple during its construction.) 8 The entrance to the lowest floor of the annex was at the right side of the temple, and stairs with intermediate landings led up to the middle story and from the middle story to the third. 9 When the temple was built to its full height, it was roofed in with rafters and boards of cedar. 10 The annex, with its lowest story five cubits high, was built all along the outside of the temple, to which it was joined by cedar beams.

11† This word of the LORD came to Solomon: 12* "As to this temple you are building—if you observe my statutes, carry out my ordinances, keep and obey all my commands, I will fulfill toward you the promise I made to your father David. 13* I will dwell in the midst of the Israelites and will not forsake my people Israel."

14 When Solomon finished building the temple, 15 its walls were lined from floor to ceiling beams with cedar paneling, and its floor was laid with fir planking. 16 At the rear of the temple a space of twenty cubits was set off by cedar partitions from the floor to the rafters, enclosing the sanctuary, the holy of holies. 17 The nave, or part of the temple in front of the sanctuary, was forty cubits long. 18 The cedar in the interior of the temple was carved in the form of gourds and open flowers; all was of cedar, and no stone was to be seen.

19† In the innermost part of the temple was located the sanctuary to house the ark of the LORD's covenant, 20† twenty cubits long, twenty wide, and twenty high. 21 Solomon overlaid the interior of the temple with pure gold. He made in front of the sanctuary a cedar altar, overlaid it with gold, and looped it with golden chains. 22 The entire temple was overlaid with gold so that it was completely covered with it; the whole altar before the sanctuary was also overlaid with gold. 23 In the sanctuary were two cherubim, each ten cubits high, made of olive wood. 24 Each wing of a cherub measured five cubits so that the space from wing tip to wing tip of each was ten cubits. 25 The cherubim were identical in size and shape, 26 and each was exactly ten cubits high. 27 The cherubim were placed in the inmost part of the temple, with their wings spread wide, so that one wing of each cherub touched a side wall while the other wing, pointing toward the middle of the room, touched the corresponding wing of the second cherub. 28 The cherubim, too, were overlaid with gold.

29 The walls on all sides of both the inner and the outer rooms had carved figures of cherubim, palm trees, and open flowers. 30 The floor of both the inner and the outer rooms was overlaid with gold. 31 At the entrance of the sanctuary, doors of olive wood were made; the doorframes had beveled posts. 32 The two doors were of olive wood, with carved figures of cherubim, palm trees, and open flowers. The doors were overlaid with gold, which was also molded to the cherubim and the palm

---

6, 1: Construction of the temple of the LORD is here paralleled in importance with the founding of the nation after the departure from Egypt. In both, God is the central figure who chose Israel as his people, and now chooses the place where his temple should be built (Dt 12, 4–18.26). The year is given in a round number, 480, which corresponds to twelve generations. The fourth year of Solomon's reign: c. 968 B.C.

6, 11ff: The word of the LORD . . . my people Israel: the oracle, which came as a climax to the completion of the work, was an expression of God's acceptance and approval. Nevertheless the fulfillment of God's promises to David and his royal descendants will depend on their observance of his ordinances and commands.

6, 19: The innermost part of the temple: the sanctuary or holy of holies reserved exclusively for the Lord. Here through his presence he dwelt as on a throne between the cherubim above the ark of the covenant (2 Kgs 6, 23–28; 2 Chr 3, 10–13). See note on Ex 25, 18ff.

6, 20: Twenty (cubits) high: it is usually supposed that the holy of holies was of this height because it had a raised floor, five cubits above the floor level of the nave, rather than a dropped ceiling. The building was twenty-five cubits high (v 2) according to the reading here followed.

6, 1: 2 Chr 3, 1.   6, 13: 1 Chr 22, 9f.
6, 12: 2 Sm 7, 13.

The Temple of Solomon

1 Kings, chap. 6

Holy of Holies

Storeroom

Storeroom

Holy Place
(Nave)

Porch

Pillar

Pillar

Steps

Sea of Bronze   Altar

to plan, in the month of Bul, the eighth month, in the eleventh year. Thus it took Solomon seven years to build it.

Building of the Palace

7 1* His own palace Solomon completed after thirteen years of construction. 2 He built the hall called the Forest of Lebanon one hundred cubits long, fifty wide, and thirty high; it was supported by four rows of cedar columns, with cedar capitals upon the columns. 3 Moreover, it had a ceiling of cedar above the beams resting on the columns; these beams numbered forty-five, fifteen to a row. 4 There were three window frames at either end, with windows in strict alignment. 5 The posts of all the doorways were rectangular, and the doorways faced each other, three at either end. 6 The porch of the columned hall he made fifty cubits long and thirty wide. The porch extended the width of the columned hall, and there was a canopy in front. 7 He also built the vestibule of the throne where he gave judgment—that is, the tribunal; it was paneled with cedar from floor to ceiling beams. 8* His living quarters were in another court, set in deeper than the tribunal and of the same construction. A palace like this tribunal was built for Pharaoh's daughter, whom Solomon had married.

9 All these buildings were of fine stones, hewn to size and trimmed front and back with a saw, from the foundation to the bonding course. 10 (The foundation was made of fine, large blocks, some ten cubits and some eight cubits. 11 Above were fine stones hewn to size, and cedar wood.) 12 The great court was enclosed by three courses of hewn stones and a bonding course of cedar beams. So also were the inner court of the temple of the LORD and the temple porch.

Furnishing of the Temple

13 King Solomon had Hiram brought from Tyre. 14 He was a bronze worker, the son of a widow from the tribe of Naphtali; his father had been from Tyre. He was endowed with skill, understanding, and knowledge of how to produce any work in bronze. He came to King Solomon and did all his metal work.

15*† Two hollow bronze columns were cast, each eighteen cubits high and twelve cubits in circumference; their metal was of four fingers' thickness. 16 There were also two capitals cast in bronze, to place on top of the columns, each of them five cubits high. 17 Two pieces of network with a chainlike mesh

trees. 33 The same was done at the entrance to the nave, where the doorposts of olive wood were rectangular. 34 The two doors were of fir wood; each door was banded by a metal strap, front and back, 35 and had carved cherubim, palm trees, and open flowers, over which gold was evenly applied.

36 The inner court was walled off by means of three courses of hewn stones and one course of cedar beams.

37 The foundations of the LORD's temple were laid in the month of Ziv 38 in the fourth year, and it was completed in all particulars, exactly according

---

† **7, 15–21:** The *two hollow bronze columns,* Jachin and Boaz (2 Chr 3, 17), stood free to the right and left of the temple porch. The names are related to God's power (Boaz) founding (Jachin) the temple and his people.

7, 1: 1 Kgs 9, 10.   7, 15: Jer 52, 21.
7, 8: 1 Kgs 3, 1.

were made to cover the (nodes of the) capitals on top of the columns, one for each capital. 18 Four hundred pomegranates were also cast; two hundred of them in a double row encircled the piece of network on each of the two capitals. 19 The capitals on top of the columns were finished wholly in a lotus pattern 20 above the level of the nodes and their enveloping network. 21 The columns were then erected adjacent to the porch of the temple, one to the right, called Jachin, and the other to the left, called Boaz. 22 Thus the work on the columns was completed.

23*† The sea was then cast; it was made with a circular rim, and measured ten cubits across, five in height, and thirty in circumference. 24 Under the brim, gourds encircled it, ten to the cubit all the way around; the gourds were in two rows and were cast in one mold with the sea. 25 This rested on twelve oxen, three facing north, three facing west, three facing south, and three facing east, with their haunches all toward the center, where the sea was set upon them. 26 It was a handbreadth thick, and its brim resembled that of a cup, being lily-shaped. Its capacity was two thousand measures.

27 Ten stands were also made of bronze, each four cubits long, four wide, and three high. 28 When these stands were constructed, panels were set within the framework. 29 On the panels between the frames there were lions, oxen, and cherubim; and on the frames likewise, above and below the lions and oxen, there were wreaths in relief.

30 Each stand had four bronze wheels and bronze axles. 32 The four wheels were below the paneling, and the axletrees of the wheels and the stand were of one piece. Each wheel was a cubit and a half high. 33 The wheels were constructed like chariot wheels; their axles, fellies, spokes, and hubs were all cast.

The four legs of each stand had cast braces, which were under the basin; they had wreaths on each side. 34 These four braces, extending to the corners of each stand, were of one piece with the stand.

35 On top of the stand there was a raised collar half a cubit high, with supports and panels which were of one piece with the top of the stand. 31 This was surmounted by a crown one cubit high within which was a rounded opening to provide a receptacle a cubit and a half in depth. There was carved work at the opening, on panels that were angular, not curved. 36 On the surfaces of the supports and on the panels, wherever there was a clear space, cherubim, lions, and palm trees were carved, as well as wreaths all around. 37 This was how the ten stands were made, all of the same casting, the same size, the same shape. 38 Ten bronze basins were then made, each four cubits in diameter with a capacity of forty measures, one basin for the top of each of the ten stands. 39 The stands were placed, five on the south side of the temple and five on the north. The sea was placed off to the southeast from the south side of the temple.

40 When Hiram made the pots, shovels, and bowls, he therewith completed all his work for King Solomon in the temple of the LORD: 41 two columns, two nodes for the capitals on top of the columns, two pieces of network covering the nodes for the capitals on top of the columns, 42 four hundred pomegranates in double rows on both pieces of network that covered the two nodes of the capitals where they met the columns, 43 ten stands, ten basins on the stands, 44 one sea, twelve oxen supporting the sea, 45 pots, shovels, and bowls. All these articles which Hiram made for King Solomon in the temple of the LORD were of burnished bronze. 46 The king had them cast in the neighborhood of the Jordan, in the clayey ground between Succoth and Zarethan. 47 Solomon did not weigh all the articles because they were so numerous; the weight of the bronze, therefore, was not determined.

48 Solomon had all the articles made for the interior of the temple of the LORD: the golden altar; the golden table on which the showbread lay; 49 the lampstands of pure gold, five to the right and five to the left before the sanctuary, with their flowers, lamps, and tongs of gold; 50 basins, snuffers, bowls, cups, and fire pans of pure gold; and hinges of gold for the doors of the inner room, or holy of holies, and for the doors of the outer room, the nave.

51* When all the work undertaken by King Solomon in the temple of the LORD was completed, he brought in the dedicated offerings of his father David, putting the silver, gold, and other articles in the treasuries of the temple of the LORD.

Dedication of the Temple

8 1* At the order of Solomon, the elders of Israel and all the leaders of the tribes, the princes in the ancestral houses of the Israelites, came to King Solomon in Jerusalem, to bring up the ark of the LORD'S covenant from the City of David [which is Zion]. 2 All the men of Israel assembled before King Solomon during the festival in the month of Ethanim (the seventh month). 3 When all the elders of Israel had arrived, the priests took up the ark; 4 they carried the ark of the LORD and the meeting tent with all the sacred vessels that were in the tent. (The priests and Levites carried them.)

---

† **7, 23–26:** *The sea . . . rested on twelve oxen:* this was a large circular tank containing about twelve thousand gallons of water.

7, 23: 2 Chr 4, 2.
7, 51: 2 Chr 5, 1.

8, 1: 2 Chr 5, 2.

5 King Solomon and the entire community of Israel present for the occasion sacrificed before the ark sheep and oxen too many to number or count. 6† The priests brought the ark of the covenant of the LORD to its place beneath the wings of the cherubim in the sanctuary, the holy of holies of the temple. 7 The cherubim had their wings spread out over the place of the ark, sheltering the ark and its poles from above. 8 The poles were so long that their ends could be seen from that part of the holy place adjoining the sanctuary; however, they could not be seen beyond. (They have remained there to this day.) 9* There was nothing in the ark but the two stone tablets which Moses had put there at Horeb, when the LORD made a covenant with the Israelites at their departure from the land of Egypt.

10 When the priests left the holy place, the cloud filled the temple of the LORD 11 so that the priests could no longer minister because of the cloud, since the LORD's glory had filled the temple of the LORD. 12* Then Solomon said, "The LORD intends to dwell in the dark cloud; 13 I have truly built you a princely house, a dwelling where you may abide forever."

14 The king turned and greeted the whole community of Israel as they stood. 15 He said to them: "Blessed be the LORD, the God of Israel, who with his own mouth made a promise to my father David and by his hand has brought it to fulfillment. It was he who said, 16 'Since the day I brought my people Israel out of Egypt, I have not chosen a city out of any tribe of Israel for the building of a temple to my honor; but I choose David to rule my people Israel.' 17* When my father David wished to build a temple to the honor of the LORD, the God of Israel, 18 the Lord said to him, 'In wishing to build a temple to my honor, you do well. 19 It will not be you, however, who will build the temple; but the son who will spring from you, he shall build the temple to my honor.' 20 And now the LORD has fulfilled the promise that he made: I have succeeded my father David and sit on the throne of Israel, as the LORD foretold, and I have built this temple to honor the LORD, the God of Israel. 21 I have provided in it a place for the ark in which is the covenant of the LORD, which he made with our fathers when he brought them out of the land of Egypt."

Solomon's Prayer

22 Solomon stood before the altar of the LORD in the presence of the whole community of Israel, and stretching forth his hands toward heaven, 23 he said, "LORD, God of Israel, there is no God like you in heaven above or on earth below; you keep your covenant of kindness with your servants who are faithful to you with their whole heart. 24 You have kept the promise you made to my father David, your servant. You who spoke that promise, have this day, by your own power, brought it to fulfillment. 25* Now, therefore, LORD, God of Israel, keep the further promise you made to my father David, your servant, saying, 'You shall always have someone from your line to sit before me on the throne of Israel, provided only that your descendants look to their conduct so that they live in my presence, as you have lived in my presence.' 26 Now, LORD, God of Israel, may this promise which you made to my father David, your servant, be confirmed.

27 "Can it indeed be that God dwells among men on earth? If the heavens and the highest heavens cannot contain you, how much less this temple which I have built! 28 Look kindly on the prayer

Holy Places

Solomon knows that the Temple will not hold God. Holy places are not cages to keep God contained. People need holy places more than God does. We gather together in public holy places to experience God's presence as a community. But we can also meet God one-on-one in private holy places, special to us alone.

Try creating a holy space in your bedroom. Clear out a corner and put in it a small table, and a chair or rug to sit on. On the table, put your Bible and an object or two to help you focus on God. You might use a candle, a special picture or statue, or something from a retreat or a special place. Try to spend a little time each day in your holy space with God.

▶ **I Kgs 8, 27–30**

1

K

G

S

---

† **8, 6–9:** The transfer of the ark of the covenant into the newly constructed temple building, and the oracle of God's acceptance (1 Kgs 9, 3–9), and his act of possession (1 Kgs 8, 10–13), constituted the temple's solemn dedication, and made of it the abiding dwelling of God among his people for which David had hoped (2 Sm 6, 12–15; 7, 1–3). The concurrence of the feast of Booths marks an appropriate transition of God's dwelling among nomadic tribes to his permanent abode among a settled people.

8, 9: Ex 34, 27; Heb 9, 4.　　8, 17: 2 Sm 7, 5.
8, 12: 2 Chr 6, 1.　　8, 25: 2 Sm 7, 12.

and petition of your servant, O LORD, my God, and listen to the cry of supplication which I, your servant, utter before you this day. 29 May your eyes watch night and day over this temple, the place where you have decreed you shall be honored; may you heed the prayer which I, your servant, offer in this place. 30 Listen to the petitions of your servant and of your people Israel which they offer in this place. Listen from your heavenly dwelling and grant pardon.

31 "If a man sins against his neighbor and is required to take an oath sanctioned by a curse, when he comes and takes the oath before your altar in this temple, 32 listen in heaven; take action and pass judgment on your servants. Condemn the wicked and punish him for his conduct, but acquit the just and establish his innocence.

33† "If your people Israel sin against you and are defeated by an enemy, and if then they return to you, praise your name, pray to you, and entreat you in this temple, 34 listen in heaven and forgive the sin of your people Israel, and bring them back to the land you gave their fathers.

35 "If the sky is closed, so that there is no rain, because they have sinned against you and you afflict them, and if then they repent of their sin, and pray, and praise your name in this place, 36 listen in heaven and forgive the sin of your servant and of your people Israel, teaching them the right way to live and sending rain upon this land of yours which you have given to your people as their heritage.

37 "If there is famine in the land or pestilence; or if blight comes, or mildew, or a locust swarm, or devouring insects; if an enemy of your people besieges them in one of their cities; whatever plague or sickness there may be, 38 if then any one [of your entire people Israel] has remorse of conscience and offers some prayer or petition, stretching out his hands toward this temple, 39 listen from your heavenly dwelling place and forgive. You who alone know the hearts of all men, render to each one of them according to his conduct; knowing their hearts, so treat them 40 that they may fear you as long as they live on the land you gave our fathers.

41 "To the foreigner, likewise, who is not of your people Israel, but comes from a distant land to honor you 42 (since men will learn of your great name and your mighty hand and your outstretched arm), when he comes and prays toward this temple, 43 listen from your heavenly dwelling. Do all that the foreigner asks of you, that all the peoples of the earth may know your name, may fear you as do your people Israel, and may acknowledge that this

temple which I have built is dedicated to your honor.

44 "Whatever the direction in which you may send your people forth to war against their enemies, if they pray to you, O LORD, toward the city you have chosen and the temple I have built in your honor, 45 listen in heaven to their prayer and petition, and defend their cause.

46* "When they sin against you (for there is no man who does not sin), and in your anger against them you deliver them to the enemy, so that their captors deport them to a hostile land, far or near, 47 may they repent in the land of their captivity and be converted. If then they entreat you in the land of their captors and say, 'We have sinned and done wrong; we have been wicked'; 48 if with their whole heart and soul they turn back to you in the land of the enemies who took them captive, pray to you toward the land you gave their fathers, the city you have chosen, and the temple I have built in your honor, 49 listen from your heavenly dwelling. 50 Forgive your people their sins and all the offenses they have committed against you, and grant them mercy before their captors, so that these will be merciful to them. 51 For they are your people and your inheritance, whom you brought out of Egypt, from the midst of an iron furnace.

52 "Thus may your eyes be open to the petition of your servant and to the petition of your people Israel. Hear them whenever they call upon you, 53 because you have set them apart among all the peoples of the earth for your inheritance, as you declared through your servant Moses when you brought our fathers out of Egypt, O Lord GOD."

54 When Solomon finished offering this entire prayer of petition to the LORD, he rose from before the altar of the LORD, where he had been kneeling with his hands outstretched toward heaven. 55 He stood and blessed the whole community of Israel, saying in a loud voice: 56 "Blessed be the LORD who has given rest to his people Israel, just as he promised. Not a single word has gone unfulfilled of the entire generous promise he made through his servant Moses. 57 May the LORD, our God, be with us as he was with our fathers and may he not forsake us nor cast us off. 58 May he draw our hearts to himself, that we may follow him in everything and keep the commands, statutes, and ordinances which he enjoined on our fathers. 59 May this prayer I have offered to the LORD, our God, be present to him day and night, that he may uphold the cause of his servant and of his people Israel as each day requires, 60 that all the peoples of the earth may know the

---

8, 33–34.46–53: These references to deportation of Israelites to a hostile land are an expansion of Solomon's prayer dating from the Babylonian exile four centuries later.

8, 46: 2 Chr 6, 36; Eccl 7, 20; 1 Jn 1, 8.

LORD is God and there is no other. 61 You must be wholly devoted to the LORD, our God, observing his statutes and keeping his commandments, as on this day."

62 The king and all Israel with him offered sacrifices before the LORD. 63 Solomon offered as peace offerings to the LORD twenty-two thousand oxen and one hundred twenty thousand sheep. Thus the king and all the Israelites dedicated the temple of the LORD. 64 On that day the king consecrated the middle of the court facing the temple of the LORD; he offered there the holocausts, the cereal offerings, and the fat of the peace offerings, because the bronze altar before the LORD was too small to hold these offerings.

65 On this occasion Solomon and all the Israelites, who had assembled in large numbers from Labo of Hamath to the wadi of Egypt, celebrated the festival before the LORD, our God, for seven days. 66 On the eighth day he dismissed the people, who bade the king farewell and went to their homes, rejoicing and happy over all the blessings the LORD had given to his servant David and to his people Israel.

Promise and Warning to Solomon

9 1 After Solomon finished building the temple of the LORD, the royal palace, and everything else that he had planned, 2* the LORD appeared to him a second time, as he had appeared to him in Gibeon. 3 The LORD said to him: "I have heard the prayer of petition which you offered in my presence. I have consecrated this temple which you have built; I confer my name upon it forever, and my eyes and my heart shall be there always. 4 As for you, if you live in my presence as your father David lived, sincerely and uprightly, doing just as I have commanded you, keeping my statutes and decrees, 5* I will establish your throne of sovereignty over Israel forever, as I promised your father David when I said, 'You shall always have someone from your line on the throne of Israel.' 6 But if you and your descendants ever withdraw from me, fail to keep the commandments and statutes which I set before you, and proceed to venerate and worship strange gods, 7 I will cut off Israel from the land I gave them and repudiate the temple I have consecrated to my honor. Israel shall become a proverb and a byword among all nations, 8* and this temple shall become a heap of ruins. Every passerby shall catch his breath in amazement, and ask, 'Why has the LORD

Catholic Connections

BLESSING THE COMMUNITY

The community is a phrase used to describe people gathered to pray together. Think of how the community is blessed at the end of Mass. With raised hands, the priest speaks with words similar to Solomon's in 1 Kgs 8, 56–61. The people are sent forth to know God's love and to do what God wants.

Let us praise God who loves us, and let us go in peace to love and serve God and one another.

▸ **1 Kgs 8, 56–61**

done this to the land and to this temple?' 9 Men will answer: 'They forsook the LORD, their God, who brought their fathers out of the land of Egypt; they adopted strange gods which they worshiped and served. That is why the LORD has brought down upon them all this evil.' "

Other Acts of the King

10 After the twenty years during which Solomon built the two houses, the temple of the LORD and the palace of the king— 11 Hiram, king of Tyre, supplying Solomon with all the cedar wood, fir wood, and gold he wished—King Solomon gave Hiram twenty cities in the land of Galilee. 12 Hiram left Tyre to see the cities Solomon had given him, but was not satisfied with them. 13 So he said, "What are these cities you have given me, my brother?" And he called them the land of Cabul, as they are called to this day. 14† Hiram, however, had sent King Solomon one hundred and twenty talents of gold.

15† This is an account of the forced labor which King Solomon levied in order to build the temple of the LORD, his palace, Millo, the wall of Jerusalem,

1

K

G

S

9, 14: *One hundred and twenty talents of gold:* approximately three million six hundred thousand dollars.
9, 15: *Millo:* probably means a filling, and may refer to an artificial earthwork or platform of stamped ground south of the temple area. It was begun by David (2 Sm 5, 9); cf 1 Kgs 9, 24; 11, 27.

9, 2: 1 Kgs 3, 5; 11, 9;   9, 5: 2 Sm 7, 12–16.
     2 Chr 7, 12.   9, 8: Dt 29, 23; Jer 22, 8.

Hazor, Megiddo, Gezer [16] (Pharaoh king of Egypt, had come up and taken Gezer and, after destroying it by fire and slaying all the Canaanites living in the city, had given it as dowry to his daughter, Solomon's wife; [17] Solomon then rebuilt Gezer), Lower Beth-horon, [18] Baalath, Tamar in the desert of Judah, [19] all his cities for supplies, cities for chariots and for horses, and whatever else Solomon decided should be built in Jerusalem, in Lebanon, and in the entire land under his dominion. [20] All the non-Israelite people who remained in the land, descendants of the Amorites, Hittites, Perizzites, Hivites, and Jebusites [21] whose doom the Israelites had been unable to accomplish, Solomon conscripted as forced laborers, as they are to this day. [22] But Solomon enslaved none of the Israelites, for they were his fighting force, his ministers, commanders, adjutants, chariot officers, and charioteers. [23] The supervisors of Solomon's works who policed the people engaged in the work numbered five hundred and fifty.

[24] As soon as Pharaoh's daughter went up from the City of David to her palace, which he had built for her, Solomon built Millo.

[25] Three times a year Solomon used to offer holocausts and peace offerings on the altar which he had built to the LORD, and to burn incense before the LORD; and he kept the temple in repair.

[26]† King Solomon also built a fleet at Ezion-geber, which is near Elath on the shore of the Red Sea in the land of Edom. [27] In this fleet Hiram placed his own expert seamen with the servants of Solomon. [28] They went to Ophir, and brought back four hundred and twenty talents of gold to King Solomon.

Visit of the Queen of Sheba

10 [1]*† The queen of Sheba, having heard of Solomon's fame, came to test him with subtle questions. [2] She arrived in Jerusalem with a very numerous retinue, and with camels bearing spices, a large amount of gold, and precious stones. She came to Solomon and questioned him on every subject in which she was interested. [3] King Solomon explained everything she asked about, and there remained nothing hidden from him that he could not explain to her.

[4] When the queen of Sheba witnessed Solomon's great wisdom, the palace he had built, [5] the food at his table, the seating of his ministers, the attendance and garb of his waiters, his banquet service, and the holocausts he offered in the temple of the LORD, she was breathless. [6] "The report I heard in my country about your deeds and your wisdom is true," she told the king. [7] "Though I did not believe the report until I came and saw with my own eyes, I have discovered that they were not telling me the half. Your wisdom and prosperity surpass the report I heard. [8] Happy are your men, happy these servants of yours, who stand before you always and listen to your wisdom. [9] Blessed be the LORD, your God, whom it has pleased to place you on the throne of Israel. In his enduring love for Israel, the LORD has made you king to carry out judgment and justice." [10] Then she gave the king one hundred and twenty gold talents, a very large quantity of spices, and precious stones. Never again did anyone bring such an abundance of spices as the queen of Sheba gave to King Solomon.

[11]† Hiram's fleet, which used to bring gold from Ophir, also brought from there a large quantity of cabinet wood and precious stones. [12] With the wood the king made supports for the temple of the LORD and for the palace of the king, and harps and lyres for the chanters. No more such wood was brought or seen to the present day.

[13] King Solomon gave the queen of Sheba everything she desired and asked for, besides such presents as were given her from Solomon's royal bounty. Then she returned with her servants to her own country.

Solomon's Wealth

[14] The gold that Solomon received every year weighed six hundred and sixty-six gold talents, [15] in addition to what came from the Tarshish fleet, from the traffic of merchants, and from all the kings of Arabia and the governors of the country. [16]* Moreover, King Solomon made two hundred shields of beaten gold (six hundred gold shekels went into each shield) [17] and three hundred bucklers of beaten gold (three minas of gold went into each buckler); and he put them in the hall of the Forest of Lebanon. [18] The king also had a large ivory throne made, and overlaid it with refined gold. [19] The throne had six steps, a back with a round top, and an arm on each side of the seat. Next to each arm stood a lion; [20] and twelve other lions stood on the steps, two to a step, one on either side of each step. Nothing like this was produced in any other kingdom. [21] In addition, all King Solomon's drinking vessels were of gold, and all the utensils in the hall of the Forest of Lebanon were of pure gold. There

---

9, 26: *Ezion-geber . . . Edom:* the first mention of maritime commerce in the Israelite kingdom (to which the land of Edom was subject after its conquest by King David; cf 2 Sm 8, 14).

10, 1: *Queen of Sheba:* women rulers among the Arabs are recorded in eighth-century-B.C. Assyrian inscriptions. Sheba was for centuries the leading principality in what is now the Yemen.

10, 11f: *Cabinet:* an unknown wood, probably fragrant.

10, 1: 2 Chr 9, 1; Mt 12, 42;   **10, 16:** 1 Kgs 14, 26.
Lk 11, 31.

was no silver, for in Solomon's time it was considered worthless. [22]† The king had a fleet of Tarshish ships at sea with Hiram's fleet. Once every three years the fleet of Tarshish ships would come with a cargo of gold, silver, ivory, apes, and monkeys. [23] Thus King Solomon surpassed in riches and wisdom all the kings of the earth. [24] And the whole world sought audience with Solomon, to hear from him the wisdom which God had put in his heart. [25] Each one brought his yearly tribute: silver or gold articles, garments, weapons, spices, horses and mules.

[26]* Solomon collected chariots and drivers; he had one thousand four hundred chariots and twelve thousand drivers; these he allocated among the chariot cities and to the king's service in Jerusalem. [27] The king made silver as common in Jerusalem as stones, and cedars as numerous as the sycamores of the foothills. [28] Solomon's horses were imported from Cilicia, where the king's agents purchased them. [29] A chariot imported from Egypt cost six hundred shekels, a horse one hundred and fifty shekels; they were exported at these rates to all the Hittite and Aramean kings.

The Sins of Solomon

11 [1]*† King Solomon loved many foreign women besides the daughter of Pharaoh (Moabites, Ammonites, Edomites, Sidonians, and Hittites), [2]* from nations with which the LORD had forbidden the Israelites to intermarry, "because," he said, "they will turn your hearts to their gods." [3] But Solomon fell in love with them. He had seven hundred wives of princely rank and three hundred concubines, and his wives turned his heart.

[4] When Solomon was old his wives had turned his heart to strange gods, and his heart was not entirely with the LORD, his God, as the heart of his father David had been. [5] By adoring Astarte, the goddess of the Sidonians, and Milcom, the idol of the Ammonites, [6] Solomon did evil in the sight of the LORD; he did not follow him unreservedly as his father David had done. [7] Solomon then built a high place to Chemosh, the idol of Moab, and to Molech, the idol of the Ammonites, on the hill opposite Jerusalem. [8] He did the same for all his foreign wives who burned incense and sacrificed to their gods. [9]* The LORD, therefore, became angry with

† **10, 22:** *Tarshish ships:* large, strong vessels for long voyages. Tarshish was the ancient Tartessus, a Phoenician colony in southern Spain, the name of which denotes a center for smelting metallic ore.

11, 1–3.7: The glorious rise of Solomon, his piety and wisdom, administrative skill and wealth, the extension of his kingdom, his prestige among neighboring rulers, his reign of peace, above all his friendship with God—these are now eclipsed by his sins of intermarriage with great numbers of pagan wives and the consequent forbidden worship of their gods (Ex 34, 11–16; Dt 7, 1–5). His construction of temples in their honor merited the punishment of loss of

PRAY IT

Solomon's Sin

Sometimes, when we think we are strongest, we are actually weakest. Solomon replaces his poverty of spirit with pride (see 1 Kgs 3, 4–14). He seems to believe that he is strong enough to go against God's command not to take foreign wives and that he can withstand the influence of their foreign gods. But Solomon falls into the sin of idolatry (worshiping other gods), breaking the Covenant.

Have you ever considered doing something that you knew was wrong? Did you tell yourself, "It won't hurt to do it just this once"? Maybe that is what Solomon said when he took his first foreign wife.

In your prayer time, reflect or journal on the following questions:

- What takes your attention away from God?
- Have you ever used the excuse, "I'm strong enough to handle this," to lead you in doing something wrong?
- Pray Ps 86, 11 to end your prayer.

▶ 1 Kgs 11, 1–8

Solomon, because his heart was turned away from the LORD, the God of Israel, who had appeared to him twice [10] (for though the LORD had forbidden him this very act of following strange gods, Solomon had not obeyed him).

[11] So the LORD said to Solomon: "Since this is what you want, and you have not kept my covenant and my statutes which I enjoined on you, I will deprive you of the kingdom and give it to your servant. [12]* I will not do this during your lifetime, however, for the sake of your father David; it is your son whom I will deprive. [13] Nor will I take away the whole kingdom. I will leave your son one tribe for the sake of my servant David and of Jerusalem, which I have chosen."

a united kingdom to his posterity, and the opposition of adversaries to himself (vv 14.23–27). Hadad the Edomite rebelled against Solomon at the beginning of his reign (v 25). Rezon of Syria established a new kingdom in Dàmascus; Jeroboam of Israel constituted the greatest threat because of his revolt from within. This threefold threat culminated in the breakup of Solomon's kingdom.

10, 26: 2 Chr 1, 14.   **11, 9:** 1 Kgs 9, 2.
11, 1: Dt 17, 17; Sir 47, 19f.   **11, 12:** 1 Kgs 12, 15.
11, 2: Ex 34, 16.

14 The LORD then raised up an adversary to Solomon: Hadad the Edomite, who was of the royal line in Edom. 15* Earlier, when David had conquered Edom, Joab, the general of the army, while going to bury the slain, put to death every male in Edom. 16 Joab and all Israel remained there six months until they had killed off every male in Edom. 17 Meanwhile, Hadad, who was only a boy, fled toward Egypt with some Edomite servants of his father. 18 They left Midian and passing through Paran, where they picked up additional men, they went into Egypt to Pharaoh, king of Egypt, who gave Hadad a house, appointed him rations, and assigned him land.

19 Hadad won great favor with Pharaoh, so that he gave him in marriage the sister of Queen Tahpenes, his own wife. 20 Tahpenes' sister bore Hadad a son, Genubath. After his weaning, the queen kept him in Pharaoh's palace, where he then lived with Pharaoh's own sons. 21 When Hadad in Egypt heard that David rested with his ancestors and that Joab, the general of the army, was dead, he said to Pharaoh, "Give me leave to return to my own country." 22 Pharaoh said to him, "What do you lack with me, that you are seeking to return to your own country?" "Nothing," he said, "but please let me go!"

23 God raised up against Solomon another adversary, in Rezon, the son of Eliada, who had fled from his lord, Hadadezer, king of Zobah, 24 when David defeated them with slaughter. Rezon gathered men about him and became leader of a band, went to Damascus, settled there, and became king in Damascus. 25 He was an enemy of Israel as long as Solomon lived; this added to the harm done by Hadad, who made a rift in Israel by becoming king over Edom.

26* Solomon's servant Jeroboam, son of Nebat, an Ephraimite from Zeredah with a widowed mother, Zeruah, also rebelled against the king. 27 This is why he rebelled. King Solomon was building Millo, closing up the breach of his father's City of David. 28 Jeroboam was a man of means, and when Solomon saw that he was also an industrious young man, he put him in charge of the entire labor force of the house of Joseph. 29* At that time Jeroboam left Jerusalem, and the prophet Ahijah the Shilonite met him on the road. The two were alone in the area, and the prophet was wearing a new cloak. 30 Ahijah took off his new cloak, tore it into twelve pieces, 31* and said to Jeroboam:

"Take ten pieces for yourself; the LORD, the God of Israel, says: 'I will tear away the kingdom from Solomon's grasp and will give you ten of the tribes. 32 One tribe shall remain to him for the sake of David my servant, and of Jerusalem, the city I have chosen out of all the tribes of Israel. 33 The ten I will give you because he has forsaken me and has worshiped Astarte, goddess of the Sidonians, Chemosh, god of Moab, and Milcom, god of the Ammonites; he has not followed my ways or done what is pleasing to me according to my statutes and my decrees, as his father David did. 34 Yet I will not take any of the kingdom from Solomon himself, but will keep him a prince as long as he lives for the sake of my servant David, whom I chose, who kept my commandments and statutes. 35 But I will take the kingdom from his son and will give it to you—that is, the ten tribes. 36 I will give his son one tribe, that my servant David may always have a lamp before me in Jerusalem, the city in which I choose to be honored. 37 I will take you; you shall reign over all that you desire and shall become king of Israel. 38 If, then, you heed all that I command you, follow my ways, and please me by keeping my statutes and my commandments like my servant David, I will be with you. I will establish for you, as I did for David, a lasting dynasty; I will give Israel to you. 39 I will punish David's line for this, but not forever.' "

40 When Solomon tried to have Jeroboam killed for his rebellion, he escaped to King Shishak, in Egypt, where he remained until Solomon's death.

41 The rest of the acts of Solomon, with all his deeds and his wisdom, are recorded in the book of the chronicles of Solomon. 42 The time that Solomon reigned in Jerusalem over all Israel was forty years. 43 Solomon rested with his ancestors; he was buried in his father's City of David, and his son Rehoboam succeeded him as king.

II: Judah and Israel to the Time of Ahab

Secession of Israel

12 1*† Rehoboam went to Shechem, where all Israel had come to proclaim him king. 3 They said to Rehoboam: 4 "Your father put on us a heavy yoke. If you now lighten the harsh service and the heavy yoke your father imposed on us, we will serve you." 5 "Come back to me in three days," he answered them. When the people had departed, 6 King Rehoboam consulted the elders who had been in his father's service while he was alive, and asked, "What answer do you advise me to give this people?" 7 They replied, "If today you will be the

---

† **12, 1:** *Shechem:* chief city of the northern tribes, where a covenant of fidelity had previously been made between the Lord and his people and a stone of witness had been erected in memory of the event (Jos 24, 25ff).

11, 15: 2 Sm 8, 14.   2 Chr 10, 15.
11, 26: 2 Chr 13, 6.   11, 31: 1 Kgs 12, 15.
11, 29: 1 Kgs 14, 2;   12, 1: 2 Chr 10, 1.

? did you KNOW?

The Kingdom of Israel Splits

When the people of Israel first came to settle in Canaan, they organized into twelve tribes, ruled by chieftains, that supported and protected one another. As Israel grew in size, it was necessary to have one central ruler who would unite the tribes into one nation. Saul was the first king of this united Israel. David followed Saul and expanded the kingdom's territory. David's son Solomon continued ruling over the expanded kingdom, and engaged in expensive building projects.

At Solomon's death, many Israelites wanted a less demanding king. They had suffered under the burden of heavy taxes and forced labor. When Solomon's son Rehoboam refused to make any changes (1 Kgs 12, 11), ten of the northern tribes pulled away and placed their own king, Jeroboam, on the throne. The northern kingdom was called Israel. The southern kingdom, composed of two tribes, was called Judah (see map 3, "The Kingdom Years"). The kingdom was now split in two, and it was never again reunited.

Saul (1020 B.C.)
|
David (1000 B.C.)
|
Solomon (961 B.C.)

Kingdom splits (931 B.C.)

JUDAH (south)	ISRAEL (north)
Capital: Jerusalem	Capital: Samaria
Twenty kings	Twenty kings
Falls to Babylonians (587 B.C.)	Falls to Assyrians (721 B.C.)
Exile to Babylon	Exile to Assyria

▸ 1 Kgs 12, 1–19

servant of this people and submit to them, giving them a favorable answer, they will be your servants forever." ⁸ But he ignored the advice the elders had given him, and consulted the young men who had grown up with him and were in his service. ⁹ He said to them, "What answer do you advise me to give this people, who have asked me to lighten the yoke my father imposed on them?" ¹⁰ The young men who had grown up with him replied, "This is what you must say to this people who have asked you to lighten the yoke your father put on them: 'My little finger is thicker than my father's body. ¹¹ Whereas my father put a heavy yoke on you, I will make it heavier. My father beat you with whips, but I will beat you with scorpions.' "

¹² On the third day all Israel came back to King Rehoboam, as he had instructed them to do. ¹³ Ignoring the advice the elders had given him, the king gave the people a harsh answer. ¹⁴ He said to them, as the young men had advised: "My father put on you a heavy yoke, but I will make it heavier. My father beat you with whips, but I will beat you with scorpions." ¹⁵* The king did not listen to the people, for the LORD brought this about to fulfill the prophecy he had uttered to Jeroboam, son of Nebat, through Ahijah the Shilonite.

¹⁶† When all Israel saw that the king did not listen to them, the people answered the king:

"What share have we in David?
We have no heritage in the son of Jesse.
To your tents, O Israel!
Now look to your own house, David."

So Israel went off to their tents, ¹⁷ but Rehoboam reigned over the Israelites who lived in the cities of Judah. ¹⁸ King Rehoboam then sent out Adoram, superintendent of the forced labor, but all Israel stoned him to death. Rehoboam managed to mount his chariot to flee to Jerusalem, ¹⁹ and Israel went into rebellion against David's house to this day. ² Jeroboam, son of Nebat, who was still in Egypt, where he had fled from King Solomon, returned from Egypt as soon as he learned this. ²⁰ When all Israel heard that Jeroboam had returned, they summoned him to an assembly and made him king over all Israel. None remained loyal to David's house except the tribe of Judah alone.

²¹ On his arrival in Jerusalem, Rehoboam gathered together all the house of Judah and the tribe of

1
K
G
S

12, 16: *What share have we in David:* even in David's time the northern tribes seemed ready to withdraw from Judah (2 Sm 20, 1). The unreasonable attitude of Rehoboam toward them intensified the discontent caused by the oppression of Solomon (v 4) and thus precipitated the establishment of a rival monarchy (v 20).

12, 15: 1 Kgs 11, 12.31.

Benjamin—one hundred eighty thousand seasoned warriors—to fight against the house of Israel, to restore the kingdom to Rehoboam, son of Solomon. 22* However, the LORD spoke to Shemaiah, a man of God: 23 "Say to Rehoboam, son of Solomon, king of Judah, and to the house of Judah and to Benjamin, and to the rest of the people: 24 'Thus says the LORD: You must not march out to fight against your brother Israelites. Let every man return home, for I have brought this about.' " They accepted this message of the LORD and gave up the expedition accordingly.

25 Jeroboam built up Shechem in the hill country of Ephraim and lived there. Then he left it and built up Penuel.

Religious Rebellion

26† Jeroboam thought to himself: "The kingdom will return to David's house. 27 If now this people go up to offer sacrifices in the temple of the LORD in Jerusalem, the hearts of this people will return to their master, Rehoboam, king of Judah, and they will kill me." 28* After taking counsel, the king made two calves of gold and said to the people: "You have been going up to Jerusalem long enough. Here is your God, O Israel, who brought you up from the land of Egypt." 29† And he put one in Bethel, the other in Dan. 30 This led to sin, because the people frequented these calves in Bethel and in Dan. 31* He also built temples on the high places and made priests from among the people who were not Levites. 32 Jeroboam established a feast in the eighth month on the fifteenth day of the month to duplicate in Bethel the pilgrimage feast of Judah, with sacrifices to the calves he had made; and he stationed in Bethel priests of the high places he had built.

Message of the Prophet from Judah

33 Jeroboam ascended the altar he built in Bethel on the fifteenth day of the eighth month, the month in which he arbitrarily chose to establish a feast for the Israelites; he was going to offer sacrifice.

13 1 A man of God came from Judah to Bethel by the word of the LORD, while Jeroboam was standing at the altar to offer sacrifice. 2* He cried out against the altar the word of the LORD: "O altar, altar, the LORD says, 'A child shall be born to the house of David, Josiah by name, who shall slaughter upon you the priests of the high places who offer sacrifice upon you, and he shall burn human bones upon you.' " 3 He gave a sign that same day and said: "This is the sign that the LORD has spoken: The altar shall break up and the ashes on it shall be strewn about."

4 When King Jeroboam heard what the man of God was crying out against the altar, he stretched forth his hand from the altar and said, "Seize him!" But the hand he stretched forth against him withered, so that he could not draw it back. 5 Moreover, the altar broke up and the ashes from it were strewn about—the sign the man of God had given as the word of the LORD. 6 Then the king appealed to the man of God. "Entreat the LORD, your God," he said, "and intercede for me that I may be able to withdraw my hand." So the man of God entreated the LORD, and the king recovered the normal use of his hand. 7 "Come home with me for some refreshment," the king invited the man of God, "and I will give you a present." 8 "If you gave me half your kingdom," the man of God said to the king, "I would not go with you, nor eat bread or drink water in this place. 9 For I was instructed by the word of the LORD not to eat bread or drink water and not to return by the way I came." 10 So he departed by another road and did not go back the way he had come to Bethel.

11 There was an old prophet living in the city, whose sons came and told him all that the man of God had done that day in Bethel. When they repeated to their father the words he had spoken to the king, 12 the father asked them, "Which way did he go?" And his sons pointed out to him the road taken by the man of God who had come from Judah. 13 Then he said to his sons, "Saddle the ass for me." When they had saddled it, he mounted 14 and followed the man of God, whom he found seated under a terebinth. When he asked him, "Are you the man of God who came from Judah?" he answered, "Yes." 15 Then he said, "Come home with me and have some bread." 16 "I cannot go back with you, and I cannot eat bread or drink water with you in this place," he answered, 17 "for I was told by the word of the LORD neither to eat bread nor drink water here, and not to go back the way I came." 18 But he said to him, "I, too, am a prophet like you, and

---

† **12, 26–32:** Jeroboam feared reunification of the divided kingdom through worship in the single temple in Jerusalem. To prevent this he encouraged shrines on the high places, and appointed false priests to supplement those of levitical descent. The golden bullocks he installed in two of his sanctuaries, though probably intended as bearers of the invisible Divine Majesty, quickly became occasions for idolatry. Thus Jeroboam caused Israel to sin, and sealed his doom and that of his royal house (1 Kgs 13, 34; 14, 7–14).

12, 29: *Bethel* and *Dan*: at the southern and northern boundaries of the separate kingdom of Israel, where sanctuaries had existed in the past (Gn 12, 8; 13, 3; 18, 10–22; 25, 1–16; Jgs 18, 1–31).

12, 22–24: 2 Chr 11, 2ff.   12, 31: 2 Chr 11, 15.
  12, 28: Tb 1, 5; Ex 32, 8.   13, 2: 2 Kgs 23, 16.

an angel told me in the word of the LORD to bring you back with me to my house and to have you eat bread and drink water." He was lying to him, however.

¹⁹ So he went back with him, and ate bread and drank water in his house. ²⁰ But while they were sitting at table, the LORD spoke to the prophet who had brought him back, ²¹ and he cried out to the man of God who had come from Judah: "The LORD says, 'Because you rebelled against the command of the LORD and did not keep the command which the LORD, your God, gave you, ²² but returned and ate bread and drank water in the place where he told you to do neither, your corpse shall not be brought to the grave of your ancestors.' "

²³ After he had eaten bread and drunk water, the ass was saddled for him, and he again ²⁴ set out. But a lion met him on the road, and killed him. His corpse lay sprawled on the road, and the ass remained standing by it, and so did the lion. ²⁵ Some passers-by saw the body lying in the road, with the lion standing beside it, and carried the news to the city where the old prophet lived. ²⁶ On hearing it, the prophet who had brought him back from his journey said: "It is the man of God who rebelled against the command of the LORD. He has delivered him to a lion, which mangled and killed him, as the LORD predicted to him." ²⁷ Then he said to his sons, "Saddle the ass for me." When they had saddled it, ²⁸ he went off and found the body lying in the road with the ass and the lion standing beside it. The lion had not eaten the body nor had it harmed the ass. ²⁹ The prophet lifted up the body of the man of God and put it on the ass, and brought it back to the city to mourn over it and to bury it. ³⁰ He laid the man's body in his own grave, and they mourned over it: "Alas, my brother!" ³¹ After he had buried him, he said to his sons, "When I die, bury me in the grave where the man of God is buried. Lay my remains beside his. ³² For the word of the LORD which he proclaimed against the altar in Bethel and against all the shrines on the high places in the cities of Samaria shall certainly come to pass."

³³ Jeroboam did not give up his evil ways after this event, but again made priests for the high places from among the common people. Whoever desired it was consecrated and became a priest of the high places. ³⁴ This was a sin on the part of the house of Jeroboam for which it was to be cut off and destroyed from the earth.

Death of Abijah

14 ¹ At that time Abijah, son of Jeroboam, took sick. ²* So Jeroboam said to his wife, "Get ready and disguise yourself so that none will recognize you as Jeroboam's wife. Then go to Shiloh, where you will find the prophet Ahijah. It is he who predicted my reign over this people. ³ Take along ten loaves, some cakes, and a jar of preserves, and go to him. He will tell you what will happen to the child." ⁴ The wife of Jeroboam obeyed. She made the journey to Shiloh and entered the house of Ahijah who could not see because age had dimmed his sight.

⁵ The LORD had said to Ahijah: "Jeroboam's wife is coming to consult you about her son, for he is sick. This is what you must tell her. When she comes, she will be in disguise." ⁶ So Ahijah, hearing the sound of her footsteps as she entered the door, said, "Come in, wife of Jeroboam. Why are you in disguise? I have been commissioned to give you bitter news. ⁷ Go, tell Jeroboam, 'This is what the LORD, the God of Israel, says: I exalted you from among the people and made you ruler of my people Israel. ⁸ I deprived the house of David of the kingdom and gave it to you. Yet you have not been like my servant David, who kept my commandments and followed me with his whole heart, doing only what pleased me. ⁹ You have done worse than all who preceded you: you have gone and made for yourself strange gods and molten images to provoke me; but me you have cast behind your back. ¹⁰* Therefore, I am bringing evil upon the house of Jeroboam: I will cut off every male in Jeroboam's line, whether slave or freeman in Israel, and will burn up the house of Jeroboam completely, as though dung were being burned. ¹¹* When one of Jeroboam's line dies in the city, dogs will devour him; when one of them dies in the field, he will be devoured by the birds of the sky. For the LORD has spoken!' ¹² So leave; go home! As you step inside the city, the child will die, ¹³ and all Israel will mourn him and bury him, for he alone of Jeroboam's line will be laid in the grave, since in him alone of Jeroboam's house has something pleasing to the LORD, the God of Israel, been found. ¹⁴ Today, at this very moment, the LORD will raise up for himself a king of Israel who will destroy the house of Jeroboam. ¹⁵ The LORD will strike Israel like a reed tossed about in the water and will pluck out Israel from this good land which he gave their fathers, scattering them beyond the River, because they made sacred poles for themselves and thus provoked the LORD. ¹⁶ He will give up Israel because of the sins Jeroboam has committed and caused Israel to commit."

¹⁷ So Jeroboam's wife started back; when she reached Tirzah and crossed the threshold of her

---

14, 2: 1 Kgs 11, 29.   14, 11: 1 Kgs 16, 4.
14, 10: 1 Kgs 15, 29.

house, the child died. [18] He was buried with all Israel mourning him, as the LORD had prophesied through his servant the prophet Ahijah.

[19] The rest of the acts of Jeroboam, with his warfare and his reign, are recorded in the book of the chronicles of the kings of Israel. [20] The length of Jeroboam's reign was twenty-two years. He rested with his ancestors, and his son Nadab succeeded him as king.

Reign of Rehoboam

[21]* Rehoboam, son of Solomon, reigned in Judah. He was forty-one years old when he became king, and he reigned seventeen years in Jerusalem, the city in which, out of all the tribes of Israel, the LORD chose to be honored. His mother was the Ammonite named Naamah.

[22] Judah did evil in the sight of the LORD, and by their sins angered him even more than their fathers had done. [23] They, too, built for themselves high places, pillars, and sacred poles, upon every high hill and under every green tree. [24] There were also cult prostitutes in the land. Judah imitated all the abominable practices of the nations whom the LORD had cleared out of the Israelites' way.

[25]† In the fifth year of King Rehoboam, Shishak, king of Egypt, attacked Jerusalem. [26]* He took everything, including the treasures of the temple of the LORD and those of the royal palace, as well as all the gold shields made under Solomon. [27] To replace them, King Rehoboam had bronze shields made, which he entrusted to the officers of the guard on duty at the entrance of the royal palace. [28] Whenever the king visited the temple of the LORD, those on duty would carry the shields, and then return them to the guardroom.

[29] The rest of the acts of Rehoboam, with all that he did, are recorded in the book of the chronicles of the kings of Judah. [30] There was constant warfare between Rehoboam and Jeroboam. [31] Rehoboam rested with his ancestors; he was buried with them in the City of David. His mother was the Ammonite named Naamah. His son Abijam succeeded him as king.

Reign of Abijam

15 [1]* In the eighteenth year of King Jeroboam, son of Nebat, Abijam became king of Judah; [2] he reigned three years in Jerusalem.

His mother's name was Maacah, daughter of Abishalom. [3] He imitated all the sins his father had committed before him, and his heart was not entirely with the LORD, his God, like the heart of his grandfather David. [4] Yet for David's sake the LORD, his God, gave him a lamp in Jerusalem, raising up his son after him and permitting Jerusalem to endure; [5]* because David had pleased the LORD and did not disobey any of his commands as long as he lived, except in the case of Uriah the Hittite.

[7]* The rest of Abijam's acts, with all that he did, are written in the book of the chronicles of the kings of Judah. [6] There was war between Abijam and Jeroboam. [8] Abijam rested with his ancestors; he was buried in the City of David, and his son Asa succeeded him as king.

Reign of Asa

[9] In the twentieth year of Jeroboam, king of Israel, Asa, king of Judah, began to reign; [10] he reigned forty-one years in Jerusalem. His grandmother's name was Maacah, daughter of Abishalom. [11] Asa pleased the LORD like his forefather David, [12] banishing the temple prostitutes from the land and removing all the idols his father had made. [13] He also deposed his grandmother Maacah from her position as queen mother, because she had made an outrageous object for Asherah. Asa cut down this object and burned it in the Kidron Valley. [14] The high places did not disappear; yet Asa's heart was entirely with the LORD as long as he lived. [15] He brought into the temple of the LORD his father's and his own votive offerings of silver, gold, and various utensils.

[16] There was war between Asa and Baasha, king of Israel, as long as they both reigned. [17]* Baasha, king of Israel, attacked Judah and fortified Ramah to prevent communication with Asa, king of Judah. [18]† Asa then took all the silver and gold remaining in the treasuries of the temple of the LORD and of the royal palace. Entrusting them to his ministers, King Asa sent them to Ben-hadad, son of Tabrimmon, son of Hezion, king of Aram, resident in Damascus. He said: [19] "There is a treaty between you and me, as there was between your father and my father. I am sending you a present of silver and gold. Go, break your treaty with Baasha, king of Israel, that he may withdraw from me." [20] Ben-hadad agreed with King Asa and sent the leaders of his

---

14, 25: *In the fifth year . . . Shishak, king of Egypt, attacked Jerusalem:* c. 926 B.C. According to 2 Chr 12, 1–12, the repentance of King Rehoboam and of the princes of Israel after the warning of the prophet Shemaiah diverted the actual attack on Jerusalem. Shishak, however, carried off the treasures of the temple of the Lord and of the king's palace (2 Chr 12, 9). A bas-relief of this Pharaoh in the temple of Aman at Karnak commemorates his conquest of some hundred and fifty Palestinian and Trans-Jordanian cities and towns.

15, 18: *Ben-hadad . . . king of Aram:* Ben-hadad I, third successor of Rezon, who had thrown off the yoke of the Israelites during the reign of Solomon and become king of Aram (11, 23f).

14, 21: 2 Chr 12, 13.	**15, 5:** 2 Sm 11, 4.
14, 26: 1 Kgs 10, 16.	**15, 7:** 2 Chr 13, 2.
15, 1: 2 Chr 13, 1f.	**15, 17:** 2 Chr 16, 1.

troops against the cities of Israel. They attacked Ijon, Dan, Abel-beth-maacah, and all Chinnereth, besides all the land of Naphtali. 21 When Baasha heard of it, he left off fortifying Ramah, and stayed in Tirzah. 22 Then King Asa summoned all Judah without exception, and they carried away the stones and beams with which Baasha was fortifying Ramah. With them King Asa built Geba of Benjamin and Mizpeh.

23 The rest of the acts of Asa, with all his valor and accomplishments, and the cities he built, are written in the book of the chronicles of the kings of Judah. In his old age, Asa had an infirmity in his feet. 24* He rested with his ancestors; he was buried in his forefather's City of David, and his son Jehoshaphat succeeded him as king.

Reign of Nadab

25 In the second year of Asa, king of Judah, Nadab, son of Jeroboam, became king of Israel; he reigned over Israel two years. 26 He did evil in the LORD's sight, imitating his father's conduct and the sin which he had caused Israel to commit. 27 Baasha, son of Ahijah, of the house of Issachar, plotted against him and struck him down at Gibbethon of the Philistines, which Nadab and all Israel were besieging. 28 Baasha killed him in the third year of Asa, king of Judah, and reigned in his stead. 29* Once he was king, he killed off the entire house of Jeroboam, not leaving a single soul to Jeroboam but destroying him utterly, according to the warning which the LORD had pronounced through his servant, Ahijah the Shilonite, 30 because of the sins Jeroboam committed and caused Israel to commit, by which he provoked the LORD, the God of Israel, to anger.

31 The rest of the acts of Nadab, with all that he did, are written in the book of the chronicles of the kings of Israel. 32 [There was war between Asa and Baasha, king of Israel, as long as they lived.]

Reign of Baasha

33 In the third year of Asa, king of Judah, Baasha, son of Ahijah, began his twenty-four-year reign over Israel in Tirzah. 34 He did evil in the LORD's sight, imitating the conduct of Jeroboam and the sin he had caused Israel to commit.

16 1 The LORD spoke against Baasha to Jehu, son of Hanani, and said: 2 "Inasmuch as I lifted you up from the dust and made you ruler of my people Israel, but you have imitated the conduct of Jeroboam and have caused my people Israel to sin, provoking me to anger by their sins, 3* I will

destroy you, Baasha, and your house; 4* I will make your house like that of Jeroboam, son of Nebat. If anyone of Baasha's line dies in the city, dogs shall devour him; if he dies in the field, he shall be devoured by the birds of the sky."

5* The rest of the acts of Baasha, with all his valor and accomplishments, are written in the book of the chronicles of the kings of Israel. 6 Baasha rested with his ancestors; he was buried in Tirzah, and his son Elah succeeded him as king. 7 [Through the prophet Jehu, son of Hanani, the LORD had threatened Baasha and his house, because of all the evil Baasha did in the sight of the LORD, provoking him to anger by his evil deeds, so that he became like the house of Jeroboam; and because he killed Nadab.]

Reign of Elah

8 In the twenty-sixth year of Asa, king of Judah, Elah, son of Baasha, began his two-year reign over Israel in Tirzah. 9 His servant Zimri, commander of half his chariots, plotted against him. As he was in Tirzah, drinking to excess in the house of Arza, superintendent of his palace in Tirzah, 10* Zimri entered; he struck and killed him in the twenty-seventh year of Asa, king of Judah, and reigned in his place. 11 Once he was seated on the royal throne, he killed off the whole house of Baasha, not sparing a single male relative or friend of his. 12 Zimri destroyed the entire house of Baasha, as the LORD had prophesied to Baasha through the prophet Jehu, 13 because of all the sins which Baasha and his son Elah committed and caused Israel to commit, provoking the LORD, the God of Israel, to anger by their idols.

14 The rest of the acts of Elah, with all that he did, are written in the book of the chronicles of the kings of Israel.

Reign of Zimri

15 In the twenty-seventh year of Asa, king of Judah, Zimri reigned seven days in Tirzah. The army was besieging Gibbethon of the Philistines 16 when they heard that Zimri had formed a conspiracy and had killed the king. So that day in the camp all Israel proclaimed Omri, general of the army, king of Israel. 17 Omri marched up from Gibbethon, accompanied by all Israel, and laid siege to Tirzah. 18 When Zimri saw the city was captured, he entered the citadel of the royal palace and burned down the palace over him. He died 19 because of the sins he had committed, doing evil in the sight of the LORD by imitating the sinful conduct of Jeroboam, thus causing Israel to sin.

15, 24: 2 Chr 17, 1.   16, 3: 1 Kgs 21, 22.   16, 5: 2 Chr 16, 1.   16, 10: 2 Kgs 9, 31.
15, 29: 1 Kgs 14, 10; 21, 22.   16, 4: 1 Kgs 14, 11.

²⁰ The rest of the acts of Zimri, with the conspiracy he carried out, are written in the book of the chronicles of the kings of Israel.

²¹ At that time the people of Israel were divided, half following Tibni, son of Ginath, to make him king, and half for Omri. ²² The partisans of Omri prevailed over those of Tibni, son of Ginath. Tibni died and Omri became king.

Reign of Omri

²³ In the thirty-first year of Asa, king of Judah, Omri became king; he reigned over Israel twelve years, the first six of them in Tirzah. ²⁴ He then bought the hill of Samaria from Shemer for two silver talents and built upon the hill, naming the city he built Samaria after Shemer, the former owner. ²⁵ But Omri did evil in the LORD's sight beyond any of his predecessors. ²⁶ He closely imitated the sinful conduct of Jeroboam, son of Nebat, causing Israel to sin and to provoke the LORD, the God of Israel, to anger by their idols.

²⁷ The rest of the acts of Omri, with all his valor and accomplishments, are written in the book of the chronicles of the kings of Israel. ²⁸ Omri rested with his ancestors; he was buried in Samaria, and his son Ahab succeeded him as king.

Reign of Ahab

²⁹ In the thirty-eighth year of Asa, king of Judah, Ahab, son of Omri, became king of Israel; he reigned over Israel in Samaria for twenty-two years. ³⁰ Ahab, son of Omri, did evil in the sight of the LORD more than any of his predecessors. ³¹ It was not enough for him to imitate the sins of Jeroboam, son of Nebat. He even married Jezebel, daughter of Ethbaal, king of the Sidonians, and went over to the veneration and worship of Baal. ³² Ahab erected an altar to Baal in the temple of Baal which he built in Samaria, ³³ and also made a sacred pole. He did more to anger the LORD, the God of Israel, than any of the kings of Israel before him.

³⁴* During his reign, Hiel from Bethel rebuilt Jericho. He lost his first-born son, Abiram, when he laid the foundation, and his youngest son, Segub, when he set up the gates, as the LORD had foretold through Joshua, son of Nun.

III: Stories of the Prophets

Drought Predicted by Elijah

17 ¹*† Elijah the Tishbite, from Tishbe in Gilead, said to Ahab: "As the LORD, the God of Israel, lives, whom I serve, during these years there shall be no dew or rain except at my word." ² The LORD then said to Elijah: ³ "Leave here, go east and hide in the Wadi Cherith, east of the Jordan. ⁴ You shall drink of the stream, and I have commanded ravens to feed you there." ⁵ So he left and did as the LORD had commanded. He went and remained by the Wadi Cherith, east of the Jordan. ⁶ Ravens brought him bread and meat in the morning, and bread and meat in the evening, and he drank from the stream.

Elijah and the Widow

⁷ After some time, however, the brook ran dry, because no rain had fallen in the land. ⁸ So the LORD said to him: ⁹ "Move on to Zarephath of Sidon and stay there. I have designated a widow there to provide for you." ¹⁰* He left and went to Zarephath. As he arrived at the entrance of the city, a widow was gathering sticks there; he called out to her, "Please bring me a small cupful of water to drink." ¹¹ She left to get it, and he called out after her, "Please bring along a bit of bread." ¹² "As the LORD, your God, lives," she answered, "I have nothing baked; there is only a handful of flour in my jar and a little oil in my jug. Just now I was collecting a couple of sticks, to go in and prepare something for myself and my son; when we have eaten it, we shall die." ¹³ "Do not be afraid," Elijah said to her. "Go and do as you propose. But first make me a little cake and bring it to me. Then you can prepare something for yourself and your son. ¹⁴ For the LORD, the God of Israel, says, 'The jar of flour shall not go empty, nor the jug of oil run dry, until the day when the LORD sends rain upon the earth.' " ¹⁵ She left and did as Elijah had said. She was able to eat for a year, and he and her son as well; ¹⁶ the jar of flour did not go empty, nor the jug of oil run dry, as the LORD had foretold through Elijah.

¹⁷ Some time later the son of the mistress of the house fell sick, and his sickness grew more severe until he stopped breathing. ¹⁸ So she said to Elijah, "Why have you done this to me, O man of God? Have you come to me to call attention to my guilt

---

17, 1: *Elijah the Tishbite:* one of the most important figures in Old Testament history. As his name indicates ("Yahweh is my God"), Elijah was the successful leader in the struggle to preserve the knowledge and worship of Yahweh against the encroaching worship of Baal introduced into Israel by Jezebel, the Tyrian wife of Ahab. The Elijah cycle of narratives includes, besides the above struggle, miracle stories, denunciations of kings, and a preparation for the

prophet's role as eschatological forerunner of the "great day of the Lord"; cf Mal 3, 23–24; Mt 17, 10–13; Lk 1, 17.

16, 34: Jos 6, 26. **17, 10:** Lk 4, 26.
17, 1: Sir 48, 3; Jas 5, 17.

and to kill my son?" ¹⁹ "Give me your son," Elijah said to her. Taking him from her lap, he carried him to the upper room where he was staying, and laid him on his own bed. ²⁰ He called out to the LORD: "O LORD, my God, will you afflict even the widow with whom I am staying by killing her son?" ²¹ Then he stretched himself out upon the child three times and called out to the LORD: "O LORD, my God, let the life breath return to the body of this child." ²² The LORD heard the prayer of Elijah; the life breath returned to the child's body and he revived. ²³ Taking the child, Elijah brought him down into the house from the upper room and gave him to his mother. "See!" Elijah said to her, "your son is alive." ²⁴ "Now indeed I know that you are a man of God," the woman replied to Elijah. "The word of the LORD comes truly from your mouth."

Elijah and the Prophets of Baal

18 ¹ Long afterward, in the third year, the LORD spoke to Elijah. "Go, present yourself to Ahab," he said, "that I may send rain upon the earth." ² So Elijah went to present himself to Ahab.

³ Now the famine in Samaria was bitter, ⁴ and Ahab had summoned Obadiah, his vizier, who was a zealous follower of the LORD. When Jezebel was murdering the prophets of the LORD, Obadiah took a hundred prophets, hid them away fifty each in two caves, and supplied them with food and drink. ⁵ Ahab said to Obadiah, "Come, let us go through the land to all sources of water and to all the streams. We may find grass and save the horses and mules, so that we shall not have to slaughter any of the beasts." ⁶ Dividing the land to explore between them, Ahab went one way by himself, Obadiah another way by himself.

⁷ As Obadiah was on his way, Elijah met him. Recognizing him, Obadiah fell prostrate and asked, "Is it you, my lord Elijah?" ⁸ "Yes," he answered. "Go tell your master, 'Elijah is here!' " ⁹ But Obadiah said, "What sin have I committed, that you are handing me over to Ahab to have me killed? ¹⁰ As the LORD, your God, lives, there is no nation or kingdom where my master has not sent in search of you. When they replied, 'He is not here,' he made each kingdom and nation swear they could not find you. ¹¹ And now you say, 'Go tell your master: Elijah is here!' ¹² After I leave you, the spirit of the LORD will carry you to some place I do not know, and when I go to inform Ahab and he does not find you, he will kill me. Your servant has revered the LORD from his youth. ¹³ Have you not been told, my lord, what I did when Jezebel was murdering

Introducing ▶ ELIJAH AND ELISHA

You didn't want to mess with Elijah and Elisha. They were take-no-prisoners kinds of prophets. According to I Kings, Elijah has 450 prophets of Baal killed after publicly humiliating them (18, 40). And when a bunch of boys call Elisha "baldy," they are attacked by bears (2 Kgs 2, 23–24).

Elijah, whose name means "Yahweh is my God," shows up in the second half of I Kings reminding the Israelites that God is their God alone, and that keeping God's Covenant means not worshiping the Canaanite baals (gods). In a dramatic story, he shows the idol-worshiping King Ahab and Queen Jezebel that God is superior to their false gods (I Kgs 18, 21–40).

Elijah was recorded as being carried to heaven in a fiery chariot (2 Kgs 2, 11) as a sign of his greatness, and he was expected to reappear before the "day of the LORD" arrived (Mal 3, 23). By New Testament times, Elijah had come to represent the prophets as Moses had come to represent the Law. Referring to Moses and Elijah was a way of summarizing everything that God had revealed before Christ.

Elisha was Elijah's disciple and successor. He plays an important role in the first half of 2 Kings. Elisha's name means "God is salvation." He was a man of wisdom and a miracle worker.

These "tough guys" also had tender hearts. Both miraculously multiplied food for widows (I Kgs 17, 16; 2 Kgs 4, 5), and both brought a dead child back to life (I Kgs 17, 22; 2 Kgs 4, 34). Elijah and Elisha are revered both for their uncompromising faith and their compassion for the "little ones."

the prophets of the LORD—that I hid a hundred of the prophets of the LORD, fifty each in two caves, and supplied them with food and drink? ¹⁴ And now you say, 'Go tell your master: Elijah is here!' He will kill me!" ¹⁵ Elijah answered, "As the LORD of hosts lives, whom I serve, I will present myself to him today."

¹⁶ So Obadiah went to meet Ahab and informed him. Ahab came to meet Elijah, ¹⁷ and when he saw Elijah, said to him, "Is it you, you disturber of Israel?" ¹⁸ "It is not I who disturb Israel," he answered, "but you and your family, by forsaking the commands of the LORD and following the Baals. ¹⁹ Now summon all Israel to me on Mount Carmel, as well as the four hundred and fifty prophets of Baal and the four hundred prophets of Asherah who eat at Jezebel's table." ²⁰ So Ahab sent to all the Israelites and had the prophets assemble on Mount Carmel.

²¹ Elijah appealed to all the people and said, "How long will you straddle the issue? If the LORD is God, follow him; if Baal, follow him." The people, however, did not answer him. ²² So Elijah said to the people, "I am the only surviving prophet of the LORD, and there are four hundred and fifty prophets of Baal. ²³ Give us two young bulls. Let them choose one, cut it into pieces, and place it on the wood, but start no fire. I shall prepare the other and place it on the wood, but shall start no fire. ²⁴ You shall call on the name of your gods, and I will call on the name of the LORD. The God who answers with fire is God." All the people answered, "Agreed!"

²⁵ Elijah then said to the prophets of Baal, "Choose one young bull and prepare it first, for there are more of you. Call upon your gods, but do not start the fire." ²⁶ Taking the young bull that was turned over to them, they prepared it and called on Baal from morning to noon, saying, "Answer us, Baal!" But there was no sound, and no one answering. And they hopped around the altar they had prepared. ²⁷ When it was noon, Elijah taunted them: "Call louder, for he is a god and may be meditating, or may have retired, or may be on a journey. Perhaps he is asleep and must be awakened." ²⁸ They called out louder and slashed themselves with swords and spears, as was their custom, until blood gushed over them. ²⁹ Noon passed and they remained in a prophetic state until the time for offering sacrifice. But there was not a sound; no one answered, and no one was listening.

³⁰ Then Elijah said to all the people, "Come here to me." When they had done so, he repaired the altar of the LORD which had been destroyed. ³¹ He took twelve stones, for the number of tribes of the sons of Jacob, to whom the LORD had said, "Your name shall be Israel." ³² He built an altar in honor of the LORD with the stones, and made a trench around the altar large enough for two seahs of grain. ³³ When he had arranged the wood, he cut up the young bull and laid it on the wood. ³⁴ "Fill four jars with water," he said, "and pour it over the holocaust and over the wood." "Do it again," he said, and they did it again. "Do it a third time," he said, and they did it a third time. ³⁵ The water flowed around the altar, and the trench was filled with the water.

³⁶ At the time for offering sacrifice, the prophet Elijah came forward and said, "LORD, God of Abraham, Isaac, and Israel, let it be known this day that you are God in Israel and that I am your servant and have done all these things by your command. ³⁷ Answer me, LORD! Answer me, that this people may know that you, LORD, are God and that you have brought them back to their senses." ³⁸ The LORD's fire came down and consumed the holocaust, wood, stones, and dust, and it lapped up the water in the trench. ³⁹ Seeing this, all the people fell prostrate and said, "The LORD is God! The LORD is God!" ⁴⁰ Then Elijah said to them, "Seize the prophets of Baal. Let none of them escape!" They were seized, and Elijah had them brought down to the brook Kishon and there he slit their throats.

⁴¹ Elijah then said to Ahab, "Go up, eat and drink, for there is the sound of a heavy rain." ⁴² So Ahab went up to eat and drink, while Elijah climbed to the top of Carmel, crouched down to the earth, and put his head between his knees. ⁴³ "Climb up and look out to sea," he directed his servant, who went up and looked, but reported, "There is nothing." Seven times he said, "Go, look again!" ⁴⁴ And the seventh time the youth reported, "There is a cloud as small as a man's hand rising from the sea." Elijah said, "Go and say to Ahab, 'Harness up and leave the mountain before the rain stops you.'" ⁴⁵ In a trice, the sky grew dark with clouds and wind, and a heavy rain fell. Ahab mounted his chariot and made for Jezreel. ⁴⁶ But the hand of the LORD was on Elijah, who girded up his clothing and ran before Ahab as far as the approaches to Jezreel.

Flight to Horeb

19 ¹ Ahab told Jezebel all that Elijah had done—that he had put all the prophets to the sword. ² Jezebel then sent a messenger to Elijah and said, "May the gods do thus and so to me if by this time tomorrow I have not done with your life what was done to each of them." ³ Elijah was afraid and fled for his life, going to Beer-sheba of Judah. He left his servant there ⁴ and went a day's journey into the desert, until he came to a broom tree and sat beneath it. He prayed for death: "This is enough, O LORD! Take my life, for I am no better than my fathers." ⁵ He lay down and fell asleep under the broom tree, but then an angel touched him and ordered him to get up and eat. [6] He looked and there at his head was a hearth cake and a jug of water. After he ate and drank, he lay down again, [7] but the angel of the LORD came back a second time, touched him, and ordered, "Get up and eat, else the journey will be too long for you!" [8] He got up, ate and drank; then strengthened by that food, he walked forty days and forty nights to the mountain of God, Horeb.

[9] There he came to a cave, where he took shelter. But the word of the LORD came to him, "Why are you here, Elijah?" [10] He answered: "I have been most zealous for the LORD, the God of hosts, but the Israelites have forsaken your covenant, torn down your altars, and put your prophets to the sword. I alone am left, and they seek to take my life." [11]† Then the LORD said, "Go outside and stand on the mountain before the LORD; the LORD will be passing by." A strong and heavy wind was rending the mountains and crushing rocks before the LORD—but the LORD was not in the wind. After the wind there was an earthquake—but the LORD was not in the earthquake. [12] After the earthquake there was fire—but the LORD was not in the fire. After the fire there was a tiny whispering sound. [13] When he heard this, Elijah hid his face in his cloak and went and stood at the entrance of the cave. A voice said to him, "Elijah, why are you here?" [14]* He replied, "I have been most zealous for the LORD, the God of hosts. But the Israelites have forsaken your covenant, torn down your altars, and put your prophets to the sword. I alone am left, and they seek to take my life." [15]† "Go, take the road back to the desert near Damascus," the LORD said to him. "When you arrive, you shall anoint Hazael as king of Aram. [16]* Then you shall anoint Jehu, son of Nimshi, as king of Israel, and Elisha, son of Shaphat of Abel-meholah, as prophet to succeed you. [17] If anyone escapes the sword of Hazael, Jehu will kill him. If he escapes the sword of Jehu, Elisha will kill him. [18]* Yet I will leave seven thousand men in Israel—all those who have not knelt to Baal or kissed him."

Call of Elisha

[19]† Elijah set out, and came upon Elisha, son of Shaphat, as he was plowing with twelve yoke of oxen; he was following the twelfth. Elijah went over

---

Looking for God

Elijah was told to meet God on the mountain. God's presence could have been in fire, an earthquake, a great wind, but God was in none of these. God was in the tiny whispering sound.

All of us have a need for God. We might not know it, but it is there: a God-shaped hole in our soul that no one and nothing else can fill. Without God, we will always feel empty.

Sometimes, we look for loud and spectacular things to fill that empty space. We buy expensive clothing or toys. Or we smoke cigarettes, drink alcohol, use other illegal drugs, or have sex without commitment. And we still feel empty.

The irony is that through all this, God is there, in the quiet depths of our heart. We need to be like Elijah—tuning out things that are not God and tuning in to God's presence. Taking quiet time to think and pray is a great start.

▶ 1 Kgs 19, 9–13

---

to him and threw his cloak over him. [20] Elisha left the oxen, ran after Elijah, and said, "Please, let me kiss my father and mother goodbye, and I will follow you." "Go back!" Elijah answered. "Have I done anything to you?" [21] Elisha left him and, taking the yoke of oxen, slaughtered them; he used the plowing equipment for fuel to boil their flesh, and gave it to his people to eat. Then he left and followed Elijah as his attendant.

Ahab's Victories over Ben-hadad

20 [1] Ben-hadad, king of Aram, gathered all his forces, and accompanied by thirty-two kings with horses and chariotry, proceeded to invest and attack Samaria. [2] He sent couriers to

---

19, 11ff: Compare these divine manifestations to Elijah with those to Moses (Ex 19, 1–23; 33, 21ff; 34, 5) on the same Mount Horeb (Sinai) (Dt 4, 10–15). Though various phenomena, such as wind, storms, earthquakes, fire (Ex 19, 18f), herald the divine presence, they do not constitute the presence itself which, like the tiny whispering sound, is imperceptible and bespeaks the spirituality of God. It was fitting that Elijah, whose mission it was to reestablish the covenant and restore the pure faith, should have returned to Horeb where the covenant was revealed to Moses and through him to the Israelite people (Ex 3, 1–4.17; 33, 18—34, 9). Moses and Elijah appeared with Christ at the time of his transfiguration (Mt 17, 1–9; Mk 9, 1–7; Lk 9, 28–36).

19, 15–17: Elijah himself carried out only the third of the commissions entrusted to him (vv 19–21); Elisha was deputed to perform the first in person (2 Kgs 8, 7–19), and the second through one of his followers (2 Kgs 9, 1–10).
19, 19–21: Elijah's act of throwing his mantle over the shoulders of Elisha expressed the divine call to share the prophetic mission. Elisha's prompt response through destruction of his plow and oxen is an example of total obedience and detachment from his former manner of living in order to promote the glory of God.

19, 14: Rom 11, 3.   19, 18: Rom 11, 4.
19, 16: 2 Kgs 9, 2.

Ahab, king of Israel, within the city, ³ and said to him, "This is Ben-hadad's message: 'Your silver and gold are mine, and your wives and your promising sons are mine.' " ⁴ The king of Israel answered, "As you say, my lord king, I and all I have are yours." ⁵ But the couriers came again and said, "This is Ben-hadad's message: 'I sent you word to give me your silver and gold, your wives and your sons. ⁶ Now, however, at this time tomorrow I will send my servants to you, and they shall ransack your house and the houses of your servants. They shall seize and take away whatever they consider valuable.' "

⁷ The king of Israel then summoned all the elders of the land and said: "Understand clearly that this man wants to ruin us. When he sent to me for my wives and sons, my silver and my gold, I did not refuse him." ⁸ All the elders and all the people said to him, "Do not listen. Do not give in." ⁹ Accordingly he directed the couriers of Ben-hadad, "Say to my lord the king, 'I will do all that you demanded of your servant the first time. But this I cannot do.' " The couriers left and reported this. ¹⁰ Ben-hadad then sent him the message, "May the gods do thus and so to me if there is enough dust in Samaria to make handfuls for all my followers." ¹¹ The king of Israel replied, "Tell him, 'It is not for the man who is buckling his armor to boast as though he were taking it off.' " ¹² Ben-hadad was drinking in the pavilions with the kings when he heard this reply. "Prepare the assault," he commanded his servants; and they made ready to storm the city.

¹³ Then a prophet came up to Ahab, king of Israel, and said: "The LORD says, 'Do you see all this huge army? When I deliver it up to you today, you will know that I am the LORD.' " ¹⁴ But Ahab asked, "Through whom will it be delivered up?" He answered, "The LORD says, 'Through the retainers of the governors of the provinces.' " Then Ahab asked, "Who is to attack?" He replied, "You are." ¹⁵ So Ahab called up the retainers of the governors of the provinces, two hundred thirty-two of them. Behind them he mustered all the Israelite soldiery, who numbered seven thousand. ¹⁶ They marched out at noon, while Ben-hadad was drinking heavily in the pavilions with the thirty-two kings who were his allies. ¹⁷ When the retainers of the governors of the provinces marched out first, Ben-hadad received word that some men had marched out of Samaria. ¹⁸ He answered, "Whether they have come out for peace or for war, in any case take them alive." ¹⁹ But when these had come out of the city—the soldiers of the governors of the provinces with the army following them— ²⁰ each of them struck down his man. The Arameans fled with Israel pursuing them,

while Ben-hadad, king of Aram, escaped on a chariot steed. ²¹ The king of Israel went out, took the horses and chariots, and inflicted a severe defeat on Aram.

²²† Then the prophet went up to the king of Israel and said to him: "Go, regroup your forces. Mark well what you do, for at the beginning of the year the king of Aram will attack you." ²³ On the other hand, the servants of the king of Aram said to him: "Their gods are gods of mountains. That is why they defeated us. But if we fight them on level ground, we shall be sure to defeat them. ²⁴ This is what you must do: Take the kings from their posts and put prefects in their places. ²⁵ Mobilize an army as large as the army that has deserted you, horse for horse, chariot for chariot. Let us fight them on level ground, and we shall surely defeat them." He took their advice and did this.

²⁶ At the beginning of the year, Ben-hadad mobilized Aram and went up to Aphek to fight against Israel. ²⁷ The Israelites, too, were called to arms and supplied with provisions; then they went out to engage the foe. The Israelites, encamped opposite them, seemed like a couple of small flocks of goats, while Aram covered the countryside. ²⁸ A man of God came up and said to the king of Israel: "The LORD says, 'Because Aram has said the LORD is a god of mountains, not a god of plains, I will deliver up to you all this large army, that you may know I am the LORD.' " ²⁹ They were encamped opposite each other for seven days. On the seventh day battle was joined, and the Israelites struck down one hundred thousand foot soldiers of Aram in one day. ³⁰ The survivors, twenty-seven thousand of them, fled into the city of Aphek, and there the wall collapsed. Ben-hadad, too, fled, and took refuge within the city, in an inside room.

³¹ His servants said to him: "We have heard that the kings of the land of Israel are merciful kings. Allow us, therefore, to garb ourselves in sackcloth, with cords around our heads, and go out to the king of Israel. Perhaps he will spare your life." ³² So they dressed in sackcloth girded at the waist, and wearing cords around their heads, they went to the king of Israel. "Your servant Ben-hadad pleads for his life," they said. "Is he still alive?" the king asked. "He is my brother." ³³ Hearing this as a good omen, the men quickly took him at his word and said, "Ben-hadad is your brother." He answered, "Go and get him." When Ben-hadad came out to him, the king had him mount his chariot. ³⁴ Ben-hadad said to him, "I will restore the cities which my father took from your father, and you may make yourself bazaars in Damascus, as my father did in Samaria." "On these

---

20, 22: *At the beginning of the year:* in the spring.

terms," Ahab replied, "I will set you free." So he made an agreement with him and then set him free.

³⁵ One of the guild prophets was prompted by the LORD to say to his companion, "Strike me." But he refused to strike him. ³⁶ Then he said to him, "Since you did not obey the voice of the LORD, a lion will kill you when you leave me." When they parted company, a lion came upon him and killed him. ³⁷ The prophet met another man and said, "Strike me." The man struck him a blow and wounded him. ³⁸ The prophet went on and waited for the king on the road, having disguised himself with a bandage over his eyes. ³⁹ As the king was passing, he called out to the king and said, "Your servant went into the thick of the battle, and suddenly someone turned and brought me a man and said, 'Guard this man. If he is missing, you shall have to pay for his life with your life or pay out a talent of silver.' ⁴⁰ But while your servant was looking here and there, the man disappeared." The king of Israel said to him, "That is your sentence. You have decided it yourself." ⁴¹ He immediately removed the bandage from his eyes, and the king of Israel recognized him as one of the prophets. ⁴²* He said to him: "The LORD says, 'Because you have set free the man I doomed to destruction, your life shall pay for his life, your people for his people.' " Disturbed and angry, the king of Israel went off homeward and entered Samaria.

Seizure of Naboth's Vineyard

21 ¹ Some time after this, as Naboth the Jezreelite had a vineyard in Jezreel next to the palace of Ahab, king of Samaria, ² Ahab said to Naboth, "Give me your vineyard to be my vegetable garden, since it is close by, next to my house. I will give you a better vineyard in exchange, or, if you prefer, I will give you its value in money." ³ "The LORD forbid," Naboth answered him, "that I should give you my ancestral heritage." ⁴ Ahab went home disturbed and angry at the answer Naboth the Jezreelite had made to him: "I will not give you my ancestral heritage." Lying down on his bed, he turned away from food and would not eat.

⁵ His wife Jezebel came to him and said to him, "Why are you so angry that you will not eat?" ⁶ He answered her, "Because I spoke to Naboth the Jezreelite and said to him, 'Sell me your vineyard, or, if you prefer, I will give you a vineyard in ex-

change.' But he refused to let me have his vineyard." ⁷ "A fine ruler over Israel you are indeed!" his wife Jezebel said to him. "Get up. Eat and be cheerful. I will obtain the vineyard of Naboth the Jezreelite for you."

⁸ So she wrote letters in Ahab's name and, having sealed them with his seal, sent them to the elders and to the nobles who lived in the same city with Naboth. ⁹ This is what she wrote in the letters: "Proclaim a fast and set Naboth at the head of the people. ¹⁰ Next, get two scoundrels to face him and accuse him of having cursed God and king. Then take him out and stone him to death." ¹¹ His fellow citizens—the elders and the nobles who dwelt in his city—did as Jezebel had ordered them in writing, through the letters she had sent them. ¹² They proclaimed a fast and placed Naboth at the head of the people. ¹³ Two scoundrels came in and confronted him with the accusation, "Naboth has cursed God and king." And they led him out of the city and stoned him to death. ¹⁴ Then they sent the information to Jezebel that Naboth had been stoned to death.

¹⁵ When Jezebel learned that Naboth had been stoned to death, she said to Ahab, "Go on, take possession of the vineyard of Naboth the Jezreelite which he refused to sell you, because Naboth is not alive, but dead." ¹⁶ On hearing that Naboth was dead, Ahab started off on his way down to the vineyard of Naboth the Jezreelite, to take possession of it.

¹⁷ But the LORD said to Elijah the Tishbite: ¹⁸ "Start down to meet Ahab, king of Israel, who rules in Samaria. He will be in the vineyard of Naboth, of which he has come to take possession. ¹⁹*† This is what you shall tell him, 'The LORD says: After murdering, do you also take possession? For this, the LORD says: In the place where the dogs licked up the blood of Naboth, the dogs shall lick up your blood, too.' " ²⁰† "Have you found me out, my enemy?" Ahab said to Elijah. "Yes," he answered. "Because you have given yourself up to doing evil in the LORD'S sight, ²¹* I am bringing evil upon you: I will destroy you and will cut off every male in Ahab's line, whether slave or freeman, in Israel. ²²* I will make your house like that of Jeroboam, son of Nebat, and like that of Baasha, son of Ahijah, because of how you have provoked me by leading Israel into sin." ²³* (Against Jezebel, too,

---

† **21, 19:** The response of Ahab to this divine judgment is described in v 27, and the consequences are given in vv 28–29, and in 2 Kgs 9, 21–26.

21, 20–26: In these verses the Judean editor of the Books of Kings substitutes, for the message of Elijah prepared for in v 19, a sweeping and definitive judgment against the whole family of Ahab in the same terms as were used against the families of Jeroboam I (1 Kgs 14, 9–11) and Baasha (1 Kgs 16, 2–4). This judgment is the fruit of later theological reflection; it is not occasioned directly by the crime

against Naboth, but by the idolatry of Ahab and Jezebel. The judgment on Jezebel herself (v 23) may have been uttered by Elijah during the Naboth episode; it finds its fulfillment in 2 Kgs 9, 36–37. Still another theological explanation for the death of Ahab is given by the north Israelite writer of 1 Kgs 20, 35–42 above.

20, 42: 1 Kgs 22, 35.   21, 22: 1 Kgs 15, 29; 16, 3.
21, 19: 1 Kgs 22, 38.   21, 23: 2 Kgs 9, 36.
21, 21: 2 Kgs 9, 8.

the LORD declared, "The dogs shall devour Jezebel in the district of Jezreel.") 24 "When one of Ahab's line dies in the city, dogs will devour him; when one of them dies in the field, the birds of the sky will devour him." 25 Indeed, no one gave himself up to the doing of evil in the sight of the LORD as did Ahab, urged on by his wife Jezebel. 26 He became completely abominable by following idols, just as the Amorites had done, whom the LORD drove out before the Israelites.

27 When Ahab heard these words, he tore his garments and put on sackcloth over his bare flesh. He fasted, slept in the sackcloth, and went about subdued. 28 Then the LORD said to Elijah the Tishbite, 29* "Have you seen that Ahab has humbled himself before me? Since he has humbled himself before me, I will not bring the evil in his time. I will bring the evil upon his house during the reign of his son."

Campaign against Ramoth-gilead

22 1* Three years passed without war between Aram and Israel. 2 In the third year, however, King Jehoshaphat of Judah came down to the king of Israel, 3 who said to his servants, "Do you not know that Ramoth-gilead is ours and we are doing nothing to take it from the king of Aram?" 4 He asked Jehoshaphat, "Will you come with me to fight against Ramoth-gilead?" Jehoshaphat answered the king of Israel, "You and I are as one, and your people and my people, your horses and my horses as well." 5 Jehoshaphat also said to the king of Israel, "Seek the word of the LORD at once."

6 The king of Israel gathered together the prophets, about four hundred of them, and asked, "Shall I go to attack Ramoth-gilead or shall I refrain?" "Go up," they answered. "The LORD will deliver it over to the king." 7 But Jehoshaphat said, "Is there no other prophet of the LORD here whom we may consult?" 8 The king of Israel answered, "There is one other through whom we might consult the LORD, Micaiah, son of Imlah; but I hate him because he prophesies not good but evil about me." Jehoshaphat said, "Let not your majesty speak of evil against you."

9 So the king of Israel called an official and said to him, "Get Micaiah, son of Imlah, at once." 10 The king of Israel and King Jehoshaphat of Judah were seated, each on his throne, clothed in their robes of state on a threshing floor at the entrance of the gate of Samaria, and all the prophets were prophesying

before them. 11 Zedekiah, son of Chenaanah, made himself horns of iron and said, "The LORD says, 'With these you shall gore Aram until you have destroyed them.'" 12 The other prophets prophesied in a similar vein, saying: "Go up to Ramoth-gilead; you shall succeed. The LORD will deliver it over to the king."

13 The messenger who had gone to call Micaiah said to him, "Look now, the prophets are unanimously predicting good for the king. Let your word be the same as any of theirs; predict good." 14 "As the LORD lives," Micaiah answered, "I shall say whatever the LORD tells me."

15 When he came to the king, the king said to him, "Micaiah, shall we go to fight against Ramoth-gilead, or shall we refrain?" "Go up," he answered, "you shall succeed! The LORD will deliver it over to the king." 16 But the king answered him, "How many times must I adjure you to tell me nothing but the truth in the name of the LORD?" 17 So Micaiah said:

> "I see all Israel
> scattered on the mountains,
> like sheep without a shepherd,
> and the LORD saying, 'These have no master!
> Let each of them go back home in peace.'"

18 The king of Israel said to Jehoshaphat, "Did I not tell you he prophesies not good but evil about me?" 19† Micaiah continued: "Therefore hear the word of the LORD: I saw the LORD seated on his throne, with the whole host of heaven standing by to his right and to his left. 20 The LORD asked, 'Who will deceive Ahab, so that he will go up and fall at Ramoth-gilead?' And one said this, another that, 21 until one of the spirits came forth and presented himself to the LORD, saying, 'I will deceive him.' The LORD asked, 'How?' 22 He answered, 'I will go forth and become a lying spirit in the mouths of all his prophets.' The LORD replied, 'You shall succeed in deceiving him. Go forth and do this.' 23 So now, the LORD has put a lying spirit in the mouths of all these prophets of yours, but the LORD himself has decreed evil against you."

24 Thereupon Zedekiah, son of Chenaanah, came up and slapped Micaiah on the cheek, saying, "Has the spirit of the LORD, then, left me to speak with you?" 25 "You shall find out," Micaiah replied, "on that day when you retreat into an inside room to

---

22, 19–23: The prophet Micaiah uses as a last resort to deter Ahab from his foolhardy design of fighting against Ramoth-gilead the literary device of describing false prophets as messengers of a lying spirit which God, after holding counsel with his angels, permits to deceive them.

21, 29: 2 Kgs 9, 26.   22, 1: 2 Chr 18, 1.

hide." ²⁶ The king of Israel then said, "Seize Micaiah and take him back to Amon, prefect of the city, and to Joash, the king's son, ²⁷ and say, 'This is the king's order: Put this man in prison and feed him scanty rations of bread and water until I return in safety.' " ²⁸† But Micaiah said, "If ever you return in safety, the LORD has not spoken through me."

²⁹ The king of Israel and King Jehoshaphat of Judah went up to Ramoth-gilead, ³⁰ and the king of Israel said to Jehoshaphat, "I will disguise myself and go into battle, but you put on your own clothes." So the king of Israel disguised himself and entered the fray. ³¹ In the meantime the king of Aram had given his thirty-two chariot commanders the order, "Do not fight with anyone at all except the king of Israel." ³² When the chariot commanders saw Jehoshaphat, they cried out, "That must be the king of Israel!" and shifted to fight him. But Jehoshaphat shouted his battle cry, ³³ and the chariot commanders, aware that he was not the king of Israel, gave up pursuit of him. ³⁴ Someone, however, drew his bow at random, and hit the king of Israel between the joints of his breastplate. He ordered his charioteer, "Rein about and take me out of the ranks, for I am disabled." ³⁵* The battle grew fierce during the day, and the king, who was propped up in his chariot facing the Arameans, died in the evening. The blood from his wound flowed to the bottom of the chariot. ³⁶ At sunset a cry went through the army, "Every man to his city, every man to his land, ³⁷ for the king is dead!" So they went to Samaria, where they buried the king. ³⁸* When the chariot was washed at the pool of Samaria, the dogs licked up his blood and harlots bathed there, as the LORD had prophesied.

³⁹ The rest of the acts of Ahab, with all that he did, including the ivory palace and all the cities he built, are recorded in the book of the chronicles of the kings of Israel. ⁴⁰ Ahab rested with his ancestors, and his son Ahaziah succeeded him as king.

Reign of Jehoshaphat

⁴¹ Jehoshaphat, son of Asa, began to reign over Judah in the fourth year of Ahab, king of Israel. ⁴² Jehoshaphat was thirty-five years old when he began to reign, and he reigned twenty-five years in Jerusalem. His mother's name was Azubah, daughter of Shilhi. ⁴³ He followed all the ways of his father Asa unswervingly, doing what was right in the LORD'S sight. ⁴⁴ Nevertheless, the high places did not disappear, and the people continued to sacrifice and to burn incense on the high places. ⁴⁵ Jehoshaphat also made peace with the king of Israel. ⁴⁶ The rest of the acts of Jehoshaphat, with his prowess, what he did and how he fought, are recorded in the book of the chronicles of the kings of Judah.

⁴⁷ He removed from the land the rest of the cult prostitutes who had remained in the reign of his father Asa. ⁴⁸ There was no king in Edom, but an appointed regent. ⁴⁹ Jehoshaphat made Tarshish ships to go to Ophir for gold; but in fact the ships did not go, because they were wrecked at Ezion-geber. ⁵⁰ Then Ahaziah, son of Ahab, said to Jehoshaphat, "Let my servants accompany your servants in the ships." But Jehoshaphat would not agree. ⁵¹ Jehoshaphat rested with his ancestors; he was buried in his forefathers' City of David. His son Jehoram succeeded him as king.

Reign of Ahaziah

⁵²† Ahaziah, son of Ahab, began to reign over Israel in Samaria in the seventeenth year of Jehoshaphat, king of Judah; he reigned two years over Israel. ⁵³ He did evil in the sight of the LORD, behaving like his father, his mother, and Jeroboam, son of Nebat, who caused Israel to sin. ⁵⁴ He served and worshiped Baal, thus provoking the LORD, the God of Israel, just as his father had done.

22, 28: A note in the Hebrew text after this verse attributes to Micaiah ben Imlah the first words of the book of a different Micaiah, the minor prophet of Moresheth.

22, 52: *Seventeenth year:* so the present Hebrew text. More consistent with 2 Kgs 1, 17 would be a date in the twenty-fourth year of Jehoshaphat for Ahab's death; see note on 2 Kgs 1, 1.

22, 35: 1 Kgs 20, 42.   **22, 38:** 1 Kgs 21, 19.

2 Kings

Chap. 25

I: The Kingdoms of Israel and Judah

Ahaziah Consults Baalzebub

1 1* After Ahab's death, Moab rebelled against Israel. 2† Ahaziah had fallen through the lattice of his roof terrace at Samaria and had been injured. So he sent out messengers with the instructions: "Go and inquire of Baalzebub, the god of Ekron, whether I shall recover from this injury."

3 Meanwhile, the angel of the LORD said to Elijah the Tishbite: "Go, intercept the messengers of Samaria's king, and ask them, 'Is it because there is no God in Israel that you are going to inquire of Baalzebub, the god of Ekron?' 4 For this, the LORD says: 'You shall not leave the bed upon which you lie; instead, you shall die.' " And with that, Elijah departed. 5 The messengers then returned to Ahaziah, who asked them, "Why have you returned?" 6 "A man came up to us," they answered, "who said to us, 'Go back to the king who sent you and tell him: The LORD says, Is it because there is no God in Israel that you are sending to inquire of Baalzebub,

the god of Ekron? For this you shall not leave the bed upon which you lie; instead, you shall die.' " 7 The king asked them, "What was the man like who came up to you and said these things to you?" 8*† "Wearing a hairy garment," they replied, "with a leather girdle about his loins." "It is Elijah the Tishbite!" he exclaimed.

Death of Two Captains

9 Then the king sent a captain with his company of fifty men after Elijah. The prophet was seated on a hilltop when he found him. "Man of God," he ordered, "the king commands you to come down." 10* "If I am a man of God," Elijah answered the captain, "may fire come down from heaven and consume you and your fifty men." And fire came down from heaven and consumed him and his fifty men. 11 Ahaziah sent another captain with his company of fifty men after Elijah. "Man of God," he called out to Elijah, "the king commands you to come down immediately." 12† "If I am a man of God," Elijah answered him, "May fire come down

---

† **1, 2:** *Baalzebub:* in this form, "Baal of flies." The name in the Hebrew text is a derisive alteration of Baalzebul, "Prince Baal." The best New Testament evidence supports the latter form in Mt 10, 25; Lk 11, 15. Later associations with Aramaic *beeldebaba*, "enemy," gave the ancient name its connotation of "devil."

1, 8: *Hairy garment:* a sign of ascetical and prophetic calling, imitated by John the Baptizer; see Mt 3, 4; Mk 1, 6.

1, 12: *Divine fire:* literally, "fire of God," which in Hebrew sounds quite like man of God. The play on words is the basis for

Elijah's alleged retort. This story was told among the people to enhance the dignity of the prophet and to reflect the power of God whom he served. The mercy which God extends even to the wicked is described in Wis 11, 17—12, 22, and the prophet Elijah was well aware of it (1 Kgs 21, 28f).

*

1, 1: 2 Kgs 3, 4–27.
1, 8: Zec 13, 4.
1, 10: Lv 10, 2; Sir 48, 3f; Lk 9, 54f.

from heaven and consume you and your fifty men."
And divine fire came down from heaven, consuming him and his fifty men.

Death of the King

13 Again, for the third time, Ahaziah sent a captain with his company of fifty men. When the third captain arrived, he fell to his knees before Elijah, pleading with him. "Man of God," he implored him, "let my life and the lives of these fifty men, your servants, count for something in your sight! 14 Already fire has come down from heaven, consuming two captains with their companies of fifty men. But now, let my life mean something to you!" 15 Then the angel of the LORD said to Elijah, "Go down with him; you need not be afraid of him."

16* So Elijah left and went down with him and stated to the king: "Thus says the LORD: 'Because you sent messengers to inquire of Baalzebub, the god of Ekron, you shall not leave the bed upon which you lie; instead you shall die.'"

17† Ahaziah died in fulfillment of the prophecy of the LORD spoken by Elijah. Since he had no son, his brother Joram succeeded him as king, in the second year of Jehoram, son of Jehoshaphat, king of Judah. 18 The rest of the acts of Ahaziah are recorded in the book of chronicles of the kings of Israel.

Elijah and Elisha

2 1† When the LORD was about to take Elijah up to heaven in a whirlwind, he and Elisha were on their way from Gilgal. 2 "Stay here, please," Elijah said to Elisha. "The LORD has sent me on to Bethel." "As the LORD lives, and as you yourself live," Elisha replied, "I will not leave you." So they went down to Bethel, 3 where the guild prophets went out to Elisha and asked him, "Do you know that the LORD will take your master from over you today?" "Yes, I know it," he replied. "Keep still."

4 Then Elijah said to him, "Stay here, please, Elisha, for the LORD has sent me on to Jericho." "As the LORD lives, and as you yourself live," Elisha

ELIJAH, PROPHET OF GOD IN SOLIDARITY WITH THE PEOPLE!

HISPANIC
¡Elías, profeta de Dios en el pueblo, solidaridad con el pueblo!

Elijah was a passionate prophet who read the history of the monarchy (Israel's kings) from the perspective of God. He saw division in the people of Israel. On the one hand were the kings, the noblemen, and the leaders of the army; on the other hand were the peasants, the widows, and the persecuted prophets. The Covenant had been broken. Elijah denounced the unfaithfulness of Queen Jezebel and Kings Ahab and Ahaziah. They had introduced idolatry in the form of the false god Baal, who favored the powerful and allowed injustices.

Elijah's faithfulness to the Covenant and his solidarity with the poor led him to speak against kings and queens, to fight false prophets, and to intervene in national affairs. The powerful rulers wanted to kill him and silence his voice. After his dramatic departure (2 Kgs 2, 11), the people never forgot him; they always expected his return.

■ If you saw today's world through the prism that Elijah used to view the world of his time, what would you see? Who would you support with your words and actions? Who would you challenge?

■ Through your Baptism, you are called to be a prophet. As a prophet, how can you promote justice in society?

---

† **1, 17:** *Joram:* in the Second Book of Kings the name Joram *(yoram),* alternately Jehoram *(yehoram),* appears in numerous passages to designate both the king of Judah, son and successor of Jehoshaphat (848–841 B.C.), and the contemporary king of Israel, son of Ahab (852–841 B.C.). For the convenience of the reader in distinguishing these two kings, the longer form, Jehoram, is used to designate the king of Judah and the shorter form, Joram, to designate the king of Israel. See note on 2 Kgs 3, 1.

2, 1: *Gilgal:* commonly identified with Jiljulieh, about seven miles north of Bethel, and different from the Gilgal in Dt 11, 30 near Shechem, and that in Jos 4 and 5, *passim,* near Jericho.

1, 16: Sir 48, 6.

replied, "I will not leave you." [5] They went on to Jericho, where the guild prophets approached Elisha and asked him, "Do you know that the LORD will take your master from over you today?" "Yes, I know it," he replied. "Keep still."

[6] Elijah said to Elisha, "Please stay here; the LORD has sent me on to the Jordan." "As the LORD lives, and as you yourself live," Elisha replied, "I will not leave you." And so the two went on together. [7] Fifty of the guild prophets followed, and when the two stopped at the Jordan, stood facing them at a distance. [8]* Elijah took his mantle, rolled it up and struck the water, which divided, and both crossed over on dry ground.

Elisha Succeeds Elijah

[9]† When they had crossed over, Elijah said to Elisha, "Ask for whatever I may do for you, before I am taken from you." Elisha answered, "May I receive a double portion of your spirit." [10]* "You have asked something that is not easy," he replied. "Still, if you see me taken up from you, your wish will be granted; otherwise not." [11]* As they walked on conversing, a flaming chariot and flaming horses came between them, and Elijah went up to heaven in a whirlwind. [12]*† When Elisha saw it happen he cried out, "My father! my father! Israel's chariots and drivers!" But when he could no longer see him, Elisha gripped his own garment and tore it in two.

[13]* Then he picked up Elijah's mantle which had fallen from him, and went back and stood at the bank of the Jordan. [14] Wielding the mantle which had fallen from Elijah, he struck the water in his turn and said, "Where is the LORD, the God of Elijah?" When Elisha struck the water it divided and he crossed over.

[15] The guild prophets in Jericho, who were on the other side, saw him and said, "The spirit of Elijah rests on Elisha." They went to meet him, bowing to

the ground before him. [16]* "Among your servants are fifty brave men," they said. "Let them go in search of your master. Perhaps the spirit of the LORD has carried him away to some mountain or some valley." "Do not send them," he answered. [17] However, they kept urging him, until he was embarrassed and said, "Send them." So they sent the fifty men, who searched for three days without finding him. [18] When they returned to Elisha in Jericho, where he was staying, he said to them, "Did I not tell you not to go?"

Healing of the Water

[19] Once the inhabitants of the city complained to Elisha, "The site of the city is fine indeed, as my lord can see, but the water is bad and the land unfruitful." [20] "Bring me a new bowl," Elisha said, "and put salt into it." When they had brought it to him, [21] he went out to the spring and threw salt into it, saying, "Thus says the LORD, 'I have purified this water. Never again shall death or miscarriage spring from it.' " [22] And the water has stayed pure even to this day, just as Elisha prophesied.

The Prophet's Curse

[23]† From there Elisha went up to Bethel. While he was on the way, some small boys came out of the city and jeered at him. "Go up, baldhead," they shouted, "go up, baldhead!" [24] The prophet turned and saw them, and he cursed them in the name of the LORD. Then two she-bears came out of the woods and tore forty-two of the children to pieces.

[25] From there he went to Mount Carmel, and thence he returned to Samaria.

Campaign of Joram against Moab

3 [1]† Joram, son of Ahab, became king of Israel in Samaria [in the eighteenth year of Jehoshaphat, king of Judah, and he reigned for twelve

---

2, 9: *Double portion of your spirit:* as the first-born son inherited a double portion of his father's property (Dt 21, 17), so Elisha asks to inherit from Elijah his spirit of prophecy in the degree befitting his principal disciple. In Nm 11, 17.25, God bestows some of the spirit of Moses on others.

2, 12: *My father:* a religious title accorded prophetic leaders; cf 2 Kgs 6, 21; 8, 9. *Israel's chariots and drivers:* Elijah was worth more than a whole army in defending Israel and the true religion. King Joash of Israel uses the same phrase of Elisha himself (2 Kgs 13, 14).

2, 23f: This story, like the one about Elijah and the captains (ch 1), is preserved for us in Scripture to convey a popular understanding of the dignity of the prophet. Told in popular vein, it becomes a caricature, in which neither Elisha nor the bears behave in character. See note on 2 Kgs 1, 12 and the contrasting narrative in ch 4.

3, 1: The sequence of the reigns between Ahab and Jehu of Israel may be reconstructed as follows: Jehoshaphat of Judah outlived Ahab by a short time, so that Ahaziah of Israel was his contemporary. Jehoram of Judah succeeded his father Jehoshaphat while Ahaziah of Israel was still alive. Jehoram (Joram) of Israel became king, following his brother Ahaziah, in the second year of Jehoram of Judah (2 Kgs 1, 17); this is one datum on which the earliest Greek evidence and the standard Hebrew text are in agreement.

The two Jehorams were contemporary for much of their reigns; Jehoram of Judah was succeeded by Ahaziah something more than a year before Jehu did away with the rulers of both kingdoms (2 Kgs 9, 1–29).

The Moabite campaign of 2 Kgs 3, 4–27 is thus best placed under the two Kings Jehoram, before the Edomite rebellion mentioned in 2 Kgs 8, 20. In the received Hebrew text, Jehoshaphat has been made the Judahite protagonist in the campaign against Moab as a tribute to his piety; this assimilates the story of 2 Kgs 3 to that of 1 Kgs 22, but creates difficulties in the chronology which the extant data leave party unresolved. An older practice for stories of the Israelite kings was to leave them and their fellow kings without identification by name; cf 2 Kgs 6, 8—7, 20. The name of Jehoshaphat has been omitted from a number of places in 2 Kgs 3–8, in this translation; cf 1 Kgs 22, 51.

2, 8: Ex 14, 16.22.　　　　　**2, 12:** 2 Kgs 13, 14; Sir 48,
2, 10: Nm 11, 17.25.　　　　　　9.12.
2, 11: Gn 5, 24; 1 Mc 2, 58;　　**2, 13:** 1 Kgs 19, 19.
　　　Acts 1, 9.　　　　　　　**2, 16:** 1 Kgs 18, 12.

years]. ² He did evil in the LORD'S sight, though not as much as his father and mother. He did away with the pillar of Baal, which his father had made, ³ but he still clung to the sin to which Jeroboam, son of Nebat, had lured Israel; this he did not give up.

⁴ Now Mesha, king of Moab, who raised sheep, used to pay the king of Israel as tribute a hundred thousand lambs and the wool of a hundred thousand rams. ⁵ But when Ahab died, the king of Moab had rebelled against the king of Israel. ⁶ Joram as king mustered all Israel, and when he set out on a campaign from Samaria, ⁷* he sent the king of Judah the message: "The king of Moab is in rebellion against me. Will you join me in battle against Moab?" "I will," he replied. "You and I shall be as one, your people and mine, and your horses and mine as well." ⁸ They discussed the route for their attack, and settled upon the route through the desert of Edom.

⁹ So the king of Israel set out, accompanied by the king of Judah and the king of Edom. After their roundabout journey of seven days the water gave out for the army and for the animals with them. ¹⁰ "Alas!" exclaimed the king of Israel. "The LORD has called together these three kings to put them in the grasp of Moab." ¹¹* But the king of Judah asked, "Is there no prophet of the LORD here through whom we may inquire of the LORD?" One of the officers of the king of Israel replied, "Elisha, son of Shaphat, who poured water on the hands of Elijah, is here." ¹² "He has the word of the LORD," the king of Judah agreed. So the kings of Israel, Judah, and Edom went down to Elisha. ¹³ "What do you want with me?" Elisha asked the king of Israel. "Go to the prophets of your father and to the prophets of your mother." "No," the king of Israel replied. "The LORD has called these three kings together to put them in the grasp of Moab." ¹⁴* Then Elisha said, "As the LORD of hosts lives, whom I serve, were it not that I respect the king of Judah, I should neither look at you nor notice you at all. ¹⁵ Now get me a minstrel."

When the minstrel played, the power of the LORD came upon Elisha ¹⁶ and he announced: "Thus says the LORD, 'Provide many catch basins in this wadi.' ¹⁷ For the LORD says, 'Though you will see neither wind nor rain, yet this wadi will be filled with water for you, your livestock, and your pack animals to drink.' ¹⁸ And since the LORD does not consider this enough, he will also deliver Moab into your grasp.

¹⁹* You shall destroy every fortified city, fell every fruit tree, stop up all the springs, and ruin every fertile field with stones."

²⁰* In the morning, at the time of the sacrifice, water came from the direction of Edom and filled the land. ²¹ Meanwhile, all Moab heard that the kings had come to give them battle; every man capable of bearing arms was called up and stationed at the border. ²²† Early that morning, when the sun shone on the water, the Moabites saw the water at a distance as red as blood. ²³ "This is blood!" they exclaimed. "The kings have fought among themselves and killed one another. Quick! To the spoils, Moabites!" ²⁴ But when they reached the camp of Israel, the Israelites rose up and attacked the Moabites, who fled from them. They ranged through the countryside striking down the Moabites, and ²⁵*† destroying the cities; each of them cast stones onto every fertile field till they had loaded it down; all the springs they stopped up and every useful tree they felled. Finally only Kir-hareseth was left behind its stone walls, and the slingers had surrounded it and were attacking it. ²⁶ When he saw that he was losing the battle, the king of Moab took seven hundred swordsmen to break through to the king of Aram, but he failed. ²⁷*† So he took his firstborn, his heir apparent, and offered him as a holocaust upon the wall. The wrath against Israel was so great that they gave up the siege and returned to their own land.

The Widow's Oil

4 ¹*† A certain woman, the widow of one of the guild prophets, complained to Elisha: "My husband, your servant, is dead. You know that he was a God-fearing man, yet now his creditor has come to take my two children as his slaves." ² "How can I help you?" Elisha answered her. "Tell me what you have in the house." "This servant of yours has nothing in the house but a jug of oil," she replied. ³ "Go out," he said, "borrow vessels from all your neighbors—as many empty vessels as you can. ⁴ Then come back and close the door on yourself and your children; pour the oil into all the vessels, and as each is filled, set it aside." ⁵ She went and did so, closing the door on herself and her children. As they handed her the vessels, she would pour in oil. ⁶ When all the vessels were filled, she said to her son, "Bring me another vessel." "There is none left," he answered her. And

---

3, 22: *Red as blood:* possibly caused by the red sandstone of the Wadi Zered (Dt 2, 13), south of Moab.

3, 25: *Kir-hareseth:* modern Kerak, east of the Dead Sea; cf Is 16, 7.11; Jer 48, 31.36.

3, 27: *The wrath against Israel:* probably the wrath of Chemosh, the Moabite god to whom the child was offered. He was feared by the Israelites who lost heart on foreign soil.

4, 1: *His creditor . . . slaves:* Hebrew law permitted the selling of wife and children as chattels for debt; cf. Ex 21, 7; Am 2, 6; 8, 6; Is 50.

3, 7: 1 Kgs 22, 4.
3, 11: 1 Kgs 22, 7.
3, 14: 1 Kgs 18, 15.
3, 19: Dt 20, 19.
3, 20: 1 Kgs 18, 29.
3, 25: Jb 5, 23.
3, 27: Jgs 11, 30f.
4, 1: 1 Kgs 17, 8–16.

4, 1—7

then the oil stopped. ⁷ She went and told the man of God, who said, "Go and sell the oil to pay off your creditor; with what remains, you and your children can live."

Elisha and the Shunammite

⁸ One day Elisha came to Shunem, where there was a woman of influence, who urged him to dine with her. Afterward, whenever he passed by, he used to stop there to dine. ⁹ So she said to her husband, "I know that he is a holy man of God. Since he visits us often, ¹⁰ let us arrange a little room on the roof and furnish it for him with a bed, table, chair, and lamp, so that when he comes to us he can stay there." ¹¹ Some time later Elisha arrived and stayed in the room overnight. ¹² Then he said to his servant Gehazi, "Call this Shunammite woman." He did so, and when she stood before Elisha, ¹³ he told Gehazi, "Say to her, 'You have lavished all this care on us; what can we do for you? Can we say a good word for you to the king or to the commander of the army?'" She replied, "I am living among my own people." ¹⁴ Later Elisha asked, "Can something be done for her?" "Yes!" Gehazi answered. "She has no son, and her husband is getting on in years." ¹⁵ "Call her," said Elisha. When she had been called, and stood at the door, ¹⁶* Elisha promised, "This time next year you will be fondling a baby son." "Please, my lord," she protested, "you are a man of God; do not deceive your servant." ¹⁷ Yet the woman conceived, and by the same time the

following year she had given birth to a son, as Elisha promised.

¹⁸* The day came when the child was old enough to go out to his father among the reapers. ¹⁹ "My head hurts!" he complained to his father. "Carry him to his mother," the father said to a servant. ²⁰ The servant picked him up and carried him to his mother; he stayed with her until noon, when he died in her lap. ²¹ The mother took him upstairs and laid him on the bed of the man of God. Closing the door on him, she went out ²² and called to her husband, "Let me have a servant and a donkey. I must go quickly to the man of God, and I will be back." ²³ "Why are you going to him today?" he asked. "It is neither the new moon nor the sabbath." But she bade him good-bye, ²⁴ and when the donkey was saddled, said to her servant: "Lead on! Do not stop my donkey unless I tell you to." ²⁵ She kept going till she reached the man of God on Mount Carmel. When he spied her at a distance, the man of God said to his servant Gehazi: "There is the Shunammite! ²⁶† Hurry to meet her, and ask if all is well with her, with her husband, and with the boy." "Greetings," she replied. ²⁷ But when she reached the man of God on the mountain, she clasped his feet. Gehazi came near to push her away, but the man of God said: "Let her alone, she is in bitter anguish; the LORD hid it from me and did not let me know." ²⁸ "Did I ask my lord for a son?" she cried out. "Did I not beg you not to deceive me?" ²⁹† "Gird your loins," Elisha said to Gehazi, "take my staff with you and be off; if you meet anyone, do not greet him, and if anyone greets you, do not answer. Lay my staff upon the boy." ³⁰ But the boy's mother cried out: "As the LORD lives and as you yourself live, I will not release you." So he started to go back with her.

³¹* Meanwhile, Gehazi had gone on ahead and had laid the staff upon the boy, but there was no sound or sign of life. He returned to meet Elisha and informed him that the boy had not awakened. ³² When Elisha reached the house, he found the boy lying dead. ³³* He went in, closed the door on them both, and prayed to the LORD. ³⁴ Then he lay upon the child on the bed, placing his mouth upon the child's mouth, his eyes upon the eyes, and his hands upon the hands. As Elisha stretched himself over the child, the body became warm. ³⁵* He arose, paced up and down the room, and then once more lay down upon the boy, who now sneezed seven times and opened his eyes. ³⁶ Elisha sum-

---

4, 26: *Greetings:* the conventional answer to Gehazi's question, which tells him nothing.

4, 29: *Do not greet him:* the profuse exchange of compliments among Orientals meeting and greeting one another consumed time. Urgency necessitated their omission, as our Lord counseled his disciples (Lk 10, 4).

4, 16: Gn 18, 10.
4, 18: 1 Kgs 17, 17–24.
4, 31–36: Acts 20, 10ff.

4, 33: 1 Kgs 17, 21–23.
4, 35: Heb 11, 35.

moned Gehazi and said, "Call the Shunammite." She came at his call, and Elisha said to her, "Take your son." [37] She came in and fell at his feet in gratitude; then she took her son and left the room.

The Poisoned Stew

[38] When Elisha returned to Gilgal, there was a famine in the land. Once, when the guild prophets were seated before him, he said to his servant, "Put the large pot on, and make some vegetable stew for the guild prophets." [39] Someone went out into the field to gather herbs and found a wild vine, from which he picked a clothful of wild gourds. On his return he cut them up into the pot of vegetable stew without anybody's knowing it. [40] The stew was poured out for the men to eat, but when they began to eat it, they exclaimed, "Man of God, there is poison in the pot!" And they could not eat it. [41] "Bring some meal," Elisha said. He threw it into the pot and said, "Serve it to the people to eat." And there was no longer anything harmful in the pot.

Multiplication of Loaves

[42] A man came from Baal-shalishah bringing the man of God twenty barley loaves made from the first-fruits, and fresh grain in the ear. "Give it to the people to eat," Elisha said. [43] But his servant objected, "How can I set this before a hundred men?" "Give it to the people to eat," Elisha insisted. "For thus says the LORD, 'They shall eat and there shall be some left over.'" [44] And when they had eaten, there was some left over, as the LORD had said.

Cure of Naaman

5 [1] Naaman, the army commander of the king of Aram, was highly esteemed and respected by his master, for through him the LORD had brought victory to Aram. But valiant as he was, the man was a leper. [2] Now the Arameans had cap-

tured from the land of Israel in a raid a little girl, who became the servant of Naaman's wife. [3] "If only my master would present himself to the prophet in Samaria," she said to her mistress, "he would cure him of his leprosy." [4] Naaman went and told his lord just what the slave girl from the land of Israel had said. [5] "Go," said the king of Aram. "I will send along a letter to the king of Israel." So Naaman set out, taking along ten silver talents, six thousand gold pieces, and ten festal garments. [6] To the king of Israel he brought the letter, which read: "With this letter I am sending my servant Naaman to you, that you may cure him of his leprosy."

7* When he read the letter, the king of Israel tore his garments and exclaimed: "Am I a god with power over life and death, that this man should send someone to me to be cured of leprosy? Take note! You can see he is only looking for a quarrel with me!" 8 When Elisha, the man of God, heard that the king of Israel had torn his garments, he sent word to the king: "Why have you torn your garments? Let him come to me and find out that there is a prophet in Israel."

9 Naaman came with his horses and chariots and stopped at the door of Elisha's house. 10* The prophet sent him the message: "Go and wash seven times in the Jordan, and your flesh will heal, and you will be clean." 11 But Naaman went away angry, saying, "I thought that he would surely come out and stand there to invoke the LORD his God, and would move his hand over the spot, and thus cure the leprosy. 12† Are not the rivers of Damascus, the Abana and the Pharpar, better than all the waters of Israel? Could I not wash in them and be cleansed?" With this, he turned about in anger and left.

13 But his servants came up and reasoned with him. "My father," they said, "if the prophet had told you to do something extraordinary, would you not have done it? All the more now, since he said to you, 'Wash and be clean,' should you do as he said." 14* So Naaman went down and plunged into the Jordan seven times at the word of the man of God. His flesh became again like the flesh of a little child, and he was clean.

15 He returned with his whole retinue to the man of God. On his arrival he stood before him and said, "Now I know that there is no God in all the earth, except in Israel. Please accept a gift from your servant." 16 "As the LORD lives whom I serve, I will not take it," Elisha replied; and despite Naaman's urging, he still refused. 17† Naaman said: "If you will not accept, please let me, your servant, have two muleloads of earth, for I will no longer offer holocaust or sacrifice to any other god except to the LORD. 18 But I trust the LORD will forgive your servant this: when my master enters the temple of Rimmon to worship there, then I, too, as his adjutant, must bow down in the temple of Rimmon. May the LORD forgive your servant this." 19† "Go in peace," Elisha said to him.

20 Naaman had gone some distance when Gehazi, the servant of Elisha, the man of God, thought to himself: "My master was too easy with this Aramean Naaman, not accepting what he brought. As the LORD lives, I will run after him and get something out of him." 21 So Gehazi hurried after Naaman. Aware that someone was running after him, Naaman alighted from his chariot to wait for him. "Is everything all right?" he asked. 22 "Yes," Gehazi replied, "but my master sent me to say, 'Two young men have just come to me, guild prophets from the hill country of Ephraim. Please give them a talent of silver and two festal garments.' " 23 "Please take two talents," Naaman said, and pressed them upon him. He tied up these silver talents in bags and gave them, with the two festal garments, to two of his servants, who carried them before Gehazi. 24 When they reached the hill, Gehazi took what they had, carried it into the house, and sent the men on their way.

25 He went in and stood before Elisha his master, who asked him, "Where have you been, Gehazi?" He answered, "Your servant has not gone anywhere." 26 But Elisha said to him: "Was I not present in spirit when the man alighted from his chariot to wait for you? Is this a time to take money or to take garments, olive orchards or vineyards, sheep or cattle, male or female servants? 27* The leprosy of Naaman shall cling to you and your descendants forever." And Gehazi left Elisha, a leper white as snow.

Recovery of the Lost Ax

6 1 The guild prophets once said to Elisha: "There is not enough room for us to continue to live here with you. 2 Let us go to the Jordan, where by getting one beam apiece we can build ourselves a place to live." "Go," Elisha said. 3 "Please agree to accompany your servants," one of them requested. "Yes, I will come," he replied.

4 So he went with them, and when they arrived at the Jordan they began to fell trees. 5 While one of them was felling a tree trunk, the iron axhead slipped into the water. "O master," he cried out, "it was borrowed!" 6 "Where did it fall?" asked the man of God. When he pointed out the spot, Elisha cut off a stick, threw it into the water, and brought the iron to the surface. 7 "Pick it up," he said. And the man reached down and grasped it.

---

†
5, 12: *Wash in them and be cleansed:* typical of the ambiguity in ritual healing or cleanliness. The muddy waters of the Jordan are no match hygienically for the mountain spring waters of Damascus; ritually, it is the other way around.

5, 17: *Two mule-loads of earth:* Israelite earth on which to erect in Aram an altar to the God of Israel.

5, 19: *Go in peace:* Elisha understands and approves the situation of Naaman who, though a proselyte as regards belief in and worship

of the God of Israel, is required by his office to assist his master, the king, worshiping in the pagan temple of Rimmon.

5, 7: Gn 30, 2; 1 Sm 2, 6; Jn   **5, 14:** Lk 4, 27.
    5, 21.   **5, 27:** Ex 4, 6; Nm 12, 10.
5, 10: Jn 9, 7.

Aramean Ambush

8 When the king of Aram was waging war on Israel, he would make plans with his servants to attack a particular place. 9 But the man of God would send word to the king of Israel, "Be careful! Do not pass by this place, for Aram will attack there." 10 So the king of Israel would send word to the place which the man of God had indicated, and alert it; then they would be on guard. This happened several times.

11 Greatly disturbed over this, the king of Aram called together his officers. "Will you not tell me," he asked them, "who among us is for the king of Israel?" 12 "No one, my lord king," answered one of the officers. "The Israelite prophet Elisha can tell the king of Israel the very words you speak in your bedroom." 13 "Go, find out where he is," he said, "so that I may take him captive."

Blinded Aramean Soldiers

Informed that Elisha was in Dothan, 14 he sent there a strong force with horses and chariots. They arrived by night and surrounded the city. 15 Early the next morning, when the attendant of the man of God arose and went out, he saw the force with its horses and chariots surrounding the city. "Alas!" he said to Elisha. "What shall we do, my lord?" 16 "Do not be afraid," Elisha answered. "Our side outnumbers theirs." 17* Then he prayed, "O LORD, open his eyes, that he may see." And the LORD opened the eyes of the servant, so that he saw the mountainside filled with horses and fiery chariots around Elisha.

18 When the Arameans came down to get him, Elisha prayed to the LORD, "Strike this people blind, I pray you." And in answer to the prophet's prayer the LORD struck them blind. 19 Then Elisha said to them: "This is the wrong road, and this is the wrong city. Follow me! I will take you to the man you want." And he led them to Samaria. 20 When they entered Samaria, Elisha prayed, "O LORD, open their eyes that they may see." The LORD opened their eyes, and they saw that they were inside Samaria. 21 When the king of Israel saw them, he asked, "Shall I kill them, my father?" 22† "You must not kill them," replied Elisha. "Do you slay those whom you have taken captive with your sword or bow? Serve them bread and water. Let them eat and drink, and then go back to their master." 23 The king spread a great feast for them. When they had

eaten and drunk he sent them away, and they went back to their master. No more Aramean raiders came into the land of Israel.

Siege of Samaria

24 After this, Ben-hadad, king of Aram, mustered his whole army and laid siege to Samaria. 25 Because of the siege the famine in Samaria was so severe that an ass's head sold for eighty pieces of silver, and a fourth of a kab of wild onion for five pieces of silver.

26 One day, as the king of Israel was walking on the city wall, a woman cried out to him, "Help, my lord king!" 27 "No," he replied, "the LORD help you! Where could I find help for you: from the threshing floor or the winepress?" 28* Then the king asked her, "What is your trouble?" She replied: "This woman said to me, 'Give up your son that we may eat him today; then tomorrow we will eat my son.' 29 So we boiled my son and ate him. The next day I said to her, 'Now give up your son that we may eat him.' But she hid her son." 30* When the king heard the woman's words, he tore his garments. And as he was walking on the wall, the people saw that he was wearing sackcloth underneath, next to his skin.

31 "May God do thus and so to me," the king exclaimed, "if the head of Elisha, son of Shaphat, stays on him today!" 32 Meanwhile, Elisha was sitting in his house in conference with the elders. The king had sent a man ahead before he himself should come to him. Elisha had said to the elders: "Do you know that this son of a murderer is sending someone to cut off my head? When the messenger comes, see that you close the door and hold it fast against him. His master's footsteps are echoing behind him." 33 While Elisha was still speaking, the king came down to him and said, "This evil is from the LORD. Why should I trust in the LORD any longer?"

7 1† Elisha said: "Hear the word of the LORD! Thus says the LORD, 'At this time tomorrow a seah of fine flour will sell for a shekel, and two seahs of barley for a shekel, in the market of Samaria.' " 2* But the adjutant on whose arm the king leaned, answered the man of God, "Even if the LORD were to make windows in heaven, how could this happen?" "You shall see it with your own eyes," Elisha said, "but you shall not eat of it."

2 KGS

6, 22: *With your sword or bow:* since the king would not slay prisoners who had surrendered to his power, much less should he slay prisoners captured by God's power. By Oriental custom they became guests within Samaria's walls.

7, 1: *Market:* literally "gate," the principal place of trading in ancient walled cities in time of peace.

6, 17: 2 Kgs 7, 6; Ps 67, 18.
6, 28: Dt 28, 53–57.
6, 30: 1 Kgs 20, 31; 21, 27.
7, 2: 2 Kgs 7, 17; Ps 78, 23;
Is 24, 18.

The Lepers at the Gate

³* At the city gate were four lepers who were deliberating, "Why should we sit here until we die? ⁴ If we decide to go into the city, we shall die there, for there is famine in the city. If we remain here, we shall die too. Come, let us desert to the camp of the Arameans. If they spare us, we live; if they kill us, we die." ⁵ At twilight they left for the Arameans; but when they reached the edge of the camp, no one was there. ⁶*† The LORD had caused the army of the Arameans to hear the sound of chariots and horses, the din of a large army, and they had reasoned among themselves, "The king of Israel has hired the kings of the Hittites and the kings of the borderlands to fight us." ⁷ Then in the twilight they fled, abandoning their tents, their horses, and their asses, the whole camp just as it was, and fleeing for their lives.

⁸ After the lepers reached the edge of the camp, they went first into one tent, ate and drank, and took silver, gold, and clothing from it, and went out and hid them. Back they came into another tent, took things from it, and again went out and hid them. ⁹ Then they said to one another: "We are not doing right. This is a day of good news, and we are keeping silent. If we wait until morning breaks, we shall be blamed. Come, let us go and inform the palace."

¹⁰ They came and summoned the city gatekeepers. "We went to the camp of the Arameans," they said, "but no one was there—not a human voice, only the horses and asses tethered, and the tents just as they were left." ¹¹ The gatekeepers announced this and it was reported within the palace. ¹² Though it was night, the king got up; he said to his servants: "Let me tell you what the Arameans have done to us. Knowing that we are in famine, they have left their camp to hide in the field, hoping to take us alive and enter our city when we leave it." ¹³ One of his servants, however, suggested: "Since those who are left in the city are no better off than all the throng that has perished, let some of us take five of the abandoned horses and send scouts to investigate."

End of the Siege

¹⁴ They took two chariots, and horses, and the king sent them to reconnoiter the Aramean army. "Go and find out," he ordered. ¹⁵ They followed the Arameans as far as the Jordan, and the whole route was strewn with garments and other objects that the Arameans had thrown away in their haste. The messengers returned and told the king.

¹⁶ The people went out and plundered the camp of the Arameans; and then a seah of fine flour sold for a shekel and two seahs of barley for a shekel, as the LORD had said.

¹⁷ The king put in charge of the gate the officer who was his adjutant; but the people trampled him to death at the gate, just as the man of God had predicted when the king visited him. ¹⁸ Thus was fulfilled the prophecy of the man of God to the king, "Two seahs of barley will sell for a shekel, and one seah of fine flour for a shekel at this time tomorrow at the gate of Samaria." ¹⁹ The adjutant had answered the man of God, "Even if the LORD were to make windows in heaven, how could this happen?" And Elisha had replied, "You shall see it with your own eyes, but you shall not eat of it." ²⁰ And that is what happened to him, for the people trampled him to death at the gate.

Prediction of Famine

8 ¹* Elisha once said to the woman whose son he had restored to life: "Get ready! Leave with your family and settle wherever you can, because the LORD has decreed a seven-year famine which is coming upon the land." ² The woman got ready and did as the man of God said, setting out with her family and settling in the land of the Philistines for seven years. ³ At the end of the seven years, the woman returned from the land of the Philistines and went out to the king to claim her house and her field. ⁴ The king was talking with Gehazi, the servant of the man of God. "Tell me," he said, "all the great things that Elisha has done." ⁵ Just as he was relating to the king how his master had restored a dead person to life, the very woman whose son Elisha had restored to life came to the king to claim her house and field. "My lord king," Gehazi said, "this is the woman, and this is that son of hers whom Elisha restored to life." ⁶† The king questioned the woman, and she told him her story. With that the king placed an official at her disposal, saying, "Restore all her property to her, with all that the field produced from the day she left the land until now."

Death of Ben-hadad Foretold

⁷ Elisha came to Damascus at a time when Ben-hadad, king of Aram, lay sick. When he was told that the man of God had come there, ⁸ the king said to Hazael, "Take a gift with you and go call on the man of God. Have him consult the LORD as to whether I shall recover from this sickness." ⁹ Hazael went to visit him, carrying a present, and with

---

7, 6: *Kings of the borderlands:* from Musur in Anatolia rather than Egypt.

8, 6: *An official:* Literally "eunuch," and perhaps actually so in this instance.

7, 3: Lv 13, 46.   2 Sm 5, 24.
7, 6f: 2 Kgs 6, 17; 19, 35f;   8, 1: 2 Kgs 4, 36.

forty camel loads of the best goods of Damascus. On his arrival, he stood before the prophet and said, "Your son Ben-hadad, king of Aram, has sent me to ask you whether he will recover from his sickness." ¹⁰ "Go and tell him," Elisha answered, "that he will surely recover. However, the LORD has showed me that he will in fact die." ¹¹ Then he stared him down until Hazael became ill at ease. The man of God wept, ¹²* and Hazael asked, "Why are you weeping, my lord?" Elisha replied, "Because I know the evil that you will inflict upon the Israelites. You will burn their fortresses, you will slay their youth with the sword, you will dash their little children to pieces, you will rip open their pregnant women."

¹³*† Hazael exclaimed, "How can a dog like me, your servant, do anything so important?" "The LORD has showed you to me as king over Aram," replied Elisha.

¹⁴ Hazael left Elisha and returned to his master. "What did Elisha tell you?" asked Ben-hadad. "He told me that you would surely recover," replied Hazael. ¹⁵ The next day, however, Hazael took a cloth, dipped it in water, and spread it over the king's face, so that he died. And Hazael reigned in his stead.

Reign of Jehoram of Judah

¹⁶† In the fifth year of Joram, son of Ahab, king of Israel, Jehoram, son of Jehoshaphat, king of Judah, became king. ¹⁷* He was thirty-two years old when he began to reign, and he reigned eight years in Jerusalem. ¹⁸ He conducted himself like the kings of Israel of the line of Ahab, since the sister of Ahab was his wife; and he did evil in the LORD's sight. ¹⁹* Even so, the LORD was unwilling to destroy Judah, because of his servant David. For he had promised David that he would leave him a lamp in the LORD's presence for all time. ²⁰ During Jehoram's reign, Edom revolted against the sovereignty of Judah and chose a king of its own. ²¹ Thereupon Jehoram with all his chariots crossed over to Zair. He arose by night and broke through the Edomites when they had surrounded him and the commanders of his chariots. Then his army fled homeward. ²²* To this day Edom has been in revolt against the rule of Judah. Libnah also revolted at that time. ²³ The rest of the acts of Jehoram, with all that he did, are recorded in the book of the chronicles of the kings of Judah. ²⁴ Jehoram rested with

did you KNOW?

Grading Kings

As you read the remaining chapters of Second Kings, notice that the author gives a kind of report card for each of the rulers of Israel and Judah. Jehoram, for example, receives an F: "He did evil in the LORD's sight" (8, 18). Josiah receives an A: "He pleased the LORD and conducted himself unswervingly" (22, 2). The author, who wrote after the fall of both kingdoms, provides a theological reason for Israel's and Judah's failure. Because most of the rulers continually violated God's law, they were largely responsible for the fall of the kingdoms.

his ancestors and was buried with them in the City of David. His son Ahaziah succeeded him as king.

Accession of Ahaziah

²⁵† Ahaziah, son of Jehoram, king of Judah, became king in the twelfth year of Joram, son of Ahab, king of Israel. ²⁶ He was twenty-two years old when he began his reign, and he reigned one year in Jerusalem. His mother's name was Athaliah; she was the daughter of Omri, king of Israel. ²⁷ He conducted himself like the house of Ahab, doing evil in the LORD's sight as they did, since he was related to them by marriage. ²⁸* He joined Joram, son of Ahab, in battle against Hazael, king of Aram, at Ramoth-gilead, where the Arameans wounded Joram. ²⁹ King Joram returned to Jezreel to be healed of the wounds which the Arameans had inflicted on him at Ramah in his battle against Hazael, king of Aram. Then Ahaziah, son of Jehoram, king of Judah, went down to Jezreel to visit him there in his illness.

Anointing of Jehu

9 ¹* The prophet Elisha called one of the guild prophets and said to him: "Gird your loins, take this flask of oil with you, and go to Ramoth-gilead. ²* When you get there, look for Jehu, son of

---

8, 13: A dog . . . your servant: Hazael feigns humility (1 Sm 24, 14; 2 Sm 9, 8), without attending to the crimes he would commit after usurping the royal power as the prophet predicts. Anything so important: literally "a great deed" for a patriotic Syrian.

8, 16: Jehoram of Judah succeeded his father Jehoshaphat during the reign of Ahaziah of Israel. See note on 2 Kgs 3, 1.

8, 25: Twelfth year of Joram: i.e., of Israel, who probably reigned only eight years.

8, 12: 2 Kgs 13, 7.
8, 13: 2 Kgs 15, 16; 1 Kgs 19, 15.
8, 17ff: 2 Chr 21, 5ff.
8, 19: 2 Sm 7, 11–16; 21, 17; 1 Kgs 11, 36; 15, 4;
2 Chr 21, 7.
8, 22: Gn 27, 40; 2 Chr 21, 8ff.
8, 28: 2 Kgs 9, 14f.
9, 1: 1 Kgs 21, 29; Hos 1, 4.
9, 2: 1 Kgs 19, 16.

Jehoshaphat, son of Nimshi. Enter and take him away from his companions into an inner chamber. 3* From the flask you have, pour oil on his head, and say, 'Thus says the LORD: I anoint you king over Israel.' Then open the door and flee without delay." 4 The young man (the guild prophet) went to Ramoth-gilead. 5 When he arrived, the commanders of the army were in session. "I have a message for you, commander," he said. "For which one of us?" asked Jehu. "For you, commander," he answered. 6 Jehu got up and went into the house. Then the young man poured the oil on his head and said, "Thus says the LORD, the God of Israel: 'I anoint you king over the people of the LORD, over Israel. 7† You shall destroy the house of Ahab your master; thus will I avenge the blood of my servants the prophets, and the blood of all the other servants of the LORD shed by Jezebel, 8* and by all the rest of the family of Ahab. I will cut off every male in Ahab's line, whether slave or freeman in Israel. 9 I will deal with the house of Ahab as I dealt with the house of Jeroboam, son of Nebat, and with the house of Baasha, son of Ahijah. 10 Dogs shall devour Jezebel at the confines of Jezreel, so that no one can bury her.' " Then he opened the door and fled.

11 When Jehu rejoined his master's servants, they asked him, "Is all well? Why did that madman come to you?" "You know that kind of man and his talk," he replied. 12 But they said, "Not at all! Come, tell us." So he told them what the young man had said to him, and finally, "Thus says the LORD: 'I anoint you king over Israel.' " 13* At once each took his garment, spread it under Jehu on the bare steps, blew the trumpet, and cried out, "Jehu is king!"

14* Thus Jehu, son of Jehoshaphat, son of Nimshi, formed a conspiracy against Joram. Joram, with all Israel, had been besieging Ramoth-gilead against Hazael, king of Aram, 15 but had returned to Jezreel to be healed of the wounds the Arameans had inflicted on him in the battle against Hazael, king of Aram.

Murder of Joram

"If you are truly with me," Jehu said, "see that no one escapes from the city to report in Jezreel." 16 Then Jehu mounted his chariot and drove to Jezreel, where Joram lay ill and Ahaziah, king of Judah, had come to visit him.

17 The watchman standing on the tower in Jezreel saw the troop of Jehu coming and reported, "I see chariots." "Get a driver," Joram said, "and send him

to meet them and to ask whether all is well." 18 So a driver went out to meet him and said, "The king asks whether all is well." "What does it matter to you how things are?" Jehu said. "Get behind me." The watchman reported to the king, "The messenger has reached them, but is not returning."

19 Joram sent a second driver, who went to them and said, "The king asks whether all is well." "What does it matter to you how things are?" Jehu replied. "Get behind me."

20 The watchman reported, "The messenger has reached them, but is not returning. The driving is like that of Jehu, son of Nimshi, in its fury." 21 "Prepare my chariot," said Joram. When they had done so, Joram, king of Israel, and Ahaziah, king of Judah, set out, each in his own chariot, to meet Jehu. They reached him near the field of Naboth the Jezreelite. 22† When Joram recognized Jehu, he asked, "Is all well, Jehu?" "How can all be well," Jehu replied, "as long as the many fornications and witchcrafts of your mother Jezebel continue?" 23 Joram reined about and fled, crying to Ahaziah, "Treason, Ahaziah!" 24 But Jehu drew his bow and shot Joram between the shoulders, so that the arrow went through his heart and he collapsed in his chariot. 25* Then Jehu said to his adjutant Bidkar, "Take him and throw him into the field of Naboth the Jezreelite. For I remember that when we were driving teams behind his father Ahab, the LORD delivered this oracle against him: 26 'As surely as I saw yesterday the blood of Naboth and the blood of his sons,' says the LORD, 'I will repay you for it in that very plot of ground, says the LORD.' So now take him into this plot of ground, in keeping with the word of the LORD."

Death of Ahaziah

27* Seeing what was happening, Ahaziah, king of Judah, fled toward Beth-haggan. Jehu pursued him, shouting, "Kill him too!" And they pierced him as he rode through the pass of Gur near Ibleam. He continued his flight as far as Megiddo and died there. 28 His servants brought him in a chariot to Jerusalem and buried him in the tomb of his ancestors in the City of David. 29 Ahaziah had become king of Judah in the eleventh year of Joram, son of Ahab.

Death of Jezebel

30 When Jezebel learned that Jehu had arrived in Jezreel, she shadowed her eyes, adorned her hair,

---

9, 7–10: The editors of the Books of Kings have here added to the prophet's message the same type of indictment and sanctions against the family of Ahab as were invoked against the dynasties of Jeroboam (1 Kgs 14, 10f), Baasha (1 Kgs 16, 3f), and Ahab on a previous occasion (1 Kgs 21, 21–24).

9, 22: *Fornications and witchcrafts:* the worship of foreign gods.

9, 3: 1 Kgs 19, 16.
9, 8ff: 1 Kgs 14, 10f; 16, 3f; 21, 21–24.
9, 13: Mt 21, 8.
9, 14f: 2 Kgs 8, 28f; 1 Kgs 22, 3f.
9, 25f: 1 Kgs 21, 9–16.
9, 27ff: 2 Chr 22, 7ff.

and looked down from her window. 31* As Jehu came through the gate, she cried out, "Is all well, Zimri, murderer of your master?" 32 Jehu looked up to the window and shouted, "Who is on my side? Anyone?" At this, two or three eunuchs looked down toward him. 33 "Throw her down," he ordered. They threw her down, and some of her blood spurted against the wall and against the horses. Jehu rode in over her body 34 and, after eating and drinking, he said: "Attend to that accursed woman and bury her; after all, she was a king's daughter." 35 But when they went to bury her, they found nothing of her but the skull, the feet, and the hands. 36* They returned to Jehu, and when they told him, he said, "This is the sentence which the LORD pronounced through his servant Elijah the Tishbite: 'In the confines of Jezreel dogs shall eat the flesh of Jezebel. 37 The corpse of Jezebel shall be like dung in the field in the confines of Jezreel, so that no one can say: This was Jezebel.' "

Killing of Ahab's Descendants

10 1* Ahab had seventy descendants in Samaria. Jehu prepared letters and sent them to the city rulers, to the elders, and to the guardians of Ahab's descendants in Samaria. 2 "Since your master's sons are with you," he wrote, "and you have the chariots, the horses, a fortified city, and the weapons, when this letter reaches you 3 decide which is the best and the fittest of your master's offspring, place him on his father's throne, and fight for your master's house." 4 They were overcome with fright and said, "If two kings could not withstand him, how can we?" 5 So the vizier and the ruler of the city, along with the elders and the guardians, sent this message to Jehu: "We are your servants, and we will do everything you tell us. We will proclaim no one king; do whatever you think best." 6 So Jehu wrote them a second letter: "If you are on my side and will obey me, count the heads of your master's sons and come to me in Jezreel at this time tomorrow." [The seventy princes were in the care of prominent men of the city, who were rearing them.]

7 When the letter arrived, they took the princes and slew all seventy of them, put their heads in baskets, and sent them to Jehu in Jezreel. 8 "They have brought the heads of the princes," a messenger came in and told him. "Pile them in two heaps at the entrance of the city until morning," he ordered. 9 Going out in the morning, he stopped and said to all the people: "You are not responsible, and although I conspired against my lord and slew him,

yet who killed all these? 10* Know that not a single word which the LORD has spoken against the house of Ahab shall go unfulfilled. The LORD has accomplished all that he foretold through his servant Elijah." 11* Thereupon Jehu slew all who were left of the family of Ahab in Jezreel, as well as all his powerful supporters, intimates, and priests, leaving him no survivor.

Ahaziah's Kinsmen

12* Then he set out for Samaria, and at Betheked-haroim on the way, 13 he came across kinsmen of Ahaziah, king of Judah. "Who are you?" he asked. "We are kinsmen of Ahaziah," they replied. "We are going down to visit the princes and the family of the queen mother." 14 "Take them alive," Jehu ordered. They were taken alive, forty-two in number, then slain at the pit of Beth-eked. Not one of them was spared.

Jehu in Samaria

15* When he had left there, Jehu met Jehonadab, son of Rechab, on the road. He greeted him and asked, "Are you sincerely disposed toward me, as I am toward you?" "Yes," replied Jehonadab. "If you are," continued Jehu, "give me your hand." Jehonadab gave him his hand, and Jehu drew him up into his chariot. 16 "Come with me," he said, "and see my zeal for the LORD." And he took him along in his own chariot.

17 When he arrived in Samaria, Jehu slew all who remained there of Ahab's line, doing away with them completely and thus fulfilling the prophecy which the LORD had spoken to Elijah.

Baal's Temple Destroyed

18* Jehu gathered all the people together and said to them: "Ahab served Baal to some extent, but Jehu will serve him yet more. 19 Now summon for me all Baal's prophets, all his worshipers, and all his priests. See that no one is absent, for I have a great sacrifice for Baal. Whoever is absent shall not live." This Jehu did as a ruse, so that he might destroy the worshipers of Baal. 20 Jehu said further, "Proclaim a solemn assembly in honor of Baal." They did so, 21 and Jehu sent word of it throughout the land of Israel. All the worshipers of Baal without exception came into the temple of Baal, which was filled to capacity. 22* Then Jehu said to the custodian of the wardrobe, "Bring out the garments for all the worshipers of Baal." When he had brought out the garments for them, 23 Jehu, with Jehonadab, son of Rechab, entered the temple of Baal and

2

K
G
S

9, 31: 1 Kgs 16, 9ff.
9, 36: 1 Kgs 21, 23.
10, 1: Jgs 9, 5; 1 Kgs 15, 29;
16, 11.
10, 10: 1 Kgs 21, 17–24.29.
10, 11: Hos 1, 4.
10, 12ff: 2 Chr 22, 8f.
10, 15: 1 Chr 2, 55; Jer 35, 1–11.
10, 18: 1 Kgs 16, 30ff.
10, 22: 1 Kgs 16, 32.

said to the worshipers of Baal, "Search and be sure that there is no worshiper of the LORD here with you, but only worshipers of Baal." 24 Then they proceeded to offer sacrifices and holocausts. Now Jehu had stationed eighty men outside with this warning, "If one of you lets anyone escape of those whom I shall deliver into your hands, he shall pay life for life." 25 As soon as he finished offering the holocaust, Jehu said to the guards and officers, "Go in and slay them. Let no one escape." So the guards and officers put them to the sword and cast them out. Afterward they went into the inner shrine of the temple of Baal, 26 took out the stele of Baal, and burned the shrine. 27 Then they smashed the stele of Baal, tore down the building, and turned it into a latrine, as it remains today.

28 Thus Jehu rooted out the worship of Baal from Israel. 29* However, he did not desist from the sins which Jeroboam, son of Nebat, had caused Israel to commit, as regards the golden calves at Bethel and at Dan. 30* The LORD said to Jehu, "Because you have done well what I deem right, and have treated the house of Ahab as I desire, your sons to the fourth generation shall sit upon the throne of Israel." 31 But Jehu was not careful to observe wholeheartedly the law of the LORD, the God of Israel, since he did not desist from the sins which Jeroboam caused Israel to commit.

32* At that time the LORD began to dismember Israel. Hazael defeated the Israelites throughout their territory 33 east of the Jordan (all the land of Gilead, of the Gadites, Reubenites and Manassehites), from Aroer on the river Arnon up through Gilead and Bashan.

34 The rest of the acts of Jehu, his valor and all his accomplishments, are written in the book of the chronicles of the kings of Israel. 35 Jehu rested with his ancestors and was buried in Samaria. His son Jehoahaz succeeded him as king. 36 The length of Jehu's reign over Israel in Samaria was twenty-eight years.

Rule of Athaliah

11 1* When Athaliah, the mother of Ahaziah, saw that her son was dead, she began to kill off the whole royal family. 2† But Jehosheba, daughter of King Jehoram and sister of Ahaziah, took Joash, his son, and spirited him away, along with his nurse, from the bedroom where the princes were about to be slain. She concealed him from Athaliah, and so he did not die. 3 For six years he remained hidden in the temple of the LORD, while Athaliah ruled the land.

4* But in the seventh year, Jehoiada summoned the captains of the Carians and of the guards. He had them come to him in the temple of the LORD, exacted from them a sworn commitment, and then showed them the king's son. 5 He gave them these orders: "This is what you must do: the third of you who come on duty on the sabbath shall guard the king's palace; 6 another third shall be at the gate Sur; and the last third shall be at the gate behind the guards. 7 The two of your divisions who are going off duty that week shall keep guard over the temple of the LORD for the king. 8 You shall surround the king, each with drawn weapons, and if anyone tries to approach the cordon, kill him; stay with the king, whatever he may do."

9* The captains did just as Jehoiada the priest commanded. Each one with his men, both those going on duty for the sabbath and those going off duty that week, came to Jehoiada the priest. 10* He gave the captains King David's spears and shields, which were in the temple of the LORD. 11 And the guards, with drawn weapons, lined up from the southern to the northern limit of the enclosure, surrounding the altar and the temple on the king's behalf. 12* Then Jehoiada led out the king's son and put the crown and the insignia upon him. They proclaimed him king and anointed him, clapping their hands and shouting, "Long live the king!"

13* Athaliah heard the noise made by the people, and appeared before them in the temple of the LORD. 14† When she saw the king standing by the pillar, as was the custom, and the captains and trumpeters near him, with all the people of the land rejoicing and blowing trumpets, she tore her garments and cried out, "Treason, treason!" 15 Then Jehoiada the priest instructed the captains in command of the force: "Bring her outside through the ranks. If anyone follows her," he added, "let him die by the sword." He had given orders that she should not be slain in the temple of the LORD. 16 She was led out forcibly to the horse gate of the royal palace, where she was put to death.

17* Then Jehoiada made a covenant between the LORD as one party and the king and the people as the other, by which they would be the LORD's people; and another covenant, between the king and the people. 18 Thereupon all the people of the land went to the temple of Baal and demolished it. They shattered its altars and images completely, and slew

---

11, 2: *Jehosheba* was the wife of Jehoida, the high priest; cf 2 Chr 22, 11.
11, 14: *By the pillar:* see note on 2 Chr 23, 13.

10, 29: 1 Kgs 12, 28f.
10, 30: 2 Kgs 15, 12ff.
10, 32: Am 1, 3.
11, 1: Jgs 9, 5.
11, 4–8: 2 Chr 23, 1–7.
11, 9–12: 2 Chr 23, 8–11.
11, 10ff: 2 Sm 8, 7; 1 Kgs 1, 33f.
11, 12: 2 Sm 1, 10.
11, 13–16: 2 Chr 23, 12–15.
11, 17–20: 2 Chr 23, 16–21.

Mattan, the priest of Baal, before the altars. After appointing a detachment for the temple of the LORD, Jehoiada [19] with the captains, the Carians, the guards, and all the people of the land, led the king down from the temple of the LORD through the guards' gate to the palace, where Joash took his seat on the royal throne. [20] All the people of the land rejoiced and the city was quiet, now that Athaliah had been slain with the sword at the royal palace.

Reign of Joash

12 [1]* Joash was seven years old when he became king. [2] Joash began to reign in the seventh year of Jehu, and he reigned forty years in Jerusalem. His mother, who was named Zibiah, was from Beer-sheba. [3] Joash did what was pleasing to the LORD as long as he lived, because the priest Jehoiada guided him. [4] Still, the high places did not disappear; the people continued to sacrifice and to burn incense there.

[5]* For the priests Joash made this rule: "All the funds for sacred purposes that are brought to the temple of the LORD—the census tax, personal redemption money, and whatever funds are freely brought to the temple of the LORD— [6] the priests may take for themselves, each from his own clients. However, they must make whatever repairs on the temple may prove necessary." [7] Nevertheless, as late as the twenty-third year of the reign of King Joash, the priests had not made needed repairs on the temple. [8] Accordingly, King Joash summoned the priest Jehoiada and the other priests. "Why do you not repair the temple?" he asked them. "You must no longer take funds from your clients, but you shall turn them over for the repairs." [9]* So the priests agreed that they would neither take funds from the people nor make the repairs on the temple.

[10] The priest Jehoiada then took a chest, bored a hole in its lid, and set it beside the stele, on the right as one entered the temple of the LORD. The priests who guarded the entry would put into it all the funds that were brought to the temple of the LORD. [11] When they noticed that there was a large amount of silver in the chest, the royal scribe [and the priest] would come up, and they would melt down all the funds that were in the temple of the LORD, and weigh them. [12] The amount thus realized they turned over to the master workmen in the temple of the LORD. They in turn would give it to the carpenters and builders working in the temple of the LORD, [13] and to the lumbermen and stone cutters,

and for the purchase of the wood and hewn stone used in repairing the breaches, and for any other expenses that were necessary to repair the temple. [14] None of the funds brought to the temple of the LORD were used there to make silver cups, snuffers, basins, trumpets, or any gold or silver article. [15] Instead, they were given to the workmen, and with them they repaired the temple of the LORD. [16] Moreover, no reckoning was asked of the men who were provided with the funds to give to the workmen, because they held positions of trust. [17] The funds from guilt-offerings and from sin-offerings, however, were not brought to the temple of the LORD; they belonged to the priests.

[18]* Then King Hazael of Aram mounted a siege against Gath. When he had taken it, Hazael decided to go on to attack Jerusalem.* [19] But King Jehoash of Judah took all the dedicated offerings presented by his forebears, Jehoshaphat, Jehoram, and Ahaziah, kings of Judah, as well as his own, and all the gold there was in the treasuries of the temple and the palace, and sent them to King Hazael of Aram, who then led his forces away from Jerusalem. [20] The rest of the acts of Joash, with all that he did, are recorded in the book of the chronicles of the kings of Judah. [21] Certain of his officials entered into a plot against him and killed him at Beth-millo. [22] Jozacar, son of Shimeath, and Jehozabad, son of Shomer, were the officials who killed him. He was buried in his forefathers' City of David, and his son Amaziah succeeded him as king.

Reign of Jehoahaz of Israel

13 [1] In the twenty-third year of Joash, son of Ahaziah, king of Judah, Jehoahaz, son of Jehu, began his seventeen-year reign over Israel in Samaria. [2] He did evil in the LORD's sight, conducting himself like Jeroboam, son of Nebat, and not renouncing the sin he had caused Israel to commit. [3] The LORD was angry with Israel and for a long time left them in the power of Hazael, king of Aram, and of Ben-hadad, son of Hazael. [4]* Then Jehoahaz entreated the LORD, who heard him, since he saw the oppression to which the king of Aram had subjected Israel. [5]† So the LORD gave Israel a savior, and the Israelites, freed from the power of Aram, dwelt in their own homes as formerly. [6]*† Nevertheless, they did not desist from the sins which the house of Jeroboam had caused Israel to commit, but persisted in them. The sacred pole also remained standing in Samaria. [7] No soldiers were left

2
K
G
S

13, 5: *A savior:* by this language, typical of the Book of Judges (Jgs 3, 9.15), Jeroboam II of Israel is meant; cf 2 Kgs 14, 27.
13, 6: *Sacred pole:* see note on Ex 34, 13.

12, 1f: 2 Chr 24, 1f.
12, 5–8: 2 Chr 24, 5–10.
12, 9–16: 2 Chr 24, 11–14.
12, 18: 2 Kgs 8, 12.
12, 18–22: 2 Chr 24, 23–27.
13, 4: 2 Kgs 14, 26f.
13, 6: Ex 34, 13.

to Jehoahaz, except fifty horsemen with ten chariots and ten thousand foot soldiers, since the king of Aram had destroyed them and trampled them like dust. 8 The rest of the acts of Jehoahaz, with all his valor and accomplishments, are recorded in the book of the chronicles of the kings of Israel. 9 Jehoahaz rested with his ancestors and was buried in Samaria. His son Joash succeeded him as king.

Reign of Joash of Israel

10 In the thirty-seventh year of Joash, king of Judah, Jehoash, son of Jehoahaz, began his sixteen-year reign over Israel in Samaria. 11 He did evil in the sight of the LORD; he did not desist from any of the sins which Jeroboam, son of Nebat, had caused Israel to commit, but persisted in them. 12*† [The rest of the acts of Joash, the valor with which he fought against Amaziah, king of Judah, and all his accomplishments, are recorded in the book of the chronicles of the kings of Israel. 13 Joash rested with his ancestors, and Jeroboam occupied the throne. Joash was buried with the kings of Israel in Samaria.]

14*† When Elisha was suffering from the sickness of which he was to die, King Joash of Israel went down to visit him. "My father, my father!" he exclaimed, weeping over him. "Israel's chariots and horsemen!" 15 "Take a bow and some arrows," Elisha said to him. When he had done so, 16† Elisha said to the king of Israel, "Put your hand on the bow." As the king held the bow, Elisha placed his hands over the king's hands 17 and said, "Open the window toward the east." He opened it, Elisha said, "Shoot," and he shot. The prophet exclaimed, "The LORD's arrow of victory! The arrow of victory over Aram! You will completely conquer Aram at Aphec." 18 Then he said to the king of Israel, "Take the arrows," which he did. Elisha said to him, "Strike the ground!" He struck the ground three times and stopped. 19 Angry with him, the man of God said: "You should have struck five or six times; you would have defeated Aram completely. Now, you will defeat Aram only three times."

20 Elisha died and was buried. At the time, bands of Moabites used to raid the land each year. 21* Once some people were burying a man, when suddenly they spied such a raiding band. So they cast the dead man into the grave of Elisha, and everyone went off. But when the man came in contact with the bones of Elisha, he came back to life and rose to his feet.

22 King Hazael of Aram oppressed Israel during the entire reign of Jehoahaz. 23* But the LORD was merciful with Israel and looked on them with compassion because of his covenant with Abraham, Isaac, and Jacob. He was unwilling to destroy them or to cast them out from his presence. 24 So when King Hazael of Aram died and his son Ben-hadad succeeded him as king, 25 Joash, son of Jehoahaz, took back from Ben-hadad, son of Hazael, the cities which Hazael had taken in battle from his father Jehoahaz. Joash defeated Ben-hadad three times, and thus recovered the cities of Israel.

Amaziah of Judah

14 1† In the second year of Joash, son of Jehoahaz, king of Israel, Amaziah, son of Joash, king of Judah, began to reign. 2* He was twenty-five years old when he became king, and he reigned twenty-nine years in Jerusalem. His mother, whose name was Jehoaddin, was from Jerusalem. 3 He pleased the LORD, yet not like his forefather David, since he did just as his father Joash had done. 4 Thus the high places did not disappear, but the people continued to sacrifice and to burn incense on them. 5* When Amaziah had the kingdom firmly in hand, he slew the officials who had murdered the king, his father. 6* But the children of the murderers he did not put to death, obeying the LORD's command written in the book of the law of Moses, "Fathers shall not be put to death for their children, nor shall children be put to death for their fathers; each one shall die for his own sin."

7* Amaziah slew ten thousand Edomites in the Salt Valley, and took Sela in battle. He renamed it Joktheel, the name it has to this day.

8* Then Amaziah sent messengers to Jehoash, son of Jehoahaz, son of Jehu, king of Israel, with this challenge, "Come, let us meet face to face." 9 King Jehoash of Israel sent this reply to the king of Judah: "The thistle of Lebanon sent word to the cedar of Lebanon, 'Give your daughter to my son in marriage,' but an animal of Lebanon passed by and trampled the thistle underfoot. 10 You have indeed

---

13, 12f: The conclusion to the reign of Joash is given again in 2 Kgs 14, 15f, where it is more appropriate.

13, 14: *My father, my father:* the king expresses here the same sentiments as those with which Elisha addressed Elijah.

13, 16–19: Symbolic acts similar to these are seen in Ex 17, 8ff; Jos 8, 18ff; Ez 4, 1ff.

14, 1f: *In the second year . . . twenty-nine years in Jerusalem:* the reigns of the kings of Judah between Athaliah and Ahaz are assigned too many years in all to correspond to the reigns in Israel from Jehu to the fall of Samaria. It seems probable that Amaziah was murdered as soon as his son Azaiah was old enough to rule, and that Amazi-

ah's reign was nearer nineteen than twenty-nine years. The correlation, in 2 Kgs 15, 1, of the beginning of Azariah's reign with the 27th year of Jeroboam II can hardly be correct; and the sixteen-year reign of Joatham of Judah (2 Kgs 15, 33) consisted for the most part of a regency during the illness of his father (2 Kgs 15, 5).

13, 12: 2 Kgs 14, 8–16.
13, 14: 2 Kgs 2, 12.
13, 21: Sir 48, 14.
13, 23: Dt 9, 27.
14, 2f: 2 Chr 25, 1f.
14, 5f: 2 Chr 25, 3f.

14, 6: Dt 24, 16; Ez 18, 20.
14, 7: 2 Sm 8, 13f; 2 Chr 25, 11.
14, 8: 2 Kgs 13, 12; Jgs 9, 8–15.

conquered Edom, and you have become ambitious. Enjoy your glory, but stay at home! Why involve yourself and Judah with you in misfortune and failure?"

[11] But Amaziah would not listen. King Jehoash of Israel then advanced, and he and King Amaziah of Judah met in battle at Beth-shemesh of Judah. [12] Judah was defeated by Israel, and all the Judean soldiery fled homeward. [13] King Jehoash of Israel captured Amaziah, son of Jehoash, son of Ahaziah, king of Judah, at Beth-shemesh. He went on to Jerusalem where he tore down four hundred cubits of the city wall, from the Gate of Ephraim to the Corner Gate. [14] He took all the gold and silver and all the utensils there were in the temple of the LORD and in the treasuries of the palace, and hostages as well. Then he returned to Samaria. [15]* The rest of the acts of Jehoash, his valor, and how he fought Amaziah, king of Judah, are recorded in the book of the chronicles of the kings of Israel. [16] Jehoash rested with his ancestors; he was buried in Samaria with the kings of Israel. His son Jeroboam succeeded him as king.

[17]† Amaziah, son of Joash, king of Judah, survived Jehoash, son of Jehoahaz, king of Israel, by fifteen years. [18] The rest of the acts of Amaziah are written in the book of the chronicles of the kings of Judah. [19] When a conspiracy was formed against him in Jerusalem, he fled to Lachish. But he was pursued to Lachish and killed there. [20] He was brought back on horses and buried with his ancestors in the City of David in Jerusalem. [21]*† Thereupon all the people of Judah took the sixteen-year-old Azariah and proclaimed him king to succeed his father Amaziah. [22] It was Azariah who rebuilt Elath and restored it to Judah, after King Amaziah rested with his ancestors.

Jeroboam II of Israel

[23] In the fifteenth year of Amaziah, son of Joash, king of Judah, Jeroboam, son of Joash, king of Israel, began his forty-one-year reign in Samaria. [24] He did evil in the sight of the LORD; he did not desist from any of the sins which Jeroboam, son of Nebat, had caused Israel to commit. [25]† He restored the boundaries of Israel from Labo-of-Hamath to the sea of the Arabah, just as the LORD, the God of Israel, had prophesied through his servant, the prophet Jonah, son of Amittai, from Gath-hepher. [26]* For the LORD saw the very bitter affliction of Israel, where there was neither slave nor freeman, no

one at all to help Israel. [27] Since the LORD had not determined to blot out the name of Israel from under the heavens, he saved them through Jeroboam, son of Joash. [28] The rest of the acts of Jeroboam, his valor and all his accomplishments, how he fought with Damascus and turned back Hamath from Israel, are recorded in the book of the chronicles of the kings of Israel. [29] Jeroboam rested with his ancestors, the kings of Israel, and his son Zechariah succeeded him as king.

Azariah of Judah

15 [1]*† Azariah, son of Amaziah, king of Judah, became king in the twenty-seventh year of Jeroboam, king of Israel. [2] He was sixteen years old when he began to reign, and he reigned fifty-two years in Jerusalem. His mother, whose name was Jecholiah, was from Jerusalem. [3] He pleased the LORD just as his father Amaziah had done. [4] Yet the high places did not disappear; the people continued to sacrifice and to burn incense on them. [5]* The LORD afflicted the king, and he was a leper to the day of his death. He lived in a house apart, while Jotham, the king's son, was vizier and regent for the people of the land. [6] The rest of the acts of Azariah, and all his accomplishments, are recorded in the book of the chronicles of the kings of Judah. [7] Azariah rested with his ancestors, and was buried with them in the City of David. His son Jotham succeeded him as king.

Zechariah of Israel

[8] In the thirty-eighth year of Azariah, king of Judah, Zechariah, son of Jeroboam, was king of Israel in Samaria for six months. [9] He did evil in the sight of the LORD as his fathers had done, and did not desist from the sins which Jeroboam, son of Nebat, had caused Israel to commit. [10] Shallum, son of Jabesh, conspired against Zechariah, attacked and killed him at Ibleam, and reigned in his place. [11] The rest of the acts of Zechariah are recorded in the book of the chronicles of the kings of Israel. [12]* Thus the LORD's promise to Jehu, "Your descendants to the fourth generation shall sit upon the throne of Israel," was fulfilled.

Shallum of Israel

[13] Shallum, son of Jabesh, became king in the thirty-ninth year of Uzziah, king of Judah; he reigned one month in Samaria. [14] Menahem, son of Gadi, came up from Tirzah to Samaria, where he attacked

---

14, 17: See note on 2 Kgs 14, 1f.
14, 21: *Azariah:* also called Uzziah in many texts.
14, 25: *Sea of the Arabah:* the Dead Sea. *Jonah:* see note on Jon 1, 1.
15, 1: *Twenty-seventh year:* see note on 2 Kgs 14, 1f.

14, 15: 2 Kgs 13, 12f.
14, 21: 2 Chr 26, 1f.
14, 26: 2 Kgs 13, 4f; 1 Kgs 14, 10.
15, 1ff: 2 Chr 26, 3f.
15, 5ff: 2 Chr 26, 21ff.
15, 12: 2 Kgs 10, 30.

and killed Shallum, son of Jabesh, and reigned in his place. [15] The rest of the acts of Shallum, and the fact of his conspiracy, are recorded in the book of the chronicles of the kings of Israel. [16] At that time, Menahem punished Tappuah, all the inhabitants of the town and of its whole district, because on his way from Tirzah they did not let him in. He punished them even to ripping open all the pregnant women.

Menahem of Israel

[17] In the thirty-ninth year of Azariah, king of Judah, Menahem, son of Gadi, began his ten-year reign over Samaria. [18] He did evil in the sight of the LORD, not desisting from the sins which Jeroboam, son of Nebat, had caused Israel to commit. During his reign, [19]† Pul, king of Assyria, invaded the land, and Menahem gave him a thousand talents of silver to have his assistance in strengthening his hold on the kingdom. [20] Menahem secured the money to give to the king of Assyria by exacting it from all the men of substance in the country, fifty silver shekels from each. The king of Assyria did not remain in the country but withdrew. [21] The rest of the acts of Menahem, and all his accomplishments, are recorded in the book of the chronicles of the kings of Israel. [22] Menahem rested with his ancestors, and his son Pekahiah succeeded him as king.

Pekahiah of Israel

[23] In the fiftieth year of Azariah, king of Judah, Pekahiah, son of Menahem, began his two-year reign over Israel in Samaria. [24] He did evil in the sight of the LORD, not desisting from the sins which Jeroboam, son of Nebat, had caused Israel to commit. [25] His adjutant Pekah, son of Remaliah, who had with him fifty men from Gilead, conspired against him, killed him within the palace stronghold in Samaria, and reigned in his place. [26] The rest of the acts of Pekahiah, and all his accomplishments, are recorded in the book of the chronicles of the kings of Israel.

Pekah of Israel

[27]† In the fifty-second year of Azariah, king of Judah, Pekah, son of Remaliah, began his twenty-year reign over Israel in Samaria. [28] He did evil in the sight of the LORD, not desisting from the sins which Jeroboam, son of Nebat, had caused Israel to commit. [29] During the reign of Pekah, king of Israel, Tiglath-pileser, king of Assyria, came and took Ijon,

Abel-beth-maacah, Janoah, Kedesh, Hazor, all the territory of Naphtali, Gilead, and Galilee, deporting the inhabitants to Assyria. [30] Hoshea, son of Elah, conspired against Pekah, son of Remaliah; he attacked and killed him, and reigned in his place [in the twentieth year of Jotham, son of Uzziah]. [31] The rest of the acts of Pekah, and all his accomplishments, are recorded in the book of the chronicles of the kings of Israel.

Jotham of Judah

[32]* In the second year of Pekah, son of Remaliah, king of Israel, Jotham, son of Uzziah, king of Judah, began to reign. [33] He was twenty-five years old when he became king, and he reigned sixteen years in Jerusalem. His mother's name was Jerusha, daughter of Zadok. [34] He pleased the LORD, just as his father Uzziah had done. [35]† Nevertheless the high places did not disappear and the people continued to sacrifice and to burn incense on them. It was he who built the Upper Gate of the temple of the LORD. [36] The rest of the acts of Jotham, and all his accomplishments, are recorded in the book of the chronicles of the kings of Judah. [37] It was at that time that the LORD first loosed Rezin, king of Aram, and Pekah, son of Remaliah, against Judah. [38] Jotham rested with his ancestors and was buried with them in his forefather's City of David. His son Ahaz succeeded him as king.

Ahaz of Judah

16 [1]* In the seventeenth year of Pekah, son of Remaliah, Ahaz, son of Jotham, king of Judah, began to reign. [2] Ahaz was twenty years old when he became king, and he reigned sixteen years in Jerusalem. He did not please the LORD, his God, like his forefather David, [3]* but conducted himself like the kings of Israel, and even immolated his son by fire, in accordance with the abominable practice of the nations whom the LORD had cleared out of the way of the Israelites. [4]* Further, he sacrificed and burned incense on the high places, on hills, and under every leafy tree.

[5]* Then Rezin, king of Aram, and Pekah, son of Remaliah, king of Israel, came up to Jerusalem to attack it. Although they besieged Ahaz, they were unable to conquer him. [6]* At the same time the king of Edom recovered Elath for Edom, driving the Judeans out of it. The Edomites then entered Elath, which they have occupied until the present.

15, 19: *Pul:* the Babylonian throne name of the Assyrian Tiglath-pileser III; cf 2 Kgs 15, 29.

15, 27: The *twenty* years here ascribed to Pekah are an impossibility; the calculation which made his reign, of five years at most, appear so long may have been based on the attempt to give Jotham of Judah a full sixteen-year reign independently of his regency. See 2 Kgs 16, 1 and the note on 2 Kgs 14, 1f.

15, 35: *The Upper Gate:* also the Gate of Benjamin; cf Jer 20, 2; Ez 9, 2.

15, 32–38: 2 Chr 27, 1–4.7–9.   16, 4: Dt 12, 2.
16, 1–4: 2 Chr 28, 1–4.   16, 5: 2 Chr 28, 5f.
  16, 3: Lv 18, 21.   16, 6: 2 Chr 28, 17.

7* Meanwhile, Ahaz sent messengers to Tiglath-pileser, king of Assyria, with the plea: "I am your servant and your son. Come up and rescue me from the clutches of the king of Aram and the king of Israel, who are attacking me." 8* Ahaz took the silver and gold that were in the temple of the LORD and in the palace treasuries and sent them as a present to the king of Assyria, 9† who listened to him and moved against Damascus, which he captured. He deported its inhabitants to Kir and put Rezin to death.

10 King Ahaz went to Damascus to meet Tiglath-pileser, king of Assyria. When he saw the altar in Damascus, King Ahaz sent to Uriah the priest a model of the altar and a detailed design of its construction. 11 Uriah the priest built an altar according to the plans which King Ahaz sent him from Damascus, and had it completed by the time the king returned home. 12 On his arrival from Damascus, the king inspected this altar, then went up to it and offered sacrifice on it, 13* burning his holocaust and cereal-offering, pouring out his libation, and sprinkling the blood of his peace-offerings on the altar. 14 The bronze altar that stood before the LORD he brought from the front of the temple—that is, from the space between the new altar and the temple of the Lord—and set it on the north side of his altar. 15*† "Upon the large altar," King Ahaz commanded Uriah the priest, "burn the morning holocaust and the evening cereal-offering, the royal holocaust and cereal-offering, as well as the holocausts, cereal-offerings, and libations of the people. You must also sprinkle on it all the blood of holocausts and sacrifices. But the old bronze altar shall be mine for consultation." 16 Uriah the priest did just as King Ahaz had commanded. 17* King Ahaz detached the frames from the bases and removed the lavers from them; he also took down the bronze sea from the bronze oxen that supported it, and set it on a stone pavement. 18† In deference to the king of Assyria he removed from the temple of the LORD the emplacement which had been built in the temple for a throne, and the outer entrance for the king. 19* The rest of the acts of Ahaz are recorded in the book of the chronicles of the kings of Judah. 20 Ahaz rested

with his ancestors and was buried with them in the City of David. His son Hezekiah succeeded him as king.

Hoshea of Israel

17 1 In the twelfth year of Ahaz, king of Judah, Hoshea, son of Elah, began his nine-year reign over Israel in Samaria. 2 He did evil in the sight of the LORD, yet not to the extent of the kings of Israel before him. 3*† Shalmaneser, king of Assyria, advanced against him, and Hoshea became his vassal and paid him tribute. 4 But the king of Assyria found Hoshea guilty of conspiracy for sending envoys to the king of Egypt at Sais, and for failure to pay the annual tribute to his Assyrian overlord. 5 For this, the king of Assyria arrested and imprisoned Hoshea; he then occupied the whole land and attacked Samaria, which he besieged for three years. 6*† In the ninth year of Hoshea, the king of Assyria took Samaria, and deported the Israelites to Assyria, settling them in Halah, at the Habor, a river of Gozan, and in the cities of the Medes.

7 This came about because the Israelites sinned against the LORD, their God, who had brought them up from the land of Egypt, from under the domination of Pharaoh, king of Egypt, and because they venerated other gods. 8 They followed the rites of the nations whom the LORD had cleared out of the way of the Israelites [and the kings of Israel whom they set up]. 9 They adopted unlawful practices toward the LORD, their God. They built high places in all their settlements, the watchtowers as well as the walled cities. 10* They set up pillars and sacred poles for themselves on every high hill and under every leafy tree. 11 There, on all the high places, they burned incense like the nations whom the LORD had sent into exile at their coming. They did evil things that provoked the LORD, 12 and served idols, although the LORD had told them, "You must not do this."

13 And though the LORD warned Israel and Judah by every prophet and seer, "Give up your evil ways and keep my commandments and statutes, in accordance with the entire law which I enjoined on your fathers and which I sent you by my servants

---

†
16, 9: Firmly dated events bearing on chapters 16 through 20 are: the fall of Damascus (16, 9) in 732 B.C., the fall of Samaria (18, 9–11) in 721 B.C., and Sennacherib's invasion of Judah (18, 13) in 701 B.C., which is equated both in Kings and in Is 36, 1 with the 14th year of Hezekiah. These data make it necessary to credit Ahaz with at least a twenty-year reign, between 735 and c. 715 B.C., and to exclude the correlations between Hoshea of Israel and Hezekiah in chapter 18.

If the 14th-year correspondence for 701 B.C. is given up, other arrangements are possible. The alleged ages of Jotham (15, 33), Ahaz (16, 2), and Hezekiah (18, 2) at their successive accessions to the throne do not argue for an early date for Hezekiah; but one or more of these may be artificial. Azariah (15, 1–7; Is 6, 1) was still on the throne of Judah in 743 B.C.

16, 15: *For consultation:* perhaps the introduction into Judah of the Babylonian practice of omen sacrifices; cf Ez 21, 16.
16, 18: *Emplacement . . . for a throne, and the outer entrance for the king:* signs of sovereignty for the Hebrew kings.
17, 3: *Shalmaneser:* son and successor of Tiglath-pileser.
17, 6: *The king of Assyria:* Shalmaneser's successor and usurper, Sargon II.

16, 7: 2 Chr 28, 16.	**16, 19:** 2 Chr 28, 26f.
16, 8: 2 Chr 28, 21.	**17, 3:** 2 Kgs 18, 9; Tb 1, 2.
16, 13: 2 Chr 28, 23.	**17, 6:** 2 Kgs 18, 10f.
16, 15: Ex 29, 38f; Nm 28, 3f.	**17, 10:** Ex 23, 24; 34, 13; Dt
16, 17: 2 Chr 28, 24.	12, 2.

did you KNOW?

The First Captivity

The Second Book of Kings describes two captivities and exiles. The first one is the Assyrian conquest of the northern kingdom, Israel, which occurred in 721 B.C. (see map 4, "The Assyrian Empire"). According to the author of 2 Kings, Israel fell first because its kings and people were even less faithful to God than the kings and people of Judah, the southern kingdom. Notice that the Assyrian conquest is described in the briefest detail (17, 5–6), but the reasons for it are described in great detail (verses 7–18).

▶ 2 Kgs 17, 5–18

the prophets," ¹⁴* they did not listen, but were as stiff-necked as their fathers, who had not believed in the LORD, their God. ¹⁵* They rejected his statutes, the covenant which he had made with their fathers, and the warnings which he had given them. The vanity they pursued, they themselves became: they followed the surrounding nations whom the LORD had commanded them not to imitate. ¹⁶* They disregarded all the commandments of the LORD, their God, and made for themselves two molten calves; they also made a sacred pole and worshiped all the host of heaven, and served Baal. ¹⁷* They immolated their sons and daughters by fire, practiced fortune-telling and divination, and sold themselves into evildoing in the LORD's sight, provoking him ¹⁸ till, in his great anger against Israel, the LORD put them away out of his sight. Only the tribe of Judah was left.

¹⁹ Even the people of Judah, however, did not keep the commandments of the LORD, their God, but followed the rites practiced by Israel. ²⁰ So the LORD rejected the whole race of Israel. He afflicted them and delivered them over to plunderers, finally casting them out from before him. ²¹* When he tore Israel away from the house of David, they made Jeroboam, son of Nebat, king: he drove the Israelites away from the LORD, causing them to commit a great sin. ²² The Israelites imitated Jeroboam in all the sins he committed, nor would they desist from them. ²³* Finally, the LORD put Israel away out of his sight as he had foretold through all his servants, the prophets; and Israel went into exile from their native soil to Assyria, an exile lasting to the present.

²⁴ The king of Assyria brought people from Babylon, Cuthah, Avva, Hamath, and Sepharvaim, and settled them in the cities of Samaria in place of the Israelites. They took possession of Samaria and dwelt in its cities. ²⁵ When they first settled there, they did not venerate the LORD, so he sent lions among them that killed some of their number. ²⁶ A report reached the king of Assyria: "The nations whom you deported and settled in the cities of Samaria do not know how to worship the God of the land, and he has sent lions among them that are killing them, since they do not know how to worship the God of the land." ²⁷ The king of Assyria gave the order, "Send back one of the priests whom I deported, to go there and settle, to teach them how to worship the God of the land." ²⁸ So one of the priests who had been deported from Samaria returned and settled in Bethel, and taught them how to venerate the LORD.

²⁹* But these peoples began to make their own gods in the various cities in which they were living; in the shrines on the high places which the Samaritans had made, each people set up gods. ³⁰ Thus the Babylonians made Marduk and his consort; the men of Cuth made Nergal; the men of Hamath made Ashima; ³¹ the men of Avva made Nibhaz and Tartak; and the men of Sepharvaim immolated their children by fire to their city gods, King Hadad and his consort Anath. ³²* They also venerated the LORD, choosing from their number priests for the high places, who officiated for them in the shrines on the high places. ³³ But, while venerating the LORD, they served their own gods, following the worship of the nations from among whom they had been deported.

³⁴*† To this day they worship according to their ancient rites. [They did not venerate the LORD nor observe the statutes and regulations, the law and commandments, which the LORD enjoined on the descendants of Jacob, whom he had named Israel. ³⁵* When he made a covenant with them, he commanded them: "You must not venerate other gods, nor worship them, nor serve them, nor offer sacrifice to them. ³⁶ The LORD, who brought you up

---

17, 34–40: *They did not . . . earlier manner:* this passage is an adaptation of language denouncing the Israelites to make it applicable to the later Samaritan sect of postexilic times. The original bearing of the discourse (vv 13–15) can be seen by reading it between vv 22 and 23. Cf also 2 Kgs 18, 12.

17, 14: Jer 25, 5; Dt 9, 13.	26–33.
17, 15: Jer 2, 5.	17, 23: Jer 25, 9.
17, 16: 1 Kgs 12, 28; Ex 34,	17, 29: Jn 4, 9.
13; Dt 4, 19; 17, 2f.	17, 32: 1 Kgs 12, 31.
17, 17: Lv 18, 21; Dt 18, 10.	17, 34: Gn 32, 29.
17, 21: 1 Kgs 12, 19f; 12,	17, 35: Ex 20, 3ff.

from the land of Egypt with great power and out-stretched arm: him shall you venerate, him shall you worship, and to him shall you sacrifice. ³⁷ You must be careful to observe forever the statutes and regulations, the law and commandment, which he wrote for you, and you must not venerate other gods. ³⁸ The covenant which I made with you, you must not forget; you must not venerate other gods. ³⁹ But the LORD, your God, you must venerate; it is he who will deliver you from the power of all your enemies." ⁴⁰ They did not listen, however, but continued in their earlier manner.] ⁴¹ Thus these nations venerated the LORD, but also served their idols. And their sons and grandsons, to this day, are doing as their fathers did.

II: The Kingdom of Judah after 721 B.C.

Hezekiah

18 ¹* In the third year of Hoshea, son of Elah, king of Israel, Hezekiah, son of Ahaz, king of Judah, began to reign. ² He was twenty-five years old when he became king, and he reigned twenty-nine years in Jerusalem. His mother's name was Abi, daughter of Zechariah. ³ He pleased the LORD, just as his forefather David had done. ⁴* It was he who removed the high places, shattered the pillars, and cut down the sacred poles. He smashed the bronze serpent called Nehushtan which Moses had made, because up to that time the Israelites were burning incense to it. ⁵ He put his trust in the LORD, the God of Israel; and neither before him nor after him was there anyone like him among all the kings of Judah. ⁶ Loyal to the LORD, Hezekiah never turned away from him, but observed the commandments which the LORD had given Moses. ⁷ The LORD was with him, and he prospered in all that he set out to do. He rebelled against the king of Assyria and did not serve him. ⁸ He also subjugated the watchtowers and walled cities of the Philistines, all the way to Gaza and its territory.

⁹† In the fourth year of King Hezekiah, which was the seventh year of Hoshea, son of Elah, king of Israel, Shalmaneser, king of Assyria, attacked Samaria, laid siege to it, ¹⁰* and after three years captured it. In the sixth year of Hezekiah, the ninth year of Hoshea, king of Israel, Samaria was taken.

¹¹ The king of Assyria then deported the Israelites to Assyria and settled them in Halah, at the Habor, a river of Gozan, and in the cities of the Medes. ¹²* This came about because they had not heeded the warning of the LORD, their God, but violated his covenant, not heeding and not fulfilling the commandments of Moses, the servant of the LORD.

Invasion of Sennacherib

¹³*† In the fourteenth year of King Hezekiah, Sennacherib,† king of Assyria, went on an expedition against all the fortified cities of Judah and captured them. ¹⁴ Hezekiah, king of Judah, sent this message to the king of Assyria at Lachish: "I have done wrong. Leave me, and I will pay whatever tribute you impose on me." The king of Assyria exacted three hundred talents of silver and thirty talents of gold from Hezekiah, king of Judah. ¹⁵ Hezekiah paid him all the funds there were in the temple of the LORD and in the palace treasuries. ¹⁶* He broke up the door panels and the uprights of the temple of the LORD which he himself had ordered to be overlaid with gold, and gave the gold to the king of Assyria.

¹⁷*† The king of Assyria sent the general, the lord chamberlain, and the commander from Lachish with a great army to King Hezekiah at Jerusalem. They went up, and on their arrival in Jerusalem, stopped at the conduit of the upper pool on the highway of the fuller's field. ¹⁸* They called for the king, who sent out to them Eliakim, son of Hilkiah, the master of the palace; Shebnah the scribe; and the herald Joah, son of Asaph. ¹⁹ The commander said to them, "Tell Hezekiah, 'Thus says the great king, the king of Assyria: On what do you base this confidence of yours? ²⁰ Do you think mere words substitute for strategy and might in war? On whom, then, do you rely, that you rebel against me? ²¹* This Egypt, the staff on which you rely, is in fact a broken reed which pierces the hand of anyone who leans on it. That is what Pharaoh, king of Egypt, is to all who rely on him. ²² But if you say to me, We rely on the LORD, our God, is not he the one whose high places and altars Hezekiah has removed, commanding Judah and Jerusalem to worship before this altar in Jerusalem?'

²³ "Now, make a wager with my lord, the king of Assyria: I will give you two thousand horses if you can put riders on them. ²⁴ How then can you re-

---

† **18, 9:** See note on 2 Kgs 16, 9.
   18, 13—20, 11: Duplication of Is 36, 1—38, 8.21.22.
   18, 13: *Sennacherib* succeeded Sargon II as king of Assyria. His Judean campaign was waged in 701 B.C. See note on 2 Kgs 16, 9.
   18, 17: *General, the lord chamberlain . . . commander:* the text lists three major functionaries by their Assyrian titles, of which only the first, more nearly "lord lieutenant," is military in origin; the commander was technically the king's chief butler.

* **18, 1ff:** 2 Chr 28, 27; 29, 1f.
   18, 4: Ex 23, 24; 34, 13; Nm 21, 9; Dt 12, 2; 2 Chr 31, 1; Wis 16, 6; Jn 3, 14.
   18, 10f: 2 Kgs 17, 6; Tb 1, 2.
   18, 12: 2 Kgs 17, 7–18.
   18, 13: 2 Chr 32, 1ff; Sir 48, 18; Is 36, 1.
   18, 16: 1 Kgs 6, 20–22.
   18, 17: 2 Chr 32, 9; Is 36, 1ff.
   18, 18: Is 22, 13–25.
   18, 21: Is 30, 1–7; 31, 1–3; Ez 29, 6–7.

pulse even one of the least servants of my lord, relying as you do on Egypt for chariots and horsemen? 25 Was it without the LORD's will that I have come up to destroy this place? The LORD said to me, 'Go up and destroy that land!' "

26 Then Eliakim, son of Hilkiah, and Shebnah and Joah said to the commander: "Please speak to your servants in Aramaic; we understand it. Do not speak to us in Judean within earshot of the people who are on the wall."

27 But the commander replied: "Was it to your master and to you that my lord sent me to speak these words? Was it not rather to the men sitting on the wall, who, with you, will have to eat their own excrement and drink their urine?" 28 Then the commander stepped forward and cried out in a loud voice in Judean, "Listen to the words of the great king, the king of Assyria. 29 Thus says the king: 'Do not let Hezekiah deceive you, since he cannot deliver you out of my hand. 30 Let not Hezekiah induce you to rely on the LORD, saying, The LORD will surely save us; this city will not be handed over to the king of Assyria. 31 Do not listen to Hezekiah, for the king of Assyria says: Make peace with me and surrender! Then each of you will eat of his own vine and of his own fig-tree, and drink the water of his own cistern, 32 until I come to take you to a land like your own, a land of grain and wine, of bread and orchards, of olives, oil and fruit syrup. Choose life, not death. Do not listen to Hezekiah when he would seduce you by saying, The LORD will rescue us. 33 Has any of the gods of the nations ever rescued his land from the hand of the king of Assyria? 34* Where are the gods of Hamath and Arpad? Where are the gods of Sepharvaim, Hena, and Avva? Where are the gods of the land of Samaria? 35 Which of the gods for all these lands ever rescued his land from my hand? Will the LORD then rescue Jerusalem from my hand?' " 36 But the people remained silent and did not answer him one word, for the king had ordered them not to answer him.

37 Then the master of the palace, Eliakim, son of Hilkiah, Shebnah the scribe, and the herald Joah, son of Asaph, came to Hezekiah with their garments torn, and reported to him what the commander had said.

Hezekiah and Isaiah

19 1* When King Hezekiah heard this, he tore his garments, wrapped himself in sackcloth, and went into the temple of the LORD. 2 He sent Eliakim, the master of the palace, Sheb-

nah the scribe, and the elders of the priests, wrapped in sackcloth, to tell the prophet Isaiah, son of Amoz, 3† "Thus says Hezekiah: 'This is a day of distress, of rebuke, and of disgrace. Children are at the point of birth, but there is no strength to bring them forth. 4 Perhaps the LORD, your God, will hear all the words of the commander, whom his master, the king of Assyria, sent to taunt the living God, and will rebuke him for the words which the LORD, your God, has heard. So send up a prayer for the remnant that is here.' " 5 When the servants of King Hezekiah had come to Isaiah, 6* he said to them, "Tell this to your master: 'Thus says the LORD: Do not be frightened by the words you have heard, with which the servants of the king of Assyria have blasphemed me. 7 I am about to put in him such a spirit that, when he hears a certain report, he will return to his own land, and there I will cause him to fall by the sword.' "

8 When the commander, on his return, heard that the king of Assyria had withdrawn from Lachish, he found him besieging Libnah. 9 The king of Assyria heard a report that Tirhakah, king of Ethiopia, had come out to fight against him. Again he sent envoys to Hezekiah with this message: 10 "Thus shall you say to Hezekiah, king of Judah: 'Do not let your God on whom you rely deceive you by saying that Jerusalem will not be handed over to the king of Assyria. 11 You have heard what the kings of Assyria have done to all other countries: they doomed them! Will you, then, be saved? 12* Did the gods of the nations whom my fathers destroyed save them? Gozan, Haran, Rezeph, or the Edenites in Telassar? 13* Where are the king of Hamath, the king of Arpad, or the kings of the cities Sepharvaim, Hena and Avva?' "

14* Hezekiah took the letter from the hand of the messengers and read it; then he went up to the temple of the LORD, and spreading it out before him, 15* he prayed in the LORD's presence: "O LORD, God of Israel, enthroned upon the cherubim! You alone are God over all the kingdoms of the earth. You have made the heavens and the earth. 16 Incline your ear, O LORD, and listen! Open your eyes, O LORD, and see! Hear the words of Sennacherib which he sent to taunt the living God. 17 Truly, O LORD, the kings of Assyria have laid waste the nations and their lands, 18* and cast their gods into the fire; they destroyed them because they were not gods, but the work of human hands, wood and stone. 19* Therefore, O LORD, our God, save us from the power of this man, that all the kingdoms of the earth may know that you alone, O LORD, are God."

19, 3: See note on Is 37, 3.

18, 34: 2 Kgs 17, 24.
19, 1–7: Is 37, 1–7.
19, 6: Is 10, 5–19.
19, 12: 2 Kgs 17, 6.

19, 13: 2 Kgs 18, 34.
19, 14–19: 2 Chr 32, 20; Is 37, 14–20.
19, 15: Ex 25, 18.
19, 18: Jer 10, 3.
19, 19: 1 Kgs 18, 24.

Punishment of Sennacherib

20 Then Isaiah, son of Amoz, sent this message to Hezekiah: "Thus says the LORD, the God of Israel, in answer to your prayer for help against Sennacherib, king of Assyria: I have listened! **21**† This is the word the LORD has spoken concerning him:

" 'She despises you, laughs you to scorn,
    the virgin daughter Zion!
Behind you she wags her head,
    daughter Jerusalem.
22 Whom have you insulted and blasphemed,
    against whom have you raised your voice
And lifted up your eyes on high?
    Against the Holy One of Israel!
23 Through your servants you have insulted the
    LORD.
You said: With my many chariots
I climbed the mountain heights,
    the recesses of Lebanon;
I cut down its lofty cedars,
    its choice cypresses;
I reached the remotest heights,
    its forest park.
24 I dug wells and drank water in foreign lands;
I dried up with the soles of my feet
    all the rivers of Egypt.
25 " 'Have you not heard?
    Long ago I prepared it,
From days of old I planned it.
    Now I have brought it to pass:
That you should reduce fortified cities
    into heaps of ruins,
26 While their inhabitants, shorn of power,
    are dismayed and ashamed,
Becoming like the plants of the field, like the
    green growth,
like the scorched grass on the housetops.
27* I am aware whether you stand or sit;
    I know whether you come or go,
28   and also your rage against me.
Because of your rage against me
    and your fury which has reached my ears,
I will put my hook in your nose
    and my bit in your mouth,
    and make you return the way you came.
29 " 'This shall be a sign for you:
    this year you shall eat the aftergrowth,
    next year, what grows of itself;
But in the third year, sow and reap,
    plant vineyards and eat their fruit!

30   The remaining survivors of the house of Judah
    shall again strike root below
    and bear fruit above.
31   For out of Jerusalem shall come a remnant,
    and from Mount Zion, survivors.
    The zeal of the LORD of hosts shall do this.'

32 "Therefore, thus says the LORD concerning the king of Assyria: 'He shall not reach this city, nor shoot an arrow at it, nor come before it with a shield, nor cast up siege-works against it. **33** He shall return by the same way he came, without entering the city, says the LORD. **34*** I will shield and save this city for my own sake, and for the sake of my servant David.' "

35* That night the angel of the LORD went forth and struck down one hundred and eighty-five thousand men in the Assyrian camp. Early the next morning, there they were, all the corpses of the dead. **36** So Sennacherib, the king of Assyria, broke camp, and went back home to Nineveh.

37 When he was worshiping in the temple of his god Nisroch, his sons Adrammelech and Sharezer slew him with the sword and fled into the land of Ararat. His son Esar-haddon reigned in his stead.

Hezekiah's Illness

20 **1*** In those days, when Hezekiah was mortally ill, the prophet Isaiah, son of Amoz, came and said to him: "Thus says the LORD: 'Put your house in order, for you are about to die; you shall not recover.' " **2** He turned his face to the wall and prayed to the LORD: **3** "O LORD, remember how faithfully and wholeheartedly I conducted myself in your presence, doing what was pleasing to you!" And Hezekiah wept bitterly.

4 Before Isaiah had left the central courtyard, the word of the LORD came to him: **5** "Go back and tell Hezekiah, the leader of my people: 'Thus says the LORD, the God of your forefather David: I have heard your prayer and seen your tears. I will heal you. In three days you shall go up to the LORD's temple; **6** I will add fifteen years to your life. I will rescue you and this city from the hand of the king of Assyria; I will be a shield to this city for my own sake, and for the sake of my servant David.' "

7 Isaiah then ordered a poultice of figs to be brought and applied to the boil, that he might recover. **8** Then Hezekiah asked Isaiah, "What is the sign that the LORD will heal me and that I shall go up to the temple of the LORD on the third day?" **9** Isaiah replied, "This will be the sign for you from the LORD that he will do what he has promised: Shall the shadow go forward or back ten steps?"

19, 21–31: vv 21–28 are addressed to Sennacherib, vv 29–31 to Judah.

19, 27: Ps 139, 2f.
19, 34: 2 Sm 7, 12; Hos 1, 7.
19, 35: Sir 48, 21; 2 Chr 32, 21f; Is 37, 36–38;

1 Mc 7, 41; 2 Mc 8, 19.
20, 1–9: 2 Chr 32, 24; Is 38, 1–8.

10 "It is easy for the shadow to advance ten steps," Hezekiah answered. "Rather, let it go back ten steps." 11 So the prophet Isaiah invoked the LORD, who made the shadow retreat the ten steps it had descended on the staircase to the terrace of Ahaz.

12*† At that time, when Merodach-baladan, son of Baladan, king of Babylon, heard that Hezekiah had been ill, he sent letters and gifts to him. 13 Hezekiah was pleased at this, and therefore showed the messengers his whole treasury, his silver, gold, spices and fine oil, his armory, and all that was in his storerooms; there was nothing in his house or in all his realm that Hezekiah did not show them.

14 Then Isaiah the prophet came to King Hezekiah and asked him: "What did these men say to you? Where did they come from?" "They came from a distant land, from Babylon," replied Hezekiah. 15 "What did they see in your house?" the prophet asked. "They saw everything in my house," answered Hezekiah. "There is nothing in my storerooms that I did not show them."

16 Then Isaiah said to Hezekiah: "Hear the word of the LORD: 17 The time is coming when all that is in your house, and everything that your fathers have stored up until this day, shall be carried off to Babylon; nothing shall be left, says the LORD. 18 Some of your own bodily descendants shall be taken and made servants in the palace of the king of Babylon."

19 Hezekiah replied to Isaiah, "The word of the LORD which you have spoken is favorable." For he thought, "There will be peace and security in my lifetime."

20*† The rest of the acts of Hezekiah, all his valor, and his construction of the pool and conduit by which water was brought into the city, are written in the book of the chronicles of the kings of Judah. 21 Hezekiah rested with his ancestors and his son Manasseh succeeded him as king.

Reign of Manasseh

21 1* Manasseh was twelve years old when he began to reign, and he reigned fifty-five years in Jerusalem. His mother's name was Hephzibah. 2 He did evil in the sight of the LORD, following the abominable practices of the nations whom the LORD had cleared out of the way of the Israelites. 3* He rebuilt the high places which his father Hezekiah had destroyed. He erected altars to Baal, and also set up a sacred pole, as Ahab, king of Israel, had done. He worshiped and served the whole host of heaven. 4 He built altars in the temple of the LORD, about which the LORD had said, "I will establish my name in Jerusalem"— 5* altars for the whole host of heaven, in the two courts of the temple.

6 He immolated his son by fire. He practiced soothsaying and divination, and reintroduced the consulting of ghosts and spirits. He did much evil in the LORD's sight and provoked him to anger.

7* The Asherah idol he had made, he set up in the temple, of which the LORD had said to David and to his son Solomon: "In this temple and in Jerusalem, which I have chosen out of all the tribes of Israel, I shall place my name forever. 8 I will not in future allow Israel to be driven off the land I gave their fathers, provided that they are careful to observe all I have commanded them, the entire law which my servant Moses enjoined upon them." 9 But they did not listen, and Manasseh misled them into doing even greater evil than the nations whom the LORD had destroyed at the coming of the Israelites.

10 Then the LORD spoke through his servants the prophets: 11* "Because Manasseh, king of Judah, has practiced these abominations and has done greater evil than all that was done by the Amorites before him, and has led Judah into sin by his idols, 12 therefore thus says the LORD, the God of Israel: 'I will bring such evil on Jerusalem and Judah that, whenever anyone hears of it, his ears shall ring. 13* I will measure Jerusalem with the same cord as I did Samaria, and with the plummet I used for the house of Ahab. I will wipe Jerusalem clean as one wipes a dish, wiping it inside and out. 14 I will cast off the survivors of my inheritance and deliver them into enemy hands, to become a prey and a booty for all their enemies, 15 because they have done evil in my sight and provoked me from the day their fathers came forth from Egypt until today.' "

16 In addition to the sin which he caused Judah to commit, Manasseh did evil in the sight of the LORD, shedding so much innocent blood as to fill the length and breadth of Jerusalem. 17* The rest of the acts of Manasseh, the sin he committed and all that he did, are written in the book of the chronicles of the kings of Judah. 18 Manasseh rested with his ancestors and was buried in his palace garden, the garden of Uzza. His son Amon succeeded him as king.

20, 12–19: Duplication of Is 39, 1–8.
20, 20: *Pool and conduit:* Hezekiah's tunnel; cf 2 Chr 32, 30.

20, 12f: Is 39, 1f; 2 Chr 32, 27ff.　　**20, 20:** 2 Chr 32, 30; Sir 48, 17.

21, 1–10: 2 Chr 33, 1–10.
21, 3: 2 Kgs 17, 16; 1 Kgs 18, 4; 16, 32f.
21, 5: Lv 18, 21.
21, 7: 2 Sm 7, 13; 1 Kgs 8,　　**16;** 9, 3.
21, 11: 1 Kgs 21, 26; Jer 15, 4.
21, 13: Is 34, 11; Am 7, 7–9; Lam 2, 8.
21, 17: 2 Chr 33, 18ff.

Reign of Amon

19* Amon was twenty-two years old when he began to reign, and he reigned two years in Jerusalem. His mother's name was Meshullemeth, daughter of Haruz of Jotbah. 20 He did evil in the sight of the LORD, as his father Manasseh had done. 21 He followed exactly the path his father had trod, serving and worshiping the idols his father had served. 22 He abandoned the LORD, the God of his fathers, and did not follow the path of the LORD. 23 Subjects of Amon conspired against him and slew the king in his palace, 24 but the people of the land then slew all who had conspired against King Amon, and proclaimed his son Josiah king in his stead. 25 The rest of the acts that Amon did are written in the book of the chronicles of the kings of Judah. 26 He was buried in his own grave in the garden of Uzza, and his son Josiah succeeded him as king.

Reign of Josiah

22 1* Josiah was eight years old when he began to reign, and he reigned thirty-one years in Jerusalem. His mother's name was Jedidah, daughter of Adaiah of Bozkath. 2 He pleased the LORD and conducted himself unswervingly just as his ancestor David had done.

3*† In his eighteenth year, King Josiah sent the scribe Shaphan, son of Azaliah, son of Meshullam, to the temple of the LORD with orders to 4* go to the high priest Hilkiah and have him smelt down the precious metals that had been donated to the temple of the Lord, which the doorkeepers had collected from the people. 5 They were to be consigned to the master workmen in the temple of the LORD, who should then pay them out to the carpenters, builders, and lumbermen making repairs on the temple, 6 and for the purchase of wood and hewn stone for the temple repairs. 7 No reckoning was asked of them regarding the funds consigned to them, because they held positions of trust.

The Book of the Law

8 The high priest Hilkiah informed the scribe Shaphan, "I have found the book of the law in the temple of the LORD." Hilkiah gave the book to Shaphan, who read it. 9 Then the scribe Shaphan went to the king and reported, "Your servants have smelted down the metals available in the temple and have consigned them to the master workmen in the temple of the LORD." 10 The scribe Shaphan also informed the king that the priest Hilkiah had

Josiah Brings Back the Ways of God

What happened to the Covenant? What happened to the Israelites' true traditions and prayer rituals? After worshiping false gods for so long, it seems as if people just forgot about the Covenant! Then in 2 Kgs 22, 8, Hilkiah discovers an old book, King Josiah reads it, and a religious reform is started. Josiah's reform is an effort to know and obey God's law and to restore worship to the one, true God. The holy days and holy ways of God are back—at least for a while (see also 2 Chronicles, chapters 34–35).

Reading can be powerful. Christians have a tremendous tradition of spiritual writings that inspire and renew faith. Spiritual autobiographies like *The Confessions of St. Augustine; The Story of a Soul,* by Saint Thérèse of Lisieux; and *The Seven Storey Mountain,* by Thomas Merton, are classics. You might try starting with entertaining fictional books with a strong spiritual message, like the seven volumes of *The Chronicles of Narnia,* by C. S. Lewis, or the *Joshua* books, by Joseph F. Girzone. For other suggestions of spiritual writings you might enjoy, ask a parent, youth minister, teacher, or pastor.

▸ **2 Kings, chapters 22–23**

given him a book, and then read it aloud to the king. 11* When the king had heard the contents of the book of the law, he tore his garments 12 and issued this command to Hilkiah the priest, Ahikam, son of Shaphan, Achbor, son of Micaiah, the scribe Shaphan, and the king's servant Asaiah: 13 "Go, consult the LORD for me, for the people, for all Judah, about the stipulations of this book that has been found, for the anger of the LORD has been set furiously ablaze against us, because our fathers did not obey the stipulations of this book, nor fulfill our written obligations."

22, 3: *Shaphan:* head of a prominent family in the reign of Josiah, secretary to the king, bearer and reader of the newfound book of the law (vv 3–13; 2 Chr 34, 8f.15–20). He and his sons favored the reform of King Josiah and supported the prophet Jeremiah; cf Jer 26, 24.

21, 19–26: 2 Chr 33, 21–25.   22, 4–7: 2 Kgs 12, 11–16.
      22, 1f: 2 Chr 34, 1f.   22, 11–20: 2 Chr 34, 19–28.
22, 3–13: 2 Chr 34, 8–21.

14 So Hilkiah the priest, Ahikam, Achbor, Shaphan, and Asaiah betook themselves to the Second Quarter in Jerusalem, where the prophetess Huldah resided. She was the wife of Shallum, son of Tikvah, son of Harhas, keeper of the wardrobe. When they had spoken to her, 15 she said to them, "Thus says the LORD, the God of Israel: 'Say to the man who sent you to me, 16 Thus says the LORD: I will bring upon this place and upon its inhabitants all the evil that is threatened in the book which the king of Judah has read. 17 Because they have forsaken me and have burned incense to other gods, provoking me by everything to which they turn their hands, my anger is ablaze against this place and it cannot be extinguished.'

18 "But to the king of Judah who sent you to consult the LORD, give this response: 'Thus says the LORD, the God of Israel: As for the threats you have heard, 19 because you were heartsick and have humbled yourself before the LORD when you heard my threats that this place and its inhabitants would become a desolation and a curse; because you tore your garments and wept before me; I in turn have listened, says the LORD. 20 I will therefore gather you to your ancestors; you shall go to your grave in peace, and your eyes shall not see all the evil I will bring upon this place.' " This they reported to the king.

23 1* The king then had all the elders of Judah and of Jerusalem summoned together before him. 2 The king went up to the temple of the LORD with all the men of Judah and all the inhabitants of Jerusalem: priests, prophets, and all the people, small and great. He had the entire contents of the book of the covenant that had been found in the temple of the LORD, read out to them. 3 Standing by the column, the king made a covenant before the LORD that they would follow him and observe his ordinances, statutes and decrees with their whole hearts and souls, thus reviving the terms of the covenant which were written in this book. And all the people stood as participants in the covenant.

4* Then the king commanded the high priest Hilkiah, his vicar, and the doorkeepers to remove from the temple of the LORD all the objects that had been made for Baal, Asherah, and the whole host of heaven. He had these burned outside Jerusalem on the slopes of the Kidron and their ashes carried to Bethel. 5* He also put an end to the pseudo-priests whom the kings of Judah had appointed to burn incense on the high places in the cities of Judah and in the vicinity of Jerusalem, as well as those who burned incense to Baal, to the sun, moon, and signs of the Zodiac, and to the whole host of heaven. 6* From the temple of the LORD he also removed the sacred pole, to the Kidron Valley, outside Jerusalem; there he had it burned and beaten to dust, which was then scattered over the common graveyard. 7*† He tore down the apartments of the cult prostitutes which were in the temple of the LORD, and in which the women wove garments for the Asherah.

8* He brought in all the priests from the cities of Judah, and then defiled, from Geba to Beer-sheba, the high places where they had offered incense. He also tore down the high place of the satyrs, which was at the entrance of the Gate of Joshua, governor of the city, to the left as one enters the city gate. 9 The priests of the high places could not function at the altar of the LORD in Jerusalem; but they, along with their relatives, ate the unleavened bread.

10*† The king also defiled Topheth in the Valley of Ben-hinnom, so that there would no longer be any immolation of sons or daughters by fire in honor of Molech. 11† He did away with the horses which the kings of Judah had dedicated to the sun; these were at the entrance of the temple of the LORD, near the chamber of Nathan-melech the eunuch, which was in the large building. The chariots of the sun he destroyed by fire. 12* He also demolished the altars made by the kings of Judah on the roof (the roof terrace of Ahaz), and the altars made by Manasseh in the two courts of the temple of the LORD. He pulverized them and threw the dust into the Kidron Valley. 13*† The king defiled the high places east of Jerusalem, south of the Mount of Misconduct, which Solomon, king of Israel, had built in honor of Astarte, the Sidonian horror, of Chemosh, the Moabite horror, and of Milcom, the idol of the Ammonites. 14* He broke to pieces the pillars, cut down the sacred poles, and filled the places where they had been with human bones. 15* Likewise the altar which was at Bethel, the high place

---

23, 7: *Cult prostitutes:* of both sexes; cf 1 Kgs 14, 24.

23, 10: *Topheth . . . by fire:* condemned by Deuteronomic law and denounced by Jeremiah (Dt 12, 31; Jer 7, 29ff; Jer 19).

23, 11: *Large building:* to the west of the temple area (1 Chr 26, 18), named in the Hebrew by an Egyptian name for a similar construction.

23, 13: *Mount of Misconduct:* a paranomasia on "Mount of Olives" (in Hebrew *Maschit/mishcheh*) as suggested by the Targum. Cf Vulgate, "Mount of Offense." *Horror . . . idol:* in all three phrases here the Hebrew uses a pejorative designation meaning "abomination."

23, 1–5: 2 Chr 34, 29–33.
23, 4: 2 Chr 34, 3–5; Sir 49, 3.
23, 5: Dt 17, 3ff.
23, 6: Dt 16, 21; 1 Kgs 14, 23.
23, 7: 1 Kgs 14, 24; Dt 23, 18f.
23, 8: Dt 12, 2f.
23, 10: Lv 18, 21.
23, 12: 2 Kgs 21, 5.
23, 13: 1 Kgs 11, 7.
23, 14: Dt 16, 21f; 1 Kgs 14, 23.
23, 15: 1 Kgs 12, 31f; 13, 32.

built by Jeroboam, son of Nebat, who caused Israel to sin—this same altar and high place he tore down, breaking up the stones and grinding them to powder, and burning the Asherah. [16] When Josiah turned and saw the graves there on the mountainside, he ordered the bones taken from the graves and burned on the altar, and thus defiled it in fulfillment of the word of the LORD which the man of God had proclaimed as Jeroboam was standing by the altar on the feast day. When the king looked up and saw the grave of the man of God who had proclaimed these words, [17] he asked, "What is that tombstone I see?" The men of the city replied, "It is the grave of the man of God who came from Judah and predicted the very things you have done to the altar of Bethel." [18]*† "Let him be," he said, "let no one move his bones." So they left his bones undisturbed together with the bones of the prophet who had come from Samaria.

[19]* Josiah also removed all the shrines on the high places near the cities of Samaria which the kings of Israel had erected, thereby provoking the LORD; he did the very same to them as he had done in Bethel. [20] He slaughtered upon the altars all the priests of the high places that were at the shrines, and burned human bones upon them. Then he returned to Jerusalem.

[21]* The king issued a command to all the people to observe the Passover of the LORD, their God, as it was prescribed in that book of the covenant. [22] No Passover such as this had been observed during the period when the Judges ruled Israel, or during the entire period of the kings of Israel and the kings of Judah, [23] until the eighteenth year of King Josiah, when this Passover of the LORD was kept in Jerusalem.

[24]*† Further, Josiah did away with the consultation of ghosts and spirits, with the household gods, idols, and all the other horrors to be seen in the land of Judah and in Jerusalem, so that he might carry out the stipulations of the law written in the book that the priest Hilkiah had found in the temple of the LORD. [25]* Before him there had been no king who turned to the LORD as he did, with his whole heart, his whole soul, and his whole strength, in accord with the entire law of Moses; nor could any after him compare with him.

[26] Yet, because of all the provocations that Manasseh had given, the LORD did not desist from his fiercely burning anger against Judah. [27]* The LORD said: "Even Judah will I put out of my sight as I did Israel. I will reject this city, Jerusalem, which I chose, and the temple of which I said, 'There shall my name be.'"

[28]* The rest of the acts of Josiah, with all that he did, are written in the book of the chronicles of the kings of Judah. [29]* In his time Pharaoh Neco, king of Egypt, went up toward the river Euphrates to the king of Assyria. King Josiah set out to confront him, but was slain at Megiddo at the first encounter. [30]† His servants brought his body on a chariot from Megiddo to Jerusalem, where they buried him in his own grave. Then the people of the land took Jehoahaz, son of Josiah, anointed him, and proclaimed him king to succeed his father.

Reign of Jehoahaz

[31]* Jehoahaz was twenty-three years old when he began to reign, and he reigned three months in Jerusalem. His mother, whose name was Hamutal, daughter of Jeremiah, was from Libnah. [32] He did evil in the sight of the LORD, just as his forebears had done. [33]† Pharaoh Neco took him prisoner at Riblah in the land of Hamath, thus ending his reign in Jerusalem. He imposed a fine upon the land of a hundred talents of silver and a talent of gold. [34] Pharaoh Neco then appointed Eliakim, son of Josiah, king in place of his father Josiah; he changed his name to Jehoiakim. Jehoahaz he took away with him to Egypt, where he died. [35] Jehoiakim gave the silver and gold to Pharaoh, but taxed the land to raise the amount Pharaoh demanded. He exacted the silver and gold from the people of the land, from each proportionately, to pay Pharaoh Neco.

Reign of Jehoiakim

[36]* Jehoiakim was twenty-five years old when he began to reign, and he reigned eleven years in Jerusalem. His mother's name was Zebidah, daughter of Pedaiah, from Rumah. [37] He did evil in the sight of the LORD, just as his forebears had done.

24

[1]* During his reign Nebuchadnezzar, king of Babylon, moved against him, and Jehoiakim became his vassal for three years. Then

---

23, 18: From Samaria: more narrowly, from Bethel; cf 1 Kgs 13, 31f.
23, 24: Household gods . . . idols: teraphim. See note on Gn 31, 19.
23, 30.35: People of the land: in this period, the phrase referred to "landed gentry"; in later times it meant "the poor." Cf 2 Kgs 24, 14.
23, 33: A talent of gold: some manuscripts of the Greek and Syriac texts have "ten talents."

23, 18: 1 Kgs 13, 31.
23, 19: 2 Chr 34, 6f.
23, 21: Dt 16, 1–8; 2 Chr 35, 1ff.18f.
23, 24: 2 Kgs 21, 6; Gn 31, 19; Dt 18, 11; Jgs 18, 14.
23, 25: Dt 6, 5.
23, 27: 2 Kgs 24, 2.
23, 28: 2 Chr 35, 26f.
23, 29: 2 Chr 35, 20–24.
23, 31: 2 Chr 36, 2f.
23, 36f: 2 Chr 36, 4f.
24, 1–5: 2 Chr 36, 6ff.

Jehoiakim turned and rebelled against him. 2* The LORD loosed against him bands of Chaldeans, Arameans, Moabites, and Ammonites; he loosed them against Judah to destroy it, as the LORD had threatened through his servants the prophets. 3 This befell Judah because the LORD had stated that he would inexorably put them out of his sight for the sins Manasseh had committed in all that he did; 4* and especially because of the innocent blood he shed, with which he filled Jerusalem, the LORD would not forgive.

5* The rest of the acts of Jehoiakim, with all that he did, are written in the book of the chronicles of the kings of Judah. 6 Jehoiakim rested with his ancestors, and his son Jehoiachin succeeded him as king. 7 The king of Egypt did not again leave his own land, for the king of Babylon had taken all that belonged to the king of Egypt from the wadi of Egypt to the Euphrates River.

Reign of Jehoiachin

8† Jehoiachin was eighteen years old when he began to reign, and he reigned three months in Jerusalem. His mother's name was Nehushta, daughter of Elnathan of Jerusalem. 9 He did evil in the sight of the LORD, just as his forebears had done.

10* At that time the officials of Nebuchadnezzar, king of Babylon, attacked Jerusalem, and the city came under siege. 11 Nebuchadnezzar, king of Babylon, himself arrived at the city while his servants were besieging it. 12 Then Jehoiachin, king of Judah, together with his mother, his ministers, officers, and functionaries, surrendered to the king of Babylon, who, in the eighth year of his reign, took him captive. 13* He carried off all the treasures of the temple of the LORD and those of the palace, and broke up all the gold utensils that Solomon, king of Israel, had provided in the temple of the LORD, as the LORD had foretold. 14 He deported all Jerusalem: all the officers and men of the army, ten thousand in number, and all the craftsmen and smiths. None were left among the people of the land except the poor. 15* He deported Jehoiachin to Babylon, and also led captive from Jerusalem to Babylon the king's mother and wives, his functionaries, and the chief men of the land. 16 The king of Babylon also led captive to Babylon all seven thousand men of the army, and a thousand craftsmen and smiths, all of them trained soldiers. 17 In place of Jehoiachin, the king of Babylon appointed his uncle Mattaniah king, and changed his name to Zedekiah.

Reign of Zedekiah

18* Zedekiah was twenty-one years old when he became king, and he reigned eleven years in Jerusalem. His mother's name was Hamutal, daughter of Jeremiah of Libnah. 19 He also did evil in the sight of the LORD, just as Jehoiakim had done. 20* The LORD's anger befell Jerusalem and Judah till he cast them out from his presence. Thus Zedekiah rebelled against the king of Babylon.

25 1*† In the tenth month of the ninth year of Zedekiah's reign, on the tenth day of the month, Nebuchadnezzar, king of Babylon, and his whole army advanced against Jerusalem, encamped around it, and built siege walls on every side. 2 The siege of the city continued until the eleventh year of Zedekiah. 3 On the ninth day of the fourth month, when famine had gripped the city, and the people had no more bread, 4 the city walls were breached. Then the king and all the soldiers left the city by night through the gate between the two walls which was near the king's garden. Since

did you KNOW?
The Fall of Jerusalem

The second conquest and exile described in 2 Kings (see "The First Captivity," 17, 5–18, for the first) involves the southern kingdom, Judah. Judah was conquered by the Babylonians in 587 B.C., which is why that event is often referred to as the Babylonian Exile (see map 5, "The Babylonian Empire"). The author of Kings implies that the kingdom of Judah lasted longer than the kingdom of Israel because it had faithful reformer kings like Hezekiah and Josiah. The fall of Judah was particularly devastating because both Jerusalem, David's city, and the Temple, the central place of worship, were destroyed. The whole Book of Lamentations is an expression of the sorrow and grief the people experienced as a result.

▸ 2 Kgs 25, 1–21

24, 8: *He reigned three months:* in the year 597 B.C.
25, 1–30: This chapter parallels Jer 39 and 52; see notes to those parts of Jeremiah.

24, 2: 2 Kgs 23, 27.
24, 4: 2 Kgs 21, 16.
24, 5: 2 Chr 36, 8.
24, 10: 2 Chr 36, 10; Dn 1, 1f.
24, 13: 2 Kgs 20, 17; Is 39, 6.
24, 15: Est A, 3; 2, 6.
24, 18: 2 Chr 36, 9; Jer 37, 1f; 52, 1ff.
24, 20: 2 Kgs 22, 17; 23, 27.
25, 1–21: Jer 39, 1–10; 52, 4–28.

the Chaldeans had the city surrounded, they went in the direction of the Arabah. 5 But the Chaldean army pursued the king and overtook him in the desert near Jericho, abandoned by his whole army.

6 The king was therefore arrested and brought to Riblah to the king of Babylon, who pronounced sentence on him. 7 He had Zedekiah's sons slain before his eyes. Then he blinded Zedekiah, bound him with fetters, and had him brought to Babylon.

8 On the seventh day of the fifth month (this was in the nineteenth year of Nebuchadnezzar, king of Babylon), Nebuzaradan, captain of the bodyguard, came to Jerusalem as the representative of the king of Babylon. 9* He burned the house of the LORD, the palace of the king, and all the houses of Jerusalem; every large building was destroyed by fire. 10 Then the Chaldean troops who were with the captain of the guard tore down the walls that surrounded Jerusalem.

11† Then Nebuzaradan, captain of the guard, led into exile the last of the people remaining in the city, and those who had deserted to the king of Babylon, and the last of the artisans. 12 But some of the country's poor, Nebuzaradan, captain of the guard, left behind as vinedressers and farmers.

13* The bronze pillars that belonged to the house of the LORD, and the wheeled carts and the bronze sea in the house of the LORD, the Chaldeans broke into pieces; they carried away the bronze to Babylon. 14* They took also the pots, the shovels, the snuffers, the bowls, the pans and all the bronze vessels used for service. 15 The fire-holders and the bowls which were of gold or silver the captain of the guard also carried off. 16 The weight in bronze of the two pillars, the bronze sea, and the wheeled carts, all of them furnishings which Solomon had made for the house of the LORD, was never calculated. 17* Each of the pillars was eighteen cubits high; a bronze capital five cubits high surmounted each pillar, and a network with pomegranates encircled the capital, all of bronze; and so for the other pillar, as regards the network.

18 The captain of the guard also took Seraiah the high priest, Zephaniah the second priest, and the three keepers of the entry. 19 And from the city he took one courtier, a commander of soldiers, five men in the personal service of the king who were still in the city, the scribe of the army commander, who mustered the people of the land, and sixty of the common people still remaining in the city. 20 The captain of the guard, Nebuzaradan, arrested these and brought them to the king of Babylon at Riblah; 21 the king had them struck down and put to death in Riblah, in the land of Hamath. Thus was Judah exiled from her land.

Governorship of Gedaliah

22* As for the people whom he had allowed to remain in the land of Judah, Nebuchadnezzar, king of Babylon, appointed as their governor Gedaliah, son of Ahikam, son of Shaphan. 23 Hearing that the king of Babylon had appointed Gedaliah governor, all the army commanders with their men came to him at Mizpah: Ishmael, son of Nethaniah, Johanan, son of Kareah, Seraiah, son of Tanhumeth the Netophathite, and Jaazaniah, from Bethmaacah. 24 Gedaliah gave the commanders and their men his oath. "Do not be afraid of the Chaldean officials," he said to them. "Remain in the country and serve the king of Babylon, and all will be well with you."

25 But in the seventh month Ishmael, son of Nethaniah, son of Elishama, of royal descent, came with ten men, attacked Gedaliah and killed him, along with the Jews and Chaldeans who were in Mizpah with him. 26 Then all the people, great and small, left with the army commanders and went to Egypt for fear of the Chaldeans.

Release of Jehoiachin

27* In the thirty-seventh year of the exile of Jehoiachin, king of Judah, on the twenty-seventh day of the twelfth month, Evil-merodach, king of Babylon, in the inaugural year of his own reign, raised up Jehoiachin, king of Judah, from prison. 28 He spoke kindly to him and gave him a throne higher than that of the other kings who were with him in Babylon. 29 Jehoiachin took off his prison garb and ate at the king's table as long as he lived. 30 The allowance granted him by the king was a perpetual allowance, in fixed daily amounts, for as long as he lived.

---

† **25, 11:** *Those who had deserted:* perhaps on the advice of Jeremiah; cf Jer 38, 2f.

25, 9: 2 Chr 36, 19; Ps 74, 7.
25, 13: 2 Kgs 16, 17; 1 Kgs 7, 15–39; 2 Chr 3, 15; 36, 18; Jer 27, 19.
25, 14: 1 Kgs 7, 48ff.
25, 17: 1 Kgs 7, 15; Jer 52, 21ff.
25, 22–26: Jer 40, 5.7—41, 1–3.
25, 27–30: Jer 52, 31–34.

Have you ever had a friendly disagreement with someone over the interpretation of a movie? Did you each emphasize different aspects of the movie to support your interpretation? The First and Second Books of Chronicles are another interpretation of the history of the people of Israel. These books downplay the Covenant and emphasize the importance of institutional ritual and worship of God.

In-depth

The Chronicler is the name given to the unknown author (or authors) of 1 and 2 Chronicles. The Chronicler, writing after the Israelites returned from the Exile in Babylon, has a unique perspective, so unique that he almost never mentions the Sinai Covenant or Moses (central themes throughout other parts of the Old Testament). Because the Israelites cannot have their own king, the Chronicler emphasizes a new type of reign, one governed by priests instead of kings.

The Chronicler uses two types of material—genealogies and lively sermons —to summarize Israel's history from the Creation to around 525 B.C. But he primarily focuses on Kings David and Solomon. They are praised extensively because of their role in centralizing worship in Jerusalem and building the Temple. Many of the negative stories about David from 2 Samuel—such as his affair with Bathsheba—are not even mentioned. The Chronicler wants nothing to tarnish the people's memory of an ideal kingdom that might one day be restored.

Second Chronicles also focuses on the southern kingdom of Judah and ignores the northern kingdom of Israel after Solomon's death. This may well be due to a bias of the priestly class in Jerusalem against the religious practice of the northern tribes. This bias lasted into Jesus' time.

The goal of 1 and 2 Chronicles was to give the Israelites hope for the future after returning from the Exile. The Chronicler reminded them that if they maintained their religious practices and worship of God, they would continue to be God's people.

At a Glance

I. Genealogical Tables (1 Chr 1, 1—9, 34).

II. The History of David (1 Chr 9, 35—29, 30).

I. The Reign of Solomon (2 Chr 1, 1—9, 31).

II. The Monarchy before Hezekiah (2 Chr 10, 1—27, 9).

III. Reforms of Hezekiah and Josiah (2 Chr 28, 1—36, 1).

IV. End of the Kingdom (2 Chr 36, 2–23).

Quick Facts

Period Covered
Creation to the end of the Babylonian captivity

Author
a Levite cantor and scribe writing after the return to Jerusalem around 400 B.C.

Theme
Israel can secure its future by continuing its worship in the pattern established by David.

The First and Second Books of Chronicles

Chronicles

1 Chronicles

I: Genealogical Tables

From Adam to Abraham

1 1*† Adam, Seth, Enosh, 2* Kenan, Mahalalel, Jared, 3* Enoch, Methuselah, Lamech, 4* Noah, Shem, Ham, and Japheth. 5* The descendants of Japheth were Gomer, Magog, Madai, Javan, Tubal, Meshech, and Tiras. 6 The descendants of Gomer were Ashkenaz, Riphath, and Togarmah. 7 The descendants of Javan were Elishah, Tarshis, the Kittim, and the Rodanim.

8* The descendants of Ham were Cush, Mesraim, Put, and Canaan. 9 The descendants of Cush were Seba, Havilah, Sabta, Raama, and Sabteca. The descendants of Raama were Sheba and Dedan. 10 Cush became the father of Nimrod, who was the first to be a conqueror on the earth. 11* Mesraim became the father of the Ludim, Anamim, Lehabim, Naphtuhim, 12 Pathrusim, Casluhim, and Caphtorim, from whom the Philistines sprang. 13 Canaan became the father of Sidon, his first-born, and Heth, 14 and the Jebusite, the Amorite, the Girgashite, 15 the Hivite, the Arkite, the Sinite, 16 the Arvadite, the Zemarite, and the Hamathite.

17* The descendants of Shem were Elam, Asshur, Arpachshad, Lud, and Aram. The descendants of Aram were Uz, Hul, Gether, and Mash. 18 Arpachshad became the father of Shelah, and Shelah became the father of Eber. 19 Two sons were born to Eber; the first was named Peleg (for in his time the world was divided), and his brother was Joktan. 20 Joktan became the father of Almodad, Sheleph, Hazarmaveth, Jerah, 21 Hadoram, Uzal, Diklah, 22 Ebal, Abimael, Sheba, 23 Ophir, Havilah, and Jobab; all these were the sons of Joktan.

24* Shem, Arpachshad, Shelah, 25 Eber, Peleg, Reu, 26 Serug, Nahor, Terah, 27* Abram, who was Abraham.

From Abraham to Jacob

28* The sons of Abraham were Isaac and Ishmael. 29* These were their descendants:

Nebaioth, the first-born of Ishmael, then Kedar, Adbeel, Mibsam, 30 Mishma, Dumah, Massa, Hadad, Tema, 31 Jetur, Naphish, and Kedemah. These were the descendants of Ishmael.

---

† **1, 1—9, 34:** The Chronicler set as his task the retelling, from his particular viewpoint, of the story of God's people from the beginning to his own day. Since his primary interest was the history of David and the Davidic dynasty of Judah, he presents through mere genealogical lists a summary of what preceded the reign of Saul, David's predecessor in the kingdom. The sources for these genealogies are mostly the canonical Hebrew Scriptures that were already in their present form in his time. The cross references in this book indicate in each case the scriptural sources used.

1, 1: 1 Chr 4, 25f; Gn 5, 3.6.9.
1, 2ff: Gn 5, 9–32; 10, 2ff.
1, 3: Gn 4, 25.
1, 4: Gn 5, 32; 6, 10; 9, 18.
1, 5ff: Gn 10, 2ff.
1, 8: Gn 10, 8.
1, 11–16: Gn 10, 13–18.
1, 17–23: Gn 10, 22–29; 11, 10–18.
1, 24–27: Gn 11, 10–26; Lk 3, 34ff.
1, 27: Gn 17, 5; Neh 9, 7.
1, 28: Gn 16, 11.15; 21, 2f; Gal 4, 22f; Heb 11, 11.
1, 29ff: Gn 25, 13–16.

32* The descendants of Keturah, Abraham's concubine: she bore Zimran, Jokshan, Medan, Midian, Ishbak, and Shuah. The sons of Jokshan were Sheba and Dedan. 33 The descendants of Midian were Ephah, Epher, Hanoch, Abida, and Eldaah. All these were the descendants of Keturah.

34* Abraham became the father of Isaac. The sons of Isaac were Esau and Israel.

35* The sons of Esau were Eliphaz, Reuel, Jeush, Jalam, and Korah. 36 The sons of Eliphaz were Teman, Omar, Zephi, Gatam, Kenaz, [Timna,] and Amalek. 37 The sons of Reuel were Nahath, Zerah, Shammah, and Mizzah.

38* † The descendants of Seir were Lotan, Shobal, Zibeon, Anah, Dishon, Ezer, and Dishan. 39 The sons of Lotan were Hori and Homam; Timna was the sister of Lotan. 40 The sons of Shobal were Alian, Manahath, Ebal, Shephi, and Onam. The sons of Zibeon were Aiah and Anah. 41 The sons of Anah: Dishon. The sons of Dishon were Hemdan, Eshban, Ithran, and Cheran. 42 The sons of Ezer were Bilhan, Zaavan, and Jaakan. The sons of Dishan were Uz and Aran.

43* The kings who reigned in the land of Edom before they had Israelite kings were the following: Bela, son of Beor, the name of whose city was Ninhabah. 44* When Bela died, Jobab, son of Zerah, from Bozrah, succeeded him. 45* When Jobab died, Husham, from the land of the Temanites, succeeded him. 46 Husham died and Hadad, son of Bedad, succeeded him. He overthrew the Midianites on the Moabite plateau, and the name of his city was Avith. 47 Hadad died and Samlah of Masrekah succeeded him. 48 Samlah died and Shaul from Rehoboth-han-nahar succeeded him. 49 When Shaul died, Baalhanan, son of Achbor, succeeded him. 50 Baalhanan died and Hadad succeeded him. The name of his city was Pai, and his wife's name was Mehetabel. She was the daughter of Matred, who was the daughter of Mezahab. 51* After Hadad died. . . .

These were the chiefs of Edom: the chiefs of Timna, Aliah, Jetheth, 52 Oholibamah, Elah, Pinon, 53 Kenaz, Teman, Mibzar, 54 Magdiel, and Iram were the chiefs of Edom.

2 1* These were the sons of Israel: Reuben, Simeon, Levi, Judah, Issachar, Zebulun, 2* Dan, Joseph, Benjamin, Naphtali, Gad, and Asher.

Judah

3* † The sons of Judah were: Er, Onan, and Shelah; these three were born to him of Bathshua, a Canaanite woman. But Judah's first-born, Er, was wicked in the sight of the LORD, so he killed him. 4* Judah's daughter-in-law Tamar bore him Perez and Zerah, so that he had five sons in all.

5* The sons of Perez were Hezron and Hamul. 6* The sons of Zerah were Zimri, Ethan, Heman, Calcol, and Darda—five in all. 7* The sons of Zimri: Carmi. The sons of Carmi: Achar, who brought trouble upon Israel by violating the ban. 8 The sons of Ethan: Azariah. 9* † The sons born to Hezron were Jerahmeel, Ram, and Chelubai.

10* † Ram became the father of Amminadab, and Amminadab became the father of Nahshon, a prince of the Judahites. 11* Nahshon became the father of Salma. Salma became the father of Boaz. 12 Boaz became the father of Obed. Obed became the father of Jesse. 13* Jesse became the father of Eliab, his first-born, of Abinadab, the second son, Shimea, the third,* 14 Nethanel, the fourth, Raddai, the fifth, 15 Ozem, the sixth, and David, the seventh. 16* Their sisters were Zeruiah and Abigail. Zeruiah had three sons: Abishai, Joab, and Asahel. 17* Abigail bore Amasa, whose father was Jether the Ishmaelite.

18* † By his wife Azubah, Caleb, son of Hezron, became the father of a daughter, Jerioth. Her sons were Jesher, Shobab, and Ardon. 19* When Azubah died, Caleb married Ephrath, who bore him Hur. 20* Hur became the father of Uri, and Uri became the father of Bezalel. 21* Then Hezron had relations with the daughter of Machir, the father of Gilead, having married her when he was sixty years old. She bore him Segub. 22* Segub became the father of

---

†
1, 38: *Seir:* another name for Esau (v 35) or Edom (v 43).

2, 3—4, 23: For two reasons, the Chronicler places the genealogy of the tribe of Judah before that of the other tribes, giving it also at greater length than the others: because of his interest in David and because in the Chronicler's time the people of God were almost exclusively Jews. Both David and the Jews were of the tribe of Judah.

2, 9: *Chelubai:* a variant form of the name Caleb (vv 18.42), distinct from Chelub of 1 Chr 4, 11.

2, 10–17: Immediate ancestors of David. A similar list is given in Ru 4, 19–22; each list, independent of the other, derives from a common source.

2, 18–24: Descendants of Caleb. In 1 Chr 4, 15, as is often the case in the Pentateuch (Nm 13, 6; 14, 6.30; 26, 65; etc.), Caleb is called son of Jephunneh. Here he is called son of Hezron, perhaps because the Calebites were reckoned as part of the clan of the Hezronites.
*

1, 32f: Gn 25, 1–4.   32, 28f; Mt 1, 2; Lk 3,
1, 34: Gn 21, 2f; 25, 19.25f.   34.

1, 35ff: Gn 36, 4f.10–13.15ff.   22, 20.
1, 38–42: Gn 36, 20–28.   **2, 9:** Rv 4, 19; Mt 1, 3.
1, 43–54: Gn 36, 31–43.   **2, 10:** Rv 4, 19; Mt 1, 4.
  1, 44: Is 34, 6; 63, 1; Jer 49,   **2, 11f:** Nm 1, 7; Rv 4, 20f; Mt
    13.22.   1, 4f.
  1, 45: Gn 36, 11; Jb 2, 11; Jer   **2, 13f:** 1 Sm 16, 6–13; 17,
    49, 7.20.   13f.
1, 51–54: Gn 36, 40–43.   **2, 13:** 2 Chr 11, 18.
  2, 1: Gn 29, 32–35; 30,   **2, 16:** 2 Sm 2, 18.
    18.20; 35, 23.   **2, 17:** 2 Sm 17, 25; 19, 14;
  2, 2: Gn 30, 6.8.11.13.24;   20, 4–13.
    35, 18.24ff.   **2, 18:** 1 Chr 2, 24.
  2, 3: 1 Chr 4, 21; Gn 38,   **2, 19:** 1 Chr 2, 24.
    1–5; 46, 12.   **2, 20:** Ex 24, 14; 31, 2; 35,
  2, 4: Gn 38, 7.13–30; 46,   30; 2 Chr 1, 5.
    12; Rv 4, 12.18; Mt   **2, 21:** Nm 26, 29; 27, 1; 32,
    1, 3.   32; Jos 13, 31; Jgs 5,
  2, 5: Gn 46, 12.   14.
  2, 6: 1 Kgs 5, 11.   **2, 22:** Nm 32, 41; 1 Kgs 4,
  2, 7: Jos 7, 1.18ff.24f.   13.

Jair, who possessed twenty-three cities in the land of Gilead. 23* Geshur and Aram took from them the villages of Jair, that is, Kenath and its towns, sixty cities in all, which had belonged to the sons of Machir, the father of Gilead. 24* After the death of Hezron, Caleb had relations with Ephrathah, the widow of his father Hezron, and she bore him Ashhur, the father of Tekoa.

25*† The sons of Jerahmeel, the first-born of Hezron, were Ram, the first-born, then Bunah, Oren, and Ozem, his brothers. 26 Jerahmeel also had another wife, Atarah by name, who was the mother of Onam. 27 The sons of Ram, the first-born of Jerahmeel, were Maaz, Jamin, and Eker. 28 The sons of Onam were Shammai and Jada. The sons of Shammai were Nadab and Abishur. 29 Abishur's wife, who was named Abihail, bore him Ahban and Molid. 30 The sons of Nadab were Seled and Appaim. Seled died without sons. 31* The sons of Appaim: Ishi. The sons of Ishi: Sheshan. The sons of Sheshan: Ahlai. 32 The sons of Jada, the brother of Shammai, were Jether and Jonathan. Jether died without sons. 33 The sons of Jonathan were Peleth and Zaza. These were the descendants of Jerahmeel. 34 Sheshan, who had no sons, only daughters, had an Egyptian slave named Jarha. 35 Sheshan gave his daughter in marriage to his slave Jarha, and she bore him Attai. 36 Attai became the father of Nathan. Nathan became the father of Zabad. 37 Zabad became the father of Ephlal. Ephlal became the father of Obed. 38 Obed became the father of Jehu. Jehu became the father of Azariah. 39 Azariah became the father of Helez. Helez became the father of Eleasah. 40 Eleasah became the father of Sismai. Sismai became the father of Shallum. 41 Shallum became the father of Jekamiah. Jekamiah became the father of Elishama.

42† The descendants of Caleb, the brother of Jerahmeel: [Mesha] his first-born, who was the father of Ziph. Then the sons of Mareshah, who was the father of Hebron. 43 The sons of Hebron were Korah, Tappuah, Rekem, and Shema. 44 Shema became the father of Raham, who was the father of Jorkeam. Rekem became the father of Shammai. 45 The sons of Shammai: Maon, who was the father of Beth-zur. 46 Ephah, Caleb's concubine, bore Haran, Moza, and Gazez. Haran became the father of Gazez. 47 The sons of Jahdai were Regem, Jotham, Geshan, Pelet, Ephah, and Shaaph. 48 Maacah, Caleb's concubine, bore Sheber and Tirhanah. 49* She also bore Shaaph, the father of Madmannah, Sheva, the father of Machbenah, and the father of Gibea. Achsah was Caleb's daughter.

50† These were descendants of Caleb, sons of Hur, the first-born of Ephrathah: Shobal, the father of Kiriath-jearim, 51 Salma, the father of Bethlehem, and Hareph, the father of Bethgader. 52 The sons of Shobal, the father of Kiriath-jearim, were Reaiah, half the Manahathites, 53* and the clans of Kiriath-jearim: the Ithrites, the Puthites, the Shumathites, and the Mishraites. From these the people of Zorah and the Eshtaolites derived. 54 The descendants of Salma were Bethlehem, the Netophathites, Atrothbeth-Joab, half the Manahathites, and the Zorites. 55* The clans of the Sopherim dwelling in Jabez were the Tirathites, the Shimeathites, and the Sucathites. They were the Kenites, who came from Hammath of the ancestor of the Rechabites.

3 1*† The following were the sons of David who were born to him in Hebron: the first-born, Amnon, by Ahinoam of Jezreel; the second, Daniel,† by Abigail of Carmel; 2 the third, Absalom, son of Maacah, who was the daughter of Talmai, king of Geshur; the fourth, Adonijah, son of Haggith; 3 the fifth, Shephatiah, by Abital; the sixth, Ithream, by his wife Eglah. 4* Six in all were born to him in Hebron, where he reigned seven years and six months. Then he reigned thirty-three years in Jerusalem, 5*† where the following were born to him: Shimea, Shobab, Nathan, Solomon—four by Bathsheba, the daughter of Ammiel,* 6 Ibhar, Elishua, Eliphelet, 7 Nogah, Nepheg, Japhia, 8 Elishama, Eliada, and Eliphelet—nine. 9* All these were sons of David, in addition to other sons by concubines; and Tamar was their sister.

10*† The son of Solomon was Rehoboam, whose son was Abijah, whose son was Asa, whose son was Jehoshaphat,* 11* whose son was Joram, whose son was Ahaziah, whose son was Joash, 12* whose son was Amaziah, whose son was Azariah, whose son was Jotham, 13* whose son was Ahaz, whose son

---

2, 25–41: The Jerahmeelites were a clan in the Negeb of Judah.
2, 42–49: Another list, dating from preexilic times, of the Calebites, a clan that inhabited the south of Judah.
2, 50–55: The Hurites, a clan dwelling to the south and west of Jerusalem and related to the Calebites.
3, 1–9: David's sons.
3, 1: *Daniel:* called Chileab in 2 Sm 3, 3.
3, 5: *Shimea:* called Shammua in 2 Sm 5, 14. *Ammiel:* called Eliam in 2 Sm 11, 3.
3, 10–16: The kings of Judah from Solomon to the destruction of Jerusalem by the Babylonians.

2, 23: Dt 3, 14; Jos 13, 30; Jgs 10, 4.
2, 24: 1 Chr 2, 19; 2 Sm 14, 2; 2 Chr 11, 6.
2, 25: 1 Sm 27, 10; 30, 29; Jb 32, 2.
2, 31: 1 Chr 4, 20.
2, 49: Jos 15, 16; Jgs 1, 12.
2, 53: Jgs 18, 2.
2, 55: Nm 24, 21; Jgs 1, 16; 4, 11; 1 Sm 15, 6.
3, 1–4: 2 Sm 3, 2–5.
3, 4: 2 Sm 2, 11; 5, 5.
3, 5–8: 2 Sm 5, 14ff.
3, 5: 2 Sm 5, 5.
3, 9: 2 Sm 13, 1f.
3, 10–17: Mt 1, 7–12.
3, 10: 1 Kgs 11, 43; 14, 31; 15, 1.8.24; 2 Chr 9, 31; 12, 16; 13, 23; 17, 1.
3, 11: 1 Kgs 22, 51; 2 Chr 21, 1; 22, 1; 24, 1.27.
3, 12: 2 Kgs 12, 21; 14, 21; 15, 7; 2 Chr 25, 1; 26, 1.23; 27, 1.
3, 13: 2 Kgs 15, 38; 16, 20; 20, 21; 2 Chr 28, 1.27; 32, 33.

did you KNOW?

Genealogies

Look at all these names! Our present-day interest in family trees obviously has ancient roots. The first nine chapters of 1 Chronicles consist entirely of family trees—or genealogies—tracing the history of Israel from Adam to Saul. In a culture where not only money and identity but also the offices of priest and king passed from one generation to another, it was essential to be able to trace one's bloodline.

The many genealogies of the Old Testament answer important questions: How were the various tribes related to one another? Who were a particular tribe's ancestors? What right did a certain group or person have to the office of priest or king? The Chronicler lists the genealogies of David and Levi in considerable detail. The kingship and the priesthood were clearly of special interest to him.

▶ **1 Chronicles, chapters 1–9**

was Hezekiah, whose son was Manasseh, ¹⁴* whose son was Amon, whose son was Josiah. ¹⁵*† The sons of Josiah were: the first-born, Johanan; the second, Jehoiakim; the third, Zedekiah; the fourth, Shallum. ¹⁶* The sons of Jehoiakim were: Jeconiah, his son; Zedekiah, his son.

¹⁷*† The sons of Jeconiah the captive were: Shealtiel, ¹⁸† Malchiram, Pedaiah, Shenazzar, Jekamiah, Shama, and Nedabiah. ¹⁹† The sons of Pedaiah were Zerubbabel and Shimei. The sons of Zerubbabel were Meshullam and Hananiah; Shelomith was their sister. ²⁰ The sons of Meshullam were Hashubah, Ohel, Berechiah, Hasadiah, Jushab-hesed—five. ²¹ The sons of Hananiah were Pelatiah, Jeshaiah, Rephaiah, Arnan, Obadiah, and Shecaniah. ²²* The sons of Shecaniah were Shemiah, Hattush, Igal, Bariah, Neariah, Shaphat—six. ²³ The sons of Neariah were Elioenai, Hizkiah, and Azrikam—three. ²⁴ The sons of Elioenai were Hodaviah, Eliashib, Pelaiah, Akkub, Johanan, Delaiah, and Anani—seven.

¹*† The descendants of Judah were: Perez, Hezron, Carmi, Hur, and Shobal. ² Reaiah, the son of Shobal, became the father of Jahath, and Jahath became the father of Ahumai and Lahad. These were the clans of the Zorathites.

³ These were the descendants of Hareph, the father of Etam: Jezreel, Ishma, and Idbash; their sister was named Hazzelelponi. ⁴ Penuel was the father of Gedor, and Ezer the father of Hushah. These were the descendants of Hur, the first-born of Ephrathah, the father of Bethlehem.

⁵* Ashhur, the father of Tekoa, had two wives, Helah and Naarah. ⁶ Naarah bore him Ahuzzam, Hepher, the Temenites and the Ahashtarites. These were the descendants of Naarah. ⁷ The sons of Helah were Zereth, Izhar, Ethnan, and Koz. ⁸ Koz became the father of Anub and Zobebah, as well as of the clans of Aharhel, son of Harum. ⁹ Jabez was the most distinguished of the brothers. His mother had named him Jabez, saying, "I bore him with pain." ¹⁰ Jabez prayed to the God of Israel: "Oh, that you may truly bless me and extend my boundaries! Help me and make me free of misfortune, without pain!" And God granted his prayer.

¹¹ Chelub, the brother of Shuhah, became the father of Mehir, who was the father of Eshton. ¹² Eshton became the father of Beth-rapha, Paseah, and Tehinnah, the father of the city of Nahash. These were the men of Recah.

¹³* The sons of Kenaz were Othniel and Seraiah. The sons of Othniel were Hathath and Meonothai; ¹⁴ Meonothai became the father of Ophrah. Seraiah became the father of Joab, the father of Geharashim, so called because they were craftsmen. ¹⁵* The sons of Caleb, son of Jephunneh, were Ir,

---

† **3, 15:** *Shallum:* the same as Jehoahaz, Josiah's successor; cf Jer 22, 11.

3, 17–24: The descendants of King Jechoniah up to the time of the Chronicler. If twenty-five years are allowed to each generation, the ten generations between Jechoniah and Anani (the last name on the list) would bring the birth of the latter to about 405 B.C.—an important item in establishing the approximate date of the Chronicler.

3, 18: *Shenazzar:* presumably the same as Sheshbazzar of Ezr 1, 8.11; 5, 14ff, the prince of Judah who was the first Jewish governor of Judah after the exile. Both forms of the name probably go back to the Babylonian name *Sin-ab-ussar* signifying, "O [god] Sin, protect [our] father!"

3, 19: *Zerubbabel:* here called the son of Pedaiah, though elsewhere (Hg 1, 12.14; 2, 2.23; Ezr 3, 2.8; 5, 2; Neh 12, 1) called son of Shealtiel. The latter term may merely mean that Zerubbabel succeeded Shealtiel as head of the house of David.

4, 1–43: The southern tribes.

3, 14: 2 Kgs 21, 18.26; 2 Chr 33, 20.25.	**3, 22:** Neh 3, 29.
3, 15: 2 Kgs 23, 34; 24, 17; 2 Chr 36, 4.10.	**4, 1:** 1 Chr 2, 4f.7.9.50; Gn 38, 29; 46, 12; Mt 1, 3.
3, 16: 2 Kgs 24, 6.17; 2 Chr 36, 8.10.	**4, 5:** 1 Chr 2, 24.
3, 17.19: Ezr 2, 2; 3, 2.8; 5, 2; Sir 49, 11; Hg 1, 1.12.14; Mt 1, 12f; Lk 3, 27.	**4, 13:** Jos 15, 17; Jgs 1, 13; 3, 9.11.
	4, 15: Nm 13, 6; 14, 6; 32, 12; Jos 14, 6.14.

Elah, and Naam. The sons of Elah were . . . and Kenaz. ¹⁶ The sons of Jehallelel were Ziph, Ziphah, Tiria, and Asarel. ¹⁷* The sons of Ezrah were Jether, Mered, Epher, and Jalon. Jether became the father of Miriam, Shammai, and Ishbah, the father of Eshtemoa. [. . . . . .] ¹⁸ His (Mered's) Egyptian wife bore Jared, the father of Gedor, Heber, the father of Soco, and Jekuthiel, the father of Zanoah. These were the sons of Bithiah, the daughter of Pharaoh, whom Mered married. ¹⁹ The sons of his Jewish wife, the sister of Naham, the father of Keilah, were Shimon the Garmite and Ishi the Maacathite. ²⁰ The sons of Shimon were Amnon, Rinnah, Benhanan, and Tilon. The son of Ishi was Zoheth and the son of Zoheth. . . .

²¹* The descendants of Shelah, son of Judah, were: Er, the father of Lecah; Laadah, the father of Mareshah; the clans of the linen weavers' guild in Beth-ashbea; ²² Jokim; the men of Cozeba; and Joash and Saraph, who held property in Moab, but returned to Bethlehem. [These are events of old.] ²³ They were potters and inhabitants of Netaim and Gederah, where they lived in the king's service.

Simeon

²⁴* The sons of Simeon were Nemuel, Jamin, Jachin, Zerah, and Shaul, ²⁵ whose son was Shallum, whose son was Mibsam, whose son was Mishma. ²⁶ The descendants of Mishma were his son Hammuel, whose son was Zaccur, whose son was Shimei. ²⁷ Shimei had sixteen sons and six daughters. His brothers, however, did not have many sons, and as a result all their clans did not equal the number of the Judahites.

²⁸* They dwelt in Beer-sheba, Moladah, Hazarshual, ²⁹ Bilhah, Ezem, Tolad, ³⁰ Bethuel, Hormah, Ziklag, ³¹ Beth-marcaboth, Hazar-susim, Bethbiri, and Shaaraim. Until David came to reign, these were their cities ³² and their villages. Etam, also, and Ain, Rimmon, Tochen, and Ashan—five cities, ³³ together with all their outlying villages as far as Baal. Here is where they dwelt, and so it was inscribed of them in their family records.

³⁴ Meshobab, Jamlech, Joshah, son of Amaziah, ³⁵ Joel, Jehu, son of Joshibiah, son of Seraiah, son of Asiel, ³⁶ Elioenai, Jaakobath, Jeshohaiah, Asaiah, Adiel, Jesimiel, Benaiah, ³⁷ Ziza, son of Shiphi, son of Allon, son of Jedaiah, son of Shimri, son of Shemaiah— ³⁸* these just named were princes in their clans, and their ancestral houses spread out to such

an extent ³⁹† that they went to the approaches of Gedor, east of the valley, seeking pasture for their flocks. ⁴⁰ They found abundant and good pastures, and the land was spacious, quiet, and peaceful. ⁴¹* They who have just been listed by name set out during the reign of Hezekiah, king of Judah, and attacked the tents of Ham (for Hamites dwelt there formerly) and also the Meunites who were there. They pronounced against them the ban that is still in force and dwelt in their place because they found pasture there for their flocks.

⁴² Five hundred of them (the Simeonites) went to Mount Seir under the leadership of Pelatiah, Neariah, Rephaiah, and Uzziel, sons of Ishi. ⁴³* They attacked the surviving Amalekites who had escaped, and have resided there to the present day.

Reuben

5 ¹*† The sons of Reuben, the first-born of Israel. (He was indeed the first-born, but because he disgraced the couch of his father his birthright was given to the sons of Joseph, son of Israel, so that he is not listed in the family records according to birthright. ²* Judah, in fact, became powerful among his brothers, so that the ruler came from him, though the birthright had been Joseph's.) ³* The sons of Reuben, the first-born of Israel, were Hanoch, Pallu, Hezron, and Carmi. ⁴ His son was Joel, whose son was Shemaiah, whose son was Gog, whose son was Shimei, ⁵ whose son was Micah, whose son was Reaiah, whose son was Baal, ⁶* whose son was Beerah, whom Tiglath-pileser, the king of Assyria, took into exile; he was a prince of the Reubenites. ⁷ His brothers who belonged to his clans, when they were listed in the family records according to their descendants, were: Jeiel, the chief, and Zechariah, ⁸* and Bela, son of Azaz, son of Shema, son of Joel. The Reubenites lived in Aroer and as far as Nebo and Baal-meon; ⁹* toward the east they dwelt as far as the desert which extends from the Euphrates River, for they had much livestock in the land of Gilead. ¹⁰* During the reign of Saul they waged war with the Hagrites, and when they had defeated them they occupied their tents throughout the region east of Gilead.

Gad

¹¹* The Gadites lived alongside them in the land of Bashan as far as Salecah. ¹²* Joel was chief,

---

† 4, 39: *Gedor:* in the Greek, Gerar, no doubt correct.
5, 1–26: The Transjordan tribes.

4, 17: 1 Sm 30, 28.
4, 21: 1 Chr 2, 3; Gn 38, 5;
   46, 12; Nm 26, 20.
4, 24: Gn 46, 10; Ex 6, 15;
   Nm 26, 12f.
4, 28–32: Jos 19, 2–8.
4, 38: Nm 1, 2.
4, 41: 2 Kgs 18, 1f; 2 Chr
   29, 1.
4, 43: Ex 17, 8.14; Dt 25,

17ff; 1 Sm 14, 48; 15,
   3.7f; 2 Sm 8, 12.
5, 1: Gn 35, 22; 48,
   5.15–22; 49, 3f; Dt
   33, 6.
5, 2: 1 Chr 28, 4; Gn 49, 8ff.
5, 3: Gn 46, 9; Ex 6, 14;
   Nm 26, 5f.
5, 6: 2 Kgs 15, 29.
5, 8: Jos 13, 9.16f; Nm 32,
   3.38.
5, 9: Jos 22, 9.
5, 10: Ps 83, 6.
5, 11: Jos 13, 11.24–28.
5, 12: Gn 46, 16.

Shapham was second in command, and Janai was judge in Bashan. [13] Their brothers, corresponding to their ancestral houses, were: Michael, Meshullam, Sheba, Jorai, Jacan, Zia, and Eber—seven. [14] These were the sons of Abihail, son of Huri, son of Jaroah, son of Gilead, son of Michael, son of Jeshishai, son of Jahdo, son of Buz. [15] Ahi, son of Abdiel, son of Guni, was the head of their ancestral houses. [16] They dwelt in Gilead, in Bashan and its towns, and in all the pasture lands of Sirion to the borders. [17] All were listed in the family records in the time of Jotham, king of Judah, and of Jeroboam, king of Israel.

[18] The Reubenites, Gadites, and half-tribe of Manasseh were warriors, men who bore shield and sword and who drew the bow, trained in warfare—forty-four thousand seven hundred and sixty men fit for military service. [19]* When they waged war against the Hagrites and against Jetur, Naphish, and Nodab, [20]* they received help so that they mastered the Hagrites and all who were with them. For during the battle they called on God, and he heard them because they had put their trust in him. [21] Along with one hundred thousand men they also captured their livestock: fifty thousand camels, two hundred fifty thousand sheep, and two thousand asses. [22]* Many had fallen in battle, for victory is from God; and they took over their dwelling place until the time of the exile.

East Manasseh

[23] The numerous members of the half-tribe of Manasseh lived in the land of Bashan as far as Baal-hermon, Senir, and Mount Hermon. [24] The following were the heads of their ancestral houses: Epher, Ishi, Eliel, Azriel, Jeremiah, Hodaviah, and Jahdiel—men who were warriors, famous men, and heads over their ancestral houses.

[25]* However, they offended the God of their fathers by lusting after the gods of the natives of the land, whom God had cleared out of their way. [26]*† Therefore the God of Israel incited against them the anger of Pul, king of Assyria, and of Tiglath-pileser, king of Assyria, who deported the Reubenites, the Gadites, and the half-tribe of Manasseh and brought them to Halah, Habor, and Hara, and to the river Gozan, where they have remained to this day.

Levi

[27]*† The sons of Levi were Gershon, Kohath, and Merari. [28]* The sons of Kohath were Amram, Izhar, Hebron, and Uzziel. [29]* The children of Amram were Aaron, Moses, and Miriam. The sons of Aaron were Nadab, Abihu, Eleazar, and Ithamar. [30]† Eleazar, became the father of Phinehas. Phinehas became the father of Abishua. [31] Abishua became the father of Bukki. Bukki became the father of Uzzi. [32] Uzzi became the father of Zerahiah. Zerahiah became the father of Meraioth. [33] Meraioth became the father of Amariah. Amariah became the father of Ahitub. [34] Ahitub became the father of Zadok. Zadok became the father of Ahimaaz. [35] Ahimaaz became the father of Azariah. Azariah became the father of Johanan. [36] Johanan became the father of Azariah, who served as priest in the temple Solomon built in Jerusalem. [37] Azariah became the father of Amariah. Amariah became the father of Ahitub. [38] Ahitub became the father of Zadok. Zadok became the father of Shallum. [39] Shallum became the father of Hilkiah. Hilkiah became the father of Azariah. [40] Azariah became the father of Seraiah. Seraiah became the father of Jehozadak. [41] Jehozadak was one of those who went into the exile which the LORD inflicted on Judah and Jerusalem through Nebuchadnezzar.

6 [1]* The sons of Levi were Gershon, Kohath, and Merari. [2]* The sons of Gershon were named Libni and Shimei. [3]* The sons of Kohath were Amram, Izhar, Hebron, and Uzziel. [4]* The sons of Merari were Mahli and Mushi.

The following were the clans of Levi, distributed according to their ancestors: [5] of Gershon: his son Libni, whose son was Jahath, whose son was Zimmah, [6] whose son was Joah, whose son was Iddo, whose son was Zerah, whose son was Jetherai.

[7] The descendants of Kohath were: his son Amminadab, whose son was Korah, whose son was Assir, [8] whose son was Elkanah, whose son was Ebiasaph, whose son was Assir, [9] whose son was Tahath, whose son was Uriel, whose son was Uzziah, whose son was Shaul. [10] The sons of Elkanah were Amasai and Ahimoth, [11] whose son was Elkanah, whose son was Zophai, whose son was Nahath, [12] whose son was Eliab, whose son was Jeroham, whose son was Elkanah, whose son was

---

5, 26: *Pul:* the name which the Assyrian king Tiglath-pileser III (745–727 B.C.) took as king of Babylon.

5, 27—6, 66: The tribe of Levi. The list gives special prominence to Levi's son Kohath, from whom were descended both the Aaronite priests (1 Chr 5, 28–41) and the leading group of temple singers (1 Chr 6, 18–23).

5, 30–41: The line of preexilic priests. The list seems to be confused in vv 36ff, which repeat the names, mostly in inverse order, that occur in vv 34f. A similar but shorter list is given, with variations, in Ezr 7, 1–5.

5, 19: 1 Chr 1, 31; 5, 10; Gn 25, 15; Ps 83, 6.
5, 20: Dt 33, 20f.
5, 22: Nm 32, 39; Dt 3, 8ff; Jgs 3, 3.
5, 25: Ex 34, 14ff; 2 Kgs 17, 7.
5, 26: 2 Kgs 15, 9.29; 17, 6.
5, 27: 1 Chr 6, 1; 23, 6; Gn 46, 11; Ex 6, 16; Nm 26, 57.

5, 28: 1 Chr 6, 3; Ex 6, 18.
5, 29: Ex 6, 20; Nm 26, 59f.
6, 1: 1 Chr 5, 27; 23, 6; Gn 46, 11; Ex 6, 16; Nm 26, 57.
6, 2: Ex 6, 17.
6, 3: 1 Chr 6, 18; Nm 3, 19; 26, 59.
6, 4: 1 Chr 6, 14; Ex 6, 19; Nm 3, 20; 26, 58.

Samuel. [13] The sons of Samuel were Joel, the first-born, and Abijah, the second.

[14]* The descendants of Merari were Mahli, whose son was Libni, whose son was Shimei, whose son was Uzzah, [15] whose son was Shimea, whose son was Haggiah, whose son was Asaiah.

[16]† The following were entrusted by David with the choir services in the LORD's house from the time when the ark had obtained a permanent resting place. [17] They served as singers before the Dwelling of the meeting tent until Solomon built the temple of the LORD in Jerusalem, and they performed their services in an order prescribed for them. [18] Those who so performed are the following, together with their descendants.

Among the Kohathites: Heman, the chanter, son of Joel, son of Samuel, [19] son of Elkanah, son of Jeroham, son of Eliel, son of Toah, [20] son of Zuth, son of Elkanah, son of Mahath, son of Amasi, [21] son of Elkanah, son of Joel, son of Azariah, son of Zephaniah, [22]* son of Tahath, son of Assir, son of Ebiasaph, son of Korah, [23] son of Izhar, son of Kohath, son of Levi, son of Israel.

[24] His brother Asaph stood at his right hand. Asaph was the son of Berechiah, son of Shimea, [25] son of Michael, son of Baaseiah, son of Malchi-jah, [26] son of Ethni, son of Zerah, son of Adaiah, [27]* son of Ethan, son of Zimmah, son of Shimei, [28] son of Jahath, son of Gershon, son of Levi.

[29] Their brothers, the Merarites, stood at the left: Ethan, son of Kishi, son of Abdi, son of Malluch, [30] son of Hashabiah, son of Amaziah, son of Hilki-ah, [31] son of Amzi, son of Bani, son of Shemer, [32]* son of Mahli, son of Mushi, son of Merari, son of Levi.

[33]* Their brother Levites were appointed to all other services of the Dwelling of the house of God. [34]* However, it was Aaron and his descendants who burnt the offerings on the altar of holocausts and on the altar of incense; they alone had charge of the holy of holies and of making atonement for Israel, as Moses, the servant of God, had ordained.

[35] These were the descendants of Aaron: his son Eleazer, whose son was Phinehas, whose son was Abishua, [36] whose son was Bukki, whose son was Uzzi, whose son was Zerahiah, [37] whose son was Meraioth, whose son was Amariah, whose son was Ahitub, [38] whose son was Zadok, whose son was Ahimaaz.

[39]† The following were their dwelling places to which their encampment was limited. To the de-scendants of Aaron who belonged to the clan of the Kohathites, since the first lot fell to them, [40] was assigned Hebron with its adjacent pasture lands in the land of Judah, [41] although the open country and the villages belonging to the city had been given to Caleb, the son of Jephunneh. [42] There were assigned to the descendants of Aaron: Hebron, a city of asylum, Libnah with its pasture lands, Jattir with its pasture lands, Eshtemoa with its pasture lands, [43] Holon with its pasture lands, Debir with its pasture lands, [44] Ashan with its pasture lands, Jetta with its pasture lands, and Beth-shemesh with its pasture lands. [45] Also from the tribe of Benjamin: Gibeon with its pasture lands, Geba with its pasture lands, Almon with its pasture lands, Anathoth with its pasture lands. In all, they had thirteen cities with their pasture lands. [49] The Israelites assigned these cities with their pasture lands to the Levites, [50] designating them by name and assigning them by lot from the tribes of the Judahites, Simeonites, and Benjaminites.

[46] The other Kohathites obtained ten cities by lot for their clans from the tribe of Ephraim, from the tribe of Dan, and from the half-tribe of Manasseh. [47] The clans of the Gershonites obtained thirteen cities from the tribes of Issachar, Asher, and Naphtali, and from the half-tribe of Manasseh in Bashan. [48] The clans of the Merarites obtained twelve cities by lot from the tribes of Reuben, Gad, and Zebulun.

[51] The clans of the Kohathites obtained cities by lot from the tribe of Ephraim. [52] They were assigned: Shechem in the mountain region of Ephraim, a city of asylum, with its pasture lands, Gezer with its pasture lands, [53] Kibzaim with its pasture lands, and Beth-horon with its pasture lands. [54] From the tribe of Dan: Elteke with its pasture lands, Gibbethon with its pasture lands, Aijalon with its pasture lands, and Gath-rimmon with its pasture lands. [55] From the half-tribe of Manasseh: Taanach with its pasture lands and Ibleam with its pasture lands. These belonged to the rest of the Kohathite clan.

[56] The clans of the Gershonites received from the half-tribe of Manasseh: Golan in Bashan with its pasture lands and Ashtaroth with its pasture lands. [57] From the tribe of Issachar: Kedesh with its pasture lands, Daberath with its pasture lands, [58] Ramoth with its pasture lands, and Engannim with its pasture lands. [59] From the tribe of Asher: Mashal with its pasture lands, Abdon with its pasture lands, [60] Hilkath with its pasture lands, and

---

† **6, 16–32:** The origin of the choir services performed by the levitical families in the postexilic temple at the time of the Chronicler is here attributed to David, somewhat as all the laws in the Pentateuch are attributed to Moses.
 6, 39–66: Regarding the nature of the rights of Levites in the cities assigned to them, see note on Jos 21, 1.

* **6, 14:** 1 Chr 6, 4; Ex 6, 19; Nm 3, 20; 26, 58.
6, 22: Ex 6, 24.
6, 27: 1 Chr 6, 2.5.
6, 32: Ex 6, 19; Nm 26, 58.
6, 33: 1 Chr 15, 17.19; 16, 41f; 2 Chr 5, 12.
6, 34: 1 Chr 16, 39f.

Rehob with its pasture lands. 61 From the tribe of Naphtali: Kedesh in Galilee with its pasture lands, Hammon with its pasture lands, and Kiriathaim with its pasture lands.

62 The rest of the Merarites received from the tribe of Zebulun: Jokneam with its pasture lands, Kartah with its pasture lands, Rimmon with its pasture lands, and Tabor with its pasture lands. 63 Across the Jordan at Jericho [that is, east of the Jordan] they received from the tribe of Reuben: Bezer in the desert with its pasture lands, Jahzah with its pasture lands, 64 Kedemoth with its pasture lands, and Mephaath with its pasture lands. 65 From the tribe of Gad: Ramoth in Gilead with its pasture lands, Mahanaim with its pasture lands, 66 Heshbon with its pasture lands, and Jazer with its pasture lands.

Issachar

7 1*† The sons of Issachar were Tola, Puah, Jashub, and Shimron: four. 2* The sons of Tola were Uzzi, Rephaiah, Jeriel, Jahmai, Ibsam, and Shemuel, warrior heads of the ancestral houses of Tola. Their kindred numbered twenty-two thousand six hundred in the time of David. 3 The sons of Uzzi: Izarahiah. The sons of Izarahiah were Michael, Obadiah, Joel, and Isshiah. All five of these were chiefs. 4 Their kindred, by ancestral houses, numbered thirty-six thousand men in organized military troops, since they had more wives and sons 5 than their fellow tribesmen. In all the clans of Issachar there was a total of eighty-seven thousand warriors in their family records.

Benjamin

6* The sons of Benjamin were Bela, Becher, and Jediael—three. 7 The sons of Bela were Ezbon, Uzzi, Uzziel, Jerimoth, and Iri—five. They were heads of their ancestral houses and warriors. Their family records listed twenty-two thousand and thirty-four. 8* The sons of Becher were Zemirah, Joash, Eliezer, Elioenai, Omri, Jeremoth, Abijah, Anathoth, and Alemeth—all these were sons of Becher. 9 Their family records listed twenty thousand two hundred of their kindred who were heads of their ancestral houses and warriors. 10 The sons of Jediael: Bilhan. The sons of Bilhan were Jeush, Benjamin, Ehud, Chenaanah, Zethan, Tarshish, and Ahishahar. 11* All these were descendants of Jediael, heads of ancestral houses and warriors. They numbered seventeen thousand two hundred men fit for military service . . . Shupham and Hupham.

Dan, Naphtali and Manasseh

12* The sons of Dan: Hushim. 13 The sons of Naphtali were Jahziel, Guni, Jezer, and Shallum. These were descendants of Bilhah. 14* The sons of Manasseh, whom his Aramean concubine bore: she bore Machir, the father of Gilead.* 15* Machir took a wife whose name was Maacah; his sister's name was Molecheth. Manasseh's second son was named Zelophehad, but to Zelophehad only daughters were born. 16 Maacah, Machir's wife, bore a son whom she named Peresh. He had a brother named Sheresh, whose sons were Ulam and Rakem. 17 The sons of Ulam: Bedan. These were the descendants of Gilead, the son of Machir, the son of Manasseh. 18 His sister Molecheth bore Ishhod, Abiezer, and Mahlah. 19 The sons of Shemida were Ahian, Shechem, Likhi, and Aniam.

Ephraim

20* The sons of Ephraim: Shuthelah, whose son was Bered, whose son was Tahath, whose son was Eleadah, whose son was Tahath, 21 whose son was Zabad. Ephraim's son Shuthelah, and Ezer and Elead, who were born in the land, were slain by the inhabitants of Gath because they had gone down to take away their livestock. 22 Their father Ephraim mourned a long time, but after his kinsmen had come and comforted him, 23* he visited his wife, who conceived and bore a son whom he named Beriah, since evil had befallen his house. 24 He had a daughter, Sheerah, who built lower and upper Beth-horon and Uzzen-sheerah. 25 Zabad's son was Rephah, whose son was Resheph, whose son was Telah, whose son was Tahan, 26* whose son was Ladan, whose son was Ammihud, whose son was Elishama, 27 whose son was Nun, whose son was Joshua.

28* Their property and their dwellings were in Bethel and its towns, Naaran to the east, Gezer and its towns to the west, and also Shechem and its towns as far as Ayyah and its towns. 29* Manasseh, however, had possession of Beth-shean and its towns, Taanach and its towns, Megiddo and its towns, and Dor and its towns. In these dwelt the descendants of Joseph, the son of Israel.

Asher

30* The sons of Asher were Imnah, Iishvah, Ishvi, and Beriah; their sister was Serah. 31 Beriah's sons were Heber and Malchiel, who was the father of Birzaith. 32 Heber became the father of Japhlet, Shomer, Hotham, and their sister Shua. 33 The sons

---

7, 1–40: The northern tribes.

7, 1: Gn 46, 13.
7, 2: Nm 26, 23f; Jgs 10, 1.
7, 6: 1 Chr 6, 6; Gn 46, 21; Nm 26, 38.
7, 8: 1 Chr 7, 8.
7, 11: Nm 26, 39.
7, 12f: Gn 46, 24; Nm 26, 48f.

7, 14–19: Nm 26, 29–32.
7, 14: Nm 26, 29; Jos 17, 1.
7, 15: Nm 26, 33; Jos 17, 3.
7, 20: Nm 26, 35.
7, 23: 1 Chr 8, 13.
7, 26: Nm 1, 10; 2, 18; 7, 48;

10, 22.
7, 28: Gn 12, 8; 1 Kgs 9, 16.
7, 29: Jos 17, 11.
7, 30: Gn 46, 17; Nm 26, 44ff.

of Japhlet were Pasach, Bimhal, and Ashvath; these were the sons of Japhlet. 34 The sons of Shomer were Ahi, Rohgah, Jehubbah, and Aram. 35 The sons of his brother Hotham were Zophah, Imna, Shelesh, and Amal. 36 The sons of Zophah were Suah, Harnepher, Shual, Beri, Imrah, 37 Bezer, Hod, Shamma, Shilshah, Ithran, and Beera. 38 The sons of Jether were Jephunneh, Pispa, and Ara. 39 The sons of Ulla were Arah, Hanniel, and Rizia. 40 All these were descendants of Asher, heads of ancestral houses, distinguished men, warriors, and chiefs among the princes. Their family records numbered twenty-six thousand men fit for military service.

Benjamin

8 1*† Benjamin became the father of Bela, his first-born, Ashbel, the second son, Aharah, the third, 2 Nohah, the fourth, and Rapha, the fifth. 3 The sons of Bela were Addar and Gera, the father of Ehud. 4* The sons of Ehud were Abishua, Naaman, Ahoah, 5 Gera, Shephuphan, and Huram. 6 These were the sons of Ehud, family heads over those who dwelt in Geba and were deported to Manahath. 7 Also Naaman, Ahijah, and Gera. The last, who led them into exile, became the father of Uzza and Ahihud. 8 Shaharaim became a father on the Moabite plateau after he had put away his wives Hushim and Baara. 9 By his wife Hodesh he became the father of Jobab, Zibia, Mesha, Malcam, 10 Jeuz, Sachia, and Mirmah. These were his sons, family heads. 11 By Hushim he became the father of Abitub and Elpaal. 12* The sons of Elpaal were Eber, Misham, Shemed, who built Ono and Lod with its nearby towns, 13 Beriah, and Shema. They were family heads of those who dwelt in Aijalon, and they put the inhabitants of Gath to flight. 14 Their brethren were Elpaal, Shashak, and Jeremoth. 15 Zebadiah, Arad, Eder, 16 Michael, Ishpah, and Joha were the sons of Beriah. 17 Zebadiah, Meshullam, Hizki, Heber, 18 Ishmerai, Izliah, and Jobab were the sons of Elpaal. 19 Jakim, Zichri, Zabdi, 20 Elienai, Zillethai, Eliel, 21 Adaiah, Beraiah, and Shimrath were the sons of Shimei. 22 Ishpan, Eber, Eliel, 23 Abdon, Zichri, Hanan, 24 Hananiah, Elam, Anthothijah, 25 Iphdeiah, and Penuel were the sons of Shashak. 26 Shamsherai, Shehariah, Athaliah, 27 Jaareshiah, Elijah, and Zichri were the sons of Jeroham. 28 These were family heads over their kindred, chiefs who dwelt in Jerusalem.

29* In Gibeon dwelt Jeiel, the founder of Gibeon, whose wife's name was Maacah; 30 also his first-born son, Abdon, and Zur, Kish, Baal, Ner, Nadab, 31 Gedor, Ahio, Zecher, and Mikloth. 32 Mikloth became the father of Shimeah. These, too, dwelt with their relatives in Jerusalem, opposite their fellow tribesmen. 33* Ner became the father of Kish, and Kish became the father of Saul. Saul became the father of Jonathan, Malchishua, Abinadab, and Eshbaal.* 34* The son of Jonathan was Meribbaal, and Meribbaal became the father of Micah. 35 The sons of Micah were Pithon, Melech, Tarea, and Ahaz. 36* Ahaz became the father of Jehoaddah, and Jehoaddah became the father of Alemeth, Azmaveth, and Zimri. Zimri became the father of Moza. 37* Moza became the father of Binea, whose son was Raphah, whose son was Eleasah, whose son was Azel. 38 Azel had six sons, whose names were Azrikam, his first-born, Ishmael, Sheariah, Azariah, Obadiah, and Hanan; all these were the sons of Azel. 39 The sons of Eshek, his brother, were Ulam, his first-born, Jeush, the second son, and Eliphelet, the third. 40 The sons of Ulam were combat archers, and many were their sons and grandsons: one hundred and fifty. All these were the descendants of Benjamin.

9 1* Thus all Israel was inscribed in its family records which are recorded in the book of the kings of Israel.

Now Judah had been carried in captivity to Babylon because of its rebellion. 2*† The first to settle again in their cities and dwell there were certain lay Israelites, the priests, the Levites, and the temple slaves.*

Jerusalemites

3 In Jerusalem lived Judahites and Benjaminites; also Ephraimites and Manassehites. 4 Among the Judahites was Uthai, son of Ammihud, son of Omri, son of Imri, son of Bani, one of the descendants of Perez, son of Judah. 5 Among the Shelanites were Asaiah, the first-born, and his sons. 6 Among the Zerahites were Jeuel and six hundred and ninety of their brethren. 7 Among the Benjaminites were Sallu, son of Meshullam, son of Hodaviah, son of Hassenuah; 8 Ibneiah, son of Jeroham; Elah, son of Uzzi, son of Michri; Meshullam, son of Shephatiah, son of Reuel, son of Ibnijah. 9 Their kindred of various families were nine hundred and fifty-six. All those named were heads of their ancestral houses.

8, 1–40: A second, variant list of the Benjaminites, with special prominence given to Saul's family (vv 33–40).
9, 2–34: The inhabitants of Jerusalem after the exile. A similar list, with many variants in the names, is given in Neh 11, 3–24.

8, 29–32: 1 Chr 9, 35–38.   9, 1: 2 Chr 16, 11; 20, 34;
8, 33–38: 1 Chr 9, 39–44.   25, 26; 27, 7; 33, 18;
8, 33: 1 Chr 10, 2; 1 Sm 9, 1;   36, 8.
     14, 49.51; 31, 2.   9, 2–22: Neh 11, 3–19.
8, 34: 2 Sm 4, 4; 9, 6.10.12.   9, 2: Ezr 2, 70; 7, 7; Neh
8, 36: 1 Chr 9, 42.   11, 3.
8, 37: 1 Chr 9, 43.

8, 1: 1 Chr 7, 6; Gn 46, 21;   8, 4: Jgs 3, 15.
     Nm 26, 38ff.   8, 12: Neh 11, 35.

10 Among the priests were Jedaiah; Jehoiarib; Jachin; 11 Azariah, son of Hilkiah, son of Meshullam, son of Zadok, son of Meraioth, son of Ahitub, the ruler of the house of God; 12 Adaiah, son of Jeroham, son of Pashhur, son of Malchijah; Maasai, son of Adiel, son of Jahzerah, son of Meshullam, son of Meshillemith, son of Immer. 13 Their brethren, heads of their ancestral houses, were one thousand seven hundred and sixty, valiant for the work of the service of the house of God.

14 Among the Levites were Shemaiah, son of Hasshub, son of Azrikam, son of Hashabiah, one of the descendants of Merari; 15 Bakbakkar; Heresh; Galal; Mattaniah, son of Mica, son of Zichri, a descendant of Asaph; 16 Obadiah, son of Shemaiah, son of Galal, a descendant of Jeduthun; and Berechiah, son of Asa, son of Elkanah, whose family lived in the villages of the Netophathites.

17 The gatekeepers were Shallum, Akkub, Talmon, Ahiman, and their brethren; Shallum was the chief. 18 Previously they had stood guard at the king's gate on the east side; now they became gatekeepers for the encampments of the Levites. 19 Shallum, son of Kore, son of Ebiasaph, a descendant of Korah, and his brethren of the same ancestral house of the Korahites had as their assigned task the guarding of the threshold of the tent, just as their fathers had guarded the entrance to the encampment of the LORD. 20* Phinehas, son of Eleazar, had been their chief in times past—the LORD be with him! 21* Zechariah, son of Meshelemiah, guarded the gate of the meeting tent. 22 In all, those who were chosen for gatekeepers at the threshold were two hundred and twelve. They were inscribed in the family records of their villages. David and Samuel the seer had established them in their position of trust. 23 Thus they and their sons kept guard over the gates of the house of the LORD, the house which was then a tent. 24* The gatekeepers were stationed at the four sides, to the east, the west, the north, and the south. 25* Their kinsmen who lived in their own villages took turns in assisting them for seven-day periods, 26 while the four chief gatekeepers were on constant duty. These were the Levites who also had charge of the chambers and treasures of the house of God. 27 At night they lodged about the house of God, for it was in their charge and they had the duty of opening it each morning.

28 Some of them had charge of the liturgical equipment, tallying it as it was brought in and taken out. 29 Others were appointed to take care of the utensils and all the sacred vessels, as well as the fine flour, the wine, the oil, the frankincense, and the spices. 30* It was the sons of priests, however, who mixed the spiced ointments. 31* Mattithiah, one of the Levites, the first-born of Shallum the Koreite, was entrusted with preparing the cakes. 32* Benaiah the Kohathite, one of their brethren, was in charge of setting out the showbread each sabbath.

33 These were the chanters and the gatekeepers, family heads over the Levites. They stayed in the chambers when free of duty, for day and night they had to be ready for service. 34 These were the levitical family heads over their kindred, chiefs who dwelt in Jerusalem.

II: The History of David

Genealogy of Saul

35* In Gibeon dwelt Jeiel, the founder of Gibeon, whose wife's name was Maacah. 36 His first-born son was Abdon; then came Zur, Kish, Baal, Ner, Nadab, 37 Gedor, Ahio, Zechariah, and Mikloth. 38 Mikloth became the father of Shimeam. These, too, with their brethren, dwelt opposite their brethren in Jerusalem. 39 Ner became the father of Kish, and Kish became the father of Saul. Saul became the father of Jonathan, Malchishua, Abinadab, and Eshbaal. 40 The son of Jonathan was Meribbaal, and Meribbaal became the father of Micah. 41 The sons of Micah were Pithon, Melech, Tahrea, and Ahaz. 42 Ahaz became the father of Jehoaddah, and Jehoaddah became the father of Alemeth, Azmaveth, and Zimri. Zimri became the father of Moza. 43 Moza became the father of Binea, whose son was Rephaiah, whose son was Eleasah, whose son was Azel. 44 Azel had six sons, whose names were Azrikam, his first-born, Ishmael, Sheariah, Azariah, Obadiah, and Hanan; these were the sons of Azel.

His Death and Burial

10 1* Now the Philistines were at war with Israel; the Israelites fled before the Philistines, and a number of them fell, slain on Mount Gilboa. 2 The Philistines pressed hard after Saul and his sons. When the Philistines had killed Jonathan, Abinadab, and Malchishua, sons of Saul, 3 the whole fury of the battle descended upon Saul. Then the archers found him, and wounded him with their arrows.

4 Saul said to his armor-bearer, "Draw your sword and thrust me through with it, that these uncircumcised may not come and maltreat me." But the armor-bearer, in great fear, refused. So Saul took his own sword and fell on it; 5 and seeing him dead,

---

9, 20: Ex 6, 25; Nm 25, 7.11; Jgs 20, 28.
9, 21: 1 Chr 26, 2.14.
9, 24: 1 Chr 26, 13.
9, 25: 2 Chr 23, 4f.
9, 30: Ex 30, 22–33.
9, 31f: 1 Chr 23, 29; Lv 2, 1ff; 6, 13ff; 7, 11.
9, 32: Ex 25, 30; Lv 24, 5–8.
9, 35–44: 1 Chr 8, 29–38.
10, 1–12: 1 Sm 31, 1–13.

the armor-bearer also fell on his sword and died. 6 Thus, with Saul and his three sons, his whole house died at one time. 7 When all the Israelites who were in the valley saw that Saul and his sons had died in the rout, they left their cities and fled; thereupon the Philistines came and occupied them.

8 On the following day, when the Philistines came to strip the slain, they found Saul and his sons where they had fallen on Mount Gilboa. 9 They stripped him, cut off his head, and took his armor; these they sent throughout the land of the Philistines to convey the good news to their idols and their people. 10 His armor they put in the house of their gods, but his skull they impaled on the temple of Dagon.

11 When all the inhabitants of Jabesh-gilead had heard what the Philistines had done to Saul, 12* its warriors rose to a man, recovered the bodies of Saul and his sons, and brought them to Jabesh. They buried their bones under the oak of Jabesh, and fasted seven days.

13*† Thus Saul died because of his rebellion against the LORD in disobeying his command, and also because he had sought counsel of a necromancer, 14* and had not rather inquired of the LORD. Therefore the LORD slew him, and transferred his kingdom to David, the son of Jesse.

David Is Made King

11 1* Then all Israel gathered about David in Hebron, and they said: "Surely, we are of the same bone and flesh as you. 2* Even formerly, when Saul was still the king, it was you who led Israel in all its battles. And now the LORD, your God, has said to you, 'You shall shepherd my people Israel and be ruler over them.' " 3* Then all the elders of Israel came to the king at Hebron, and there David made a covenant with them in the presence of the LORD; and they anointed him king over Israel, in accordance with the word of the LORD as revealed through Samuel.

Jerusalem Captured

4* Then David and all Israel went to Jerusalem, that is, Jebus, where the natives of the land were called Jebusites. 5 The inhabitants of Jebus said to David, "You shall not enter here." David nevertheless captured the fortress of Zion, which is the City of David. 6* David said, "Whoever strikes the Jebusites first shall be made the chief commander." Joab, the son of Zeruiah, was the first to go up; and so he became chief. 7 David took up his residence in the fortress, which thenceforth was called the City of David. 8* He rebuilt the city on all sides, from the Millo all the way around, while Joab restored the rest of the city. 9 David became more and more powerful, for the LORD of hosts was with him.

David's Warriors

10* These were David's chief warriors who, together with all Israel, supported him in his reign in order to make him true king, even as the LORD had commanded concerning Israel. 11† Here is the list of David's warriors:

Ishbaal, the son of Hachamoni, chief of the Three. He brandished his spear against three hundred, whom he slew in a single encounter.

12* Next to him Eleazar, the son of Dodo the Ahohite, one of the Three warriors. 13* He was with David at Pasdammim, where the Philistines had massed for battle. The plowland was fully planted with barley, but its defenders were retreating before the Philistines. 14 He made a stand on the sown ground, kept it safe, and cut down the Philistines. Thus the LORD brought about a great victory.

15* Three of the Thirty chiefs went down to the rock, to David, who was in the cave of Adullam while the Philistines were encamped in the valley of Rephaim. 16 David was then in the stronghold, and a Philistine garrison was at Bethlehem. 17 David expressed a desire: "Oh, that someone would give me a drink from the cistern that is by the gate at Bethlehem!" 18 Thereupon the Three broke through the encampment of the Philistines, drew water from the cistern by the gate at Bethlehem, and carried it back to David. But David refused to drink it. Instead, he poured it out as a libation to the LORD, 19 saying, "God forbid that I should do such a thing! Could I drink the blood of these men who risked their lives?" For at the risk of their lives they brought it; and so he refused to drink it. Such deeds as these the Three warriors performed.

20*† Abishai, the brother of Joab. He was the chief of the Thirty; he brandished his spear against three hundred, and slew them. Thus he had a reputation like that of the Three.* 21 He was twice as

---

10, 13f: The Chronicler's comment on why Saul met his tragic end: he had disobeyed the Lord's command given through the prophet Samuel (1 Sm 15, 3–9), and had sought counsel of a necromancer (1 Sm 28, 6–19), contrary to the Mosaic law against necromancy (Dt 18, 10f).

11, 11f: The Three: the Chronicler names only two of them: Ishbaal and Eleazar. According to 2 Sm 23, 8–12, the Three were Ishbaal, Eleazar, and Shammah.

11, 20: The Thirty: listed by name in vv 26–47. The list given in 2 Sm 23, 8–39 often differs in names and spellings; for the numbers, see the note there.

10, 12: 2 Sm 2, 5.
10, 13: Dt 18, 10ff; 1 Sm 13, 13f; 15, 3.11.26.
10, 14: 1 Sm 15, 28; 2 Sm 3, 9f.
11, 1–9: 2 Sm 5, 1–10.
11, 2: 1 Sm 18, 5.13–16.30; 19, 8.
11, 3: 1 Sm 16, 1.13; 2 Sm 2, 4.
11, 4: Jos 15, 8; Jgs 1, 21; 19, 10f.

11, 6: 2 Sm 2, 13ff; 8, 16.
11, 8: 1 Kgs 9, 15.24; 11, 27; 2 Chr 32, 5.
11, 10–41: 2 Sm 23, 8–39.
11, 12: 1 Chr 27, 4.
11, 13: 1 Sm 17, 1.
11, 15: 1 Chr 14, 9; 2 Sm 5, 18.22.
11, 20f: 2 Sm 23, 18f.
11, 20: 1 Chr 18, 12; 1 Sm 26, 6ff; 2 Sm 16, 9; 18, 2; 21, 17.

famous as any of the Thirty and became their commander, but he did not attain to the Three.

²² Benaiah, the son of Jehoiada, a valiant man of mighty deeds, from Kabzeel. He killed the two sons of Ariel of Moab, and also, on a snowy day, he went down and killed the lion in the cistern. ²³ He likewise slew the Egyptian, a huge man five cubits tall. The Egyptian carried a spear that was like a weaver's heddle-bar, but he came against him with a staff, wrested the spear from the Egyptian's hand, and killed him with his own spear. ²⁴ Such deeds as these of Benaiah, the son of Jehoiada, gave him a reputation like that of the Three. ²⁵* He was more famous than any of the Thirty, but he did not attain to the Three. David put him in charge of his bodyguard.

²⁶* Also these warriors: Asahel, the brother of Joab; Elhanan, son of Dodo, from Bethlehem; ²⁷ Shammoth, from En-harod; Helez, from Palti; ²⁸ Ira, son of Ikkesh, from Tekoa; Abiezer, from Anathoth; ²⁹* Sibbecai, from Husha; Ilai, from Ahoh; ³⁰* Maharai, from Netophah; Heled, son of Baanah, from Netophah; ³¹* Ithai, son of Ribai, from Gibeah of Benjamin; Benaiah, from Pirathon; ³² Hurai, from the valley of Gaash; Abiel, from Betharabah; ³³ Azmaveth, from Bahurim; Eliahba, from Shaalbon; ³⁴ Jashen the Gunite; Jonathan, son of Shagee, from En-harod; ³⁵ Ahiam, son of Sachar, from En-harod; Elipheleth, son of ³⁶ Ahasabi, from Beth-maacah; Ahijah, from Gilo; ³⁷ Hezro, from Carmel; Naarai, the son of Ezbai; ³⁸ Joel, brother of Nathan, from Rehob, the Gadite; ³⁹ Zelek the Ammonite; Naharai, from Beeroth, the armor-bearer of Joab, son of Zeruiah; ⁴⁰ Ira, from Jattir; Gareb, from Jattir; ⁴¹ Uriah the Hittite; Zabad, son of Ahlai, ⁴² and, in addition to the Thirty, Adina, son of Shiza, the Reubenite, chief of the tribe of Reuben; ⁴³ Hanan, from Beth-maacah; Joshaphat the Mithnite; ⁴⁴ Uzzia, from Ashterath; Shama and Jeiel, sons of Hotham, from Aroer; ⁴⁵ Jediael, son of Shimri, and Joha, his brother, the Tizite; ⁴⁶ Eliel the Mahavite; Jeribai and Joshaviah, sons of Elnaam; Ithmah, from Moab; ⁴⁷ Eliel, Obed, and Jaasiel the Mezobian.

David's Early Followers

12 ¹* The following men came to David in Ziklag while he was still under banishment from Saul, son of Kish; they, too, were among the warriors who helped him in his battles. ² They were archers who could use either the right or the left hand, both in slinging stones and in shooting arrows with the bow. They were some of Saul's kinsmen, from Benjamin. ³* Ahiezer was their chief, along with Joash, both sons of Shemaah of Gibeah; also Jeziel and Pelet, sons of Azmaveth; Beracah; Jehu, from Anathoth; ⁴ Ishmaiah the Gibeonite, a warrior on the level of the Thirty, and in addition to their number: ⁵ Jeremiah; Jahaziel; Johanan; Jozabad, from Gederah; ⁶ Eluzai; Jerimoth; Bealiah; Shemariah; Shephatiah the Haruphite; ⁷ Elkanah, Isshiah, Azarel, Joezer, and Ishbaal, who were Korahites; ⁸ Joelah, finally, and Zebadiah, sons of Jeroham, from Gedor.

⁹* Some of the Gadites also went over to David when he was at the stronghold in the wilderness. They were valiant warriors, experienced soldiers equipped with shield and spear, who bore themselves like lions, and were as swift as the gazelles on the mountains. ¹⁰ Ezer was their chief, Obadiah was second, Eliab third, ¹¹ Mishmannah fourth, Jeremiah fifth, ¹² Attai sixth, Eliel seventh, ¹³ Johanan eighth, Elzabad ninth, ¹⁴ Jeremiah tenth, and Machbannai eleventh. ¹⁵ These Gadites were army commanders, the lesser placed over hundreds and the greater over thousands. ¹⁶ It was they who crossed over the Jordan when it was overflowing both its banks in the first month, and dispersed all who were in the valleys to the east and to the west.

¹⁷ Some Benjaminites and Judahites also came to David at the stronghold. ¹⁸ David went out to meet them and addressed them in these words: "If you come peacefully, to help me, I am of a mind to have you join me. But if you have come to betray me to my enemies though my hands have done no wrong, may the God of our fathers see and punish you."

¹⁹ Then spirit enveloped Amasai, the chief of the Thirty, who spoke:

"We are yours, O David,
  we are with you, O son of Jesse.
Peace, peace to you,
  and peace to him who helps you;
  your God it is who helps you."

So David received them and placed them among the leaders of his troops.

²⁰ Men from Manasseh also deserted to David when he came with the Philistines to battle against Saul. However, he did not help the Philistines, for their lords took counsel and sent him home, saying, "At the cost of our heads he will desert to his master Saul." ²¹ As he was returning to Ziklag, therefore, these deserted to him from Manasseh: Adnah, Jozabad, Jediael, Michael, Jozabad, Elihu, and Zillethai, chiefs of thousands of Manasseh. ²² They

helped David by taking charge of his troops, for they were all warriors and became commanders of his army. 23 And from day to day men kept coming to David's help until there was a vast encampment, like an encampment of angels.

The Assembly at Hebron

24 This is the muster of the detachments of armed troops that came to David at Hebron to transfer to him Saul's kingdom, as the LORD had ordained. 25† Judahites bearing shields and spears: six thousand eight hundred armed troops. 26 Of the Simeonites, warriors fit for battle: seven thousand one hundred. 27 Of the Levites: four thousand six hundred, 28 along with Jehoiada, leader of the line of Aaron, with another three thousand seven hundred, 29 and Zadok, a young warrior, with twenty-two princes of his father's house. 30 Of the Benjaminites, the brethren of Saul: three thousand—until this time, most of them had held their allegiance to the house of Saul. 31 Of the Ephraimites: twenty thousand eight hundred warriors, men renowned in their ancestral houses. 32 Of the half-tribe of Manasseh: eighteen thousand, designated by name to come and make David king. 33 Of the Issacharites, their chiefs who were endowed with an understanding of the times and who knew what Israel had to do: two hundred chiefs, together with all their brethren under their command. 34 From Zebulun, men fit for military service, set in battle array with every kind of weapon for war: fifty thousand men rallying with a single purpose. 35 From Naphtali: one thousand captains, and with them, armed with shield and lance, thirty-seven thousand men. 36 Of the Danites, set in battle array: twenty-eight thousand six hundred. 37 From Asher, fit for military service and set in battle array: forty thousand. 38 From the other side of the Jordan, of the Reubenites, Gadites, and the half-tribe of Manasseh, men equipped with every kind of weapon of war: one hundred and twenty thousand.

39 All these soldiers, drawn up in battle order, came to Hebron with the resolute intention of making David king over all Israel. The rest of Israel was likewise of one mind to make David king. 40 They remained with David for three days, feasting and drinking, for their brethren had prepared for them. 41 Moreover, their neighbors from as far as Issachar, Zebulun, and Naphtali came bringing food on asses, camels, mules, and oxen—provisions in great quantity of meal, pressed figs, raisins, wine, oil, oxen, and sheep. For there was rejoicing in Israel.

Transfer of the Ark

13 1* After David had taken counsel with his commanders of thousands and of hundreds, that is to say, with every one of his leaders, 2* he said to the whole assembly of Israel: "If it seems good to you, and is so decreed by the LORD our God, let us summon the rest of our brethren from all the districts of Israel, and also the priests and the Levites from their cities with pasture lands, that they may join us; 3 and let us bring the ark of our God here among us, for in the days of Saul we did not visit it." 4 And the whole assembly agreed to do this, for the idea was pleasing to all the people.

5*† Then David assembled all Israel, from Shihor of Egypt to Labo of Hamath, to bring the ark of God from Kiriath-jearim. 6* David and all Israel went up to Baalah, that is, to Kiriath-jearim, of Judah, to bring back the ark of God, which was known by the name "LORD enthroned upon the cherubim." 7 They transported the ark of God on a new cart from the house of Abinadab; Uzzah and Ahio were guiding the cart, 8 while David and all Israel danced before God with great enthusiasm, amid songs and music on lyres, harps, tambourines, cymbals, and trumpets.

9† As they reached the threshing floor of Chidon, Uzzah stretched out his hand to steady the ark, for the oxen were upsetting it. 10 Then the LORD became angry with Uzzah and struck him; he died there in God's presence, because he had laid his hand on the ark. 11† David was disturbed because the LORD's anger had broken out against Uzzah. Therefore that place has been called Perez-uzza even to this day.

12 David was now afraid of God, and he said, "How can I bring the ark of God with me?" 13 Therefore he did not take the ark back with him to the City of David, but he took it instead to the house of Obed-edom the Gittite. 14* The ark of God remained in the house of Obed-edom with his family for three months, and the LORD blessed Obed-edom's household and all that he possessed.

David in Jerusalem

14 1* Hiram, king of Tyre, sent envoys to David along with masons and carpenters,

---

12, 25–38: The Chronicler fills out the pageantry of joyous occasions in keeping with his much later appreciation of the significance of the event in the history of God's people: the numbers in attendance at David's crowning in Hebron (cf 2 Sm 5, 1ff) are recounted in the same spirit of enthusiasm which in v 23 compares David's band of desert freebooters to a numerous encampment of angels.
13, 5: *Shihor Of Egypt:* the eastern branch of the Nile delta. *Labo of Hamath:* in southern Syria.
13, 9: *Chidon:* in 2 Sm 6, 6, Nodan.

13, 11: *Perez-uzza:* A Hebrew term meaning "the breaking out against Uzza."

13, 1–14: 2 Sm 6, 1–11.   2 Sm 6, 1–11.
13, 2: Nm 35, 1ff; Jos 14, 4; 21, 2ff.   **13, 6:** Jos 15, 9; 18, 14; 1 Sm 4, 4; 7, 1.
13, 5: 1 Chr 15, 3; Jos 13, 3.5; 1 Sm 6, 21; 7, 1f;   **13, 14:** 1 Chr 26, 4f.
14, 1–16: 2 Sm 5, 11–25.

and cedar wood to build him a house.* ² David now understood that the LORD had truly confirmed him as king over Israel, for his kingdom was greatly exalted for the sake of his people Israel. ³* David took other wives in Jerusalem and became the father of more sons and daughters. ⁴ These are the names of those who were born to him in Jerusalem: Shammua, Shobab, Nathan, Solomon, ⁵ Ibhar, Elishua, Elpelet, ⁶ Nogah, Nepheg, Japhia, ⁷ Elishama, Beeliada, and Eliphelet.

The Philistine Wars

⁸ When the Philistines had heard that David was anointed king over all Israel, they went up in unison to seek him out. But when David heard of this, he marched out against them. ⁹* Meanwhile the Philistines had come and raided the valley of Rephaim. ¹⁰ David inquired of God, "Shall I advance against the Philistines, and will you deliver them into my power?" The LORD answered him, "Advance, for I will deliver them into your power." ¹¹ They advanced, therefore, to Baal-perazim, and David defeated them there. Then David said, "God has used me to break through my enemies just as water breaks through a dam." Therefore that place was called Baal-perazim. ¹²* The Philistines had left their gods there, and David ordered them to be burnt.

¹³ Once again the Philistines raided the valley, ¹⁴ and again David inquired of God. But God answered him: "Do not try to pursue them, but go around them and come upon them from the direction of the mastic trees. ¹⁵ When you hear the sound of marching in the tops of the mastic trees, then go forth to battle, for God has already gone before you to strike the army of the Philistines." ¹⁶ David did as God commanded him, and they routed the Philistine army from Gibeon to Gezer.

¹⁷ Thus David's fame was spread abroad through every land, and the LORD made all the nations fear him.

The Ark Brought to Jerusalem

15 ¹ David built houses for himself in the City of David and prepared a place for the ark of God, pitching a tent for it there. ²* At that time he said, "No one may carry the ark of God except the Levites, for the LORD chose them to carry the ark of the LORD and to minister to him forever." ³* Then David assembled all Israel in Jerusalem to bring the ark of the LORD to the place which he had prepared for it. ⁴ David also called together the sons of Aaron and the Levites: ⁵ of the sons of Kohath, Uriel, their chief, and one hundred and twenty of his brethren; ⁶ of the sons of Merari, Asaiah, their chief, and two hundred and twenty of his brethren; ⁷ of the sons of Gershon, Joel, their chief, and one hundred and thirty of his brethren; ⁸ of the sons of Elizaphan, Shemaiah, their chief, and two hundred of his brethren; ⁹ of the sons of Hebron, Eliel, their chief, and eighty of his brethren; ¹⁰ of the sons of Uzziel, Amminadab, their chief, and one hundred and twelve of his brethren.

¹¹* David summoned the priests Zadok and Abiathar, and the Levites Uriel, Asaiah, Joel, Shemaiah, Eliel, and Amminadab, ¹²* and said to them: "You, the heads of the levitical families, must sanctify yourselves along with your brethren and bring the ark of the LORD, the God of Israel, to the place which I have prepared for it. ¹³* Because you were not with us the first time, the wrath of the LORD our God burst upon us, for we did not seek him aright." ¹⁴ Accordingly, the priests and the Levites sanctified themselves to bring up the ark of the LORD, the God of Israel. ¹⁵* The Levites bore the ark of God on their shoulders with poles, as Moses had ordained according to the word of the LORD.

¹⁶* David commanded the chiefs of the Levites to appoint their brethren as chanters, to play on musical instruments, harps, lyres, and cymbals, to make a loud sound of rejoicing. ¹⁷* Therefore the Levites appointed Heman, son of Joel, and, among his brethren, Asaph, son of Berechiah; and among the sons of Merari, their brethren, Ethan, son of Kushaiah; ¹⁸ and, together with these, their brethren of the second rank: the gatekeepers Zechariah, Uzziel, Shemiramoth, Jehiel, Unni, Eliab, Benaiah, Maaseiah, Mattithiah, Eliphelehu, Mikneiah, Obed-edom, and Jeiel. ¹⁹ The chanters, Heman, Asaph, and Ethan, sounded brass cymbals. ²⁰† Zechariah, Uzziel, Shemiramoth, Jehiel, Unni, Eliab, Maaseiah, and Benaiah played on harps set to "Alamoth." ²¹ But Mattithiah, Eliphelehu, Mikneiah, Obed-edom, and Jeiel led the chant on lyres set to "the eighth." ²²* Chenaniah was the chief of the Levites in the chanting; he directed the chanting, for he was skillful. ²³ Berechiah and Elkanah were gatekeepers before the ark. ²⁴* The priests, Shebaniah, Joshaphat, Nethanel, Amasai, Zechariah, Benaiah, and Eliezer, sounded the trumpets before the ark of

---

15, 20: *Alamoth:* a musical term (literally, "young women") of uncertain meaning, occurring also in Ps 46, 1, where it is rendered as virgins. Perhaps it may mean something like "soprano," whereas the term "eighth" (Hebrew *sheminith*, v 21) may then mean "bass"; cf Pss 6, 1; 12, 1.

14, 1: 1 Kgs 5, 1; 2 Chr 2, 3.
14, 3–7: 1 Chr 3, 5–8; 2 Sm 5,

13–16.
14, 9: 1 Chr 11, 15.

14, 12: Dt 7, 5.25.
  15, 2: Nm 1, 50; 7, 9; Dt 10, 8; 31, 25; 1 Sm 6, 15; Jos 3, 8.
  15, 3: 1 Chr 13, 5; 2 Sm 6, 15.17.
  15, 11: 1 Chr 16, 39; 2 Sm 8, 17; 15, 29.35.
  15, 12: 2 Chr 29, 5.15.34; 30, 3.15.24.

15, 13: 1 Chr 13, 3.
15, 15: Ex 25, 13ff; Nm 1, 50; 7, 9; 2 Chr 35, 3.
15, 16: 1 Chr 13, 8; 16, 5; 2 Chr 5, 12; 29, 25; Neh 12, 27.
15, 17: 1 Chr 6, 31–47; 25, 1–8.
15, 22: 1 Chr 26, 29.
15, 24: Nm 10, 8; Jos 6, 4ff.

God. Obed-edom and Jeiel were also gatekeepers before the ark.

25* Thus David, the elders of Israel, and the commanders of thousands went to bring up the ark of the covenant of the LORD with joy from the house of Obed-edom. 26* While the Levites, with God's help, were bearing the ark of the covenant of the LORD, seven bulls and seven rams were sacrificed. 27* David was clothed in a robe of fine linen, as were all the Levites who carried the ark, the singers, and Chenaniah, the leader of the chant; David was also wearing a linen ephod. 28 Thus all Israel brought back the ark of the covenant of the LORD with joyful shouting, and to the sound of horns, trumpets, and cymbals, and the music of harps and lyres. 29* But as the ark of the covenant of the LORD was entering the City of David, Michal, daughter of Saul, looked down from her window, and when she saw King David leaping and dancing, she despised him in her heart.

16 1* They brought in the ark of God and set it within the tent which David had pitched for it. Then they offered up holocausts and peace offerings to God.* 2 When David had finished offering up the holocausts and peace offerings, he blessed the people in the name of the LORD, 3 and distributed to every Israelite, to every man and to every woman, a loaf of bread, a piece of meat, and a raisin cake.

The Ministering Levites

4* He now appointed certain Levites to minister before the ark of the LORD, to celebrate, thank, and praise the LORD, the God of Israel. 5 Asaph was their chief, and second to him were Zechariah, Uzziel, Shemiramoth, Jehiel, Mattithiah, Eliab, Benaiah, Obed-edom, and Jeiel. These were to play on harps and lyres, while Asaph was to sound the cymbals, 6 and the priests Benaiah and Jahaziel were to be the regular trumpeters before the ark of the covenant of God.

7 Then, on that same day, David appointed Asaph and his brethren to sing for the first time these praises of the LORD:

8*†Give thanks to the LORD, invoke his name;
    make known among the nations his
        deeds.
9   Sing to him, sing his praise,
        proclaim all his wondrous deeds.

10   Glory in his holy name;
        rejoice, O hearts that seek the LORD!
11   Look to the LORD in his strength;
        seek to serve him constantly.
12   Recall the wondrous deeds that he
            has wrought,
        his portents, and the judgments he
            has uttered,
13   You descendants of Israel, his servants,
        sons of Jacob, his chosen ones!

14   He, the LORD, is our God;
        throughout the earth his judgments prevail.
15   He remembers forever his covenant
        which he made binding for a
            thousand generations—
16   Which he entered into with Abraham
        and by his oath to Isaac;
17   Which he established for Jacob by statute,
        for Israel as an everlasting covenant,
18   Saying, "To you will I give the land of Canaan
        as your alloted inheritance."

19   When they were few in number,
        a handful, and strangers there,
20   Wandering from nation to nation,
        from one kingdom to another people,
21   He let no one oppress them,
        and for their sake he rebuked kings:
22   "Touch not my anointed,
        and to my prophets do no harm."

23*   Sing to the LORD, all the earth,
        announce his salvation, day after day.
24   Tell his glory among the nations;

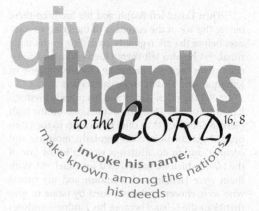

give thanks to the LORD, 16, 8
invoke his name;
make known among the nations
his deeds

16, 8–36: A hymn composed of parts, with textual variants, from several Psalms; vv 8–22 = Ps 105, 1–15; vv 23–33 = Ps 96, 1–13; vv 34–36 = Ps 106, 1.47f.

15, 25–29: 2 Sm 6, 12–16.
  15, 26: 2 Sm 6, 17; 2 Chr 29, 21.
  15, 27: 1 Sm 2, 18; 2 Sm 6, 14.
  15, 29: 2 Sm 6, 20ff.

16, 1–3: 2 Sm 6, 17ff.
  16, 1: 1 Chr 15, 1.
  16, 4: Sir 47, 9.
  16, 8–22: Ps 105, 1–15.
  16, 23–33: Ps 96, 1–13.

among all peoples, his wondrous deeds.

25 For great is the LORD and highly to be praised;
and awesome is he, beyond all gods.

26 For all the gods of the nations are things
of nought,
but the LORD made the heavens.

27 Splendor and majesty go before him;
praise and joy are in his holy place.

28 Give to the LORD, you families of nations,
give to the LORD glory and praise;

29 Give to the LORD the glory due his name!
Bring gifts, and enter his presence;
worship the LORD in holy attire.

30 Tremble before him, all the earth;
he has made the world firm, not to
be moved.

31 Let the heavens be glad and the earth rejoice;
let them say among the nations: The LORD
is king.

32 Let the sea and what fills it resound;
let the plains rejoice and all that is in them!

33 Then shall all the trees of the forest exult
before the LORD, for he comes:
he comes to rule the earth.

34* Give thanks to the LORD, for he is good,
for his kindness endures forever;

35 And say, "Save us, O God, our savior,
gather us and deliver us from the nations,
That we may give thanks to your holy name
and glory in praising you."

36 Blessed be the LORD, the God of Israel,
through all eternity!
Let all the people say, Amen! Alleluia.

37 Then David left Asaph and his brethren there before the ark of the covenant of the LORD to minister before the ark regularly according to the daily ritual; 38* he also left there Obed-edom and sixty-eight of his brethren, including Obed-edom, son of Jeduthun, and Hosah, to be gatekeepers.

39* But the priest Zadok and his priestly brethren he left before the Dwelling of the LORD on the high place at Gibeon, 40* to offer holocausts to the LORD on the altar of holocausts regularly, morning and evening, and to do all that is written in the law of the LORD which he has decreed for Israel. 41* With them were Heman and Jeduthun and the others who were chosen and designated by name to give thanks to the LORD, "because his kindness endures

Catholic Connections

RITUAL PRAYER

King David established times of regular, ritual prayer at the ark. Regular, ritual prayer is a practice of many of the world's great religions and, in the eyes of the Chronicler, is a key ingredient of true religious practice. Catholics also have ancient traditions of regular, ritual prayer. (Regular, in this instance, does not mean "ordinary," but rather "at certain, established times.") We start the day with prayer, we end the day with prayer, we have special blessings for special occasions, and we gather to celebrate the Eucharist each week. Regular, ritual prayer helps to remind us of God's presence and of our identity as God's people.

How do you pray? Do you pray regularly? Do you have any personal rituals as part of your prayer life?

▶ 1 Chr 16, 37–43

forever," 42* with trumpets and cymbals for accompaniment, and instruments for the sacred chant. The sons of Jeduthun kept the gate.

43* Then all the people departed, each to his own home, and David returned to bless his household.

The Oracle of Nathan

17 1* After David had taken up residence in his house, he said to Nathan the prophet, "See, I am living in a house of cedar, but the ark of the covenant of the LORD dwells under tentcloth."* 2 Nathan replied to David, "Do, therefore, whatever you desire, for God is with you."

3 But that same night the word of God came to Nathan: 4* "Go and tell my servant David, Thus says the LORD: It is not you who are to build a house for me to dwell in. 5 For I have never dwelt in a

16, 34ff: Ps 106, 1.47f.
16, 38: 1 Chr 15, 24.
16, 39: 1 Kgs 3, 4.
16, 40: Ex 29, 38–42; Lv 6, 9;

Nm 28, 3.6; 2 Chr 13,
11.
16, 41: 2 Chr 5, 12; 7, 3.6; 20,
21; Ezr 3, 11.

16, 42: 2 Chr 29, 27.
16, 43: 2 Sm 6, 19f.
17, 1–27: 2 Sm 7, 1–29.
17, 1: 1 Chr 15, 1;

2 Sm 5, 11.
17, 4: 1 Chr 28, 3; 1 Kgs 8,
19.

house, from the time when I led Israel onward, even to this day, but I have been lodging in tent or pavilion ⁶ as long as I have wandered about with all of Israel. Did I ever say a word to any of the judges of Israel whom I commanded to guide my people, such as, 'Why have you not built me a house of cedar?' ⁷* Therefore, tell my servant David, Thus says the LORD of hosts: I took you from the pasture, from following the sheep, that you might become ruler over my people Israel. ⁸ I was with you wherever you went, and I cut down all your enemies before you. I will make your name great like that of the greatest on the earth. ⁹ I will assign a place for my people Israel and I will plant them in it to dwell there henceforth undisturbed; nor shall wicked men ever again oppress them, as they did at first, ¹⁰ and during all the time when I appointed judges over my people Israel. And I will subdue all your enemies. Moreover, I declare to you that I, the LORD, will build you a house; ¹¹* so that when your days have been completed and you must join your fathers, I will raise up your offspring after you who will be one of your own sons, and I will establish his kingdom. ¹²* He it is who shall build me a house, and I will establish his throne forever. ¹³* I will be a father to him, and he shall be a son to me, and I will not withdraw my favor from him as I withdrew it from him who preceded you; ¹⁴ but I will maintain him in my house and in my kingdom forever, and his throne shall be firmly established forever."

¹⁵ All these words and this whole vision Nathan related exactly to David.

David's Thanksgiving

¹⁶ Then David came in and sat in the LORD's presence, saying: "Who am I, O LORD God, and what is my family, that you should have brought me as far as I have come? ¹⁷* And yet, even this you now consider too little, O God! For you have made a promise regarding your servant's family reaching into the distant future, and you have looked on me as henceforth the most notable of men, O LORD God. ¹⁸ What more can David say to you? You know your servant. ¹⁹ O LORD, for your servant's sake and in keeping with your purpose, you have done this great thing. ²⁰* O LORD, there is no one like you and there is no God but you, just as we have always understood.

²¹* "Is there, like your people Israel, whom you redeemed from Egypt, another nation on earth whom a god went to redeem as his people? You won for yourself a name for great and awesome deeds by driving out the nations before your people. ²² You made your people Israel your own forever, and you, O LORD, became their God. ²³ Therefore, O LORD, may the promise that you have uttered concerning your servant and his house remain firm forever. Bring about what you have promised, ²⁴ that your renown as LORD of hosts, God of Israel, may be great and abide forever, while the house of David, your servant, is established in your presence.

²⁵* "Because you, O my God, have revealed to your servant that you will build him a house, your servant has made bold to pray before you. ²⁶ Since

Where Do We Place God?

How the world loves boxes and containers and compartments! Remember the old saying, A place for everything and everything in its place? There is something comforting in knowing that everything is where it should be.

Don't we often try to put God away in a special place? Isn't it more convenient to think of God as residing "up there" in the tabernacle or sanctuary? Perhaps that is why in I Chr 17, 4–6, God seems less than enthusiastic about David's desire to build a temple. The danger is clear: identify God with a building, however grand and beautiful, and in people's minds, God *stays* there.

When we enter a chapel or a church, we become reverent, sensing that we are in the presence of God. And, indeed, we are. But we need to remember that we do not leave God behind when we step out of that structure. Simply put, God cannot and will not be confined, despite our best efforts.

Our God walks with us. God's place is everywhere.

How can you practice living in the constant presence of God?

▸ I Chr 17, 1–15

17, 7: 1 Sm 16, 11.
17, 11: 2 Sm 7, 12f.
17, 12: 1 Chr 22, 10; 28, 6.10.
17, 13: 2 Sm 7, 14.
17, 17: 2 Sm 7, 19.
17, 20: Sir 36, 4.
17, 21: Dt 4, 7; 2 Sm 7, 23.
17, 25: 2 Sm 7, 27.

you, O LORD, are truly God and have promised this good thing to your servant, ²⁷* and since you have deigned to bless the house of your servant, so that it will remain forever—since it is you, O LORD, who blessed it, it is blessed forever."

David's Victories

18 ¹* After this, David defeated the Philistines and subdued them; and he took Gath and its towns away from the control of the Philistines. ² He also defeated Moab, and the Moabites became his subjects, paying tribute.

³ David then defeated Hadadezer, king of Zobah toward Hamath, when the latter was on his way to set up his victory stele at the river Euphrates. ⁴* David took from him twenty thousand foot soldiers, one thousand chariots, and seven thousand horsemen. Of the chariot horses, David hamstrung all but one hundred. ⁵ The Arameans of Damascus came to the aid of Hadadezer, king of Zobah, but David also slew twenty-two thousand of their men. ⁶ Then David set up garrisons in the Damascus region of Aram, and the Arameans became his subjects, paying tribute. Thus the LORD made David victorious in all his campaigns.

⁷ David took the golden shields that were carried by Hadadezer's attendants and brought them to Jerusalem. ⁸* He likewise took away from Tibhath and Cun, cities of Hadadezer, large quantities of bronze, which Solomon later used to make the bronze sea and the pillars and the vessels of bronze.

⁹ When Tou, king of Hamath, heard that David had defeated the entire army of Hadadezer, king of Zobah, ¹⁰* he sent his son Hadoram to wish King David well and to congratulate him on having waged a victorious war against Hadadezer; for Hadadezer had been at war with Tou. He also sent David gold, silver and bronze utensils of every sort. ¹¹ These also King David consecrated to the LORD along with all the silver and gold that he had taken from the nations: from Edom, Moab, the Ammonites, the Philistines, and Amalek.

¹²* Abishai, the son of Zeruiah, also slew eighteen thousand Edomites in the Valley of Salt. ¹³ He set up garrisons in Edom, and all the Edomites became David's subjects. Thus the LORD made David victorious in all his campaigns.

David's Officials

¹⁴* David reigned over all Israel and dispensed justice and right to all his people. ¹⁵* Joab, son of Zeruiah, was in command of the army; Jehoshaphat, son of Ahilud, was herald; ¹⁶*† Zadok, son of Ahitub, and Ahimelech, son of Abiathar, were priests; Shavsha was scribe; ¹⁷*† Benaiah, son of Jehoiada, was in command of the Cherethites and the Pelethites; and David's sons were the chief assistants to the king.

Campaigns against Ammon

19 ¹* Afterward Nahash, king of the Ammonites, died and his son succeeded him as king. ² David said, "I will show kindness to Hanun, the son of Nahash, for his father treated me with kindness." Therefore he sent envoys to him to comfort him over the death of his father. But when David's servants had entered the land of the Ammonites to comfort Hanun, ³ the Ammonite princes said to Hanun, "Do you think David is doing this—sending you these consolers—to honor your father? Have not his servants rather come to you to explore the land, spying it out for its overthrow?" ⁴ Thereupon Hanun seized David's servants and had them shaved and their garments cut off half-way at the hips. Then he sent them away. ⁵ When David was informed of what had happened to his men, he sent messengers to meet them, for the men had been greatly disgraced. "Remain at Jericho," the king told them, "until your beards have grown again; and then you may come back here."

⁶ When the Ammonites realized that they had put themselves in bad odor with David, Hanun and the Ammonites sent a thousand talents of silver to hire chariots and horsemen from Aram Naharaim, from Aram-maacah, and from Zobah. ⁷ They hired thirty-two thousand chariots along with the king of Maacah and his army, who came and encamped before Medeba. The Ammonites also assembled from their cities and came out for war.

⁸ When David heard of this, he sent Joab and his

---

† **18, 16:** *Zadok . . . and Ahimelech, son of Abiathar, were priests:* as in the Chronicler's source, 2 Sm 8, 17. But according to 2 Sm 15, 24.29.35; 17, 15; 19, 11; 20, 25, and even 1 Chr 15, 11, it was Abiathar who shared the priestly office with Zadok, and he remained in this office even during the early years of Solomon's reign (1 Kgs 2, 26; 4, 4). Moreover, according to 1 Sm 22, 20; 23, 6; 30, 7, Ahimelech was the father, not the son, of Abiathar. If the text Ahimelech, son of Abiathar, is not due to a scribal change, one must assume that Abiathar had a son who was named after his grandfather and who shared the priestly office with his father during the last years of David's reign.

18, 17: *David's sons were the chief assistants to the king:* in the parallel passage, 2 Sm 8, 18, which was the Chronicler's source,

David's sons were priests. The change is characteristic of the Chronicler, for whom only Aaron's descendants could be priests.

17, 27: Nm 22, 6.
18, 1-13: 2 Sm 8, 1-14.
  18, 4: 2 Sm 8, 14; Jos 11, 6.9.
  18, 8: 2 Sm 8, 8; 1 Kgs 7, 15.23.27.
  18, 10: 2 Sm 8, 10.
  18, 12: 2 Sm 8, 13; 2 Kgs 14, 7.

18, 14-17: 2 Sm 8, 15-18.
  18, 15: 1 Chr 11, 6; 2 Sm 8, 16; 1 Kgs 4, 3.
  18, 16: 1 Chr 24, 3.6.31; 2 Sm 8, 17.
  18, 17: 1 Chr 11, 22; 2 Sm 8, 18; 1 Kgs 1, 38.44.
19, 1-19: 2 Sm 10, 1-19.

whole army of warriors against them. ⁹ The Ammonites marched out and lined up for battle at the gate of the city, while the kings who had come to their help remained apart in the open field. ¹⁰* When Joab saw that there was a battle line both in front of and behind him, he chose some of the best fighters among the Israelites and set them in array against the Arameans; ¹¹* the rest of the army, which he placed under the command of his brother Abishai, then lined up to oppose the Ammonites. ¹² And he said: "If the Arameans prove too strong for me, you must come to my help; and if the Ammonites prove too strong for you, I will save you. ¹³ Hold steadfast and let us show ourselves courageous for the sake of our people and the cities of our God; then may the LORD do what seems best to him." ¹⁴ Joab therefore advanced with his men to engage the Arameans in battle; but they fled before him. ¹⁵ And when the Ammonites saw that the Arameans had fled, they also took to flight before his brother Abishai, and reentered the city. Joab then returned to Jerusalem.

¹⁶ Seeing themselves vanquished by Israel, the Arameans sent messengers to bring out the Arameans from the other side of the River, with Shophach, the general of Hadadezer's army, at their head. ¹⁷ When this was reported to David, he gathered all Israel together, crossed the Jordan, and met them. With the army of David drawn up to fight the Arameans, they gave battle. ¹⁸ But the Arameans fled before Israel, and David slew seven thousand of their chariot fighters and forty thousand of their foot soldiers; he also killed Shophach, the general of the army. ¹⁹ When the vassals of Hadadezer saw themselves vanquished by Israel, they made peace with David and became his subjects. After this, the Arameans refused to come to the aid of the Ammonites.

20 ¹ At the beginning of the following year, the time when kings go to war, Joab led the army out in force, laid waste the land of the Ammonites, and went on to besiege Rabbah, while David himself remained in Jerusalem. When Joab had attacked Rabbah and destroyed it, ²* David took the crown of Milcom from the idol's head. It was found to weigh a talent of gold; and it contained precious stones, which David wore on his own head.

He also brought out a great amount of booty from the city. ³ He deported the people of the city and set them to work with saws, iron picks, and axes. Thus David dealt with all the cities of the Ammonites. Then he and his whole army returned to Jerusalem.

Victories over the Philistines

⁴* Afterward there was another battle with the Philistines, at Gezer. At that time, Sibbecai the Hushathite slew Sippai, one of the descendants of the Raphaim, and the Philistines were subdued.* ⁵*† Once again there was war with the Philistines, and Elhanan, the son of Jair, slew Lahmi, the brother of Goliath of Gath, whose spear shaft was like a weaver's heddle-bar.

⁶ In still another battle, at Gath, they encountered a giant, also a descendant of the Raphaim, who had six fingers to each hand and six toes to each foot; twenty-four in all. ⁷ He defied Israel, and Jonathan, the son of Shimea, David's brother, slew him. ⁸ These were the descendants of the Raphaim of Gath who died at the hands of David and his servants.

David's Census; the Plague

21 ¹*† A satan rose up against Israel, and he enticed David into taking a census of Israel.* ² David therefore said to Joab and to the other generals of the army, "Go, find out the number of the Israelites from Beer-sheba to Dan, and report back to me that I may know their number." ³ But Joab replied: "May the LORD increase his people a hundredfold! My lord king, are not all of them my lord's subjects? Why does my lord seek to do this thing? Why will he bring guilt upon Israel?" ⁴ However, the king's command prevailed over Joab, who departed and traversed all of Israel, and then returned to Jerusalem. ⁵ Joab reported the result of the census to David: of men capable of wielding a sword, there were in all Israel one million one hundred thousand, and in Judah four hundred and seventy thousand. ⁶* Levi and Benjamin, however, he did not include in the census, for the king's command was repugnant to Joab. ⁷ This command displeased God, who began to punish Israel. ⁸ Then David said to God, "I have sinned greatly in doing this thing. Take away your servant's guilt, for I have acted very foolishly."

20, 5: *Elhanan . . . slew Lahmi, the brother of Goliath:* the Chronicler thus solves the difficulty of the apparent contradiction between 1 Sm 17, 49ff (David killed Goliath) and 2 Sm 21, 19 (Elhanan killed Goliath).

21, 1: *A satan:* in the parallel passage of 2 Sm 24, 1, the Lord's anger. The change in the term reflects the changed theological outlook of postexilic Israel, when evil could no longer be attributed directly to God. At an earlier period the Hebrew word *satan* ("adversary" or, especially in a court of law, "accuser"), when not used of men, designated an angel who accused men before God (Jb

1, 6–12; 2, 1–7; Zec 3, 1f). Here, as in later Judaism (Wis 2, 24) and in the New Testament, satan, or the "devil" (from the Greek translation of the word), designates an evil spirit who tempts men to wrongdoing.

19, 10: 1 Chr 20, 23; 1 Kgs 2, 28.34.
19, 11: 1 Chr 23, 18f.
20, 2f: 2 Sm 12, 30f.
20, 4–8: 2 Sm 21, 18–22.
20, 4: 1 Chr 11, 29; 27, 11.
20, 5: 1 Chr 11, 26; 1 Sm 17, 4.23.
21, 1–7: 2 Sm 24, 1–25.
21, 1: 1 Zec 3, 1f.
21, 6: 1 Chr 27, 24; Nm 1, 49.

9* Then the LORD spoke to Gad, David's seer, in these words: 10 "Go, tell David: Thus says the LORD: I offer you three alternatives; choose one of them, and I will inflict it on you." 11 Accordingly, Gad went to David and said to him: "Thus says the LORD: Decide now— 12 will it be three years of famine; or three months of fleeing your enemies, with the sword of your foes ever at your back; or three days of the LORD'S own sword, a pestilence in the land, with the LORD'S destroying angel in every part of Israel? Therefore choose: What answer am I to give him who sent me?" 13 Then David said to Gad: "I am in dire straits. But I prefer to fall into the hand of the LORD, whose mercy is very great, than into the hands of men."

14 Therefore the LORD sent pestilence upon Israel, and seventy thousand men of Israel died. 15* God also sent an angel to destroy Jerusalem; but as he was on the point of destroying it, the LORD saw and decided against the calamity, and said to the destroying angel, "Enough now! Stay your hand!"

Ornan's Threshing Floor

The angel of the LORD was then standing by the threshing floor of Ornan the Jebusite. 16 When David raised his eyes, he saw the angel of the LORD standing between earth and heaven, with a naked sword in his hand stretched out against Jerusalem. David and the elders, clothed in sackcloth, prostrated themselves face to the ground, 17 and David prayed to God: "Was it not I who ordered the census of the people? I am the one who sinned, I did this wicked thing. But these sheep, what have they done? O LORD, my God, strike me and my father's family, but do not afflict your people with this plague!"

18* Then the angel of the LORD commanded Gad to tell David to go up and erect an altar to the LORD on the threshing floor of Ornan the Jebusite. 19 David went up at Gad's command, given in the name of the LORD. 20 While Ornan was threshing wheat, he turned around and saw the king, and his four sons who were with him, without recognizing them. 21 But as David came on toward him, he looked up and saw that it was David. Then he left the threshing floor and bowed down before David, his face to the ground. 22 David said to Ornan: "Sell me the ground of this threshing floor, that I may build on it an altar to the LORD. Sell it to me at its full price, that the plague may be stayed from the people." 23 But Ornan said to David: "Take it as your own, and let my lord the king do what seems best to him. See, I also give you the oxen for the holocausts, the threshing sledges for the wood, and the wheat for the cereal offering. I give it all to you." 24 But King David replied to Ornan: "No! I will buy it from you properly, at its full price. I will not take what is yours for the LORD, nor offer up holocausts that cost me nothing." 25† So David paid Ornan six hundred shekels of gold for the place.

Altar of Holocausts

26* David then built an altar there to the LORD, and offered up holocausts and peace offerings. When he called upon the LORD, he answered him by sending down fire from heaven upon the altar of holocausts. 27 Then the LORD gave orders to the angel to return his sword to its sheath.

28 Once David saw that the LORD had heard him on the threshing floor of Ornan the Jebusite, he continued to offer sacrifices there. 29* The Dwelling

True Repentance

Think of a time when you said, "I'm sorry," just because you felt you had to. Now, think of a time when you were truly sorry for causing harm to others by doing something God has commanded you not to do. There is a big difference between going through the motions of repentance and being truly repentant before others and before God. For example, David sinned by ordering a census to count his people (1 Chr 21, 2). He accepted a consequence that he hoped would be the easiest (verse 13). But when he saw the harm he had caused, he became truly repentant and asked God's mercy upon the Israelites (verse 17).

Repentance requires true sorrow and asking God to change our heart. It leads to an active response to make amends with God and with the church. Such repentance is called reconciliation, and Catholics celebrate it in the sacrament of Reconciliation.

▸ 1 Chr 21, 1–17

21, 25: *Six hundred shekels of gold:* about 10,000 dollars. According to 2 Sm 24, 24, David paid 50 shekels of silver, about 20 dollars, for Ornan's threshing floor; but for the Chronicler the site of the temple was much more precious than that.

21, 9: 1 Chr 29, 29; 1 Sm 9,
  9; 2 Chr 29, 25.
21, 15: Gn 6, 6; Ex 32, 14;
  2 Sm 24, 16; Jon 3, 10.
21, 18: 2 Chr 3, 1.

21, 26: Lv 9, 24; Jgs 6, 21;
  1 Kgs 18, 38; 2 Chr 7,
  1; 2 Mc 2, 10ff.
21, 29: 1 Chr 16, 39; 1 Kgs 8,
  4; 2 Chr 1, 8.

of the LORD, which Moses had built in the desert, and the altar of holocausts were at that time on the high place at Gibeon. 30 But David could not go there to worship God, for he was fearful of the sword of the angel of the LORD. 1*† Therefore David said, "This is the house of the LORD God, and this is the altar of holocausts for Israel."

Material for the Temple

22 2*† David then ordered that all the aliens who lived in the land of Israel be brought together, and he appointed them stonecutters to hew out stone blocks for building the house of God. 3* He also laid up large stores of iron to make nails for the doors of the gates, and clamps, together with so much bronze that it could not be weighed, 4* and cedar trees without number. The Sidonians and Tyrians brought great stores of cedar logs to David, 5* who said: "My son Solomon is young and immature; but the house that is to be built for the LORD must be made so magnificent that it will be renowned and glorious in all countries. Therefore I will make preparations for it." Thus before his death David laid up materials in abundance.

Charge to Solomon

6 Then he called for his son Solomon and commanded him to build a house for the LORD, the God of Israel. 7* David said to Solomon: "My son, it was my purpose to build a house myself for the honor of the LORD, my God. 8 But this word of the LORD came to me: 'You have shed much blood, and you have waged great wars. You may not build a house in my honor, because you have shed too much blood upon the earth in my sight. 9*† However, a son is to be born to you. He will be a peaceful man, and I will give him rest from all his enemies on every side. For Solomon shall be his name, and in his time I will bestow peace and tranquility on Israel. 10* It is he who shall build a house in my honor; he shall be a son to me, and I will be a father to him, and I will establish the throne of his kingship over Israel forever.' 11 Now, my son, the

LORD be with you, and may you succeed in building the house of the LORD your God, as he has said you shall. 12 May the LORD give you prudence and discernment when he brings you to rule over Israel, so that you keep the law of the LORD, your God. 13* Only then shall you succeed, if you are careful to observe the precepts and decrees which the LORD gave Moses for Israel. Be brave and steadfast; do not fear or lose heart. 14*† See, with great effort I have laid up for the house of the LORD a hundred thousand talents of gold, a million talents of silver, and bronze and iron in such great quantities that they cannot be weighed. I have also stored up wood and stones, to which you must add. 15 Moreover, you have available an unlimited supply of workmen, stonecutters, masons, carpenters, and every kind of craftsman 16 skilled in gold, silver, bronze, and iron. Set to work, therefore, and the LORD be with you!"

Charge to the Leaders

17 David also commanded all of Israel's leaders to help his son Solomon: 18* "Is not the LORD your God with you? Has he not given you rest on every side? Indeed, he has delivered the occupants of the land into my power, and the land is subdued before the LORD and his people. 19* Therefore, devote your hearts and souls to seeking the LORD your God. Proceed to build the sanctuary of the LORD God, that the ark of the covenant of the LORD and God's sacred vessels may be brought into the house built in honor of the LORD."

The Levitical Classes

23 1* When David had grown old and was near the end of his days, he made his son Solomon king over Israel. 2 He then gathered together all the leaders of Israel, together with the priests and the Levites.

3* The Levites thirty years old and above were counted, and their total number was found to be thirty-eight thousand men. 4 Of these, twenty-four thousand were to direct the service of the house of the LORD, six thousand were to be officials and judges, 5* four thousand were to be gatekeepers,

---

21, 1: This belongs to ch 22.
22, 2ff: According to 1 Kgs 5, 15–32, it was Solomon who made the material preparations for building the temple, even though David had wished to do so (1 Kgs 5, 17ff). The Chronicler, however, sought to have David, who was Israel's ideal king, more closely connected with Israel's most sacred sanctuary, the temple of Jerusalem.
22, 9: The Hebrew word for peace, *shalom*, is reflected in the name Solomon, in Hebrew, *Shelomo*. A contrast is drawn here between Solomon, the peaceful man, and David, who waged great wars (v 8). David was prevented from building the temple, not only because all his time was taken up in waging war (1 Kgs 5, 17), but also because he shed much blood (v 8), and in the eyes of the Chronicler this made him ritually unfit for the task.
22, 14: *A hundred thousand talents of gold:* about 3,775 tons of gold. *A million talents of silver:* about 37,750 tons of silver. The fantastically exaggerated figures are intended merely to stress the

inestimable value of the temple as the center of Israelite worship. More modest figures are given in 1 Kgs 9, 14.28; 10, 10.14.

21, 1: 1 Chr 21, 18.26.28;	6.23; Jos 1, 6f.9; 1 Kgs
2 Chr 3, 1.	2, 2f.
22, 2ff: 1 Kgs 5, 31f; 9, 20f;	**22, 14:** 1 Chr 29, 2ff.
2 Chr 2, 16f.	**22, 18:** 1 Chr 23, 25; Jos 21,
22, 3: 1 Chr 18, 8; 1 Kgs	44; 23, 1; 2 Sm 7, 1.
7, 47.	**22, 19:** 1 Kgs 8, 6.21; 2 Chr 5,
22, 4: 1 Chr 10, 27; Ezr 3, 7.	7; 6, 11.
22, 5: 1 Chr 29, 1.	**23, 1:** 1 Chr 28, 5; 1 Kgs 1,
22, 7–10: 1 Chr 17, 1–14; 28,	30.
2–7; 2 Sm 7, 1–16;	**23, 3:** Nm 4, 3.23.30.35.39.
1 Kgs 5, 3ff; 8, 17–21.	43.47; 8, 23–26; 2 Chr
22, 9: 2 Sm 12, 24.	31, 17.
22, 10: Heb 1, 5.	**23, 5:** 1 Chr 9, 22.
22, 13: 1 Chr 28, 7.20; Dt 31,	

and four thousand were to praise the LORD with the instruments which David had devised for praise. 6* David divided them into classes according to the sons of Levi: Gershon, Kohath, and Merari.

7 To the Gershonites belonged Ladan and Shimei. 8* The sons of Ladan: Jehiel the chief, then Zetham and Joel; three in all. 9 The sons of Shimei were Shelomoth, Haziel, and Haran; three. These were the heads of the families of Ladan. 10 The sons of Shimei were Jahath, Zizah, Jeush, and Beriah; these were the sons of Shimei, four in all. 11 Jahath was the chief and Zizah was second to him; but Jeush and Beriah had not many sons, and therefore they were classed as a single family, fulfilling a single office.

12* The sons of Kohath: Amram, Izhar, Hebron, and Uzziel; four in all. 13* The sons of Amran were Aaron and Moses. Aaron was set apart to be consecrated as most holy, he and his sons forever, to offer sacrifice before the LORD, to minister to him, and to bless his name forever. 14 As for Moses, however, the man of God, his sons were counted as part of the tribe of Levi. 15* The sons of Moses were Gershon and Eliezer. 16* The sons of Gershon: Shubael the chief. 17 The sons of Eliezer were Rehabiah the chief—Eliezer had no other sons, but the sons of Rehabiah were very numerous. 18 The sons of Izhar: Shelomith the chief. 19* The sons of Hebron: Jeriah, the chief, Amariah, the second, Jahaziel, the third, and Jekameam, the fourth. 20* The sons of Uzziel: Micah, the chief, and Isshiah, the second.

21* The sons of Merari: Mahli and Mushi. The sons of Mahli: Eleazar and Kish. 22* Eleazar died leaving no sons, only daughters; the sons of Kish, their kinsmen, married them. 23* The sons of Mushi: Mahli, Eder, and Jeremoth; three in all.

24* These were the sons of Levi according to their ancestral houses, the family heads as they were enrolled one by one according to their names. They performed the work of the service of the house of the LORD from twenty years of age upward, 27 for David's final orders were to enlist the Levites from the time they were twenty years old.

25* David said: "The LORD, the God of Israel, has given rest to his people, and has taken up his dwelling in Jerusalem. 26* Henceforth the Levites need not carry the Dwelling or any of its furnishings or equipment. 28 Rather, their duty shall be to assist the sons of Aaron in the service of the house of the

LORD, having charge of the courts, the chambers, and the preservation of everything holy: they shall take part in the service of the house of God. 29* They shall also have charge of the showbread, of the fine flour for the cereal offering, of the wafers of unleavened bread, and of the baking and mixing, and of all measures of quantity and size. 30* They must be present every morning to offer thanks and to praise the LORD, and likewise in the evening; 31* and at every offering of holocausts to the LORD on sabbaths, new moons, and feast days, in such numbers as are prescribed, they must always be present before the LORD. 32* They shall observe what is prescribed for them concerning the meeting tent, the sanctuary, and the sons of Aaron, their brethren, in the service of the house of the LORD."

The Priestly Classes

24 1* The descendants of Aaron also were divided into classes. The sons of Aaron were Nadab, Abihu, Eleazar, and Ithamar. 2* Nadab and Abihu died before their father, leaving no sons; therefore only Eleazar and Ithamar served as priests. 3* David, with Zadok, a descendant of Eleazar, and Ahimelech, a descendant of Ithamar, assigned the functions for the priestly service. 4 But since the descendants of Eleazar were found to be more numerous than those of Ithamar, the former were divided into sixteen groups, and the latter into eight groups, each under its family head. 5 Their functions were assigned impartially by lot, for there were officers of the holy place, and officers of the divine presence, descended both from Eleazar and from Ithamar. 6*† The scribe Shemaiah, son of Nethanel, a Levite, made a record of it in the presence of the king, and of the leaders, of Zadok the priest, and of Ahimelech, son of Abiathar, and of the heads of the ancestral houses of the priests and of the Levites, listing two successive family groups from Eleazar before each one from Ithamar.

7* The first lot fell to Jehoiarib, the second to Jedaiah, 8 the third to Harim, the fourth to Seorim, 9 the fifth to Malchijah, the sixth to Mijamin, 10* the seventh to Hakkoz, the eighth to Abijah, 11 the ninth to Jeshua, the tenth to Shecaniah, 12 the eleventh to Eliashib, the twelfth to Jakim, 13 the thirteenth to Huppah, the fourteenth to Ishbaal, 14 the fifteenth to Bilgah, the sixteenth to Immer, 15 the seventeenth to Hezir, the eighteenth to Hap-

---

† **24, 6:** *Ahimelech, son of Abiathar:* see note on 1 Chr 18, 16.

23, 6: 1 Chr 6, 1.16–30; 26, 1–19; Ex 6, 16; Nm 3, 17; 26, 57.
23, 8: 1 Chr 26, 21f; 29, 8.
23, 12: 1 Chr 26, 23; Ex 6, 18; Nm 3, 19; 26, 23ff.
23, 13: 1 Chr 6, 49; Ex 6, 20; 28, 1; Nm 6, 23.

23, 15: Ex 2, 22; 18, 3f.
23, 16: 1 Chr 26, 24.
23, 19: 1 Chr 24, 23.
23, 20: 1 Chr 24, 24f.
23, 21: 1 Chr 6, 29; 24, 26.28f; Ex 6, 19; Nm 3, 20.33.
23, 22: 1 Chr 24, 28f.
23, 23: 1 Chr 6, 47; 24, 30.

23, 24: 2 Chr 31, 17; Ezr 3, 8.
23, 25: 1 Chr 22, 18; Ps 132, 13.
23, 26: 1 Chr 15, 15; 2 Chr 35, 3.
23, 29: 1 Chr 9, 29.31f; Lv 2, 1.4f; 24, 5–8.
23, 30: Nm 28, 3–8.
23, 31: Nm 28, 2–29.39.
23, 32: Nm 3, 6–9; 18, 2–5.
24, 1: Ex 6, 23; Nm 3, 2ff;

26, 60.
24, 2: Lv 10, 1–7.12; Nm 3, 2.4.
24, 3: 1 Chr 18, 16; 2 Sm 8, 17; 2 Chr 8, 14.
24, 6: 1 Chr 18, 16; 2 Sm 8, 17.
24, 7–10: 1 Chr 9, 10ff; Ezr 2, 36ff; Neh 7, 39ff; 11, 10ff.
24, 10: Lk 1, 5.

pizzez, 16 the nineteenth to Pethahiah, the twentieth to Jehezkel, 17 the twenty-first to Jachin, the twenty-second to Gamul, 18 the twenty-third to Delaiah, the twenty-fourth to Maaziah. 19* This was the appointed order of their service when they functioned in the house of the LORD in keeping with the precepts given them by Aaron, their father, as the LORD, the God of Israel, had commanded him.

Other Levites

20* Of the remaining Levites, there were Shubael, of the descendants of Amram, and Jehdeiah, of the descendants of Shubael; 21 Isshiah, the chief, of the descendants of Rehabiah; 22 Shelomith of the Izharites, and Jahath of the descendants of Shelomith. 23 The descendants of Hebron were Jeriah, the chief, Amariah, the second, Jahaziel, the third, Jekameam, the fourth. 24 The descendants of Uzziel were Micah; Shamir, of the descendants of Micah; 25 Isshiah, the brother of Micah; and Zechariah, a descendant of Isshiah. 26 The descendants of Merari were Mahli, Mushi, and the descendants of his son Uzziah. 27 The descendants of Merari through his son Uzziah: Shoham, Zaccur, and Ibri. 28 Descendants of Mahli were Eleazar, who had no sons, 29 and Jerahmeel, of the descendants of Kish. 30 The descendants of Mushi were Mahli, Eder, and Jerimoth.

These were the descendants of the Levites according to their ancestral houses. 31* They too, in the same manner as their relatives, the descendants of Aaron, cast lots in the presence of King David, Zadok, Ahimelech, and the heads of the priestly and levitical families; the more important family did so in the same way as the less important one.

The Singers

25 1* David and the leaders of the liturgical cult set apart for service the descendants of Asaph, Heman, and Jeduthun, as singers of inspired song to the accompaniment of lyres and harps and cymbals.

This is the list of those who performed this service: 2† Of the sons of Asaph: Zaccur, Joseph, Nethaniah, and Asharelah, sons of Asaph, under the direction of Asaph, who sang inspired songs under the guidance of the king. 3 Of Jeduthun, these sons of Jeduthun: Gedaliah, Zeri, Jeshaiah, Shimei, Hashabiah, and Mattithiah; six, under the direction

of their father Jeduthun, who sang inspired songs to the accompaniment of a lyre, to give thanks and praise to the LORD. 4 Of Heman, these sons of Heman: Bukkiah, Mattaniah, Uzziel, Shubael, and Jerimoth; Hananiah, Hanani, Eliathah, Giddalti, Romamti-ezer, Joshbekashah, Mallothi, Hothir, and Mahazioth. 5* All these were the sons of Heman, the king's seer in divine matters; to enhance his prestige, God gave Heman fourteen sons and three daughters. 6* All these, whether of Asaph, Jeduthun, or Heman, were under their fathers' direction in the singing in the house of the LORD to the accompaniment of cymbals, harps and lyres, serving in the house of God, under the guidance of the king. 7 Their number, together with that of their brethren who were trained in singing to the LORD, all of them skilled men, was two hundred and eighty-eight. 8* They cast lots for their functions equally, young and old, master and pupil alike.

9 The first lot fell to Asaph, the family of Joseph; he and his sons and his brethren were twelve. Gedaliah was the second; he and his brethren and his sons were twelve. 10 The third was Zaccur, his sons, and his brethren: twelve. 11 The fourth fell to Izri, his sons, and his brethren: twelve. 12 The fifth was Nethaniah, his sons, and his brethren: twelve. 13 The sixth was Bukkiah, his sons, and his brethren: twelve. 14 The seventh was Jesarelah, his sons, and his brethren: twelve. 15 The eighth was Jeshaiah, his sons, and his brethren: twelve. 16 The ninth was Mattaniah, his sons, and his brethren: twelve. 17 The tenth was Shimei, his sons, and his brethren: twelve. 18 The eleventh was Uzziel, his sons, and his brethren: twelve. 19 The twelfth fell to Hashabiah, his sons, and his brethren: twelve. 20 The thirteenth was Shubael, his sons, and his brethren: twelve. 21 The fourteenth was Mattithiah, his sons, and his brethren: twelve. 22 The fifteenth fell to Jeremoth, his sons, and his brethren: twelve. 23 The sixteenth fell to Hananiah, his sons, and his brethren: twelve. 24 The seventeenth fell to Joshbekashah, his sons, and his brethren: twelve. 25 The eighteenth fell to Hanani, his sons, and his brethren: twelve. 26 The nineteenth fell to Mallothi, his sons, and his brethren: twelve. 27 The twentieth fell to Eliathah, his sons, and his brethren: twelve. 28 The twenty-first fell to Hothir, his sons, and his brethren: twelve. 29 The twenty-second fell to Giddalti, his sons, and his brethren: twelve. 30 The

---

25, 2–31: This list of twenty-four classes of temple singers balances the list of the twenty-four classes of priests (1 Chr 24, 4–19). The last nine names in 1 Chr 25, 4, which seem to form a special group, appear to have been originally fragments or incipits of hymns. With some slight changes in the vocalization, the names would mean: "Have mercy on me, O LORD," "Have mercy on me," "You are my God," "I magnify," "I extol the help of . . . ," "Sitting in adversity," "I have fulfilled," "He made abundant," and "Visions."

24, 19: 2 Chr 23, 8.
24, 20–31: 1 Chr 23, 7–23.
24, 31: 1 Chr 25, 8; 26, 13.
25, 1: 1 Chr 6, 31ff; 15,
    16f.19; 16, 37; 2 Chr

5, 12; 35, 15; Neh 12,
    27.45.
25, 5: 2 Chr 35, 15.
25, 6: 1 Chr 15, 16.
25, 8: 1 Chr 24, 31.

twenty-third fell to Mahazioth, his sons, and his brethren: twelve. 31 The twenty-fourth fell to Romamti-ezer, his sons, and his brethren: twelve.

Classes of Gatekeepers

26 1* As for the classes of gatekeepers. Of the Korahites was Meshelemiah, the son of Kore, one of the sons of Abiasaph. 2 Meshelemiah's sons: Zechariah, the first-born, Jediael, the second son, Zebadiah, the third, Jathniel, the fourth, 3 Elam, the fifth, Jehohanan, the sixth, Eliehoenai, the seventh. 4 Obed-edom's sons: Shemaiah, the first-born, Jehozabad, a second son, Joah, the third, Sachar, the fourth, Nethanel, the fifth, 5 Ammiel, the sixth, Issachar, the seventh, Peullethai, the eighth, for God blessed him. 6 To his son Shemaiah were born sons who ruled over their family, for they were warriors. 7 The sons of Shemaiah were Othni, Rephael, Obed, and Elzabad; also his brethren who were men of might, Elihu and Semachiah. 8 All these were of the sons of Obed-edom, who, together with their sons and their brethren, were mighty men, fit for the service. Of Obed-edom, sixty-two. 9 Of Meshelemiah, eighteen sons and brethren, mighty men.

10* Hosah, a descendant of Merari, had these sons: Shimri, the chief (for though he was not the first-born, his father made him chief), 11 Hilkiah, the second son, Tebaliah, the third, Zechariah, the fourth. All the sons and brethren of Hosah were thirteen.

12 To these classes of gatekeepers, under their chief men, were assigned watches in the service of the house of the LORD, for each group in the same way. 13 They cast lots for each gate, the small and the large families alike. 14* When the lot was cast for the east side, it fell to Meshelemiah. Then they cast lots for his son Zechariah, a prudent counselor, and the north side fell to his lot. 15 To Obed-edom fell the south side, and to his sons the storehouse. 16 To Hosah fell the west side with the Shallecheth gate at the ascending highway. For each family, watches were established. 17 On the east, six watched each day, on the north, four each day, on the south, four each day, and at the storehouse they were two and two; 18† as for the large building on the west, there were four at the highway and two at the large building. 19 These were the classes of the gatekeepers, descendants of Kore and Merari.

Treasurers

20* Their brother Levites superintended the stores for the house of God and the stores of votive offerings. 21* Among the descendants of Ladan the Gershonite, the family heads were descendants of Jehiel: the descendants of Jehiel, 22* Zetham and his brother Joel, who superintended the treasures of the house of the LORD. 23 From the Amramites, Izharites, Hebronites, and Uzzielites, 24 Shubael, son of Gershon, son of Moses, was chief superintendent over the treasures. 25* His associate pertained to Eliezer, whose son was Rehabiah, whose son was Jeshaiah, whose son was Joram, whose son was Zichri, whose son was Shelomith. 26* This Shelomith and his brethren superintended all the stores of the votive offerings dedicated by King David, the heads of the families, the commanders of thousands and of hundreds, and the commanders of the army, 27 from the booty they had taken in the wars, for the enhancement of the house of the LORD. 28 Also, whatever Samuel the seer, Saul, son of Kish, Abner, son of Ner, Joab, son of Zeruiah, and all others had consecrated, was under the charge of Shelomith and his brethren.

Magistrates

29* Among the Izharites, Chananiah and his sons were in charge of Israel's civil affairs as officials and judges. 30* Among the Hebronites, Hashabiah and his brethren, one thousand seven hundred police officers, had the administration of Israel on the western side of the Jordan in all the work of the LORD and in the service of the king. 31* Among the Hebronites, Jerijah was their chief according to their family records. In the fortieth year of David's reign search was made, and there were found among them outstanding officers at Jazer of Gilead. 32 His brethren were also police officers, two thousand seven hundred heads of families. King David appointed them to the administration of the Reubenites, the Gadites, and the half-tribe of Manasseh in everything pertaining to God and to the king.

Army Commanders

27 1† This is the list of the Israelite family heads, commanders of thousands and of hundreds, and other officers who served the king in all that pertained to the divisions, of twenty-four

---

26, 18: The large building (in the Hebrew text Parbar): see note on 2 Kgs 23, 11.

27, 1–15: This list of army commanders is similar to, but distinct from, the list of David's warriors as given in 1 Chr 11, 10–47. The schematic enumeration of the soldiers as presented here is, no doubt, artificial and grossly exaggerated (12 x 24,000 = 288,000 men!), unless the Hebrew word (eleph) for thousand is understood as designating a military unit of much smaller size; see note on 1 Chr 12, 25–38.

26, 1: 1 Chr 9, 19; 2 Chr 8, 14; 23, 19; 35, 15; Neh 12, 45.
26, 10: 1 Chr 16, 38.
26, 14: 1 Chr 9, 24.
26, 20: 1 Chr 28, 12; 1 Kgs 7, 51.
26, 21: 1 Chr 23, 7f; 29, 8.
26, 22ff: 1 Chr 23, 8.12.16.
26, 25: 1 Chr 23, 17f; 24, 21.
26, 26: 2 Sm 8, 11.
26, 29: 1 Chr 23, 4.
26, 30: 1 Chr 27, 17; Neh 11, 15f.
26, 31: 1 Chr 23, 19; 29, 27; Jos 13, 25.

thousand men each, that came and went month by month throughout the year.

2 Over the first division for the first month was Ishbaal, son of Zabdiel, and in his division were twenty-four thousand men; 3 a descendant of Perez, he was chief over all the commanders of the army for the first month. 4* Over the division of the second month was Eleazar, son of Dodo, from Ahoh, and in his division were twenty-four thousand men. 5* The third army commander, chief for the third month, was Benaiah, son of Jehoiada the priest, and in his division were twenty-four thousand men. 6 This Benaiah was a warrior among the Thirty and over the Thirty. His son Ammizabad was over his division. 7* Fourth, for the fourth month, was Asahel, brother of Joab, and after him his son Zebadiah, and in his division were twenty-four thousand men. 8 Fifth, for the fifth month, was the commander Shamhuth, a descendant of Zerah, and in his division were twenty-four thousand men. 9 Sixth, for the sixth month, was Ira, son of Ikkesh, from Tekoa, and in his division were twenty-four thousand men. 10 Seventh, for the seventh month, was Helles, from Beth-pheleth, of the sons of Ephraim, and in his division were twenty-four thousand men. 11*Eighth, for the eighth month, was Sibbecai the Hushathite, a descendant of Zerah, and in his division were twenty-four thousand men. 12 Ninth, for the ninth month, was Abiezer from Anathoth, of Benjamin, and in his division were twenty-four thousand men. 13 Tenth, for the tenth month, was Maharai from Netophah, a descendant of Zerah, and in his division were twenty-four thousand men. 14 Eleventh, for the eleventh month, was Benaiah the Pirathonite, of Ephraim, and in his division were twenty-four thousand men. 15 Twelfth, for the twelfth month, was Heldai the Netophathite, of the family of Othniel, and in his division were twenty-four thousand men.

Tribal Heads

16 Over the tribes of Israel, for the Reubenites the leader was Eliezer, son of Zichri; for the Simeonites, Shephatiah, son of Maacah; 17 for Levi, Hashabiah, son of Kemuel; for Aaron, Zadok; 18* for Judah, Eliab, one of David's brothers; for Issachar, Omri, son of Michael; 19 for Zebulun, Ishmaiah, son of Obadiah; for Naphtali, Jeremoth, son of Azriel; 20 for the sons of Ephraim, Hoshea, son of Azaziah;

for the half-tribe of Manasseh, Joel, son of Pedaiah; 21 for the half-tribe of Manasseh in Gilead, Iddo, son of Zechariah; for Benjamin, Jaasiel, son of Abner; 22 for Dan, Azarel, son of Jeroham. These were the commanders of the tribes of Israel.

23* David did not count those who were twenty years of age or younger, for the LORD had promised to multiply Israel like the stars of the heavens. 24* Joab, son of Zeruiah, began to take the census, but he did not complete it, for because of it wrath fell upon Israel. Therefore the number did not enter into the book of chronicles of King David.

Overseers

25* Over the treasures of the king was Azmaveth, the son of Adiel. Over the stores in the country, the cities, the villages, and the towers was Jonathan, son of Uzziah. 26 Over the farm workers who tilled the soil was Ezri, son of Chelub. 27 Over the vineyards was Shimei from Ramah, and over their produce for the wine cellars was Zabdi the Shiphmite. 28 Over the olive trees and sycamores of the foothills was Baal-hanan the Gederite, and over the stores of oil was Joash. 29 Over the cattle that grazed in Sharon was Shitrai the Sharonite, and over the cattle in the valleys was Shaphat, the son of Adlai; 30 over the camels was Obil the Ishmaelite; over the she-asses was Jehdeiah the Meronothite; 31 and over the flocks was Jaziz the Hagrite. All these were the overseers of King David's possessions.

David's Court

32 Jonathan, David's uncle and a man of intelligence, was counselor and scribe; he and Jehiel, the son of Hachmoni, were tutors of the king's sons. 33* Ahithophel was also the king's counselor, and Hushai the Archite was the king's confidant. 34† After Ahithophel came Jehoiada, the son of Benaiah, and Abiathar. The commander of the king's army was Joab.

The Assembly at Jerusalem

28 1* David assembled at Jerusalem all the leaders of Israel, the heads of the tribes, the commanders of the divisions who were in the service of the king, the commanders of thousands and of hundreds, the overseers of all the king's estates and possessions, and his sons, together with the courtiers, the warriors, and every important

---

† **27, 34:** *After Ahithophel:* after his suicide (2 Sm 17, 23). Jehoiada then succeeded him as the king's officer. *Abiathar:* the priest. The Chronicler does not mention his office because he regards only the Zadokites as legitimate high priests.

27, 4: 1 Chr 9, 37; 11, 12;
       2 Sm 23, 9.
27, 5f: 1 Chr 11, 22ff; 18, 17;
       2 Sm 23, 20ff.
27, 7: 2 Sm 2, 18; 23, 24.
27, 11: 1 Chr 11, 29; 20, 4;
       2 Sm 21, 18.
27, 18: 1 Chr 2, 13.

27, 23: 1 Chr 22, 17.
27, 24: 2 Sm 24, 10.
27, 25: 2 Sm 23, 31.
27, 33: 2 Sm 15, 12.32–37;
       16, 16–19.23; 17,
       5–16.23.
28, 1: 1 Chr 27, 2–22.25–31;
       11, 10ff.

man. ²*† King David rose to his feet and said: "Hear me, my brethren and my people. It was my purpose to build a house of repose myself for the ark of the covenant of the LORD, the footstool for the feet of our God; and I was preparing to build it. ³ But God said to me, 'You may not build a house in my honor, for you are a man who fought wars and shed blood.' ⁴* However, the LORD, the God of Israel, chose me from all my father's family to be king over Israel forever. For he chose Judah as leader, then one family of Judah, that of my father; and finally, among all the sons of my father, it pleased him to make me king over all Israel. ⁵* And of all my sons—for the LORD has given me many sons—he has chosen my son Solomon to sit on the LORD's royal throne over Israel. ⁶* For he said to me: 'It is your son Solomon who shall build my house and my courts, for I have chosen him for my son, and I will be a father to him. ⁷ I will establish his kingdom forever, if he perseveres in keeping my commandments and decrees as he keeps them now.' ⁸* Therefore in the presence of all Israel, the assembly of the LORD, and in the hearing of our God, I exhort you to keep and to carry out all the commandments of the LORD, your God, that you may continue to possess this good land and afterward leave it as an inheritance to your children forever.

⁹* "As for you, Solomon, my son, know the God of your father and serve him with a perfect heart and a willing soul, for the LORD searches all hearts and understands all the mind's thoughts. If you seek him, he will let himself be found by you; but if you abandon him, he will cast you off forever. ¹⁰ See, then! The LORD has chosen you to build a house as his sanctuary. Take courage and set to work."

Temple Plans Given to Solomon

¹¹* Then David gave to his son Solomon the pattern of the portico and of the building itself, with its storerooms, its upper rooms and inner chambers, and the room with the propitiatory. ¹² He provided also the pattern for all else that he had in mind by way of courts for the house of the LORD, with the surrounding compartments for the stores for the house of God and the stores of the votive offerings, ¹³ as well as for the divisions of the priests and Levites, for all the work of the service of the house

of the LORD, and for all the liturgical vessels of the house of the LORD. ¹⁴ He specified the weight of gold to be used in the golden vessels for the various services and the weight of silver to be used in the silver vessels for the various services; ¹⁵* likewise for the golden lampstands and their lamps he specified the weight of gold for each lampstand and its lamps, and for the silver lampstands he specified the weight of silver for each lampstand and its lamps, depending on the use to which each lampstand was to be put. ¹⁶ He specified the weight of gold for each table to hold the showbread, and the silver for the silver tables; ¹⁷ the pure gold to be used for the forks and pitchers; the amount of gold for each golden bowl and the silver for each silver bowl; ¹⁸*† the refined gold, and its weight, to be used for the altar of incense; and, finally, gold for what would suggest a chariot throne: the cherubim that spread their wings and covered the ark of the covenant of the LORD. ¹⁹ He had successfully committed to writing the exact specifications of the pattern, because the hand of the LORD was upon him.

²⁰* Then David said to his son Solomon: "Be firm and steadfast; go to work without fear or discouragement, for the LORD God, my God, is with you. He will not fail you or abandon you before you have completed all the work for the service of the house of the LORD. ²¹* The classes of the priests and Levites are ready for all the service of the house of God; they will help you in all your work with all those who are eager to show their skill in every kind of craftsmanship. Also the leaders and all the people will do everything that you command."

Offerings for the Temple

29 ¹* King David then said to the whole assembly: "My son Solomon, whom alone God has chosen, is still young and immature; the work, however, is great, for this castle is not intended for man, but for the LORD God. ²* For this reason I have stored up for the house of my God, as far as I was able, gold for what will be made of gold, silver for what will be made of silver, bronze for what will be made of bronze, iron for what will be made of iron, wood for what will be made of wood, onyx stones and settings for them, carnelian and mosaic stones, every other kind of precious stone,

28, 2: *The ark . . . the footstool . . . of our God:* the Lord, who was invisibly enthroned upon the cherubim that were associated with the ark of the covenant at Shiloh and later in the Jerusalem temple, had the ark as his footstool; cf Pss 99, 5; 132, 7. The propitiatory (1 Chr 28, 11) and the chariot throne (1 Chr 28, 18) reflect the different circumstances of the postexilic community, for whom only the place of the ark was a focal point of worship, though the ark itself was no longer present.
28, 18: *Chariot throne:* probably suggested by Ez 1, 4–24; 10, 1–22.

28, 2f: 1 Chr 17, 4; 22, 7ff;
 2 Sm 7, 5; 1 Kgs 5, 3;
 Ps 132, 3–7.
28, 4: 1 Chr 17, 23; Gn 49,
 8ff; 1 Sm 16, 6–13.
28, 5: 1 Chr 3, 1–9; 14, 3–7;
 22, 9; 23, 1; Wis 9, 7.
28, 6: 1 Chr 17, 11ff; 22, 9f;
 2 Sm 7, 12f.
28, 8: Dt 4, 5.
28, 9: 1 Chr 29, 17; 2 Chr
15, 2; 1 Kgs 8, 61.
28, 11: Ex 25, 9.40; 26, 30.
28, 15: Ex 25, 31–37.
28, 18: Ex 25, 18–22; 30,
 1–10; 1 Kgs 6, 23–28.
28, 20: 1 Chr 22, 13.16; Jos
 1, 5.
28, 21: Ex 36, 1–5.
29, 1: 1 Chr 22, 5; 28, 5.
29, 2: 1 Chr 22, 14.

Asian American

God's Name

As David neared the end of his life and reign, he blessed God's name in the midst of the people. The Israelites, who believed in one God, were surrounded by other cultures who believed in many different gods, both good and evil. The name of the Israelites' one God was sacred and precious to them, and they often associated God's name with power, glory, majesty, and victory over all creation.

In Hmong, the name of God is Huab Tais Ntuj, which can be translated as Highest One or Emperor Spirit or Overriding Spirit. The Hmong culture developed as a subculture within the Central Highlands of China. The Hmong believed in different spirits, both good and evil, angelic and demonic. So, in naming God Highest Emperor, overriding all other spirits, they clearly also developed a belief in one God with power over all creation.

▸ 1 Chr 29, 10–22

and great quantities of marble. ³ But now, because of the delight I take in the house of my God, in addition to all that I stored up for the holy house, I give to the house of my God my personal fortune in gold and silver: ⁴* three thousand talents of Ophir gold, and seven thousand talents of refined silver, for overlaying the walls of the rooms, ⁵* for the various utensils to be made of gold and silver, and for every work that is to be done by artisans. Now, who else is willing to contribute generously this day to the LORD?"

⁶* Then the heads of the families, the leaders of the tribes of Israel, the commanders of thousands and of hundreds, and the overseers of the king's affairs came forward willingly ⁷* and contributed for the service of the house of God five thousand talents and ten thousand darics of gold, ten thousand talents of silver, eighteen thousand talents of

bronze, and one hundred thousand talents of iron. ⁸* Those who had precious stones gave them into the keeping of Jehiel the Gershonite for the treasury of the house of the LORD. ⁹* The people rejoiced over these free-will offerings, which had been contributed to the LORD wholeheartedly. King David also rejoiced greatly.

David's Prayer

¹⁰ Then David blessed the LORD in the presence of the whole assembly, praying in these words:

"Blessed may you be, O LORD,
   God of Israel our father,
   from eternity to eternity.

¹¹   "Yours, O LORD, are grandeur and power,
   majesty, splendor, and glory.
For all in heaven and on earth is yours;
   yours, O LORD, is the sovereignty;
   you are exalted as head over all.

¹²* "Riches and honor are from you,
   and you have dominion over all.
In your hand are power and might;
   it is yours to give grandeur and strength
      to all.

¹³   Therefore, our God, we give you thanks
   and we praise the majesty of your name."

¹⁴ "But who am I, and who are my people, that we should have the means to contribute so freely? For everything is from you, and we only give you what we have received from you. ¹⁵* For we stand before you as aliens: we are only your guests, like all our fathers. Our life on earth is like a shadow that does not abide. ¹⁶ O LORD our God, all this wealth that we have brought together to build you a house in honor of your holy name comes from you and is entirely yours. ¹⁷ I know, O my God, that you put hearts to the test and that you take pleasure in uprightness. With a sincere heart I have willingly given all these things, and now with joy I have seen your people here present also giving to you generously. ¹⁸* O LORD, God of our fathers Abraham, Isaac, and Israel, keep such thoughts in the hearts and minds of your people forever, and direct their hearts toward you. ¹⁹ Give to my son Solomon a wholehearted desire to keep your commandments, precepts, and statutes, that he may carry out all these plans and build the castle for which I have made preparation."

29, 4: 2 Chr 9, 10; 1 Kgs 9,
   28; 10, 11.
29, 5: Ex 25, 2; 35, 5f.
29, 6: 1 Chr 27, 1.25–31;

28, 1.
29, 7: Ezr 2, 69; 8, 27; Neh
   7, 70ff.
29, 8: 1 Chr 23, 8; 26, 21.

29, 9: 2 Kgs 12, 4.
29, 12: 2 Chr 20, 6; Wis 6, 3.
29, 15: Lv 25, 23; Wis 2, 5;

5, 9.
29, 18: Ex 3, 6.15f; 4.5; 1 Kgs
   18, 36.

20 Then David besought the whole assembly, "Now bless the LORD your God!" And the whole assembly blessed the LORD, the God of their fathers, bowing down and prostrating themselves before the LORD and before the king. 21 On the following day they offered sacrifices and holocausts to the LORD, a thousand bulls, a thousand rams, and a thousand lambs, together with their libations and many other sacrifices for all Israel; 22 and on that day they ate and drank in the LORD's presence with great rejoicing.

Solomon Anointed

† Then for a second time they proclaimed David's son Solomon king, and they anointed him as the LORD's prince, and Zadok as priest. 23* Thereafter Solomon sat on the throne of the LORD as king in place of his father David; he prospered, and all Israel obeyed him. 24 All the leaders and warriors, and also all the other sons of King David, swore allegiance to King Solomon. 25* And the LORD exalted Solomon greatly in the eyes of all Israel, giving him a glorious reign such as had not been enjoyed by any king over Israel before him.

Death of David

26 Thus David, the son of Jesse, had reigned over all Israel. 27* The time that he reigned over Israel was forty years: in Hebron he reigned seven years, and in Jerusalem thirty-three. 28* He died at a ripe old age, rich in years and wealth and glory, and his son Solomon succeeded him as king.

29* Now the deeds of King David, first and last, can be found written in the history of Samuel the seer, the history of Nathan the prophet, and the history of Gad the seer, 30 together with the particulars of his reign and valor, and of the events that affected him and all Israel and all the kingdoms of the surrounding lands.

29, 22: *For a second time:* the first time is referred to in 1 Chr 23, 1. Here there is a solemn public ratification of David's earlier appointment of Solomon as his successor.

29, 23: 1 Chr 28, 5; 2 Chr 9, 8; 1 Kgs 2, 10ff.
29, 25: 2 Chr 1, 12; 1 Kgs 3, 13.
29, 27: 2 Sm 5, 5; 1 Kgs 2, 11.
29, 28: 1 Chr 23, 1.
29, 29: 1 Chr 21, 9; 1 Sm 22, 5.

2 Chronicles

For background on this book, see the introduction to 1 and 2 Chronicles on page 410.

Chap. 3

I: The Reign of Solomon

Solomon at Gibeon

1 ¹ Solomon, son of David, strengthened his hold on the kingdom, for the LORD, his God, was with him, constantly making him more renowned. ² He sent a summons to all Israel, to the commanders of thousands and of hundreds, the judges, the princes of all Israel, and the family heads; ³* and, accompanied by the whole assembly, he went to the high place at Gibeon, because the meeting tent of God, made in the desert by Moses, the LORD's servant, was there. ⁴ (The ark of God, however, David had brought up from Kiriath-jearim to Jerusalem, where he had provided a place and pitched a tent for it.) ⁵*† The bronze altar made by Bezalel, son of Uri, son of Hur, he put in front of the LORD's Dwelling on the high place. There Solomon and the assembly consulted the LORD, ⁶ and Solomon offered sacrifice in the LORD's presence on the bronze altar at the meeting tent; he offered a thousand holocausts upon it.

⁷ That night God appeared to Solomon and said to him, "Make a request of me, and I will grant it to you." ⁸ Solomon answered God: "You have shown great favor to my father David, and you have allowed me to succeed him as king. ⁹ Now, LORD God, may your promise to my father David be fulfilled, for you have made me king over a people as numerous as the dust of the earth. ¹⁰ Give me, therefore, wisdom and knowledge to lead this people, for otherwise who could rule this great people of yours?" ¹¹ God then replied to Solomon: "Since this has been your wish and you have not asked for riches, treasures and glory, nor for the life of those who hate you, nor even for a long life for yourself, but have asked for wisdom and knowledge in order to rule my people over whom I have made you king, ¹² wisdom and knowledge are given you; but I will also give you riches, treasures and glory, such as kings before you never had, nor will those have them who come after you."

Solomon's Wealth

¹³ Solomon returned to Jerusalem from the high place at Gibeon, from the meeting tent, and became king over Israel. ¹⁴* He gathered together chariots and drivers, so that he had one thousand four hundred chariots and twelve thousand drivers he

---

† **1, 5:** *The bronze altar . . . the LORD's Dwelling:* the Chronicler justifies Solomon's worship at the high place of Gibeon. He pictures *the LORD's Dwelling,* i.e., the Mosaic meeting tent, and *the bronze altar* made at Moses' command (Ex 31, 1–9) as still at Gibeon after David had removed the ark of the covenant from there to a new tent in Jerusalem (1 Chr 15, 1.25; 16, 1). The altar made by Bezalel is described as being of acacia wood plated with bronze (Ex 27, 1f).

Solomon later made an all-bronze altar for the temple in Jerusalem (2 Chr 4, 1).

* **1, 3–12:** 1 Kgs 3, 4–15; 1 Chr 21, 29.
1, 5: Ex 27, 1f; 31, 2; 1 Chr
2, 20.
1, 14: 2 Chr 9, 25; 10, 26–29.

?did you KNOW?

Wisdom and the Torah

What a deal for Solomon! God tells him to ask for anything and Solomon will have it (2 Chr 1, 7). Solomon prays to be wise (verse 10), which pleases God, because it indicates Solomon's desire to rule God's people according to God's will. But what is wisdom? For the Chronicler, wisdom is ultimately living one's life in conformity with God's instruction, or the Torah (see Dt 17, 8–11). Wisdom is evident in the person who worships God correctly and lives a moral life in keeping with the Law, and in the king who governs justly. To learn more about the Israelites' view of wisdom, take a look at the wisdom books in the next section of the Old Testament. For a New Testament perspective, see Lk 2, 41–52; 1 Cor 1, 18–31.

▶ 2 Chr 1, 7–12

could station in the chariot cities and with the king in Jerusalem. ¹⁵* The king made silver and gold as common in Jerusalem as stones, while cedars became as numerous as the sycamores of the foothills. ¹⁶*† Solomon also imported horses from Egypt and Cilicia. The king's agents would acquire them by purchase from Cilicia, ¹⁷* and would then bring up chariots from Egypt and export them at six hundred silver shekels, with the horses going for a hundred and fifty shekels. At these rates they served as middlemen for all the Hittite and Aramean kings.

Preparations for the Temple

¹⁸ Solomon gave orders for the building of a house to honor the LORD and also of a house for his own royal estate.

2 ¹* He conscripted seventy thousand men to carry stone and eighty thousand to cut the stone in the mountains, and over these he placed

three thousand six hundred overseers. ²* Moreover, Solomon sent this message to Huram, king of Tyre: "As you dealt with my father David, sending him cedars to build a house for his dwelling, so deal with me. ³* I intend to build a house for the honor of the LORD, my God, and to consecrate it to him, for the burning of fragrant incense in his presence, for the perpetual display of the showbread, for holocausts morning and evening, and for the sabbaths, new moons, and festivals of the LORD, our God: such is Israel's perpetual obligation. ⁴ And the house I intend to build must be large, for our God is greater than all other gods. ⁵* Yet who is really able to build him a house, since the heavens and even the highest heavens cannot contain him? And who am I that I should build him a house, unless it be to offer incense in his presence? ⁶ Now, send me men skilled at work in gold, silver, bronze and iron, in purple, crimson, and violet fabrics, and who know how to do engraved work, to join the craftsmen who are with me in Judah and Jerusalem, whom my father David appointed. ⁷ Also send me boards of cedar, cypress and cabinet wood from Lebanon, for I realize that your servants know how to cut the wood of the Lebanon. My servants will labor with yours ⁸ in order to prepare for me a great quantity of wood, since the house I intend to build must be lofty and wonderful. ⁹* I will furnish as food for your servants, the hewers who cut the wood, twenty thousand kors of wheat, twenty thousand kors of barley, twenty thousand measures of wine, and twenty thousand measures of oil."

¹⁰ Huram, king of Tyre, wrote an answer which he sent to Solomon: "Because the LORD loves his people, he has placed you over them as king." ¹¹* He added: "Blessed be the LORD, the God of Israel, who made heaven and earth, for having given King David a wise son of intelligence and understanding, who will build a house for the LORD and also a house for his royal estate. ¹²* I am now sending you a craftsman of great skill, Huram-abi, ¹³† son of a Danite woman and of a father from Tyre; he knows how to work with gold, silver, bronze and iron, with stone and wood, with purple, violet, fine linen and crimson, and also how to do all kinds of engraved work and to devise every type of artistic work that may be given him and your craftsmen and the craftsmen of my lord David your father. ¹⁴* And now, let my lord send to his servants the wheat, barley, oil and wine

---

1, 16f: *Egypt . . . Cilicia:* it seems likely that the horses came from Cilicia and the chariots from Egypt. Some read the source of these data in 1 Kgs 10, 28f as containing the name (Musur) of a mountain district north of Cilicia, rather than of Egypt; but the author of Chronicles surely understood Egypt; cf 2 Chr 9, 28.

2, 13: *A Danite woman:* a widow of the tribe of Naphtali (1 Kgs 7, 14). The Danites had settled in the northern section of Naphtali's territory (Jgs 18, 27ff). Bezalel's fellow craftsman was of the tribe of Dan (Ex 31, 6).

1, 15: 1 Kgs 10, 27.
1, 16: 1 Kgs 10, 28.
1, 17: 1 Kgs 10, 29.
  2, 1: 2 Chr 2, 17; 5, 29f.
2, 2–9: 1 Kgs 5, 15–20; 1 Chr 14, 1.
  2, 3: Lv 24, 5–8;

Nm 28–29.
2, 5: 2 Chr 6, 18.
2, 9: 1 Kgs 5, 25; Ezr 3, 7.
2, 11: 1 Kgs 5, 21.
2, 12f: 1 Kgs 7, 13f; Ex 31, 1–5.
2, 14f: 1 Kgs 5, 22–26.

2 Chronicles

For background on this book, see the introduction to 1 and 2 Chronicles on page 410.

Chap. 3

I: The Reign of Solomon

Solomon at Gibeon

1 ¹ Solomon, son of David, strengthened his hold on the kingdom, for the LORD, his God, was with him, constantly making him more renowned. ² He sent a summons to all Israel, to the commanders of thousands and of hundreds, the judges, the princes of all Israel, and the family heads; ³* and, accompanied by the whole assembly, he went to the high place at Gibeon, because the meeting tent of God, made in the desert by Moses, the LORD'S servant, was there. ⁴ (The ark of God, however, David had brought up from Kiriath-jearim to Jerusalem, where he had provided a place and pitched a tent for it.) ⁵*† The bronze altar made by Bezalel, son of Uri, son of Hur, he put in front of the LORD'S Dwelling on the high place. There Solomon and the assembly consulted the LORD, ⁶ and Solomon offered sacrifice in the LORD'S presence on the bronze altar at the meeting tent; he offered a thousand holocausts upon it.

⁷ That night God appeared to Solomon and said to him, "Make a request of me, and I will grant it to you." ⁸ Solomon answered God: "You have shown great favor to my father David, and you have allowed me to succeed him as king. ⁹ Now, LORD God, may your promise to my father David be fulfilled, for you have made me king over a people as numerous as the dust of the earth. ¹⁰ Give me, therefore, wisdom and knowledge to lead this people, for otherwise who could rule this great people of yours?" ¹¹ God then replied to Solomon: "Since this has been your wish and you have not asked for riches, treasures and glory, nor for the life of those who hate you, nor even for a long life for yourself, but have asked for wisdom and knowledge in order to rule my people over whom I have made you king, ¹² wisdom and knowledge are given you; but I will also give you riches, treasures and glory, such as kings before you never had, nor will those have them who come after you."

Solomon's Wealth

¹³ Solomon returned to Jerusalem from the high place at Gibeon, from the meeting tent, and became king over Israel. ¹⁴* He gathered together chariots and drivers, so that he had one thousand four hundred chariots and twelve thousand drivers he

---

1, 5: *The bronze altar . . . the LORD'S Dwelling:* the Chronicler justifies Solomon's worship at the high place of Gibeon. He pictures *the LORD'S Dwelling,* i.e., the Mosaic meeting tent, and *the bronze altar* made at Moses' command (Ex 31, 1–9) as still at Gibeon after David had removed the ark of the covenant from there to a new tent in Jerusalem (1 Chr 15, 1.25; 16, 1). The altar made by Bezalel is described as being of acacia wood plated with bronze (Ex 27, 1f).

Solomon later made an all-bronze altar for the temple in Jerusalem (2 Chr 4, 1).

1, 3–12: 1 Kgs 3, 4–15; 1 Chr 21, 29.
1, 5: Ex 27, 1f; 31, 2; 1 Chr

2, 20.
1, 14: 2 Chr 9, 25; 10, 26–29.

did you KNOW?

Wisdom and the Torah

What a deal for Solomon! God tells him to ask for anything and Solomon will have it (2 Chr 1, 7). Solomon prays to be wise (verse 10), which pleases God, because it indicates Solomon's desire to rule God's people according to God's will. But what is wisdom? For the Chronicler, wisdom is ultimately living one's life in conformity with God's instruction, or the Torah (see Dt 17, 8–11). Wisdom is evident in the person who worships God correctly and lives a moral life in keeping with the Law, and in the king who governs justly. To learn more about the Israelites' view of wisdom, take a look at the wisdom books in the next section of the Old Testament. For a New Testament perspective, see Lk 2, 41–52; I Cor 1, 18–31.

▶ 2 Chr I, 7–12

could station in the chariot cities and with the king in Jerusalem. ¹⁵* The king made silver and gold as common in Jerusalem as stones, while cedars became as numerous as the sycamores of the foothills. ¹⁶*† Solomon also imported horses from Egypt and Cilicia. The king's agents would acquire them by purchase from Cilicia, ¹⁷* and would then bring up chariots from Egypt and export them at six hundred silver shekels, with the horses going for a hundred and fifty shekels. At these rates they served as middlemen for all the Hittite and Aramean kings.

Preparations for the Temple

¹⁸ Solomon gave orders for the building of a house to honor the LORD and also of a house for his own royal estate.

2 ¹* He conscripted seventy thousand men to carry stone and eighty thousand to cut the stone in the mountains, and over these he placed

three thousand six hundred overseers. ²* Moreover, Solomon sent this message to Huram, king of Tyre: "As you dealt with my father David, sending him cedars to build a house for his dwelling, so deal with me. ³* I intend to build a house for the honor of the LORD, my God, and to consecrate it to him, for the burning of fragrant incense in his presence, for the perpetual display of the showbread, for holocausts morning and evening, and for the sabbaths, new moons, and festivals of the LORD, our God: such is Israel's perpetual obligation. ⁴ And the house I intend to build must be large, for our God is greater than all other gods. ⁵* Yet who is really able to build him a house, since the heavens and even the highest heavens cannot contain him? And who am I that I should build him a house, unless it be to offer incense in his presence? ⁶ Now, send me men skilled at work in gold, silver, bronze and iron, in purple, crimson, and violet fabrics, and who know how to do engraved work, to join the craftsmen who are with me in Judah and Jerusalem, whom my father David appointed. ⁷ Also send me boards of cedar, cypress and cabinet wood from Lebanon, for I realize that your servants know how to cut the wood of the Lebanon. My servants will labor with yours ⁸ in order to prepare for me a great quantity of wood, since the house I intend to build must be lofty and wonderful. ⁹* I will furnish as food for your servants, the hewers who cut the wood, twenty thousand kors of wheat, twenty thousand kors of barley, twenty thousand measures of wine, and twenty thousand measures of oil."

¹⁰ Huram, king of Tyre, wrote an answer which he sent to Solomon: "Because the LORD loves his people, he has placed you over them as king." ¹¹* He added: "Blessed be the LORD, the God of Israel, who made heaven and earth, for having given King David a wise son of intelligence and understanding, who will build a house for the LORD and also a house for his royal estate. ¹²* I am now sending you a craftsman of great skill, Huram-abi, ¹³† son of a Danite woman and of a father from Tyre; he knows how to work with gold, silver, bronze and iron, with stone and wood, with purple, violet, fine linen and crimson, and also how to do all kinds of engraved work and to devise every type of artistic work that may be given him and your craftsmen and the craftsmen of my lord David your father. ¹⁴* And now, let my lord send to his servants the wheat, barley, oil and wine

---

1, 16f: *Egypt . . . Cilicia:* it seems likely that the horses came from Cilicia and the chariots from Egypt. Some read the source of these data in 1 Kgs 10, 28f as containing the name (Musur) of a mountain district north of Cilicia, rather than of Egypt; but the author of Chronicles surely understood Egypt; cf 2 Chr 9, 28.
2, 13: *A Danite woman:* a widow of the tribe of Naphtali (1 Kgs 7, 14). The Danites had settled in the northern section of Naphtali's territory (Jgs 18, 27ff). Bezalel's fellow craftsman was of the tribe of Dan (Ex 31, 6).

1, 15: 1 Kgs 10, 27.
1, 16: 1 Kgs 10, 28.
1, 17: 1 Kgs 10, 29.
2, 1: 2 Chr 2, 17; 5, 29f.
2, 2–9: 1 Kgs 5, 15–20; 1 Chr 14, 1.
2, 3: Lv 24, 5–8;
Nm 28–29.
2, 5: 2 Chr 6, 18.
2, 9: 1 Kgs 5, 25; Ezr 3, 7.
2, 11: 1 Kgs 5, 21.
2, 12f: 1 Kgs 7, 13f; Ex 31, 1–5.
2, 14f: 1 Kgs 5, 22–26.

which he has promised. [15]* For our part, we will cut trees on Lebanon, as many as you need, and float them down to you at the port of Joppa, whence you may take them up to Jerusalem."

[16]* Thereupon Solomon took a census of all the alien men who were in the land of Israel (following the census David his father had taken of them), who were found to number one hundred fifty-three thousand six hundred. [17]* Of these he made seventy thousand carriers and eighty thousand cutters in the mountains, and three thousand six hundred overseers to keep the people working.

Building of the Temple

3 [1]*† Then Solomon began to build the house of the LORD in Jerusalem on Mount Moriah, which had been pointed out to his father David, on the spot which David had selected, the threshing-floor of Ornan the Jebusite. [2] He began to build in the second month of the fourth year of his reign. [3]* These were the specifications laid down by Solomon for building the house of God: the length was sixty cubits according to the old measure, and the width was twenty cubits; [4]*† the porch which lay before the nave along the width of the house was also twenty cubits, and it was twenty cubits high. He overlaid its interior with pure gold. [5]* The nave he overlaid with cypress wood which he covered with fine gold, embossing on it palms and chains. [6] He also decorated the building with precious stones. [7] The house; its beams and thresholds, as well as its walls and its doors, he overlaid with gold, and he engraved cherubim upon the walls. (The gold was from Parvaim.) [8]* He also made the room of the holy of holies. Its length corresponded to the width of the house, twenty cubits, and its width was also twenty cubits. He overlaid it with fine gold to the amount of six hundred talents. [9] The weight of the nails was fifty gold shekels. The upper chambers he likewise covered with gold.

[10]* For the room of the holy of holies he made two cherubim of carved workmanship, which were then overlaid with gold. [11] The wings of the cherubim spanned twenty cubits: [12] one wing of each cherub, five cubits in length, extended to a wall of the building, while the other wing, also five cubits in length, touched the corresponding wing of the second cherub. [13] The combined wingspread of the two cherubim was thus twenty cubits. They stood upon their own feet, facing toward the nave. [14]*† He made the veil of violet, purple, crimson and fine linen, and had cherubim embroidered upon it.

[15]* In front of the building he set two columns thirty-five cubits high; the capital topping each was of five cubits. [16] He worked out chains in the form of a collar with which he encircled the capitals of the columns, and he made a hundred pomegranates which he set on the chains. [17] He set up the columns to correspond with the nave, one for the right side and the other for the left, and he called the one to the right Jachin and the one to the left Boaz.

4 [1]* Then he made a bronze altar twenty cubits long, twenty cubits wide and ten cubits high. [2]* He also made the molten sea. It was perfectly round, ten cubits in diameter, five in depth, and thirty in circumference; [3]† below the rim a ring of figures of oxen encircled the sea, ten to the cubit, all the way around; there were two rows of these cast in the same mold with the sea. [4] It rested on twelve oxen, three facing north, three west, three south, and three east, with their haunches all toward the center; the sea rested on their backs. [5]† It was a handbreadth thick, and its brim was made like that of a cup, being lily-shaped. It had a capacity of three thousand measures.

[6]* Then he made ten basins for washing, placing five of them to the right and five to the left. Here were cleansed the victims for the holocausts; but the sea was for the priests to wash in.

[7]* He made the lampstands of gold, ten of them as was prescribed, and placed them in the nave, five to the right and five to the left. [8]* He made ten tables and had them set in the nave, five to the right and five to the left; and he made a hundred golden bowls. [9]* He made the court of the priests and the

---

3, 1: *Mount Moriah:* the height in the land of Moriah (Gn 22, 2). This is the only place in the Bible where the temple mount is identified with the site where Abraham was to sacrifice Isaac.

3, 4: *The porch . . . twenty cubits high:* this measurement, not given in the Books of Kings, is here based on a variant Greek text that may be a later revision. The received Hebrew text says, "one hundred and twenty cubits high." The height of the two freestanding columns adjacent to the porch (1 Kgs 7, 15–16) is nearly doubled by the Chronicler (2 Chr 3, 15).

3, 14: *The veil:* at the entrance of the holy of holies, as also in the Mosaic meeting tent (Ex 26, 31f). Solomon's temple had doors at this place (1 Kgs 6, 31). Apparently there was a veil here in the temple of the Chronicler's time as there was also in Herod's temple (Mt 27, 51; Mk 15, 38; Lk 23, 45).

4, 3: *Oxen:* in 1 Kgs 7, 24 this double row of ornaments is described as being gourds. The text of Kings available to the Chronicler

may have been faulty on this point as the words are similar in sound. In 2 Chr 4, 16 the forks correspond in a similar way to bowls in the text of 1 Kings (7, 40).

4, 5: *Three thousand measures:* according to 1 Kgs 7, 26, "two thousand measures."

2, 15: Ezr 3, 7.
2, 16f: 1 Chr 22, 2.
2, 17: 2 Chr 2, 1.
3, 1f: Gn 22, 2; 1 Kgs 6, 1; 1 Chr 21, 22–26.
3, 3: 1 Kgs 6, 2.
3, 4: 1 Kgs 6, 3; Ez 40, 48.
3, 5: 1 Kgs 6, 15; Ez 41, 1.
3, 8: 1 Kgs 6, 16f.20; Ez 41, 3.
3, 10–31: 1 Kgs 6, 23–27.
3, 14: Mt 27, 51.

3, 15ff: 1 Kgs 7, 15–22; Ez 40, 49.
4, 1: Ez 43, 13–17.
4, 2–5: 1 Kgs 7, 23–26; Ez 43, 13.
4, 6: 1 Kgs 7, 38f; Ez 40, 38.
4, 7: 1 Kgs 7, 49.
4, 8: 1 Kgs 7, 50; 1 Chr 28, 16.
4, 9: 1 Kgs 7, 12.

great courtyard and the gates of the courtyard; the gates he overlaid with bronze. 10* The sea was placed off to the southeast from the right side of the temple.

11* Huram also made the pots, the shovels and the bowls. Huram thus completed the work he had to do for King Solomon in the house of God: 12 two columns, two nodes for the capitals topping these two columns, and two networks covering the nodes of the capitals topping the columns; 13 also four hundred pomegranates for the two networks, with two rows of pomegranates to each network, to cover the two nodes of the capitals topping the columns. 14 He made the stands, and the basins on the stands; 15 one sea, and the twelve oxen under it; 16 likewise the pots, the shovels and the forks. Huram-abi made all these articles for King Solomon from polished bronze for the house of the LORD. 17 The king had them cast in the Jordan region, in the clayey ground between Succoth and Zeredah. 18 Solomon made all these vessels, so many in number that the weight of the bronze was not ascertained.

19 Solomon had all these articles made for the house of God: the golden altar, the tables on which the showbread lay, 20 the lampstands and their lamps of pure gold which were to burn according to prescription before the sanctuary, 21 flowers, lamps and gold tongs [this was the purest gold], 22 snuffers, bowls, cups and firepans of pure gold. As for the entry to the house, its inner doors to the holy of holies, as well as the doors to the nave, were of gold.

Dedication of the Temple

5 1* When all the work undertaken by Solomon for the temple of the LORD had been completed, he brought in the dedicated offerings of his father David, putting the silver, the gold and all the other articles in the treasuries of the house of God. 2 At Solomon's order the elders of Israel and all the leaders of the tribes, the princes of the Israelite ancestral houses, came to Jerusalem to bring up the ark of the LORD'S covenant from the City of David (which is Zion). 3 All the men of Israel assembled before the king during the festival of the seventh month. 4*† When all the elders of Israel had arrived, the Levites took up the ark, 5 and they carried the ark and the meeting tent with all the sacred vessels that were in the tent; it was the levitical priests who carried them.

6 King Solomon and the entire community of Israel gathered about him before the ark were sacrificing sheep and oxen so numerous that they could not be counted or numbered. 7 The priests brought the ark of the covenant of the LORD to its place beneath the wings of the cherubim in the sanctuary, the holy of holies of the temple. 8 The cherubim had their wings spread out over the place of the ark, sheltering the ark and its poles from above. 9† The poles were long enough so that their ends could be seen from that part of the holy place nearest the sanctuary; however, they could not be seen beyond. The ark has remained there to this day. 10 There was nothing in it but the two tablets which Moses put there on Horeb, the tablets of the covenant which the LORD made with the Israelites at their departure from Egypt.

11 When the priests came out of the holy place (all the priests who were present had purified themselves without reference to the rotation of their various classes), 12 the Levites who were singers, all who belonged to Asaph, Heman, Jeduthun, and their sons and brothers, clothed in fine linen, with cymbals, harps and lyres, stood east of the altar, and with them a hundred and twenty priests blowing trumpets.

13 When the trumpeters and singers were heard as a single voice praising and giving thanks to the LORD, and when they raised the sound of the trumpets, cymbals and other musical instruments to "give thanks to the LORD, for he is good, for his mercy endures forever," the building of the LORD'S temple was filled with a cloud. 14* The priests could not continue to minister because of the cloud, since the LORD's glory filled the house of God.

6 1* Then Solomon said: "The LORD intends to dwell in the dark cloud. 2 I have truly built you a princely house and dwelling, where you may abide forever." 3* Turning about, the king greeted the whole community of Israel as they stood. 4 He said: "Blessed be the LORD, the God of Israel, who with his own mouth made a promise to my father David and by his own hands brought it to fulfillment. He said: 5 'Since the day I brought my people out of the land of Egypt, I have not chosen any city from among all the tribes of Israel for the building of a temple to my honor, nor have I chosen any man to be commander of my people Israel; 6 but now I choose Jerusalem, where I shall be honored,

---

5, 4: *The Levites:* The parallel passage in 1 Kgs 8, 3 has the priests; but see 2 Chr 5, 5, where the Deuteronomic term levitical priests is used, as also in 2 Chr 23, 18; 30, 27.

5, 9: *The ark has remained there to this day:* the Chronicler must have copied this from his source (1 Kgs 8, 8) without reflecting that the ark was lost in the Babylonian destruction of Jerusalem; cf 2 Mc 2, 4–8.

4, 10: 1 Kgs 7, 39.
4, 11–22: 1 Kgs 7, 40–51.
5, 1–14: 1 Kgs 7, 51—8, 13.
5, 4f: 2 Chr 35, 3.

5, 14: 2 Chr 7, 2; 1 Kgs 8, 10f.
6, 1f: 1 Kgs 8, 12f.
6, 3–11: 1 Kgs 8, 14–21.

and I choose David to rule my people Israel.' [7] My father David wished to build a temple to the honor of the LORD, the God of Israel, [8] but the LORD said to him: 'In wishing to build a temple to my honor, you do well. [9] However, you shall not build the temple; rather, your son whom you will beget shall build the temple to my honor.'

[10] "Now the LORD has fulfilled the promise that he made. I have succeeded my father David and have taken my seat on the throne of Israel, as the LORD foretold, and I have built the temple to the honor of the LORD, the God of Israel. [11] And I have placed there the ark, in which abides the covenant of the LORD which he made with the Israelites."

Solomon's Prayer

[12]* Solomon then took his place before the altar of the LORD in the presence of the whole community of Israel and stretched forth his hands. [13]† He had made a bronze platform five cubits long, five cubits wide, and three cubits high, which he had placed in the middle of the courtyard. Having ascended it, Solomon knelt in the presence of the whole of Israel and stretched forth his hands toward heaven. [14] Thus he prayed: "LORD, God of Israel, there is no god like you in heaven or on earth; you keep your covenant and show kindness to your servants who are wholeheartedly faithful to you. [15] You have kept the promise you made to my father David, your servant. With your own mouth you spoke it, and by your own hand you have brought it to fulfillment this day. [16] Now, therefore, LORD, God of Israel, keep the further promise you made to my father David, your servant, when you said, 'You shall always have someone from your line to sit before me on the throne of Israel, provided only that your descendants look to their conduct so as always to live according to my law, even as you have lived in my presence.' [17] Now, LORD, God of Israel, may this promise which you made to your servant David be confirmed.

[18] "Can it indeed be that God dwells with mankind on earth? If the heavens and the highest heavens cannot contain you, how much less this temple which I have built! [19] Look kindly on the prayer and petition of your servant, O LORD, my God, and listen to the cry of supplication your servant makes before you. [20] May your eyes watch day and night over this temple, the place where you have decreed you shall be honored; may you heed the prayer which I your servant offer toward this place. [21] Listen to the petitions of your servant and

of your people Israel which they direct toward this place. Listen from your heavenly dwelling, and when you have heard, pardon.

[22] "When any man sins against his neighbor and is required to take an oath of execration against himself, and when he comes for the oath before your altar in this temple, [23] listen from heaven: take action and pass judgment on your servants, requiting the wicked man and holding him responsible for his conduct, but absolving the innocent and rewarding him according to his virtue. [24] When your people Israel have sinned against you and are defeated by the enemy, but afterward they return and praise your name, and they pray to you and entreat you in this temple, [25] listen from heaven and forgive the sin of your people Israel, and bring them back to the land which you gave them and their fathers. [26] When the sky is closed so that there is no rain, because they have sinned against you, but then they pray toward this place and praise your name, and they withdraw from sin because you afflict them, [27] listen in heaven and forgive the sin of your servants and of your people Israel. But teach them the right way to live, and send rain upon your land which you gave your people as their heritage. [28] When there is famine in the land, when there is pestilence, or blight, or mildew, or locusts, or caterpillars; when their enemies besiege them at any of their gates; whenever there is a plague or sickness of any kind; [29] when any Israelite of all your people offers a prayer or petition of any kind, and in awareness of his affliction and pain, stretches out his hands toward this temple, [30] listen from your heavenly dwelling place, and forgive. Knowing his heart, render to everyone according to his conduct, for you alone know the hearts of men. [31] So may they fear you and walk in your ways as long as they live on the land you gave our fathers.

[32] "For the foreigner, too, who is not of your people Israel, when he comes from a distant land to honor your great name, your mighty power, and your outstretched arm, when they come in prayer to this temple, [33] listen from your heavenly dwelling place, and do whatever the foreigner entreats you, that all the peoples of the earth may know your name, fearing you as do your people Israel, and knowing that this house which I have built is dedicated to your honor.

[34] "When your people go forth to war against their enemies, wherever you send them, and pray to you in the direction of this city and of the

---

6, 13: This verse is not found in the Chronicler's source; cf 1 Kgs 8, 22f. He has Solomon praying on a bronze platform . . . in the middle of the courtyard because at the time of the Chronicler only the priests prayed before the altar.

6, 12–41: 1 Kgs 8, 22–53.

house I have built to your honor, ³⁵ listen from heaven to their prayer and petition, and defend their cause. ³⁶ When they sin against you (for there is no man who does not sin), and in your anger against them you deliver them to the enemy, so that their captors deport them to another land, far or near, ³⁷ when they repent in the land where they are captive and are converted, when they entreat you in the land of their captivity and say, 'We have sinned and done wrong; we have been wicked,' ³⁸ and with their whole heart and with their whole soul they turn back to you in the land of those who hold them captive, when they pray in the direction of their land which you gave their fathers, and of the city you have chosen, and of the house which I have built to your honor, ³⁹ listen from your heavenly dwelling place, hear their prayer and petitions, and uphold their cause. Forgive your people who have sinned against you. ⁴⁰ My God, may your eyes be open and your ears attentive to the prayer of this place. ⁴¹ And now,

> "Advance, LORD God, to your resting place,
> you and the ark of your majesty.
> May your priests, LORD God, be clothed with salvation,
> may your faithful ones rejoice in good things.
> ⁴² LORD God, reject not the plea of your anointed,
> remember the devotion of David, your servant."

7 ^{1*} When Solomon had ended his prayer, fire came down from heaven and consumed the holocaust and the sacrifices, and the glory of the LORD filled the house. ^{2*} But the priests could not enter the house of the LORD, for the glory of the LORD had filled the house of the LORD. ³ All the Israelites looked on while the fire came down and the glory of the LORD was upon the house, and they fell down upon the pavement with their faces to the earth and adored, praising the LORD, "for he is good, for his mercy endures forever." ^{4*} The king and all the people were offering sacrifices before the LORD. ^{5*} King Solomon offered as sacrifice twenty-

two thousand oxen, and one hundred twenty thousand sheep.

End of the Dedication

^{6*} Thus the king and all the people dedicated the house of God. The priests were standing at their stations, as were the Levites, with the musical instruments of the LORD which King David had made for "praising the LORD, for his mercy endures forever," when David used them to accompany the hymns. Across from them the priests blew the trumpets and all Israel stood.

^{7*} Then Solomon consecrated the middle part of the court which lay before the house of the LORD; there he offered the holocausts and the fat of the peace offerings, since the bronze altar which Solomon had made could not hold the holocausts, the cereal offerings and the fat.

^{8*} On this occasion Solomon and with him all Israel, who had assembled in very large numbers from Labo of Hamath to the Wadi of Egypt, celebrated the festival for seven days. ^{9*†} On the eighth day they held a special meeting, for they had celebrated the dedication of the altar for seven days and the feast for seven days. ¹⁰ On the twenty-third day of the seventh month he sent the people back to their tents, rejoicing and glad at heart at the good things the LORD had done for David, for Solomon, and for his people Israel. ^{11*} Solomon completed the house of the LORD and the royal palace; he successfully accomplished everything he had planned to do in regard to the house of the LORD and his own house.

God's Promise to Solomon

¹² The LORD appeared to Solomon during the night and said to him: "I have heard your prayer, and I have chosen this place for my house of sacrifice. ¹³ If I close heaven so that there is no rain, if I command the locust to devour the land, if I send pestilence among my people, ¹⁴ and if my people, upon whom my name has been pronounced, humble themselves and pray, and seek my presence and turn from their evil ways, I will hear them from heaven and pardon their sins and revive their land. ¹⁵ Now my eyes shall be open and my ears attentive to the prayer of this place. ¹⁶ And now I have chosen and consecrated this house that my name may be there forever; my eyes and my heart also shall be there always.

---

^{7, 9f:} *The feast:* of Booths, celebrated on the fifteenth day of the seventh month and followed by a solemn octave lasting through the twenty-second day (Lv 23, 33–36; Nm 29, 12–35); the people are therefore sent home on the twenty-third day (v 10). The festival (v 8) for the dedication of the altar and of the temple lasted for seven days before the feast of Booths, from the seventh to the fourteenth day. According to 1 Kgs 8, 65f, the people are dismissed at the end of these seven days.

7, 1–10: 1 Kgs 8, 54–66; Jgs 6, 21; 1 Chr 21, 26; 2 Mc 2, 10.
7, 2: 2 Chr 5, 14; Ex 24, 16; 1 Kgs 8, 10f.
7, 4: 2 Chr 5, 13; 1 Kgs 8, 62; Ps 136, 1.
7, 5: 1 Kgs 8, 62f.
7, 6: Nm 10, 8.10; Ps 136, 1.
7, 7: 1 Kgs 8, 64.
7, 8: 1 Kgs 8, 65.
7, 9f: 1 Kgs 8, 66.
7, 11–22: 1 Kgs 9, 1–9.

17 "As for you, if you live in my presence as your father David did, doing all that I have commanded you and keeping my statutes and ordinances, 18 I will establish your royal throne as I covenanted with your father David when I said, 'There shall never be lacking someone of yours as ruler in Israel.' 19 But if you turn away and forsake my statutes and commands which I placed before you, if you proceed to venerate and worship strange gods, 20 then I will uproot the people from the land I gave them; I will cast from my sight this house which I have consecrated to my honor, and I will make it a proverb and a byword among all peoples. 21 This temple which is so exalted— everyone passing by it will be amazed and ask: 'Why has the LORD done this to this land and to this house?' 22 And men will answer: 'They forsook the LORD, the God of their fathers, who brought them out of the land of Egypt, and they adopted strange gods and worshiped them and served them. That is why he has brought down upon them all this evil.' "

Public Works

8 1* After the twenty years during which Solomon built the house of the LORD and his own house, 2† he built up the cities which Huram had given him, and settled Israelites there. 3 Then Solomon went to Hamath of Zoba and conquered it. 4† He built Tadmor in the desert region and all the supply cities, which he built in Hamath. 5* He built Upper Beth-horon and Lower Beth-horon, fortified cities with walls, gates and bars; 6 also Baalath, all the supply cities belonging to Solomon, and all the cities for the chariots, the cities for the horsemen, and whatever else Solomon decided should be built in Jerusalem, in the Lebanon, and in the entire land under his dominion. 7 All the people that remained of the Hittites, Amorites, Perizzites, Hivites, and Jebusites, who were not of Israel— 8 that is, their descendants remaining in the land, whom the Israelites had not destroyed— Solomon subjected to forced labor, as they continue to this day. 9 But Solomon did not enslave the Israelites for his works. They became soldiers, commanders of his warriors, and commanders of his chariots and his horsemen. 10 They were also King Solomon's two hundred and fifty overseers who had charge of the people.

Solomon's Piety

11 Solomon brought the daughter of Pharaoh up from the City of David to the palace which he had built for her, for he said, "No wife of mine shall dwell in the house of David, king of Israel, for the places where the ark of the LORD has come are holy."

12 In those times Solomon offered holocausts to the LORD upon the altar of the LORD which he had built in front of the porch, 13* as was required day by day according to the command of Moses, and in particular on the sabbaths, at the new moons, and on the fixed festivals three times a year: on the feast of the Unleavened Bread, the feast of Weeks and the feast of Booths.

14* And according to the ordinance of his father David he appointed the various classes of the priests for their service, and the Levites according to their functions of praise and ministry alongside the priests, as the daily duty required. The gatekeepers of the various classes stood guard at each gate, since such was the command of David, the man of God. 15 There was no deviation from the king's command in any respect relating to the priests and Levites or the treasuries. 16 All of Solomon's work was carried out successfully from the day the foundation of the house of the LORD was laid until the house of the LORD had been completed in every detail.

Glories of the Court

17* In those times Solomon went to Ezion-geber and to Elath on the seashore of the land of Edom. 18* Huram, through his servants, sent him ships and crewmen acquainted with the sea, who accompanied Solomon's servants to Ophir and brought back from there four hundred and fifty talents of gold to King Solomon.

9 1* When the queen of Sheba heard of Solomon's fame, she came to Jerusalem to test him with subtle questions, accompanied by a very numerous retinue and by camels bearing spices, much gold, and precious stones. She came to Solomon and questioned him on every subject in which she was interested. 2 Solomon explained to her everything she asked about, and there remained nothing hidden from Solomon that he could not explain to her.

8, 2: *The cities which Huram had given him:* according to 1 Kgs 9, 10–14, Solomon had ceded the cities as payment for the timber and gold received from Tyre. But since Huram was dissatisfied, he may have returned the cities to Solomon.

8, 4: *Tadmor:* later known as Palmyra, an important caravan city in the Syrian desert. The parallel passage in 1 Kgs 9, 18 has Tamar, in southern Judah; cf Ez 47, 19; 48, 28. But Solomon may well have fortified Tadmor against the Arameans.

8, 1f: 1 Kgs 9, 10f.
8, 5–12: 1 Kgs 9, 18–25.
8, 13: 1 Kgs 9, 25; Ex 23, 14; Nm 28–29.
8, 14: 1 Chr 23–26; Neh 12, 46.
8, 17: 1 Kgs 9, 26; Mt 12, 42; Lk 11, 31.
8, 18: 1 Kgs 9, 27f.
9, 1: 1 Kgs 10, 1f; Mt 12, 42; Lk 11, 31.

Chap. 9

3 When the queen of Sheba witnessed Solomon's wisdom, the palace he had built, 4 the food at his table, the seating of his ministers, the attendance of his servants and their dress, his cupbearers and their dress, and the holocausts he offered in the house of the LORD, it took her breath away. 5 "The account I heard in my country about your deeds and your wisdom is true," she told the king. 6 "Yet I did not believe the report until I came and saw with my own eyes. I have discovered that they did not tell me the half of your great wisdom; you have surpassed the stories I heard. 7 Happy are your men, happy these servants of yours, who stand before

you always and listen to your wisdom. 8 Blessed be the LORD, your God, who has been so pleased with you as to place you on his throne as king for the LORD, your God. Because your God has so loved Israel as to will to make it last forever, he has appointed you over them as king to administer right and justice." 9 Then she gave the king one hundred and twenty gold talents and a very large quantity of spices, as well as precious stones. There was no other spice like that which the queen of Sheba gave to King Solomon.

10 The servants of Huram and of Solomon who brought gold from Ophir also brought cabinet wood and precious stones. 11 With the cabinet wood the king made stairs for the temple of the LORD and the palace of the king; also lyres and harps for the chanters. The like of these had not been seen before in the land of Judah.

12 King Solomon gave the queen of Sheba everything she desired and asked him for, more than she had brought to the king. Then she returned to her own country with her servants.

13* The gold that Solomon received each year weighed six hundred and sixty-six gold talents, 14 in addition to what was collected from travelers and what the merchants brought. All the kings of Arabia also, and the governors of the country, brought gold and silver to Solomon.

15 Moreover, King Solomon made two hundred large shields of beaten gold, six hundred shekels of beaten gold going into each shield, 16 and three hundred bucklers of beaten gold, three hundred shekels of gold going into each buckler; these the king put in the hall of the Forest of Lebanon.

Money Talks

You can't take it with you.
How often have we heard this statement? We know it's true. Yet we are so easily impressed with wealth and riches. King Solomon, whose wealth is described in 2 Chr 9, 13–28, would be right at home in our world, which seems so taken with the rich and the famous.

The Chronicler seems to suggest that Solomon's wealth is a sign of his being blessed by God (see 1, 12). And some Jews and Christians still see wealth as a sign of God's blessing. But we need to remember Jesus' words, "For where your treasure is, there also will your heart be" (Mt 6, 21), and "Blessed are you who are poor, / for the kingdom of God is yours" (Lk 6, 20). Jesus saw that the accumulation of wealth in his time was frequently the result of injustice (see "The Greed Trap," Lk 12, 13–21). Simply put, Jesus probably would not have approved of Solomon's wealth. How do you view wealth? What is your attitude toward poor people?

▶ 2 Chr 9, 13–28

[17] King Solomon also made a large ivory throne which he overlaid with fine gold. [18] The throne had six steps; a footstool of gold was fastened to it, and there was an arm on each side of the seat, with two lions standing beside the arms. [19] Twelve other lions also stood there, one on either side of each step. Nothing like this had ever been produced in any other kingdom. [20] Furthermore, all of King Solomon's drinking vessels were of gold, and all the utensils in the hall of the Forest of Lebanon were of pure gold; silver was not considered of value in Solomon's time. [21] For the king had ships that went to Tarshish with the servants of Huram. Once every three years the fleet of Tarshish would return with a cargo of gold and silver, ivory, apes and monkeys. [22] Thus King Solomon surpassed all the other kings of the earth in riches as well as in wisdom.

[23] All the kings of the earth sought audience with Solomon, to hear from him the wisdom which God had put in his heart. [24] Year in and year out, each one would bring his tribute—silver and gold articles, garments, weapons, spices, horses and mules. [25] Solomon also had four thousand stalls of horses, chariots, and twelve thousand horsemen, which he assigned to the chariot cities and to the king in Jerusalem. [26] He was ruler over all the kings from the River to the land of the Philistines and down to the border of Egypt. [27] The king made silver as common in Jerusalem as stones, while cedars became as numerous as the sycamores of the foothills. [28]† Horses were imported for Solomon from Egypt and from all the lands.

The Death of Solomon

[29]* The rest of the acts of Solomon, first and last, are written, as is well known, in the acts of Nathan the prophet, in the prophecy of Ahijah the Shilonite, and in the visions of Iddo the seer which concern Jeroboam, son of Nebat. [30] Solomon reigned in Jerusalem over all Israel for forty years. [31] He rested with his ancestors; he was buried in his father's City of David, and his son Rehoboam succeeded him as king.

II: The Monarchy before Hezekiah

Division of the Kingdom

10 [1]*† Rehoboam went to Shechem, for all Israel had come to Shechem to proclaim him king. [2] When Jeroboam, son of Nebat, heard of this in Egypt where he had fled from King Solomon, he returned from Egypt. [3] Jeroboam was summoned to the assembly, and he and all Israel said to Rehoboam: [4] "Your father laid a heavy yoke upon us. If you now lighten the harsh service and the heavy yoke that your father imposed on us, we will serve you." [5] "In three days," he answered them, "come back to me."

When the people had departed, [6] King Rehoboam consulted the elders who had been in the service of his father during Solomon's lifetime, asking, "What answer do you advise me to give this people?" [7] They replied, "If you will deal kindly with this people and give in to them, acceding to their request, they will be your servants forever." [8] But he ignored the advice the elders had given him and consulted the young men who had grown up with him and were in his service. [9] He said to them, "What answer do you advise me to give this people, who have asked me to lighten the yoke my father imposed on them?" [10] The young men who had grown up with him replied: "This is the answer you should give to this people who have said to you, 'Your father laid a heavy yoke upon us, but do you lighten our yoke'; this you should say to them: 'My little finger is thicker than my father's body. [11] Whereas my father put a heavy yoke on you, I will make it heavier! My father beat you with whips, but I will beat you with scorpions!'"

[12] On the third day, Jeroboam and all the people came back to King Rehoboam as he had instructed them to do. [13] Ignoring the advice the elders had given him, the king gave them a harsh answer, [14] speaking to them according to the advice of the young men: "My father laid a heavy yoke on you, but I will make it heavier! My father beat you with whips, but I will beat you with scorpions." [15]* The king would not listen to the people, for this turn of events was divinely ordained to fulfill the prophecy the LORD had uttered to Jeroboam, the son of Nebat, through Ahijah the Shilonite.

[16]* When all Israel saw that the king would not listen to them, the people answered the king,

"What share have we in David?
  We have no heritage in the son of Jesse.
Everyone to your tents, O Israel!
  Now look to your own house, David!"

So all Israel went off to their tents. [17] Rehoboam, therefore, reigned over only those Israelites who lived in the cities of Judah. [18] King Rehoboam then

---

9, 28: See note on 2 Chr 1, 16f.
10, 1: *All Israel:* as in the original source (1 Kgs 12, 1), the northern tribes, distinct from Judah and Benjamin. Contrast the Chronicler's own terms, those Israelites who lived in the cities of Judah (v 17), and all the Israelites [literally, all Israel] in Judah and Benjamin (2 Chr 11, 3).

9, 29ff: 1 Kgs 11, 41ff.
10, 1–14: 1 Kgs 12, 1–14.
10, 15: 1 Kgs 11, 29–39;
12, 15.
10, 16–19: 1 Kgs 12, 16–19.

sent out Hadoram, who was superintendent of the forced labor, but the Israelites stoned him to death. Rehoboam himself managed to mount his chariot and flee to Jerusalem. ¹⁹ Thus Israel has been in rebellion against David's house to this day.

11 ¹* On his arrival in Jerusalem Rehoboam gathered together the house of Judah and Benjamin, a hundred and eighty thousand seasoned warriors, to have them fight against Israel and restore the kingdom to him. ² However, the word of the LORD came to Shemiah, a man of God: ³ "Say to Rehoboam, son of Solomon, king of Judah, and to all the Israelites in Judah and Benjamin: ⁴ Thus says the LORD: You must not march out to fight against your brothers. Let every man return home, for what has occurred I have brought about.' " They obeyed this message of the LORD and gave up the expedition against Jeroboam.

Rehoboam's Works

⁵† Rehoboam took up residence in Jerusalem and built fortified cities in Judah. ⁶ He built up Bethlehem, Etam, Tekoa, ⁷ Beth-zur, Soco, Adullam, ⁸ Gath, Mareshah, Ziph, ⁹ Adoraim, Lachish, Azekah, ¹⁰ Zorah, Aijalon, and Hebron; these were fortified cities in Judah and Benjamin. ¹¹ Then he strengthened the fortifications and put commanders in them, with supplies of food, oil and wine. ¹² In every city were shields and spears, and he made them very strong. Thus Judah and Benjamin remained his.

Refugees from the North

¹³ Now the priests and Levites throughout Israel presented themselves to him from all parts of their land, ¹⁴* for the Levites left their assigned pasture lands and their holdings and came to Judah and Jerusalem, because Jeroboam and his sons repudiated them as priests of the LORD. ¹⁵* In their place, he himself appointed priests for the high places and satyrs and calves he had made. ¹⁶ After them, all those of the Israelite tribes who firmly desired to seek the LORD, the God of Israel, came to Jerusalem to sacrifice to the LORD, the God of their fathers. ¹⁷ Thus they strengthened the kingdom of Judah and made Rehoboam, son of Solomon, prevail for three years; for they walked in the way of David and Solomon three years.

Rehoboam's Family

¹⁸ Rehoboam took to himself as wife Mahalath, daughter of Jerimoth, son of David and of Abihail,

daughter of Eliab, son of Jesse. ¹⁹ She bore him sons: Jehush, Shemariah and Zaham. ²⁰* After her, he married Maacah, daughter of Absalom, who bore him Abijah, Attai, Ziza and Shelomith. ²¹ Rehoboam loved Maacah, daughter of Absalom, more than all his other wives and concubines; he had taken eighteen wives and sixty concubines, and he fathered twenty-eight sons and sixty daughters. ²² Rehoboam constituted Abijah, son of Maacah, commander among his brothers, for he intended to make him king. ²³ He acted prudently, distributing various of his sons throughout all the districts of Judah and Benjamin, in all the fortified cities; and he furnished them with copious provisions and sought an abundance of wives for them.

His Apostasy

12 ¹* After Rehoboam had consolidated his rule and had become powerful, he abandoned the law of the LORD, he and all Israel with him. ²* Thus it happened that in the fifth year of King Rehoboam, Shishak, king of Egypt, attacked Jerusalem, for they had been unfaithful to the LORD. ³† He came up with twelve hundred chariots and sixty thousand horsemen, and there was no counting the army that came with him from Egypt—Libyans, Sukkites and Ethiopians. ⁴ They captured the fortified cities of Judah and came as far as Jerusalem. ⁵* Then Shemaiah the prophet came to Rehoboam and the commanders of Judah who had gathered at Jerusalem because of Shishak, and said to them: "Thus says the LORD: 'You have abandoned me, and therefore I have abandoned you to the power of Shishak.' "

⁶ However, the commanders of Israel and the king humbled themselves, saying, "The LORD is just." ⁷ When the LORD saw that they had humbled themselves, the word of the LORD came to Shemaiah: "Because they have humbled themselves, I will not destroy them; I will give them some deliverance, and my wrath shall not be poured out upon Jerusalem through Shishak. ⁸ But they shall be his servants, that they may know what it is to serve me and what it is to serve earthly kingdoms." ⁹* Therefore Shishak, king of Egypt, attacked Jerusalem and carried off the treasures of the temple of the LORD and of the king's palace. He took everything, including the gold bucklers that Solomon had made. ¹⁰ (To replace them, King Rehoboam made bronze bucklers, which he entrusted to the officers of the guard on duty at the entrance of the royal palace. ¹¹ Whenever the king visited the temple of the LORD, the troops would come bearing them, and

---

11, 5–12: These verses, though not found in 1 Kings, are apparently based on a reliable, ancient source.
12, 3: *Sukkites:* foreign mercenaries in the Egyptian army.

11, 1–4: 1 Kgs 12, 21–24.   **12, 1:** 1 Kgs 11, 4; 14, 22.
11, 14: 1 Kgs 12, 32.   **12, 2:** 1 Kgs 14, 25.
11, 15: 1 Kgs 12, 32; Lv 17, 7. **12, 5:** 2 Chr 11, 2.
11, 20: 1 Kgs 15, 2.   **12, 9ff:** 1 Kgs 14, 25–28.

Selling Out

LIVE IT!

King Rehoboam, son of Solomon, sold out and abandoned the law of the
LORD after he thought his rule was secure (2 Chr 12, 1). The Chronicler tells us
that the LORD abandoned Rehoboam to the Egyptians because of this. Fortunately, Rehoboam and his officers repented, and the LORD showed mercy on them.

It is tempting to compromise our values in order to succeed and become popular, even
though doing this ends up hurting the people around us. Maybe you have experienced some
success like Rehoboam and figure you can have even more if you just bend the rules a bit.
Maybe you feel life has given you a rotten deal and the only way to get ahead is to forget
your principles. But before you sell out, think again. Ultimately, abandoning your good and
holy principles won't get you ahead; it will only lead to your downfall.

▶ 2 Chr 12, 1–12

---

then they would return them to the guardroom.)
[12] Because he had humbled himself, the anger of
the LORD turned from him so that it did not destroy
him completely; and in Judah, moreover, good
deeds were found.

[13] King Rehoboam consolidated his power in
Jerusalem and continued to rule; he was forty-one
years old when he became king, and he reigned seventeen years in Jerusalem, the city in which, out of
all the tribes of Israel, the LORD chose to be honored. Rehoboam's mother was named Naamah, an
Ammonite. [14] He did evil, for he had not truly resolved to seek the LORD. [15] The acts of Rehoboam,
first and last, are written, as is well known, in the
history of Shemaiah the prophet and of Iddo the
seer [his family record]. There was war continually
between Rehoboam and Jeroboam. [16] Rehoboam
rested with his ancestors; he was buried in the City
of David. His son Abijah succeeded him as king.

War between Abijah and Jeroboam

13 [1] In the eighteenth year of King Jeroboam, Abijah became king of Judah;
[2] he reigned three years in Jerusalem. His mother
was named Michaiah, daughter of Uriel of Gibeah.
There was war between Abijah and Jeroboam.

[3] Abijah joined battle with a force of four hundred thousand picked warriors, while Jeroboam
lined up against him in battle with eight hundred
thousand picked and valiant warriors. [4] Abijah
stood on Mount Zemaraim, which is in the highlands of Ephraim, and said: "Listen to me, Jeroboam and all Israel! [5] Do you not know that the
LORD, the God of Israel, has given the kingdom of
Israel to David forever, to him and to his sons, by a
covenant made in salt? [6] Yet Jeroboam, son of

Nebat, the servant of Solomon, son of David, has
stood up and rebelled against his lord! [7] Worthless
men, scoundrels, joined him and overcame Rehoboam, son of Solomon, when Rehoboam was
young and unthinking, and no match for them.
[8] But now, do you think you are a match for the
kingdom of the LORD commanded by the sons of
David, simply because you are a huge multitude
and have with you the golden calves which Jeroboam made you for gods?

[9] "Have you not expelled the priests of the LORD,
the sons of Aaron, and the Levites, and made for
yourselves priests like the peoples of foreign lands?
Everyone who comes to consecrate himself with a
young bull and seven rams becomes a priest of no-
gods. [10] But as for us, the LORD is our God, and we
have not forsaken him. The priests ministering to
the LORD are sons of Aaron, and the Levites also
have their offices. [11] They burn holocausts to the
LORD and fragrant incense morning after morning
and evening after evening; they display the showbread on the pure table, and the lamps of the gold-
en lampstand burn evening after evening; for we
observe our duties to the LORD, our God, but you
have abandoned him. [12] See, God is with us, at our
head, and his priests are here with trumpets to
sound the attack against you. Do not battle against
the LORD, the God of your fathers, O Israelites, for
you will not succeed!"

[13] But Jeroboam had an ambush go around them
to come at them from the rear; so that while his army
faced Judah, his ambush lay behind them. [14] When
Judah turned and saw that they had to battle on both
fronts, they cried out to the LORD and the priests
sounded the trumpets. [15] Then the men of Judah
shouted; and when they did so, God defeated

13, 4–12: This is a free composition of the Chronicler to show
that this was a religious, rather than a political, war.

12, 13: 1 Kgs 14, 21.
12, 15f: 1 Kgs 14, 29ff.

13, 1f: 1 Kgs 15, 1f.
13, 6: 1 Kgs 11, 26.

Jeroboam and all Israel before Abijah and Judah. 16 The Israelites fled before Judah, and God delivered them into their hands. 17 Abijah and his people inflicted a severe defeat upon them; five hundred thousand picked men of Israel fell slain. 18 The Israelites were subdued on that occasion and the Judahites were victorious because they relied on the LORD, the God of their fathers. 19 Abijah pursued Jeroboam and took cities from him: Bethel and its dependencies, Jeshanah and its dependencies, and Ephron and its dependencies. 20 Jeroboam did not regain power during the time of Abijah; the LORD struck him down and he died, 21 while Abijah continued to grow stronger. He took to himself fourteen wives and fathered twenty-two sons and sixteen daughters.

Death of Abijah

22* The rest of Abijah's acts, his deeds and his words, are written in the midrash of the prophet Iddo. 23 Abijah rested with his ancestors; they buried him in the City of David. His son Asa succeeded him as king. During his time, ten years of peace began in the land.

Asa the Reformer

14 1* Asa did what was good and pleasing to the LORD, his God, 2 removing the heathen altars and the high places, breaking to pieces the sacred pillars, and cutting down the sacred poles. 3 He commanded Judah to seek the LORD, the God of their fathers, and to observe the law and its commands. 4 He removed the high places and incense stands from all the cities of Judah, and under him the kingdom had peace. 5 He built fortified cities in Judah, for the land had peace and no war was waged against him during these years, because the LORD had given him peace. 6 He said to Judah: "Let us build these cities and surround them with walls, towers, gates and bars. The land is still ours, for we have sought the LORD, our God; we sought him, and he has given us rest on every side." So they built and prospered.

The Ethiopian Invasion

7† Asa had an army of three hundred thousand shield- and lance-bearers from Judah, and two hundred and eighty thousand from Benjamin who carried bucklers and were archers, all of them valiant warriors. 8* Zerah the Ethiopian moved against them with a force of one million men and three hundred chariots, and he came as far as Mareshah. 9 Asa went out to meet him and set himself in battle array in the valley of Zephathah, near Mareshah. 10* Asa called upon the LORD, his God, praying: "O LORD, there is none like you to help the powerless against the strong. Help us, O LORD, our God, for we rely on you, and in your name we have come against this multitude. You are the LORD, our God; let no man prevail against you." 11* And so the LORD defeated the Ethiopians before Asa and Judah, and they fled. 12 Asa and those with him pursued them as far as Gerar, and the Ethiopians fell until there were no survivors, for they were crushed before the LORD and his army, which carried away enormous spoils. 13 Then the Judahites conquered all the cities around Gerar, for the fear of the LORD was upon them; they despoiled all the cities, for there was much booty in them. 14 They attacked also the tents of the cattle-herders and carried off a great number of sheep and camels. Then they returned to Jerusalem.

Cult Reform

15 1 Upon Azariah, son of Oded, came the spirit of God. 2* He went forth to meet Asa and said to him: "Hear me, Asa and all Judah and Benjamin! The LORD is with you when you are with him, and if you seek him he will be present to you; but if you abandon him, he will abandon you. 3 For a long time Israel had no true God, no priest-teacher and no law, 4* but when in their distress they turned to the LORD, the God of Israel, and sought him, he was present to them. 5 In that former time there was no place for anyone to go or come, but there were many terrors upon the inhabitants of the lands. 6* Nation crushed nation and city crushed city, for God destroyed them by every kind of adversity. 7* But as for you, be strong and do not relax, for your work shall be rewarded."

8 When Asa heard these words and the prophecy [Oded the prophet], he was encouraged to remove the detestable idols from the whole land of Judah and Benjamin and from the cities he had taken in the highlands of Ephraim, and to restore the altar of the LORD which was before the vestibule of the LORD. 9 Then he convened all Judah and Benjamin, together with those of Ephraim, Manasseh and Simeon who sojourned with them; for many had fled to him from Israel when they saw that the LORD, his God, was with him. 10† They gathered at

---

14, 7–14: An Ethiopian invasion of Judah is mentioned only in 1 Chronicles. This account may be a legend contrived to show how the pious King Asa was rewarded through divine assistance. There may, however, have been an incursion of nomads from the Negeb at this time; cf vv 13f.

15, 10ff: With this description of a covenant ceremony in the third month of a year beginning in the spring, the Chronicler lays a

13, 22f: 2 Chr 12, 15; 1 Kgs 7ff.
14, 1f: 2 Chr 33, 15; Ex 23, 24; 34, 13; 1 Kgs 15, 11f.
14, 8: 2 Chr 16, 8.
14, 10: 2 Chr 32, 8.
14, 11: Pss 20, 7f; 60, 11f.
15, 2: Jer 29, 13f; Hos 3, 4f.
15, 4: Dt 4, 29f.
15, 6: Is 19, 2.
15, 7: Is 7, 4; Jer 31, 16.

Keep On Turning

LIVE IT!

Conversion.

A very important word for Christians. Its Latin root means "to turn around." We turn from sin and toward God, as individuals and as a people. In 2 Chr 15, 8–15, we read about King Asa and his people hearing the words of the prophet Azariah and then turning away from idols and turning back to God.

Conversion is not a one-time event. It is a process all of us go through again and again as our faith and understanding grow. We are reminded of that especially during the season of Lent. On Ash Wednesday, as individuals and as a community, we hear the words, "Turn away from sin and be faithful to the gospel" (*The Sacramentary*, p. 77). The Israelites went through the same thing. Again and again, they were called to turn back to God.

If we are committed to following Jesus, conversion is a lifelong process of deepening our faith. Where are you most in need of conversion? Where is our nation most in need of conversion?

▸ 2 Chr 15, 8–15

Jerusalem in the third month of the fifteenth year of Asa's reign, [11] and sacrificed to the LORD at that time seven hundred oxen and seven thousand sheep of the booty they had brought. [12] They entered into a covenant to seek the LORD, the God of their fathers, with all their heart and soul; [13]* and everyone who would not seek the LORD, the God of Israel, was to be put to death, whether small or great, whether man or woman. [14] They swore to the LORD with a loud voice, with shouting and with trumpets and horns. [15]* All Judah rejoiced over the oath, for they had sworn with their whole heart and sought him with complete desire, so that he was present to them. And the LORD gave them rest on every side.

[16]* Maacah, the mother of King Asa, he deposed as queen mother because she had made an outrageous object for Asherah; Asa cut this down, smashed it, and burnt it in the Kidron Valley. [17] Although the high places did not disappear from Israel, yet Asa's heart was undivided as long as he lived. [18] He brought into the house of God his father's votive offerings and his own: silver, gold, and various utensils. [19] There was no war until the thirty-fifth year of Asa's reign.

Asa's Infidelity

16 [1]* In the thirty-sixth year of Asa's reign, Baasha, king of Israel, attacked Judah and fortified Ramah to prevent any communication with Asa, king of Judah. [2] Asa then brought out silver and gold from the treasuries of the temple of the LORD and of the royal palace and sent them to Ben-hadad, king of Aram, who lived in Damascus, with this message: [3] "There is a treaty between you and me, as there was between your father and my father. See, I am sending you silver and gold. Go, break your treaty with Baasha, king of Israel, that he may withdraw from me." [4] Ben-hadad agreed to King Asa's request and sent the leaders of his troops against the cities of Israel. They attacked Ijon, Dan, Abel-maim, and all the store cities of Naphtali. [5] When Baasha heard of it, he left off fortifying Ramah; he stopped his work. [6] Then King Asa commandeered all of Judah to carry away the stone and wood with which Baasha had been fortifying Ramah, and with them he fortified Geba and Mizpah.

[7]† At that time Hanani the seer came to Asa, king of Judah, and said to him: "Because you relied on the king of Aram and did not rely on the LORD, your God, the army of the king of Aram has escaped your hand. [8]* Were not the Ethiopians and Libyans a vast army, with great numbers of chariots and drivers? And yet, because you relied on the LORD, he delivered them into your power. [9]* The eyes of the LORD roam over the whole earth, to encourage those who are devoted to him wholeheartedly. You have acted foolishly in this matter, for from now on you will have wars." [10] But Asa became angry with the seer and imprisoned him in the stocks, so greatly was he enraged at him over this. Asa also oppressed some of his people at this time.

---

† foundation for celebrating the ancient feast of Pentecost (Weeks) as the time for a solemn renewal of the people's covenant with God on Mount Sinai; see Ex 19, 1ff; Lv 23, 16 and the note there. This is also the background for Pentecost as the "birthday of the Church."
16, 7: *The king of Aram . . . escaped:* according to the Lucianic

recension, "the king of Israel escaped": this may well be the original reading; Asa was friendly with Aram.

*
15, 13: Neh 10, 30.   16, 1–6: 1 Kgs 15, 16–21.
15, 15: Dt 4, 29.   16, 8: 2 Chr 14, 8–14.
15, 16ff: 1 Kgs 15, 13ff. 16, 9: Ps 33, 13ff.

11* Now the acts of Asa, first and last, can be found recorded in the book of the kings of Judah and Israel. 12 In the thirty-ninth year of his reign, Asa contracted a serious disease in his feet. But even in his sickness he did not seek the LORD, but only the physicians. 13 Asa rested with his ancestors; he died in the forty-first year of his reign. 14 They buried him in the tomb he had hewn for himself in the City of David, having laid him upon a couch which was filled with spices and various kinds of aromatics compounded into an ointment. They also burned a very great funeral pyre for him.

Zeal of Jehoshaphat for the Law

17 1* His son Jehoshaphat succeeded him as king and strengthened his hold against Israel. 2 He placed armed forces in all the fortified cities of Judah, and put garrisons in the land of Judah and in the cities of Ephraim which his father Asa had taken. 3† The LORD was with Jehoshaphat, for he walked in the ways his father had pursued in the beginning, and he did not consult the Baals. 4 Rather, he sought the God of his father and observed his commands, and not the practices of Israel. 5 As a result, the LORD made his kingdom secure, and all Judah gave Jehoshaphat gifts, so that he enjoyed great wealth and glory. 6* Thus he was encouraged to follow the LORD's ways, and again he removed the high places and the sacred poles from Judah.

7 In the third year of his reign he sent his leading men, Ben-hail, Obadiah, Zechariah, Nethanel and Micaiah, to teach in the cities of Judah. 8* With them he sent the Levites Shemaiah, Nethaniah, Zebadiah, Asahel, Shemiramoth, Jehonathan, Adonijah and Tobijah, together with the priests Elishama and Jehoram. 9* They taught in Judah, having with them the book containing the law of the LORD; they traveled through all the cities of Judah and taught among the people.

His Power

10 Now the fear of the LORD was upon all the kingdoms of the countries surrounding Judah, so that they did not war against Jehoshaphat. 11 Some of the Philistines brought Jehoshaphat gifts and a tribute of silver; and the Arabs also brought him a flock of seven thousand seven hundred rams and seven thousand seven hundred he-goats.

12 Jehoshaphat grew steadily greater. He built strongholds and store cities in Judah. 13 He carried out many works in the cities of Judah, and he had soldiers, valiant warriors, in Jerusalem. 14 This was

their mustering according to their ancestral houses. Of Judah, the commanders of thousands: Adnah the commander, and with him three hundred thousand valiant warriors. 15 Next to him, Jehohanan the commander, and with him two hundred eighty thousand. 16 Next to him, Amasiah, son of Zichri, who offered himself to the LORD, and with him two hundred thousand valiant warriors. 17 From Benjamin: Eliada, a valiant warrior, and with him two hundred thousand armed with bow and buckler. 18 Next to him, Jozabad, and with him one hundred and eighty thousand equipped for war. 19 These were at the service of the king; in addition were those whom the king had placed in the fortified cities throughout all Judah.

Alliance with Israel

18 1* Jehoshaphat therefore had wealth and glory in abundance; but he became related to Ahab by marriage. 2 After some years he went down to Ahab at Samaria; Ahab offered numerous sheep and oxen for him and the people with him, and persuaded him to go up against Ramoth-gilead. 3 Ahab, king of Israel, asked Jehoshaphat, king of Judah, "Will you come with me to Ramoth-gilead?" "You and I are as one," was his answer; "your people and my people as well. We will be with you in the battle." 4 But Jehoshaphat also said to the king of Israel, "Seek the word of the LORD at once."

The Prophets

5 The king of Israel gathered his prophets, four hundred in number, and asked them, "Shall we go to attack Ramoth-gilead, or shall I refrain?" "Go up," they answered. "God will deliver it over to the king." 6 But Jehoshaphat said, "Is there no other prophet of the LORD here whom we may consult?" 7 The king of Israel answered Jehoshaphat, "There is still another through whom we may consult the LORD, but I hate him, for he prophesies not good but always evil about me. That is Micaiah, son of Imlah." Jehoshaphat said, "Let not your Majesty speak of evil against you." 8 So the king of Israel called an official, to whom he said, "Get Micaiah, son of Imlah, at once." 9 The king of Israel and King Jehoshaphat of Judah were seated each on his throne, clothed in their robes of state on a threshing floor at the entrance of the gate of Samaria, and all the prophets were prophesying before them.

10 Zedekiah, son of Chenaanah, made iron horns for himself and said: "The LORD says, 'With these you shall gore Aram until you have destroyed them.' " 11 The other prophets prophesied in the

---

†
17, 3: *The LORD was with Jehoshaphat:* along with Hezekiah and Josiah, Jehoshaphat was one of the Chronicler's favorite kings.

*
16, 11–14: 1 Kgs 15, 23f.   17, 8: 2 Chr 19, 8.
17, 1: 1 Kgs 15, 24.   17, 9: Ezr 7, 25.
17, 6: 2 Chr 20, 33; Ex 34, 13.   18, 1–34: 1 Kgs 22, 1–35.

same vein, saying: "Go up to Ramoth-gilead. You shall succeed; the LORD will deliver it over to the king." [12]† The messenger who had gone to call Micaiah said to him: "Look now, the prophets unanimously predict good for the king. Let your word, like each of theirs, predict good." [13] "As the LORD lives," Micaiah answered, "I will say what my God tells me."

[14] When he came to the king, the king said to him, "Micaiah, shall we go to fight against Ramoth-gilead, or shall I refrain?" "Go up," he answered, "and succeed; they will be delivered into your power." [15] But the king said to him, "How many times must I adjure you to tell me nothing but the truth in the name of the LORD?" [16] Then Micaiah answered:

"I see all Israel
    scattered on the mountains,
like sheep without a shepherd,
    and the LORD saying, 'These have
        no master!
Let each of them go back home in peace.' "

[17] The king of Israel said to Jehoshaphat, "Did I not tell you that he prophesies no good about me, but only evil?" [18] But Micaiah continued: "Therefore hear the word of the LORD: I saw the LORD seated on his throne, with the whole host of heaven standing by to his right and to his left. [19] The LORD asked, 'Who will deceive Ahab, king of Israel, so that he will go up and fall at Ramoth-gilead?' And one said this, another that, [20] until a spirit came forward and presented himself to the LORD, saying, 'I will deceive him.' The LORD asked, 'How?' [21] He answered, 'I will go forth and become a lying spirit in the mouths of all his prophets.' The LORD agreed: 'You shall succeed in deceiving him. Go forth and do this.' [22] So now the LORD has put a lying spirit in the mouths of these your prophets, but the LORD himself has decreed evil against you."

[23] Thereupon Zedekiah, son of Chenaanah, came up and slapped Micaiah on the cheek, saying, "Which way did the spirit of the LORD go when he left me to speak to you?" [24] "You shall find out," Micaiah replied, "on that day when you enter an innermost chamber to hide." [25] The king of Israel then said: "Seize Micaiah and take him back to Amon, prefect of the city, and to Joash the king's son, [26] and say, 'This is the king's order: Put this man in prison and feed him scanty rations of bread

and water until I return in safety!' " [27]† But Micaiah said, "If ever you return in safety, the LORD has not spoken through me." And he said, "Hear, O peoples, all of you!"

Ahab's Death

[28] The king of Israel and King Jehoshaphat of Judah went up to Ramoth-gilead [29] and the king of Israel said to Jehoshaphat, "I will go into battle disguised, but you put on your own clothes." So the king of Israel disguised himself and they entered the fray. [30] Meanwhile, the king of Aram had given his chariot commanders the order, "Fight with no one, small or great, except the king of Israel." [31] When the commanders saw Jehoshaphat, they exclaimed, "That must be the king of Israel!" and shifted to fight him. But Jehoshaphat cried out and the LORD helped him; God induced them to leave him. [32] The chariot commanders became aware that he was not the king of Israel and gave up their pursuit of him. [33]* Someone, however, drew his bow at random and hit the king of Israel between the joints of his breastplate. He ordered his charioteer, "Rein about and take me out of the ranks, for I am disabled." [34] The battle grew fierce during the day, and the king of Israel braced himself up on his chariot facing the Arameans until evening. He died as the sun was setting.

Jehoshaphat Rebuked

19 [1] King Jehoshaphat of Judah returned in safety to his house in Jerusalem. [2]† Jehu the seer, son of Hanani, met King Jehoshaphat and said to him: "Should you help the wicked and love those who hate the LORD? For this reason, wrath is upon you from the LORD. [3] Yet some good things are to be found in you, since you have removed the sacred poles from the land and have been determined to seek God."

Judges Appointed

[4] Jehoshaphat dwelt in Jerusalem; but he went out again among the people from Beer-sheba to the highlands of Ephraim and brought them back to the LORD, the God of their fathers. [5] He appointed judges in the land, in all the fortified cities of Judah, city by city, [6]* and he said to them: "Take care what you do, for you are judging, not on behalf of man, but on behalf of the LORD; he judges with you. [7]* And now, let the fear of the LORD be upon you. Act carefully, for with the LORD, our God, there is

---

18, 12–22: See note on 1 Kgs 22, 19–23.
18, 27: *"Hear, O peoples, all of you!":* this quotation, which appears in some texts of 1 Kgs 22, 28, ascribes to the prophets Micaiah ben Imlah the opening words of the prophetic utterance of Micah of Moresheth (Mi 1, 2), a century later.

19, 2: *Jehu the seer, son of Hanani:* hardly the same seer as Jehu, son of Hanani, who prophesied against Baasha almost 50 years earlier (1 Kgs 16, 1).

18, 33: 2 Chr 35, 23; 1 Kgs   19, 6: Dt 1, 16ff; 16, 19f.
        22, 34.   19, 7: Dt 10, 17.

no injustice, no partiality, no bribe-taking." 8* In Jerusalem also, Jehoshaphat appointed some Levites and priests and some of the family heads of Israel to judge in the name of the LORD and to settle quarrels among the inhabitants of Jerusalem. 9 He gave them this command: "You shall act faithfully and wholeheartedly in the fear of the LORD. 10* And in every dispute that your brethren living in their cities bring to you, whether it concerns bloodguilt or questions of law, command, statutes, or judgments, warn them lest they become guilty before the LORD and his wrath come upon you and your brethren. Do that and you shall be guiltless. 11 See now, Amariah is high priest over you in everything that pertains to the LORD, and Zebadiah, son of Ishmael, is leader of the house of Judah in all that pertains to the king; and the Levites will be your officials. Act firmly, and the LORD will be with the good."

Invasion from Edom

20 1† After this the Moabites, the Ammonites, and with them some Meunites came to fight against Jehoshaphat. 2 The message was brought to Jehoshaphat: "A great multitude is coming against you from across the sea, from Edom; they are already in Hazazon-tamar" (which is Engedi). 3 Jehoshaphat was frightened, and he hastened to consult the LORD. He proclaimed a fast for all Judah. 4* Then Judah gathered to seek help from the LORD; from every one of the cities of Judah they came to seek the LORD.

Prayer of Jehoshaphat

5 Jehoshaphat stood up in the assembly of Judah and Jerusalem in the house of the LORD before the new court, 6* and he said: "LORD, God of our fathers, are you not the God in heaven, and do you not rule over all the kingdoms of the nations? In your hand is power and might, and no one can withstand you. 7* Was it not you, our God, who drove out the inhabitants of this land before your people Israel and gave it forever to the descendants of Abraham, your friend? 8 They have dwelt in it and they built in it a sanctuary to your honor, saying, 9 'When evil comes upon us, the sword of judgment, or pestilence, or famine, we will stand before this house and before you, for your name is in this house, and we will cry out to you in our affliction, and you will hear and save!' 10* And now, see the Ammonites, Moabites, and those of Mount Seir whom you did not allow Israel to invade when they came from the land of Egypt, but instead they passed them by and did not destroy them. 11 See how they are now repaying us by coming to drive us out of the possession you have given us. 12 O our God, will you not pass judgment on them? We are powerless before this vast multitude that comes against us. We are at a loss what to do, hence our eyes are turned toward you."

Victory Prophesied

13 All Judah was standing before the LORD, with their little ones, their wives, and their young sons. 14 And the spirit of the LORD came upon Jahaziel, son of Zechariah, son of Benaiah, son of Jeiel, son of Mattaniah, a Levite of the clan of Asaph, in the midst of the assembly, 15 and he said: "Listen, all of Judah, inhabitants of Jerusalem, and King Jehoshaphat! The LORD says to you: 'Do not fear or lose heart at the sight of this vast multitude, for the battle is not yours but God's. 16 Go down against them tomorrow. You will see them coming up by the ascent of Ziz, and you will come upon them at the end of the wadi which opens on the wilderness of Jeruel. 17* You will not have to fight in this encounter. Take your places, stand firm, and see how the LORD will be with you to deliver you, Judah and Jerusalem. Do not fear or lose heart. Tomorrow go out to meet them, and the LORD will be with you.' " 18 Then Jehoshaphat knelt down with his face to the ground, and all Judah and the inhabitants of Jerusalem fell down before the LORD in worship. 19 Levites from among the Kohathites and Korahites rose to sing the praises of the LORD, the God of Israel, in a resounding chorus.

The Invaders Destroyed

20* In the early morning they hastened out to the wilderness of Tekoa. As they were going out, Jehoshaphat halted and said: "Listen to me, Judah and inhabitants of Jerusalem! Trust in the LORD, your God, and you will be found firm. Trust in his prophets and you will succeed." 21*† After consulting with the people, he appointed some to sing to the LORD and some to praise the holy Appearance

---

20, 1–30: Although the account here seems to be a free composition of the Chronicler, there is probably a basis in fact for it; there could well have been a raid of nomads against Judah in the reign of Jehoshaphat, similar to Zerah's attack on Asa (2 Chr 14, 8–14). The story may also, in some way, be connected with the campaign of Israel and Judah against Moab through the territory of Edom (2 Kgs 3, 4–27).

20, 21: *Holy Appearance:* the Lord, who is with the Israelite army

(v 17), manifests himself (the same language is in Ps 29, 2) in bringing Israel the victory (Ex 14, 14.24).

* **19, 8:** 2 Chr 17, 8f; Dt 17, 8–13; Ps 122, 3ff.
19, 10: Nm 35, 19.
20, 4: Jer 36, 6; Jb 1, 14.
20, 6: 2 Chr 32, 7; Dt 4, 39.
20, 7: Dn 3, 35.
20, 10: Dt 2, 4f.9f.18f.
20, 17: Is 8, 10.
20, 20: Is 7, 9.
20, 21: Ps 136, 1.

as it went forth at the head of the army. They sang: "Give thanks to the LORD, for his mercy endures forever." 22 At the moment they began their jubilant hymn, the LORD laid an ambush against the Ammonites, Moabites, and those of Mount Seir who were coming against Judah, so that they were vanquished. 23* For the Ammonites and Moabites set upon the inhabitants of Mount Seir and completely exterminated them. And when they had finished with the inhabitants of Seir, they began to destroy each other.

24 When Judah came to the watchtower of the desert and looked toward the throng, they saw only corpses fallen on the ground, with no survivors. 25 Jehoshaphat and his people came to take plunder, and they found an abundance of cattle and personal property, garments and precious vessels. They took so much that they were unable to carry it all; they were three days taking the spoil, so great was it. 26† On the fourth day they held an assembly in the Valley of Beracah—for there they blessed the LORD; therefore that place has ever since been called the Valley of Beracah. 27 Then all the men of Judah and Jerusalem, with Jehoshaphat at their head, turned back toward Jerusalem celebrating the joyful victory the LORD had given them over their enemies. 28 They came to Jerusalem, to the house of the LORD, with harps, lyres and trumpets. 29 And the fear of God came upon all the kingdoms of the surrounding lands when they heard how the LORD had fought against the enemies of Israel. 30 Thereafter Jehoshaphat's kingdom enjoyed peace, for his God gave him rest on every side.

Jehoshaphat's Other Deeds

31* Thus Jehoshaphat reigned over Judah. He was thirty-five years old when he became king, and he reigned twenty-five years in Jerusalem. His mother was named Azubah, daughter of Shilhi. 32 He followed the path of his father Asa unswervingly, doing what was right in the LORD'S sight. 33 But the high places were not removed, nor as yet had the people fixed their hearts on the God of their fathers.

34 The rest of the acts of Jehoshaphat, first and last, can be found written in the chronicle of Jehu, son of Hanani, which is inserted in the book of the kings of Israel. 35 After this, King Jehoshaphat of Judah allied himself with King Ahaziah of Israel, who did evil. 36* He joined with him in building

ships to sail to Tarshish; the fleet was built at Eziongeber. 37 But Eliezer, son of Dodavahu from Mareshah, prophesied against Jehoshaphat, saying, "Because you have joined with Ahaziah, the LORD will shatter your work." And the ships were wrecked and were unable to sail to Tarshish.

21

1* Jehoshaphat rested with his ancestors; he was buried with them in the City of David. Jehoram, his son, succeeded him as king. 2 His brothers, sons of Jehoshaphat, were Azariah, Jehiel, Zechariah, Azariah, Michael and Shephatiah; all these were sons of King Jehoshaphat of Judah. 3 Their father gave them numerous gifts of silver, gold and precious objects, together with fortified cities in Judah, but the kingship he gave to Jehoram because he was the first-born.

Evil Deeds of Jehoram

4 When Jehoram had come into his father's kingdom and had consolidated his power, he put to the sword all his brothers and also some of the princes of Israel. 5* Jehoram was thirty-two years old when he became king, and he reigned eight years in Jerusalem. 6† He conducted himself like the kings of Israel of the line of Ahab, because one of Ahab's daughters was his wife. He did evil in the sight of the LORD, 7* but the LORD would not destroy the house of David because of the covenant he had made with David and because of his promise to give him and his sons a lamp for all time.

8* During his time Edom revolted against the sovereignty of Judah; they chose a king of their own. 9 Thereupon Jehoram crossed over with his officers and all the chariots he had. He arose by night and broke through the Edomites when they had surrounded him and the commanders of his chariots. 10 However, Edom has continued in revolt against the sovereignty of Judah down to the present time. Libnah also revolted at that time against Jehoram's sovereignty because he had forsaken the LORD, the God of his fathers. 11 He also set up high places in the mountains of Judah; he led the inhabitants of Jerusalem into idolatry and seduced Judah.

Retribution

12† He received a letter from the prophet Elijah with this message: Thus says the LORD, the God of your ancestor David: 'Because you have not followed the path of your father Jehoshaphat, nor of

---

20, 26: *Beracah:* the Hebrew word for "blessing."
21, 6: *One of Ahab's daughters:* Athaliah. In 2 Chr 22, 2 (and in its source, 2 Kgs 8, 26) she is called Omri's daughter; but this should probably be understood in the sense of granddaughter.
21, 12: *Elijah:* the only mention by the Chronicler of this prophet of the northern kingdom of Israel. It is doubtful that Elijah was still living in the reign of Jehoram of Judah; in any case, the attribution

of the letter to him is most likely an imaginative filling out of the narration.

20, 23: Jos 6, 17; Ez 38, 21.　21, 7: 1 Kgs 11, 36; 2 Kgs 8,
20, 31–34: 1 Kgs 22, 41–45.　　　19.
　20, 36f: 1 Kgs 22, 48f.　21, 8ff: Gn 27, 40; 2 Kgs 8,
　21, 1: 1 Kgs 22, 51.　　　20ff.
21, 5ff: 2 Kgs 8, 17ff.

did you KNOW?

The Role of the Prophet

The letter from Elijah to King Jehoram discussed in 2 Chr 21, 12–15 underscores the principal role of the Hebrew prophet: to be God's voice, the one who speaks for God. Although many early figures are called prophets, including Moses and Deborah, the classical prophet—*nabi'* in Hebrew—appeared later in Israelite history. The primary function of the prophet was not to foretell the future, but to announce God's judgment, to confront those who violated God's law, and to console those who suffered. In short, the prophets were the conscience of the Israelite nation.

▶ 2 Chr 21, 12–15

Asa, king of Judah, 13 but instead have walked in the way of the kings of Israel and have led Judah and the inhabitants of Jerusalem into idolatry, as did the house of Ahab, and also because you have murdered your brothers of your father's house who were better than you, 14 the LORD will strike your people, your children, your wives, and all that is yours with a great plague; 15 and you shall have severe pains from a disease in your bowels, while your bowels issue forth because of the disease, day after day.' "

16 Then the LORD stirred up against Jehoram the animosity of the Philistines and of the Arabs who bordered on the Ethiopians. 17 They came up against Judah, invaded it, and carried away all the wealth found in the king's palace, along with his sons and his wives; there was left to him only one son, Jehoahaz, his youngest. 18 After these events, the LORD afflicted him with an incurable disease of the bowels. 19 As time went on until a period of two years had elapsed, his bowels issued forth because of the disease and he died in great pain. His people did not make a pyre for him like that of his fathers. 20* He was thirty-two years old when he became king, and he reigned eight years in Jerusalem. He departed unloved and was buried in the City of David, but not in the tombs of the kings.

Ahaziah

22 1* Then the inhabitants of Jerusalem made Ahaziah, his youngest son, king in his stead, since all the older sons had been slain by the band that had come into the fort with the Arabs. Thus Ahaziah, son of Jehoram, reigned as king of Judah. 2 He was twenty-two years old when he became king, and he reigned one year in Jerusalem. His mother was named Athaliah, daughter of Omri. 3 He, too, followed the ways of the house of Ahab, because his mother counseled him to act sinfully. 4 To his own destruction, he did evil in the sight of the LORD, as did the house of Ahab, since they were his counselors after the death of his father.

5 He was also following their counsel when he accompanied Jehoram, son of Ahab, king of Israel, to battle against Hazael, king of Aram, at Ramoth-gilead. There Jehoram was wounded by the Arameans. 6 He returned to Jezreel to be healed of the wounds he had received at Rama in his battle against Hazael, king of Aram. Because of this illness, Ahaziah, son of Jehoram, king of Judah, went down to visit Jehoram, son of Ahab, in Jezreel. 7* Now it was willed by God for Ahaziah's downfall that he should join Jehoram, for after his arrival he rode out with Jehoram to Jehu, son of Nimshi, whom the LORD had anointed to cut down the house of Ahab. 8* While Jehu was executing judgment on the house of Ahab, he also encountered the princes of Judah and the nephews of Ahaziah who were his attendants, and he slew them. 9*† Then he looked for Ahaziah himself. They caught him where he was hiding in Samaria and brought him to Jehu, who put him to death. They buried him, for they said, "He was the grandson of Jehoshaphat, who sought the LORD with his whole heart." There remained in Ahaziah's house no one powerful enough to wield the kingship.

Usurpation of Athaliah

10* When Athaliah, mother of Ahaziah, learned that her son was dead, she proceeded to kill off all the royal offspring of the house of Judah. 11 But Jehosheba, a royal princess, secretly took Ahaziah's son Joash from among the king's sons who were about to be slain, and put him and his nurse in a bedroom. In this way Jehosheba, who was the daughter of King Jehoram, a sister of Ahaziah, and wife of Jehoiada the priest, hid the child from Athaliah's sight, so that she did not put him to death. 12 For six years he remained hidden with them in the house of God, while Athaliah ruled over the land.

---

† **22, 9:** This account of the death of Ahaziah of Judah is not derived from 2 Kgs 9, 27f, with which it is at variance.

21, 20: 2 Kgs 8, 24.   22, 8: 2 Kgs 10, 12ff.
22, 1–6: 2 Kgs 8, 24–29.   22, 9: 2 Kgs 9, 27f.
22, 7: 2 Kgs 9, 21; 10, 12ff.   22, 10ff: 2 Kgs 11, 1ff.

Athaliah Overthrown

23 ¹* In the seventh year, Jehoiada took courage and entered a conspiracy with certain captains: Azariah, son of Jehoram; Ishmael, son of Jehohanan; Azariah, son of Obed; Masseiah, son of Adaiah; and Elishaphat, son of Zichri. ² They journeyed about Judah, gathering the Levites from all the cities of Judah and also the heads of the Israelite families. When they had come to Jerusalem, ³ the whole assembly made a covenant with the king in the house of God. Jehoiada said to them: "Here is the king's son who must reign, as the LORD promised concerning the sons of David. ⁴ This is what you must do: a third of your number, both priests and Levites, who come in on the sabbath must guard the thresholds, ⁵ another third must be at the king's palace, and the final third at the Foundation Gate, when all the people will be in the courts of the LORD's temple. ⁶ Let no one enter the LORD's house except the priests and those Levites who are ministering. They may enter because they are holy; but all the other people must observe the prescriptions of the LORD. ⁷ The Levites shall surround the king on all sides, each with his weapon drawn. Whoever tries to enter the house must be slain. Stay with the king wherever he goes."

⁸* The Levites and all Judah did just as Jehoiada the priest commanded. Each brought his men, those who were to come in on the sabbath as well as those who were to depart on the sabbath, since Jehoiada the priest had not dismissed any of the divisions. ⁹ Jehoiada the priest gave the captains the spears, shields and bucklers of King David which were in the house of God. ¹⁰ He stationed all the people, each with his spear in hand, from the southern to the northern extremity of the enclosure, around the altar and the temple on the king's behalf. ¹¹ Then they brought out the king's son, set the crown and the insignia upon him, and made him king. Jehoiada and his sons anointed him, and they cried, "Long live the king!"

¹² When Athaliah heard the din of the people running and acclaiming the king, she went to the people in the temple of the LORD. ¹³† She looked, and there was the king standing beside his pillar at the entrance, the officers and the trumpeters around him, and all the people of the land rejoicing and blowing trumpets, while the singers with their musical instruments were leading the acclaim. Athaliah

tore her garments and cried out, "Treason! treason!" ¹⁴ Then Jehoiada the priest sent out the captains who were in command of the army; he said to them: "Take her outside through the ranks, and if anyone tries to follow her, let him die by the sword. For," the priest continued, "you must not put her to death in the LORD's temple." ¹⁵ So they seized her, and when she arrived at the entrance to the Horse Gate of the palace, they put her to death there.

¹⁶ Then Jehoiada made a covenant between himself and all the people and the king, that they should be the LORD's people. ¹⁷ And all the people went to the temple of Baal and tore it down. They smashed its altars and images, and they slew Mattan, the priest of Baal, before the altars. ¹⁸* Then Jehoiada gave the charge of the LORD's temple into the hands of the levitical priests, to whom David had assigned turns in the temple for offering the holocausts of the LORD, as is written in the law of Moses, with rejoicing and song, as David had provided. ¹⁹ Moreover, he stationed guards at the gates of the LORD's temple, so that no one unclean in any respect might enter. ²⁰ Then he took the captains, the nobles, the rulers among the people, and all the people of the land, and led the king out of the LORD's house. When they had come within the upper gate of the king's house, they seated the king upon the royal throne. ²¹ All the people of the land rejoiced and the city was quiet, now that Athaliah had been put to death by the sword.

The Temple Restored

24 ¹* Joash was seven years old when he became king, and he reigned forty years in Jerusalem. His mother, named Zibiah, was from Beer-sheba. ² Joash did what was pleasing to the LORD as long as Jehoiada the priest lived. ³ Jehoiada provided him with two wives, and he became the father of sons and daughters.

⁴ After some time, Joash decided to restore the LORD's temple. ⁵† He called together the priests and Levites and said to them: "Go out to all the cities of Judah and collect money from all Israel that you may repair the house of your God over the years. You must hasten this affair." But the Levites did not hasten. ⁶* Then the king summoned Jehoiada, who was in charge, and said to him: "Why have you not required the Levites to bring in from Judah and Jerusalem the tax levied by Moses, the servant of the

---

† **23, 13:** *Beside his pillar:* the king had a special place in the eastern gateway of the temple court that contained the altar of holocausts. He occupied this place on feasts and sabbaths at the time of the statutory offerings, or when he made freewill offerings of his own; cf 2 Kgs 11, 4 and also Ez 46, 1–8 for a later reflection of this.

24, 5: *Collect money:* according to 2 Kgs 12, 5, the people themselves brought the money to the temple; it consisted, at least in part, of voluntary contributions. At the time of the Chronicler (see Neh

10, 32) there was a fixed head tax for the upkeep of the temple (2 Chr 34, 9), based on Ex 30, 12–16. This was still in force in New Testament times (Mt 17, 24f).

23, 1–17.19ff: 2 Kgs 11, 4–20.   24, 1–14: 2 Kgs 12, 1–13.
   23, 8: 2 Kgs 11, 9; 1 Chr 24,   24, 6: Ex 25, 1–9; Neh 10,
     19.   33.
   23, 18: 1 Chr 23, 13.

LORD, and by the assembly of Israel, for the tent of the testimony?" 7 For the wicked Athaliah and her sons had damaged the house of God and had even turned over to the Baals the dedicated resources of the LORD's temple.

8* At the king's command, therefore, they made a chest, which they put outside the gate of the LORD's temple. 9* They had it proclaimed throughout Judah and Jerusalem that the tax which Moses, the servant of God, had imposed on Israel in the desert should be brought to the LORD. 10 All the princes and the people rejoiced; they brought what was asked and cast it into the chest until it was filled. 11 Whenever the chest was brought to the royal officials by the Levites and they saw that it contained much money, the royal scribe and an overseer for the high priest came, emptied the chest, then took it back and returned it to its place. This they did day after day until they had collected a large sum of money. 12 Then the king and Jehoiada gave it to the workmen in charge of the labor on the LORD's temple, who hired masons and carpenters to restore the temple, and also iron- and bronze-smiths to repair it. 13 The workmen labored, and the task of restoration progressed under their hands. They restored the house of God according to its original form, and reinforced it. 14 After they had finished, they brought the rest of the money to the king and to Jehoiada, who had it made into utensils for the LORD's temple, utensils for the service and the holocausts, and basins and other gold and silver utensils. They offered holocausts in the LORD's temple continually throughout the lifetime of Jehoiada. 15 Jehoiada lived to a ripe old age; he was a hundred and thirty years old when he died. 16 He was buried in the City of David with the kings, because he had done good in Israel, in particular with respect to God and his temple.

Apostasy of King Joash

17 After the death of Jehoiada, the princes of Judah came and paid homage to the king, and the king then listened to them. 18* They forsook the temple of the LORD, the God of their fathers, and began to serve the sacred poles and the idols; and because of this crime of theirs, wrath came upon Judah and Jerusalem. 19 Although prophets were sent to them to convert them to the LORD, the people would not listen to their warnings. 20 Then the spirit of God possessed Zechariah, son of Jehoiada the priest. He took his stand above the people and said to them: "God says, 'Why are you transgressing the LORD's commands, so that you cannot prosper? Be-

cause you have abandoned the LORD, he has abandoned you.' " 21 But they conspired against him, and at the king's order they stoned him to death in the court of the LORD's temple. 22 Thus King Joash was unmindful of the devotion shown him by Jehoiada, Zechariah's father, and slew his son. And as he was dying, he said, "May the LORD see and avenge."

Retribution

23* At the turn of the year a force of Arameans came up against Joash. They invaded Judah and Jerusalem, did away with all the princes of the people, and sent all their spoil to the king of Damascus. 24* Though the Aramean force came with few men, the LORD surrendered a very large force into their power, because Judah had abandoned the LORD, the God of their fathers. So punishment was meted out to Joash. 25* After the Arameans had departed from him, leaving him in grievous suffering, his servants conspired against him because of the murder of the son of Jehoiada the priest. They killed him on his sickbed. He was buried in the City of David, but not in the tombs of the kings.

26 These conspired against him: Zabad, son of Shimeath from Ammon, and Jehozabad, son of Shimrith from Moab. 27* Of his sons, and the great tribute imposed on him, and of his rebuilding of the house of God, there is a written account in the midrash of the book of the kings. His son Amaziah succeeded him as king.

Campaign in Edom

25 1* Amaziah was twenty-five years old when he became king, and he reigned twenty-nine years in Jerusalem. His mother, named Jehoaddan, was from Jerusalem. 2 He did what was pleasing in the sight of the LORD, though not wholeheartedly. 3 After he had strengthened his hold on the kingdom, he slew those of his servants who had killed the king, his father; 4* but he did not put their children to death, for he acted according to what is written in the law, in the Book of Moses, as the LORD commanded: "Fathers shall not be put to death for their children, nor children for their fathers; but only for his own guilt shall a man be put to death."

5 Amaziah mustered Judah and placed them, out of all Judah and Benjamin according to their ancestral houses, under leaders of thousands and of hundreds. When he had counted those of twenty years and over, he found them to be three hundred thousand picked men fit for war, capable of handling

---

24, 8: 2 Chr 34, 9.
24, 9: Ex 30, 13.
24, 18: Ex 34, 13.

24, 23: 2 Kgs 12, 17f.
24, 24: Dt 32, 30.
24, 25f: 2 Kgs 12, 21f.

24, 27: 2 Kgs 12, 19.22.
25, 1–4: 2 Kgs 14, 1–6.

25, 4: Dt 24, 16; 2 Kgs 14, 5f; Ez 18, 20.

lance and shield. 6 He also hired a hundred thousand valiant warriors from Israel for a hundred talents of silver. 7 But a man of God came to him and said: "O king, let not the army of Israel go with you, for the LORD is not with Israel, with any Ephraimite. 8 Instead, go on your own, strongly prepared for the conflict; otherwise the LORD will defeat you in the face of the enemy. It is God who has the power to reinforce or to defeat." 9 Amaziah answered the man of God, "But what is to be done about the hundred talents that I paid for the troops of Israel?" The man of God replied, "The LORD can give you much more than that." 10 Amaziah then disbanded the troops that had come to him from Ephraim, and sent them home. They, however, became furiously angry with Judah, and returned home blazing with resentment.

11* Amaziah now assumed command of his army. They proceeded to the Valley of Salt, and there they killed ten thousand men of Seir. 12 The Judahites also brought back another ten thousand alive, whom they led to the summit of the Rock and then cast down, so that they were all crushed. 13 Meanwhile, the mercenaries whom Amaziah had dismissed from battle service with him raided the cities of Judah from Samaria to Beth-horon. They killed three thousand of the inhabitants and took away much booty.

Infidelity of Amaziah

14 When Amaziah returned from his conquest of the Edomites he brought back with him the gods of the people of Seir, which he set up as his own gods; he bowed down before them and offered sacrifice to them. 15 Then the anger of the LORD blazed out against Amaziah, and he sent a prophet to him who said: "Why have you had recourse to this people's gods that could not save their own people from your hand?" 16 While he was still speaking, however, the king said to him: "Have you been made the king's counselor? Be silent! Why should it be necessary to kill you?" Therefore the prophet desisted. "I know, however," he said, "that God has let you take counsel to your own destruction, because you have done this thing and have refused to hear my counsel."

Retribution

17* Having taken counsel, King Amaziah of Judah sent messengers to Joash, son of Jehoahaz, son of Jehu, the king of Israel, saying, "Come, let us meet each other face to face." 18* King Joash of Israel sent this reply to King Amaziah of Judah: "The thistle of the Lebanon sent a message to the cedar of the Lebanon, saying, 'Give your daughter to my son for his wife.' But the wild beasts of the Lebanon passed by and trampled the thistle down. 19 You are thinking, 'See, I have beaten Edom!', and thus ambition makes you proud. Remain at home. Why involve yourself, and Judah with you, in misfortune and failure?" 20 But Amaziah would not listen, for God had determined to hand them over because they had had recourse to the gods of Edom.

21 Therefore King Joash of Israel advanced and he and King Amaziah met in battle at Bethshemesh of Judah. 22 There Judah was defeated by Israel, and all the Judean soldiers fled homeward. 23 King Joash of Israel captured Amaziah, king of Judah, son of Joash, son of Jehoahaz, at Bethshemesh and brought him to Jerusalem. Then he tore down the wall of Jerusalem from the Ephraim Gate to the Corner Gate, a distance of four hundred cubits. 24† He took away all the gold and silver and all the vessels he found in the house of God with Obed-edom, together with the treasures of the palace, and hostages as well. Then he returned to Samaria.

25* Amaziah, son of Joash, king of Judah, survived Joash, son of Jehoahaz, king of Israel, by fifteen years. 26 The rest of the acts of Amaziah, first and last, can be found written, as is well known, in the book of the kings of Judah and Israel. 27 Now from the time that Amaziah ceased to follow the LORD, a conspiracy was formed against him in Jerusalem; hence he fled to Lachish. But they pursued him to Lachish and put him to death there. 28† They brought him back on horses and buried him with his ancestors in the City of Judah.

The Works of Uzziah

26 1* All the people of Judah chose Uzziah, though he was but sixteen years of age, and proclaimed him king to succeed his father Amaziah. 2 He rebuilt Elath and restored it to Judah; this was after King Amaziah had gone to rest with his ancestors. 3 Uzziah was sixteen years old when he became king, and he reigned fifty-two years in Jerusalem. His mother, named Jecoliah, was from Jerusalem. 4 He pleased the LORD, just as his father Amaziah had done.

---

† **25, 24:** *With Obed-edom:* possibly a reference to the priest of an Edomite false worship (cf v 14), if not to a levitical family of gatekeepers; cf 1 Chr 15, 18; 26, 12–15.

25, 28: *The City of Judah:* in the parallel passage of 2 Kgs 14, 20, the City of David. The Chronicler is referring, by this term, to the capital of Judah, Jerusalem.

---

* **25, 11:** 2 Kgs 14, 7.   2 Kgs 14, 9.
25, 17–24: 2 Kgs 14, 8–14.   **25, 25–28:** 2 Kgs 14, 17–20.
   25, 18: Jgs 9, 7–15;   **26, 1–4:** 2 Kgs 14, 21f; 15, 1ff.

5*† He was prepared to seek God as long as Zechariah lived, who taught him to fear God; and as long as he sought the LORD, God made him prosper. 6* He went out and fought the Philistines and razed the walls of Gath, Jabneh and Ashdod [and built cities in the district of Ashdod and in Philistia]. 7 God helped him against the Philistines, against the Arabs who dwelt in Gurbaal, and against the Meunites. 8 The Ammonites paid tribute to Uzziah and his fame spread as far as Egypt, for he grew stronger and stronger. 9 Moreover, Uzziah built towers in Jerusalem at the Corner Gate, at the Valley Gate, and at the Angle, and he fortified them. 10 He built towers in the desert and dug numerous cisterns, for he had many cattle. He had plowmen in the foothills and the plains, and vinedressers in the highlands and the garden land. He was a lover of the soil.

11 Uzziah also had a standing army of fit soldiers divided into bands according to the number in which they were mustered by Jeiel the scribe and Maaseiah the recorder, under the command of Hananiah, one of the king's officials. 12 The entire number of family heads over these valiant warriors was two thousand six hundred, 13 and at their disposal was a mighty army of three hundred seven thousand five hundred fighting men of great valor to help the king against his enemies. 14 Uzziah provided for them—for the entire army—bucklers, lances, helmets, breastplates, bows and slingstones. 15 He also built machines in Jerusalem, devices contrived to stand on the towers and at the angles of the walls to shoot arrows and cast large stones. His fame spread far and wide, and his power was ascribed to the marvelous help he had received.

Pride and Fall

16 But after he had become strong, he became proud to his own destruction and broke faith with the LORD, his God. He entered the temple of the LORD to make an offering on the altar of incense. 17 But Azariah the priest, and with him eighty other priests of the LORD, courageous men, followed him. 18* They opposed King Uzziah, saying to him: "It is not for you, Uzziah, to burn incense to the LORD, but for the priests, the sons of Aaron, who have been consecrated for this purpose. Leave the sanctuary, for you have broken faith and no longer have a part in the glory that comes from the LORD God." 19* Uzziah, who was holding a censer for burning the incense, became angry, but at the moment he showed his anger to the priests, while they were looking at him in the house of the LORD beside the altar of incense, leprosy broke out on his forehead. 20 Azariah the chief priest and all the other priests examined him, and when they saw that his forehead was leprous, they expelled him from the temple. He himself fled willingly, for the LORD had afflicted him. 21* King Uzziah remained a leper to the day of his death. As a leper he dwelt in a segregated house, for he was excluded from the house of the LORD. Therefore his son Jotham was regent of the palace and ruled the people of the land.

22 The prophet Isaiah, son of Amos, wrote the rest of the acts of Uzziah, first and last. 23 Uzziah rested with his ancestors; he was buried with them in the field adjoining the royal cemetery, for they said, "He was a leper." His son Jotham succeeded him as king.

Jotham

27 1* Jotham was twenty-five years old when he became king, and he reigned sixteen years in Jerusalem. His mother was named Jerusa, daughter of Zadok. 2 He pleased the LORD just as his father Uzziah had done, though he did not enter the temple of the LORD; the people, however, continued to act sinfully.

3 He built the upper gate of the LORD's house and had much construction done on the wall of Ophel. 4 Moreover, he built cities in the hill country of Judah, and in the forest land he set up fortresses and towers. 5 He fought with the king of the Ammonites and conquered them. That year the Ammonites paid him one hundred talents of silver, together with ten thousand kors of wheat and ten thousand of barley. They brought the same to him also in the second and in the third year. 6 Thus Jotham continued to grow strong because he lived resolutely in the presence of the LORD, his God. 7* The rest of the acts of Jotham, his wars and his activities, can be found written in the book of the kings of Israel and Judah. 8 He was twenty-five years old when he became king, and he reigned sixteen years in Jerusalem. 9 Jotham rested with his ancestors and was buried in the City of David, and his son Ahaz succeeded him as king.

III: Reforms of Hezekiah and Josiah

Impiety of Ahaz

28 1* Ahaz was twenty years old when he became king, and he reigned sixteen years in Jerusalem. He did not please the LORD as his forefather David had done, 2 but conducted himself

---

26, 5: *Zechariah:* this person, not otherwise identified, is referred to in language suggesting a pious layman rather than a priest or prophet; cf 2 Chr 29, 1.

26, 5: 2 Chr 24, 2.
26, 6: Am 1, 8.
26, 18: Ex 30, 7.
26, 19: Nm 12, 10.
26, 21ff: 2 Kgs 15, 5ff;

Lv 13, 46; Nm 19, 20.
27, 1–3: 2 Kgs 15, 32–35.
27, 7–9: 2 Kgs 15, 36ff.
28, 1–4: 2 Kgs 16, 1–4.

like the kings of Israel and even made molten idols of the Baals. ³* Moreover, he offered sacrifice in the Valley of Ben-hinnom, and immolated his sons by fire according to the abominable practice of the nations which the LORD had cleared out before the Israelites. ⁴ He offered sacrifice and incense on the high places, on hills, and under every leafy tree.

Retribution

⁵* Therefore the LORD, his God, delivered him into the power of the king of Aram. The Arameans defeated him and carried away captive a large number of his people, whom they brought to Damascus. He was also delivered into the power of the king of Israel, who defeated him with great slaughter. ⁶ For Pekah, son of Remaliah, slew one hundred and twenty thousand of Judah in a single day, all of them valiant men, because they had abandoned the LORD, the God of their fathers. ⁷ Zichri, an Ephraimite warrior, killed Maaseiah, the king's son, and Azrikam, the master of the palace, and also Elkanah, who was second to the king. ⁸ The Israelites took away as captives two hundred thousand of their brethren's wives, sons and daughters; they also took from them much plunder, which they brought to Samaria.

The Prophecy of Oded

⁹ In Samaria there was a prophet of the LORD by the name of Oded. He went out to meet the army returning to Samaria and said to them: "It was because the LORD, the God of your fathers, was angry with Judah that he delivered them into your hands. You, however, have slaughtered them with a fury that has reached up to heaven. ¹⁰ And now you are planning to make the children of Judah and Jerusalem your slaves and bondwomen. Are not you yourselves, therefore, guilty of a crime against the LORD, your God? ¹¹ Now listen to me: send back the captives you have carried off from among your brethren, for the burning anger of the LORD is upon you."

¹² At this, some of the Ephraimite leaders, Azariah, son of Johanan, Berechiah, son of Meshillemoth, Jehizkiah, son of Shallum, and Amasa, son of Hadlai, themselves stood up in opposition to those who had returned from the war. ¹³ They said to them: "Do not bring the captives here, for what you propose will make us guilty before the LORD and increase our sins and our guilt. Our guilt is already great, and there is a burning anger upon Is-

rael." ¹⁴ Therefore the soldiers left their captives and the plunder before the princes and the whole assembly. ¹⁵* Then the men just named proceeded to help the captives. All of them who were naked they clothed from the booty; they clothed them, put sandals on their feet, gave them food and drink, anointed them, and all who were weak they set on asses. They brought them to Jericho, the city of palms, to their brethren. Then they returned to Samaria.

Further Sins of Ahaz

¹⁶* At that time King Ahaz sent an appeal for help to the kings of Assyria. ¹⁷* The Edomites had returned, attacked Judah, and carried off captives. ¹⁸ The Philistines too had raided the cities of the foothills and the Negeb of Judah; they captured Beth-shemesh, Aijalon, Gederoth, Soco and its dependencies, Timnah and its dependencies, and Gimzo and its dependencies, and occupied them. ¹⁹† For the LORD had brought Judah low because of Ahaz, king of Israel, who let Judah go its own way and proved utterly faithless to the LORD. ²⁰* Tilgath-pilneser, king of Assyria, did indeed come to him, but to oppress him rather than to help him. ²¹* Though Ahaz plundered the LORD'S house and the houses of the king and the princes to make payment to the king of Assyria, it availed him nothing.

²² While he was already in distress, the same King Ahaz became even more unfaithful to the LORD. ²³* He sacrificed to the gods of Damascus who had defeated him, saying, "Since it was the gods of the kings of Aram who helped them, I will sacrifice to them that they may help me also." However, they only caused further disaster to him and to all Israel. ²⁴* Ahaz gathered up the utensils of God's house and broke them in pieces. He closed the doors of the LORD'S house and had altars made for himself in every corner of Jerusalem. ²⁵ In every city throughout Judah he set up high places to offer sacrifice to other gods. Thus he angered the LORD, the God of his fathers.

²⁶* The rest of his deeds and his activities, first and last, can be found written in the book of the kings of Judah and Israel. ²⁷ Ahaz rested with his ancestors and was buried in Jerusalem—in the city, for they did not bring him to the tombs of the kings of Israel. His son Hezekiah succeeded him as king.

28, 19: *Ahaz, king of Israel:* in the period of the divided kingdom the term king of Israel would elsewhere mean "king of the northern Kingdom of Israel."

28, 3: 2 Kgs 16, 3; Lv 18, 21.
28, 5: 2 Kgs 16, 5; Is 7, 1–9.
28, 15: Lk 10, 25–37.
28, 16: 2 Kgs 16, 7.

28, 17: 2 Kgs 16, 6.
28, 20: 2 Kgs 16, 10; Is 7, 17–20; 8, 5–8.
28, 21: 2 Kgs 16, 8.
28, 23: 2 Kgs 16, 12f;
Is 10, 20.
28, 24: 2 Chr 29, 3; 30, 14; 2 Kgs 16, 17.
28, 26f: 2 Kgs 16, 19f.

2
CHR

Reforms of Hezekiah

29 [1]* Hezekiah was twenty-five years old when he became king, and he reigned twenty-nine years in Jerusalem. His mother was named Abia, daughter of Zechariah. [2] He pleased the LORD just as his forefather David had done. [3]* It was he who, in the first month of the first year of his reign, opened the doors of the LORD'S house and repaired them. [4] He summoned the priests and Levites, gathered them in the open space to the east, [5] and said to them: "Listen to me, you Levites! Sanctify yourselves now and sanctify the house of the LORD, the God of your fathers, and clean out the filth from the sanctuary. [6] Our fathers acted faithlessly and did evil in the eyes of the LORD, our God. They abandoned him, turned away their faces from the LORD'S dwelling, and turned their backs on him. [7]* They also closed the doors of the vestibule, extinguished the lamps, and refused to burn incense and offer holocausts in the sanctuary to the honor of the God of Israel. [8]* Therefore the anger of the LORD has come upon Judah and Jerusalem; he has made them an object of terror, astonishment and mockery, as you see with your own eyes. [9] For our fathers, as you know, fell by the sword, and our sons, our daughters and our wives have been taken captive because of this. [10] Now, I intend to make a covenant with the LORD, the God of Israel, that his burning anger may withdraw from us. [11] My sons, be not negligent any longer, for it is you whom the LORD has chosen to stand before him, to minister to him, to be his ministers and to offer incense."

[12] Then the Levites arose: Mahath, son of Amasai, and Joel, son of Azariah, descendants of the Kohathites; of the sons of Merari: Kish, son of Abdi, and Azariah, son of Jehallel; of the Gershonites: Joah, son of Zimmah, and Eden, son of Joah; [13] of the sons of Elizaphan: Shimri and Jeuel; of the sons of Asaph: Zechariah and Mattaniah; [14] of the sons of Heman: Jehuel and Shimei; of the sons of Jeduthun: Shemiah and Uzziel. [15] They gathered their brethren together and sanctified themselves; then they came as the king had ordered, to cleanse the LORD'S house in keeping with his words.

[16] The priests entered the interior of the LORD'S house to cleanse it; and whatever they found in the LORD'S temple that was unclean they brought out to the court of the LORD'S house, where the Levites took it from them and carried it out to the Kidron Valley. [17] They began the work of consecration on the first day of the first month, and on the eighth day of the month they arrived at the vestibule of the LORD; they consecrated the LORD'S house during eight days, and on the sixteenth day of the first month, they had finished. [18] Then they went inside to King Hezekiah and said: "We have cleansed the entire house of the LORD, the altar of holocausts with all its utensils, and the table for the showbread with all its utensils. [19] All the articles which King Ahaz during his reign had thrown away because of his apostasy, we have restored and consecrated, and they are now before the LORD'S altar."

The Rite of Expiation

[20] Then King Hezekiah hastened to convoke the princes of the city and went up to the LORD'S house. [21] Seven bulls, seven rams, seven lambs and seven he-goats were brought for a sin offering for the kingdom, for the sanctuary, and for Judah, and he ordered the sons of Aaron, the priests, to offer them on the altar of the LORD. [22] They slaughtered the bulls, and the priests collected the blood and cast it

Renewing Your Prayer Life

Hezekiah was one of Judah's reformer kings. Before he became king, the people had neglected the Temple in Jerusalem for a long time. At the beginning of Hezekiah's reign, the Temple needed some intense effort to get it back in order.

Sometimes, our prayer life suffers from neglect too. We get busy and do not take enough time to pray, or forget to pray altogether. When we decide to commit ourselves to regular prayer, it may take some intense effort to get rid of our bad habits.

Imagine your prayer life as being like the Temple. How does it look? Is it in need of a little dusting? full of cobwebs? ready for major renovation? What steps can you take to make sure you do not neglect your prayer life?

▸ 2 Chr 29, 1–11

29, 1ff: 2 Kgs 18, 1ff.   29, 8f: Lv 26, 32f; Dt 28, 25;
29, 3: 2 Chr 28, 24.   Jer 25, 18.
29, 7: 2 Kgs 16, 15.

on the altar. Then they slaughtered the rams and cast the blood on the altar; then they slaughtered the lambs and cast the blood on the altar. 23 Then the he-goats for the sin offering were led before the king and the assembly, who laid their hands upon them. 24 The priests then slaughtered them and offered their blood on the altar to atone for the sin of all Israel; for "The holocaust and the sin offering," the king had said, "is for all Israel."

25 He stationed the Levites in the LORD's house with cymbals, harps and lyres according to the prescriptions of David, of Gad the king's seer, and of Nathan the prophet; for the prescriptions were from the LORD through his prophets. 26 The Levites were stationed with the instruments of David, and the priests with the trumpets. 27 Then Hezekiah ordered the holocaust to be sacrificed on the altar, and in the same instant that the holocaust began, they also began the song of the LORD, to the accompaniment of the trumpets and the instruments of David, king of Israel. 28 The entire assembly prostrated itself, and they continued to sing the song and to sound the trumpets until the holocaust had been completed. 29 As the holocaust was completed, the king and all who were with him knelt and prostrated themselves. 30 King Hezekiah and the princes then commanded the Levites to sing the praises of the LORD in the words of David and of Asaph the seer. They sang praises till their joy was full, then fell down and prostrated themselves.

31 Hezekiah now spoke out this command: "You have undertaken a work for the LORD. Approach, and bring forward the sacrifices and thank offerings for the house of the LORD." Then the assembly brought forward the sacrifices and thank offerings and all the holocausts which were free-will offerings. 32 The number of holocausts that the assembly brought forward was seventy oxen, one hundred rams, and two hundred lambs: all of these as a holocaust to the LORD. 33 As consecrated gifts there were six hundred oxen and three thousand sheep. 34* Since the priests were too few in number to be able to skin all the victims for the holocausts, their brethren the Levites assisted them until the task was completed and the priests had sanctified themselves; the Levites, in fact, were more willing than the priests to sanctify themselves. 35 Also, the holocausts were many, along with the fat of the peace offerings and the libations for the holocausts. Thus the service of the house of the LORD was reestablished. 36 Hezekiah and all the people rejoiced over what God had reestablished for the people, and at how suddenly this had been done.

Invitation to the Passover

30 1* Hezekiah sent a message to all Israel and Judah, and even wrote letters to Ephraim and Manasseh saying that they should come to the house of the LORD in Jerusalem to celebrate the Passover in honor of the LORD, the God of Israel. 2* The king, his princes, and the entire assembly in Jerusalem had agreed to celebrate the Passover during the second month, 3 for they could not celebrate it at the time of the restoration: the priests had not sanctified themselves in sufficient numbers, and the people were not gathered at Jerusalem. 4 When this proposal had been approved by the king and the entire assembly, 5 they issued a decree to be proclaimed throughout all Israel from Beer-sheba to Dan, that everyone should come to Jerusalem to celebrate the Passover in honor of the LORD, the God of Israel; for not many had kept it in the manner prescribed. 6 Accordingly the couriers, with the letters written by the king and his princes, traversed all Israel and Judah, and at the king's command they said: "Israelites, return to the LORD, the God of Abraham, Isaac and Israel, that he may return to you, the remnant left from the hands of the Assyrian kings. 7* Be not like your fathers and your brethren who proved faithless to the LORD, the God of their fathers, so that he delivered them over to desolation, as you yourselves now see. 8 Be not obstinate, as your fathers were; extend your hands to the LORD and come to his sanctuary that he has consecrated forever, and serve the LORD, your God, that he may turn away his burning anger from you. 9* For when you return to the LORD, your brethren and your children will find mercy with their captors and return to this land; for merciful and compassionate is the LORD, your God, and he will not turn away his face from you if you return to him."

10 So the couriers passed from city to city in the land of Ephraim and Manasseh and as far as Zebulun, but they were derided and scoffed at. 11 Nevertheless, some from Asher, Manasseh and Zebulun humbled themselves and came to Jerusalem. 12 In Judah, however, the power of God brought it about that the people were of one mind to carry out the command of the king and the princes in accordance with the word of the LORD. 13 Thus many people gathered in Jerusalem to celebrate the feast of Unleavened Bread in the second month; it was a very great assembly.

The Passover Celebrated

14* They proceeded to take down the altars that were in Jerusalem; also they removed all the altars

---

of incense and cast them into the Kidron Valley. 15 They slaughtered the Passover on the fourteenth day of the second month. The priests and Levites, touched with shame, sanctified themselves and brought holocausts into the house of the LORD. 16 They stood in the places prescribed for them according to the law of Moses, the man of God. The priests sprinkled the blood given them by the Levites; 17* for many in the assembly had not sanctified themselves, and the Levites were in charge of slaughtering the Passover victims for all who were unclean and therefore could not consecrate them to the LORD. 18 The greater part of the people, in fact, chiefly from Ephraim, Manasseh, Issachar and Zebulun, had not cleansed themselves. Nevertheless they ate the Passover, contrary to the prescription; for Hezekiah prayed for them, saying, "May the LORD, who is good, grant pardon to 19 everyone who has resolved to seek God, the LORD, the God of his fathers, though he be not clean as holiness requires." 20 The LORD heard Hezekiah and spared the people.

21 Thus the Israelites who were in Jerusalem celebrated the feast of Unleavened Bread with great rejoicing for seven days, and the Levites and the priests sang the praises of the LORD day after day with all their strength. 22 Hezekiah spoke encouragingly to all the Levites who had shown themselves well skilled in the service of the LORD. And when they had completed the seven days of festival, slaying peace offerings and singing praises to the LORD, the God of their fathers, 23 the whole assembly agreed to celebrate another seven days. With joy, therefore, they continued the festivity seven days longer. 24 King Hezekiah of Judah had contributed a thousand bulls and seven thousand sheep to the assembly, and the princes had contributed to the assembly a thousand bulls and ten thousand sheep. The priests sanctified themselves in great numbers, 25 and the whole assembly of Judah rejoiced, together with the priests and Levites and the rest of the assembly that had come from Israel, as well as the sojourners from the land of Israel and those that lived in Judah. 26 There was great rejoicing in Jerusalem, for since the days of Solomon, son of David, king of Israel, there had not been the like in the city. 27 Then the levitical priests rose and blessed the people; their voice was heard and their prayer reached heaven, God's holy dwelling.

Liturgical Reform

31 1* After all this was over, those Israelites who had been present went forth to the cities of Judah and smashed the sacred pillars, cut down the sacred poles, and tore down the high places and altars throughout Judah, Benjamin, Ephraim and Manasseh, until all were destroyed. Then the Israelites returned to their various cities, each to his own possession.

2 Hezekiah reestablished the classes of the priests and the Levites according to their former classification, assigning to each priest and Levite his proper service, whether in regard to holocausts or peace offerings, thanksgiving or praise, or ministering in the gates of the encampment of the LORD. 3* From his own wealth the king allotted a portion for holocausts, those of morning and evening and those on sabbaths, new moons and festivals, as prescribed in the law of the LORD. 4 He also commanded the people living in Jerusalem to provide the support of the priests and Levites, that they might devote themselves entirely to the law of the LORD.

5* As soon as the order was promulgated, the Israelites brought, in great quantities, the best of their grain, wine, oil and honey, and all the produce of the fields; they gave a generous tithe of everything. 6* Israelites and Judahites living in other cities of Judah also brought in tithes of oxen, sheep, and things that had been consecrated to the LORD, their God; these they brought in and set out in heaps. 7† It was in the third month that they began to establish these heaps, and they completed them in the seventh month. 8 When Hezekiah and the princes had come and seen the heaps, they blessed the LORD and his people Israel. 9 Then Hezekiah questioned the priests and the Levites concerning the heaps, 10* and the priest Azariah, head of the house of Zadoc, answered him, "Since they began to bring the offerings to the house of the LORD, we have eaten to the full and have had much left over, for the LORD has blessed his people. This great supply is what was left over."

11 Hezekiah then gave orders that chambers should be constructed in the house of the LORD. When this had been done, 12 the offerings, tithes and consecrated things were deposited there in safekeeping. The overseer of these things was Conaniah the Levite, and his brother Shimei was second in charge. 13 Jehiel, Azaziah, Nathan, Asahel, Jerimoth, Jozabad, Eliel, Ismachiah, Mahath and Bena-

---

31, 7: *Third month . . . seventh month:* between the feast of Pentecost and that of Booths, an interval without rain in Palestine, at the end of which the problem of storage (v 11) would become more urgent.

30, 17: 2 Chr 35, 6.
31, 1: 2 Chr 34, 3f; 2 Kgs 18, 4.
31, 3: 1 Chr 29, 3; Ez 45, 17; Nm 28—29.
31, 5: Nm 18, 8–24; Dt 14, 22f.
31, 6: Nm 12, 44–47; 13, 10–13.
31, 10: Lv 25, 19–22.

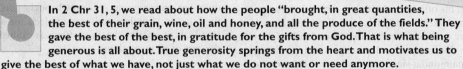

Giving the Best of the Best

In 2 Chr 31, 5, we read about how the people "brought, in great quantities, the best of their grain, wine, oil and honey, and all the produce of the fields." They gave the best of the best, in gratitude for the gifts from God. That is what being generous is all about. True generosity springs from the heart and motivates us to give the best of what we have, not just what we do not want or need anymore.

The word *tithe* appears in this verse. For the Israelites, to tithe meant to give 10 percent of one's earnings as a tax for the upkeep of the Temple. Some Christians continue the spirit of tithing by giving 10 percent of all they earn to the church and other charities. They are offering God their best, the firstfruits of their labor (see Lk 21, 1–4 and Acts 4, 32–37).

We all need to search our heart and continue this tradition of offering our best back to God—not because it makes us look good and gives us "extra points" with God, but because it comes from our gratitude for the gifts we have received.

▸ 2 Chr 31, 2–10

---

iah were supervisors subject to Conaniah and his brother Shimei by appointment of King Hezekiah and of Azariah, the prefect of the house of God. ¹⁴ Kore, the son of Imnah, a Levite and the keeper of the eastern gate, was in charge of the free-will gifts made to God; he distributed the offerings made to the LORD and the most holy of the consecrated things. ¹⁵ Under him in the priestly cities were Eden, Miniamin, Jeshua, Shemaiah, Amariah and Shecaniah, who faithfully made the distribution to their brethren, great and small alike, according to their classes.

¹⁶* There was also a register by ancestral houses of males thirty years of age and over, for all priests who were eligible to enter the house of the LORD according to the daily rule to fulfill their service in the order of their classes. ¹⁷* The priests were inscribed in their family records according to their ancestral houses, and the Levites of twenty years and over according to their various offices and classes. ¹⁸ A distribution was also made to all who were inscribed in the family records, for their little ones, wives, sons and daughters—thus for the entire assembly, since they were to sanctify themselves by sharing faithfully in the consecrated things. ¹⁹ The sons of Aaron, the priests who lived on the lands attached to their cities, had in every city men designated by name to distribute portions to every male among the priests and to every Levite listed in the family records.

²⁰ This Hezekiah did in all Judah. He did what was good, upright and faithful before the LORD, his God. ²¹* Everything that he undertook, for the service of the house of God or for the law and the commandments, was to do the will of his God. He did this wholeheartedly, and he prospered.

Invasion of Sennacherib

32 ¹* But after he had proved his fidelity by such deeds, Sennacherib, king of Assyria, came. He invaded Judah, besieged the fortified cities, and proposed to take them by storm. ² When Hezekiah saw that Sennacherib was coming with the intention of attacking Jerusalem, ³ he decided in counsel with his princes and warriors to stop the waters of the springs outside the city. When they had pledged him their support, ⁴* a large crowd was gathered which stopped all the springs and also the running stream in the valley nearby. For they said, "Why should the kings of Assyria come and find an abundance of water?" ⁵* He then looked to his defenses: he rebuilt the wall where it was broken down, raised towers upon it, and built another wall outside. He strengthened the Millo of the City of David and had a great number of spears and shields prepared. ⁶ Then he appointed army commanders over the people. He gathered them together in his presence in the open space at the gate of the city and encouraged them with these words: ⁷* "Be brave and steadfast; do not be afraid or dismayed because of the king of Assyria and all the throng that is coming with him, for there is more with us than with him. ⁸* For he has only an arm of flesh, but we have the LORD, our God, to help us and to fight our battles." And the people took confidence from the words of King Hezekiah of Judah.

31, 16: 1 Chr 23, 3f.
31, 17: 1 Chr 23, 6–24.
31, 21: Ps 119, 2f.
32, 1: 2 Kgs 18, 13.
32, 4: Is 22, 9.11.
32, 5: Neh 2, 17f.
32, 7: 2 Chr 14, 10;
20, 6–12.
32, 8: Is 31, 3.

Threat of Sennacherib

9* After this, while Sennacherib, king of Assyria, himself remained at Lachish with all his forces, he sent his officials to Jerusalem with this message for King Hezekiah of Judah, and all the Judahites who were in Jerusalem: 10 "King Sennacherib of Assyria has this to say: On what are you relying, while you remain under siege in Jerusalem? 11 Has not Hezekiah deceived you, delivering you over to a death of famine and thirst, by his claim that 'the LORD, our God, will save us from the grasp of the king of Assyria'? 12 Has not this same Hezekiah removed his high places and altars and commanded Judah and Jerusalem, 'You shall prostrate yourselves before one altar only, and on it alone you shall offer incense'? 13 Do you not know what my fathers and I have done to all the peoples of other lands? Were the gods of the nations in those lands able to save their lands from my hand? 14 Who among all the gods of those nations which my fathers put under the ban was able to save his people from my hand? Will your god, then, be able to save you from my hand? 15 Let not Hezekiah mislead you further and deceive you in any such way. Do not believe him! Since no other god of any other nation or kingdom has been able to save his people from my hand or the hands of my fathers, how much the less shall your god save you from my hand!"

16 His officials said still more against the LORD God and against his servant Hezekiah, 17* for he had written letters to deride the LORD, the God of Israel, speaking of him in these terms: "As the gods of the nations in other lands have not saved their people from my hand, neither shall Hezekiah's god save his people from my hand." 18 In a loud voice they shouted in the Judean language to the people of Jerusalem who were on the wall, to frighten and terrify them so that they might capture their city. 19 They spoke of the God of Israel as though he were one of the gods of the other peoples of the earth, a work of human hands. 20* But because of this, King Hezekiah and the prophet Isaiah, son of Amos, prayed and called out to heaven.

Defeat of Sennacherib

21* Then the LORD sent an angel, who destroyed every valiant warrior, leader and commander in the camp of the Assyrian king, so that he had to return shamefaced to his own country. And when he entered the temple of his god, some of his own offspring struck him down there with the sword.

22 Thus the LORD saved Hezekiah and the inhabitants of Jerusalem from the hand of Sennacherib, king of Assyria, as from every other power; he gave them rest on every side. 23* Many brought gifts for the LORD to Jerusalem and costly objects for King Hezekiah of Judah, who thereafter was exalted in the eyes of all the nations.

Hezekiah's Other Deeds

24* In those days Hezekiah became mortally ill. He prayed to the LORD, who answered him by giving him a sign. 25 Hezekiah, however, did not then discharge his debt of gratitude, for he had become proud. Therefore anger descended upon him and upon Judah and Jerusalem. 26* But then Hezekiah humbled himself for his pride—both he and the inhabitants of Jerusalem; and therefore the LORD did not vent his anger on them during the time of Hezekiah.

27* Hezekiah possessed very great wealth and glory. He had treasuries made for his silver, gold, precious stones, spices, jewels, and other precious things of all kinds; 28 also storehouses for the harvest of grain, for wine and oil, and barns for the various kinds of cattle and for the flocks. 29 He built cities for himself, and he acquired sheep and oxen in great numbers, for God gave him very great riches. 30* This same Hezekiah stopped the upper outflow of water from Gihon and led it underground westward to the City of David. Hezekiah prospered in all his undertakings. 31 Nevertheless, in respect to the ambassadors [princes] sent to him from Babylon to investigate the sign that had occurred in the land, God forsook him to test him, that he might know all that was in his heart.

32 The rest of Hezekiah's acts, including his pious works, can be found written in the Vision of the Prophet Isaiah, son of Amos, and in the book of the kings of Judah and Israel. 33† Hezekiah rested with his ancestors; he was buried at the approach to the tombs of the descendants of David. All Judah and the inhabitants of Jerusalem paid him honor at his death. His son Manasseh succeeded him as king.

Impiety of Manasseh

33 1* Manasseh was twelve years old when he became king, and he reigned fifty-five years in Jerusalem. 2 He did evil in the sight of the LORD, following the abominable practices of the nations whom the LORD had cleared out of the way of the Israelites. 3 He rebuilt the high places which his

---

† **32, 33:** *The approach to the tombs:* literally, "the ascent of the tombs," which may mean "the upper section of the tombs," their most prominent and honored place.

32, 9–20: 2 Kgs 18, 17–37; Is 36, 1–22.   **32, 17:** 2 Kgs 19, 9–13; Is 37, 9–13.

32, 20: 2 Kgs 19, 14–19; Is 37, 14–20.
32, 21: 2 Kgs 19, 35ff; Is 37, 36ff.
32, 23: 2 Chr 14, 6.
32, 24: 2 Kgs 20, 1–11;

Is 38, 1–8.
32, 26.31: 2 Kgs 20, 12–19; Is 39, 1–8.
32, 27f: 2 Kgs 20, 13; Is 39, 2.
32, 30: 2 Kgs 20, 20f.
33, 1: 2 Kgs 21, 1–9.

Perseverance in Leadership

LIVE IT!

King Hezekiah persevered and prospered. He had many riches and provided for the people in his kingdom. One great accomplishment was a tunnel he had dug under the City of David (2 Chr 32, 30). The tunnel allowed the springs of Gihon to flow into the city so that the people had easier access to the water.

That tunnel, more than seventeen hundred feet long, was carved through the stone. Today, it would not take much to complete such a task, but in Hezekiah's time, it was done little by little with simple tools.

A great leader needs perseverance. People can get discouraged and lose heart when faced with difficult tasks. A good leader provides the encouragement and vision to get the job done. Who is an encouraging leader in your life? How do you encourage other people you work or go to school or live with?

▶ **2 Chr 32, 27–33**

father Hezekiah had torn down, erected altars for the Baals, made sacred poles, and prostrated himself before the whole host of heaven and worshiped them. 4 He even built altars in the temple of the LORD, of which the LORD had said, "In Jerusalem shall my name be forever": 5 he built altars to the whole host of heaven in the two courts of the LORD's house. 6 It was he, too, who immolated his sons by fire in the Valley of Ben-hinnom. He practiced augury, divination and magic, and appointed necromancers and diviners of spirits, so that he provoked the LORD with the great evil that he did in his sight. 7 He placed an idol that he had carved in the house of God, of which God had said to David and his son Solomon: "In this house and in Jerusalem which I have chosen from all the tribes of Israel I shall place my name forever. 8 I will not again allow Israel's feet to leave the land which I assigned to your fathers, provided they are careful to observe all that I commanded them, keeping the whole law and the statutes and the ordinances given by Moses." 9 Manasseh misled Judah and the inhabitants of Jerusalem into doing even greater evil than the nations which the LORD had destroyed at the coming of the Israelites. 10 The LORD spoke to Manasseh and his people, but they paid no attention.

His Conversion

11*† Therefore the LORD brought against them the army commanders of the Assyrian king; they took Manasseh with hooks, shackled him with chains, and transported him to Babylon. 12 In this distress, he began to appease the LORD, his God. He humbled himself abjectly before the God of his fathers 13† and prayed to him. The LORD let himself be won over: he heard his prayer and restored him to his kingdom in Jerusalem. Then Manasseh understood that the LORD is indeed God.

14 Afterward he built an outer wall for the City of David to the west of Gihon in the valley, extending to the Fish Gate and encircling Ophel; he built it very high. He stationed army officers in all the fortified cities of Judah. 15* He removed the foreign gods and the idol from the LORD's house and all the altars he had built on the mount of the LORD's house and in Jerusalem, and he cast them outside the city. 16 He restored the altar of the LORD, and sacrificed on it peace offerings and thank offerings, and commanded Judah to serve the LORD, the God of Israel. 17 Though the people continued to sacrifice on the high places, they now did so to the LORD, their God.

18* The rest of the acts of Manasseh, his prayer to his God, and the words of the seers who spoke to him in the name of the LORD, the God of Israel, can be found written in the chronicles of the kings of Israel. 19 His prayer and how his supplication was heard, all his sins and his infidelity, the sites where he built high places and erected sacred poles and carved images before he humbled himself, all can be found written down in the history of his seers. 20 Manasseh rested with his ancestors and was buried in his own palace. His son Amon succeeded him as king.

33, 11: There is no evidence elsewhere for an imprisonment of King Manasseh in Babylon. However, according to the Assyrian inscriptions, he paid tribute to the Assyrian kings Esarhaddon (680–669 B.C.) and Asshurbanipal (668–627 B.C.). He may well have been obliged to go to Nineveh to take the oath of allegiance as vassal to the king of Assyria.

33, 13: *And prayed to him:* these words led an unknown writer to compose the apocryphal "Prayer of Manasseh," which is added as an appendix to many editions of the Vulgate Bible and is used in the public prayers of the church.

33, 11: Jb 36, 7f; Ez 19, 9.   **33, 18.20:** 2 Kgs 21, 17f.   **33, 15:** 2 Chr 14, 2.

Amon

21* Amon was twenty-two years old when he became king, and he reigned two years in Jerusalem. 22 He did evil in the sight of the LORD, just as his father Manasseh had done. Amon offered sacrifice to all the idols which his father Manasseh had made, and worshiped them. 23 Moreover, he did not humble himself before the LORD as his father Manasseh had done; on the contrary, Amon only increased his guilt. 24 His servants conspired against him and put him to death in his own house. 25 But the people of the land slew all those who had conspired against King Amon, and then they, the people of the land, made his son Josiah king in his stead.

Reforms of Josiah

34 1* Josiah was eight years old when he became king, and he reigned thirty-one years in Jerusalem. 2 He pleased the LORD, following the path of his ancestor David. 3*† In the eighth year of his reign, while he was still a youth, he began to seek after the God of his forefather David, and in his twelfth year he began to purge Judah and Jerusalem of the high places, the sacred poles and the carved and molten images. 4 In his presence, the altars of the Baals were destroyed; the incense stands erected above them were torn down; the sacred poles and the carved and molten images were shattered and beaten into dust, which was strewn over the tombs of those who had sacrificed to them; 5 and the bones of the priests he burned upon their altars. Thus he purged Judah and Jerusalem. 6 He did likewise in the cities of Manasseh, Ephraim, Simeon, and in the ruined villages of the surrounding country as far as Naphtali; 7 he destroyed the altars, broke up the sacred poles and carved images and beat them into dust, and tore down the incense stands throughout the land of Israel. Then he returned to Jerusalem.

The Temple Restored

8* In the eighteenth year of his reign, in order to cleanse the temple as well as the land, he sent Shaphan, son of Azaliah, Maaseiah, the ruler of the city, and Joah, son of Joahaz, the chamberlain, to restore the house of the LORD, his God. 9* They came to Hilkiah the high priest and turned over the money brought to the house of God which the Levites, the guardians of the threshold, had collected from Manasseh, Ephraim, and all the remnant

of Israel, as well as from all of Judah, Benjamin, and the inhabitants of Jerusalem. 10 They turned it over to the master workmen in the house of the LORD, and these in turn used it to pay the workmen in the LORD's house who were restoring and repairing the temple. 11 They also gave it to the carpenters and the masons to buy hewn stone and timber for the tie beams and rafters of the buildings which the kings of Judah had allowed to fall into ruin. 12 The men worked faithfully at their tasks; their overseers were Jahath and Obadiah, Levites of the line of Merari, and Zechariah and Meshullam, of the Kohathites, who directed them. All those Levites who were skillful with musical instruments 13 were in charge of the men who carried the burdens, and they directed all the workers in every kind of labor. Some of the other Levites were scribes, officials and gatekeepers.

The Finding of the Law

14* When they brought out the money that had been deposited in the house of the LORD, Hilkiah the priest found the book of the law of the LORD given through Moses. 15 He reported this to Shaphan the scribe, saying, "I have found the book of the law in the house of the LORD." Hilkiah gave the book to Shaphan, 16 who brought it to the king at the same time that he was making his report to him. He said, "Your servants are doing everything that has been entrusted to them; 17 they have turned into bullion the metals deposited in the LORD's house and have handed it over to the overseers and the workmen." 18 Then Shaphan the scribe announced to the king, "Hilkiah the priest has given me a book." And Shaphan read from it before the king.

19 When the king heard the words of the law, he tore his garments 20 and issued this command to Hilkiah, to Ahikam, son of Shaphan, to Abdon, son of Michah, to Shaphan the scribe, and to Asaiah, the king's servant: 21 "On behalf of myself and those who are left in Israel and Judah, go, consult the LORD concerning the words of the book that has been found. For the anger of the LORD has been set furiously ablaze against us, since our fathers have not kept the word of the LORD and have not done all that is written in this book." 22 Then Hilkiah and the other men from the king went to the prophetess Huldah, the wife of Shallum, son of Tokhath, son of Hasrah, the guardian of the wardrobe; she dwelt

---

34, 3: *In his twelfth year:* c. 628 B.C., the year after Asshurbanipal's death, when Judah could free itself from Assyrian domination. From 2 Kgs 22, 1—23, 25 alone, one might think that Josiah's reform began only after the discovery of the book of the law in the temple, in the eighteenth year of his reign. But the Chronicler is no doubt right in placing the beginning of the reform at an earlier period. The

very repair of the temple, which led to the finding of the book of the law, must have been occasioned by a cultic reform.

33, 21–25: 2 Kgs 21, 19–26.　　　**34, 8–13:** 2 Kgs 22, 3–7.
34, 1f: 2 Kgs 22, 1f.　　　　　　　**34, 9:** 2 Chr 24, 8f.
34, 3–7: 2 Chr 14, 1–4; 31, 1;　　**34, 14–28:** 2 Kgs 22, 8–20.
　2 Kgs 23, 4–20.

in Jerusalem, in the new quarter. They spoke to her as they had been instructed, 23 and she said to them: "Thus says the LORD, the God of Israel: 'Tell the one who sent you to me, 24 The LORD says: I am prepared to bring evil upon this place and upon its inhabitants, all the curses written in the book that has been read before the king of Judah. 25 Because they have abandoned me and have offered incense to other gods, provoking me by every deed that they have performed, my anger is ablaze against this place and cannot be extinguished.'

26 "But to the king of Judah who sent you to consult the LORD, give this response: 'Thus says the LORD, the God of Israel, concerning the threats you have heard: 27 Because you were heartsick and have humbled yourself before God on hearing his words spoken against this place and its inhabitants; because you have humbled yourself before me, have torn your garments, and have wept before me, I in turn have listened—so declares the LORD. 28 I will gather you to your ancestors and you shall be taken to your grave in peace. Your eyes shall not see all the evil I will bring upon this place and upon its inhabitants.' "

They brought back this message to the king.

Renewal of the Covenant

29* The king now convened all the elders of Judah and Jerusalem. 30 He went up to the house of the LORD with all the men of Judah and the inhabitants of Jerusalem, the priests, the Levites, and all the people, great and small; and he had read aloud to them the entire text of the book of the covenant that had been found in the house of the LORD. 31† Standing at his post, the king made a covenant before the LORD to follow the LORD and to keep his commandments, decrees, and statutes with his whole heart and soul, thus observing the terms of the covenant written in this book. 32 He thereby committed all who were of Jerusalem and Benjamin, and the inhabitants of Jerusalem conformed themselves to the covenant of God, the God of their fathers. 33* Josiah removed every abominable thing from all the territory belonging to the Israelites, and he obliged all who were in Israel to serve the LORD, their God. During his lifetime they did not desert the LORD, the God of their fathers.

The Passover

35 1* Josiah celebrated in Jerusalem a Passover to honor the LORD; the Passover sacrifice was slaughtered on the fourteenth day of the first month.* 2 He reappointed the priests to their duties and encouraged them in the service of the LORD's house. 3* He said to the Levites who were to instruct all Israel, and who were consecrated to the LORD: "Put the holy ark in the house built by Solomon, son of David, king of Israel. It shall no longer be a burden on your shoulders. Serve now the LORD, your God, and his people Israel. 4 Prepare yourselves in your ancestral houses and your classes according to the prescriptions of King David of Israel and his son Solomon. 5* Stand in the sanctuary according to the divisions of the ancestral houses of your brethren, the common people, so that the distribution of the Levites and the families may be the same. 6* Slay the Passover sacrifice, sanctify yourselves, and be at the disposition of your brethren, that all may be carried out according to the word of the LORD given through Moses."

7* Josiah contributed to the common people a flock of lambs and kids, thirty thousand in number, each to serve as a Passover victim for any who were present, and also three thousand oxen; these were from the king's property. 8* His princes also gave a free-will gift to the people, the priests and the Levites. Hilkiah, Zechariah and Jehiel, prefects of the house of God, gave to the priests two thousand six hundred Passover victims together with three hundred oxen. 9 Conaniah and his brothers Shemaiah, Nethanel, Hashabiah, Jehiel and Jozabad, the rulers of the Levites, contributed to the Levites five thousand Passover victims, together with five hundred oxen.

10 When the service had been arranged, the priests took their places, as did the Levites in their classes according to the king's command. 11 The Passover sacrifice was slaughtered, whereupon the priests sprinkled some of the blood and the Levites proceeded to the skinning. 12 They separated what was destined for the holocaust and gave it to various groups of the ancestral houses of the common people to offer to the LORD, as is prescribed in the book of Moses. They did the same with the oxen. 13* They cooked the Passover on the fire as prescribed, and also cooked the sacred meals in pots, cauldrons and pans, then brought them quickly to all the common people. 14 Afterward they prepared the Passover for themselves and for the priests. Indeed the priests, the sons of Aaron, were busy offering holocausts and the fatty portions until night; therefore the Levites prepared for themselves and for the priests, the sons of Aaron. 15 The singers, the sons of Asaph, were at their posts as prescribed by David: Asaph, Heman and

†
34, 31: *Standing at his post:* see note on 2 Chr 23, 13.

34, 29–32: 2 Kgs 23, 1ff.
34, 33: 2 Kgs 23, 4–20.
35, 1–19: 2 Kgs 23, 21ff.
35, 1: Ex 12, 1–28;

2 Kgs 23, 21.
35, 3: 2 Chr 5, 4; 1 Chr 15,
12.15.
35, 5: 1 Chr 24—26.
35, 6: 2 Chr 30, 17.
35, 7: Ex 12, 5.
35, 8: Nm 7, 1–83.
35, 13: Nm 12, 8f.

Jeduthun, the king's seer. The gatekeepers were at every gate; there was no need for them to leave their stations, for their brethren, the Levites, prepared for them. ¹⁶ Thus the entire service of the LORD was arranged that day so that the Passover could be celebrated and the holocausts offered on the altar of the LORD, as King Josiah had commanded. ¹⁷ The Israelites who were present on that occasion kept the Passover and the feast of the Unleavened Bread for seven days. ¹⁸* No such Passover had been observed in Israel since the time of the prophet Samuel, nor had any king of Israel kept a Passover like that of Josiah, the priests and Levites, all of Judah and Israel that were present, and the inhabitants of Jerusalem. ¹⁹ It was in the eighteenth year of Josiah's reign that this Passover was observed.

Josiah's Reign Ends

²⁰ After Josiah had done all this to restore the temple, Neco, king of Egypt, came up to fight at Carchemish on the Euphrates, and Josiah went out to intercept him. ²¹ Neco sent messengers to him, saying: "What quarrel is between us, king of Judah? I have not come against you this day, for my war is with another kingdom, and God has told me to hasten. Do not interfere with God who is with me, as otherwise he will destroy you." ²² But Josiah would not withdraw from him, for he had sought a pretext for fighting with him. Therefore he would not listen to the words of Neco that came from the mouth of God, but went out to fight in the plain of Megiddo. ²³* Then the archers shot King Josiah, who said to his servants, "Take me away, for I am seriously wounded." ²⁴ His servants removed him from his own chariot, placed him in another he had in reserve, and brought him to Jerusalem, where he died. He was buried in the tombs of his ancestors, and all Judah and Jerusalem mourned him. ²⁵† Jeremiah also composed a lamentation over Josiah, which is recited to this day by all the male and female singers in their lamentations over Josiah. These have been made obligatory for Israel, and can be found written in the Lamentations.

²⁶* The rest of the chronicle of Josiah, his pious deeds in regard to what is written in the law of the LORD, and his acts, first and last, can be found written in the book of the kings of Israel and Judah.

36 ¹* The people of the land took Jehoahaz, son of Josiah, and made him king in Jerusalem in his father's stead.

IV: End of the Kingdom

Jehoahaz

² Jehoahaz was twenty-three years old when he became king, and he reigned three months in Jerusalem. ³ The king of Egypt deposed him in Jerusalem and fined the land one hundred talents of silver and a talent of gold. ⁴ Then the king of Egypt made his brother Eliakim king over Judah and Jerusalem, and changed his name to Jehoiakim. Neco took his brother Jehoahaz away and brought him to Egypt.

Jehoiakim

⁵* Jehoiakim was twenty-five years old when he became king, and he reigned eleven years in Jerusalem. He did evil in the sight of the LORD, his God. ⁶*† Nebuchadnezzar, king of Babylon, came up against him and bound him with chains to take him to Babylon. ⁷ Nebuchadnezzar also carried away to Babylon some of the vessels of the house of the LORD and put them in his palace in Babylon. ⁸* The rest of the acts of Jehoiakim, the abominable things that he did, and what therefore happened to him, can be found written in the book of the kings of Israel and Judah. His son Jehoiachin succeeded him as king.

Jehoiachin

⁹* Jehoiachin was eighteen years old when he became king, and he reigned three months [and ten days] in Jerusalem. He did evil in the sight of the LORD. ¹⁰*† At the turn of the year, King Nebuchadnezzar sent for him and had him brought to Babylon, along with precious vessels from the temple of the LORD. He made his brother Zedekiah king over Judah and Jerusalem.

Zedekiah

¹¹* Zedekiah was twenty-one years old when he became king, and he reigned eleven years in Jerusalem. ¹²* He did evil in the sight of the LORD, his God, and he did not humble himself before the

---

† **35, 25:** The reference to a lamentation over Josiah composed by Jeremiah is not found either in 2 Kgs or Jer; but see note on Zec 12, 11. *Their lamentations:* probably a reference to the canonical Book of Lamentations.

36, 6: *Nebuchadnezzar . . . bound him with chains to take him to Babylon:* the Chronicler does not say that Jehoiakim was actually taken to Babylon. According to 2 Kgs 24, 1–6, Jehoiakim revolted after being Nebuchadnezzar's vassal for three years; he died in Jerusalem before the Babylonian king could reach the city. However, Dn 1, 1f, apparently based on 2 Chr 36, 6f, speaks of Jehoiakim's deportation to Babylon.

36, 10: *His brother Zedekiah:* Zedekiah was actually the brother of Jehoiakim and the uncle of Jehoiachin (2 Kgs 24, 17; Jer 37, 1), though scarcely older than his nephew (2 Kgs 24, 8.18; 2 Chr 36, 9.11).

35, 18f: 2 Kgs 23, 22f.
35, 23: 2 Chr 18, 33f.
35, 26: 2 Kgs 23, 28.
36, 1–4: 2 Kgs 23, 30–34; 1 Chr 3, 15f.
36, 5: 2 Kgs 23, 36f; Jer 22, 18f.
36, 6: 2 Kgs 24, 1f.
36, 8: 2 Kgs 24, 5.
36, 9: 2 Kgs 24, 8f.
36, 10: 2 Kgs 24, 10–16.
36, 11: 2 Kgs 24, 18ff; Jer 52, 1ff.
36, 12: Jer 37, 1ff.

prophet Jeremiah, who spoke the word of the LORD. ¹³* He also rebelled against King Nebuchadnezzar, who had made him swear by God. He became stiff-necked and hardened his heart rather than return to the LORD, the God of Israel. ¹⁴ Likewise all the princes of Judah, the priests and the people added infidelity to infidelity, practicing all the abominations of the nations and polluting the LORD's temple which he had consecrated in Jerusalem.

Dissolution of Judah

¹⁵* Early and often did the LORD, the God of their fathers, send his messengers to them, for he had compassion on his people and his dwelling place. ¹⁶* But they mocked the messengers of God, despised his warnings, and scoffed at his prophets, until the anger of the LORD against his people was so inflamed that there was no remedy. ¹⁷* Then he brought up against them the king of the Chaldeans, who slew their young men in their own sanctuary building, sparing neither young man nor maiden, neither the aged nor the decrepit; he delivered all of them over into his grip. ¹⁸* All the utensils of the house of God, the large and the small, and the

treasures of the LORD's house and of the king and his princes, all these he brought to Babylon. ¹⁹* They burnt the house of God, tore down the walls of Jerusalem, set all its palaces afire, and destroyed all its precious objects. ²⁰ Those who escaped the sword he carried captive to Babylon, where they became his and his sons' servants until the kingdom of the Persians came to power. ²¹ All this was to fulfill the word of the LORD spoken by Jeremiah: "Until the land has retrieved its lost sabbaths, during all the time it lies waste it shall have rest while seventy years are fulfilled."

Decree of Cyrus

²²*† In the first year of Cyrus, king of Persia, in order to fulfill the word of the LORD spoken by Jeremiah, the LORD inspired King Cyrus of Persia to issue this proclamation throughout his kingdom, both by word of mouth and in writing: ²³ "Thus says Cyrus, king of Persia: 'All the kingdoms of the earth the LORD, the God of heaven, has given to me, and he has also charged me to build him a house in Jerusalem, which is in Judah. Whoever, therefore, among you belongs to any part of his people, let him go up, and may his God be with him!' "

Stiff Necks

It happened so quickly. I was waiting at a stoplight when the car behind me slammed into my car and my neck snapped back. Whiplash! It hurt, but it didn't seem very serious. I was much more upset at the damage that had been done to my car. But by the next morning, I was in agony. I could barely move my head, and my neck was stiff and sore. By the end of the day, my neck was in a brace, and I was taking pain medication.

Now I understand a little better why the Bible so often uses the metaphor of stiff-necked people (2 Chr 36, 13). To be unable or unwilling to turn their heads deprives people of the ability to look toward God. They just keep looking straight ahead as if it were not possible to look in any other direction. You miss out on a lot if you don't or can't look from side to side, believe me!

How often have you refused to turn toward God, or to gain a new perspective on life?

▶ 2 Chr 36, 11–14

36, 22f: The words of these verses are identical with those of Ezr 1, 1–3a. Originally Ezra-Nehemiah formed the last part of the single work of the Chronicler, of which 1 and 2 Chronicles formed the first part. But when Ezra-Nehemiah was regarded as a natural sequence to the Books of Samuel and of Kings, it was separated from 1 and 2 Chronicles and placed before them. Thus, 1 and 2 Chronicles became the last part of the Hebrew Bible. To prevent this work from ending on a note of doom, Ezr 1, 1–3a was repeated as 2 Chr 36, 22f.

36, 13: 2 Kgs 25, 1; Jer 52, 4; Ex 17, 13–16.	**36, 17:** Lam 1, 15; 5, 11–14.
36, 15: Jer 7, 25; Heb 1, 1.	**36, 18:** 2 Kgs 25, 14f.
36, 16: Mt 23, 34ff.	**36, 19:** 2 Kgs 25, 9f; Lam 2, 8.
	36, 22: Ezr 1, 1ff.

The Books of Ezra and Nehemiah

Imagine the worst vacation ever. The car breaks down twice, you are sick almost the whole time, and the weather is awful. You can't wait to get home—but when you walk in the front door, the house is trashed. Now, imagine how the Israelites felt. They didn't just have a bad vacation; they spent fifty years as captives in a foreign land. When they finally returned home, they faced the overwhelming task of rebuilding Jerusalem and starting their new life. Fortunately, they had Ezra and Nehemiah to help lead and encourage them.

At a Glance

I. The Return from Exile (Ezr 1, 1—6, 22).

II. The Deeds of Ezra (Ezr 7, 1—10, 44).

I. The Deeds of Nehemiah (Neh 1, 1—7, 72).

II. Promulgation of the Law (Neh 8, 1—13, 31).

In-depth

In 587 B.C., the land of Judah and the city of Jerusalem were conquered by the Babylonians, and many Israelites were exiled to Babylon. The Books of Ezra and Nehemiah pick up the story with the return of some Israelites from Babylon to Judah in 538 B.C. The two books were originally a single work, perhaps written in their final form by the same person (or persons) who wrote 1 and 2 Chronicles.

Ezra, a descendant of Israelite priests, was born in Babylonian captivity and became a priest. Because priests couldn't exercise their religious functions during the Exile, they dedicated themselves to studying the Scriptures. Eventually, Ezra was sent to Judah by the Persian emperor Artaxerxes to restore Israel's faithfulness to God. Ezra appointed scribes and judges to establish civil and moral order in the new community returned from Exile.

Nehemiah was a Jewish cupbearer for Emperor Artaxerxes (a cupbearer tastes the contents of whatever the emperor drinks to assure it is not poisoned). When Nehemiah heard reports of Jerusalem's poverty and ruin, he persuaded the emperor to appoint him governor of Judah to help rebuild the city. Nehemiah turned out to be a gifted governor. Under Nehemiah's direction, Jerusalem's walls were rebuilt, and economic and social reforms helped restore order and hope to the community.

Ezra and Nehemiah's leadership was extremely important to Israel as the people returned and began the difficult task of rebuilding Jerusalem. The need to save the faith and customs of the Israelites led to a strict observance of the Law and the beginnings of modern Judaism.

Quick Facts

Period Covered
from the Exiles' return to Jerusalem through Nehemiah's tenure as governor of Judah, from 538 to about 400 B.C.

Author
a scribe (the Chronicler) drawing on Ezra's and Nehemiah's memoirs and other sources

Themes
the return of the Israelites from captivity, the rebuilding of Jerusalem and the Temple

Ezra

I: The Return from Exile

The Decree of Cyrus

1 ¹*† In the first year of Cyrus, king of Persia, in order to fulfill the word of the LORD spoken by Jeremiah, the LORD inspired King Cyrus of Persia to issue this proclamation throughout his kingdom, both by word of mouth and in writing: ² "Thus says Cyrus, king of Persia: 'All the kingdoms of the earth the LORD, the God of heaven, has given to me, and he has also charged me to build him a house in Jerusalem, which is in Judah. ³ Whoever, therefore, among you belongs to any part of his people, let him go up, and may his God be with him! ⁴ Let everyone who has survived, in whatever place he may have dwelt, be assisted by the people of that place with silver, gold, goods, and cattle, together with free will offerings for the house of God in Jerusalem.' "

⁵ Then the family heads of Judah and Benjamin and the priests and Levites—everyone, that is, whom God had inspired to do so—prepared to go up to build the house of the LORD in Jerusalem. ⁶* All their neighbors gave them help in every way, with silver, gold, goods, and cattle, and with many precious gifts besides all their free-will offerings. ⁷ King Cyrus, too, had the utensils of the house of the LORD brought forth which Nebuchadnezzar had taken away from Jerusalem and placed in the house of his god. ⁸† Cyrus, king of Persia, had them brought forth by the treasurer Mithredath, and counted out to Sheshbazzar, the prince of Judah. ⁹ This was the inventory: sacks of goldware, thirty; sacks of silverware, one thousand and twenty-nine; ¹⁰ golden bowls, thirty; silver bowls, four hundred and ten; other ware, one thousand pieces. ¹¹† Total of the gold- and silverware: five thousand four hundred pieces. All these Sheshbazzar took with him when the exiles were brought back from Babylon to Jerusalem.

Census of the Province

2 ¹*† These are the inhabitants of the province who returned from the captivity of the exiles, whom Nebuchadnezzar, king of Babylon, had carried away to Babylon, and who came back to Jerusalem and Judah, each man in his own city ² (those who returned with Zerubbabel, Jeshua, Nehemiah,

---

1, 1: *In the first year of Cyrus:* as sovereign over the world empire which began with his conquest of Babylon; that is, 538 B.C.

1, 8: *Sheshbazzar:* very probably the fourth son of Jehoiachin, king of Judah, taken captive to Babylon in 598 B.C., listed in 1 Chr 3, 18 as Senneser; if so, he was the uncle of Zerubbabel (Ezr 3, 2ff); see note on 1 Chr 3, 18.

1, 11: *Total . . . five thousand four hundred pieces:* either this figure or the figures given for one or more of the items listed (vv 9f) have been corrupted in the transmission of the text.

2, 1–67: As it now stands, this list is an expanded form of the lists of returned captives from the sixth century B.C.; see Neh 7, 6–72, where it reappears.

1, 1ff: 2 Chr 36, 22f; Jer 25, 11f; 29, 10; Zec 1, 12.
1, 6: Ex 3, 22; 11, 2; 12, 35.
2, 1: Neh 7, 6–67.

The Spirit of Giving

LIVE IT!

It was Christmas Eve, and Sally was depressed because she had little to give her three children for Christmas. The father of Sally's children had left suddenly one day, and each day since had been a struggle. The children each had a gift that they wanted from Santa, and Sally could not afford what they were hoping for. Friends and family had offered to help, but she was too proud to accept their charity.

As Sally and the children headed home after church, Sally's heart was heavy because she knew her children would be disappointed. But when they arrived home, they found a pile of presents in the middle of the living room. The children had each received their special gift. Sally never found out who was responsible for this special Christmas.

For the Jews returning to Jerusalem, the task of rebuilding Jerusalem must have seemed overwhelming. King Cyrus understood this and asked that family, friends, and neighbors help by giving whatever they could. Who has been there to help you when you have felt completely overwhelmed? How do you offer help to others?

▸ Ezr 1, 6–11

Seraiah, Reelaiah, Mordecai, Bilshan, Mispereth, Bigvai, Rehum, and Baanah):

The census of the men of Israel: ³ sons of Parosh, two thousand one hundred and seventy-two; ⁴ sons of Shephatiah, three hundred and seventy-two; ⁵ sons of Arah, seven hundred and seventy-five; ⁶ sons of Pahath-moab, who were sons of Jeshua and Joab, two thousand eight hundred and twelve; ⁷ sons of Elam, one thousand two hundred and fifty-four; ⁸ sons of Zattu, nine hundred and forty-five; ⁹ sons of Zaccai, seven hundred and sixty; ¹⁰ sons of Bani, six hundred and forty-two; ¹¹ sons of Bebai, six hundred and twenty-three; ¹² sons of Azgad, one thousand two hundred and twenty-two; ¹³ sons of Adonikam, six hundred and sixty-six; ¹⁴ sons of Bigvai, two thousand and fifty-six; ¹⁵ sons of Adin, four hundred and fifty-four; ¹⁶ sons of Ater, who were sons of Hezekiah, ninety-eight; ¹⁷ sons of Bezai, three hundred and twenty-three; ¹⁸ sons of Jorah, one hundred and twelve; ¹⁹ sons of Hashum, two hundred and twenty-three; ²⁰ sons of Gibeon, ninety-five; ²¹ sons of Bethlehem, one hundred and twenty-three; ²² men of Netophah, fifty-six; ²³ men of Anathoth, one hundred and twenty-eight; ²⁴ men of Beth-azmaveth, forty-two; ²⁵ men of Kiriath-jearim, Chephirah, and Beeroth, seven hundred and forty-three; ²⁶ men of Ramah and Geba, six hundred and twenty-one; ²⁷ men of Michmas, one hundred and twenty-two; ²⁸ men of Bethel and Ai, two hundred and twenty-three; ²⁹ sons of Nebo, fifty-two; ³⁰ sons of Magbish, one hundred and fifty-six; ³¹ sons of the other Elam, one thousand two hundred and fifty-four; ³² sons of Harim, three hundred and twenty; ³³ sons of Lod, Hadid, and Ono, seven hundred and twenty-five; ³⁴ sons of Jericho, three hundred and forty-five; ³⁵ sons of Senaah, three thousand six hundred and thirty.

³⁶ The priests: sons of Jedaiah, who were of the house of Jeshua, nine hundred and seventy-three; ³⁷ sons of Immer, one thousand and fifty-two; ³⁸ sons of Pashhur, one thousand two hundred and forty-seven; ³⁹ sons of Harim, one thousand and seventeen.

⁴⁰* The Levites: sons of Jeshua, Kadmiel, Binnui, and Hodaviah, seventy-four.

⁴¹ The singers: sons of Asaph, one hundred and twenty-eight.

⁴² The gatekeepers: sons of Shallum, sons of Ater, sons of Talmon, sons of Akkub, sons of Hatita, sons of Shobai, one hundred and thirty-nine in all.

⁴³ The temple slaves: sons of Ziha, sons of Hasupha, sons of Tabbaoth, ⁴⁴ sons of Keros, sons of Siaha, sons of Padon, ⁴⁵ sons of Lebanah, sons of Hagabah, sons of Akkub, ⁴⁶ sons of Hagab, sons of Shamlai, sons of Hanan, ⁴⁷ sons of Giddel, sons of Gahar, sons of Reaiah, ⁴⁸ sons of Rezin, sons of Nekoda, sons of Gazzam, ⁴⁹ sons of Uzza, sons of Paseah, sons of Besai, ⁵⁰ sons of Asnah, sons of the Meunites, sons of the Nephusites, ⁵¹ sons of Bakbuk, sons of Hakupha, sons of Harhur, ⁵² sons of Bazluth, sons of Mehida, sons of Harsha, ⁵³ sons of Barkos, sons of Sisera, sons of Temah, ⁵⁴ sons of Neziah, sons of Hatipha.

⁵⁵ Descendants of the slaves of Solomon: sons of Sotai, sons of Hassophereth, sons of Peruda, ⁵⁶ sons of Jaalah, sons of Darkon, sons of Giddel, ⁵⁷ sons of Shephatiah, sons of Hattil, sons of Pochereth-hazzebaim, sons of Ami. ⁵⁸ The total of the temple slaves and the descendants of the slaves of Solomon was three hundred and ninety-two.

*

2, 40: Neh 12, 24.

⁵⁹ The following who returned from Tel-melah, Tel-harsha, Cherub, Addan, and Immer were unable to prove that their ancestral houses and their descent were Israelite: ⁶⁰ sons of Delaiah, sons of Tobiah, sons of Nekoda, six hundred and fifty-two. ⁶¹* Also, of the priests: sons of Habaiah, sons of Hakkoz, sons of Barzillai (he had married one of the daughters of Barzillai the Gileadite and became known by his name). ⁶² These men searched their family records, but their names could not be found written there; hence they were degraded from the priesthood, ⁶³† and His Excellency ordered them not to partake of the most holy foods until there should be a priest bearing the Urim and Thummim.

⁶⁴ The entire assembly taken together came to forty-two thousand three hundred and sixty, ⁶⁵ not counting their male and female slaves, who were seven thousand three hundred and thirty-seven. They also had two hundred male and female singers. ⁶⁶ Their horses were seven hundred and thirty-six, their mules two hundred and forty-five, ⁶⁷ their camels four hundred and thirty-five, their asses six thousand seven hundred and twenty.

⁶⁸ When they arrived at the house of the LORD in Jerusalem, some of the family heads made free-will offerings for the house of God, to rebuild it in its place. ⁶⁹ According to their means they contributed to the treasury for the temple service: sixty-one thousand drachmas of gold, five thousand minas of silver, and one hundred garments for the priests. ⁷⁰ The priests, the Levites, and some of the common people took up residence in Jerusalem; but the singers, the gatekeepers, and the temple slaves dwelt in their cities. Thus all the Israelites dwelt in their cities.

Restoration of the Altar

3 ¹*† Now when the seventh month came, after the Israelites had settled in their cities, the people gathered at Jerusalem as one man. ² Then Jeshua, son of Jozadak, together with his brethren the priests, and Zerrubbabel, son of Shealtiel, together with his brethren, set about rebuilding the altar of the God of Israel in order to offer on it the holocausts prescribed in the law of Moses, the man of God. ³* Despite their fear of the peoples of the land, they replaced the altar on its foundations and

offered holocausts to the LORD on it, both morning and evening. ⁴* They also kept the feast of Booths in the manner prescribed, and they offered the daily holocausts in the proper number required for each day. ⁵ Thereafter they offered the established holocaust, the sacrifices prescribed for the new moons and all the festivals sacred to the LORD, and those which anyone might offer as a free-will gift to the LORD. ⁶ From the first day of the seventh month they began to offer holocausts to the LORD, though the foundation of the temple of the LORD had not yet been laid.

Founding of the Temple

⁷* Then they hired stonecutters and carpenters, and sent food and drink and oil to the Sidonians and Tyrians that they might ship cedar trees from the Lebanon to the port of Joppa, as Cyrus, king of Persia, had authorized. ⁸ In the year after their coming to the house of God in Jerusalem, in the second month, Zerubbabel, son of Shealtiel, and Jeshua, son of Jozadak, together with the rest of their brethren, the priests and Levites and all who had come from the captivity to Jerusalem, began by appointing the Levites twenty years of age and over to supervise the work on the house of the LORD. ⁹ Jeshua and his sons and brethren, with Kadmiel and Binnui, son of Henadad, and their sons and their brethren, the Levites, stood as one man to supervise those who were engaged in the work on the house of God. ¹⁰* When the builders had laid the foundation of the LORD'S temple, the vested priests with the trumpets and the Levites, sons of Asaph, were stationed there with the cymbals to praise the LORD in the manner laid down by David, king of Israel. ¹¹* They alternated in songs of praise and thanksgiving to the LORD, "for he is good, for his kindness to Israel endures forever"; and all the people raised a great shout of joy, praising the LORD because the foundation of the LORD'S house had been laid. ¹²* Many of the priests, Levites, and family heads, the old men who had seen the former house, cried out in sorrow as they watched the foundation of the present house being laid. Many others, however, lifted up their voices in shouts of joy, ¹³* and no one could distinguish the sound of the joyful shouting from the sound of those who were

---

2, 63: *His Excellency:* the deputy of the Persian government; from the context, he was one of the Jewish exile leaders. Nehemiah as governor receives the same title (Neh 8, 9; 10, 2). *Urim and Thummim:* see note on Ex 28, 30.

3, 1f: *The seventh month:* Tishri (September–October), apparently of 538 B.C.; cf Ezr 1, 1; 4, 5. In this case, it was Sheshbazzar who erected the first altar, since he began the work on the foundations of the temple in Jerusalem; cf Ezr 5, 16. It was in the second year of Darius I, i.e., in 520 B.C., that Jeshua and Zerubbabel resumed the work on the temple that had been temporarily interrupted (Ezr 4, 24–5, 1; Hg 1, 1; 2, 1). The Chronicler or a later editor of the text here attributes to them the beginning of the work which, in reality,

they merely completed. *Shealtiel:* the oldest son of King Jehoiachin of Judah and the brother of Sheshbazzar (1 Chr 3, 18f); Zerubbabel was therefore the grandson of Jehoiachin; see note on Ezr 1, 8.

2, 61: 2 Sm 17, 27; 19, 32f;
  1 Kgs 2, 7.
3, 1: Neh 7, 73—8, 1.
3, 3: 1 Kgs 8, 64; Dn 9, 25.
3, 4: Ex 23, 16; Nm 28,
  3–8.
3, 7: 1 Chr 22, 4;

2 Chr 2, 9.
3, 10: Ezr 2, 41.
3, 11: Pss 100, 5; 136; Jer 33,
  11.
3, 12: Hg 2, 3.
3, 13: Tb 14, 5.

EZR

weeping; for the people raised a mighty clamor which was heard afar off.

Holy Tears

Ezra 3, 12 tells us that many of the older Israelites who remembered the first Temple wept at the grand celebration that marked its rebirth. Were they shedding tears of joy that the Temple was being built again? Or were they shedding tears of sorrow over what they had lost and never regained? Most likely, they were doing both.

Weeping can be a holy and healing part of life. Unfortunately, some people believe that strong men and women never cry. But tears are appropriate on many occasions: the loss of a dear friend or family member, a reconciliation with someone after a long separation, and the moment we recognize we have sinned and hurt someone deeply, to name a few. We should bring our tears to God in prayer. They will turn into holy tears as God's healing love enters our life.

▸ **Ezr 3, 10–13**

Samaritan Interference

4 ¹ When the enemies of Judah and Benjamin heard that the exiles were building a temple for the LORD, the God of Israel, ² they approached Zerubbabel and the family heads and said to them, "Let us build with you, for we seek your God just as you do, and we have sacrificed to him since the days of Esarhaddon, king of Assyria, who had us brought here." ³ But Zerubbabel, Jeshua, and the rest of the family heads of Israel answered them, "It is not your responsibility to build with us a house for our God, but we alone must build it for the LORD, the God of Israel, as King Cyrus of Persia has commanded us." ⁴ Thereupon the people of the land set out to intimidate and dishearten the people of Ju-

dah so as to keep them from building. ⁵† They also suborned counselors to work against them and thwart their plans during the remaining years of Cyrus, king of Persia, and until the reign of Darius, king of Persia.

Later Hostility

⁶ Also at the beginning of the reign of Ahashuerus they prepared a written accusation against the inhabitants of Judah and Jerusalem.

⁷† Again, in the time of Artaxerxes, Mithredath wrote in concert with Tabeel and the rest of his fellow officials to Artaxerxes, king of Persia. The document was written in Aramaic and was accompanied by a translation. [Aramaic:]

⁸† Then Rehum, the governor, and Shimshai, the scribe, wrote the following letter against Jerusalem to King Artaxerxes: ⁹ "Rehum, the governor, Shimshai, the scribe, and their fellow judges, officials, and agents from among the Persian, Urukian, Babylonian, Susian (that is, Elamite), ¹⁰ and the other peoples whom the great and illustrious Assurbanipal transported and settled in the city of Samaria and elsewhere in the province West-of-Euphrates, as follows. . . ." ¹¹ This is a copy of the letter that they sent to him:

"To King Artaxerxes, your servants, the men of West-of-Euphrates, as follows: ¹² Let it be known to the king that the Jews who came up from you to us have arrived at Jerusalem and are now rebuilding this rebellious and evil city. They are raising up its walls, and the foundations have already been laid. ¹³ Now let it be known to the king that if this city is rebuilt and its walls are raised up again, they will no longer pay taxes, tributes, or tolls; thus it can only result in harm to the throne. ¹⁴ Now, since we partake of the salt of the palace, we ought not simply to look on while the king is being dishonored. Therefore we have sent this message to inform you, O king, ¹⁵ so that inquiry may be made in the historical records of your fathers. In the historical records you can discover and verify that this city is a rebellious city which has proved fatal to kings and provinces, and that sedition has been fostered there since ancient times. For that reason this city was destroyed. ¹⁶ We inform you, O king, that if this city is rebuilt and its walls are raised up again, by that very fact you will no longer own any part of West-of-Euphrates."

4, 5: *Darius:* Darius I (521–485 B.C.). The temple-building narrative continues in Ezr 4, 24. In between (Ezr 4, 6–23) is a series of notes about the opposition to the returned exiles voiced at the Persian court in the early fifth century B.C., after the temple had been reestablished.

4, 7: *Aramaic:* this word in the original text seems to be a note indicating a change of language from Hebrew to Aramaic, which in

fact takes place here. The Aramaic section ends with Ezr 6, 18, but again in Ezr 7, 12–26 a royal letter is cited in Aramaic.

4, 8–23: The central question here is the rebuilding of the fortification walls of Jerusalem, not the building of the temple. The interruption of work on the city wall some time before 445 B.C. was the occasion for the coming of Nehemiah to Palestine (Neh 1, 1–4; 2, 1–5). *Artaxerxes:* Artaxerxes I (464–423 B.C.).

17 The king sent this answer: "To Rehum, the governor, Shimshai, the scribe, and their fellow officials living in Samaria and elsewhere in the province West-of-Euphrates, greetings and the following: 18 The communication which you sent us has been read plainly in my presence. 19 When at my command inquiry was made, it was verified that from ancient times this city has risen up against kings and that rebellion and sedition have been fostered there. 20 Powerful kings were once in Jerusalem who ruled over all West-of-Euphrates, and taxes, tributes, and tolls were paid to them. 21 Give orders, therefore, that will stop the work of these men. This city may not be rebuilt until a further decree has been issued by me. 22 Take care that you do not neglect this matter, lest the evil grow to the detriment of the throne."

23* As soon as a copy of King Artaxerxes' letter had been read before Rehum, the governor, Shimshai, the scribe, and their fellow officials, they went in all haste to the Jews in Jerusalem and stopped their work by force of arms.

Rebuilding of the Temple

24† Thus it was that the work on the house of God in Jerusalem was halted. This inaction lasted until the second year of the reign of Darius, king of Persia.

5 1*† Then the prophets Haggai and Zechariah, son of Iddo, began to prophesy to the Jews in Judah and Jerusalem in the name of the God of Israel. 2 Thereupon Zerubbabel, son of Shealtiel, and Jeshua, son of Jozadak, began again to build the house of God in Jerusalem, with the prophets of God giving them support. 3 At that time there came to them Tattenai, governor of West-of-Euphrates, and Shethar-bozenai, and their fellow officials, who asked of them: "Who issued the decree for you to build this house and raise this edifice? 4 What are the names of the men who are building this structure?" 5 But their God watched over the elders of the Jews so that they were not hindered, until a report could go to Darius and then a written order be sent back concerning this matter.

6 A copy of the letter sent to King Darius by Tattenai, governor of West-of-Euphrates, and Shethar-bozenai, and their fellow officials from West-of-Euphrates; 7 they sent him a report in which was written the following:

"To King Darius, all good wishes! 8 Let it be known to the king that we have visited the province of Judah and the house of the great God: it is being rebuilt of cut stone and the walls are being reinforced with timber; the work is being carried on diligently and is making good progress under their hands. 9 We then questioned the elders, addressing to them the following words: 'Who issued the decree for you to build this house and raise this edifice?' 10 We also asked them their names, to report them to you in a list of the men who are their leaders. 11 This was their answer to us: 'We are the servants of the God of heaven and earth, and we are rebuilding the house built here long years ago, which a great king of Israel built and finished. 12 But because our fathers provoked the wrath of the God of heaven, he delivered them into the power of the Chaldean, Nebuchadnezzar, king of Babylon, who destroyed this house and led the people captive to Babylon. 13 However, in the first year of Cyrus, king of Babylon, King Cyrus issued a decree for the rebuilding of this house of God. 14 Moreover, the gold and silver utensils of the house of God which Nebuchadnezzar had taken from the temple in Jerusalem and carried off to the temple in Babylon, King Cyrus ordered to be removed from the temple in Babylon and consigned to a certain Sheshbazzar, whom he named governor. 15 And he commanded him: Take these utensils and deposit them in the temple of Jerusalem, and let the house of God be rebuilt on its former site. 16 Then this same Sheshbazzar came and laid the foundations of the house of God in Jerusalem. Since that time the building has been going on, and it is not yet completed.' 17 Now, if it please the king, let a search be made in the royal archives of Babylon to discover whether a decree really was issued by King Cyrus for the rebuilding of this house of God in Jerusalem. And may the king's pleasure in this matter be communicated to us."

The Decree of Darius

6 1 Thereupon King Darius issued an order to search the archives in which the Babylonian records were stored away; 2* and in Ecbatana, the stronghold in the province of Media, a scroll was found containing the following text: "Memorandum. 3 In the first year of King Cyrus, King Cyrus issued a decree: The house of God in Jerusalem. The house is to be rebuilt as a place for offering sacrifices and bringing burnt offerings. Its height is to be sixty cubits and its width sixty cubits. 4 It shall have

---

4, 24: *The second year . . . of Darius:* 520 B.C.; it marks the beginning of the successful restoration of the temple, which was accomplished within the five years following (Ezr 5, 1—6, 18).

5, 1: *The prophets Haggai and Zechariah:* two of the Minor Prophets, whose books record their role in the encouragement of this work.

4, 23: Neh 1, 3.
5, 1: Hg 1, 14—2, 9;
Zec 4, 9.
6, 2—12: Ezr 1, 4—11.

three courses of cut stone for each one of timber. The costs are to be borne by the royal palace. [5] Also, the gold and silver utensils of the house of God which Nebuchadnezzar took from the temple of Jerusalem and brought to Babylon are to be sent back: to be returned to their place in the temple of Jerusalem and deposited in the house of God.

did you KNOW?

The Second Temple

The first Temple, built during Solomon's reign, was destroyed in 587 B.C. when the southern kingdom of Judah was conquered by the Babylonians. The Persian king, Cyrus II, conquered Babylon in 539 B.C. and a year later liberated the Jewish exiles in Babylon. He also decreed that the Temple in Jerusalem be rebuilt (Ezr 6, 3). Between the years 520 and 515 the second Temple was rebuilt in Jerusalem. The second Temple was an essential aspect of the Israelites' rebuilding of their life, culture, and religion after the Babylonian Exile. This Temple, rather than a king, became the central focus of Jewish identity.

[6] "Now, therefore, Tattenai, governor of West-of-Euphrates, and Shethar-bozenai, and you, their fellow officials in West-of-Euphrates, do not interfere in that place. [7] Let the governor and the elders of the Jews continue the work on that house of God; they are to rebuild it on its former site. [8] I also issue this decree concerning your dealing with these elders of the Jews in the rebuilding of that house of God: From the royal revenue, the taxes of West-of-Euphrates, let these men be repaid for their expenses, in full and without delay. [9] Whatever else is required—young bulls, rams, and lambs for holocausts to the God of heaven, wheat, salt, wine, and oil, according to the requirements of the priests who are in Jerusalem—is to be delivered to them day by day without fail, [10] that they may continue to offer sacrifices of pleasing odor to the God of heaven and pray for the life of the king and his sons. [11] I also issue this decree: If any man violates

this edict, a beam is to be taken from his house, and he is to be lifted up and impaled on it; and his house is to be reduced to rubble for this offense. [12] And may the God who causes his name to dwell there overthrow every king or people who may undertake to alter this or to destroy this house of God in Jerusalem. I, Darius, have issued this decree; let it be carefully executed."

[13] Then Tattenai, the governor of West-of-Euphrates, and Shethar-bozenai, and their fellow officials carried out fully the instructions King Darius had sent them. [14] The elders of the Jews continued to make progress in the building, supported by the message of the prophets, Haggai and Zechariah, son of Iddo. They finished the building according to the command of the God of Israel and the decrees of Cyrus and Darius [and of Artaxerxes, king of Persia]. [15] They completed this house on the third day of the month Adar, in the sixth year of the reign of King Darius. [16] The Israelites—priests, Levites, and the other returned exiles—celebrated the dedication of this house of God with joy. [17] For the dedication of this house of God, they offered one hundred bulls, two hundred rams, and four hundred lambs, together with twelve he-goats as a sin-offering for all Israel, in keeping with the number of the tribes of Israel. [18] Finally, they set up the priests in their classes and the Levites in their divisions for the service of God in Jerusalem, as is prescribed in the book of Moses.

The Passover

[19]* The exiles kept the Passover on the fourteenth day of the first month. [20] The Levites, every one of whom had purified himself for the occasion, sacrificed the Passover for the rest of the exiles, for their brethren the priests, and for themselves. [21]* The Israelites who had returned from the exile partook of it together with all those who had separated themselves from the uncleanness of the peoples of the land to join them in seeking the LORD, the God of Israel. [22]† They joyfully kept the feast of Unleavened Bread for seven days, for the LORD had filled them with joy by making the king of Assyria favorable to them, so that he gave them help in their work on the house of God, the God of Israel.

II: The Deeds of Ezra

Ezra the Scribe

7 [1]† After these events, during the reign of Artaxerxes, king of Persia, Ezra, son of Seraiah, son

---

6, 22: *Assyria:* used here in a broad sense for the Persian Empire.
7, 1–8: The date of Ezra's journey to Palestine is not known with certainty. The seventh year of King Artaxerxes I would be 458 B.C., and the present order of the text suggests that date. The narratives of

Ezra and Nehemiah make it seem to many, however, that the arrival of Nehemiah in 445 B.C. should precede that of Ezra. If so, Ezra may

6, 19–22: Ex 12, 1–20.   6, 21: Ps 47, 9.

of Azariah, son of Hilkiah, 2 son of Shallum, son of
Zadok, son of Ahitub, 3 son of Amariah, son of Azariah, son of Meraioth, 4 son of Zerahiah, son of
Uzzi, son of Bukki, 5 son of Abishua, son of Phinehas, son of Eleazar, son of the high priest Aaron—
6* this Ezra came up from Babylon. He was a scribe,
well-versed in the law of Moses which was given by
the LORD, the God of Israel. Because the hand of the
LORD, his God, was upon him, the king granted
him all that he requested.

7 Some of the Israelites and some priests, Levites,
singers, gatekeepers, and temple slaves also came
up to Jerusalem in the seventh year of King Artaxerxes. 8 Ezra came to Jerusalem in the fifth month
of that seventh year of the king. 9 On the first day of
the first month he resolved on the journey up from
Babylon, and on the first day of the fifth month he
arrived at Jerusalem, for the favoring hand of his
God was upon him. 10* Ezra had set his heart on
the study and practice of the law of the LORD and
on teaching statutes and ordinances in Israel.

The Decree of Artaxerxes

11 This is a copy of the rescript which King Artaxerxes gave to Ezra the priest-scribe, the scribe of the
text of the LORD's commandments and statutes
for Israel:

12* "Artaxerxes, king of kings, to Ezra the priest,
scribe of the law of the God of heaven (then, after
greetings): 13 I have issued this decree, that anyone
in my kingdom belonging to the people of Israel, its
priests or Levites, who is minded to go up to
Jerusalem with you, may do so. 14 You are the envoy
from the king and his seven counselors to supervise
Judah and Jerusalem in respect of the law of your
God which is in your possession, 15 and to bring
with you the silver and gold which the king and his
counselors have freely contributed to the God of Israel, whose dwelling is in Jerusalem, 16 as well as all
the silver and gold which you may receive throughout the province of Babylon, together with the free-
will offerings which the people and priests freely
contribute for the house of their God in Jerusalem.
17 You must take care, therefore, to use this money
to buy bulls, rams, lambs, and the cereal offerings
and libations proper to these, and offer them on the
altar of the house of your God in Jerusalem. 18 You
and your brethren may do whatever seems best to
you with the remainder of the silver and gold, con-
formably to the will of your God. 19 The utensils
consigned to you for the service of the house of
your God you are to deposit before the God of

Jerusalem. 20 Whatever else you may be required to
supply for the needs of the house of your God, you
may draw from the royal treasury. 21 I, Artaxerxes
the king, issue this decree to all the treasurers of
West-of-Euphrates: Whatever Ezra the priest, scribe
of the law of the God of heaven, requests of you,
dispense to him accurately, 22 within these limits:
silver, one hundred talents; wheat, one hundred
kors; wine, one hundred baths; oil, one hundred
baths; salt, without limit. 23 Let everything that is
ordered by the God of heaven be carried out exactly for the house of the God of heaven, that wrath
may not come upon the realm of the king and his
sons. 24 We also inform you that it is not permitted
to impose taxes, tributes, or tolls on any priest,
Levite, singer, gatekeeper, temple slave, or any other
servant of that house of God.

25*† "As for you, Ezra, in accordance with the
wisdom of your God which is in your possession,
appoint magistrates and judges to administer justice to all the people in West-of-Euphrates, to all,
that is, who know the laws of your God. Instruct
those who do not know these laws. 26 Whoever
does not obey the law of your God and the law of
the king, let strict judgment be executed upon him,
whether death, or corporal punishment, or a fine
on his goods, or imprisonment."

Ezra and His Companions

27 Blessed be the LORD, the God of our fathers,
who thus disposed the mind of the king to glorify
the house of the LORD in Jerusalem, 28* and who let
me find favor with the king, with his counselors,
and with all the most influential royal officials. I
therefore took courage and, with the hand of the
LORD, my God, upon me, I gathered together Israelite family heads to make the return journey
with me.

8 1 This is the list of the family heads who returned with me from Babylon during the reign
of King Artaxerxes:

2 Of the sons of Phinehas, Gershon; of the sons
of Ithamar, Daniel; of the sons of David, Hattush,
3 son of Shecaniah; of the sons of Parosh, Zechariah, and with him one hundred and fifty males were
enrolled; 4 of the sons of Pahath-moab, Eliehoenai,
son of Zerahiah, and with him two hundred males;
5 of the sons of Zattu, Shecaniah, son of Jahaziel,
and with him three hundred males; 6 of the sons
of Adin, Ebed, son of Jonathan, and with him
fifty males; 7 of the sons of Elam, Jeshaiah, son of

† be thought to have come in 398 B.C., the seventh year of King Artaxerxes II. Others argue for the thirty-seventh year of Artaxerxes I,
that is, 428 B.C.; this would suppose that the date given in the text
has suffered in transmission.
7, 25: *The wisdom of your God:* the Mosaic law; cf vv 6, 14.

7, 6: Ezr 7, 28; 8, 18; Neh   **7, 12–17:** Ezr 1, 2ff.
    2, 8.18.   **7, 25:** 2 Chr 17, 9.
7, 10: Ps 119, 45.   **7, 28:** Ezr 7, 6.

Athaliah, and with him seventy males; [8] of the sons of Shephatiah, Zebadiah, son of Michael, and with him eighty males; [9] of the sons of Joab, Obadiah, son of Jehiel, and with him two hundred and eighteen males; [10] of the sons of Bani, Shelomith, son of Josiphiah, and with him one hundred and sixty males; [11] of the sons of Bebai, Zechariah, son of Bebai, and with him twenty-eight males; [12] of the sons of Azgad, Johanan, son of Hakkatan, and with him one hundred and ten males; [13] of the sons of Adonikam, younger sons, whose names were Eliphelet, Jeiel, and Shemaiah, and with them sixty males; [14] of the sons of Bigvai, Uthai, son of Zakkur, and with him seventy males.

The Journey to Jerusalem

[15]† I had them assemble by the river that flows toward Ahava, where we made camp for three days. There I perceived that both laymen and priests were present, but I could not discover a single Levite. [16] Therefore I sent Eliezer, Ariel, Shemaiah, Jarib, Elnathan, Nathan, Zechariah, and Meshullam, wise leaders, [17] with a command for Iddo, the leader in the place Casiphia, instructing them what to say to Iddo and his brethren, and to the temple slaves in Casiphia, in order to procure for us ministers for the house of our God. [18]* They sent to us—for the favoring hand of our God was upon us—a well-instructed man, one of the sons of Mahli, son of Levi, son of Israel, namely Sherebiah, with his sons and brethren, eighteen men. [19] They also sent us Hashabiah, and with him Jeshaiah, sons of Merari, and their brethren and their sons, twenty men. [20]* Of the temple slaves (those whom David and the princes appointed to serve the Levites) there were two hundred and twenty. All these men were enrolled by name.

[21] Then I proclaimed a fast, there by the river of Ahava, that we might humble ourselves before our God to petition from him a safe journey for ourselves, our children, and all our possessions. [22]* For I would have been ashamed to ask the king for troops and horsemen to protect us against enemies along the way, since we had said to the king, "The favoring hand of our God is upon all who seek him, but his mighty wrath is against all who forsake him." [23] So we fasted, and prayed to our God for this, and our petition was granted. [24] Next I selected twelve of the priestly leaders along with Sherebiah, Hashabiah, and ten of their brethren, [25] and I weighed out before them the silver and the gold and the utensils offered for the house of our God by the king, his counselors, his officials, and all the Israelites of that region. I consigned it to them in these amounts: [26] silver, six hundred and fifty talents; silver utensils, one hundred; gold, one hundred talents; [27] twenty golden bowls valued at a thousand darics; two vases of excellent polished bronze, as precious as gold. [28] I addressed them in these words: "You are consecrated to the LORD, and the utensils are also consecrated; the silver and the gold are a free-will offering to the LORD, the God of your fathers. [29] Keep good watch over them till you weigh them out in Jerusalem in the presence of the chief priests and Levites and the family leaders of Israel, in the chambers of the house of the LORD." [30] The priests and the Levites then took over the silver, the gold, and the utensils that had been weighted out, to bring them to Jerusalem, to the house of our God.

[31] We set out for Jerusalem from the river of Ahava on the twelfth day of the first month. The hand of our God remained upon us, and he protected us from enemies and bandits along the way. [32] Thus we arrived at Jerusalem, where we first rested for three days. [33] On the fourth day, the silver, the gold, and the utensils were weighed out in the house of our God and consigned to the priest Meremoth, son of Uriah, who was assisted by Eleazar, son of Phinehas; they were assisted by the Levites Jozabad, son of Jeshua, and Noadiah, son of Binnui. [34] Everything was in order as to number and weight, and the total weight was registered. At that same time, [35] those who had returned from the captivity, the exiles, offered as holocausts to the God of Israel twelve bulls for all Israel, ninety-six rams, seventy-seven lambs, and twelve goats as sin-offerings: all these as a holocaust to the LORD. [36]† Finally, the orders of the king were presented to the king's satraps and to the governors in West-of-Euphrates, who gave their support to the people and to the house of God.

Denunciation of Mixed Marriages

9 [1]* When these matters had been concluded, the leaders approached me with this report: "Neither the Israelite laymen nor the priests nor the Levites have kept themselves aloof from the peoples of the land and their abominations [Canaanites, Hittites, Perizzites, Jebusites, Ammonites, Moabites, Egyptians, and Amorites]; [2] for they have taken some of their daughters as wives for themselves and

---

† **8, 15:** *Ahava:* a town at an unidentified site in Babylonia. The river that flowed toward it was probably a branch or canal of the Euphrates.
8, 36: The story of Ezra's mission is seemingly continued from this point by Neh 7, 72b—8, 18, which may be read before Ezr 9, 1.

8, 18: Ezr 7, 6.
8, 20: Ezr 2, 43.
8, 22: Neh 2, 9.
9, 1f: Dt 7, 1; Neh 9, 2.

their sons, and thus they have desecrated the holy race with the peoples of the land. Furthermore, the leaders and rulers have taken a leading part in this apostasy!"

Ezra's Exhortation

3* When I had heard this thing, I tore my cloak and my mantle, plucked hair from my head and beard, and sat there stupefied. 4* Around me gathered all who were in dread of the sentence of the God of Israel on this apostasy of the exiles, while I remained motionless until the evening sacrifice. 5 Then, at the time of the evening sacrifice, I rose in my wretchedness, and with cloak and mantle torn I fell on my knees, stretching out my hands to the LORD, my God.

6* I said: "My God, I am too ashamed and confounded to raise my face to you, O my God, for our wicked deeds are heaped up above our heads and our guilt reaches up to heaven. 7† From the time of our fathers even to this day great has been our guilt, and for our wicked deeds we have been delivered over, we and our kings and our priests, to the will of the kings of foreign lands, to the sword, to captivity, to pillage, and to disgrace, as is the case today.

8* "And now, but a short time ago, mercy came to us from the LORD, our God, who left us a remnant and gave us a stake in his holy place; thus our God has brightened our eyes and given us relief in our servitude. 9* For slaves we are, but in our servitude our God has not abandoned us; rather, he has turned the good will of the kings of Persia toward us. Thus he has given us new life to raise again the

house of our God and restore its ruins, and has granted us a fence in Judah and Jerusalem. 10 But now, O our God, what can we say after all this? For we have abandoned your commandments, 11* which you gave through your servants the prophets: the land which you are entering to take as your possession is a land unclean with the filth of the peoples of the land, with the abominations with which they have filled it from one end to the other in their uncleanness. 12* Do not, then, give your daughters to their sons in marriage, and do not take their daughters for your sons. Never promote their peace and prosperity; thus you will grow strong, enjoy the produce of the land, and leave it as an inheritance to your children forever.

13 "After all that has come upon us for our evil deeds and our great guilt—though you, our God, have made less of our sinfulness than it deserved and have allowed us to survive as we do— 14 shall we again violate your commandments by intermarrying with these abominable peoples? Would you not become so angered with us as to destroy us without remnant or survivor? 15 O LORD, God of Israel, you are just; yet we have been spared, the remnant we are today. Here we are before you in our sins. Because of all this, we can no longer stand in your presence."

The People's Response

10 1 While Ezra prayed and acknowledged their guilt, weeping and prostrate before the house of God, a very large assembly of Israelites gathered about him, men, women, and children;

EZR

Who Belongs, and Who Does Not?

LIVE IT!

In Ezra, chapters 9–10, Ezra tells the people to reject their foreign wives and children. Nehemiah does the same in Neh 13, 23–27. This probably strikes us as harsh, but we can try to understand the Israelites' situation. Only a remnant of the Israelites was left to re-establish Israel's identity. History had taught the Israelites that intermarriage led to a watering down of their faith and of the people's loyalty to their religious practices. The only way to survive as a people was to separate themselves from outsiders.

This separation led to an even greater animosity between the Jews from Judah and their cousins in faith, the Samaritans. We see some of this prejudice in the Gospels (see Jn 4, 1–42 and "Discrimination in Jesus' Time," Lk 10, 25–37). Christians have had similar separations throughout our history. Today, the church teaches us to be faithful to our beliefs but also to be open to others who believe differently and discover together what we have in common.

▸ Ezra, chapters 9–10

9, 7: After this verse, the next part of the prayer attributed to Ezra is perhaps to be found in Neh 9, 6–37, which may be read as leading up to Ezr 9, 8–15.

9, 3: Ps 119, 136.
9, 4: Is 66, 2.
9, 6: Ps 38, 4.
9, 8: Is 4, 3.

9, 9: Ps 106, 46.
9, 11: Lv 18, 24f; Ez 36, 17.
9, 12: Dt 7, 3.

and the people wept profusely. 2 Then Shecaniah, the son of Jehiel, one of the sons of Elam, made this appeal to Ezra: "We have indeed betrayed our God by taking as wives foreign women of the peoples of the land. Yet even now there remains a hope for Israel. 3 Let us therefore enter into a covenant before our God to dismiss all our foreign wives and the children born of them, in keeping with what you, my lord, advise, and those who fear the commandments of our God. Let the law be observed! 4 Rise, then, for this is your duty! We will stand by you, so have courage and take action!"

5 Ezra rose to his feet and demanded an oath from the chiefs of the priests, from the Levites and from all Israel that they would do as had been proposed; and they swore it. 6† Then Ezra retired from his place before the house of God and entered the chamber of Johanan, son of Eliashib, where he spent the night neither eating food nor drinking water, for he was in mourning over the betrayal by the exiles. 7 A proclamation was made throughout Judah and Jerusalem that all the exiles should gather together in Jerusalem, 8 and that whoever failed to appear within three days would, according to the judgment of the leaders and elders, suffer the confiscation of all his possessions, and himself be excluded from the assembly of the exiles.

9† All the men of Judah and Benjamin gathered together in Jerusalem within the three-day period: it was in the ninth month, on the twentieth day of the month. All the people, standing in the open place before the house of God, were trembling both over the matter at hand and because it was raining. 10 Then Ezra, the priest, stood up and said to them: "Your unfaithfulness in taking foreign women as wives has added to Israel's guilt. 11* But now, give praise to the LORD, the God of your fathers, and do his will: separate yourselves from the peoples of the land and from these foreign women." 12 In answer, the whole assembly cried out with a loud voice: "Yes, it is our duty to do as you say! 13 But the people are numerous and it is the rainy season, so that we cannot remain out-of-doors; besides, this is not a task that can be performed in a single day or even two, for those of us who have sinned in this regard are many. 14 Let our leaders represent the whole assembly; then let all those in our cities who have taken foreign women

for wives appear at appointed times, accompanied by the elders and magistrates of each city in question, till we have turned away from us our God's burning anger over this affair." 15 Only Jonathan, son of Asahel, and Jahzeiah, son of Tikvah, were against this proposal, with Meshullam and Shabbethai the Levite supporting them.

The Guilty

16† The exiles did as agreed. Ezra appointed as his assistants men who were family heads, one for each family, all of them designated by name. They held sessions to examine the matter, beginning with the first day of the tenth month. 17 By the first day of the first month they had passed judgment on all the men who had taken foreign women for wives.

18 Among the priests, the following were found to have taken foreign women for wives: Of the sons of Jeshua, son of Jozadak, and his brethren: Maaseiah, Eiezer, Jarib, and Gedaliah. 19 They pledged themselves to dismiss their wives, and as a guilt-offering for their guilt they gave a ram from the flock. 20 Of the sons of Immer: Hanani and Zebadiah; 21 of the sons of Harim: Maaseiah, Elijah, Shemaiah, Jehiel, and Uzziah; 22 of the sons of Pashhur: Elioenai, Maaseiah, Ishmael, Nethanel, Jozabad, and Elasah.

23* Of the Levites: Jozabad, Shemei, Kelaiah (also called Kelita), Pethahiah, Judah, and Eliezer.

24 Of the singers: Eliashib and Zakkur; of the gatekeepers: Shallum, Te'em, and Uri.

25 Among the other Israelites: Of the sons of Parosh: Ramiah, Izziah, Malchijah, Mijamin, Eleazar, Malchijah, and Benaiah; 26 of the sons of Elam: Mattaniah, Zechariah, Jehiel, Abdi, Jeremoth, and Elijah; 27 of the sons of Zattu: Elioenai, Eliashib, Mattaniah, Jeremoth, Zabad, and Aziza; 28 of the sons of Bebai: Jehohanan, Hananiah, Zabbai, and Athlai; 29 of the sons of Bani: Meshullam, Malluch, Adaiah, Jashub, Sheal, and Jeremoth; 30 of the sons of Pahath-moab: Adna, Chelal, Benaiah, Maaseiah, Mattaniah, Bezalel, Binnui, and Manasseh; 31 of the sons of Harim: Eliezer, Isshijah, Malchijah, Shemaiah, Shimeon, 32 Benjamin, Malluch, Shemariah; 33 of the sons of Hashum: Mattenai, Mattattah, Zabad, Eliphelet, Jeremai, Manasseh, Shimei; 34 of the sons of Begui: Maadai, Amram, Uel, 35 Benaiah, Bedeiah, Cheluhi, 36 Vani-

---

10, 6: *Johanan, son of Eliashib:* actually, the grandson of Eliashib; the father of Johanan was Eliashib's son Joiada (Neh 12, 10f, 22). Since Eliashib was high priest at the time of Nehemiah (Neh 3, 1. 20f; 13, 4.7) and Johanan, if not yet high priest, was at least old enough to have his own separate quarters (chamber) in the temple at the time of Ezra, it is practically certain that Nehemiah's activity in Jerusalem must have preceded that of Ezra.

10, 9: *Ninth month:* Chislev (November–December), during the

"early rains" in Palestine. Since the assembly took place *in the open . . . all the people . . . were trembling . . . because it was raining.*

10, 16f: The work of the committee lasted three months, from the first day of the tenth month, Tebet (December–January), to the first day of the first month, Nisan (March–April), of the following Jewish year.

10, 11: Neh 9, 2.   10, 23: Neh 8, 7; 10, 11.

ah, Meremoth, Eliashib, ³⁷ Mattaniah, Mattenai, and Jaasu; ³⁸ of the sons of Binnui: Shimei, ³⁹ Shelemiah, Nathan, and Adaiah; ⁴⁰ of the sons of Zachai: Shashai, Sharai, ⁴¹ Azarel, Shelemiah, Shemariah, ⁴² Shallum, Amariah, Joseph; ⁴³ of the sons of Nebo: Jeiel, Mattithiah, Zabad, Zebina, Jaddai, Joel, Benaiah.

⁴⁴† All these had taken foreign wives; but they sent them away, both the women and their children.

10, 44: The account of the problem of mixed marriages at the time of Ezra is continued in Neh 9, 1–5; this may be read immediately after Ezr 10, 44, though the date given in Neh 9, 1 fits more precisely after Ezr 10, 15; cf Hg 2, 10–14.

EZR

Nehemiah

For background on this book, see the introduction to Ezra and Nehemiah on page 472.

I: The Deeds of Nehemiah

Nehemiah's Vocation

1 ¹† The words of Nehemiah, the son of Hacaliah.

In the month Chislev of the twentieth year, I was in the citadel of Susa ² when Hanani, one of my brothers, came with other men from Judah. I asked them about the Jews, the remnant preserved after the captivity, and about Jerusalem, ³ and they answered me: "The survivors of the captivity there in the province are in great distress and under reproach. Also, the wall of Jerusalem lies breached, and its gates have been gutted with fire." ⁴ When I heard this report, I began to weep and continued mourning for several days; I fasted and prayed before the God of heaven.

⁵* I prayed: "O LORD, God of heaven, great and awesome God, you who preserve your covenant of mercy toward those who love you and keep your commandments, ⁶* may your ear be attentive, and your eyes open, to heed the prayer which I, your servant, now offer in your presence day and night for your servants the Israelites, confessing the sins which we of Israel have committed against you, I

and my father's house included. ⁷* Grievously have we offended you, not keeping the commandments, the statutes, and the ordinances which you committed to your servant Moses. ⁸* But remember, I pray, the promise which you gave through Moses, your servant, when you said: 'Should you prove faithless, I will scatter you among the nations; ⁹ but should you return to me and carefully keep my commandments, even though your outcasts have been driven to the farthest corner of the world, I will gather them from there, and bring them back to the place which I have chosen as the dwelling place for my name.' ¹⁰* They are your servants, your people, whom you freed by your great might and your strong hand. ¹¹*† O LORD, may your ear be attentive to my prayer and that of all your willing servants who revere your name. Grant success to your servant this day, and let him find favor with this man"—for I was cupbearer to the king.

Appointment by the King

2 ¹ In the month Nisan of the twentieth year of King Artaxerxes, when the wine was in my charge, I took some and offered it to the king. As I had never before been sad in his presence, ² the

---

1, 1: The first mission of Nehemiah, from the twentieth year of Artaxerxes I, lasted from the spring (Neh 2, 1) of 445 B.C. until 433 B.C. (Neh 5, 14). It is recounted in Neh 1, 1—6, 15; 12, 27–43; 6, 16—7, 5; 11, 1–21, which may be read in that order.

1, 11: *Cupbearer to the king:* an important official in the royal household. Because Nehemiah could appear in the queen's pres-

ence (Neh 2, 6), it is commonly presumed that he was a eunuch; but this is not necessarily so.

1, 5: Dt 7, 9.12; Dn 9, 4.	**1, 8f:** Dt 30, 1–5.
1, 6: 2 Chr 6, 40.	**1, 10:** Dt 9, 29.
1, 7: Dn 3, 29f.	**1, 11:** Ps 118, 25.

Nehemiah Prepares for Action

Do you ever watch the news and think, Why bother trying to make the world a better place? Christians are called to social action—action for justice, action to make the world a better place. But social sin can scare Christians away from social action. Social sin—such as poverty, racism, violence, materialism, and indifference—seems too big for any individual to do much about. In the overwhelming face of social sin, it is easy to say, "I give up."

But then we have Nehemiah's example. When Nehemiah heard of the results of Israel's collective sin, he could have said, "I give up." Instead, he turned to God in fasting and prayer. Fasting and prayer help us focus on what is important. Fasting and prayer help us remember that God calls us only to be faithful in taking action. Let God worry about the results.

In your prayer, reflect or journal on the following questions:

- What social issue are you concerned about?
- What can you fast from to help yourself gain a new perspective on that issue? (You can fast from many things: food, television, a particular activity, a particular place.)
- What group can you get involved with to address this concern?
- What do you need to bring to God in prayer?

▶ Nehemiah, chapter 1

king asked me, "Why do you look sad? If you are not sick, you must be sad at heart." Though I was seized with great fear, [3] I answered the king: "May the king live forever! How could I not look sad when the city where my ancestors are buried lies in ruins, and its gates have been eaten out by fire?" [4] The king asked me, "What is it, then, that you wish?" I prayed to the God of heaven [5] and then answered the king: "If it please the king, and if your servant is deserving of your favor, send me to Judah, to the city of my ancestors' graves, to rebuild it." [6] Then the king, and the queen seated beside him, asked me how long my journey would take and when I would return. I set a date that was acceptable to him, and the king agreed that I might go.

[7] I asked the king further: "If it please the king, let letters be given to me for the governors of West-of-Euphrates, that they may afford me safe-conduct till I arrive in Judah; [8]* also a letter for Asaph, the keeper of the royal park, that he may give me wood for timbering the gates of the temple-citadel and for the city wall and the house that I shall occupy." The king granted my requests, for the favoring hand of my God was upon me. [9]* Thus I proceeded to the governors of West-of-Euphrates and presented the king's letters to them. The king also sent with me army officers and cavalry.

[10]† When Sanballat the Horonite and Tobiah the Ammonite slave had heard of this, they were very much displeased that someone had come to seek the welfare of the Israelites.

Circuit of the City

[11] When I had arrived in Jerusalem, I first rested there for three days. [12] Then I set out by night with only a few other men (for I had not told anyone what my God had inspired me to do for Jerusalem) and with no other animals but my own mount. [13]† I rode out at night by the Valley Gate, passed by the Dragon Spring, and came to the Dung Gate, observing how the walls of Jerusalem lay in ruins and its gates had been eaten out by fire. [14] Then I passed over to the Spring Gate and to the King's Pool. Since there was no room here for my mount to pass with me astride, [15] I continued on foot up the wadi by

---

2, 10: *Sanballat the Horonite:* the governor of the province of Samaria (Neh 3, 33f), apparently a native of one of the Beth-horons. A letter from the Jews living at Elephantine in southern Egypt, dated 408–407 B.C., mentions "Delayah and Shelemyah, the sons of Sanballat, the governor of Samaria." Although his own name was Babylonian—Sin-uballit, i.e., "Sin (the moon god) has given life"—two sons had names referring to Yahweh. *Tobiah the Ammonite slave:* the governor of the province of Ammon in Transjordan. His honorary title, "servant" (in Hebrew, *ebed*), i.e., of the king, could also be understood as slave, and Nehemiah no doubt meant it in this derogatory sense. The Tobiads remained a powerful family even in Maccabean times (2 Mc 3, 11). Sanballat and Tobiah together with Geshem the Arab (Neh 2, 19; 6, 1f), who was probably in charge of Edom and the regions to the south and southeast of Judah, opposed

the rebuilding of Jerusalem's walls on political grounds; the city was the capital of a rival province.

2, 13ff: Nehemiah left Jerusalem by the Valley Gate near the northwestern end of the old City of David and went south down the Tyropoean Valley toward the Dragon Spring (or the En-rogel of Jos 15, 7; 18, 16; 2 Sm 17, 17; 1 Kgs 1, 9, now known as Job's Well) at the juncture of the Valley of Hinnom and the Kidron Valley; he then turned north at the Dung Gate (or the Potsherd Gate of Jer 19, 2) at the southern end of the city and proceeded up the wadi, that is, the Kidron Valley, passing the Spring Gate (at the Spring of Gihon) and the King's Pool (unidentified); finally he turned west and then south to his starting point.

2, 8: Ezr 7, 6.   **2, 9:** Ezr 8, 22.

night, inspecting the wall all the while till I once more reached the Valley Gate, by which I went back in. 16 The magistrates knew nothing of where I had gone or what I was doing, for as yet I had disclosed nothing to the Jews, neither to the priests, nor to the nobles, nor to the magistrates, nor to the others who would be concerned about the matter.

Rebuilding Jerusalem's Walls

17 Afterward I said to them: "You see the evil plight in which we stand: how Jerusalem lies in ruins and its gates have been gutted by fire. Come, let us rebuild the wall of Jerusalem, so that we may no longer be an object of derision!" 18* Then I explained to them how the favoring hand of my God had rested upon me, and what the king had said to me. They replied, "Let us be up and building!" And they undertook the good work with vigor.

19 On hearing of this, Sanballat the Horonite, Tobiah the Ammonite slave, and Geshem the Arab mocked us and ridiculed us. "What is this that you are about?" they asked. "Are you rebelling against the king?" 20† My answer to them was this: "It is the God of heaven who will grant us success. We, his servants, shall set about the rebuilding; but for you there is to be neither share nor claim nor memorial in Jerusalem."

List of Workers†

3 1* Eliashib the high priest and his priestly brethren took up the task of rebuilding the Sheep Gate. They timbered it and set up its doors, its bolts, and its bars, then continued the rebuilding to the Tower of Hananel. 2 At their side the men of Jericho were rebuilding, and next to them was Zaccur, son of Imri. 3* The Fish Gate was rebuilt by the sons of Hassenaah; they timbered it and set up its doors, its bolts, and its bars. 4 At their side Meremoth, son of Uriah, son of Hakkoz, carried out the work of repair; next to him was Meshullam, son of Berechiah, son of Meshezabel; and next to him was Zadok, son of Baana. 5 Next to him the Tekoites carried out the work of repair; however, some of their outstanding men would not submit to the labor asked by their lords. 6 The New City Gate was repaired by Joiada, son of Paseah; and Meshullam, son of Besodeiah; they timbered it and set up its doors, its bolts, and its bars. 7 At their side were Melatiah the Gibeonite, Jadon the Meronothite, and the men of Gibeon and of Mizpah, who were

under the jurisdiction of the governor of West-of-Euphrates. 8† Next to them the work of repair was carried out by Uzziel, son of Harhaiah, a member of the goldsmiths' guild, and at his side was Hananiah, one of the perfumers' guild. They restored Jerusalem as far as the wall of the public square. 9 Next to them the work of repair was carried out by Rephaiah, son of Hur, leader of half the district of Jerusalem, 10 and at his side was Jedaiah, son of Harumaph, who repaired opposite his own house. Next to him Hattush, son of Hashabneiah, carried out the work of repair. 11 The adjoining sector, as far as the Oven Tower, was repaired by Malchijah, son of Harim, and Hasshub, of Pahath-moab. 12 At their side the work of repair was carried out by Shallum, son of Hallohesh, leader of half the district of Jerusalem, by himself and his daughters. 13 The Valley Gate was repaired by Hanun and the inhabitants of Zanoah; they rebuilt it and set up its doors, its bolts, and its bars. They also repaired a thousand cubits of the wall up to the Dung Gate. 14 The Dung Gate was repaired by Malchijah, son of Rechab, leader of the district of Beth-haccherem; he rebuilt it and set up its doors, its bolts, and its bars. 15 The Spring Gate was repaired by Shallum, son of Colhozeh, leader of the district of Mizpah; he rebuilt it, roofed it over, and set up its doors, its bolts, and its bars. He also repaired the wall of the Aqueduct Pool near the king's garden as far as the steps that lead down from the City of David. 16 After him, the work of repair was carried out by Nehemiah, son of Azbuk, leader of half the district of Beth-zur, to a place opposite the tombs of David, as far as the artificial pool and the barracks.

17 After him, the Levites carried out the work of repair: Rehum, son of Bani. Next to him, for his own district, was Hashabiah, leader of half the district of Keilah. 18 After him, their brethren carried out the work of repair: Binnui, son of Henadad, leader of half the district of Keilah; 19 next to him Ezer, son of Jeshua, leader of Mizpah, who repaired the adjoining sector, the Corner, opposite the ascent to the arsenal. 20 After him, Baruch, son of Zabbai, repaired the adjoining sector from the Corner to the entrance of the house of Eliashib, the high priest. 21 After him, Meremoth, son of Uriah, son of Hakkoz, repaired the adjoining sector from the entrance of Eliashib's house to the end of the house.

22 After him, the work of repair was carried out

2, 20: *Neither share nor claim nor memorial:* although Sanballat and Tobiah were Yahwist, Nehemiah would not let them participate in any of the rights of the religious community in Jerusalem.

3, 1–32: The construction work on the gates and walls of the city is described in counterclockwise direction, beginning and ending at the Sheep Gate (to the north of the temple). The exact sites of many of the topographical points mentioned are uncertain.

3, 8: *Wall of the public square:* that is, the section of wall bound-

ing the place of assembly outside the Gate of Ephraim, or New City Gate; cf Neh 3, 6; 8, 16.

2, 18: Ezr 7, 6.   3, 3: Ezr 2, 35; Zep 1, 10.
3, 1: Jer 31, 38.

by the priests, men of the surrounding country. [23] After them, Benjamin and Hasshub carried out the repair in front of their houses; after them, Azariah, son of Maaseiah, son of Ananiah, made the repairs alongside his house. [24] After him, Binnui, son of Henadad, repaired the adjoining sector from the house of Azariah to the Corner [that is, to the Angle]. [25] After him, Palal, son of Uzai, carried out the work of repair opposite the Corner and the tower projecting from the Upper Palace at the quarters of the guard. After him, Pedaiah, son of Parosh, carried out the work of repair [26] to a point opposite the Water Gate on the east, and the projecting tower. [27] After him, the Tekoites repaired the adjoining sector opposite the great projecting tower, to the wall of Ophel [the temple slaves were dwelling on Ophel].

[28] Above the Horse Gate the priests carried out the work of repair, each before his own house. [29]* After them Zadok, son of Immer, carried out the repair before his house, and after him the repair was carried out by Shemaiah, son of Shecaniah, keeper of the East Gate. [30] After him, Hananiah, son of Shelemiah, and Hanun, the sixth son of Zalaph, repaired the adjoining sector; after them, Meshullam, son of Berechiah, repaired the place opposite his own lodging. [31] After him, Malchijah, a member of the goldsmiths' guild, carried out the work of repair as far as the quarters of the temple slaves and the merchants, before the Gate of Inspection and as far as the upper chamber of the Angle. [32] Between the upper chamber of the Angle and the Sheep Gate, the goldsmiths and the merchants carried out the work of repair.

Opposition from Judah's Foes

[33] When Sanballat heard that we were rebuilding the wall, it roused his anger and he became very much incensed. He ridiculed the Jews, [34] saying in the presence of his brethren and the troops of Samaria: "What are these miserable Jews trying to do? Will they complete their restoration in a single day? Will they recover these stones, burnt as they are, from the heaps of dust?" [35] Tobiah the Ammonite was beside him, and he said: "It is a rubble heap they are building. Any fox that attacked it would breach their wall of stones!" [36] Take note, O our God, how we were mocked! Turn back their derision upon their own heads and let them be carried away to a land of captivity! [37]* Hide not their crime and let not their sin be blotted out in your sight, for they insulted the builders to their face! [38] We, however, continued to build the wall, which was soon filled in and completed up to half its height. The people worked with a will.

4 [1] When Sanballat, Tobiah, the Arabs, the Ammonites, and the Ashdodites heard that the restoration of the walls of Jerusalem was progressing—for the gaps were beginning to be closed up—they became extremely angry. [2] Thereupon they all plotted together to come and fight against Jerusalem and thus to throw us into confusion. [3] We prayed to our God and posted a watch against

Nehemiah's Strength

Many young people have traumatic experiences, such as the divorce of their parents, domestic and community violence, the death of a parent or sibling, prejudice, and poverty. Some young people come through these experiences as victims, unable to take any control of their life. Others take the attitude If you can't beat them, join them, and become cynical, violent, or antisocial. But some rise above their hurt to live a happy and healthy life. What can account for the difference in people's reactions?

Perhaps Nehemiah provides a clue. He was confronted by cynical people (Neh 3, 33–35) and violent people (4, 1–3). But he trusted in something bigger than himself. "It is the God of heaven who will grant us success" (2, 20), he proclaimed to those with negative attitudes.

Prayer and faith in God gave Nehemiah strength to take action in difficult times. They can work for us too. Don't let life's traumas make you powerless. Don't let them make you cynical and part of the problem. Pray and have faith, and you too will have the strength to meet your problems with action.

▸ Neh 3, 33—4, 17

3, 29: Ez 40, 6.   3, 37: Jer 18, 23.

them day and night for fear of what they might do. [4] Meanwhile the Judahites were saying:

> "Slackened is the bearers' strength,
>   there is no end to the rubbish;
> Never shall we be able
>   the wall to rebuild."

[5] Our enemies thought, "Before they are aware of it or see us, we shall come into their midst, kill them, and put an end to the work."

[6] When the Jews who lived near them had come to us from one place after another, and had told us ten times over that they were about to attack us, [7] I stationed guards down below, behind the wall, near the exposed points, assigning them by family groups with their swords, their spears, and their bows. [8] I made an inspection, then addressed these words to the nobles, the magistrates, and the rest of the people: "Have no fear of them! Keep in mind the LORD, who is great and to be feared, and fight for your brethren, your sons and daughters, your wives and your homes." [9] When our enemies became aware that we had been warned and that God had upset their plan, we all went back, each to his own task at the wall.

[10]* From that time on, however, only half my able men took a hand in the work, while the other half, armed with spears, bucklers, bows, and breastplates, stood guard behind the whole house of Judah [11] as they rebuilt the wall. The load carriers, too, were armed; each did his work with one hand and held a weapon with the other. [12] Every builder, while he worked, had his sword girt at his side. Also, a trumpeter stood beside me, [13] for I had said to the nobles, the magistrates, and the rest of the people: "Our work is scattered and extensive, and we are widely separated from one another along the wall; [14] wherever you hear the trumpet sound, join us there; our God will fight with us." [15] Thus we went on with the work, half of the men with spears at the ready, from daybreak till the stars came out.

[16] At the same time I told the people to spend the nights inside Jerusalem, each man with his own attendant, so that they might serve as a guard by night and a working force by day. [17] Neither I, nor my kinsmen, nor any of my attendants, nor any of the bodyguard that accompanied me took off his clothes; everyone kept his weapon at his right hand.

Antisocial Conduct

5 [1]* Then there rose a great outcry of the common people and their wives against certain of their fellow Jews. [2] Some said: "We are forced to pawn our sons and daughters in order to get grain to eat that we may live." [3] Others said: "We are forced to pawn our fields, our vineyards, and our houses, that we may have grain during the famine." [4] Still others said: "To pay the king's tax we have borrowed money on our fields and our vineyards. [5]* And though these are our own kinsmen and our children are as good as theirs, we have had to reduce our sons and daughters to slavery, and violence has been done to some of our daughters! Yet we can do nothing about it, for our fields and our vineyards belong to others."

Nehemiah's Action

[6] I was extremely angry when I heard the reasons they had for complaint. [7]† After some deliberation, I called the nobles and magistrates to account, saying to them, "You are exacting interest from your own kinsmen!" I then rebuked them severely, [8]* saying to them: "As far as we were able, we bought back our fellow Jews who had been sold to Gentiles; you, however, are selling your own brothers, to have them bought back by us." They remained silent, for they could find no answer. [9] I continued: "What you are doing is not good. Should you not walk in the fear of our God, and put an end to the derision of our Gentile enemies? [10] I myself, my kinsmen, and my attendants have lent the people money and grain without charge. Let us put an end to this usury! [11] I ask that you return to them this very day their fields, their vineyards, their olive groves, and their houses, together with the interest on the money, the grain, the wine, and the oil that you have lent them." [12] They answered: "We will return everything and exact nothing further from them. We will do just what you ask." Then I called for the priests and had them administer an oath to these men that they would do as they had promised. [13] I also shook out the folds of my garment, saying, "Thus may God shake from his home and his fortune every man who fails to keep this promise, and may he thus be shaken out and emptied!" And the whole assembly answered, "Amen," and praised the LORD. Then the people did as they had promised.

Nehemiah's Lack of Self-Interest

[14] Moreover, from the time that King Artaxerxes appointed me governor in the land of Judah, from his twentieth to his thirty-second year—during these twelve years neither I nor my brethren lived from the governor's allowance. [15] The earlier gover-

---

5, 7: *You are exacting interest from your own kinsmen!:* contrary to the Mosaic law (Dt 23, 20).

4, 10: Ps 149, 6.
5, 1f: Jer 34, 8–22.

5, 5: Ez 21, 7; Lv 25, 39.
5, 8: Lv 25, 48.

Hunger Pains

LIVE IT!

"I'm hungry."

"Yeah, I'm starved. Let's go get something to eat."

How many times have we uttered those words or heard them said? It's so easy. If we're hungry, we eat. If we're thirsty, we grab something to drink. If we're not feeling well, we get something to make us feel better. We forget sometimes that our way of doing things is the exception in the world, not the rule. Right now, people in this country and in the rest of the world are starving and have no idea where their next meal is coming from.

When Nehemiah's people were hungry, he saw the problem right away. The problem was not a lack of food. It was that some people were using their wealth and influence to control who got the food (Neh 5, 7–8). Nehemiah took the radical step of demanding that the powerful and wealthy stop taking advantage of those less well off. He demanded that the wealthy restore the money and property that they had taken from others through unjust taking of interest (verses 10–11).

Experts tell us that much the same is true today. People are starving not because food is scarce but because political and economic conditions prevent them from getting the food. If only we could be like Nehemiah and demand that the powerful and wealthy reform. Well, you know what? We can! We can educate ourselves and speak out through letters and phone calls to elected officials. And while we are calling for society to change, let's volunteer at a neighborhood pantry or soup kitchen to help feed the poor people in our own backyard.

▸ Nehemiah, chapter 5

NEH

---

nors, my predecessors, had laid a heavy burden on the people, taking from them each day forty silver shekels for their food; then too, their men oppressed the people. But I, because I feared God, did not act thus. ¹⁶ Moreover, though I had acquired no land of my own, I did my part in this work on the wall, and all my men were gathered there for the work. ¹⁷ Though I set my table for a hundred and fifty persons, Jews and magistrats, as well as those who came to us from the nations round about, ¹⁸ and though the daily preparations were made at my expense—one beef, six choice muttons, poultry—besides all kinds of wine in abundance every ten days, despite this I did not claim the governor's allowance, for the labor lay heavy upon this people. ¹⁹ Keep in mind, O my God, in my favor all that I did for this people.

Plots against Nehemiah

6 ¹ When it had been reported to Sanballat, Tobiah, Geshem the Arab, and our other enemies that I had rebuilt the wall and that there was no breach left in it (though up to that time I had not yet set up the doors in the gates), ² Sanballat and Geshem sent me this message: "Come, let us hold council together at Caphirim in the plain of Ono." They were planning to do me harm. ³ However, I sent messengers to them with this reply: "I am engaged in a great enterprise and am unable to come

down; why should the work stop, while I leave it to come down to you?" ⁴ Four times they sent me this same proposal, and each time I gave the same reply. ⁵ Then, the fifth time, Sanballat sent me the same message by one of his servants, who bore an unsealed letter ⁶ containing this text: "Among the nations it has been reported—Geshem is witness to this—that you and the Jews are planning a rebellion; that for this reason you are rebuilding the wall; and that you are to be their king"—and so on. ⁷ "Also, that you have set up prophets in Jerusalem to proclaim you king of Judah. Now, since matters like these must reach the ear of the king, come, let us hold council together." ⁸ I sent him this answer: "Nothing of what you report has taken place; rather, it is the invention of your own mind." ⁹ They were all trying to frighten us, thinking, "Their hands will slacken in the work, and it will never be completed." But instead, I now redoubled my efforts.

¹⁰ I went to the house of Shemaiah, son of Delaiah, son of Mehetabel, who was unable to go about, and he said:

"Let us meet in the house of God,
  inside the temple building;
  let us lock the doors of the temple.
For men are coming to kill you;
  by night they are coming coming to
    kill you."

¹¹ My answer was: "A man like me take flight? Can a man like me enter the temple to save his life? I will not go!" ¹² For on consideration it was plain to me that God had not sent him; rather, because Tobiah and Sanballat had bribed him, he voiced this prophecy concerning me ¹³ that I might act on it out of fear and commit this sin. Then they would have had a shameful story with which to discredit me. ¹⁴* Keep in mind Tobiah and Sanballat, O my God, because of these things they did; keep in mind as well Noadiah the prophetess and the other prophets who were trying to frighten me.

Conclusion of the Work

¹⁵† The wall was finished on the twenty-fifth day of Elul; it had taken fifty-two days. ¹⁶* When all our enemies had heard of this, and all the nations round about had taken note of it, our enemies lost much face in the eyes of the nations, for they knew that it was with our God's help that this work had been completed. ¹⁷† At that same time, however, many letters were going to Tobiah from the nobles of Judah, and Tobiah's letters were reaching them, ¹⁸ for many in Judah were in league with him, since he was the son-in-law of Shecaniah, son of Arah, and his son Jehohanan had married the daughter of Meshullam, son of Berechiah. ¹⁹ Thus they would praise his good deeds in my presence and relate to him whatever I said; and Tobiah sent letters trying to frighten me.

7 ¹ When the wall had been rebuilt, I had the doors set up, and the gatekeepers [and the singers and the Levites] were put in charge of them. ² Over Jerusalem I placed Hanani, my brother, and Hananiah, the commander of the citadel, who was a more trustworthy and God-fearing man than most. ³ I said to them: "The gates of Jerusalem are not to be opened until the sun is hot, and while the sun is still shining they shall shut and bar the doors. Appoint as watchmen the inhabitants of Jerusalem, some at their watch posts, and others before their own houses."

Census of the Province

⁴ Now the city was quite wide and spacious, but its population was small, and none of the houses had been rebuilt. ⁵ When my God had put it into my mind to gather together the nobles, the magistrates, and the common people, and to examine their family records, I came upon the family list of those who had returned in the earliest period. There I found the following written:

⁶*† These are the inhabitants of the province who returned from the captivity of the exiles whom Nebuchadnezzar, king of Babylon, had carried away, and who came back to Jerusalem and Judah, each man to his own city ⁷ (those who returned with Zerubbabel, Jeshua, Nehemiah, Azariah, Raamiah, Nahamani, Mordecai, Bilshan, Mispereth, Bigvai, Nehum, and Baanah).

The census of the men of Israel: ⁸ sons of Parosh, two thousand one hundred and seventy-two; ⁹ sons of Shephatiah, three hundred and seventy-two; ¹⁰ sons of Arah, six hundred and fifty-two; ¹¹ sons of Pahath-moab who were sons of Jeshua and Joab, two thousand eight hundred and eighteen; ¹² sons of Elam, one thousand two hundred and fifty-four; ¹³ sons of Zattu, eight hundred and forty-five; ¹⁴ sons of Zaccai, seven hundred and sixty; ¹⁵ sons of Binnui, six hundred and forty-eight; ¹⁶ sons of Bebai, six hundred and twenty-eight; ¹⁷ sons of Azgad, two thousand three hundred and twenty-two; ¹⁸ sons of Adonikam, six hundred and sixty-seven; ¹⁹ sons of Bigvai, two thousand and sixty-seven; ²⁰ sons of Adin, six hundred and fifty-five; ²¹ sons of Ater who were sons of Hezekiah, ninety-eight; ²² sons of Hashum, three hundred and twenty-eight; ²³ sons of Bezai, three hundred and twenty-four; ²⁴ sons of Hariph, one hundred and twelve; ²⁵ sons of Gibeon, ninety-five; ²⁶ men of Bethlehem and Netophah, one hundred and eighty-eight; ²⁷ men of Anathoth, one hundred and twenty-eight; ²⁸ men of Beth-azmaveth, forty-two; ²⁹ men of Kiriath-jearim, Chephirah, and Beeroth, seven hundred and forty-three; ³⁰ men of Ramah and Geba, six hundred and twenty-one; ³¹ men of Michmas, one hundred and twenty-two; ³² men of Bethel and Ai, one hundred and twenty-three; ³³ men of Nebo, fifty-two; ³⁴ sons of another Elam, one thousand two hundred and fifty-four; ³⁵ sons of Harim, three hundred and twenty; ³⁶ sons of Jericho, three hundred and forty-five; ³⁷ sons of Lod, Hadid, and Ono, seven hundred and twenty-one; ³⁸ sons of Senaah, three thousand nine hundred and thirty.

³⁹ The priests: sons of Jedaiah who were of the house of Jeshua, nine hundred and seventy-three; ⁴⁰ sons of Immer, one thousand and fifty-two; ⁴¹ sons of Pashhur, one thousand two hundred and forty-seven; ⁴² sons of Harim, one thousand and seventeen.

---

† **6, 15:** *Elul:* the sixth month (August–September). *Fifty-two days:* according to Josephus (*Antiquities* XI, v 8), the rebuilding of the walls of Jerusalem by Nehemiah took two years and four months, which seems more probable.

6, 17ff: These verses should be read immediately after v 14.
7, 6–72a: See note on Ezr 2, 1–67.

6, 14: Jer 23, 9–40;   6, 16: Ps 118, 22f; 127, 1.
Zec 13, 3.   7, 6–72: Ezr 2, 1–70.

43 The Levites: sons of Jeshua, Kadmiel, Binnui, Hodeviah, seventy-four.

44 The singers: sons of Asaph, one hundred and forty-eight.

45 The gatekeepers: sons of Shallum, sons of Ater, sons of Talmon, sons of Akkub, sons of Hatita, sons of Shobai, one hundred and thirty-eight.

46 The temple slaves: sons of Ziha, sons of Hasupha, sons of Tabbaoth, 47 sons of Keros, sons of Sia, sons of Padon, 48 sons of Lebana, sons of Hagaba, sons of Shalmai, 49 sons of Hanan, sons of Giddel, sons of Gahar, 50 sons of Reaiah, sons of Rezin, sons of Nekoda, 51 sons of Gazzam, sons of Uzza, sons of Paseah, 52 sons of Besai, sons of the Meunites, sons of the Nephusites, 53 sons of Bakbuk, sons of Hakupha, sons of Harhur, 54 sons of Bazlith, sons of Mehida, sons of Harsha, 55 sons of Barkos, sons of Sisera, sons of Temah, 56 sons of Neziah, sons of Hatipha.

57 Descendants of the slaves of Solomon: sons of Sotai, sons of Sophereth, sons of Perida, 58 sons of Jaala, sons of Darkon, sons of Giddel, 59 sons of Shephatiah, sons of Hattil, sons of Pocherethhazzebaim, sons of Amon. 60 The total of the temple slaves and the descendants of the slaves of Solomon was three hundred and ninety-two.

61 The following who returned from Telmelah, Tel-harsha, Cherub, Addon, and Immer were unable to prove that their ancestral houses and their descent were Israelite: 62 sons of Delaiah, sons of Tobiah, sons of Nekoda, six hundred and forty-two. 63 Also, of the priests: sons of Hobaiah, sons of Hakkoz, sons of Barzillai (he had married one of the daughters of Barzillai the Gileadite and became known by his name). 64 These men searched their family records, but their names could not be found written there; hence they were degraded from the priesthood, 65† and His Excellency ordered them not to partake of the most holy foods until there should be a priest bearing the Urim and Thummim.

66 The entire assembly taken together came to forty-two thousand three hundred and sixty, 67 not counting their male and female slaves, who were seven thousand three hundred and thirty-seven. They also had two hundred male and female singers. Their horses were seven hundred and thirty-six, their mules two hundred and forty-five, 68 their camels four hundred and thirty-five, their asses six thousand seven hundred and twenty.

69 Certain of the family heads contributed to the service. His Excellency put into the treasury one thousand drachmas of gold, fifty basins, thirty garments for priests, and five hundred minas of silver. 70 Some of the family heads contributed to the treasury for the temple service: twenty thousand drachmas of gold and two thousand two hundred minas of silver. 71 The contributions of the rest of the people amounted to twenty thousand drachmas of gold, two thousand minas of silver, and sixty-seven garments for priests.

72 The priests, the Levites, the gatekeepers, the singers, the temple slaves, and all Israel took up residence in their cities.

II: Promulgation of the Law

Ezra Reads the Law†

8 * Now when the seventh month came, 1 the whole people gathered as one man in the open space before the Water Gate, and they called upon Ezra the scribe to bring forth the book of the law of Moses which the LORD prescribed for Israel. 2 On the first day of the seventh month, therefore, Ezra the priest brought the law before the assembly, which consisted of men, women, and those children old enough to understand. 3 Standing at one end of the open place that was before the Water Gate, he read out of the book from daybreak till midday, in the presence of the men, the women, and those children old enough to understand; and all the people listened attentively to the book of the law. 4 Ezra the scribe stood on a wooden platform that had been made for the occasion; at his right side stood Mattithiah, Shema, Anaiah, Uriah, Hilkiah, and Maaseiah, and on his left Pedaiah, Mishael, Malchijah, Hashum, Hashbaddanah, Zechariah, Meshullam. 5 Ezra opened the scroll so that all the people might see it (for he was standing higher up than any of the people); and, as he opened it, all the people rose. 6 Ezra blessed the LORD, the great God, and all the people, their hands raised high, answered, "Amen, amen!" Then they bowed down and prostrated themselves before the LORD, their faces to the ground. 7* [The Levites Jeshua, Bani, Sherebiah, Jamin, Akkub, Shabbethai, Hodiah, Maaseiah, Kelita, Azariah, Jozabad, Hanan, and Pelaiah explained the law to the people, who remained in their places.] 8* Ezra read plainly from the book of the law of God, interpreting it so that all could understand what was read. 9 Then [Nehemiah, that is, His Excellency, and] Ezra the priestscribe [and the Levites who were instructing the

7, 65.69: His Excellency: see note on Ezr 2, 63.

7, 72b—8, 18: To be read after Ezr 8, 36. The gloss mentioning Nehemiah in v 9 was inserted in this Ezra section after the dislocation of several parts of Ezra-Nehemiah had occurred. There is no clear evidence of a simultaneous presence of Nehemiah and Ezra in Jerusalem; Neh 12, 26 and 12, 36 are also scribal glosses.

8, 1: Ezr 3, 1.   8, 8: Ezr 7, 6.
8, 7: Neh 10, 11.

people] said to all the people: "Today is holy to the LORD your God. Do not be sad, and do not weep"— for all the people were weeping as they heard the words of the law. 10* He said further: "Go, eat rich foods and drink sweet drinks, and allot portions to those who had nothing prepared; for today is holy to our LORD. Do not be saddened this day, for rejoicing in the LORD must be your strength!" 11 [And the Levites quieted all the people, saying, "Hush, for today is holy, and you must not be saddened."] 12 Then all the people went to eat and drink, to distribute portions, and to celebrate with great joy, for they understood the words that had been expounded to them.

The Feast of Booths

13 On the second day, the family heads of the whole people and also the priests and the Levites gathered around Ezra the scribe and examined the words of the law more closely. 14* They found it written in the law prescribed by the LORD through Moses that the Israelites must dwell in booths during the feast of the seventh month; 15* and that they should have this proclamation made throughout their cities and in Jerusalem: "Go out into the hill country and bring in branches of olive trees, oleasters, myrtle, palm, and other leafy trees, to make booths, as the law prescribes." 16 The people went out and brought in branches with which they made booths for themselves, on the roofs of their houses, in their courtyards, in the courts of the house of God, and in the open spaces of the Water Gate and the Gate of Ephraim. 17 Thus the entire assembly of the returned exiles made booths and dwelt in them. Now the Israelites had done nothing of this sort from the days of Jeshua, son of Nun, until this occasion; therefore there was very great joy. 18 Ezra read from the book of the law of God day after day, from the first day to the last. They kept the feast for seven days, and the solemn assembly on the eighth day, as was required.

Confession of the People

9 1*† On the twenty-fourth day of this month, the Israelites gathered together fasting and in sackcloth, their heads covered with dust. 2* Those of Israelite descent separated themselves from all who were of foreign extraction, then stood forward and confessed their sins and the guilty deeds of their fathers. 3 When they had taken their places, they read from the book of the law of the LORD

Catholic Connections

GATHERING TO PRAY

It is good for us to gather as church and worship God.

Notice how the event described in Neh 8, 1–12 sounds similar to some parts of the Mass. The people gather, read and reflect, renew a covenant with God, and offer a great "Amen, Amen!" Finally, they are blessed to go forth and share what they have with one another.

Several times, the people at this event heard, "Today is holy." We set aside Sunday as a holy day, a Sabbath day. What do you do to make this day holy? Can you do something to make it even more special?

▸ Neh 8, 1–12

their God, for a fourth part of the day, and during another fourth part they made their confession and prostrated themselves before the LORD their God. 4 Standing on the platform of the Levites were Jeshua, Binnui, Kadmiel, Shebaniah, Bunni, Sherebiah, Bani, and Chenani, who cried out to the LORD their God with a loud voice. 5* The Levites Jeshua, Kadmiel, Bani, Hashabneiah, Sherebiah, Hodiah, Shebaniah, and Pethahiah said,

"Arise, bless the LORD, your God,
    from eternity to eternity!"

The Israelites answered with the blessing,

"Blessed is your glorious name,
    and exalted above all blessing and praise."

6† Then Ezra said: "It is you, O LORD, you are the only one; you made the heavens, the highest heav-

---

9, 1–5: This is a continuation of the account concerning the problem of mixed marriages at the time of Ezra; it should be read immediately after Ezr 10, 44.

9, 6–37: The prayer of Ezra which began in Ezr 9, 6f is here continued; see note on Ezr 9, 7.

8, 10: Est 9, 19.
8, 14: Ex 23, 14; Lv 23, 33–36.
8, 15: Ps 118, 27.
9, 1: Dn 9, 3.
9, 2: Ezr 9, 1f; 10, 11.
9, 5: Dn 2, 20; 3, 52.

ens and all their host, the earth and all that is upon it, the seas and all that is in them. To all of them you give life, and the heavenly hosts bow down before you.

⁷* "You, O LORD, are the God who chose Abram, who brought him out from Ur of the Chaldees, and named him Abraham. ⁸* When you had found his heart faithful in your sight, you made the covenant with him to give to him and his posterity the land of the Canaanites, Hittites, Amorites, Perizzites, Jebusites, and Girgashites. These promises of yours you fulfilled, for you are just.

⁹* "You saw the affliction of our fathers in Egypt,
   you heard their cry by the Red Sea;
¹⁰* You worked signs and wonders
     against Pharoah,
  against all his servants and the people of
     his land,
Because you knew of their insolence
     toward them;
  thus you made for yourself a name even to
     this day.
¹¹* The sea you divided before them,
   on dry ground they passed through the
     midst of the sea;
Their pursuers you hurled into the depths,
   like a stone into the mighty waters.
¹²* With a column of cloud you led them by day,
   and by night with a column of fire,
To light the way of their journey,
   the way in which they must travel.
¹³* On Mount Sinai you came down,
   you spoke with them from heaven;
You gave them just ordinances, firm laws,
   good statutes, and commandments;
¹⁴* Your holy sabbath you made known to them,
   commandments, statutes, and law you
     prescribed for them,
   by the hand of Moses your servant.

ARISE, bless the LORD, your God, from eternity to eternity!

9, 5

¹⁵* Food from heaven you gave them in
   their hunger,
  water from a rock you sent them in
   their thirst.
You bade them enter and occupy the land
  which you had sworn with upraised hand
   to give them.

¹⁶ "But they, our fathers, proved to be insolent; they held their necks stiff and would not obey your commandments. ¹⁷* They refused to obey and no longer remembered the miracles you had worked for them. They stiffened their necks and turned their heads to return to their slavery in Egypt. But you are a God of pardons, gracious and compassionate, slow to anger and rich in mercy; you did not forsake them. ¹⁸* Though they made for themselves a molten calf, and proclaimed, 'Here is your God who brought you up out of Egypt,' and were guilty of great effronteries, ¹⁹ yet in your great mercy you did not forsake them in the desert. The column of cloud did not cease to lead them by day on their journey, nor did the column of fire by night cease to light for them the way by which they were to travel.

²⁰* "Your good spirit you bestowed on them, to give them understanding; your manna you did not withhold from their mouths, and you gave them water in their thirst. ²¹* Forty years in the desert you sustained them: they did not want; their garments did not become worn, and their feet did not become swollen. ²²* You gave them kingdoms and peoples, which you divided up among them as border lands. They possessed the land of Sihon, king of Heshbon, and the land of Og, king of Bashan.

²³* "You made their children as numerous as the stars of the heavens, and you brought them into the land which you had commanded their fathers to enter and possess. ²⁴ The sons went in to take possession of the land, and you humbled before them the Canaanite inhabitants of the land and delivered them over into their power, their kings as well as the peoples of the land, to do with them as they would. ²⁵* They captured fortified cities and fertile land; they took possession of houses filled with all good things, cisterns already dug, vineyards, olive groves, and fruit trees in abundance. They could eat and have their fill, fatten and feast themselves on your immense good gifts.

²⁶* "But they were contemptuous and rebellious: they cast your law behind their backs, they slew your prophets who bore witness against them in

9, 7: Gn 12, 1; 17, 5.
9, 8: Gn 15, 18f.
9, 9: Ex 2, 23f.
9, 10: Ex 7–11; 14.
9, 11: Ex 15, 5.10.
9, 12: Ex 13, 21f.
9, 13: Ex 19–20.
9, 14: Ex 20, 8.
9, 15: Ex 16, 4; 17, 1f.
9, 17: Nm 14, 1–4; Ex 34, 6;
Dn 9, 9.
9, 18: Ex 32, 4.
9, 20: Dt 2, 7.
9, 21: Dt 8, 4.
9, 22: Nm 21, 21–35;
Dt 1, 4; 2, 26—3, 11.
9, 23: Dt 1, 10.
9, 25: Dt 3, 5; 6, 10f; 11, 11;
32, 15.
9, 26: Wis 2, 10–20.

order to bring them back to you, and they were guilty of great effronteries. 27* Therefore you delivered them into the power of their enemies, who oppressed them. But in the time of their oppression they would cry out to you, and you would hear them from heaven, and according to your great mercy give them saviors to deliver them from the power of their enemies.

28 "As soon as they had relief, they would go back to doing evil in your sight. Then again you abandoned them to the power of their enemies, who crushed them. Then they cried out to you, and you heard them from heaven and delivered them according to your mercy, many times over. 29* You bore witness against them, in order to bring them back to your law. But they were insolent and would not obey your commandments; they sinned against your ordinances, from which men draw life when they practice them. They turned stubborn backs, stiffened their necks, and would not obey. 30 You were patient with them for many years, bearing witness against them through your spirit, by means of your prophets; still they would not listen. Thus you delivered them over into the power of the peoples of the lands. 31 Yet in your great mercy you did not completely destroy them and you did not forsake them, for you are a kind and merciful God.

32* "Now, therefore, O our God, great, mighty, and awesome God, you who in your mercy preserve the covenant, take into account all the disasters that have befallen us, our kings, our princes, our priests, our prophets, our fathers, and your entire people, from the time of the kings of Assyria until this day! 33* In all that has come upon us you have been just, for you kept faith while we have done evil. 34 Yes, our kings, our princes, our priests, and our fathers have not kept your law; they paid no attention to your commandments and the obligations of which you reminded them. 35 While they were yet in their kingdom, in the midst of the many good things that you had given them and in the wide and fertile land that you had spread out before them, they did not serve you nor did they turn away from their evil deeds. 36 But, see, we today are slaves; and as for the land which you gave our fathers that they might eat its fruits and good things—see, we have become slaves upon it! 37 Its rich produce goes to the kings whom you set over us because of our sins, who rule over our bodies and our cattle as they please. We are in great distress!"

Agreement of the People

10 1*† In view of all this, we are entering into a firm pact, which we are putting into writing. On the sealed document appear the names of our princes, our Levites, and our priests.

2 On the sealed document: His Excellency Nehemiah, son of Hacaliah, and Zedekiah.

3 Seraiah, Azariah, Jeremiah, 4 Pashhur, Amariah, Malchijah, 5 Hattush, Shebaniah, Malluch, 6 Harim, Meremoth, Obadiah, 7 Daniel, Ginnethon, Baruch, 8 Meshullam, Abijah, Mijamin, 9 Maaziah, Bilgai, Shemaiah: these are the priests.

10 The Levites: Jeshua, son of Azaniah; Binnui, of the sons of Henadad; Kadmiel; 11* and their brethren Shebaniah, Hodiah, Kelita, Pelaiah, Hanan, 12 Mica, Rehob, Hashabiah, 13 Zaccur, Sherebiah, Shebaniah, 14 Hodiah, Bani, Beninu.

15 The leaders of the people: Parosh, Pahath-moab, Elam, Zattu, Bani, 16 Bunni, Azgad, Bebai, 17 Adonijah, Bigvai, Adin, 18 Ater, Hezekiah, Azzur, 19 Hodiah, Hashum, Bezai, 20 Hariph, Anathoth, Nebai, 21 Magpiash, Meshullam, Hazir, 22 Meshezabel, Zadok, Jaddua, 23 Pelatiah, Hanan, Anaiah, 24 Hoshea, Hananiah, Hasshub, 25 Hallohesh, Pilha, Shobek, 26 Rehum, Hashabnah, Maaseiah, 27 Ahiah, Hanan, Anan, 28 Malluch, Harim, Baanah.

Provisions of the Pact

29 The rest of the people, priests, Levites, gatekeepers, singers, temple slaves, and all others who have separated themselves from the peoples of the lands in favor of the law of God, with their wives, their sons, their daughters, all who are of the age of discretion, 30* join with their brethren who are their princes, and with the sanction of a curse take this oath to follow the law of God which was given through Moses, the servant of God, and to observe carefully all the commandments of the LORD, our Lord, his ordinances and his statutes.

31* Agreed, that we will not marry our daughters to the peoples of the land, and that we will not take their daughters for our sons.

32* When the peoples of the land bring in merchandise or any kind of grain for sale on the sabbath day, we will not buy from them on the sabbath or on any other holy day. We will forgo the seventh year, as well as every kind of debt.

33* We impose these commandments on ourselves: to give a third of a shekel each year for the service of the house of our God, 34 for the show-

---

10, 1–40: This section belongs to the Nehemiah narrative rather than to that of Ezra. It is best read after Neh 13, 31. *In view of all this:* considering the situation described in Neh 13, 4–31.

9, 27: Dn 9, 19.
9, 29: Lv 18, 5; Dt 30, 16; 32, 47.
9, 32: Lam 5.
9, 33: Dn 3, 27; 9, 14.
10, 1: Neh 12, 12–26.
10, 11: Ezr 10, 23.
10, 30: Neh 13, 23–27.
10, 31: Neh 13, 15–22.
10, 32: Neh 5, 1–13; Ex 20, 8; Lv 25, 2–7.
10, 33: 2 Chr 24, 6.9f; Lv 24, 5–9.

bread, for the daily cereal offering, for the daily holocaust, for the sabbaths, new moons, and festivals, for the holy offerings, for sin offerings to make atonement for Israel, and for every service of the house of our God. 35* We, priests, Levites, and people, have determined by lot concerning the procurement of wood: it is to be brought to the house of our God by each of our family houses at stated times each year, to be burnt on the altar of the LORD, our God, as the law prescribes. 36* We have agreed to bring each year to the house of the LORD the first fruits of our fields and of our fruit trees, of whatever kind; 37 also, as is prescribed in the law, to bring to the house of our God, to the priests who serve in the house of our God, the first-born of our children and our animals, including the first-born of our flocks and herds. 38* The first batch of our dough, and our offerings of the fruit of every tree, of wine and of oil, we will bring to the priests, to the chambers of the house of our God. The tithe of our fields we will bring to the Levites; they, the Levites, shall take the tithe in all the cities of our service. 39 An Aaronite priest shall be with the Levites when they take the tithe, and the Levites shall bring the tithe of the tithes to the house of our God, to the chambers of the treasury. 40 For to these chambers the Israelites and Levites bring the offerings of grain, wine, and oil; there also are housed the utensils of the sanctuary, and the ministering priests, the gatekeepers, and the singers. We will not neglect the house of our God.

Repeopling of Jerusalem

11 1*† The leaders of the people took up residence in Jerusalem, and the rest of the people cast lots to bring one man in ten to reside in Jerusalem, the holy city, while the other nine would remain in the other cities. 2 The people applauded all those men who willingly agreed to take up residence in Jerusalem.

The Residents of Jerusalem

3* These are the heads of the province who took up residence in Jerusalem. (In the cities of Judah dwelt lay Israelites, priests, Levites, temple slaves, and the descendants of the slaves of Solomon, each man on the property he owned in his own city.) 4 In Jerusalem dwelt both Judahites and Benjaminites. Of the Judahites: Athaiah, son of Uzziah, son of Zechariah, son of Amariah, son of Shephatiah, son of Mehallalel, of the sons of Perez; 5 Maa-

seiah, son of Baruch, son of Colhozeh, son of Hazaiah, son of Adaiah, son of Joiarib, son of Zechariah, a son of the Shelanites. 6 The total of the sons of Perez who dwelt in Jerusalem was four hundred and sixty-eight valiant men.

7 These were the Benjaminites: Sallu, son of Meshullam, son of Joed, son of Pedaiah, son of Kolaiah, son of Maaseiah, son of Ithiel, son of Jeshaiah, 8 and his brethren, warriors, nine hundred and twenty-eight in number. 9 Joel, son of Zichri, was their commander, and Judah, son of Hassenuah, was second in charge of the city.

10 Among the priests were: Jedaiah; Joiarib; Jachin; 11 Seraiah, son of Hilkiah, son of Meshullam, son of Zadok, son of Meraioth, son of Ahitub, the ruler of the house of God, 12 and their brethren who carried out the temple service, eight hundred and twenty-two; Adaiah, son of Jeroham, son of Pelaliah, son of Amzi, son of Zechariah, son of Pashhur, son of Malchijah, 13 and his brethren, family heads, two hundred and forty-two; and Amasai, son of Azarel, son of Ahzai, son of Meshillemoth, son of Immer, 14 and his brethren, warriors, one hundred and twenty-eight. Their commander was Zabdiel, son of Haggadol.

15 Among the Levites were Shemaiah, son of Hasshub, son of Azrikam, son of Hashabiah, son of Bunni; 16 Shabbethai and Jozabad, levitical chiefs who were placed over the external affairs of the house of God; 17 Mattaniah, son of Micah, son of Zabdi, son of Asaph, director of the psalms, who led the thanksgiving at prayer; Bakbukiah, second in rank among his brethren; and Abda, son of Shammua, son of Galal, son of Jeduthun. 18 The total of the Levites in the holy city was two hundred and eighty-four.

19 The gatekeepers were Akkub, Talmon, and their brethren, who kept watch over the gates; one hundred and seventy-two in number.

20 The rest of Israel, including priests and Levites, were in all the other cities of Judah, each man in his inheritance.

21 The temple slaves lived on Ophel. Ziha and Gishpa were in charge of the temple slaves.

22* The prefect of the Levites in Jerusalem was Uzzi, son of Bani, son of Hashabiah, son of Mattaniah, son of Micah; he was one of the sons of Asaph, the singers appointed to the service of the house of God — 23 for they had been appointed by royal decree, and there was a fixed schedule for the singers assigning them their daily duties.

24 Pethahiah, son of Meshezabel, a descendant of

NEH

11, 1–19: This list of the family heads who lived in Jerusalem at the time of Nehemiah is best read after Neh 7, 72a. It is basically the same as that given in 1 Chr 9, 2–17, but there are many differences between the two lists.

10, 35: Neh 13, 31.
10, 36f: Ex 13, 1.11ff;
    Dt 26, 1.
10, 38: Neh 13, 10–14;

Nm 18, 21.24ff.
11, 1: Neh 7, 4.
11, 3–19: 1 Chr 9, 2–34.
11, 22: 2 Chr 20, 14.

Zerah, son of Judah, was royal deputy in all affairs that concerned the people.

The Other Cities

25 As concerns their villages in the country: Judahites lived in Kiriath-arba and its dependencies, in Dibon and its dependencies, in Jekabzeel and its villages, 26 in Jeshua, Moladah, Beth-pelet, 27 in Hazar-shual, in Beer-sheba and its dependencies, 28 in Ziklag, in Meconah and its dependencies, 29 in En-rimmon, Zorah, Jarmuth, 30 Zanoah, Adullam, and their villages, Lachish and its countryside, Azekah and its dependencies. They were settled from Beer-sheba to Ge-hinnom.

31 Benjaminites were in Geba, Michmash, Aija, Bethel and its dependencies, 32 Anathoth, Nob, Ananiah, 33 Hazor, Ramah, Gittaim, 34 Hadid, Zeboim, Neballat, 35 Lod, Ono, and the Valley of the Artisans.

36 Some sections of the Levites from Judah settled in Benjamin.

Priests and Levites under Zerubbabel

12 1* The following are the priests and Levites who returned with Zerubbabel, son of Shealtiel, and Jeshua: Seraiah, Jeremiah, Ezra, 2 Amariah, Malluch, Hattush, 3 Shecaniah, Rehum, Meremoth, 4 Iddo, Ginnethon, Abijah, 5 Mijamin, Maadiah, Bilgah, 6 Shemaiah, and Joiarib, Jedaiah, 7 Sallu, Amok, Hilkiah, Jedaiah. These were the priestly heads and their brethren in the days of Jeshua.

8 The Levites were Jeshua, Binnui, Kadmiel, Sherebiah, Judah, Mattaniah; the last-mentioned, together with his brethren, was in charge of the hymns, 9 while Bakbukiah and Unno and their brethren ministered opposite them by turns.

High Priests

10† Jeshua became the father of Joiakim, Joiakim became the father of Eliashib, and Eliashib became the father of Joiada. 11 Joiada became the father of Johanan, and Johanan became the father of Jaddua.

Priests and Levites under Joiakim

12* In the days of Joiakim these were the priestly family heads: for Seraiah, Meraiah; for Jeremiah,

Hananiah; 13 for Ezra, Meshullam; for Amariah, Jehohanan; 14 for Malluch, Jonathan; for Shebaniah, Joseph; 15 for Harim, Adna; for Meremoth, Helkai; 16 for Iddo, Zechariah; for Ginnethon, Meshullam; 17 for Abijah, Zichri; for Miamin, . . . ; for Maadiah, Piltai; 18 for Bilgah, Shammua; for Shemaiah, Jehonathan; 19 and for Joiarib, Mattenai; for Jedaiah, Uzzi; 20 for Sallu, Kallai; for Amok, Eber; 21 for Hilkiah, Hashabiah; for Jedaiah, Nethanel.

22 In the time of Eliashib, Joiada, Johanan, and Jaddua, the family heads of the priests were written down in the Book of Chronicles, up until the reign of Darius the Persian. 23 The sons of Levi: the family heads were written down in the Book of Chronicles, up until the time of Johanan, the son of Eliashib.

24* The heads of the Levites were Hashabiah, Sherebiah, Jeshua, Binnui, Kadmiel. Their brethren who stood opposite them to sing praises and thanksgiving in fulfillment of the command of David, the man of God, one section opposite the other, 25* were Mattaniah, Bakbukiah, Obadiah.

Meshullam, Talmon, and Akkub were gatekeepers. They kept watch over the storerooms at the gates.

26 All these lived in the time of Joiakim, son of Jeshua, son of Jozadak [and in the time of Nehemiah the governor and of Ezra the priest-scribe].

Dedication of the City Wall

27† At the dedication of the wall of Jerusalem, the Levites were sought out wherever they lived and were brought to Jerusalem to celebrate a joyful dedication with thanksgiving hymns and the music of cymbals, harps, and lyres. 28 The levitical singers gathered together from the region about Jerusalem, from the villages of the Netophathites, 29 from Beth-gilgal, and from the plains of Geba and Azmaveth (for the singers had built themselves settlements about Jerusalem). 30 The priests and Levites first purified themselves, then they purified the people, the gates, and the wall.

31 I had the princes of Judah mount the wall, and I arranged two great choirs. The first of these proceeded to the right, along the top of the wall, in the direction of the Dung Gate, 32 followed by Hoshaiah and half the princes of Judah, 33 along with Azariah, Ezra, Meshullam, 34 Judah, Benjamin, She-

---

† **12, 10f:** Jeshua, the high priest when Zerubbabel was governor, i.e., the last decades of the sixth century B.C. (Hg 1, 1.12.14; 2, 2.4). He was the grandfather of Eliashib, the high priest at least in the early period of Nehemiah's governorship, i.e., 445–433 B.C. (Ezr 10, 6; Neh 3, 1.20f; 13, 4.7). Eliashib, in turn, was the grandfather of Johanan, a grown man, if not yet a high priest, at the time of Ezra, i.e., c. 400 B.C. (Ezr 10, 6, and note). According to Josephus (*Antiquities* XI, v), whose testimony here is doubtful, Jaddua, son of Johanan, died as an old man about the same time that Alexander the Great died, i.e., 323 B.C. If this list of the postexilic high priests, at least as far as Johanan, comes, as seems probable (cf v 23), from the Chron-

icler himself and not from a later scribe, it is of prime importance for dating the Chronicler's work in the first decades of the fourth century B.C.

12, 27–43: The dedication of the wall of Jerusalem took place, no doubt, soon after the restoration of the wall and its gates had been completed. Therefore, this section is best read after Neh 6, 15.

12, 1–6: Neh 12, 12–22.   12, 24: Ezr 2, 40.
12, 12–22: Neh 10, 3–9; 12, 1–6.   12, 25: Neh 11, 17.

maiah, and Jeremiah, [35] priests with the trumpets, and also Zechariah, son of Jonathan, son of Shemaiah, son of Mattaniah, son of Micaiah, son of Zaccur, son of Asaph, [36] and his brethren Shemaiah, Azarel, Milalai, Gilalai, Maai, Nethanel, Judah, and Hanani, with the musical instruments of David, the man of God. [Ezra the scribe was at their head.] [37] At the Spring Gate they went straight up by the steps of the City of David and continued along the top of the wall above the house of David until they came to the Water Gate on the east.

[38] The second choir proceeded to the left, followed by myself and the other half of the princes of the people, along the top of the wall past the Oven Tower as far as the Broad Wall, [39] then past the Ephraim Gate [the New City Gate], the Fish Gate, the Tower of Hananel, and the Hundred Tower, as far as the Sheep Gate [and they came to a halt at the Prison Gate].

[40] The two choirs took up a position in the house of God; I, too, who had with me half the magistrates, [41] the priests Eliakim, Maaseiah, Minjamin, Micaiah, Elioenai, Zechariah, Hananiah, with the trumpets, [42] and Maaseiah, Shemaiah, Eleazar, Uzzi, Jehohanan, Malchijah, Elam, and Ezer. The singers were heard under the leadership of Jezrahiah. [43] Great sacrifices were offered on that day, and there was rejoicing over the great feast of the LORD in which they shared. The women and the children joined in, and the rejoicing at Jerusalem could be heard from afar off.

Offerings for Priests and Levites

[44]*† At that time men were appointed over the chambers set aside for stores, offerings, first fruits, and tithes; in them they were to collect from the fields of the various cities the portions legally assigned to the priests and Levites. For Judah rejoiced in its appointed priests and Levites [45] who carried out the ministry of their God and the ministry of purification (as did the singers and the gatekeepers) in accordance with the prescriptions of David and of Solomon, his son. [46]* For the heads of the families of the singers and the hymns of praise and thanksgiving to God came down from the days of David and Asaph in times of old. [47]* Thus all Israel, in the days of Zerubbabel [and in the days of Ne-

hemiah], gave the singers and the gatekeepers their portions, according to their daily needs. They made their consecrated offering to the Levites, and the Levites made theirs to the sons of Aaron.

Separation from Aliens

13 [1]*† At that time, when there was reading from the book of Moses in the hearing of the people, it was found written there that "no Ammonite or Moabite may ever be admitted into the assembly of God; [2]* for they would not succor the Israelites with food and water, but they hired Balaam to curse them, though our God turned the curse into a blessing." [3]* When they had heard the law, they separated from Israel every foreign element.

Reform in the Temple

[4]† Before this, the priest Eliashib, who had been placed in charge of the chambers of the house of our God and who was an associate of Tobiah, [5]* had set aside for the latter's use a large chamber in which had previously been stored the cereal offerings, incense and utensils, the tithes in grain, wine, and oil allotted to the Levites, singers, and gatekeepers, and the offerings due the priests. [6]† During all this time I had not been in Jerusalem, for in the thirty-second year of Artaxerxes, king of Babylon, I had gone back to the king. After due time, however, I asked leave of the king [7] and returned to Jerusalem, where I discovered the evil thing that Eliashib had done for Tobiah, in setting aside for him a chamber in the courts of the house of God. [8] This displeased me very much, and I had all of Tobiah's household goods thrown outside the chamber. [9] Then I gave orders to purify the chambers, and I had them replace there the utensils of the house of God, the cereal offerings, and the incense.

[10] I learned, too, that the portions due the Levites were no longer being given, so that the Levites and the singers who should have been carrying out the services had deserted, each man to his own field. [11] I took the magistrates to task, demanding, "Why is the house of God abandoned?" Then I brought the Levites together and had them resume their stations. [12]* All Judah once more brought in the tithes

---

† **12, 44–47:** This account of the provisions made for the temple services is apparently a composition of the Chronicler. *At that time:* a mere connective; no particular time is meant, but the account fits best after that of the restoration of the temple (Ezr 6, 13–18) in the days of Zerubbabel (v 47). The gloss mentioning Nehemiah is not in the ancient Greek version.

13, 1ff: These verses were composed by the Chronicler to serve as an introduction to the reforms that Nehemiah instituted during his second mission in Jerusalem (vv 4–31). The part of the book of Moses read to the people is freely quoted here from Dt 23, 3–6.

13, 4–31: This is part of the "Memoirs of Nehemiah"; it is continued in Neh 10, 1–40.

13, 6: *After due time:* It is not known when Nehemiah returned to Jerusalem or how long his second period of activity there lasted, but it probably ended before Ezra came to Palestine; see note on Ezr 7, 1–8.

12, 44f: 1 Chr 23–26; 2 Chr 8, 14.
12, 46: 2 Chr 29, 30; 35, 15.
12, 47: Neh 13, 10f; 10, 39; Nm 18, 26.
13, 1ff: Dt 23, 3–6.
13, 2: Nm 22–24.
13, 3: Neh 13, 23–28.
13, 5: Neh 12, 44.
13, 12: Neh 10, 38f; 12, 44f.47; 2 Chr 31, 6.

of grain, wine, and oil to the storerooms; 13 and in charge of the storerooms I appointed the priest Shelemiah, Zadok the scribe, and Pedaiah, one of the Levites, together with Hanan, son of Zaccur, son of Mattaniah, as their assistant; for these men were held to be trustworthy. It was their duty to make the distribution to their brethren. 14 Remember this to my credit, O my God! Let not the devotion which I showed for the house of my God and its services be forgotten!

Sabbath Observance

15* In those days I perceived that men in Judah were treading the winepresses on the sabbath; that they were bringing in sheaves of grain, loading them on their asses, together with wine, grapes, figs, and every other kind of burden, and bringing them to Jerusalem on the sabbath day. I warned them to sell none of these victuals. 16 In Jerusalem itself the Tyrians who were resident there were importing fish and every other kind of merchandise and selling it to the Judahites on the sabbath. 17 I took the nobles of Judah to task, demanding of them: "What is this evil thing that you are doing, profaning the sabbath day? 18 Did not your fathers act in this same way, with the result that our God has brought all this evil upon us and upon this city? Would you add to the wrath against Israel by once more profaning the sabbath?"

19 When the shadows were falling on the gates of Jerusalem before the sabbath, I ordered the doors to be closed and forbade them to be reopened till after the sabbath. I posted some of my own men at the gates so that no burden might enter on the sabbath day. 20 The merchants and sellers of various kinds of merchandise spent the night once or twice outside Jerusalem, 21 but then I warned them, saying to them: "Why do you spend the night alongside the wall? If you keep this up, I will lay hands

on you!" From that time on, they did not return on the sabbath. 22 Then I ordered the Levites to purify themselves and to go and watch the gates, so that the sabbath day might be kept holy. This, too, remember in my favor, O my God, and have mercy on me in accordance with your great mercy!

Mixed Marriages

23* Also in those days I saw Jews who had married Ashdodite, Ammonite, or Moabite wives. 24† Of their children, half spoke Ashdodite, and none of them knew how to speak Jewish; and so it was in regard to the languages of the various other peoples. 25 I took them to task and cursed them; I had some of them beaten and their hair pulled out; and I adjured them by God: "You shall not marry your daughters to their sons nor take any of their daughters for your sons or for yourselves! 26* Did not Solomon, the king of Israel, sin because of them? Though among the many nations there was no king like him, and though he was beloved of his God and God had made him king over all Israel, yet even he was made to sin by foreign women. 27 Must it also be heard of you that you have done this same very great evil, betraying our God by marrying foreign women?"

28* One of the sons of Joiada, son of Eliashib the high priest, was the son-in-law of Sanballat the Horonite! I drove him from my presence. 29 Remember against them, O my God, how they defiled the priesthood and the covenant of the priesthood and the Levites!

30 Thus I cleansed them of all foreign contamination. I established the various functions for the priests and Levites, so that each had his appointed task. 31* I also provided for the procurement of wood at stated times and for the first fruits. Remember this in my favor, O my God!

13, 24: *Ashdodite:* the language spoken at Ashdod, more likely an Aramaic rather than a Philistine dialect. *Jewish:* Hebrew as spoken in postexilic Judah.

13, 15: Neh 10, 32; Ex 20, 8.
13, 23: Neh 10, 31; 13, 1ff; Dt 23, 3.
13, 26: 1 Kgs 11, 1–13.
13, 28: Neh 2, 10; 13, 4f.7ff.
13, 31: Neh 10, 35f.

Good people suffering, love that must overcome a frightening obstacle, an undercover angel—the Book of Tobit has it all. Part fairy tale, part love story, this book will bring a smile to your face and perhaps a tear to your eye. Enjoy!

In-depth

For the author of the Book of Tobit, understanding God's will was not difficult. The conviction that God rewards good people, especially those who have experienced great suffering, is evident on every page. In the story, the faithful Tobit, who is blinded after doing a good deed, and the virtuous Sarah, who is ridiculed because she has had seven husbands die on their wedding night, pray for death because of their suffering and humiliation. In answer to their prayers, God sends the angel Raphael to lead Tobit's son Tobias on a journey to Sarah's town. The story ends happily—but you will have to read it yourself to find out exactly how.

The Book of Tobit is a novel, that is, a fiction book. The author was writing at a time when the Jews were governed by oppressive Greek rulers, and the people needed the reassurance of this happy tale. They had not forgotten the fall of Jerusalem or the Exile in Babylon, and Israel's suffering weighed heavily on them. What was the advantage of following God's law if all they had to look forward to was more suffering? (Belief in an afterlife had not yet developed among the Jewish people.) The book assured the faithful that God would eventually reward them: it was just a matter of time.

Although the book's miraculous answers may seem too simple to modern-day readers, its insistence on God's presence in human life and God's concern for those who suffer remains as important as ever. All people—even Christians who believe in life after death—need encouragement to face the challenges of this world with faith and hope.

At a Glance

I. **Tobit's Ordeals (1, 3—3, 6).**

II. **Sarah's Plight (3, 7–17).**

III. **Tobiah's Journey and Marriage to Sarah (4, 1—9, 6).**

IV. **Tobiah's Return; Cure of Tobit's Blindness (10, 1—11, 18).**

V. **Raphael Reveals His Identity (12, 1–22).**

VI. **Tobit's Song of Praise (13, 1–18).**

VII. **Epilogue (14, 1–15).**

Quick Facts

Setting
although fictional, the book reflects the historical situation of Israelites deported from Israel to Nineveh in 721 B.C.

Author
unknown, writing sometime in the second century B.C.

Theme
In time, God will aid the faithful who suffer.

Of Note
Raphael is one of only three angels named in the Bible; the others are Michael and Gabriel.

The Book of *Tobit*

Tobit

Tobit

1 ¹† This book tells the story of Tobit, son of Tobiel, son of Hananiel, son of Aduel, son of Gabael of the family of Asiel, of the tribe of Naphtali, ²*† who during the reign of Shalmaneser, king of Assyria, was taken captive from Thisbe, which is south of Kedesh Naphtali in upper Galilee, above and to the west of Asser, north of Phogor.

I: Tobit's Ordeals

His Virtue

³ I, Tobit, have walked all the days of my life on the paths of truth and righteousness. I performed many charitable works for my kinsmen and my people who had been deported with me to Nineveh, in Assyria. ⁴ When I lived as a young man in my own country, Israel, the entire tribe of my forefather Naphtali had broken away from the house of David and from Jerusalem. This city had been singled out of all Israel's tribes, so that they all might offer sacrifice in the place where the temple, God's

dwelling, had been built and consecrated for all generations to come. ⁵*† All my kinsmen, like the rest of the tribe of my forefather Naphtali, used to offer sacrifice on all the mountains of Galilee as well as to the young bull which Jeroboam, king of Israel, had made in Dan.

⁶*† I, for my part, would often make the pilgrimage alone to Jerusalem for the festivals, as is prescribed for all Israel by perpetual decree. Bringing with me the first fruits of the field and the firstlings of the flock, together with a tenth of my income and the first shearings of the sheep,* I would hasten to Jerusalem ⁷* and present them to the priests, Aaron's sons, at the altar. To the Levites who were doing service in Jerusalem I would give the tithe of grain, wine, olive oil, pomegranates, figs, and other fruits. And except for sabbatical years, I used to give a second tithe in money, which each year I would go and disburse in Jerusalem. ⁸ The third tithe I gave to orphans and widows, and to converts who were living with the Israelites. Every third year I would bring them this offering, and we

---

[†] **1, 1:** *Tobit:* in the fragments of the book found at Qumran, is given as Tobi, an abbreviated form of Tobiyah (v 9; Ezr 2, 60) or of Tobiyabu (2 Chr 17, 8), a name which means "Yahweh is good." Tobiel, "God is good"; Hananiel, "God is merciful." The book abounds in theophoric names.

1, 2: *Shalmaneser V (727–722 B.C.):* began the siege of Samaria; the inhabitants of the northern kingdom were taken into captivity by his successor, Sargon II (722–705). *Thisbe* and *Phogor:* towns of Galilee that have not been identified; *Thisbe* in Gilead was perhaps the birthplace of Elijah. *Kedesh:* cf Jos 20, 7. *Asser:* Hazor (Jos 11, 1).

1, 5: Jeroboam established sanctuaries in *Dan* and Bethel so that the people would no longer go to Jerusalem for the festivals. The gold

statues of bulls which he placed in the sanctuaries were considered the throne of Yahweh; but the people soon came to worship the images themselves. Jeroboam also encouraged the high places or hilltop shrines (1 Kgs 12, 26–33).

1, 6ff: *Perpetual decree:* Dt 12, 11.13–14. Refusing to worship at Jeroboam's shrines, the faithful Tobit continued to bring his offerings to Jerusalem; see 2 Chr 11, 16. For the various tithes, cf Nm 18, 20–32; 2 Chr 31, 4–6; Dt 14, 22–29; 26, 12f.

*

1, 2: 2 Kgs 17, 3; 18, 9ff.	**1, 6:** Dt 16, 16.
1, 5: 1 Kgs 12, 26–32.	**1, 7f:** Nm 18, 12f.24; Dt 14, 22–29; 18, 4f.
1, 6: Ex 23, 14f.17; 34, 23.	

ate it in keeping with the decree of the Mosaic law and the commands of Deborah, the mother of my father Tobiel; for when my father died, he left me an orphan.

⁹ When I reached manhood, I married Anna, a woman of our own lineage. By her I had a son whom I named Tobiah. ¹⁰* Now after I had been deported to Nineveh, all my brothers and relatives ate the food of heathens, ¹¹ but I refrained from eating that kind of food. ¹² Because of this wholehearted service of God, ¹³* the Most High granted me favor and status with Shalmaneser, so that I became purchasing agent for all his needs. ¹⁴† Every now and then until his death I would go to Media to buy goods for him. I also deposited several pouches containing a great sum of money with my kinsman Gabael, son of Gabri, who lived at Rages, in Media. ¹⁵† But when Shalmaneser died and his son Sennacherib succeeded him as king, the roads to Media became unsafe, so I could no longer go there.

Courage in Burying the Dead

¹⁶ During Shalmaneser's reign I performed many charitable works for my kinsmen and my people. ¹⁷*† I would give my bread to the hungry and my clothing to the naked. If I saw one of my people who had died and been thrown outside the walls of Nineveh, I would bury him. ¹⁸ I also buried anyone whom Sennacherib slew when he returned as a fugitive from Judea during the days of judgment decreed against him by the heavenly King because of the blasphemies he had uttered. In his rage he killed many Israelites, but I used to take their bodies by stealth and bury them; so when Sennacherib looked for them, he could not find them. ¹⁹ But a certain citizen of Nineveh informed the king that it was I who buried the dead. When I found out that the king knew all about me and wanted to put me to death, I went into hiding; then in my fear I took to flight. ²⁰ Afterward, all my property was confiscated; I was left with nothing. All that I had was taken to the king's palace, except for my wife Anna and my son Tobiah.

²¹*† But less than forty days later the king was as-

The Case of the Missing Books

The Book of Tobit is treated differently in some versions of the Bible. Some put it in a section of books separated from the rest of the Old Testament. Some do not include it at all. We can find an explanation to this puzzle if we look back in time.

Sometime in the second or third century B.C., Jewish scholars translated the Scriptures from Hebrew and Aramaic into Greek. Many Jews living throughout the Mediterranean world spoke Greek, which had become a common language in that area at the time. For Greek-speaking Jews, this translation, called the Septuagint, was the Bible that they used. As most of the early Christians spoke Greek, including Jews such as Paul, the Septuagint was adopted by the Church as its Bible (Old Testament).

After the destruction of the Jerusalem temple by the Romans in A.D. 70, leading rabbis strove to reorganize Jewish worship, which could no longer center on the temple in Jerusalem. They reviewed the existing editions of the Bible and developed an official list of thirty-one holy books. They rejected certain books contained in the Greek Sepuagint for which there was no existing original Hebrew or Aramaic text, such as Tobit, Judith, 1 and 2 Maccabees, Wisdom, Sirach, Baruch, and additions to the Books of Esther and Daniel.

Many centuries later, the Christian reformer Martin Luther used the Jewish canon of the Old Testament in his translation of the Bible. He placed the additional books in a separate section, entitling them the Apocrypha (from the Greek for "hidden"). The Catholic church and the Orthodox churches continue to use the fuller Greek canon, preferring the term *deuterocanonical* (from the Greek for "second canon") for the disputed books.

1, 14: *A great sum of money:* literally, "ten silver talents," about ten thousand dollars. *Rages:* modern Rai, about five miles southeast of Teheran. *Media:* the northwestern part of modern Iran.

1, 15: *Sennacherib* (705–681 B.C.): the son of Sargon (722–705 B.C.); neither was descended from Shalmaneser. Inconsistencies such as this point to the fact that the Book of Tobit is a religious novel (see Introduction; also notes on 5, 6 and 14, 15).

1, 17–18: Tobit risked his own life to bury the dead. Deprivation of burial was viewed with horror by the Jews. Cf Tb 4, 3–4; 6, 15; 14, 12–13.

1, 21: *Esarhaddon:* 681–669 B.C. *Ahiqar:* a hero of ancient folklore, known for his outstanding wisdom. The Story (or Wisdom) of Ahiqar was very popular in antiquity and is extant in many different forms: Aramaic, Syriac, Armenian, Arabic (Arabian Nights), Greek (Aesop's Fables), Slavonic, Ethiopic, and Romanian. The sacred au-

thor makes Tobit the uncle of the famous Ahiqar in order to enhance Tobit's own prestige. See note on Tb 14, 10.

1, 10: Lv 11: Dt 14, 3–21;	**1, 17:** Jb 31, 16–20.
Acts 15, 29; 1 Cor 8,	**1, 21:** 2 Kgs 19, 37; 2 Chr
7ff.	32, 21; Sir 48, 21; Is
1, 13: Dn 2, 48f.	37, 38; 2 Mc 8, 19.

sassinated by two of his sons, who then escaped into the mountains of Ararat. His son Esarhaddon, who succeeded him as king, placed Ahiqar, my brother Anael's son, in charge of all the accounts of his kingdom, so that he took control over the entire administration. ²² Then Ahiqar interceded on my behalf, and I was able to return to Nineveh. For under Sennacherib, king of Assyria, Ahiqar had been chief cupbearer, keeper of the seal, administrator, and treasurer; and Esarhaddon reappointed him. He was a close relative—in fact, my nephew.

2 ¹*† Thus under King Esarhaddon I returned to my home, and my wife Anna and my son Tobiah were restored to me. Then on our festival of Pentecost, the feast of Weeks, a fine dinner was prepared for me, and I reclined to eat. ²† The table was set for me, and when many different dishes were placed before me, I said to my son Tobiah: "My son, go out and try to find a poor man from among our kinsmen exiled here in Nineveh. If he is a sincere worshiper of God, bring him back with you, so that he can share this meal with me. Indeed, son, I shall wait for you to come back."

³ Tobiah went out to look for some poor kinsman of ours. When he returned he exclaimed, "Father!" I said to him, "What is it, son?" He answered, "Father, one of our people has been murdered! His body lies in the market place where he was just strangled!" ⁴ I sprang to my feet, leaving the dinner untouched; and I carried the dead man from the street and put him in one of the rooms, so that I might bury him after sunset. ⁵*† Returning to my own quarters, I washed myself and ate my food in sorrow. ⁶* I was reminded of the oracle pronounced by the prophet Amos against Bethel:

"Your festivals shall be turned
    into mourning,
And all your songs into lamentation."

⁷ And I wept. Then at sunset I went out, dug a grave, and buried him.

⁸ The neighbors mocked me, saying to one another: "Will this man never learn! Once before he was hunted down for execution because of this very

thing; yet now that he has escaped, here he is again burying the dead!"

Tobit's Blindness

⁹ That same night I bathed, and went to sleep next to the wall of my courtyard. Because of the heat I left my face uncovered. ¹⁰† I did not know there were birds perched on the wall above me, till their warm droppings settled in my eyes, causing cataracts. I went to see some doctors for a cure, but the more they anointed my eyes with various salves, the worse the cataracts became, until I could see no more. For four years I was deprived of eyesight, and all my kinsmen were grieved at my condition. Ahiqar, however, took care of me for two years, until he left for Elymais.

¹¹ At that time my wife Anna worked for hire at weaving cloth, the kind of work women do. ¹²† When she sent back the goods to their owners, they would pay her. Late in winter she finished the cloth and sent it back to the owners. They paid her the full salary, and also gave her a young goat for the table. ¹³ On entering my house the goat began to bleat. I called to my wife and said: "Where did this goat come from? Perhaps it was stolen! Give it back to its owners; we have no right to eat stolen food!" ¹⁴*† But she said to me, "It was given to me as a bonus over and above my wages." Yet I would not believe her; and told her to give it back to its owners. I became very angry with her over this. So she retorted: "Where are your charitable deeds now? Where are your virtuous acts? See! Your true character is finally showing itself!"

3 ¹ Grief-stricken in spirit, I groaned and wept aloud. Then with sobs I began to pray:

Tobit's Prayer for Death

²* "You are righteous, O Lord,
    and all your deeds are just;
All your ways are mercy and truth;
    you are the judge of the world.
³* And now, O Lord, may you be mindful
    of me,
    and look with favor upon me.
Punish me not for my sins,

2, 1: *The feast of Weeks:* also called by its Greek name Pentecost, was celebrated fifty days after the Passover. Cf Lv 23, 15–21; Dt 16, 9–12.

2, 2: Almsgiving and charity to the poor are important virtues taught by the book (Tb 4, 7–11.16f; 12, 8f; 14, 10f).

2, 5: *I washed myself:* because of ritual defilement from touching a corpse (Nm 19, 11–13).

2, 10: *Cataracts:* literally, "white scales, or films." *Elymais:* the Greek name of ancient Elam, a district northeast of the head of the Persian Gulf.

2, 12: *Late in winter:* literally, "seventh of Dystros," the Mace-

donian month which corresponds to the Jewish month of Shebat (January–February). *For the table:* literally, "for the hearth"; the gift had probably been made in view of some springtime festival like the Jewish Purim.

2, 14: Anna's sharp rebuke calls to mind the words of Job's wife (Jb 2, 9).

2, 1: Lv 23, 15–21; Nm 28, 26–31; Dt 16, 9–12.	2, 14: Jb 2, 9.
2, 5: Nm 19, 11–22.	3, 2: Pss 25, 10; 119, 137; Dn 3, 27.
2, 6: Am 8, 10; 1 Mc 1, 39.	3, 3: Ex 34, 7.

nor for my inadvertent offenses,
nor for those of my fathers.

"They sinned against you,
4* and disobeyed your commandments.
So you handed us over to plundering, exile,
and death,
till we were an object lesson, a byword,
a reproach
in all the nations among whom you
scattered us.

5 "Yes, your judgments are many and true
in dealing with me as my sins
and those of my fathers deserve.
For we have not kept your commandments,
nor have we trodden the paths of truth
before you.

6*† "So now, deal with me as you please,
and command my life breath to be taken
from me,
that I may go from the face of the earth
into dust.
It is better for me to die than to live,
because I have heard insulting calumnies,
and I am overwhelmed with grief.

"Lord, command me to be delivered from
such anguish;
let me go to the everlasting abode;
Lord, refuse me not.
For it is better for me to die
than to endure so much misery in life,
and to hear these insults!"

II: Sarah's Plight

Sarah Falsely Accused

7† On the same day, at Ecbatana in Media, it so
happened that Raguel's daughter Sarah also had to
listen to abuse, from one of her father's maids.
8† For she had been married to seven husbands, but
the wicked demon Asmodeus killed them off before
they could have intercourse with her, as it is prescribed for wives. So the maid said to her: "You are
the one who strangles your husbands! Look at you!

You have already been married seven times, but you
have had no joy with any one of your husbands.
9 Why do you beat us? Because your husbands are
dead? Then why not join them! May we never see a
son or daughter of yours!"

10* That day she was deeply grieved in spirit. She
went in tears to an upstairs room in her father's
house with the intention of hanging herself. But she
reconsidered, saying to herself: "No! People would
level this insult against my father: 'You had only
one beloved daughter, but she hanged herself because of ill fortune!' And thus would I cause my father in his old age to go down to the nether world
laden with sorrow. It is far better for me not to hang

PRAY IT?

Praying for Death?

Tobit and Sarah are at the end of their
rope. They have experienced such suffering and disgrace that life no longer has
any meaning for them. They know suicide
is wrong, so they each pray that God will
send death to end their suffering and humiliation (Tb 3, 6.10).

It is not uncommon for people who
are very sick or in great pain or very old
to pray for death, like Tobit. Unfortunately, young people who have experienced
great loss or trauma often wish for death
too, like Sarah. No one can completely
explain the mystery of why we—both
young and old—suffer. But through our
loving actions and prayers, we can support one another in our suffering.

What people do you know who are
suffering to the point of despair? Take a
few moments every day to remember
those people in prayer, and call or write
to let them know you are thinking of
them.

▶ Tobit, chapter 3

3, 6: *It is better for me to die than to live*: in his distress Tobit uses
the words of the petulant Jonah (Jon 4, 3.8), who wished to die because God did not destroy the hated Ninevites. In similar circumstances, Moses (Nm 11, 15), Elijah (1 Kgs 19, 4), and Job (Jb 7, 15)
also prayed for death. *Everlasting abode*: a reference to Sheol, the
dismal abode of the dead from which no one returns (Jb 7, 9–10;
14, 12; Is 26, 14). The revelation of a blessed immortality had not yet
been made. See note on Tb 4, 6.
3, 7: From here on, the story is told in the third person. V 7
relates one of the several marvelous coincidences which the story-
teller uses to heighten interest; see also vv 16.17; 4, 1; 5, 4. *Ec-*

batana: Hamadan in modern Iran; this was the capital of ancient
Media. *Raguel*: "friend of God."
3, 8: *Asmodeus*: in Persian *aeshma daeva*, "demon of wrath,"
adopted into Aramaic with the sense of "the Destroyer." He will be
subdued (Tb 8, 3) by Raphael (v 17), "God heals."

3, 4: Dt 28, 15; Bar 1,   4; Jb 7, 15; Jon 4, 3.8.
  16–22; 2, 4f; 3, 8; Dn   3, 10: Tb 6, 15; Gn 37, 35;
  9, 5f.   42, 38; 44, 29.31.
3, 6: Nm 11, 15; 1 Kgs 19,

myself, but to beg the Lord to have me die, so that I need no longer live to hear such insults."

¹¹† At that time, then, she spread out her hands, and facing the window, poured out this prayer:*

Sarah's Prayer for Death

"Blessed are you, O Lord, merciful God!
Forever blessed and honored is your
   holy name;
may all your works forever bless you.
¹² And now, O Lord, to you I turn my face
   and raise my eyes.
¹³ Bid me to depart from the earth,
   never again to hear such insults.

¹⁴ "You know, O Master, that I am innocent
   of any impure act with a man,
¹⁵ And that I have never defiled my own name
   or my father's name in the land of
    my exile.

"I am my father's only daughter,
   and he has no other child to make his heir,
Nor does he have a close kinsman or
    other relative
whom I might bide my time to marry.
I have already lost seven husbands;
   why then should I live any longer?
But if it please you, Lord, not to slay me,
   look favorably upon me and have pity on me;
never again let me hear these insults!"

An Answer to Prayer

¹⁶ At that very time, the prayer of these two suppliants was heard in the glorious presence of Almighty God. ¹⁷*† So Raphael was sent to heal them both: to remove the cataracts from Tobit's eyes, so that he might again see God's sunlight; and to marry Raguel's daughter Sarah to Tobit's son Tobiah, and then drive the wicked demon Asmodeus from her. For Tobiah had the right to claim her before any other who might wish to marry her.

In the very moment that Tobit returned from the courtyard to his house, Raguel's daughter Sarah came downstairs from her room.

III: Tobiah's Journey and Marriage to Sarah

A Father's Instruction

4 ¹ That same day Tobit remembered the money he had deposited with Gabael at Rages in Media, and he thought, ² "Now that I have asked for death, why should I not call my son Tobiah and let him know about this money before I die?" ³*† So he called his son Tobiah; and when he came, he said to him: "My son, when I die, give me a decent burial. Honor your mother, and do not abandon her as long as she lives. Do whatever pleases her, and do not grieve her spirit in any way. ⁴ Remember, my son, that she went through many trials for your sake while you were in her womb. And when she dies, bury her in the same grave with me.

⁵ "Through all your days, my son, keep the Lord in mind, and suppress every desire to sin or to break his commandments. Perform good works all the days of your life, and do not tread the paths of wrongdoing. ⁶*† For if you are steadfast in your service, your good works will bring success, not only to you, but also to all those who live uprightly.

⁷* "Give alms from your possessions. Do not turn your face away from any of the poor, and God's face will not be turned away from you. ⁸ Son, give alms in proportion to what you own. If you have great wealth, give alms out of your abundance; if you have but little, distribute even some of that. But do not hesitate to give alms; ⁹* you will be storing up a goodly treasure for yourself against the day of adversity. ¹⁰ Almsgiving frees one from death, and keeps one from going into the dark abode. ¹¹* Alms are a worthy offering in the sight of the Most High for all who give them.

¹²* "Be on your guard, son, against every form of immorality, and above all, marry a woman of the lineage of your forefathers. Do not marry a stranger who is not of your father's tribe, because we are sons of the prophets. My boy, keep in mind Noah, Abraham, Isaac, and Jacob, our fathers from of old: all of them took wives from among their own kinsmen and were blessed in their children. Remember

---

3, 11: *Facing the window:* that is, looking toward Jerusalem; cf Dn 6, 11: *Blessed are you* and "Blessed be God" are traditional openings of Jewish prayers (Tb 8, 5.15; 11, 14; 13, 1).

3, 17: *Tobiah had the right:* according to the patriarchal custom of marriage within the family group. Tobiah was Sarah's closest eligible relative (Tb 6, 12). Cf Tb 4, 12–13; Gn 24.

4, 3–19: A collection of maxims which parallel those in the wisdom literature, especially Proverbs and Sirach (see Introduction): duties toward parents (3–4); cf also Tb 14, 13; perseverance in virtue and avoidance of evil (5–6.14b); necessity and value of almsgiving and charity (7–11.16–17); marriage to a kinsman (12–13a); industry (13b); prompt payment of wages (14a); the golden rule (15a); temperance (15b); docility (18); prayer (19).

4, 6: Before the revelation of retribution for all men in the after-

life—a doctrine taught in the Book of Wisdom—Old Testament man believed that virtue guaranteed earthly prosperity, and sin earthly disaster (cf Dt 28).

3, 11: 1 Kgs 8, 44.48; Pss 28, 2; 134, 2; Dn 6, 11.
3, 17: Tb 4, 12f; 6, 12f; Gn 24, 3f.
4, 3: Ex 20, 12; Prv 23, 22; Sir 7, 27.
4, 6: Tb 13, 6; Jn 3, 21; Eph 4, 15.
4, 7f: Tb 12, 8ff; Dt 15,

7f.11; Prv 19, 17; Sir 4, 1–6; 14, 13; Lk 14, 13; 1 Jn 3, 17.
4, 9: Mt 6, 20f.
4, 11: Sir 3, 30; 29, 12.
4, 12: Tb 3, 15.17; 6, 12; Gn 11, 29.31; 25, 20; 28, 1–4; 29, 15–30; Ex 34, 16; Dt 7, 3; Jgs 14, 3.

that their posterity shall inherit the land. ¹³ Therefore, my son, love your kinsmen. Do not be so proudhearted toward your kinsmen, the sons and daughters of your people, as to refuse to take a wife for yourself from among them. For in such arrogance there is ruin and great disorder. Likewise, in worthlessness there is decay and dire poverty, for worthlessness is the mother of famine.

¹⁴* "Do not keep with you overnight the wages of any man who works for you, but pay him immediately. If you thus behave as God's servant, you will receive your reward. Keep a close watch on yourself, my son, in everything you do, and discipline yourself in all your conduct. ¹⁵* Do to no one what you yourself dislike. Do not drink wine till you become

Give Food to the Hungry

In China, whenever you see a friend, it is customary to ask whether he or she has eaten a meal yet. If your friend responds, "No, I haven't eaten yet," it may mean that his or her last meal was yesterday or even the day before that. Then, you invite your friend to your home and share whatever food you have. This custom goes back to the great famine of China (1958–59), when people were dying of starvation and even eating tree bark.

Tobit gives his son good advice when he instructs him to share his food with the hungry and his clothing with the poor (Tb 4, 16). Read Mt 25, 31–46 to hear how seriously Jesus wants us to follow this advice.

▸ Tb 4, 16

drunk, nor let drunkenness accompany you on your way.

¹⁶* "Give to the hungry some of your bread, and to the naked some of your clothing. Whatever you have left over, give away as alms; and do not begrudge the alms you give. ¹⁷*† Be lavish with your bread and wine at the burial of the virtuous, but do not share them with sinners.

¹⁸ "Seek counsel from every wise man, and do not think lightly of any advice that can be useful. ¹⁹*† At all times bless the Lord God, and ask him to make all your paths straight and to grant success to all your endeavors and plans. For no pagan nation possesses good counsel, but the Lord himself gives all good things. If the Lord chooses, he raises a man up; but if he should decide otherwise, he casts him down to the deepest recesses of the nether world. So now, my son, keep in mind my commandments, and never let them be erased from your heart.

²⁰ "And now, son, I wish to inform you that I have deposited a great sum of money with Gabri's son Gabael at Rages in Media. ²¹* Do not be discouraged, my child, because of our poverty. You will be a rich man if you fear God, avoid all sin, and do what is right before the Lord your God."

The Angel Raphael

5 ¹ Then Tobiah replied to his father Tobit: "Everything that you have commanded me, father, I will do. ² But how shall I be able to obtain the money from him, since he does not know me nor do I know him? What can I show him to make him recognize me and trust me, so that he will give me the money? I do not even know which roads to take for the journey into Media!" ³† Tobit answered his son Tobiah: "We exchanged signatures on a document written in duplicate; I divided it into two parts, and each of us kept one; his copy I put with the money. Think of it, twenty years have already passed since I deposited that money! So now, my son, find yourself a trustworthy man who will make the journey with you. We will, of course, give him a salary when you return; but get back that money from Gabael."

⁴*† Tobiah went to look for someone acquainted with the roads who would travel with him to Media. As soon as he went out, he found the angel

---

4, 17: Tobit counsels his son either to give alms in honor of the dead, or, more probably, to give the "bread of consolation" to the family of the deceased. Cf Jer 16, 7; Ez 24, 17.

4, 19: Prayer is the foundation of a moral life.

5, 3: *Document:* in Greek *cheirographon.* In the Middle Ages, notably in England, a deed and its duplicate were written on one piece of parchment, with the Latin word *chirographum* inscribed across the top of the sheet or between the two copies of the text. The document was then cut in two in either a straight or a wavy line, the parts being given to the persons concerned. Perhaps this procedure derived from the present verse of Tobit. Duplicate documents,

usually one open and the other sealed, are well known from the ancient Near East.

5, 4: *He did not know:* the theme of an angel in disguise occurs frequently in folklore as well as in the Old Testament (Gn 18; cf Heb 13, 2).

4, 14: Lv 19, 13; Dt 24, 15. **4, 17:** Jer 16, 7; Lk 14, 13.
4, 15: Mt 7, 12; Lk 6, 31. **4, 19:** Dt 4, 6; Ps 119, 10.
4, 16: Dt 15, 10; Is 58, 7; Mt 25, 35f; 2 Cor 9, 7. **4, 21:** 1 Tm 6, 6ff.
5, 4: Heb 13, 2.

Raphael standing before him, though he did not know that this was an angel of God. ⁵ Tobiah said to him, "Who are you, young man?" He replied, "I am an Israelite, one of your kinsmen. I have come here to work." Tobiah said, "Do you know the way to Media?" ⁶† The other replied: "Yes, I have been there many times. I know the place well and I know all the routes. I have often traveled to Media; I used to stay with our kinsman Gabael, who lives at Rages in Media. It is a good two days' travel from Ecbatana to Rages, for Rages is situated at the mountains, Ecbatana out on the plateau." ⁷* Tobiah said to him, "Wait for me, young man, till I go back and tell my father; for I need you to make the journey with me. I will, of course, pay you." ⁸ Raphael replied, "Very well, I will wait for you; but do not be long."

⁹ Tobiah went back to tell his father Tobit what had happened. He said to him, "I have just found a man who is one of our own Israelite kinsmen!" Tobit said, "Call the man, so that I may find out what family and tribe he comes from, and whether he is trustworthy enough to travel with you, son." Tobiah went out to summon the man saying, "Young man, my father would like to see you."

¹⁰† When Raphael entered the house, Tobit greeted him first. Raphael said, "Hearty greetings to you!" Tobit replied: "What joy is left for me any more? Here I am, a blind man who cannot see God's sunlight, but must remain in darkness, like the dead who no longer see the light! Though alive, I am among the dead. I can hear a man's voice, but I cannot see him." Raphael said, "Take courage! God has healing in store for you; so take courage!" Tobit then said: "My son Tobiah wants to go to Media. Can you go with him to show him the way? I will of course pay you, brother." Raphael answered: "Yes, I can go with him, for I know all the routes. I have often traveled to Media and crossed all its plains and mountains; so I know every road well." ¹¹ Tobit asked, "Brother, tell me, please, what family and tribe are you from?" ¹²* Raphael said: "Why? Do you need a tribe and a family? Or are you looking for a hired man to travel with your son?" Tobit replied, "I wish to know truthfully whose son you are, brother, and what your name is."

¹³† Raphael answered, "I am Azariah, son of Hananiah the elder, one of your own kinsmen." ¹⁴ Tobit exclaimed: "Welcome! God save you, brother! Do not be provoked with me, brother, for wanting to learn the truth about your family. So it turns out that you are a kinsman, and from a noble and good line! I knew Hananiah and Nathaniah, the two sons of Shemaiah the elder; with me they used to make the pilgrimage to Jerusalem, where we would worship together. No, they did not stray from the right path; your kinsmen are good men. You are certainly of good lineage, and welcome!"

¹⁵† Then he added: "For each day you are away I will give you the normal wages, plus expenses for you and for my son. If you go with my son, ¹⁶ I will even add a bonus to your wages!" Raphael replied: "I will go with him; have no fear. In good health we shall leave you, and in good health we shall return to you, for the way is safe." ¹⁷ Tobit said, "God bless you, brother." Then he called his son and said to him: "My son, prepare whatever you need for the journey, and set out with your kinsman. May God in heaven protect you on the way and bring you back to me safe and sound; and may his angel accompany you for safety, my son."

Before setting out on his journey, Tobiah kissed his father and mother. Tobit said to him, "Have a safe journey." ¹⁸ But his mother began to weep. She said to Tobit: "Why have you decided to send my child away? Is he not the staff to which we cling, ever there with us in all that we do? ¹⁹ I hope more money is not your chief concern! Rather let it be a ransom for our son! ²⁰ What the Lord has given us to live on is certainly enough for us." ²¹ Tobit reassured her: "Have no such thought. Our son will leave in good health and come back to us in good health. Your own eyes will see the day when he returns to you safe and sound. ²²† So, no such thought; do not worry about them, my love. For a good angel will go with him, his journey will be successful, and he will return unharmed." ¹† Then she stopped weeping.

Journey to Rages

6 ² When the boy left home, accompanied by the angel, the dog followed Tobiah out of the house and went with him. The travelers walked till nightfall, and made camp beside the Tigris River.

5, 6: *It is a good two days' travel from Ecbatana to Rages:* Alexander's army took eleven days in forced marches to cover this distance, about 180 miles. The author is merely using popular impressions about faraway places; he is not teaching geography. (See notes on Tb 1, 15; 3, 7 and Introduction.)

5, 10: *Hearty greetings* and *what joy* form a wordplay on the Greek verb *chairein,* "to greet" and "to be joyful."

5, 13–14: *Azariah,* "Yahweh helps"; *Hananiah,* "Yahweh is merciful"; *Nathaniah,* "Yahweh gives"; *Shemaiah,* "Yahweh hears."

5, 15: *The normal wages:* literally, "a drachma," about seventeen cents, a day's wage for a workingman.

5, 22: *My love:* literally, "sister," a term of endearment applied to one's wife; cf Tb 7, 11.15; 8, 4.21; 10, 6.13; Song 4, 9.10.12; 5, 1f. *A good angel:* a reference to the guardian angel, though Tobit does not know, of course, that Raphael himself, disguised as Azariah, is the good angel in this case.

5, 1: *Then . . . weeping:* this verse belongs to ch 6.

5, 7: Tb 12, 2.   **5, 12:** Jgs 13, 17f.

3 Now when the boy went down to wash his feet in the river, a large fish suddenly leaped out of the water and tried to swallow his foot. He shouted in alarm. 4 But the angel said to him, "Take hold of the fish and don't let it get away!" The boy seized the fish and hauled it up on the shore. 5† The angel then told him: "Cut the fish open and take out its gall, heart, and liver, and keep them with you; but throw away the entrails. Its gall, heart, and liver make useful medicines." 6 After the lad had cut the fish open, he put aside the gall, heart, and liver. Then he broiled and ate part of the fish; the rest he salted and kept for the journey.

Raphael's Instructions

7 Afterward they traveled on together till they were near Media. The boy asked the angel this question: "Brother Azariah, what medicinal value is there in the fish's heart, liver, and gall?" 8 He answered: "As regards the fish's heart and liver, if you burn them so that the smoke surrounds a man or a woman who is afflicted by a demon or evil spirit, the affliction will leave him completely, and no demons will ever return to him again. 9 And as for the gall, if you rub it on the eyes of a man who has cataracts, blowing into his eyes right on the cataracts, his sight will be restored."

10 When they had entered Media and were getting close to Ecbatana, 11 Raphael said to the boy, "Brother Tobiah!" He answered, "Yes, what is it?" Raphael continued: "Tonight we must stay with Raguel, who is a relative of yours. He has a daughter named Sarah, 12* but no other child. Since you are Sarah's closest relative, you before all other men have the right to marry her. Also, her father's estate is rightfully yours to inherit. Now the girl is sensible, courageous, and very beautiful; and her father loves her dearly." 13† He continued: "Since you have the right to marry her, listen to me, brother. Tonight I will ask the girl's father to let us have her as your bride. When we return from Rages, we will hold the wedding feast for her. I know that Raguel cannot keep her from you or let her become engaged to another man; that would be a capital crime according to the decree in the Book of Moses, and he knows that it is your right, before all other men, to marry his daughter. So heed my words, brother; tonight we must speak for the girl, so that we may have her engaged to you. And when we return from Rages, we will take her and bring her back with us to your house."

14 Tobiah objected, however: "Brother Azariah, I have heard that this woman has already been married seven times, and that her husbands died in their bridal chambers. On the very night they approached her, they dropped dead. And I have heard it said that it was a demon who killed them. 15* So now I too am afraid of this demon. Because he loves her, he does not harm her; but he does slay any man who wishes to come close to her. I am my father's only child. If I should die, I would bring my father and mother down to their grave in sorrow over me. And they have no other son to bury them!"

16 Raphael said to him: "Do you not remember your father's orders? He commanded you to marry a woman from your own family. So now listen to me, brother; do not give another thought to this demon, but marry Sarah. I know that tonight you shall have her for your wife! 17 When you go into the bridal chamber, take the fish's liver and heart, and place them on the embers for the incense. 18† As soon as the demon smells the odor they give off, he will flee and never again show himself near her. Then when you are about to have intercourse with her, both of you first rise up to pray. Beg the Lord of heaven to show you mercy and grant you deliverance. But do not be afraid, for she was set apart for you before the world existed. You will save her, and she will go with you. And I suppose that you will have children by her, who will take the place of brothers for you. So do not worry."

When Tobiah heard Raphael say that she was his kinswoman, of his own family's lineage, he fell deeply in love with her, and his heart became set on her.

At the House of Raguel

7 1 When they entered Ecbatana, Tobiah said, "Brother Azariah, lead me straight to our kinsman Raguel." So he brought him to the house of Raguel, whom they found seated by his courtyard gate. They greeted him first. He said to them, "Greetings to you too, brothers! Good health to you, and welcome!" When he brought them into his home, 2 he said to his wife Edna, "This young man looks just like my kinsman Tobit!" 3 So Edna asked them, "Who are you, brothers?" They answered, "We are of the exiles from Naphtali at Nineveh." 4 She said, "Do you know our kinsman Tobit?" They answered, "Indeed we do!" She asked, "Is he well?" 5 They answered, "Yes, he is alive and well." Then Tobiah exclaimed, "He is my father!" 6 Raguel sprang up and kissed him, shedding tears

---

6, 5: *Its gall . . . medicines:* belief in the healing power of these organs was common among the physicians of antiquity.

6, 13: *Raguel . . . Book of Moses:* Nm 36, 6–8 prescribed marriage within the ancestral tribe, but no death penalty is mentioned.

6, 18: *Rise up to pray:* prayer is needed to drive out the demon.

6, 12: Tb 4, 12f; Nm 36, 8.   6, 15: Tb 3, 10.

of joy. ⁷ But when he heard that Tobit had lost his eyesight, he was grieved and wept aloud. He said to Tobiah: "My child, God bless you! You are the son of a noble and good father. But what a terrible misfortune that such a righteous and charitable man should be afflicted with blindness!" He continued to weep in the arms of his kinsman Tobiah. ⁸ His wife Edna also wept for Tobit; and even their daughter Sarah began to weep.

Marriage of Tobiah and Sarah

⁹ Afterward, Raguel slaughtered a ram from the flock and gave them a cordial reception. When they had bathed and reclined to eat, Tobiah said to Raphael, "Brother Azariah, ask Raguel to let me marry my kinswoman Sarah." ¹⁰ Raguel overheard the words; so he said to the boy: "Eat and drink and be merry tonight, for no man is more entitled to marry my daughter Sarah than you, brother. Besides, not even I have the right to give her to anyone but you, because you are my closest relative. But I will explain the situation to you very frankly. ¹¹ I have given her in marriage to seven men, all of whom were kinsmen of ours, and all died on the very night they approached her. But now, son, eat and drink. I am sure the Lord will look after you both." Tobiah answered, "I will eat or drink nothing until you set aside what belongs to me."

Raguel said to him: "I will do it. She is yours according to the decree of the Book of Moses. Your marriage to her has been decided in heaven! Take your kinswoman; from now on you are her love, and she is your beloved. She is yours today and ever after. And tonight, son, may the Lord of heaven prosper you both. May he grant you mercy and peace." ¹²* Then Raguel called his daughter Sarah, and she came to him. He took her by the hand and gave her to Tobiah with the words: "Take her according to the law. According to the decree written in the Book of Moses she is your wife. Take her and bring her back safely to your father. And may the God of heaven grant both of you peace and prosperity." ¹³* He then called her mother and told her to bring a scroll, so that he might draw up a marriage contract stating that he gave Sarah to Tobiah as his wife according to the decree of the Mosaic law. Her mother brought the scroll, and he drew up the contract, to which they affixed their seals.

¹⁴ Afterward they began to eat and drink. ¹⁵ Later Raguel called his wife Edna and said, "My love, prepare the other bedroom and bring the girl there."

¹⁶ She went and made the bed in the room, as she was told, and brought the girl there. After she had cried over her, she wiped away the tears and said: ¹⁷ "Be brave, my daughter. May the Lord of heaven grant you joy in place of your grief. Courage, my daughter." Then she left.

Expulsion of the Demon

8 ¹ When they had finished eating and drinking, the girl's parents wanted to retire. They brought the young man out of the dining room and led him into the bedroom. ²† At this point Tobiah, mindful of Raphael's instructions, took the fish's liver and heart from the bag which he had with him, and placed them on the embers for the incense. ³† The demon, repelled by the odor of the fish, fled into Upper Egypt; Raphael pursued him there and bound him hand and foot. Then Raphael returned immediately.

⁴ When the girl's parents left the bedroom and closed the door behind them, Tobiah arose from bed and said to his wife, "My love, get up. Let us pray and beg our Lord to have mercy on us and to grant us deliverance." ⁵* She got up, and they started to pray and beg that deliverance might be theirs. He began with these words:

"Blessed are you, O God of our fathers;
　　praised be your name forever and ever.
Let the heavens and all your creation
　　praise you forever.
⁶* You made Adam and you gave him his
　　wife Eve
　　to be his help and support;
　　and from these two the human
　　race descended.
You said, 'It is not good for the man to
　　be alone;
　　let us make him a partner like himself.'
⁷ Now, Lord, you know that I take this wife
　　of mine
　　not because of lust,
　　but for a noble purpose.
Call down your mercy on me and on her,
　　and allow us to live together to a happy
　　old age."

⁸ They said together, "Amen, amen," ⁹ and went to bed for the night.

But Raguel got up and summoned his servants. With him they went out to dig a grave, ¹⁰ for he

---

8, 2f: The manner of coping with demonic influences among the ancients seems quaint to us. However, the fish here is part of the story, and not a recipe for exorcism. It is clear that the author places primary emphasis on the value of prayer to God (Tb 6, 18; 8, 4–8), on the role of the angel as God's agent, and on the pious dispositions of Tobiah.

8, 3: *Into Upper Egypt:* to the desert there. The desert was considered the dwelling place of demons. Cf Is 13, 21; 34, 14; Mt 4, 1; 12, 43.

7, 12: Gn 24, 50f.　　　　8, 5: Dn 3, 26.
7, 13: Tb 6, 12.　　　　　8, 6: Gn 2, 18–23.

LIVE IT!

Angels Among Us

Many older Catholics were taught as children that they were to leave a bit of space on their chair for their guardian angel. We smile at that story, partly because it was a creative way to make angels real in the lives of children, and partly because it points to a truth about God's presence in our life.

In the fictional story of Tobit, we meet the angel Raphael. In other parts of the Bible, angels serve primarily as God's messengers. But Raphael is much more than a messenger. He disguises himself as a kindly but unknown relative who guides Tobias to the secrets he needs to know to relieve both Tobit's and Sarah's suffering.

The truth is that many angels are around us. Most of us have heard stories about kind strangers who appear seemingly out of nowhere to help and then disappear. Our seat may not have a lot of room for an angel, but our world certainly does. They remind us that God is with us, protecting us and guiding us.

Have you or someone you know been touched by an angel? In return, why don't you look for opportunities to be someone else's "angel"?

---

said, "I must do this, because if Tobiah should die, we would be subjected to ridicule and insult." [11] When they had finished digging the grave, Raguel went back into the house and called his wife, [12] saying, "Send one of the maids in to see whether Tobiah is alive or dead, so that if necessary we may bury him without anyone's knowing about it." [13] She sent the maid, who lit a lamp, opened the bedroom door, went in, and found them sound asleep together. [14] The maid went out and told the girl's parents that Tobiah was alive, and that there was nothing wrong. [15] Then Raguel praised the God of heaven in these words:

"Blessed are you, O God, with every holy and
     pure blessing!
Let all your chosen ones praise you;
let them bless you forever!
[16] Blessed are you, who have made
     me glad;
what I feared did not happen.
Rather you have dealt with us
according to your great mercy.
[17] Blessed are you, for you were merciful
toward two only children.
Grant them, Master, mercy and
     deliverance,
and bring their lives to fulfillment
with happiness and mercy."

[18] Then he told his servants to fill in the grave before dawn.

Wedding Feast

[19] He asked his wife to bake many loaves of bread; he himself went out to the herd and picked out two steers and four rams which he ordered to be slaughtered. So the servants began to prepare the feast. [20]† He summoned Tobiah and made an oath in his presence, saying: "For fourteen days you shall not stir from here, but shall remain here eating and drinking with me; and you shall bring joy to my daughter's sorrowing spirit. [21] Take, to begin with, half of whatever I own when you go back in good health to your father; the other half will be yours when I and my wife die. Be of good cheer, my son! I am your father, and Edna is your mother; and we belong to you and to your beloved now and forever. So be happy, son!"

The Money Recovered

9 [1] Then Tobiah called Raphael and said to him: [2] "Brother Azariah, take along with you four servants and two camels and travel to Rages. Go to Gabael's house and give him this bond. Get the money and then bring him along with you to the wedding celebration. [4] For you know that my father is counting the days. If I should delay my return by a single day, I would cause him intense grief. [3] You witnessed the oath that Raguel has sworn; I cannot violate his oath." [5] So Raphael, together with the four servants and two camels, traveled to Rages in Media, where they stayed at Gabael's house. Raphael gave Gabael his bond and told him about Tobit's son Tobiah, and that he had married and

---

8, 20: *For fourteen days:* because of the happy, and unexpected, turn of events, Raguel doubles the time of the wedding feast. When Tobiah returns home, the usual seven-day feast is held (Tb 11, 18). Cf Jgs 14, 12.

was inviting him to the wedding celebration. Gabael promptly checked over the sealed money-bags, and they placed them on the camels.

6 The following morning they got an early start and traveled to the wedding celebration. When they entered Raguel's house, they found Tobiah reclining at table. He sprang up and greeted Gabael, who wept and blessed him, exclaiming: "O noble and good child, son of a noble and good, upright and charitable man, may the Lord grant heavenly blessing to you and to your wife, and to your wife's father and mother. Blessed be God, because I have seen the very image of my cousin Tobit!"

IV: Tobiah's Return; Cure of Tobit's Blindness

Anxiety of the Parents

10 1 Meanwhile, day by day, Tobit was keeping track of the time Tobiah would need to go and to return. When the number of days was reached and his son did not appear, 2 he said, "I wonder what has happened. Perhaps he has been detained there; or perhaps Gabael is dead, and there is no one to give him the money." 3 And he began to worry. 4 His wife Anna said, "My son has perished and is no longer among the living!" And she began to weep aloud and to wail over her son: 5 "Alas, my child, light of my eyes, that I let you make this journey!" 6 But Tobit kept telling her: "Hush, do not think about it, my love; he is safe! Probably they have to take care of some unexpected business there. The man who is traveling with him is trustworthy, and is one of our own kinsmen. So do not worry over him, my love. He will be here soon." 7* But she retorted, "Stop it, and do not lie to me! My child has perished!" She would go out and keep watch all day at the road her son had taken, and she ate nothing. At sunset she would go back home to wail and cry the whole night through, getting no sleep at all.

Departure from Ecbatana

Now at the end of the fourteen-day wedding celebration which Raguel had sworn to hold for his daughter, Tobiah went to him and said: "Please let me go, for I know that my father and mother do not believe they will ever see me again. So I beg you, father, let me go back to my father. I have already told you how I left him." 8 Raguel said to Tobiah: "Stay, my child, stay with me I am sending messengers to your father Tobit, and they will give him news of you." 9 But Tobiah insisted, "No, I beg you to let me go back to my father."

10 Raguel then promptly handed over to Tobiah Sarah his wife, together with half of all his property: male and female slaves, oxen and sheep, asses and camels, clothing, money, and household goods. 11 Bidding them farewell, he let them go. He embraced Tobiah and said to him: "Good-bye, my son. Have a safe journey. May the Lord of heaven grant prosperity to you and to your wife Sarah. And may I see children of yours before I die!" 12 Then he kissed his daughter Sarah and said to her: "My daughter, honor your father-in-law and your mother-in-law, because from now on they are as much your parents as the ones who brought you into the world. Go in peace, my daughter; let me hear good reports about you as long as I live." Finally he said good-bye to them and sent them away.

13 Then Edna said to Tobiah: "My child and beloved kinsman, may the Lord bring you back safely, and may I live long enough to see children of you and of my daughter Sarah before I die. Before the Lord, I entrust my daughter to your care. Never cause her grief at any time in your life. Go in peace, my child. From now on I am your mother, and Sarah is your beloved. May all of us be prosperous all the days of our lives." She kissed them both and sent them away in peace.

14 When Tobiah left Raguel, he was full of happiness and joy, and he blessed the Lord of heaven and earth, the King of all, for making his journey so successful. Finally he said good-bye to Raguel and his wife Edna, and added, "May I honor you all the days of my life!"

Homeward Journey

11 1 Then they left and began their return journey. When they were near Kaserin, just before Nineveh, 2 Raphael said: "You know how we left your father. 3 Let us hurry on ahead of your wife to prepare the house while the rest of the party are still on the way." 4 So they both went on ahead and Raphael said to Tobiah, "Have the gall in your hand!" And the dog ran along behind them.

5 Meanwhile, Anna sat watching the road by which her son was to come. 6 When she saw him coming, she exclaimed to his father, "Tobit, your son is coming, and the man who traveled with him!"

7 Raphael said to Tobiah before he reached his father: "I am certain that his eyes will be opened. 8 Smear the fish gall on them. This medicine will make the cataracts shrink and peel off from his eyes; then your father will again be able to see the light of day."

10, 7: Gn 45, 26.

Sight Restored

9* Then Anna ran up to her son, threw her arms around him, and said to him, "Now that I have seen you again, son, I am ready to die!" And she sobbed aloud. 10 Tobit got up and stumbled out through the courtyard gate. Tobiah went up to him 11 with the fish gall in his hand, and holding him firmly, blew into his eyes. "Courage, father," he said. 12 Next he smeared the medicine on his eyes, 13 and it made them smart. Then, beginning at the corners of Tobit's eyes, Tobiah used both hands to peel off the cataracts. When Tobit saw his son, he threw his arms around him 14 and wept. He exclaimed, "I can see you, son, the light of my eyes!" Then he said:

"Blessed be God,
and praised be his great name,
and blessed be all his holy angels.
May his holy name be praised
throughout all the ages,
15* Because it was he who scourged me,
and it is he who has had mercy on me.
Behold, I now see my son Tobiah!"

Then Tobit went back in, rejoicing and praising God with full voice. Tobiah told his father that his journey had been a success; that he had brought back the money; and that he had married Raguel's daughter Sarah, who would arrive shortly, for she was approaching the gate of Nineveh.

16 Rejoicing and praising God, Tobit went out to the gate of Nineveh to meet his daughter-in-law. When the people of Nineveh saw him walking along briskly, with no one leading him by the hand, they were amazed. 17 Before them all Tobit proclaimed how God had mercifully restored sight to his eyes. When Tobit reached Sarah, the wife of his son Tobiah, he greeted her: "Welcome, my daughter! Blessed be your God for bringing you to us, daughter! Blessed are your father and your mother. Blessed is my son Tobiah, and blessed are you, daughter! Welcome to your home with blessing and joy. Come in, daughter!" That day there was joy for all the Jews who lived in Nineveh. 18 Ahiqar and his nephew Nadab also came to rejoice with Tobit. They celebrated Tobiah's wedding feast for seven happy days, and he received many gifts.

V: Raphael Reveals His Identity

Raphael's Wages

12 1† When the wedding celebration came to an end, Tobit called his son Tobiah and said to him, "Son, see to it that you give what is due to the man who made the journey with you; give him a bonus too." 2* Tobiah said: "Father, how much shall I pay him? It would not hurt me at all to give him half of all the wealth he brought back with me. 3 He led me back safe and sound; he cured my wife; he brought the money back with me; and he cured you. How much of a bonus should I give him?" 4 Tobit answered, "It is only fair, son, that he should receive half of all that he brought back." 5 So Tobiah called Raphael and said, "Take as your wages half of all that you have brought back, and go in peace."

Exhortation

6† Raphael called the two men aside privately and said to them: "Thank God! Give him the praise and the glory. Before all the living, acknowledge the many good things he has done for you, by blessing and extolling his name in song. Before all men, honor and proclaim God's deeds, and do not be slack in praising him. 7 A king's secret it is prudent to keep, but the works of God are to be declared and made known. Praise them with due honor. Do good, and evil will not find its way to you. 8*† Prayer and fasting are good, but better than either is almsgiving accompanied by righteousness. A little with righteousness is better than abundance with wickedness. It is better to give alms than to store up gold; 9* for almsgiving saves one from death and expiates every sin. Those who regularly give alms shall enjoy a full life; 10 but those habitually guilty of sin are their own worst enemies.

Raphael's Identity

11 "I will now tell you the whole truth; I will conceal nothing at all from you. I have already said to you, 'A king's secret it is prudent to keep, but the works of God are to be made known with due honor.' 12*† I can now tell you that when you, Tobit, and Sarah prayed, it was I who presented and read the record of your prayer before

---

12, 1–5: *Tobit* and *his son* generously agree to give Azariah far more than the wages agreed upon in Tb 5, 15–16.

12, 6–10: In the fashion of a wisdom teacher, *Raphael* gives the two men a short exhortation similar to the one Tobit gave his son in Tb 4, 3–19.

12, 6f: The Jews considered the duty of praising God their most esteemed privilege. Without praise of God, life was meaningless. Cf Is 38, 16–20.

12, 8: *Prayer . . . fasting . . . almsgiving . . . righteousness:* these, together with the proper attitude toward wealth, are treated in great detail by Christ our Lord in the Sermon on the Mount (Mt 6).

12, 12.15: *Raphael* is one of the seven specially designated intercessors who present man's prayers to God. Angelology was developing in this period. The names of two other angels are given in the Bible: Gabriel (Dn 8, 16; 9, 21; Lk 1, 19.26) and Michael (Dn 10, 13.21; 12, 1; Jude 9; Rv 12, 7).

11, 9: Gn 33, 4; 45, 14; 46, 29f; Lk 15, 20.
11, 15: Tb 13, 2; Dt 32, 39; 1 Sm 2, 6.
12, 2: Tb 5, 3.7.15f.
12, 8: Tb 4, 7–11; Sir 29, 8–13.
12, 9: Dn 4, 24.
12, 12: Jb 33, 23f; Acts 10, 4; Rv 8, 3f.

the Glory of the Lord; and I did the same thing when you used to bury the dead. 13 When you did not hesitate to get up and leave your dinner in order to go and bury the dead, 14† I was sent to put you to the test. At the same time, however, God commissioned me to heal you and your daughter-in-law Sarah. 15* I am Raphael, one of the seven angels who enter and serve before the Glory of the Lord."

16 Stricken with fear, the two men fell to the ground. 17 But Raphael said to them: "No need to fear; you are safe. Thank God now and forever. 18 As for me, when I came to you it was not out of any favor on my part, but because it was God's will. So continue to thank him every day; praise him with song. 19 Even though you watched me eat and drink, I did not really do so; what you were seeing was a vision. 20* So now get up from the ground and praise God. Behold, I am about to ascend to him who sent me; write down all these things that have happened to you." 21 When Raphael ascended, they rose to their feet and could no longer see him. 22 They kept thanking God and singing his praises; and they continued to acknowledge these marvelous deeds which he had done when the angel of God appeared to them.

VI: Tobit's Song of Praise

13 1*† Then Tobit composed this joyful prayer:

Blessed be God who lives forever,
  because his kingdom lasts for all ages.
2* For he scourges and then has mercy;
  he casts down to the depths of
      the netherworld,
  and he brings up from the great abyss.
No one can escape his hand.

3 Praise him, you Israelites, before the Gentiles,
  for though he has scattered you among them,
4 he has shown you his greatness even there.
Exalt him before every living being,
  because he is the Lord our God,
  our Father and God forever.
5* He scourged you for your iniquities,
  but will again have mercy on you all.
He will gather you from all the Gentiles
  among whom you have been scattered.

6* When you turn back to him with all
      your heart,

HOPE FOR THE FAITHFUL!

When the Jews lived under the influence of Greek culture, there was a great need for hope. The story of Tobit and Tobias, whose names mean "goodness" and "God is good," was written to give hope to those who continue to be faithful to God, even in difficult times.

Tobit is the model of the good Israelite at all times and places. God's saving actions for him and his family symbolize God's actions toward Israel. In this spirit, before his death, Tobit sings a beautiful hymn in thanksgiving for God's goodness and with hope in the triumph of Jerusalem over its oppressors.
- Recognize the goodness of God in your life and the way in which you fail God.
- Take a moment to pray in Tobit's style. Praise God for the blessings in your life; ask forgiveness for the times you have failed God; give thanks for the times God has answered your prayers in a wiser way than what you had asked for. Pray not only for yourself but for all people, with hope for the triumph of God's love and peace over the egoism, hatred, and violence so common today.

▶ Tobit, chapter 13

12, 14: *I was sent . . . test:* God often sends trials to purify his faithful servants further. Cf Jb 1–2.
13, 1–18: Tobit's hymn of praise (cf Ex 15, 1–18; Jdt 16, 1–17) is divided into two parts. The first part (vv 1–8) is a song of praise that echoes themes from the hymns and psalms of the kingdom; the second (vv 9–18) is addressed to Jerusalem in the style of the prophets who spoke of a new and ideal Jerusalem (Is 60); cf Rv 21.

12, 15: Lk 1, 19; Rv 8, 2.
12, 20: Jgs 13, 20.
13, 1: Tb 3, 11; 8, 5.15; 1 Chr 29, 10; Dn 3, 26.
13, 2: Tb 11, 15; 13, 9; Dt 32, 39; 1 Sm 2, 6; Wis 16, 13.
13, 5: Dt 30, 3; Neh 1, 9.
13, 6: Dt 30, 2.

to do what is right before him,
Then he will turn back to you,
  and no longer hide his face from you.

So now consider what he has done for you,
  and praise him with full voice.
Bless the Lord of righteousness,
  and exalt the King of the ages.

In the land of my exile I praise him,
  and show his power and majesty to a
    sinful nation.
"Turn back, you sinners! do the right
    before him:
  perhaps he may look with favor upon you
    and show you mercy.

7 "As for me, I exalt my God,
  and my spirit rejoices in the King
    of heaven.
8 Let all men speak of his majesty,
  and sing his praises in Jerusalem."

9*†O Jerusalem, holy city,
  he scourged you for the works of
    your hands,
  but will again pity the children of
    the righteous.
10* Praise the Lord for his goodness,
  and bless the King of the ages,
  so that his tent may be rebuilt in you
    with joy.
May he gladden within you all who
    were captives;
  all who were ravaged may he cherish
    within you
  for all generations to come.

11* A bright light will shine to all parts of
    the earth;
  many nations shall come to you from afar,
And the inhabitants of all the limits of
    the earth,
  drawn to you by the name of the Lord God,
Bearing in their hands their gifts for the King
    of heaven.
Every generation shall give joyful praise
    in you,
  and shall call you the chosen one,
    through all ages forever.

12* Accursed are all who speak a harsh word
    against you;

accursed are all who destroy you
  and pull down your walls,
And all who overthrow your towers
  and set fire to your homes;
  but forever blessed are all those who build
    you up.

13 Go, then, rejoice over the children of
    the righteous,
  who shall all be gathered together
    and shall bless the Lord of the ages.
14* Happy are those who love you,
  and happy those who rejoice in
    your prosperity.

Happy are all the men who shall grieve
    over you,
  over all your chastisements,
For they shall rejoice in you
  as they behold all your joy forever.

15 My spirit blesses the Lord, the great King;
16* Jerusalem shall be rebuilt as his home
    forever.
Happy for me if a remnant of my
    offspring survive
  to see your glory and to praise the King
    of heaven!

The gates of Jerusalem shall be built with
    sapphire and emerald,
  and all your walls with precious stones.
The towers of Jerusalem shall be built
    with gold,
  and their battlements with pure gold.
17 The streets of Jerusalem shall be paved
    with rubies and stones of Ophir;
18 The gates of Jerusalem shall sing hymns
    of gladness,
  and all her houses shall cry out, "Alleluia!"

"Blessed be God who has raised you up!
  may he be blessed for all ages!"
For in you they shall praise his holy
    name forever.

The end of Tobit's hymn of praise.

VII: Epilogue

Parting Advice

14 ¹Tobit died peacefully at the age of a
hundred and twelve, and received an

13, 9: *Works of your hands:* idols.

13, 9: Tb 11, 15; Mi 7, 19; Rv 21.

13, 10: Is 44, 26.28; Am 9, 11;   13, 12: Bar 4, 31f.
  Zec 1, 16.   13, 14: Ps 122, 6; Is 66, 10.
13, 11: Is 2, 3f; 9, 1; 49, 6; 60,   13, 16: Tb 14, 5; Is 54, 11–13;
  1; Mi 4, 2; Zec 8, 22.   62, 2; Rv 21, 10–21.

honorable burial in Nineveh. ² He was sixty-two years old when he lost his eyesight, and after he recovered it he lived in prosperity, giving alms and continually blessing God and praising the divine Majesty.

³* Just before he died, he called his son Tobiah and Tobiah's seven sons, and gave him this command: "Son, take your children ⁴*† and flee into Media, for I believe God's word which was spoken by Nahum against Nineveh. It shall all happen, and shall overtake Assyria and Nineveh; indeed, whatever was said by Israel's prophets, whom God commissioned, shall occur. Not one of all the oracles shall remain unfulfilled, but everything shall take place in the time appointed for it. So it will be safer in Media than in Assyria or Babylon. For I know and believe that whatever God has spoken will be accomplished. It shall happen, and not a single word of the prophecies shall prove false.

"As for our kinsmen who dwell in Israel, they shall all be scattered and led away into exile from the Good Land. The entire country of Israel shall become desolate; even Samaria and Jerusalem shall become desolate! God's temple there shall be burnt to the ground and shall be desolate for a while. ⁵*† But God will again have mercy on them and bring them back to the land of Israel. They shall rebuild the temple, but it will not be like the first one, until the era when the appointed times shall be completed. Afterward all of them shall return from their exile, and they shall rebuild Jerusalem with splendor. In her the temple of God shall also be rebuilt; yes, it will be rebuilt for all generations to come, just as the prophets of Israel said of her. ⁶*† All the nations of the world shall be converted and shall offer God true worship; all shall abandon their idols which have deceitfully led them into error, ⁷* and shall bless the God of the ages in righteousness. Because all the Israelites who are to be saved in those days will truly be mindful of God, they shall be gathered together and go to Jerusalem; in security shall they dwell forever in the land of Abraham, which will be given over to them. Those who sincerely love God shall rejoice, but those who

become guilty of sin shall completely disappear from the land.

⁹ "Now, children, I give you this command: serve God faithfully and do what is right before him; you must tell your children to do what is upright and to give alms, to be mindful of God and at all times to bless his name sincerely and with all their strength.

⁸ "Now, as for you, my son, depart from Nineveh; do not remain here. ¹⁰*† The day you bury your mother next to me, do not even stay overnight within the confines of the city. For I see that people here shamelessly commit all sorts of wickedness and treachery. Think, my son, of all that Nadab did to Ahiqar, the very one who brought him up: Ahiqar went down alive into the earth! Yet God made Nadab's disgraceful crime rebound against him. Ahiqar came out again into the light, but Nadab went into the everlasting darkness, for he had tried to kill Ahiqar. Because Ahiqar had given alms to me, he escaped from the deadly trap Nadab had set for him. But Nadab himself fell into the deadly trap, and it destroyed him. ¹¹ So, my children, note well what almsgiving does, and also what wickedness does—it kills! But now my spirit is about to leave me."

Death of Tobit and Tobiah

¹²* They placed him on his bed and he died; and he received an honorable burial. When Tobiah's mother died, he buried her next to his father. He then departed with his wife and children for Media, where he settled in Ecbatana with his father-in-law Raguel. ¹³ He took respectful care of his aging father-in-law and mother-in-law; and he buried them at Ecbatana in Media. Then he inherited Raguel's estate as well as that of his father Tobit. ¹⁴ He died at the venerable age of a hundred and seventeen. ¹⁵† But before he died, he heard of the destruction of Nineveh and saw its effects. He witnessed the exile of the city's inhabitants when Cyaxares, king of Media, led them captive into Media. Tobiah praised God for all that he had done against the citizens of Nineveh and Assyria. Before dying he rejoiced over Nineveh's destruction, and he blessed the Lord God forever and ever. Amen.

14, 4f: *Nahum:* one of the minor prophets, whose book contains oracles of doom against *Nineveh.* Here, in keeping with the period to which he assigns his story, the sacred author makes Tobit speak as if the punishment of *Nineveh,* the destruction of Jerusalem (587 B.C.), the exile from Judah and the return, would all take place in the future. The technique of using the facts of past history as seemingly future predictions, is a frequent device of apocalyptic writers. *The Good Land:* a favorite name for the promised land. Cf Dt 1, 35; 3, 25; 4, 21.22.

14, 5: *Until the era . . . completed:* a reference to the advent of messianic times, in which a new, more perfect temple was to be expected. Cf Heb 9, 1–14.

14, 6: Conversion of the Gentiles is also to come in the messianic era.

14, 10: *Nadab:* In the story of *Ahiqar,* the hero *Ahiqar,* chancel-

lor under the Assyrian kings Sennacherib and Esarhaddon, adopts his nephew *Nadab* and prepares him to become his successor. But *Nadab* treacherously plots to have his uncle put to death. *Ahiqar* hides in a friend's house, and is finally vindicated (came out again into the light) when *Nadab's* scheme is discovered. Thereupon *Nadab* is thrown into a dungeon where he dies (went into everlasting darkness). It was *Ahiqar's* almsgiving that delivered him from death; see note on Tb 2, 2.

14, 15: *Cyaxares:* Nabopolassar, king of Babylon, and *Cyaxares* conquered and destroyed *Nineveh* in 612 B.C.; see note on Tb 1, 15.

14, 3: Gn 47, 29f.	Ex 34, 28; 37, 25;
14, 4: Na 2, 2—3, 19.	39, 26.
14, 5: Neh 12, 27; Jer 31, 38.	**14, 10:** Tb 1, 21f.
14, 6: Tb 45, 14; Is 60, 1–4.	**14, 12:** Tb 4, 4.
14, 7: Is 60, 21; Jer 32, 37;	

Do you like to cheer for the underdog? If so, you are like most people. Whether in a law court, on a football field, or in politics, we get a thrill from seeing the high and mighty toppled by a courageous and determined underdog. This theme is evident in some of the most popular stories of the Old Testament: a group of Hebrew slaves escapes from Pharaoh's army; the teenage David topples the giant Goliath; the prophet Daniel escapes injury in the lions' den. Judith's story is another in which the little people —against all odds—somehow come out on top.

At a Glance

I. Peril of the Jews (1, 1—7, 32).

II. Deliverance of the Jews (8, 1—14, 10).

III. Victory (14, 11—16, 25).

In-depth

As the Book of Judith opens, the mighty Assyrian army is on the march against Jerusalem. To block the advance, the citizens of the small town of Bethulia are asked by the high priest to resist the army's movement. With little hope of success but a great deal of courage, the Bethulians accept the challenge. When they are at the point of surrender, a childless widow named Judith steps forward. Putting all her trust in "the God of the lowly, the helper of the oppressed, the supporter of the weak, the protector of the forsaken, the savior of those without hope" (Jdt 9, 11), she bravely delivers her nation from certain defeat.

The story of Judith must have presented a challenge to the male-dominated world of the Israelites. As a childless widow, Judith would have had little social standing. Yet she succeeds where the king, the priests, and the leaders of the city fail. It is interesting that the name Judith is probably not even a proper name. It simply means "Jewish woman." In a sense, Judith stands for all the Jewish women of the past who have served God through their faith, courage, and decisive action.

Because of its many historical errors, the Book of Judith is clearly a fictional work. With remarkable storytelling flair, the author underlines one of the major elements of Hebrew faith: "O LORD, great are you and glorious, / wonderful in power and unsurpassable" (16, 13). This was the kind of faith that the underdog people of God needed as they faced the growing might of the Roman Empire.

Quick Facts

Setting
a fictional book without a clear historical setting

Author
unknown, writing at the end of the second or the beginning of the first century B.C.

Themes
a woman of faith and courage, God's saving power

The Book of Judith

Judith

Chap. 10

I: Peril of the Jews

War against the Medes

1 ¹ It was the twelfth year of the reign of Nebuchadnezzar, king of the Assyrians in the great city of Nineveh. At that time Arphaxad ruled over the Medes in Ecbatana. ² Around this city he built a wall of blocks of stone, each three cubits in height and six in length. He made the wall seventy cubits high and fifty thick. ³ At the gates he raised towers of a hundred cubits, with a thickness of sixty cubits at the base. ⁴ The gateway he built to a height of seventy cubits, with an opening forty cubits wide for the passage of his chariot forces and the marshaling of his infantry. ⁵ Then King Nebuchadnezzar waged war against King Arphaxad in the vast plain, in the district of Ragae. ⁶† To him there rallied all the inhabitants of the mountain region, all who dwelt along the Euphrates, the Tigris, and the Hydaspes, and King Arioch of the Elamites, in the plain. Thus many nations came together to resist the people of Cheleoud.

Ultimatum to the West

⁷ Now Nebuchadnezzar, king of the Assyrians, sent messengers to all the inhabitants of Persia, and to all those who dwelt in the West: to the inhabitants of Cilicia and Damascus, Lebanon and Anti-Lebanon, to all who dwelt along the seacoast, ⁸ to the peoples of Carmel, Gilead, Upper Galilee, and the vast plain of Esdraelon, ⁹ to all those in Samaria and its cities, and west of the Jordan as far as Jerusalem, Bethany, Chelous, Kadesh, and the River of Egypt; to Tahpanhes, Raamses, all the land of Goshen, ¹⁰ Tanis, Memphis and beyond, and to all the inhabitants of Egypt as far as the borders of Ethiopia.

¹¹ But the inhabitants of all that land disregarded the summons of Nebuchadnezzar, king of the Assyrians, and would not go with him to the war. They were not afraid of him but regarded him as a lone individual opposed to them, and turned away his envoys empty-handed, in disgrace. ¹²† Then Nebuchadnezzar fell into a violent rage against all that land, and swore by his throne and his kingdom that he would avenge himself on all the territories of Cilicia and Damascus and Syria, and also destroy with his sword all the inhabitants of Moab, Ammon, the whole of Judea, and those living anywhere in Egypt as far as the borders of the two seas.

Defeat of Arphaxad

¹³ In the seventeenth year he proceeded with his army against King Arphaxad, and was victorious in his campaign. He routed the whole force of Arphax-

---

1, 6: *Cheleoud:* probably the Chaldeans are meant.
1, 12: *The two seas:* the ancient rulers in Mesopotamia often des-
ignated the limits of their realm as extending from the Upper Sea (the Mediterranean) to the Lower Sea (the Persian Gulf).

ad, his entire cavalry and all his chariots, ¹⁴ and took possession of his cities. He pressed on to Ecbatana and took its towers, sacked its marketplaces, and turned its glory into shame. ¹⁵ Arphaxad himself he overtook in the mountains of Ragae, ran him through with spears, and utterly destroyed him. ¹⁶* Then he returned home with all his numerous, motley horde of warriors; and there he and his army relaxed and feasted for a hundred and twenty days.

Council of War against the West

2 ¹ In the eighteenth year, on the twenty-second day of the first month, there was a discussion in the palace of Nebuchadnezzar, king of the Assyrians, about taking revenge on the whole world, as he had threatened. ² He summoned all his ministers and nobles, laid before them his secret plan, and urged the total destruction of those countries. ³ They decided to do away with all those who had refused to comply with the order he had issued.

⁴ When he had completed his plan, Nebuchadnezzar, king of the Assyrians, summoned Holofernes, general in chief of his forces, second to himself in command, and said to him: ⁵* "Thus says the great king, the lord of all the earth: Go forth from my presence, take with you men of proven valor, a hundred and twenty thousand infantry and twelve thousand cavalry, ⁶ and proceed against all the land of the West, because they did not comply with the order I issued. ⁷† Tell them to have earth and water ready, for I will come against them in my wrath; I will cover all the land with the feet of my soldiers, to whom I will deliver them as spoils. ⁸ Their slain shall fill their ravines and wadies, the swelling torrent shall be choked with their dead; ⁹ and I will deport them as exiles to the very ends of the earth.

¹⁰ "You go before me and take possession of all their territories for me. If they surrender to you, guard them for me till the day of their punishment. ¹¹ As for those who resist, show them no quarter, but deliver them up to slaughter and plunder in each country you occupy. ¹²† For as I live, and by the strength of my kingdom, what I have spoken I will accomplish by my power. ¹³ Do not disobey a single one of the orders of your lord; fulfill them exactly as I have commanded you, and do it without delay."

Campaign of Holofernes

¹⁴ So Holofernes left the presence of his lord, and summoned all the princes, and the generals and officers of the Assyrian army. ¹⁵ He mustered a hundred and twenty thousand picked troops, as his lord had commanded, and twelve thousand mounted archers, ¹⁶ and grouped them into a complete combat force. ¹⁷ He took along a very large number of camels, asses, and mules for their baggage; innumerable sheep, cattle, and goats for their food supply; ¹⁸ abundant provisions for each man, and much gold and silver from the royal palace.

¹⁹ Then he and his whole army proceeded on their expedition in advance of King Nebuchadnezzar, to cover all the western region with their chariots and cavalry and regular infantry. ²⁰* A huge, irregular force, too many to count, like locusts or the dust of the earth, went along with them.

²¹ After a three-day march from Nineveh, they reached the plain of Bectileth, and from Bectileth they next encamped near the mountains to the north of Upper Cilicia. ²² From there Holofernes took his whole force, the infantry, calvary, and chariots, and marched into the mountain region. ²³† He devastated Put and Lud, and plundered all the Rassisites and the Ishmaelites on the border of the desert toward the south of Chaldea.

²⁴ Then, following the Euphrates, he went through Mesopotamia, and battered down every fortified city along the Wadi Abron, until he reached the sea. ²⁵ He seized the territory of Cilicia, and cut down everyone who resisted him. Then he proceeded to the southern borders of Japheth, toward Arabia. ²⁶ He surrounded all the Midianites, burned their tents, and plundered their sheepfolds. ²⁷ Descending to the plain of Damascus at the time of the wheat harvest, he set fire to all their fields, destroyed their flocks and herds, despoiled their cities, devastated their plains, and put all their youths to the sword.

²⁸ The fear and dread of him fell upon all the inhabitants of the coastland, upon those in Sidon and Tyre, and those who dwelt in Sur and Ocina, and the inhabitants of Jamnia. Those in Azotus and Ascalon also feared him greatly.

Submission of the West

3 ¹ They therefore sent messengers to him to sue for peace in these words: ² "We, the servants of

---

2, 7: *Earth and water:* in the Persian period, the offering of these to a conqueror was a symbolic gesture of unconditional surrender.
2, 12: *As I live:* in the Old Testament, an oath proper to divinity; cf Dt 32, 40. Nebuchadnezzar is making himself equal to God; see Jdt 6, 2. *By my power:* literally "by my hand." The hand of Nebuchadnezzar raised in opposition to God and to his people is the occasion for Judith's intervention by a woman's hand; cf Jdt 9, 9f; Is 10, 5–14.

2, 23: *Put and Lud:* the same as the "Put and Lud" mentioned in Ez 30, 5 as allies of Egypt, and in Ez 27, 10 as supplying mercenary soldiers to Tyre. Here they seem inserted to embellish the narrative with assonance and prophetic associations rather than to indicate definite localities.

1, 16: Est 1, 3f.   **2, 20:** Jgs 7, 12.
2, 5f: Est 3, 8f.

J
D
T

Nebuchadnezzar the great king, lie prostrate before you; do with us as you will. ³ Our dwellings and all our wheat fields, our flocks and herds, and all our encampments are at your disposal; make use of them as you please. ⁴ Our cities and their inhabitants are also at your service; come and deal with them as you see fit."

⁵ After the spokesmen had reached Holofernes and given him this message, ⁶ he went down with his army to the seacoast, and stationed garrisons in the fortified cities; from them he impressed picked troops as auxiliaries. ⁷ The people of these cities and all the inhabitants of the countryside received him with garlands and dancing to the sound of timbrels. ⁸* Nevertheless, he devastated their whole territory and cut down their sacred groves, for he had been commissioned to destroy all the gods of the earth, so that every nation might worship Nebuchadnezzar alone, and every people and tribe invoke him as a god. ⁹ At length Holofernes reached Esdraelon in the neighborhood of Dothan, the approach to the main ridge of the Judean mountains; ¹⁰† he set up his camp between Geba and Scythopolis, and stayed there a whole month to refurbish all the equipment of his army.

Israelite Defense

¹ When the Israelites who dwelt in Judea heard of all that Holofernes, commander in chief of Nebuchadnezzar, king of the Assyrians, had done to the nations, and how he had despoiled all their temples and destroyed them, ² they were in extreme dread of him, and greatly alarmed for Jerusalem and the temple of the LORD, their God. ³† Now, they had lately returned from exile, and only recently had all the people of Judea been gathered together, and the vessels, the altar, and the temple been purified from profanation. ⁴ So they sent word to the whole region of Samaria, to Kona, Beth-horon, Belmain, and Jericho, to Choba and Aesora, and to the valley of Salem. ⁵ The people there posted guards on all the summits of the high mountains, fortified their villages, and since their fields had recently been harvested, stored up provisions in preparation for war.

⁶† Joakim, who was high priest in Jerusalem in those days, wrote to the inhabitants of Bethulia

[and Betomesthaim], which is on the way to Esdraelon, facing the plain near Dothan, ⁷ and instructed them to keep firm hold of the mountain passes, since these offered access to Judea. It would be easy to ward off the attacking forces, as the defile was only wide enough for two abreast. ⁸† The Israelites carried out the orders given them by Joakim, the high priest, and the senate of the whole people of Israel, which met in Jerusalem.

Prayer and Penance

⁹ All the men of Israel cried to God with great fervor and did penance— ¹⁰*† they, along with their wives, and children, and domestic animals. All their resident aliens, hired laborers, and slaves also girded themselves with sackcloth. ¹¹† And all the Israelite men, women, and children who lived in Jerusalem prostrated themselves in front of the temple building, with ashes strewn on their heads, displaying their sackcloth covering before the LORD. ¹²* The altar, too, they draped in sackcloth; and with one accord they cried out fervently to the God of Israel not to allow their children to be seized, their wives to be taken captive, the cities of their inheritance to be ruined, or the sanctuary to be profaned and mocked for the nations to gloat over.

¹³* The LORD heard their cry and had regard for their distress. For the people observed a fast of many days' duration throughout Judea, and before the sanctuary of the LORD Almighty in Jerusalem. ¹⁴ The high priest Joakim, and all the priests in attendance on the LORD who served his altar, were also girded with sackcloth as they offered the daily holocaust, the votive offerings, and the free-will offerings of the people. ¹⁵ With ashes upon their turbans, they cried to the LORD with all their strength to look with favor on the whole house of Israel.

Council against the Israelites

¹ It was reported to Holofernes, commander in chief of the Assyrian army, that the Israelites were ready for battle, and had blocked the mountain passes, fortified the summits of all the higher peaks, and placed roadblocks in the plains. ² In great anger he summoned all the rulers of the Moabites, the generals of the Ammonites, and all the satraps of the seacoast ³ and said to them: "Now

3, 10: *Geba:* perhaps originally "Gelboe," the mountain range near the eastern end of which lay Scythopolis, the Greek name for ancient Beth-shean (Jos 17, 11).

4, 3: *Returned from exile . . . profanation:* these allusions are variously attributed—to the Persian period (538–323 B.C.), or even to a condition in the days of Antiochus Epiphanes (175–164 B.C.).

4, 6: *Joakim, who was high priest:* see Bar 1, 7 and the footnote on Bar 1, 8f; this name for a high priest cannot be used in dating the events in Judith.

4, 8: The organization of the Jewish nation as subject to a high priest and a senate, or council of elders, was proper to the Greek

period (after 323 B.C.), and is reflected in the coinage of John Hyrcanus (135–104 B.C.).

4, 10: *Domestic animals:* see note on Jon 3, 8.

4, 11: *Prostrated themselves in front of the temple building:* for a parallel to this ceremony of entreaty, see Jl 1, 13f; 2, 15ff, and the note on Jl 2, 17.

3, 8: Ex 34, 13.   4, 12: Est 4, 1f.
3, 10f: Jon 3, 7f.   4, 13: Est 4, 16.

JDT

tell me, you Canaanites, what sort of people is this that dwells in the mountains? Which cities do they inhabit? How large is their army? In what does their power and strength consist? Who has set himself up as their king and the leader of their army? 4 Why have they refused to come out to meet me along with all the other inhabitants of the West?"

Achior's Speech

5* Then Achior, the leader of all the Ammonites, said to him: "My lord, hear this account from your servant; I will tell you the truth about this people that lives near you [that inhabits this mountain region]; no lie shall escape your servant's lips.

6† "These people are descendants of the Chaldeans. 7* They formerly dwelt in Mesopotamia, for they did not wish to follow the gods of their forefathers who were born in the land of the Chaldeans. 8 Since they abandoned the way of their ancestors, and acknowledged with divine worship the God of heaven, their forefathers expelled them from the presence of their gods. So they fled to Mesopotamia and dwelt there a long time. 9* Their God bade them leave their abode and proceed to the land of Canaan. Here they settled, and grew very rich in gold, silver, and a great abundance of livestock. 10* Later, when famine had gripped the whole land of Canaan, they went down into Egypt. They stayed there as long as they found sustenance, and grew into such a great multitude that the number of their race could not be counted. 11* The king of Egypt, however, rose up against them, shrewdly forced them to labor at brickmaking, oppressed and enslaved them. 12 But they cried to their God, and he struck the land of Egypt with plagues for which there was no remedy. When the Egyptians expelled them, 13* God dried up the Red Sea before them, 14 and led them along the route to Sinai and Kadesh-barnea. First they drove out all the inhabitants of the desert; 15* then they settled in the land of the Amorites, destroyed all the Heshbonites by main force, crossed the Jordan, and took possession of the whole mountain region. 16* They expelled the Canaanites, the Perizzites, the Jebusites, the Shechemites, and all the Gergesites; and they lived in these mountains a long time.

17* "As long as the Israelites did not sin in the sight of their God, they prospered, for their God, who hates wickedness, was with them. 18* But

when they deviated from the way he prescribed for them, they were ground down steadily, more and more, by frequent wars, and finally taken as captives into foreign lands. The temple of their God was razed to the ground, and their cities were occupied by their enemies. 19 But now that they have returned to their God, they have come back from the Dispersion wherein they were scattered, and have repossessed Jerusalem, where their sanctuary is, and have settled again in the mountain region which was unoccupied.

20* "So now, my lord and master, if these people are at fault, and are sinning against their God, and if we verify this offense of theirs, then we shall be able to go up and conquer them. 21 But if they are not a guilty nation, then your lordship should keep his distance; otherwise their LORD and God will shield them, and we shall become the laughing-stock of the whole world."

22 Now when Achior had concluded his recommendation, all the people standing round about the tent murmured; and the officers of Holofernes and all the inhabitants of the seacoast and of Moab alike said he should be cut to pieces. 23 "We are not afraid of the Israelites," they said, "for they are a powerless people, incapable of a strong defense. 24* Let us therefore attack them; your great army, Lord Holofernes, will swallow them up."

Holofernes' Answer

6 1 When the noise of the crowd surrounding the council had subsided, Holofernes, commander in chief of the Assyrian army, said to Achior, in the presence of the whole throng of coastland peoples, of the Moabites, and of the Ammonite mercenaries: 2* "Who are you, Achior, to prophesy among us as you have done today, and to tell us not to fight against the Israelites because their God protects them? What god is there beside Nebuchadnezzar? He will send his force and destroy them from the face of the earth. Their God will not save them; 3* but we, the servants of Nebuchadnezzar, will strike them down as one man, for they will be unable to withstand the force of our cavalry. 4* We will overwhelm them with it, and the mountains shall be drunk with their blood, and their plains filled with their corpses. Not a trace of them shall survive our attack: they shall utterly perish, says King Nebuchadnezzar, lord of all the earth;

5, 6–9: Achior outlines the early history of the Hebrews, whose forefather, Abraham, first lived in Ur of the Chaldeans (Gn 11, 28) and then migrated to Haran (Gn 11, 31) in Aram Naharaim (Gn 24, 10), which was called Mesopotamia by the Greeks. The gods of their forefathers were the pagan deities worshiped by Abraham's relatives (Jos 24, 2).

5, 5: Jdt 11, 9–19.
5, 7: Gn 11, 31.
5, 9: Gn 11, 31—12, 5.
5, 10: Gn 42, 1–5; 46, 1–7;
    Ex 1, 7.
5, 11f: Ex 5, 4–21; 7, 1–9.
5, 13f: Ex 14, 21f.29.
5, 15: Nm 21, 21–32; Jos 2,
    10.
5, 16: Dt 7, 1.
5, 17f: Dt 28—30; Ps 106,
    40–46; Is 59, 7.
5, 18: 2 Kgs 25.
5, 20f: Jdt 8, 18ff; 11, 10.
5, 24: Jdt 6, 2; 9, 7; 16, 2.
6, 2: Jdt 3, 8; 9, 7.
6, 3: Is 36, 18ff.
6, 4: Jdt 6, 17.

for he has spoken, and his words shall not remain unfulfilled. 5 As for you, Achior, you Ammonite mercenary, for saying these things in a moment of perversity you shall not see my face after today, until I have taken revenge on this race of people from Egypt. 6* Then at my return, the sword of my army or the spear of my servants will pierce your sides, and you shall fall among their slain. 7 My servants will now conduct you to the mountain region, and leave you at one of the towns along the ascent. 8 You shall not die till you are destroyed together with them. 9 If you still cherish the hope that they will not be taken, then there is no need for you to be downcast. I have spoken, and my words shall not prove false in any respect."

Achior in Bethulia

10 Then Holofernes ordered the servants who were standing by in his tent to seize Achior, conduct him to Bethulia, and hand him over to the Israelites. 11 So the servants took him in custody and brought him out of the camp into the plain. From there they led him into the mountain region till they reached the springs below Bethulia. 12 When the men of the city saw them, they seized their weapons and ran out of the city to the crest of the ridge; and all the slingers blocked the ascent of Holofernes' servants by hurling stones upon them. 13 So they took cover below the mountain, where they bound Achior and left him lying at the foot of the mountain; then they returned to their lord.

14 The Israelites came down to him from their city, loosed him, and brought him into Bethulia. They haled him before the rulers of the city, 15 who in those days were Uzziah, son of Micah of the tribe of Simeon, Chabris, son of Gothoniel, and Charmis, son of Melchiel. 16 They then convened all the elders of the city; and all their young men, as well as the women, gathered in haste at the place of assembly. They placed Achior in the center of the throng, and Uzziah questioned him about what had happened. 17 He replied by giving them an account of what was said in the council of Holofernes, and of all his own words among the Assyrian officers, and of all the boasting threats of Holofernes against the house of Israel.

18 At this the people fell prostrate and worshiped God; and they cried out: 19† "Lord, God of heaven, behold their arrogance! Have pity on the lowliness of our people, and look with favor this day on those

who are consecrated to you." 20 Then they reassured Achior and praised him highly. 21 Uzziah brought him from the assembly to his home, where he gave a banquet for the elders. That whole night they called upon the God of Israel for help.

Siege of Bethulia

7 1 The following day Holofernes ordered his whole army, and all the allied troops that had come to his support, to move against Bethulia, seize the mountain passes, and engage the Israelites in battle. 2 That same day all their fighting men went into action. Their forces numbered a hundred and seventy thousand infantry and twelve thousand horsemen, not counting the baggage train or the men who accompanied it on foot—a very great army. 3 They encamped at the spring in the valley near Bethulia, and spread out in breadth toward Dothan as far as Balbaim, and in length from Bethulia to Cyamon, which faces Esdraelon.

4 When the Israelites saw how many there were, they said to one another in great dismay: "Soon they will devour the whole country. Neither the high mountains nor the valleys and hills can support the mass of them." 5† Yet they all seized their weapons, lighted fires on their bastions, and kept watch throughout the night.

6 On the second day Holofernes led out all his cavalry in the sight of the Israelites who were in Bethulia. 7 He reconnoitered the approaches to their city and located their sources of water; these he seized, stationing armed detachments around them, while he himself returned to his troops.

8 All the commanders of the Edomites and all the leaders of the Ammonites, together with the generals of the seacoast, came to Holofernes and said: 9 "Sir, listen to what we have to say, that there may be no losses among your troops. 10* These Israelites do not rely on their spears, but on the height of the mountains where they dwell; it is not easy to reach the summit of their mountains. 11 Therefore, sir, do not attack them in regular formation; thus not a single one of your troops will fall. 12 Stay in your camp, and spare all your soldiers. Have some of your servants keep control of the source of water that flows out at the base of the mountain, 13* for that is where the inhabitants of Bethulia get their water. Then thirst will begin to carry them off, and they will surrender their city. Meanwhile, we and our men will go up to the summits of the nearby

---

† **6, 19:** The Latin Vulgate (6, 15) has a longer form of this prayer: "Lord, God of heaven and earth, behold their arrogance; regard our lowliness and look with favor on your people; show that you do not abandon those who trust in you, but that you humble those who trust in themselves and glory in their own strength."

7, 5: *Lighted fires on their bastions:* to serve as signals for alerting the neighboring towns. Reference to fire signals in time of siege is

made in the Lachish ostraca at the beginning of the sixth century B.C. *Kept watch throughout the night:* to prevent a surprise attack.

6, 6: Jdt 5, 22.   **7, 13:** Ex 5, 21.
7, 10: 1 Kgs 20, 23.28.

mountains, and encamp there to guard against anyone's leaving the city. 14 They and their wives and children will languish with hunger, and even before the sword strikes them they will be laid low in the streets of their city. 15 Thus you will render them dire punishment for their rebellion and their refusal to meet you peacefully."

16 Their words pleased Holofernes and all his ministers, and he ordered their proposal to be carried out. 17 Thereupon the Moabites moved camp, together with five thousand Assyrians. They encamped in the valley, and held the water supply and the springs of the Israelites. 18 The Edomites and the Ammonites went up and encamped in the mountain region opposite Dothan; and they sent some of their men to the south and to the east opposite Egrebel, near Chusi, which is on Wadi Mochmur. The rest of the Assyrian army was encamped in the plain, covering the whole countryside. Their enormous store of tents and equipment was spread out in profusion everywhere.

19* The Israelites cried to the LORD, their God, for they were disheartened, since all their enemies had them surrounded, and there was no way of slipping through their lines. 20 The whole Assyrian camp, infantry, chariots, and cavalry, kept them thus surrounded for thirty-four days. All the reservoirs of water failed the inhabitants of Bethulia, 21 and the cisterns ran dry, so that on no day did they have enough to drink, but their drinking water was rationed. 22 Their children fainted away, and the women and youths were consumed with thirst and were collapsing in the streets and gateways of the city, with no strength left in them.

23 All the people, therefore, including youths, women, and children, went in a crowd to Uzziah and the rulers of the city. They set up a great clamor and said before the elders: 24 "God judge between you and us! You have done us grave injustice in not making peace with the Assyrians. 25 There is no help for us now! Instead, God has sold us into their power by laying us prostrate before them in thirst and utter exhaustion. 26 Therefore, summon them and deliver the whole city as booty to the troops of Holofernes and to all his forces; 27 we would be better off to become their prey. We should indeed be made slaves, but at least we should live, and not have to behold our little ones dying before our eyes and our wives and children breathing out their souls. 28 We adjure you by heaven and earth, and by our God, the LORD of our forefathers, who is punishing us for our sins and

those of our forefathers, to do as we have proposed, this very day."

29 All in the assembly with one accord broke into shrill wailing and loud cries to the LORD their God. 30 But Uzziah said to them, "Courage, my brothers! Let us wait five days more for the LORD our God, to show his mercy toward us; he will not utterly forsake us. 31 But if those days pass without help coming to us, I will do as you say." 32 Then he dispersed the men to their posts, and they returned to the walls and towers of the city; the women and children he sent to their homes. Throughout the city they were in great misery.

II: Deliverance of the Jews

Judith

8 1 † Now in those days Judith, daughter of Merari, son of Joseph, son of Oziel, son of Elkiah, son of Ananias, son of Gideon, son of Raphain, son of Ahitob, son of Elijah, son of Hilkiah, son of Eliab, son of Nathanael, son of Salamiel, son of Sarasadai, son of Simeon, son of Israel, heard of this. 2 Her husband, Manasseh, of her own tribe and clan, had died at the time of the barley harvest. 3 While he was in the field supervising those who bound the sheaves, he suffered sunstroke; and he died of this illness in Bethulia, his native city. He was buried with his forefathers in the field between Dothan and Balamon. 4 The widowed Judith remained three years and four months at home, 5† where she set up a tent for herself on the roof of her house. She put sackcloth about her loins and wore widow's weeds. 6* She fasted all the days of her widowhood, except sabbath eves and sabbaths, new moon eves and new moons, feastdays and holidays of the house of Israel. 7 She was beautifully formed and lovely to behold. Her husband, Manasseh, had left her gold and silver, servants and maids, livestock and fields, which she was maintaining. 8 No one had a bad word to say about her, for she was a very God-fearing woman.

Her Words to the Elders

9 When Judith, therefore, heard of the harsh words which the people, discouraged by their lack of water, had spoken against their ruler, and of all that Uzziah had said to them in reply, swearing that he would hand over the city to the Assyrians at the end of five days, 10 she sent the maid who was in charge of all her things to ask Uzziah, Chabris, and Charmis, the elders of the city, to visit her. 11 When

J
D
T

---

†

8, 1: *Salamiel, son of Sarasadai:* head of the tribe of Simeon during the wanderings of the Israelites in the desert (Nm 1, 6).

8, 5: *A tent:* erected by Judith on the roof of her house (v 5); it was here that the elders came to confer with her (v 11).

7, 19: Ps 106, 6.   8, 6: Lk 2, 37.

AFRICAN AMERICAN

The Principle of *Kujichagulia*

"That man over there says that women need to be helped into carriages, and lifted over ditches, and to have the best place everywhere. Nobody ever helps me into carriages, or over mud puddles, or gives me any best place! And ain't I a woman?" (Sojourner Truth, 1851)

When people who are abused cower quietly in corners, injustice lives on. Bent heads, muffled voices, and terrified spirits invite wrongs to continue.

Judith was a biblical heroine who refused to let her role be determined by others. As a woman and a widow, she had little social standing in ancient Israel. Yet, she did not let this keep her from speaking out and challenging the community leaders to action.

Sojourner Truth was a modern hero who refused to keep quiet despite being mistreated and devalued. Her womanhood was slighted, and her personhood was trampled, yet she traveled America to tell all who would listen about the evils of slavery.

The Kwanzaa principle of *kujichagulia* (see "Kwanzaa as a Way of Life," Dt 10, 12–22), or self-determination, sometimes requires us to stand up and speak out. Silence can be compliance. Thank God for the gift of boldness of speech! It gives us the power to speak the truth even in the most oppressive situations.

Dear God, give me the boldness of Judith and Sojourner Truth to address the wrongs of this world. Amen.

▶ Jdt 8, 9–36

they came, she said to them: "Listen to me, you rulers of the people of Bethulia. What you said to the people today is not proper. When you promised to hand over the city to our enemies at the end of five days unless within that time the LORD comes to

our aid, you interposed between God and yourselves this oath which you took. 12* Who are you, then, that you should have put God to the test this day, setting yourselves in the place of God in human affairs? 13 It is the LORD Almighty for whom you are laying down conditions; will you never understand anything? 14* You cannot plumb the depths of the human heart or grasp the workings of the human mind; how then can you fathom God, who has made all these things, discern his mind, and understand his plan?

"No, my brothers, do not anger the LORD our God. 15 For if he does not wish to come to our aid within the five days, he has it equally within his power to protect us at such time as he pleases, or to destroy us in the face of our enemies. 16 It is not for you to make the LORD our God give surety for his plans.

"God is not man that he should be moved
        by threats,
    nor human, that he may be given an ultimatum.

17 "So while we wait for the salvation that comes from him, let us call upon him to help us, and he will hear our cry if it is his good pleasure. 18* For there has not risen among us in recent generations, nor does there exist today, any tribe, or clan, or town, or city of ours that worships gods made by hands, as happened in former days. 19* It was for such conduct that our forefathers were handed over to the sword and to pillage, and fell with great destruction before our enemies. 20 But since we acknowledge no other god but the LORD, we hope that he will not disdain us or any of our people. 21 If we are taken, all Judea will fall, our sanctuary will be plundered, and God will make us pay for its profanation with our life's blood. 22 For the slaughter of our kinsmen, for the taking of exiles from the land, and for the devastation of our inheritance, he will lay the guilt on our heads. Wherever we shall be enslaved among the nations, we shall be a mockery and a reproach in the eyes of our masters. 23 Our enslavement will not be turned to our benefit, but the LORD our God will maintain it to our disgrace.

24 "Therefore, my brothers, let us set an example for our kinsmen. Their lives depend on us, and the defense of the sanctuary, the temple, and the altar rests with us. 25* Besides all this, we should be grateful to the LORD our God, for putting us to the test, as he did our forefathers. 26 Recall how he dealt with Abraham, and how he tried Isaac, and all that happened to Jacob in Syrian Mesopotamia while he

8, 12: Jb 38, 2; 40, 2.7f;
42, 3.
8, 14: Jb 41, 3; Prv 14, 10;

Wis 9, 13; Is 40, 13;
Rom 11, 33f; 1 Cor 2,
11

8, 18: Jdt 5, 20f; 11, 10.
8, 19: Pss 78, 56f; 106, 13f;
Jer 7, 16–20; 14, 7.

8, 25f: Gn 22, 1–12; 29,
22–30.

was tending the flocks of Laban, his mother's brother. 27* Not for vengeance did the LORD put them in the crucible to try their hearts, nor has he done so with us. It is by way of admonition that he chastises those who are close to him."

Uzziah's Response

28 Then Uzziah said to her: "All that you have said was spoken with good sense, and no one can gainsay your words. 29 Not today only is your wisdom made evident, but from your earliest years all the people have recognized your prudence, which corresponds to the worthy dispositions of your heart. 30 The people, however, were so tortured with thirst that they forced us to speak to them as we did, and to bind ourselves by an oath that we cannot break. 31 But now, God-fearing woman that you are, pray for us that the LORD may send rain to fill up our cisterns, lest we be weakened still further."

32 Then Judith said to them: "Listen to me! I will do something that will go down from generation to generation among the descendants of our race. 33 Stand at the gate tonight to let me pass through with my maid; and within the days you have specified before you will surrender the city to our enemies, the LORD will rescue Israel by my hand. 34 You must not inquire into what I am doing, for I will not tell you until my plan has been accomplished." 35 Uzziah and the rulers said to her, "Go in peace, and may the LORD God go before you to take vengeance upon our enemies!" 36 Then they withdrew from the tent and returned to their posts.

The Prayer of Judith

9 1 * Judith threw herself down prostrate, with ashes strewn upon her head, and wearing nothing over her sackcloth. While the incense was being offered in the temple of God in Jerusalem that evening, Judith prayed to the LORD with a loud voice: 2*† "LORD, God of my forefather Simeon! You put a sword into his hand to take revenge upon the foreigners who had immodestly loosened the maiden's girdle, shamefully exposed her thighs, and disgracefully violated her body. This they did, though you forbade it. 3† Therefore you had their rulers slaughtered; and you covered with their blood the bed in which they lay deceived, the same bed that had felt the shame of their own deceiving. You smote the slaves together with their princes, and the princes together with their servants. 4 Their

Catholic Connections

THE BODY PRAYER

To pray, Judith prostrated herself, which means she lay face down on the ground. This position demonstrates humility and surrender. Judith also wore ashes and sackcloth, additional symbols of repentance and sorrow.

You will see this prayer posture on Good Friday, when the priests lie down on the floor at the beginning of the service. It is a sign of reverence and humility as we remember in a special way Jesus' sacrifice on the cross. You will see priest and deacon candidates prostrate themselves during the ordination ceremony as a sign of humility and their dependence on God's strength to carry out their ministry—a sign not just for themselves but for the whole Christian community.

▶ Jdt 9, 1

wives you handed over to plunder, and their daughters to captivity; and all the spoils you divided among your favored sons, who burned with zeal for you, and in their abhorrence of the defilement of their kinswoman, called on you for help.

5* "O God, my God, hear me also, a widow. It is you who were the author of those events and of what preceded and followed them. The present, also, and the future you have planned. Whatever you devise comes into being; 6* the things you decide on come forward and say, 'Here we are!' All your ways are in readiness, and your judgment is made with foreknowledge.

7* "Here are the Assyrians, a vast force, priding themselves on horse and rider, boasting of the power of their infantry, trusting in shield and spear, bow and sling. They do not know that

---

9, 2: *The maiden:* Dinah, Jacob's daughter, who was violated by Shechem, the Hivite (Gn 34, 2).

9, 3: Because Shechem had deceived and violated Dinah, her brothers, Simeon and Levi, tricked Shechem and the men of his city into being circumcised, and then slew them while they were confined to bed from the circumcision; cf Gn 34, 13–29.

8, 27: Dt 4, 7.
9, 1: Ex 30, 7f; Ps 141, 2.
9, 2: Gn 34.
9, 5: Is 44, 7.

9, 6: Jb 38, 35; Is 46, 9–13; Bar 3, 35.
9, 7f: Jdt 5, 23; 6, 2; 16, 2.

8   " 'You, the LORD, crush warfare;
      Lord is your name.'

"Shatter their strength in your might, and crush their force in your wrath; for they have resolved to profane your sanctuary, to defile the tent where your glorious name resides, and to overthrow with iron the horns of your altar. 9* See their pride, and send forth your wrath upon their heads. Give me, a widow, the strong hand to execute my plan. 10 With the guile of my lips, smite the slave together with the ruler, the ruler together with his servant; crush their pride by the hand of a woman.

11 "Your strength is not in numbers, nor does your power depend upon stalwart men; but you are the God of the lowly, the helper of the oppressed, the supporter of the weak, the protector of the forsaken, the savior of those without hope.

12 "Please, please, God of my forefather, God of the heritage of Israel, LORD of heaven and earth, Creator of the waters, King of all you have created, hear my prayer! 13* Let my guileful speech bring wound and wale on those who have planned dire things against your covenant, your holy temple, Mount Zion, and the homes your children have inherited. 14 Let your whole nation and all the tribes know clearly that you are the God of all power and might, and that there is no other who protects the people of Israel but you alone."

Judith's Departure

10 ¹ As soon as Judith had thus concluded, and ceased her invocation to the God of Israel, ² she rose from the ground. She called her maid and they went down into the house, which she used only on sabbaths and feast days. 3* She took off the sackcloth she had on, laid aside the garments of her widowhood, washed her body with water, and anointed it with rich ointment. She arranged her hair and bound it with a fillet, and put on the festive attire she had worn while her husband, Manasseh, was living. 4* She chose sandals for her feet, and put on her anklets, bracelets, rings, earrings, and all her other jewelry. Thus she made herself very beautiful, to captivate the eyes of all the men who should see her.

5* She gave her maid a leather flask of wine and a cruse of oil. She filled a bag with roasted grain, fig cakes, bread and cheese; all these provisions she wrapped up and gave to the maid to carry.

6 Then they went out to the gate of the city of Bethulia and found Uzziah and the elders of the city, Chabris and Charmis, standing there. 7 When these men saw Judith transformed in looks and differently dressed, they were very much astounded at her beauty and said to her, 8 "May the God of our fathers bring you to favor, and make your undertaking a success, for the glory of the Israelites and the exaltation of Jerusalem."

Judith bowed down to God. Then she said to them, 9 "Order the gate of the city opened for me, that I may go to carry out the business we discussed." So they ordered the youths to open the gate for her as she requested. 10 When they did so, Judith and her maid went out. The men of the city kept her in view as she went down the mountain and crossed the valley; then they lost sight of her.

Judith Captured

11 As Judith and her maid walked directly across the valley, they encountered the Assyrian outpost. 12† The men took her in custody and asked her, "To what people do you belong? Where do you come from, and where are you going?" She replied: "I am a daughter of the Hebrews, and I am fleeing from them, because they are about to be delivered up to you as prey. 13* I have come to see Holofernes, the general in chief of your forces, to give him a trustworthy report; I will show him the route by which he can ascend and take possession of the whole mountain district without a single one of his men suffering injury or loss of life."

14 When the men heard her words and gazed upon her face, which appeared wondrously beautiful to them, they said to her, 15 "By coming down thus promptly to see our master, you have saved your life. Now go to his tent; some of our men will accompany you to present you to him. 16 When you stand before him, have no fear in your heart; give him the report you speak of, and he will treat you well." 17 So they detailed a hundred of their men as an escort for her and her maid, and these conducted them to the tent of Holofernes.

18 When the news of her arrival spread among the tents, a crowd gathered in the camp. They came and stood around her as she waited outside the tent of Holofernes, while he was being informed about her. 19 They marveled at her beauty, regarding the Israelites with wonder because of her, and they said to one another, "Who can despise this people that has such women among them? It is not wise to leave one man of them alive, for if any were to be spared they could beguile the whole world."

10, 12f: The deceitful means used by Judith against Holofernes, here and in Jdt 11, 5–19, are to be judged in the light of the moral concepts of Old Testament times; cf Gn 27, 1–25; 34, 13–29; 37, 32ff; Jos 2, 1–7; Jgs 4, 17–22.

9, 9: Ps 33, 16.
9, 13: Jdt 10, 4; 11, 20.23; 16, 6.9.
10, 3: Jdt 8, 6ff.
10, 4: Jdt 9, 13.
10, 5: Jdt 12, 2.
10, 13: Jdt 11, 5f.

JDT

Judith Meets Holofernes

[20] The guard of Holofernes and all his servants came out and ushered her into the tent. [21] Now Holofernes was reclining on his bed under a canopy with a netting of crimson and gold, emeralds and other precious stones. [22] When they announced her to him, he came out to the antechamber, preceded by silver lamps; [23] and when Holofernes and his servants beheld Judith, they all marveled at the beauty of her face. She threw herself down prostrate before him, but his servants raised her up.

11 [1] Then Holofernes said to her: "Take courage, lady; have no fear in your heart! Never have I harmed anyone who chose to serve Nebuchadnezzar, king of all the earth. [2] Nor would I have raised my spear against your people who dwell in the mountain region, had they not despised me and brought this upon themselves. [3] But now tell me why you fled from them and came to us. In any case, you have come to safety. Take courage! Your life is spared tonight and for the future. [4] No one at all will harm you. Rather, you will be well treated, as are all the servants of my lord, King Nebuchadnezzar."

[5]* Judith answered him: "Listen to the words of your servant, and let your handmaid speak in your presence! I will tell no lie to my lord this night, [6] and if you follow out the words of your handmaid, God will give you complete success, and my lord will not fail in any of his undertakings. [7]* By the life of Nebuchadnezzar, king of all the earth, and by the power of him who has sent you to set all creatures aright! not only do men serve him through you; but even the wild beasts and the cattle and the birds of the air, because of your strength, will live for Nebuchadnezzar and his whole house. [8] Indeed, we have heard of your wisdom and sagacity, and all the world is aware that throughout the kingdom you alone are competent, rich in experience, and distinguished in military strategy.

[9]* "As for Achior's speech in your council, we have heard of it. When the men of Bethulia spared him, he told them all he had said to you. [10]* So then, my lord and master, do not disregard his word, but bear it in mind, for it is true. For our people are not punished, nor does the sword prevail against them, except when they sin against their God. [11] But now their guilt has caught up with them by which they bring the wrath of their God upon them whenever they do wrong; so that my lord will not be repulsed and fail, but death will overtake them. [12] Since their food gave out and all

their water ran low, they decided to kill their animals, and determined to consume all the things which God in his laws forbade them to eat. [13] They decreed that they would use up the first fruits of grain and the tithes of wine and oil which they had sanctified and reserved for the priests who minister in the presence of our God in Jerusalem: things which no layman should even touch with his hands. [14] They have sent messengers to Jerusalem to bring back to them authorization from the council of the elders; for the inhabitants there have also done these things. [15] On the very day when the response reaches them and they act upon it, they will be handed over to you for destruction.

[16] "As soon as I, your handmaid, learned all this, I fled from them. God has sent me to perform with you such deeds that people throughout the world will be astonished on hearing of them. [17] Your handmaid is, indeed, a God-fearing woman, serving the God of heaven night and day. Now I will remain with you, my lord; but each night your handmaid will go out to the ravine and pray to God. He will tell me when the Israelites have committed their crimes. [18] Then I will come and let you know, so that you may go out with your whole force, and not one of them will be able to withstand you. [19] I will lead you through Judea, till you come to Jerusalem, and there I will set up your judgment seat. You will drive them like sheep that have no shepherd, and not even a dog will growl at you. This was told me, and announced to me in advance, and I in turn have been sent to tell you."

[20]* Her words pleased Holofernes and all his servants; they marveled at her wisdom and exclaimed, [21] "No other woman from one end of the world to the other looks so beautiful and speaks so wisely!" [22] Then Holofernes said to her: "God has done well in sending you ahead of your people, to bring victory to our arms, and destruction to those who have despised my lord. [23]* You are fair to behold, and your words are well spoken. If you do as you have said, your God will be my God; you shall dwell in the palace of King Nebuchadnezzar, and shall be renowned throughout the earth."

Judith's Conduct

12 [1] Then he ordered them to lead her into the room where his silverware was kept, and bade them set a table for her with his own delicacies to eat and his own wine to drink. [2]* But Judith said, "I will not partake of them, lest it be an occasion of sin; but I shall be amply supplied from the things I brought with me." [3] Holofernes asked her: "But if your provisions give out, where shall we

11, 5f: Jdt 10, 13.　　　　　　　Dn 2, 38.
11, 7: Jer 27, 6; Bar 3, 16f;　　　11, 9f: Jdt 5, 5.

11, 10: Jdt 5, 21; 8, 18.　　　　11, 23: Jdt 9, 13.
11, 20: Jdt 9, 13.　　　　　　　12, 2: Jdt 10, 5; Dn 1, 8.

get more of the same to provide for you? None of your people are with us." ⁴ Judith answered him, "As surely as you, my lord, live, your handmaid will not use up her supplies till the LORD accomplishes by my hand what he has determined."

⁵ Then the servants of Holofernes led her into the tent, where she slept till midnight. In the night watch just before dawn, she rose ⁶ and sent this message to Holofernes, "Give orders, my lord, to let your handmaid go out for prayer." ⁷ So Holofernes ordered his bodyguard not to hinder her. Thus she stayed in the camp three days. Each night she went out to the ravine of Bethulia, where she washed herself at the spring of the camp. ⁸ After bathing, she besought the LORD, the God of Israel, to direct her way for the triumph of his people. ⁹ Then she returned purified to the tent, and remained there until her food was brought to her toward evening.

Holofernes' Banquet

¹⁰† On the fourth day Holofernes gave a banquet for his servants alone, to which he did not invite any of the officers. ¹¹ And he said to Bagoas, the eunuch in charge of his household: "Go and persuade this Hebrew woman in your care to come and to eat and drink with us. ¹² It would be a disgrace for us to have such a woman with us without enjoying her company. If we do not entice her, she will laugh us to scorn."

¹³ So Bagoas left the presence of Holofernes, and came to Judith and said, "So fair a maiden should not be reluctant to come to my lord to be honored by him, to enjoy drinking wine with us, and to be like one of the Assyrian women who live in the palace of Nebuchadnezzar." ¹⁴ She replied, "Who am I to refuse my lord? Whatever is pleasing to him I will promptly do. This will be a joy for me till the day of my death."

¹⁵ Thereupon she proceeded to put on her festive garments and all her feminine adornments. Meanwhile her maid went ahead and spread out on the ground for her in front of Holofernes the fleece Bagoas had furnished for her daily use in reclining at her dinner. ¹⁶ Then Judith came in and reclined on it. The heart of Holofernes was in rapture over her, and his spirit was shaken. He was burning with the desire to possess her, for he had been biding his time to seduce her from the day he saw her. ¹⁷ Holofernes said to her, "Drink and be merry with us!" ¹⁸ Judith replied, "I will gladly drink, my lord, for at no time since I was born have I ever enjoyed life as much as I do today." ¹⁹ She then took the things her maid had prepared, and ate and drank in his presence. ²⁰ Holofernes, charmed by her, drank a great quantity of wine, more than he had ever drunk on one single day in his life.

Dead Drunk!

Have you ever wondered why people get drunk? Why would anyone want to drink enough alcohol to pass out? Getting drunk has lots of negative consequences, and getting very drunk can even be fatal.

In the Book of Judith, chapter 13 Judith takes advantage of Holofernes' drunkenness to kill him. She gives the term *dead drunk* a whole new meaning. If you do not believe that getting drunk can destroy your life, then think again. It doesn't take a widow with a sword to help drunkenness destroy your life.

▶ Jdt 12, 15—13, 10

12, 10: *Banquet for his servants alone . . . officers:* Holofernes invited the officials of his household, but not the officers of his army who were needed for military duty.

13

¹ When it grew late, his servants quickly withdrew. Bagoas closed the tent from the outside and excluded the attendants from their master's presence. They went off to their beds, for they were all tired from the prolonged banquet. ² Judith was left alone in the tent with Holofernes, who lay prostrate on his bed, for he was sodden with wine. ³ She had ordered her maid to stand outside the bedroom and wait, as on the other days, for her to come out; she said she would be going out for her prayer. To Bagoas she had said this also.

Beheading of Holofernes

⁴ When all had departed, and no one, small or great, was left in the bedroom, Judith stood by Holofernes' bed and said within herself: "O LORD, God of all might, in this hour look graciously on my undertaking for the exaltation of Jerusalem; ⁵ now is the time for aiding your heritage and for carrying out my design to shatter the enemies who have risen against us." ⁶ She went to the bedpost near the head of Holofernes, and taking his sword from it, ⁷ drew close to the bed, grasped the hair of his head, and said, "Strengthen me this day, O God of Israel!" ⁸* Then with all her might she struck him twice in the neck and cut off his head. ⁹ She rolled his body off the bed and took the canopy from its supports. Soon afterward, she came out and handed over the head of Holofernes to her maid, ¹⁰ who put it into her food pouch; and the two went off together as they were accustomed to do for prayer.

The Return to Bethulia

They passed through the camp, and skirting the ravine, reached Bethulia on the mountain. As they approached its gates, ¹¹ Judith shouted to the guards from a distance: "Open! Open the gate! God, our God, is with us. Once more he has made manifest his strength in Israel and his power against our enemies; he has done it this very day." ¹² When the citizens heard her voice, they quickly descended to their city gate and summoned the city elders. ¹³ All the people, from the least to the greatest, hurriedly assembled, for her return seemed unbelievable. They opened the gate and welcomed the two women. They made a fire for light; and when they gathered around the two, ¹⁴ Judith urged them with a loud voice: "Praise God, praise him! Praise God, who has not withdrawn his mercy from the house of Israel, but has shattered our enemies by my hand this very night." ¹⁵* Then she took the head out of the pouch, showed it to them, and said: "Here is the head of Holofernes, general in charge of the Assyri-

did you KNOW?

Is God a Fan of Violence?

Is it hard to believe that God strengthened Judith to cut off Holofernes' head (Jdt 13, 7–8)? Or that God was angry at Saul for not destroying Agag and his possessions (1 Sm 15, 18–19)? Or that Jephthah had to sacrifice his daughter because of a vow he had made (Jdg 11, 29–40)? The violence portrayed in the Old Testament is often horrifying, especially when the Old Testament authors view it as part of God's will.

In the ancient world, tribes and nations viewed their gods as the leaders of their armies. The Hebrews were no exception. One of God's oldest titles is "LORD, God of hosts" (Ps 89, 9; Is 6, 3); the image is of an almighty warrior who fought on Israel's side (see Ex 15, 3; 1 Sm 14, 23). The enemies of Israel were seen as God's enemies, and their destruction as God's will. The military victories of Joshua, Saul, and David were understood as proof of heaven's blessing on the nation.

Later in history, as the Israelites experienced one agonizing defeat after another and the prophets challenged them to consider God's love for all nations, a new understanding of God's will began to develop in certain Jewish circles. Later prophets spoke of beating "swords into plowshares" (Is 2, 4), of making "a covenant of peace" (Ez 37, 26), of seeking "to do the right and to love goodness, / and to walk humbly with your God" (Mi 6, 8). From their own painful history, the Chosen People started to see that war and violence always meant unspeakable suffering for many, and they began to question whether holy war was part of God's will.

▸ Jdt 13, 1–10

an army, and here is the canopy under which he lay in his drunkenness. The LORD struck him down by the hand of a woman. ¹⁶ As the LORD lives, who has protected me in the path I have followed, I swear

J
D
T

---

that it was my face that seduced Holofernes to his ruin, and that he did not sin with me to my defilement or disgrace."

17 All the people were greatly astonished. They bowed down and worshiped God, saying with one accord, "Blessed are you, our God, who today have brought to nought the enemies of your people." 18* Then Uzziah said to her: "Blessed are you, daughter, by the Most High God, above all the women on earth; and blessed be the LORD God, the creator of heaven and earth, who guided your blow at the head of the chief of our enemies. 19 Your deed of hope will never be forgotten by those who tell of the might of God. 20 May God make this redound to your everlasting honor, rewarding you with blessings, because you risked your life when your people were being oppressed, and you averted our disaster, walking uprightly before our God." And all the people answered, "Amen! Amen!"

Judith's Counsel

14 1 Then Judith said to them: "Listen to me, my brothers. Take this head and hang it on the parapet of your wall. 2 At daybreak, when the sun rises on the earth, let each of you seize his weapons, and let all the able-bodied men rush out of the city under command of a captain, as if about to go down into the plain against the advance guard of the Assyrians, but without going down. 3 They will seize their armor and hurry to their camp to awaken the generals of the Assyrian army. When they run to the tent of Holofernes and do not find him, panic will seize them, and they will flee before you. 4 Then you and all the other inhabitants of the whole territory of Israel will pursue them and strike them down in their tracks. 5 But before doing this, summon for me Achior the Ammonite, that he may see and recognize the one who despised the house of Israel and sent him here to meet his death."

Achior Summoned

6† So they called Achior from the house of Uzziah. When he came and saw the head of Holofernes in the hand of one of the men in the assembly of the people, he fell forward in a faint. 7 Then, after they lifted him up, he threw himself at the feet of Judith in homage, saying: "Blessed are you in every tent of Judah; and in every foreign nation, all who hear of you will be struck with terror. 8 But now, tell me all that you did during these days." So Judith told him, in the presence of the people, all that she had been doing from the day she left till the time

she began speaking to them. 9 When she finished her account, the people cheered loudly, and their city resounded with shouts of joy. 10 Now Achior, seeing all that the God of Israel had done, believed firmly in him. He had the flesh of his foreskin circumcised, and he has been united with the house of Israel to the present day.

III: Victory

Consternation in the Camp

11 At daybreak they hung the head of Holofernes on the wall. Then all the Israelite men took up their arms and went to the slopes of the mountain. 12 When the Assyrians saw them, they notified their captains; these, in turn, went to the generals and division leaders and all their other commanders. 13 They came to the tent of Holofernes and said to the one in charge of all his things, "Waken our master, for the slaves have dared come down to give us battle, to their utter destruction." 14 Bagoas went in, and knocked at the entry of the tent, presuming that he was sleeping with Judith. 15 As no one answered, he parted the curtains, entered the bedroom, and found him lying on the floor, a headless corpse. 16 He broke into a loud clamor of weeping, groaning, and howling, and rent his garments. 17 Then he entered the tent where Judith had her quarters; and, not finding her, he rushed out to the troops and cried: 18* "The slaves have duped us! A single Hebrew woman has brought disgrace on the house of King Nebuchadnezzar. Here is Holofernes headless on the ground!"

19 When the commanders of the Assyrian army heard these words, they rent their tunics and were seized with consternation. Loud screaming and howling arose in the camp.

15 1 On hearing what had happened, those still in their tents were amazed, 2 and overcome with fear and trembling. No one kept ranks any longer; they scattered in all directions, and fled along every road, both through the valley and in the mountains. 3 Those also who were stationed in the mountain district around Bethulia took to flight. Then all the Israelite warriors overwhelmed them.

Pursuit

4 Uzziah sent messengers to Betomasthaim, to Choba and Kona, and to the whole country of Israel to report what had happened, that all might fall upon the enemy and destroy them. 5 On hearing

---

14, 6–10: In recognizing the head of Holofernes, whom he had known personally, Achior was so overcome with the evidence of the Lord's power exerted through a woman that he believed in the God of Israel.

13, 18: Jgs 5, 24; Lk 1, 28.42.
14, 18: Jdt 13, 15; 16, 5–9; Jgs 9, 54.

this, all the Israelites, with one accord, attacked them and cut them down as far as Choba. Even those from Jerusalem and the rest of the mountain region took part in this, for they too had been notified of the happenings in the camp of their enemies. The Gileadites and the Galileans struck the enemy's flanks with great slaughter, even beyond Damascus and its territory. 6 The remaining inhabitants of Bethulia swept down on the camp of the Assyrians, plundered it, and acquired great riches. 7* The Israelites who returned from the slaughter took possession of what was left, till the towns and villages in the mountains and on the plain were crammed with the enormous quantity of booty they had seized.

8* The high priest Joakim and the elders of the Israelites, who dwelt in Jerusalem, came to see for themselves the good things that the LORD had done for Israel, and to meet and congratulate Judith. 9† When they had visited her, all with one accord blessed her, saying:

"You are the glory of Jerusalem,
    the surpassing joy of Israel;
    you are the splendid boast of our people.
10   With your own hand you have done all this;
    you have done good to Israel,
        and God is pleased with what you
            have wrought.
    May you be blessed by the LORD Almighty
        forever and ever!"

And all the people answered, "Amen!"
11 For thirty days the whole populace plundered the camp, giving Judith the tent of Holofernes, with all his silver, his couches, his dishes, and all his furniture, which she accepted. She harnessed her mules, hitched her wagons to them, and loaded these things on them.
12* All the women of Israel gathered to see her; and they blessed her and performed a dance in her honor. She took branches in her hands and distributed them to the women around her, 13 and she and the other women crowned themselves with garlands of olive leaves. At the head of all the people, she led the women in the dance, while the men of Israel followed in their armor, wearing garlands and singing hymns.

Hymn of Praise

14 Judith led all Israel in this song of thanksgiving, and the people swelled this hymn of praise:

16 1* "Strike up the instruments,
        a song to my God with timbrels,
    chant to the LORD with cymbals;
    Sing to him a new song,
        exalt and acclaim his name.
2*   For the LORD is God; he crushes warfare,
        and sets his encampment among
            his people;
    he snatched me from the hands of my
        persecutors.

3   "The Assyrian came from the mountains of
        the north,
    with the myriads of his forces he came;
    Their numbers blocked the torrents, their
        horses covered the hills.
4   He threatened to burn my land,
        put my youths to the sword,
    Dash my babes to the ground,
        make my children a prey,
        and seize my virgins as spoil.

5*   "But the LORD Almighty thwarted them,
        by a woman's hand he confounded them.
6*   Not by youths was their mighty one
            struck down,
        nor did titans bring him low,
        nor huge giants attack him;
    But Judith, the daughter of Merari,

Judith Leads the Prayer-Song

In the Book of Judith, chapter 16, Judith sings praises to God and leads the people in a holy celebration after victory over the enemy.

Notice the similarity to Miriam's song (Exodus, chapter 15), Deborah's song (Judges, chapter 5), and even Tobit's song (Tobit, chapter 13).

Singing, dancing, and retelling special stories go hand in hand with praising God.

▶ Jdt 16, 1–20

JDT

† **15, 9:** *You are the glory of Jerusalem, the surpassing joy of Israel; you are the splendid boast of our people:* these words are used in the liturgy of the Church in regard to the Blessed Virgin Mary.

15, 7: Est 9, 5.16.
15, 8: Est 9, 10.
15, 12: Ex 15, 20f; Jgs 11, 34;
    1 Sm 18, 6; Jer 31, 4.13.
16, 1: Pss 81, 2f; 135, 1ff;
    149, 1ff.
16, 2: Jdt 5, 23; 6, 2; 9.7f;
    Ex 15; 3; Ps 46, 10.
16, 5: Jdt 14, 8.
16, 6: Jdt 9, 13.

by the beauty of her countenance
     disabled him.
7   She took off her widow's garb
     to raise up the afflicted in Israel.
   She anointed her face with fragrant oil;
8   with a fillet she fastened her tresses
     and put on a linen robe to beguile him.
9* Her sandals caught his eyes,
     and her beauty captivated his mind.
   The sword cut through his neck.

10 "The Persians were dismayed at her daring,
     the Medes appalled at her boldness.
11 When my lowly ones shouted, they
        were terrified;
     when my weaklings cried out,
        they trembled;
     at the sound of their war cry, they took
        to flight.
12 The sons of slave girls pierced them through;
     the supposed sons of rebel mothers cut
        them down;
     they perished before the ranks of
        my LORD.

13* "A new hymn I will sing to my God.
     O LORD, great are you and glorious,
     wonderful in power and unsurpassable.
14* Let your every creature serve you;
     for you spoke, and they were made,
   You sent forth your spirit, and they
        were created;
     no one can resist your word.
15* The mountains to their bases, and the seas,
        are shaken;
     the rocks, like wax, melt before your
        glance.

   "But to those who fear you,
     you are very merciful.
16* Though the sweet odor of every sacrifice is
     a trifle,

and the fat of all holocausts but little in
     your sight,
   one who fears the LORD is forever great.

17*† "Woe to the nations that rise against
        my people!
   The LORD Almighty will requite them;
     in the day of judgment he will
        punish them:
   He will send fire and worms into their flesh,
     and they shall burn and suffer forever."

Thanksgiving

18 The people then went to Jerusalem to worship God; when they were purified, they offered their holocausts, free-will offerings, and gifts. 19* Judith dedicated, as a votive offering to God, all the things of Holofernes that the people had given her, as well as the canopy that she herself had taken from his bedroom. 20 For three months the people continued their celebration in Jerusalem before the sanctuary, and Judith remained with them.

Judith's Renown

21 When those days were over, each one returned to his inheritance. Judith went back to Bethulia and remained on her estate. For the rest of her life she was renowned throughout the land. 22 Many wished to marry her, but she gave herself to no man all the days of her life from the time of the death and burial of her husband, Manasseh. 23* She lived to be very old in the house of her husband, reaching the advanced age of a hundred and five. She died in Bethulia, where they buried her in the tomb of her husband, Manasseh; 24 and the house of Israel mourned her for seven days. Before she died, she distributed her goods to the relatives of her husband, Manasseh, and to her own relatives; and to the maid she gave her freedom.
25*† During the life of Judith and for a long time after her death, no one again disturbed the Israelites.

16, 17: *Fire and worms into their flesh:* see footnote on Is 66, 24.
16, 25: The Vulgate adds: "The feast day of this victory was adopted by the Hebrews into the calendar of their holy days, and has been celebrated by the Jews from that time to the present." However, there is no other evidence of such a festivity; and it is the ancient feast of Passover to which the narrative is especially suited.

16, 9: Jdt 9, 13.
16, 13: Ps 144, 9.
16, 14: Pss 33, 9; 104, 30;
   148, 5.
16, 15: Jgs 5, 5; Ps 97, 5.
16, 16: Ps 86, 11; Sir 34,
   13–17.
16, 17: Is 66, 24.
16, 19: Nm 31, 48–54; Dt 13,
   13–18; Jos 6, 18f.
16, 23: Gn 23, 19; 49, 29–32.
16, 25: Jgs 3, 11.30; 5, 31; 8,
   28.

Most of us cannot understand what would possess a group of people to plot the complete destruction of another group of people. Yet, in our own time, ethnic groups have been targeted for extinction through wars, concentration camps, and death squads. The Book of Esther is the story of a genocidal plot against a Jewish population and how that plot was prevented by Mordecai and his courageous cousin Esther.

In-depth

In the five centuries before Jesus, many of the Jewish people who were uprooted from their homeland had to be on the lookout for their safety. Several of the late Old Testament books—Sirach, Tobit, and Daniel—reflect the challenges that these emigrant Jews had to face. The fictional story of Queen Esther belongs to this group. Like Joseph in Egypt, Esther rose to a position of power in a foreign government. When a plot was hatched to destroy the Jews, she used her influence with the king of Persia to save her people. Each year, Esther's victory is celebrated in the Jewish feast of Purim (Est 9, 18–32)—the feast of little people who have triumphed over larger forces.

Like Daniel, the Book of Esther has come down to us in two versions: the Hebrew and the Greek. The difference in style between these two versions is obvious:

- The shorter Hebrew text is clearly fictional and does not even mention God's name. The Greek text, a later reworking of the Hebrew, adds sections to bring out the religious dimension of the story and to make the book appear more historical.

- The Hebrew version emphasizes the human actors; the Greek version, the divine Actor. The two versions stress different aspects of the same truth: God is the savior of the Chosen People (Greek), but works through human beings to achieve that goal (Hebrew).

In the present translation, the portions preceded by the letters A through F indicate the underlying Greek additions referred to above. The regular chapter numbers apply to the Hebrew text. Despite the confusing numbering, the book reads as a unified story; it's full of action and has a happy ending. What is more, it challenges us to recognize in our hatred of others the seeds of unthinkable destruction.

Quick Facts

Setting
Persia after the Babylonian Exile

Authors
Hebrew version. unknown, probably writing in the late fourth century B.C.
Greek version. unknown, writing about two centuries later

Themes
God's love for the little ones, the origin of the feast of Purim

Of Note
Catholic Bibles include the Greek version of Esther, inserted as additions A to F.

The Book of Esther

531

Esther

Chap. D

I: Prologue

Dream of Mordecai

A [1*†] In the second year of the reign of the great King Ahasuerus, on the first day of Nisan, Mordecai, son of Jair, son of Shimei, son of Kish, of the tribe of Benjamin, had a dream. [2] He was a Jew residing in the city of Susa, a prominent man who served at the king's court, [3*] and one of the captives whom Nebuchadnezzar, king of Babylon, had taken from Jerusalem with Jeconiah, king of Judah.

[4*†] This was his dream. There was noise and tumult, thunder and earthquake—confusion upon the earth. [5] Two great dragons came on, both poised for combat. They uttered a mighty cry, [6] and at their cry every nation prepared for war, to fight against the race of the just. [7] It was a dark and gloomy day. Tribulation and distress, evil and great confusion, lay upon the earth. [8] The whole race of the just were dismayed with fear of the evils to come upon them, and were at the point of destruc-tion. [9*] Then they cried out to God, and as they cried, there appeared to come forth a great river, a flood of water from a little spring. [10] The light of the sun broke forth; the lowly were exalted and they de-voured the nobles.

[11] Having seen this dream and what God intend-ed to do, Mordecai awoke. He kept it in mind, and tried in every way, until night, to understand its meaning.

The Plot Discovered

[12*] Mordecai lodged at the court with Bagathan and Thares, two eunuchs of the king who were court guards. [13] He overheard them plotting, inves-tigated their plans, and discovered that they were preparing to lay hands on King Ahasuerus. So he informed the king about them, [14] and the king had the two eunuchs questioned and, upon their con-fession, put to death. [15] Then the king had these things recorded; Mordecai, too, put them into writ-ing. [16*†] The king also appointed Mordecai to serve at the court, and rewarded him for his actions.

A, 1: *King Ahasuerus:* Xerxes I (485–464 B.C.). *Mordecai:* a Bab-ylonian name, after the God Marduk. The genealogy of Mordecai is designed to reflect opposition to Israel's enemy, as narrated in 1 Sm 15, 7ff, where Saul (whose father's name was Kish, of the Tribe of Benjamin) conquered Agag the Amalekite; in A, 17 Haman is said to be the son of an Agagite. Further emphasis on the Benjaminite-Agagite opposition can be seen in Shimei, the Benjaminite who reviled David (2 Sm 16, 5ff). Jair appears to be the minor Judge, a Transjordan Manassehite (Jgs 10, 3). The chronology of the book would make Mordecai well over one hundred years old, since he was deported with Jehoiachin about 598 B.C.; cf Est 2, 5f.

A, 4: The interpretation of this dream is given in Est F, 1–6.
A, 16: *Rewarded him:* this reward comes only later; see the se-quence of events from the Hebrew text of Esther at 2, 22f, and 6, 3, below.

A, 1: Est 2, 5.	**A, 4ff:** Est F, 2.4ff.
A, 3: Est 2, 6; 2 Kgs 24, 15;	**A, 9f:** Est F, 3.
2 Chr 36, 9f; Jer 22,	**A, 12–15:** Est 2, 21ff; 6, 1ff.
24ff; 24, 1; 29, 1f.	**A, 16:** Est 6, 3.

[17]*† Haman, however, son of Hammedatha the Agagite, who was in high honor with the king, sought to harm Mordecai and his people because of the two eunuchs of the king.

II: Elevation of Esther

The Banquet of Ahasuerus

1 [1]† During the reign of Ahasuerus—this was the Ahasuerus who ruled over a hundred and twenty-seven provinces from India to Ethiopia—[2]† while he was occupying the royal throne in the stronghold of Susa, [3]* in the third year of his reign, he presided over a feast for all his officers and ministers: the Persian and Median aristocracy, the nobles, and the governors of the provinces. [4] For as many as a hundred and eighty days, he displayed the glorious riches of his kingdom and the resplendent wealth of his royal estate.

[5] At the end of this time the king gave a feast of seven days in the garden court of the royal palace for all the people, great and small, who were in the stronghold of Susa. [6] There were white cotton draperies and violet hangings, held by cords of crimson byssus from silver rings on marble pillars. Gold and silver couches were on the pavement, which was of porphyry, marble, mother-of-pearl, and colored stones. [7] Liquor was served in a variety of golden cups, and the royal wine flowed freely, as befitted the king's munificence. [8] By ordinance of the king the drinking was unstinted, for he had instructed all the stewards of his household to comply with the good pleasure of everyone.

[9]† Queen Vashti also gave a feast for the women inside the royal palace of King Ahasuerus.

Deposal of Vashti

[10]* On the seventh day, when the king was merry with wine, he instructed Mehuman, Biztha, Harbona, Bigtha, Abagtha, Zethar, and Carkas, the seven eunuchs who attended King Ahasuerus, [11] to bring Queen Vashti into his presence wearing the royal crown, that he might display her beauty to the populace and the officials, for she was lovely to behold. [12] But Queen Vashti refused to come at the royal order issued through the eunuchs. At this the king's wrath flared up, and he burned with fury.

[13] He conferred with the wise men versed in the law, because the king's business was conducted in general consultation with lawyers and jurists. [14]* He summoned Carshena, Shethar, Admatha, Tarshish, Meres, Marsena and Memucan, the seven Persian and Median officials who were in the king's personal service and held first rank in the realm, [15] and asked them, "What is to be done by law with Queen Vashti for disobeying the order of King Ahasuerus issued through the eunuchs?"

[16] In the presence of the king and of the officials, Memucan answered: "Queen Vashti has not wronged the king alone, but all the officials and the populace throughout the provinces of King Ahasuerus. [17] For the queen's conduct will become known to all the women, and they will look with disdain upon their husbands when it is reported, 'King Ahasuerus commanded that Queen Vashti be ushered into his presence, but she would not come.' [18] This very day the Persian and Median ladies who hear of the queen's conduct will rebel against all the royal officials, with corresponding disdain and rancor. [19]*† If it please the king, let an irrevocable royal decree be issued by him and inscribed among the laws of the Persians and Medes, forbidding Vashti to come into the presence of King Ahasuerus and authorizing the king to give her royal dignity to one more worthy than she. [20] Thus, when the decree which the king will issue is published throughout his realm, vast as it is, all wives will honor their husbands, from the greatest to the least."

[21] This proposal found acceptance with the king and the officials, and the king acted on the advice of Memucan. [22]† He sent letters to all the royal provinces, to each province in its own script and to each people in its own language, to the effect that every man should be lord in his own home.

Esther Made Queen

2 [1] After this, when King Ahasuerus' wrath had cooled, he thought over what Vashti had done and what had been decreed against her. [2] Then the king's personal attendants suggested: "Let beautiful young virgins be sought for the king. [3] Let the king appoint commissaries in all the provinces of his realm to bring together all beautiful young virgins to the harem in the stronghold of Susa. Under the

---

A, 17: *Haman . . . the Agagite:* opposed Mordecai the Benjaminite, by whom, however, he was overcome (Est 9, 9f), just as King Agag the Amalekite, was conquered by King Saul ancestor of Mordecai (1 Sm 15, 7ff).

1, 1: *From India to Ethiopia:* from western India to Upper Egypt, the greatest extent of the Persian Empire achieved under Darius the Great, father of Ahasuerus.

1, 2: *Susa:* ancient capital of Elam (Gn 14, 1); under the Achamenid kings, one of the two capitals of the Persian Empire. The other was Persepolis, the summer palace of the kings.

1, 9: *Queen Vashti:* Herodotus (Histories 7, 61) relates that the wife of Ahasuerus was Amestris.

1, 19: *Irrevocable royal decree:* the historian Siculus indicates that such a concept of irrevocable laws existed in the time of Darius III (335–331 B.C.), the last of the Persian kings, cf Est 8, 8.

1, 22: *To each province . . . script and to each people . . . language:* many languages were spoken in the Persian Empire, the principal ones being Persian, Elamite, Babylonian, Aramaic, Phoenician, Egyptian, and Greek. Each of them had its own script.

A, 17: Est 3, 1–15; B, 1–7; E, 13.   1, 3: Jdt 1, 16.   1, 10: Dn 5, 1.   1, 14: Ezr 7, 14.   1, 19: Est 8, 5.8; Dn 6, 8f.

did you KNOW?

Diaspora Jews

The fictional story of Esther implies that Mordecai and Esther were members of the Diaspora. The Greek word *diaspora* means "scattered abroad." It refers to the Jews who lived outside of Palestine. When the Babylonians destroyed Jerusalem (587 B.C.), many of the Jews who were forced to leave the land of Israel decided to settle in various Greco-Roman cities and not return home. They maintained their Jewish identity by adapting the language and customs of their new home into their Jewish traditions. The Diaspora Jews were responsible for the translation of the Hebrew Bible into Greek, a translation called the Septuagint.

care of the royal eunuch Hegai, custodian of the women, let cosmetics be given them. ⁴ Then the girl who pleases the king shall reign in place of Vashti." This suggestion pleased the king, and he acted accordingly.

⁵ There was in the stronghold of Susa a certain Jew named Mordecai, son of Jair, son of Shimei, son of Kish, a Benjaminite, ⁶* who had been exiled from Jerusalem with the captives taken with Jeconiah, king of Judah, whom Nebuchadnezzar, king of Babylon, had deported. ⁷*† He was foster father to Hadassah, that is, Esther, his cousin; for she had lost both father and mother. The girl was beautifully formed and lovely to behold. On the death of her father and mother, Mordecai had taken her as his own daughter.

⁸ When the king's order and decree had been obeyed and many maidens brought together to the stronghold of Susa under the care of Hegai, Esther also was brought in to the royal palace under the care of Hegai, custodian of the women. ⁹ The girl pleased him and won his favor. So he promptly furnished her with cosmetics and provisions. Then picking out seven maids for her from the royal

palace, he transferred both her and her maids to the best place in the harem. ¹⁰ Esther did not reveal her nationality or family, for Mordecai had commanded her not to do so.

¹¹ Day by day Mordecai would walk about in front of the court of the harem, to learn how Esther was faring and what was to become of her.

¹² Each girl went in turn to visit King Ahasuerus after the twelve months' preparation decreed for the women. Of this period of beautifying treatment, six months were spent with oil of myrrh, and the other six months with perfumes and cosmetics. ¹³ Then, when the girl was to visit the king, she was allowed to take with her from the harem to the royal palace whatever she chose. ¹⁴* She would go in the evening and return in the morning to a second harem under the care of the royal eunuch Shaashgaz, custodian of the concubines. She could not return to the king unless he was pleased with her and had her summoned by name.

¹⁵ As for Esther, daughter of Abihail and adopted daughter of his nephew Mordecai, when her turn came to visit the king, she did not ask for anything but what the royal eunuch Hegai, custodian of the women, suggested. Yet she won the admiration of all who saw her. ¹⁶ Esther was led to King Ahasuerus in his palace in the tenth month, Tebeth, in the seventh year of his reign. ¹⁷ The king loved Esther more than all other women, and of all the virgins she won his favor and benevolence. So he placed the royal diadem on her head and made her queen in place of Vashti. ¹⁸† Then the king gave a great feast in honor of Esther to all his officials and ministers, granting a holiday to the provinces and bestowing gifts with royal bounty.

The Plot Discovered

¹⁹*† [To resume: From the time the virgins had been brought together, and while Mordecai was passing his time at the king's gate, ²⁰ Esther had not revealed her family or nationality, because Mordecai had told her not to; and Esther continued to follow Mordecai's instructions, just as she had when she was being brought up by him. ²¹*† And during the time that Mordecai spent at the king's gate, Bagathan and Thares, two of the royal eunuchs who guarded the entrance, had plotted in anger to lay hands on King Ahasuerus. ²² When the plot became known to Mordecai, he told Queen Esther, who in

---

2, 7: *Hadassah* (the feminine form of hadas, myrtle), was the name by which this woman would be known among her Jewish compatriots. Esther is a variant of the name of the Babylonian goddess Ishtar.

2, 18: *A holiday:* or perhaps, "a remission of taxes."

2, 19–23: This is a resumption, in a slightly different form, of the story already told in Est A, 12–15.

2, 21: *Mordecai . . . at the king's gate:* to exercise watchful care for Esther. Some understand this to mean that Mordecai was stationed at the gate to render royal service; cf Est A, 2.

2, 6: Est A, 3; 2 Kgs 24, 15; 2 Chr 36, 9f; Jer 22, 24ff; 24, 1; 29, 1f.
2, 7: Est 2, 15.
2, 14: Est 2, 19f; 4, 11.16.
2, 19f: Est 2, 14.
2, 21ff: Est A, 12–15; 6, 1ff.

turn informed the king for Mordecai. [23]† The matter was investigated and verified, and both of them were hanged on a gibbet. This was written in the annals for the king's use.]

III: Haman's Plot Against the Jews

Mordecai Refuses To Honor Haman

3 [1]* After these events King Ahasuerus raised Haman, son of Hammedatha the Agagite, to high rank, seating him above all his fellow officials. [2]*† All the king's servants who were at the royal gate would kneel and bow down to Haman, for that is what the king had ordered in his regard. Mordecai, however, would not kneel and bow down. [3]* The king's servants who were at the royal gate said to Mordecai, "Why do you disobey the king's order?" [4] When they had reminded him day after day and he would not listen to them, they informed Haman, to see whether Mordecai's explanation was acceptable, since he had told them that he was a Jew.

Haman's Reprisal

[5] When Haman observed that Mordecai would not kneel and bow down to him, he was filled with anger. [6] Moreover, he thought it was not enough to lay hands on Mordecai alone. Since they had told Haman of Mordecai's nationality, he sought to destroy all the Jews, Mordecai's people, throughout the realm of King Ahasuerus. [7]*† In the first month, Nisan, in the twelfth year of King Ahasuerus, the *pur*, or lot, was cast in Haman's presence, to determine the day and the month for the destruction of Mordecai's people on a single day, and the lot fell on the thirteenth day of the twelfth month, Adar.

Decree against the Jews

[8]* Then Haman said to King Ahasuerus: "Dispersed among the nations throughout the provinces of your kingdom, there is a certain people living apart, with laws differing from those of every other people. They do not obey the laws of the king, and so it is not proper for the king to tolerate them. [9]* If it please the king, let a decree be issued to destroy them; and I will deliver to the procurators ten thousand silver talents for deposit in the royal treasury." [10]*† The king took the signet ring from his hand and gave it to Haman, son of Hammedatha the Agagite, the enemy of the Jews. [11] "The silver you may keep," the king said to Haman, "but

Body Count

> **Genocide.** Such a frightening word. The complete destruction of a people. This is what King Ahasuerus plots in the Book of Esther: to destroy all the Jews in his kingdom. Fortunately, he does not succeed.
>
> In our time, we know only too well that the past two centuries have been marked by many attempts to exterminate whole groups of people. The most systematic and ambitious of these attempts was that of Adolf Hitler and the Third Reich. Six million Jews were put to death in Nazi concentration camps, along with four million other "undesirables." Yet, we in the Americas need to look no farther than our own shores. Many Native American peoples were slaughtered simply because they were defending their homes and way of life. Others were wiped out by diseases brought by European settlers in the name of progress, civilization, and Christianity.
>
> Such atrocities begin with a them-and-us attitude. The first step is to set apart a group of people and blame them for whatever is going wrong. The second is to give them a label, like "savages" or "communists," to make them seem less human and easier to destroy. The ghosts of too many victims of genocide remind us that the only accurate pronoun to describe our human family is *we*.
>
> ▶ Est 3, 1–7

2, 23: *Hanged on a gibbet:* impaled, perhaps, after the Babylonian manner.

3, 2: *Mordecai . . . would not kneel and bow down:* in order not to render to man, the homage which he regarded as belonging to God alone; cf Est C, 5ff.

3, 7: *Pur:* a Babylonian word which the Hebrew translates as goral, "lot." This word is preserved in the text because its plural, purim, became the name of the feast of Purim commemorating the deliverance of the Jews; cf Est 9, 24.26.

3, 10: *Signet ring:* a ring containing a seal which was impressed on documents to authenticate them. By giving this ring to Haman, the king bestowed on him the power to authenticate royal decrees.

3, 1: Est B, 3; 5, 11; E, 11.
3, 2: Est C, 5; 5, 9.13; 6, 10.12.
3, 3: Est 4, 16.
3, 7: Est 9, 24ff; F, 10.
3, 8: Est 3, 13; B, 4; E, 24; Dn 3, 8–12; Wis 2, 14f.
3, 9: Est 7, 4.
3, 10: Gn 41, 42.

EST

as for this people, do with them whatever you please."

¹² So the royal scribes were summoned; and on the thirteenth day of the first month they wrote, at the dictation of Haman, an order to the royal satraps, the governors of every province, and the officials of every people, to each province in its own script and to each people in its own language. It was written in the name of King Ahasuerus and sealed with the royal signet ring. ¹³* Letters were sent by couriers to all the royal provinces, that all the Jews, young and old, including women and children, should be killed, destroyed, wiped out in one day, the thirteenth day of the twelfth month, Adar, and that their goods should be seized as spoil.

B ¹ This is a copy of the letter:

"The great King Ahasuerus writes to the satraps of the hundred and twenty-seven provinces from India to Ethiopia, and the governors subordinate to them, as follows: ²* When I came to rule many peoples and to hold sway over the whole world, I determined not to be carried away with the sense of power, but always to deal fairly and with clemency; to provide for my subjects a life of complete tranquillity; and by making my government humane and effective as far as the borders, to restore the peace desired by all men. ³* When I consulted my counselors as to how this might be accomplished, Haman, who excels among us in wisdom, who is outstanding for constant devotion and steadfast loyalty, and who has gained the second rank in the kingdom, ⁴* brought it to our attention that, mixed in with all the races throughout the world, there is one people of bad will, which by its laws is opposed to every other people and continually disregards the decrees of kings, so that the unity of empire blamelessly designed by us cannot be established.

⁵ "Having noted, therefore, that this most singular people is continually at variance with all men, lives by divergent and alien laws, is inimical to our interests, and commits the worst crimes, so that stability of government cannot be obtained, ⁶*† we hereby decree that all those who are indicated to you in the letters of Haman, who is in charge of the administration and is a second father to us, shall, together with their wives and children, be utterly destroyed by the swords of their enemies, without any pity or mercy, on the fourteenth day of the twelfth month, Adar, of the current year; ⁷ so that when these peo-

ple, whose present ill will is of long standing, have gone down into the nether world by a violent death on one same day, they may at last leave our affairs stable and undisturbed for the future."

(3) ¹⁴ A copy of the decree to be promulgated as law in every province was published to all the peoples, that they might be prepared for that day. ¹⁵ The couriers set out in haste at the king's command; meanwhile, the decree was promulgated in the stronghold of Susa. The king and Haman then sat down to feast, but the city of Susa was thrown into confusion.

Esther's Aid Sought by Mordecai

4 ¹* When Mordecai learned all that was happening, he tore his garments, put on sackcloth and ashes, and walked through the city, crying out loudly and bitterly, ² till he came before the royal gate, which no one clothed in sackcloth might enter. ³ (Likewise in each of the provinces, wherever the king's legal enactment reached, the Jews went into deep mourning, with fasting, weeping, and lament; they all slept on sackcloth and ashes.)

⁴ Queen Esther's maids and eunuchs came and told her. Overwhelmed with anguish, she sent garments for Mordecai to put on, so that he might take off his sackcloth; but he refused. ⁵ Esther then summoned Hathach, one of the king's eunuchs whom he had placed at her service, and commanded him to find out what this action of Mordecai meant and the reason for it. ⁶ So Hathach went out to Mordecai in the public square in front of the royal gate, ⁷ and Mordecai told him all that had happened, as well as the exact amount of silver Haman had promised to pay to the royal treasury for the slaughter of the Jews. ⁸ He also gave him a copy of the written decree for their destruction which had been promulgated in Susa, to show and explain to Esther. He was to instruct her to go to the king; she was to plead and intercede with him in behalf of her people. ⁸† "Remember the days of your lowly estate," Mordecai had him say, "when you were brought up in my charge; for Haman, who is second to the king, has asked for our death. ⁹ Invoke the LORD and speak to the king for us: save us from death."

Hathach returned to Esther and told her what Mordecai had said. ¹⁰ Then Esther replied to Hathach and gave him this message for Mordecai: ¹¹* "All the servants of the king and the people of his provinces know that any man or woman who

---

B, 6: *Fourteenth day:* the Hebrew text, as in Est 2, 13 above, and the Greek text here translated do not agree on the day of the month specified by the king; in fact, a two-day celebration is decreed in chapter 9, and the 13th, 14th and 15th of Adar are all mentioned; see Est 9, 15.18.

4, 8: This verse belongs to chapter B.

3, 13: Est B, 6; 7, 4.
B, 2: Est E, 8f.
B, 3: Est 3, 1; 5, 11; E, 11.
B, 4: Est 3, 8; E, 24.
B, 6: Est 3, 13; 7, 4; E, 11ff.
4, 1: Jdt 4, 12.
4, 11: Est 2, 14; 4, 12; D, 12.

?did you KNOW?

The Silent Women of the Bible

"Mordecai went away and did exactly as Esther had commanded" (Est C, I). What a surprise: to hear of a man in the ancient world taking orders from a woman! Esther, like Judith, has an exceptional role in the Old Testament. Many other important women are not even named: Jephthah's daughter, Samson's mother, and Job's wife, for instance. Even the Hebrew women whose names have become famous—Sarah, Rebekah, Rachel, Miriam, Bathsheba—played second fiddle to their more famous husbands. They depended on indirect influence or trickery to get what they wanted.

In the biblical world, a woman was defined by her relationships with men. Before marriage, she belonged to her father's household and had no status outside of it. Once married, a woman left her father's family and joined the family of her husband. If her husband died, she remained in the new family, rearing children for her deceased spouse or, if childless, marrying a brother-in-law. Although many women undoubtedly lived happily under this system, many others just as surely suffered abuse or felt oppressed. The stories of Lot's daughters (Gn 19, 8) and the woman of Gibeah (Jgs 19, 22–30) testify to this horrifying truth.

A system of scriptural interpretation that was developed during recent decades attempts to give voice to the many silent, forgotten, abused women of the Bible. More and more biblical scholars reread the familiar stories, searching for quiet messages that have long been overlooked. All of us—males and females alike—can benefit from this effort to listen to the voices of these women who have been silenced for so many centuries.

▶ Est 4, 15—C, I

goes to the king in the inner court without being summoned, suffers the automatic penalty of death, unless the king extends to him the golden scepter, thus sparing his life. Now as for me, I have not been summoned to the king for thirty days."

[12] When Esther's words were reported to Mordecai, [13] he had this reply brought to her: "Do not imagine that because you are in the king's palace, you alone of all the Jews will escape. [14]† Even if you now remain silent, relief and deliverance will come to the Jews from another source; but you and your father's house will perish. Who knows but that it was for a time like this that you obtained the royal dignity?"

[15] Esther sent back to Mordecai the response: [16]* "Go and assemble all the Jews who are in Susa; fast on my behalf, all of you, not eating or drinking, night or day, for three days. I and my maids will also fast in the same way. Thus prepared, I will go to the king, contrary to the law. If I perish, I perish!"

Prayer of Mordecai

Mordecai went away and did exactly as Esther had commanded. [1] Recalling all that the LORD had done, he prayed to him [2] and said: "O Lord God, almighty King, all things are in your power, and there is no one to oppose you in your will to save Israel. [3] You made heaven and earth and every wonderful thing under the heavens. [4] You are LORD of all, and there is no one who can resist you, LORD. [5]* You know all things. You know, O LORD, that it was not out of insolence or pride or desire for fame that I acted thus in not bowing down to the proud Haman. [6] Gladly would I have kissed the soles of his feet for the salvation of Israel. [7] But I acted as I did so as not to place the honor of man above that of God. I will not bow down to anyone but you, my LORD. It is not out of pride that I am acting thus. [8] And now, LORD God, King, God of Abraham, spare your people, for our enemies plan our ruin and are bent upon destroying the inheritance that was yours from the beginning. [9] Do not spurn your portion, which you redeemed for yourself out of Egypt. [10] Hear my prayer; have pity on your inheritance and turn our sorrow into joy: thus we shall live to sing praise to your name, O LORD. Do not silence those who praise you."

[11] All Israel, too, cried out with all their strength, for death was staring them in the face.

Prayer of Esther

[12]* Queen Esther, seized with mortal anguish, likewise had recourse to the LORD. [13] Taking off her

E
S
T.

---

† **4, 14:** *From another source:* very probably Mordecai refers to divine aid; the Greek additions (C) are explicit about this.

* **4, 16:** Est C, 12f.   **C, 12f:** Est 4, 16.
C, 5ff: Est 3, 2; 5, 9.

splendid garments, she put on garments of distress and mourning. In place of her precious ointments she covered her head with dirt and ashes. She afflicted her body severely; all her festive adornments were put aside, and her hair was wholly disheveled.

14 Then she prayed to the LORD, the God of Israel, saying: "My LORD, our King, you alone are God. Help me, who am alone and have no help but you, 15* for I am taking my life in my hand. 16* As a child I was wont to hear from the people of the land of my forefathers that you, O LORD, chose Israel from among all peoples, and our fathers from among all their ancestors, as a lasting heritage, and that you fulfilled all your promises to them. 17 But now we have sinned in your sight, and you have delivered us into the hands of our enemies, 18 because we worshiped their gods. You are just, O LORD. 19 But now they are not satisfied with our bitter servitude, but have undertaken 20 to do away with the decree you have pronounced, and to destroy your heritage; to close the mouths of those who praise you, and to extinguish the glory of your temple and your altar; 21 to open the mouths of the heathen to acclaim their false gods, and to extol an earthly king forever.

22 "O LORD, do not relinquish your scepter to those that are nought. Let them not gloat over our ruin, but turn their own counsel against them and make an example of our chief enemy. 23 Be mindful of us, O LORD. Manifest yourself in the time of our distress and give me courage, King of gods and Ruler of every power. 24 Put in my mouth persuasive words in the presence of the lion and turn his heart to hatred for our enemy, so that he and those who are in league with him may perish. 25 Save us by your power, and help me, who am alone and have no one but you, O LORD.

"You know all things. 26 You know that I hate the glory of the pagans, and abhor the bed of the uncircumcised or of any foreigner. 27 You know that I am under constraint, that I abhor the sign of grandeur which rests on my head when I appear in public; abhor it like a polluted rag, and do not wear it in private. 28† I, your handmaid, have never eaten at the table of Haman, nor have I graced the banquet of the king or drunk the wine of libations. 29 From the day I was brought here till now, your handmaid has had no joy except in you, O LORD, God of Abraham. 30 O God, more powerful than all, hear the voice of those in despair. Save us from the power of the wicked, and deliver me from my fear."

Esther Is Received by the King

D 1 On the third day, putting an end to her prayers, she took off her penitential garments and arrayed herself in her royal attire. 2 In making her state appearance, after invoking the all-seeing God and savior, she took with her two maids; 3 on the one she leaned gently for support, 4 while the other followed her, bearing her train. 5 She glowed with the perfection of her beauty and her countenance was as joyous as it was lovely, though her heart was shrunk with fear. 6 She passed through all the portals till she stood face to face with the king, who was seated on his royal throne, clothed in full robes of state, and covered with gold and precious stones, so that he inspired great awe. 7 As he looked up, his features ablaze with the height of majestic anger, the queen staggered, changed color, and leaned weakly against the head of the maid in front of her. 8 But God changed the king's anger to gentleness. In great anxiety he sprang from his throne, held her in his arms until she recovered, and comforted her with reassuring words. 9 "What is it, Esther?" he said to her. "I am your brother. Take courage! 10 You shall not die because of this general decree of ours. 11 Come near!" 12* Raising the golden scepter, he touched her neck with it, embraced her, and said, "Speak to me."

13 She replied: "I saw you, my lord, as an angel of God, and my heart was troubled with fear of your majesty. 14 For you are awesome, my lord, though your glance is full of kindness." 15 As she said this, she fainted. 16 The king became troubled and all his attendants tried to revive her.

5 1† [Now on the third day, Esther put on her royal garments and stood in the inner courtyard, looking toward the royal palace, while the king was seated on his royal throne in the audience chamber, facing the palace doorway. 2 He saw Queen Esther standing in the courtyard, and made her welcome by extending toward her the golden staff which he held. She came up to him, and touched the top of the staff.]

3* Then the king said to her, "What is it, Queen Esther? What is your request? Even if it is half of my kingdom, it shall be granted you." 4 "If it please your majesty," Esther replied, "come today with Haman to a banquet I have prepared." 5 And the king ordered, "Have Haman make haste to fulfill the wish of Esther."

First Banquet of Esther

So the king went with Haman to the banquet Esther had prepared. 6* During the drinking of the

---

C, 28: *Wine of libations:* offered in sacrifice to the gods.
5, 1f: The Hebrew text here translated is a short form of the account already given in Greek.

C, 15: Est 4, 16.
C, 16: Dt 4, 20; 7, 6; 9, 29; 14, 2; 26, 18; 32, 9.
D, 12: Est 4, 11.
5, 3: Est 5, 6; 7, 2; 9, 12.
5, 6: Est 5, 3.

wine, the king said to Esther, "Whatever you ask for shall be granted, and whatever request you make shall be honored, even if it is for half my kingdom." 7 Esther replied: "This is my petition and request: 8 if I have found favor with the king and if it pleases your majesty to grant my petition and honor my request, come with Haman tomorrow to a banquet which I shall prepare for you; and then I will do as you ask."

Haman's Plot against Mordecai

9* That day Haman left happy and in good spirits. But when he saw that Mordecai at the royal gate did not rise, and showed no fear of him, he was filled with anger toward him. 10 Haman restrained himself, however, and went home, where he summoned his friends and his wife Zeresh. 11* He recounted the greatness of his riches, the large number of his sons, and just how the king had promoted him and placed him above the officials and royal servants. 12 "Moreover," Haman added, "Queen Esther invited no one but me to the banquet with the king; again tomorrow I am to be her guest, with the king. 13* Yet none of this satisfies me as long as I continue to see the Jew Mordecai sitting at the royal gate." 14* His wife Zeresh and all his friends said to him, "Have a gibbet set up, fifty cubits in height, and in the morning ask the king to have Mordecai hanged on it. Then go to the banquet with the king in good cheer." This suggestion pleased Haman, and he had the gibbet erected.

IV: Vindication of the Jews

Mordecai's Reward from the King

6 1 That night the king, unable to sleep, asked that the chronicle of notable events be brought in. While this was being read to him, 2* the passage occurred in which Mordecai reported Bagathan and Teresh, two of the royal eunuchs who guarded the entrance, for seeking to lay hands on King Ahasuerus. 3* The king asked, "What was done to reward and honor Mordecai for this?" The king's attendants replied, "Nothing was done for him."

4* "Who is in the court?" the king asked. Now Haman had entered the outer court of the king's palace to suggest to the king that Mordecai should be hanged on the gibbet he had raised for him. 5 The king's servants answered him, "Haman is waiting in the court." "Let him come in," the king said. 6 When Haman entered, the king said to him, "What should be done for the man whom the king wishes to reward?" Now Haman thought to himself, "Whom would the king more probably wish to reward than me?" 7 So he replied to the king: "For the man whom the king wishes to reward 8 there should be brought the royal robe which the king wore and the horse on which the king rode when the royal crown was placed on his head. 9* The robe and the horse should be consigned to one of the noblest of the king's officials, who must clothe the man the king wishes to reward, have him ride on the horse in the public square of the city, and cry out before him, 'This is what is done for the man whom the king wishes to reward.' " 10* Then the king said to Haman: "Hurry! Take the robe and horse as you have proposed, and do this for the Jew Mordecai, who is sitting at the royal gate. Do not omit anything you proposed." 11 So Haman took the robe and horse, clothed Mordecai, had him ride in the public square of the city, and cried out before him, "This is what is done for the man whom the king wishes to reward."

12* Mordecai then returned to the royal gate, while Haman hurried home, his head covered in grief. 13 When he told his wife Zeresh and all his friends everything that had happened to him, his advisers and his wife Zeresh said to him, "If Mordecai, before whom you are beginning to decline, is of the Jewish race, you will not prevail against him, but will surely be defeated by him."

Esther's Second Banquet

14 While they were speaking with him, the king's eunuchs arrived and hurried Haman off to the banquet Esther had prepared.

7 1 So the king and Haman went to the banquet with Queen Esther. 2* Again, on this second day, during the drinking of the wine, the king said to Esther, "Whatever you ask, Queen Esther, shall be granted you. Whatever request you make shall be honored, even for half the kingdom." 3 Queen Esther replied: "If I have found favor with you, O king, and if it pleases your majesty, I ask that my life be spared, and I beg that you spare the lives of my people. 4* For my people and I have been delivered to destruction, slaughter, and extinction. If we were to be sold into slavery I would remain silent, but as it is, the enemy will be unable to compensate for the harm done to the king." 5* "Who and where," said King Ahasuerus to Queen Esther, "is the man who has dared to do this?" 6 Esther replied, "The enemy oppressing us is this wicked Haman." At this, Haman was seized with dread of the king and queen.

5, 9: Est 3, 2f; C, 5ff; 6, 10.12.
5, 11: Est 3, 1; B, 3; E, 11; 9, 6–10.
5, 13: Est 3, 2f; 6, 10, 12.
5, 14: Est 6, 4; 7, 9f.
6, 2: Est A, 12ff; 2, 21ff.
6, 3: Est A, 16.
6, 4: Est 5, 14; 7, 9f.
6, 9: Gn 41, 42f; 1 Kgs 1, 33; Dn 5, 29.
6, 10: Est 2, 21; 3, 2f; 5, 9.13.
6, 12: Est 2, 21; 3, 2f; 5, 9.13.
7, 2: Est 5, 3.
7, 4: Est 3, 13; B, 6.
7, 5: Est 3, 8f.

7 The king left the banquet in anger and went into the garden of the palace, but Haman stayed to beg Queen Esther for his life, since he saw that the king had decided on his doom. 8 When the king returned from the garden of the palace to the banquet hall, Haman had thrown himself on the couch on which Esther was reclining; and the king exclaimed, "Will he also violate the queen while she is with me in my own house!" Scarcely had the king spoken, when the face of Haman was covered over.

Punishment of Haman

9* Harbona, one of the eunuchs who attended the king, said, "At the house of Haman stands a gibbet fifty cubits high. Haman prepared it for Mordecai, who gave the report that benefited the king." The king answered, "Hang him on it." 10 So they hanged Haman on the gibbet which he had made ready for Mordecai, and the anger of the king abated.

8 1* That day King Ahasuerus gave the house of Haman, enemy of the Jews, to Queen Esther; and Mordecai was admitted to the king's presence, for Esther had revealed his relationship to her. 2* The king removed his signet ring from Haman, and transferred it into the keeping of Mordecai; and Esther put Mordecai in charge of the house of Haman.

The Second Royal Decree

3 In another audience with the king, Esther fell at his feet and tearfully implored him to revoke the harm done by Haman the Agagite, and the plan he had devised against the Jews. 4 The king stretched forth the golden scepter to Esther. So she rose and, standing in his presence, 5* said: "If it pleases your majesty and seems proper to you, and if I have found favor with you and you love me, let a document be issued to revoke the letters which that schemer Haman, son of Hammedatha the Agagite, wrote for the destruction of the Jews in all the royal provinces. 6 For how can I witness the evil that is to befall my people, and how can I behold the destruction of my race?"

7 King Ahasuerus then said to Queen Esther and to the Jew Mordecai: "Now that I have given Esther the house of Haman, and they have hanged him on the gibbet because he attacked the Jews, 8*† you in turn may write in the king's name what you see fit concerning the Jews and seal the letter with the roy-

al signet ring." For whatever is written in the name of the king and sealed with the royal signet ring cannot be revoked.

9 At that time, on the twenty-third day of the third month, Sivan, the royal scribes were summoned. Exactly as Mordecai dictated, they wrote to the Jews and to the satraps, governors, and officials of the hundred and twenty-seven provinces from India to Ethiopia: to each province in its own script and to each people in its own language, and to the Jews in their own script and language. 10 These letters, which he wrote in the name of King Ahasuerus and sealed with the royal signet ring, he sent by mounted couriers riding thoroughbred royal steeds. 11* In these letters the king authorized the Jews in each and every city to group together and defend their lives, and to kill, destroy, wipe out, along with their wives and children, every armed group of any nation or province which should attack them, and to seize their goods as spoil 12 throughout the provinces of King Ahasuerus, on a single day, the thirteenth of the twelfth month, Adar.

E 1 The following is a copy of the letter:

"King Ahasuerus the Great to the governors of the provinces in the hundred and twenty-seven satrapies from India to Ethiopia, and to those responsible for our interests: Greetings! 2 "Many have become the more ambitious the more they were showered with honors through the bountiful generosity of their patrons. 3 Not only do they seek to do harm to our subjects; incapable of bearing such greatness, they even begin plotting against their own benefactors. 4 Not only do they drive out gratitude from among men; with the arrogant boastfulness of those to whom goodness has no meaning, they suppose they will escape the vindictive judgment of the all-seeing God.

5 "Often, too, the fair speech of friends entrusted with the administration of affairs has induced many placed in authority to become accomplices in the shedding of innocent blood, and has involved them in irreparable calamities 6 by deceiving with malicious slander the sincere good will of rulers. 7 This can be verified in the ancient stories that have been handed down to us, but more fully when one considers the wicked deeds perpetrated in your midst by the pestilential influence of those undeserving of authority. 8* We must provide for the future, so as to render the kingdom undisturbed and peaceful for all men, 9 taking advantage of changing

---

† **8, 8:** *Whatever is written . . . cannot be revoked:* the king cannot directly grant Esther's request (v 5) to revoke the previous decree against the Jews because of the irrevocable character of the laws of the Medes and Persians (Est 1, 19; Dn 6, 9); but he empowers Esther to issue a new decree in his name which renders the earlier decree without effect; cf Est 3, 12f.

7, 9f: Est 5, 14; 6, 4.
8, 1: Est 9, 1; Prv 11, 8; 26, 27; Mt 7, 2.
8, 2: Prv 13, 22; Dn 2, 48f.
8, 5: Est 1, 19.
8, 8: Est 1, 19.
8, 11f: Est 9, 1–4.
E, 8f: Est B, 2.

conditions and deciding always with equitable treatment matters coming to our attention.

¹⁰† "For instance, Haman, son of Hammedatha, a Macedonian, certainly not of Persian blood, and very different from us in generosity, was hospitably received by us. ¹¹* He so far enjoyed the good will which we have toward all peoples that he was proclaimed 'father of the king,' before whom everyone was to bow down; he attained the rank second to the royal throne. ¹² But, unequal to this dignity, he strove to deprive us of kingdom and of life; ¹³* and by weaving intricate webs of deceit, he demanded the destruction of Mordecai, our savior and constant benefactor, and of Esther, our blameless royal consort, together with their whole race. ¹⁴ For by such measures he hoped to catch us defenseless and to transfer the rule of the Persians to the Macedonians. ¹⁵ But we find that the Jews, who were doomed to extinction by this arch-criminal, are not evildoers, but rather are governed by very just laws ¹⁶ and are the children of the Most High, the living God of majesty, who has maintained the kingdom in a flourishing condition for us and for our forebears.

¹⁷ "You will do well, then, to ignore the letter sent by Haman, son of Hammedatha, ¹⁸* for he who composed it has been hanged, together with his entire household, before the gates of Susa. Thus swiftly has God, who governs all, brought just punishment upon him.

¹⁹ "You shall exhibit a copy of this letter publicly in every place, to certify that the Jews may follow their own laws, ²⁰ and that you may help them on the day set for their ruin, the thirteenth day of the twelfth month, Adar, to defend themselves against those who attack them. ²¹ For God, the ruler of all, has turned that day for them from one of destruction of the chosen race into one of joy. ²² Therefore, you too must celebrate this memorable day among your designated feasts with all rejoicing, ²³ so that both now and in the future it may be, for us and for loyal Persians, a celebration of victory, and for those who plot against us a reminder of destruction.

²⁴* "Every city and province, without exception, that does not observe this decree shall be ruthlessly destroyed with fire and sword, so that it will be left not merely untrodden by men, but even shunned by wild beasts and birds forever."

(8) ¹³† A copy of the letter to be promulgated as law in each and every province was published among all the peoples, so that the Jews might be prepared on that day to avenge themselves on their enemies. ¹⁴ Couriers mounted on royal steeds sped forth in haste at the king's order, and the decree was promulgated in the stronghold of Susa.

¹⁵* Mordecai left the king's presence clothed in a royal robe of violet and of white cotton, with a large crown of gold and a cloak of crimson byssus. The city of Susa shouted with joy, ¹⁶ and there was splendor and merriment for the Jews, exultation and triumph. ¹⁷* In each and every province and in each and every city, wherever the king's order arrived, there was merriment and exultation, banqueting and feasting for the Jews. And many of the peoples of the land embraced Judaism, for they were seized with a fear of the Jews.

Victory of the Jews

9 ¹* When the day arrived on which the order decreed by the king was to be carried out, the thirteenth day of the twelfth month, Adar, on which the enemies of the Jews had expected to become masters of them, the situation was reversed: the Jews became masters of their enemies. ² The Jews mustered in their cities throughout the provinces of King Ahasuerus to attack those who sought to do them harm, and no one could withstand them, but all peoples were seized with a fear of them. ³ Moreover, all the officials of the provinces, the satraps, governors, and royal procurators supported the Jews from fear of Mordecai; ⁴ for Mordecai was powerful in the royal palace, and the report was spreading through all the provinces that he was continually growing in power.

⁵* The Jews struck down all their enemies with the sword, killing and destroying them; they did to their enemies as they pleased. ⁶* In the stronghold of Susa, the Jews killed and destroyed five hundred men. ⁷ They also killed Parshandatha, Dalphon, Aspatha, ⁸ Porathai, Adalia, Aridatha, ⁹ Parmashta, Arisai, Aridai, and Vaizatha, ¹⁰*† the ten sons of Haman, son of Hammedatha, the foe of the Jews. However, they did not engage in plundering.

¹¹ On the same day, when the number of those killed in the stronghold of Susa was reported to the king, ¹² he said to Queen Esther: "In the stronghold

---

† **E, 10:** *Macedonian:* a redactor of the book in the Hellenistic period used the designation Macedonian, here and in v 14, to express, after Macedonia's conquest of Persia, the most odious kind of man that a Persian ruler could be supposed to think of; the Hebrew text, for a similar reason, called Haman an Agagite. See note on Est A, 17.

8, 13: *Avenge themselves on their enemies:* partly in self-defense (Est E, 20), and partly to express the fact that the extreme cruelty designed against the Jews by their enemies now recoiled upon the latter as a punishment. Cf 9, 1f.

9, 10: *They did not engage in plundering:* in contrast to the Israelites who fought Agag (1 Sm 15, 9); cf also vv 15f.

E, 11: Est B, 3.6.
E, 13: Est A, 17.
E, 18: Est 7, 10; 9, 14.
E, 24: Est 3, 8f; B, 4.
8, 15: Dn 5, 7.
8, 17: Est 9, 27.
9, 1f: Est 8, 11f.
9, 5: Jdt 15, 6.
9, 6–10: Est 5, 11; B, 3; E, 11.
9, 10: Est 9, 15; Jdt 15, 7.11.

of Susa the Jews have killed and destroyed five hundred men, as well as the ten sons of Haman. What must they have done in the other royal provinces! You shall again be granted whatever you ask, and whatever you request shall be honored." [13] So Esther said, "If it pleases your majesty, let the Jews in Susa be permitted again tomorrow to act according to today's decree, and let the ten sons of Haman be hanged on gibbets." [14]* The king then gave an order to this effect, and the decree was published in Susa. So the ten sons of Haman were hanged, [15]*† and the Jews in Susa mustered again on the fourteenth of the month of Adar and killed three hundred men in Susa. However, they did not engage in plundering.

[16]*† The other Jews, who dwelt in the royal provinces, also mustered and defended themselves, and obtained rest from their enemies. They killed seventy-five thousand of their foes, without engaging in plunder, [17] on the thirteenth day of the month of Adar. On the fourteenth of the month they rested, and made it a day of feasting and rejoicing.

[18] (The Jews in Susa, however, mustered on the thirteenth and fourteenth of the month. But on the fifteenth they rested, and made it a day of feasting and rejoicing.) [19] That is why the rural Jews, who dwell in villages, celebrate the fourteenth of the month of Adar as a day of rejoicing and feasting, a holiday on which they send gifts of food to one another.

The Feast of Purim

[20] Mordecai recorded these events and sent letters to all the Jews, both near and far, in all the provinces of King Ahasuerus. [21] He ordered them to celebrate every year both the fourteenth and the fifteenth of the month of Adar [22] as the days on which the Jews obtained rest from their enemies and as the month which was turned for them from sorrow into joy, from mourning into festivity. They were to observe these days with feasting and gladness, sending food to one another and gifts to the poor. [23]* The Jews took upon themselves for the future this observance which they instituted at the written direction of Mordecai.

[24]* Haman, son of Hammedatha the Agagite, the foe of all the Jews, had planned to destroy them and had cast the *pur*, or lot, for the time of their defeat

and destruction. [25]* Yet, when Esther entered the royal presence, the king ordered in writing that the wicked plan Haman had devised against the Jews should instead be turned against Haman and that he and his sons should be hanged on gibbets. [26] And so these days have been named Purim after the word *pur.*

Thus, because of all that was contained in this letter, and because of what they had witnessed and experienced in this affair, [27]* the Jews established and took upon themselves, their descendants, and all who should join them, the inviolable obligation of celebrating these two days every year in the manner prescribed by this letter, and at the time appointed. [28] These days were to be commemorated and kept in every generation, by every clan, in every province, and in every city. These days of Purim were never to fall into disuse among the Jews, nor into oblivion among their descendants.

did you KNOW?

Purim

The feast of Purim ("lots" in Hebrew) commemorates the legendary victory of Queen Esther and Mordecai. A minor festival in the Jewish calendar, Purim is celebrated in late winter and is marked by the exchange of gifts and the sharing of meals.

▶ Est 9, 20–32

[29]† Queen Esther, daughter of Abihail and of Mordecai the Jew, wrote to confirm with full authority this second letter about Purim, [30]* when Mordecai sent documents concerning peace and security to all the Jews in the hundred and twenty-seven provinces of Ahasuerus' kingdom. [31]† Thus were established, for their appointed time, these days of Purim which Mordecai the Jew and Queen

---

9, 15: This second slaughter explains the two dates (13th and 14th) of the Purim celebration by Jews in Susa (v 18).
9, 16: *Seventy-five thousand:* according to the Greek text this number was fifteen thousand.
9, 29: *Queen Esther, daughter of Abihail and of Mordecai:* the natural offspring of Abihail and adopted daughter of Mordecai; cf Est 2, 15. *This second letter:* for the burden of this letter see Est 9, 20ff. It was endorsed by Queen Esther. The first letter, written in the king's name, is referred to in Est 8, 9.
9, 31: *Fasting and supplication:* as the Jews had previously un-

dertaken the duty of fasting and supplication to prevent the impending disaster, they now observe days of festival to commemorate their deliverance—in both cases (cf Est 4, 3.15f) at the request of Mordecai and Esther.

9, 14: Est 7, 10; E, 18.	**9, 24ff:** Est 3, 7; F, 10.
9, 15: Est 9, 10.	**9, 25:** Est 6, 5–13.
9, 16: Jdt 15, 6.	**9, 27:** Est 8, 12.17.
9, 23: Est 9, 29.	**9, 30:** Est 9, 23–26.

Esther had designated for the Jews, just as they had previously enjoined upon themselves and upon their race the duty of fasting and supplication. [32] The command of Esther confirmed these prescriptions for Purim and was recorded in the book.

10 [1] King Ahasuerus laid tribute on the land and on the islands of the sea. [2] All the acts of his power and valor, as well as a detailed account of the greatness of Mordecai, whom the king promoted, are recorded in the chronicles of the kings of Media and Persia. [3]* The Jew Mordecai was next in rank to King Ahasuerus, in high standing among the Jews, and was regarded with favor by his many brethren, as the promoter of his people's welfare and the herald of peace for his whole race.

V: Epilogue

Mordecai's Dream Fulfilled

F [1]* Then Mordecai said: "This is the work of God. [2] I recall the dream I had about these very things, and not a single detail has been left unfulfilled— [3] the tiny spring that grew into a river, the light of the sun, the many waters. The river is Esther, whom the king married and made queen. [4] The two dragons are myself and Haman. [5] The nations are those who assembled to destroy the name of the Jews, [6] but my people is Israel, who cried to God and was saved.

"The LORD saved his people and delivered us from all these evils. God worked signs and great wonders, such as have not occurred among the nations. [7]† For this purpose he arranged two lots: one for the people of God, the second for all the other nations. [8] These two lots were fulfilled in the hour, the time, and the day of judgment before God and among all the nations. [9]* God remembered his people and rendered justice to his inheritance.

[10]† "Gathering together with joy and happiness before God, they shall celebrate these days on the fourteenth and fifteenth of the month Adar throughout all future generations of his people Israel."

F, 7: *Two lots:* in this passage of the Greek text, which gives a more religious interpretation of the feast, the two lots are drawn by God to determine, respectively, the destiny of Israel and that of the nations. In Est 3, 7 above, translated from the Hebrew text, the feast is called Purim because of the lots which Aman cast to determine the day for the extinction of the Jews.

F, 10: The Greek text of Esther contains a postscript as follows: In the fourth year of the reign of Ptolemy and Cleopatra, Dositheus, who said he was a priest and Levite, and his son Ptolemy brought the present letter of Purim, saying that it was genuine and that Lysimachus, son of Ptolemy, of the community of Jerusalem, had translated it. The date referred to in this postscript is most probably 78–77 B.C., in the reign of Ptolemy XII and Cleopatra V.

10, 3: 2 Mc 15, 14.
F, 1–6: Est A, 4–10.

F, 9: Est 3, 7; 9, 17f.21.24–28.

Have you ever listened as two fighting siblings tell their parents about a conflict? Usually, each child blames the other one and protests his or her complete innocence. Sometimes you have to wonder if they are even talking about the same fight. In a similar way, the author of 1 Maccabees, reporting on the Jewish resistance to the persecution of the Seleucid (Greek) rulers, tells one version of the story. The book defends the violent resistance of the family of Mattathias. Second Maccabees, on the other hand, has a broader perspective in telling of other forms of Jewish resistance.

At a Glance

I. **Introduction: Hellenism in Asia Minor (1, 1–9).**

II. **The Maccabean Revolt (1, 10—2, 70).**

III. **Leadership of Judas Maccabeus (3, 1—9, 22).**

IV. **Leadership of Jonathan (9, 23—12, 53).**

V. **Simon, High Priest and Ethnarch (13, 1—16, 24).**

In-depth

The writer of 1 Maccabees has a clear purpose in mind: to defend the family of Mattathias, whose sons—the Maccabees—held positions of authority in the Jewish community. The most famous of them, Judas Maccabeus, led the Jews in a successful revolt (167–164 B.C.) against the Greek persecution—an incredible feat given the military might of the Greeks. After Judas's death, his brothers and nephews held positions of power, and Israel remained free from foreign domination for the next hundred years.

For traditional Jews, the power of the Maccabees posed a problem: because Mattathias's bloodline could be traced to neither King David nor Aaron the priest, by what right had his descendants assumed kingly and priestly authority? Against such criticism, the author of 1 Maccabees tries to prove that God's plan was accomplished through Mattathias's family.

The interpretation of Jewish history contained in 1 Maccabees invites us to believe in God's choice of Mattathias's sons as saviors of the nation. Even more important, it invites us to believe in the utter reliability of God: "And so, consider this from generation to generation, that none who hope in him shall fail in strength" (2, 61).

Quick Facts

Period Covered
from 175 to 134 B.C.

Author
unknown, writing around 100 B.C.

Theme
God brings Israel to freedom through the family of Mattathias.

Of Note
First Maccabees is not found in some Protestant Bibles (see "The Case of the Missing Books," near Tb 1, 16).

1 Maccabees

I: Introduction: Hellenism In Asia Minor

Conquests and Death of Alexander

1 [1]*† After Alexander the Macedonian, Philip's son, who came from the land of Kittim, had defeated Darius, king of the Persians and Medes, he became king in his place, having first ruled in Greece. [2] He fought many campaigns, captured fortresses, and put kings to death. [3] He advanced to the ends of the earth, gathering plunder from many nations; the earth fell silent before him, and his heart became proud and arrogant. [4] He collected a very strong army and conquered provinces, nations, and rulers, and they became his tributaries. [5] But after all this he took to his bed, realizing that he was going to die. [6] He therefore summoned his officers, the nobles, who had been brought up with him from his youth, to divide his kingdom among them while he was still alive. [7]† Alexander had reigned twelve years when he died.

[8] So his officers took over his kingdom, each in his own territory, [9] and after his death they all put on royal crowns, and so did their sons after them for many years, causing much distress over the earth.

II: The Maccabean Revolt

Pact between Jews and Gentiles

[10]*† There sprang from these a sinful offshoot, Antiochus Epiphanes, son of King Antiochus, once a hostage at Rome. He became king in the year one hundred and thirty-seven of the kingdom of the Greeks.

[11]* In those days there appeared in Israel men who were breakers of the law, and they seduced many people, saying: "Let us go and make an alliance with the Gentiles all around us; since we separated from them, many evils have come upon us." [12] The proposal was agreeable; [13]* some from among the people promptly went to the king, and he authorized them to introduce the way of living of the Gentiles. [14]† Thereupon they built a gymnasium

---

1, 1: *Land of Kittim:* Greece. The name referred originally to inhabitants of Kiti, capital of the isle of Cyprus, then to any Cypriots (Is 23, 1; Jer 2, 10), later to Greeks in general, and finally even to Romans. See note on Dn 11, 30. *Darius:* Darius III, Codoman (336–331 B.C.).
1, 7: *Twelve years:* 336–323 B.C.
1, 10: *The year one hundred and thirty-seven:* Antiochus IV seized the throne in September, 175 B.C. Dates are given in this book according to the Seleucid era, which however was reckoned in two different ways. Antiochians considered this date to be October, 312 B.C. (Syrian calendar), while Babylonians and Jewish priests accepted April, 311 B.C. as the commencement of the era (temple calendar). The author of 1 Mc dates political events by the Syrian

calendar but religious events by the temple calendar. Accordingly, the civil New Year occurred variously in September or October, the religious New Year in March or April.
1, 14: *Gymnasium:* symbol and center of athletic and intellectual life, it was the chief instrument of Hellenistic propaganda. Jewish youth were attracted by sports and encouraged to join youth clubs. They received training in military skills and in the duties of citizens. Through participation in the intellectual life, many were gradually won over to paganism.

1, 1–10: Dn 8, 20ff; 11, 3f.21.   1, 11: 2 Mc 4, 9–17.
1, 10: 2 Mc 4, 7.   1, 13ff: 2 Mc 4, 7–17.

in Jerusalem according to the Gentile custom. 15* They covered over the mark of their circumcision and abandoned the holy covenant; they allied themselves with the Gentiles and sold themselves to wrongdoing.

Egyptian Campaign of Antiochus

16 When his kingdom seemed secure, Antiochus proposed to become king of Egypt, so as to rule over both kingdoms. 17*† He invaded Egypt with a strong force, with chariots and elephants, and with a large fleet, 18 to make war on Ptolemy, king of Egypt. Ptolemy was frightened at his presence and fled, leaving many casualties. 19 The fortified cities in the land of Egypt were captured, and Antiochus plundered the land of Egypt.

Persecution of the Jews

20*† After Antiochus had defeated Egypt in the year one hundred and forty-three, he returned and went up to Israel and to Jerusalem with a strong force. 21 He insolently invaded the sanctuary and took away the golden altar, the lampstand for the light with all its fixtures, 22 the offering table, the cups and the bowls, the golden censers, the curtain, the crowns, and the golden ornament on the façade of the temple. He stripped off everything, 23 and took away the gold and silver and the precious vessels; he also took all the hidden treasures he could find. 24 Taking all this, he went back to his own country, after he had spoken with great arrogance and shed much blood.

25 And there was great mourning for Israel, in
    every place where they dwelt,
26   and the rulers and the elders groaned.
    Virgins and young men languished,
    and the beauty of the women was disfigured.
27 Every bridegroom took up lamentation,
    she who sat in the bridal
      chamber mourned,
28 And the land was shaken on account of
    its inhabitants,
    and all the house of Jacob was covered
      with shame.

29* Two years later, the king sent the Mysian commander to the cities of Judah, and he came to Jerusalem with a strong force. 30 He spoke to them deceitfully in peaceful terms, and won their trust. Then he attacked the city suddenly, in a great onslaught, and destroyed many of the people in Israel. 31 He plundered the city and set fire to it, demolished its houses and its surrounding walls, 32 took captive the women and children, and seized the cattle. 33*† Then they built up the City of David with a high, massive wall and strong towers, and it became their citadel. 34 There they installed a sinful race, perverse men, who fortified themselves inside it, 35 storing up weapons and provisions, and depositing there the plunder they had collected from Jerusalem. And they became a great threat.

36   The citadel became an ambush against
      the sanctuary,
      and a wicked adversary to Israel at all times.
37   And they shed innocent blood around
      the sanctuary;
      they defiled the sanctuary.
38   Because of them the inhabitants of Jerusalem
      fled away,
      and she became the abode of strangers.
    She became a stranger to her own offspring,
      and her children forsook her.
39* Her sanctuary was as desolate as a wilderness;
      her feasts were turned into mourning,
    Her sabbaths to shame,
      her honor to contempt.
40   Her dishonor was as great as her glory
      had been,
    and her exaltation was turned
      into mourning.

Prohibitions against Religion

41 Then the king wrote to his whole kingdom that all should be one people, 42 each abandoning his particular customs. All the Gentiles conformed to the command of the king, 43 and many Israelites were in favor of his religion; they sacrificed to idols and profaned the sabbath.

44* The king sent messengers with letters to Jerusalem and to the cities of Judah, ordering them to follow customs foreign to their land: 45 to prohibit holocausts, sacrifices, and libations in the sanctuary, to profane the sabbaths and feast days, 46* to desecrate the sanctuary and the sacred minis-

---

† **1, 17:** *Elephants:* an important part of Seleucid armament. About 300 B.C. Seleucus I, founder of the dynasty, procured five hundred of them from India; cf 1 Mc 6, 34–37.

1, 20: *Defeated Egypt in the year one hundred and forty-three:* 169 B.C. No mention is made in 1 Maccabees of the second expedition to Egypt a year later, described in 2 Mc 5, 1.11. Dn 11, 25.29 records both.

1, 33: *City of David:* not Mount Zion on the eastern hill of Jerusalem, which David captured from the Jebusites (2 Sm 5, 7), but a new fortress built on the western hill and overlooking the temple and its courts on Mount Zion. It was occupied for twenty-six years by the Syro-Macedonian garrison, together with apostate Jews, and was a continual threat to the temple and the Jewish people (v 36); cf 1 Mc 13, 49ff.

1, 15: 1 Cor 7, 18.
1, 17: 2 Mc 5, 1; Dn 11, 25–28.
1, 20–24: 2 Mc 5, 11–21.
1, 29–32: 2 Mc 5, 24ff.
1, 33: 1 Mc 6, 18.
1, 39f: Tb 2, 6; Am 8, 10.
1, 44–63: 2 Mc 6, 1–11.
1, 46: 2 Mc 6, 2; Dn 9, 27.

ters, to build pagan altars and temples and shrines, 47 to sacrifice swine and unclean animals, 48 to leave their sons uncircumcised, and to let themselves be defiled with every kind of impurity and abomination, 49 so that they might forget the law and change all their observances. 50* Whoever refused to act according to the command of the king should be put to death.

51 Such were the orders he published throughout his kingdom. He appointed inspectors over all the people, and he ordered the cities of Judah to offer sacrifices, each city in turn. 52 Many of the people, those who abandoned the law, joined them and committed evil in the land. 53 Israel was driven into hiding, wherever places of refuge could be found.

54*† On the fifteenth day of the month Chislev, in the year one hundred and forty-five, the king erected the horrible abomination upon the altar of holocausts, and in the surrounding cities of Judah they built pagan altars. 55 They also burnt incense at the doors of houses and in the streets. 56† Any scrolls of the law which they found they tore up and burnt. 57* Whoever was found with a scroll of the covenant, and whoever observed the law, was condemned to death by royal decree. 58 So they used their power against Israel, against those who were caught, each month, in the cities. 59 On the twenty-fifth day of each month they sacrificed on the altar erected over the altar of holocausts. 60* Women who had had their children circumcised were put to death, in keeping with the decree, 61 with the babies hung from their necks; their families also and those who had circumcised them were killed. 62 But many in Israel were determined and resolved in their hearts not to eat anything unclean; 63* they preferred to die rather than to be defiled with unclean food or to profane the holy covenant; and they did die. Terrible affliction was upon Israel.

Mattathias and His Sons

2 1† In those days Mattathias, son of John, son of Simeon, a priest of the family of Joarib, left Jerusalem and settled in Modein. 2* He had five sons: John, who was called Gaddi; 3 Simon, who was called Thassi; 4 Judas, who was called Maccabeus; 5 Eleazar, who was called Avaran; and Jonathan, who was called Apphus. 6 When he saw the sacrileges that were being committed in Judah and in Jerusalem, 7 he said: "Woe is me! Why was I

born to see the ruin of my people and the ruin of the holy city, and to sit idle while it is given into the hands of enemies, and the sanctuary into the hands of strangers?

8   "Her temple has become like a man disgraced,
9*   her glorious ornaments have been carried
      off as spoils,
    Her infants have been murdered in her streets,
      her young men by the sword of the enemy.
10   What nation has not taken its share of
      her realm,
    and laid its hand on her possessions?
11   All her adornment has been taken away.
    From being free, she has become a slave.
12   We see our sanctuary and our beauty
    and our glory laid waste,
    And the Gentiles have defiled them!
13   Why are we still alive?"

14 Then Mattathias and his sons tore their garments, put on sackcloth, and mourned bitterly.

Pagan Worship Refused

15 The officers of the king in charge of enforcing the apostasy came to the city of Modein to organize the sacrifices. 16 Many of Israel joined them, but Mattathias and his sons gathered in a group apart. 17 Then the officers of the king addressed Mattathias: "You are a leader, an honorable and great man in this city, supported by sons and kinsmen. 18† Come now, be the first to obey the king's command, as all the Gentiles and the men of Judah and those who are left in Jerusalem have done. Then you and your sons shall be numbered among the King's Friends, and shall be enriched with silver and gold and many gifts." 19 But Mattathias answered in a loud voice: "Although all the Gentiles in the king's realm obey him, so that each forsakes the religion of his fathers and consents to the king's orders, 20 yet I and my sons and my kinsmen will keep to the covenant of our fathers. 21 God forbid that we should forsake the law and the commandments. 22 We will not obey the words of the king nor depart from our religion in the slightest degree."

23 As he finished saying these words, a certain Jew came forward in the sight of all to offer sacrifice on the altar in Modein according to the king's order. 24 When Mattathias saw him, he was filled with

---

1, 54: *Fifteenth day of the month Chislev, in the year one hundred and forty-five:* early December, 167 B.C. *Horrible abomination:* in the original Hebrew, a contemptuous pun on the title "Lord of heaven" given to the god Zeus Olympios, to whom an image or perhaps an altar was erected upon the altar of holocausts in the temple of Jerusalem; cf Dn 9, 27; 11, 31.
1, 56f: *Scrolls of the law:* one or more of the first five books of the Old Testament.
2, 1: *Modein:* a village twenty miles northwest of Jerusalem.

2, 18: *The King's Friends:* a regular order of nobility at Hellenistic courts. The various grades are frequently mentioned in this book: Friends, Chief Friends, Kinsmen.

1, 50: 2 Mc 6, 18—7, 41.   1, 60f: 2 Mc 6, 10.
1, 54: 1 Mc 6, 7; Dn 9, 27;   1, 63: 2 Mc 6, 10.
    11, 31.   2, 2: 1 Chr 24, 7.
1, 57: 2 Mc 2, 14.   2, 9: Lam 2, 11.21.

Religious Persecution

The Jews were facing a societal attack on their faith. But Mattathias and his sons chose to fight the official and cultural pressure to turn away from their faith.
          Are there times when you feel persecuted because of your belief in God? In what subtle ways does contemporary society ridicule people with religious beliefs? If you were to be persecuted because of your religion, how would you respond?

▸ **1 Mc 2, 19–22**

zeal; his heart was moved and his just fury was aroused; he sprang forward and killed him upon the altar. 25 At the same time, he also killed the messenger of the king who was forcing them to sacrifice, and he tore down the altar. 26* Thus he showed his zeal for the law, just as Phinehas did with Zimri, son of Salu.

27 Then Mattathias went through the city shouting, "Let everyone who is zealous for the law and who stands by the covenant follow after me!" 28* Thereupon he fled to the mountains with his sons, leaving behind in the city all their possessions. 29† Many who sought to live according to righteousness and religious custom went out into the desert to settle there, 30 they and their sons, their wives and their cattle, because misfortunes pressed so hard on them.

31 It was reported to the officers and soldiers of the king who were in the City of David, in Jerusalem, that certain men who had flouted the king's order had gone out to the hiding places in the desert. 32* Many hurried out after them, and having caught up with them, camped opposite and prepared to attack them on the sabbath. 33 "Enough of this!" the pursuers said to them. "Come out and obey the king's command, and your lives will be spared." 34 But they replied, "We will not come out, nor will we obey the king's command to profane the sabbath." 35 Then the enemy attacked them at once; 36 but they did not retaliate; they neither threw stones, nor blocked up their own hiding places. 37 They said, "Let us all die without reproach; heaven and earth are our witnesses that you destroy us unjustly." 38 So the officers and soldiers attacked them on the sabbath, and they died with their wives, their children and their cattle, to the number of a thousand persons.

39 When Mattathias and his friends heard of it,

they mourned deeply for them. 40 "If we all do as our kinsmen have done," they said to one another, "and do not fight against the Gentiles for our lives and our traditions, they will soon destroy us from the earth." 41 On that day they came to this decision: "Let us fight against anyone who attacks us on the sabbath, so that we may not all die as our kinsmen died in the hiding places."

42† Then they were joined by a group of Hasideans, valiant Israelites, all of them devout followers of the law. 43 And all those who were fleeing from the disaster joined them and supported them. 44* They gathered an army and struck down sinners in their anger and lawbreakers in their wrath, and the survivors fled to the Gentiles for safety. 45 Mattathias and his friends went about and tore down the pagan altars; 46 they also forcibly circumcised any uncircumcised boys whom they found in the territory of Israel. 47 They put to flight the arrogant, and the work prospered in their hands. 48 They saved the law from the hands of the Gentiles and of the kings and did not let the sinner triumph.

Death of Mattathias

49 When the time came for Mattathias to die, he said to his sons: "Arrogance and scorn have now grown strong; it is a time of disaster and violent anger. 50 Therefore, my sons, be zealous for the law and give your lives for the covenant of our fathers.

51   "Remember the deeds that our fathers did in
          their times,
          and you shall win great glory and an
          everlasting name.
52*   Was not Abraham found faithful in trial,
          and it was reputed to him as uprightness?
53*   Joseph, when in distress, kept
          the commandment,

2, 29: *The desert:* the sparsely inhabited mountain country southward from Jerusalem and west of the Dead Sea. It was an arid region with some perennial springs and a fair amount of rain in winter.
2, 42: *Hasideans:* in Hebrew *hasidim,* "pious ones," a religious group devoted to the strict observance of the law. They were the forerunners of both the Pharisees and the Essenes. They first supported

the Maccabean movement, but subsequently opposed it, regarding it as too political.

2, 26: 1 Mc 2, 54; Nm 25, 6–14.	**2, 44:** Is 63, 3.
2, 28: 2 Mc 5, 27.	**2, 52:** Gn 15, 6; 22, 1ff.
2, 32–38: 2 Mc 6, 11.	**2, 53:** Gn 39, 7–10; 41, 39–43.

and he became master of Egypt.
54* Phinehas our father, for his burning
    zeal,
    received the covenant of an
    everlasting priesthood.
55* Joshua, for executing his commission,
    became a judge in Israel.
56* Caleb, for bearing witness before
    the assembly,
    received an inheritance in the land.
57* David, for his piety,
    received as a heritage a throne of
    everlasting royalty.
58* Elijah, for his burning zeal for the law,
    was taken up to heaven.
59* Hananiah, Azariah and Mishael, for
    their faith,
    were saved from the fire.
60* Daniel, for his innocence,
    was delivered from the jaws of lions.
61 And so, consider this from generation
    to generation,
    that none who hope in him shall fail
    in strength.
62 Do not fear the words of a sinful man,
    for his glory ends in corruption
    and worms.
63 Today he is exalted, and tomorrow he is not
    to be found,
    because he has returned to his dust,
    and his schemes have perished.
64 Children! be courageous and strong in
    keeping the law,
    for by it you shall be glorified.

65 "Here is your brother Simeon who I know is a wise man; listen to him always, and he will be a father to you. 66 And Judas Maccabeus, a warrior from his youth, shall be the leader of your army and direct the war against the nations. 67 You shall also gather about you all who observe the law, and you shall avenge the wrongs of your people. 68 Pay back the Gentiles what they deserve, and observe the precepts of the law."

69 Then he blessed them, and he was united with his fathers. 70† He died in the year one hundred and forty-six, and was buried in the tombs of his fathers in Modein, and all Israel mourned him greatly.

III: Leadership of Judas Maccabeus

Defeat of Apollonius and Seron

3 1 Then his son Judas, who was called Maccabeus, took his place. 2 All his brothers and all who had joined his father supported him, and they carried on Israel's war joyfully.

3* He spread abroad the glory of his people,
    and put on his breastplate like a giant.
He armed himself with weapons of war;
    he planned battles and protected the camp
    with his sword.
4 In his actions he was like a lion,
    like a young lion roaring for prey.
5 He pursued the wicked, hunting them out,
    and those who troubled his people he
    destroyed by fire.
6 The lawbreakers were cowed by fear of him,
    and all evildoers were dismayed.
By his hand redemption was
    happily achieved,
7 and he afflicted many kings;
He made Jacob glad by his deeds,
    and his memory is blessed forever.
8 He went about the cities of Judah
    destroying the impious there.
He turned away wrath from Israel
9 and was renowned to the ends of the earth;
    he gathered together those who
    were perishing.

10† Then Apollonius gathered the Gentiles, together with a large army from Samaria, to fight against Israel. 11 When Judas learned of it, he went out to meet him and defeated and killed him. Many fell wounded, and the rest fled. 12 Their possessions were seized and the sword of Apollonius was taken by Judas, who fought with it the rest of his life.

13 But Seron, commander of the Syrian army, heard that Judas had gathered many about him, an assembly of faithful men ready for war. 14 So he said, "I will make a name for myself and win glory in the kingdom by defeating Judas and his followers, who have despised the king's command." 15 And again a large company of renegades advanced with him to help him take revenge on the Israelites. 16† When he reached the ascent of Beth-horon, Judas went out to meet him with a few

---

2, 70: In the year one hundred and forty-six: 166 B.C.
3, 10: Apollonius: the Mysian commander mentioned in 1 Mc 1, 29 and in 2 Mc 5, 24.
3, 16: Beth-horon: the famous pass leading up from the coastal plain to the Judean hill country. Here Joshua won an important battle (Jos 10, 10f), and in 66 A.D. a Roman force under Cestius was trapped and massacred.

2, 54: Nm 25, 10–13; Sir 45, 28ff.
2, 55: Jos 1, 2.5.
2, 56: Nm 13, 30; 14, 6–9. 24; Jos 14, 14.
2, 57: 2 Sm 2, 4; 7, 16.
2, 58: 1 Kgs 19, 10.14; 2 Kgs 2, 11.
2, 59: Dn 3, 50.
2, 60: Dn 6, 23; 14, 31–42.
3, 3: 2 Mc 8, 5.

men. ¹⁷ But when they saw the army coming against them, they said to Judas: "How can we, few as we are, fight such a mighty host as this? Besides, we are weak today from fasting." ¹⁸ But Judas said: "It is easy for many to be overcome by a few; in the sight of Heaven there is no difference between deliverance by many or by few; ¹⁹* for victory in war does not depend upon the size of the army, but on strength that comes from Heaven. ²⁰ With great presumption and lawlessness they come against us to destroy us and our wives and children and to despoil us; ²¹ but we are fighting for our lives and our laws. ²²† He himself will crush them before us; so do not be afraid of them." ²³ When he finished speaking, he rushed suddenly upon Seron and his army, who were crushed before him. ²⁴*† He pursued Seron down the descent of Beth-horon into the plain. About eight hundred of their men fell, and the rest fled to the country of the Philistines. ²⁵ Then Judas and his brothers began to be feared, and dread fell upon the Gentiles about them. ²⁶ His fame reached the king, and all the Gentiles talked about the battles of Judas.

Regency of Lysias

²⁷ When Antiochus heard about these events, he was angry; so he ordered a muster of all the forces of his kingdom, a very strong army. ²⁸ He opened his treasure chests, gave his soldiers a year's pay, and commanded them to be prepared for anything. ²⁹ He then found that this exhausted the money in his treasury; moreover the income from the province was small, because of the dissension and distress he had brought upon the land by abolishing the laws which had been in effect from of old. ³⁰ He feared that, as had happened more than once, he would not have enough for his expenses and for the gifts that he had previously given with a more liberal hand than the preceding kings. ³¹ Greatly perplexed, he decided to go to Persia and levy tribute on those provinces, and so raise a large sum of money. ³² He left Lysias, a nobleman of royal blood, in charge of the king's affairs from the Euphrates River to the frontier of Egypt, ³³ and commissioned him to take care of his son Antiochus until his own return. ³⁴ He entrusted to him half of the army, and the elephants, and gave him instruc-

tions concerning everything he wanted done. As for the inhabitants of Judea and Jerusalem, ³⁵ Lysias was to send an army against them to crush and destroy the power of Israel and the remnant of Jerusalem and efface their memory from the land. ³⁶ He was to settle foreigners in all their territory and distribute their land by lot.

³⁷† The king took the remaining half of the army and set out from Antioch, his capital, in the year one hundred and forty-seven; he crossed the Euphrates River and advanced inland.

The Victories of Judas

³⁸*† Lysias chose Ptolemy, son of Dorymenes, and Nicanor and Gorgias, capable men among the King's Friends,* ³⁹ and with them he sent forty thousand men and seven thousand cavalry to invade the land of Judah and ravage it according to the king's orders. ⁴⁰† Setting out with all their forces, they came and pitched their camp near Emmaus in the plain. ⁴¹ When the merchants of the country heard of their fame, they came to the camp, bringing fetters and a large sum of silver and gold, to buy the Israelites as slaves. A force from Idumea and from Philistia joined with them.

⁴² Judas and his brothers saw that the situation had become critical now that armies were encamped within their territory; they knew of the orders which the king had given to destroy and utterly wipe out the people. ⁴³ So they said to one another, "Let us restore our people from their ruined estate, and fight for our people and our sanctuary!"

⁴⁴ The assembly gathered together to prepare for battle and to pray and implore mercy and compassion.

⁴⁵   Jerusalem was uninhabited, like a desert;
     not one of her children entered or
       came out.
   The sanctuary was trampled on,
       and foreigners were in the citadel;
       it was a habitation of Gentiles.
   Joy had disappeared from Jacob,
       and the flute and the harp were silent.

⁴⁶*† Thus they assembled and went to Mizpah near Jerusalem, because there was formerly at Miz-

---

3, 22: *He himself:* out of reverence for God, the author of 1 Maccabees prefers to use this and other expressions, such as "Heaven," instead of the divine name. Cf 1 Mc 3, 50.

3, 24: *About eight hundred:* the figures given in this book for strength of armies and number of casualties are not to be taken literally. In accordance with biblical usage, they indicate rather the importance of the battle described or the greatness of the victory.

3, 37: This expedition, in the spring of 165 B.C., resulted in failure; cf ch 6.

3, 38: *Nicanor:* the leader of another attack against the Jews four years later. He was finally killed by Judas; cf 1 Mc 7, 26–46.

3, 40: *Emmaus:* probably not the village mentioned in Lk 24, 13, but a settlement about twenty miles west of Jerusalem at the edge of the hill country.

3, 46: . . . *Mizpah a place of prayer for Israel:* a holy place established of old eight miles north and slightly west of Jerusalem. It was here that Samuel began to judge the Israelites (1 Sm 7, 5–11; 10, 17).

3, 19: 1 Sm 14, 16.
3, 24: Jos 10, 10.
3, 38–44: 2 Mc 8, 8–15.
3, 38f: 1 Mc 7, 26; 2 Mc 4,

45; 8, 8f; 10, 14.
3, 46ff: 1 Sm 7, 5f; 2 Mc 8,
16–23.

pah a place of prayer for Israel. ⁴⁷ That day they fasted and wore sackcloth; they sprinkled ashes on their heads and tore their clothes. ⁴⁸† They unrolled the scroll of the law, to learn about the things for which the Gentiles consulted the images of their idols. ⁴⁹*† They brought with them the priestly vestments, the first fruits, and the tithes; and they brought forward the nazirites who had completed the time of their vows. ⁵⁰ And they cried aloud to Heaven: "What shall we do with these men, and where shall we take them? ⁵¹ For your sanctuary has been trampled on and profaned, and your priests are in mourning and humiliation. ⁵² Now the Gentiles are gathered together against us to destroy us. You know what they plot against us. ⁵³ How shall we be able to resist them unless you help us?" ⁵⁴ Then they blew the trumpets and cried out loudly.

⁵⁵ After this Judas appointed officers among the people, over thousands, over hundreds, over fifties, and over tens. ⁵⁶* He proclaimed that those who were building houses, or were just married, or were planting vineyards, and those who were afraid, could each return to his home, according to the law. ⁵⁷ Then the army moved off, and they camped to the south of Emmaus. ⁵⁸ Judas said: "Arm yourselves and be brave; in the morning be ready to fight these Gentiles who have assembled against us to destroy us and our sanctuary. ⁵⁹* It is better for us to die in battle than to witness the ruin of our nation and our sanctuary. Whatever Heaven wills, he will do."

4 ¹ Now Gorgias took five thousand infantry and a thousand picked cavalry, and this detachment set out at night ² in order to attack the camp of the Jews and take them by surprise. Some men from the citadel were their guides. ³ Judas heard of it, and himself set out with his soldiers to attack the king's army at Emmaus, ⁴ while the latter's forces were still scattered away from the camp. ⁵ During the night Gorgias came into the camp of Judas, and found no one there; so he began to hunt for them in the mountains, saying, "They are fleeing from us."

⁶ But at daybreak Judas appeared in the plain with three thousand men, who lacked such armor and swords as they would have wished. ⁷ They saw the army of the Gentiles, strong and breastplated, flanked with cavalry, and made up of expert soldiers. ⁸ Judas said to the men with him: "Do not be afraid of their numbers or dread their attack. ⁹* Remember how our fathers were saved in the Red Sea, when Pharaoh pursued them with an army. ¹⁰* So now let us cry to Heaven in the hope that he will favor us, remember his covenant with our fathers, and destroy this army before us today. ¹¹ All the Gentiles shall know that there is One who redeems and delivers Israel."

¹² When the foreigners looked up and saw them marching toward them, ¹³ they came out of their camp for battle, and the men with Judas blew the trumpet. ¹⁴ The battle was joined and the Gentiles were defeated and fled toward the plain. ¹⁵† Their whole rearguard fell by the sword, and they were pursued as far as Gazara and the plains of Judea, to Azotus and Jamnia. About three thousand of their men fell.

¹⁶ When Judas and the army returned from the pursuit, ¹⁷ he said to the people: "Do not be greedy for the plunder, for there is a fight ahead of us, ¹⁸ and Gorgias and his army are near us on the mountain. But now stand firm against our enemies and overthrow them. Afterward you can freely take the plunder."

¹⁹ As Judas was finishing this speech, a detachment appeared, looking down from the mountain. ²⁰ They saw that their army had been put to flight and their camp was being burned. The smoke that could be seen indicated what had happened. ²¹ When they realized this, they were terrified; and when they also saw the army of Judas in the plain ready to attack, ²²† they all fled to Philistine territory.

²³ Then Judas went back to plunder the camp, and his men collected much gold and silver, violet and crimson cloth, and great treasure. ²⁴* As they returned, they were singing hymns and glorifying Heaven, "for he is good, for his mercy endures forever." ²⁵ Thus Israel had a great deliverance that day.

Victory over Lysias

²⁶* But those of the foreigners who had escaped went and told Lysias all that had occurred. ²⁷ When he heard it he was disturbed and discouraged, because things in Israel had not turned out as he intended and as the king had ordered.

²⁸ So the following year he gathered together

3, 48: *To learn . . . idols:* favorable omens for the coming battle. A contrast is intended between the idol worship of the pagans and the consultation of the word of God by the Jews; cf 2 Mc 8, 23.

3, 49: *Nazirites:* see note on Nm 6, 1ff.

4, 15: *Gazara:* Gezer of the Hebrew Bible, five miles northwest of Emmaus: *Azotus,* Hebrew Ashdod, lay to the southwest; and *Jamnia,* Hebrew Jabneel (Jos 15, 11) or Jabneh (2 Chr 26, 6), to the west of Gazara.

4, 22: *Philistine territory:* the coastal cities of southern Palestine,

traditionally hostile to Jerusalem. Jamnia in particular was an important base for the Seleucid power.

3, 49: Nm 6, 2–5.
3, 56: Dt 20, 5–8; Jgs 7, 3.
3, 59: 1 Mc 2, 21f.
4, 9: Ex 14, 21ff.
4, 10: 1 Mc 2, 21.
4, 24: Ps 118, 1ff.29.
4, 26–35: 2 Mc 11, 1–12.

sixty thousand picked men and five thousand cavalry, to subdue them. ²⁹† They came into Idumea and camped at Beth-zur, and Judas met them with ten thousand men. ³⁰* Seeing that the army was strong, he prayed thus:

"Blessed are you, O Savior of Israel, who broke the rush of the mighty one by the hand of your servant David and delivered the camp of the Philistines into the hand of Jonathan, the son of Saul, and his armor-bearer. ³¹ Give this army into the hands of your people Israel; make them ashamed of their troops and their cavalry. ³² Strike them with fear, weaken the boldness of their strength, and let them tremble at their own destruction. ³³ Strike them down by the sword of those who love you, that all who know your name may hymn your praise."

³⁴ Then they engaged in battle, and about five thousand of Lysias' men fell in hand-to-hand fighting. ³⁵† When Lysias saw his ranks beginning to give way, and the increased boldness of Judas, whose men were ready either to live or to die bravely, he withdrew to Antioch and began to recruit mercenaries so as to return to Judea with greater numbers.

Purification of the Temple

³⁶*† Then Judas and his brothers said, "Now that our enemies have been crushed, let us go up to purify the sanctuary and rededicate it." ³⁷ So the whole army assembled, and went up to Mount Zion. ³⁸* They found the sanctuary desolate, the altar desecrated, the gates burnt, weeds growing in the courts as in a forest or on some mountain, and the priests' chambers demolished. ³⁹ Then they tore their clothes and made great lamentation; they sprinkled their heads with ashes ⁴⁰ and fell with their faces to the ground. And when the signal was given with trumpets, they cried out to Heaven.

⁴¹ Judas appointed men to attack those in the citadel, while he purified the sanctuary. ⁴² He chose blameless priests, devoted to the law; ⁴³ these purified the sanctuary and carried away the stones of the Abomination to an unclean place. ⁴⁴* They deliberated what ought to be done with the altar of holocausts that had been desecrated. ⁴⁵* The happy thought came to them to tear it down, lest it be a lasting shame to them that the Gentiles had defiled it; so they tore down the altar. ⁴⁶ They stored the stones in a suitable place on the temple hill, until a

prophet should come and decide what to do with them. ⁴⁷* Then they took uncut stones, according to the law, and built a new altar like the former one. ⁴⁸ They also repaired the sanctuary and the interior of the temple and purified the courts. ⁴⁹* They made new sacred vessels and brought the lampstand, the altar of incense, and the table into the temple. ⁵⁰* Then they burned incense on the altar and lighted the lamps on the lampstand, and these illuminated the temple. ⁵¹ They also put loaves on the table and hung up the curtains. Thus they finished all the work they had undertaken.

⁵²† Early in the morning on the twenty-fifth day of the ninth month, that is, the month of Chislev, in the year one hundred and forty-eight, ⁵³* they arose and offered sacrifice according to the law on the new altar of holocausts that they had made. ⁵⁴ On the anniversary of the day on which the Gentiles had defiled it, on that very day it was reconsecrated with songs, harps, flutes, and cymbals. ⁵⁵ All the people prostrated themselves and adored and praised Heaven, who had given them success.

⁵⁶ For eight days they celebrated the dedication of the altar and joyfully offered holocausts and sac-

?did you KNOW?

Hanukkah

Hanukkah, or the feast of dedication, is a joyful eight-day celebration in the month of Chislev (December). On each night of the festival, a candle is lit in joyful remembrance of the Maccabees' rededication of the Temple in Jerusalem after it was robbed and desecrated by Antiochus IV Epiphanes (1 Mc 4, 56). Even more deeply, the candlelight symbolizes the gratitude of the Jewish people for the survival, often against great odds, of their age-old faith.

▸ 1 Mc 4, 52–59

4, 29: *Beth-zur:* an important frontier city in the mountain area, fifteen miles southwest of Jerusalem. Its inhabitants were sympathetic to the Maccabees and refused to receive Lysias.

4, 35: According to 2 Mc 11, 13–15, peace negotiations followed between Lysias and Judas.

4, 36: *The sanctuary:* the whole temple area with its walls, courts and outbuildings, to be distinguished from the temple proper, the oblong edifice with porch, main room and inner shrine.

4, 52: *Twenty-fifth day of the ninth month . . . in the year one hundred and forty-eight:* December 14, 164 B.C.

4, 30: 1 Sm 17, 48ff.	**4, 47:** Ex 20, 25.
4, 36–59: 2 Mc 10, 1–8.	**4, 49:** Ex 25, 23–39; 30, 1–6.
4, 38: Ps 74, 2–7.	**4, 50:** Ex 30, 7ff.
4, 44: 1 Kgs 8, 64.	**4, 53.56:** Ex 30, 10; Ez 43,
4, 45: 1 Mc 6, 7.	18–27.

rifices of deliverance and praise. [57] They ornamented the façade of the temple with gold crowns and shields; they repaired the gates and the priests' chambers and furnished them with doors. [58] There was great joy among the people now that the disgrace of the Gentiles was removed. [59]*† Then Judas and his brothers and the entire congregation of Israel decreed that the days of the dedication of the altar should be observed with joy and gladness on the anniversary every year for eight days, from the twenty-fifth day of the month Chislev.

[60] At that time they built high walls and strong towers around Mount Zion, to prevent the Gentiles from coming and trampling over it as they had done before. [61] Judas also placed a garrison there to protect it, and likewise fortified Beth-zur, that the people might have a stronghold facing Idumea.

Punishment of Hostile Acts

5 [1]*† When the Gentiles round about heard that the altar had been rebuilt and the sanctuary consecrated as before, they were very angry. [2] So they decided to destroy the descendants of Jacob who were among them, and they began to massacre and persecute the people. [3]*† Then Judas attacked the sons of Esau at Akrabattene in Idumea, because they were blockading Israel; he defeated them heavily, overcame and despoiled them. [4]† He also remembered the malice of the sons of Baean, who had become a snare and a stumblingblock to the people by ambushing them along the roads. [5] He forced them to take refuge in towers, which he besieged; he vowed their annihilation and burned down the towers along with all the persons in them. [6]† Then he crossed over to the Ammonites, where he found a strong army and a large body of people with Timothy as their leader. [7] He fought many battles with them, routed them, and struck them down. [8] After seizing Jazer and its villages, he returned to Judea.

Liberation of Galilean Jews

[9] The Gentiles in Gilead assembled to attack and destroy the Israelites who were in their territory; these then fled to the stronghold of Dathema. [10] They sent a letter to Judas and his brothers saying: "The Gentiles around us have combined against us to destroy us, [11] and they are preparing to come and seize this stronghold to which we have fled. Timothy is the leader of their army. [12] Come at once and rescue us from them, for many of us have fallen. [13]* All our kinsmen who were among the Tobiads have been killed; the Gentiles have carried away their wives and children and their goods, and they have slain there about a thousand men."

[14] While they were reading this letter, suddenly other messengers, in torn clothes, arrived from Galilee to deliver a similar message: [15]† that the inhabitants of Ptolemais, Tyre, and Sidon, and the whole of Gentile Galilee had joined forces to destroy them. [16] When Judas and the people heard this, a great assembly convened to consider what they should do for their unfortunate kinsmen who were being attacked by enemies.

[17] Judas said to his brother Simon: "Choose men for yourself, and go, rescue your kinsmen in Galilee; I and my brother Jonathan will go to Gilead."

[18] In Judea he left Joseph, son of Zechariah, and Azariah, leader of the people, with the rest of the army to guard it. [19] "Take charge of these people," he commanded them, "but do not fight against the Gentiles until we return." [20] Three thousand men were allotted to Simon, to go into Galilee, and eight thousand men to Judas, for Gilead.

[21] Simon went into Galilee and fought many battles with the Gentiles. They were crushed before him, [22] and he pursued them to the very gate of Ptolemais. About three thousand men of the Gentiles fell, and he gathered their spoils. [23] He took with him the Jews who were in Galilee and in Arbatta, with their wives and children and all that they had, and brought them to Judea with great rejoicing.

Rescue in Gilead

[24]* Judas Maccabeus and his brother Jonathan crossed the Jordan and marched for three days through the desert. [25]† There they met some Nabateans, who received them peacefully and told them all that had happened to the Jews in Gilead: [26] "Many of them have been imprisoned in Bozrah,

---

4, 59: *Days of the dedication . . . Chislev:* institution of the feast of Hannukah, also called the feast of Dedication (Jn 10, 22). Josephus Flavius calls it the feast of Lights.
5, 1: The events of this chapter occurred within the year 163 B.C.
5, 3: *Akrabattene:* a district southwest of the Dead Sea.
5, 4: *Sons of Baean:* 2 Mc 10, 15–23 calls them simply Idumeans.
5, 6ff: This summary anticipates the order of events and would fit better between vv 36 and 37. It corresponds to 2 Mc 12, 17–23. The action was probably a reprisal for the massacre referred to in v 13. Timothy was the Seleucid governor of Transjordan. *Jazer:* a town on the road from the Jordan to Amman.
5, 15: *Ptolemais:* Hebrew Acco (Jgs 1, 31), modern Acre, on the coast north of Haifa.

5, 25: *Nabateans:* an Arab people who acquired wealth and power as caravan merchants in the final two centuries B.C. They settled down, established Petra as their capital, and for a time controlled all of Transjordan, even as far as Damascus. It was from a Nabatean governor that St. Paul escaped about 38 A.D. (2 Cor 11, 32f).

4, 59: Jn 10, 22.　　　　　5, 13: 2 Mc 12, 17.
5, 1f: 1 Mc 13, 6.　　　　　5, 24–36: 2 Mc 12, 10ff.
5, 3ff: 2 Mc 10, 15–23.

in Bosor near Alema, in Chaspho, Maked, and Carnaim"—all of these are large, fortified cities— [27] "and some have been imprisoned in the other cities of Gilead. Tomorrow their enemies plan to attack the strongholds and to seize and destroy all these people in one day."

[28] Thereupon Judas suddenly changed direction with his army, marched across the desert to Bozrah, and captured the city. He slaughtered all the male population, took all their possessions, and set fire to the city. [29] He led his army from that place by night, and they marched toward the stronghold of Dathema. [30] When morning came, they looked ahead and saw a countless multitude of people, with ladders and devices for capturing the stronghold, and beginning to attack the people within. [31] When Judas perceived that the struggle had begun and that the noise of the battle was resounding to heaven with trumpet blasts and loud shouting, [32] he said to the men of his army, "Fight for our kinsmen today."

[33] He came up behind them with three columns blowing their trumpets and shouting in prayer. [34] When the army of Timothy realized that it was Maccabeus, they fell back before him, and he inflicted on them a crushing defeat. About eight thousand of their men fell that day. [35] Then he turned toward Alema and attacked and captured it; he killed all the male population, plundered the place, and burned it down. [36] From there he moved on and took Chaspho, Maked, Bosor, and the other cities of Gilead.

[37]* After these events Timothy assembled another army and camped opposite Raphon, on the other side of the stream. [38] Judas sent men to spy on the camp, and they reported to him: "All the Gentiles around us have rallied to him, making a very large force; [39] they have also hired Arabs to help them, and have camped beyond the stream, ready to attack you." So Judas went forward to attack them.

[40]* As Judas and his army were approaching the running stream, Timothy said to the officers of his army: "If he crosses over to us first, we shall not be able to resist him; he will certainly defeat us. [41] But if he is afraid and camps on the other side of the river, we will cross over to him and defeat him."

[42] But when Judas reached the running stream, he stationed the officers of the people beside the stream and gave them this order: "Do not allow any man to pitch a tent; all must go into battle." [43] He was the first to cross to the attack, with all the people behind him, and the Gentiles were crushed before them; they threw away their arms and fled to the temple enclosure at Carnaim. [44]* The Jews captured that city and burnt the enclosure with all who were in it. So Carnaim was subdued, and Judas met with no more resistance.

[45] Then he assembled all the Israelites, great and small, who were in Gilead, with their wives and children and their goods, a great crowd of people, to go into the land of Judah. [46]*† When they reached Ephron, a large and strongly fortified city along the way, they found it impossible to encircle it on either the right or the left; they would have to march right through it. [47]* But the men in the city shut them out and blocked up the gates with stones. [48] Then Judas sent them his peaceful message: "We wish to cross your territory in order to reach our own; no one will harm you; we will only march through." But they would not open to him.

[49] So Judas ordered a proclamation to be made in the camp that everyone make an attack from the place where he was. [50] When the men of the army took up their positions, he assaulted the city all that day and night, and it was delivered to him. [51] He slaughtered every male, razed and plundered the city, and passed through it over the slain.

[52] Then they crossed the Jordan to the great plain in front of Beth-shan; [53] and Judas kept rounding up the stragglers and encouraging the people the whole way, until he reached the land of Judah. [54] They ascended Mount Zion in joy and gladness and offered holocausts, because not one of them had fallen; they returned in safety.

Joseph and Azariah Defeated

[55] During the time that Judas and Jonathan were in the land of Gilead, and Simon his brother was in Galilee opposite Ptolemais, [56] Joseph, son of Zechariah, and Azariah, the leaders of the army, heard about the brave deeds and the fighting that they were doing. [57] They said, "Let us also make a name for ourselves by going out and fighting against the Gentiles around us."

[58] They gave orders to the men of their army who were with them, and marched toward Jamnia. [59] But Gorgias and his men came out of the city to meet them in battle. [60] Joseph and Azariah were beaten, and were pursued to the frontiers of Judea, and about two thousand Israelites fell that day. [61] It was a bad defeat for the people, because they had not obeyed Judas and his brothers, thinking that they would do brave deeds. [62] But they did not belong to the family of those men to whom it was granted to achieve Israel's salvation. [63] The valiant

---

5, 37–44: 2 Mc 12, 20–26.
  5, 40: 1 Sm 14, 9f.
  5, 44: 2 Mc 12, 21.

5, 46–54: 2 Mc 12, 27–31.
  5, 47: Nm 20, 17–21; 21, 21–25.

Judas and his brothers were greatly renowned in all Israel and among all the Gentiles, wherever their name was heard; 64 and men gathered about them and praised them.

65† Then Judas and his brothers went out and attacked the sons of Esau in the country toward the south; he took Hebron and its villages, and he destroyed its strongholds and burned the towers around it. 66 He then set out for the land of the Philistines and passed through Marisa. 67 At that time some priests fell in battle who had gone out rashly to fight in their desire to distinguish themselves. 68 Judas then turned toward Azotus in the land of the Philistines. He destroyed their altars and burned the statues of their gods; and after plundering their cities he returned to the land of Judah.

Defeat and Death of Antiochus IV

6 1*† As King Antiochus was traversing the inland provinces, he heard that in Persia there was a city called Elymais, famous for its wealth in silver and gold, 2 and that its temple was very rich, containing gold helmets, breastplates, and weapons left there by Alexander, son of Philip, king of Macedon, the first king of the Greeks. 3 He went therefore and tried to capture and pillage the city. But he could not do so, because his plan became known to the people of the city 4 who rose up in battle against him. So he retreated and in great dismay withdrew from there to return to Babylon.

5 While he was in Persia, a messenger brought him news that the armies sent into the land of Judah had been put to flight; 6 that Lysias had gone at first with a strong army and been driven back by the Israelites; that they had grown strong by reason of the arms, men, and abundant possessions taken from the armies they had destroyed; 7* that they had pulled down the Abomination which he had built upon the altar in Jerusalem; and that they had surrounded with high walls both the sanctuary, as it had been before, and his city of Beth-zur.

8 When the king heard this news, he was struck with fear and very much shaken. Sick with grief because his designs had failed, he took to his bed. 9 There he remained many days, overwhelmed with sorrow, for he knew he was going to die. 10 So he called in all his Friends and said to them: "Sleep has departed from my eyes, for my heart is

sinking with anxiety. 11 I said to myself: 'Into what tribulation have I come, and in what floods of sorrow am I now! 12 Yet I was kindly and beloved in my rule.' But I now recall the evils I did in Jerusalem, when I carried away all the vessels of gold and silver that were in it, and for no cause gave orders that the inhabitants of Judah be destroyed. 13 I know that this is why these evils have overtaken me; and now I am dying, in bitter grief, in a foreign land."

14 Then he summoned Philip, one of his Friends, and put him in charge of his whole kingdom. 15 He gave him his crown, his robe, and his signet ring, so that he might guide the king's son Antiochus and bring him up to be king. 16† King Antiochus died in Persia in the year one hundred and forty-nine.

The Citadel Besieged

17*† When Lysias learned that the king was dead, he set up the king's son Antiochus, whom he had reared as a child, to be king in his place; and he gave him the title Eupator.

18* The men in the citadel were hemming in Israel around the sanctuary, continually trying to harm them and to strengthen the Gentiles. 19 But Judas planned to destroy them, and called all the people together to besiege them. 20† So in the year one hundred and fifty they assembled and stormed the citadel, for which purpose he constructed catapults and other devices. 21 Some of the besieged escaped, joined by impious Israelites; 22 they went to the king and said:

"How long will you fail to do justice and avenge our kinsmen? 23 We agreed to serve your father and to follow his orders and obey his edicts. 24 And for this the sons of our people have become our enemies; they have put to death as many of us as they could find and have plundered our estates. 25 They have acted aggressively not only against us, but throughout their whole territory. 26 Look! They have now besieged the citadel in Jerusalem in order to capture it, and they have fortified the sanctuary and Beth-zur. 27 Unless you quickly forestall them, they will do even worse things than these, and you will not be able to stop them."

Campaign against Judas

28* When the king heard this he was angry, and he called together all his Friends, the officers of his

5, 65: Sons of Esau: Idumeans.
6, 1: Elymais: the mountainous region of Elam, north of the Persian Gulf. This section continues the story from 1 Mc 3, 37 and pertains to events preceding those in 1 Mc 4, 37ff.
6, 16: The year one hundred and forty-nine: September 22, 164, to October 9, 163 B.C. A Babylonian list of the Seleucid kings indicates that Antiochus died in November or early December of 164.
6, 17: The king's son Antiochus: Antiochus V Eupator, then about nine years old. He was in Antioch, still in the charge of Lysias, who proceeded to govern and wage wars in his name. Both were put to

death two years later, when Demetrius, brother of Antiochus IV, arrived to claim the kingship; cf 1 Mc 7, 1ff.
6, 20: The year one hundred and fifty: October, 163, to September, 162 B.C.

6, 1–13: 2 Mc 1, 12–17; 9, 1–29.
6, 7: 1 Mc 1, 54; 4, 41ff.60f.
6, 17: 2 Mc 10, 10f.
6, 18: 1 Mc 1, 33ff.
6, 28–54: 2 Mc 13, 1–23.

army, and the commanders of the cavalry.* ²⁹ Mercenary forces also came to him from other kingdoms and from the islands of the seas. ³⁰ His army numbered a hundred thousand foot-soldiers, twenty thousand cavalry, and thirty-two elephants trained for war. ³¹ They passed through Idumea and camped before Beth-zur. For many days they attacked it; they constructed siege-devices, but the besieged made a sortie and burned these, and they fought bravely.

³² Then Judas marched away from the citadel and moved his camp to Beth-zechariah, on the way to the king's camp. ³³ The king, rising before dawn, moved his force hastily along the road to Beth-zechariah; and the armies prepared for battle, while the trumpets sounded. ³⁴ They made the elephants drunk on grape and mulberry wine to provoke them to fight. ³⁵ The beasts were distributed along the phalanxes, each elephant having assigned to it a thousand men in coats of mail, with bronze helmets, and five hundred picked cavalry. ³⁶ These anticipated the beast wherever it was; and wherever it moved, they moved too and never left it. ³⁷ A strong wooden tower covering each elephant, and fastened to it by a harness, held, besides the Indian mahout, three soldiers who fought from it. ³⁸ The remaining cavalry were stationed on one or the other of the two flanks of the army, to harass the enemy and to be protected from the phalanxes. ³⁹ When the sun shone on the gold and bronze shields, the mountains gleamed with their brightness and blazed like flaming torches. ⁴⁰ Part of the king's army extended over the heights, while some were on low ground, but they marched forward steadily and in good order. ⁴¹ All who heard the noise of their numbers, the tramp of their marching, and the clashing of the arms, trembled; for the army was very great and strong.

⁴² Judas with his army advanced to fight, and six hundred men of the king's army fell. ⁴³* Eleazar, called Avaran, saw one of the beasts bigger than any of the others and covered with royal armor, and he thought the king must be on it. ⁴⁴ So he gave up his life to save his people and win an everlasting name for himself. ⁴⁵ He dashed up to it in the middle of the phalanx, killing men right and left, so that they fell back from him on both sides. ⁴⁶ He ran right under the elephant and stabbed it in the belly, killing it. The beast fell to the ground on top of him, and he died there.

⁴⁷ When the Jews saw the strength of the royal army and the ardor of its forces, they retreated from them. ⁴⁸* A part of the king's army went up to

A Just War

did you KNOW?

Have you ever believed in something so strongly that you could justify a war to protect it? The Maccabees did, and they led a violent resistance against terrible religious persecution.

The Catholic church teaches that "all citizens and all governments are obliged to work for the avoidance of war" (*Catechism*, no. 2308). But it also teaches that there can be occasions for legitimate defense by military force (no. 2309), or what is sometimes called a just war. The criteria for a just war are as follows:

- All other means to avoid war must be exhausted.
- The damage done by the aggressor must be grave and certain.
- There must be serious prospects of success.
- The use of arms must not produce evils that are greater than the evil to be eliminated.

No Catholic Christian can participate in good conscience in any war that does not meet all these criteria.

War is not the answer; peace is. But at times in history, some Christians have felt that the only response to a grave injustice was violent resistance. However, no Christian is obligated to fight in a war if doing so goes against his or her conscience—although he or she may be required to serve the community in some other way—and nonviolent resistance is always an option (see "Nonviolent Resistance," near 2 Mc 7, 42).

Jerusalem to attack them, and the king established camps in Judea and at Mount Zion. ⁴⁹*† He made peace with the men of Beth-zur, and they evacuated the city, because they had no food there to enable them to stand a siege, for that was a sabbath year in the land. ⁵⁰ The king took Beth-zur and stationed a garrison there to hold it. ⁵¹ For many days he besieged the sanctuary, setting up artillery and ma-

---

6, 49: *A sabbath year in the land:* when sowing and reaping were prohibited (Ex 23, 10f; Lv 25, 2–7). The year without a harvest (autumn of 164 to autumn of 163) was followed by a food shortage.

6, 28ff: 2 Mc 13, 1f.
6, 43: 2 Mc 13, 15.

6, 48f: 2 Mc 13, 22–23.
6, 49: Lv 25, 2.

chines, fire-throwers, catapults and mechanical bows for shooting arrows and slingstones. 52 The Jews countered by setting up machines of their own, and kept up the fight a long time. 53 But there were no provisions in the storerooms, because it was the seventh year, and the tide-over provisions had been eaten up by those who had been rescued from the Gentiles and brought to Judea. 54 Few men remained in the sanctuary; the rest scattered, each to his own home, for the famine was too much for them.

Peace Treaty

55* Lysias heard that Philip, whom King Antiochus, before his death, had appointed to train his son Antiochus to be king, 56 had returned from Persia and Media with the army that accompanied the king, and that he was seeking to take over the government. 57* So he hastily resolved to withdraw. He said to the king, the leaders of the army, and the soldiers: "We are growing weaker every day, our provisions are scanty, the place we are besieging is strong, and it is our duty to take care of the affairs of the kingdom. 58 Therefore let us now come to terms with these men, and make peace with them and all their nation. 59 Let us grant them freedom to live according to their own laws as formerly; it was on account of their laws, which we abolished, that they became angry and did all these things."

60 The proposal found favor with the king and the leaders; he sent peace terms to the Jews, and they accepted. 61 So the king and the leaders swore an oath to them, and on these terms they evacuated the fortification. 62 But when the king entered Mount Zion and saw how the place was fortified, he broke the oath he had sworn and gave orders for the encircling wall to be destroyed. 63 Then he departed in haste and returned to Antioch, where he found Philip in possession of the city. He fought against him and took the city by force.

Expedition of Bacchides and Alcimus

7 1*† In the year one hundred and fifty-one, Demetrius, son of Seleucus, set out from Rome, arrived with a few men in a city on the seacoast, and began to rule there. 2 As he was preparing to enter the royal palace of his ancestors, the soldiers seized Antiochus and Lysias to bring them to him. 3 When he was informed of this, he said, "Do not show me

their faces." 4 So the soldiers killed them, and Demetrius sat on the royal throne.

5† Then all the lawless and impious men of Israel came to him. They were led by Alcimus, who desired to be high priest. 6 They made this accusation to the king against the people: "Judas and his brothers have destroyed all your friends and have driven us out of our country. 7 So now, send a man whom you trust to go and see all the havoc Judas has done to us and to the king's land, and let him punish them and all their supporters."

8 Then the king chose Bacchides, one of the King's Friends, governor of West-of-Euphrates, a great man in the kingdom, and faithful to the king. 9* He sent him and the impious Alcimus, to whom he granted the high priesthood, with orders to take revenge on the Israelites. 10 They set out and, on arriving in the land of Judah with a great army, sent messengers who spoke deceitfully to Judas and his brothers in peaceful terms. 11 But these paid no attention to their words, seeing that they had come with a great army. 12 A group of scribes, however, gathered about Alcimus and Bacchides to ask for a just agreement. 13* The Hasideans were the first among the Israelites to seek peace with them, 14 for they said, "A priest of the line of Aaron has come with the army, and he will not do us any wrong." 15 He spoke with them peacefully and swore to them, "We will not try to injure you or your friends." 16 So they trusted him. But he arrested sixty of them and killed them in one day, according to the text of Scripture:

17* "The flesh of your saints they have strewn,
    and their blood they have shed round
        about Jerusalem,
    and there was no one to bury them."

18 Then fear and dread of them came upon all the people, who said: "There is no truth or justice among them; they violated the agreement and the oath that they swore."

19† Bacchides withdrew from Jerusalem and pitched his camp in Beth-zaith. He had many of the men arrested who deserted to him, throwing them into the great pit. 20 He handed the province over to Alcimus, leaving troops to help him, while he himself returned to the king.

---

† **7, 1ff:** *The year one hundred and fifty-one:* the spring of 161 B.C. Demetrius, son of Seleucus, was the lawful heir to the kingdom; but when only nine years old, he was taken as a hostage at Rome in place of his uncle, who ruled as Antiochus IV Epiphanes. At the age of twenty-five Demetrius fled secretly from Rome and, with the support of the Syrians, overcame his rival Antiochus V and put him to death. *The royal palace:* at Antioch.

7, 5f: *Alcimus:* a renegade Jew hostile to the Maccabees, who became high priest after the death of Menelaus (2 Mc 14, 3). He received confirmation in his office from the new King Demetrius (v 9),

and brought malicious charges against Judas and his brothers and the people (v 6). He wrought more evils on the Israelites than the Gentiles had done (v 23).

7, 19: *Beth-zaith:* about three miles north of Beth-zur and twelve miles south of Jerusalem.

6, 55–63: 2 Mc 13, 23–26.   7, 9ff: 2 Mc 14, 46.
6, 57: 2 Mc 11, 13ff.   7, 13f: 1 Mc 2, 42.
7, 1–7: 2 Mc 14, 1–11.   7, 17: Ps 79, 1ff.

²¹ Alcimus spared no pains to maintain his high priesthood, ²² and all those who were disturbing their people gathered about him. They took possession of the land of Judah and caused great distress in Israel. ²³ When Judas saw all the evils that Alcimus and his men were bringing upon the Israelites, more than even the Gentiles had done, ²⁴ he went about all the borders of Judea and took revenge on the men who had deserted, preventing them from going out into the country. ²⁵ But when Alcimus saw that Judas and his followers were gaining strength and realized that he could not oppose them, he returned to the king and accused them of grave crimes.

Defeat of Nicanor

²⁶* Then the king sent Nicanor, one of his famous officers, who was a bitter enemy of Israel, with orders to destroy the people. ²⁷† Nicanor came to Jerusalem with a large force and deceitfully sent to Judas and his brothers this peaceable message: ²⁸ "Let there be no fight between me and you. I will come with a few men to meet you peaceably."

²⁹ So he came to Judas, and they greeted one another peaceably. But Judas' enemies were prepared to seize him. ³⁰* When he became aware that Nicanor had come to him with treachery in mind, Judas was afraid and would not meet him again. ³¹† When Nicanor saw that his plan had been discovered, he went out to fight Judas near Capharsalama. ³² About five hundred men of Nicanor's army fell; the rest fled to the City of David.

³³* After this, Nicanor went up to Mount Zion. Some of the priests from the sanctuary and some of the elders of the people came out to greet him peaceably and to show him the holocaust that was being offered for the king. ³⁴† But he mocked and ridiculed them, defiled them, and spoke disdainfully. ³⁵ In a rage he swore: "If Judas and his army are not delivered to me at once, when I return victorious I will burn this temple down." He went

away in great anger. ³⁶* The priests, however, went in and stood before the altar and the sanctuary. They wept and said: ³⁷ "You have chosen this house to bear your name, to be a house of prayer and petition for your people. ³⁸ Take revenge on this man and his army, and let them fall by the sword. Remember their blasphemies, and do not let them continue."

³⁹ Nicanor left Jerusalem and pitched his camp at Beth-horon, where the Syrian army joined him. ⁴⁰† But Judas camped in Adasa with three thousand men. Here Judas uttered this prayer: ⁴¹* "When they who were sent by the king blasphemed, your angel went out and killed a hundred and eighty-five thousand of them. ⁴²* In the same way, crush this army before us today, and let the rest know that Nicanor spoke wickedly against your sanctuary; judge him according to his wickedness."

⁴³* The armies met in battle on the thirteenth day of the month Adar. Nicanor's army was crushed, and he himself was the first to fall in the battle. ⁴⁴ When his army saw that Nicanor was dead, they threw down their arms and fled. ⁴⁵ The Jews pursued them a day's journey, from Adasa to near Gazara, blowing the trumpets behind them as signals. ⁴⁶ From all the surrounding villages of Judea people came out and closed in on them. They hemmed them in, and all the enemies fell by the sword; not a single one escaped.

⁴⁷ Then the Jews collected the spoils and the booty; they cut off Nicanor's head and his right arm, which he had lifted up so arrogantly. These they brought to Jerusalem and displayed there. ⁴⁸ The people rejoiced greatly, and observed that day as a great festival. ⁴⁹† They decreed that it should be observed every year on the thirteenth of Adar. ⁵⁰† And for a short time the land of Judah was quiet.

Treaty with the Romans

8 ¹† Judas had heard of the reputation of the Romans. They were valiant fighters and acted

---

† **7, 27:** *Nicanor . . . deceitfully sent to Judas:* a more favorable picture of Nicanor, as an honest man who became a personal friend of Judas, is given in 2 Mc 14, 17–25. Their friendship was broken by the intrigues of Alcimus (2 Mc 14, 26–30).

7, 31: *Caphar-salama:* a village seven miles north-northwest of Jerusalem, on the road leading to Beth-horon.

7, 34: *Defiled them:* spitting on the priests caused them to become legally defiled.

7, 40: *Adasa:* a village southeast of Caphar-salama.

7, 49: *The thirteenth of Adar:* March 27, 160 B.C. This day in the Jewish calendar was called the "Day of Nicanor" (2 Mc 15, 36), but it was not long celebrated by the Jews.

7, 50: *A short time:* about one month following the death of Nicanor. After that began the attack of Bacchides resulting in the death of Judas (1 Mc 9, 1–18).

8, 1: This chapter contains the account of the embassy which Judas sent to Rome, probably before the death of Nicanor, to conclude

a treaty of alliance between Rome and the Jewish nation. Without precise chronology, the pertinent data are gathered into a unified whole.

The image of the Roman Republic greatly impressed the smaller Eastern peoples seeking support against their overlords (1–16), because of Roman success in war (2–11) and effective aid to their allies (12–13). Numerous interventions by Rome in the politics of the Near East bear witness to its power and prestige in the second century B.C. Cf 1 Mc 1, 10; 7, 2; 12, 3; 15, 15–24; 2 Mc 11, 34. With the Roman control of Palestine in 63 B.C., the Republic and later the Empire became heartily detested. The eulogy of Rome in this chapter is one of the reasons why 1 Maccabees was not preserved by the Palestinian Jews of the century that followed.

7, 26f: 1 Mc 3, 38; 2 Mc 8, 9;	7, 36: Jl 2, 17.
14, 12f.	7, 41f: 2 Mc 8, 19; 15, 22ff.
7, 30: 2 Mc 14, 30.	7, 42: Is 37, 36ff.
7, 33–38: 2 Mc 14, 31–36.	7, 43: 2 Mc 15, 25–35.

amiably to all who took their side. They established a friendly alliance with all who applied to them. [2]† He was also told of their battles and the brave deeds that they had performed against the Gauls, conquering them and forcing them to pay tribute. [3] They had gotten possession of the silver and gold mines in Spain, [4] and by planning and persistence had conquered the whole country, although it was very remote from their own. They had crushed the kings who had come against them from the far corners of the earth and had inflicted on them severe defeat, and the rest paid tribute to them every year. [5]† Philip and Perseus, king of the Macedonians, and the others who opposed them in battle had been overwhelmed and subjugated. [6]† Antiochus the Great, king of Asia, who had fought against them with a hundred and twenty elephants and with cavalry and chariots and a very great army, had been defeated by them. [7] They had taken him alive and obliged him and the kings who succeeded him to pay a heavy tribute, to give hostages and a section of [8]† Lycia, Mysia, and Lydia from among their best provinces. The Romans took these from him and gave them to King Eumenes. [9]† When the men of Greece had planned to come and destroy them, [10] the Romans discovered it, and sent against the Greeks a single general who made war on them. Many were wounded and fell, and the Romans took their wives and children captive. They plundered them, took possession of their land, tore down their strongholds and reduced them to slavery even to this day. [11] All the other kingdoms and islands that had ever opposed them they destroyed and enslaved; [12] with their friends, however, and those who relied on them, they maintained friendship. They had conquered kings both far and near, and all who heard of their fame were afraid of them. [13] In truth, those whom they desired to help to a kingdom became kings, and those whom they wished to depose they deposed; and they were greatly exalted. [14] Yet with all this, none of them put on a crown or wore purple as a display of grandeur. [15] They had made for themselves a senate

house, and every day three hundred and twenty men took counsel, deliberating on all that concerned the people and their well-being. [16]† They entrusted their government to one man every year, to rule over their entire country, and they all obeyed that one, and there was no envy or jealousy among them.

[17]* So Judas chose Eupolemus, son of John, son of Accos, and Jason, son of Eleazar, and sent them to Rome to establish an alliance of friendship with them. [18] He did this to get rid of the yoke, for it was obvious that the kingdom of the Greeks was subjecting Israel to slavery. [19] After making a very long journey to Rome, the envoys entered the senate and spoke as follows: [20] "Judas, called Maccabeus, and his brothers, with the Jewish people, have sent us to you to make a peaceful alliance with you, and to enroll ourselves among your allies and friends." [21] The proposal pleased the Romans, [22]*† and this is a copy of the reply they inscribed on bronze tablets and sent to Jerusalem, to remain there with the Jews as a record of peace and alliance:

[23] "May it be well with the Romans and the Jewish nation at sea and on land forever; may sword and enemy be far from them. [24] But if war is first made on Rome, or any of its allies in any of their dominions, [25] the Jewish nation will help them wholeheartedly, as the occasion shall demand; [26] and to those who wage war they shall not give nor provide grain, arms, money, or ships; this is Rome's decision. They shall fulfill their obligations without receiving any recompense. [27] In the same way, if war is made first on the Jewish nation, the Romans will help them willingly, as the occasion shall demand, [28] and to those who are attacking them there shall not be given grain, arms, money, or ships; this is Rome's decision. They shall fulfill their obligations without deception. [29] On these terms the Romans have made an agreement with the Jewish people. [30] But if both parties hereafter decide to add or take away anything, they shall do as they choose, and whatever they shall add or take away shall be valid.

†——
8, 2: *Gauls:* probably the Celts of northern Italy and southern France, subdued by the Romans in 222 B.C., and again in 200–191 B.C.; but perhaps also those in Asia Minor (the Galatians), whom the Romans defeated in 189 B.C.

8, 5: *Philip:* Philip V of Macedonia, defeated by a Graeco-Roman alliance at Cynoscephalae in 197 B.C. Perseus, his son, was defeated at Pydna in 168 B.C., and died a prisoner. With this, the kingdom of Macedonia came to an end.

8, 6: *Antiochus:* Antiochus III, greatest of the Seleucid kings. He was defeated at Magnesia in 190 B.C. By the Treaty of Apamea in 189, he was obliged to pay Rome a crushing indemnity of 15,000 talents. It was the weakening of Antiochene power and the growing military and economic influence of Rome that led Antiochus IV to adopt the policy of political, religious and cultural unification of Syria and Palestine.

8, 8: *Lycia, Mysia:* regions in western Asia Minor. These names are restored here by conjectural emendation; the Greek text has "India, Media," most likely through scribal error. *Eumenes:* Eumenes II

(197–158), king of Pergamum, an ally of Rome who benefited greatly from Antiochus' losses.

8, 9f: The revolt of the Achaean League, inserted here, occurred in 146 B.C., after Judas' time. It was crushed by the Roman consul Lucius Mummius and marked the end of Greek independence. The author regards all Greeks as the enemies of God.

8, 16: *They entrusted their government to one man:* actually the Roman Republic always had two consuls as joint heads of the government. Presumably, a single one dealt with embassies and answered letters, hence the impression the Jews received; cf 1 Mc 15, 16.

8, 22: *The reply . . . on bronze tablets and sent to Jerusalem:* the decree of the Senate would be inscribed on bronze and kept in the Roman Capitol, with only a copy in letter form sent to Jerusalem. The translation of the decree into Hebrew and then into Greek, as found here in 1 Maccabees, may have occasioned this error.

*——
8, 17: 1 Mc 12, 1f; 15, 15–22.   8, 22: 1 Mc 14, 18.

31 "Moreover, concerning the wrongs that King Demetrius has done to them, we have written to him thus: 'Why have you made your yoke heavy upon our friends and allies the Jews? 32 If they complain about you again, we will do them justice and make war on you by land and sea.' "

Invasion of Judah

9 1 When Demetrius heard that Nicanor and his army had fallen in battle, he again sent Bacchides and Alcimus into the land of Judah, along with the right wing of his army. 2† They took the road to Galilee, and camping opposite the ascent at Arbela, they captured it and killed many people. 3† In the first month of the year one hundred and fifty-two, they encamped against Jerusalem. 4 Then they set out for Berea with twenty thousand men and two thousand cavalry. 5 Judas, with three thousand picked men, had camped at Elasa. 6 When his men saw the great number of the troops, they were very much afraid, and many slipped away from the camp, until only eight hundred men remained.

7 As Judas saw that his army was melting away just when the battle was imminent, he was panic-stricken, because he had no time to gather them together. 8 But in spite of his discouragement, he said to those who remained: "Let us go forward to meet our enemies; perhaps we can put up a good fight against them." 9 They tried to dissuade him, saying: "We certainly cannot. Let us save our lives now, and come back with our kinsmen, and then fight against them. Now we are too few." 10 But Judas said: "Far be it from me to do such a thing as to flee from them! If our time has come, let us die bravely for our kinsmen and not leave a stain upon our glory!"

Death of Judas

11 Then the army of Bacchides moved out of camp and took its position for combat. The cavalry were divided into two squadrons, and the slingers and the archers came on ahead of the army, and all the valiant men were in the front line. 12 Bacchides was on the right wing. Flanked by the two squadrons, the phalanx attacked as they blew their trumpets. Those who were on Judas' side also blew their trumpets. 13 The earth shook with the noise of the armies, and the battle raged from morning until evening. 14 Seeing that Bacchides was on the right, with the main force of his army, Judas, with all the most stouthearted rallying to him, 15† drove back the right wing and pursued them as far as the mountain slopes. 16 But when the men on the left wing saw that the right wing was driven back, they turned and followed Judas and his men, taking them in the rear. 17 The battle was fought desperately, and many on both sides fell wounded. 18 Then Judas fell, and the rest fled.

19 Jonathan and Simon took their brother Judas and buried him in the tomb of their fathers at Modein. 20 All Israel bewailed him in great grief. They mourned for him many days, and they said, 21* "How the mighty one has fallen, the savior of Israel!" 22 The other acts of Judas, his battles, the brave deeds he performed, and his greatness have not been recorded; but they were very many.

IV: Leadership of Jonathan

Bacchides and Jonathan

23 After the death of Judas, the transgressors of the law raised their heads in every part of Israel, and all kinds of evildoers appeared. 24 In those days there was a very great famine, and the country deserted to them. 25 Bacchides chose impious men and made them masters of the country. 26 These sought out and hunted down the friends of Judas and brought them to Bacchides, who punished and derided them. 27 There had not been such great distress in Israel since the time prophets ceased to appear among the people.

28 Then all the friends of Judas came together and said to Jonathan: 29 "Since your brother Judas died, there has been no one like him to oppose our enemies, Bacchides and those who are hostile to our nation. 30 Now therefore we have chosen you today to be our ruler and leader in his place, and to fight our battle." 31 From that moment Jonathan accepted the leadership, and took the place of Judas his brother.

32 When Bacchides learned of it, he sought to kill him. 33† But Jonathan and his brother Simon and all the men with him discovered this, and they fled to the desert of Tekoa and camped by the waters of the pool of Asphar.

9, 2: *They took the road . . . Arbela, they captured it*: this passage is restored, in part, by conjectural emendation. The present Greek text could be translated, "They took the road to Gilgal, and camping opposite Mesaloth at Arbela, they captured it." But Arbela (modern Khirbet Irbid) was in Galilee—on a high hill overlooking the western shore of the Sea of Galilee. Gilgal, on the contrary, was in the Jordan valley near Jericho. "Mesaloth" is probably a corrupt form of a Hebrew word meaning "steps, ascent."

9, 3: *The first month of the year one hundred and fifty-two*: April/May 160 B.C., by the temple calendar.

9, 15: *As far as the mountain slopes*: conjectural emendation. The Greek text has "as far as Mount Azotus"; this is most unlikely. Apparently the Greek translator mistook the Hebrew word *ashdot*, "slopes," for *asdod*, "Azotus."

9, 33: *Tekoa*: Home of the prophet Amos in the wild country above the Dead Sea, southeast of Jerusalem.

9, 34: Omitted, it is a dittography of verse 43.

9, 21: 2 Sam 1, 27.

LIVE IT!

What Makes a Hero?

History is full of heroes, those bigger-than-life men and women like Judas Maccabeus who have made a difference because of their courageous acts and their willingness to take risks that frighten other people. What makes someone a hero? Is each of us capable of heroism?

Someone we have grown up with, who now seems ordinary, could one day be a hero. None of us knows when we could be called on to do something heroic. We need an openness to God's call and a willingness to take a risk—to let go of our fears and to reach deep within ourselves for courage and strength. You may amaze yourself at what you can accomplish in extraordinary situations. The stuff of heroes, of great and brave persons such as Judas Maccabeus, is already within us. We need only to believe in ourselves and believe that God is with us.

You may not end up in a history book or be memorialized in a statue, but you can make a difference in the life of one or perhaps many people. What really counts is to be a hero in the eyes of God.

▸ I Mc 9, 19–22

35*† Jonathan sent his brother as leader of the convoy to ask permission of his friends, the Nabateans, to deposit with them their great quantity of baggage. 36† But the sons of Jambri from Medaba made a raid and seized and carried off John and everything he had. 37 After this, word was brought to Jonathan and his brother Simon: "The sons of Jambri are celebrating a great wedding, and with a large escort they are bringing the bride, the daughter of one of the great princes of Canaan, from Nadabath." 38 Remembering the blood of John their brother, they went up and hid themselves under cover of the mountain. 39 They watched, and suddenly saw a noisy crowd with baggage; the bridegroom and his friends and kinsmen had come out to meet the bride's party with tambourines and musicians and much equipment. 40 The Jews rose up against them from their ambush and killed them. Many fell wounded, and after the survivors fled toward the mountain, all their spoils were taken. 41 Thus the wedding was turned into mourning, and the sound of music into lamentation. 42 Having taken their revenge for the blood of their brother, the Jews returned to the marshes of the Jordan.

43 When Bacchides heard of it, he came on the sabbath to the banks of the Jordan with a large force. 44 Then Jonathan said to his companions, "Let us get up now and fight for our lives, for today is not like yesterday and the day before. 45† The battle is before us, and behind us are the waters of the Jordan on one side, marsh and thickets on the other, and there is no way of escape. 46 Cry out now to Heaven for deliverance from our enemies." 47 When they joined battle, Jonathan raised his arm to strike Bacchides, but Bacchides backed away from him. 48 Jonathan and his men jumped into the Jordan and swam across to the other side, but the enemy did not pursue them across the Jordan. 49 A thousand men on Bacchides' side fell that day.

50† On returning to Jerusalem, Bacchides built strongholds in Judea: the Jericho fortress, as well as Emmaus, Beth-horon, Bethel, Timnath, Pharathon, and Tephon, with high walls and gates and bars. 51 In each he put a garrison to oppose Israel. 52 He fortified the city of Beth-zur, Gazara and the citadel, and put soldiers in them and stores of provisions. 53* He took as hostages the sons of the leaders of the country and put them in custody in the citadel at Jerusalem.

54† In the year one hundred and fifty-three, in the second month, Alcimus ordered the wall of the inner court of the sanctuary to be torn down, thus destroying the work of the prophets. But he only began to tear it down. 55 Just at that time he had a stroke, and his work was interrupted; his mouth was closed and he was paralyzed, so that he could no longer utter a word to give orders concerning his house. 56 Finally he died in great agony. 57 Seeing that Alcimus was dead, Bacchides returned to the king, and the land of Judah was quiet for two years.

---

† 9, 35: *Jonathan sent his brother:* this was John who was called Gaddi (1 Mc 2, 2; cf 9, 36.38).

9, 36: *Medaba:* northeast of the Dead Sea.

9, 45: Jonathan's force was apparently trapped in one of the many oxbows of the lower Jordan. Bacchides had crossed and caught them still on the east bank.

9, 50: These sites constitute a ring on the edges of the province of Judea.

9, 54: *In the year . . . second month:* May 159 B.C.

*

9, 35: 1 Mc 5, 25.   9, 53: 1 Mc 10, 9.

1
M
C

58 Then all the transgressors of the law held a council and said: "Jonathan and his companions are living in peace and security. Now then, let us have Bacchides return, and he will capture all of them in a single night." 59 So they went and took counsel with him. 60 When Bacchides was setting out with a large force, he sent letters secretly to all his allies in Judea, telling them to seize Jonathan and his companions. They were not able to do this, however, because their plot became known. 61 In fact, Jonathan's men seized about fifty of the men of the country who were ringleaders in the mischief and put them to death. 62† Then Jonathan and Simon and their companions withdrew to Bethbasi in the desert; they rebuilt and strengthened its fortifications that had been demolished. 63 When Bacchides learned of this, he gathered together his whole force and sent word to those who were in Judea. 64 He came and pitched his camp before Bethbasi, and constructing siege-machines, he fought against it for many days.

65 Leaving his brother Simon in the city, Jonathan, accompanied by a small group of men, went out into the field. 66 He struck down Odomera and his kinsmen and the sons of Phasiron in their encampment; these men had set out to go up to the siege with their forces. 67 Simon and his men then sallied forth from the city and set fire to the machines. 68 They fought against Bacchides, and he was beaten. This caused him great distress. Because the enterprise he had planned came to naught, 69 he was angry with the lawless men who had advised him to invade the province. He killed many of them and resolved to return to his own country.

70 Jonathan learned of this and sent ambassadors to make peace with him and to obtain the release of the prisoners. 71 He agreed to do as Jonathan had asked. He swore an oath to him that he would never try to injure him for the rest of his life; 72 and he released the prisoners he had previously taken from the land of Judah. He returned to his own country and never came into their territory again.

73† Then the sword ceased in Israel. Jonathan settled in Michmash; he began to judge the people, and he destroyed the impious in Israel.

Revolt of Alexander

10 1† In the year one hundred and sixty, Alexander, who was called Epiphanes,

son of Antiochus, came up and took Ptolemais. He was accepted and began to reign there. 2 When King Demetrius heard of it, he mustered a very large army and marched out to engage him in combat. 3 Demetrius sent a letter to Jonathan written in peaceful terms, to pay him honor; 4 for he said: "Let us be the first to make peace with him, before he makes peace with Alexander against us, 5 since he will remember all the wrongs we have done to him, his brothers, and his nation."

6 So Demetrius authorized Jonathan, as his ally, to gather an army and procure arms; and he ordered that the hostages in the citadel be released to him. 7 Accordingly Jonathan went up to Jerusalem and read the letter to all the people. The men in the citadel 8 were struck with fear when they heard that the king had given him authority to gather an army. 9* They released the hostages to Jonathan, and he gave them back to their parents. 10 Thereafter Jonathan dwelt in Jerusalem, and began to build and restore the city. 11 He ordered the workmen to build the walls and encircle Mount Zion with square stones for its fortification, which they did. 12 The foreigners in the strongholds that Bacchides had built, took flight; 13 each one of them left his place and returned to his own country. 14 Only in Beth-zur did some remain of those who had abandoned the law and the commandments, for they used it as a place of refuge.

Jonathan Supports Alexander

15 King Alexander heard of the promises that Demetrius had made to Jonathan; he was also told of the battles and valiant deeds of Jonathan and his brothers and the troubles that they had endured. 16 He said, "Shall we ever find another man like him? Let us now make him our friend and ally." 17 So he sent Jonathan a letter written in these terms: 18 "King Alexander sends greetings to his brother Jonathan. 19 We have heard of you, that you are a mighty warrior and worthy to be our friend. 20* We have therefore appointed you today to be high priest of your nation; you are to be called the King's Friend, and you are to look after our interests and preserve amity with us." He also sent him a purple robe and a crown of gold.

21† Jonathan put on the sacred vestments in the seventh month of the year one hundred and sixty at the feast of Booths, and he gathered an army and

---

9, 62: *Bethbasi:* two miles east of Bethlehem, and six miles north of Tekoa.

9, 73: *Began to judge:* exercise the governing authority as in the book of Judges. With Jerusalem and the garrison towns (v 50) firmly in Seleucid hands, Jonathan's freedom of action was greatly restricted. Michmash, southeast of Bethel, famous for the exploit of the former Jonathan, son of Saul; cf 1 Sm 14.

10, 1: *The year one hundred and sixty:* 152 B.C. *Alexander . . . Antiochus:* Alexander Balas claimed to be a son of Antiochus IV. He

had the backing of the Romans, who had never forgiven Demetrius for becoming king without their permission. The latter meanwhile had become unpopular with his own people as well as with the Jews.

10, 21: *Jonathan . . . feast of Booths:* Jonathan began to discharge the office of high priest October 23–30, 152 B.C. For seven years after the death of Alcimus there had been no high priest in Jerusalem.

10, 9: 1 Mc 9, 53.   10, 20: 1 Mc 2, 18.

procured many arms. 22 When Demetrius heard of these things, he was distressed and said: 23 "Why have we allowed Alexander to get ahead of us by gaining the friendship of the Jews and thus strengthening himself? 24 I too will write them conciliatory words and offer dignities and gifts, so that they may be an aid to me."

25 So he sent them this message: "King Demetrius sends greetings to the Jewish nation. 26 We have heard how you have kept the treaty with us and continued in our friendship and not gone over to our enemies, and we are glad. 27 Continue, therefore, to keep faith with us, and we will reward you with favors in return for what you do in our behalf. 28 We will grant you many exemptions and will bestow gifts on you.

29* "I now free you, as I also exempt all the Jews, from the tribute, the salt tax, and the crown levies. 30*† Instead of collecting the third of the grain and the half of the fruit of the trees that should be my share, I renounce the right from this day forward. Neither now nor in the future will I collect them from the land of Judah or from the three districts annexed from Samaria. 31 Let Jerusalem and her territory, her tithes and her tolls, be sacred and free from tax. 32 I also yield my authority over the citadel in Jerusalem, and I transfer it to the high priest, that he may put in it such men as he shall choose to guard it. 33 Every one of the Jews who has been carried into captivity from the land of Judah into any part of my kingdom I set at liberty without ransom; and let all their taxes, even those on their cattle, be canceled. 34 Let all feast days, sabbaths, new moon festivals, appointed days, and the three days that precede each feast day, and the three days that follow, be days of immunity and exemption for every Jew in my kingdom. 35 Let no man have authority to exact payment from them or to molest any of them in any matter.

36 "Let thirty thousand Jews be enrolled in the king's army and allowances be given them, as is due to all the king's soldiers. 37 Let some of them be stationed in the king's principal strongholds, and of these let some be given positions of trust in the affairs of the kingdom. Let their superiors and their rulers be taken from among them, and let them follow their own laws, as the king has commanded in the land of Judah.

38 "Let the three districts that have been added to Judea from the province of Samaria be incorporated with Judea so that they may be under one man

and obey no other authority than the high priest. 39 Ptolemais and its confines I give as a present to the sanctuary in Jerusalem for the necessary expenses of the sanctuary. 40 I make a yearly personal grant of fifteen thousand silver shekels out of the royal revenues, from appropriate places. 41 All the additional funds that the officials did not hand over as they had done in the first years, shall henceforth be handed over for the services of the temple. 42 Moreover, the dues of five thousand silver shekels that used to be taken from the revenue of the sanctuary every year shall be canceled, since these funds belong to the priests who perform the services. 43 Whoever takes refuge in the temple of Jerusalem or in any of its precincts, because of money he owes the king, or because of any other debt, shall be released, together with all the goods he possesses in my kingdom. 44 The cost of rebuilding and restoring the structures of the sanctuary shall be covered out of the royal revenue. 45 Likewise the cost of building the walls of Jerusalem and fortifying it all around, and of building walls in Judea, shall be donated from the royal revenue."

46 When Jonathan and the people heard these words, they neither believed nor accepted them, for they remembered the great evil that Demetrius had done in Israel, and how sorely he had afflicted them. 47 They therefore decided in favor of Alexander, for he had been the first to address them peaceably, and they remained his allies for the rest of his life.

48 King Alexander gathered together a large army and encamped opposite Demetrius. 49 The two kings joined battle, and when the army of Demetrius fled, Alexander pursued him, and overpowered his soldiers. 50 He pressed the battle hard until sunset, and Demetrius fell that day.

Treaty of Ptolemy and Alexander

51 Alexander sent ambassadors to Ptolemy, king of Egypt, with this message: 52 "Now that I have returned to my realm, taken my seat on the throne of my fathers, and established my rule by crushing Demetrius and gaining control of my country— 53 for I engaged him in battle, defeated him and his army, and recovered the royal throne— 54 let us now establish friendship with each other. Give me your daughter for my wife; and as your son-in-law, I will give to you and to her gifts worthy of you."

55 King Ptolemy answered in these words: "Happy the day on which you returned to the land of

---

† It was taken for granted that the king, though a Gentile, had the power to appoint one. The Maccabees, though a priestly family, were not of the line of Zadok, and some in Israel regarded Jonathan's tenure as a usurpation.

10, 30: *The three districts annexed from Samaria:* mentioned by

name in 1 Mc 11, 34. The present Greek text, by a scribal error, has added "and Galilee" after "Samaria."

*
10, 29: 1 Mc 11, 28f.35.   **10, 30:** 1 Mc 11, 28.34.

your fathers and took your seat on their royal throne! 56 I will do for you what you have written; but meet me in Ptolemais, so that we may see each other, and I will become your father-in-law as you have proposed."

57† So Ptolemy with his daughter Cleopatra set out from Egypt and came to Ptolemais in the year one hundred and sixty-two. 58 There King Alexander met him, and Ptolemy gave him his daughter Cleopatra in marriage. Their wedding was celebrated at Ptolemais with great splendor according to the custom of kings.

59 King Alexander also wrote to Jonathan to come and meet him. 60* So he went with pomp to Ptolemais, where he met the two kings and gave them and their friends silver and gold and many gifts and thus won their favor. 61 Some pestilent Israelites, transgressors of the law, united against him to accuse him, but the king paid no heed to them. 62 He ordered Jonathan to be divested of his ordinary garments and to be clothed in royal purple; and so it was done. 63 The king also had him seated at his side. He said to his magistrates: "Go with him to the center of the city and make a proclamation that no one is to bring charges against him on any grounds or be troublesome to him in any way."

64* When his accusers saw the honor paid to him in the proclamation, and the purple with which he was clothed, they all fled. 65 The king also honored him by numbering him among his Chief Friends and made him military commander and governor of the province. 66 So Jonathan returned in peace and happiness to Jerusalem.

Victory over Apollonius

67† In the year one hundred and sixty-five, Demetrius, son of Demetrius, came from Crete to the land of his fathers. 68 When King Alexander heard of it he was greatly troubled, and returned to Antioch. 69 Demetrius appointed Apollonius governor of Coelesyria. Having gathered a large army, Apollonius pitched his camp at Jamnia. From there he sent this message to Jonathan the high priest:

70 "You are the only one who resists us. I am laughed at and put to shame on your account. Why are you displaying power against us in the mountains? 71 If you have confidence in your forces, come down now to us in the plain, and let us test each other's strength there; the city forces are on my side. 72 Inquire and learn who I am and who the others are who are helping me. Men say that you cannot make a stand against us because your fathers were twice put to flight in their own land. 73 Now you too will be unable to withstand our cavalry and such a force as this in the plain, where there is not a stone or a pebble or a place to flee."

74 When Jonathan heard the message of Apollonius, he was roused. Choosing ten thousand men, he set out from Jerusalem, and Simon his brother joined him to help him. 75 He pitched camp near Joppa, but the men in the city shut him out because Apollonius had a garrison there. When the Jews besieged it, 76† the men of the city became afraid and opened the gates, and so Jonathan took possession of Joppa.

77 When Apollonius heard of it, he drew up three thousand horsemen and an innumerable infantry. He marched on Azotus as though he were going on through the country, but at the same time he advanced into the plain, because he had such a large number of horsemen to rely on. 78 Jonathan followed him to Azotus, and they engaged in battle. 79 Apollonius, however, had left a thousand cavalry in hiding behind them. 80 When Jonathan discovered that there was an ambush behind him, his army was surrounded. From morning until evening they showered his men with arrows. 81 But his men held their ground, as Jonathan had commanded, whereas the enemy's horses became tired out. 82 When the horsemen were exhausted, Simon attacked the phalanx, overwhelmed it and put it to flight. 83 The horsemen too were scattered over the plain. The enemy fled to Azotus and entered Bethdagon, the temple of their idol, to save themselves. 84* But Jonathan burned and plundered Azotus with its neighboring towns, and destroyed by fire both the temple of Dagon and the men who had taken refuge in it. 85 Those who fell by the sword, together with those who were burned alive, came to about eight thousand men. 86 Then Jonathan left there and pitched his camp at Ashkalon, and the people of that city came out to meet him with great pomp. 87 He and his men then returned to Jerusalem, laden with much booty. 88 When King Alexander heard of these events, he accorded new honors to Jonathan. 89† He sent him a gold buckle, such as is usually given to King's Kinsmen; he also gave him Ekron and all its territory as a possession.

Alliance of Demetrius and Ptolemy

11 1 The king of Egypt gathered his forces, as numerous as the sands of the seashore,

---

10, 57: *Cleopatra:* Cleopatra Thea, then about fifteen years old. She later married Demetrius II, and later still, his brother Antiochus VII. *The year one hundred and sixty-two:* 151/150 B.C.

10, 67: *The year one hundred and sixty-five:* 147 B.C. *Demetrius:* Demetrius II Nicator.

10, 76: *Joppa:* about forty miles northwest of Jerusalem. For the first time the Maccabees took possession of a seaport; nominally it was on behalf of King Alexander.

10, 89: *Kinsmen:* a class higher than Chief Friends.

* 10, 60: 1 Mc 2, 18.
10, 64f: 1 Mc 2, 18; 11, 27.
10, 84: 1 Mc 11, 4; 1 Sm 5, 2–5.

and many ships; and he sought by deceit to take Alexander's kingdom and add it to his own. ² He entered Syria with peaceful words, and the people in the cities opened their gates to welcome him, as King Alexander had ordered them to do, since Ptolemy was his father-in-law. ³ But when Ptolemy entered the cities, he stationed garrison troops in each one. ⁴* When he reached Azotus, he was shown the temple of Dagon destroyed by fire, Azotus and its suburbs demolished, corpses lying about, and the charred bodies of those burned by Jonathan in the war and stacked up along his route. ⁵ To prejudice the king against Jonathan, he was told what the latter had done; but the king said nothing. ⁶ Jonathan met the king with pomp at Joppa, and they greeted each other and spent the night there. ⁷† Jonathan accompanied the king as far as the river called Eleutherus and then returned to Jerusalem.

⁸† Plotting evil against Alexander, King Ptolemy took possession of the cities along the seacoast as far as Seleucia-by-the-Sea. ⁹ He sent ambassadors to King Demetrius, saying: "Come, let us make a pact with each other; I will give you my daughter whom Alexander has married, and you shall reign over your father's kingdom. ¹⁰† I regret that I gave him my daughter, for he has sought to kill me." ¹¹ His real reason for accusing Alexander, however, was that he coveted Alexander's kingdom. ¹² After taking his daughter away and giving her to Demetrius, Ptolemy broke with Alexander; their enmity became open. ¹³ Then Ptolemy entered Antioch and assumed the crown of Asia; he thus wore two crowns on his head, that of Egypt and that of Asia.

Deaths of Alexander and Ptolemy

¹⁴ King Alexander was in Cilicia at that time, because the people of that region had revolted. ¹⁵ When Alexander heard the news, he came to challenge Ptolemy in battle. Ptolemy marched out and met him with a strong force and put him to flight. ¹⁶ Alexander fled to Arabia to seek protection. King Ptolemy's triumph was complete ¹⁷ when the Arab Zabdiel cut off Alexander's head and sent it to Ptolemy. ¹⁸ But three days later King Ptolemy

himself died, and his men in the fortified cities were killed by the inhabitants of the strongholds. ¹⁹† Thus Demetrius became king in the year one hundred and sixty-seven.

Pact with Demetrius

²⁰ At that time Jonathan gathered together the men of Judea to attack the citadel in Jerusalem, and they set up many machines against it. ²¹ Some transgressors of the law, enemies of their own nation, went to the king and informed him that Jonathan was besieging the citadel. ²² When Demetrius heard this, he was furious, and set out immediately for Ptolemais. He wrote to Jonathan to discontinue the siege and to meet him for a conference at Ptolemais as soon as possible.

²³ On hearing this, Jonathan ordered the siege to continue. He selected some elders and priests of Israel and exposed himself to danger ²⁴ by going to the king at Ptolemais. He brought with him silver, gold apparel, and many other presents, and found favor with the king. ²⁵ Although some impious men of his own nation brought charges against him, ²⁶ the king treated him just as his predecessors had done and showed him great honor in the presence of all his Friends. ²⁷ He confirmed him in the high priesthood and in all the honors he had previously held, and had him enrolled among his Chief Friends.

²⁸* Jonathan asked the king to exempt Judea and the three districts of Samaria from tribute, promising him in return three hundred talents. ²⁹ The king agreed and wrote the following letter to Jonathan about all these matters:

³⁰*† "King Demetrius sends greetings to his brother Jonathan and to the Jewish nation. ³¹† We are sending you, for your information, a copy of the letter that we wrote to Lasthenes our kinsman concerning you. ³² 'King Demetrius sends greetings to his father Lasthenes. ³³ Because of the good will they show us, we have decided to bestow benefits on the Jewish nation, who are our friends and who observe their obligations to us. ³⁴*† Therefore we confirm their possession, not only of the territory of Judea, but also of the three districts of Aphairema, Lydda,

---

11, 7: *Eleutherus:* modern Nahr el-Kebir, the northern border of modern Lebanon; in the second century B.C. the northern limit of Coelesyria.

11, 8: *Seleucia-by-the-Sea:* at the mouth of the Orontes, the port city of Antioch.

11, 10: *I regret . . . to kill me:* according to Josephus, Ammonius, a friend of Alexander, had tried to assassinate Ptolemy, and the latter claimed that Alexander was the instigator, thus calumniating him to gain his kingdom (v 11).

11, 19: *The year one hundred and sixty-seven:* 146/145 B.C. The two deaths (vv 17–18) occurred in the summer of 145 B.C.

11, 30: *Brother:* this title and *father* in v 32 are honorific titles used of the Kinsmen.

11, 31: *Lasthenes:* leader of the mercenary troops who had come

with Demetrius from Crete. He was now the young king's chief minister and was apparently responsible for the disastrous policy (v 38) of disbanding the national army.

11, 34: *Aphairema:* the Ophrah of Jos 18, 23; 1 Sm 23, 6; the Ephron of 2 Chr 13, 19; and the Ephraim of Jn 11, 54—modern et-Taiyibeh, five miles northeast of Bethel. *Lydda:* the Lod of the post-exilic Jews (Ez 2, 33; Neh 11, 35) and the hometown of Aeneas, who was cured by Peter (Acts 9, 32ff). It is ten miles southeast of Joppa. *Ramathaim:* the Ramathaim-zophim of 1 Sm 1, 1, and the Arimathea of Mt 27, 57—modern Rentis, nine miles northeast of Lydda.

11, 4: 1 Mc 10, 84.   **11, 30–37:** 1 Mc 10, 26–45.
11, 28: 1 Mc 10, 29; 11, 34.   **11, 34f:** 1 Mc 10, 29; 11, 28.

and Ramathaim. These districts, together with all their dependencies, were transferred from Samaria to Judea in favor of all those who offer sacrifices for us in Jerusalem instead of paying the royal taxes that formerly the king received from them each year from the produce of the soil and the fruit of the trees. 35 From this day on we grant them release from payment of all other things that would henceforth be due to us, that is, of tithes and tribute and of the tax on the salt pans and the crown tax. 36 Henceforth none of these provisions shall ever be revoked. 37 Be sure, therefore, to have a copy of these instructions made and given to Jonathan, that it may be displayed in a conspicuous place on the holy hill.' "

The Intrigue of Trypho

38 When King Demetrius saw that the land was peaceful under his rule and that he had no opposition, he dismissed his entire army, every man to his home, except the foreign troops which he had hired from the islands of the nations. So all the soldiers who had served under his predecessors hated him. 39* When a certain Trypho, who had previously belonged to Alexander's party, saw that all the troops were grumbling at Demetrius, he went to Imalkue the Arab, who was bringing up Alexander's young son Antiochus. 40 Trypho kept urging Imalkue to hand over the boy to him, that he might make him king in his father's place. During his stay there of many days, he told him of all that Demetrius had done and of the hatred that his soldiers had for him.

Jonathan Aids Demetrius

41 Meanwhile Jonathan sent the request to King Demetrius to withdraw his troops from the citadel of Jerusalem and from the other strongholds, for they were constantly hostile to Israel. 42 Demetrius, in turn, sent this word to Jonathan: "I will not only do this for you and your nation, but I will greatly honor you and your nation when I find the opportunity. 43 Do me the favor, therefore, of sending men to fight for me, because all my troops have revolted." 44 So Jonathan sent three thousand good fighting men to him at Antioch. When they came to the king, he was delighted over their arrival, 45 for the populace, one hundred and twenty thousand strong, had massed in the center of the city in an attempt to kill him. 46 But he took refuge in the

palace, while the populace gained control of the main streets and began to fight. 47 So the king called the Jews to his aid. They all rallied around him and spread out through the city. On that day they killed about a hundred thousand men in the city, 48 which, at the same time, they set on fire and plundered on a large scale. Thus they saved the king's life. 49 When the populace saw that the Jews held the city at their mercy, they lost courage and cried out to the king in supplication, 50 "Give us your terms and let the Jews stop attacking us and our city." So they threw down their arms and made peace. 51 The Jews thus gained glory in the eyes of the king and all his subjects, and they became renowned throughout his kingdom. Finally they returned to Jerusalem with much spoil.

52 But when King Demetrius was sure of his royal throne, and the land was peaceful under his rule, 53 he broke all his promises and became estranged from Jonathan. Instead of rewarding Jonathan for all the favors he had received from him, he caused him much trouble.

Alliance with Trypho

54* After this, Trypho returned and brought with him the young boy Antiochus, who became king and wore the royal crown. 55 All the soldiers whom Demetrius had discharged rallied around Antiochus and fought against Demetrius, who was routed and fled. 56 Trypho captured the elephants and occupied Antioch. 57 Then young Antiochus wrote to Jonathan: "I confirm you in the high priesthood and appoint you ruler over the four districts and wish you to be one of the King's Friends." 58* He also sent him gold dishes and a dinner service, gave him the right to drink from gold cups, to dress in royal purple, and to wear a gold buckle. 59† Likewise, he made Jonathan's brother Simon governor of the region from the Ladder of Tyre to the frontier of Egypt.

60† Jonathan set out and traveled through West-of-Euphrates and its cities, and all the forces of Syria espoused his cause as allies. When he arrived at Ashkalon, the citizens welcomed him with pomp. 61 But when he set out for Gaza, the people of Gaza locked their gates against him. So he besieged it and burned and plundered its suburbs. 62 Then the people of Gaza appealed to him for mercy, and he granted them peace. He took the sons of their chief men as hostages and sent them to Jerusalem. He then traveled on through the province as far as Damascus.

11, 59: *Ladder of Tyre:* modern Ras en-Naquurah, on the border between Lebanon and Israel, where the mountains reach the sea, so that the coastal road must ascend in a series of steps.
11, 60: *West-of-Euphrates:* refers here to the territory of Palestine and Coelesyria, but not Upper Syria; cf 1 Mc 3, 32; 7, 8.

11, 39: 1 Mc 12, 39.   11, 58: 1 Mc 2, 18.
11, 54: 1 Mc 11, 39; 12, 39.

War with Demetrius

63 Jonathan heard that the generals of Demetrius had come with a strong force to Kadesh in Galilee, intending to remove him from office. 64 So he went to meet them, leaving his brother Simon in the province. 65 Simon besieged Beth-zur, attacked it for many days, and blockaded the inhabitants. 66 When they sued for peace, he granted it to them. He expelled them from the city, took possession of it, and put a garrison there.

67† Meanwhile, Jonathan and his army pitched their camp near the waters of Gennesaret, and at daybreak they went to the plain of Hazor. 68 There, in front of him on the plain, was the army of the foreigners. This army attacked him in the open, having first detached an ambush against him in the mountains. 69 Then the men in ambush rose out of their places and joined in the battle. 70 All of Jonathan's men fled; no one stayed except the army commanders Mattathias, son of Absalom, and Judas, son of Chalphi. 71 Jonathan tore his clothes, threw earth on his head, and prayed. 72 Then he went back to the combat and so overwhelmed the enemy that they took to flight. 73 Those of his men who were running away saw it and returned to him; and with him they pursued the enemy as far as their camp in Kadesh, where they pitched their own camp. 74 Three thousand of the foreign troops fell on that day. Then Jonathan returned to Jerusalem.

Alliances with Rome and Sparta

12 1* When Jonathan saw that the times favored him, he sent selected men to Rome to confirm and renew his friendship with the Romans. 2 He also sent letters to Sparta and other places for the same purpose.

3 After reaching Rome, the men entered the senate chamber and said, "The high priest Jonathan and the Jewish people have sent us to renew the earlier friendship and alliance between you and them." 4 The Romans gave them letters addressed to the authorities in the various places, requesting them to provide the envoys with safe conduct to the land of Judah.

5 This is a copy of the letter that Jonathan wrote to the Spartans: 6 "Jonathan the high priest, the senate of the nation, the priests, and the rest of the Jewish people send greetings to their brothers the Spartans. 7*† Long ago a letter was sent to the high

priest Onias from Arius, who then reigned over you, stating that you are our brothers, as the attached copy shows. 8 Onias welcomed the envoy with honor and received the letter, which clearly referred to alliance and friendship. 9*† Though we have no need of these things, since we have for our encouragement the sacred books that are in our possession, 10 we have ventured to send word to you for the renewal of brotherhood and friendship, so as not to become strangers to you altogether; a long time has passed since your mission to us. 11 We, on our part, have never ceased to remember you in the sacrifices and prayers that we offer on our feasts and other appropriate days, as it is right and proper to remember brothers. 12 We likewise rejoice in your renown. 13 But many hardships and wars have beset us, and the kings around us have attacked us. 14 We did not wish to be troublesome to you and to the rest of our allies and friends in these wars; 15 with the help of Heaven for our support, we have been saved from our enemies, and they have been humbled. 16* So we have chosen Numenius, son of Antiochus, and Antipater, son of Jason, and we have sent them to the Romans to renew our former friendship and alliance with them. 17 We have also ordered them to come to you and greet you, and to deliver to you our letter about the renewal of our brotherhood. 18 Therefore kindly send us an answer on this matter."

19 This is a copy of the letter that was sent to Onias: 20* "Arius, king of the Spartans, sends greetings to Onias the high priest. 21 A document has been found stating that the Spartans and the Jews are brothers; both nations descended from Abraham. 22 Now that we have learned this, kindly write to us about your welfare. 23 We, on our part, are informing you that your cattle and your possessions are ours, and ours are yours. We have, therefore, given orders that you should be told of this."

Demetrius Repelled

24 Jonathan heard that the generals of Demetrius had returned to attack him with a stronger army than before. 25† He set out from Jerusalem and went into the country of Hamath to meet them, giving them no time to enter his province. 26 The spies he had sent into their camp came back and reported that the enemy had made ready to attack the Jews that very night. 27 Therefore, when the sun set,

---

11, 67: *Plain of Hazor:* the site of the ancient Canaanite city (Jos 11, 10), ten miles north of the Lake of Gennesaret.

12, 7: *Onias:* Onias I, high priest from 323–300 or 290 B.C. *Arius:* Arius I, king from 309 to 265 B.C. The letter was sent long ago, i.e., a century and a half before.

12, 9: *The sacred books . . . in our possession:* a reference to "the law, the prophets and other books," as mentioned in the Prologue to Sirach (v 1), after 132 B.C.

12, 25: *Country of Hamath:* the Seleucid territory of Upper Syria northeast of Coelesyria and separated from it by the Eleutherus River. The latter territory was under the command of Jonathan (1 Mc 11, 59f).

12, 1: 1 Mc 8, 17.   **12, 16:** 1 Mc 14, 22; 15, 15.
12, 7: 1 Mc 12, 20–23.   **12, 20–23:** 1 Mc 12, 6f.
12, 9: Rom 15, 4.

Jonathan ordered his men to be on guard and to remain armed, ready for combat, throughout the night. He also set outposts all around the camp. 28 When the enemy heard that Jonathan and his men were ready for battle, their hearts sank with fear and dread. They lighted fires and then withdrew. 29 But because Jonathan and his men were watching the lights burning, they did not know what had happened until morning. 30 Then Jonathan pursued them, but he could not overtake them, for they had crossed the river Eleutherus. 31 So Jonathan turned aside against the Arabs who are called Zabadeans, overwhelming and plundering them. 32 Then he marched on to Damascus and traversed that whole region.

33 Simon also set out and went as far as Ashkalon and its neighboring strongholds. He then turned to Joppa and occupied it, 34 for he heard that its men had intended to hand over this stronghold to the supporters of Demetrius. He left a garrison there to guard it.

35 When Jonathan returned, he assembled the elders of the people, and with them he made plans for building strongholds in Judea, 36 for making the walls of Jerusalem still higher, and for erecting a high barrier between the citadel and the city, that would isolate the citadel and so prevent its garrison from commerce with the city. 37 The people therefore worked together on building up the city, for part of the east wall above the ravine had collapsed. The quarter called Chaphenatha was also repaired. 38 Simon likewise built up Adida in the Shephelah, and strengthened its fortifications by providing them with gates and bars.

Capture of Jonathan

39* Trypho was determined to become king of Asia, assume the crown, and do away with King Antiochus. 40 But he was afraid that Jonathan would not permit him, but would fight against him. Looking for a way to seize and kill him, he set out and reached Beth-shan. 41 Jonathan marched out against him with forty thousand picked fighting men and came to Beth-shan. 42 But when Trypho saw that Jonathan had arrived with a large army, he was afraid to offer him violence. 43 Instead, he received him with honor, introduced him to all his friends, and gave him presents. He also ordered his friends and soldiers to obey him as they would himself. 44 Then he said to Jonathan: "Why have you put all your soldiers to so much trouble when we are not at war? 45 Pick out a few men to stay with you, send the rest back home, and then come with me to Ptolemais. I will hand it over to you together

with other strongholds and their garrisons, as well as the officials, then I will leave and go home. That is why I came here."

46 Jonathan believed him and did as he said. He dismissed his troops, and they returned to the land of Judah. 47 But he kept with him three thousand men, of whom he sent two thousand to Galilee while one thousand accompanied him. 48 Then as soon as Jonathan had entered Ptolemais, the men of the city closed the gates and seized him; all who had entered with him, they killed with the sword.

49† Trypho sent soldiers and cavalry to Galilee and the Great Plain to destroy all Jonathan's men. 50 These, upon learning that Jonathan had been captured and his companions killed, encouraged one another and went out in compact body ready to fight. 51 As their pursuers saw that they were ready to fight for their lives, they turned back. 52 Thus all these men of Jonathan came safely into the land of Judah. They mourned over Jonathan and his men, and were in great fear, and all Israel fell into deep mourning.

53* All the nations round about sought to destroy them. They said, "Now that they have no leader to help them, let us make war on them and wipe out their memory from among men."

V: Simon, High Priest and Ethnarch

Simon, Leader of the Jews

13 1 When Simon heard that Trypho was gathering a large army to invade and ravage the land of Judah, 2 and saw that the people were in dread and terror, he went up to Jerusalem. There he assembled the people ³ and exhorted them in these words: "You know what I, my brothers, and my father's house have done for the laws and the sanctuary; what battles and disasters we have been through. ⁴ It was for the sake of these, for the sake of Israel, that all my brothers have perished, and I alone am left. ⁵ Far be it from me, then, to save my own life in any time of distress, for I am not better than my brothers. ⁶* Rather will I avenge my nation and the sanctuary, as well as your wives and children, for all the nations out of hatred have united to destroy us."

⁷ As the people heard these words, their spirit was rekindled. ⁸ They shouted in reply: "You are our leader in place of your brothers Judas and Jonathan. ⁹ Fight our battles, and we will do everything that you tell us." ¹⁰ So Simon mustered all the men able to fight, and quickly completing the walls of Jerusalem, fortified it on every side. ¹¹ He sent Jonathan, son of Absalom, to Joppa with a large force; Jonathan drove out the occupants and remained there.

Deceit and Treachery of Trypho

¹² Then Trypho moved from Ptolemais with a large army to invade the land of Judah, bringing Jonathan with him as prisoner. ¹³ But Simon pitched his camp at Adida, facing the plain. ¹⁴ When Trypho learned that Simon had succeeded his brother Jonathan, and that he intended to fight him, he sent envoys to him with this message: ¹⁵ "We have detained your brother Jonathan on account of the money that he owed the royal treasury in connection with the offices that he held. ¹⁶ Therefore, if you send us a hundred talents of silver, and two of his sons as hostages to guarantee that when he is set free he will not revolt against us, we will release him."

¹⁷ Although Simon knew that they were speaking deceitfully to him, he gave orders to get the money and the boys, for fear of provoking much hostility among the people, who might say ¹⁸ that Jonathan perished because Simon would not send Trypho the money and the boys. ¹⁹ So he sent the boys and the hundred talents; but Trypho broke his promise and would not let Jonathan go. ²⁰† Next he began to invade and ravage the country. His troops went around by the road that leads to Adora, but Simon and his army moved along opposite him everywhere he went. ²¹ The men in the citadel sent messengers to Trypho, urging him to come to them by way of

the desert, and to send them provisions. ²² Although Trypho got all his cavalry ready to go, there was a heavy fall of snow that night, and he could not go. So he left for Gilead. ²³† When he was approaching Baskama, he had Jonathan killed and buried there. ²⁴ Then Trypho returned to his own country.

Jonathan's Tomb

²⁵ Simon sent for the remains of his brother Jonathan, and buried him in Modein, the city of his fathers. ²⁶ All Israel bewailed him with solemn lamentation, mourning over him for many days. ²⁷ Then Simon erected over the tomb of his father and his brothers a monument of stones, polished front and back, and raised high enough to be seen at a distance. ²⁸ He set up seven pyramids facing one another for his father and his mother and his four brothers. ²⁹ For the pyramids he devised a setting of big columns, on which he carved suits of armor as a perpetual memorial, and next to the armor he placed carved ships, which could be seen by all who sailed the sea. ³⁰ This tomb which he built at Modein is there to the present day.

Pact between Simon and Demetrius

³¹ Trypho dealt treacherously with the young King Antiochus. He killed him ³² and assumed the kingship in his place, putting on the crown of Asia. Thus he brought much evil on the land. ³³ Simon, on his part, built up the strongholds of Judea, strengthening their fortifications with high towers, thick walls, and gates with bars, and he stored up provisions in the fortresses. ³⁴ Simon also sent chosen men to King Demetrius with the request that he grant the land a release from taxation, for all that Trypho did was to plunder the land. ³⁵ In reply, King Demetrius sent him the following letter:

³⁶ "King Demetrius sends greetings to Simon the high priest, the friend of kings, and to the elders and the Jewish people. ³⁷ We have received the gold crown and the palm branch that you sent. We are willing to be on most peaceful terms with you and to write to our official to grant you release from tribute. ³⁸ Whatever we have guaranteed to you remains in force, and the strongholds that you have built shall remain yours. ³⁹ We remit any oversights and defaults incurred up to now, as well as the crown tax that you owe. Any other tax that may have been collected in Jerusalem shall no longer be collected there. ⁴⁰ If any of you are qualified for enrollment in our service, let them be enrolled. Let there be peace between us."

13, 20f: The invaders made a wide flanking movement to invade Judea from the south. *Adora* was a few miles southwest of Beth-zur. They would avoid Beth-zur itself and other strongholds of the Maccabees by following the way of the desert.

13, 23: *Baskama:* northeast of the Sea of Galilee.

* 13, 6: 1 Mc 5, 2; 12, 53.

[41]† Thus in the year one hundred and seventy, the yoke of the Gentiles was removed from Israel, [42] and the people began to write in their records and contracts, "In the first year of Simon, high priest, governor, and leader of the Jews."

Capture of Gazara and the Citadel

[43]*† In those days Simon besieged Gazara and surrounded it with troops. He made a siege machine, pushed it up against the city, and attacked and captured one of the towers. [44] The men who had been on the siege machine jumped down into the city and caused a great tumult there. [45] The men of the city, joined by their wives and children, went up on the wall, with their garments rent, and cried out in loud voices, begging Simon to grant them peace. [46] "Do not treat us according to our evil deeds," they said, "but according to your mercy."

[47] So Simon came to terms with them and did not destroy them. He made them leave the city, however, and he purified the houses in which there were idols. Then he entered the city with hymns and songs of praise. [48] After removing from it everything that was impure, he settled there men who observed the law. He improved its fortifications and built himself a residence.

[49] The men in the citadel in Jerusalem were prevented from going out into the country and back for the purchase of food; they suffered greatly from hunger, and many of them died of starvation. [50] They finally cried out to Simon for peace, and he gave them peace. He expelled them from the citadel and cleansed it of impurities. [51]*† On the twenty-third day of the second month, in the year one hundred and seventy-one, the Jews entered the citadel with shouts of jubilation, waving of palm branches, the music of harps and cymbals and lyres, and the singing of hymns and canticles, because a great enemy of Israel had been destroyed. [52] Simon decreed that this day should be celebrated every year with rejoicing. He also strengthened the fortifications of the temple hill alongside the citadel, and he and his companions dwelt there. [53]† Seeing that his son John was now a grown man, Simon made him commander of all his soldiers, with his residence in Gazara.

Capture of Demetrius

14 [1]† In the year one hundred and seventy-two, King Demetrius assembled his army and marched into Media to obtain help so that he could fight Trypho. [2]† When Arsaces, king of Persia and Media, heard that Demetrius had invaded his territory, he sent one of his generals to take him alive. [3] The general went forth and defeated the army of Demetrius; he captured him and brought him to Arsaces, who put him in prison.

Glory of Simon

[4]* The land was at rest all the days of Simon,
who sought the good of his nation.
His people were delighted with his power
and his magnificence throughout his reign.
[5]   As his crowning glory he captured the port
of Joppa
and made it a gateway to the isles of
the sea.
[6]* He enlarged the borders of his nation
and gained control of the country.
[7]   He took many enemies prisoners of war
and made himself master of Gazara,
Beth-zur, and the citadel.
He cleansed the citadel of its impurities;
there was no one to withstand him.
[8]* The people cultivated their land in peace;
the land yielded its produce
and the trees of the field their fruit.
[9]* Old men sat in the squares,
all talking about the good times,
while the young men wore the glorious
apparel of war.
[10]   He supplied the cities with food
and equipped them with means of defense,
till his glorious name reached the ends of
the earth.
[11]* He brought peace to the land,
and Israel was filled with happiness.
[12]* Every man sat under his vine and his fig tree,
with no one to disturb him.
[13]   No one was left to attack them in their land;
the kings in those days were crushed.
[14]   He strengthened all the lowly among
his people

---

† **13, 41:** *The year one hundred and seventy:* March, 142, to April, 141 B.C., by the temple calendar.
13, 43: *Gazara:* a key position in the Shephelah, fortified by Bacchides in 160 B.C.; cf 1 Mc 9, 52.
13, 51: *The twenty-third day of the second month:* June 3, 141 B.C.
13, 53: *John:* John Hyrcanus, who was to succeed his father as ruler and high priest; cf 1 Mc 16, 23f.
14, 1: *The year one hundred and seventy-two:* 141–140 B.C. The expedition began most probably in the spring of 140.
14, 2: *Arsaces:* Arsaces VI, also called Mithridates I, the Parthian

king (171–138 B.C.). Parthians had overrun Persia and now held Babylonia, both of which had hitherto belonged to the Seleucid empire. The Greeks and Macedonians in these countries had appealed to Demetrius for help.

* **13, 43:** 2 Mc 10, 32–38.   **14, 8:** Zec 8, 12.
13, 51: 1 Mc 1, 36.   **14, 9:** Zec 8, 4f.
14, 4: 1 Mc 3, 3–9.   **14, 11:** Lv 26, 6.
14, 6: Ex 34, 24.   **14, 12:** Mi 4, 4; Zec 3, 10.

and was zealous for the law;
    he suppressed all the lawless and
        the wicked.
15 He made the temple splendid
        and enriched its equipment.

Alliance with Rome and Sparta

16† When people heard in Rome and even in Sparta that Jonathan had died, they were deeply grieved. 17 But when the Romans heard that his brother Simon had been made high priest in his place and was master of the country and the cities, 18* they sent him inscribed tablets of bronze to renew with him the friendship and alliance that they had established with his brothers Judas and Jonathan. 19 These were read before the assembly in Jerusalem.

20 This is a copy of the letter that the Spartans sent: "The rulers and the citizens of Sparta send greetings to Simon the high priest, the elders, the priests, and the rest of the Jewish people, our brothers. 21 The envoys you sent to our people have informed us of your glory and fame, and we were happy that they came. 22* In accordance with what they said we have recorded the following in the public decrees: Since Numenius, son of Antiochus, and Antipater, son of Jason, envoys of the Jews, have come to us to renew their friendship with us, 23 the people have voted to receive the men with honor, and to deposit a copy of their words in the public archives, so that the people of Sparta may have a record of them. A copy of this decree has been made for Simon the high priest."

24* After this, Simon sent Numenius to Rome with a great gold shield weighing a thousand minas, to confirm the alliance with the Romans.

Decree of Honor

25 When the people heard of these things, they said, "How can we thank Simon and his sons? 26 He and his brothers and his father's house have stood firm and repulsed Israel's enemies. They have thus preserved its liberty." So they made an inscription on bronze tablets, which they affixed to pillars on Mount Zion. 27† The following is a copy of the inscription:

"On the eighteenth day of Elul, in the year one hundred and seventy-two, that is, the third year under Simon the high priest in Asaramel, 28 in a great assembly of priests, people, rulers of the nation, and elders of the country, the following proclamation was made:

29 " 'Since there have often been wars in our country, Simon, son of the priest Mattathias, descendant of Joarib, and his brothers have put themselves in danger and resisted the enemies of their nation, so that their sanctuary and law might be maintained, and they have thus brought great glory to their nation. 30 After Jonathan had rallied his nation and become their high priest, he was gathered to his kinsmen. 31 When the enemies of the Jews sought to invade and devastate their country and to lay hands on their temple, 32 Simon rose up and fought for his nation, spending large sums of his own money to equip the men of his nation's armed forces and giving them their pay. 33 He fortified the cities of Judea, especially the frontier city of Bethzur, where he stationed a garrison of Jewish soldiers, and where previously the enemy's arms had been stored. 34 He also fortified Joppa by the sea and Gazara on the border of Azotus, a place previously occupied by the enemy; these cities he resettled with Jews, and furnished them with all that was necessary for their restoration. 35 When the Jewish people saw Simon's loyalty and the glory he planned to bring to his nation, they made him their leader and high priest because of all he had accomplished and the loyalty and justice he had shown his nation. In every way he sought to exalt his people.

36 " 'In his time and under his guidance they succeeded in driving the Gentiles out of their country, especially those in the City of David in Jerusalem, who had built for themselves a citadel from which they used to sally forth to defile the environs of the temple and inflict grave injury on its purity. 37 In this citadel he stationed Jewish soldiers, and he strengthened its fortifications for the defense of the land and the city, while he also raised the wall of Jerusalem to a greater height. 38 Consequently, King Demetrius confirmed him in the high priesthood, 39* made him one of his Friends, and conferred the highest honors on him. 40 He had indeed heard that the Romans had addressed the Jews as friends, allies, and brothers and that they had received Simon's envoys with honor.

41 " 'The Jewish people and their priest have, therefore, made the following decisions. Simon shall be their permanent leader and high priest until a true prophet arises. 42 He shall act as governor general over them, and shall have charge of the temple, to make regulations concerning its functions and concerning the country, its weapons and

---

14, 16: The embassy to *Rome* and *Sparta* was sent soon after Simon's accession to power, and the replies were received before Demetrius' expedition (vv 1–3) — probably in 142 B.C.
  14, 27: *Eighteenth day of Elul:* September 13, 140 B.C. *Asaramel:* a Hebrew name meaning "court of the people of God."

14, 18: 1 Mc 8, 22.   **14, 24:** 1 Mc 12, 16; 15, 15.
14, 22: 1 Mc 12, 16; 15, 15.   **14, 39f:** 1 Mc 2, 18.

strongholds; ⁴³ he shall be obeyed by all. All contracts made in the country shall be dated by his name. He shall have the right to wear royal purple and gold ornaments. ⁴⁴ It shall not be lawful for any of the people or priests to nullify any of these decisions, or to contradict the orders given by him, or to convene an assembly in the country without his consent, to be clothed in royal purple or wear an official gold brooch. ⁴⁵ Whoever acts otherwise or violates any of these prescriptions shall be liable to punishment.

⁴⁶ " 'All the people approved of granting Simon the right to act in accord with these decisions, ⁴⁷† and Simon accepted and agreed to act as high priest, governor general, and ethnarch of the Jewish people and priests and to exercise supreme authority over all.' "

⁴⁸ It was decreed that this inscription should be engraved on bronze tablets, to be set up in a conspicuous place in the precincts of the temple, ⁴⁹ and that copies of it should be deposited in the treasury, where they would be available to Simon and his sons.

Letter of Antiochus

15 ¹† Antiochus, son of King Demetrius, sent a letter from the islands of the sea to Simon, the priest and ethnarch of the Jews, and to all the nation, ² which read as follows:

"King Antiochus sends greetings to Simon, the priest and ethnarch, and to the Jewish nation. ³ Whereas certain villains have gained control of the kingdom of my ancestors, I intend to reclaim it, that I may restore it to its former state. I have recruited a large number of mercenary troops and equipped warships ⁴ to make a landing in my country and take revenge on those who have ruined it and laid waste many cities in my realm.

⁵ "Now, therefore, I confirm to you all the tax exemptions that the kings before me granted you and whatever other privileges they conferred on you. ⁶ I authorize you to coin your own money, as legal tender in your country. ⁷ Jerusalem and its temple shall be free. All the weapons you have prepared and all the strongholds you have built and now occupy shall remain in your possession. ⁸ All debts, present or future, due to the royal treasury shall be canceled for you, now and for all time. ⁹ When we recover our kingdom, we will greatly honor you and your

nation and the temple, so that your glory will be manifest in all the earth."

¹⁰† In the year one hundred and seventy-four, Antiochus invaded the land of his ancestors, and all the troops rallied to him, so that few were left with Trypho. ¹¹† Pursued by Antiochus, Trypho fled to Dor, by the sea, ¹² realizing what a mass of troubles had come upon him now that his soldiers had deserted him. ¹³ Antiochus encamped before Dor with a hundred and twenty thousand infantry and eight thousand horsemen. ¹⁴ While he invested the city, his ships closed in along the coast, so that he blockaded it by land and sea and let no one go in or out.

Roman Alliance Renewed

¹⁵* Meanwhile, Numenius and his companions left Rome with letters such as this addressed to various kings and countries:

¹⁶† "Lucius, Consul of the Romans, sends greetings to King Ptolemy. ¹⁷ Certain envoys of the Jews, our friends and allies, have come to us to renew their earlier alliance of friendship. They had been sent by Simon the high priest and the Jewish people, ¹⁸* and they brought with them a gold shield worth a thousand minas. ¹⁹ Therefore we have decided to write to various kings and countries, that they are not to harm them, or wage war against them or their cities or their country, and are not to assist those who fight against them. ²⁰ We have also decided to accept the shield from them. ²¹ If, then, any troublemakers from their country take refuge with you, hand them over to Simon the high priest, so that he may punish them according to their law."

²²† The consul sent similar letters to Kings Demetrius, Attalus, Ariarthes and Arsaces; ²³ to all the countries—Sampsames, Sparta, Delos, Myndos, Sicyon, Caria, Samos, Pamphylia, Lycia, Halicarnassus, Rhodes, Phaselis, Cos, Side, Aradus, Gortyna, Cnidus, Cyprus, and Cyrene. ²⁴ A copy of the letter was also sent to Simon the high priest.

Hostility of Antiochus

²⁵ When King Antiochus was encamped before Dor, he assaulted it continuously both with troops and with the siege machines he had made. He blockaded Trypho by preventing anyone from going in or out. ²⁶ Simon sent to Antiochus' support two thousand elite troops, together with gold and

---

^{14, 47:} *Ethnarch:* a subaltern ruler over a racial group whose office needed confirmation by a higher authority within the empire.

^{15, 1:} *Antiochus:* Antiochus VII Sidetes, son of Demetrius I, and younger brother of Demetrius II, now a prisoner of the Parthians. At the age of twenty he set out from the island of Rhodes to take his brother's place and drive out the usurper Trypho.

^{15, 10:} *The year one hundred and seventy-four:* 138 B.C.

^{15, 11:} *Dor, by the sea:* a fortress on the Palestinian coast, fifteen miles south of Carmel.

^{15, 16:} *Lucius:* perhaps Lucius Caecilius Metellus, consul in 142 B.C., or Lucius Calpurnius Piso, consul in 140–139 B.C. This document pertains to Simon's first year as leader.

^{15, 22:} *Attalus:* Attalus II of Pergamum, reigned 159–138 B.C. *Ariarthes:* Ariarthes V of Cappadocia, reigned 162–130 B.C. *Arsaces:* see note on 1 Mc 14, 2.

15, 15: 1 Mc 8, 17; 12, 16; 14, 22.24.

15, 18: 1 Mc 14, 24.

silver and much equipment. 27 But he refused to accept the aid; in fact, he broke all the agreements he had previously made with Simon and became hostile toward him.

28 He sent Athenobius, one of his Friends, to confer with Simon and say: "You are occupying Joppa and Gazara and the citadel of Jerusalem; these are cities of my kingdom. 29 You have laid waste their territories, done great harm to the land, and taken possession of many districts in my realm. 30 Therefore, give up the cities you have seized and the tribute money of the districts outside the territory of Judea of which you have taken possession; 31 or instead, pay me five hundred talents of silver for the devastation you have caused and five hundred talents more for the tribute money of the cities. If you do not do this, we will come and make war on you."

32 So Athenobius, the king's Friend, came to Jerusalem, and on seeing the splendor of Simon's court, the gold and silver plate on the sideboard, and the rest of his rich display, he was amazed. When he gave him the king's message, 33 Simon said to him in reply:

"We have not seized any foreign land; what we took is not the property of others, but our ancestral heritage which for a time had been unjustly held by our enemies. 34 Now that we have the opportunity, we are holding on to the heritage of our ancestors. 35 As for Joppa and Gazara, which you demand, the men of these cities were doing great harm to our people and laying waste our country; however, we are willing to pay you a hundred talents for these cities."

36 Athenobius made no reply, but returned to the king in anger. When he told him of Simon's words, of his splendor, and of all he had seen, the king fell into a violent rage.

Victory over Cendebeus

37† Trypho had gotten aboard a ship and escaped to Orthosia. 38 Then the king appointed Cendebeus commander in chief of the seacoast, and gave him infantry and cavalry forces. 39† He ordered him to move his troops against Judea and to fortify Kedron and strengthen its gates, so that he could launch attacks against the Jewish people. Meanwhile the king went in pursuit of Trypho. 40 When Cendebeus came to Jamnia, he began to harass the people and to make incursions into Judea, where he took people captive or massacred them. 41 As the king ordered, he fortified Kedron and stationed horsemen

and infantry there, so that they could go out and patrol the roads of Judea.

16 1 John then went up from Gazara and told his father Simon what Cendebeus was doing. 2 Simon called his two oldest sons, Judas and John, and said to them: "I and my brothers and my father's house have fought the battles of Israel from our youth until today, and many times we succeeded in saving Israel. 3 I have now grown old, but you, by the mercy of Heaven, have come to man's estate. Take my place and my brother's, and go out and fight for our nation; and may the help of Heaven be with you!"

4 John then mustered in the land twenty thousand warriors and horsemen. Setting out against Cendebeus, they spent the night at Modein, 5 rose early, and marched into the plain. There, facing them, was an immense army of foot soldiers and horsemen, and between the two armies was a stream. 6 John and his men took their position against the enemy. Seeing that his men were afraid to cross the stream, John crossed first. When his men saw this, they crossed over after him. 7 Then he divided his infantry into two corps and put his cavalry between them, for the enemy's horsemen were very numerous. 8 They blew the trumpets, and Cendebeus and his army were put to flight; many of them fell wounded, and the rest fled toward the stronghold. 9 It was then that John's brother Judas fell wounded; but John pursued them until Cendebeus reached Kidron, which he had fortified. 10 Some took refuge in the towers on the plain of Azotus, but John set fire to these, and about two thousand of the enemy perished. He then returned to Judea in peace.

Murder of Simon and His Sons

11 Ptolemy, son of Abubus, had been appointed governor of the plain of Jericho, and he had much silver and gold, 12 being the son-in-law of the high priest. 13 But he became ambitious and sought to get control of the country. So he made treacherous plans to do away with Simon and his sons. 14† As Simon was inspecting the cities of the country and providing for their needs, he and his sons Mattathias and Judas went down to Jericho in the year one hundred and seventy-seven, in the eleventh month (that is, the month Shebat). 15† The son of Abubus gave them a deceitful welcome in the little stronghold called Dok which he had built. While serving them a sumptuous banquet, he had his men

---

15, 37: *Orthosia:* a port between Tripoli and the Eleutherus River.
15, 39: *Kedron:* a few miles southeast of Jamnia and facing the fortress of Gazara held by John Hyrcanus.

16, 14: *In the year one hundred and seventy-seven, in the eleventh month:* January-February, 134 B.C., by the temple calendar.
16, 15: *Dok:* a fortress built on a cliff three miles northwest of Jericho, near modern Ain Duq.

hidden there. 16 Then, when Simon and his sons had drunk freely, Ptolemy and his men sprang up, weapons in hand, rushed upon Simon in the banquet hall, and killed him, his two sons, and some of his servants. 17 By this vicious act of treason he repaid good with evil.

18 Then Ptolemy wrote an account of this and sent it to the king, asking that troops be sent to help him and that the country be turned over to him. 19 He sent other men to Gazara to do away with John. To the army officers he sent letters inviting them to come to him so that he might present them with silver, gold, and gifts. 20 He also sent others to seize Jerusalem and the mount of the temple. 21 But someone ran ahead and brought word to John at Gazara that his father and his brothers had perished, and that Ptolemy had sent men to kill him also. 22 On hearing this, John was utterly astounded. When the men came to kill him, he had them arrested and put to death, for he knew what they meant to do. 23† Now the rest of the history of John, his wars and the brave deeds he performed, his rebuilding of the walls, and his other achievements— 24 these things are recorded in the chronicle of his pontificate, from the time that he succeeded his father as high priest.

16, 23f: John Hyrcanus was ruler and high priest from 134 B.C. till his death in 104 B.C. These verses suggest that the book was written, or at least completed, only after he died.

When you are suffering, what is your first response? to escape? to look for relief? to cry out in pain? These are normal and healthy responses: no well-adjusted person chooses to suffer willingly. Sometimes, though, people inflict unspeakable suffering on one another, especially through violence such as rape and torture. What meaning could there be in such suffering? In response, 2 Maccabees insists that God will vindicate all those who suffer innocently at the hands of the unjust.

At a Glance

I. Letters to the Jews in Egypt (1, 1—2, 18).

II. Author's Preface (2, 19–32).

III. Heliodorus' Attempt To Profane the Temple (3, 1–40).

IV. Profanation and Persecution (4, 1—7, 42).

V. Victories of Judas and Purification of the Temple (8, 1—10, 8).

VI. Renewed Persecution (10, 9—15, 36).

VII. Epilogue (15, 37–39).

In-depth

In 167 B.C., the Jewish people faced a new persecution under the Seleucid (Greek) king Antiochus IV Epiphanes. In an effort to unify the many different peoples under his rule, Antiochus imposed his own language, customs, and religion on all of them, including the Jews. Second Maccabees covers some of the same history as First Maccabees but with different purposes: to show the variety of ways the Jews resisted persecution and to give hope to persecuted Jews in the author's time.

The Book of Job had already struggled with the mystery of human suffering and concluded that only God could understand it. Not content with this answer, the author of 2 Maccabees presses forward with new insights:

Quick Facts

Period Covered
from 180 to 161 B.C.

Author
someone around 100 B.C., summarizing a lost work by Jason of Cyrene

Themes
differing responses to persecution, the just and suffering

Of Note
Second Maccabees is not found in every translation of the Old Testament (see "The Case of the Missing Books," near Tb 1, 16).

■ In the famous story of the martyrdom of a Jewish mother and her seven sons (7, 1–42), 2 Maccabees talks about the resurrection of the dead.

■ In chapter 12, the value of praying for the dead is commended.

■ In chapter 15, the book speaks confidently of the prayers of the saints in heaven for those on earth.

Second Maccabees is less concerned with the facts of history than with the meaning of history. It insists that whenever God's faithful people suffer, they can be assured of receiving justice—if not in this life, then in the resurrection. The book shows how the Jewish faith continued to develop as it faced the sometimes painful events of history.

2 Maccabees

I: Letters to the Jews In Egypt

First Letter 124 B.C.

1 ¹ The Jews in Jerusalem and in the land of Judea send greetings to their brethren, the Jews in Egypt, and wish them true peace! ² May God bless you and remember his covenant with his faithful servants, Abraham, Isaac and Jacob. ³ May he give to all of you a heart to worship him and to do his will readily and generously. ⁴ May he open your heart to his law and his commandments and grant you peace. ⁵ May he hear your prayers, and be reconciled to you, and never forsake you in time of adversity. ⁶ Even now we are praying for you here.

⁷*† In the reign of Demetrius, the year one hundred and sixty-nine, we Jews wrote to you during the trouble and violence that overtook us in these years after Jason and his followers had revolted against the holy land and the kingdom, ⁸*† setting fire to the gatehouse and shedding innocent blood.

But we prayed to the LORD, and our prayer was heard; we offered sacrifices and fine flour; we lighted the lamps and set out the loaves of bread. ⁹† We are now reminding you to celebrate the feast of Booths in the month of Chislev. ¹⁰† Dated in the year one hundred and eighty-eight.

Festival Letter 164 B.C.

The people of Jerusalem and Judea, the senate, and Judas send greetings and good wishes to Aristobulus, counselor of King Ptolemy and member of the family of the anointed priests, and to the Jews in Egypt. ¹¹† Since we have been saved by God from grave dangers, we give him great thanks for having fought on our side against the king; ¹²* it was he who drove out those who fought against the holy city. ¹³† When their leader arrived in Persia with his seemingly irresistible army, they were cut to pieces in the temple of the goddess Nanea through a deceitful stratagem employed by Nanea's priests.

1, 7: *Demetrius:* Demetrius II, king of Syria (145–139, 129–125 B.C.). *The year one hundred and sixty-nine* of the Seleucid era, 143 B.C. Regarding the dates in 1 and 2 Maccabees, see note on 1 Mc 1, 10. On the troubles caused by Jason and his revolt against the kingdom, i.e., the rule of the legitimate high priest, see 2 Mc 4, 7–22.
1, 8: *Our prayer was heard:* in the ultimate victory of the Maccabees.
1, 9: *Feast of Booths in the month of Chislev:* really the feast of the Dedication of the temple (2 Mc 10, 1–8), celebrated on the twenty-fifth of Chislev (Nov.-Dec.). Its solemnity resembles that of the true feast of Booths (Lv 23, 33–43), celebrated on the fifteenth of Tishri (Sept.-Oct.); cf 2 Mc 1, 18.

1, 10: 124 B.C. The date pertains to the preceding, not the following letter. *King Ptolemy:* Ptolemy VI Philometor, ruler of Egypt from 180 to 145 B.C.; he is mentioned also in 1 Mc 1, 18; 10, 51–59.
1, 11f: *The king:* Antiochus IV of Syria, the bitter persecutor of the Jews, who, as leader of the Syrian army that invaded Persia, perished there in 164 B.C.
1, 13: *Nanea:* an oriental goddess comparable to Artemis of the Greeks.

1, 7: 2 Mc 4, 7–20.	**1, 12–17:** 2 Mc 9, 1–29; 1 Mc 6,
1, 8: 1 Mc 4, 38.	1–13.

¹⁴† On the pretext of marrying the goddess, Antiochus with his Friends had come to the place to get its great treasures by way of dowry. ¹⁵ When the priests of the Nanaeon had displayed the treasures, Antiochus with a few attendants came to the temple precincts. As soon as he entered the temple, the priests locked the doors. ¹⁶ Then they opened a hidden trapdoor in the ceiling, hurled stones at the leader and his companions and struck them down. They dismembered the bodies, cut off their heads and tossed them to the people outside. ¹⁷ Forever blessed be our God, who has thus punished the wicked!

¹⁸† We shall be celebrating the purification of the temple on the twenty-fifth day of the month Chislev, so we thought it right to inform you that you too may celebrate the feast of Booths and of the fire that appeared when Nehemiah, the rebuilder of the temple† and the altar, offered sacrifices. ¹⁹† When our fathers were being exiled to Persia, devout priests of the time took some of the fire from the altar and hid it secretly in the hollow of a dry cistern, making sure that the place would be unknown to anyone. ²⁰ Many years later, when it so pleased God, Nehemiah, commissioned by the king of Persia, sent the descendants of the priests who had hidden the fire to look for it. ²¹ When they informed us that they could not find any fire, but only muddy water, he ordered them to scoop some out and bring it. After the material for the sacrifices had been prepared, Nehemiah ordered the priests to sprinkle with the water the wood and what lay on it. ²² When this was done and in time the sun, which had been clouded over, began to shine, a great fire blazed up, so that everyone marveled. ²³ While the sacrifice was being burned, the priests recited a prayer, and all present joined in with them, Jonathan leading and the rest responding with Nehemiah.

²⁴ The prayer was as follows: "LORD, LORD God, creator of all things, awesome and strong, just and merciful, the only king and benefactor, ²⁵ who alone are gracious, just, almighty, and eternal, Israel's savior from all evil, who chose our forefathers and sanctified them: ²⁶ accept this sacrifice on behalf of all your people Israel and guard and sanctify your heritage. ²⁷ Gather together our scattered people, free those who are the slaves of the Gentiles, look kindly on those who are despised and detested, and let the Gentiles know that you are our God. ²⁸ Punish those who tyrannize over us and arrogantly mistreat us. ²⁹* Plant your people in your holy place, as Moses promised."

³⁰ Then the priests began to sing hymns. ³¹ After the sacrifice was burned, Nehemiah ordered the rest of the liquid to be poured upon large stones. ³² As soon as this was done, a flame blazed up, but its light was lost in the brilliance cast from a light on the altar. ³³ When the event became known and the king of the Persians was told that, in the very place where the exiled priests had hidden the fire, a liquid was found with which Nehemiah and his people had burned the sacrifices, ³⁴ the king, after verifying the fact, fenced the place off and declared it sacred. ³⁵ To those on whom the king wished to bestow favors he distributed the large revenues he received there. ³⁶† Nehemiah and his companions called the liquid nephthar, meaning purification, but most people named it naphtha.

2 ¹† You will find in the records, not only that Jeremiah the prophet ordered the deportees to take some of the aforementioned fire with them, ²* but also that the prophet, in giving them the law, admonished them not to forget the commandments of the LORD or be led astray in their thoughts, when seeing the gold and silver idols and their ornaments. ³ With other similar words he urged them not to let the law depart from their hearts. ⁴*† The same document also tells how the prophet, following a divine revelation, ordered that the tent and the ark should accompany him and how he went off to the mountain which Moses climbed to see God's inheritance. ⁵ When Jeremiah arrived there, he found a room in a cave in which he put the tent, the ark, and the altar of incense; then he blocked up the entrance. ⁶ Some of those who followed him came up intending to mark the path, but they could not find it. ⁷ When Jeremiah heard of this, he reproved them: "The place is to remain unknown

---

1, 14–17: A different account of the death of Antiochus IV is given in 2 Mc 9, 1–29, and another variant account in 1 Mc 6, 1–16. The writer of this letter had probably heard a distorted rumor of the king's death. This fact and other indications show that the letter was written very soon after Antiochus IV died, hence in 164 B.C.

1, 18–36: This purely legendary account of Nehemiah's miraculous fire is incorporated in the letter because of its connection with the temple and its rededication.

1, 18: *Nehemiah, the rebuilder of the temple:* he rebuilt the walls of Jerusalem, but the temple had been rebuilt by Zerubbabel almost a century before.

1, 19: *Persia:* actually Babylonia, which later became part of the Persian Empire.

1, 36: By a play on words, the Greek term *naphtha* (petroleum) is assimilated to some Semitic word, perhaps *nephthar,* meaning "loosened."

2, 1–8: This legendary account of how Jeremiah hid the sacred tent (which was not mentioned after the time of Solomon!), the ark and the altar is given for the purpose of explaining why the postexilic temple was the legitimate place of worship even without these sacred objects.

2, 4: *The mountain:* Nebo; cf Dt 34, 1.

1, 29: 2 Mc 2, 18; Dt 30, 3ff.   2, 4f: Dt 32, 49; 34, 1; Rv
2, 2: Bar 6, 3–72.   11, 19.

until God gathers his people together again and shows them mercy. 8*† Then the LORD will disclose these things, and the glory of the LORD will be seen in the cloud, just as it appeared in the time of Moses and when Solomon prayed that the Place might be gloriously sanctified."

9 It is also related how Solomon in his wisdom offered a sacrifice at the dedication and the completion of the temple. 10* Just as Moses prayed to the LORD and fire descended from the sky and consumed the sacrifices, so Solomon also prayed and fire came down and burned up the holocausts. 11*† Moses had said, "Because it had not been eaten, the sin offering was burned up." 12 Solomon also celebrated the feast in the same way for eight days.

13† Besides these things, it is also told in the records and in Nehemiah's Memoirs how he collected the books about the kings, the writings of the prophets and of David, and the royal letters about sacred offerings. 14* In like manner Judas also collected for us the books that had been scattered because of the war, and we now have them in our possession. 15 If you need them, send messengers to get them for you.

16 As we are about to celebrate the feast of the purification of the temple, we are writing to you requesting you also to please celebrate the feast. 17 It is God who has saved all his people and has restored to all of them their heritage, the kingdom, the priesthood, and the sacred rites, 18* as he promised through the law. We trust in God, that he will soon have mercy on us and gather us together from everywhere under the heavens to his holy Place, for he has rescued us from great perils and has purified his Place.

II: Author's Preface

19 This is the story of Judas Maccabeus and his brothers, of the purification of the great temple, the dedication of the altar, 20† the campaigns against Antiochus Epiphanes and his son Eupator, 21 and of the heavenly manifestations accorded to the heroes who fought bravely for Judaism, so that, few as they were, they seized the whole land, put to flight the barbarian hordes, 22 regained possession of the world-famous temple, liberated the city, and re-

established the laws that were in danger of being abolished, while the LORD favored them with all his generous assistance. 23 All this, which Jason of Cyrene set forth in detail in five volumes, we will try to condense into a single book.

Purpose and Method

24 In view of the flood of statistics, and the difficulties encountered by those who wish to plunge into historical narratives where the material is abundant, 25 we have aimed to please those who prefer simple reading, as well as to make it easy for the studious who wish to commit things to memory, and to be helpful to all. 26 For us who have taken upon ourselves the labor of making this digest, the task, far from being easy, is one of sweat and of sleepless nights, 27 just as the preparation of a festive banquet is no light matter for one who thus seeks to give enjoyment to others. Similarly, to win the gratitude of many we will gladly endure these inconveniences, 28 while we leave the responsibility for exact details to the original author, and confine our efforts to giving only a summary outline. 29 As the architect of a new house must give his attention to the whole structure, while the man who undertakes the decoration and the frescoes has only to concern himself with what is needed for ornamentation, so I think it is with us. 30 To enter into questions and examine them thoroughly from all sides is the task of the professional historian; 31 but the man who is making an adaptation should be allowed to aim at brevity of expression and to omit detailed treatment of the matter. 32 Here, then, we shall begin our account without further ado; it would be nonsense to write a long preface to a story and then abbreviate the story itself.

III: Heliodorus' Attempt to Profane the Temple†

Treachery of Simon

3 1* While the holy city lived in perfect peace and the laws were strictly observed because of the piety of the high priest Onias† and his hatred of evil, 2 the kings themselves honored the Place and glorified the temple with the most magnificent

---

2, 8: *The Place:* the temple of Jerusalem.

2, 11: The statement attributed here to Moses seems to be based on Lv 10, 16–20.

2, 13: *Nehemiah's Memoirs:* a lost apocryphal work.

2, 20: For the account of the campaigns against Antiochus IV Epiphanes, see 2 Mc 4, 7—10, 9; and for the account of those against his son Antiochus V Eupator, see 2 Mc 10, 10 —13, 26.

3, 1–40: This legendary episode about Heliodorus is recounted here for the purpose of stressing the inviolability of the temple of

Jerusalem; its later profanation was allowed by God because of the people's sins; cf 2 Mc 5, 17f.

3, 1: *The high priest Onias:* Onias III, who was priest from 196 to 175 B.C., and died in 171 B.C. He was the son of Simon, whose praises are sung in Sir 50, 1–21.

2, 8: 1 Kgs 8, 11.	2, 14: 1 Mc 1, 57.
2, 10: Lv 9, 23f; 2 Chr 7, 1.	2, 18: Dt 30, 3ff.
2, 11: Lv 10, 16–20.	3, 1ff: 2 Mc 5, 19f; 15, 12.

gifts. ³† Thus Seleucus, king of Asia, defrayed from his own revenues all the expenses necessary for the sacrificial services. ⁴*† But a certain Simon, of the priestly course of Bilgah, who had been appointed superintendent of the temple, had a quarrel with the high priest about the supervision of the city market. ⁵ Since he could not prevail against Onias, he went to Apollonius of Tarsus, who at that time was governor of Coelesyria and Phoenicia, ⁶ and reported to him that the treasury in Jerusalem was so full of untold riches that the total sum of money was incalculable and out of all proportion to the cost of the sacrifices, and that it would be possible to bring it all under the control of the king.

Mission of Heliodorus

⁷ When Apollonius had an audience with the king, he informed him about the riches that had been reported to him. The king chose his minister Heliodorus and sent him with instructions to expropriate the aforesaid wealth. ⁸ So Heliodorus immediately set out on his journey, ostensibly to visit the cities of Coelesyria and Phoenicia, but in reality to carry out the king's purpose. ⁹ When he arrived in Jerusalem and had been graciously received by the high priest of the city, he told him about the information that had been given, and explained the reason for his presence, and he asked if these things were really true. ¹⁰* The high priest explained that part of the money was a care fund for widows and orphans, ¹¹† and a part was the property of Hyrcanus, son of Tobias, a man who occupied a very high position. Contrary to the calumnies of the impious Simon, the total amounted to four hundred talents of silver and two hundred of gold. ¹² He added that it was utterly unthinkable to defraud those who had placed their trust in the sanctity of the Place and in the sacred inviolability of a temple venerated all over the world. ¹³ But because of the orders he had from the king, Heliodorus said that in any case the money must be confiscated for the royal treasury. ¹⁴ So on the day he had set he went in to take an inventory of the funds.

Anguish of the Faithful

There was great distress throughout the city. ¹⁵ Priests prostrated themselves in their priestly robes before the altar, and loudly begged him in heaven who had given the law about deposits to keep the deposits safe for those who had made

them. ¹⁶ Whoever saw the appearance of the high priest was pierced to the heart, for the changed color of his face manifested the anguish of his soul. ¹⁷ The terror and bodily trembling that had come over the man clearly showed those who saw him the pain that lodged in his heart. ¹⁸ People rushed out of their houses in crowds to make public supplication, because the Place was in danger of being profaned. ¹⁹ Women, girded with sackcloth below their breasts, filled the streets; maidens secluded indoors ran together, some to the gates, some to the walls, others peered through the windows, ²⁰ all of them with hands raised toward heaven, making supplication. ²¹ It was pitiful to see the populace variously prostrated in prayer and the high priest full of dread and anguish.

Divine Intervention

²² While they were imploring the almighty LORD to keep the deposits safe and secure for those who had placed them in trust, ²³ Heliodorus went on with his plan. ²⁴ But just as he was approaching the treasury with his bodyguards, the LORD of spirits who holds all power manifested himself in so striking a way that those who had been bold enough to follow Heliodorus were panic-stricken at God's power and fainted away in terror. ²⁵ There appeared to them a richly caparisoned horse, mounted by a dreadful rider. Charging furiously, the horse attacked Heliodorus with its front hoofs. The rider was seen to be wearing golden armor. ²⁶ Then two other young men, remarkably strong, strikingly beautiful, and splendidly attired, appeared before him. Standing on each side of him, they flogged him unceasingly until they had given him innumerable blows. ²⁷ Suddenly he fell to the ground, enveloped in great darkness. Men picked him up and laid him on a stretcher. ²⁸ The man who a moment before had entered that treasury with a great retinue and his whole bodyguard was carried away helpless, having clearly experienced the sovereign power of God. ²⁹ While he lay speechless and deprived of all hope of aid, due to an act of God's power, ³⁰ the Jews praised the LORD who had marvelously glorified his holy Place; and the temple, charged so shortly before with fear and commotion, was filled with joy and gladness, now that the almighty LORD had manifested himself.

³¹ Soon some of the companions of Heliodorus begged Onias to invoke the Most High, praying that

---
3, 3: *Seleucus:* Seleucus IV Philopator, who reigned from 187 to 175 B.C.
3, 4: *Bilgah:* a priestly family mentioned in Neh 12, 5.18.
3, 11: *Son of Tobias:* a member of the Tobiad family of Transjor-

dan (Neh 2, 10; 6, 17ff; 13, 4–8). Hyrcanus' father was Joseph, whose mother was the sister of the high priest Onias II.
*
3, 4: 2 Mc 4, 23.   **3, 10:** Dt 14, 29.

2
M
C

the life of the man who was about to expire might be spared. ³² Fearing that the king might think that Heliodorus had suffered some foul play at the hands of the Jews, the high priest offered a sacrifice for the man's recovery. ³³ While the high priest was offering the sacrifice of atonement, the same young men in the same clothing again appeared and stood before Heliodorus. "Be very grateful to the high priest Onias," they told him. "It is for his sake that the LORD has spared your life. ³⁴ Since you have been scourged by Heaven, proclaim to all men the majesty of God's power." When they had said this, they disappeared.

Testimony of Heliodorus

³⁵ After Heliodorus had offered a sacrifice to the LORD and made most solemn vows to him who had spared his life, he bade Onias farewell, and returned with his soldiers to the king. ³⁶ Before all men he gave witness to the deeds of the most high God that he had seen with his own eyes. ³⁷ When the king asked Heliodorus who would be a suitable man to be sent to Jerusalem next, he answered: ³⁸ "If you have an enemy or a plotter against the government, send him there, and you will receive him back well-flogged, if indeed he survives at all; for there is certainly some special divine power about the Place. ³⁹ He who has his dwelling in heaven watches over that Place and protects it, and he strikes down and destroys those who come to harm it." ⁴⁰ This was how the matter concerning Heliodorus and the preservation of the treasury turned out.

IV: Profanation and Persecution

Onias Appeals to the King

4 ¹ The Simon mentioned above as the informer about the funds against his own country, made false accusations that it was Onias who threatened Heliodorus and instigated the whole miserable affair. ² He dared to brand as a plotter against the government the man who was a benefactor of the city, a protector of his compatriots, and a zealous defender of the laws. ³ When Simon's hostility reached such a point that murders were being committed by one of his henchmen, ⁴ Onias saw that the opposition was serious and that Apollonius, son of Menestheus, the governor of Coelesyria and Phoenicia, was abetting Simon's wickedness. ⁵ So he had recourse to the king, not as an accuser of his countrymen, but as a

PRAY IT

Arrogance

Arrogance seems to run in the family of Simon. First, Simon seeks to embarrass the high priest, Onias, because of a minor disagreement (2 Mc 3, 1–14). When that fails, he falsely accuses Onias of a crime (4, 1–6). Several years later, Simon's brother bribes his way into power (verses 23–29).

We have all encountered arrogant people who think that they can do no wrong, and when they do err, cover it up by attacking others. Many of us are intimidated by such people and resent that we felt talked down to or easily dismissed as unimportant. So, how should we respond to arrogant people? The most obvious solution is to ignore them. If that is not possible, then we need to react to them calmly and confidently. Finally, we should keep them in our prayers. Their arrogance can be masking an insecurity or a hurt that needs God's healing touch.

In your prayer, reflect or journal on the following questions:
- Who intimidates you by her or his arrogant behavior?
- How could you respond in a loving and just way?
- What do you need to bring to God in prayer?

▶ 2 Mc 3, 1—4, 29

man looking to the general and particular good of all the people. ⁶ He saw that, unless the king intervened, it would be impossible to have a peaceful government, and that Simon would not desist from his folly.

Jews Led by Jason To Apostatize

⁷*† But Seleucus died, and when Antiochus surnamed Epiphanes succeeded him on the throne, Onias' brother Jason obtained the high priesthood by corrupt means: ⁸ in an interview, he promised the king three hundred and sixty talents of silver, as

---

4, 7: *Seleucus died:* he was murdered by Heliodorus. Antiochus Epiphanes was his younger brother. Onias' brother showed his love

for the Greek way of life (v 10) by changing his Hebrew name Joshua, or Jesus, to the Greek name Jason.

4, 7: 2 Mc 1, 7; 1 Mc 1, 10.

well as eighty talents from another source of income. 9† Besides this he agreed to pay a hundred and fifty more, if he were given authority to establish a gymnasium and a youth club for it and to enroll men in Jerusalem as Antiochians.

10 When Jason received the king's approval and came into office, he immediately initiated his countrymen into the Greek way of life. 11*† He set aside the royal concessions granted to the Jews through the mediation of John, father of Eupolemus (that Eupolemus who would later go on an embassy to the Romans to establish a treaty of friendship with them); he abrogated the lawful institutions and introduced customs contrary to the law. 12*† He quickly established a gymnasium at the very foot of the acropolis, where he induced the noblest young men to wear the Greek hat. 13 The craze for Hellenism and foreign customs reached such a pitch, through the outrageous wickedness of the ungodly pseudo-high-priest Jason, 14 that the priests no longer cared about the service of the altar. Disdaining the temple and neglecting the sacrifices, they hastened, at the signal for the discus-throwing, to take part in the unlawful exercises on the athletic field. 15 They despised what their ancestors had regarded as honors, while they highly prized what the Greeks esteemed as glory. 16 Precisely because of this, they found themselves in serious trouble: the very people whose manner of life they emulated, and whom they desired to imitate in everything, became their enemies and oppressors. 17 It is no light matter to flout the laws of God, as the following period will show.

18 When the quinquennial games were held at Tyre in the presence of the king, 19 the vile Jason sent envoys as representatives of the Antiochians of Jerusalem, to bring there three hundred silver drachmas for the sacrifice to Hercules. But the bearers themselves decided that the money should not be spent on a sacrifice, as that was not right, but should be used for some other purpose. 20† So the contribution destined by the sender for the sacrifice to Hercules was in fact applied, by those who brought it, to the construction of triremes.

21† When Apollonius, son of Menestheus, was sent to Egypt for the coronation of King Philome-

tor, Antiochus learned that the king was opposed to his policies; so he took measures for his own security. 22 After going to Joppa, he proceeded to Jerusalem. There he was received with great pomp by Jason and the people of the city, who escorted him with torchlights and acclamations; following this, he led his army into Phoenicia.

Menelaus Supplants Jason

23† Three years later Jason sent Menelaus, brother of the aforementioned Simon, to deliver the money to the king, and to obtain decisions on some important matters. 24 When he had been introduced to the king, he flattered him with such an air of authority that he secured the high priesthood for himself, outbidding Jason by three hundred talents of silver. 25 He returned with the royal commission, but with nothing that made him worthy of the high priesthood; he had the temper of a cruel tyrant and the rage of a wild beast. 26 Then Jason, who had cheated his own brother and now saw himself cheated by another man, was driven out as a fugitive to the country of the Ammonites.

27 Although Menelaus had obtained the office, he did not make any payments of the money he had promised to the king, 28 in spite of the demand of Sostratus, the commandant of the citadel, whose duty it was to collect the taxes. For this reason, both were summoned before the king. 29 Menelaus left his brother Lysimachus as his substitute in the high priesthood, while Sostratus left Crates, commander of the Cypriots, as his substitute.

Murder of Onias

30† While these things were taking place, the people of Tarsus and Mallus rose in revolt, because their cities had been given as a gift to Antiochis, the king's mistress. 31 The king, therefore, went off in haste to settle the affair, leaving Andronicus, one of his nobles, as his deputy. 32 Then Menelaus, thinking this a good opportunity, stole some gold vessels from the temple and presented them to Andronicus; he had already sold some other vessels in Tyre and in the neighboring cities. 33 When Onias had clear evidence of the facts, he made a public protest, after withdrawing to the inviolable sanctuary at

---

4, 9: *Youth club:* an educational institution in which young men were trained both in Greek intellectual culture and in physical fitness. *Antiochians:* honorary citizens of Antioch, a Hellenistic city of the Seleucid Kingdom that had a corporation of such Antiochians, who enjoyed certain political and commercial privileges.

4, 11: *Eupolemus:* one of the two envoys sent to Rome by Judas Maccabeus (1 Mc 8, 17).

4, 12: Since the *gymnasium,* where the youth exercised naked (Greek *gymnos*), lay in the Tyropoeon Valley to the east of the citadel, it was directly next to the temple on its eastern side. *The Greek hat:* a wide-brimmed hat, traditional headgear of Hermes,

the patron god of athletic contests; it formed part of the distinctive costume of the members of the "youth club."

4, 20: *Triremes:* war vessels with three banks of oars.

4, 21: *Philometor:* Ptolemy VI, king of Egypt, c. 172 to c. 145 B.C.

4, 23: *Menelaus:* Jewish high priest from c. 172 to his execution in 162 B.C. (2 Mc 13, 3–8).

4, 30: *Mallus:* a city of Cilicia (v 36) in southeastern Asia Minor, about thirty miles east of Tarsus.

4, 11: 1 Mc 8, 17.   4, 12: 1 Mc 1, 14.

Daphne, near Antioch. [34] Thereupon Menelaus approached Andronicus privately and asked him to lay hands on Onias. So Andronicus went to Onias, and by treacherously reassuring him through sworn pledges with right hands joined, persuaded him, in spite of his suspicions, to leave the sanctuary. Then, without any regard for justice, he immediately put him to death.

[35] As a result, not only the Jews, but many people of other nations as well, were indignant and angry over the unjust murder of the man. [36]† When the king returned from the region of Cilicia, the Jews of the city, together with the Greeks who detested the crime, went to see him about the murder of Onias. [37] Antiochus was deeply grieved and full of pity; he wept as he recalled the prudence and noble conduct of the deceased. [38] Inflamed with anger, he immediately stripped Andronicus of his purple robe, tore off his other garments, and had him led through the whole city to the very place where he had committed the outrage against Onias; and there he put the murderer to death. Thus the LORD rendered him the punishment he deserved.

Riot against Lysimachus

[39]† Many sacrilegious thefts had been committed by Lysimachus in the city with the connivance of Menelaus. When word was spread that a large number of gold vessels had been stolen, the people assembled in protest against Lysimachus. [40] As the crowds, now thoroughly enraged, began to riot, Lysimachus launched an unjustified attack against them with about three thousand armed men under the leadership of Auranus, a man as advanced in folly as he was in years. [41] Reacting against Lysimachus' attack, the people picked up stones or pieces of wood or handfuls of the ashes lying there and threw them in wild confusion at Lysimachus and his men. [42] As a result, they wounded many of them and even killed a few, while they put all the rest to flight. The sacrilegious thief himself they slew near the treasury.

[43] Charges about this affair were brought against Menelaus. [44]† When the king came to Tyre, three men sent by the senate presented to him the justice of their cause. [45]* But Menelaus, seeing himself on the losing side, promised Ptolemy, son of Do-

rymenes, a substantial sum of money if he would win the king over. [46] So Ptolemy retired with the king under a colonnade, as if to get some fresh air, and persuaded him to change his mind. [47] Menelaus, who was the cause of all the trouble, the king acquitted of the charges, while he condemned to death those poor men who would have been declared innocent even if they had pleaded their case before Scythians. [48] Thus, those who had prosecuted the case for the city, for the people, and for the sacred vessels, quickly suffered unjust punishment. [49] For this reason, even some Tyrians were indignant over the crime and provided sumptuously for their burial. [50] But Menelaus, thanks to the covetousness of the men in power, remained in office, where he grew in wickedness and became the chief plotter against his fellow citizens.

Sedition and Death of Jason

5 [1]*† About this time Antiochus sent his second expedition into Egypt. [2]* It then happened that all over the city, for nearly forty days, there appeared horsemen charging in midair, clad in garments interwoven with gold—companies fully armed with lances [3] and drawn swords; squadrons of cavalry in battle array, charges and countercharges on this side and that, with brandished shields and bristling spears, flights of arrows and flashes of gold ornaments, together with armor of every sort. [4] Therefore all prayed that this vision might be a good omen.

[5]† But when a false rumor circulated that Antiochus was dead, Jason gathered fully a thousand men and suddenly attacked the city. As the defenders on the walls were forced back and the city was finally being taken, Menelaus took refuge in the citadel. [6] Jason then slaughtered his fellow citizens without mercy, not realizing that triumph over one's own kindred was the greatest failure, but imagining that he was winning a victory over his enemies, not his fellow countrymen. [7] Even so, he did not gain control of the government, but in the end received only disgrace for his treachery, and once again took refuge in the country of the Ammonites. [8]† At length he met a miserable end. Called to account before Aretas, king of the Arabs, he fled from city to city, hunted by all men, hated as a transgressor of the

---

†

4, 36: *The city:* Antioch. But some understand the Greek to mean "each city."

4, 39: *The city:* Jerusalem. Menelaus was still in Syria.

4, 44: *The senate:* the council of Jewish elders at Jerusalem; cf 1 Mc 12, 6.

5, 1: *Second expedition:* the first invasion of Egypt by Antiochus in 169 B.C. (1 Mc 1, 16–20) is not mentioned in 2 Maccabees, unless the coming of the Syrian army to Palestine (2 Mc 4, 21f) is regarded as the first invasion. The author of 2 Maccabees apparently combines the first pillage of Jerusalem in 169 B.C. after Antiochus' first invasion

of Egypt (1 Mc 1, 20–28; cf 2 Mc 5, 5ff) with the second pillage of the city two years later (167 B.C.), following the king's second invasion of Egypt in 168 B.C. (1 Mc 1, 29–35; cf 2 Mc 5, 24ff).

5, 5: *Jason:* brother of Onias III, was claimant of the high priesthood (2 Mc 4, 7–10). Later he was supplanted by Menelaus who drove him into Transjordan (2 Mc 4, 26).

5, 8: *Aretas:* King Aretas I of the Nabateans; cf 1 Mc 5, 25.

---

*

4, 45: 2 Mc 8, 8; 1 Mc 3, 38.   **5, 2f:** 2 Mc 3, 24ff; 10, 29f;
5, 1: 1 Mc 1, 17.   11, 8.

laws, abhorred as the butcher of his country and his countrymen. After being driven into Egypt, [9] he crossed the sea to the Spartans, among whom he hoped to find protection because of his relations with them. There he who had exiled so many from their country perished in exile; [10] and he who had cast out so many to lie unburied went unmourned himself with no funeral of any kind or any place in the tomb of his ancestors.

The City Ravaged

[11]* When these happenings were reported to the king, he thought that Judea was in revolt. Raging like a wild animal, he set out from Egypt and took Jerusalem by storm. [12] He ordered his soldiers to cut down without mercy those whom they met and to slay those who took refuge in their houses. [13] There was a massacre of young and old, a killing of women and children, a slaughter of virgins and infants. [14] In the space of three days, eighty thousand were lost, forty thousand meeting a violent death, and the same number being sold into slavery. [15] Not satisfied with this, the king dared to enter the holiest temple in the world; Menelaus, that traitor both to the laws and to his country, served as guide. [16] He laid his impure hands on the sacred vessels and gathered up with profane hands the votive offerings made by other kings for the advancement, the glory, and the honor of the Place. [17]* Puffed up in spirit, Antiochus did not realize that it was because of the sins of the city's inhabitants that the Lord was angry for a little while and hence disregarded the holy Place. [18] If they had not become entangled in so many sins, this man, like Heliodorus, who was sent by King Seleucus to inspect the treasury, would have been flogged and turned back from his presumptuous action as soon as he approached. [19]*† The Lord, however, had not chosen the people for the sake of the Place, but the Place for the sake of the people. [20] Therefore, the Place itself, having shared in the people's misfortunes, afterward participated in their good fortune; and what the Almighty had forsaken in his anger was restored in all its glory, once the great Sovereign became reconciled.

[21]* Antiochus carried off eighteen hundred talents from the temple, and hurried back to Antioch. In his arrogance he planned to make the land navigable and the sea passable on foot, so carried away was he with pride. [22]† But he left governors to harass the nation: at Jerusalem, Philip, a Phrygian by birth, and in character more cruel than the man who appointed him; [23]† at Mount Gerizim, Andronicus; and besides these, Menelaus, who lorded it over his fellow citizens worse than the others did. Out of hatred for the Jewish citizens, [24]*† the king sent Apollonius, commander of the Mysians, at the head of an army of twenty-two thousand men, with orders to kill all the grown men and sell the women and young men into slavery. [25] When this man arrived in Jerusalem, he pretended to be peacefully disposed and waited until the holy day of the sabbath; then, finding the Jews refraining from work, he ordered his men to parade fully armed. [26] All those who came out to watch, he massacred, and running through the city with armed men, he cut down a large number of people.

[27]* But Judas Maccabeus with about nine others withdrew to the wilderness where he and his companions lived like wild animals in the hills, continuing to eat what grew wild to avoid sharing the defilement.

The Temple Desecrated

6 [1]* Not long after this the king sent an Athenian senator to force the Jews to abandon the customs of their ancestors and live no longer by the laws of God; [2]*† also to profane the temple in Jerusalem and dedicate it to Olympian Zeus, and that on Mount Gerizim to Zeus the Hospitable, as the inhabitants of the place requested. [3] This intensified the evil in an intolerable and utterly disgusting way. [4]† The Gentiles filled the temple with debauchery and revelry; they amused themselves with prostitutes and had intercourse with women even in the sacred court. They also brought into the temple things that were forbidden, [5] so that the altar was covered with abominable offerings prohibited by the laws.

†
5, 19: Man is more important than even the most sacred institutions; cf Mk 2, 27.
5, 22: *Philip, a Phrygian by birth:* the Philip of 2 Mc 6, 11 and 8, 8, but probably not the same as Philip the regent of 2 Mc 9, 29 and 1 Mc 6, 14.
5, 23: *Mount Gerizim:* the sacred mountain of the Samaritans at Shechem; cf 2 Mc 6, 2.
5, 24: *Apollonius:* the Mysian commander of 1 Mc 1, 29; mentioned also in 2 Mc 3, 5; 4, 4.
6, 2: *Olympian Zeus:* equated with the Syrian Baal *shomem* ("the lord of the heavens"), a term which the Jews rendered as "*Shiqqus*

shomem," horrible abomination (Dn 9, 27; 11, 31; 12, 11; 1 Mc 1, 54).
6, 4: *Amused themselves with prostitutes:* as in the fertility cults of the ancient Near East; see notes on Bar 6, 10.42f.

5, 11–21: 1 Mc 1, 20–24.	5, 21: 1 Mc 1, 23f.
5, 17: 2 Mc 6, 12–16; 7, 16–19.32–38.	5, 24ff: 1 Mc 1, 29f.
5, 19ff: 2 Mc 3, 1ff; 1 Chr 17, 9; Mk 2, 27.	5, 27: 1 Mc 2, 28.
	6, 1–11: 1 Mc 1, 44–63.
	6, 2: 1 Mc 1, 46; Dn 9, 27.

Abolition of the Law

⁶ A man could not keep the sabbath or celebrate the traditional feasts, nor even admit that he was a Jew. ⁷† Moreover, at the monthly celebration of the king's birthday the Jews had, from bitter necessity, to partake of the sacrifices, and when the festival of Dionysus was celebrated, they were compelled to march in his procession, wearing wreaths of ivy.

⁸ At the suggestion of the citizens of Ptolemais, a decree was issued ordering the neighboring Greek cities to act in the same way against the Jews: oblige them to partake of the sacrifices, ⁹ and put to death those who would not consent to adopt the customs of the Greeks. It was obvious, therefore, that disaster impended. ¹⁰* Thus, two women who were arrested for having circumcised their children were publicly paraded about the city with their babies hanging at their breasts and then thrown down from the top of the city wall. ¹¹* Others, who had assembled in nearby caves to observe the sabbath in secret, were betrayed to Philip and all burned to death. In their respect for the holiness of that day, they had scruples about defending themselves.

Purpose of Divine Judgment

¹²* Now I beg those who read this book not to be disheartened by these misfortunes, but to consider that these chastisements were meant not for the ruin but for the correction of our nation. ¹³ It is, in fact, a sign of great kindness to punish sinners promptly instead of letting them go for long. ¹⁴* Thus, in dealing with other nations, the LORD patiently waits until they reach the full measure of their sins before he punishes them; but with us he has decided to deal differently, ¹⁵ in order that he may not have to punish us more severely later, when our sins have reached their fullness. ¹⁶ He never withdraws his mercy from us. Although he disciplines us with misfortunes, he does not abandon his own people. ¹⁷ Let these words suffice for recalling this truth. Without further ado we must go on with our story.

Martyrdom of Eleazar

¹⁸*† Eleazar, one of the foremost scribes, a man of advanced age and noble appearance, was being forced to open his mouth to eat pork. ¹⁹ But preferring a glorious death to a life of defilement, he spat out the meat, and went forward of his own accord to the instrument of torture, ²⁰ as men ought to do who have the courage to reject the food which it is unlawful to taste even for love of life. ²¹ Those in charge of that unlawful ritual meal took the man aside privately, because of their long acquaintance with him, and urged him to bring meat of his own

Teaching by Example

Second Maccabees tells the story of Eleazar, a dignified, elderly scribe who has followed God his whole life. Rather than compromise his principles, Eleazar courageously accepts death by torture. He knows that his example will influence younger people (6, 28). His example gives others courage (verse 31).

Young people watch and learn. An old television commercial showed a father and son driving along in a car. The son had a toy steering wheel in front of him and imitated his father's driving. When the father turned the wheel, so did the son. When the father switched the turn signal, so did the son.

Then the father pulled a cigarette from a pack. He lit it and began smoking. The next scene showed the son going for the pack of cigarettes.

The next time you find yourself struggling to make the right choice, think about the example you might be giving to someone younger than you.

▸ 2 Mc 6, 18–31

---

† **6, 7:** *Dionysus:* called also Bacchus the god of the grape harvest and of wine; ivy was one of his symbols.

6, 18—7, 42: The stories of Eleazar and of the mother and her seven sons, among the earliest models of "martyrology," were understandably popular among the Christians of the early centuries. Written originally to encourage God's people in times of persecu-

tion, they add gruesome details to the record of tortures, and place long speeches in the mouths of the martyrs.

*
6, 10: 1 Mc 1, 60f.
6, 11: 1 Mc 2, 32–38.
6, 12–16: 2 Mc 5, 17; 7.

16–19.32–38.
6, 14: Wis 11, 9f; 12, 2.22.
6, 18: Lv 11, 7f; Heb 11, 35.

providing, such as he could legitimately eat, and to pretend to be eating some of the meat of the sacrifice prescribed by the king; 22 in this way he would escape the death penalty, and be treated kindly because of their old friendship with him. 23 But he made up his mind in a noble manner, worthy of his years, the dignity of his advanced age, the merited distinction of his gray hair, and of the admirable life he had lived from childhood; and so he declared that above all he would be loyal to the holy laws given by God.

He told them to send him at once to the abode of the dead, explaining: 24 "At our age it would be unbecoming to make such a pretense; many young men would think the ninety-year-old Eleazar had gone over to an alien religion. 25 Should I thus dissimulate for the sake of a brief moment of life, they would be led astray by me, while I would bring shame and dishonor on my old age. 26 Even if, for the time being, I avoid the punishment of men, I shall never, whether alive or dead, escape the hands of the Almighty. 27 Therefore, by manfully giving up my life now, I will prove myself worthy of my old age, 28 and I will leave to the young a noble example of how to die willingly and generously for the revered and holy laws."

He spoke thus, and went immediately to the instrument of torture. 29 Those who shortly before had been kindly disposed, now became hostile toward him because what he had said seemed to them utter madness. 30 When he was about to die under the blows, he groaned and said: "The LORD in his holy knowledge knows full well that, although I could have escaped death, I am not only enduring terrible pain in my body from this scourging, but also suffering it with joy in my soul because of my devotion to him." 31 This is how he died, leaving in his death a model of courage and an unforgettable example of virtue not only for the young but for the whole nation.

Martyrdom of a Mother and Her Sons

7 1* It also happened that seven brothers with their mother were arrested and tortured with whips and scourges by the king, to force them to eat pork in violation of God's law. 2 One of the brothers, speaking for the others, said: "What do you expect to achieve by questioning us? We are ready to die rather than transgress the laws of our ancestors." 3 At that the king, in a fury, gave orders to have pans and caldrons heated. 4 While they were being quickly heated, he commanded his executioners to cut out the tongue of the one who had spoken for

the others, to scalp him and cut off his hands and feet, while the rest of his brothers and his mother looked on. 5 When he was completely maimed but still breathing, the king ordered them to carry him to the fire and fry him. As a cloud of smoke spread from the pan, the brothers and their mother encouraged one another to die bravely, saying such words as these: 6* "The LORD God is looking on, and he truly has compassion on us, as Moses declared in his canticle, when he protested openly with the words, 'And he will have pity on his servants.' "

7 When the first brother had died in this manner, they brought the second to be made sport of. After tearing off the skin and hair of his head, they asked him, "Will you eat the pork rather than have your

I Will Sacrifice Myself

If I were a bird
and able to fly afar,
I would like to be a white dove
to guide the people to freedom.
If I were the cloud in the sky,
I would shelter and bring rains
to the rice field.
If I were a grain of sand
I would throw myself down
to make a path for the people.
I will sacrifice my life
for the suffering people.
I would sacrifice myself
no matter how many times
I would have to die.

(From Maren C. Tirabassi and
Kathy Wonson Eddy, editors,
Gifts of Many Cultures, p. 208)

This song was written by a twenty-two-year-old Thai student. He was later shot and killed by police officers at a demonstration against the return of a corrupt leader. His love for Thailand echoes the love of the mother and her seven sons for God and their Jewish faith in chapter 7 of 2 Maccabees.

▶ **2 Maccabees, chapter 7**

7, 1: Jer 15, 9.   7, 6: Dt 32, 36.

body tortured limb by limb?" [8] Answering in the language of his forefathers, he said, "Never!" So he too in turn suffered the same tortures as the first. [9]*† At the point of death he said: "You accursed fiend, you are depriving us of this present life, but the King of the world will raise us up to live again forever. It is for his laws that we are dying."

[10] After him the third suffered their cruel sport. He put out his tongue at once when told to do so, and bravely held out his hands, [11]* as he spoke these noble words: "It was from Heaven that I received these; for the sake of his laws I disdain them; from him I hope to receive them again." [12] Even the king and his attendants marveled at the young man's courage, because he regarded his sufferings as nothing.

[13] After he had died, they tortured and maltreated the fourth brother in the same way. [14] When he was near death, he said, "It is my choice to die at the hands of men with the God-given hope of being restored to life by him; but for you, there will be no resurrection to life."

[15] They next brought forward the fifth brother and maltreated him. [16]* Looking at the king, he said: "Since you have power among men, mortal though you are, do what you please. But do not think that our nation is forsaken by God. [17] Only wait, and you will see how his great power will torment you and your descendants."

[18] After him they brought the sixth brother. When he was about to die, he said: "Have no vain illusions. We suffer these things on our own account, because we have sinned against our God; that is why such astonishing things have happened to us. [19]* Do not think, then, that you will go unpunished for having dared to fight against God."

[20] Most admirable and worthy of everlasting remembrance was the mother, who saw her seven sons perish in a single day, yet bore it courageously because of her hope in the LORD. [21] Filled with a noble spirit that stirred her womanly heart with manly courage, she exhorted each of them in the language of their forefathers with these words: [22] "I do not know how you came into existence in my womb; it was not I who gave you the breath of life, nor was it I who set in order the elements of which each of you is composed. [23] Therefore, since it is the Creator of the universe who shapes each man's beginning, as he brings about the origin of everything, he, in his mercy, will give you back both breath and life, because you now disregard yourselves for the sake of his law."

[24] Antiochus, suspecting insult in her words, thought he was being ridiculed. As the youngest brother was still alive, the king appealed to him, not with mere words, but with promises on oath, to make him rich and happy if he would abandon his ancestral customs: he would make him his Friend and entrust him with high office. [25] When the youth paid no attention to him at all, the king appealed to the mother, urging her to advise her boy to save his life. [26] After he had urged her for a long time, she went through the motions of persuading her son. [27] In derision of the cruel tyrant, she leaned over close to her son and said in their native language: "Son, have pity on me, who carried you in my womb for nine months, nursed you for three years, brought you up, educated and supported you to your present age. [28]† I beg you, child, to look at the heavens and the earth and see all that is in them; then you will know that God did not make them out of existing things; and in the same way the human race came into existence. [29] Do not be afraid of this executioner, but be worthy of your brothers and accept death, so that in the time of mercy I may receive you again with them."

[30] She had scarcely finished speaking when the youth said: "What are you waiting for? I will not obey the king's command. I obey the command of the law given to our forefathers through Moses. [31] But you, who have contrived every kind of affliction for the Hebrews, will not escape the hands of God. [32]* We, indeed, are suffering because of our sins. [33] Though our living LORD treats us harshly for a little while to correct us with chastisements, he will again be reconciled with his servants. [34] But you, wretch, vilest of all men! do not, in your insolence, concern yourself with unfounded hopes, as you raise your hand against the children of Heaven. [35] You have not yet escaped the judgment of the almighty and all-seeing God. [36] My brothers, after enduring brief pain, have drunk of never-failing life, under God's covenant, but you, by the judgment of God, shall receive just punishments for your arrogance. [37] Like my brothers, I offer up my body and my life for our ancestral laws, imploring God to show mercy soon to our nation, and by afflictions and blows to make you confess that he alone is God. [38] Through me and my brothers, may there be an end to the wrath of the Almighty that has justly

---

7, 9: *The King of the world will raise us up:* here, and in vv 11.14.23.29.36, belief in the future resurrection of the body, at least for the just, is clearly stated; cf also 2 Mc 12, 44; 14, 46; Dn 12, 2.

7, 28: *God did not make them out of existing things:* that is, God made all things solely by his omnipotent will and his creative word; cf Heb 11, 3.

7, 9: 2 Mc 12, 44; 14, 46.
7, 11: 2 Mc 12, 43ff.
7, 16–19: 2 Mc 5, 17; 6, 12–16.
7, 19: Acts 5, 39.
7, 32.38: 2 Mc 5, 17; 6, 12–16; 17, 16–19.

fallen on our whole nation." [39] At that, the king became enraged and treated him even worse than the others, since he bitterly resented the boy's contempt. [40]* Thus he too died undefiled, putting all his trust in the LORD. [41] The mother was last to die, after her sons.

[42] Enough has been said about the sacrificial meals and the excessive cruelties.

V: Victories of Judas and Purification of the Temple

Judas Maccabeus

8 [1]* Judas Maccabeus and his companions entered the villages secretly, summoned their kinsmen, and by also enlisting others who remained faithful to Judaism, assembled about six thousand men. [2] They implored the LORD to look kindly upon his people, who were being oppressed on all sides; to have pity on the temple, which was profaned by godless men; [3] to have mercy on the city, which was being destroyed and about to be leveled to the ground; to hearken to the blood that cried out to him; [4] to remember the criminal slaughter of innocent children and the blasphemies uttered against his name; and to manifest his hatred of evil. [5]* Once Maccabeus got his men organized, the Gentiles could not withstand him, for the LORD'S wrath had now changed to mercy. [6] Coming unexpectedly upon towns and villages, he would set them on fire. He captured strategic positions, and put to flight a large number of the enemy. [7] He preferred the nights as being especially helpful for such attacks. Soon the fame of his valor spread everywhere.

First Victory over Nicanor

[8]*† When Philip saw that Judas was gaining ground little by little and that his successful advances were becoming more frequent, he wrote to Ptolemy, governor of Coelesyria and Phoenicia, to come to the aid of the king's government. [9]* Ptolemy promptly selected Nicanor, son of Patroclus, one of the Chief Friends, and sent him at the head of at least twenty thousand armed men of various nations to wipe out the entire Jewish race. With him he associated Gorgias, a professional military commander, well-versed in the art of war. [10] Nicanor planned to raise the two thousand talents of tribute owed by the king to the Romans by selling captured Jews into slavery. [11] So he immediately sent word to the coastal cities, inviting them to buy Jewish slaves

and promising to deliver ninety slaves for a talent— little did he dream of the punishment that was to fall upon him from the Almighty.

8, 8–29.34ff: This account of the campaign of *Nicanor* and *Gorgias* against Judas is paralleled, with certain differences, in 1 Mc 3, 38—4, 24.

7, 40f: Heb 11, 35.
8, 1–7: 2 Mc 5, 27; 1 Mc 3, 10–26.

8, 5ff: 1 Mc 3, 3–9.
8, 8: 2 Mc 4, 45; 1 Mc 3, 38.
8, 9: 1 Mc 7, 26.

¹² When Judas learned of Nicanor's advance and informed his companions about the approach of the army, ¹³ the cowardly and those who lacked faith in God's justice deserted and got away. ¹⁴ But the others sold everything they had left, and at the same time besought the LORD to deliver those whom the ungodly Nicanor had sold before even meeting them. ¹⁵ They begged the LORD to do this, if not for their sake, at least for the sake of the covenants made with their forefathers, and because they themselves bore his holy, glorious name. ¹⁶ Maccabeus assembled his men, six thousand strong, and exhorted them not to be panic-stricken before the enemy, nor to fear the large number of the Gentiles attacking them unjustly, but to fight courageously, ¹⁷ keeping before their eyes the lawless outrage perpetrated by the Gentiles against the holy Place and the affliction of the humiliated city, as well as the subversion of their ancestral way of life. ¹⁸ "They trust in weapons and acts of daring," he said, "but we trust in almighty God, who can by a mere nod destroy not only those who attack us, but the whole world." ¹⁹* He went on to tell them of the times when help had been given their ancestors: both the time of Sennacherib, when a hundred and eighty-five thousand of his men were destroyed, ²⁰ and the time of the battle in Babylonia against the Galatians, when only eight thousand Jews fought along with four thousand Macedonians; yet when the Macedonians were hard pressed, the eight thousand routed one hundred and twenty thousand and took a great quantity of booty, because of the help they received from Heaven. ²¹ With such words he encouraged them and made them ready to die for their laws and their country.

Then Judas divided his army into four, ²²† placing his brothers, Simon, Joseph, and Jonathan, each over a division, assigning to each fifteen hundred men. ²³* (There was also Eleazar.) After reading to them from the holy book and giving them the watchword, "The Help of God," he himself took charge of the first division and joined in battle with Nicanor. ²⁴ With the Almighty as their ally, they killed more than nine thousand of the enemy, wounded and disabled the greater part of Nicanor's army, and put all of them to flight. ²⁵ They also seized the money of those who had come to buy them as slaves. When they had pursued the enemy

for some time, ²⁶ they were obliged to return by reason of the late hour. It was the day before the sabbath, and for that reason they could not continue the pursuit. ²⁷ They collected the enemy's arms and stripped them of their spoils, and then observed the sabbath with fervent praise and thanks to the LORD who kept them safe for that day on which he let descend on them the first dew of his mercy. ²⁸ After the sabbath, they gave a share of the booty to the persecuted and to widows and orphans; the rest they divided among themselves and their children. ²⁹ When this was done, they made supplication in common, imploring the merciful LORD to be completely reconciled with his servants.

Timothy and Bacchides Defeated

³⁰ They also challenged the forces of Timothy and Bacchides, killed more than twenty thousand of them, and captured some very high fortresses. They divided the enormous plunder, allotting half to themselves and the rest to the persecuted, to orphans, widows, and the aged. ³¹ They collected the enemies' weapons and carefully stored them in suitable places; the rest of the spoils they carried to Jerusalem. ³² They also killed the commander of Timothy's forces, a most wicked man, who had done great harm to the Jews. ³³ While celebrating the victory in their ancestral city, they burned both those who had set fire to the sacred gates and Callisthenes, who had taken refuge in a little house; so he received the reward his wicked deeds deserved.

Humiliation of Nicanor

³⁴* The accursed Nicanor, who had brought the thousand slave dealers to buy the Jews, ³⁵ after being humbled through the LORD's help by those whom he had thought of no account, laid aside his fine clothes and fled alone across country like a runaway slave, until he reached Antioch. He was eminently successful in destroying his own army. ³⁶ So he who had promised to provide tribute for the Romans by the capture of the people of Jerusalem testified that the Jews had a champion, and that they were invulnerable for the very reason that they followed the laws laid down by him.

Punishment and Death of Antiochus

9 ¹*† About that time Antiochus retreated in disgrace from the region of Persia. ² He had

---

8, 22: *Joseph:* called John in 1 Mc 2, 2; 9, 36.38. This paragraph interrupts the story of Nicanor's defeat, which is resumed in v 34. The purpose of the author apparently is to group together the defeats suffered by the Syrians on various occasions. Battles against Timothy are recounted in 1 Mc 5, 37–44 and 2 Mc 12, 10–25; against Bacchides in 1 Mc 7, 8–20.

9, 1–28: In order to keep together the various accounts of God's

punishment of the persecutors of his people, the author places here the stories of Antiochus' illness and death (in actuality the king died only after the purification of the temple; cf 1 Mc 4, 36–59; 6, 1–16; 2 Mc 10, 1–8); of Judas' campaigns in Idumea and Transjordan

8, 19: 2 Mc 15, 22; 2 Kgs 19, 35; Is 37, 36.
8, 23: 1 Mc 3, 48.
8, 34f: 2 Mc 8, 23f; 1 Mc 7, 26.
9, 1–29: 2 Mc 1, 12–17; 1 Mc 6, 1–13.

entered the city called Persepolis and attempted to rob the temple and gain control of the city. Thereupon the people had swift recourse to arms, and Antiochus' men were routed, so that in the end Antiochus was put to flight by the natives and forced to beat a shameful retreat. ³ On his arrival in Ecbatana, he learned what had happened to Nicanor and to Timothy's forces. ⁴ Overcome with anger, he planned to make the Jews suffer for the injury done by those who had put him to flight. Therefore he ordered his charioteer to drive without stopping until he finished the journey.

Yet the condemnation of Heaven rode with him, since he said in his arrogance, "I will make Jerusalem the common graveyard of the Jews as soon as I arrive there." ⁵* So the all-seeing LORD, the God of Israel, struck him down with an unseen but incurable blow; for scarcely had he uttered those words when he was seized with excruciating pains in his bowels and sharp internal torment, ⁶ a fit punishment for him who had tortured the bowels of others with many barbarous torments. ⁷ Far from giving up his insolence, he was all the more filled with arrogance. Breathing fire in his rage against the Jews, he gave orders to drive even faster. As a result he hurtled from the dashing chariot, and every part of his body was racked by the violent fall. ⁸* Thus he who previously, in his superhuman presumption, thought he could command the waves of the sea, and imagined he could weigh the mountaintops in his scales, was now thrown to the ground and had to be carried on a litter, clearly manifesting to all the power of God. ⁹* The body of this impious man swarmed with worms, and while he was still alive in hideous torments, his flesh rotted off, so that the entire army was sickened by the stench of his corruption. ¹⁰ Shortly before, he had thought that he could reach the stars of heaven, and now, no one could endure to transport the man because of this intolerable stench.

¹¹ At last, broken in spirit, he began to give up his excessive arrogance, and to gain some understanding, under the scourge of God, for he was racked with pain unceasingly. ¹² When he could no longer bear his own stench, he said, "It is right to be subject to God, and not to think one's mortal self divine." ¹³ Then this vile man vowed to the LORD,

who would no longer have mercy on him, ¹⁴ that he would set free the holy city, toward which he had been hurrying with the intention of leveling it to the ground and making it a common graveyard; ¹⁵ he would put on perfect equality with the Athenians all the Jews, whom he had judged not even worthy of burial, but fit only to be thrown out with their children to be eaten by vultures and wild animals; ¹⁶ he would adorn with the finest offerings the holy temple which he had previously despoiled; he would restore all the sacred vessels many times over; and would provide from his own revenues the expenses required for the sacrifices. ¹⁷ Besides all this, he would become a Jew himself and visit every inhabited place to proclaim there the power of God. ¹⁸ But since God's punishment had justly come upon him, his sufferings were not lessened, so he lost hope for himself and wrote the following letter to the Jews in the form of a supplication. It read thus:

¹⁹† "To my esteemed Jewish citizens, Antiochus, their king and general, sends hearty greetings and best wishes for their health and happiness. ²⁰ If you and your children are well and your affairs are going as you wish, I thank God very much, for my hopes are in heaven. ²¹ Now that I am ill, I recall with affection the esteem and good will you bear me. On returning from the regions of Persia, I fell victim to a troublesome illness; so I thought it necessary to form plans for the general welfare of all. ²² Actually, I do not despair about my health, since I have great hopes of recovering from my illness. ²³ Nevertheless, I know that my father, whenever he went on campaigns in the hinterland, would name his successor, ²⁴ so that, if anything unexpected happened or any unwelcome news came, the people throughout the realm would know to whom the government had been entrusted, and so not be disturbed. ²⁵† I am also bearing in mind that the neighboring rulers, especially those on the borders of our kingdom, are on the watch for opportunities and waiting to see what will happen. I have therefore appointed as king my son Antiochus, whom I have often before entrusted and commended to most of you, when I made hurried visits to the outlying provinces. I have written to him the letter copied below. ²⁶ Therefore I beg and entreat each of you to

---

†
(cf 2 Mc 5, 1–51; 2 Mc 10, 14–38); and of the first expedition of Lysias (1 Mc 4, 26–35; 2 Mc 11, 1–15).
  9, 19–27: Despite the statement in v 18, this letter is not really a supplication. It is rather a notification to all the king's subjects of the appointment of his son as his successor and a request that they be loyal to the new king. Apparently the same letter, which has every appearance of being authentic, was sent to the various peoples

throughout the kingdom, with only a few words of address changed for each group.
  9, 25: *The letter copied below:* not included in the text of 2 Maccabees.
*
  9, 5: Acts 12, 20–23.   Is 40, 12.
  9, 8: Jb 38, 8–11; Ps 65, 6f;   **9, 9:** Acts 12, 23.

remember the general and individual benefits you have received, and to continue to show good will toward me and my son. ²⁷ I am confident that, following my policy, he will treat you with mildness and kindness in his relations with you."

²⁸ So this murderer and blasphemer, after extreme sufferings, such as he had inflicted on others, died a miserable death in the mountains of a foreign land. ²⁹ His foster brother Philip brought the body home; but fearing Antiochus' son, he later withdrew into Egypt, to Ptolemy Philometor.

Purification of Temple and City

10 ¹* When Maccabeus and his companions, under the LORD'S leadership, had recovered the temple and the city, ² they destroyed the altars erected by the Gentiles in the marketplace and the sacred enclosures. ³† After purifying the temple, they made a new altar. Then, with fire struck from flint, they offered sacrifice for the first time in two years, burned incense, and lighted lamps. They also set out the showbread. ⁴ When they had done this, they prostrated themselves and begged the LORD that they might never again fall into such misfortunes, and that if they should sin at any time, he might chastise them with moderation and not hand them over to blasphemous and barbarous Gentiles. ⁵ On the anniversary of the day on which the temple had been profaned by the Gentiles, that is, the twenty-fifth of the same month Chislev, the purification of the temple took place. ⁶ The Jews celebrated joyfully for eight days as on the feast of Booths, remembering how, a little while before, they had spent the feast of Booths living like wild animals in caves on the mountains. ⁷ Carrying rods entwined with leaves, green branches and palms, they sang hymns of grateful praise to him who had brought about the purification of his own Place. ⁸ By public edict and decree they prescribed that the whole Jewish nation should celebrate these days every year.

VI: Renewed Persecution

Death of Ptolemy

⁹* Such was the end of Antiochus surnamed Epiphanes. ¹⁰ Now we shall relate what happened under Antiochus Eupator, the son of that godless man, and shall give a summary of the chief evils caused by the wars. ¹¹ When Eupator succeeded to

the kingdom, he put a certain Lysias in charge of the government as commander in chief of Coelesyria and Phoenicia. ¹²† Ptolemy, surnamed Macron, had taken the lead in treating the Jews fairly because of the previous injustice that had been done them, and he endeavored to have peaceful relations with them. ¹³ As a result, he was accused before Eupator by the King's Friends. In fact, on all sides he heard himself called a traitor for having abandoned Cyprus, which Philometor had entrusted to him, and for having gone over to Antiochus Epiphanes. Since he could not command the respect due to his high office, he ended his life by taking poison.

Victory over the Idumeans

¹⁴† When Gorgias became governor of the region, he employed foreign troops and used every opportunity to attack the Jews. ¹⁵* At the same time the Idumeans, who held some important strongholds, were harassing the Jews; they welcomed fugitives from Jerusalem and endeavored to continue the war. ¹⁶ Maccabeus and his companions, after public prayers asking God to be their ally, moved quickly against the strongholds of the Idumeans. ¹⁷ Attacking vigorously, they gained control of the places, drove back all who manned the walls, and cut down those who opposed them, killing as many as twenty thousand men. ¹⁸ When at least nine thousand took refuge in two very strong towers, containing everything necessary to

---

10, 3: *Two years:* three years according to 1 Mc 1, 54 and 4, 52.
10, 12: *Ptolemy Macron:* son of Dorymenes (2 Mc 4, 45), was formerly hostile to the Jews (2 Mc 6, 8).
10, 14–23: Probably the same campaign of Judas against the Idumeans that is mentioned in 1 Mc 5, 1–3.

10, 1–8: 1 Mc 4, 36–59.   **10, 15–23:** 1 Mc 5, 3ff.
  10, 9: 2 Mc 2, 21; 1 Mc 6, 17.

sustain a siege, ¹⁹ Maccabeus left Simon and Joseph, along with Zacchaeus and his men, in sufficient numbers to besiege them, while he himself went off to places where he was more urgently needed. ²⁰ But some of the men in Simon's force who were money lovers let themselves be bribed by some of the men in the towers; on receiving seventy thousand drachmas, they allowed a number of them to escape. ²¹ When Maccabeus was told what had happened, he assembled the rulers of the people and accused those men of having sold their kinsmen for money by setting their enemies free to fight against them. ²² So he put them to death as traitors, and without delay captured the two towers. ²³ As he was successful at arms in all his undertakings, he destroyed more than twenty thousand men in the two strongholds.

Victory over Timothy

²⁴† Timothy, who had previously been defeated by the Jews, gathered a tremendous force of foreign troops and collected a large number of cavalry from Asia; then he appeared in Judea, ready to conquer it by force. ²⁵ At his approach, Maccabeus and his men made supplication to God, sprinkling earth upon their heads and girding their loins in sackcloth. ²⁶* Lying prostrate at the foot of the altar, they begged him to be gracious to them, and to be an enemy to their enemies, and a foe to their foes, as the law declares.

²⁷ After the prayer, they took up their arms and advanced a considerable distance from the city, halting when they were close to the enemy. ²⁸† As soon as dawn broke, the armies joined battle, the one having as pledge of success and victory not only their valor but also their reliance on the LORD, and the other taking fury as their leader in the fight.

²⁹* In the midst of the fierce battle, there appeared to the enemy from the heavens five majestic men riding on golden-bridled horses, who led the Jews on. ³⁰ They surrounded Maccabeus, and shielding him with their own armor, kept him from being wounded. They shot arrows and hurled thunderbolts at the enemy, who were bewildered and blinded, thrown into confusion and routed. ³¹ Twenty-five hundred of their foot soldiers and six hundred of their horsemen were slain. ³²* Timothy, however, fled to a well-fortified stronghold called Gazara, where Chaereas was in command. ³³ For four days Maccabeus and his men eagerly besieged the fortress. ³⁴ Those inside, relying on the strength of the place, kept repeating outrageous blasphemies and uttering abominable words. ³⁵ When the fifth day dawned, twenty young men in the army of Maccabeus, angered over such blasphemies, bravely stormed the wall and with savage fury cut down everyone they encountered. ³⁶ Others who climbed up the same way swung around on the defenders, taking the besieged in the rear; they put the towers to the torch, spread the fire and burned the blasphemers alive. Still others broke down the gates and let in the rest of the troops, who took possession of the city. ³⁷† Timothy had hidden in a cistern, but they killed him, along with his brother Chaereas, and Apollophanes. ³⁸ On completing these exploits, they blessed, with hymns of grateful praise, the LORD who shows great kindness to Israel and grants them victory.

Defeat of Lysias

11 ¹*† Very soon afterward, Lysias, guardian and kinsman of the king and head of the government, being greatly displeased at what had happened, ² mustered about eighty thousand infantry and all his cavalry and marched against the Jews. His plan was to make Jerusalem a Greek settlement; ³ to levy tribute on the temple, as he did on the sanctuaries of the other nations; and to put the high priesthood up for sale every year. ⁴ He did not take God's power into account at all, but felt exultant confidence in his myriads of foot soldiers, his thousands of horsemen, and his eighty elephants. ⁵ So he invaded Judea, and when he reached Beth-zur, a fortified place about twenty miles from Jerusalem, launched a strong attack against it. ⁶* When Maccabeus and his men learned that Lysias was besieging the strongholds, they and all the people begged the LORD with lamentations and tears to send a good angel to save Israel. ⁷ Maccabeus himself was the first to take up arms, and he exhorted the others to join him in risking their lives to help their kinsmen. Then they resolutely set out together. ⁸* Suddenly, while they were still near Jerusalem, a horseman appeared at their head, clothed in white garments and brandishing gold weapons. ⁹ Then all of them together thanked God for his mercy, and

10, 24: Timothy . . . previously . . . defeated by the Jews: as recounted in 2 Mc 8, 30ff.
10, 28: As soon as dawn broke: the same battle at dawn as in 1 Mc 5, 30–34.
10, 37: Timothy . . . they killed: apparently, the same Timothy is still alive in 2 Mc 12, 2.18–25. The present passage is not in chronological order, Gazara, v 32 (Gezer) was not captured by the Jews until much later (cf 1 Mc 9, 50ff; 13, 53).

11, 1–12: The defeat of Lysias at Beth-zur probably occurred before the purification of the temple; cf 1 Mc 4, 26–35.

10, 26: Ex 23, 22.   **11, 1–12:** 1 Mc 4, 26–35.
10, 29f: 2 Mc 3, 24ff; 5, 2f; 10,   **11, 6:** Ex 23, 20.
     29f; 11, 8.   **11, 8:** 2 Mc 3, 24ff; 5, 2f; 10,
10, 32: 1 Mc 13, 43–48.   29f.

their hearts were filled with such courage that they were ready to assault not only men, but the most savage beasts, yes, even walls of iron. ¹⁰ Now that the LORD had shown his mercy toward them, they advanced in battle order with the aid of their heavenly ally. ¹¹ Hurling themselves upon the enemy like lions, they laid low eleven thousand foot soldiers and sixteen hundred horsemen, and put all the rest to flight. ¹² Most of those who got away were wounded and stripped of their arms, while Lysias himself escaped only by shameful flight.

Peace with the Syrians

¹³* But Lysias was not a stupid man. He reflected on the defeat he had suffered, and came to realize that the Hebrews were invincible because the mighty God was their ally. He therefore sent a message ¹⁴ persuading them to settle everything on just terms, and promising to persuade the king also, and to induce him to become their friend. ¹⁵ Maccabeus, solicitous for the common good, agreed to all that Lysias proposed; and the king, on his part, granted in behalf of the Jews all the written requests of Maccabeus to Lysias.

Official Letters

¹⁶ These are the terms of the letter which Lysias wrote to the Jews: "Lysias sends greetings to the Jewish people. ¹⁷ John and Absalom, your envoys, have presented your signed communication and asked about the matters contained in it. ¹⁸ Whatever had to be referred to the king I called to his attention, and the things that were acceptable he has granted. ¹⁹ If you maintain your loyalty to the government, I will endeavor to further your interests in the future. ²⁰ On the details of these matters I have authorized my representatives, as well as your envoys, to confer with you. ²¹† Farewell." The year one hundred and forty-eight, the twenty-fourth of Dioscorinthius.

²² The king's letter read thus: "King Antiochus sends greetings to his brother Lysias. ²³ Now that our father has taken his place among the gods, we wish the subjects of our kingdom to be undisturbed in conducting their own affairs. ²⁴ We understand that the Jews do not agree with our father's policy concerning Greek customs but prefer their own way of life. They are petitioning us to let them retain

their own customs. ²⁵ Since we desire that this people too should be undisturbed, our decision is that their temple be restored to them and that they live in keeping with the customs of their ancestors. ²⁶ Accordingly, please send them messengers to give them our assurances of friendship, so that, when they learn of our decision, they may have nothing to worry about but may contentedly go about their own business."

²⁷ The king's letter to the people was as follows: "King Antiochus sends greetings to the Jewish senate and to the rest of the Jews. ²⁸ If you are well, it is what we desire. We too are in good health. ²⁹ Menelaus has told us of your wish to return home and attend to your own affairs. ³⁰ Therefore, those who return by the thirtieth of Xanthicus will have our assurance of full permission ³¹ to observe their dietary laws and other laws, just as before, and none of the Jews shall be molested in any way for faults committed through ignorance. ³² I have also sent Menelaus to reassure you. ³³† Farewell." In the year one hundred and forty-eight, the fifteenth of Xanthicus.

³⁴ The Romans also sent them a letter as follows: "Quintus Memmius and Titus Manius, legates of the Romans, send greetings to the Jewish people. ³⁵ Whatever Lysias, kinsman of the king, has granted you, we also approve. ³⁶ But the matters on which he passed judgment should be submitted to the king. As soon as you have considered them, send someone to us with your decisions so that we may present them to your advantage, for we are on our way to Antioch. ³⁷ Make haste, then, to send us those who can inform us of your intentions. ³⁸† Farewell." In the year one hundred and forty-eight, the fifteenth of Xanthicus.

Persecution Renewed

12 ¹ After these agreements were made, Lysias returned to the king, and the Jews went about their farming. ²† But some of the local governors, Timothy and Apollonius, son of Gennaeus, as also Hieronymus and Demophon, to say nothing of Nicanor, the commander of the Cyprians, would not allow them to live in peace.

³ Some people of Joppa also committed this outrage: they invited the Jews who lived among them,

---

11, 21: *The year one hundred and forty-eight:* 164 B.C. The reading of the name of the month and its position in the calendar are uncertain.
11, 33: The date, which is the same as the date of the Romans' letter (v 38) cannot be correct. The king's letter must be connected with the peace treaty of the year 149 of the Seleucid era, i.e., 163 B.C. Perhaps the mention of the month of Xanthicus in the body of the letter (v 30) caused the date of the Romans' letter to be transferred to this one.

11, 38: The date is April 12, 164 B.C.
12, 2: *Apollonius, son of Gennaeus:* not the Apollonius who was the son of Menestheus (2 Mc 4, 21). *Nicanor:* probably distinct from the Nicanor of 2 Mc 14, 2.

11, 13–33: 1 Mc 6, 57–61.

together with their wives and children, to embark on boats which they had provided. There was no hint of enmity toward them: ⁴ this was done by public vote of the city. When the Jews, not suspecting treachery and wishing to live on friendly terms, accepted the invitation, the people of Joppa took them out to sea and drowned at least two hundred of them.

Activity of Judas

⁵ As soon as Judas heard of the barbarous deed perpetrated against his countrymen, he summoned his men; ⁶ and after calling upon God, the just judge, he marched against the murderers of his kinsmen. In a night attack he set the harbor on fire, burnt the boats, and put to the sword those who had taken refuge there. ⁷ When the gates of the town were shut, he withdrew, intending to come back later and wipe out the entire population of Joppa.

⁸ On hearing that the men of Jamnia planned to give like treatment to the Jews who lived among them, ⁹ he attacked the Jamnian populace by night, setting fire to the harbor and the fleet, so that the glow of the flames was visible as far as Jerusalem, thirty miles away.

¹⁰*† When the Jews had gone about a mile from there in the campaign against Timothy, they were attacked by Arabs numbering at least five thousand foot soldiers, and five hundred horsemen. ¹¹ After a hard fight, Judas and his companions, with God's help, were victorious. The defeated nomads begged Judas to make friends with them and promised to supply the Jews with cattle and to help them in every other way. ¹² Realizing that they could indeed be useful in many respects, Judas agreed to make peace with them. After the pledge of friendship had been exchanged, the Arabs withdrew to their tents.

¹³ He also attacked a certain city called Caspin, fortified with earthworks and ramparts and inhabited by a mixed population of Gentiles. ¹⁴ Relying on the strength of their walls and their supply of provisions, the besieged treated Judas and his men with contempt, insulting them and even uttering blasphemies and profanity. ¹⁵* But Judas and his men invoked the aid of the great Sovereign of the world, who, in the day of Joshua, overthrew Jericho without battering-ram or siege machine; then they furiously stormed the ramparts. ¹⁶ Capturing the city by the will of God, they inflicted such indescribable slaughter on it that the adjacent pool,

which was about a quarter of a mile wide, seemed to be filled with the blood that flowed into it.

¹⁷*† When they had gone on some ninety miles, they reached Charax,* where there were certain Jews known as Toubiani. ¹⁸ But they did not find Timothy in that region, for he had already departed from there without having done anything except to leave behind in one place a very strong garrison. ¹⁹ But Dositheus and Sosipater, two of Maccabeus' captains, marched out and destroyed the force of more than ten thousand men that Timothy had left in the stronghold. ²⁰ Meanwhile, Maccabeus divided his army into cohorts, with a commander over each cohort, and went in pursuit of Timothy, who had a force of a hundred and twenty thousand foot soldiers and twenty-five hundred horsemen. ²¹ When Timothy learned of the approach of Judas, he sent on ahead of him the women and children, as well as the baggage, to a place called Karnion, which was hard to besiege and even hard to reach because of the difficult terrain of that region. ²² But when Judas' first cohort appeared, the enemy was overwhelmed with fear and terror at the manifestation of the All-seeing. Scattering in every direction, they rushed away in such headlong flight that in many cases they wounded one another, pierced by the swords of their own men. ²³ Judas pressed the pursuit vigorously, putting the sinners to the sword and destroying as many as thirty thousand men.

²⁴ Timothy himself fell into the hands of the men under Dositheus and Sosipater; but with great cunning, he asked them to spare his life and let him go, because he had in his power the parents and relatives of many of them, and could make these suffer. ²⁵ When he had fully confirmed his solemn pledge to restore them unharmed, they let him go for the sake of saving their brethren.

Further Successes

²⁶† Judas then marched to Karnion and the shrine of Atargatis, where he killed twenty-five thousand people. ²⁷* After the defeat and destruction of these, he moved his army to Ephron, a fortified city inhabited by people of many nationalities. Robust young men took up their posts in defense of the walls, from which they fought valiantly; inside were large supplies of machines and missiles. ²⁸ But the Jews, invoking the Sovereign who forcibly shatters the might of his enemies, got possession of the

---

12, 10: *From there:* not from the aforesaid Jamnia (vv 8f) or Joppa (vv 3–7), but from a place in Transjordan; vv 10–26 parallel the account given in 1 Mc 5, 9–13.24–54 of Judas' campaign in northern Transjordan.

12, 17: *Certain Jews known as Toubiani:* because they lived "in the land of Tob" (1 Mc 5, 13).

12, 26: *Atargatis:* a Syrian goddess, represented by the body of a fish.

12, 10–16: 1 Mc 5, 24–36.   **12, 17:** 1 Mc 5, 13.
12, 15: Jos 6, 1–21.   **12, 27–31:** 2 Mc 5, 45–54.
12, 17–26: 1 Mc 5, 37–44.

city and slaughtered twenty-five thousand of the people in it. 29† Then they set out from there and hastened on to Scythopolis, seventy-five miles from Jerusalem. 30 But when the Jews who lived there testified to the good will shown by the Scythopolitans and to their kind treatment even in times of adversity, 31 Judas and his men thanked them and exhorted them to be well disposed to their race in the future also. Finally they arrived in Jerusalem, shortly before the feast of Weeks.

32 After this feast called Pentecost, they lost no time in marching against Gorgias, governor of Idumea, 33 who opposed them with three thousand foot soldiers and four hundred horsemen. 34 In the ensuing battle, a few of the Jews were slain. 35† A man called Dositheus, a powerful horseman and one of Bacenor's men, caught hold of Gorgias, grasped his military cloak and dragged him along by main strength, intending to capture the vile wretch alive, when a Thracian horseman attacked Dositheus and cut off his arm at the shoulder. Then Gorgias fled to Marisa. 36 After Esdris and his men had been fighting for a long time and were weary, Judas called upon the LORD to show himself their ally and leader in the battle. 37 Then, raising a battle cry in his ancestral language, and with songs, he charged Gorgias' men when they were not expecting it and put them to flight.

Expiation for the Dead

38 Judas rallied his army and went to the city of Adullam. As the week was ending, they purified themselves according to custom and kept the sabbath there. 39 On the following day, since the task had now become urgent, Judas and his men went to gather up the bodies of the slain and bury them with their kinsmen in their ancestral tombs. 40* But under the tunic of each of the dead they found amulets sacred to the idols of Jamnia, which the law forbids the Jews to wear. So it was clear to all that this was why these men had been slain. 41 They all therefore praised the ways of the LORD, the just judge who brings to light the things that are hidden. 42† Turning to supplication, they prayed that the sinful deed might be fully blotted out. The noble Judas warned the soldiers to keep themselves

free from sin, for they had seen with their own eyes what had happened because of the sin of those who had fallen. 43 He then took up a collection among all his soldiers, amounting to two thousand silver drachmas, which he sent to Jerusalem to provide for an expiatory sacrifice. In doing this he acted in a very excellent and noble way, inasmuch as he had the resurrection of the dead in view; 44 for if he were not expecting the fallen to rise again, it would have been useless and foolish to pray for them in death. 45 But if he did this with a view to the splendid reward that awaits those who had gone to rest in godliness, it was a holy and pious thought. 46 Thus he made atonement for the dead that they might be freed from this sin.

The Syrians Invade Judea

13 1† In the year one hundred and forty-nine, Judas and his men learned that Antiochus Eupator was invading Judea with a large force, 2*† and that with him was Lysias, his guardian, who was in charge of the government. They led a Greek army of one hundred and ten thousand foot soldiers, fifty-three hundred horsemen, twenty-two elephants, and three hundred chariots armed with scythes.

Death of Menelaus

3 Menelaus also joined them, and with great duplicity kept urging Antiochus on, not for the welfare of his country, but in the hope of being established in office. 4*† But the King of kings aroused the anger of Antiochus against the scoundrel. When the king was shown by Lysias that Menelaus was to blame for all the trouble, he ordered him to be taken to Beroea and executed there in the customary local method. 5† There is at that place a tower seventy-five feet high, full of ashes, with a circular rim sloping down steeply on all sides toward the ashes. 6 A man guilty of sacrilege or notorious for certain other crimes is brought up there and then hurled down to destruction. 7 In such a manner was Menelaus, the transgressor of the law, fated to die; he was deprived even of decent burial. 8 It was altogether just that he who had committed so many sins against the altar with its pure fire and ashes should meet his death in ashes.

---

† **12, 29:** *Scythopolis:* the Greek name of the city of Beth-shan; cf 1 Mc 5, 52.
12, 35: *One of Bacenor's men:* certain ancient witnesses to the text have "one of the Toubiani"; cf v 17.
12, 42–46: This is the earliest statement of the doctrine that prayers (v 42) and sacrifices (v 43) for the dead are beneficial. The statement is made here, however, only for the purpose of proving that Judas believed in the resurrection of the just (2 Mc 7, 9.14.23.36). That is, he believed that expiation could be made for certain sins of otherwise good men—soldiers who had given their lives for God's cause. Thus, they could share in the resurrection. His belief was similar to, but not quite the same as, the Catholic doctrine of purgatory.

13, 1: *In the year one hundred and forty-nine:* 163–162 B.C.
13, 2: *They led:* the Greek means literally "Each (of them) led," but it is unlikely that the author meant the already immense numbers to be doubled; the numbers are similar to those in 1 Mc 6, 30.
13, 4: *Beroea:* the Greek name of Aleppo.
13, 5: *Ashes:* probably smoldering ashes; the tower resembles the ancient Persian fire towers.

12, 40: Dt 7, 25.   13, 4: 1 Tm 6, 15; Rv 17, 14;
13, 2: 1 Mc 6, 30.   19, 16.